Also from Visible Ink Press

Real Ghosts, Restless Spirits, and Haunted Places

The UFO Book:
Encyclopedia of the Extraterrestrial

The Vampire Book:
The Encyclopedia of the Undead, 2nd edition

The Werewolf Book:
The Encyclopedia of Shape-Shifting Beings

VideoHound's Cult Flicks and Trash Pics, 2nd edition

VideoHound's Dragon:
Asian Action & Cult Flicks

VideoHound's Groovy Movies:
Far-out Films of the Psychedelic Era

VideoHound's Horror Show:
999 Hair-Raising, Hellish, and Humorous Movies

VideoHound's Sci-Fi Experience:
Your Quantum Guide to the Video Universe

Please visit Visible Ink Press at visibleink.com.

The Superhero Book

The Superhero Book

The Ultimate Encyclopedia of Comic-Book Icons and Hollywood Heroes

Edited by Gina Misiroglu

with David A. Roach

Detroit

The Ultimate Encyclopedia of Comic-Book Icons and Hollywood Heroes

Contents

Contents

Contents

Introduction

"LEAPING OVER SKYSCRAPERS, RUNNING FASTER THAN AN EXPRESS TRAIN, SPRINGING GREAT DISTANCES AND HEIGHTS, LIFTING AND SMASHING TREMENDOUS WEIGHTS, POSSESSING AN IMPENETRABLE SKIN--THESE ARE THE AMAZING ATTRIBUTES WHICH SUPERMAN, SAVIOR OF THE HELPLESS AND OPPRESSED, AVAILS HIMSELF OF AS HE BATTLES THE FORCES OF EVIL AND INJUSTICE."

--SUPERMAN, *ACTION COMICS*, 1939

Superhuman strength. Virtual invulnerability. Motivated to defend the world from evildoers. A secret identity. And a penchant for looking good in long underwear. These are the traits that define the quintessential superhero: those characters whose impossible feats graced the pages of comic books during comics' Golden and Silver Ages. They are Batman, Captain America, Captain Marvel, Spider-Man, Superman, Wonder Woman, and dozens of others—with names like Ant-Man, Daredevil, Hawkman, the Human Torch, the Spectre, the Spirit, and Sub-Mariner—whose death-defying acts and altruistic motives have come to characterize heroism for generations of fans.

Though these characters repeatedly saved planet Earth from the well-laid plans of supervillains, larger-than-life aliens, and Nazi infiltrators, by the mid–twentieth century, heroes had evolved from the All-American boy fantasy to multidimensional characters that clearly reflected the dreams and fears of modern society. By the end of the twentieth century, the real world had become a darker place, necessitating a new kind of hero. Popular heroes of yesteryear were reinvented to meet the demands of a new age. The popular culture witnessed the rise of the anti-hero, a fresh breed of brazen, gritty adventurer that includes the likes of Elektra, the Punisher, and Wolverine. Heroes that aren't typically defined as *super*—Buffy, Hellboy, Sandman, and Spawn—became associated with the word because they possessed superhuman qualities and identified with their audience in unique ways.

At this time, too, the superhero's presence in mass media became stronger than ever, with the Batman and Superman live-action film franchises of the 1980s preparing audiences for the entrée of superhero films like *Spider-Man 1* and *2* and two X-Men adventures, which consistently made worldwide top-grossing films lists. Mega-merchandising machines like the Ninja Turtles and the Powerpuff Girls enjoyed previously unheard-of success, helping to round out a burgeoning market filled with independents like the spunky neo-feminist Action Girl, anime favorite Sailor Moon, and even Cutey Bunny, the world's first African-American rabbit superheroine. Characters continued to show up on consumer products as varied as hair barrettes and lunchboxes, and they began to make new inroads into the videogame, trading-card, and book markets. One well-known hero even starred in his own "got milk?" ad campaign.

But who exactly are these mask-wearing, cape-donning men and women? What are their strengths and weaknesses? Secret identities? Who are their arch-enemies? When and where did the characters first appear and how have they changed through the years? *The Superhero Book*—the ultimate A–Z compendium of everyone's favorite superheroes and their mythology, sidekicks, villains, love interests, superpowers, vulnerabilities, and modus operandi—attempts to answer these questions and more as it explores many of pop culture's favorite icons. Within its pages lie almost 300 entries on superheroes mainstream and counterculture, famous and forgotten, best and worst—including classics like Green Lantern and Plastic Man, cult favorites like the Rocketeer and Madman, and timeless entities like the X-Men. You'll be reminded why you love them (who wouldn't want to fly like Superman for just one day?), why they were chosen to save the world ("We shall call you Captain America, son! Because like you—America shall gain the strength and will to safeguard our shores"), what they do for their day jobs (world traveler Oliver Queen ... Hollywood star and America's sweetheart Linda Turner ... billionaire playboy Bruce Wayne … college student and freelance photographer Peter Parker), and their very human *faux pas* (as the Flash, he could outrun the wind, but as alter ego Barry Allen he was hard-pressed to show up for a date on time!).

Because this encyclopedia is as much a reference on modern mythology as it is a chronicling of the superhero genre in America, the book discusses the cultural phenomenon of each character and its various incarnations in the popular culture. "In the Media" entries supplement many of the more commercial heroes' write-ups. Themed topics for discussion include African-American heroes, alternative futures, anime and manga, atomic heroes, camp and comedy heroes, civilian heroes, feminism, funny animal heroes, multiculturalism, one-hit wonders, sidekicks and protégés, superheroes with disabilities, superheroines, supernatural heroes, superpatriots, team-ups and crossovers, and World War II and the superhero in America. Each significant era of the superhero is explored—the Golden Age (1938–1954), the Silver Age (1956–1969), the Bronze Age (1970–1979), and the Modern Age (1980–present)—providing the reader with a perspective of the hero over the twentieth century and beyond. And creators, comic-book companies, and merchandising efforts all take their rightful place in the history of hero-making.

Why do all this? The bottom line is, we need our heroes. Psychologist Carl Jung (*Man and His Symbols,* 1964) and myth-maker Joseph Campbell (*The Hero with a Thousand Faces,* 1949) both explored society's need for heroes, though many prefer the edited version. Upon gazing at Batman and Robin approaching Gotham City in their Batcopter in *Batman: The Movie* (1966), Ordinary Joe said it best when he declared, "It gives a fella a good feeling to know they're up there doing their job." In a world not quite right, heroes provide a solution. Though scholars have long noted that superheroes fulfill our longing to honor the heroes of legend and myth, it really goes beyond that. They satisfy our "inner hero." Superheroes embody "the ancient longing of mankind for a mighty protector, a helper, guide or guardian angel who offers miraculous deliverance to mortals," observed Reinhold Reitberger and Wolfgang Fuchs in their *Comics: Anatomy of a Mass Medium* (1972). Frank Miller, artist extraordinaire of Daredevil, put it a bit differently when he said, "It's very comforting to know that there's a god-like figure going around making things right. That's a lot of what superheroes are about."

That's not all the outspoken Miller has had to say. Regarding the prospects for the superhero genre's health into the new millennium,

Miller told the *Village Voice* in 2002, "The president talks incessantly about evil. I don't think melodrama is dead." Indeed, in the era of action-movie heroes winning governorships and military missions against opponents with designations like "Dr. Germ," comics have struck a chord again—even if nowadays they deal with gray skepticism about government motives as often as they deal in black-and-white portrayals of heroic firepower. Comics have emerged from an industrywide sales slump since September 11, 2001. Even though they were generating notice in prestigious quarters before then—with a Pulitzer Prize for Michael Chabon's novel about the comic-book medium's pioneers, *The Amazing Adventures of Kavalier & Clay* (2000), for example—the current cultural currency of blockbuster superhero films and widely covered events like Miller's *Dark Knight Strikes Again* series show that the costumed variety of comic book still has a lot to tell America about the state of its soul.

Noted cartoonist Jules Feiffer once said that if superheroes joined the more numerous supervillains, they would fill the skies like locusts. This truism prompts a note about selecting the superheroes, particularly those created in the first half of the twentieth century: Out of the tens of thousands of comic books that make up the Golden and Silver Ages, hundreds of them contain costumed heroes. Even following the strictest criteria of a superhero or superheroine—he or she wears a costume/mask and has special powers and/or a secret identity—a complete listing of every hero would be prohibitive. Therefore, the table of contents reflects the most diverse listing of American superheroes (or those from other countries that have had a U.S. presence) possible—those that are among the best loved, historically significant, or most representative of a type of hero.

Generally speaking, most heroes follow what Robert C. Harvey in his *Art of the Comic Book* (1996) calls "the superhero formula" as established by Superman in his *Action Comics* debut in 1938. He or she has an altruistic mission, possesses superpowers or advanced mental or physical skills, wears an iconic costume, and functions within a dual identity, the "civilian" one of which is concealed. Following these criteria, *The Superhero Book* naturally eliminates entries for one-off or obscure characters, as well as those that would more precisely be defined as cowboys, magicians, detectives, spacemen, or jungle men, though some thematic entries do touch on these character types. In addition, the characters of Japanese manga and anime don't follow the rigid conventions of the early American superheroes, though readers may be surprised to find more similarities than are typically acknowledged.

The ground gets muddier for the later heroes, those of the Bronze and Modern Ages, since they break away from the "strict criteria" that can easily be applied to the earlier heroes. Here, some artistic license has been applied to their selection. May of these later protagonists possess qualities customarily considered nonheroic, or "anti-heroic," their motivations for superheroic acts being not always selfless or clear. To further broaden the definition, they may not always wear a costume, possess superpowers, or function in the real world with a civilian identity, yet the popular culture considers them heroes primarily because there is a strong heroic identity associated with the character. Rather than argue whether certain borderline characters fit the mold, the book chooses to include them and lets the reader draw his or her own conclusions.

These qualifiers aside, the goal of *The Superhero Book* is straightforward: to pay homage to the heroes who have, in whatever minor or major way, influenced our lives.

—Gina Misiroglu, Los Angeles, 2004

Acknowledgments

The list of people who made this book possible is too long to reproduce here. Regardless, I am indebted to every person who contributed words of wisdom, research time, comic books, and sheer encouragement at various points in this endeavor. A thank-you of superheroic proportions is due to Peter Coogan, Jon Cooke, Robert Graff, Michael Gross, Robert Huffman, George Khoury, Denis Kitchen, John Morrow, and Randall W. Scott. Contributing writers Michael Eury, Andy Mangels, Mike Martin, Adam McGovern, Marc McKenzie, Frank Plowright, and David A. Roach tirelessly and cheerfully penned entries into the wee hours of the night. Many of these kind souls provided images as well, or directed me to art sources that otherwise would have remained untouchable. And Adam McGovern did double-duty as the book's copyeditor, playing an invaluable production role and certainly helping the book's readability. Jeff Mayse dipped into his coveted comics collections for me, and ComicSmash!, my friendly neighborhood comic-book store (www.comicsmash.com), helped put the finishing touches on the book's image requirements. Comic-book companies, including AC Comics, Dark Horse, and Image, were models of professionalism and patience. An extra-special thanks goes to my team at Visible Ink Press, without whom this encyclopedic volume simply would not have been: dream-of-a-publisher Martin Connors, super–managing editor Christa Gainor, preproduction guru Bob Huffman, art director Mary Claire Krzewinski, salesman extraordinaire Roger Jänecke, typesetter Jake Di Vita, indexer Brad Morgan (and his superteam, Jim Craddock, T. J. Craddock, and Dee Morgan), and proofreaders Dawn DesJardins, Jennifer Moore, and Terri Schell. I cannot say enough kind words about this publishing house and its creative team.

Contributors

Editor

Gina Misiroglu (GM) is a fourteen-year veteran of the West Coast publishing industry, specializing in the development and editing of popular culture, biography, and film-related titles. Misiroglu is the author of *The Handy Politics Answer Book* (2002); *Girls Like Us: 40 Extraordinary Women Celebrate Girlhood in Story, Poetry, and Song* (1999), winner of the New York Public Library's "Best Book for Teens" Award; and *Imagine: The Spirit of Twentieth-Century American Heroes* (1999). Misiroglu has worked on a number of film and TV tie-in titles, and she is the co-author of *Space Jammin': Bugs and Michael Hit the Big Screen* (1997). Misiroglu resides in Los Angeles, where superheroes can be spied on almost every street corner.

Co-Editor

David Roach (DAR) is a comic-book illustrator and writer based in Wales, United Kingdom. In addition to his post as associate editor of the U.S.-based magazine *Comic Book Artist,* which is dedicated to the historic representation of comic-book characters, Roach actively illustrates for several UK companies, including 2000 AD, Panini, and Marvel. In the United States, he has drawn and inked heroes for DC Comics, Dark Horse Comics, Topps, and the gaming company Wizards of the Coast. Roach is co-editor of *The Warren Companion: The Definitive Compendium to the Great Comics of Warren Publishing* (2001) and the revised edition of the *Slings and Arrows Comic Guide* (2003). He is a regular contributor to *Comic Book Artist* and *Comics International.*

Contributing Writers

Guided into a life of superhero fandom by his heroic idol Adam "Batman" West, **Michael Eury (ME)** has co-created and/or written comics and cartoon properties for Nike, Toys R Us, Warner Bros. Worldwide Publishing, the Microsoft Network, the "First Flight" Centennial, DC Comics, Marvel Comics, Dark Horse Comics, Archie Comics, and *Cracked* magazine. A former editor for DC and Dark Horse, Eury edited the ambitious, award-winning loose-leaf encyclopedia *Who's Who in the DC Universe,* and he is currently editing and co-writing the bimonthly comic-book magazine *Back Issue.* Eury has authored two published books, *Captain Action: The Original Super-Hero Action Figure* (2002) and *Dick Giordano: Changing Comics, One Day at a Time* (2003), and writes hero histories for the packages of Bowen Designs' Marvel Comics mini-busts.

Andy Mangels (AM) is a best-selling author and co-author of more than a dozen books, including *Star Trek* and *Roswell* novels, and the books *Animation on DVD: The Ultimate Guide* (2003) and *Star Wars: The Essential Guide to Characters* (1995). He is an award-winning comic-book anthology editor and has written comics for almost two decades. He has also written thousands of articles for entertainment and lifestyle magazines and newspapers in the United States, England, and Italy, mostly about film and television. A national award–winning activist in the gay community, Mangels lives in Portland, Oregon, with his partner, Don, and their dog, Bela. His favorite superheroes are Wonder Woman, Aquaman, Green Arrow, Hawkman, and the Teen Titans.

Michael A. Martin (MAM)'s obsession with comics began more than three decades ago at a spinner-rack in Santa Claus Lane, California. Years after this origin tale, Martin schlepped the funnies to the direct-sales market, first for Marvel Comics and later for Dark Horse Comics. In 1996, he began collaborating with Andy Mangels on scripts for Marvel's *Star Trek: Deep Space 9* comics. That same year, Martin's solo original short fiction began appearing in *The Magazine of Fantasy & Science Fiction.* He has co-authored (also with Mangels) several *Star Trek* novels and shorter pieces of *Star Trek* fiction for Pocket Books, as well as a trio of novels based on the late, lamented *Roswell* television series. He has written for *Star Trek Monthly,* Atlas Editions, *Dreamwatch,* Grolier Books, WildStorm, Platinum Studios, *Gobshite Quarterly,* and Gareth Stevens, Inc., for whom he has penned six *World Almanac Library of the States* nonfiction books.

Writing about action heroes wasn't **Adam McGovern (AMC)**'s choice; being named after one himself (Detective Adam Flint from the classic police drama *Naked City*), it was his destiny. Since then he's fulfilled it by writing about comic books, cartoons, and other popular culture for such outlets as the *Village Voice, Yahoo! Internet Life* magazine, TotalTV Online, *Comic Book Artist,* and *The Jack Kirby Collector,* among many others. He also edited *MusicHound World: The Essential Album Guide* for Visible Ink Press in 2000. Corporate copywriting and nonprofit arts consulting help support his comic-book habit and prolong what was already a somewhat enduring adolescence.

A longtime comic-book fan, **Marc McKenzie (MM)** became interested in Japanese animation after watching *Robotech* in the late 1980s. At the same time, the first English translations of Japanese manga were starting to appear in America, and McKenzie quickly took an interest in such titles as Masaomi Kanzaki's *Heavy Metal Warrior Xenon,* Kazuya Kudo and Ryoichi Ikegami's *Mai, the Psychic Girl,* Kaoru Shintani's *Area 88,* Yoshihisa Tagami's *Grey,* and Masamune Shirow's *Appleseed.* After earning a degree in biology from St. Peter's College in Jersey City, New Jersey, he went on to study computer animation at the Art Institute of Philadelphia. Now a freelance artist, McKenzie resides in Hillsborough, New Jersey. Related to anime and manga, he has written for the websites the Slush Factory and Silver Bullet Comic Books, and he has created artwork for the 2003 Otakon anime convention.

Frank Plowright (FP) is best known to the comics community as co-organizer of the United Kingdom's longest-running comic convention, UKCAC. An established freelance writer, Plowright is editor of the revised edition of the *Slings and Arrows Comic Guide* (2003), which reviews more than 5,000 comic-book series from the 1930s to the present.

AC Comics Heroes

Along with Pacific, First, and Eclipse Comics, AC Comics was a pioneer of the independent direct market for color comics in the early 1980s, distributing comics directly to a new network of specialty shops. While the other three companies are long gone and many indie publishers are now known for steering clear of superheroes, preferring not to compete with industry giants Marvel and DC Comics' specialty, AC Comics publisher Bill Black built his company on costumed characters and it prospers to this day. Having already created an interwoven universe of supertypes in his black-and-white Paragon Publications line of the 1970s, Black began bringing them to comic-shop shelves in full color, starting with the very first official AC Comics publication (or "Americomics" as the company was called until 1984), *Fun Comics* #4.

Superstrong, invulnerable, and puzzled as to where he came from, Captain Paragon (who would eventually drop the military modifier from his name) burst forth from that issue in red, white, and blue glory, as did the sensuous sorceress Nightfall (almost immediately changed to Nightveil), the dimension-hopping yellow-and-green adventurer Commando D, and the stellar-powered alien super-heroine Stardust. These heroes would continue for dozens of epic adventures.

Throughout 1983 and 1984, a plethora of costumed crime fighters were sent into the spotlight in a superhero tryout title called *Americomics*. The dark and ghostly avenger known as the Shade appeared in the pages of *Americomics* #1, along with the unique cloned multi-hero Captain Freedom, quickly followed by the indomitable street fighter known as the Scarlet Scorpion. Others appeared in additional titles, including galaxy-roamer Bolt (*Bolt & Starforce Six* #1), who demonstrates the power of flight, near-invulnerability (including the ability to exist in airless space), and the skill of firing tremendously powerful bolts of pure energy, and Astron and Astra (*Astron Venture Comics* #1), members of a group of para-dimensional police officers. In addition to Black's original characters, selected creators were encouraged to showcase their own concepts, including Jerry Ordway, John Beatty, and Jim Sanders II. These outside contributions met with varying degrees of success, although Rik Levins' Dragonfly and Don Secrease's Colt enjoyed long and popular runs at AC.

Changing market conditions toward the end of 1984 led to using a short-term strategy that turned into AC's biggest success, when the sudden popularity of black-and-white books prompted Black to edit together some existing stories to create a new superhero book, *Femforce*. Composed of beautiful, strong, and competent heroines inspired by Good Girl art characters from long-defunct companies in comics' Golden Age (1938–1954), the team of Miss (soon to become Ms.) Victory, the Blue Bulleteer, Rio Rita, and She-Cat crashed the scene in their own fifty-two-page special with a World War II–era adventure in which they battled Nazi supercriminals Lady Luger and Fritz Voltzman. It was a smashing success, and plans were immediately made for an ongoing color series, which appeared by spring of 1985. The girls of *Femforce* proved popular and enduring, the title becoming one of the longest-running comics of any kind ever spawned by the independent comics market.

After striking gold with Femforce, the company began to reprint long-forgotten comic-book material in near-perfect full-story black-and-white editions. Starting with the squarebound, trade paperback *Golden Age Greats* series, and continuing through the ongoing *Men of Mystery* comic, dozens of classic superheroes have been brought before a new comic-reading audience. Golden Age heroes like the Black Terror, Commando Yank, Golden Lad, the Flame, Captain Flash, Cat-Man, the Green Lama, Pyroman, Miss Masque, the Owl, Black Venus, Captain Wings, the Eagle, Yankee Girl, the Fighting Yank, Black Cobra, Rocketman, Dynamic Man, the Grim Reaper, and countless others round out the AC hero universe. All told, superheroes from more than a dozen former publishers have been showcased in AC's comics, and the company has intriguingly woven those characters into a number of brand-new stories.

As the comic-book medium hit some of its hardest economic times ever in the mid-1990s, AC continued to thrive, with a booming online and mail-order business that rivals and in some cases surpasses its comic-shop presence. With its impressive output, longevity, and creative marketing (not to mention its role as an early showcase for some of today's most popular comics artists, including Ord-

way and Erik Larsen), AC Comics stands as a leading haven for the superhero in an often-harsh publishing world. —*GM*

Action Girl

Erica Smith is a student at Hayley High, located in a small town on the West Coast, some time in the near future. A bit bored and frustrated with the usual issues surrounding adolescence and trying to make her way in life, Smith discovers the costume and personal effects of a forgotten crime-fighting female aviator of the 1940s, Action Girl. Inspired by the Amelia Earhart–like story of Action Girl's life and bravery, Smith decides to assume the hero's name and identity herself. Clad in the original Action Girl's vintage jacket with an "AG" logo on the chest, to-the-knee wrestling boots, and flared skirt, Smith becomes the costumed crime fighter's successor, leaving the confines of her bedroom hideout to fight against typical teenage angst. Her signature quote: "Action is everything!"

Action Girl was created by writer/artist Sarah Dyer, who started various Action Girl projects in 1992 "as a desire to see self-published work by women profiled." Although Smith first appeared as a non-superhero alter ego of Dyer herself in various fanzines and Dyer's own *Action Girl Newsletter* during the early 1990s, it was not until 1995 that Action Girl appeared as a superhero, in Dyer's self-published *Action Girl Comics* #2. Dyer quickly introduced Action Girl's support team, friends Jenna, Lilia, and Marina, who collectively make up "Team Action," as well as a cool "signal ring" that Jenna created so that Action Girl could call upon her comrades in times of need. With no superpowers except for superheroic determination, the group has battled the Go-Go Gang, the Catgirls from Mars, and Neutrina (who eventually reformed and joined Team Action as Ultra Girl).

Action Girl is often aided by her ally, fellow high-school student Flying Girl, created by Elizabeth

Action Girl #7 © & ™ 1996 Sarah Dyer.
COVER ART BY SARAH DYER.

"practical, small-scale action" (as one reviewer termed it), the girl-friendly heroes being a refreshing departure from the very adult-themed mainstream superheroine fare of the day. "Girls naturally responded to the empowerment undertones of the comic, but guys seemed to really embrace it as something that was not didactic, anti-male, or exclusivist," observed Dyer. Every issue of the comic features paper-doll cutouts, with hip wardrobe additions such as thrift-store-bought Doc Martens. While the comic has showcased the work of some forty writers and artists, the creators other than Dyer who have contributed to Action Girl stories are Watasin and artist Elim Mak. —GM

Adam Strange

Among the many things gripping the imaginations of children in the late 1950s were the emerging superheroes of the Silver Age of comics (1956–1969) and the beginnings of the space race. DC Comics decided to combine those two interests by launching a pair of space heroes in its tryout comic book *Showcase.* The first to appear was the futuristic spaceman, Space Ranger, while the second (who premiered in *Showcase* #17 in late 1958) was Adam Strange, overseen by longtime science fiction fan and editor Julius Schwartz. His first choice as artist was Carmine Infantino, but, as Infantino was currently entertaining the troops in Korea, Mike Sekowsky was drafted in for the three *Showcase* issues. When these proved popular, Strange moved over to the *Mystery in Space* comic, where he enjoyed a run of fifty issues, most of them drawn by Infantino and written by the prolific Gardner Fox.

Strange is first seen deep in the Andes, searching for lost cities, when some sort of beam suddenly transports him light years across the universe to the planet Rann, where he is confronted by those science-fiction staples, the pretty girl and the raging monster. Having dispatched the beast, Strange and his maiden-in-distress (rejoicing in the

Watasin. Flying Girl is Ginnie Exupery, Action Girl's best friend and one true confidante. Watasin has taken time to flesh out their friendship—devoting an entire story to the girls discussing their motivations as heroes—Action Girl having chosen her profession, Flying Girl reluctantly pursuing it. As a birthday present, Flying Girl introduces Action Girl to the power of flight by taking her to a vertical wind tunnel (as depicted on the cover of *Action Girl* #7 [1996]).

Action Girl Comics, a comic anthology created to showcase the work of women comic-book writers and artists, drew a surprisingly mixed fan base. Fans of both genders responded to the display of suitably off-worldly name Alanna) travel to the nearest city with her father, a scientist called Sardath. It turns out that the transporter ray—a zeta-beam—was only intended to contact far-off planets and that Strange's precipitous arrival on Rann was accidental. Unfortunately, the effect of the beam wears off after a while, and Strange is zapped back to Earth, but he has by then developed a taste for saving far-off worlds (and far-off girls called Alanna). So each story for the next six years begins with Strange whizzing around the world to catch the next zeta-beam and zoom off back to Rann.

Probably no comic series better typifies the hope and optimism of the postwar "new frontier" than Adam Strange under Fox and Infantino. Even his costume—a sleek red suit with aerodynamic jet pack and a shark-fin on his cowl (rather resembling the tail fins popular on cars of the late 1950s and early 1960s)—seemed to be emblematic of the era. Infantino's art was dynamic, slick, and very stylish, and the strip was littered with the sort of stark, elegant, and futuristic cities that architect Frank Lloyd Wright would have been proud of. Strange himself was the thinking man's superhero, preferring to use his intellect rather than his fists to defeat the menace of the week (although having his own ray gun also came in handy).

And menaces there certainly were. Seemingly every time that Strange beamed down he was confronted by a panicking Alanna, describing yet another world-shattering horror, be it Jakarta the Dust Devil (a sort of sentient dust storm); a living, tentacled world; or Ulthoon the living tornado. A particularly entertaining alien race were the cube-headed Vantorians, who struck terror into their enemies with their deadly vacuum cleaners. For much of his run, Strange seemed to exist in a fictional world of his own, though he did share a villain—the insect-eyed Konjar Ro—with DC's superhero team the Justice League, resulting in a memorable meeting with those adventurers.

Although the strip had a devoted following, it was never a massive seller, and when Fox and Infantino were moved over to revive the failing *Detective Comics* the strip nose-dived in popularity. It struggled on for a further ten issues before being replaced by the ludicrous Ultra the Multi-Alien, and Strange was banished to a life of occasional guest spots and the odd backup series. In a touching 1970s issue of *The Justice League,* Strange and Alanna finally got married, and many years later the pair appeared in a few issues of Alan Moore's revolutionary *Swamp Thing* comic. That brief revival prompted an ill-conceived, darker 1990 miniseries that was not well received by fans, and perhaps showed that the feature was very much a product of a more innocent time, with no place in a more cynical real world. —*DAR*

African-American Heroes

In 1990, DC Comics editorial director Dick Giordano was asked by one of his young staff editors why virtually all of the DC superheroes were white: "Because they were created in the 1940s by Jews and Italians who wrote and drew what they knew," he replied.

FROM INVISIBILITY TO COMIC RELIEF

Superhero comic books have mirrored societal trends since their inception, and when the medium originated in the late 1930s, African Americans cast no reflection: Segregation made blacks invisible to most whites.

When African Americans did appear in the early comics, they were abhorrently stereotyped with wide eyes and exaggerated pink lips, portrayed as easily frightened to elicit a chuckle from the white reader, and characterized as utterly dependent upon their Caucasian benefactors. The cover of *The Spirit* #1

(1944) promised "action, thrills, and *laughs*," the latter provided by black sidekick Ebony White, nervously tiptoeing through a graveyard while sticking close to his protective mentor, the white Spirit. Timely (later Marvel) Comics' kid team the Young Allies included an African-American teen named Whitewash Jones—the "comic relief" equivalent of Buckwheat from the *Our Gang* (a.k.a. "The Little Rascals") theatrical shorts—who was frequently rescued by white heroes Bucky and Toro. No black sidekick was more offensive than Spirit-clone Midnight's aide Gabby, the talking monkey, drawn in some stories to resemble a chimp-sized black person with a tail.

Other portrayals of people of color depicted them in subservience. A black butler answering the door in the Vision story in *Marvel Mystery Comics* #13 (1940) announced to white visitors, "Ise sorry, gennilmun, de doctor is pow'ful busy, experuh-mintin'!" Lothar, the aide to comic-strip hero Mandrake the Magician, "served for many years as the dumb, faithful factotum of the intelligent white man," wrote Reinhold Reitberger and Wolfgang Fuchs in their book *Comics: Anatomy of a Mass Medium* (1972). "This black man, dressed in a lion skin and wearing a fez, could be trusted at first to perform only the simplest of tasks for the intellectual Mandrake."

Sidekicks and servants aside, the integration of white and black Americans was mostly avoided during comics' Golden Age (1938–1954). DC Comics, however, published at least two stories in the later Golden Age that included early attempts at enlightenment. *World's Finest Comics* #17 (1945) shows African-American World War II servicemen on leave being denied service in a "white-only" restaurant, and in *Batman* #57 (1950), the hero stops a fight between a white man and a black man. But instances such as these were rare. African Americans remained in the background, if seen at all, in comic books of the late 1940s and 1950s, although a handful of titles specifically targeted a black audience: *All-Negro Comics* (1947), *Negro Heroes* (1947–1948), and *Negro Romance* (1950).

THE FIRST BLACK SUPERHERO

During the early Silver Age (1956–1969), African Americans were nonexistent in the pages of DC Comics' superhero series like *Superman, The Flash,* or *Green Lantern*. Remarked historian Bradford W. Wright in his tome *Comic Book Nation* (2001), "Handsome superheroes resided in clean, green suburbs and modern, even futuristic cities with shimmering glass skyscrapers, no slums, and populations of well-dressed white people." The burgeoning Marvel universe, commencing from the release of *Fantastic Four* #1 (1961), occasionally depicted a token person of color amid Manhattan crowd scenes, or in an urban school class with Peter (Spider-Man) Parker. By 1965, war—"the great leveler," according to Reitberger and Fuchs—afforded African Americans equality in the fictional realm of war comics, with black soldiers like Jackie Johnson (from the Sgt. Rock series in DC's *Our Army at War*) and Gabriel Jones (from Marvel's *Sgt. Fury and His Howling Commandos*) valiantly fighting alongside whites in stories set during World War II.

Marvel made history by introducing the Black Panther in *Fantastic Four* #52 (1966). Whether the comic's writer, Stan Lee, intentionally named the hero after the militant civil rights group, the Black Panthers, is uncertain. The Panther—actually Prince T'Challa of the affluent, industrialized African nation of Wakanda—was highly educated, extremely noble, and amazingly lithe, becoming a colleague of the Fantastic Four's resident brain, Reed Richards (a.k.a. the immodestly nicknamed Mr. Fantastic). The Black Panther broke the color barrier for African Americans in the world of superheroes and was portrayed as an admirable role model for readers of any race. The impact of his introduction, however, was not apparent from an examination of the cover: The Black Panther's full facemask provided no hint as to his ethnicity.

Though the 1966 premiere of the Black Panther is regarded as acutely influential from a long-term historical perspective, the hero appeared sporadically at first, and no other African-American

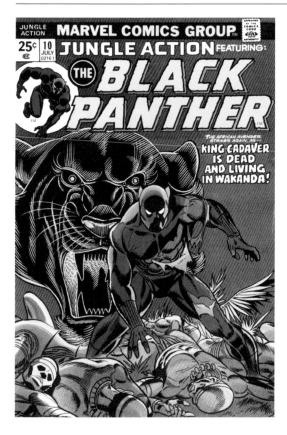

Jungle Action #10 © 1974 Marvel Comics.
COVER ART BY GIL KANE AND FRANK GIACOIA.

the Black Panther into the roster of Marvel's mighty superteam—and this time, the color of T'Challa's skin was clearly evident on the cover (and in the interiors), as his facemask was modified to reveal his nose, mouth, and chin. Scribe Roy Thomas dropped the "Black" from the hero's name to distance Marvel's Panther from the militant group, and showed no fear in chronicling white America's distrust of people of color. When T'Challa arrived at Avengers headquarters to report for duty, he discovered three of his new teammates apparently dead, and he was suspected of and arrested for the crime by Caucasian operatives of the covert organization S.H.I.E.L.D. The Panther was soon cleared, and his fellow Avengers, unlike S.H.I.E.L.D., were colorblind, accepting T'Challa with no hesitation.

Then came the Falcon, a black hero flying into *Captain America* #117 (1969). Behind his feathered fighting togs was Harlem social worker Sam Wilson, who guest-starred with Marvel's "Star-Spangled Sentinel" before actually becoming his teammate, sharing cover co-billing. Noteworthy is the fact that Captain America, the superheroic embodiment of American ideals, was the first white superhero to partner with a black superhero; he also endorsed the Black Panther's membership in the Avengers. Cap's actions tacitly endorsed racial equality, imprinting the mores of many of Marvel's readers.

"Alienated superheroes like the Hulk and the Silver Surfer especially empathized with African Americans," historian Wright observed. "The green Hulk befriends an impoverished black teenager and explains to him, 'World hates us … both of us! … Because we're different!'" African Americans were now a part of the Marvel universe. Outside of the occasional in-house public-service announcement extolling racial harmony, however, DC's world—its superheroes, its supporting cast, and its incidental background characters—was almost exclusively white.

But DC was about to receive a wake-up call.

superheroes followed his lead. The comics industry was experiencing a superhero boom during the mid-1960s and regarded black superheroes as a financially risky venture given the social unrest playing out on college campuses and in American streets of the day. Yet through the actions of real-life activists, most notably the Reverend Dr. Martin Luther King Jr.—the greatest African-American hero of the decade—a blending of cultures was transpiring across America, warmly welcomed by the progressive, vehemently resisted by the ignorant, and violently opposed by the bigoted.

Avengers #52 (1968) took the next giant step for African-American heroes in comics by admitting

THE RELEVANCE MOVEMENT

Writer Denny O'Neil grabbed DC Comics and its readers by their collective collar and forced them to address racism in the landmark *Green Lantern/Green Arrow* #76 (1970). A haggard old African-American man asked the following of Green Lantern, the power-ring-wielding, conservative cosmic cop:

> I been readin' about you ... how you work for the *blue skins* ... and how on a planet someplace you helped out the *orange skins* ... and you done considerable for the *purple skins*! Only there's *skins* you never bothered with—! ... The *black* skins! I want to know ... *how come*?! Answer me *that*, Mr. *Green Lantern*!

On the 2003 History Channel documentary, *Comic Book Superheroes: Unmasked,* O'Neil revealed his rationale behind that speech: "It was too late for my generation, but if you get a real smart twelve-year-old, and get him thinking about racism," then change can be effected.

A "relevance" movement swept DC's comics, and people of color at last gained visibility. "It's *important* that I live the next *24 hours* as a *black woman*!" asserted Metropolis' star reporter to the Man of Steel as Lois Lane—now with brown skin and an Afro hairdo—exited a pigmentation-altering "body mold." This scene played out on the cover of *Superman's Girl Friend Lois Lane* #106 (1970), in a tale titled "I Am Curious (Black)," described by writer Les Daniels in his book, *Superman: The Complete History* (1998), as a "well-intentioned but unsuccessful story, inexplicably named after a sexually explicit film." DC had better results with the introduction of John Stewart, the African-American "substitute" Green Lantern, first seen in *Green Lantern/Green Arrow* #87 (1972). Stewart so extolled "Black Power" that *GL/GA* #87's cover blurb touted, "Introducing an unforgettable new character who really means it when he warns ... 'Beware My Power.'" Even DC's romance titles, long the home for fairy tales starring spoiled white debu-

tantes, printed love stories featuring black women (often social workers) and men.

One "relevant" moment in a DC comic ignited a firestorm of controversy. In *Teen Titans* #26 (1970), Mal Duncan, a black member of the Titans, was given an innocent farewell kiss by his teammate Lilith—who was white. "This was a superhero group, and Mal and Lilith were friendly—why wouldn't she kiss him good-bye?" thought Giordano, the editor of that issue, in his recollections in his biography, *Dick Giordano: Changing Comics, One Day at a Time* (2003). When others at DC objected to the scene prior to its publication, Giordano instructed the colorist to color the scene monochromatically, to call less attention to it. "Regardless of its hue, it made some readers see red," observed Giordano biographer Michael Eury. Some readers wrote hate mail to the editor—including a death threat!—but a flood of supportive letters validated Giordano's gutsy interracial encounter.

Outside of comics, doors were opening for African Americans in popular culture. Primetime television introduced series featuring black leads, including *Julia* (1968–1971) and *Sanford and Son* (1972–1977). The interracial friendship of real-life Chicago Bears football stars was chronicled in the tearjerker telefilm *Brian's Song* (1971), starring Billy Dee Williams as Gayle Sayers and James Caan as Brian Piccolo. "Blaxploitation"—a trend of low-budget movies starring black action heroes—became popular through vehicles like *Shaft* (1971) and *Superfly* (1972).

I'M BLACK AND I'M PROUD

Marvel Comics once again took a momentous stride forward by producing the first comic-book series starring an African-American superhero: *Luke Cage, Hero for Hire* #1 (1972). "Lucas" was a streetwise black man unjustly incarcerated and given superpowers—superstrength and ultra-dense skin—in a scientific "experiment" intended to destroy him. He punched his way through the stone walls of jail and, as a free man, sold his augmented talents as a mercenary. With his Afro, open-shirted funky disco outfit, and bad-ass attitude, Cage was Shaft as a superhero—the cover to his first issue, in fact, was blatantly inspired by the montage motif so common among blaxploitation movie posters. He eventually called himself "Power Man," beginning in issue #17 of his magazine. (Nicolas Coppola, a young fan of *Luke Cage, Hero for Hire,* was so enamored of the character that he took his name, and is better known as Academy Award–winning actor Nicolas Cage.)

Luke Cage, Hero for Hire trailblazed a trend: Marvel broadened its universe with new black superheroes. *Tomb of Dracula* #10 premiered the vampire slayer Blade, a human/vampire crossbreed with a mission to destroy Deacon Frost, the vampire that killed his mother as she was giving birth to him. Blade rode the wave of 1970s superhero blax-ploitation, then retreated into the void until several 1990s revivals and a successful 2000s franchise of live-action movies. Brother Voodoo, first seen in *Strange Tales* #169 (1973), mixed the supernatural with superheroics. He was Jericho Drumm, a U.S.-schooled physician who returned to his native Haiti to avenge his brother's death by using occult powers. The Black Panther leapt into his own series beginning with *Jungle Action* #5 (1974), in an acclaimed collab-oration by writer Don McGregor and African-American artist Billy Graham. This duo handled provocative subject matter, including T'Challa's war with the Ku Klux Klan (issues #19–#23 [1975–1976]). Despite its innovation, *Jungle Action* was canceled in 1976 and replaced with the hero's own title, produced by the legendary Jack Kirby, who, unfortunately, made *Black Panther* (1977–1979) a routine superhero comic.

Storm, the African weather-controlling goddess, moved to the U.S. to join Marvel's menagerie of mutants in *Giant-Size X-Men* #1 (1975), and black scientist Bill Foster became a ten-foot superhero in the short-lived series *Black Goliath* (1975–1976). Discounting Storm's inclusion in the popular *X-Men* series, these titles failed to attract their target audi-ence—black readers—and carried marginal appeal to whites of the era. Only Cage's comic survived past the 1970s, and did so by incorporating a white co-star, Iron Fist. Penned commentator Aylze Jama-Everett in the irreverent magazine *BadAzz MoFo* vol. 2 #3 (1998), "There are just more white geeks in America than black. And sadly, little cracker geeks ain't down with brothers and sisters kicking honky ass on a monthly basis."

Just when the 1970s black-hero boom was dying, DC joined in with its own African-American headliner. *Black Lightning* #1 (1977) starred Jeffer-son Pierce, an inner-city high-school teacher in the "Suicide Slum" district of Superman's berg, Metrop-olis. To help clean up the community's drug traffic—and to give teens in the 'hood an empowering role model—Pierce donned a voltage-generating belt, a blue bodysuit with stylized yellow lightning bolts, and a white mask (with an Afro attached!) and took to the streets as Black Lightning. His title was dis-connected after eleven issues, falling prey to the 1978 "DC Implosion," a collapse brought on by an overaggressive expansion the year prior.

THE CULTURAL BLEND

The shackles had been broken, and beginning in the 1980s African Americans were regularly depicted as superheroes. Cyborg, a black teen whose nearly destroyed body had been outfitted with cybernetics, premiered in *The New Teen Titans* #1 (1980). New Orleans Police Captain Monica Ram-beau acquired the ability to become living energy as Captain Marvel in *The Amazing Spider-Man Annual* #16 (1982), but later changed her heroic name to Photon. In a storyline running from 1979 to 1985 in the pages of Marvel's *Iron Man,* white industrialist Tony Stark, secretly Iron Man, succumbed so deeply to alcoholism that his best friend, African American Jim Rhodes, temporarily replaced him in the super-charged armor. Black Lightning returned, not as a solo character, but as a team member, in DC's *Batman and the Outsiders/The Outsiders* (1983–1988). Other people of color came and went through myriad series, some as heroes, some as supporting cast members or villains.

Since the 1980s, black superheroes have occasionally received their own comics. Notable examples include the four-issue *Black Panther* miniseries (1988) that addresses apartheid; *Green Lantern: Mosaic* (1992–1993), starring John Stewart; DC's *Steel* (1994–1998), a *Superman* spinoff; a monthly *Black Panther* series (1998–2003) examining Wakanda's role in a volatile and vastly changing global landscape; and several attempts to revive Power Man, including the hard-hitting, graphically shocking Marvel "MAX" interpretation *Cage* (2002). The mainstream media took note when Marvel published a provocative miniseries, *Truth* (2003), which revealed that the "super-soldier serum" that created Captain America had actually been tested on black GIs, one of whom had a secret career predating the Captain's. This was followed by a series (telling the story of the secret Captain America's son) that did not cause a stir with the general public but was more anticipated in fan circles: *The Crew* (2003), by popular *Black Panther* writer Christopher Priest, is unusual both for starring a black and Latino superteam and for its unflinchingly realistic look at modern race and class relations.

In the early 1990s, a group of African-American comic-book writers and artists banded together to produce superhero comics starring multicultural (largely black) characters, presenting "a range of characters within each ethnic group, which means that we couldn't do just one book," explained Dwayne McDuffie, one of the partners involved, in *DC Comics: Sixty Years of the World's Favorite Comic Book Heroes.* "We had to do a series of books and we had to present a view of the world that's wider than the world we've seen before." Under the DC Comics–published imprint Milestone Media, a handful of series were released, spanning several years of publication. Milestone titles included *Icon* (1993–1997), *Hardware* (1993–1997), *The*

Blood Syndicate (1993–1996), and *Static* (1993–1997). Arguably the most famous African-American superhero is Spawn. Published by Image Comics, *Spawn* #1 (1992) sold 1.7 million copies and made its creator, Todd McFarlane, a wealthy superstar.

African-American heroes have been visible in films and on television since the 1970s. Black Vulcan, inspired by DC's Black Lightning, appeared in TV's animated *All New Super Friends Hour* (1977), and Cyborg was among the cast of *Super Powers Team: Galactic Guardians* (1985). *Meteor Man* (1994), starring Robert Townsend as an African-American caped superman, and *Blankman* (1994), a superhero satire featuring comedian Damon Wayans, failed to attract large box-office receipts. A similar sad fate was met by the Fox network's one-season show *M.A.N.T.I.S.* (1994–1995), starring Carl Lumly as an exoskeletoned super-scientist in moody adventures. A live-action theatrical version of *Spawn* (1997) was followed by made-for-video sequels and an HBO animated series. Basketball star Shaquille "Shaq" O'Neal portrayed DC's iron man in the poorly reviewed theatrical *Steel* (1997). Townsend returned to tights as the "Bronze Eagle" in the Disney Channel telemovie *Up, Up, and Away!* (2000), featuring a family of black superheroes. Wesley Snipes sizzled on the big screen as Marvel's martial artist/vampire slayer in *Blade* (1998), *Blade II* (2002), and *Blade: Trinity* (2004). And Green Lantern John Stewart is among the most popular heroes on the Cartoon Network's *Justice League* (2001–present). *—ME*

Alpha Flight

"One side, super heroes … This is a job only we can handle!" So says the team of Canadian heroes on the front cover of *Alpha Flight* #1 (August 1983). A spinoff from the ultra-popular *X-Men* series where the characters had first appeared, the members of Alpha Flight were the creation of writer/artist John Byrne.

They were also the first non-American superteam to garner their own title at Marvel Comics.

The first member of *Alpha Flight* to appear was Weapon Alpha in *X-Men* #109 (February 1978). In that story, a man named James MacDonald Hudson, garbed in a costume based on the Canadian flag, attempts to retrieve Wolverine (whom he calls "Weapon X") and return him to Canada. Defeated, Hudson returns in *X-Men* #120–#121 (April–May 1979) with a team of heroes called Alpha Flight, and they face off against the X-Men. This time, Hudson calls himself "Vindicator," and he is accompanied by Sasquatch, Snowbird, Aurora, Northstar, and Shaman. The X-Men learn that, prior to joining them, Wolverine had been involved with Alpha Flight in Canada. The mutant heroes would later meet their Canadian counterparts again to stop the mystical beast Wendigo in *X-Men* #139–#140 (November–December 1980).

It would be another few years until the full story of Alpha Flight began to unspool in their own series. There, it was revealed that Hudson was a brilliant engineer who had developed a superpowered armored suit and helmet that allowed him to channel Earth's magnetic fields to fly and project force fields and concussive blasts. Stealing the suit from his employers who wanted to use the suit for evil goals, Hudson sought refuge with the Canadian government. The Canadian Ministry of Defense soon put Hudson in charge of Department H, a top-secret project. Inspired by the formation of the Fantastic Four, Hudson began to assemble superpowered individuals to protect the Great White North. After his first recruit—Wolverine—left Canada, Hudson decided to lead the team as Vindicator, though he later chose the name Guardian.

Hudson's wife, Heather McNeil Hudson, had been his research assistant prior to their marriage, and she assisted him with Alpha Flight duties. When Hudson was apparently killed, she took on the battle-suit and powers of Guardian, renaming herself Vindicator. She remained the team leader on and off throughout its many adventures, until the resurrection of James Hudson.

Northstar and Aurora were orphaned twin brother and sister Jean-Paul and Jeanne-Marie Beaubier. Raised separately, they were unaware of the fact that they were superpowered mutants until they were teenagers. Jeanne-Marie had a difficult childhood and developed a split personality, with one side of her very uninhibited, and the other side deeply religious. Jean-Paul had fared better, becoming an Olympic skiing champion (perhaps through the use of his mutant powers), but he too held a secret: He was homosexual. The Beaubiers were reunited by Hudson as members of Alpha Flight, where they discovered that their similar powers—flight and superspeed—were accented when they touched hands; then they could create brilliant bursts of light.

Sasquatch was Walter Langkowski, an ex-football player who became a doctor specializing in gamma radiation transformations, such as that experienced by Bruce Banner into the Hulk. Bombarding himself with radiation from his own experiments, Langkowski became able to transform himself at will to a ten-feet-tall orange-furred creature who had superstrength and stamina.

Snowbird was Narya, a demigod born to the Eskimo goddess Nelvanna. Raised on Earth by Shaman, Narya had the ability to transform into any white-colored animal from the arctic north of Canada. Narya eventually assumed the identity of Anne McKenzie, who worked for the Royal Canadian Mounted Police as a records officer. Shaman was Michael Twoyoungmen, a Native North American who had rejected the magical ways of his lineage to become a medical doctor. After the death of his wife and grandfather—and an estrangement from his daughter—Twoyoungmen began to study the mystical arts of the Saracee (née Sarcee) Indian tribespeople. He eventually became a powerful magician.

Hudson's Department H supported not only Alpha Flight, but subsidiary groups as well; training in the lower ranks were other newer heroes as part of Beta Flight, and completely new recruits as Gamma Flight. Two Beta members graduated to Alpha Flight in the first issue of their comic. Puck was Eugene Milton Judd, a gymnastic strongman and ex-soldier-of-fortune who had been cursed with both long life and the shrinking of his body to dwarf-size. Marrina was Marrina Smallwood, a yellow-skinned amphibious girl who could breathe underwater and swim at great speeds.

Over the years, the Alpha Flight team—headquartered in British Columbia—went through an astonishing number of permutations. Beta and Gamma members joined, including the robotic Box, Shaman's magical daughter Talisman, insane mutant Wild Child/Wildheart, hard-skinned Diamond Lil, armored blaster Windshear, mind-controllers Purple Girl and Murmur, brothers Radius and Flex who could control force fields and metals, and many others. Characters were killed (Guardian, Marrina, Snowbird, Sasquatch, Box), were resurrected (Guardian, Marrina, Snowbird, Sasquatch), went insane and were cured (Aurora, Wild Child), lost their children (Snowbird), experienced debilitating sicknesses (Northstar, Diamond Lil), were cloned (Guardian), and even changed sexes (Sasquatch)! Additionally, the Canadian government disbanded and reinstated Alpha Flight several times, and Department H itself became corrupted. Villains they fought included the Master of the World, Omega Flight, Wendigo, Ranaq the Great Devourer, the Dream Queen, Gilded Lily, and others.

As a comic book series, *Alpha Flight* was at its best under creator Byrne, but he left the series with issue #28 (November 1985), telling readers in a text piece, "I've finally told all the *Alpha Flight* stories I have to tell." A succession of writers and artists have guided the book through the years, with the most famous being newcomer Jim Lee, who made his Marvel art debut on *Alpha Flight* #51 (November 1987). *Alpha Flight* was canceled in March 1994 with issue #130, but it was revived again for a second series in August 1997 by writer Steve Seagle. This incarnation didn't last quite as long, and it was canceled with issue #20 (March 1999), a victim of Marvel's bankruptcy cutbacks as much as the book's own depressed sales.

Although the series is best remembered for featuring Marvel's first gay superhero, Northstar, and for being Canadian, Alpha Flight has continued to appear in today's Marvel universe. A trio of two-pack *Alpha Flight* action figures were released in 1999 by Toy Biz, and the characters made their first animated appearance in a second-season episode of Fox's animated *X-Men* series in November 1993. In 2002, Northstar joined the cast of *Uncanny X-Men* with issue #414 (December 2002), while Aurora and Wild Child became cast members of *Weapon X* with issue #1 (November 2002). Given *Alpha Flight's* popularity among fans, it was no surprise when the announcement came that Canada's premiere superhero team would once again push aside other heroes to regain its own ongoing series in 2004. *—AM*

Alternative Futures

Hailing from the hinterlands of science fiction, the superhero genre has a history of asking speculative questions about the future. During the 1960s, a time when the promise of the burgeoning space age contrasted sharply with cold war nuclear fears, DC Comics pioneered the exploration of possible futures. Some of these "imaginary stories"—an awkward term that DC used to describe stories set outside of canonical continuity—offer tantalizing glimpses into worlds that might, or might not, one day come to pass.

One of the more memorable of these appeared in *Superman* vol. 1 #181 (1965). Set in 2965, the story introduced Clar Ken, a direct descendant of the original Man of Steel. Ken, who bears an astonishing resemblance to his famous forebear, wears his ancestor's indestructible costume, and has even inherited some of his powers, such as X-ray vision. The latest in a long line of interplanetary policemen descended from the first Superman, Ken swears to use his super powers "to uphold the principles of democracy and the enforcement of the law … never for selfish or evil ends!"

DC's Silver Age (1956–1969) was replete with such upbeat forecasts, a fact perhaps best exemplified by the Legion of Super-Heroes, a team of thirtieth-century superpowered teenagers that first saw action in *Adventure Comics* #247 (1958). The magnetic-powered Cosmic Boy, the electrically gifted Lightning Lad, and the telepathic Saturn Girl travel backward in time to offer a teenage Superman (Superboy) membership in their group. This encounter inaugurated nearly half a century of Legion stories, which depicted the peaceful, advanced civilization of Earth—and of the United Planets, to which it belongs—that holds sway a millennium hence (though this thirtieth century appears to be lateral to and separate from the one inhabited by the aforementioned Clar Ken). As Utopian as this world appeared, however, it still produced more than enough supervillains and would-be world-beaters to keep the Legionnaires (not to mention generations of comics writers) extremely busy.

DC's thirtieth century yielded a wealth of alternative-future stories. *Adventure Comics* #355 (1967) introduced adult versions of the Legionnaires, setting up prophetic expectations about the destinies of the teenage teammates. In a 1970s version of Legion continuity—the group's history is occasionally subject to retroactive revision (known as "retconning")—in *Superboy* vol. 1 #217 (1976), Laurel Kent, another remote descendant of Superman, tried unsuccessfully to join the team; her sole power, invulnerability, was considered redundant. In an earlier Legion timeline, a set of teenage twins descended from the Flash (a.k.a. Barry Allen) were

offered slots on the Legion roster, but they had to decline membership when their superspeed powers turned out not to be permanent (*Adventure Comics* #373, 1968). Much later, DC published an interstellar Arthurian epic set in a decidedly non-Legion-oriented thirtieth century: *Camelot 3000,* a twelve-issue miniseries (1982–1985) by writer Mike W. Barr and illustrator Brian Bolland.

The inconsistencies between DC's proliferating alternative futures became most apparent with the advent of Jack Kirby's *Kamandi* (1972–1978); inspired by the *Planet of the Apes* films, this series depicts a nuclear war–ravaged Earth of several centuries hence, where mute, bestial humans are ruled by sentient tigers, gorillas, and other nonhuman animals. Here, Superman's indestructible costume is a relic of an extinguished and all-but-forgotten heroic age (*Kamandi* #29, 1975), rather than a revered Kent family heirloom handed down from father to son for a millennium. In a similar super-dream gone sour, DC's twenty-fifth century was home to a time-traveling malefactor known as Professor Zoom; this self-styled "Reverse-Flash" (who debuted in *The Flash* #139, 1963) wore a yellow-and-red Flash costume (the negative image of the original) during his many battles against the Scarlet Speedster. The mutually exclusive futures inhabited by Clar Ken, the Legion of Super-Heroes, the Reverse-Flash, and Kamandi serve to underscore the time-honored science-fictional notion that the future is fluid, and not fixed. In DC's far-flung future(s), anything is possible; for example, in the year 85,271 A.D., J'onn J'onzz the Martian Manhunter still protects the Red Planet from cosmic menaces (*Martian Manhunter* vol. 2 #1,000,000, 1998).

DC introduced yet another strand in its complex alternative-future tapestry in *World's Finest Comics* #215 (1973), in which the teenage sons of Superman and Batman debuted as a recurring feature. Although DC never specifically mentioned the time frame of these stories, the "Super-Sons" were clearly the product of a possible future, since neither Superman nor Batman were then portrayed as old enough (or married enough!) to have nearly adult offspring. This wasn't the first time comics audiences read about possible future offspring of the Caped Crusader or his supporting cast. In *Batman* #145 ("The Son of the Joker," 1962), a future Bruce Wayne passed the cape and cowl down to an adult Dick Grayson, whose sidekick was the teenage son of the selfsame Bruce Wayne. Each member of this "Dynastic Duo" wore a large yellow Roman-numeral "II" on his chest as they chased a second-generation Joker. DC attempted to resolve its many incompatible might-be worlds with *Crisis on Infinite Earths* (1985–1986), a twelve-issue miniseries that hit the "reset button" on vast swaths of DC's past, present, and future; the Legion of Super-Heroes was among the alternative futures to make the cut (with the retroactively eliminated Superboy shunted into an alternate "pocket universe"), while Kamandi's dystopia did not.

Though rival publisher Marvel Comics took great pains to maintain a coherent, companywide continuity, it too presented several competing alternative futures. All of these were justified by the conceit of an infinitely branching multiverse capable of holding any number of possible worlds. But this tidy temporal resolution did not prevent the time-traveling Kang the Conqueror (a.k.a. Rama-Tut, who first appeared in 1963's *Fantastic Four* #19) from imperiling the entire skein of history. Like DC's Legionnaires, Kang originated in a possible thirtieth century, from which he traveled backward in time to conquer ancient Egypt (as Rama-Tut), and later subjugated Earth of 4,000 A.D. before attempting an assault on the twentieth and twenty-first centuries. Marvel's Guardians of the Galaxy, a superteam that fought to free humanity from the tyrannical yoke of the reptile-like alien Badoon, came from an alternate thirty-first century (*Marvel Super-Heroes* vol. 1 #18, 1969, and later series in the 1970s and 1990s).

Marvel's notion of an infinitely branching multiverse may have reached its apotheosis with the advent of the first *What If?* series (1977), which showed what might have happened had contingency caused certain pivotal superhero adventures to turn out differently. *What If?* asked and answered such questions as, "What if the Avengers had never assembled?" (*What If?* #3, 1977), "What if Conan the Barbarian came to the twentieth century?" (*What If?* #13, 1979), "What if Spider-Man's clone had survived?" (*What If?* #30, 1981), and "What if Daredevil's girlfriend Elektra hadn't died?" (*What If?* #35, 1982). *What If?* was renowned for stories depicting how small changes in past and present events might snowball into future catastrophes, sometimes leading to the destruction of Earth or even the annihilation of the universe itself. The series concluded in 1984 after a 47-issue run, and a second *What If?* series replaced it in 1989, generating 114 issues until its cancellation in 1998.

During the 1980s and 1990s, the alternative futures that appeared in superhero comics became progressively darker and more sophisticated. In Marvel's *Uncanny X-Men* #141 and #142 (1981), writer Chris Claremont and artist John Byrne treated audiences (as well as the X-Men themselves) to a glimpse of a future in which the Earth's superpowered mutants (hero and villain alike) have been hunted to near-extinction by hysterical politicians and a relentless army of giant androids called Sentinels, a cautionary scenario (titled "Days of Future Past") that has been referenced many times since both in the comics and in the *X-Men* feature film series that that began in 2000.

In DC's *Batman: The Dark Knight Returns* (1986) and its sequel *The Dark Knight Strikes Back* (2001–2002), writer-artist Frank Miller presents a future Gotham City so crime-infested that it draws a retired Caped Crusader back into action, with a vengeance; Miller's speculative dystopia not only transforms Batman and Superman from the amiable partners seen in decades of *World's Finest Comics* stories into adversaries and ideological opposites, it also lets slip the dogs of nuclear war. In Marvel's *The Incredible Hulk: Future Imperfect* miniseries (two issues, 1993), writer Peter David and artist George Pérez bring the Hulk into an alternative future in which an older, meaner Hulk (known as the Maestro) rules the world as a brutal dictator.

DC's *Elseworlds* publishing program, introduced in 1989 with a Victorian-era Batman tale titled *Gotham by Gaslight,* places familiar DC superheroes in unfamiliar times and places, both past and future. Writer-artist John Byrne tipped his hat to the speculative Batman dynasty first posited in *Batman* #145 (1962) in an *Elseworlds* miniseries titled *Superman and Batman: Generations* (1999). This story traces the crime-fighting careers and personal lives of both of DC's marquee superheroes, from 1929 until nearly a millennium later. By that time, Superman, Batman, and Lana Lang are all still alive, and dozens of generations of hypothetical future Kent and Wayne offspring have come and gone. Many of these super-descendants spend years wearing the costumes and performing the duties established by their legendary ancestors. (In the grand DC tradition of clashing continuities, Byrne presented yet another future Superman in Byrne's short-lived non-*Elseworlds* series *Lab Rats* [2002]. The eponymous team of unwanted teens sent on government suicide missions tests a time machine that brings them to a destroyed Earth dominated by a despotic, amnesiac Superman—who regains his memory in time to prevent the apocalyptic event that had created his timeline: the very launch of the Lab Rats' experimental vehicle.) Perhaps the most significant *Elseworlds* alternative future is the *Kingdom Come* miniseries (four issues, 1996), in which writer Mark Waid and painter Alex Ross serve up an apocalyptic battle royale between two factions of an aging Justice League of America; though the climactic confrontation nearly destroys the world, the series ends on a decidedly hopeful, forward-looking note.

A number of new alternative superheroic futures have been advanced over the past several years, most of them taking the tone of *Kingdom Come*'s grimmer sequences. Marvel's *2099* line (1992–1998) covered successors to several of the company's most popular characters in a corrupt and dangerous future. The occasional series *The End* (2002–present) fast-forwards to tell the sad final stories of various Marvel favorites. A more upbeat Marvel future is seen in the "MC-2" series of comics, which are rooted in a storyline about the daughter of Mary Jane Watson and Peter (Spider-Man) Parker (born in 1997's *The Amazing Spider-Man* vol. 1 #418, then relegated to an alternate reality by Marvel's 1998 "continuity reboot"), who inherits her father's arachnid abilities (*What If?* vol. 2 #105, 1998). In a subsequent series of her own, the girl—named May Parker in honor of her father's beloved Aunt May—grows up and enters the family business of costumed crime fighting (*Spider-Girl,* 1998–present). Like DC's revisionist *Crisis on Infinite Earths* more than a decade earlier, Marvel's 1998 "reboot" of its superhero continuity set up yet another new alternative future—one that is even now slowly mapping itself out, month by month and issue by issue.

For both Marvel and DC, the concept of alternative realities is something that goes both ways—and even sideways. *Concurrent* timelines have been prominent in comics ever since DC introduced "Earth-2" in the 1960s (with *Flash* vol. 1 #123, 1961) as a home for its heroes from the Golden Age of comics (1938–1954). This was followed by several other "Earths" to house the heroes from companies that DC acquired over the years (including the original Captain Marvel and other Fawcett Comics characters). This profusion of worlds was another reason DC decided to clean things up with the *Crisis* storyline. Marvel has had its share of such worlds too, including the alternate Earth on which the Squadron Supreme (a clever pastiche of DC's Justice League) operate, and "Counter-Earth," a replica planet on the opposite side of the sun where the mystical hero Adam Warlock had an odd series of Christ-like struggles in the early 1970s. For the mid-1990s "Heroes Reborn" event, a number of Marvel's characters spent twelve months in an alternate dimension not unlike the established Marvel universe, yet different enough to set up the year-long experiment of handing over several of the company's most famous features (including *Captain America* and *Iron Man*) to the star creators who had defected to form Image Comics a few years earlier.

These worlds overlap with Marvel's main continuity as did DC's many Earths, though Marvel also has had several stand-alone cosmos. These include the late 1980s *New Universe* line of comics about ordinary (and costume-less) people gaining strange powers (and, it must have been hoped, attracting audiences beyond the usual comics fan); and the Ultimate Marvel line (2000–present) of familiar heroes reinvented for the twenty-first century with a hip, *Smallville*-style spin. In 2001 and 2002 DC even broke its own taboo against such parallel presents with the *Just Imagine* line of DC stars overhauled by Marvel founder Stan Lee. The two companies have combined for an occasional imprint, the "Amalgam" line, featuring one-shot appearances of characters spliced together from each stable's stars (Superboy plus Spider-Man equaling Spider-Boy, etc.), set in a mix-and-match parallel dimension and done in affectionate 1960s/1970s-pastiche styles. In 2003 Marvel even introduced a parallel past, in the Renaissance-era series *1602,* featuring centuries-old versions of the Marvel cast with mysterious ties to the best-known incarnations.

As the twenty-first century loomed, Marvel advanced what is arguably its most ambitious alternate-future scenario: *Earth X* (thirteen issues, 1999 and 2000), followed by *Universe X* (twelve issues and several one-shots, 2000–2001), and *Paradise X* (another lengthy miniseries with its own specials and offshoots [2002–2003]). *Earth X* shows readers the world in the aftermath of a mutant plague, which gave everyone on the planet superheroic abilities as a side effect. But instead of ushering in a new "golden age," the phenomenon precipitates global famine, economic decline, and political upheavals that confound U.S. president Norman Osborn (Spider-Man's nemesis the Green Goblin back in the "real" world); a widowed, overweight, unmasked Spider-Man; a good-guy version of

Venom (who is actually Spider-Man's daughter May, bonded with her dad's old enemy the Venom symbiote); and a Captain Britain who now rules the British Isles as King Britain. These series chart a course into a fascinating-yet-frightening future that remains, for better or worse, merely one among many possible worlds. —*MAM*

America's Best Comics Heroes

The Internet-era axiom that "in the future, everyone will be famous to fifteen people" rings especially true—and can sting especially sharply—for fans and creators of the comic-book artform. By the mid-1990s, the man acknowledged by many as the medium's all-time finest scripter, Alan Moore, found that such acclaim brought no career security. Having authored the 1986 miniseries *Watchmen* (with artist Dave Gibbons), one of the few superhero sagas to register as legitimate literature and also an enduring favorite of hardcore fans, by 1996 Moore's position in pop-culture history was secure but his footing in the present was by no means certain. At that time, comics entrepreneur Rob Liefeld had hired Moore to reimagine a group of heroes Liefeld originally launched for Image Comics and later relocated to his own companies (first Maximum and then Awesome). These characters—including the Superman-ish hero Supreme and the Wonder Woman wannabe Glory—were in the affectionate/ironic archetype mode that Moore had pioneered, and his handling of the characters for the three companies brought the approach to further heights.

But the heights quickly proved Icarus-like; Awesome landed in the same historical dustbin as many Liefeld ventures, casting Moore adrift, leaving a number of his scripts never illustrated, and turning those that were into instant collectors' rarities. But like the transformative traumas of superhero lore (nuclear accidents, planetary explosions, bad business plans), the experience ultimately put Moore—and his fans—in enhanced circumstances. By mid-1999 Moore had launched an imprint of his own, America's Best Comics (ABC), under successful indie upstart WildStorm (with a "firewall" promised between Moore and the editorial edicts of DC Comics, which acquired WildStorm from Image soon after Moore joined but had alienated him some time before). With characteristic ambition, Moore imagined not just isolated adventure comics but a whole alternate universe across several titles; with sadder-but-wiser pragmatism, he and his artist collaborators ceded ownership of almost all their new characters at the start in exchange for a more immediately lucrative work-for-hire deal.

Nonetheless, Moore's publishers understood the prestige his presence conferred, and the relatively free artistic hand he was given benefited publisher, author, collaborators, and readers alike throughout his time on the titles. The line debuted with the unlikely runaway hit *The League of Extraordinary Gentleman* (with artist Kevin O'Neill), known by the general public for the 2003 live-action movie version which, remarkably, was optioned for film before an issue of the comic ever came out. A kind of *Wild Wild West* by way of *Masterpiece Theatre,* the book is a dark farce in which a gamut of literary characters—from *Dracula*'s Mina Harker to the Invisible Man—interact with each other and with real-life events in a satirical swirl of the history readers think they know and the classics they don't really remember. The book spawned a surprising subgenre of Victorian-era action strips (from Cliffhanger's *Steampunk* to Vertigo's *Barnum!*) and a second series of its own in addition to the movie.

Though ostensibly unconnected to ABC's other books, Moore and O'Neill's 1890s terminators set the tone for the rest of the line: Moore went back to the very DNA of the American action hero for his models, basing the new characters on pulp adventures and even earlier popular lore, or on equally uncharted (or at least long-neglected) precincts of popular entertainment. The main single-character series were *Tom Strong* (with artist Chris Sprouse) and *Promethea* (with artist J. H. Williams III). Tom Strong is a benevolent warrior-wiseman in the Doc Savage mold from which Superman himself was cast; Promethea, a kind of self-made muse, is a spirit of creativity with roots in personified patron saints from pagan myth (Athena) to pre–World War II patriotic mascots (Britannia, Columbia).

Also in the first batch of ABC titles was *Top Ten* (with artists Zander Cannon and Gene Ha), a superhero-team book with the twist of being a self-described *Hill Street Blues* in spandex; and *Tomorrow Stories,* an anthology of short stories concerning several characters: *Greyshirt* (with artist Rick Veitch), a mysterious detective whose trickily designed stories paid homage to Will Eisner's *Spirit; Cobweb* (with artist Melinda Gebbie), an aristocratic femme fatale drifting through homoerotic fables more reminiscent of a surrealist journal than a comic; *Jack B. Quick, Boy Inventor* (with artist Kevin Nowland), an unlikely theoretical-physics sitcom centered around a hellish rural Harry Potter; *The First American* (with artist Jim Baikie), a patriotic-hero spoof recalling the halcyon days of early *MAD* magazine; and *Splash Brannigan* (with artist Hilary Barta), an outlandish burlesque of both the "elemental" strain of superheroes (Human Torch, Iceman, etc.) and the shape-shifting school (Plastic Man, Metamorpho, etc.), in the person of a sentient splotch of ink.

As time went on, *Top Ten* and *Tomorrow Stories* were retired for a variety of miniseries and one-shots, and another book featuring the line's most popular hero, *Tom Strong's Terrific Tales* (2002–2004). That book included ABC's one clunker, *Jonni Future* (written by Steve Moore—no relation—with artist Arthur Adams), a beautifully drawn but narratively tiresome softcore-porn space-opera. The specials included a one-shot for Tom Strong's daughter Tesla, *The Many Worlds of Tesla Strong* (written by Peter Hogan, 2003); several-issue stints for Greyshirt (written by Veitch, 2001–2002) and

Top Ten's character Smax (2003–2004); and *Terra Obscura* (written by Moore and Hogan with art by Yanick Paquette, 2003), an intriguing B-movie superhero saga featuring the cult-favorite characters of the widely forgotten 1940s Nedor line (public-domain properties also still published by—pardon the confusion—AC Comics).

Lovingly executed in a multitude of pastiche styles from across the history of pop culture, the books brim with imagination and charm both nostalgic and fresh. Moore's fascination with historical permutations of heroic archetypes reaches full flower here. Tom Strong is the product of wonky genetic and social engineering à la Philip Wylie's *Gladiator;* raised by a tyrannical Victorian father in a gravity-enhanced chamber to develop unnatural strength in normal settings (while being schooled with equal boot-camp intensity), Strong emerges as a brawny boy science genius when Dad's scheme is wiped out by a volcanic eruption in the secluded Caribbean setting he's chosen for it. Adopted by a wise but unstereotypical tropical tribe, Strong develops a heart to match his mind, traveling to his ancestral America to become the benefactor of the utopian Millennium City. The tribe's mythical "goloka root" that slows his age is a handy device for century-spanning adventures that dispense elegantly with the contrived immortality of most action heroes, while allowing Moore and his artists to picture their star in a plethora of period homages and send-ups.

Similarly, *Promethea* portrays a recurring archetype who stretches back to eighteenth-century potboilers and forward through later pulps and comics. Researching the character for a pop-literature class, young college student Sophie Bangs discovers that there is actually a lineage of women who have invoked and then channeled Promethea through their own creative activities as writers or artists (and that Bangs herself will be the next one to do so). The character lives in the Immateria, a kind of heaven for all creatures of the imagination, and is a benevolent creative force sometimes manifesting in the real world. This background allowed for more

The Many Worlds of Tesla Strong #1 © 2003 America's Best Comics/DC Comics.
COVER ART BY BRUCE TIMM.

dazzling stylistic variety and historic sweep, and for spiritual storylines far from the common fisticuffs of standard superheroics. A kind of vernacular holy book, the series ranks among Moore's masterworks.

In its first five years, the ABC line earned just about every award available in the medium (including multiple Eisners from 2000–2003), attracting acclaim and generating controversy (a Cobweb story reportedly ridiculing the Church of Scientology was spiked by DC; an entire issue of the *League* was pulped for its reproduction of a Victorian ad for a feminine-hygiene product with "Marvel" in its name, no doubt to the bafflement even of DC's main competitor). Along the way, many of comics' most prestigious artists (from Jerry Ordway to Kyle Baker) had made cameo contributions, whole worlds had been created (Moore is a major practitioner of setting-as-character, from *Greyshirt*'s natural-gas-powered modern metropolis to *Top Ten*'s citywide retirement community for surplus superheroes), and plentiful new possibilities for the medium had been glimpsed.

In 2003, Moore made the bombshell announcement that he would be entering semi-retirement and shutting down the line, making comics history one last time by actually writing an apocalypse for the entire ABC world (the medium's first voluntary closure of a company). Weary of an underappreciated artform's economic grind, but with financial security ironically enhanced by its merchandizing to other media—the royalties from two film adaptations he refused to ever watch (*The League* and *From Hell*)—Moore intends to concentrate on novels, his ongoing ritualistic recording and performance-art work, and occasional comics at greater leisure. Timing this transition for his fiftieth birthday, it was what he needed to top the notorious announcement of his debut as a professional magician for his fortieth. Having dwelt in comics' future for so long, it's only fair that he should get a rest—and give the industry a chance to catch up—before he's ready for his next trick. —*AMC*

Anime and Manga

For American fans, the year 1963 marks an important date in the history of anime (Japanese animation) and manga (Japanese comics). It was in that year that *Astro Boy*—the English-language version of the anime *Tetsuwan Atom*—first premiered on American television. In the forty-plus years since Astro's arrival, anime and manga have grown from an underground murmur to a major cultural phenomenon. Even though both are still regarded as a "niche" market, it is an indisputable fact that they are here to stay.

Many American fans (or *otaku*) of the two mediums are drawn to the diversity of genres present in both—science fiction, fantasy, horror, action-adventure, and comedy—but the best anime and manga showcase strong artwork and complex storylines and character studies that often stand head and shoulders above most contemporary American animation and comic books.

Superheroes are present in both anime and manga, but while many creators were influenced by American comics and animation at first (especially during the occupation of Japan following World War II), during the 1960s and into the 1970s they sought to break away from traditional renditions and give their characters more depth and complexity—a trend that has continued to today. During the mid–twentieth century there was also a move to create storylines of equal complexity, with plots that went beyond the typical "good versus evil." There was a greater effort to explore the characters and their motivations. A prominent example is the five-member Gatchaman team from the anime *Science Ninja Team Gatchaman*. While the team sported costumes that would not look out of place in an American comic, they were also complex characters, with strengths and weaknesses that were fully brought out, not downplayed. There were major story arcs that *Gatchaman* followed, and not every episode had an "all is well again" ending. This was a sharp contrast to the animated superhero adventures shown on American television during the 1970s, and it explains why *Gatchaman* was heavily edited when it arrived in the United States under the title *Battle of the Planets*.

ANIME BEGINNINGS

Anime first arrived in the United States in 1961 with the release of three films: *Magic Boy* (originally titled *Sasuke*), *Panda and the Magic Serpent* (originally titled *White Snake Enchantress*), and *Alakazam the Great*. It was not until Fred Ladd produced an English-language version of Osamu Tezuka's *Tetsuwan Atom*—renamed *Astro Boy*—in

1963 that anime was first broadcast on American television. *Astro Boy* was the first full-length animated series made for Japanese television, and many consider it Tezuka's most important work. Tezuka engaged the growing fandom in the United States and continued his prolific career until his death in 1989. Tezuka himself had been influenced by American films and animation (especially the works of the Fleischer Brothers and Walt Disney), and he single-handedly began the modern era of animation and manga in Japan.

If *Astro Boy* marked the starting point for anime in the United States, then *Speed Racer* (1967) was the next key development. Originally *Mach Go Go Go* in Japan, the series focused on the adventures of a young racecar driver named Speed Racer. From the start, the series—the first animated series in Japan to be produced in color—garnered fans with its blend of action, adventure, fast cars, and offbeat characters. Peter Fernandez, who had previously worked on *Astro Boy* with Fred Ladd, took on the duties of transforming *Mach Go Go Go* into *Speed Racer.* That Speed himself had no superpowers did not matter to fans; it was his youth and humanity that set him apart from popular costumed heroes of the time. He did not need to hide his identity behind a mask. Unlike other animated programs at the time, Speed's adventures are still fondly remembered, and in the ensuing years interest in the character has not waned.

Another hero reached American shores in the late 1960s, but he was in full-color live-action—and larger than life. Tsuburaya Productions' *Ultraman* would set the standard for live-action "superhero versus monster of the week" action in Japan, and he would also gain popularity in America among fans of Toho Studios' *Godzilla* films (and the subsequent live-action monster films spawned by Toho's most popular character, such as Mothra and the Gamera series of films, which were not produced by Toho). *Ultraman* became the first of a popular franchise that included movies, television shows, comics, and merchandise—in both Japan and America. The live-action hero spawned a new genre—the *sentai* genre. No less than three attempts have been made to create an Ultraman series in America—one animated, the latter two live-action. Though that particular Ultraman series never came about, one popular example of the *sentai* genre, *Kyoryu Sentai Zyuranger,* was adapted into English with an American cast and achieved major success as *Mighty Morphin' Power Rangers.*

ANIME'S SECOND WAVE

American and Japanese superheroes are similar in some respects—some operate solo, some in teams; the majority wear costumes. And many choose to have civilian identities, changing into their superhero identities in times of need. In Japan, the phenomenon of *henshin* ("change" or "transformation") was a popular theme in the works of the late Shotaro Ishinomori during the late 1960s and early 1970s; his major works at that time, *Cyborg 009* and *Jinzo Ningen Kikaider* (Artificial Human Kikaider) featured cybernetic or fully robotic heroes that would change from civilian guise into "superpower" mode at the push of a button (sometimes together with a particular word or phrase). A key difference is that many of his characters felt ostracized from society because of their powers and sought ways to regain their lost humanity.

Tatsunoko Productions' *Science Ninja Team Gatchaman* (1972) shook anime to its core by focusing on the concept of the team. While *Cyborg 009* did feature a team of superheroes, *Gatchaman* introduced elements that would remain a staple of anime for years. The series itself was the first of the popular "Tatsunoko Heroes" shows that would bring a new take on anime superheroes in the 1970s. The four series of the "Tatsunoko heroes"—*Gatchaman, Casshan, Hurricane Polymar,* and *Space Knight Tekkaman*—featured more action and darker themes than superhero adventures in the United States. The storylines were more sophisticated, the characters were more fully fleshed out, and the villains spared no expense in finding new and more destructive ways to end the lives of the heroes. *Gatchaman* proved to be one of the most influential anime of the 1970s, together with *Space Cruiser Yamato* (1974) and *Mobile Suit Gundam* (1979). While the latter two were not superhero dramas—both were science fiction—like *Gatchaman,* there was a greater focus on the characters.

Americans got their first taste of this new wave of anime superheroes when *Gatchaman* was released in the United States in October 1978. Retitled (and re-edited) as *Battle of the Planets,* the series attracted many fans despite editing that removed excessive violence and the insertion of the new character 7-Zark-7, a robotic character resembling *Star Wars*' R2-D2. More than twenty years later, *Battle of the Planets* still has a place in the hearts of many.

The first stirrings of organized anime fandom in the United States began to grow in the 1970s with the establishment of the Cartoon/Fantasy Organization, and in 1980 Fred Patten's article "TV Animation in Japan" was published in the third issue of the now-defunct magazine *Fanfare.* The article was, at that time, the most thorough overview of the history of television animation in Japan. Patten not only gave a historical overview of anime, but also offered comparisons and contrasts to animation produced in the United States.

Anime continued to be imported and adapted for American audiences throughout the 1980s, but the editing and dubbing left much to be desired. One notable exception was 1985's *Robotech,* a combination of three unrelated science-fiction anime from Japan. Both lauded and condemned, *Robotech* gained a fan following that praised the show for its strong storytelling, characters, and uncompromising look at war, love, and the human condition. Since *Robotech*'s premiere, the following anime superheroes have dominated the American marketplace: *Dragon Ball* (and its major characters like Goku, Vegeta, and Piccolo), *Ronin Warriors,* and

Sailor Moon. Others have appeared, such as *Cardcaptors* (the English-language version of *Card Captor Sakura*), but the changes that accompanied its export to the States caused much controversy. Anime superhero programs have steadily made their way to American television, most notably *Saint Seiya* (retitled *Knights of the Zodiac*) and *Android Kikaider* (the English-language version of the 2000–2001 anime *Jinzo Ningen Kikaider*).

Titles such as Go Nagai's *Devilman* and Yoshiki Takaya's *Bio-Booster Armor Guyver* were released uncut on home video in the United States, since their darker themes and violence would have prevented them from being shown on syndicated television.

MANGA ROOTS

With anime firmly in place in the hearts of an American audience, the 1980s saw the arrival of translated Japanese manga in the United States. The independent comic-book companies First Publishing, Viz, Eclipse, and Lead Publishing began releasing translated versions of such titles as *Lone Wolf and Cub, Mai the Psychic Girl, Dagger of Kamui,* and *Golgo 13.* Marvel Comics produced a translated (and computer-colored) version of Katsuhiro Otomo's groundbreaking manga *Akira;* the 1988 animated film based on the manga captured the attention of American film critics and received rave reviews. In addition, the publication of Frederik L. Schodt's *Manga! Manga! The World of Japanese Comics* in 1983 was a seminal event; the book was the first to take Western readers into the world of manga. Well received by critics in the United States and around the world, the book placed Schodt in the position of becoming the leading American expert on Japanese pop culture. *Manga! Manga!* did not focus on any superheroes per se, but it was a powerful showcase of manga's diversity. Osamu Tezuka penned the foreword to the book.

Since the 1980s, the following manga superhero properties have landed on the American landscape, some with major merchandising programs that helped propel these heroes to star status: *Mai, the Psychic Girl,* a series whose title character deals with teen angst and a sinister organization; *Cobra,* an action-packed science-fiction adventure with a hero who is a former space pirate; and *Bio-Booster Armor Guyver,* a science-fiction story featuring a teen who gains the power of a unique alien battle armor. Both *Guyver* and Masaomi Kanzaki's *Heavy Metal Warrior Xenon* leaned more in the direction of science fiction, and they took different approaches with similar themes. *Fist of the North Star* (created by Buronson and Tetsuo Hara) is primarily a post-apocalyptic story, and its protagonist Kenshiro is master of a literally explosive martial art technique. Likewise, Yoshihisa Tagami's *Grey* is a science-fiction tale set in a dystopian future, but the title character is a tough soldier who ends the series as a cyborg—and a reluctant savior of humanity. The original manga for *Dragon Ball* and *Sailor Moon* debuted in the United States in the 1990s, greeting an audience already familiar with the characters.

FURTHER DEVELOPMENTS

The 1990s saw a virtual explosion of anime and manga in the United States. Anime conventions became popular, drawing increasing numbers of attendees. The popularity of videogames and assorted merchandise—for example, games such as the *Final Fantasy* series and *Chrono Trigger,* the Playstation and Dreamcast videogame consoles, and videogame consoles from Nintendo and Microsoft—helped increase awareness of the medium. More titles were released than ever before, with a greater effort on behalf of publishing companies to import more popular titles from Japan. The home-video market proved to be extremely successful for anime because titles could be released unedited, with the choice between a subtitled or English-dubbed version. For the first time, Americans also saw the remaining Tatsunoko heroes—albeit in the remakes of the venerable heroes created by Tatsunoko Productions.

During this decade, the phenomenally popular *Dragon Ball* and *Sailor Moon* were broadcast on television in the United States, with controversial editing done to both programs. Such editing, however, was unavoidable; broadcast standards in Japan allowed anime to explore darker, more mature themes—but the perception of animation as a "kids' medium" still existed in America. By the end of the 1990s, more companies were releasing anime and manga in the United States than at any time before. These included A.D. Vision, Central Park Media, Animeigo, TOKYOPOP, Urban Vision, and Viz; Pioneer and Bandai created their own distribution companies in the United States as well. Manga also moved from the comic-book shop into major bookstores such as Borders and Barnes & Noble.

The rising popularity of anime and manga in the United States led to an interesting cross-cultural exchange. American comic-book artists were influenced by the artwork and storytelling of both mediums and began to create their own manga-flavored works. Ben Dunn (*Ninja High School*), Adam Warren (*Dirty Pair*), Fred Perry (*Gold Digger*), Tim Eldred (*Broid*), Lea Hernandez (*Clockwork Angels*), Colleen Doran (*A Distant Soil*), and Richard and Wendy Pini (*Elfquest*) were part of the first wave that began in the 1980s. Frank Miller (*The Dark Knight Returns*) created the miniseries *Ronin* (which ran from 1983 to 1984) and championed the English-language version of Kazuya Koike and Goseki Kojima's classic manga *Lone Wolf and Cub.* In the following decade, these artists—along with Joe Madureira (*Battle Chasers*), Humberto Ramos (*Out There*), Pat Lee's (*Darkminds*), Dreamwave Studios, and others—worked on major American superhero titles, among them *X-Men, Gen 13, Spider-Man,* and *Fantastic Four.* In 2002, Marvel Comics introduced the "Marvel Mangaverse," a limited series that reimagined the major characters of the Marvel universe—among them Spider-Man, the Avengers, and the X-Men—through a manga-influenced lens.

In the same year, Top Cow began a twelve-issue *Battle of the Planets* comic. With art direction by

Alex Ross (*Kingdom Come*), writing by Munier Sharri-eff (*Battle Chasers*), and art by Wilson Tortosa, this new comic introduced the series to a fresh genera-tion of fans while receiving praise from older ones. And while not a superhero in the traditional sense, Neil Gaiman's Sandman became the basis of the best-selling book *Sandman: The Dream Hunters* (1999), a joint project between Gaiman and artist Yoshitaka Amano. Amano also illustrated the mini-series *Elektra and Wolverine: The Redeemer* (2001).

In Japan, artists influenced by American super-heroes and comic-book artists began their own suc-cessful careers. Ryoichi Ikegami (*Mai, the Psychic Girl*) counted Neil Adams as a major influence, and even drew a manga version of *Spider-Man* in the early 1970s; Akira Toriyama used elements of *Superman* in the wildly popular series *Dragon Ball* (1985–1995). Yukito Kishiro (*Battle Angel Alita*) was heavily influenced by Frank Miller in his series *Ashen Victor* (1999). Juzo Tokoro created the manga *Shadows of Spawn* (1998) under the super-vision of Todd McFarlane (*Spawn*).

The late 1990s saw Japanese artists working on popular American superhero comics. Katsuhiro Otomo created the short comic "The Third Mask" for the fourth issue of the *Batman: Black and White* anthology series (1996). Koichi Ohata co-wrote and penciled the 1995 comic-book adaptation of his popular OVA (Original Video Animation, direct-to-video series) *M.D. Geist* for Central Park Media Comics. Tsutome Nihei (*Blame!*) wrote and illustrat-ed a five-issue miniseries for Marvel titled *Wolver-ine: Snikt!* (2003). Yet no manga artist has gone further than Kia Asamiya (*Silent Mobius*). Asamiya, a fan of the work of Mike Mignola (*Hellboy*), became the first manga artist to illustrate a major ongoing title when he became the artist on *The Uncanny X-Men* with writer Chuck Austen in late 2002. While his run on the series was only a few issues, Asamiya had already made inroads; he created the cover art for *Fantastic Four* #59 (2002) and wrote and illustrated *Batman: Child of Dreams* for Kodan-sha (under the supervision of DC Comics) in 2000.

Asamiya's rendition of the Dark Knight was brought to the United States in 2002 and received critical acclaim. Max Allan Collins (*Road to Perdition*) adapted the graphic novel into English—but Collins himself was influenced by *Lone Wolf and Cub* when he wrote *Road to Perdition* (1998). And, after nearly fifty years, Tezuka's original *Tetsuwan Atom* manga saw release in America, albeit under the title more familiar to Americans: *Astro Boy.*

The ultimate expression of American interest in anime and manga was the 1999 science-fiction blockbuster motion picture *The Matrix*. Writer/direc-tors Larry and Andy Wachowski combined elements of manga, anime, American comic books, super-heroes, science fiction, and Hong Kong cinema and philosophy into a film that stunned audiences with never-before-seen visual effects and storytelling. The film led to two sequels that were released in 2003; the sequels had a much more prominent anime and manga influence, drawing inspiration from works such as *Ghost in the Shell* and *Akira*. There was even *The Animatrix,* a joint American-Japanese project that showcased a collection of nine animated stories set in the universe of the film. Director Yoshiyuki Tomino (*Mobile Suit Gun-dam*) commented of the original *Matrix* film in the March 2000 issue of *Animerica,* "It was a movie, but it used anime techniques and methodology. I was pleased to see someone breaking new ground in this respect."

TO BE CONTINUED ...

What will the future bring? Will interest in the superheroes of anime and manga (or the mediums themselves, for that matter) fade away? Will the cross-cultural exchange of ideas and techniques continue between Japan and the United States? New superhero titles continue to arrive on American shores; in 2003, they included *Sadamitsu the Destroyer, Idol Fighter Su-Chi-Pai, Project Arms,* and *B'Tx*. Two classic titles also arrived: the *Saint Seiya* anime (retitled *Knights of the Zodiac*) and Ishinomori's manga *Cyborg 009*—as well as the 2001 *Cyborg 009* anime series. It will take time to see how fans and the general public receive these titles. One fact is clear, however: Anime and manga from Japan have introduced Americans to superheroes and storytelling that are different from, and yet strikingly similar to, the pantheon of superheroes created in the United States. —*MM*

Ant-Man

Marvel's superhero revolution has been so successful that it is hard to imagine a time when the company was unsure about how to handle them, but in its early years there were a few strips that never quite caught on. One of these was Ant-Man, although, over the years, he has remained in the public eye through a succession of name—and size—changes. Dr. Henry ("Hank") Pym was first introduced in a short Stan Lee/Jack Kirby story called "The Man in the Ant Hill!" (in *Tales to Astonish* #27) in early 1962, barely two months after *Fantastic Four* #1; this makes him Marvel's second superhero. The tale recounts how intrepid (not to say reckless) scientist Hank Pym discovers a serum that can shrink him to the size of an ant; essentially, this plot device was little different from those used in the many mystery stories that the company was churning out at the time. However, later that year (in *Tales to Astonish* #33) Pym returns, this time with a stylish red costume and a "cybernetic" helmet that allows him to communicate with and control ants, as well as amplify his voice when he is shrunken so that humans can hear him. With a supply of shrinking fluids (later capsules) in his belt, he is ready to tackle crime as Ant-Man.

This faintly ludicrous premise inspired a number of enjoyably wacky stories—as long as Lee and Kirby were aboard. However, issues by lesser hands were a pale shadow of the company's top features, such as *Fantastic Four* or *Spider-Man.* From a contemporary perspective, nevertheless, there is much to enjoy in the series' parade of outrageous villains, including Egghead (whose head was, indeed, ovoid), the Porcupine, El Toro, the Scarlet Beetle, the Human Top, and the infamously stupid Living Eraser. *Tales to Astonish* #44 introduced the partner, love interest, and part-time damsel-in-distress Janet Van Dyne, a.k.a. the Wasp. She was gifted with shrinking powers, wings, and stingers by a smitten Pym. In late 1963 the pair were founding members of the Avengers, in whose comic book they would find much of their success over the following decades. One month later, Pym underwent the first of many transformations.

In issue #49 of *Tales to Astonish,* Pym discovered that, by adjusting his serum, he could grow rather than shrink, and so Giant-Man was born. Several issues later, the strip introduced a group of kids called the Giant-Man and Wasp Fan Club, but in reality the strip was in trouble and in issue #70 was replaced by the Sub-Mariner, just as Ant-Man and the Wasp had been replaced in *The Avengers* #15 by the Scarlet Witch and Quicksilver. After a year in the wilderness, the pair returned and became *Avengers* regulars throughout the 1960s, but all this shrinking and growing were taking their toll on poor old Pym, who first changed his name to Goliath and then had a mental breakdown, reappearing as the mad, bad, and dangerous-to-know Yellowjacket. Undeterred by her beau's raging schizophrenia, the Wasp promptly married Pym/Yellowjacket and, even though he soon returned to normal, the seeds of future trouble were sown.

For the rest of that decade, Yellowjacket and the Wasp were occasional stars in the Avengers, while Clint Barton, a.k.a. Hawkeye, "borrowed" Pym's growth serum and became a new, barechested Goliath. In the early 1970s, the pair went on an extended "research" leave of absence, although Pym starred in a brief run in *Marvel Feature* (issues #4–#10 in 1972) as Ant-Man, before returning to the group with issue #137. Though Pym seemed content to be Yellowjacket, his lab assistant Bill Foster briefly became the size-changing

Black Goliath for five issues of his own comic. The 1980s were a less happy time for the couple, with the Wasp becoming ever more prominent in the Avengers while Pym gradually went around the bend (again) in his lab. In a sequence of events starting in *The Avengers* #213, Hank had a nervous breakdown, hit Van Dyne, was court-martialed by the team, framed by Egghead for stealing some nuclear devices, jailed, freed, divorced, retired, un-retired, and finally inducted in the West Coast Avengers (as depressed scientist-in-residence).

Meanwhile, someone at Marvel noticed that there was currently no one in their line called Ant-Man, and so a new one duly appeared in two issues of *Marvel Premiere* (issues #47 and #48, in 1981). This new incarnation was Scott Lang, who had turned to crime to support his family and had been jailed for three years, during which his wife divorced him. On his release, he found work with Stark Industries but stole one of Pym's old Ant-Man costumes to rescue the one doctor who could save his critically ill daughter (and who had rather inconveniently been kidnapped). Following his first successful outing as Ant-Man, Lang was given the suit permanently by a very understanding Pym and has since gone on to guest appearances in *Avengers, Rom, Iron Man, Silver Surfer,* and *Alias.* After quitting his job with Stark Industries, he was hired by the Fantastic Four to replace Reed Richards when that character temporarily disappeared (in *Fantastic Four* #388). Following Reed's inevitable return, Lang became something of a glorified computer repairman for the team before joining the Heroes for Hire for a couple of years in the late 1990s (and appearing as mentor and rival to his grown-up, Wasp-like daughter Cassie—a.k.a. "Stinger"—in the parallel-future Avengers book *A-Next*). Like the original Ant-Man, Lang's powers are not really significant enough to sustain a solo series, but he makes a decent team player and his own insecurity and self-doubt make him an engaging character.

As far as Pym is concerned, the late 1980s saw him begin to rebuild his life and, for a while, he used his abilities (now made inherent after such prolonged use of his various potions and gases) to shrink or enlarge other objects before gaining the confidence to become a superhero again. In due time, he rejoined the Avengers as Giant-Man, once more changed his name to Goliath, and gradually became reconciled with the Wasp. Post-millennial developments have seen the inevitable third mental breakdown and the reappearance of Yellowjacket. Although this time Yellowjacket initially occupied a separate body, he and Pym were eventually merged together again and now, as Yellowjacket, he remains a central character in the Avengers. While never a major figure in the comics world, Pym has enjoyed something of a cult following, particularly as Ant-Man, which has resulted in a well-received book collection of his *Tales to Astonish* years (in 2002) and the occasional action figure and statue. His sole brush with the mass media was in the 1999–2000 Fox *Avengers* television cartoon, where he appeared simply as scientist Dr. Hank Pym. —*DAR*

Anti-communism: *See* **Fighting American; Golden Age of Superheroes (1938–1954); Superpatriots**

Anti-drug Series

In an October 1970 article for *New York* magazine titled "The Radicalization of the Superheroes," Marvel Comics writer and editor-in-chief Stan Lee said, "I feel that comics could do much good as far as helping kids avoid the danger of drugs." Less than a year later, Lee would make history with the same sentiment. "I got a letter from the Department of Health, Education and Welfare," Lee recalled, "which said, in essence, that they recognized the great influence that Marvel Comics and Spider-Man have on young people. And they thought it would really be very beneficial if we created a story warning kids about the dangerous effects of drug addiction."

The comics industry's self-censoring Comics Code Authority would not allow the depiction of drugs under its 1954 Comics Code, so a comic that broached the subject would have to do so without its seal of approval. Lee forged ahead with a novel Spider-Man story about the dangers of drugs, which he fought to publish in *The Amazing Spider-Man* vol. 1 #96 (May 1971). In this issue, Spider-Man rescues an African-American youth who, under the influence of drugs and imagining he can fly, jumps from a sky-scraper. Later in the story, as alter ego Peter Parker, the hero muses, "My life as Spider-Man is probably as dangerous as any—but I'd rather face a hundred supervillains than toss it away by getting hooked on hard drugs! 'Cause that's one fight you can't win!"

The first issue published by a comic-book com-pany without code approval since the code's incep-tion, *Spider-Man* #96 (and subsequent issues #97 [June] and #98 [July]) challenged the code to revise its language. And revise it did. The Comics Code's new language stated, "Narcotics addiction shall not be presented except as a vicious habit." With the adoption of the more lax standards, DC editor Carmine Infantino went on record in a 1971 *New York Times* article with his support of the code's new attitude: "I think this can prove that the medi-um that was considered junk for one generation will be jewel for the next. It can explore the social ills for the younger generation and help them decide how to direct their lives." It didn't take long for DC to follow in Marvel's footsteps—publishing *Green Lantern/Green Arrow* #85 in September 1971, which boldly portrays the Neal Adams–rendered Green Arrow sidekick, Speedy, shooting up drugs on the issue's front cover. The tagline? "DC attacks youths' greatest problem … drugs!"

In fact, over the course of more than a dozen issues, under the hand of writer Denny O'Neil and artist Neal Adams, *Green Lantern/Green Arrow* would tackle more than drugs in their forging of a larger comics-industry movement known as "rele-vance." Beginning in May 1970 with *Green Lantern/Green Arrow* #76, frank discussion of vari-

Green Lantern/Green Arrow #86 © 1971 DC Comics.
COVER ART BY NEAL ADAMS.

ous American social and cultural topics *du jour* took place inside *Green Lantern/Green Arrow*'s pages—including prejudice, Native American rights, women's liberation, ecological waste, consumerism, overpopulation, and campus unrest. Said O'Neil of the series, "It was superheroes questioning them-selves for the first time." This critically acclaimed approach to realism in superhero comics had come to its natural conclusion by the mid-1970s, as the readership tired of having superheroes confront social ills instead of the standard fare of mad scien-tists and alien invaders. However, with more atten-tion to narrative impact than social obligation, such themes have returned sporadically but prominently in the decades since, with the recurrent alcoholism of Iron Man's secret identity Tony Stark and the abused childhood of the Hulk's alter ego Bruce Banner being just two of the best known. —*GM*

Anti-heroes

"A fitting ending for his kind," the hero remarked without compunction, as the adversary he had just assaulted flailed toward a grisly demise into a vat of acid. This was, surprisingly, the Batman, at the conclusion of his first story—"The Case of the Chemical Syndicate"—in *Detective Comics* #27 (May 1939). Granted, his foe, a murderous "rat" named Stryker, certainly deserved a comeuppance, but Batman's action was shockingly excessive. By conventional standards, heroes do not kill.

Nor did Batman for long: In under a year his editors at DC Comics forced the character's creator, Bob Kane, to align Batman with the law—"The whole moral climate changed," Kane said; "You couldn't kill or shoot villains"—and paired him with a buoyant Boy Wonder, Robin. For decades Batman was a costumed cop and a father figure, before being returned to his foreboding roots as an anti-hero, beginning in the 1970s in a "creature of the night" movement orchestrated by writer Denny O'Neil and artist Neal Adams.

By definition, an anti-hero is a protagonist possessing qualities customarily considered non-heroic. An anti-hero may exhibit personality flaws such as self-absorption or pity, emotional extremes like rage or introversion, a distrust of accepted values, or a lack of social decorum. Conversely, a hero cut from the traditional cloth is altruistic and dedicated to righting wrongs while following the letter of the law.

Literary authors have long been enamored of anti-heroes: Mark Twain's Huckleberry Finn, for example, was a mischievous runaway who broke the law to liberate a slave. On radio dramas and in pulp magazines of the early twentieth century, the Shadow frightened criminals with his unholy, disembodied laugh, leaving a trail of corpses behind as he exacted justice, and the Green Hornet perpetuated the myth of his mob alliance to sting gangsters in entrapment ploys. In film and on television, anti-heroes are common, from the suave but roguish James Bond, to Clint Eastwood as the gun-slinging "Man with No Name" in the movie *The Good, the Bad, and the Ugly* (1966), to Michael Chiklis' Vic Mackley, the brutal L.A. cop in the TV drama *The Shield* (2002–present). These anti-heroes engage in actions that are illegal, rebellious, or scandalous, but their motivations for doing so resonate with readers and viewers.

Sometimes, the line demarcating anti-heroism and villainy is blurred. The two sides are divided, however, by the understanding that the anti-hero is driven to attain a higher ideal. There's a little "bad" in everyone, be it the result of original sin or an innate desire to nurture self-indulgence. Hence, the popularity of anti-heroes: Their methods may be taboo, but their goals are (usually) laudable.

Namor, the pompous undersea superhero better known as the Sub-Mariner, was Marvel Comics' first anti-hero, premiering in 1939. The offspring of a human sea captain and a denizen of an aquatic race, Namor harbored venomous hatred toward the "surface dwellers" for underwater bombings that nearly exterminated his people (his very first story in *Marvel Comics* #1 concluded with the caption "And so Namor, the Avenging Son, faces the surface men of the world, in what promises to be mortal combat!"). With his awesome strength, his ability to fly (thanks to tiny wings on his ankles), his command of the seas, and his unbridled rage, Sub-Mariner regularly attacked the city of New York, toppling bridges and destroying buildings. During a momentous 1941 clash with the Human Torch, Namor flooded Manhattan with a massive tidal wave. These heinous measures never categorized the Sub-Mariner as a villain, however; as Peter Sanderson observes in his book *Marvel Universe*

(1996), "Readers understood that he abided by his own moral code, according to which he was a lone avenger and defender of his people." Once the United States became involved in World War II, Namor directed his ire toward the Axis powers, even rescuing Allied seamen. In 1962, after an absence from comics along with many other superheroes, Sub-Mariner returned to attack New York. Over time his hostility quelled, although readers of Marvel comics can never be sure if this unpredictable anti-hero will resurface as friend or foe.

Amazing Man, Centaur Publications' barely remembered superhero first seen in September 1939, was not adverse to stealing police vehicles and dropping bombs during his initial appearances, but, like Batman, was soon watered down and paired with a sidekick named Tommy the Amazing Kid.

Materializing in DC's *More Fun Comics* #52 (1940), the Spectre was the next anti-hero to appear in comic books. The Spectre was actually Jim Corrigan, a hard-edged gumshoe who was the victim of a gangland execution. Corrigan was turned away from the Pearly Gates by an ethereal voice: "Your mission on Earth is unfinished … You shall remain earthbound battling crime on your world, with supernatural powers …" For the first phase of his career in the early to mid-1940s, the Spectre was essentially a "ghostly guardian" who fought criminals with a bizarre array of occult abilities; he returned in the mid-1960s to tackle magical menaces. In an early 1970s revival by writer Michael Fleischer and artist Jim Aparo, the Spectre became a wrathful spirit, disposing of evildoers in an array of ghastly manners that included conjuring a giant pair of scissors to cut a man in half. This anti-heroic interpretation of the Spectre has propelled him through several revivals in the decades that followed.

MLJ Publications, best known for its wholesome line of comics starring teenage Archie Andrews and his friends, uncharacteristically published the adventures of two anti-heroes during comics' Golden Age (1938–1954). The first was the Comet (1940–1941), a volatile chemist named John Dickering who created a gas that enabled him to fly. The Comet also wielded destructive eye beams, which he used to disable and sometimes slaughter his foes. After seventeen stories, the Comet was waylaid by mobsters and murdered. His brother Bob swore to avenge his slain sibling as the cowled and cloaked Hangman (1941–1944). The Hangman terrified his prey by projecting his symbol, a noose, against a wall or even a foe's face, and he was merciless in his missions. Both of these bleak anti-heroes originally appeared in a comic book titled, oddly enough, *Pep Comics.*

Shortly after the end of World War II, superhero comics suffered a precipitous plunge in popularity and most fell by the wayside. Cultural climates shifted as the United States lived in paranoia of the spread of Communism and of nuclear war. Heroes of that era represented traditional values, from Superman's "truth, justice, and the American way" to the old-fashioned prairie righteousness (shoot the bad guy) of popular Western TV shows and comic books. Then came Stan Lee.

In 1961 Lee had written and edited various Marvel Comics series for twenty years and was creatively depleted, ready to find another job. A corporate mandate to produce a superhero *team* (based on rival DC Comics' renewed success with the Justice League) inspired him to give the medium one last chance and create something different: superheroes with "real" personalities. With *Fantastic Four* #1 (1961), Lee and his partner, artist Jack Kirby, introduced the "FF," a family of four often quarrelsome figures banding together as a force for good. While none of these characters were anti-heroes in the strictest sense, the FF's success encouraged Lee and Kirby to combine monster and superhero into one anti-heroic form with their next creation.

"Is he *man* or *monster* or … is he *both?*" queried the cover copy of *The Incredible Hulk* #1 (1962). The Hulk, "the strongest man of all time!!!"

as that same cover proclaimed, was a green-skinned behemoth (although *gray* in his first tale) who was actually a meek but repressed scientist named Dr. Bruce Banner. Banner was exposed to a devastating blast of gamma radiation, which should have killed him but instead gave him an even worse fate: Whenever his anger consumed him, Banner would transform into the rampaging creature of rage, the Hulk. Like the Frankenstein Monster, the Hulk just wanted to be left alone, but the U.S. Army had other ideas, their efforts to apprehend the Hulk always goading him into destructive retribution. The dichotomy between Banner and the Hulk was originally portrayed as a Jekyll-and-Hyde switch, but in the comics of the 1980s it was given deeper significance by writer Bill Mantlo. Mantlo established that Banner experienced physical abuse as a child and repressed his rage for years, that anger later exploding uncontrollably as his Hulk persona. Director Ang Lee nurtured this concept when he brought the emerald anti-hero to the big screen in the blockbuster film *The Hulk* (2003). In the 2000s Bruce Jones, writer of Marvel's *The Incredible Hulk,* regularly explores the mental anguish suffered by Banner when contemplating the annihilation caused by his alter ego.

Throughout the 1960s Stan Lee continued to create a "Marvel Age" of problem-plagued superheroes, but competitor DC Comics simply followed tradition with altruistic characters—until Deadman. In *Strange Adventures* #205 (1967), sharp-tongued, arrogant circus aerialist Boston Brand was shot to death while performing a trapeze act. Like the Spectre, Brand, as Deadman, was assigned an after-life mission: to find his killer. Tough to do, given his disembodied form. Deadman's self-absorption in his search for his assassin made his motivation anti-heroic, although Brand experienced some level of redemption during his journeys, frequently using his eerie ability to possess humans' bodies to assist those in need.

Also in 1967, Charlton Comics took a radical step with one of its "action heroes." In creator/artist Steve Ditko's "Question" backup series in *Blue Beetle* #4, the Question willingly permitted his enemy to drown by refusing to rescue him. Dick Giordano, the comic's editor, admitted in his biography, *Dick Giordano: Changing Comics, One Day at a Time* (2003), "That was over the top for the time. I thought, 'we're trying to be different, we're trying to be bold,' so it didn't bother me." This story kindled bitter controversy and vehement letters. While Marvel's Hulk was an anti-hero by circumstance, Charlton's Question was one by choice. DC Comics acquired the rights to Ditko's creation in the 1980s and produced a critically acclaimed series starring the anti-hero (*The Question,* 1987–1990).

Marvel Comics introduced a pair of characters in 1974 that would ultimately reshape the mold for superheroes. In *The Amazing Spider-Man* #129, "Spidey" was targeted by a black-clad, heavily armed combatant with a white skull shirt insignia: the Punisher. Originally conceived as a relentless hired gun ("It's *you* again! Won't you ever *quit?*" asked Spider-Man as the Punisher dogged him; "Not while you're still *alive,* punk!" was his answer as he kicked Spidey in the head), the Punisher was soon converted into an anti-hero, a dangerous enemy of organized crime whose methods were sometimes more brutal than his enemies'. In November 1974 the Hulk encountered a "gaudily garbed gentleman" with "claws beared, teeth clenched, his face awash with almost feral *fury*": Wolverine. Brandishing retractable claws forged of the unbreakable metal adamantium, Wolverine's "natural inclination was to disembowel an antagonist without a second thought," notes Les Daniels in *Marvel: Five Fabulous Decades of the World's Greatest Comics* (1992). Wolverine struggles to resist his untamed proclivities, although he has killed foes in the past.

It is interesting to note that both the Punisher and Wolverine premiered during the year that U.S. president Richard Nixon resigned from office due to his role in the Watergate scandal. The American people, particularly its youth, had grown jaded by a leader who lied to them. Readers knew exactly where they stood with visceral heroes like Wolverine and the Punisher: There was no talk, no compromise, no manipulation, only quick, decisive action. This attitude similarly played out on the silver screen in two prominent film franchises, the *Death Wish* movies starring Charles Bronson as a vigilante mopping up street crime, and the *Dirty Harry* series with Clint Eastwood as the no-nonsense San Francisco cop packing a .45 magnum and little patience.

Frank Miller's Elektra continued this trend. Introduced in Marvel's *Daredevil* #168 (1981), Elektra, superhero Daredevil's former lover, is an assassin for hire, proficiently trained in martial arts. Her marks are always evildoers, but her flair for carnage puts her on the opposite side of the law from Daredevil. Her brazen methods and uniqueness immediately resonated with readers. In the 2000s Elektra stars in her own monthly Marvel comic series, and actress Jennifer Garner portrayed the assassin in the live-action film *Daredevil* (2003), with the prospect of a spinoff *Elektra* film franchise. Shortly after Elektra's debut, Sylvester Stallone's vigilante war vet Rambo drew first blood in a 1982 film, followed by two sequels. Americans were held captive by anti-heroes.

1986 was a pivotal year for anti-heroes in superhero comics. Elektra creator Miller distinguished himself with his gritty reinterpretation of DC's first anti-hero in *Batman: The Dark Knight Returns* (1986), in which a grizzled, older Batman emerged from retirement and adopted extreme measures to battle rampant crime in Gotham City. DC Comics also published Alan Moore and Dave Gibbons' *Watchmen* beginning that year, a twelve-issue series exploring the darker side of superheroes. In the mid-1980s Marvel published a limited series titled *Squadron Supreme,* a thinly disguised riff on DC's *Justice League* about a band of superheroes who benevolently ruled the world, until one of their legion led a rebellion to unseat their power.

Many new characters who have originated since the mid-1980s exhibit anti-heroism rather than standard heroism. From Matt Wagner's engine of aggression, Grendel, to DC's "greatest mass murderer ever known," Lobo, anti-heroes represent the new breed. By the 1990s they became the norm: Image Comics published the hell-born Spawn and raucous teams Youngblood and WildC.A.T.S, Dark Horse Comics' X and Ghost blasted away bad guys without thinking twice, and even the classic heroes were altered to reflect the times, including Superman, who was butchered in 1992 and rose from the dead with a black uniform and a meaner attitude (though this was one of the few such grim reinventions that didn't last for long).

The ultimate commentary on this shift in the heroic ideal was made by author Mark Waid and painter Alex Ross in their four-issue DC Comics miniseries *Kingdom Come* (1996). *Kingdom Come* envisions a near future where the conventional superhero is outmoded and a new wave of anti-heroes, many of whom are descendants of older heroes, have inherited the earth, spoiling it in the process. The series evolved into a cataclysmic conflict between the old guard and the new blood.

Beyond comics, the heroes of mass-media pop culture also reflects a brazen, take-no-prisoners attitude: Witness Tomb Raider Lara Croft of video game and movie fame, as adept with guns as she is with archaeology, and the violent, feisty anti-heroes that pepper most Japanese manga and anime series.

A devastating real-life catastrophe on September 11, 2001, helped restore some semblance of time-honored principles into the world of superheroes. Terrorist attacks on United States soil inspired a resurgence of altruism, reflected in the comics medium with new leases on life for paragons like Captain America and Superman. Those and a few other examples aside, anti-heroes, with their human foibles and penchant for swift reprisals, remain the norm. This is unlikely to change, unless human nature's unspoken impulse for permanent retribution changes as well. —*ME*

Aquaman

Although he was not the first aquatic superhero, Aquaman is the only one who has been in print almost continuously since his creation in 1941. Aquaman, also nicknamed King of the Seven Seas, first swam onto the scene in *More Fun* #73, one of several creations of legendary DC Comics editor Mort Weisinger, with art by Paul Norris. The creators covered Aquaman's origin in a mere three panels: His father, an undersea explorer named Tom Curry, discovers the ruins of long-lost Atlantis and sets up home there. From the books and records of that ancient civilization, he teaches his son, Arthur Curry, how to live and breathe underwater (not to mention swim through the ocean at 100 miles per hour), and how to communicate with and control the many denizens of the deep. Later on, the comic reveals that Aquaman's mother had been an Atlantean herself, truly solidifying Aquaman as a man of the sea. His one true weakness, however, is that he cannot survive for more than one hour without water. But since even the slightest contact with water keeps him alive, the Marine Marvel can also enjoy the life of a crime fighter on land.

In 1945, Aquaman moved from *More Fun* to *Adventure Comics,* where he stayed until 1961, one of only five superheroes from comics' Golden Age (1938–1954) to remain in print throughout the 1950s. While he started life battling Nazis, most of his strips in this later period were peopled with petty criminals, or helpless fish in need of rescuing. As superheroes came back into vogue by that decade's end, the strip was revamped and a young companion, plucky boy-hero Aqualad, was introduced. Affectionately dubbed "Tadpole" and "Little Sardine," Aqualad learns the ways of the deep from Aquaman, joining his mentor in many undersea adventures. In 1961, Aquaman starred in four issues of *Showcase,* which led the next year to his own solo comic and an ongoing membership in the Justice League of America.

Aquaman #36 © 1967 DC Comics.
COVER ART BY NICK CARDY.

Throughout the 1960s, Aquaman was a stalwart of DC's superhero lineup—albeit a somewhat middle-aged one. *Showcase* stories had revealed that he was in fact the king of Atlantis, and most of his later strips dealt with threats to the kingdom from other aquatic races, weird beasts, and alien invaders. In short order, he met and wed Mera, a water-dwelling girl from another dimension, and the pair quickly produced Aquababy. Not to be outdone, Aqualad acquired his own love interest, Aquagirl, and became a founding member of the Teen Titans. With solid writing from Bob Haney and elegant art by Nick Cardy, the *Aquaman* comic was always well crafted, but perhaps lacking in excitement. During this period, Aquaman jumped from print into various cartoon shows—first during the 1967–1968 CBS season with *Aquaman* (voiced by Bud Collyer, who voiced Superman for radio and television) and then in 1970 on *The Superman/Aquaman Hour. Aquaman* comics published at the end of the 1960s saw a punchier, more ecologically inclined approach from Steve Skeates and Jim Aparo, but the comic was canceled in 1971 and Aquaman was reduced to regular appearances with the Justice League.

However, a few years later, following the sudden cancellation of the controversial Spectre strip in *Adventure Comics,* Aquaman was rushed back, along with his last creative team, to fill the gap. This led to a short-lived revival of his own comic, which culminated in the unexpected and shocking murder of Aquababy by arch-villain Black Manta. In time, cancellation was followed by backup slots and a starring role in the long-running (1973–1986) *Super Friends* cartoon series, and to the present day DC has managed to keep the character in the public eye in one way or another.

Following the death of their son, Mera and Aquaman parted company, and the 1980s and 1990s witnessed a gradual hardening of the hero's personality, and even grittier stories. One (of many) 1980s miniseries introduced a new, camouflaged costume to replace his old, fish-scale-covered, green-and-orange getup. This run led to a regular series in 1991. Its ecological theme proved no more popular than the previous, late 1960s attempt, but a third series in 1994 met with more success. In a reflection of the current popularity of violent antiheroes, Aquaman now grew his hair long, sported a straggly beard, lost his left hand, and had it replaced by a harpoon! Mera and Aqualad were back on the scene but Aquaman's main love interest was Dolphin, a previously obscure water-breathing girl from the pages of *Showcase* some twenty years earlier. At seventy-five issues, this was the title's longest run, and it was followed after a year's break by a fourth series in 2002. It now seems that Aquaman has been forced into exile following a coup, and is reduced to living in freshwater areas, where he has

acquired magical powers (and a replacement left hand) from the Lady of the Lake. Whatever changes the character may go through in the new millennium, it now seems certain that he will be a regular newsstand presence for years to come. —*DAR*

Aquatic Heroes

Visionaries as diverse as novelist Jules Verne and oceanographer Jacques Costeau have captivated readers and viewers with accounts, imagined and real, of the beauty beneath the sea. Yet horrors exist in the murky depths, evolutionary atrocities, mutated monstrosities, and oceanic overlords that can only be vanquished by the defenders of the deep: the aquatic heroes.

The most legendary of their nautical number—Marvel Comics' Prince Namor, better known as the Sub-Mariner, and DC Comics' Aquaman, at one time the King of the Seven Seas—originally swam in opposite currents. The imperious Sub-Mariner loathed surface dwellers, routinely attacking sailors (particularly Nazi submarines during World War II) and the city of New York. Antithetically, the accommodating Aquaman aided endangered seamen and protected coastal (and other) communities from sea-spawned dangers, such as "The Creature that Devoured Detroit," an algae-monster oozing from polluted waters in *Aquaman* #56 (1971). The line dividing the two ebbed with passing years: Sub-Mariner's hostility waned and he formed apprehensive partnerships with landlubbers, while Aquaman's surmounting vortex of misfortunes embittered him.

Subsea adversaries have plagued the watery worlds of both heroes. Sub-Mariner's rogues' gallery includes the Shark, a sharp-toothed pirate who jets the waters in a shark-shaped ship; U-Man, a pariah from Namor's oceanic home, Atlantis; the Man-Eating Monsters, aquatic aliens who inhabit the forms of earthly sharks; Dr. Dorcas, a psychotic biologist commanding an army of mutant "Men-Fish"; and the fin-cowled Tiger Shark, an Olympic swimmer-turned-supervillain. Aquaman has clashed with the Human Flying Fish, a gimmick-enhanced thief plundering both sky and sea in his garish yellow-and-purple gear; the Fisherman, who reels in loot; the Ocean Master, Aquaman's demented half-brother who simulates his sibling's ability to breathe underwater with a seashell-shaped helmet; the Black Manta, one of Aquaman's fiercest foes, responsible for the death of his son Aquababy; the hideous water witch Gamemnae; and the Thirst, a sea-devouring mud-golem.

According to superhero lore, there are undersea kingdoms filled with water-breathing humanoids. Sub-Mariner and Aquaman both hail from their respective publishers' versions of Atlantis, the fabled sunken continent now a vibrant oceanic city. Marvel's Atlantis contains blue-skinned inhabitants, including the late Lady Dorma, Sub-Mariner's wife. DC's Atlantis has spawned bipedal inhabitants and a race of mermen and mermaids. Migrating there was the estranged wife of Aquaman, Mera, a native of a watery dimension where denizens manipulate the density of H_2O (Mera commands "hard-water" powers). Lori Lemaris, a mermaid, attended college on the surface world and hid her fishtail in a specially constructed wheelchair; she met and fell in love with classmate Clark Kent (Superman). During her youth, the Silver Age (1956–1969) Wonder Woman dated Merboy (alternately called Mer-Boy). Wonder Woman's maritime encounters did not end with her seafaring suitor: The Amazing Amazon's classic 1966 Aurora model kit depicted the heroine roping a hostile octopus with her magic lasso, and a (comic) book-and-record set released by Peter Pan Records in 1978 pitted Wonder Woman against the jaws of a great white shark.

Both Sub-Mariner and Aquaman splashed into comics during its celebrated Golden Age (1938–1954). They were not alone. First seen in Eastern Color's *Reg'lar Fellers Heroic Comics* #1 (1940), scientist Bob Blake creates a chemical that enables him to transmute himself into living water

and uses his uncanny abilities—which include cascading through pipes and exiting through faucets, changing himself into a geyser, and creating waves and waterspouts—as Hydroman, a goggled crusader who wears, curiously, a see-through shirt. Hydroman safeguarded American shores and skies from invading Japanese, and sometimes teamed with a young sidekick named Rainbow Boy. Hydroman's name and powers were arrogated by a Spider-Man villain in 1981 who, in the 2000s, literally drizzles on thrill seekers in the interactive 3-D Spider-Man amusement-park ride at Universal's Islands of Adventure in Orlando, Florida.

Marvel Comics introduced the Fin in the pages of *Daring Mystery* #7 (1941). This costumed crime fighter, originally naval officer Peter Noble, survives a deep-sea calamity and discovers he can live underwater, a gift afforded him by "some strange whim of Mother Nature." Donning a tan wetsuit with a shark-fin headpiece, the Fin wielded his steel-piercing mystical cutlass against Nazis and other marine menaces for a few issues before sinking into limbo. Noteworthy is the fact that three of the Golden Age's aquatic heroes—Sub-Mariner, Hydroman, and the Fin—were illustrated by the same man, artist Bill Everett.

The family of Everett's most famous aquatic superhero expanded when Namora, Sub-Mariner's cousin, dove into her own series in 1948 as part of Marvel's unsuccessful attempt to spotlight a line of superheroine comics. This "Sea Beauty" was more jovial than her raucous relative, relishing her morning swims ("This *really* works up a good appetite!") but paddling into cancellation after a mere three issues. Decades later, another Sub-Mariner relative, Namorita, was part of the teenage superteam called the New Warriors.

In 1960, Aquaman met Garth, a young boy exiled from Atlantis due to a genetic defect—his purple eyes, considered a foreboding omen among his people. Befriended by the Sea King, the boy became his sidekick Aqualad. More recently, Aqualad has mastered Atlantean sorcery and is now known as Tempest. His first girlfriend, Tula (a.k.a. Aquagirl), died heroically, and Garth later married the undersea adventuress named Dolphin, a character originally introduced in a superhero "romance" tale as a mysterious sea nymph with whom a sailor fell in love, in *Showcase* #79 (1968).

Marvel's Triton is one of the Inhumans, a shunned race of beings mutated by the mysterious Terrigen Mist. Green-skinned and scaly, this gilled explorer is adept in the ocean's depths but cannot exist outside of water, requiring a water-immersing body harness when surfacing. Stingray is another Marvel aquatic hero, an oceanographer named Walter Newell whose red-and-white super-suit's "glider-membrane cape" enables him to soar through the skies and the waters, and imbues him with enhanced strength and the ability to fire electrical "stings." He has been known to operate from an island headquarters he calls his Hydrobase.

Tower Comics' *Undersea Agent* (1966–1967) is actually Lieutenant Davey Jones, part of an aquatic-based espionage force called U.N.D.E.R.S.E.A. This Davey Jones apparently owns a locker stuffed with uniforms: He changed costumes throughout his six-issue run, his gear ranging from a midnight-blue wetsuit with a bubble helmet to more colorful variations (orange with red boots, red with blue fins, and green with red fins). Undersea Agent and his team thwarted the tyrannical Dr. Fang, who mocked the heroes on the cover of their first issue: "Those fools! Who do they think they are, to try to overcome the invincible Dr. Fang?" Jones' underwater world was besieged by oceanic oddities such as jade-skinned barbarians with tridents, a dog-faced shark that bites through subs, and a giant robot.

Similar grotesqueries challenged DC Comics' Sea Devils, a thinly disguised aquatic version of Marvel's Fantastic Four. Led by Dane Dorrance, the Sea Devils encountered giant octopi—tentacled terrors that have populated heroic fiction for

Thrill-O-Rama #2 © 1966 Harvey Comics.
COVER ART BY GEORGE TUSKA AND JOE SIMON.

decades—as well as an assemblage of undersea rogues like Captain X, Manosaur, Mr. Neptune, the Human Tidal Wave, and Octopus Man. The thirty-five-issue run of *Sea Devils* (1961–1967) is best remembered among collectors for its photo-realistic illustrations by Russ Heath, whose stunning covers employed an artistic technique appropriately called a "wash" effect.

Other seaworthy stalwarts have paddled in and out of superhero adventures, including Harvey Comics' Pirana, an aquatic James Bond in an emerald wetsuit whose high-tech arsenal (a scuba gun, his "toss-net," and his aqua-plane) enabled him to checkmate "the world's most brilliant villain," Brainstorm; the Amphibian (a.k.a. Amphibion), an Aquaman pastiche appearing in Marvel's supergroup the Squadron Supreme; Mark Harris, a gilled hybrid with webbed hands and feet, portrayed by actor Patrick Duffy in the short-lived live-action television series *The Man from Atlantis* (1977); Manta, an animated TV superhero (on CBS's *Tarzan and the Super 7* [1978]), whose ability to communicate with fish led to litigation by DC Comics citing copyright infringement of Aquaman; Moray, the wife of Manta; the Little Mermaid, the Danish do-gooder from DC's Global Guardians whose legs can mutate into a fishtail; Fathom, the water-based superheroine from Bill Willingham's Elementals; Marrina, a yellow-skinned alien who migrated from her overpopulated world to Earth and joined forces with Marvel's Canadian-based superteam Alpha Flight; and Abe Sapien, the amphibian ally of Mike Mignola's occult hero Hellboy.

In DC's *Firestorm the Nuclear Man* vol. 2 #90 (1989), the water elemental Naiad is introduced. Radical environmentalist Mai Miyazaki single-handedly protests an oil spill when a rigger's crewman fires a flare toward her. Engulfed in flames, Mai abandons ship, and Maya, the spirit of the Earth, magically makes her one with the sea. Now Naiad, Mai is living water and can summon—or even become—waves, tsunamis, or whirlpools. In 2003, DC introduced the Lady of the Lake as the concierge of the unexplored "Secret Sea," a peculiar realm where Aquaman now resides. The Lady of the Lake regenerated Aquaman's missing hand, which he lost in battle, with an appendage made of water.

Lastly, many non-aquatic heroes have battled demons from the deep. Captain Marvel wrestled an angry tiger shark on the cover of *Whiz Comics* #19 (1941), and the little-known superhero Master Key was entangled by a humongous eel in *Scoop Comics* #2 (1942). DC's Shark was a sea creature that climbed the evolutionary ladder after radiation exposure, becoming a humanoid with heightened mental capabilities, which he used to combat Green Lantern, Superman, Aquaman, and the entire Justice League of America. Luke Cage, Marvel's "Hero

for Hire" also known as Power Man, clashed with a scaly scalawag calling himself Mr. Fish, as well as a street enforcer named Piranha Jones. Even the Legion of Super-Heroes, the superteens living 1,000 years in the future, combated an amphibious mutant called Devil-Fish before learning that the creature, who lacked the ability to communicate with them, was not their enemy. —*ME*

Archie Heroes

Archie Comics is best known for the superheroic feat of continuing to thrive while the rest of the comics industry slumps, outpacing other companies by still selling millions annually and appearing at point-of-sale in supermarkets throughout the United States while most of its competition is consigned to the specialty comic shop. But the imprint that has prospered from tales of the ageless all-American teen and his madcap pals has at times also fearlessly pursued the caped crime fighter market, heeding the call of the genre's cyclical booms.

Archie Comics began in 1939 as MLJ, one of many pulp-magazine publishers that saw gold in them thar colorful costumes. Though obscure today and minor by any measure, the company scored a surprising number of firsts. For instance, MLJ debuted the original patriotic superhero, the Shield, in 1940, fourteen months before (and with an almost identical origin to) Captain America, who is widely remembered as the first and best of the type.

At the same time, MLJ brought out the Comet, an early and forgotten brainchild of the now-revered Plastic Man creator Jack Cole. The Comet discovers a gas much lighter than hydrogen and injects it into his veins (don't try this at home, kids), gaining the ability to fly and the unfortunate side effect of rays that shoot uncontrollably from his eyes but are restrained by a special visor—an unlikely "power" lifted verbatim, and much more profitably, by Marvel Comics for the X-Men team-leader Cyclops decades later.

Steel Sterling, who in 1940 acquired the strength of that metal by coating himself in a special chemical and leaping naked into a molten vat of the stuff (don't even think about it, kids), was actually comics' first character to be called "The Man of Steel," and MLJ also featured perhaps the first death of a superhero and the first "outing" of a secret identity. (Such subjects would become preoccupations in the mid-1980s, with DC Comics' infamous fan phone-in contest to decide if the Joker should kill Robin, and in the early 2000s, with Marvel's lengthy storyline on the tabloid revelation of Daredevil's alter ego.)

In 1941 the Comet was murdered by vengeful gangsters, becoming likely the first star in superhero history to die—or at least to stay dead; the medium has seen many costumed resurrections, and, with the ghostly crusader Mr. Justice, MLJ was one of several companies to feature heroes who *started* dead. (MLJ broke even on the Comet's demise, using the event to inspire his brother to become 1941's answer to Charles Bronson, the Hangman.) A different costumed vigilante, the Black Hood, demoted himself to street-clothes detective after a villain unmasked him in 1946, though for the preceding six years this most generic of superheroes had enjoyed a surprising degree of renown, not only headlining comics but starring briefly in his own pulp magazine and radio show.

But even this fame, like that of all the MLJ heroes, was fleeting; the ingratiating Archie was introduced in the back pages of *Pep Comics* (then the Shield and Hangman's domain) in 1941, and by 1945 he was the runaway hit that put all of MLJ's heroes into retreat (even taking over the name of the company in that year). It would be almost two decades before the costumes would come out of storage.

When DC rang in comics' Silver Age (1956–1969) by revising and revamping characters like the Flash and Green Lantern in the mid- to late 1950s, Archie Comics was the first competitor to follow suit, with a retooled Shield (adapted by Cap-

tain America's own creators, Joe Simon and Jack Kirby, as *The Double Life of Private Strong*). This comic was soon followed by *The Fly* (whose alter ego rubs a magic ring to gain all the powers of the insect world) in 1959 and *The Jaguar* (whose alter ego, um, rubs a magic belt to gain all the powers of the animal kingdom) in 1961. Marvel Comics had a lot more success stealing DC's thunder, while the "Archie Adventure Series" books bit the dust within a few years or even a few issues.

Regardless, Archie Comics tried again with the "Mighty Comics Group" line in 1965, hiring, of all people, Superman co-creator Jerry Siegel to script several series in the campy fashion of the day. The Fly was renamed Fly-Man; his counterpart Fly-Girl appeared; the Shield's son showed up in his dad's costume; the Black Hood and the Comet came out of retirement (or, in the Comet's case, death); and the Hangman and another 1940s MLJ hero, the Wizard, were economically repurposed as supervillains. There were occasional walk-ons by many MLJ alums, and the company even licensed an unappetizingly costumed superhero version of the classic pulp avenger the Shadow.

Capitalizing on the hip humor and hyperbole of early 1960s Marvel Comics and the *Batman* television show while lacking their wit and quality, Archie's "Mighty" titles did have a breathless, show-must-go-on exuberance that gives them a certain crude charm and admirable audacity. If nothing else, they tell a crucial part of comics history, as indicators of how insatiable the market for superheroes once was—though these books in particular were history themselves by 1967.

Later, Archie Comics met a mid-1980s superhero boomlet with a fitful revival of its own costumed heroes, which lasted two years, from 1983 to 1985. First through the Red Circle imprint (1983–1984), a banner under which Archie had published respected occult-themed thrillers in the 1970s, and then through a return of the Archie Adventure Series (1984–1985), the company revived the Fly (and his original name), the Comet, both versions of the Shield, and the Mighty Crusaders (a catchall superteam of the Archie heroes first seen in the Mighty Comics days). Some of comics history's biggest names passed through the short-lived line (including Jack Kirby and Jim Steranko, who did covers, and Carmine Infantino, who did interior art on *The Comet*), but the comics' style seems to have surpassed their substance, and they rank among the medium's least remembered.

In the early 1990s, comics companies were eager to feed another fleeting superhero craze, fueled by a speculation boom among collectors. Feeling new to many readers while providing publishers with at least some kind of commercial pedigree, the Archie heroes briefly came to the rescue again, being licensed by DC Comics for the stand-alone "!mpact" line (1991–1993). The familiar names were wheeled out with slightly unfamiliar (but none too innovative) origins and alter egos, including a Jaguar retooled to be a woman were-cat (like Marvel's Tigra), a Black Hood book in which the mystical headgear is more the star than its wearers (like Dark Horse's *The Mask*), a Comet powered by the explosion of a damaged radio antenna (?), several confusing generations of Shields, and so forth. The books generally suffered from the quantity-over-quality aesthetic that prevailed at the time, and, with only the comics-addict to sustain them, died off as the casual mass audience did. (Ironically, the rights to these characters hadn't been forthcoming a few years before, when a rising writer named Alan Moore wanted them for a little DC proposal that came to be called *Watchmen*.)

The Archie heroes occasionally cameo with America's favorite teen and appear on his website to stand guard over their own copyrights, but the company remains most amazing for the ordinary. —*AMC*

Astro Boy

Doctor Osamu Tezuka was not the first person in Japan to work on manga, nor was he the first person to create an animated work in Japan. Likewise, his most well-known character, Atom—renamed Astro Boy in the United States—was not his first creation. Nor was Astro Boy the first robot character created in Japan. Despite this, both Tezuka and Astro would go on to redefine manga and animation in Japan, influencing future manga artists and creating a new era of Japanese animation that would continue into the twenty-first century to worldwide accolades.

Born in 1928, Tezuka began his career as a manga artist during the post–World War II years in then-occupied Japan. Although a medical student, he was also an artist, a passion he had nurtured since childhood. He counted among his influences American movies, especially the animated works of Walt Disney and Max Fleischer. Tezuka would frequently cite the films of these men—the classic 1942 Disney film *Bambi,* for instance—as factors in his decision to pursue comics and later animation. He would go on to receive his medical degree, but would never practice. His first major work was 1947's *Shin Takarajima* (New Treasure Island), a Japanese sensation with an art style that gave readers the impression they were watching a movie, not reading a comic. Tezuka's works over the next forty years included *Metropolis* (1949), *Jungle Emperor* (1950), *Black Jack* (1973–1978), *Hi no Tori* (The Phoenix; begun in 1954), and *Adolph* (1983). He worked in all genres, from horror to science fiction to comedy, and he even created the first full-length *shojo* ("girls comic") title in 1953—*Princess Knight*.

Despite the large volume of his works, whether manga or animated, none became as popular as Tezuka's creation *Tetsuwan Atom* (Mighty Atom). In 1952, *Tetsuwan Atom* appeared in the comic magazine S*honen.* The story opens in the year 2003. Atom is a robot boy built by Dr. Tenma; the grieving scientist is attempting to replace his son Tobio, who was killed in a tragic car accident. Sadly, despite the robot's efforts to become more human, Tenma rejects him. Sent off to a robot merchant, the robot is sold to a circus and given the name "Atom." He is later found and adopted by the kind Professor Ochanomizu, and here begin his adventures.

Tetsuwan Atom ran for sixteen years and its success was immediate. In late 1962, Mushi Productions—the animated studio founded by Tezuka—began work on an animated series for *Tetsuwan Atom*. The black-and-white series first premiered on January 1, 1963, on the Fuji television network and ran for 193 episodes. It was not the first animated series to appear on Japanese television (that honor belonged to *Otagi Cartoon Calender*), but it would become the first animated series from Japan to be broadcast in the United States. The man chiefly responsible for this was producer Fred Ladd, who worked on adapting 104 episodes for NBC. Ladd would be instrumental in bringing over several series from Japan to the United States, including *Gigantor*. One of Ladd's assistants in the endeavor was Peter Fernandez, who would later go on to work on the anime classic *Speed Racer*. The *Tetsuwan Atom* series was renamed *Astro Boy* and began airing on American television in September 1963.

As a robot character, Astro ushered in a new era of robots in both manga and anime, and led to a new love and acceptance of robots in Japan. As a robot, Astro followed ten "laws," similar to Isaac Asimov's "Three Laws of Robotics." His powers came not from magic but from technology (no doubt Tezuka's scientific background was a tremendous asset). He could fly using jets in his feet and could also journey into space; he could speak sixty languages and had searchlights for eyes. While he was a peacemaker first, Astro could defend himself with superstrength and machine guns in his rear. His "heart" was a computer, but his power came from an internal atomic fusion reactor. In a country forever in the shadow of Hiroshima and Nagasaki, Tezuka took the initiative of using nuclear power for peace, not destruction. His strong respect for life was evident in Astro's mission of working for peace; this went beyond typical "good versus evil" battles. With his big eyes, black trunks, red boots, and metallic hair, Astro had a distinctive look that

Astro Boy #1 © 2002 Tezuka Productions.
COVER ART BY OSAMU TEZUKA.

intrigued Japanese and American viewers alike (and was even the subject of one episode of Bill Watterson's comic strip *Calvin and Hobbes*).

Astro's success in his native land caused Tezuka's stature in Japan to grow. His tremendous output and influence earned him the title of *manga no kami-sama*—literally, "God of Comics." In 1980, Tezuka won the Ink Pot Award at the San Diego Comic Convention. Astro's animated adventures featured the early efforts of several animators who would go on to successful careers as directors. Among them were Yoshiyuki Tomino (*Mobile Suit Gundam*), Rin Taro (*Galaxy Express 999*), Osamu Dezaki (*Space Adventure Cobra*), and Noburo Ishiguro (*Space Cruiser Yamato, Macross*). Tezuka also influenced new generations of manga artists, some of whom worked with him as assistants. Among them were Shotaro Ishinomori (*Cyborg 009*), Reiji Matsumoto (*Space Pirate Captain Harlock*), and Buichi Terasawa (*Cobra, Midnight Eye Goku*). Even American artists such as Wendy Pini (*Elfquest*) and Scott McCloud (*Zot!, Understanding Comics*) count Tezuka as a major influence.

In 1980, Tezuka brought Astro back to television, this time through Tezuka Productions (Mushi Productions had gone bankrupt several years earlier). This time, Noburo Ishiguro would direct the fifty-two-episode series, now in color and called *Shin Tetsuwan Atom* (New Mighty Atom). The show was now set in 2030, and Tezuka had a more direct hand in the scripts. A new character was added, a robot girl named Uran (Astro Girl in the American version). During the 1990s, the anime distributor The Right Stuf International released the original black-and-white series on video in the United States. Manga Entertainment released the newer series in 2002 under the title of *Astro Boy New Adventures.* A new animated series produced by Sony Pictures and Tezuka Productions began airing in Japan in April 2003 (to coincide with the date given for Astro's construction—April 7, 2003), with a dubbed version airing in the United States on the Kids' WB! network in early 2004. An all-computer-generated, American-produced Astro Boy movie has been discussed since 1999 but still had no definite release date as of early 2004.

While there had been an *Astro Boy* comic released by Gold Key in 1965, it had been heavily redrawn and reedited from an original Tezuka story. Now Comics published a monthly Astro Boy series in 1987 with Michael Dimpsey writing and Ken Steacy (*Tempus Fugitive*) and Rodney Dunn providing the art. Fred Patten also assisted with the plot. It was not until 2002 that the original *Tetsuwan Atom* manga was released in the United States through Dark Horse Comics and Studio Proteus. Now titled *Astro Boy,* the translation was done by Frederick L. Schodt (*Manga! Manga! The World of Japanese Comics*), who had been a close friend of Tezuka's and worked as a translator for him. The translated manga ran for over fifteen volumes.

Sadly, Tezuka would not see this new flurry of interest in Astro Boy in the American popular culture; he died in 1989 from complications due to stomach cancer. However, Tezuka's legacy has lived on in new animated works based on his manga—including Astro Boy. And in the actual, real-world field of robotics, Astro has also had a profound effect. In Japan, many entered the field because they had seen or read Astro's adventures as children. Both America and Japan have pursued the construction of new, advanced robots, but in Japan, there has been a movement toward more humanoid-shaped machines. Among the results of this effort were the P-series robots built by Honda; the successor of these robots was Asimo, a fully mobile, walking humanoid robot that was unveiled in 2002. In August 2003, the Atom Project was proposed by a group of Japanese researchers, with the ultimate goal being the creation of a humanoid robot with the emotional, physical, and mental capacity of a five-year-old human child. —*MM*

Astro City

Astro City is the preeminent city in America, and the hub of superpowered activities on Earth. But how do its residents view their superheroic protectors and the villains they oppose, as well as assorted aliens, monsters, and other menaces? And how do the heroes themselves feel about their lives when they aren't fighting crime? These themes are explored in *Astro City,* a comic-book series created by writer Kurt Busiek in August 1995 for Image Comics imprint WildStorm (and originally titled *Kurt Busiek's Astro City*). Busiek worked with interior artist Brent Anderson and cover painter Alex Ross to create a world that was the opposite in theory from the "realistic" comics of the 1990s. Instead of examining what superheroes would be like in the real world, he posed the question, "What would the world be like if superheroes were commonplace?"

Astro City has many archetypal heroes, but their private lives—and interaction with the world around them—is richer than in many comic-book series. The Superman-like Samaritan flies from rescue to rescue, never able to enjoy the sensation of flight except in his dreams. Winged Victory prioritizes those she will aid: women first, men second. The superpowered Astra, ten-year-old daughter and member of The First Family, wants to learn to play hopscotch and go to school with normal kids. Jack-in-the-Box uses toys to fight crime but worries about his own upcoming child. Dark avenger the Confessor hides a startling secret from everyone, including his teen sidekick, Altar Boy. An ex-villain named Steeljack gets out of prison and tries to resume a normal life, despite his silver skin. A cartoon anthropomorphic lion brought to life experiences the ups and downs of Hollywood stardom.

Not only the heroes are under the spotlight in Astro City. As he did in his landmark series Marvels—in which he examined the history of Marvel Comics heroes through the eyes of a newspaperman—Busiek often uses ordinary people and their perceptions to tell about the world of Astro City. Whether it is a newspaper reporter who cannot prove the astonishing adventure he witnessed with Silver Agent and the Honor Guard, a thief who discovers Jack-in-the-Box's identity and imagines what the knowledge could do for him, a second-generation immigrant girl who finds the monster-filled Shadow Hill neighborhood more comforting than the gleaming city, or a father concerned about moving his family to Astro City because of the super-violence, the ordinary citizens of this metropolis make as much of an impact in Astro City stories as do the heroes.

The Astro City series also features many homages to past comic-book creators. Street, store, and building names are rife with comic book

Astro City #1 © 1995 Juke Box Productions.
COVER ART BY ALEX ROSS.

connections. Binderbeck Plaza, the heart of Astro City, is named after the creators of Captain Marvel, Otto Binder and C. C. Beck, while Iger Square, Grandenetti Avenue, and Feldstein's Bar & Grill refer to artists Jerry Iger and Jerry Grandenetti, and EC Comics/*MAD* magazine editor Al Feldstein.

Since its inception, Astro City has had an irregular publishing schedule, but given its anthology format, the wait for issues is not as difficult as for serialized storylines. Four hardcover collections and trade paperbacks of Astro City are available, and the series (under various names, including the five-issue Astro City: Local Heroes miniseries in 2003–2004) is ongoing from DC Comics' WildStorm/Homage imprint. A short-lived series of *Astro City* action figures was also released in 1999 by Toy Vault, and Bowen Designs released a Samaritan statue in April 1999. —*AM*

Atlas Comics: *See* **Bronze Age of Superheroes (1970–1979); Cat Heroes; Insect Heroes**

The Atom

There has always been a place in comics for the little guy, and few came any smaller than DC's Atom—or rather, both of them! The first Atom premiered in *All-American Comics* #19 in late 1940 and very soon afterward began appearing as a member of the Justice Society in *All Star Comics.* The young Al Pratt, a student at Calvin College, is tired of being teased about his diminutive stature and, to impress his sweetheart Mary James, vows to transform his body into something more presentable. Through intensive training with former boxing champ Joe Morgan, he is soon immensely powerful. After donning a brown-and-yellow weightlifting costume (complete with straps and buckles), with a blue cowl and cape, the Atom starts a one-man crusade against crime and injustice.

Without doubt, the Atom was one of the most uncomplicated characters of the Golden Age of comics (1938–1954); he had no superpowers, secret hideouts, sidekick, weaponry, or gimmicks. What the strip had, particularly when drawn by the gritty Joe Gallacher, was a sort of down-at-the-heels honesty, as the hero took on a variety of hoodlums and gangsters in a succession of short, punchy yarns. Considering how basic the feature's premise was, it is surprising that the Atom was to prove so enduring, but he outlasted many of his more flamboyant colleagues. He starred in over fifty issues of *All-American Comics* and, when he was ignominiously displaced from that title by Inky, Winky and Noddy (!), he moved right on over to *Flash Comics* for a few more years' worth of strips. In *All Star Comics* he was to prove one of the most enduring members of

Showcase #35 © 1961 DC Comics.
COVER ART BY GIL KANE AND MURPHY ANDERSON.

the Justice Society of America, starring in almost every story until the comic's demise in 1951. By this time, he had undergone a radical revamp in which he had somehow acquired "atomic strength" and sported a new costume, topped off with a fin on his head.

Al Pratt's Atom was next seen, along with the rest of the Justice Society, a decade later in the 1960s, but he was only an occasional participant in their adventures, perhaps because another Atom had been created in his absence. Following the success of the Flash and Green Lantern, DC editor Julius Schwartz was looking for another Golden Age character to revamp when artist Gil Kane brought in some new designs for the Atom. Kane was inspired by Quality Comics' Dollman, and his Atom update was similarly a hero who could shrink himself down to an almost microscopic size. Over three issues of *Showcase* in 1961 and 1962, Schwartz, Kane, and writer Gardner Fox introduced physics professor Ray Palmer, whose experiments with fragments of a white dwarf star enable him to shrink almost at will. After discovering that his best size is six inches, Palmer dons the requisite red-and-blue superhero costume and embarks on a clandestine career as a crime fighter.

Schwartz and Fox had a solid background in science fiction, and consequently the Atom's adventures were frequently based on some sort of scientific conundrum or another, be it a natural disaster or a trip back in time to meet Jules Verne or Edgar Allen Poe. When shrunk, the Atom had increased physical strength but was still something of a lightweight compared to heavy-hitters such as Superman or Wonder Woman, and so his villains, like Jason Woodroe the Plant Master or the stripey-costumed Chronos, also tended to be second rate. In civilian life, Ray Palmer was courting the pretty lawyer Jean Loring, but the pair acted more like a middle-aged couple than young lovers, and the feature as a whole was beautifully illustrated but ultimately rather dry. After thirty-eight issues of his own title (including two guest appearances from his Golden Age counterpart) and six more co-headlining with Hawkman, the Atom was relegated to a backup slot in *Action Comics.*

Throughout the 1960s and 1970s, the Atom (by now married to Loring) was a regular member of the Justice League of America, and that seemed to be enough for most fans, few of whom were clamouring for a new Atom comic. However, Gil Kane still fondly remembered his creation and, together with writer Jan Strnad, brought out a miniseries, *Sword of the Atom,* in 1983. After finding out that his wife was having an affair, Palmer flew out to the Amazon, where he discovered a tribe of minute, yellow-skinned barbarians, which he promptly joined. This new direction, which continued in a series of specials throughout the 1980s, owed more to Conan

than a regular superhero book and was surprisingly well written. However, a subsequent 1988 regular series was a more pedestrian retread of the 1960s, and interest once more died out.

The 1990s brought an appearance in the *Zero Hour* miniseries and a rather unexpected transformation: the now resolutely middle-aged Palmer was bizarrely changed into a seventeen-year-old. The teenage Palmer did the only logical thing a teenage superhero could do: He joined DC's all-purpose kid group, the Teen Titans. In 1997, the Justice League was relaunched with its original 1960s lineup including, of course, the Atom, and it is there that he continues to appear to this day, with his temporary youthful transformation apparently forgotten by everyone, including the comic's creators. —*DAR*

Atomic Heroes

It is no exaggeration to say that the advent of the nuclear age changed the world as we knew it, and the world of comics echoed that sense of wonder and uncertainty. Initially, the atomic bomb was seen as a positive development, at least as far as the war effort was concerned, and comics were quick to exploit this (in fact, some even speculate that Burtis Publishing's *Atomic Bomb* #1 pre-dates the Hiroshima bomb). The first significant atomic superhero was Atomic Man, who debuted in a 1943 issue of Prize Publishing's *Headline Comics*. Atomic Man dispatched underworld hoods with a quick zap of his fingers, but it could be argued that his most notable features were his peculiarly Aztec-style helmet and the fact that he wore a skirt. Atomic Man was not, however, unique: Other titles such as *Atoman, Atomic Thunderbolt,* and two separate *Atomic Comics* appeared in 1946.

Even at this early date there was ambivalence and uncertainty about the bomb. On one side there were broadly positive "atomic" stories in strips as diverse as those of Superman, the Shadow, Mid-

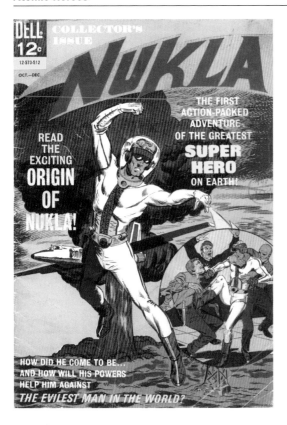

Nukla #1 © 1965 Dell.
COVER ART BY DICK GIORDANO AND SAL TRAPANI.

night, Robin, Superduck (in which the cantankerous mallard makes his own A-bomb) and Pyroman, who was shown on the cover of *Startling Comics* #41 jubilantly hugging his own atom bomb. On the other hand, the horror and anxiety resulting from the devastation caused in Hiroshima and Nagasaki were reflected in a 1946 Captain Marvel story in which all manner of countries nuke each other into oblivion, leaving the Captain the last man alive on the planet. But this was only an imaginary story, so that's all right, then.

After this initial flurry of atomic activity, publishers turned their attention elsewhere until cold war proliferation and the Korean War in particular put the red menace firmly on the map. Apocalyptic tomes, such as Ace's *World War III* and *Atomic War,* and ACG's *Commander Battle and His Atomic Sub,* reflected the hysteria and paranoia of the early 1950s, and inevitably the superhero books got mixed up in that turmoil, too. Unlike the 1940s, however, this time around it was atomic villains who started popping up, such as Doll Man's foe the Radioactive Man, Plastic Man's Mr. Fission, and Airboy's Living Fuse. By and large, mainstream superheroes (those few that were left in the 1950s) stayed untouched by the genre, with the exception of a unique bunch of costumed heroes from the reliably eccentric Charlton Comics. For reasons known only to itself, the company decided that the world was crying out for cute costumed critters with an atomic bent, and so Atomic Mouse, Atomic Rabbit (later changed to Atomic Bunny), and Atom the Cat hit the stands. Each minuscule marvel had his own unique way of charging up: Atomic Mouse guzzled uranium pills before flying into action, and Atomic Rabbit ate irradiated Carrot Cubes, while Atom the Cat merely needed to eat a fish! As bizarre as it might seem, Charlton appeared to have hit upon something, with Atomic Mouse thrilling fans for an astonishing ten years before hanging up his cape in 1963. By that time, the rest of the industry had learned to love the bomb—well, almost.

Once again, Charlton led the way when in 1960 their top artist, Steve Ditko, introduced Captain Atom in the pages of *Space Adventures.* Air Force scientist Captain Adam is blown to smithereens in a rocket accident, but mysteriously reconstitutes himself as the atomic-powered (and very shiny) Captain Atom. A few years later, Dell's Nukla had an almost identical origin, except that he is shot down by the reds, while over at Gold Key Dr. Solar, Man of the Atom, was an irradiated scientist who ends up with great powers, green skin, and a lousy costume.

Clearly, atomic power possessed an awe-inspiring force but carried with it a terrible price. Nowhere was this better reflected than at the newly resurgent Marvel Comics of the 1960s. Whereas writers had traditionally fallen back on magic, mad scientists, or courage, determination, and a snazzy costume for their heroes' origins, Marvel's Stan Lee seized on the infinite mutations of radiation. The Fantastic Four, for example, were created when their rocket flew through a storm of cosmic rays; the Incredible Hulk was transformed by gamma rays from a "G-bomb" during a test explosion; young Peter Parker became Spider-Man after a bite from a radioactive spider; and Daredevil's extraordinary senses developed after he was hit and blinded by a radioactive canister. The X-Men were a group of teenage mutants gathered together by Professor X. While the cause of their mutation is never specified, the side effects of radiation were becoming better known at that time and so it is no great stretch of the imagination to see these characters, too (who would later be called "children of the atom"), as nuclear heroes. Another Marvel character that makes it into the nuclear club through unusual qualifications is Hyperion, a Superman pastiche the first of whose several origins over the years involved him escaping a doomed planet (just like Superman's Krypton) that turns out to be the first atom ever split by Earth scientists!

The growing ambivalence and fear about nuclear power were reflected in Lee's "heroes with problems." Because of their powers and appearance, the X-Men, Spider-Man, and the Fantastic Four's Thing became outcasts from society. The Hulk's alter ego, Bruce Banner, not only became an emerald monster but also lost control of his mind, while Daredevil's powers must have been scant consolation for the loss of his sight. After the nuclear 1960s, Marvel's later heroes were again frequently mutants of various types, and the publisher's atomic heroes came to dominate the industry. Over at rival DC Comics, on the other hand, radiation and mutation rarely raised their ugly heads—with one notable exception. The Atomic Knights, who debuted in *Strange Adventures* in 1960, were six indomitable heroes in a post-nuclear-war 1986 (!) who walked around in medieval suits of armor, which supposedly protected them against radiation.

Some fifteen years later, that same postwar future was revisited in a short-lived Hercules title that starred the Greek god of legend, mutants, armies, talking apes, and the self-same Atomic Knights.

However, as the threat of global nuclear war has receded and distrust of "peaceful" nuclear power has increased, the subject has largely disappeared from comics. One exception was 1978's Firestorm, the Nuclear Man, who was created by a bomb in a nuclear reactor. He rejoiced in the ability to throw atomic fireballs and had hair of fire. Tellingly, before the explosion young Ronnie Raymond had been protesting against nuclear power, an indication that comics and society had moved a long way from the brave new world of 1945 and the Atomic Man. (The distance is also measured by Bongo Comics' buffoonish Radioactive Man and Fallout Boy, a retro parody of optimistic atomic heroes appearing in what's billed as "Bart Simpson's Favorite Comic.") Post–Three Mile Island atomic characters have tended to be villains, such as Ghost Rider's Nuclear Man and Superman's the Atomic Skull ("the man with the self-destruct mind"!), though Marvel's mutants still dominate both the company and the marketplace. Since contemporary superheroes are increasingly realistic, the days of ludicrous mutations and nuclear-powered rabbits may be long gone, but atomic energy has a lengthy half-life and the atomic heroes will probably be around for a long time to come, too. —*DAR*

The Authority

"We are the Authority. Behave." So admonished Jenny Sparks, the leader of the superpowered group known as the Authority, after the group had substantially altered the political and physical aspects of an alternate Earth. In those words, she gave the dichotomy of the comic-book series *The Authority*, published by WildStorm Comics. By implication, she was telling the people of Earth that the group would force them to behave, but the Authority itself did not behave. Winning the day at any cost, the Authority protected humankind while making decisions about its future.

Many members of the Authority had previously been members of the United Nations–sponsored superhero team Stormwatch, but when that team dissolved (and the *Stormwatch* series was canceled in 1998), a new group was formed. The Authority is headquartered aboard the Carrier, an immense ship that can travel between dimensions on the edge of "the Bleed," but which likes to stick close to Earth. The Carrier can open "doors," allowing the team to teleport almost anywhere in the known world.

Utilizing her vast experience and wielding electrical powers, Sparks was the one-hundred-year-old leader of the team until her death at midnight on December 31, 1999. She was then replaced by Jenny Quantum, a fast-growing, precocious infant who was adopted by Apollo and Midnighter, a pair of gay heroes in a committed relationship.

Apollo's powers are akin to Superman's. He can fly at tremendous speed, has enhanced strength and heat vision, can survive in space, and is powered by absorbing sunlight. Midnighter is as dark as Apollo is light. Essentially Batman-like, Midnighter is a scrappy fighter dressed in black leather who is capable of analyzing fights in a way that allows him to win most of the time.

The Engineer is Angela Spica, a woman whose blood is actually mechanical, allowing her to control machinery and morph her body's protective covering to include weaponry. She is the second Engineer; the other multi-generational hero in the group is the Doctor. Latest in a long line of shamanistic magicians, the Doctor can converse with all the Doctors before him (of which Albert Einstein and Jesus Christ are two), and can magically transmute matter into living material such as trees or flowers.

Jack Hawksmoor and Swift make up the rest of the team. Hawksmoor can channel the spirit of cities, allowing himself to merge with concrete streets and steel buildings, and to utilize their strength. The winged Swift (Shen Li-Min) is a huntress, viciously attacking from the air. Over the course of their adventures, the team members face an array of villains, including evil Asian clone-maker Kaizen Gamorra, British soldiers from an alternate Earth known as Sliding Albion, a group of characters resembling Marvel Comics' Avengers (if they were rapists and murderers), and more.

The first twelve issues of *The Authority* (May 1999–April 2000) were written by Warren Ellis and drawn by Bryan Hitch and Paul Neary. They quickly established that they were telling grand tales on a big canvas; the first four-part storyline had Moscow wiped out by hundreds of superpowered clones, then London and Los Angeles attacked as well. A second four-part story saw the Earth being invaded from an alternate dimension, while the third four-parter revealed that Earth was actually created by an alien being that now wanted to reclaim it. In essence, the Authority had to face "God" and stop it.

Under Ellis, Hitch, and Neary, *The Authority* became both a sales success and a critical success, but the team left the series en masse with issue #12 in April 2000. Coming on board was writer Mark Millar, aided by artist Frank Quitely (and other guest artists as needed). *The Authority* soon took a nastier turn; instead of grand, huge storylines and heroic actions, the Authority were now merciless and political, facing fewer cosmic evils and determined to change the world as they saw fit. Millar's dialogue was coarser as well, and his stories tended toward lots of violence, mayhem, rape, and taboo-breaking. Millar even managed to offend fans of one of the comics world's patron saints, super-artist Jack Kirby; in one storyline, Millar's Kirby-like Jacob Krigstein character is the villain. Another storyline completely replaced the Authority with new, similar characters, who were even more debased than their predecessors. The real Authority, thankfully, returned by the end of that arc.

By early 2001, Quitely quit the book—multiple issues had required fill-in artists already—and Art

Adams stepped aboard, but *The Authority* was mired in controversy (although sales stayed high). When news was leaked that pages from *The Authority* were being censored after the September 11 attacks—removed or changed were political scenes, extreme gore, and over-the-top debasement—the series' already shaky publishing schedule became disrupted further. A completed forty-eight-page *The Authority: Widescreen* special was indefinitely postponed due to some scenes rife with devastation in New York City.

Millar's run on *The Authority* finally ended with an extremely delayed issue #29 (July 2002)—an issue that featured a comics industry first: a gay wedding—and with the exception of some one-shots and specials, the series disappeared. Despite the uncertainty about the series' future, corporate synergy did allow for a set of four *Authority* action figures to be released by DC Direct in August 2002.

In July 2003, WildStorm and DC revived *The Authority* as an ongoing monthly series, under the new creative team of writer Robbie Morrison and artists Dwayne Turner and Sal Regla. In late 2003, the creative team of writer Ed Brubaker and hot artist Jim Lee was announced. A role-playing game based on the series has been tapped for 2004 release. Whether *The Authority* can regain its status as both a best-seller and a genre-buster remains to be seen. —*AM*

The Avengers

In 1963 Marvel Comics was riding an unprecedented wave of sustained success with series such as *The Fantastic Four, The Amazing Spider-Man,* and *The Uncanny X-Men,* two of which featured superhero teams. But rival publisher DC Comics (coyly referred to by Marvel writer/editor Stan Lee as "the Distinguished Competition") had already struck paydirt three years earlier with *Justice League of America,*

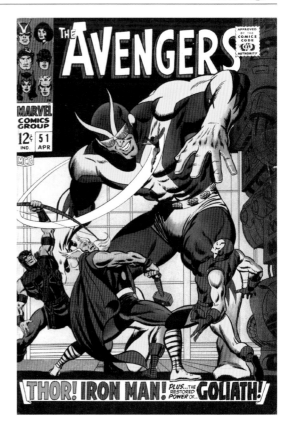

The Avengers #51 © 1968 Marvel Comics.
COVER ART BY JOHN BUSCEMA.

which presented the company's best-selling heroes operating together as a crime-fighting team. Marvel's initial response to the Justice League of America (JLA) had been 1961's *The Fantastic Four,* which consisted of heroes created from whole cloth (with the exception of a second-generation Human Torch), because Marvel had no preexisting heroes then capable of competing with the likes of DC's Superman, Batman, Wonder Woman, the Flash, and Green Lantern. A mere two years later, the publishing landscape had changed considerably in Marvel's favor, enabling Lee and artist Jack Kirby to assemble enough successful Marvel headliners to form a supergroup title in the JLA mold with *The Avengers* (whose first issue bore a September 1963 cover date).

The Avengers, however, was anything but a carbon copy of *Justice League of America,* whose members exhibited a stilted uniformity, at times seeming almost interchangeable. Marvel's new team not only showed real diversity, but also owed its existence largely to the machinations of a villain. Loki, the Norse god of evil, maneuvers his half-brother, the thunder god Thor (from the pages of *Journey into Mystery*), into a battle against the Hulk (whose first six-issue *Incredible Hulk* series had concluded with its March 1963 issue), a fracas that also attracts the attention of Iron Man (who debuted in March 1963's *Tales of Suspense* #39), Ant-Man, and his crime-fighting partner and paramour, the Wasp (both of whom maintained an address in *Tales to Astonish*). Although this *ad hoc* quartet at first believes the Hulk to be the villain responsible for an act of railway sabotage, Loki quickly emerges as the real culprit and suffers a decisive defeat. Before the heroes disperse to their respective titles, Ant-Man suggests that they make their association a permanent one, and the Avengers (a name suggested by the Wasp) is born. Even the notably antisocial Hulk agrees to become part of this new crime-fighting quintet, hoping that by keeping such heroic company he will discourage the military from continually hounding him.

In the mastheads of many Avengers stories of the 1970s, the group's origin and subsequent history are aptly encapsulated: "And there came a day unlike any other, when Earth's mightiest heroes and heroines found themselves united against a common threat! On that day, the Avengers were born—to fight the foes no single super hero could withstand! Through the years, their roster has prospered, changing many times, but their glory has never been denied! Heed the call, then—for now, the Avengers Assemble!" Indeed, the aforementioned roster changes begin almost immediately, with the departure of the Hulk (*The Avengers* #2, 1963) and the induction of Captain America after his recovery from the block of ice in which he had been frozen since the end of the World War II (issue #4, 1964). Captain America (whose 1950s incarnation is conveniently ignored) suffers tremendous angst because of his displacement in time and agonizes over the wartime death of his kid sidekick Bucky Barnes; this poignant characterization, and the contrast between Cap's steadfast patriotism and the hot-headedness of some of his younger teammates, swiftly become two of the group's essential dramatic foci—as does the return of the Nazi Baron Zemo, Captain America's arch-foe, and his Masters of Evil, a collection of superpowered opponents already familiar to the other Avengers.

With issue #16 (1965), the original Avengers roster is replaced entirely by newcomers (though overseen by Captain America). "One great thing about the Avengers team," Lee recalled, "is the fact that we could always change the lineup of heroes. Over the years, we've probably had every one of our heroes, and villains too, appearing in *The Avengers* from time to time. As you might imagine, my biggest problem was finding things for them to avenge, month after month."

The Avengers distinguished itself from *Justice League of America* in another important respect: It questioned the idea of heroism itself. While the JLA members were all unambiguous good guys—so much so that they were virtually indistinguishable from one another, except by their costumes—more than a few Avengers started their careers on the wrong side of the thin spandex line that separates hero from villain. When Thor, Giant-Man (the former Ant-Man, who would later change his name again to Goliath), and the Wasp simultaneously leave the team, Captain America finds himself heading a new squad of Avengers: Hawkeye, an accomplished archer in the mold of DC's Green Arrow; Quicksilver, a mutant speedster reminiscent of DC's Flash; and the Scarlet Witch (Quicksilver's sister), a young woman with the power to alter probabilities using an inborn "hex power," thus making seemingly impossible things occur when necessary.

The recruitment of these characters was a daring editorial choice, and it would have been unheard of in a staid organization like the Justice League. Hawkeye, after all, had formerly been a super-criminal, a part of Iron Man's rogues' gallery (*Tales of Suspense* #57, 1964); Quicksilver and the Scarlet Witch had been (reluctant) members of the self-described Brotherhood of Evil Mutants, a group headed by their father Magneto (*X-Men* vol. 1 #4, 1964). This development helped foster a sense that anything was possible in the burgeoning Marvel universe, the feeling that all human beings possess capacities for both good and evil, and that no one has to be beyond redemption. This notion is reinforced years later when Wonder Man (introduced as a villain in *The Avengers* #9) returns from the dead as a hero and takes his place in the Avengers' ranks (*The Avengers* #151, 1976). Adding further realism and ambiguity to the mix is the fact that not every superhero desires Avengers membership; when the team extends an invitation to Spider-Man (*The Avengers* #11, 1964), he declines it. Reflecting the rise of feminism in the 1970s, the Wasp would return to the group, eventually becoming a competent Avengers leader and putting the lie to her early 1960s airhead persona.

From its inception *The Avengers* was a hit, and the series' initial success doubtless owes much to the power-packed, *sui generis* renderings of Kirby, who had not only co-created Captain America with writer Joe Simon in 1941, but had also collaborated with Lee on such Marvel mainstay titles as *The Fantastic Four, The Incredible Hulk,* and *Journey into Mystery* (featuring Thor). Kirby illustrated *The Avengers* throughout its first year; with issue #9 (September 1964), Iron Man artist Don Heck (from *Tales of Suspense*) ably took over the penciling reins (though Kirby filled in as penciler on issues #14–#16, and did the page layouts for other second-year *Avengers* issues), while Lee continued with the writing chores until he handed the series off to Roy Thomas (issue #35, December 1966). Over the next several years, Thomas worked with such notable Marvel artists as the aforementioned Heck, John Buscema, George Tuska, Gene Colan, Barry

Smith, Sal Buscema, Frank Giacoia, Rich Buckler, and Neal Adams, whose brief run on the title in 1971 (issues #93–#96), during the war between the galactic empires of the Skrulls and the Kree (alien races created by Lee and Kirby and first seen in *The Fantastic Four*), is widely regarded as among the finest Avengers work ever done.

Under Thomas' direction (with writing assists from noted fantasist Harlan Ellison in issues #88 [1971] and #101 [1972]), Avengers story arcs became increasingly complex and characterization-oriented, flowering into a superpowered melodrama of operatic proportions. Among the many notable characters introduced during Thomas' tenure are such team members as the Vision (an emotionally tortured android with optic-blast powers and the ability to turn intangible), and such villains as the Grim Reaper (the vengeance-crazed brother of Wonder Man) and Ultron (a world-conquering robot who sought to destroy his creator, Henry Pym, the former Ant-Man). Thomas left the series after issue #104 (1972), to be succeeded by Steve Englehart (author of a seminal time-travel arc involving the villain Kang the Conqueror and his time-displaced doppelgangers Rama-Tut and Immortus), Gerry Conway, Jim Shooter (Conway's and Shooter's Avengers runs are also distinguished by the stunning and highly detailed artwork of George Pérez), Steve Gerber, Tom DeFalco (a future Marvel editor-in-chief), David Michelinie, Mark Gruenwald, Steven Grant, Roger Stern, Bill Mantlo, and John Byrne.

During the 1970s and 1980s, the Avengers' membership roles would turn over completely several times while growing exponentially (despite orders from Marvel's fictitious federal government that the group be downsized dramatically in 1979), encompassing such major and minor Marvel heroes as the Beast (from *X-Men*), the Black Panther, Starfox, Hellcat (Patsy Walker), Mantis (Englehart's "Celestial Madonna," whose destiny was to give birth to the most powerful being in the universe), the Black Knight, the She-Hulk, the Sub-Mariner, Tigra, the Black Widow, and even the nineteenth-century Western hero known as the Two-Gun Kid. This relentless expansion isn't surprising, however, given the special government security-clearance status and the weekly thousand-dollar salary (courtesy of Iron Man's Stark International munitions firm) afforded to members by the late 1970s. By the 1990s all the original members of the Fantastic Four—and even the chronic non-joiner, Spider-Man—had become either reserve or inactive Avengers.

By the mid-1980s, the New York–based team had grown to such unwieldy proportions—despite the inactive status of most members—that a second squad was formed in Los Angeles, under the initial leadership of Hawkeye (1984's *West Coast Avengers* limited series, and the ongoing *West Coast Avengers* [later *Avengers West Coast*] monthly series, which ran from 1985 to 1994). In 1989 a self-styled "wannabe" team known as the Great Lakes Avengers—consisting of oddball, previously unknown fourth-stringers such as Mr. Immortal, Dinah Soar, Big Bertha, Flat Man, and Doorman—came into being in 1989 (*West Coast Avengers* #46), but never achieved official standing with either of the bicoastal teams.

In late 1995 Marvel released *Last Avengers,* a two-issue series (written by Peter David and drawn by Ariel Olivetti) that puts paid to many decades-long continuity arcs and boasts a high Avengers body count, killing off Captain America, Thor, Hercules, the Vision, the Scarlet Witch, and others. But this was far from the end of the line for the Assemblers, who resurfaced in the latest volume of their ongoing saga in February 1998 (*The Avengers* vol. 3). From that point, fan-favorite writer and Silver Age (1956–1969) scholar Kurt Busiek (who made his reputation penning 1994's superb, Alex Ross–illustrated *Marvels* miniseries) chronicled most of the team's adventures in its main title for four years, collaborating with artists such as George Pérez, Carlos Pacheco, Jerry Ordway, Stuart Immonen, Norm Breyfogle, Richard Howell, Mark Bagley, John Romita Jr., Steve Epting, Alan Davis, Manuel Garcia, Brent Anderson, Ivan Reis, Kieron Dwyer, Patrick

Zircher, and Yanick Paquette before leaving the series in the hands of writer Geoff Johns in October 2002 with *Avengers* vol. 3 #57 (writer Chuck Austen took over in vol. 3 #77, March 2004). The 1990s was also replete with *Avengers* miniseries and other ancillary titles executed by various creative teams, including the hugely popular, time-spanning *Avengers Forever* (1999). In 2002, writer Mark Millar and artist Bryan Hitch collaborated on an alternately grim and satirical reinvention of the series for Marvel's "Ultimate" line, suitably retitled *The Ultimates,* which immediately became one of comics' best-selling and most critically acclaimed series. Also in the new millennium, Busiek and Pérez teamed up to create the long-awaited *JLA/Avengers* intercompany crossover miniseries (2003), which after two decades of false starts finally brings the Avengers together with the DC Comics superteam that inspired it in the first place.

Like the comics business itself, the Avengers team (of whichever coast) has had its ups and downs over the course of four decades. At times it has been a brilliant dramatic showcase, at others a veritable Island of Misfit Heroes for characters unable to sustain themselves in other, more focused titles. The constant, almost meteorological transformations in the Avengers' membership roles, and the concomitant evolution of new, hitherto-unconsidered character-driven story possibilities, are likely to continue alternately pleasing, surprising, and frustrating eager audiences for many decades to come—at least so long as the nefarious deeds of unnumbered costumed bad guys continue to require Avenging. —*MAM*

Azrael

In 1992, publisher DC Comics was faced with a dilemma: how to match, or better yet, *surpass* the phenomenal success of their just-released "Death of Superman" storyline. Their solution: Create a new Batman. Debuting in writer Dennis O'Neil and artist Joe Quesada's four-issue miniseries *Batman: Sword of Azrael* #1 (October 1992) is Jean Paul Valley, who, while in the womb, is genetically conditioned toward physical perfection by the malevolent Order of St. Dumas, an errant sect dating back to the Crusades. Brainwashed and combatively trained throughout his youth, Valley obediently succeeds his late father—an assassin for the Order—donning Dad's formidable crimson-and-gold habiliment and fiery swords and assuming his destiny as the Avenging Angel, Azrael.

But the Order was in for a surprise: Their newest executioner possessed a powerful force of will. Azrael was excommunicated from the Order after saving the life of Bruce (Batman) Wayne. When Batman's back was broken by Bane, a crime lord boasting drug-enhanced strength, Wayne selected Valley as his successor. Such a move had previously been unthinkable; DC had several different Flashes and Green Lanterns—and even a string of Robins—but the idea of replacing Wayne as the alter ego of Batman was as unlikely as ... killing Superman. This unprecedented event earned DC Comics extensive media coverage and huge sales. Readers who had previously ignored Batman, thinking the character too familiar, now jumped on board. In a gesture showing that its new Batman was no fly-by-night, DC Comics had "Az-Bat," as the character was colloquially nicknamed, co-star with the Punisher in a 1994 DC/Marvel Comics crossover.

While Wayne's Batman was designed to strike fear into criminals' hearts, Valley's Batman pushed that concept to a dangerous extreme. An unstable psychotic whose addled mind allowed him to speak with the specter of St. Dumas, Valley, armed with Bat-blade-firing gauntlets, repeatedly crossed the line, even killing an adversary, thereby breaking the original Batman's code to preserve life. As soon as he was able, Wayne reappeared as Batman, bolstered by his true protégés Nightwing (Dick Grayson) and the new Robin (Tim Drake), and fought his surrogate to repossess the "mantle of the Bat."

No longer the Batman, Valley once again became Azrael and in February 1995 spun off into his own monthly series, *Azrael: Agent of the Bat.* Author/co-creator O'Neil explored Valley's personal and religious redemption (ground he had similarly covered three decades prior in the legendary *Green Lantern/Green Arrow* series), leading Azrael, aided by St. Dumas refugees Nomoz and Sister Lilhy, on a mission to overthrow the Order. Despite occasional crossovers with other titles in the Batman franchise, *Azrael* ran out of steam and was canceled with its one hundredth issue in early 2003, but not before Valley had mended his relationship with the Dark Knight. —*ME*

Bad Girl Art

The genre of "Bad Girl art" that emerged in the 1990s comic-book world was named in contrast to the long-standing tradition of "Good Girl art," which was popular during comics' Golden Age (1938–1954) and featured sexy, pin-up heroines such as Sheena, Queen of the Jungle, and early superheroines like Phantom Lady and Lady Luck. Bad Girl art was birthed out of a trend in comics, film, and other media toward strong, positive women heroes with an attitude (think *Alien*'s Ellen Ripley and Lara Croft, Tomb Raider). Early precursors of today's Bad Girl art include Warren Publishing's dark 1970s temptress Vampirella and Frank Miller's 1980s assassin Elektra. In the 1990s and the new millennium these bad babes include the likes of Chaos! Comics' Lady Death (often cited by comic-book historians as the character that ignited the trend); Rob Liefeld's Glory and Avengelyne; London Nights' Razor; Image Comics' Witchblade; Dark Horse's Ghost and Barb Wire; Crusade Comics' Shi; and a revamped and resurrected Elektra. Bad Girl art has also permeated the superhero mainstream, as seen in DC's *Catwoman* title and Marvel's *Mystique* miniseries.

These heroines mete out punishment clad in sexually provocative outfits—often nothing more than a few pieces of tattered cloth, leather, and spikes—wielding bladed weapons, a don't-mess-with-me attitude, and (often) occult powers. Embodying the themes of bondage, eroticism, vengeance, and violence, their renderings are the most extreme portrayals of the superheroine yet to grace comics' pages. Frequently, theological or occult themes are a part of these character's origins, including archetypes such as demons, fallen or militant angels, or vampires. Artistically, they are often portrayed as women with exaggerated physical attributes, struck in provocative poses, soaked in blood, sweat, or tears. In light of the popularity of extreme superheroines, Bad Girl art continues to proliferate in the pages of Image, Chaos!, Ground Zero, and London Night comics, as well as the more traditional publishing houses. —GM

The Badger

It can be argued that only those with very extreme personalities would don masks and tights to wage war on crime. Although neurotic superheroes like Spider-Man, intermittent multiple-personality sufferers such as the

Hulk, or borderline psychopaths like the Punisher aren't unique in comics, superheroes whose costumed personae arise solely from a psychiatric disorder are rare indeed. The costumed martial-arts expert known as the Badger is one such hero.

The creation of writer Mike Baron (co-creator of Nexus with artist Steve Rude), the Badger debuted in 1983 in *Badger* vol. 1 #1 (Capital Comics). "The Badger is Norbert Sykes," reads the series' splash-page origin boilerplate, "a Vietnam veteran suffering from an extremely rare multiple personality disorder: seven great personalities in one. The personality most frequently inhabited by Norbert, indeed almost exclusively preferred, is the Badger, a self-styled crime fighter who rides the highways and byways of America, meting out bloody justice to jaywalkers, ticket scalpers, [and] indifferent teenaged fast food clerks—in fact, any damn body he feels like because he's CRAZY!"

The seeds of the Badger's madness are sewn during Sykes' childhood, during which he is repeatedly abused by his psychopathic stepfather, Larry. As a young man, the emotionally fragile Sykes serves in Vietnam, where his months-long captivity at the hands of the Viet Cong brings him a vision of God as a badger named Myrtle, who grants him the ability to talk to animals, Dr. Doolittle–style. Traumatized, Sykes begins manifesting multiple personalities in addition to plain old Norbert Sykes.

Sykes' seventh personality—that of the martial-arts savvy, self-styled crime fighter who calls himself the Badger—apparently emerges only after Sykes returns to the United States. Arrested for beating up some street punks, the Badger is committed to an insane asylum, where he meets fellow inmate Hammaglystwythkbrngxxaxolotl (also known as Hamilton J. Thorndyke, or simply "Ham" for short), a fifth-century Welsh druid with the power to control the weather, among other arcane skills. Ham shows the Badger how to "fake sanity" long enough to secure his release; in fairly short order, both men are discharged from the institution and take up residence in Ham's forbidding castle, locat-

ed just south of Barneveld, Wisconsin, and purchased with the huge fortune Ham has amassed over the centuries. The Badger becomes Ham's employee, performing numerous odd jobs, using the "dozens of obscure, esoteric, arcane, not to mention abstruse martial arts" he has mastered.

Although the premiere issue of *Badger* (1983) boasted the cleanly delineated art of Steve Rude, Capital Comics (which went on to become one of the largest direct-market comics distributors of the 1980s and 1990s) couldn't make a go of the series. Luckily First Comics, a larger independent publisher co-founded by Mike Gold, gave the series a home beginning with issue #5 (1984). *Badger* continued at First until its seventieth issue (1991), when the company folded. Baron wrote the series for its entire run, and his uniquely hilarious (and sometimes poignant) scripts displayed his self-declared enthusiasm both for kung fu adventure and the antics of Carl Barks' Uncle Scrooge McDuck. The Badger made guest appearances in *Nexus* vol. 1 #45–#50 (First Comics, 1988) and starred in a four-issue miniseries titled *Badger Goes Berserk* (First Comics, 1989), as well as in a new "first issue" (1991's *Badger* vol. 2 #1), which retold the character's origin. In addition, the Badger headlined a large-format graphic novel titled *Hexbreaker* (First Comics, 1988).

In addition to Ham, the Badger developed a fascinating, unique, and far-ranging supporting cast over the years, including such allies as Mavis Davis, a female martial artist (and fellow talker-to-the-animals) who becomes the Badger's wife; Daisy Fields, Norbert Sykes' personal psychotherapist and Ham's secretary; Jim Wonktendonk, another Nam veteran; Connie Ammerperson, an African-American lesbian cab driver and feminist activist; Fuzzbuster, an owl who helps the Badger avoid speeding tickets; the Yak and the Yeti, a pair of large, ancient, hairy, and often foul-tempered creatures straight out of Tibetan myth; the Wombat, an Australian Vietnam veteran (as crazy and costumed as the Badger) who is the self-styled protector of all animals; Riley Thorpe, the originator of a martial-arts system called Jabber-wocky ("some say it's my jabber, some say it's my walk") and one of the Badger's closest associates; and Lamont, a figure-skating buffalo who likes to hoof-race and is self-conscious about his hairstyle.

Numbering among the Badger's many bizarre nemeses are Hodag, a former Green Beret turned neo-Nazi kook (Sykes is no fan of Nazis); Lord Weterlackus (alias Slotman), a powerful demon lord who draws strength from blood sacrifices; the Roach Wrangler, a former exterminator capable of raising insect armies; Dr. Buick Riviera, an insane, demon-powered, martial artist/physician who uses snakes and other animals as hand-to-hand weapons; Count Kohler, who can turn ordinary humans into demons; Ron Dorgan, a martial artist capable of delivering a "death touch"; and Lannier Lutefisk, a Badger impersonator who actually takes Sykes' place for a whole issue (*Badger* vol. 1 #65).

When First Comics disappeared, so did the Badger. Then the headcase hero eventually resurfaced at Dark Horse Comics with a pair of mini-series: *Badger: Zen Pop Funny-Animal Version* (two issues, 1994) and *Badger: Shattered Mirror* (four issues, 1994). Three years later, Baron took his emotionally challenged hero to Image Comics in another attempt to helm an ongoing Badger series. But this comic lasted only eleven issues, either because of the industry's general sales slump, or because late 1990s audiences were unreceptive to over-the-top superheroics based on mental illness. To those who would find offense in Norbert Sykes' insanity-fueled adventures, however, the Badger would no doubt send one of his trademark verbal barbs: "Critics are grinks and groinks." —*MAM*

Bartman

Fox's long-running animated television series *The Simpsons* (1990–present) is replete with references to superhero comics, from Bartman (the ersatz superhero persona of America's favorite bad boy, Bart Simpson) and the stereotypically slovenly "Comic Book Guy" who runs the Android's Dungeon comic shop, to cameo appearances of the cast of the 1960s *Batman* television show, to the revelation that the fictitious nuclear-enabled muscleman called Radioactive Man has been the country's most influential superhero for about half a century (or so it is told in the fictitious and geographically inscrutable town of Springfield).

In 1993 Bongo Comics (spearheaded by Steve and Cindy Vance, Bill Morrison, and *Simpsons* creator Matt Groening) underscored the cultural importance of Radioactive Man—Bartman's principal inspiration—by actually publishing some of the atomic hero's key adventures, the very comics read by Bart Simpson, Milhouse Van Houten, Martin Prince, and the rest of the superhero fans of the Simpsonverse. Among these four-color snapshots of Radioactive Man's decades-long evolution are: the sought-after November 1952 *Radioactive Man* premiere issue (1993), which includes an origin story that lampoons the Incredible Hulk, Superman, Batman, 1950s red-baiting, and the Comics Code Authority; May 1962's *Radioactive Man* #88 (1994), which lovingly skewers Stan Lee, Jack Kirby, and superheroes' teenage sidekicks; August 1972's *Radioactive Man* #216 (1994), which parodies the prosocial "relevance" of DC's *Green Lantern/Green Arrow* ("Jeepers!" exclaims a shocked Man of Atoms, "My sidekick *Fallout Boy* is a dirty *Hippy!*"); October 1980's 412th-issue sendup of Chris Claremont and John Byrne's "Dark Phoenix" X-Men saga (1994); January 1986's 679th-issue jab at Marvel's *Punisher,* DC's *Watchmen,* and *The Dark Knight Returns* (1994); January 1995's watershed *Radioactive Man* #1,000 (1994), which aims its barbs squarely at Todd McFarlane and the Image Comics aesthetic; and the Summer 1968 *Radioactive Man 80 Page Colossal* edition (1995), showcasing such gems of Silver Age camp as "Radioactive Man, Teen Idol," "The 1,001 Faces of Radioactive Ape," and a tale of the Radioactive

Man of the far-flung future year of 1995. (Since the late 1990s, a regular if infrequent *Radioactive Man* series has been gently massacring the remaining eras and styles of comics history.)

Subject to such powerful pop-cultural currents, it is no surprise that Bart Simpson would aspire to become a superhero himself, in the guise of Bartman. Bart first donned the purple cape and cowl on a second-season television episode titled "Three Men and a Comic Book" (1991), in an unsuccessful attempt to win a discount admission to a comic-book convention. Despite this ignominious genesis—and in spite of a complete lack of superpowers, crime-fighting equipment, Batman-style training, or realistic prospects of maintaining a secret identity—Bartman managed to make a go of superheroics (at least in his own mind). Two years later, a one-shot comic book titled *Simpsons Comics and Stories* marked the advent of Bongo Comics and finally brought Bartman to the medium that had inspired him in the first place. In a story titled "There Shall Come … a Bartman!!" (written by Steve and Cindy Vance and illustrated by Bill Morrison and Mike Anderson), Bartman befriends Radioactive Man's elderly creator by preventing the venerable nuclear hero from being killed off by his rapacious publisher as a sales gimmick—thereby making a comment on the stampede of speculation, hoarding, and dumping precipitated by DC's decision to (temporarily) kill Superman.

Bartman's first adventure proved popular enough to justify granting the spiky-haired, underachieving superhero a *Bartman* miniseries (1993–1995), featuring stories by Gary Glasberg, Bill Morrison, Jan Strnad, and Steve Vance, with art by Tim Bavington, Chris Clements, Luis Escobar, Jim Massara, Phil Ortiz, and Cindy Vance. During the series' six-issue run, Bartman stops the Comic Book Guy and school bullies Jimbo Jones, Dolph, and Kearny from scamming comics fans by adding fake "enhancements" to comic book covers; encounters the Penalizer (a Punisher pastiche); has an existential crisis that leads him to quit the hero business temporarily, in an homage to Peter Park-

er's historic super-sabbatical from *The Amazing Spider-Man* #50 (1967); transforms the family pet into "Bart Dog, the Canine Crusader," evoking shades of Ace the Bat-Hound from Batman stories of the 1950s; and fights alongside Radioactive Man himself against the entire population of Springfield after a nuclear mishap sends the townsfolk on a superpowered rampage that began in *Simpsons Comics* #5. In *Bartman* #5 (1995) Bart's sisters Lisa and Maggie swing into costumed action as Lisa the Conjurer and the Great Maggeena while Bartman is briefly sidelined by a sprained ankle.

Though Bartman has not seen much action during recent years, his fortunes might well change in the not-too-distant future. "I think there is a possibility of bringing Bartman back," Bongo Entertainment Group creative director Bill Morrison commented in 2003. "We're actually planning a couple of Bartman stories for upcoming issues of *Bart Simpson Comics*. We may decide to come out with a revived *Bartman* comic." In the meantime, back issues of *Bartman* and trade paperback reprints of the miniseries continue to be snapped up by enthusiastic Bartophiles. And comicdom waits eagerly for the famous Bart Signal to slice across the night sky of Springfield. —*MAM*

Batgirl

Batgirl was created to attract a demographic. The ratings of ABC-TV's *Batman* series were slipping during its second season (1966–1967), and the show's producers brainstormed a "Batgirl" to lure young girls (and lustful men) to the show for its third. Dancer/actress Yvonne Craig was hired for the role, clad in a form-fitting, purple-and-gold Batsuit, and while her high-kicking antics may have ignited some awakenings in the young boys watching, she couldn't save the series: Ratings continued to slump and *Batman* was canceled in 1968 after its third season.

DC Comics, publisher of the Batman comics franchise that inspired the TV show, had, during the program's run, imitated its success by adding camp humor and pop-art sound effects to the comic books. When DC's higher-ups caught wind of a Batgirl joining the show's cast, they gave Julius "Julie" Schwartz, editor of *Batman* and *Detective Comics,* the mandate to create an all-new Batgirl for the comics (a teenage heroine calling herself Bat-Girl [alter ego Betty Kane] had premiered in *Batman* #139 in April 1961 and made a few scattered appearances before fading into oblivion). The result was "The Million Dollar Debut of Batgirl!" in *Detective Comics* #359, January 1967. Behind the bat-eared cowl was Barbara Gordon, a stunning redhead whose good looks and shapely figure belied the physical stereotype of her profession: librarian. The daughter of Gotham City police commissioner James Gordon, Barbara was headed to the Policemen's Masquerade Ball, wearing a black-yellow-and-blue Batgirl costume of her own design, when she by chance encountered a kidnapping attempt. Killer Moth, one of the more outrageous villains to harass Gotham City, was abducting millionaire Bruce Wayne when this masked "Batgirl," energized by an adrenaline rush, burst onto the scene and rescued Wayne. Thrilled by this exploit, Barbara maintained her Batgirl identity and continued to fight crime, ignoring the protestations of Batman, who feared that Batgirl's inexperience may bring her harm on the dangerous streets of Gotham.

Through a number of guest appearances in DC comic books in 1967 and 1968, Batgirl was portrayed in a manner considered sexist by contemporary social standards: Much of her arsenal was carried in a Batpurse attached to her utility belt, a *Detective* cover depicted her distracted by a run in her nylon stockings, and she even got into a cat-fight with Catwoman! But by the early 1970s, Batgirl had matured, using her keen intellect, athletic dexterity, and burgeoning detective skills to solve petty and not-so-petty thefts. Soon, Barbara Gordon relocated to Washington, D.C., as a congresswoman, occasionally appearing as Batgirl in the nation's capital and even teaming with former Boy Wonder Robin, with

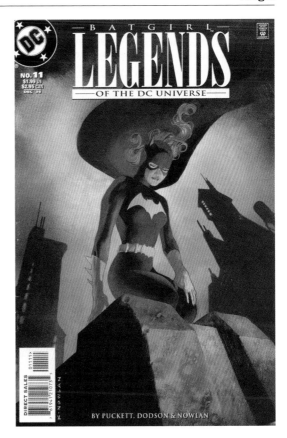

Legends of the DC Universe #11 © 1998 DC Comics. COVER ART BY KEVIN NOWLAN.

the hint of a romance between the two. But as Batman comic books grew grimmer throughout the 1970s and 1980s, Batgirl's existence weakened Batman's, and Barbara Gordon hung up her cowl, despite being merchandized by a variety of toy manufacturers, still craving that girl demographic.

By the time Gordon resurfaced in 1988 in the one-shot comic *Batman: The Killing Joke,* retroactive continuity revisions had now made her the niece—not the daughter—of Commissioner Gordon. In that story, the Joker, Batman's most maniacal foe, exacted revenge on his enemy by rampaging against those close to him. The Joker shot Barbara, leaving her a paraplegic confined to a wheelchair.

Some readers at the time accused DC Comics of misogyny, as this brutal attack on Batgirl closely followed the poignant but violent death of Supergirl in DC's *Crisis on Infinite Earths.* But this tragic moment actually heralded Barbara Gordon's reemergence. In *Suicide Squad* #23 (January 1989), Barbara became Oracle, a behind-the-scenes crusader whose development of a vast computer information network, along with her photographic memory and her uncanny hacking abilities, enabled her to ferret out information to help other heroes. In addition to aiding the Suicide Squad, Batman, and others, Oracle ultimately bonded with Black Canary and the Huntress as the Birds of Prey. A new Batgirl was introduced in *Batman* #567 (July 1999), a mute teenage drifter befriended by Barbara Gordon. It was soon disclosed that this girl was actually Cassandra Cain, daughter of the notorious assassin David Cain, who had expertly trained his offspring in martial arts and other modes of combat. The intervention of Oracle and Batman helped reshape Cassandra's destiny, and now she heroically prowls the streets of Gotham as the new Batgirl.

In tandem with and contrary to DC Comics' continuity, Barbara Gordon as Batgirl has continued a mainstream profile on the small and large screens. In animation, Batgirl appeared in several shows, including *The Batman/Superman Hour* (1968–1969), *The Adventures of Batman and Robin* (1969–1970), and *The New Adventures of Batman* (1977). She didn't reappear on television until Fox's second season of *Batman: The Animated Series,* where she made her debut in the two-part "Shadow of the Bat" (September 13–14, 1993), and became a semi-regular on that series and its later incarnations, *The Adventures of Batman & Robin* (1994–1997, Fox) and *The New Batman/Superman Adventures* (1997–1999, the WB). She arrived on the big screen in summer 1997's live-action film *Batman & Robin,* in which Alicia Silverstone played the superheroine (albeit altered to Barbara *Wilson,* the niece of Bruce Wayne's butler Alfred). Batgirl also appeared in the direct-to-video animated films

Batman & Mr. Freeze: SubZero (March 1998) and *Batman: Mystery of the Batwoman* (October 2003), as well as in much older form in the futuristic TV spin-off cartoon *Batman Beyond* (1998–2001). Actress Dina Meyer was cast as Barbara Gordon/Oracle (with flashbacks to her Batgirl career) in the short-lived *Birds of Prey* live-action series, on the WB network from fall 2002 through early 2003. —*ME*

Batman

Creature of the night. Caped cubmaster. Quipping crime fighter. Masked detective. Vengeful vigilante. At various times throughout his illustrious career, Batman has been all of the above, adapting to shifting social climes while enduring as one of the most recognizable pop-culture icons ever.

Cartoonist Bob Kane compensated for his limited artistic talent with his uninhibited imagination—and unabashed mimicry. Inspired by a host of influences—Leonardo da Vinci's "ornithopter" design, Douglas Fairbanks' swashbuckling outing in *The Mark of Zorro* (1920), and pulp heroes the Shadow and the Spider, among others—Kane sketched a black-masked, red-costumed bat-man, an image refined by recommendations from his silent partner, writer Bill Finger, into the black-and-grey version of the hero soon to become famous as Batman. While Kane, to this day, remains the sole credited creator of Batman, Finger's contributions cannot be overlooked. By his own admission, Kane offered the *look* of the dark prowler, but Finger provided the *story.*

The origin of DC Comics' Batman (which wasn't revealed to readers until the character's seventh appearance) is a now-familiar fable rooted in tragedy. As prosperous physician Thomas Wayne, his social butterfly wife Martha, and their young son Bruce exit a Gotham City movie house after a nighttime showing of *The Mark of Zorro,* they are robbed by a thief brandishing a pistol. Dr. Wayne valiantly attempts to protect his wife, but the panicky gunman murders the adult Waynes as their grief-stricken son watches. The lad dedicates his very existence to avenging his parents' murders by "spending the rest of my life warring on all criminals." After years of training his mind and body to perfection, Wayne, having inherited his father's millions, mulls over a crime-fighting disguise that will terrorize lawbreakers. A bat flaps through an open window, and Wayne deems it an omen. The origin's end caption heralds, "And thus is born this weird avenger of the dark … this avenger of evil. The Batman."

Premiering in May 1939 in *Detective Comics* #27, the Batman became a sudden sensation. In his earliest adventures, Batman (alternately called "Bat-Man" until the hyphen was dropped for consistency) was quite brutal: He tossed a thug off of a rooftop and executed a vampire by shooting him with a silver bullet. Batman's violent methods earned him an enemy: police commissioner James Gordon. Gordon, a mainstay of Batman's mythos since the character's very first story, sicced the Gotham Police Department on this peculiar winged troublemaker, until later forming an uneasy alliance with the Batman after it became obvious they were playing on the same team.

As Batman's acclaim swelled, the character's publisher recoiled, fearful that the sinister elements in the comic book would be emulated by its young audience. DC eliminated Batman's use of firearms and extreme force—never again would Batman take a life. Just under a year after the hero's debut, DC softened him even more in *Detective* #38 (April 1940) by introducing Robin the Boy Wonder. Robin—actually Dick Grayson, a circus aerialist—observes the mob-ordered murder of his parents and becomes the ward of a sympathetic Wayne, who trains the lad as his crime-fighting ally. *Detective*'s sales briskly escalated with Robin's inclusion. The Boy Wonder, exuberant and wisecracking, had a profound influence on the brooding Batman. The former "weird avenger" stepped smoothly into the role of father figure.

Batman Family #17 © 1978 DC Comics.
COVER ART BY MICHAEL KALUTA.

While maintaining the lead spot in *Detective,* Batman was awarded his own title in the spring of 1940, with artists Jerry Robinson and Sheldon Moldoff signing on to help illustrate the additional material (but never signing their stories, due to Kane's creator's deal). *Batman* #1 introduced two villains who would become integral components of the character's history: the sneering clown prince of crime, the Joker, and the sultry princess of plunder, the Catwoman (although she was called "The Cat" during her initial appearance). Batman and Robin were soon challenged by a growing contingent of odd antagonists: The frightful Scarecrow, the larcenous Penguin, and the puzzling Riddler were just some of the rogues who repeatedly took on this "Dynamic Duo." When not battling their bizarre rogues' gallery, Batman and Robin were mopping up mobsters or unearthing clues to crimes in mysteries that challenged the reader to play along as armchair detectives.

Batman and Robin's synchronized acrobatics and deductive mastery dazzled readers, as did their arsenal: They each sported utility belts containing the tools of their trade, including Batarangs (bat-winged boomerangs), Bat-ropes (for climbing and swinging), microcameras and tape recorders, gas pellets, acetylene torches, bolas, respirators, first-aid kits, penlights, and Bat-cuffs. For transportation, the Dynamic Duo hit the streets in their Batmobile, the skies in their Batplane, and the sea in their Bat-boat, an armada warehoused in the secret Batcave beneath the hero's grand home, Wayne Manor. By 1942, Commissioner Gordon—in a full reversal from the days when he ordered his officers to fire upon the Batman—was summoning the hero into action by illuminating the nighttime skies of Gotham City with the Bat-signal.

The Dynamic Duo's burgeoning popularity could not be contained in two magazines alone. They soon appeared in DC's *World's Best* (later *World's Finest*) *Comics,* and in 1943 swung into their own newspaper strip, a medium in which they encountered their first defeat—at the hands of a hero who would soon be their ally, Superman. Many newspapers declined to carry the *Batman* daily and Sunday strips since they were already running the *Superman* feature, cutting short Batman and Robin's first excursion into the funnypapers after a mere two years. Nonetheless, Batman didn't hold a grudge: He and Robin guest starred on several episodes of the radio program *The Adventures of Superman* in the mid-1940s.

Straying even further from Batman's grim roots, DC introduced a comic-relief character in *Batman* #16 (1943): a gentleman's gentleman named Alfred Pennyworth. The son of the butler of Bruce Wayne's father, Alfred surprised Wayne and Grayson by showing up on their doorstep—and surprised them even *more* when he discovered their Batman and Robin guises. The humorous element was quickly abandoned and Alfred became the Dynamic Duo's valuable and trusted aide.

Unlike DC's and Marvel Comics' patriotic paragons, Superman and Captain America, Batman did very little for the war effort in the 1940s other than hawk bonds on his covers. Flag waving and Nazi bashing were not his forte—he and Robin invested their energies in keeping American citizens safe at home. In addition to their comics appearances, they segued into movie theaters in two serials, *Batman* (1943) and *The New Adventures of Batman and Robin* (1949).

As most superheroes were put out to pasture after World War II, Batman was one of three DC Comics characters to maintain his own series, the others being Superman and Wonder Woman. Survivors Superman and Batman even joined forces as "Your Two Favorite Heroes—Together" in the pages of *World's Finest.* Despite Batman's resiliency (and the emergence of popular artist Dick Sprang, whose interpretation of the Joker remains one of the classic renditions of the character), the 1950s were unkind to the cowled crime fighter and his sidekick. The science-fiction craze that mushroomed out of the atomic age injected concepts into the Batman comic books ill-suited to their street-level milieu: Time travel, mutations of Batman and Robin, invading aliens, and giant insects were common themes.

The biggest threat facing Batman and Robin in the 1950s, however, was real-life psychiatrist Fredric Wertham. In his scathing book *Seduction of the Innocent* (1954), Dr. Wertham charged that the comic-book industry was morally corrupting its impressionable young readers, impeaching Batman and Robin in particular for flaunting a gay lifestyle. Wertham wrote, "They live in sumptuous quarters, with beautiful flowers in large vases, and have a butler. It is like a wish dream of two homosexuals living together." Granted, our hero didn't have much luck with women—Wayne zipped through a throng of beauties like Julie Madison, Vicki Vale, and Kathy Kane, and Batman was tantalized by femme fatale Catwoman and, on a couple of instances, even Superman's girlfriend, Lois Lane—but if DC's writers and editors intended the Dynamic Duo's relationship as a gay metaphor, it's a secret that has remained closeted. In response to Wertham's damaging allegations and ensuing parental and U.S. Senate criticism, DC Comics built a wholesome "Batman Family" with the Caped Crusader as its pointy-eared patriarch. Soon Batman and Robin were joined by Batwoman and Ace the Bat-Hound, as well as Bat-Girl and even the magical imp Bat-Mite. Batman's ghoulish adversaries were either neutered or discarded from the series. For years, DC produced a kinder, gentler Batman—and readers defected. *Batman* and *Detective Comics* were on the brink of cancellation.

Editor Julius "Julie" Schwartz, who launched the Silver Age of comics (1956–1969) through his renovations of Golden Age (1938–1954) favorites the Flash, Green Lantern, and the Justice Society of America (reworked in 1960 as the Justice *League,* a team that counted Batman among its eminent roster), was tapped by DC to work his magic on Batman. Enter the "New Look" era in 1964: Schwartz updated the appearance of the hero by adding a yellow oval to Batman's chest insignia; hired *Flash* illustrator Carmine Infantino to modernize the artwork; evicted the codependent Batman Family, except for Robin; and excised the silly sci-fi gimmickry that had strangled the character for more than ten years. Detective mysteries became the norm, Batman's rogues' gallery reappeared (with new additions like Blockbuster), and Robin was franchised out for membership in a junior Justice League called the Teen Titans. The only bad call Schwartz made was the elimination of Alfred: Batman's butler died in 1964 and was replaced by Grayson's Aunt Harriet, Schwartz's volley to counter Wertham's contentions of a decade earlier, but that decision was soon reversed and Alfred was resurrected.

On January 12, 1966, ABC premiered a live-action *Batman* television series starring handsome Adam West as a swaggering Batman/Wayne and unseasoned newcomer Burt Ward as an effervescent Robin/Grayson. *Batman* bubbled with flashy costumes and sets (at a time when color television was relatively new), pop-art sound-effect graphics ("Pow!" "Zowie!"), a surfin' soundtrack by Neal Hefti, and guest appearances by popular celebrities as villains. The show's flamboyant action enthralled kids, while its campy humor amused their parents. *Batman,* which aired twice a week (the first night's cliff-hanger would be resolved "tomorrow night, same Bat-time, same Bat-channel," as the narrator promised), was not only an immediate hit, it birthed a national phenomenon. America went "Bat" crazy: West as Batman appeared on major magazine covers including *Life* and *TV Guide,* Ward as Robin became a teen heartthrob, an unprecedented wave of Bat-merchandise was sold to boys *and* girls, the *Batman* newspaper strip resumed, and a theatrical movie was churned out for the summer of 1966. DC plastered Batman on as many comics as possible—the hero usurped *Justice League* and *World's Finest* covers from his partners, and Batman team-ups took over the title *The Brave and the Bold.* The entire genre of superheroes benefited from this Bat-mania, with costumed crime fighters new and old taking over the airwaves, comics racks, and toy shelves for a few years. ABC's *Batman* returned for two more seasons, but ratings sagged each year (despite the introduction of Yvonne Craig in season three as Batgirl, a character also inserted into the comics), and the show was axed in 1968, although Batman segued to Saturday-morning television in September 1968 as part of the animated *The Batman/Superman Hour.*

The inflated comic-book sales DC enjoyed from the television show's hit status quickly deflated once it left the air. Batman needed another shot in the arm. Artist Neal Adams' photo-realistic illustrations and experimental layouts on the Deadman series in DC's *Strange Adventures* had made him comics' "it" boy. With the Batman/Deadman pairing in *The Brave and the Bold* #79 (1968), Adams began a stint on that team-up title that would, with each issue, revitalize the look of Batman: the hero's batears began to grow longer, his brow became more menacingly furrowed, his cape engulfed comics panels like flowing batwings, and his escapades always took place at night—even when scripter Bob Haney called for a daytime scene! Adams took it upon himself to restore Batman to his roots as a foreboding nocturnal force—he was "the" Batman again. Editor Schwartz noticed, and recruited Adams to the main Bat-titles.

Other changes were transpiring at the same time: In late 1969, Dick Grayson left home for college (and his own adventures as Robin the *Teen Wonder*), and Wayne and Alfred temporarily boarded up the mansion and relocated into a highrise in the heart of Gotham. New and frightening foes like Man-Bat and Ra's al Ghul appeared, Two-Face returned from limbo, and the Joker was transformed from a clownish buffoon into a homicidal maniac. Throughout the 1970s, writers like Dennis O'Neil, Steve Englehart, and Len Wein, and dynamic artists including Adams, Dick Giordano, and Marshall Rogers produced gothic, atmospheric masterpieces that are still lauded by readers over thirty years later. Batman overcame a sales slump in the early 1970s and was again being exploited by DC by the mid-1970s: *The Joker, Man-Bat,* and *The Batman Family* joined DC's lineup. Batman's romantic life became a captivating soap opera; Batman cavorted with Talia, the vivacious but villainous daughter of his new foe al Ghul, and Wayne fell in love with the natty Silver St. Cloud, who actually deduced his dual identity by recognizing Bruce's chin in the Batmask. While Batman was the "Dark-night Detective" in DC's comics, television wouldn't allow the light-hearted interpretation of the hero to die: Witness ABC's kid-friendly *Super Friends* (beginning in 1973 and running, in various incarnations, until the mid-1980s) and CBS's *The New*

Adventures of Batman (1977, featuring the voices of West and Ward). A puffy West and Ward even donned their colorful costumes once again in 1978 for a pair of campy one-hour television specials called *Legends of the Super-Heroes* (also featuring the Flash, Green Lantern, the Riddler, and other good and bad guys).

This didn't faze DC's comic-book Batman, however. In the 1980s, his comics explored grimmer themes: Batman became a vampire, blew off his Justice League pals and formed the Outsiders, and encountered freakish new villains like the bone-crushing Killer Croc. By 1984, Grayson had hung up his red Robin tunic to become Nightwing, and troubled teen Jason Todd was introduced as the new—and rebellious—Boy Wonder. Batman's most influential moment of the decade occurred with *Batman: The Dark Knight Returns* (1986), a four-issue miniseries by writer/artist Frank Miller and inker Klaus Janson. Set in the near future, *Dark Knight* portrayed a grizzled, booze-addled Bruce Wayne crawling out of retirement to restore order to a chaotic Gotham as the Batman. Miller's gritty take on Batman established a template for other writers and artists to follow. Batman comics grew somber, and sometimes graphically startling: The manic Joker debased and nearly killed Commissioner Gordon and Batgirl in *Batman: The Killing Joke* (1988), and *did* kill the new Robin—echoing reader demand from a phone-in contest—in *Batman* #428 (1988). A new Robin, Tim Drake, entered the canon the following year, as did another Tim, real-life movie director Tim Burton.

Burton, a wild-haired, cartoonish figure himself, was fascinated by fantasy: His earliest cinematic efforts included *Frankenweenie* (1984) and *Pee-Wee's Big Adventure* (1985). So when he took on the project of bringing Batman to the big screen, comics fans were thrilled … until they learned of his casting choice. Michael Keaton, a quirky actor slight of build and best known for comedy roles in *Mr. Mom* (1983) and Burton's own *Beetlejuice* (1988), was chosen by the director to play Wayne and Batman. A delegation of comics fans demanded Keaton's removal from the project. Burton was convinced, however, that the wild look in Keaton's eyes would give him the edge to portray the obsessed hero. Box-office receipts proved him right: *Batman* (1989), which included Jack Nicholson as the Joker and Kim Basinger as love interest Vicki Vale, was the year's megahit, spawning a wave of Bat-merchandise the likes of which had not been seen since 1966.

1992 was Batman's next pivotal year. Burton and Keaton were back in theaters with *Batman Returns,* inspiring a television cartoon spinoff that fall: the *noir*-ish *Batman: The Animated Series.* In the comics, a brutish crime lord called Bane deposed Gotham's guardian by snapping Batman's spine and triumphantly pitching him off a rooftop. During his convalescence, Wayne was replaced by a psychotically violent surrogate Batman named Jean Paul Valley (a.k.a. Azrael). Once healed, the true Batman overcame Valley and resumed "the mantle of the Bat." Even the leveling of Gotham City by an earthquake in DC's serialized storyline "No Man's Land" (1999) could not stop the hero. Bolstered by a convoy of comic-book titles and specials, a perennial line of action figures (more than one hundred variations of Batman figures have been produced since the 1990s), an enduring television presence (the 1966 *Batman* series aired weekly on TV Land in 2004, and *Batman: The Animated Series* continued for years, inspiring the futuristic *Batman Beyond* and the superteam *Justice League* cartoon shows), and live-action movies (Val Kilmer and George Clooney played Batman in two additional film sequels, and Warner Bros. is aggressively developing a reintroduction of the Batman film franchise), the Dark Knight shows no signs of age.

Since his 1939 debut, Batman has repeatedly proved that while he may suffer setbacks, he is undefeatable. He represents our fears, and inspires us to conquer them. And he will inevitably continue to do so for decades to come. —*ME*

Batman in the Media

Although he began his comic-book career as a creature of the night, Batman has been portrayed on television and film as both a dark avenger and a campy crime-fighting clown. Artist Bob Kane was influenced by Douglas Fairbanks' look in *The Mark of Zorro* (1920) and the villainous cloaked character in *The Bat* (1926) when he designed Batman, and as he and writer Bill Finger further developed the character following his May 1939 debut, cinematic influences continued. Although sidekick Robin was introduced in 1940 without specific media inspirations, the look of arch-villain the Joker was transferred almost verbatim from the eerie smiling appearance of Conrad Veidt in *The Man Who Laughs* (1927).

FILM-SERIAL BEGINNINGS

In 1943, just four years after his comic debut, Batman was brought to the masses in a film serial. Columbia had the rights to both Superman and Batman, but they chose to film the non-superpowered hero first. Film serials were short films that played in movie theaters every week, each ending in a cliffhanger so that audiences would return the following week to see the next chapter.

The fifteen-chapter *Batman* serial debuted on July 16, 1943, starring Lewis Wilson as Batman and Douglas Croft as Robin. The damsel-in-distress of the piece was Linda Page, played by Shirley Patterson, while Caucasian actor J. Carroll Naish pushed racial boundaries (and, a later generation of viewers would agree, crossed the line into stereotype) as the villainous Japanese spy Dr. Daka. While trying to steal radium to fuel his atomic disintegrator, Daka uses a mind-control device on the residents of Gotham City, turning them into "zombies."

Since the serial was shot in black-and-white, the colors of Batman and Robin's costumes were irrelevant, but they looked very similar to the comic designs, even if Batman's ears more closely resembled horns. The serial was dull at times—largely due to both Wilson's and Croft's performances and a meandering script—but it did firmly establish the Batcave (which was utilized more in publisher DC's comics thereafter).

In 1945, Batman and Robin both made regular guest-appearances on the *Superman* radio show, often played by Matt Crowley and Ronald Liss, respectively. A few aborted attempts at a solo *Batman* radio series were made, but the Dark Knight's next appearance was back in the serials. Following the success of their first *Superman* serial in 1948, Columbia chose to go back to the Batcave, with *Superman's* director, Spencer Bennet, at the helm.

Batman and Robin, a fifteen-chapter serial (also known as *The Return of Batman*) premiered in theaters on May 26, 1949. This time, Robert Lowery played Batman and John Duncan played Robin. In this outing, they faced the Wizard (Leonard Penn), who uses a top-secret remote control device to take command of planes, trains, and automobiles, then uses a stolen "neutralizer" and a zone of invisibility, all to commit dastardly crimes such as stealing diamonds. The serial includes Vicki Vale (Jane Adams), who had recently been introduced in the comics, but it is a lackluster production in almost every sense. The cliff-hangers are poorly written, the acting is mediocre, the costumes are bad, the music is weak, and even the director seems to have lost interest in his own product.

Batman retreated to the pages of comics for another fifteen years, at which time the first serial was re-edited and re-released under the title *An Evening with Batman and Robin* (1965). The press materials for the re-release called it "The Greatest Serial Ever Filmed," and quoted a review that noted that it was "two high-camp folk heroes in a marathon of fist-fights, zombies, & ravenous alligators!" It was that camp element that would become the public's prime association with Batman for the next several years.

FORAYS INTO TELEVISION

Television network ABC acquired the rights for a live-action *Batman* series shortly after the serial was re-released (one legend has it that an executive was inspired by a print of the film he saw at Hugh Hefner's Chicago Playboy mansion), and work on a pilot began in fall 1965. Producer William Dozier and his crew decided on a style for the series that would mimic the elements of the comic in a way that stayed true to them and made fun of them at the same time. Cameras were tilted for an askew perspective, colors were brightened, deadpan narration was employed, and most famously, animated sound effects of "Biff! Bam! Pow!" were superimposed on the screen during fight scenes.

Although Lyle Waggoner originally read for the dual role of Bruce Wayne/Batman, the part went to fellow small-screen bit-parter Adam West, who proved perfect at staying in completely serious character no matter what wackiness ensued around him. Newcomer Burt Ward was youthful partner Dick Grayson/Robin, whose expressions were generally preceded by the adjective "Holy," as in "Holy Priceless Collection of Etruscan Snoods!" Genteel Alan Napier was butler Alfred, while befuddled Commissioner Gordon and Chief O'Hara were played by Neil Hamilton and Stafford Repp, respectively.

Debuting mid-season on January 12, 1966, *Batman* was an almost immediate success. Each half-hour show was a two-parter, with the first part ending in a cliff-hanger and the conclusion airing the following night. It was a bold experiment, and it paid off handsomely in ratings and merchandising;

Opposite: Michael Keaton portrays the Dark Night in *Batman Returns.*

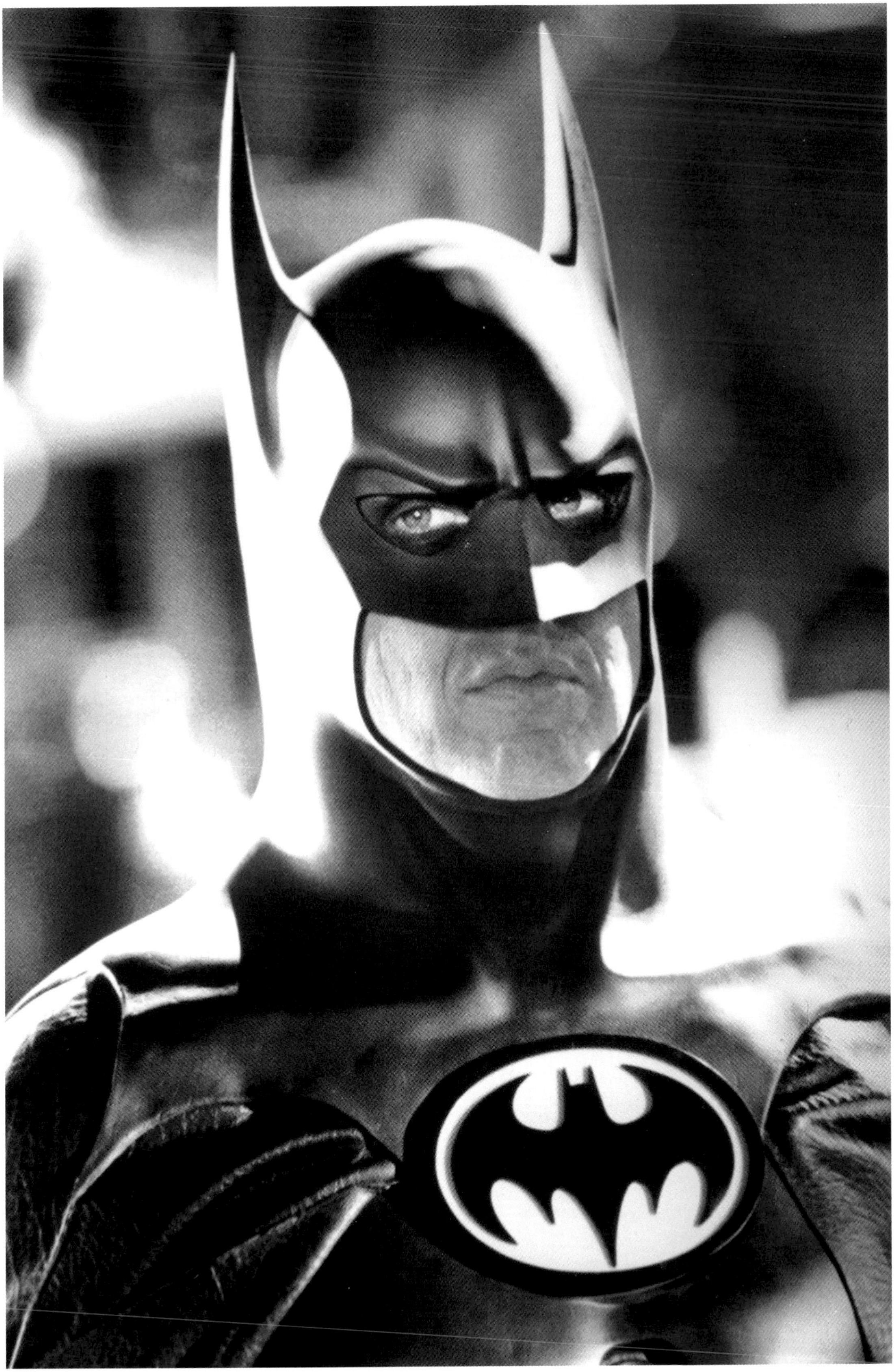

even the theme song by Neal Hefti hit the music charts. Additionally, big-name actors wanted to be a part of the series, enabling the producers to cast villains and bit parts more easily. Villains included the Riddler (Frank Gorshin [who would get an Emmy nomination for the role], and John Astin), the Joker (Cesar Romero), the Penguin (Burgess Meredith), Catwoman (Julie Newmar, Lee Meriwether, Eartha Kitt), Mr. Freeze (George Sanders, Otto Preminger), Bookworm (Roddy McDowall), Ma Parker (Shelley Winters), Egghead (Vincent Price), Chandell (Liberace), Siren (Joan Collins), and many more.

Batman was popular enough that, between the first and second seasons, a feature film was shot utilizing much of the series' cast as Batman and Robin faced their four toughest villains: the Penguin, the Joker, the Riddler (Gorshin), and Catwoman (Meriwether). *Batman* was released by Twentieth Century Fox on August 3, 1966, further fueling the Bat-craze sweeping the country. A Batcopter and Batboat were created for the film, and were later utilized in addition to the Batmobile on the series. Other Bat-vehicles and Bat-gadgets include the Batcycle; the Batmobile's micro-TV Batscanner; the Bat-charger launcher; and various Batcave accessories, including the navigational aid computer and the "complete anti-criminal eye-pattern master file." Although a scene with Shark-Repellent Batspray is funny, perhaps the most memorable scene in the film involves Batman trying to get rid of an explosive device on a crowded pier. "Some days you just can't get rid of a bomb," he intones, deadpan.

Fearing then-significant concerns that Batman and Robin would be perceived as homosexual, two female characters were added to the TV series. Aunt Harriet Cooper (Madge Blake) was introduced into the household of stately Wayne Manor, and—following an eight-minute presentation pilot which was filmed to test the character—femme sidekick Batgirl (a luminous Yvonne Craig) followed in the series' third season in fall 1967. Batgirl, who debuted in comic-book form only a few months

before, had actually been created as an advance tie-in to what the TV producers had in mind.

But by the third season, even Batgirl could not help save the *Batman* series, which had been experiencing a significant drop in viewership during year two. ABC cut the series back to one night a week, and on March 14, 1968, ended *Batman* with its 120th episode. Although NBC expressed an interest in reviving the series, by the time they made clear overtures to Twentieth Century Fox, ABC had already scrapped the sets. *Batman* almost immediately entered the syndication market, where it has been an ultra-popular television staple for more than thirty years.

ANIMATION

Six months after the live-action *Batman* series ended, CBS debuted a Filmation animated series of adventures in *The Batman/Superman Hour*. Each episode featured one seven-minute story, as well as a two-part fourteen-minute show. The tone of the tales was slightly less campy than the live series, though the villainous deathtraps were just as elaborate. Antagonists included Joker, Penguin, Catwoman, Scarecrow, Riddler, Mr. Freeze, and others. Olan Soule voiced Batman, with Casey Kasem (before his radio stardom) voicing Robin, and Jane Webb handling vocal chores for Batgirl. Ted Knight lent his tones to almost all of the villains, as well as Commissioner Gordon and the Narrator. From 1969 to 1970, the Bat-stories were split off into their own series, titled *The Adventures of Batman and Robin.* During this period, Filmation also animated five brief *Batman* segments for Children's Television Workshop's *Sesame Street* series, some of which featured Joker and Penguin.

The animated Batman wasn't off the air for too long after the Filmation series ended. In 1972, Hanna-Barbera was producing *The New Scooby-Doo Movies* for CBS. Each episode found the familiar gang of mystery-solvers teaming up with celebrities, both real—such as Sonny and Cher or the Three Stooges—and fictional. Batman and Robin guest-starred in two episodes, helping the Scooby Gang foil the dastardly plans of Joker and Penguin. Interestingly enough, Casey Kasem provided the voices for both Shaggy and Robin, while Olan Soule again voiced Batman. The shows were a warm-up for Hanna-Barbera, who thought that a crime-fighting team of superheroes should work in animation as well as it did in the comics.

On September 8, 1973, ABC-TV debuted *Super Friends,* a new Hanna-Barbera series that teamed Superman, Batman, Wonder Woman, Robin, and Aquaman to fight crime. The group was accompanied on their adventures by teenagers Wendy and Marvin, and their pet, Wonder Dog (in the comics, Wendy was retroactively written to be Bruce Wayne's niece). Soule and Kasem stayed on to provide the Dynamic Duo's voices. The series was a relative success, and its sixteen episodes stayed in rotation on ABC until fall 1977, when the format was revamped and new characters were added to create *The All New Super Friends Hour.*

It wasn't until 1978's revamp, *Challenge of the Super Friends,* that any Batman villains showed up in the *Super Friends* milieu. Joining in with the Legion of Doom were Scarecrow and Riddler, certainly not the most powerful of Batman's rogues' gallery. Riddler would pop up again in 1980's *The Super Friends Hour,* but it wasn't until the 1985 incarnation of the series, *The Super Powers Team: Galactic Guardians* (which saw Adam West take over Batman's vocal duties from Olan Soule) that other Bat-villains came into play. Penguin would reappear, as would Joker (as a member of the Wild Cards gang), but it was in an episode titled "The Fear" that ground was broken. In the episode, Scarecrow subjects Batman to a fear device and puts him in Crime Alley, the place where his parents were murdered. The show marked the first time in Batman's near-fifty-year history that his origin had been addressed in any medium other than print.

Even while he was appearing as a regular in the various *Super Friends* series, the animated Bat-

man was also showing up on another network. In early 1977, Filmation produced *The New Adventures of Batman* for CBS. The sixteen episodes found Batman, Robin, and Batgirl joined in their crime-fighting adventures by a fifth-dimensional imp known as Bat-Mite. Villains ranged from known characters such as Joker, Catwoman, Penguin, Mr. Freeze, and Clayface to newcomers like Sweet Tooth, Professor Bubbles, Electro, and Chameleon (the latter two unrelated to Marvel Comics villains of the same names). Adam West and Burt Ward were reunited for the lead character voices, though Filmation didn't really tout the reunion in any advertising or marketing campaigns.

In the fall of 1977, CBS teamed the Caped Crusader with the King of the Jungle for *The Batman/Tarzan Adventure Hour,* though no new episodes were produced. The following year the series became *Tarzan and the Super 7,* and that title lasted until 1980 when it was changed to *Batman and the Super 7* (on NBC). Having rebroadcast the *Batman* episodes to death, the network finally retired the series in the fall of 1981. Bat-Mite would eventually make his reappearance in the comics.

Batman and Robin made one further appearance on television in the 1970s, when Hanna-Barbera produced two hour-long live-action specials for NBC. *Legends of the Super-Heroes* was the overall title, but "The Challenge" aired January 18, 1979 and "The Roast" aired January 25, 1979. Not only did Adam West and Burt Ward reprise their famous roles, but so did Frank Gorshin as Riddler. Even the Batmobile made an appearance. Most interestingly, the specials also saw the first live-action appearance of the Huntress, who in the comics was the daughter of the Earth-Two Batman and Catwoman! The specials were tremendously campy, and never re-aired.

THE DARK KNIGHT ON FILM AND TV

Film producers Jon Peters and Peter Guber had been trying for years to get a Batman film on track in

Hollywood, and in the late 1980s they finally found the key to their film with director Tim Burton, whose dark sensibilities gelled with the grittier *Batman* comics of the post–*Dark Knight Returns* era. With a script by Sam Hamm and Warren Skaaren, production designer Anton Furst began creating stunning gothic sets for Gotham City at Pinewood Studios in London. The Warner Bros. film was slated to be a big-budget affair, and although few in the potential audience quibbled with Kim Basinger's casting as Vicki Vale, nor with Jack Nicholson as Joker, it was the man behind the Batmask that gave fans pause. Michael Keaton had been primarily known for his comedic roles, and fans were apoplectic when his casting as Batman was announced.

The $40 million *Batman* was released on June 23, 1989, with a huge media campaign behind it. Accepting Keaton wholeheartedly, fans were also agog at how seriously the film took the comic-book mythos, even if it did tweak Batman's origin so that Joker was involved. The film grossed over $250 million worldwide, and merchandising ran into the multi-million dollars. A sequel was immediately greenlighted, and Burton decided to up the ante in terms of strangeness and characters alike.

Batman Returns flew into theaters on June 12, 1992, but the story was darker than its predecessor and merchandisers were not happy. Danny DeVito played a creepy Penguin whose deformities caused him to be abandoned by his parents, while Michelle Pfeiffer played much-abused Selina Kyle, who becomes the sexually liberated Catwoman over the course of the film. Pfeiffer had gotten the role when first choice Annette Bening dropped out due to pregnancy; before the part had been recast, however, actress Sean Young forced her way onto the Warner Bros. lot in a Catwoman costume, demanding to see Tim Burton about the role. He hid behind a desk rather than face Young, and she later went on talk shows to discuss the matter.

One character who would have been in *Batman Returns* was Robin, and the role was actually cast and costumed—with a twist. Young actor Marlon Wayans was set to play an African-American Robin, but the character was completely excised from the script before Wayans could film any scenes. Burton felt the movie was overstuffed with characters as written, and the cutting of Robin streamlined the film more.

Although it was the highest-grossing film of 1992, *Batman Returns* "only" made $163 million at the box office, and merchandising revenue was severely depressed. Warner now wanted a new vision for the films, one that would be brighter and more merchandising- and kid-friendly. Tim Burton exited talks for a sequel, and with him went Michael Keaton. Ironically, Burton's dark vision for the Caped Crusader was already being played out in a format that did appeal to younger and older audiences alike.

In 1990, several animators at Warner Bros. produced a three-minute test pilot of *Batman,* done in a style they called "Dark Deco." Eventually the concept sold to Fox, and work began on the new *Batman: The Animated Series.* When the show started airing on September 5, 1992, *Batman: TAS* wowed audiences and critics alike. The stories were gloomy and dark, the villains were nasty, and Batman was brooding. The look of the series was particularly gorgeous, utilizing Art Deco architecture and character designs on darkened or black backgrounds, with heavy airbrushed effects. The animated Gotham City now seemed as if it could *only* exist at night, and its protector was right at home among the jutting spires and stone gargoyles.

Producers Bruce Timm and Eric Radomski were responsible for much of *Batman: TAS*'s visual look, while Alan Burnett came in to serve as story editor and co-producer. Burnett had previously worked on *The Super Powers Team: Galactic Guardians,* and he hired writer Paul Dini to come aboard as well. The stories the production crew created included many classic and newer *Batman* comic villains, as well as supporting cast members and storylines lifted directly from the pages of the comics themselves.

Batman: TAS's voice cast was excellent, led by Kevin Conroy in the lead role. Loren Lester played

Dick Grayson/Robin, while Melissa Gilbert and Tara Charendoff took on the role of Batgirl/Barbara Gordon. Once Grayson became Nightwing, the new Robin/Tim Drake was played by Mathew Valencia. The villain roster was once again filled with familiar Hollywood names: Mark Hamill (Joker); Adrienne Barbeau (Catwoman); Ron Perlman (Clayface); Richard Moll (Two-Face); Roddy McDowall (The Mad Hatter); David Warner (Ra's Al Ghul); and Helen Slater (Talia), among others. One episode even paid tribute to an older hero in Gotham—the Grey Ghost—and the producers cast Adam West in the vocal role.

Batman: The Animated Series quickly became one of the most critically acclaimed animated series in television history, winning numerous Emmy Awards and a generation of faithful viewers. Seventy episodes were produced in the original show. In September 1994, the series moved to Saturday mornings and adopted a more kid-friendly tone, becoming *The Adventures of Batman & Robin.* Fifteen more new episodes were produced, mixed in with older reruns. The last new show aired in the fall of 1995, but repeats continued for a while thereafter.

In 1997, the series jumped from Fox to the fledgling WB! network, becoming even more stylized along the way. The show was paired with Superman episodes as *The New Batman/Superman Adventures,* and a final thirteen episodes were produced, airing through early 1999.

While the animated series was showing, several feature-length productions were created. *Batman: Mask of the Phantasm* was the first Batman animated theatrical release, premiering on Christmas Day of 1993. A direct-to-video story called *Batman & Mr. Freeze: SubZero* was released on March 17, 1998, while *The Batman/Superman Movie* was actually a video compilation of three October 1997 *Superman* TV episodes that guest-starred Batman.

Even as the animated Batman was pleasing fans, critics, and merchandisers alike, the feature-film franchise was gearing up for a pair of sequels. Joel Schumacher directed *Batman Forever* (1995)

and *Batman & Robin* (1997), with a heavy-handed campy tone that laid on a thick homoerotic element to the series. Replacing Keaton in *Forever* was Val Kilmer, and George Clooney stepped into the cape and cowl for *Batman & Robin.* Marlon Wayans wasn't called back for Robin's role, and instead, Chris O'Donnell donned the rubber body-suit in both films. Alicia Silverstone as Batgirl joined the Dynamic Duo in *Batman & Robin,* but as in the TV series, the character's inclusion came too late to help the franchise's sagging box office.

Batman Forever utilized comedian Jim Carrey as Riddler and Tommy Lee Jones as Two-Face, but neither was served by the slapdash script, nor Schumacher's penchant for letting them run completely over the top with their characterizations. The campy tone and dialogue worsened for *Batman & Robin,* wherein Uma Thurman played a seductive Poison Ivy and Arnold Schwarzenegger played a leaden Mr. Freeze. Both films were savaged by the critics and fans, and after *Batman & Robin* underperformed at the box office, Schumacher even publicly admitted to having hurt the *Batman* film franchise.

No matter how the films fared at the box office, Warner was not about to let the *successful* part of its *Batman* franchise fall completely. In January 1999, the WB debuted *Batman Beyond,* a futuristic animated series in which a young boy named Terry McGinnis discovers the secrets of Batman fifty years into Gotham City's future. Now, using a high-tech costume—and being coached by the crotchety recluse Bruce Wayne—Terry fights crime as the Batman of the future. By its end in 2001, fifty-two episodes of *Batman Beyond* were produced.

In December 2000, a direct-to-video animated feature called *Batman Beyond: Return of the Joker* was released. Warner had planned an earlier street date, but after political pressure about violence aimed at young audiences, the studio decided to re-edit the film. In 2002, an uncut version of the film was released on DVD, rated PG-13 for violence.

In December 2001, Batman began to appear in *Justice League,* a half-hour animated series on the Cartoon Network. There, he occasionally battles familiar Bat-villains like Joker and Clayface, although more often he joins his super-colleagues to battle other menaces. As with all of the other Warner-produced cartoons since 1990, Kevin Conroy provides the voice of Batman, while Mark Hamill is the Joker. Batman guest-starred with the Justice League on two episodes of WB's *Static Shock* cartoon in 2003, and that year also saw Robin appear on Cartoon Network's *Teen Titans* series and the release of the direct-to-video feature *Batman: Mystery of the Batwoman.*

In March 2003, CBS aired *Return to the Batcave: The Misadventures of Adam and Burt,* a telefilm comedy reuniting Adam West, Burt Ward, Frank Gorshin, Julie Newmar, and a handful of other *Batman* TV veterans in a story that told of their "real-life" misadventures filming the 1960s series. Warner Bros. executives are still planning on Batman returning to the live-action scene. Versions of a TV series featuring a teenage Bruce Wayne have been discussed, as has his appearance on the hit series *Smallville.* Multiple movie scripts have been written for a new Batman film, with scenarios including the popular 1980s comics storyline *Batman: Year One,* a modern Batman, and the futuristic *Batman Beyond* all being considered.

In September 2003, Christian Bale (*American Psycho*) was announced as the next actor to play a big-screen Batman, for director Christopher Nolan (*Memento*) and scripter David Goyer (*Blade*), with filming of the "early days of Batman" story to begin in the spring of 2004. A return to animation was also in the works, with *The Batman* announced in February 2004 for Kids WB! and Cartoon Network. Set to debut in the fall of that year, the show focuses on the earliest days of Batman's career and his first clashes against his formidable rogues' gallery. The roofs of Gotham City may be silent for the time being, but the dark night shadows hold the promise of more Bat-adventures in the future. —*AM*

Batman Villains

Since his debut in *Detective Comics* #29 (1939), Batman has battled the most infamous and imaginative rogues' gallery in comics. It didn't begin that way, however. In the Dark Knight's initial outings, creator/artist Bob Kane and writer Bill Finger accentuated the cowled hero, not his adversaries, pitting him against generic gangsters, clichéd evil masterminds, and vampires. Near the end of Batman's inaugural year of publication, in *Detective Comics* #36 (1940), the hero encountered his first scoundrel of note: Professor Hugo Strange. In his early appearances, Strange smothered Gotham City with fog, mutated mental patients into monsters, and even lashed Batman with a bullwhip, his sinister antics raising the badness bar for all Bat-villains to come.

Batman #1 (Spring 1940) introduced "The Cat," soon to be re-dubbed Catwoman, the slinky "princess of plunder" who would soon become one of Batman's greatest foes, and the Joker. With his pallid pigmentation, green hair, and baleful smile, the Joker's frightfulness extended beyond his ghastly looks: This homicidal harlequin exterminated foes and associates alike with a poison that froze his victims' faces in hideous grins. Also debuting in 1940, horror-movie star Basil Karlo (a thinly disguised homage to Boris Karloff) embarked upon a career of serial killings in the guise that made him famous on film: Clayface. As the readers' world became gripped by a war that produced real-life genocidal menaces, Batman's creators were challenged to envision larger-than-life villains: Jonathan Crane was so scarred by childhood taunts over his gangly appearance that he adopted the guise of a cornfield Scarecrow and made Batman quake in his boots with his terror-inducing gas. The impeccably dressed racketeer the Penguin waddled into Gotham abetted by a flock of feathered fiends and an armada of deadly umbrellas. Half of district attorney Harvey Dent's visage was so gruesomely deformed by a gangster's acid attack that he became Jekyll and Hyde in one man, and as the schizoid Two-Face unleashed a crime career in which each action was predicated on the flip of a coin. The Riddler compulsively taunted Batman and his junior partner Robin the Boy Wonder with conundrums that contained clues to his forthcoming crimes. Jervis Tetch fancied himself the Mad Hatter from *Alice in Wonderland* and nearly toppled the Dynamic Duo with hypnotic devices concealed within his chapeau. Other villains bowing in the 1940s, like the rotund Tweedledee and Tweedledum and seafaring Tiger Shark, didn't fare as well and soon vanished from view.

In the 1950s, U.S. Senate hearings over comics' graphic story content, and the ensuing comics industry–created "Comics Code" that mandated what comics publishers could and couldn't publish, forced Batman to stray from his dark roots into silliness, and his villains followed suit. The grisly Joker was sanitized into the "Clown Prince of Crime," the Penguin was similarly softened for comic relief, and Catwoman temporarily sheathed her claws and slinked into inactivity, as did Two-Face. Villains premiering during that decade were uninspired and gimmick-ridden, like Killer Moth, Firefly, the Terrible Trio (the Fox, the Shark, and the Vulture, thugs wearing Mardi Gras–like animal heads), and Calendar Man. Only the icy Mr. Freeze, called "Mr. Zero" in his 1959 debut, proved chilling enough to develop staying power with readers.

By the early 1960s, the Batman franchise was in sad shape, and the Dynamic Duo's rogues' gallery appeared infrequently, with alien invaders, lampoons of movie monsters, and, once again, mundane mobsters becoming the norm. Yet one memorable new villain managed to ooze out of this mire: ne'er-do-well Matt Hagen became the new Clayface, a formidable shape-shifter, after wading in a shimmering pool of an unexplained liquid. In 1964, sagging sales led DC Comics to give Batman a much-needed facelift in a movement called the "New Look," orchestrated by editor Julius Schwartz. Artist Carmine Infantino provided a sleeker, more

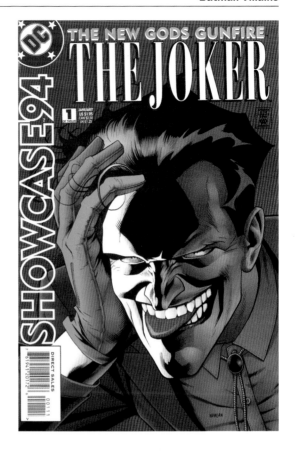

Showcase 94 #1 © 1994 DC Comics.
COVER ART BY KEVIN NOWLAN.

stylized interpretation of Batman and Robin, and the stories incorporated more crime-detection and scientific elements. Joker, Penguin, Riddler, Catwoman, and Scarecrow returned to active duty, joined by a heinous host of new foes: the brutish Blockbuster, whose rage could only be quelled by the face of Bruce Wayne, Batman's alter ego; the psychedelic Spellbinder; the captivating Poison Ivy, whose intoxicating allure divided the Dynamic Duo; and international crimelord Dr. Tzin-Tzin.

During the heyday of ABC's *Batman* television show (1966–1968), being cast as a guest Bat-villain was a coveted Hollywood gig, and Tinseltown's luminaries vied for roles. Mainstay menaces from the comic books were present—the Joker (Cesar Romero), the Riddler (Frank Gorshin and, temporarily, John Astin), and the Penguin (Burgess Meredith), among others—and new antagonists were created, including Egghead (Vincent Price), King Tut (Victor Buono), and the Siren (Joan Collins).

Batman experienced a comic-book renaissance in the 1970s. Writers Frank Robbins and Denny O'Neil returned the hero to his original "creature of the night" status, and the villains became more startling as well. Man-Bat, a biologist whose goal of emulating Batman bore freakish results, first flapped his wings in 1970. Ra's al Ghul, a global terrorist empowered with immortality from regular dips in the "Lazurus Pit," deduced the hero's Wayne identity and chose the "Detective" (as he called Batman) as his successor. Batman refused, of course, despite the temptation of al Ghul's fetching daughter Talia. And the ominous old guard got nastier: The Joker resumed murdering victims with a smile and Two-Face, more demented than ever, returned from limbo.

By the 1980s, Batman's rogues were no longer mere costumed thieves: They were now full-fledged psychopaths, incarcerated at (and systematically escaping from) Arkham Asylum, an institution for the criminally insane. Newer villains were introduced—including the shocking Electrocutioner, devilish siblings Night-Slayer and Nocturna, a female Clayface (who later joined her predecessors as the Mudpack), and the vigilante Anarky—but they lacked the longevity of two new threats: the reptilian-skinned Killer Croc and the mousy mobster Ventriloquist (who voiced crime commands through his dummy Scarface). Still, no Bat-villain better epitomized the grim-and-gritty 1980s than the good old Joker, who ended the decade by shooting and paralyzing Barbara (Batgirl) Gordon, murdering the second Robin, and usurping the screen from the title star (in a *tour de force* by actor Jack Nicholson) in Tim Burton's hit film *Batman* (1989).

By the 1990s, the traditional superhero—in comics and in other media—was no more. In his place stood the anti-hero, the dark avenger whose methods for apprehending adversaries were often as violent as his foes'. Batman had jumpstarted this movement twenty years prior and continued the trend through that decade and into the 2000s, differentiated from other anti-heroes by his pledge to preserve human life. His contemporary enemies share no such vow—newer foes often leave a trail of bodies in their wake. Witness Bane (whose "Venom"-enhanced strength enabled him to break Batman's back); Nicholas Scratch, Orca, and assassins Brutale and Cain; retreads like Charaxes (a mutated Killer Moth); the new Spellbinder; and yet another Clayface. The breakthrough Bat-baddie of the 1990s was the Joker's girlfriend Harley Quinn, originally created for television's *Batman: The Animated Series* (1992). Quinn proved so popular she was added to DC Comics continuity, even receiving her own monthly series in 2000.

That long-running *Batman* cartoon series included a legion of Bat-villains, the most popular of which was the Joker, voiced by Mark Hamill. On the big screen, the continuation of the *Batman* franchise lured box-office giants to the roles of Bat-rogues: Danny DeVito as the Penguin and Michelle Pfeiffer as Catwoman in *Batman Returns* (1992); Tommy Lee Jones as Two-Face and Jim Carrey as the Riddler in *Batman Forever* (1995); and Arnold Schwarzenegger as Mr. Freeze and Uma Thurman as Poison Ivy in *Batman & Robin* (1997). The Dark Knight's foes, particularly the Joker, have been heavily merchandized since the mid-1960s in everything from action figures to children's underwear. —*ME*

Batman's Weapons and Gadgets

Perhaps no other costumed crime fighter claims all the weapons, tools, and gadgets that DC Comics' Batman possesses. And for good reason: Unlike most superheroes, Batman does not have any innate superhuman abilities. Instead, he fights with a martial arts expertise that might make Jet Li flinch, the high-tech gadgetry of James Bond, a host of otherworldly weapons, custom-designed vehicles, and razor-sharp detective skills, his ability to deductively reason tantamount to master sleuth Hercule Poirot. The Dark Knight's equipment is often black or midnight blue, bearing a bat insignia.

His utility belt—a fundamental part of the Caped Crusader's costume and the backbone of his crime-fighting arsenal—contains the stuff of boys' wildest imaginings. Containers hold every conceivable apparatus, from fingerprint equipment to a palm-top communicator, complete with encrypted cell phone and e-mail capabilities. Batman's notorious Bat-rope is drawn out of the lining of his utility belt, much like the line on a fishing reel. Because this silken cord is as "strong as steel," it can easily be used as a lasso, or for scaling skyscrapers and swinging from rooftops. Historian Michael L. Fleisher noted that the utility belt has been used on "easily a thousand occasions" throughout Batman's long career, its various contents—changed over the years and composed of dozens if not hundreds of implements—used to "rescue him from life-and-death situations and help him apprehend criminals." First introduced as part of Batman's costume in 1939 and last overhauled during the "No Man's Land" story arc of 1999 in order to accommodate more weapons and supplies for an earthquake-ridden Gotham City, the utility belt is counted among Batman's strongest crime-fighting assets.

Tucked neatly within Batman's utility belt are various Batarang compartments, first introduced into Batman's staple of battle supplies in September 1939. While the Batarang can be pulled from his belt instantly and thrown and retrieved with Green Beret–like accuracy, Batman also developed, in 1946, a Batarang gun, for firing the Batarang over especially long distances. The

Batarang has had many variations, including the magnetic Batarang, the seeing-eye Batarang (which contains a miniature camera), the flash-bulb Batarang (for illuminating a subject or temporarily blinding an evil-doer), and the bomb Batarang (armed with explosives and always useful in a pinch). Used consistently throughout the history of Batman comics, Batarangs have also gone Hollywood in the live-action *Batman* TV series of the 1960s and live-action feature films of the late 1980s and early 1990s.

Other Bat-gadgets created by Batman over the years include the entangling Bat-bolo; the Batpoon, a harpoon with Bat-rope attached; Bat-grenades; and a Bat glass cutter. Bat-darts were also a favorite accessory of the Dark Knight in the late 1950s and, like other items in Batman's arsenal, come and go as needed. Green-tinted infrared goggles allow Batman to see in the dark "just like a real bat" (proclaimed *Detective Comics* #37) and magnifying goggles allow him to see distant objects close-up, though of late Batman relies more heavily on his ultra-tech multifunction binoculars. Shark-Repellent Batspray graced the big screen in the 1966 live-action movie *Batman,* always useful for battling deadly sea creatures that have started chewing on body parts. Likewise, the 1960s *Batman* TV show introduced the Bat-shield—a folding, shield-like device doubling as a motorcycle window and protecting the Batman and sidekick Robin—though comic-book fans will probably never see this particular Bat-gizmo in print.

During the 1950s and 1960s, Batman developed a line of gliding and scaling accessories for accessing Gotham, including glider Bat-wings that functioned much like a hang-glider; and a pair of "human jet-power units" that—when strapped to Batman and Robin's backs—allowed the heroes to soar through the air at breakneck speed. For scaling skyscrapers, Batman frequently used—what else?—specially crafted gloves and knee pads with suction cups attached. To allow the heroes to walk on water, the Dynamic Duo used "air-inflated" raft shoes. When he is not sleuthing about with his various jumplines, today's Batman prefers to travel via his technologically advanced Batmobile, bulletproof Batcycle, or Bat-humvee.

Gone are the Golden Age (1938–1954) spy-like devices like the Flying Eye, a remote-controlled bowling ball-shaped machine that could soar through the air, hover at command, and then televise what it saw and heard back to a receiver located in the Batcave. For checking out the scene of a crime and performing other investigative work, only the most advanced technology will suffice. Batman's ultra-cool Universal Tool is a lightweight, miniaturized self-contained tool kit. His Crime-Scene Kit comes complete with a multispectral, high-resolution camera, fingerprint kit, evidence-collecting bags in various sizes, and forensics software. A fingerlight, fitted with a rubberized mouth-holder to allow for hands-free use, illuminates the scene of any crime. Alter ego Bruce Wayne's WayneTech research often provides the electronics, computer chips, or other equipment necessary to make the Guardian of Gotham's sleuthing tools function.

Other members of the Bat-family have enjoyed their own gadgetry, though most accessories pale in comparison to the Dark Knight's. Robin's utility belt always ran a close second to his mentor's. As Nightwing, the costumed hero sports night-vision lenses in his mask and prefers to keep his weapons arsenal loaded in his glove gauntlets rather than a utility belt. Barbara Gordon as Batgirl wore a weapons belt, complete with a bat-insignia-decorated Batpurse—perfect for lipstick and assorted sundries. As Oracle, Gordon is Gotham's information broker, with her super-computer workstation as her most coveted accessory. In his heydey, canine crime-fighting companion Ace the Bat-Hound, in character with his black mask and bat insignia on his collar, sported a tiny two-way radio in his collar that allowed Batman and Robin to call for him once he traveled outside voice range, as well as to overhear villains' conversations once Ace had tracked them down. —*GM*

Battle of the Planets

For more than thirty years the heroes of the classic television series *Battle of the Planets* have enthralled legions of children everywhere. The band of teenagers that form the superhero group G-Force were the creation of Tatsuo Yoshida, the founder of Tatsunoko Animation and the originator of the classic 1960s anime character Speed Racer. Yoshida envisioned a show that explored the relationship between humans and science, and so named his Japanese anime series *Science Ninja Team Gatchaman.* From the moment the program premiered on primetime Japanese television in 1972, it was a smash hit. With its homeland success, it was inevitable that *Gatchaman* would invade television sets across the world. When it hit the United States in 1978 as the rechristened *Battle of the Planets,* the show was an instant success—becoming one of the most popular anime series ever to air on American television and leading the way for a massive worldwide anime revolution.

The massive box office success of *Star Wars* convinced Sandy Frank, an independent television program packager, that *Gatchaman* might be just the thing to whet the appetite of children craving more intergalactic adventures. Sparing no expense, Frank hired formidable animation veterans Jameson Brewer and Alan Dinehart to reformat the original *Gatchaman* shows for Western audiences by toning down the violent and sexual content, which Japanese audiences were accustomed to. One of most controversial characters was the villain Zoltar, who was originally portrayed as a hermaphrodite, an aspect of his persona that would never fly with American censors. Also, since the original Japanese production was earthbound, creators conceived of new animation that depicted space flight and planets. Finally, the show was given its *Star Wars*-esque name, and an empire was born.

Battle of the Planets took place in a not-so-distant future where Earth and its colonized worlds formed the Intergalactic Federation of Planets to ensure peace across the universe. When the Federation's defenses were down, an evil organization named Spectra, led by the tyrant Zoltar and his master the Luminous One, came from its decaying universe to conquer the Federation. The only thing that stood between Spectraand the Federation was a company of five teenagers named G-Force, who were sworn to serve and protect the Federation's survival with their enhanced abilities, sheer determination, and mighty Phoenix aircraft.

G-Force established the five-person team archetype that set the mold for Japanese superhero teams in shows like *The Mighty Morphin' Power Rangers* and *Voltron.* In *Battle of the Planets,* each member was unique in personality and appearance, and each had a distinctive "bird" costume along with his or her own custom vehicle. The group consisted of the stern leader Mark; the hot-headed Jason; the beautiful Princess; the comic relief Keyop; and the easygoing Tiny.

Battle of the Planets © 2002 Sandy Frank Entertainment.

The characters had extensive combat training, but also had "cerebonic implants," giving them increased strength and endurance (in the original *Gatchaman* series, the team had no implants). All the team members, with the exception of Tiny, were orphans of one sort or another—Keyop (who had a speech impediment that caused him to speak with an odd, chirping sound) was a test-tube baby, born in a laboratory. The team was lead by Chief Anderson of the Intergalactic Federation. Monitoring the team from their main headquarters, Center Neptune, was the robot 7-Zark-7. A character similar to *Star Wars*' R2-D2, Zark was created for the Stateside version of the series, to provide narration for the show and to create a bridge over the portions that had been edited.

Even though the premise of the series was slightly altered from the original, the sophisticated characterizations and strong storylines stood out for audiences used to feeding on the light and breezy Hanna Barbera–influenced animation that was abundant in the 1970s. *Battle of the Planets* became an international hit as well; the series found success in countries including Great Britain, France, Spain, Canada, and the Netherlands, accompanied by merchandise such as board games, toys, specialty magazines, and comic books.

By the mid-1980s, *Battle of the Planets* went off the air. Various incarnations of the show have enjoyed moderate success, including *G-Force,* Turner's re-edited version of the original *Gatchaman* shows, which ran on TBS briefly beginning in July 1987; but it was not until 1995 that the entire series was shown on the Cartoon Network. In the 1990s, Saban Entertainment produced another English-language version called *Eagle Riders;* however, the company used the second *Gatchaman* series, which aired in Japan in 1978.

In the 1990s and 2000s, the characters have enjoyed a resurgence in popularity thanks to a new toy line and the best-selling *Battle of the Planets* series from Top Cow Comics, with art direction by Alex Ross, and Munier Sharrieff and Wilson Tortosa handling the story and art, respectively. Beginning in October 2001, the classic episodes were released on DVD from Rhino Home Video. The DVD collection also includes the original, unedited episodes of *Gatchaman* that were used in the creation of *Battle of the Planets.* The soundtrack for the series was released on CD in early 2001. —*MM*

Big Bang Heroes

Return to the days of 1940s yesteryear when super-strong Ultiman starred in *Ultiman Comics* and *HiOc-*

tane Comics, dark detective Knight Watchman headlined *Deductive Comics,* patriotic supersoldier the Badge fought Nazis, and the Knights of Justice teamed up to undo dastardly plots. Don't remember those heroes? How about the updated 1960s supergroup Round Table of America or the teen sidekick group the Whiz Kids? What about the time when Amazonian goddess Venus had her powers removed?

If those situations and characters sound familiar, but not quite right, that's because they are a part of the fictional history of the *Big Bang Comics* line. The creation of Gary S. Carlson and Chris Ecker, *Big Bang* is the ultimate homage to the comic world's Golden Age (1938–1954) and Silver Age (1956–1969). Debuting in 1995, at a time when heroes were grim and gritty, being reinvented as gun-toting or claw-bearing murderers—and when few Golden Age reprints were being offered from any publisher—*Big Bang Comics* gave readers stories that looked, felt, and read like the comics of decades past. Occasionally, issues of the series would take a more "modern" look at the characters, but the majority of the stories were set in the era between 1939 and 1969.

In addition to those previously mentioned, other Big Bang characters included super-speedster the Blitz, Thunder Girl (who shouted a magic word to transform and gain powers of flight and strength), mystical spirit of vengeance Dr. Weird, the Beacon (whose jewel-in-a-miner's-helmet gave him light-based powers), star-powered Dr. Stellar, pill-powered Vita-Man, slinkily dressed femme fatale Shadow Lady, flaming hero the Blue Blaze, aquatic hero the Human Sub, shrinking hero the Hummingbird, and uncanny archer Robo-Hood, in addition to the aforementioned Whiz Kids (Knight Watchman's acrobatic sidekick Kid Gallahad, Blitz's quick-footed junior partner Cyclone, and Atomic Sub's water-breathing granddaughter Moray).

Big Bang villains were as familiar as the heroes they faced. Ultiman fought extradimension imp Mr. Mix-it-Up and evil genius Dexter Cortex, while Knight Watchman faced the clownish prince of

Big Bang Comics #4 © 1996 Gary Carlson and
Chris Ecker.
COVER ART BY TERRY BEATTY.

crime Pink Flamingo and shape-changer Mr. Mask.
The Badge traded blows with the zombie-like Dr.
Cadaver and the ghastly Axis spy the Yellow Peril,
but Thunder Girl's worst adversary was the brilliant-
but-wicked monkey known as Dr. Hy Q. Binana! Not
all of *Big Bang*'s characters quite so closely resembled any specific superhero or villain from the DC,
Marvel, or Fawcett Comics universes, but many
easy comparisons can be drawn.

Co-creator Gary Carlson said in a 1998 online
interview that part of the reason he set *Big Bang
Comics* so far in the past was "because the recent
comics past has been so bleak. Most of us remember when comics were fun to read." After a few characters previously appeared in Carlson's self-published *Megaton* (1983–1986), *Big Bang Comics*
#0–#4 were published by Caliber Press in
1995–1996, as well as miniseries for *Knight Watchmen* and *Dr Weird*. In 1996, Carlson brought the
series to Image Comics and restarted the series
with issue #1. There, the crew was able to utilize
Erik Larsen's Shazam-esque pastiche Mighty Man in
stories that aped C. C. Beck's *Captain Marvel*
adventures, while Jim Valentino's *Shadowhawk*
made a Silver Age appearance. Even Alan Moore's
own Silver Age pastiche characters from Image's
1963 appeared. Two highlight issues from the *Big
Bang Comics* series (#24 and #27, 1999) were
done in the style of Jim Steranko's *History of
Comics* publications, and included—amidst dozens
of fake covers—a comprehensive and believable
historical look at the *Big Bang* characters.

A low-budget direct-to-video *Knights of Justice*
film was released in summer 2000, featuring Ultiman (Mike Constantin), Thunder Girl (Sandra Kuhn),
Knight Watchmen (Allen Woodman), and newcomer
Masker (Lorin Taylor) against the evil scientist Cortex (writer/director Philip R. Cable). Further film or
television versions of the characters have been
under discussion. Knight Watchman creator Chris
Ecker has sponsored wrestlers wearing his hero's
costume. And although the final regular issue of *Big
Bang Comics* (#35) was released in 2001, further
specials have appeared: *World Class Comics, Ultiman Giant, Whiz Kids,* and *Big Bang Comics Summer Special*. Even if the stories and characters are
trapped in the past, it appears that there will continue to be *Big Bang Comics* in the future. —AM

Bird Heroes

Flight represents the ultimate freedom. Consequently, humankind has for centuries regarded the
bird as a muse for its mythology, its science, and its
fantasy. As a result, a flock of bird-based super-

heroes have soared through comic books, television, and movies.

Hawkman is the most famous of the bird heroes, originating in DC Comics' *Flash Comics* #1 (1940). His golden, winged helmet and broad feathered wingspan have prompted a host of imitators, but Hawkman himself was not the first feathered fighter in the comics—the Hawkmen of the *Flash Gordon* comic strip preceded him. Yet Hawkman endures, although his nest has been re-feathered by numerous reworkings. His companion Hawkgirl has flown alongside him since the 1940s, and in 2001 became a television star as part of the Cartoon Network's animated *Justice League* series.

Among the Hawkman clones are two young hatchlings directly connected to the Winged Wonder's lore (by way of groups he's belonged to). Golden Eagle, a long-haired teen named Charley Parker, took wing in *Justice League of America* #116 (1975) as a surrogate Hawkman in a battle with the hero's foe the Matter Master, then joined Titans West, an offshoot of the Teen Titans. Northwind, who premiered in *All-Star Squadron* #25 (1983), hails from a secret society of human/bird hybrids living in the appropriately named Feithera, a remote area of Greenland. The son of a Feitherian princess and a human anthropologist, Northwind's mixed heritage and peculiar appearance—ebon, feathery skin, golden plumage "hair," and natural wings—makes him forever a recluse outside of his homeland, although he finds kinship among the members of the supergroup Infinity, Inc. Northwind can converse with birds and commands migratory powers.

Air Man began his short flight as a superhero in Centaur Comics' *Keen Detective Funnies* #23 (1949). Drake Stevens adopts synthetic wings and a jet-pack to avenge the killing of his father—an ornithologist—and uses guns and even explosives in his aerial war on crime. His massive wingspan was an obvious takeoff on Hawkman, but Air Man's dazzlingly hued feathers of yellow, white, and red differentiate his appearance from his predecessor's more earthen image. The Owl, one of the few super-

heroes to wear a lavender costume, was first seen in Dell Comics' *Crackajack Funnies* #25 (1940). More Batman than Hawkman, the Owl is actually police investigator Nick Terry, but prowls the streets at night in his flying Owlmobile and glides through the air with his parachute cape. The Owl employs perhaps the most bizarre weapon of any superhero: His Owl-gun's "ga-ga ray" induces owl-like behavior—what a hoot! The Owl was sometimes joined in his crime-fighting endeavors by Terry's fiancée, Laura Holt, masquerading as Owl Girl. The Owl's adventures lasted under two years, and a two-issue Gold Key Comics revival in 1967–1968 failed to earn him a permanent perch.

The television superhero Birdman, a product of the Hanna-Barbera animation studios, was first seen on NBC's *Birdman and the Galaxy Trio* (1967). Brightly garbed in a yellow bodysuit with a blue cowl and blue wings, this airborne adventurer can fly, is super strong, and emits hand-generated solar beams, gifts afforded him by the Egyptian god of the sun, Ra. Operating from the volcano-based Bird Lair, Birdman and his eagle Avenger—with, occasionally, his kid sidekick Birdboy—are dispatched by the operative "Falcon 7" to thwart the threats of supervillains like Vulturo, Nitron, and Cumulus, members of the lawless league F.E.A.R. After two seasons, Birdman fluttered into occasional reruns until being resurrected in 2001 as *Harvey Birdman, Attorney at Law* as part of the Cartoon Network's Adult Swim programming.

Another cinematic crusader, Condorman, made a multimedia premiere in late 1980 in a newspaper comic strip (that lasted roughly four months), a three-issue Gold Key comic-book series, and a live-action theatrical movie starring Michael Crawford, who would later become famous in Broadway's *Phantom of the Opera.* Woody Wilkins is a comic-book artist who festoons himself in the vibrant, feathered attire of his creation, Condorman, to fully understand his character, and is recruited by a CIA agent friend to use his flying costume to protect Russian defectors from errant KGB agents. *Condorman,* the movie

(1981), attempted mass-demographic appeal by mixing a variety of genres, hence its tagline, "An action adventure romantic comedy spy story."

Black Condor is an appellation shared by two airborne comic-book superheroes. The original Black Condor, who bowed in Quality Comics' *Crack Comics* #1 (1940), was raised by a black condor and learned to fly by example. Sporting a midnight-blue ensemble of briefs, boots, and glider wings, the superhero Black Condor was ultimately purchased by DC Comics and absorbed into its universe, beginning in the 1970s with appearances in *Justice League of America* and *Freedom Fighters.* DC updated the hero in 1992, making the new Black Condor a young man given the natural power of flight through the machinations of a centuries-old sect, the Society of the Golden Wing.

Other flying bird heroes include Timely (later Marvel) Comics' Red Raven, a Golden Age (1938–1954) character wearing, as his name suggests, a crimson costume with red wings (albeit those of a bat rather than his namesake); Marvel Comics' Falcon, a red-and-white clad African-American hero whose glider wings propel him through the air; Marvel's Nighthawk, a blue-clad crusader with jet-propelled wings; Blue Eagle, a member of Marvel's Squadron Supreme, who dons anti-gravity wings to soar the heavens (in his adventures he temporarily changes his name to Cap'n Hawk and Condor); a DC heroine called Dawnstar, an "Amerind" (American Indian) member of the futuristic team the Legion of Super-Heroes, born with white wings and a foolproof tracking ability; Craig Lawson, a.k.a. Raven of Tower Comics' T.H.U.N.D.E.R. Agents, whose costumes molted from issue to issue, ranging from rocket-powered glider wings to bulletproof metal wings; Snowbird of Marvel's Alpha Flight, who morphs into Arctic creatures, including owls; and France's superhero Peregrine ("falcon" in French), who flew through Marvel's multicultural miniseries *Contest of Champions* (1982).

Not all birds are airborne, nor are all bird-named superheroes. The most famous is Robin, the partner of Batman. This Boy Wonder sports a bright red breast (his tunic), but generally takes to the air by swinging on his Bat-rope. Robin was parodied as Sparrow in the oft-reprinted "Bats-Man" story in *MAD* #105 (1966). The original version of DC's the Hawk and the Dove were teenage brothers—polar political opposites—bequeathed bird costumes and enhanced strength and nimbleness by a mysterious voice in *Showcase* #75 (1968). The Blackhawks *can* fly, but only in their planes. This international team of fighter pilots premiered in *Military Comics* #1 (1941). Prize Publications' Black Owl started his career in 1940 in a tuxedo and owl mask before adopting blue tights and a yellow bird headdress, more standard-issue superhero garb. His outfit and name aside, he bore no other bird characteristics, but managed to stay in print through 1948.

Black Canary, one of DC's street operatives called the Birds of Prey, is flightless, but at one time commanded a dizzying sonic scream called her "canary cry." Her Marvel counterpart, martial artist Bobbi Morse—better known as Mockingbird—was an agent of the espionage organization S.H.I.E.L.D. before becoming a member of the Avengers. Mockingbird is renowned for her iron "battle staves"—twin batons that, when connected, serve as a vaulting pole—and for her mockery: She frequently disconcerts her foes with derisions. Marvel's Songbird plagiarized Black Canary's cry: When she premiered in *Marvel Two-In-One* #56 (1979) she was the pro-wrestler-turned-supervillain Screaming Mimi, using her hypersonic screech to disorient opponents. She resurfaced in 1997 as Songbird, one of the team of super-fugitives called the Thunderbolts, and ultimately reformed.

Other bird-named heroes have been fly-by-nights: The Eagle, decked out in red, white, and blue with a gold eagle chest insignia, was more superpatriot than bird hero, and flitted through several Fox Features Syndicate titles in 1940 and 1941; comics' original Raven, premiering in Ace Periodicals' *Sure-Fire Lightning* #1 (1940), was essentially a copy of the Green Hornet but with a bird motif; and TV's Blue Falcon, a priggish animated superhero, played the straight man to his wacky partner, the clumsy robotic dog Dynomutt. No character better exemplifies the bird hero than Howard the Duck, writer Steve Gerber's anthropomorphic drake "trapped in a world he never made"—the Marvel universe! Howard popped into the pages of Marvel's Man-Thing series in 1973 and stuck around for several years, trying to find his place this reality of "hairless apes" (humans), fighting monsters and supervillains (and even teaming up with Spider-Man) along the way. Filmmaker George Lucas brought the character to life in the 1986 theatrical flop *Howard the Duck. —ME*

Birds of Prey

Even with a dozen or so costumed vigilantes prowling over its rooftops, Gotham City is filled with crime. Most of the heroes have had interaction with Batman, and some have even been his protégés. One such heroine was Barbara Gordon, whose career as Batgirl put many criminals behind bars. After the Joker shot her, a paraplegic Gordon refused to sink into self-pity, or accept that her crime-fighting career was over. Using money from Wayne Enterprises and other sources, the now wheelchair-bound Gordon established a base of operations in the Clocktower high above Gotham. There, utilizing an astonishing array of computers and electronics, Gordon became Oracle, an information broker who uses her databases and contacts to fight crime—not only in Gotham, but worldwide.

As leader of a rotating-membership superhero mini-group called Birds of Prey, Gordon first utilized Power Girl as an operative, but that relationship was disastrously short-lived. Oracle examined the other female superheroines whom she knew and settled upon Dinah Lance, the second-generation crime fighter known as the Black Canary. The daughter of the original Black Canary, Lance not only has consummate detective and martial arts skills, she also has a metagenetic ability to use a sonic "Canary Cry" to topple opponents and doorways alike.

Oracle has used other operatives as part of her "Birds of Prey," allying herself with the mysterious crossbow-wielding Huntress, and even an occasional male hero, such as the Blue Beetle. Although Black Canary is also involved with the Justice Society of America, she prefers to work as one of Oracle's operatives. And for Barbara Gordon, the good she does as Oracle—helping Batman, Nightwing, the Justice League, or the Birds of Prey—balances out the mobility she lost to Gotham's craziest criminal.

Gordon first appeared as Oracle in *Suicide Squad* #29 (January 1989), her new persona the re-creation of writer John Ostrander. The *Birds of Prey* concept began as a series of one-shots and miniseries in 1996, and included appearances in *Showcase* and *Green Arrow*. The concept proved popular enough that a regular *Birds of Prey* series began in January 1999.

Although a *Birds of Prey* television series was introduced in 2002, all the characters had made appearances in television and film prior to this. Batgirl was featured in the 1960s *Batman* television series and the 1997 feature film *Batman & Robin,* as well as a number of animated TV series and films from the 1960s onward. Black Canary and Huntress both made a pair of television appearances in Hanna-Barbera's two *Legends of the Super-Heroes* primetime specials on NBC (airing February 3 and 10, 1977). The campy stories had a collection of superheroes interacting with supervillains in "The Challenge" and "The Roast." Black Canary was played by the one-named Danuta (Rylko-Soderman, later a television evangelist), while Huntress was played by Barbara Joyce.

On October 9, 2002, the WB network debuted a highly advertised new live-action series called *Birds of Prey,* based loosely on the DC comic book. The narration at the show's beginning established the characters as a trio of heroines: Helena Kyle, a.k.a. Huntress (Ashley Scott), was the half-metahuman daughter of Batman and Catwoman; the former Batgirl Barbara Gordon a.k.a. Oracle (Dina Meyer) was the wheelchair-bound computer genius;

and Dinah Redmond (Rachel Skarsten) was the run-away metahuman daughter of the original Black Canary. Headquartered in the Clocktower, the trio protected New Gotham from villains of all sorts.

The series mixed a lot of concepts from the comics, including the original version of Huntress (the Batman's daughter concept that had been written out of continuity) and guest appearances by the Joker (only briefly), Harley Quinn, Lady Shiva, Clayface, and the original Black Canary. Barbara Gordon even donned her Batgirl suit a few times. Despite its high action quotient and Batman-esque promos, *Birds of Prey* only lasted for thirteen episodes, and the two-part finale aired on February 19, 2003.

The fate of the TV show has not affected the *Birds of Prey* comic book. Oracle and Black Canary—and occasionally Huntress—have withstood the biggest villain of all. If a slumping comic-book market can't hurt the Birds of Prey, how can any escapee from Arkham Asylum hope to? —*AM*

Black Canary

The Black Canary was the last major DC Comics superhero created in the Golden Age of comics (1938–1954) and, in one form or another, she has proved to be one of the most enduring. She was introduced in the pages of *Flash Comics* #86 in August 1947 as a sort of villainous Robin Hood with a femme fatale twist, guesting in the Johnny Thunder strip. The Black Canary stole from criminals but kept the money herself, though Johnny—once he had got over his lovesick attraction for her—quickly persuaded her to go straight. She soon gained a solid fan following and as a result was able to repay Johnny's devotion by taking over his slot in the comic. She also ousted him from the Justice Society of America, and became the last new member to join.

While little was initially revealed of her origins, a 1970s story described how, as a child, Dinah Drake

was relentlessly trained by her police lieutenant father to be a policewoman, only to see him die of a broken heart when she was turned down by the force. Inspired by such heroes as Batman, Drake resolved that she could best serve her father's memory by becoming a costumed crime fighter; by the time of this story, it seems that everyone thought it best to ignore her brief fling with crime. So, dressed in dark halter-top, shorts, jacket, boots, nylon stockings, and a blonde wig (her only element of disguise), Drake became the Black Canary. Armed only with her detective skills and martial arts knowledge, she proved to be quite a formidable character. In her civilian identity Drake ran a flower shop, but she seemed to spend just as much time fending off the amorous advances of boyfriend Larry Lance, a rather down-at-the-heels private eye. In a role reversal, and in welcome relief from the usual damsel-in-distress cliché, it was Lance who was frequently captured by villains and the Black Canary who had to rush in to save the day.

Written by Robert Kanigher and drawn by Carmine Infantino, the Black Canary strip ran for twelve installments—until *Flash Comics* was canceled. She also starred in twenty *Justice Society* tales up to 1951, when even that legendary strip went under. But when the Justice Society was brought back in the 1960s, as annual guests in *The Justice League,* the Black Canary was there, too, having apparently gone into semi-retirement and married Lance in the interim. Poor Lance did not last long after his wife's second stint in the team, as an encounter with a sentient star called Aquarius (in *Justice League* #74) resulted in his tragic death. A heartbroken Canary promptly jumped ship to the Justice League, to avoid the sad memories of Lance that would be brought back by seeing her old Justice Society teammates, and embarked on a long career with the League. She became romantically linked with the somewhat dissolute Green Arrow and, when he joined with Green Lantern in their groundbreaking early 1970s series, she went along as well.

Green Arrow became an archetypical anti-authority radical, and Black Canary, infused with the era's concerns, assumed advocacy of women's lib and operated with noticeably more self-assurance. Throughout the decade, she appeared both with and without Green Arrow in stories in *Adventure Comics, Action Comics,* and *World's Finest Comics,* as well as with the Justice League, and she really became an integral part of DC's lineup. The 1980s were a less encouraging time for her, however, as she settled down into the role of Green Arrow's "old lady" and a civilian life in (once more) a flower shop. In an attempt to cash in on the vogue for grittier heroes, the Green Arrow was toughened up in a 1987 miniseries, part of which involved the Black Canary being savagely attacked, tortured, and assaulted, going from powerful superheroine to victim in one ill-judged story. The violent assault also appears to have robbed her of her one superpower—a sort of sonic cry, which had been gifted her in the early battle with Aquarius that had killed her husband. In time, the romance with Green Arrow soured and the couple split.

In the mid-1990s *Zero Hour* series, DC attempted to simplify and reinvigorate its comics line and, in a confusing bit of retrofitting, editors decided that from the moment she joined the Justice League, fans had not been reading about the Black Canary of the 1940s but her daughter! However illogical this may have been, that period did indeed see a renewed interest in the character, with a short-lived solo series and a starring role in the *Birds of Prey* comic. The solo series proved to be an ill-considered attempt at (yet another) gritty reinvention, as Dinah Lance was given a wretched new costume to take on Seattle's crack dealers. By contrast, in *Birds of Prey* Lance moved to Gotham City to join Oracle, Huntress, and even Catwoman in a far more life-affirming mixture of crime-busting and *Thelma & Louise*–style empowerment. A 2002 *Birds of Prey* TV show proved to be something of a disappointment to fans, but the rest of the 2000s have been kind to the Canary, with her Birds of Prey adventures alternating with appearances in a newly reformed Justice Society. With yet another costume, two comics, and a heightened public profile, things have never been better for the Black Canary. —*DAR*

The Black Cat I

The Black Cat is responsible for several firsts in her medium: She starred in the first comic from the legendary Harvey Comics, *Pocket Comics* #1 (in August 1941), and was the first and longest-lived Harvey superhero, in addition to being the first major costumed superheroine to grace comic-book pages.

Alfred Harvey had been an editor at Fox Comics when he decided to enter the comics market as a publisher himself, starting with *Pocket Comics.* As its name suggests, this was a digest-sized title, running up to one hundred pages, which Harvey packaged together with artist Joe Simon (of Captain America fame). The comic flew off the newsstands—but not in the way that Harvey expected! Its small size made it easy to steal, and light-fingered comics fans were carrying them off in droves. However, one of Harvey's creations in that first issue, the Black Cat (drawn by Al Gabrielle), would prove to be much more satisfyingly successful.

The Black Cat's alter ego, actress Linda Turner (named after real-life actresses Linda Darnell and Lana Turner), works for a tyrannical movie director called Garboil, whom she suspects is actually a Nazi Fifth-Columnist. Inspired by her cat's instant dislike of Garboil, she decides to adopt the identity of a cat—a black cat—and dons a suitably feline costume of low-cut black swimsuit, black pointed mask, gloves, and boots. Her origin story announces her quite pointedly: "Linda Turner, Hollywood Star and America's Sweetheart, becomes bored with her ultra-sophisticated life of movie make-believe and takes to crime-fighting in her most dynamic role of all as the … BLACK CAT!"

Teaming up with pipe-smoking reporter Rick Horne, the Black Cat tracks down Garboil and his pals and smashes their spy ring. Horne soon becomes Turner's constant companion, reporting on set from her many films but secretly harboring a crush for the Black Cat—never suspecting that she and Turner are one and the same. Although not superpowered in the traditional sense of the word, Turner's years of stuntwork and Hollywood action scenes left her with an athletic physique and mastery of martial arts, making her a formidable opponent for any miscreant.

After four issues of *Pocket Comics,* Harvey switched "Hollywood's Glamorous Detective Star" over to the more conventionally sized *Speed Comics,* where she appeared throughout World War II (from issues #17 in 1942 to issue #38 in 1945), as well as in occasional strips in *All-New Comics.* Those were creditable enough stories, drawn by the likes of Jill Elgin, Bob Powell, and Arturo Caseneuve, but it was the largely forgettable Captain Freedom who was usually the title's cover star, and our heroine had to wait for the lifting of wartime paper restrictions and the creation of her own title before she could really come into her own. *Black Cat* #1 premiered in the summer of 1946 and, from issue #4, became one of the era's most attractive strips with the addition of Lee Elias on art. British artist Elias was a great talent, working in the tradition of Milton Caniff (famed creator of newspaper strips *Terry and the Pirates* and *Steve Canyon*), and he added finesse, glamour, and a touch of humor to the feature.

The postwar years were characterized by a succession of crazes for such disparate genres as

The Black Cat (circa 1940s) from *Alfred Harvey's Black Cat* (1995). ™ & © Lorne-Harvey Publications Inc.
ART BY LEE ELIAS.

romance, crime, funny animals, and horror, which Al Harvey was determined to exploit. Seeing that Westerns were suddenly in vogue, Harvey temporarily changed the comic's title to *Black Cat Western,* which saw the heroine swap her trademark motorcycle for a horse. That period lasted a mere four issues (#16–#19). Then, from issue #30, retaining the character's name but not her presence, the comic became *Black Cat Mystery,* one of several Harvey horror comics, and poor old Linda Turner was banished into limbo. After several years of astonishingly gory horror tales (drawn by Elias, Warren Kremer, Bob Powell, and others), the incoming self-censorship body, the Comics Code Authority, prompted a sudden change of direction and the title briefly reverted once more to *Black Cat Western* with its old star (for #54–#56 in 1955).

These were the last Black Cat adventures for decades, as the comic's direction was changed back to "mystery" yet again when the mid-1950s superhero boom hoped for by Marvel, Magazine Enterprises, and others failed to materialize. After sporadic anthology issues of *Black Cat Mystery* in the late 1950s, the Black Cat herself reappeared to cash in on the 1960s superhero craze, but the three issues published then were reprints, which seemed out of place among the more sophisticated Marvel comics of that era.

Of course, Harvey Comics experienced enormous success throughout the 1950s, 1960s, and 1970s with its line of wholesome children's favorites, such as *Casper the Friendly Ghost, Little Dot, Sad Sack,* and *Richie Rich.* Elements of the Harvey empire were sold off in the 1980s, resulting in the Casper and Richie Rich movies, while other properties, notably the Black Cat, stayed within the Harvey family. Under its Recollection imprint, Harvey brought out nine issues of *The Original Black Cat* (1988–1992), while its Lorne-Harvey imprint released *Black Cat: The Origins* in 1995. The latter title mixed vintage Elias reprints with stories featuring a new Black Cat: movie stunt double Kim Stone. In the comic, this new Black Cat dons her costume to star in a film about the original Black Cat. Indeed, there were rumors of a Black Cat feature film at the time, but the project proved to be a nonstarter, and neither have any further comics adventures appeared since the mid-1990s. —*DAR*

The Black Cat II

Between 1979 and 1983, Spider-Man (Peter Parker) has to face life without Mary Jane Watson, the long-time love interest whom he is destined one day to marry. During this romantic interregnum, Parker's love life begins taking a decidedly unusual direction when he encounters Felicia Hardy, the talented burglar and platinum-blonde bombshell known as the Black Cat, who debuted in 1979 in *The Amazing Spider-Man* vol. 1 #194.

The creation of writer Marv Wolfman and illustrators Keith Pollard and Frank Giacoia, the Black Cat introduced an element of emotional chaos into the life of a youthful but steadily maturing—and thus ever-more-serious—hero. The daughter of a renowned cat burglar (Walter Hardy) who follows in her father's footsteps after he is imprisoned for life, Hardy becomes infatuated with Spider-Man, even going so far as building a shrine in his honor. She decides to turn over a new leaf, earns a legal pardon for her past crimes, and even becomes the wall-crawler's partner in crime fighting, if only briefly. As her formerly adversarial relationship with Spidey blossoms into a real romance, the hero takes her into his confidence enough to share his secret identity with her. Only then does he discover that she finds Peter Parker boring; her interest is entirely in Parker's costumed persona and the freedom and excitement it represents.

At first there is nothing superhuman about Hardy's burglar skills and tricks, which include a world-class gymnast's agility, martial arts expertise, a cable device she uses for swinging from rooftops (or as a tightrope), and the "accidents" she carefully arranges to befall anyone who crosses her path (she is a black cat, after all). In the mid-1980s, after the villains the Owl and Dr. Octopus nearly kill her in an action-packed issue of *Spectacular Spider-Man* (vol. 1 #75, 1983), she becomes worried that her lack of superpowers is making her a liability to her lover and partner in crime-busting, whom she fears will dump her. During Spider-Man's brief absence from Earth during the twelve-issue *Marvel Super Heroes Secret Wars* miniseries (May 1984–April 1985), Hardy gains a genuine superpower, namely the ability to prevail against her opponents using a mutation-derived probability-altering (or "bad luck") ability. But the scientists who give the Black Cat this bizarre ability are in the employ of the villainous Kingpin, who counts on her "bad luck" to bring about Spider-Man's destruction. Hardy's ill-considered actions—and her dishonesty in keeping them a secret—ultimately doom her relationship with Spidey, although the sorcery of Dr. Strange subsequently removes her bad luck powers.

On the rebound from Spider-Man, she travels across Europe, where she has a short-lived affair with the criminal known as the Foreigner before returning to New York. After Parker marries Hardy's romantic rival Mary Jane Watson in 1987, the Black Cat's life continues to intertwine with Spidey's, at least occasionally. Hardy tries to provoke Parker into jealousy by briefly dating his former high-school rival Flash Thompson, only to find herself accidentally falling in love with Flash; when he leaves her, she is genuinely heartbroken. Surprisingly, Hardy and Watson later become good friends. Her criminal career a thing of the past, the Black Cat goes on to found her own security company, Cat's Eye Investigations (as outlined in the 1994 four-issue miniseries, *Felicia Hardy: The Black Ca*t), and still assists her former flame in his struggles against such superfoes as the new "evil" Spider-Woman, introduced in 1999, and Hydro-Man, with whom she clashed as recently as 2000.

Although the Black Cat's love relationship with Spider-Man may have been doomed from the start, a 1991 issue of Marvel's *What If?* provides an intriguing glimpse into the insuperable problems these two disparate personalities—one cautious and hyper-responsible, the other flighty and reckless—would have encountered had they married. After a quarter century or more, the Black Cat continues to enthrall and intrigue Spidey's audiences—including the filmmaker Kevin Smith (writer, producer, and director of such cult-favorite films as *Clerks, Mallrats,* and *Chasing Amy*). Smith wrote the Terry Dodson–illustrated three-issue Spider-Man/Black Cat miniseries titled *The Evil That Men Do* (August–October 2002), and plans (along with Dodson) to pen more of Felicia Hardy's sometimes legally ambiguous adventures. In the meantime, readers have the character's parallel-universe counterparts to entertain them in occasional issues of *Ultimate Spider-Man* and *Spider-Girl.* —MAM

Black Condor

Of all the publishing houses in comics' Golden Age (1938–1954), Quality Comics probably had the strongest lineup of artists, with Jack Cole, Will Eisner, Reed Crandall, and Lou Fine. While the first three of these creative forces made their names on well-known and well-written series (Plastic Man, the Spirit, and Blackhawk, respectively), Fine flitted about from feature to feature, only settling down briefly on two of Quality's new superhero strips, the Ray and the Black Condor. Quality itself was one of the earliest comics publishers, started up by ex-printer Everett "Busy" Arnold in 1937, and much of its comics material was provided by the Eisner/Iger studio. When Eisner split up the studio, he took Fine and a few others with him, and soon Fine was working directly for Arnold as one of the company's top cover artists.

After a stint on Doll Man, Fine started work on a large number of strips, including the Ray (for *Smash Comics*), Uncle Sam (in *National Comics*) and the Black Condor, which first appeared in issue #1 of *Crack Comics,* in May 1940. The Black Condor's origin owed a lot to Edgar Rice Burroughs' Tarzan, except in this case the unfortunate child was brought up by—you guessed it—condors. Dick Grey's parents are murdered by bandits while on an archaeological expedition on the steppes of Outer Mongolia. The orphaned child is picked up by a passing condor, which decides to raise him as her own. Over the years, Grey tries to imitate his condor brethren and finally discovers how to fly. Later, while looking for food, he is set upon by eagles and forced to the ground, only to be discovered by a convenient hermit called Father Pierre, who nurses him back to life and then looks after the lad. Later, the now ailing hermit, with his dying wish, urges Grey (whom he has taken to calling the Black Condor) to travel to civilization and use his amazing gift for the benefit of humankind.

Adopting a blue-and-grey costume with a hood (which he rarely wore), and with large, flapping wings of cloth beneath his arms, the Black Condor battled all sorts of wrongdoers in his first year, before (in *Crack Comics* #11) chancing upon the body of a dead senator, Tom Wright. Noticing that he and the recently deceased could pass for twins, the Condor inexplicably decides to assume the senator's identity, inheriting at a stroke a nice job in Washington and a pretty young fiancée, Wendy Foster. Only Wendy's uncle and guardian knows that the new Tom is an impostor, and he seems not to mind! As was so often the case in comics, Foster continually bemoaned the fact that Wright wasn't more like the dashing Black Condor, and she never did connect the two, despite her fiancé's paltry disguise of a pair of spectacles worn when he was out of costume.

Most of the Black Condor's later adventures revolved around the machinations of the departed senator's killer, the evil, scheming lobbyist and "industrial tyrant," Jasper Crow. On the entry of the United States into World War II, Crow conveniently became a Nazi sympathizer and the strip became flooded with German troops, spies, and insurrectionists. However, despite the unusual political backdrop to the strip, there was little to lift the Black Condor above its many rivals, except the extraordinary art of Fine, who drew the series for most of its twenty-four episodes. Fine was able to marry his superior figure-work and drawing ability with a graceful, fluid storytelling sense which was the envy of his peers. His Black Condor glided effortlessly from panel to panel in a succession of imaginative poses that inspired a whole generation of comic-book artists. When Will Eisner was drafted in 1942, Fine (a polio victim as a child and so too weak to enlist) was moved over to the more prestigious Spirit strip. Other hands, including Charles Sultan and Bob Fujitani, took over the Black Condor series in his absence, but the feature ultimately did not work without Fine and was canceled in *Crack Comics* #31 in late 1943.

After the war, Fine went on to become the highly paid illustrator that he had always dreamed of being, and Arnold's Quality Comics continued to thrive. However, by 1956 Arnold's comics empire was losing ground, and he decided to sell up to arch-rivals DC Comics, who continued publishing *Blackhawk, Robin Hood, GI Combat,* and *Heart Throbs,* but ignored the superhero characters (most of whom were long gone by that time, anyway). In 1973, newly installed *Justice League of America* writer Len Wein remembered that DC owned all those venerable Quality heroes and reintroduced some of them as a team called the Freedom Fighters. This new group consisted of Uncle Sam, Doll Man, the Ray, the Human Bomb, Phantom Lady, and the Black Condor, and they proved popular enough to spin off into their own comic in 1976.

In *The Freedom Fighters,* the Black Condor was portrayed as a slightly distant, sinister figure, but the comic was canceled before much could be made of his revamped persona. A new Black Condor appeared in 1992; this one was a Native American who underwent all sorts of medical experiments, ultimately allowing him to fly—under the tutelage of the ghost of the first Black Condor. The comic also included guest appearances by another one of Fine's past triumphs, the Ray. In spite of this, however, and the fact that artist Rags Morales was something of a Fine acolyte, the title was short-lived. In recent years, little has been seen of any of the great heroes of Lou Fine or "Busy" Arnold, except in reprint form, and it might take a collection of 1940s Black Condor strips to rekindle interest in the hero. —DAR

Black Panther

Within the course of one incredible year in the pages of Marvel Comics' *Fantastic Four,* the writer/artist duo Stan Lee and Jack Kirby created characters like the Inhumans, the Silver Surfer, Galactus, and the Black Panther—comics' first black superhero. To have debuted him in 1966 (in *Fantastic Four* #52) shows both bravery and prescience on Marvel's part and, to their credit, the

Black Panther would go on to take a central role in their comics for years to come. The Panther was T'Challa, chief of the hidden African country of Wakanda; in true comics tradition, African countries are always hidden. Wakanda was depicted as a peculiar mix of high-tech machinery and mud huts, its futuristic technology being derived from "vibranium" metal found in a meteorite. The Black Panthers had been developed as a succession of elite guards, each in turn protecting the meteorite with the aid of sacred herbs which granted them fantastic strength and agility. T'Challa was the current inheritor of the Black Panther mantle (and all-black costume). After meeting the Fantastic Four, T'Challa decides his powers would be put to best use protecting the whole world (or at least America), and so he flies off to New York, leaving his people and his rather impractical cape behind.

For the next couple of years, the character flitted about from comic to comic before joining the Avengers in 1968, where he became a mainstay for the next seven years, save for the occasional jaunt back to Africa for the odd chunk of vibranium (which handily seemed to defeat most criminals). Marvel rarely made much of the Panther's color in the 1960s but in the more radical 1970s he acquired a forthright, liberated girlfriend, Monica Lynne, and briefly became a teacher in the ghetto, while the Avengers took on the racist Sons of the Serpent. Although it seems to have been pure coincidence, Marvel could not help but note that one of their leading characters shared his name with the radical black-power movement the Black Panthers, and he briefly became the Black Leopard. One month later, however, he was back to being the Black Panther again, and in 1973 was finally granted his own strip.

"Panther's Rage" ran for two years in the wonderfully titled *Jungle Action,* written by Don McGregor and drawn for the most part by the African-American artist Billy Graham. Reflecting the times' interest in African roots and black consciousness in general, the strip returned T'Challa to a Wakanda riven by infighting and sedition, and it managed to bal-

ance superheroics with musings on colonialism and democracy. The more overtly political material was leavened by the Panther's romance with Monica, which was surprisingly passionate for the time. For the duration of the tale, the strip featured an all-black cast, something that had never been attempted in comics before, and the innovations continued in a later story, which saw the Panther take on the Ku Klux Klan in Monica's native Georgia.

Poor sales prompted Marvel to cancel *Jungle Action* before the Klan story was finished, and replace it with a new Black Panther title by his creator, Jack Kirby. This new direction was as far from the gritty realism of McGregor's tales as it is possible to imagine, as our hero encountered the likes of King Solomon's Frog, the Yeti, and the Black Musketeers. Not surprisingly, this title, too, was short-lived. Sporadic appearances over the next two decades kept the Panther in the Marvel firmament, but he was increasingly marginalized. Miniseries in 1988 and 1991 were solid if unspectacular attempts at revitalizing what was effectively a lapsed franchise. The first tackled apartheid while the second dealt with the Panther's search for his mother, but neither led to anything substantial. With black characters no longer a comics novelty, and with role models such as the characters of Milestone Comics—which had more relevance to their readers than a wealthy African king—it seemed as if the Panther had had his day.

However, out of the blue, writer Christopher Priest reintroduced the hero as part of the slightly more adult "Marvel Knights" line, in a series that was acclaimed in every venue from the fan press to *Entertainment Weekly* and continued for six years—by far the character's most successful run. For this reinvention, a now aging T'Challa returns to the urban jungle of New York armed with claws and the occasional gun, and after thirty years he once again sports a cape. In a series of hard-hitting tales, he abdicates, witnesses his daughter's murder, and ultimately passes on the mantle of the Panther to a young cop, Kasper Cole. Though the franchise is dormant once more, persistent interest in the character and perennial talk of a Black Panther film is sure to make the absence a relatively brief one. —*DAR*

Black Widow

From her introduction as a superheroine in *Tales of Suspense* #52 in 1964, the Black Widow (created by the writer/artist team of Stan Lee and Don Heck) has been an almost constant presence across a dizzying array of Marvel Comics titles, equal parts superhero and superspy. The first communist heroine to appear in comics, the Black Widow is Marvel's longest-lived solo heroine. In her first appearance, battling Iron Man, she was simply Natasha Romanoff, a Soviet spy sent on an industrial espionage mission to Stark Industries—wearing an inconspicuous veil and figure-hugging cocktail dress combination. A few issues later she was back with an embittered young circus performer, the archer Hawkeye, whom she persuaded to battle Iron Man, but he soon saw the error of his ways and joined the Avengers. Inspired by his example, she denounced her cold war masters and defected to the West, donning a black and grey fishnet costume and signing up as a member of S.H.I.E.L.D. (Supreme Headquarters International Espionage Law-Enforcement Division), Marvel's all-purpose secret intelligence agency.

Throughout much of the 1960s, the Widow was a regular guest of the Avengers, alternately joining in their adventures and pining for Hawkeye. In *The Avengers* #43, her past was fleshed out in more detail; she had been orphaned during World War II and was brought up by the grizzled mountain man Ivan Petrovich. She later married the Soviet superhero the Red Guardian, but on his "death" she joined the KGB and was trained to become its top operative. In that same issue editors revealed that the Red Guardian had been alive all along, but in the following issue's mêlée he was killed anyway. Following several rebuffed attempts to join the Avengers, she abandoned her efforts (for the next twenty years, at any rate) and struck out on her own, determined to be a solo adventuress.

Readers next met the Black Widow in *Amazing Superman* #86 (1970), sporting a revamped all-in-one, black leather catsuit and armed with all-purpose "wristshooter" wristbands (incorporating a "widow's line" wire for swinging, tear-gas pellets, and "widow's bite" electric stinger), transforming her into a groovy late 1960s heroine à la Emma Peel of TV's *The Avengers*. This appearance was immediately followed by the Widow's first solo series, a co-headlining slot (shared with the Inhumans) in *Amazing Adventures,* which revealed a new jet-setting Natasha Romanoff, complete with penthouse pad, chauffeur (Ivan), maid, and swinging parties with playboys, princes, and Jackie O. The strips were sharp, hip, and beautifully drawn by Gene Colan (among others). They pitted the Widow against slum lords, the mob, and hippie cults. However, the split-book innovation failed to win a large enough readership, and the Inhumans were granted sole ownership of the title with issue #9. Undeterred by this setback, Romanoff jumped ship to *Daredevil,* without missing a month, and there she stayed for four years, even sharing cover billing for a while.

Daredevil and the Black Widow were a good combination: two sleek, elegant figures swinging gracefully through the night sky of San Francisco; this period of the comic is fondly remembered for its sophistication. Following a change of writer, Romanoff was written out of the comic and straight into another, one of the era's less memorable teams, *The Champions* (running for seventeen issues from 1975 to 1978). Former X-Men Iceman and the Angel put the Champions together, which also included Hercules and Ghost Rider in addition to the Black Widow—a more unlikely group of superheroes would be hard to find. Following the group's inevitable break-up, the Widow appeared to go on a tour of Marvel's entire line, taking in *The Avengers* and *Daredevil* (again), *Marvel Two in One* and *Marvel Team-up,* as well as a couple of well-executed

Black Widow #1 © 1999 Marvel Comics.
COVER ART BY J. G. JONES.

archy, resulting in appearances in numerous titles, including *Forceworks* and *Captain America,* though a little of her unique background was sacrificed in the process. In 1996, the Avengers were literally spirited away to another realm, leaving the Black Widow holding the fort alone and, notwithstanding guest appearances in the new (volume 3) *Avengers* title, the end of the decade was to be one of unprecedented solo success.

Having already returned to the glamour and sex-appeal of her 1970s costume, the Black Widow made the biggest splash of her career with an immensely popular 1999 miniseries by writer Devin Grayson and artist J. G. Jones. The story placed the Widow in the shady world of international espionage, and introduced her blonde Russian counterpart Yelena Belova, a new Black Widow. The combination of Romanoff's doubts over her age and abilities, an arch-enemy worthy of the name, a succession of exciting action set pieces and Jones' beautiful artwork (which made him an instant star) was dynamite. Further miniseries followed, as well as appearances in the *Marvel Knights* superteam series and (in only slightly modified form) the popular parallel-universe Avengers comic *The Ultimates,* confirming that the Black Widow's time had finally come. —*DAR*

Blackhawk

Blackhawk was conceived before World War II, thrived during the conflict, and enjoyed a long period of success in peacetime for two comics companies: Quality and DC. The birth of the Blackhawk strip is still somewhat contentious, but it probably originated through a request for a new feature from Quality Comics boss Everett "Busy" Arnold to packager/editor/artist Will Eisner. Together with members of his studio, Chuck Cuidera, Bob Powell, and others, Eisner created a band of fighting men to counter the growing Nazi menace across the ocean. Inspired by his love of the foreign legion, Eisner conceived of a band of men from all over the globe—the Black-

solo strips in *Bizarre Adventures* #25 (1981) and *Marvel Fanfare* #10–#13 (1983), which emphasized her spying past.

A further guest slot in *Daredevil* (issue #187, 1983), under the aegis of *enfant terrible* Frank Miller, led to a harsh, 1980s-style makeover, replacing the Widow's flowing locks with a spiky buzz-cut and sacrificing her hipster belt and groovy bracelets for a grey leotard. If the ensuing decade was a relatively fallow one, then the 1990s proved spectacularly successful, initially through a lengthy run in *The Avengers*—a team she was finally allowed to join and eventually lead. Her increased visibility as an Avenger cemented her place in the Marvel hier-hawks—led by a dark man of mystery known simply as Blackhawk. The strip premiered in mid-1941 in the pages of *Military Comics* #1, in a script written and laid out by Eisner, with finished artwork by Chuck Cuidera, and it was an overnight sensation.

The story opens in blitzkrieged 1939 Warsaw, Poland, with a brave pilot struggling out of his crashed fighter plane in the wake of a dogfight with Captain Von Tepp's Nazi squadron. The downed pilot stumbles to his bombed-out house only to find his family wiped out in the bombing and, choking back his tears, he vows revenge on the evil Von Tepp and his rampaging minions. Over the following months, the mysterious man—now known by the name Blackhawk—gathers a band of daredevil freedom fighters around him (known collectively as the Blackhawks) and wages a ruthless guerrilla campaign against the Teutonic hordes across mainland Europe. The story climaxes with another aerial dogfight between Von Tepp and Blackhawk, culminating in the Nazi's death. A legend was born.

In the Golden Age of comics (1938–1954), writers rarely lingered over details or backstory, preferring to concentrate on action and spectacle. So readers never learned how Blackhawk assembled his band of happy warriors, nor indeed how he acquired the well-appointed Blackhawk Island, somewhere in the Atlantic, complete with airfield, disappearing forts, Zeppelin shed, and lighthouse. *Military Comics* #2 introduced the rest of the Blackhawks: Andre, the suave French ladies' man; Olaf, the burly Swede; Stanislaus, the brave Pole; and Hendrickson, the veteran, mustached Dutchman (who later mysteriously became a German). Other, minor Blackhawks, Boris and Zug, were jettisoned in favor of all-American boy Chuck and comic relief Chinese cook Chop-Chop, whose decidedly un-politically correct ethnic stereotyping was an unfortunate feature of the strip for many years. Blackhawk himself was, of course, a Pole (probably at the insistence of Powell, who was of Polish descent), but this was gradually forgotten and in later adventures he became a Polish American.

A typical Blackhawk adventure would feature the team flying out in their stylish, twin-engined Grumman F5F fighters (a contribution from plane-buff Cuidera) to fight some Axis threat in an exotic corner of the globe. Early strips emphasized aerial battles and owed much to pulp/radio stars such as Bill Barnes and G-8, but over time the strip became increasingly earthbound, with the gang wading into action with guns (or fists) blazing. In the dark days of the war, there were few qualms about our heroes mowing down vast swathes of the enemy, and the Blackhawks were among the most bloodthirsty and driven of comics stars. Dressed in their matching blue-and-black SS-style uniforms, complete with peaked caps, jodhpurs, and jackboots (only Blackhawk himself was allowed the embellishment of a yellow hawk insignia on his jacket), the team ironically resembled the fascist horde that they were hell-bent on defeating.

After eleven issues of *Military Comics,* Cuidera was drafted into the air force and Eisner left to concentrate on the Spirit but, despite this, the strip went from strength to strength. Reed Crandall, one of Quality's top talents, took over the art and a host of writers, including Manly Wade Wellman, Bill Woolfold, and Batman writer Bill Finger, replaced Eisner. One of the incoming writers, Dick French, was also an accomplished songwriter, and he introduced the novel twist of having the team sing celebratory songs (usually about how great they all were!) as they went into battle or after each victory. ("Over land, over sea, we fight to make men free / Of danger we don't care … We're … Blackhawks!") But it was Crandall who, more than anyone else, inspired the feature's fervid fan following with his immaculate figure work and elaborately choreographed fight scenes.

With their secret hideout, matching costumes, independent persona as a multinational squadron of fighters who are not beholden to any one country, and leader's secrecy surrounding his original identity, the Blackhawks were very much a *de facto* supergroup. Yet, whereas most superhero sales dropped as the war came to a close, the Hawks retained their readership. In 1944, the failing *Uncle Sam* title was changed (with issue #9) into a new *Blackhawk* comic, boasting book-length yarns and even a Chop-Chop solo feature. The postwar Blackhawks now turned their attention to a succession of world-conquering villains, robots, aliens, mad scientists, and *femmes fatale*. Glamorous vixens such as Madame Butterfly, Princess Sari, Amora, and Mavis, Tigress of the Sea, all bent on world domination, suddenly filled the strips and almost invariably fell in love with Blackhawk. Notable villains included Captain Squid, King Cobra and his Rattlesnake Squadron, and—their most recurring foe—the sharp-toothed Killer Shark with his squadron of amphibious Shark Planes. As self-appointed guardians of the free world, the Blackhawks were responsible for their fair share of red-baiting, as stories such as "Slavery in Siberia," "The Red Executioner," and "Stalin's Ambassador of Murder" illustrate.

Military Comics was canceled in 1950, one of many casualties of the hero implosion of the 1950s, but the *Blackhawk* title itself continued throughout the decade—the only team comic to do so. Artists such as pin-up king Bill Ward, Rudy Palais, and John Forte had all contributed to the strip but Crandall was very much the feature's star, and his departure for E.C. Comics in 1953 was a serious blow. However, his replacement, Dick Dillin, while not quite as inspired, was nevertheless a sold professional and proved to be adept at drawing the comic's endless crowd scenes. The 1950s Blackhawks still operated out of their island hideaway, now mysteriously relocated to the Pacific Ocean, but their wartime planes were traded in for sleek F90 jets.

By 1957, Quality Comics was a spent force, and the company sold (or, as in the case of *Blackhawk*, leased) their top-selling titles to DC. Fortunately, DC retained Dillin on the book, along with Chuck Cuidera on inks, and so the transition was seamless. DC's titles of that time were full of monsters, robots, and aliens, and these also began to dominate the Hawks' strip, as did a relic of the Quality days, the vast War Wheel—literally a colossal, house-crushing steel wheel, armed with gun turrets

Blackhawk #242 © 1968 DC Comics.
COVER ART BY PAT BOYETTE.

and spikes. One welcome DC innovation was a mini-skirted adventurer called Zinda, who joined the group as Lady Blackhawk (in issue #151) and made sporadic appearances throughout the 1960s. Less welcome for the purists was 1964's new look, which replaced the old stormtrooper-style uniforms with garish green-and-red costumes (#197, in 1964) and unwanted mascots such as Blackie the Hawk (a pet hawk) and Tom Thumb Blackhawk, a midget.

While never a superhero strip by the strictest definition of the term, the 1960s Blackhawks had much in common with other DC strips such as Challengers of the Unknown and the Doom Patrol, but few fans guessed how much closer they were going to get. In

1966, in the wake of the successful *Batman* TV show, DC transformed the venerable fighters into tried and true superheroes. Hendrickson donned a purple boiler-suit to become the Weapons Master, Olaf became the silver-suited Leaper (because his new suited allowed him to leap vast distances), Stan wore a suit of armor à la Marvel's Iron Man to become the Golden Centurion, Andre kept his beret but gained a fancy motorcycle to become Monsieur Machine, and Chop-Chop sported a pair of metal hands to become Dr. Hands. Poor old Chuck suffered the worst indignity: He was now the Listener, dressed in blue pajamas decorated with hundreds of pink ears. Only Blackhawk himself avoided the cloaking of an entirely new super-costume, trading in his old blue uniform for a more fashionable red version, going now by the name of the Big Eye. After the Blackhawks had battled supervillains in their new identities for two years, incoming editor Dick Giordano turned to a yellowing old plot sent in by teenage fan Marv Wolfman (future Marvel editor-in-chief and co-creator of Blade), which returned the Blackhawks to their wartime costumes and more serious approach. This was the team's best story in years, but it came too late to save the comic and, one issue later (#243 in 1968), the Hawks seemingly flew off into the sunset for the last time.

Eight years later, new DC boss Jenette Kahn oversaw a number of revivals of long-forgotten titles, one of which was *Blackhawk;* the revival picked up with issue #244. The new comic took as its inspiration the campier 1950s and 1960s DC Blackhawks, complete with bizarre villains (Anti-Man, Bio-Lord, and a returning War Wheel) and a new *femme fatale,* Duchess Ramona Fatale. The strip was set in 1976 and starred a now middle-aged band of adventurers, enjoying civilian identities as scientists and corporate bosses. None of this appealed to a new generation of fans, and so the comic was canceled six issues later.

An enjoyably fanciful team-up with Batman (in *The Brave and the Bold* #167, 1981), in a story set during World War II, rekindled interest in the Hawks and inspired a new set of wartime tales. A well-received (by old-time fans, at least) 1982 series detailed untold war adventures that were very true to the spirit of the old Quality strips. Its two-year run by Mark Evanier and Dan Spiegle was one of the feature's creative high points, as was Howard Chaykin's 1988 miniseries, but there the similarities end. Chaykin's story was a contemporary reinvention of the wartime group's exploits, led by a hard-driving, vain, Trotskyite, womanizing Blackhawk, who finally had a real name: Janos Prohaska. Mixing in such elements as gangsters, Zionists, the Spanish Civil War, television, and the atomic bomb, this was heady stuff indeed. The well-received tale led to a number of Blackhawk strips in *Action Comics* and a series in 1989 that was set in 1947 and involved the team with the CIA and the "red menace" scare.

The concept of a band of brave fighters taking on evil around the globe had enormous resonance to readers in the war-torn 1940s and the cold-war paranoia of the 1950s, and perhaps inevitably the strip was at its peak in those years. Indeed, such was the strip's popularity that it inspired a 1952 Columbia serial starring Kirk Alyn (also one of the screen's earliest Supermans) and a short-lived radio show. Sadly, any residual nostalgia for the Blackhawks or their wartime oeuvre has largely died out, and so they are unlikely to emerge as a commercial force in the twenty-first-century market. Nevertheless, a 2002 DC Archive edition reprinting their early years may yet prove to have entranced a new generation. However, younger fans have already been enjoying the legacy of the strip for years without realizing it; in the mid-1970s, editor Roy Thomas (with artist Dave Cockrum and eventual writer Len Wein) reinvented the moribund *X-Men* title as a multinational team, inspired by his affection for the Blackhawk strips of his youth. —*DAR*

Blonde Phantom

Perhaps more than any other company of the 1940s or 1950s, Marvel Comics' ethos was always to jump on any trend going and to swamp the newsstands with as much product as it could muster. The Blonde Phantom was both a response to what was happening in several areas of the marketplace and a trendsetter herself. Her first appearance came in the eleventh issue of *All-Select Comics* (Fall 1946), previously a bastion of Marvel's big three superheroes, the Human Torch, Sub-Mariner, and Captain America. She made her presence felt by entirely ousting the old heroes from the cover.

The Blonde Phantom was the brainchild of the prolific Otto Binder and was drawn by one of Marvel's top artists of the time, Syd Shores. Her strips were simplicity themselves. In civilian life, she was Louise Grant, mousy secretary to the dashing private investigator Mark Mason. Picking up tips from the cases on his desk, she donned a slinky red evening gown (open at the navel and back), let down her blond tresses, swapped her horn-rimmed spectacles for a black mask, and slipped on the highest of high-heeled slippers. Then, armed with her wits, determination, and a .45 (she had no superpowers to speak of), she sashayed off to right wrongs on America's mean streets.

The Blonde Phantom strips were an amalgam of all sorts of trends that were influencing the post–World War II market. The success of *Archie* had shown that girls were beginning to read comics in some numbers, and Marvel had exploited that with a flood of teen titles, such as *Millie the Model, Patsy Walker, Tessie the Typist, Margie,* and many others. The company had always had success with its superhero books, and so they might have imagined that a superhero for girls should be a hit. Indeed, Marvel had met with some success with earlier girl heroes, such as Miss America and Miss Fury. Another of the era's big hits was the crime genre, first established by Lev Gleason's millionselling *Crime Does Not Pay* title. So, perhaps inevitably, the Blonde Phantom's adventures were full of vicious gangsters and crazed psychopaths. Stories such as "The Devil's Playground," "Modelled for Murder," "Horror in Hollywood," and "The Man

Who Deserved to Die" indicate the sort of hardboiled fare served up in her yarns.

In true superhero fashion, Binder had a lot of fun with the Phantom's secret identity since, much in the manner of Wonder Woman and Steve Trevor, Louise Grant loved Mason, but he only had eyes for the sultry, dashing Blonde Phantom. In a reverse of the usual damsel-in-distress shtick so prevalent in the Golden Age of comics (1938–1954), it was usually the trouble-prone Mason who needed rescuing, only increasing his ardour for his beautiful rescuer. Interestingly, a little less than a year later, DC Comics came out with the Black Canary, a similarly blonde adventuress with a detective paramour in perpetual need of rescuing, though the Canary would prove to be far longer-lived than the Phantom.

After one issue in *All Select* and a plug in *Millie the Model #2* (wherein Millie dresses up in a Blonde Phantom costume and promotes Blonde Phantom perfume), the Blonde Phantom was given her own quarterly title (adopting its initial numbering from the *All-Select* series at #12). Within a year, she was starring in each issue of *Marvel Mystery Comics* as well and by mid-1948 had also gained regular backup slots in *Sub-Mariner* and *Blackstone.* By August of that year, her success inspired Marvel to launch an entire line of girls' superheroes, and the first issues of *Sun Girl, Venus,* and *Namora* were released. Coupled with Blonde Phantom's various strips and Golden Girl's emergence in the pages of *Captain America,* that gave Marvel five superheroines. Inevitably, the various heroines crossed over with each other, and the Blonde Phantom guest-starred in *Sun Girl,* but perhaps the whole experiment was overdone and, within a year, not only the heroines but also Marvel's entire superhero line was out of print.

In her two-and-a-half-year existence, the Blonde Phantom appeared in more than thirty stories spread across eight titles, but in May 1949 her own title was transformed into *Lovers* with its twentythird issue, reflecting the next trend that would dominate the newsstands for much of the coming decade: romance comics. Whereas *Venus* would live on for several more years, riding the waves of romance, mystery, and horror trends, and Namora's daughter, Namorita, would find success in the 1970s and beyond, the Blonde Phantom joined Sun Girl, Golden Girl, and Miss Fury in obscurity. —*DAR*

Blue Beetle

The Blue Beetle was the second superhero to have his own comic, and went on to more changes and publishers (six in all) than almost any other character in comics history. He also spanned the quality spectrum from excellent to absolutely awful. In 1939, Victor Fox was an accountant at DC Comics who had noticed with envy the profits coming in from the company's new Superman character. Moving to a different floor in the same building, he set up his own company, Fox Comics, and hired the Will Eisner/Jerry Iger creative shop to provide the story and artwork for his new venture. Unfortunately, their first character, Wonder Man, was immediately hit by a lawsuit from DC, and so they quickly dreamed up a new hero, the Blue Beetle. In his first appearance (drawn by Charles Nicholas in *Mystery Men Comics* #1), the Beetle was little more than a Green Hornet clone, but he was soon given a blue chain mail costume with a mask and hood topped off with antennae; the latter sadly disappeared by his fourth strip.

In his civilian identity, the Beetle was rookie cop Dan Garret, whose athletic prowess made him a powerful hero as soon as he donned his costume—though the gun he toted in the early days was probably more useful. As far as superpowers go, he really had none, although he often projected his beetle insignia on dark walls. Soon enough, he was given a girlfriend, reporter Joan Mason, and a special vitamin mixture (2X) that beefed up his muscles. The Blue Beetle briefly had his own radio show and newspaper strip, but the poor overall quality of Fox's product led the company to close shop in 1942. A few months later, the Beetle was back on

the stands, this time published by Fox's printers, Holyoke, who (historians believe) took over the character in lieu of debts. The Holyoke years saw the character gain a sidekick called Spunky but, if anything, the strip got even worse. By 1944, Victor Fox had come back into publishing and took over the comic again for a series of catastrophically awful strips in which the Beetle could suddenly fly, and also mysteriously acquired the Beetlemobile and the Beetleboat.

One of the hottest comics of the postwar years was the ultraviolent *Crime Does Not Pay,* and in 1946 Fox decided to get a piece of that action. This new direction concentrated more on the Blue Beetle's shapely girlfriend and featured a series of so-called "true crime stories," which were little more than an excuse for acres of flesh and gallons of blood. Story titles such as "Satan's Circus," "The Vanishing Nude," and "House of a Thousand Corpses" tell it all. By the end of the decade, Fox had left comics forever, but the Beetle was soon picked up by bargain-basement publisher Charlton, who brought out a few nondescript issues in 1955. Somehow, I.W. Comics got its hands on some old artwork and, in 1964, released it in two issues inexplicably retitled *The Human Fly.* That same year (are you following this?), Charlton was back again with a ten-issue run of staggeringly silly strips in which the beefed-up hero appeared to resemble the Pillsbury Doughboy.

Then something strange happened: The Blue Beetle finally starred in some good stories—very good stories, in fact. Soon after leaving his astonishingly successful *Spider-Man* comic, artist Steve Ditko moved over to Charlton and completely revamped the Beetle. Ditko's hero was now scientist Ted Kord and he had a stylish new costume, his own designer flying vehicle (in the shape of a beetle, of course) and genuinely exciting, well-drawn stories. Inexplicably, despite action scenes that rivaled Spider-Man at its best, the public simply wasn't interested, and the comic was canceled after barely a year.

Blue Beetle #3 © 1967 Charlton Comics.
COVER ART BY STEVE DITKO.

A generation later, the few fans who bought Ditko's issues were creating comics of their own, and the first of many revivals saw print in 1981 in the semi-pro Charlton *Bullseye.* A few years later, another fan publication, *Americomics,* pitted the two Blue Beetles against each other in pitched battle, before things came full circle and DC Comics, the impetus for the Beetle's creation in the first place, bought the rights to the character. For much of the 1980s, he starred in amiable yarns in his own comic and enjoyed great success in one of several incarnations of the Justice League. In true 1980s fashion, it seems that Kord used his scientific expertise to become a millionaire and

appeared to have settled down to a life of leisure. However, a 2003 miniseries—the wittily titled *Formally Known as the Justice League*—brought him out of retirement so yet another generation of fans can enjoy his adventures again. —DAR

Bronze Age of Superheroes (1970-1979)

Superheroes were in their infancy during comics' Golden Age (1938–1954), experienced growing pains during the Silver Age (1956–1969), and reached adolescence during the Bronze Age (1970–1979).

"AN EPIC FOR OUR TIMES"

During the 1960s, Marvel Comics snuck up on DC Comics and usurped the industry's number-one spot. DC's editorial director Carmine Infantino started the 1970s with both guns blazing, vowing to regain DC's market share. The biggest bullet in Infantino's holster was the illustrious Jack Kirby, the veteran artist who co-created most of Marvel's major superheroes, including Captain America, the Fantastic Four, the Hulk, and the X-Men.

After a series of teaser ads announcing that "Kirby is Coming," in 1970 Kirby began working exclusively for DC and introduced a mythic tapestry into the company's universe, a series of four interlocking series—three new books of his own design, *The New Gods, The Forever People,* and *Mister Miracle,* plus a revamp of DC's long-running *Superman's Pal Jimmy Olsen*—under the umbrella title "The Fourth World." Among its gaggle of gods, both good and evil, stood Darkseid, DC's first utterly malevolent villain. Kirby's vigorous artwork and concepts recharged DC with an energy never before seen at the company, as did his hyperbolic cover blurbs like "An Epic for Our Times" and "Don't Ask—Just Buy It!" *But not enough people are buying it,* thought DC, and Kirby's Fourth World died after two years, although the characters have continued to exist for decades. After follow-ups including *The Demon, OMAC, Sandman,* and *Kamandi, the Last Boy on Earth,* Kirby returned to Marvel.

SUPERHERO RELEVANCE

Green Lantern/Green Arrow #76 (1970) was a revolutionary step forward for DC Comics. It borrowed from Marvel Comics' propensity toward argumentative superheroes, but with "GL" and "GA," their struggles were ideological debates. GL, a power-ring-wielding intergalactic cop, represented the conservative right, while "GA was the voice of the streets, of the left," writer Denny O'Neil declared on the 2003 History Channel documentary *Comic Book Superheroes: Unmasked.* With artist Neal Adams, O'Neil took this groundbreaking series into realms political, radical, and racial, but the market was unprepared for its level of sophistication and *Green Lantern/Green Arrow* was canceled with issue #89 (1972). *Green Lantern/Green Arrow* put the industry on notice, however, proving that superheroes' exploits could involve matters beyond skirmishes with supervillains.

For the first few years of the 1970s, contemporary thematic material—dubbed "relevance" by those in the biz—became common in many DC books: Robin the Teen (formerly "Boy") Wonder left Batman for college and took on campus unrest, Barbara (Batgirl) Gordon went to Washington, D.C., to tackle crime as a congresswoman, and the Justice League of America battled polluters. Even the stilted Man of Steel got hip. *Superman* #233 (1971) started a new era for DC's flagship hero, updating his alter ego Clark Kent to a television reporter and eliminating his weakness kryptonite, but those changes were short-lived. Batman's tales, in his own series and in *Detective Comics,* shied away

from this relevance trend and veered more into gothic terrain, returning the hero to his original, baleful nature. "Batman is a loner who never shows his face in the light," stated O'Neil, the chief *Batman* writer of the 1970s, on the *Comic Book Heroes: Unmasked* program.

MARVEL BREAKS NEW GROUND

A three-issue anti-drug story Stan Lee penned for *The Amazing Spider-Man* #96 through #98 (1971) was rejected by the industry's censorship board, the Comics Code Authority (CCA). Lee lobbied Marvel publisher Martin Goodman to resist the CCA and print the issues, which Marvel did—*without* the Code's seal of approval, the first time a major comic-book publisher had exercised such defiance. The CCA, in response, relaxed some of its requirements to more adequately address societal changes.

One of those liberalizations permitted the depiction of the undead, which had been taboo since the implementation of the CCA in the mid-1950s. Marvel took full advantage of this, fostering a 1970s horror-comics fad with titles including *Ghost Rider, The Son of Satan, Man-Thing, The Tomb of Dracula,* and *Werewolf by Night*—series that occurred inside the workings of the Marvel superhero continuity (DC published its applauded *Swamp Thing* series during this period). Marvel steered two other Bronze Age industry movements: "sword and sorcery," beginning in 1970 with its adaptations and continuations of Robert E. Howard's fantasy hero Conan the Barbarian; and kung fu, through *Master of Kung Fu, Iron Fist* and others. And a cinema trend—"blaxploitation," low-budget action films starring black actors—inspired *Luke Cage, Hero for Hire* #1 (1972), the first comic book to headline an African-American superhero.

Marvel continued to build upon its Silver Age foundation of human heroes with "real" problems. Mr. Fantastic and his wife Invisible Girl of the Fantastic Four suffered marital strains. In the controversial *The Amazing Spider-Man* #121 (1973), the hero did *not* save the day, as Gwen Stacy, girlfriend of Spidey's alter ego Peter Parker, died at the hands of the villainous Green Goblin. Just eight issues later, in *The Amazing Spider-Man* #129 (1974), the beleaguered wall-crawler was targeted by the assassin-for-hire called the Punisher, and later that year, in *The Incredible Hulk* #181, the Green Goliath battled the feral Canadian superhero Wolverine. The Punisher and Wolverine were anti-heroes for a cynical generation, and would grow into superstardom.

WHAT'S OLD IS NEW AGAIN

The Bronze Age re-popularized heroes of yesterday. DC's critically acclaimed *Tarzan* comic, written, drawn, and edited by Joe Kubert for most of its run, was a minor hit, as was DC's noir interpretation of *The Shadow*. DC also obtained publishing rights for superheroes previously under the jurisdiction of Fawcett Publications and Quality Comics, the results being its *Shazam!* series (starring the original Captain Marvel) and its superteam title, *The Freedom Fighters* (with Uncle Sam, the Phantom Lady, and others). Marvel published *Doc Savage* and ultimately picked up the *Tarzan* license after DC.

One 1975 Marvel Comics revival produced unparalleled results. *Giant-Size X-Men* #1 introduced a new team of offbeat superheroes—multicultural mutants including Storm (African), Colossus (Russian), Nightcrawler (German), Sunfire (Japanese), and Wolverine (Canadian)—and began its trek toward becoming Marvel's number-one series.

Lackluster sales did not encourage many publishers to attempt superhero comics during the Bronze Age, but a few gave it the old college try: Atlas Comics produced a diverse but short-lived comics line in the mid-1970s, including superheroes Tiger-Man and the Destructor, as well as Howard Chaykin's pulpish Scorpion; and longtime player Charlton Comics published King Features' jungle hero *The Phantom* and introduced a wry superhero parody, *E-Man.*

Superman vs. the Amazing Spider-Man © 1976 DC/Marvel.
COVER ART BY ROSS ANDRU AND DICK GIORDANO.

DC VS. MARVEL

DC's Infantino-steered accomplishments narrowed the sales gap between his company and its competitor. Still, Marvel largely dominated the entire decade, although a 1976 project would unite the publishers on equal ground. *Superman vs. The Amazing Spider-Man,* a one-hundred-page, tabloid-sized special edition by Gerry Conway, Ross Andru, and Dick Giordano, mixed up DC's and Marvel's top superheroes in a momentous clash followed by "the greatest team-up of all time." Infantino worked with Marvel's Lee to nurture the bestseller, but before a sequel could be brokered, Infantino and DC parted company. Children's magazine publisher Jenette Kahn replaced him as DC's head, but her long, impressive tenure would begin on a bumpy path. The quality of DC's titles suffered later in the decade, and the company's content expansion—the highly promoted "DC Explosion" in 1977—led to a market glut and a devastating "DC Implosion" in 1978.

Both DC and Marvel benefited from multimedia visibility of their superheroes during the Bronze Age. Mego Toys' "World's Greatest Super-Heroes" eight-inch action figures funneled icons as diverse as Superman, Spider-Man, Conan, Wonder Girl, and Tarzan into a shared commercial line. Hostess Twinkies sponsored a popular series of one-page comics that appeared as house ads in Marvel and DC comics, featuring famous superheroes as product pitchmen. The Justice League ventured to animated television in ABC's *Super Friends,* and live-action superheroes Captain Marvel (in *Shazam!*), Isis, and ElectraWoman and DynaGirl starred on Saturday-morning TV. *The New Adventures of Wonder Woman, The Incredible Hulk,* and *The Amazing Spider-Man* were weekly CBS dramatic series (CBS's telemovies starring Captain America and Doctor Strange did not warrant ongoing shows), and the multi-million-dollar theatrical blockbuster *Superman: The Movie* (1978) set box-office records (for the time). Spider-Man and Superman both appeared in newspaper comic strips, and paperback novels and comics reprint editions starring DC and Marvel superheroes saw print. The merchandising of superheroes became big business, though readership of the comic books themselves continued a gradual decline.

By the end of the 1970s, most traditional outlets for comics like newsstands and drug stores stopped carrying comic books, since their low profit margin offered little incentive for shelf display. Print runs of individual titles, in many cases exceeding 1 million copies per issue during the 1940s, had slipped to several hundred thousand, at best. Television (broadcast and cable), special effects–laden movies, and the emerging video game and computer technologies now competed with comics for the young consumer's interest. Yet this most persistent of art forms, comics, stood poised to begin a path of rediscovery as the new decade dawned. —*ME*

Buffy the Vampire Slayer

Mix in equal parts sardonic humor, martial arts action, attractive cast members, monsters as metaphor, doomed romance, and feminism. Heat for seven years. Serve garnished with a stake through the undead heart, and you have the main course that was *Buffy the Vampire Slayer.* Created by Joss Whedon, the title heroine was first seen in a 1992 feature film of the same name, embodied by Kristy Swanson. Buffy was a popular cheerleader who discovered she was part of a historical line chosen to fight vampires and other spawns of evil. Trained under the eye of a Watcher (Donald Sutherland), Swanson still found time to romance bad boy Pike (Luke Perry), even as she faced down the twin perils of the school dance and the vampiric overlord Lothos (Rutger Hauer). The movie was not much of a hit, but Whedon wasn't quite willing to let his brainchild stay in the dark forever.

In March 1997, a new *Buffy the Vampire Slayer* debuted on the WB network as a limited-run series. This time, Buffy Summers (Sarah Michelle Gellar) has moved to Sunnydale with her divorced mother, Joyce (Kristine Sutherland), and tried to forget the past. That would be fine, except that Sunnydale is located on the Hellmouth, an evil portal that makes the California town a haven for vampires, demons, and other creepy things. It just so happens that the high school librarian is also a Watcher named Rupert Giles (Anthony Stewart Head), and he is as stuffy as any British librarian ever committed to celluloid. As she begins to face the terrors of school, Buffy also fights monsters ranging from demon teachers to invisible girls to the Master (Mark Metcalf), a powerful vampire. It's a good thing that her Slayer powers give her immense strength, fighting skills, and healing factors, because Buffy's battles are just beginning.

Luckily, Buffy has friends to help her. Xander Harris (Nicholas Brendon) is a good-natured nerd who is helpful despite his unfortunate crushes on women who turn out to be evil. Willow Rosenberg (Alyson Hannigan) is a brilliant computer geek with a penchant for magic and shyness. Rounding out the group of sidekicks is Cordelia Chase (Charisma Carpenter), a bitchy fashion-plate who resents helping the geeks, but is drawn into the good fight time and again. When not in the graveyard or alleys fighting ghouls, the group mostly hangs out at the underage nightclub the Bronze, where live music—and the occasional fracas against the undead—are a staple. By the end of the first mini-season, *Buffy* had established itself as a ratings hit and a critical darling. Even as hundreds of websites sprang into life on the Internet, work began on a second season.

Throughout her tenure on the show, Buffy is portrayed as an archetypal heroine with a less-than-archetypal personality. Though she has no costume, she has a distinct alter ego as a student and daughter, as well as a heroic identity as a Slayer (the name most of the monsters call her). And while her Slayer's mission is to defeat vampires specifically, and evil generally, she uses her superpowers to make sure that her mission as a teenager—shopping, dating, hanging out with friends—is protected. While her secret is unknown to her mother initially, it eventually becomes evident to most of Sunnydale High's student body that Buffy is their protector (they eventually honor her as such at the senior prom in season three).

The first year had introduced into the mix a character named Angel (David Boreanaz), a brooding black-clad loner who was really a vampire "cursed" with a soul. As season two began, Angel was both aiding Buffy and falling in love with her. Complications arose when they slept together, and his moment of true happiness forced Angel to revert to his evil vampiric self. Angel killed Giles' girlfriend, Jenny Calendar (Robia LaMorte), showing that even series semi-regulars were not immune from sudden death. Even as Buffy and the so-called

"Scooby Gang" tried to cope with Angel's bad side, they also faced fellow vamps Spike (James Marsters) and Drusilla (Juliet Landau), whose past intertwined with Angel's in the 1800s. Luckily, the heroes were regularly aided by Oz (Seth Green), a sarcastic teen rock-and-roller who was also a were-wolf and Willow's love interest.

Season three (1998–1999) featured the redemption of Angel, even as the town's demonic Mayor Wilkins (Harry Groener) planned to sacrifice Buffy's senior class of Sunnydale High in a bid to gain ultimate power. To do this, Wilkins seduced new Vampire Slayer Faith (Eliza Dushku) to the dark side. Faith was an anomaly; although only one Slayer was "called" per generation, a brief death (and resurrection) for Buffy in season one had resulted in another being called. Slayer vs. Slayer was soon set into motion, but as the season ended, controversy erupted. An episode about a teen bringing a gun to school—and the season finale about the mayor attacking the graduation ceremonies—were delayed in airing, following the Columbine school shootings.

The following year featured the cast relocating to college, while Angel, Cordelia, and Faith's Watcher Wesley Wyndham-Pryce (Alexis Denisof) relocated to a spin-off series called *Angel*. Buffy found the balance of classes and creature-fighting difficult, especially once she began to fall for muscular stud Riley Finn (Marc Blucas). Too bad then that Riley was part of the secret government group the Initiative, which was capturing and studying monsters in laboratories underneath the university! Once Riley and Buffy found out each others' secret identities, they helped each other in battle, especially against Frankenstein-like creation Adam (George Hertzberg). Also notable this season were the additions of the characters Anya (Emma Caulfield), a whiny ex-vengeance demon falling for Xander, and Tara (Amber Benson), a shy lesbian witch whose interaction with the magic-wielding Willow would intensify over time. One episode written and directed by Whedon—"Hush"—was mostly in silence, and earned the series one of its few Emmy Award nominations.

By now the public and the critics alike were aware that Emmy was not going to reward *Buffy* no matter how good it was, but at least the show won in both ratings and sales of licensed merchandise, including an ongoing Dark Horse comic-book series and spin-offs; tie-in books; calendars; apparel, action figures; and Christmas ornaments.

In its fifth season (2000–2001), *Buffy* introduced a bizarre new wrinkle with younger sister Dawn Summers (Michelle Trachtenberg), whom everyone remembered, even though viewers had never seen her before. As the season-long story arc progressed, the secret of Dawn's existence played in heavily to the evil plans of sexy villainess Glory (Clare Kramer). Relationships progressed as well: after Riley left, Buffy and Spike began a dangerous romance (he now had a microchip in his head stopping him from harming humans so he joined the fight against evil); Willow and Tara became an openly lesbian couple; and Xander and Anya planned marriage. But the show's most shocking moment came when Buffy returned home to find her mother dead. In the season's ender, Buffy would sacrifice herself to save the world from Glory's machinations.

Moving from WB to UPN after contract renegotiations, *Buffy's* darkest and most controversial year was in 2001–2002, wherein everything good began to go bad. Willow's dark magic resurrected Buffy, but her friend was less than grateful to be pulled from heaven back to hell on Earth. Buffy and Spike's relationship grew ever more destructive. Three geeks—Jonathan (Danny Strong), Warren (Adam Busch), and Andrew (Tom Lenk)—planned to use their magical and scientific knowledge to become supervillains. The eventual result of their actions was the accidental death of Tara, a storyline that proved incredibly controversial in the press and on the Internet; Whedon and producer Marti Noxon spent much time defending themselves from charges of homophobia for killing one of the two lesbian characters. Another episode, written and directed by Whedon, was a musical, with the entire cast singing and dancing under the spell of a demon. The season ended with "Dark Willow" having a black-magic meltdown that threatened all of the cast, and left one villain flayed alive!

The 2002–2003 season of *Buffy* was announced as its final one, and with rising costs, declining ratings, and series star Gellar chafing to move on to other projects, this announcement surprised few. The producers moved to lighten the mood, establishing a newly rebuilt Sunnydale High, a soul for Spike, and the return of Rupert Giles to semi-regular duty after his time away from the series. But Buffy and the Scooby Gang's troubles were not over, with an indestructible nasty preacher named Caleb (Nathan Fillion), a horde of super-strong über-vampires, and the First Evil threatening apocalypse. "Potential" Slayers began arriving in Sunnydale to train, so in case Buffy fell in battle, they could move into her place. The series ended with the destruction of the Hellmouth and Sunnydale, but also a gift from Buffy to the world; the potential in girls everywhere was magically heightened, implying that every girl could be tough and strong like the Slayers.

Throughout its seven years, *Buffy's* strength lay partially in clever plots that used the evils and monsters as metaphors for problems faced by the characters—and implicitly, the viewers. The dialogue and direction of the series were almost always top-notch, the "girl power" message was both constant and consistent, and the actors were likable and believable in their roles. *Buffy* became a cottage industry for its stars, who would appear at conventions and parlay their popularity into further roles once the series ended.

Spin-off series *Angel* continued on the WB, with Spike added as a series regular for the 2003–2004 season, the show's last. A *Buffy* animated series was in development for more than a year, but despite extensive script-writing, voice work, and design, the show was not picked up by a network. Rumors of a *Buffy* spin-off for Giles, Faith, or Willow swirled in the Hollywood hype machine, but momentum seemingly stalled on the Giles series (alternately called *Watcher* or *Rippe*), Dushku got her own Fox drama series, and Hannigan signed for a 2004 sitcom. Still, *Buffy* fans remain committed to a future for their heroines and heroes. New adventures still appear in comic book and novel form, and with the Slayer line opened for a broader group, it seems unlikely that *Buffy the Vampire Slayer* won't rise from the grave on television or film some time in the future. —AM

Bulletgirl: *See* **Bulletman; Superheroines**

Bulletman

Sensing that it had a hit on its hands with Captain Marvel, Fawcett Comics rushed out three other comics in early 1940 to capitalize on the superhero's success, but the company soon discovered that launching successful characters was not as easy as it thought. The three comics were: *Slam Bang,* starring a no-hoper called Diamond Jack; *Master Comics,* starring (appropriately enough) Master Man; and *Nickel Comics,* starring Bulletman. Fawcett soon realized that it was in trouble with these titles. *Nickel Comics* was half the price of other comics but only offered half the page count of its rivals (and, what's more, only gave the newsstand owners a tiny profit). *Master Comics* was launched as an oversized comic so that it would stand out from its competitors, but both it and *Slam Bang* were filled with second-rate strips that failed to excite their readers. So Fawcett decided to cut its losses and merged the three titles into *Master Comics* with its seventh issue (October 1940). This version finally went on to enjoy the success that the publisher had hoped for, thanks to Bulletman and Captain Marvel Junior (a late arrival, in issue #22).

Bulletman's origin, recounted in *Nickel Comics* #1, details how Jim Barr attempts to join the police force after seeing his father—a cop—gunned down by gangsters. Vowing to carry on his father's crusade against crime, Barr becomes a scientist devoted to somehow "curing" the desire for crime. Sadly, years in the laboratory weaken him and, after the inevitable rejection by the police force, it seems as if Barr will have to settle for a career in the police labs. Instead, he works up a new concoction that magically increases his physical and mental abilities, creating an Adonis-like physique and vastly amplified intelligence. Armed with this new brainpower, he creates the Gravity Regulator Helmet, a bullet-shaped, chrome headpiece that allows him to fly at great speed and also magnetically repels bullets away from him. Donning a red shirt open to the waist, yellow tights, and boots, he now adapts his nickname "Bullet" Barr to become Bulletman. In addition to being able to fly, he possesses telescopic vision.

Fawcett had a small army of second-division heroes, such as Spy Smasher, Ibis the Invincible, Minute Man, Mr. Scarlet and Pinky, Commando Yank, and Golden Arrow. While Bulletman never rose to the exalted status of Captain Marvel, he was probably the star act of these lesser-known characters. His principal writer was Fawcett's inventive workhorse Otto Binder and, with art from talents such as Jon Small, Mac Raboy, Dan Barry, Bill Ward, and Charles Sultan, the strip was an attractive feature. It came to life in April 1941 with the introduction of Bulletgirl, created (in the fine tradition of Robin, Bucky, and other sidekicks) so that Bulletman would have someone to talk to and, of course, to add a little glamour to the feature. Bulletgirl was Susan Kent, the inquisitive daughter and secretary of Police Chief Kent, and when she stumbles upon Barr's amazing alter ego, he bows to the inevitable, giving her a hit of his secret elixir and building a second bullet helmet. In 1944, the team was accompanied by Bulletboy and a dog called— you guessed it—Bulletdog, who flies thanks to the invention of an anti-gravity collar.

As the "Flying Detectives," Bulletman and Bulletgirl enjoyed a lengthy run in *Master Comics* (until issue #106, in 1949), and starred in sixteen issues of *Bulletman* (from 1941 to 1946) as well as appearing in *America's Greatest Comics, X-Mas Comics, Fawcett Miniatures,* and *Mighty Midget Comics*—a total of around 150 yarns in all. One of the first man-and-woman superhero duos, predating Hawkman and Hawkgirl, Flame and Flame Girl, and Lash Lightning and Lightning Girl, their adventures tended to be fast-moving tales with little scope for introspection or characterization. These short stories were frequently peppered with bizarre and macabre foes, including Black Mask, Dr. Weird, Mr. Murder, the Gorgon, the Black Rat, the Invisible Man, and the Black Spider. Later adventures featured a one-off team-up with Captain Marvel Junior and Minute Man as the Crime Crusaders Club. However, the strip's status was most convincingly shown with a visit from Captain Marvel himself during the lengthy fight with Captain Nazi in *Master Comics* #21 and #22.

With the cancellation of their feature in *Master Comics* #106, the pair mostly faded from view until the late 1990s, when Jerry Ordway reintroduced the Flying Detectives in *The Power of Shazam* #8 in 1995. A further appearance in issue #43, when they came out of retirement to cover for a temporarily missing Captain Marvel, has been their last appearance as of 2004. However, the Bulletman strip's legacy is more than being just one of many largely forgotten Golden Age features, since Bulletgirl was in fact one of the first superheroines in comics history, predating Wonder Woman's, Mary Marvel's, and even the Black Cat's first appearances. —*DAR*

Camp and Comedy Heroes

The earliest costumed crime fighters of comics' Golden Age (1938–1954) were dreadfully somber, not surprising given America's bleak mood during the Great Depression and World War II. It was only a matter of time, however, before someone realized that the separation of heroes and humor was unnecessary.

THE RED "TOMATO"

That someone was Sheldon Mayer. In 1940 Mayer created the Red Tornado (not to be confused with the solemn android character of the same name who appeared decades later in DC Comics' *Justice League of America*), introduced as a supporting-cast member in the "Scribbly" series in DC's *All-American Comics*. The Red Tornado was clearly not intended to be taken seriously—a running gag featured the hero being called the Red "Tomato." The Red Tornado bore another rather surprising distinction: He was secretly a *she*. Husky Ma Hunkle righted wrongs in a cobbled-together guise of red long johns, a towel as a cape, and a helmet that was once a cooking pot.

While the Red Tornado didn't pave the way for cross-dressing superheroes, Ma Hunkle leveraged an acceptance of humorous characters in other "straight" superhero comics: Fawcett's *Captain Marvel* franchise featured Mr. Tawky Tawny, a talking anthropomorphic tiger, and Green Lantern gained a portly comic-relief sidekick (Doiby Dickles). In August 1941 Quality Comics' wacky Plastic Man, a malleable FBI agent, bounced into *Police Comics* #1, joined by *his* portly comic-relief sidekick (Woozy Winks).

George Marcoux's *Supersnipe,* "The Boy with the Most Comic Books in America," was published by Street & Smith from 1942 through 1949. Supersnipe was actually shrimpy Koppy McFad, a kid so thoroughly obsessed with superheroes he pretended to be one himself. Hopping into red long underwear (did he have the same tailor as Red Tornado?) and sporting a mask and blue cape, this neighborhood protector imagined himself a strapping muscleman (McFad's tiny, child-size head was drawn onto Supersnipe's brutish body). *Supersnipe* was also the first comic book to deal with comics themselves as subject matter.

The year 1942 marked the debut of funny animal heroes, mirthful mergers of superheroes and cartoon critters. Terrytoons' Mighty Mouse and Marvel (then known as Timely) Comics' Supermouse were the first big cheeses, soon joined by Fawcett's Hoppy the Marvel Bunny (Captain Marvel as a rabbit) and Marvel's copycat Super Rabbit, plus DC's Terrific Whatzit (a takeoff of the Flash in the unlikely form of a superfast turtle).

In 1947 Superman's creators Jerry Siegel and Joe Shuster introduced Funnyman, a Danny Kaye-inspired TV comedian named Larry Davis who fought crime in a clown suit. Siegel and Shuster were prohibited from using Superman's famous name in promoting their new character, and thus *Funnyman,* who appeared in a comic book and a syndicated newspaper strip, laughed his last in 1949.

Without the war effort to sustain their adventures, most superheroes disappeared from the comics stands during the late 1940s, their titles replaced by a host of other genres that dominated the marketplace throughout the 1950s. Humor was one of those genres, and in 1952 publisher E.C. Comics launched its trailblazing *MAD* title (which originated as a color comic book before changing to a black-and-white magazine format in 1955). *MAD* skewered a handful of superheroes in send-ups including "Superduperman" (which mocked the real-life lawsuit between DC Comics and Fawcett Comics over Captain Marvel's supposed similarities to Superman), "Plastic Sam," "Bat Boy and Rubin," and "Woman Wonder." Also premiering in the 1950s were Charlton Comics' *Atomic Mouse* and its spin-offs, and the Super Turtle half-page fillers that ran in a host of DC Comics titles.

Two significant comedic superheroes premiered in the 1950s. The first was the Fighting American, Prize Comics' patriotic hero from writer Joe Simon and artist Jack Kirby. *Fighting American* is acknowledged by many comics historians as the first superhero *satire*: Its target was obvious—Marvel's Captain America, whom Simon and Kirby themselves created in 1941—and its tone was irreverent, with Communist menaces like Poison Ivan and Hotsky Trotsky plaguing the flag-clad hero and his boisterous sidekick Speedboy. The strip's flippancy

with the cold war chilled most readers, and the series ended after a mere seven issues. Revival attempts in later decades similarly failed. The second significant 1950s spoof was Herbie Popnecker, an improbable superhero first seen in ACG's *Forbidden Worlds* #73 (1958). The creation of writer Richard E. Hughes (using the pen name Shane O'Shea) and artist Ogden Whitney, Herbie was more like the stereotypical comics *reader* than a comics hero: He was comically corpulent, hopelessly boring, and universally disliked. Herbie had one thing going for him (other than his trademark lollipops, that is): secret superpowers. He embarked on a series of novel adventures, taking place everywhere from the Wild West to the depths of space. In 1965 Herbie waddled into long underwear and placed a plunger on his head as the Fat Fury.

THE CAMP CRAZE

There was no decade with more superhero parodies and comedy crime fighters than the 1960s. Politically and culturally, Americans were burdened by an unpopular war and social strife, and virtually every facet of entertainment reflected the nation's desire to escape from these dark realities. The movies and television were filled with spy spoofs, mindless farces, silly sitcoms … and *Batman.*

DC Comics' former creature of the night became a campy caped crusader in producer William Dozier's live-action ABC series *Batman* (1966–1968), starring Adam West as a know-it-all crime fighter who would go to any tongue-in-cheek length to trap his foes, including dancing the Batusi with gun molls. *Batman* was an instant ratings smash, and inspired a theatrical movie in the summer of 1966, a bonanza of merchandising, and a national superhero craze.

1960s television was overrun with funny crime fighters. *Mighty Mouse* was joined on TV by other animated superhero series like *Courageous Cat and Minute Mouse* (a Batman lampoon by the hero's creator Bob Kane), *The Mighty Heroes* (a fondly remembered super-spoof light-years from director Ralph Bakshi's edgy later work), *Atom Ant, Frankenstein Jr. and the Impossibles,* and *Underdog.* TV sitcoms featured superhero parodies—the Monkees took to the air in tights and capes in a musical fantasy sequence, and Paul Lynde as Uncle Arthur wore a Superman suit for laughs on *Bewitched.* ABC's success with *Batman* led its competitors to launch their own live-action superhero spoofs. NBC's effort was *Captain Nice,* created by Buck Henry, about a nebbish mother's boy who paled in comparison to the menaces in his home turf of Bigtown. CBS jumped into the fray with *Mr. Terrific,* featuring a gullible geek named Stanley Beamish who transformed into a superhero by popping "power pills"—the effects of which would usually wear off just when Mr. Terrific needed his abilities most. Both series debuted as mid-season replacements in January 1967, and were canceled by the end of that summer, although *Captain Nice* spun off into a one-shot comic book from Gold Key and a paperback novel written by William Johnston and published by Tempo Books.

Nowhere were superhero send-ups more common than in the comics. Many of DC's mainstream heroes had their moments of merriment. *Adventure Comics* featured "Tales of the Bizarro World," with hundreds of oddball Superman duplicates on a square-shaped planet where inhabitants did everything exactly opposite from Earthlings. DC's *Metal Men, Wonder Woman,* and *Teen Titans* comics were wildly campy, as were its eccentric new series *Metamorpho the Element Man,* "Dial 'H' for Hero" (in *The House of Mystery*), and "Ultra the Multi-Alien" (in *Mystery in Space*). DC revived the Golden Age great *Plastic Man* for a stretch, and its *Batman* comic books parroted the lunacy of the successful TV show. One of DC's most peculiar moments transpired in its team-up comic *The Brave and the Bold* #68 (1966), in which Batman momentarily transformed into Bat-Hulk, a take-off on Marvel's character (minus any lawsuit-risking green pigmentation).

DC didn't stop there. The mod teenager called Super-Hip made the scene in 1965 in *The Adven-*

Fatman the Human Flying Saucer #3 © 1967 Lightning Comics.
COVER ART BY C. C. BECK.

tures of Bob Hope (a licensed title starring the popular comedian). No DC superhero parody is better remembered than the Inferior Five, first seen in *Showcase* #62 (1966). This quintet of second-generation superheroes—Merryman, Awkwardman, Dumb Bunny, White Feather, and the Blimp—was also second-string, failing as freedom fighters in pun-filled satires of everything from serious literature to Marvel's superheroes.

DC wasn't alone in the comedy hero game. From 1966 to 1967, the teens of Archie Comics' Riverdale would temporarily gain superpowers—just long enough to ride the wave of superhero popularity—in the farcical *Archie as Pureheart the Powerful*

(with Reggie as Evilheart) and *Jughead as Captain Hero,* superhero comics that the publisher has repeatedly recycled and revived in subsequent decades. In 1967 writer Otto Binder and artist C. C. Beck, renowned for their Golden Age work on *Captain Marvel Adventures,* created *Fatman, The Human Flying Saucer* for Lightning Comics. As his name suggests, Fatman was, well, *fat,* and could transform into a flying saucer. Fatman's adventures mimicked the gentle whimsy of Captain Marvel's two decades earlier, a flavor that had grown stale by the 1960s. *Fatman* was sent to the fat farm after three issues. Walt Disney's Goofy sported red long johns (what else?) and gulped "super goobers" (which were, in actuality, peanuts) in Gold Key Comics' long-running *Super Goof.* Protecting the town of Duckberg, Super Goof's abilities—which included X-ray vision, flight, superstrength, super-hearing, super-smell, and super-suction by spinning his hands—lasted only a few minutes per peanut, forcing him to carry a constant supply. Wonder Warthog appeared throughout the 1960s in a series of underground comics, and even Harvey Comics, best known for its entry-level *Casper* and *Richie Rich* titles, tried its hand at superhero parody in 1969 with *Fruitman.*

MAD lampooned TV's *Batman* as "Bats-Man" in its "Special Summer 'Camp' Issue," #105 (1966), featuring a cover with Batman repulsed by the magazine's mascot Alfred E. Newman as Robin the Boy Wonder. The following year *MAD* also offered its own original superhero, Captain Klutz, in an all-new paperback from Signet Books, *The MAD Adventures of Captain Klutz.* Illustrated by Don Martin, Captain Klutz, secretly Ringo Fonebone, wore red long underwear (!) and became a crime fighter after reading too many comic books left him unable to do anything else. Martin brought back Captain Klutz on several occasions, his last outing being in 1983.

Marvel Comics premiered its *MAD*-like *Not Brand Echh* title in 1967, poking fun at its "Marble" Comics characters (some examples: the Mighty Thor was the "Mighty Sore," and the Silver Surfer, the "Silver Burper"), pop culture, and its "Distinguished Competition" (including a Superman burlesque called "Stupor-Man"). *Not Brand Echh* was also the home of Forbush-Man, yet another comedy hero in red flannel underwear—and, like the Red Tornado, he wore a pot over his head! Irving Forbush was originally an unseen character mentioned jokingly in Marvel letters columns, but was first depicted in *Not Brand Echh* #1 as a janitor whose goal was to collect autographs from all of the Marble superheroes. Forbush-Man became *Not Brand Echh*'s answer to *MAD*'s Alfred E. Newman. Meanwhile, Topps, the premier producer of bubble-gum trading cards, published a series of mini-comics in 1967 parodying popular comics superheroes; included in this madcap mix were *Fantastic Fear* ("The World's Greatest Scaredy-Cats"), *The Incredible Hunk* (son of the Jolly Green Giant), *Jester's League of America* (the Justice League as practical jokers), and *The Flush* (a Flash take-off with the fleet-footed hero being outrun by *Looney Tunes*' Road Runner). In an even more comedic footnote to comics history, these spoofs bear the design work of Art Spiegelman, later a Pulitzer Prize winner for the Holocaust fable *Maus.*

NOT AS GOOD AS REGULAR SUPERHEROES, BUT SLIGHTLY BETTER THAN YOU

When the superhero craze died in the late 1960s, so did the parodies and campy heroes. But not for long. In the early to mid-1970s *National Lampoon* magazine frequently spoofed comic books. Their best-remembered (and most controversial) superhero burlesque was Son-O'-God—Jesus as a superhero—divinely rendered by legendary *Batman* artist Neal Adams. Son-O'-God fought Bible-based adversaries like Antichrist, the Scarlet Woman of Babylon, and even Satan himself. *National Lampoon* also poked fun at *Batman* (as senior-citizen Batfart in *Decrepit Comics*), *Nick Fury, Agent of S.H.I.E.L.D.* (as *Gordon Liddy, Agent of*

C.R.E.E.P.), and other superheroes. *Saturday Night Live* (*SNL*) sometimes ridiculed superheroes, including a late 1970s skit set at a party thrown by Lois Lane (guest host Margot Kidder, who played Lane in the four theatrical *Superman* movies from 1978 to 1987), with *SNL* cast members Bill Murray as Superman, Dan Aykroyd as a stocky Flash, and John Belushi as a boisterous Incredible Hulk. A few 1970s Saturday morning TV cartoons featured funny heroes, including *Dynomutt, Dog Wonder* (1976), a robotic superdog partnered with the Batman takeoff Blue Falcon, and the short-lived *The Super Globetrotters* (1979), featuring basketball starts the Harlem Globetrotters as superheroes (including Meadowlark Lemon as Fluid Man and Curly Neal as Sphere Man).

Lighthearted heroes were rare on TV in the 1980s (exceptions being *The Greatest American Hero,* which debuted in 1981, and *Misfits of Science,* which debuted a few years later on NBC but only lasted fifteen episodes), but comic books were full of them. Bob Burden's eccentric *Flaming Carrot Comics,* first seen in 1979, featured a peculiar protagonist, brain-addled from reading too many comics (a recurring theme in these parodies, perhaps a cryptic warning to readers?), who wore swim flippers and a six-feet-tall carrot mask (with a flaming top!). *Flaming Carrot Comics* has continued in print, albeit sporadically, through the 2000s. In 1987 it produced a spinoff, *Mysterymen Stories,* interpreted into a live-action film in 1999 as *Mystery Men,* spotlighting a band of low-rent superheroes: Mr. Furious (Ben Stiller), the Bowler (Janeane Garofalo), and Captain Amazing (Greg Kinnear), among others. A similar film, *The Specials* (2000), featured the Weevil (Rob Lowe), the Strobe (Thomas Haden Church), and Amok (Jamie Kennedy), as well as the tagline, "Not as good as regular superheroes, but slightly better than you."

Other 1980s superspoofs: DC's *Captain Carrot and His Amazing Zoo Crew,* a superteam of funny animals, and Marvel's *Peter Porker, The Spectacular Spider-Ham,* a kid-friendly concept with Spider-Man

as a cartoon pig (it also included Captain Americat, Goose Rider, and other anthropomorphic farces on Marvel heroes). The biggest 1980s success among cartoon heroes was *Teenage Mutant Ninja Turtles* (*TMNT*), a black-and-white comic book by Kevin Eastman and Peter Laird published by Mirage Press in 1984. Its marriage of martial arts, humor, and amiable characters was instantly successful, sparking sold-out print runs and counterfeit editions. *TMNT* single-handedly incited an explosion of small-press imitators, all of which promptly disappeared. The "heroes in a half-shell" expanded beyond their comics roots into a line of perennially popular *TMNT* action figures, several animated television series, and a live-action movie franchise.

Writer/artist Keith Giffen's Ambush Bug first popped up in the Superman/Doom Patrol story in *DC Comics Presents* #52 (1982). This wiry, green-clad, antenna-wearing fruitcake—whose real name is Irwin Schwab—was conceived as an irritant to Superman. Soon the Bug, enchanted by the idea that he existed "inside" a comic book, starred in a number of miniseries and specials where he pestered other DC superheroes, lampooning their origins, their powers, and sometimes their creators. The in-jokes of the various *Ambush Bug* series were an annoyance to some members of DC's editorial staff as well. Ambush Bug made a return appearance in *Lobo Unbound* #3 (2003).

In 1989 a second-string Marvel Comics character was revitalized with humor in *The Sensational She-Hulk.* Writer/artist John Byrne had used the Incredible Hulk's cousin during his *Fantastic Four* stint a few years prior, then segued her to solo adventures. She-Hulk, like Ambush Bug, acknowledged her existence inside her comic-book reality, frequently breaking the "fourth wall" by addressing Byrne, usually in frustration over the ludicrous situations he placed her in.

Creator Jim Valentino's *normalman* enjoyed a twelve-issue run in 1984–1985 in a black-and-white series from publisher Aardvark-Vanaheim. *normalman* reversed the Superman legend by stranding its star—Norm, an average, nerdy guy—on Levram (read that name backwards), a planet exclusively populated with superheroes. Also in 1984 writer/artist Don Simpson skewered the folklore of Superman, the Fantastic Four, Tarzan, Spider-Man, and Captain America with his madcap origin of Megaton Man. Sent to Earth as the only survivor of his planet, Megaton Man was bombarded by "cataclysmic" radiation, reared by gifted kangaroos, gnawed by a radioactive frog, and empowered by "solider syrup." This ridiculously proportioned hero (gigantically broad shoulders tapering into a tiny waist) debuted in Kitchen Sink Press' *Megaton Man* #1 (1984) and appeared for a brief run, with one-shots and an online version (www.megatonman. com) following. Ben Edlund's *The Tick* appeared two years after Megaton Man's debut, spinning out of comic shop New England Comics' newsletter into his own series. An oafish powerhouse, the bulky Tick was paired with mousy Arthur, comics' only sidekick in a moth suit. Edlund sharply satirized superheroes with original characters like American Maid and the Man-Eating Cow. The character has appeared on TV in an animated series (1994–1997) and a live-action show (2001).

The diminutive do-gooder called 'Mazing Man strolled into comics with a critically acclaimed twelve-issue run beginning in January 1986. Written by Bob Rozakis and illustrated by Stephen DeSte-fano, *'Mazing Man*'s protagonist was a docile mental patient who performed good deeds for his neighbors while wearing a gold helmet and a cape. His suburban stories were quiet, slice-of-life fables with a lively supporting cast including the cynical Denton Fixx, a walking dog. *Radioactive Man* is a much noisier parody of superheroes from Bongo Comics, the publisher of a line of titles based on Matt Groening's popular animated TV series *The Simpsons*. First seen in 1994, Radioactive Man, an orange-clad, camp-inspired superhero with a lightning bolt protruding from his skull, is joined by sidekick Fallout Boy in an irregularly published series of comics that presupposes publication through the decades and parodies the pop-culture of different times. *Radioactive Man* continues to appear in the 2000s.

COMEDY HEROES 2K

For decades *MAD* magazine and its chief competitor *CRACKED* have relentlessly ridiculed superhero TV shows, movies, and comic books (and their fans). In 2002 MAD Books published the trade paperback *MAD About Super Heroes,* compiling all of *MAD*'s superhero parodies to that time including "Don Martin Looks at the Hulk," "Stuporman ZZZ" (a *Superman III* takeoff), "$-Men" (a 2001 *X-Men* movie parody), and "What if Superman Were Raised by Jewish Parents?" (In February 2004 the magazine convened some of the hottest talents in serious superhero art, from Frank Miller to Jim Lee, to illustrate "The League of Rejected Superheroes," the cover story of issue #438.) *Saturday Night Live* superhero skits have continued sporadically into the 2000s, with comedian Sinbad as DC's Black Lightning, pro wrestler the Rock as Clark Kent with a not-so-secret identity (his blue-and-red Superman uniform was clearly visible through his white dress shirt), and the animated shorts *X-Presidents* (former U.S. presidents as superheroes) and *The Ambiguously Gay Duo* among their number. Fox-TV's *In Living Color* (1990–1994) featured a recurring superhero parody: the physically challenged champion Handi-Man, portrayed by Damon Wayans. Often aided by a midget superheroine known as the Tiny Avenger, Handi-Man, whose chest insignia was a wheelchair icon, stood up for the rights of the disabled, concluding his adventures by reciting his motto, "Never underestimate the powers of the handicapped."

Comic books' content grew grimmer in the 1990s and the 2000s, with violent anti-heroes abounding, and superhero parodies largely drifted by the wayside. As a result, humor has become a subgenre in the comics medium, with small-press titles like Evan Dorkin's *Milk and Cheese,* Tony Millionaire's *The Adventures of Sock Monkey,* and Shannon Wheeler's *Too Much Coffee Man* earning loyal cult audiences. During this period, a few super-hero series have premiered appropriate satirical elements without being actual lampoons: Mike Allred's *Madman* and Arthur Adams' *Monkeyman and O'Brien,* for example. While out-and-out super-hero parodies may be rare, they do occasionally occur, in odd outings like *Archie Meets the Punisher* (1994), an anomalous crossover between Archie and Marvel Comics' death-dealing vigilante; DC's *Sergio Destroys DC* and its chief competitor's *Sergio Massacres Marvel,* both by *MAD*'s Sergio Aragones and both published in June 1996; Alan Moore's evil twin to early Marvel, *1963* (Image, 1993); DC Comics' comic-shop satire *Fanboy* (1999); filmmaker Kevin Smith's Jay and Silent Bob as *Bluntman and Chronic,* from Oni Press (1999); Image Comics' *The Pro* (2002), a super-prostitute among straight-laced Justice League send-ups; Bongo Comics' *Heroes Anonymous* (2003–2004), a superhero self-help saga; the super-workplace farce *Capes* (Image, 2003); *The B-Sides,* New Jersey's best—and only—superteam (Marvel, 2002); the irony-era Batman and Robin, "Hawk-Owl and Woody," of Marvel's *Ultimate Adventures* (2002–2004); and DC's *Bizarro Comics!* (2001), a 240-page hardcover featuring a host of avant-garde cartoonists and their twisted takes on traditional DC superheroes. Whether or not the superhero parody and comedy heroes will survive in the future depends upon the audience's ability to laugh at the material, and by extension laugh at itself. —*ME*

Camp Heroes in the Media

O, Batman, what hath thou wrought? Debuting in January 1966, ABC's goofy live-action *Batman* television series was quickly labeled "camp." When ratings exploded and *Batman* became a public darling, both networks and movie studios looked to see what they could do to tie in to the camp super-hero craze.

First out of the gate were *Rat Pfink and Boo-Boo* (1966) and *The Wild World of Batwoman* (1966), two micro-budget live-action feature films that specifically made fun of *Batman*. In *Rat Pfink,* inept rockabilly heroes Rat Pfink (Ron Haydock, credited as Vin Saxon) and sidekick Boo Boo (Titus Moede) must rescue the curvaceous Ceebee Beaumont (Carolyn Brandt) from the evil Chain Gang and Kogar the Swinging Ape. The inept hero and his sidekick race to save Beaumont on their (what else?) Pfinkcycle, their mouths uttering inept super-hero slogans like "Fight crime!" The story behind the movie title is well known in fan circles; it was accidentally misspelled and director Ray Dennis Steckler didn't have the money to correct it. The scantily clad femme cast of *Wild World* face mad scientist Professor Neon (George Mitchell, credited as George Andre) and his assistant Rat Fink (Richard Banks, no relation to Rat Pfink) as they plot dastardly evil with hallucinatory Happy Pills and an atomic-powered explosive hearing aid!

On January 9, 1967, one year after *Batman* debuted, NBC unveiled *Captain Nice* and CBS debuted *Mr. Terrific,* two half-hour camp superhero shows. Created by Buck Henry (co-creator of *Get Smart*), *Captain Nice* starred William Daniels as police chemist Carter Nash, who discovers Super Juice, an extract that gives him temporary super-powers. Wearing a red-white-and-blue outfit sewn by his mother, Captain Nice ineptly tries to stop thugs and villains, all while failing to notice the wily seductive nature of female co-worker Sgt. Candy Crane. Meanwhile, Mr. Terrific was really Stanley Beamish (Stephen Strimpell), a gas station attendant who could take super pills to gain powers for an hour, including the power of flight (if he flapped his arms). Beamish worked with the government agency Bureau of Secret Projects, while wearing a silver lamé suit and goggles. *Captain Nice* lasted fifteen episodes, while *Mr. Terrific* limped on to sixteen shows total.

While Saturday morning cartoons continued to include a wide range of humorous heroes throughout the late 1960s and 1970s, live-action counterparts were few on television or in theaters. Some movies, like *Superchick* (1971), *Infra-Man* (1976), *Supersonic Man* (1978), *The Puma Man* (1980), and *Super Fuzz* (1980), were simply inept feature films that were only "campy" because their budgets could not have fed a small family for more than a week. Featuring little-known directors with little-known actors, these films rarely applied the "super" to the concept of superhero.

Other features attempted to update the formula, diluting the camp and injecting real comedy instead. *Hero At Large* (1980) saw John Ritter portraying an actor slumming in the role of Captain Avenger to promote a film, until he actually performs heroic deeds while in costume and learns he likes it. Disney's *Condorman* (1981) followed a similar storyline, finding a cartoonist (played by later Broadway *Phantom of the Opera* star Michael Crawford) forced to become his supercharacter to help save a beautiful Russian spy. *The Return of Captain Invincible* (1983) offered Alan Arkin in the title role as a hero who was famous in the 1940s but is now an alcoholic outcast. Can he redeem himself when the world needs him, fighting Mr. Midnight and enduring the musical song-and-dance interludes?

Television once again saw the rise of a humorous live-action hero with *The Greatest American Hero* (1981–1983), in which a school teacher is given an alien supersuit to fight crime, but he loses the instruction booklet. A few years later, NBC debuted *Misfits of Science,* a funny hour-long show that found a group of superpowered young adults gathered together to fight crime at the Humanidyne science institute. The group included a tall black man who could shrink (Kevin Peter Hall), a hipster who could shoot lightning from his hands (Mark Thomas Miller), a recurring character who could freeze things (Mickey Jones), and a girl with psychic powers (the breakout star of the series, Courteney

Cox). After fifteen episodes garnered low ratings, NBC yanked the series.

Troma Studios debuted the feature film *The Toxic Avenger* in 1986. After a geek (Melvin Junko) is exposed to toxic waste, he is mutated into the monstrous superhero (Mitchell Cohen) who wears a burned tutu and wields a mop. A return to camp in a storytelling sense, *Toxic Avenger* had a low budget, but directors Michael Herz and Lloyd Kaufman made the most of everything they had. "Toxie" became a cult phenomenon, and sequels were made: *The Toxic Avenger, Part 2* (1989); *The Toxic Avenger, Part 3: The Last Temptation of Toxie* (1989); and *Citizen Toxie: The Toxic Avenger, Part 4* (2000). An animated TV series, *The Toxic Crusaders,* ran for thirteen episodes in 1991, and a spin-off film, *Sgt. Kabukiman N.Y.P.D.,* was released that same year. Both Toxie and Kabukiman are familiar sights at both the Cannes Film Festival and the San Diego Comic-Con International, where Troma hosts presentations for fans and industry insiders.

The 1990s saw a handful of superhero comedy films released that tried to make hip their camp qualities. *The Meteor Man* (1993) was written and directed by Robert Townsend, who also starred. Hit by a meteor, schoolteacher Townsend gains superpowers and tries to defend his neighborhood from the gang known as the Golden Lords. Because he is afraid of heights, Meteor Man flies only four feet off the ground, and he wears costumes created by his mother. The film includes cameos by Bill Cosby, Sinbad, Luther Vandross, and LaWanda Page—and *Batman* TV show Riddler Frank Gorshin shows up as a mobster named Byers. 1994's *Blankman,* written by and starring comedian Damon Wayans, attempted to be funnier, giving a nerd superpowered gadgets and a literal long-underwear costume (bullet-proof), accented with a cape made from his grandmother's bathrobe. As a self-appointed superhero Wayans battles thugs and robbers to keep his city safe, and awaits his first kiss from pretty Kimberly (Robin Givens).

Several more recent films have been an odd mixture of camp, irony, and superhero deconstruc-

Stephen Strimpell poses as camp hero Mr. Terrific.

tionism. *Mystery Men* (1999) was based on Bob Burden's strange superheroes from the cult series *Flaming Carrot Comics* published by Dark Horse Comics. Directed by Kinka Usher, the movie teamed a group of amateur, second-string heroes against a nemesis from their past. The all-star cast featured Ben Stiller as the very angry Mr. Furious, Janeane Garofalo as the second-generation heroine the Bowler, Hank Azaria as the silverware-wielding Blue Raja, Paul Reubens as the gas-filled Spleen, William H. Macy as the Shoveller, Kel Mitchell as the too-visible Invisible Boy, and Wes Studi as the inscrutable Sphinx, all working to stop Geoffrey Rush's Casanova Frankenstein and his goons from destroying Champion City.

The Specials (2000) followed a similar formula, though it went straight-to-video. Headquartered in a suburban house in Silver Lake, California, the world's seventh best superhero team, the Specials, include Power Chick (Kelly Coffield), Minute Man (James Gunn), and blue-skinned Amok (Jamie Kennedy). They must cope as action figure deals fall through, as well as the fallout when the Strobe (Thomas Haden Church) disbands the group after discovering that his wife, Ms. Indestructible (Paget Brewster), is having an affair with fellow hero the Weevil (Rob Lowe). Directed by Craig Maizen, the film was well received—by those few who saw it—for its smart dialogue and silly cast.

The Duo (2001) is a direct-to-video "mockumentary" in which a reporter (Marie Black) tries to make a film about two masked Texas twenty-somethings who think they're superheroes. Best Man (Bill Wise)

is vaguely gayesque and wears parts of a tuxedo, while sidekick Buddy Boy (Ryan Wickerham) can use his staring powers to warp minds and force people to incessantly hula hoop. Sure to maintain a higher profile is *The Incredibles,* a 2004 animated film from Disney about a suburban superhero family.

Although the age of camp superheroes is definitely a thing of the past, making fun of the campy superhero concept is definitely part of the appeal of *Comic Book: The Movie.* Directed by and starring *Star Wars'* Mark Hamill, the direct-to-video film (2003) follows the travails of Donald Swann, #1 fan of popular 1940s hero Commander Courage, as he attempts to film a documentary at the San Diego Comic-Con International. Real-world comic-book creators make cameos in the film, including Paul Dini, Peter David, Scott Shaw, Mark Evanier, and someone whose initials follow the dash. —*AM*

Captain Action

Captain Action, the original superhero action figure, owes his existence to Barbie. When Mattel premiered its dress-up doll in 1959, it also launched the "razor/razor blade" concept: marketing a host item (the "razor," or the Barbie doll), with supplemental accessories (the "razor blades," or Barbie's clothing). Barbie's rampant success inspired toy makers Stanley Weston and Larry Reiner to attempt a similar product for boys, the result being Hasbro's GI Joe, a generic military figure complemented by an

escalating line of combat garb and gear. GI Joe so took the nation by storm in 1964 that Weston and Reiner repackaged their idea in a superhero context, knocking on the door of Reiner's employer, Ideal Toys. And so Captain Action, a twelve-inch superhero figure with additional crime-fighting costumes (all sold separately), was launched in 1966.

Captain Action (circa 1966) © & ™ Karl Art Publishing, Inc. ART BY MURPHY ANDERSON, INKED IN 2002 OVER UNUSED 1966 PENCILS.

The original line of Captain Action uniforms consisted of Superman, Batman, Aquaman, Captain America, Sgt. Fury, Flash Gordon, the Phantom, Steve Canyon, and the Lone Ranger, popular characters representing five different licensors, a concerted effort that now seems impossible in today's competitive market. Solid sales, bolstered by a ubiquitous advertising campaign on television and in comic books, sparked an increase of product in 1967, including more costumes (with the popular Spider-Man joining the line, along with other heroes), play sets, and accessories, plus the sidekick Action Boy, also marketed with additional uniforms (Robin, Superboy, and Aqualad). Captain Action was merchandized outside of Ideal's figure line, with a card game, inflatable swim ring, and Halloween costume released.

Captain Action sales began to shrink in 1967, but not so much that Ideal abandoned the concept. In 1968, the company issued Captain Action and Action Boy in redesigned packaging and added a villain, the blue-skinned alien Dr. Evil (not to be confused with the character from the *Austin Powers* movies). DC Comics published five issues of a Captain Action comic book beginning in 1968, illustrated by Wally Wood and Gil Kane, marking the first toy-inspired comic book (over time, *Hot Wheels, The Micronauts, Rom: Spaceknight,* and others would follow, including, coincidentally, *Barbie* and *GI Joe*). Writer Jim Shooter, in *Captain Action* #1, created a true identity for Captain Action—Clive Arno (note the initials)—and provided him with a host of powers from coins imbued with the abilities of ancient gods. These efforts came too late: Captain Action toys and comics disappeared in 1969.

Yet Captain Action maintained a loyal collectors' audience. In 1995, Karl Art Publishing obtained the Captain Action copyright through the publication of a one-shot comic book. Playing Mantis, a producer of reissued baby-boomer toys, acquired the action-figure license in 1998. Captain Action and Dr. Evil reappeared, along with costumes of classic heroes and villains. Even Action Boy returned, renamed "Kid Action" due to copyright restrictions. But publishers DC and Marvel refused to grant licenses for their characters, and without the identifiable Batman, Spider-Man, and the like to support the line, Captain Action was canceled once again in 2000. While his two leases on life have failed to make him famous, Captain Action remains a nostalgic favorite, and a book celebrating his history, *Captain Action: The Original Super-Hero Action Figure,* was published in 2002. —*ME*

Captain America

Captain America may not be the first patriotic superhero—that title belongs to the Shield—but he is by far the most enduring and most widely recognized of those wrapped in the red, white, and blue. Probably more than any other character of the last sixty years, the good Captain has been rendered by artists and writers to reflect the mood of the nation. In March 1941, Captain America's creators, Joe Simon and Jack Kirby, fashioned his origin after the simplicity of a prewar America: Having been rejected by the army, effete beanpole Steve Rogers volunteers to be a guinea pig for the government's top-

secret super soldier serum. One injection from the brilliant Professor Reinstein and the pale army reject is transformed into the steel-jawed, muscle-rippling Captain America, complete with red-white-and-blue costume, winged mask, chain mail shirt, and stars-and-stripes shield. His mission is clear: "We shall call you Captain America, Son! Because like you—America shall gain the strength and will to safeguard our shores!" Reinstein gets shot and his Nazi assassins soon taste the swift, hard knuckles of the nation's newest hero. In due course, Rogers joins the army, acquires a kid sidekick—plucky regimental mascot Bucky Barnes—and embarks on a career of enthusiastic Nazi-bashing.

Simon and Kirby clearly established Captain America's identity from the very first issue they created for Marvel (then Timely) Comics, audaciously showing Cap landing a righteous haymaker on the Führer's chin—on the cover itself! Here was a hero who could protect the free world almost a year before the United States would enter World War II. And if Cap was our hero, then Rogers represented every American soldier who would soon fight for his country. The early stories were simple, straightforward tales peopled with bizarre villains such as the Hunchback of Hollywood, the Black Toad, Ivan the Terrible, and assorted fifth columnists. Chief among the bad guys was the Red Skull, a seemingly invincible Nazi whose face literally was a crimson skull, and who would return again and again. As straightforward as all that derring-do was, it was also gripping, exciting, and fast-moving, and with Kirby's dramatic art the comic was one of the most widely read titles of the Golden Age era (1938–1954).

From Captain America's beginning, audience identification and participation were central to his success. The first issue announced the creation of "The Sentinels of Liberty" Fan Club, which eager young fans could join for a modest dime, entitling them to a membership card and metal badge. The club proved so popular that the government pleaded with Marvel to wind it down; the badges were eating up too much precious metal, which could be better used in the imminent war. More significantly, in Bucky readers had a role model they could identify with: a boy much like themselves who bravely fought beside their idol with only his two sharp fists to defend himself. It wasn't long before he was given his own strip as leader of the Young Allies kid gang, who would be featured in more than forty stories in titles such as *Kid Komics* and *Marvel Mystery,* as well as in their own eponymous comic book.

By the time of Pearl Harbor, Captain America had become Marvel's top-selling title (at almost 1 million copies a month), and over the course of the war Cap and Bucky fought the Axis Powers on both fronts. After ten wonderful issues, the comic's creators were enticed away to rival company DC Comics, but their replacements—tyro writer/editor Stan Lee and various artists including Syd Shores—handled things well in their absence. In 1943 the character received the honor of his own Republic Pictures serial, *The Adventures of Captain America*—confirmation (if any were needed) of his potent iconic status. Then, at the height of Cap's popularity, disaster struck: the war ended.

After military discharge, Cap and Bucky settled into life as teacher and pupil at a New York slum school, and took the good fight to homegrown mobsters, miscreants, and monsters. But while the country had embraced superheroes in wartime, peace brought an upsurge in crime, funny animal, Western, and romance comics—everything, in fact, except superheroes. In an effort to broaden their dwindling readership, Marvel stuck a conveniently wounded Bucky into the hospital and replaced him with Cap's longtime squeeze, Betty (or Betsy, depending on the writer's mood) Ross, a.k.a. Golden Girl. Perhaps unsurprisingly, the gun-toting, high-heeled, evening gown–wearing Golden Girl failed to resonate with the stalwart Sentinels of Liberty club members, and in 1950 the comic was canceled.

Barely four years later, a very different Cap returned. Stan Lee sensed that the country, rocked by the Korean War, was in need of heroes again,

and so he reintroduced Captain America, Human Torch, and Sub-Mariner in the dubiously titled *Young Men* #24. Steve and Bucky were still at school (and still fighting the Red Skull) but the comic's subtitle said it all: This was "Captain America, Commie Smasher"—a hero for the McCarthy era. Over the course of sixteen stories, the intrepid pair beat the stuffing out of reds from Eastern Europe to Egypt and from China to Vietnam. But the public simply did not warm to them as they once had. Lee's instincts were right but he was just a little too early; a mere two years later, DC's revival of the Flash sparked off the great superhero revival of comics' Silver Age (1956–1969).

By late 1963, Marvel's own Silver Age heroes were beginning to find a large and enthusiastic audience, and with both the Torch and Sub-Mariner successfully given new life (in a revised version as a member of Lee & Kirby's Fantastic Four and as a guest-star in the same team's book, respectively), surely the time was ripe for the good Captain once more. Lee was cautious at first, starring Cap in a Human Torch story and having him turn out to be an impostor, and then reintroducing him properly in *Avengers* #4 (1964). It seems that, following a pitched battle in the dying days of World War II with the hooded Baron Zemo, in which the pair try to defuse a deadly drone aircraft, Bucky bit the dust and Cap ended up floating in the ocean in ice-induced suspended animation. (Why Cap and Bucky had seemed to still be alive in the 1950s would be explained a bit later on.) The Rip Van Winkle of comics immediately joined the Avengers, gained an ersatz Bucky in Rick Jones (with his own would-be young allies, a group of intrepid wireless hams called the Teen Brigade), fought copious colorful villains, and started brooding about the past. Within a year of his revival, he had graduated to his own strip in *Tales of Suspense,* a title he shared with Iron Man, and was well on his way to becoming an icon all over again.

However, despite all manner of merchandise and deliriously exciting art from the returning Jack

Kirby, the character would never be as popular as Marvel's powerhouse headliners Spider-Man, the Fantastic Four, or the Hulk. As an admission that the strip was at its most potent in World War II, this revival almost immediately resorted to "untold tales" of the war, and when that did not quite work Lee brought back the Red Skull and various ex-Nazis. But if it never again hit the commercial heights of the past, the strip was nevertheless a cornerstone of the "Marvel Universe" and, with Lee and Kirby at the peak of their powers, the late 1960s stories were a compelling read. In 1968 Cap graduated to his own solo comic and, despite Kirby defecting to DC (once again), the character has been published continuously ever since.

Very much a man out of time and something of an elder statesman among superheroes, the 1960s Cap was essentially an establishment figure who became the *de facto* leader of the Avengers, a part-time agent of S.H.I.E.L.D. (Marvel's James Bond-ian take on the FBI), and a father figure to Rick Jones. Indeed, for a short period in the early 1970s, Rick actually donned Bucky's costume and, although that did not quite work out, it was clear that Cap worked best with a partner. That troubled decade saw the rise of women's lib, black power, and introspection, and the strip reflected America's sense of change and uncertainty. Cap's girlfriend Sharon Carter preferred life as a jump-suited agent of S.H.I.E.L.D. to the "domestic bliss" of a married life tied to the kitchen and kids. In 1971, Captain America gained a new partner in black social worker Sam Wilson, a.k.a. the Falcon, and for a short time became an NYPD cop on the beat in Harlem's ghettoes. Perhaps most tellingly, one storyline had the Captain doing that most 1970s of things, getting on his motorcycle and heading out into the country in search of the "real" America.

By the mid-1970s, Stan Lee had left the comic, and young scripter Steve Englehart took Cap into deeper, darker waters. The 1950s Captain America and Bucky were revived (literally!) and revealed to have been government doppelgängers who had

Captain America #106 © 1968 Marvel Comics.
COVER ART BY JACK KIRBY AND FRANK GIACOIA.

themselves been put into suspended animation after their overzealous red-baiting got completely out of hand. In a lengthy tale that cleverly echoed Watergate, the "Campaign to Rejoin America's Principles" was revealed to be a cover for the evil "Secret Empire" and the government's insidious corruption horrified our hero. Sickened at what he saw as the betrayal of his country, Cap quit in disgust, briefly becoming a character called Nomad ("The Man without a Country," get it?) before his innate patriotism got the better of him. 1976 was the year of the Bicentennial, and of course Cap had to have his own take on the celebrations, fighting an underground band of neo-royalists (courtesy of Jack Kirby on his third tour of duty at Marvel).

Throughout this period, the character was a consistently merchandised property, from dolls and posters to toy cars and clothes. The Reagan years were similarly something of a disappointment for the strip. Kirby had not handled the Falcon well and, despite his potential as a counterpoint to Cap's conservatism, he was rarely more than a second stringer. After almost ninety issues as co-star, Sam Wilson was written out of the comic and faded into obscurity. Soon after that, Sharon Carter was ignominiously killed, which was a cue for the perpetually morose Captain to become ever more introspective. This search for meaning in his life culminated in Cap considering a presidential bid—perhaps the logical conclusion to a lifetime wrapped in the flag. (The Falcon entered politics a few years later, trading in his costume for life as a congressman.)

The 1980s came to be dominated by the writing of Mark Gruenwald, who stayed on the strip for an astonishing ten years and adopted a more lighthearted approach as a counterpoint to the previous decade's upheavals. The strip had always featured a number of recurring villains, including the outrageously camp French martial arts expert Batroc the Leaper, the large-headed Modok, insidious crime cartels A.I.M. and H.Y.D.R.A., and of course the ever-present Red Skull. Under Gruenwald, the villains expanded exponentially but the comic perhaps lost some of its individuality in the process. One exception to this was a witty response to recession-era cutbacks, in which the government stripped Steve Rogers of his costume, claiming that they were no longer getting their money's worth. His replacement, the Super-Patriot (later known as USAgent), soon discovered that, like the similarly ill-conceived new Coca-Cola, life as a living legend is far from easy. Inevitably, the original Cap ("Classic Cap," anyone?) returned, but the departing Gruenwald handed his successors the most poisoned of chalices by killing the character off; it seems that the super serum that had kept him going all those years had finally run out.

But there are always more comics to be printed, more movies to be made, and more merchandise to sell. It is an accepted fact, of course, that no one stays dead in comics for very long. One blood transfusion—from the Red Skull, no less—and Cap was back as good as new. So, too, was Sharon Carter, and in fact the 1990s and 2000s saw an endless series of new directions, relaunches, returns to basics, and yet more relaunches. Longtime readers have now learned to expect several inviolable certainties: that Cap will regularly pine for the dear, departed Bucky; that no matter how many painful deaths he may suffer, the Red Skull will always come back for more; that you are never more than a few issues away from a World War II flashback; and that a new direction is always around the corner. These have included the revelation that the super soldier serum was originally tested on black GIs, one of whom briefly adventured before Steve Rogers; hints that Cap was frozen on purpose by a government that feared he would oppose the bombing of Hiroshima; yet another death (in *Captain America* vol. 3 #50), his resurrection from which remains unexplained; and a new 2004 *Captain America and the Falcon* comic by acclaimed writer Christopher Priest.

Cap's current incarnation, which again unerringly taps into the zeitgeist, sees the character reinvented as a four-color foot-soldier in the fight against terrorism—albeit one facing serious moral quandaries—which only goes to show his longevity as a symbol of America itself. This superhero, who is literally wrapped in the flag, proudly symbolizes his country and will no doubt continue to do so for as long as comics are published. —*DAR*

Captain America in the Media

As war loomed in 1941, the citizens of the United States were caught in a maelstrom of patriotism. Comics creators Joe Simon and Jack Kirby wanted to translate those patriotic ideals into a superhero for Timely (later Marvel) Comics, so they created Captain America, a supersoldier dressed in the red, white, and blue of the country's flag. The shield-slinging hero was a hit, whether he was combating saboteurs and spies, or villains such as the Red Skull. It was only natural that Hollywood was set on taking its own swing at bringing Captain America to the masses.

Republic Pictures was famous for its film serials, a series of short fifteen- to twenty-minute films that played every week (usually Saturdays) in theaters. Since each chapter of the serial ended in a nail-biting cliff-hanger, children and adults alike would return each week to see how their hero escaped to triumph over evil. Since Captain America didn't fly or have any otherworldly powers, Republic knew that not only would the character be popular with the public, but a *Captain America* serial would be cheap to film as well.

Republic optioned the rights to *Captain America* in 1943. Incredibly, Timely didn't charge Republic any money for the film rights, thinking of the serial as a promotional tool rather than as merchandising! Republic filmed the fifteen-part *Captain America* serial in the fall of 1943, and debuted the first chapter on December 31 of that same year. Dick Purcell played Cap, but the script was anything but true to the comics. Instead of soldier Steve Rogers, our hero was secretly District Attorney Grant Gardner. Instead of wielding a shield against Nazis, Cap fought criminals with a gun and his fists. At least the costume was reasonably similar to its four-color counterpart, though it lacked the wings on its cowl, and the tall buccaneer-style boots.

The ultra-violent serial found Captain America fighting against the deadly Scarab, his Purple Death poison, his experimental "dynamic vibrator," and his plans to use a serum that brought the dead back to life. Seen today as one of the better superhero serials ever produced, *Captain America* did well in the theaters, but Republic had already decided to stop making superhero serials. The death of Purcell

shortly after filming sealed their decision. A few years later the serial was released, unchanged, as *The Return of Captain America.*

Captain America didn't resurface in Hollywood until 1965, when animators and producers Robert Lawrence, Grant Simmons, and Ray Patterson founded the animation company Grantray-Lawrence. They created a syndicated daily animated program for television called *The Marvel Super-Heroes;* each day spotlit a different hero with a three-part adventure. *Captain America* was Monday, *The Incredible Hulk* was Tuesday, *Iron Man* was Wednesday, *Mighty Thor* was Thursday (naturally), and *Sub-Mariner* was Friday. The *Captain America* theme song was incredibly catchy, with its lyrics that proclaimed, "When Captain America throws his mighty shield, all those who chose to oppose his shield must yield! If he's led to a fight, and the duel is due, then the red and the white and the blue will come through. When Captain America throws his mighty shield!"

To call the animation acceptable would be charitable. Through a process called Xerography, artwork was transferred directly from Marvel comic books onto animation cels. It was then given a slight movement by jiggling the cel or sliding it across a background. Occasionally, blinking eyes or moving hands would give the illusion of movement. The stories were taken from issues of *Tales of Suspense* and *The Avengers,* and were thus very faithful to their origins. Despite only one season of production, *The Marvel Super-Heroes* show was popular enough to remain in syndication for many years, and still resurfaces on the video market today.

Following the success of *The Incredible Hulk* television series in 1977, Universal optioned several Marvel superheroes for CBS telefilms. If successful, they would be used as pilots for a series. Following a *Dr. Strange* flop, Universal released a two-hour *Captain America* TV movie on January 19, 1979. The film was dreadfully slow, with many alterations from Cap's comic book origins. Now, Captain America was Steve Rogers Jr., the son of the original. Rogers Jr. (actor Reb Brown) wanted to be an artist, but when he was given the F.L.A.G. (Full Latent Ability Gain) serum developed by his late father, he became a motorcycle-riding hero for the government. His costume was radically different from the comic book outfit, and his shield was clear Plexiglas (doubling as a motorcycle windshield) with some stripes and a star.

With a plot that included a criminal mastermind who planned to blow up Phoenix, Arizona, with a neutron bomb, *Captain America* bored viewers and received low ratings, but CBS wasn't ready to give up yet. A second pilot aired in two parts, on November 23 and 24, 1979. This was alternately called *Captain America II* and *Captain America: Death Too Soon,* and featured the comic book costume and noted horror actor Christopher Lee as the mad scientist villain, Miguel. Ratings weren't enough to start a franchise, however.

Captain America next guest-starred in two episodes of the animated *Spider-Man and His Amazing Friends* show (1981–1983), teaming up with Spider-Man and other heroes to battle Kingpin, Dr. Faustus, and the Chameleon. He also appeared in the syndicated *Spider-Man* animated series during the 1981–1982 season.

Several announcements in Hollywood industry trade papers saw *Captain America* promised for more feature film action in 1984 and 1986, but it wasn't until 1989 that a new live-action film went into production from Menachem Golan's 21st Century Film Corporation. Shot in Yugoslavia, the movie starred Matt Salinger (son of writer J. D. Salinger) as Steve Rogers/Cap, and Scott Paulin as the Red Skull. The film began with a close approximation of the comics' origin story, including Cap being frozen in a block of ice after being strapped to a rocket by the Red Skull. Thawed out in the 1980s, he once again found himself facing his ancient Nazi enemy.

Although Columbia agreed to release *Captain America* to theaters in 1990, the feature was delayed for two years, eventually being sent direct-to-video in the United Kingdom in 1991 and the United States in June 1992. With a low budget and a rubbery costume for its hero, *Captain America* is not a perfect film, but it isn't quite as horrid as some reviewers have opined.

Regardless of the low profile that movie maintained, Cap has become one of those characters that can be seen everywhere in pop culture. Wyatt, one of the two counterculture heroes of the cinematic classic *Easy Rider* (1969), is better known by his nickname of "Captain America," and Captain America's name became a synonym for an ailing superpower in the Kinks' 1979 song about the post-Watergate USA, "Catch Me Now I'm Falling." When a later rock band, eventually known as Eugenius, tried to call itself Captain America, Marvel threw its mighty shield with a threatened lawsuit, though when Cap was hauled into court again in Joe Simon's high-profile early 2000s suit to reclaim the rights to the character, this superhero became one of the few to star in both the entertainment and the news media.

In the years since the *Captain America* film, the patriotic hero has appeared in a handful of animated adventures. He appeared in a flashback (with X-Men hero Wolverine) for the fifth and final season of Fox's popular *X-Men* series in 1996–1997, then alongside other World War II heroes in a three-part adventure for *Spider-Man*'s fourth season in 1997–1998. Although Fox commissioned and developed a *Captain America* animated pilot in 1998, plans did not proceed. As of 2004, Captain America's final television appearance was in several episodes of Fox Kids' *The Avengers* in the 1999–2000 season. The resilient patriotic hero has rarely stayed on ice for very long though, so new Captain America adventures are likely to come in the future. —*AM*

Captain Atom

Captain Atom holds a special place in comics history—not so much as a creation himself as for one of his creators. The Captain was the main hero from

Charlton Comics, the independent-minded, eccentric, and largely unloved publishing house from Derby, Connecticut. Captain Atom made his first appearance in 1960 in the pages of one of the company's science fiction and mystery comics, *Space Adventures* (issue #33). He preceded Marvel's more famous Fantastic Four by some twenty months and, more to the point, Steve Ditko's Spider-Man by two-and-a-half years. Ditko had been Charlton's star artist for many years and was establishing himself at Marvel at the same time, but Captain Atom marked his first significant work on a superhero and laid the foundations for his later success as one of the decade's most important artists.

Captain Atom's opening story in *Space Adventures,* by editor/writer Pat Masuli and Steve Ditko, reveals how rocket specialist and air force captain Allen Adam loses a screwdriver during some last-minute adjustments to a missile's nuclear warhead, and unwisely delays his exit by looking for the tool. Unable to leave the rocket in time, he is accidentally launched into space and blown to atoms when the missile explodes. Incredibly, he somehow manages to reconstruct himself and reappear in his military base back on Earth, shooting off radiation from every pore in his body. Military scientists quickly devise a sparkly yellow-and-red costume (with a red starburst and an atomic symbol on its chest) to contain all the radiation, and thus a new superhero—Captain Atom—is born. Captain Atom soon discovers that he can fly as fast as a rocket (100,000 miles per hour), adjust his molecular structure to walk through walls, endure temperatures as high as 10,000 degrees Centigrade, and pack enough of a punch to destroy an errant missile.

Captain Atom's origin story and powers resemble those of Doctor Solar (Gold Key Comics) and Nukla (Dell Comics), other atomic physicist types turned superheroes of the Silver Age (1956–1969). The early Captain Atom stories ranged between five and nine pages, and there were up to three adventures per issue, of three general types. In the first category, the hero was busy either helping small

Space Adventures #42 © 1961 Charlton Comics.
COVER ART BY STEVE DITKO.

children or rescuing satellites, planes, or people in distress. The second story type involved some sort of alien menace, often an extraterrestrial invasion force or glamorous space sirens, usually from Venus. The last and most common type of tale featured the hero foiling some sort of nuclear attack or sabotage attempt by an unnamed Eastern Bloc dictatorship, and indulging in the sort of violent red-baiting not seen since the days of Captain America, Commie Smasher. There was no room for characterization or supporting cast, and were it not for Ditko's art the strip would probably have remained a minor footnote in the history books.

After ten issues, Captain Atom bowed out of *Space Adventures* with issue #42, but Ditko and superheroes went on to great things and, by the mid-1960s, Charlton decided to cash in on the popularity of both by reprinting old Captain Atom strips in three issues of *Strange Suspense Stories* (#75–#77, 1965). This venture proved successful enough to prompt a new series of *Captain Atom* comics (carrying on the numbering from *Strange Suspense Stories* at #78) from writer Joe Gill and, once again, Steve Ditko—moonlighting from his Spider-Man and Dr. Strange commitments. In fact, Ditko gave up his duties on the Hulk series to return to Captain Atom.

Initially, the new Captain Atom stories were much the same as the old, with the predictable alien invasions, but Atom did get his own supervillain at last—the brightly costumed Dr. Spectro. With issue #82, incoming Charlton editor Dick Giordano shook things up a bit by introducing a new, young writer (David Kaler) and a female companion (Nightshade), while in issue #84 Atom was given a new silver-and-blue costume and a regular backup feature (the new Blue Beetle). Nightshade was, like Captain Atom, a government agent—in her case, as an expert at the martial arts—and the pair soon found themselves tackling industrial spies and supervillains such as the Ghost, Punch and Jewelee, and a returning Dr. Spectro. In civilian life, Nightshade was wealthy heiress Eve Eden, who chose to fight crime secretly after her mother's assassination. In an unusual twist, it was later revealed that her mother was a princess from a magical dimension, who was killed by aliens. By and large, the new direction was a definite improvement. Giordano had created a whole superhero line for Charlton, spanning comics as diverse as *Thunderbolt, Judo-Master, The Fightin' Five, Hercules,* and *Sarge Steel,* but sales were disappointing, and none of these comics lasted more than two years.

Captain Atom's final issue was #89 in late 1967, though the unpublished #90 was later serialized in the fanzine *Charlton Bullseye.* After a couple of reprint series from Charlton in the late 1970s, enterprising publisher Bill Black created a super-group out of the (by then defunct) Charlton heroes for a one-off adventure, in 1983. *The Sentinels of Justice* featured Captain Atom, Blue Beetle, Nightshade, and the Question. However, when *The Sentinels* reappeared two years later, it was with an entirely new line-up. By that time, Giordano had become a senior executive at DC Comics and, remembering his fondness for the old Charlton heroes, persuaded the company to buy their rights.

Consequently, in 1987 a new Captain Atom arrived on the shelves. This was Nathanial Adam, a condemned traitor who had volunteered for a military experiment involving his being placed near a detonating nuclear bomb. The explosion sent Adam into a quantum field, from which he returned twenty years later with powers and (silver) costume similar to those of the original Atom. This new Captain Atom worked covertly for Air Force intelligence under General Wade Eiling, who (strangely enough) had adopted Adam's now grown-up son at the time of the experiment. The strip was developed by writer Cary Bates and artist Pat Broderick, and it soon proved popular enough for its star to join the Justice League of America. Over the course of fifty-seven issues, the Captain battled with such villains as Plastique, Major Force, and a new Dr. Spectro, and he rubbed shoulders with Blue Beetle and Nightshade once again.

In 1991, with the series in decline, Captain Atom was penciled in as the hero-turned-bad for DC's *Armageddon 2001* series, but a leak to the fan press saved him and he became one of the comic's stars instead. However, as a government agent with a criminal background, the new Captain had none of the wholesome appeal of his predecessor, and it is no surprise that he became a founding member of the brutal Extreme Justice Group in 1995. *Extreme Justice,* which also included Maxima, Booster Gold, and Blue Beetle, was conceived as a home for heroes who felt that the Justice League was too soft on criminals, and it was a largely unloved example of the 1990s craze for darker, more violent heroes. It lasted for nineteen issues, and Captain Atom has mostly faded from view ever since. Even so, the earlier artwork of Steve Ditko will no doubt continue to create interest in the hero for years to come. —*DAR*

Captain Britain

Superheroes constantly draw upon myth and folk-lore as their archetypal source material, and the legend of King Arthur (popularized in the fifteenth century by Sir Thomas Malory's *Le Mort D'Arthur*) is one of the mythic wells to which comics creators constantly return. Created by British-born *X-Men* writer Chris Claremont and *Incredible Hulk* artist (and Cornwall resident) Herb Trimpe as the flagship character for Marvel Comics' new United Kingdom line (and debuting in *Captain Britain Weekly* vol. 1 #1, October 13, 1976), Captain Britain unambiguously draws upon the Arthurian mythos, mixed with a dollop of Captain America, a national symbol from the States (where Captain Britain would not debut until 1978, alongside Spider-Man in *Marvel Team-Up* #65 and #66). The Captain would then vanish again from the sight of American readers for another decade, except for the lucky few who stumbled across imported British comics at the local comics shop. While Captain Britain's popularity grew steadily in the United Kingdom through the first half of the 1980s (though other British heroes, such as Brian Bolland's tongue-in-cheekily ultraviolent Judge Dredd, had a decided head start), the Captain had scant opportunity to replicate that burgeoning success in America.

Thames University graduate student Brian Braddock, already a brilliant young scientist in the mode of Peter Parker (Spider-Man), is working as a research assistant at England's Darkmoor Research Centre when the facility is attacked by a super-criminal known as the Reaver. Panicked, Braddock flees on a motorcycle, but the attackers pursue him, causing a fiery crash. The mortally injured Braddock then experiences a vision in which the sorcerer Merlin

and the goddess Roma offer to make him Britain's superpowered champion. They bid him to choose between two mystic talismans, the Amulet of Right and the Sword of Might. Braddock selects the amulet, and is immediately infused with mystical energies that not only heal his injuries, but also enhance his strength, stamina, and agility, and give him the power of flight, thereby transforming him into Captain Britain, a red-garbed figure with a gold lion emblazoned across his chest (perhaps symbolizing King Richard Lion-Heart) and a Union Jack–motif mask which conceals his entire face (the costume also amplifies Braddock's physical abilities via internal microcircuitry). In addition, the patron gods of the British Isles give Braddock a staff called a "star scepter," whose mystic properties greatly enhance his hand-to-hand combat abilities.

Merlin, acting as Braddock's mentor, reveals to his charge that the Braddock family has a mystical connection to an extradimensional realm called Otherworld, located at a cosmic nexus linking every parallel Earth in the multiverse (known here as the Omniverse). Here the newly minted hero becomes the most powerful member of Merlin's Captain Britain Corps—a group charged with protecting Earth and all of its infinite parallel worlds from the forces of evil, whether magical or scientific—bringing to fruition the life's work of Braddock's late father, scientist James Braddock. "[Merlin and Roma] dipped me in magic and clothed me in science," Braddock tells his telepathic twin sister Elizabeth [Betsy] Braddock years later (*Captain Britain* vol. 2 #1, 1985). "They made me a hero. They dragged me screaming into the Omniverse … I was their creation, birthed in blood. I was Captain Britain. They made me fight. And I liked it."

Despite his initial enthusiasm for the nonstop costumed derring-do his mystic sponsors demand of him, Braddock finds it difficult to balance his personal life (his desire to be a scientist) with his superheroic responsibilities. This conflict spurs him to problem drinking, gets him killed several times (luckily these demises prove to be only temporary), and leads him to take several sabbaticals during the 1980s and 1990s. During his first leave of absence from superheroics, Braddock hands the mantle of Captain Britain off to his sister (who would years later become the X-Men's Psylocke). He resumes his costumed identity after the not-yet-ready-for-primetime Betsy is blinded by the villain Slaymaster, whom Brian then kills.

Captain Britain's early adventures achieved only spotty success. Following the cancellation of the first *Captain Britain* series in 1977, the United Kingdom's homegrown superhero found himself wandering among the various other British Marvel titles (and the aforementioned two issues of *Marvel Team-Up* in the States), landing first in the weekly *Super Spider-Man,* then guest-starring in the weekly *Hulk Comic,* in that title's *Black Knight* feature. London's *Financial Times* characterized some of the early *Captain Britain* tales as a "farrago of illiterate SF nonsense." Claremont, who was succeeded in *Captain Britain* #11 (1977) by writer Gary Friedrich, has acknowledged that something was lacking during Captain Britain's early outings: "Over the years since his debut, the poor Captain more or less floundered. Costume changes, role changes—superhero action adventure segueing sideways into outright fantasy and science fiction—but nothing ever seemed to jell."

Things began to turn around in the early 1980s when Marvel U.K. editor (later editor-in-chief) Paul Neary decided to hire some of England's most gifted young comics creators to bring *Captain Britain* to life, beginning with artist Alan Davis and writer David Thorpe in the U.K. monthly *Marvel Superheroes* magazine (1981). Davis not only redesigned Captain Britain's costume—transforming it into a more dynamic red, white, and blue while retaining and emphasizing its Union Jack aesthetic and making it "friendlier" by revealing part of the Captain's face—but also collaborated with writers such as Alan Moore (destined for enduring fame on DC's *The Saga of the Swamp Thing* and *Watchmen*) in revamping the character's mythos by injecting a compelling

balance of fantasy, realism, horror, and whimsy. Claremont has called Moore's "Jaspers Warp" storyline (beginning in 1982's *Marvel Superheroes* magazine #387), in which a madman named Jim Jaspers alters all of reality to suit himself, "one of the most emotionally powerful stories Alan Moore has ever written." After the hero had migrated yet again to *The Daredevils* and *Mighty World of Marvel,* writer Jamie Delano teamed with Davis in 1985 (beginning with *Captain Britain* vol. 2 #1), building on the character's growing success with the introduction and evolution-toward-humanity of Brian Braddock's shapeshifting werewoman lover, Meggan.

In 1988 Claremont and Davis made Captain Britain the focus of an England-based superhero team known as Excalibur (*Excalibur: The Sword is Drawn* #1), published in the United States by Marvel Comics, a development that gave the character his greatest stateside success, thanks to the group's close relationship to Marvel's immensely popular mutant characters the X-Men. Among the Captain's teammates are Meggan and several expatriate American X-Men, including Rachel Summers (the second Phoenix), Kitty Pryde (a.k.a. Shadowcat, possessed of the ability to walk through walls), and the teleporting acrobat known as Nightcrawler. During the course of the series, Captain Britain apparently resolves the old conflict between his superhero duties and his desire to do science, and eventually loses his powers while preventing the Dragons of the Crimson Dawn from opening a world-threatening dimensional portal.

Excalibur proved extremely popular with the worldwide legions of X-Men fans, though it never enabled Captain Britain to make the leap to television or film, and spawned very little in the way of licensed products, either in England or the States. Excalibur's final issue (*Excalibur* #125, 1998) presents the long-awaited wedding of Brian Braddock and Meggan on Otherworld, after which the team disbands, its American members returning home. But the Braddocks' hopes of living a normal life afterward go awry when Braddock gets involved—

along with the Captain Britain Corps and allies Psylocke, Captain U.K., Crusader X, and the Black Knight—in a battle to prevent an apparently insane Roma from destroying Otherworld as part of an attempt to conquer the entire Omniverse. The Captain frees Roma from the influence of Mastermind, the artificial intelligence (created, ironically, by Braddock's late father) that turns out to be the true culprit in this cosmic malfeasance. Braddock then accepts the Sword of Might from a grateful Roma, bringing the blade together with the Amulet of Right. Taking his place as the rightful ruler of Otherworld and the protector of the Omniverse, Captain Britain at last fulfills his Arthurian destiny, with Meggan (his Lady Guenivere) at his side. —*MAM*

Captain Canuck

In the near future of 1993, Tom Evans is a scoutmaster for the Boy Scouts when he has a close encounter with aliens. Bathed by weird alien rays, he develops powers of extra strength and speed. Already a member of the Royal Canadian Mounted Police, Evans leaves that organization to join the Canadian Intelligence Security Organization (C.I.S.O.). Costumed in a red-and-white outfit that resembles Canada's national flag, Evans is codenamed "Captain Canuck" and dispatched on missions throughout Canada and elsewhere. At times, Captain Canuck is aided by two other costumed agents, Kébec and Redcoat. Eventually, Evans resigns from the C.I.S.O., but continues doing heroic deeds as Canada's best-known superhero, fighting such villains as the manipulative George Gold, alien Nyro-Ka, and Canuck's traitorous ex-partner, Blue Fox.

Easily the best known Canadian superhero, Captain Canuck was conceptualized by artist Ron Leishman. When he met a fellow comic-book fan, Richard Comely, at church in 1972, the two worked at developing the character for a comic book. When Leishman moved away, Comely continued work on

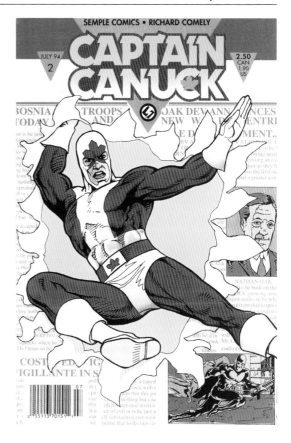

Captain Canuck Reborn #2 © 1994 Richard Comely/Semple Comics.

the hero on his own, self-publishing the debut issue of *Captain Canuck* in July 1975 under the "Comely Comix" imprint. A second and third issue appeared in 1975 and 1976, respectively, but Comely Comics folded sometime thereafter. *Captain Canuck* was revived in 1979 with the publication of issue #4, and new parent company CKR Productions (though Comely Comics still appeared on the covers). The series appeared bimonthly until April 1981's issue #14—including a 1980 *Captain Canuck Summer Special* in its run—and then abruptly halted again.

Fondly remembered by many 1970s comics readers in the United States and Canada, *Captain*

Canuck was extremely ahead of its time. Not only was it self-published and self-distributed, but it also featured high-quality paper, painted color, flexographic printing, and more innovations that wouldn't hit the American comic market until the early 1980s. Additionally, the series had quirky backup stories such as barbarian Jonn, dark hero Catman, and the fantasy adventurers in "Beyond." On the main title, Comely's art and scripts were serviceable, but he tended to interject politics and religion into his stories; for example, the Captain prayed before missions. Better were the post-#4 issues produced by Comely and artists George Freeman (who eventually took over scripting as well) and Jean-Claude St. Aubin.

The other aspect that *Captain Canuck* was known for was publicity and memorabilia. Comely managed to get tremendous press for his hero in his native Canada and in many U.S. publications throughout the comic's publishing run, although not all of it was positive. Fans could join the Captain Canuck Club (CCC) and get cards, newsletters, stickers, autographed comics, and more. For the general public, there were *Captain Canuck* T-shirts, metal plaques, patches ("crests" in Canada), pens, stickers, signed and numbered posters, and even a chance to become a shareholder in the Captain Canuck Corporation (this latter offer was announced in the original series' final issue, #14).

Various *Captain Canuck* newspaper strips appeared in some Canadian papers in 1976 and other years, but the maple leaf–clad hero didn't reappear in comics until 1993 (ironic, given that this was when the original series was set). Richard Comely relaunched the series as *Captain Canuck Reborn* with issue #0, from Semple Comics, also based in Canada. Issues were published in both English-language and French-language versions. This new Captain Canuck was Darren Oaks, and despite having no superpowers, he fought against global conspiracies. Two more issues were published in 1993–1994, while the delayed issue #3 (1996) featured reprints of the 1995–1996 syndi-

cated newspaper strip. But the series folded with that issue, and Captain Canuck has once again been retired, but he went out on the highest of notes: with a national stamp!

On October 2, 1995, the Canada Post released a set of five 45-cent stamps commemorating Canadian superheroes, following the stamps with T-shirts, mouse pads, and other merchandising. The five heroes chosen to represent the country were World War II hero Johnny Canuck, 1940s heroine Nelvana of the Northern Lights, 1984's *Northguard* martial artist heroine Fleur de Lyse, Superman (co-created by Canadian Joe Shuster), and Captain Canuck. Ahead of its time, *Captain Canuck* is still fondly remembered by fans and comics historians alike, in both the United States and Canada. *—AM*

Captain Marvel

As of 2004, there have been five Captain Marvels, the first of whom was Fawcett Comics' best-selling character and the most popular superhero of the Golden Age of comics (1938–1954). In 1966, notorious schlock publisher Myron Fass published a few issues of his own Captain Marvel, about which the less said the better. Marvel Comics' hero, on whom this entry focuses, premiered in late 1967, and it is widely thought that the company primarily wanted to copyright the name (as the publisher's success has grown, it has become increasingly proprietary over the name Marvel). Nevertheless, that first appearance of the character in *Marvel Superheroes* #12 was one of the more unusual of the 1960s.

An earlier issue of the Fantastic Four had introduced a large robot called the Sentry, which had been sent to Earth by an alien race called the Kree, who had apparently been visiting the planet for centuries. To find out what happened to their Sentry, the Kree send out an espionage unit headed by the ambitious Colonel Yon-Rogg and including the romantic couple of medic Una and Captain Mar-Vell.

The Captain is dispatched undercover to assume the role of a professor in the Cape Canaveral missile complex, where he meets beautiful security chief Carol Danvers. Donning his white and green space suit (which looks much like a superhero costume), he has all sorts of abilities, including flying and super strength, which he has much use for as he encounters all manner of monsters, villains, and alien creatures. Confusingly, in his Kree identity he is Mar-Vell but seemingly changes the spelling of his name to Marvel when indulging in superheroics.

Much of the comic's tension issued from the love triangle of Mar-Vell, Una, and Yon-Rogg, whose ruthless attitude to the natives (us!) and designs on the young nurse gradually forced the pacifist Mar-Vell against his own people. Una was killed in issue #11—an unusual event in comics at that time. Five issues later, an avenging Mar-Vell returned home, where he foiled a coup and was given even more powers, as well as a stylish new costume. But he found himself stranded in the Negative Zone, a kind of limbo.

Issue #17 saw a major change of direction, courtesy of a new creative team: Roy Thomas and Gil Kane. A spectral Captain Marvel convinces perennial boy sidekick Rick Jones to try on a pair of wrist bands (or Nega-bands), which when struck together enable him to switch places with the lad. Having initially taken the character's name from Fawcett, Marvel was now very cheekily adopting the transformation from boy to man that made Fawcett's Captain Marvel so popular. Following several periods of cancellation, Jim Starlin took over creative duties, and things started to get very cosmic. Starlin crafted an epic intergalactic battle that saw his arch-villain Thanos journeying to Earth from his home on Saturn's moon Titan, to find the Cosmic Cube and thereby take over the universe. In the granite-faced Thanos and his colorful entourage of lackeys and foes, Starlin had created an exciting cast of intergalactic characters, which would feature in Marvel for decades to come.

Captain Marvel #33 © 1974 Marvel Comics. COVER ART BY JIM STARLIN.

The Thanos saga ran from issue #25 to #35, to much acclaim, and was followed up by a bizarre story featuring Nitro (a villain who blew himself up!), after which Starlin was off to new pastures. The book carried on in a solid enough manner, including a story that de-coupled Mar-Vell and Rick, but was never as popular again. In 1977, on-again off-again romantic interest Carol Danvers was given her own, short-lived comic as Ms. Marvel, complete with cosmic powers and a more revealing version of Mar-Vell's costume (today she soldiers on as the Avenger named Warbird). The final regularly published Captain Marvel story came out in 1981, a long time from his glory days, but one year later Starlin came back for a graphic novel—Marvel's first—which wrapped up the series. His story revealed that, in fighting Nitro, Mar-Vell had been affected by radioactivity and, by the tale's end, our hero was dead from cancer.

After an appropriate period of mourning (i.e., a couple of months), Marvel, ever mindful of the dangers of letting a copyright lapse, introduced another Captain Marvel. This incarnation was statuesque African American Monica Rambeau, who could turn herself into pure energy. Following an early team-up with Spider-Man, she went on to a long spell in the Avengers (eventually being renamed Photon). As she faded from view in the 1990s, yet another Captain Marvel appeared. This time, it was Mar-Vell's previously unknown son Genis (whose growth had somehow been accelerated), complete with cosmic powers, his dad's costume, and a talent for teenage whining. (Uncharacteristically for comics heroes, Mar-Vell has stayed dead, though from the other side of the grave fans got to see a lot of him in the alternate-future series *Universe X* [2000–2001] and *Paradise X* [2002–2003], which portrayed him as a somewhat imperious self-styled messiah.) The late 1990s and early 2000s saw a number of relaunches for Genis, including a twist in which he dons a version of his father's first Kree costume, becomes incredibly powerful, and goes mad. Even Rick Jones has returned, proving that the more things change, the more they stay the same. —*DAR*

Captain Marvel Jr.

With sales of Fawcett's Captain Marvel comics increasing almost daily in the early 1940s, it is not surprising that Fawcett Comics wanted another superhero to pull in the fans. Captain Marvel Jr. grew out of one of the first intertitle crossovers, as Captain Marvel and Bulletman battled the jackbooted Captain Nazi from the pages of Master Comics to Whiz Comics and back again. In the December 1941 edition of *Whiz Comics* (#25), Captain Nazi (effectively an evil mirror image of Captain Marvel) plummets into

the sea near a small boat and, when its occupants attempt to rescue him, he hurls them into the sea, killing one and injuring the other. Well, what else would you expect from someone called Captain Nazi? Seeing that the kid is close to death, Captain Marvel takes him to the ever convenient wizard, Shazam, who transfers some of the elder Marvel's superpowers to the lad, and—voila!—up pops Captain Marvel Jr.

As conceived by editor and writer Eddie Heron with artist Mac Raboy, Junior was an athletic, almost angelic-looking fourteen-year-old boy, clad in a blue version of Captain Marvel's costume. Once restored to his civilian identity of Freddy Freeman (which happened whenever he spoke Captain Marvel's name), he was a crippled newspaper boy, selling his wares on a windy street corner, propped up on his crutches. To compound the misery of comics' own Tiny Tim, the poor lad was an orphan whose grandfather had been the old man killed by Captain Nazi, and his meagre earnings were spent on a shabby room in a nearby guesthouse. As reader identification went, it was a remarkable piece of wish fulfilment to see the poor wretch metamorphose into the god-like hero. But astute readers might also wonder why Freeman did not simply remain in his superhero form, make vast amounts of cash saving the world, and retire to a life of luxury; the idea clearly never crossed his mind.

One of the comic's great selling points was undoubtedly Raboy's elegant, exquisitely drawn artwork, which was far more realistic than that of the Captain Marvel strip. However, Raboy was such a perfectionist that he soon found it almost impossible to meet deadlines, and he hit upon the solution of pasting in photostats of previous drawings. In fact, some pages were almost entirely made up of stats, with new backgrounds provided by one of his assistants. Raboy left Fawcett in 1944 but the feature carried on, drawn by Bud Thompson, Kurt Schaffenburger, and others, in both Master Comics and Junior's own title.

Throughout the war years, Junior repeatedly tangled with Captain Nazi and amassed a gaggle of supervillains, including Dr. Eternity, the Pied Piper, and

Captain Nippon. In the postwar period, one villain came to dominate the strip: the boy scientist-gone-bad Sivana Junior, son of … oh, you guessed—Captain Marvel's arch-foe, Dr. Sivana! Sivana Junior's evil plots included potions to make himself a giant, induce insatiable hunger, or provoke unstoppable jitterbugging. As the decade progressed, however, the feature came to be dominated by the fads of the day, such as crime comics, juvenile delinquency comics, funny animal comics, and even horror. One remarkable cover memorably showed Captain Marvel Jr. being strapped to an electric chair and shot through with electricity. That is not to say that the strip was all darkness and no light, however, since our hero was just as likely to be found speeding up the revolutions of the planet Mars as fighting werewolves or gangsters.

Captain Marvel Jr.'s comic was canceled in 1953 along with the rest of Fawcett's superhero line and he lay fallow until DC Comics' revival in the 1970s, when he starred in a number of decent if unspectacular strips. In the 1990s *Power of Shazam* revival he played a somewhat more prominent role and also briefly joined the Teen Titans (decades after his birth, he was seemingly still a teenager) but, despite this longevity, his true importance might actually lie somewhere altogether more surprising. Several sources have suggested that a certain Elvis Presley was a big fan of the character and modeled his look on Junior, right down to the curls and insouciant quiff that set a generation's hearts aflutter. In Las Vegas as well, it seems that his cape was a tribute to the one Captain Marvel Jr. wore, so the look that launched a thousand imitators came from the comics—not bad for a newspaper boy on crutches. —*DAR*

Captain Marvel/Shazam!

In the pantheon of truly great original superheroes, there are Superman, Batman, Wonder Woman, Spider-Man, and the Hulk, and one other that is far less well known today: Captain Marvel. In his heyday in the 1940s, the good Captain outsold every other superhero, including Superman, and launched a vast line of comics and merchandise, as well as a decade-spanning lawsuit that ultimately brought his entire empire crashing down.

By 1940, Fawcett Comics was already one of the top publishing houses in the country and, sensing that comics were becoming the next big thing, the company decided to bring out its own superhero. Calling on staff writer Bill Parker, Fawcett initially wanted him to create six heroes, each with a different attribute, but later decided to combine all six powers into one person. Another staff member, Charles Clarence ("C. C.") Beck, was recruited from the humor magazine department and, in February 1940, Captain Marvel was born in the pages of *Whiz Comics*.

The first story opens with young, orphaned newspaper seller Billy Batson being summoned by a stranger into a nearby subway station, and in short order the boy is whisked by subway car to the end of a tunnel. Once there, the lad is confronted by a long-bearded wizard named Shazam, who has been hanging around for 3,000 years protecting the world from evil. He declares that it is now Batson's turn and, when the boy repeats the wizard's name, "Shazam!", he is transformed into a red-suited adult man with rippling muscles, a white cape, gold boots, and a lighting-flash design on his chest. The wizard instructs him that he now possesses six great powers: wisdom from Solomon, strength from Hercules, stamina from Atlas, power from Zeus, courage from Achilles, and speed from Mercury (the initials of each "donor" conveniently forming the magic word, Shazam!). Whenever Captain Marvel wishes to resume the form of Batson, he need only repeat the word and the reverse transformation will occur. Thrilled with his new body and seemingly limitless powers, the Captain travels back to the surface, failing to see the falling block of granite that inconveniently squashes the old man. Still, he need not worry, since Shazam would reappear at various points over the coming decade, seemingly none the worse for wear.

In no time at all, Captain Marvel met and defeated his first foe, the bald-headed mad scientist Dr. Sivana (in the first of many, many such battles) and, as Billy Batson, had gained a job as a radio announcer at station WHIZ. The story and art were direct, simple, and charming, and the readers loved the strip. While Superman's stories were ostensibly serious and science-based, Captain Marvel was a creation of magic, and literally anything could happen in his adventures. They were also underpinned by a wry sense of humor, as was soon proved by the introduction of the bumbling would-be superheroes, the Lieutenant Marvels. More importantly, the Captain (or "the Big Red Cheese" as he was nicknamed by Sivana) was every boy's wish fulfilment made flesh. Superman and Batman were resolutely grown-ups but Billy Batson was a kid just like his readers—apart from being able to change into a dashing superhero (a sort of omnipotent big brother or uncle figure) at the drop of a magic word. Why relate to a sidekick like Robin when you can imagine being the real thing?

Almost immediately, sales were colossal and, in early 1941, Captain Marvel was given his own title. Soon after, two spin-off characters, Captain Marvel Jr. and Mary Marvel, began appearing in other Fawcett comics. Later still, that pair spun off into their own books, while Captain Marvel himself began to crop up in such comics as *All Hero* and *America's Greatest Comics*. Then, in 1945, all three characters starred together in *Marvel Family*. By 1943, their combined titles were selling almost 3 million copies a month and the Captain Marvel comic itself was appearing twice a month. At its peak, two years later, the comic was selling an amazing 1.3 million copies per issue, and was by a substantial margin the most successful superhero comic on the stands.

The sheer quantity of product required by this demand was too much for Parker (who was, in any case, drafted in 1941) and Beck on their own, and so

Fawcett recruited a small army of creators. Writers included Rod Reed and Eddie Heron, but it was the prolific Otto Binder who was to define the true essence of Captain Marvel over the course of his 451 scripts (which were part of more than 1,000 stories in total, if you include the whole range of Marvel Family titles). The art was taken from two studios (comics factories, almost) set up by Beck and partner Pete Costanza, a third studio run by Otto Binder's brother Jack, and Fawcett's own stable of talents, including Marc Swayze. But it was Beck's simple yet perfectly realized art that best characterized the Captain, his bold and almost cartoonish approach being both exciting and humorous, and instantly accessible to even the youngest reader. Binder was only one of the thousands to recognize this, having said of Beck, "The enormous success of Captain Marvel was due primarily to the storytelling talents of Beck. He had tremendous story sense and could see ways to improve the flow of my scripts, or bolster up weak parts. I believe I wrote good stuff in general, but Beck's art made me seem a master."

Binder and Beck's finest hour was undoubtedly a serial that ran in the pages of *Whiz Comics* for two years during the darkest days of the war: "The Monster Society of Evil." The tale introduced an evil criminal genius named Mr. Mind, who gathered together a group of villains including Sivana, Captain Nazi, Mr. Banjo (now there's a name to conjure with!), King Krull, and Ibac to do battle with the Big Red Cheese. In a masterstroke that could only have worked in Captain Marvel stories, Mr. Mind turned out to be a particularly devious worm, much to the amazed delight of the readers. Another anthropomorphic favorite was a talking tiger called Mr. Tawny, who repeatedly roped the Captain into his schemes to get rich, to become a movie star, and similar escapades. A less successful development was occasional sidekick Steamboat, an unfortunately caricatured African-American boy who was widely denounced by critics and has since been airbrushed out of the comics history books.

With such rich material (and an enthusiastic audience) to draw upon, Captain Marvel was among the most merchandised of Golden Age super-heroes, probably second only to (him again!) Super-man. Throughout the 1940s, all sorts of badges, puzzles, planes, games, clothes, watches, figures, and all-purpose do-dads spewed forth from the toy companies. Fawcett itself was quick to introduce a Captain Marvel fan club in 1941 and a Mary Marvel club five years later. In 1941, Republic Pictures released the highly regarded movie serial, *The Adventures of Captain Marvel,* starring Tom Tyler and Frank Coghlan Jr.

In his many hundreds of strips, Captain Marvel tirelessly conquered an unending stream of villains, but there was one enemy even he could not defeat— his greatest rival, Superman, and the latter's litigious publisher, DC Comics. As early as 1939, DC had suc-cessfully prosecuted Fox Comics for their character Wonder Man's similarity to Superman and, as soon as it appeared that the Big Red Cheese was becom-ing a serious rival, DC turned its sights on him. From 1941 to 1953, Fawcett and DC battled it out in court, earning their lawyers a small fortune in fees before Fawcett threw in the towel, agreeing to cease publish-ing the character. It could be argued that just about every superhero owed something to the character that started the genre, and that Captain Marvel—of all of them—owed the least to the Man of Steel. However, by this point superhero sales were falling and comics in general were suffering something of a slump, following a media-led witch hunt and the arrival of the Comics Code. So Fawcett had in any case decided to shut down its entire comics division and, rather than incur further court costs, they set-tled with DC and the Captain was doomed to fly no more—or so it seemed.

For many years before the lawsuit, Captain Marvel stories were licensed all over the world, and in Brazil and Great Britain when the reprints ran out in the mid-1950s those comic publishers simply drew their own stories. In Brazil the char-acter was called Capitao Marvel, while in Britain he was renamed Marvelman and starred in hun-dreds of strips well into the 1960s. Back in the

Captain Marvel #149 © 1953 Fawcett Comics. COVER ART BY C. C. BECK.

United States, however, Captain Marvel lived on in the memories of comics fans, and throughout the 1960s he was a nostalgic figure in fanzines and convention costume parades. No one would have guessed that DC, of all companies, would turn out to be the Captain's savior, but it was indeed DC that, however ironically, licensed him from Fawcett and began publishing a new series in 1973. DC also managed to tempt C. C. Beck out of retirement to resuscitate the Captain. The only fly in the ointment was that Marvel Comics had in the meantime appropriated the name Cap-tain Marvel for one of its comics, and so the new DC comic had to have a new name; DC happily hit on *Shazam!*

However, what worked so well in the 1940s seemed not to have the same resonance in the more cynical 1970s, and the revival was not the success everyone had hoped for. Beck argued with DC over the direction of the feature, which he said the writers had failed to grasp, and he left after ten issues. He maintained that the original run had dramatic stories that had a humorous treatment, whereas this newer run was all too often played for laughs—and with stories such as "Invasion of the Salad Men" you could see his point. Still, it did reintroduce the Captain and his supporting and opposing casts to a new generation, and it undoubtedly prompted Filmation Studios to produce a *Shazam!* television show. The live-action show premiered on CBS in 1974 and ran for several seasons, starring Jackson Bostwick (and, later, John Davey) as Captain Marvel with Michael Gray as Billy Batson. A new, well, mentor character called Mentor was introduced. While it suffered from a small budget and limited special effects, it had a certain charm and is fondly remembered by fans.

What the show failed to do was help sales of the comic, even though for a while the latter tried—to little effect—to reflect the television version, albeit replacing Mentor with Uncle Marvel (a regular of Mary Marvel strips in the 1940s). A further revamp, which had a more realistic, gritty approach to the art, was similarly ineffective, and for many years the strip was relegated to backup status in comics such as *World's Finest*. Subsequent revivals in such comics as *Superpowers* and Jerry Ordway's well-crafted *Power of Shazam* series (which ran for five years from 1995 to 1999) have kept the Captain in the public eye, but have not been enormous successes financially. However, an almost imperceptible shift has granted him iconic status in DC's line-up of stars, so that he regularly appears as statues, action figures, posters, and books along with the rest of DC's characters. Star artist Alex Ross made him one of the central figures of the blockbuster *Kingdom Come* comic (1996) and in 2000 painted the lavish *Shazam—Power of Hope* oversized paper-

back book, including the Captain as one of only four DC characters to be given the honor of such an upscale comic (inevitably, Superman, Batman, and Wonder Woman were the others). A new 2004 series by acclaimed indie cartoonist Jeff Smith was the talk of comics fandom. So, while sales may never again match their 1940s heights, Captain Marvel remains an American icon to this day. —*DAR*

Captain Marvel/Shazam! in the Media

With one magic word—Shazam!—young Billy Batson could transform into the "World's Mightiest Mortal," Captain Marvel. It's fitting that a superhero whose face (popular legend has it) was designed to resemble that of film star Fred MacMurray would be brought to Hollywood quickly after his conception. The superhero genre was in its early days when Fawcett Comics staff writer Bill Parker and artist Charles Clarence ("C. C.") Beck co-created Captain Marvel (originally calling him "Captain Thunder") in 1939. His first appearance was in February 1940's *Whiz Comics #2*.

Less than a year had passed before Republic Pictures optioned the character of Captain Marvel for a movie serial. The script was written as a twelve-part storyline; like other film serials, each quarter-hour-plus segment ended in a dramatic cliffhanger designed to get the audience to return to the movie theater the following week to see how the hero managed to escape death and get to the next chapter. *The Adventures of Captain Marvel* debuted on March 28, 1941, and continued weekly thereafter for three months.

The comic-book adventures of Captain Marvel were fairly cartoony—a style that would have been impossible to reproduce with live actors—so the producers of the serial settled on a more realistic approach. They cast heroic leading man Tom Tyler as Captain Marvel, whose radio announcer alter ego Billy Batson (Frank Coghlan Jr.) is given powers by an ancient wizard named Shazam (Nigel de Brulier). He must use these powers to stop the evil villain the Scorpion before he can gain all of the crystal lenses that can be placed in a scorpion idol and provide a devastating weapon. The Scorpion is actually a member of the archeological team that Batson is a part of, and the mystery of his identity is cleverly achieved; Harry Worth and other cast members played the masked villain, but he was voiced by an uncredited (and unseen) Gerald Mohr! When the Scorpion learns Billy's secret and kidnaps Billy's girlfriend, could the days of Captain Marvel be numbered?

Helmed by a pair of directors (John English and William Whitney), *The Adventures of Captain Marvel* features an engaging storyline and some good cliff-hangers, as well as some surprising violence, such as when Captain Marvel uses a machine gun, or throws a villain off a building. But the serial's most fascinating aspect was the way in which the flying effects for Captain Marvel were created. Special effects directors Howard and Theodore Lydecker used a costumed mannequin on a wire to show Marvel flying overhead for some shots, while other scenes had stuntman Dave Sharp diving off buildings or being catapulted into the air. The serial wasn't

Jackson Bostwick (Captain Marvel) and Michael Gray (Billy Batson) in a scene from *Shazam!*

popular enough to spawn a sequel, though it was re-released as *The Return of Captain Marvel* in 1953.

Captain Marvel might have continued in some form in Hollywood had not Fawcett been sued by DC Comics over the similarity of Captain Marvel to Superman. The protracted lawsuit ran from 1941 to 1953, and the character made a final appearance in *Marvel Family Comics #89* in January 1954. Ironically, DC Comics itself would be the company to revive Captain Marvel in February 1973 with a comic-book series titled *Shazam!* (since Marvel Comics now owned the title name "Captain Marvel"). The new title posed no public-recognition problems. After all, actor Jim Nabors had already kept Captain Marvel's catchphrase alive since the spring of 1963 on the TV series *The Andy Griffith Show* and *Gomer Pyle, U.S.M.C.,* where his comic book–reading character Gomer Pyle was fond of exclaiming "Shazam!" Now, with the character back in comic-book circulation, it wasn't long before Hollywood came to see if lightning could strike again.

Under their Filmation Studios banner, producers Lou Scheimer and Norm Prescott drafted the Captain to star in a new live-action television series for CBS. This new version, which debuted in September 1974 and was also titled *Shazam!,* varied significantly from its comic-book counterpart. The narration at the start of the series gave the premise: "Chosen from among all others by the immortal elders—Solomon, Hercules, Atlas, Zeus, Achilles, Mercury—Billy Batson and his Mentor travel the highways and byways of the land on a never ending mission … to right wrongs, to develop understanding, and to seek justice for all! In time of dire need, young Billy has been granted the power by the immortals to summon awesome forces at the utterance of a single word: Shazam! A word which transforms him, in a flash, into the mightiest of mortal beings: Captain Marvel!"

Teenage Billy was played by twenty-five-year-old Michael Gray (though teen magazines always listed him as much younger), while a new character, Mentor, was portrayed by radio, film, and stage star Les Tremayne. Mentor was a grandfatherly type who often lectured Billy, but who was always helpful when needed. The role of Captain Marvel was originally played by Jackson Bostwick, although he was replaced early in the second season by a stockier John Davey. The "Elders" (as the immortals were known) would appear in each episode as barely animated heads, with voices by producers Prescott

and Scheimer. Episodes were shot quickly and cheaply—sometimes two in a week—near Sepulveda Basin in southern California.

The twenty-eight half-hour episodes that were produced of *Shazam!* were aimed squarely at pre-teen audiences. Hyper-moralistic plots depicted teens discovering the dangers of joyriding in cars, sneaking into zoos, and using drugs. Each episode would end with Captain Marvel or Billy giving out a preachy moral lesson, looking into the camera at the viewers as if lecturing them personally.

In the fall of 1975, the series became *The Shazam!/Isis Hour,* and the second half-hour was filled with the adventures of a Filmation-created heroine named Isis. Crossovers were popular, with Isis appearing in three *Shazam!* episodes, and Captain Marvel guest-starring in a trio of *Isis* adventures. *The Shazam!/Isis Hour* stayed on the air until the fall of 1977. *Shazam!* was rerun as a solo series again in 1980, and has been syndicated since then worldwide.

Perhaps the strangest appearance of Captain Marvel came in January 1979, when Hanna-Barbera produced two hour-long live-action specials for NBC. *Legends of the Superheroes* was the overall title, but "The Challenge" aired January 18, 1979, and "The Roast" aired January 25, 1979. In the shows, Captain Marvel was played by Garrett Craig (with no Billy Batson alter ego) while Howard Morris played the cackling villain Dr. Sivana. The specials were tremendously campy, and never re-aired.

In 1980, Prescott and Scheimer began work on a series for NBC, which would later be called *Hero High* when it went into syndication. The show was designed as a live-action and animated hybrid, with live actors portraying the Hero High students in musical and comedy sketches, interspersed between short animated comedy adventures. Filmation decided that the series would achieve higher ratings if a known quantity was introduced, and paired the planned series with new animated adventures of Captain Marvel.

Kid Super-Power Hour with Shazam! debuted in September 1981, and twelve half-hour segments of *Shazam!* were part of the package. This new series hewed very closely to the comic-book plots, featuring not only Mary Marvel, Captain Marvel Jr., Uncle Dudley, and Tawky Tawny, but also veteran comics villains such as Dr. Sivana, Mr. Mind, Black Adam, and Ibac. The character designs looked like C. C. Beck drawings, and both Beck and comic editor/writer E. Nelson Bridwell made animated cameos in one episode! The series ended after one season, but *Shazam!* and *Hero High* (minus the live segments) were licensed later for syndication and video release.

For a character that was once the most popular superhero of all time, Captain Marvel has been scarce beyond the printed page in the last twenty years or so. However, that may change. In late 2002, New Line Cinema announced that a *Shazam!* film project was in development with producer Michael Uslan. As of early 2004 Joel Cohen and Alec Sokolow were selected as screenwriters, reworking a first draft by William Goldman. Rumors of development of another animated *Shazam!* series also made Internet rounds in 2003. Could lightning strike again for Billy Batson and Captain Marvel? Only the future will tell. —*AM*

Captain Midnight

Many superheroes found success in radio after breaking through in pulps or comics, notably the Shadow and Superman, but Captain Midnight was one of the few who moved the other way, from radio to comics. In the wake of World War I, a number of flying aces caught the public's imagination, both real (Charles Lindbergh and Captain Frank Hawkes) and fictional (such as pulp stars G-8 and his Battle Aces, and Bill Barnes). So it made sense for the Skelly Gasoline Company to sponsor a new radio show starring a daredevil flying ace—Captain Midnight—in stories written by a couple of genuine aviators, Robert M. Burtt and Wilfred G. Moore. Captain Midnight debuted on Mutual Radio (from Chicago) on September 30, 1940.

Captain Midnight (voiced by Ed Prentiss) was Red Albright, a World War I flying ace who earned his nickname when he returned from a vital mission at the stroke of twelve midnight. Together with his adopted son Chuck Ramsey, plucky young Patsy (later replaced by another aviatrix called Joyce Ryan) and his mechanic Ichabod Mudd (also known as "Ikky"), Captain Midnight flew off to find adventure around the world. Although he didn't possess any superpowers per se, Captain Midnight possessed extraordinarily precise flying skills, able to take off from such obscure locations as a Mexican pyramid. Albright was a resourceful inventor, creating such super-gadgets as his Gliderchute (think combination glider and parachute); Code-O-Graph for deciphering top-secret assignments; "Doom Beam Torch," 'which doubled as an infrared-heat generator and a device for flashing the Captain Midnight clock symbol; and "blackout" pellets.

His nemesis was Ivan Shark, a seemingly indestructible rogue who was joined by a gang of his own, which included his daughter Fury. From 1940, Ovaltine took over sponsorship of the radio show, a successful relationship that continued for years and resulted in a torrent of merchandising, including badges, T-shirts, posters, and rings, and a fan club. On the entry of the United States into World War II, Captain Midnight was summoned by the president and given command of his own squadron of flying aces—all the better to take the fight to the Axis hordes.

The radio show was a real hit and, not surprisingly, comic-book publishers soon took note. First in the field was Dell, which ran faithful story adaptations of several Captain Midnight radio scripts in *Funnies* and *Popular Comics* in 1941. Another inevitable spin-off was the newspaper strip, which duly arrived in 1942, from the Chicago Sun Syndicate, drawn by "Jonwan." That same year saw the release of a fifteen-chapter *Captain Midnight* movie serial from Columbia Pictures, starring Dave O'Brien. If these features were all very much true to the spirit of the radio show, another development from 1942 was most certainly not. Seeing the success of the serial, Fawcett Comics launched its own interpretation of the daredevil ace.

Like its legendary Captain Marvel, Fawcett's Captain Midnight debuted in his own red costume, complete with aviator's helmet, goggles, and winged-clock insignia on his chest. Though initially quite baggy, the suit became increasingly tight-fitting over the following months, so that he was soon every inch the superhero. Although the character retained his radio comrades (albeit with Ikky soon becoming known as Sergeant Twilight), for good measure Fawcett's Captain Midnight borrowed a couple of gimmicks from his comic-book rivals. From the Black Condor he took a pair of underarm wings—his "Gliderchute," which allowed him to fly into action without bothering with his plane. From Batman he borrowed the idea of a handy utility belt, boasting blackout bombs, a doom beam radio transmitter, and a grappling hook. While the Captain and his chums usually took the fight to the Nazi and Nippon war machines, he did cultivate a few other villains along the way, including the sinister Angels and the Shark.

By the standards of the day, *Captain Midnight* was not one of the most exciting comics on the stands, but it was always competently crafted by writers such as Joe Millard and Otto Binder, with art by the Binder studio (run by Otto's brother Jack), Leonard Frank, Carl Pfeufer, and Sheldon Moldoff. With Germans and their accomplices as ready-made villains, the war years were fertile ones for the Captain, but peacetime proved more problematic, and Fawcett took the unusual step of switching the strip to a science fiction direction. Most issues from #50 (1947) on featured the space-helmeted Captain Midnight toughing it out with the Flying Saucers of Death, Xog (Evil Lord of Saturn), Dr. Osmosis, Jagga the Space Raider, and their ilk. Unconvinced readers stayed away from the comic and, in 1948, after

sixty-seven issues, the comic was retitled *Sweethearts* and headed off for more romantic pastures—without the Captain, needless to say.

The radio show was itself abandoned the following year, but Ovaltine soon switched its sponsorship to the new medium of television. A *Captain Midnight* half-hour television show ran from 1953 to 1957 on CBS and starred Richard Webb as a suitably jet-age Captain. (When the show went into syndication, Ovaltine, which owned the rights to the character, was not involved, and so the series was renamed *Jet Jackson*.) No comics were published to tie in to the *Captain Midnight* TV show, and as of 2004 no more *Captain Midnight* comics have appeared at all, though Marvel did produce a Captain Midnight health and fitness book in the late 1970s, starring a yellow-costumed hero. In retrospect, the good Captain seems to be an early example of the cross-media merchandising that is so common with characters today. From radio to comics, toys, books, newspapers, premiums, movies, and television, the character was everywhere, drafting the blueprint for licensing for years to come. —*DAR*

Card Captor Sakura

For many fans of anime and manga, the name CLAMP represents *shojo* ("girls' comics") at its best: powerful storytelling combined with beautiful artwork. Hailing from Osaka, Japan, the all-female studio CLAMP was founded in the late 1980s with seven members. Its first major work was published in 1989, and the group consists of four members— Nanase Okawa, Satsuki Igarashi, Mokona Apapa, and Mikku Nekai. This writing/art team gained even greater popularity in the 1990s, especially in light of the wave of new *shojo* titles that followed the success of Naoko Takeuchi's *Lovely Soldier Sailor Moon;* that highly successful manga and anime franchise had combined elements of *shojo* with superhero action and adventure. The titles following in its footsteps included *Revolutionary Girl Utena, Corrector Yui, Fushigi Yuugi,* and *Ayashi no Ceres* (Ceres, Celestial Legend).

CLAMP's titles would further change the face of *shojo* in Japan. Among them were *Magic Knight Reyearth,* a popular fantasy epic; *X,* a grim apocalyptic horror tale; and *Chobits,* a science-fiction comedy. With *Card Captor Sakura,* CLAMP created a title that combined elements of the "Magical Girl" *shojo* (a genre begun with the *Little Witch Sally* manga by Mitsuteru Yokoyama) and the *Pokemon* franchise. The series began in 1998 as a monthly title in *Nakayoshi* (literally, "intimate friend" or "pals") magazine and ran until 2000; more than ten volumes were published. The main audience for the manga was young, pre-teen girls, the same age as the manga's protagonist.

By all accounts, Sakura Kinomoto has a typical life—she is a ten-year-old student at Tomoeda Elementary School in Japan. She is somewhat naïve, and lives with her father Fujitaka and older brother Touya. Sakura's mother, Nadeshiko, died several years earlier. Sakura's life changes when, while investigating a strange noise in her father's basement library, she finds a book entitled "The Clow." Curious, she opens the book and discovers that it is filled with cards resembling a Tarot card set. When Sakura reads the name on the first one, "Windy," a violent wind blows away all of the cards in the book, leaving only the Windy card. Immediately following the windstorm, a small creature appears out of thin air—a creature resembling a winged teddy bear named Kerberos (better known as Kero). He tells Sakura that he is the guardian of the Clow Cards, magical items of incredible power created long ago by Clow Reed, the greatest—and most powerful—magician ever known. Each Clow Card represents a particular element or grants a certain power to the owner.

Unfortunately, Kero is not happy that Sakura caused the Clow Cards to be lost. He tells Sakura that since she lost the Cards, she is the only one who can recover them. She must become the Card

Captor. Kero gives her a magical key that transforms into a pink staff with a stylized birdlike "head" that allows her to "capture" the Clow Cards. Her best friend, the wealthy Tomoyo Daidouji, helps Sakura by creating outfits for her to wear while she pursues the Clow Cards, and also videotapes Sakura in action. While Sakura's search for the cards remains hidden from her family and her school, the arrival of Li Shaoran (an exchange student from Hong Kong) further complicates matters. Shaoran is a distant relative of Clow Reed, and feels that his family is entitled to the Clow Cards. At first, he and Sakura are rivals for possession of the Clow Cards, but they eventually forge a close friendship—with the implication that it could go further.

Throughout the series, Sakura's magical ability grows, but she also has visions of a great battle near the landmark Tokyo Tower. And Kero, without her knowledge, speaks to Yue, a character who will test the worthiness of the Card Captor with a "Final Judgment."

Card Captor Sakura's story has roots in mythology; Sakura's accidental loss of the Clow Cards parallels the story of Pandora's box, and Kero is named after Cerberus, the three-headed hound of hell. Like *Pokemon* (or a similar property, *Digimon*), where a character can use one creature to capture another (and use the captured creature's power later), so can Sakura use the powers of the Clow Cards. Each time she captures a card, it selects her as its owner. Examples of these cards include the Windy card, "Fly" (which gives Sakura's staff wings, allowing her to fly), "Dash" (which can give Sakura the power of speed), "Return" (which can temporarily give Sakura the ability to see into the past), and "Shield" (a card that can protect Sakura from magical or physical attacks).

As is the case in manga, the success of *Card Captor Sakura* led the creation of an animated series. CLAMP and Kumiko Takahashi were the main designers for the series, and Nanase Okawa and Jiro Kaneko were the main writers. Directors Akito Daichi and Morio Asaka supervised the production of the series, with animation from Madhouse (*Ninja Scroll, X*). The seventy-episode series began in 1998 on Japan's NHK satellite channel BS2. Like the manga, the series was also very popular, as was the merchandise wave that followed. Such items included a replica of Sakura's magical staff; art books featuring CLAMP and Takahashi's illustrations; and even an actual Clow Card set. Two theatrical features were also made: *Card Captor Sakura: The Movie* (1999) and *Card Captor Sakura: The Sealed Card* (2000).

Card Captor Sakura eventually made its way to the United States, beginning in 1999. At first, the Japanese publisher Kodansha published the manga in an English-language *tankobon* format (a paperback format similar to the trade paperback in the United States, with high-quality paper, color pages, and a dust jacket for a cover) as part of its "Kodansha Bilingual Comics" line. TokyoPop continued the publication of the English-language translation, first as a monthly comic, then as graphic novel collections. In 2000, the WB network began airing *Cardcaptors,* the English-dubbed version of *CCS.* Nelvana Studios worked on the dubbing for the series; unfortunately, as in the case of *Sailor Moon* five years earlier, the end result did not satisfy anime fans in America. To conform to network standards, the series was heavily edited—dialogue and names were changed (Sakura Kinomoto became Sakura Avalon), and episodes were simply dropped. The dubbed version of the series began at episode eight, after Li Shaoran arrives. In trying to make the series geared more to males—not its original audience—a great deal of back history and general information about Sakura and the Clow Cards was never revealed. Fortunately, Pioneer began releasing the original unedited *Card Captor Sakura* series, subtitled, on VHS and DVD, as well as the English dub. Both of the theatrical films were released in the United States by Pioneer on DVD in 2003. *—MM*

Casshan: Robot Hunter

"Man versus machine" is a common, long-running theme in the science fiction genre. Examples include films such as the *Matrix* trilogy, the *Terminator* films, and James P. Hogan's 1979 novel *The Two Faces of Tomorrow*. Comic books have also embraced the theme of man versus machine, with the Gold Key Comics (later Valiant Comics) series *Magnus, Robot Fighter* of the 1960s and 1990s being one major example.

Japanese animation and manga have also dealt with this theme, from the days of *Astro Boy* to more contemporary examples such as *Argento Soma.* In the 1970s, the animation studio Tatsunoko Productions used the theme of man versus machine as the starting point for the series *Jinzo Ningen Casshan* (New Style Human Casshan). *Casshan* aired on Fuji Television on October 2, 1973, and concluded on June 25, 1974, after thirty-five half-hour episodes. Part of the "Tatsunoko heroes" line of the 1970s (which included *Gatchaman, Tekkaman,* and *Hurricane Polymar*), *Casshan*'s story is a dark one. Tatsuo Yoshida (who founded Tatsunoko Productions) created the series and also performed the additional duty of character designer, along with Yoshitaka Amano. Junzo Toriumi, Akiyoshi Sakai, Takao Koyama, and Toshio Nagata were the main scriptwriters and Hiroshi Sasakawa was the series director.

Set in the future, *Casshan* opens with Dr. Kotaro Higashi working on a project to build robots to help humankind. Sadly, the scientist's good intentions are thwarted by a lighting strike on one of these machines, BK-1, which destroys the robot's moral circuits. BK-1—now known as the Black King—gathers other machines to its side and begins a war against humankind, with devastating results. Higashi's son, Tatsuya, makes the decision to fight the machines …

but he must become a machine in order to do so. Higashi augments his son with an android body, with the full knowledge that Tatsuya can never go back to being "normal." Tatsuya Higashi dies, and Casshan is born. His body is all white, with black trim and a stylized "C" on his chest. While a mask hides most of his face, it opens when he speaks. Casshan's punches and kicks can shatter the armor of any machine (or he simply rips them apart). Yet all of his powers cannot hide the angst of the young man, who has sacrificed *his* humanity to *save* humanity.

Tatsuya's dog, Friender, is also cybernetically enhanced, becoming a valuable ally, transforming into different vehicles depending upon the combat situation. A young freedom fighter, Luna, falls in love with Tatsuya, but the relationship is bittersweet, since both know that he can never be human again. Tatsuya's deceased mother returns in the form of a robot swan that often appears to give advice or valuable information.

Thanks to Casshan, the tide of war turns in favor of the human race, but in the end, the conflict comes down to the final face-off between Casshan and Black King—the two creations of the same scientist, but extreme opposites.

The original *Casshan* series never achieved the major success of *Gatchaman,* and was never released in the United States. Nonetheless, Pioneer released the series on DVD in Japan in 2001. Casshan would also appear in the video game *Tatsunoko Fight,* released for the Sony Playstation in Japan. In the early 1990s, Tatsunoko produced a four-part OVA (Original Video Animation, direct-to-video) series *New Android Casshan,* which retold the original series in a condensed manner. Hiroyuki Fukushima both directed and co-wrote the screenplay with Noboru Aikawa, and Yasuomi Umezu updated the character designs (Umezu would go on to perform similar duties on the remakes of *Gatchaman* and *Hurricane Poylmar*). The studio Artmic produced the animation; it was also one of Artmic's final projects.

In 1995, Streamline Pictures acquired the rights to the English-language version and released the series on VHS under the title of *Casshan: Robot Hunter.* The series was edited together as a two-hour movie and first premiered on American television on the Sci-Fi Channel in 1996. AD Vision re-released the OVA on DVD in 2003. —*MM*

The Cat

The Cat was launched by Marvel Comics in late 1972 in an attempt to attract the emerging women's liberation movement by featuring strong female characters. Her first issue introduced the ex-hippie-student Greer Nelson, whose policeman husband has recently been killed in a corner store hold-up. Working as an assistant to the great woman scientist Dr. Tumolo, Nelson takes part in hi-tech experiments to boost women's physical and mental potential. The experiments turn out to be funded by a sexist megalomaniac bent on creating a race of compliant superwomen, but nevertheless Greer emerges with some formidable powers. Donning a yellow catsuit with retractable claws, the Cat swings from building to building like a female Spider-Man. With an all-woman creative team of Linda Fite on scripts and Marie Severin on art, which was virtually unheard of in the 1970s, the comic was certainly distinctive. But because it was saddled with a parade of strictly B-list villains and an unresponsive, mostly male audience, the comic failed, lasting only four issues.

Of course, Marvel is famous for never letting a character go to waste, and the Cat was back a year later in a rather different guise. Foiling a kidnap attempt on Dr. Tumolo, the Cat became "fatally" injured, whereupon the good doctor revealed that she was in fact a member of a secret race of cat-people, and only their secret potions could cure her. In the process, Nelson was herself transformed into a cat-person, complete with a tail, striped fur, and real claws. Rechristened Tigra the Werewoman, she was now somewhat more flirtatious and adopted a costume of bikini and chains that was one of the most provocative in comics.

An entertaining 1976 series was short-lived, but in the 1980s Tigra became an occasional Avenger, and finally found a regular berth in the spin-off *West Coast Avengers* title. She was portrayed as an interesting combination of self-doubt and sexual allure, and eventually proved to be a popular character. But back in 1976, in the same month that Tigra's solo series had started, an issue of *The Avengers* introduced a new version of the Cat, whose roots stretched back to the earliest days of Marvel.

Patsy Walker first appeared back in 1944 in the second issue of *Miss America* comics, and within four issues had taken over the title. For twenty years the ditzy redhead's misadventures in love and work entertained the same young fans who enjoyed Archie Comics, with an early cover boasting more than 5 million readers. She was certainly no superheroine and was probably introduced into the short-lived 1970s Beast series as a bit of comic relief, but writer Steve Engelhart had other plans for her. Disgusted by her husband's career with the corporate crime organization, the Brand Corp., Walker follows the Beast to the Avengers' headquarters where she happens upon the Cat's old costume. In a flash, she dons the suit and decides to become a superheroine, this time called Hellcat (one of the names first considered for the character in 1972). Following a few less-than-inspiring outings, her creators sent her away for training but she soon reappeared in the rival group, the Defenders. Like the original Cat, the Walker version was both athletic and self-assured, though also rather reckless and irresponsible.

In comics, nothing should be taken for granted and, as the Defenders stories moved into a darker and more horror-based direction in the 1980s, things became rather strange for the ex-model—

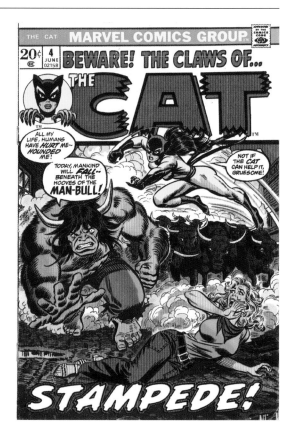

The Cat #4 © 1973 Marvel Comics.
COVER ART BY JOHN ROMITA AND TONY MORTELLARO.

from being transformed into a pink-furred demon to bumping into just about every monster in the Marvel universe. Nevertheless, this detour is no drawback in the world of superheroes and, following her sojourn with the Defenders, the Cat went on to rejoin the Avengers briefly before, in 2000, starring in her own miniseries. (This somewhat gloomy tale, covering Hellcat's literal comeback from hell, was followed by a more lighthearted return to the character's roots in a humorous *Defenders* reboot shortly afterward.)

While never the success that Marvel had hoped for, the Cat was one of the few characters that can be said to be two heroines for the price of one. —*DAR*

Cat Heroes

Cats became objects of worship in ancient Egypt because they kept the rodent population under control, but the sleek beauty and fascinating aloofness of felines have continued to mesmerize humans for centuries. Superheroes (or at least their creators) have been unable to escape the allure of cats. Catwoman's hissy fits between thievery and heroism have etched her into the public's consciousness, and Marvel Comics' Black Panther, Tigra (a.k.a. the Cat), and Black Cat have added their notches on the superhero scratching post. There are lesser-known crime fighters in cat costumes, however, some of whom still enjoy an occasional stretch in the sun, and others who have scatted into obscurity.

Consider Cat-Man, first seen in Holyoke Publishing's *Crash Comics* #4 (1940). Some fans dismiss this character as a Batman clone with a feline motif, but his novelty extends beyond imitation. Cat-Man's powers—catlike prowess, vision, reflexes, and nine lives—were naturally developed, not artificially acquired like so many superheroes of comics' Golden Age (1938–1954): He was orphaned as a child in the wilds of Burma and was raised by jungle cats. Cat-Man is also distinguished by his nubile female sidekick, the playful Kitten, whose very presence added subtle innuendos into a prudish period of comic-book history.

It is unlikely that the Lynx, Fox Features Syndicate's caped crusader with leopard-spotted trunks and a red mask, could avoid allegations of being a Batman copycat, especially with his partner, the Robin the Boy Wonder–like Blackie the Mystery Boy, at his side. Premiering in *Mystery Men* #14 (1940), the Lynx had few distinguishing characteristics and no superpowers, and was banished to comics' litter box by issue #31.

What if Catwoman's alter ego, Selina Kyle, were real—*and* a comic-book artist? Tarpe Mills, the creator of the slinky superheroine Miss Fury, was the

Tiger-Man #2 © 1975 Atlas Comics.
COVER ART BY FRANK THORNE.

closest imaginable personification of a true-life Kyle—*without* Catwoman's criminal tendencies. Mills was vivacious and lovely, a socialite who owned many cats as pets.

DC Comics' Wildcat was first seen in *Sensation Comics* #1 (1942), an issue better known for featuring the second appearance of Wonder Woman. Inside Wildcat's midnight-blue bodysuit—with floppy cat ears, a catlike face application (with whiskers!), and clawed feet—is professional pugilist Ted Grant. In his origin story, this pummeling heavyweight parlays his muscle into superheroics, being inspired to action by the Golden Age Green Lantern. Wildcat later joined the Justice Society of America, and has sporadically appeared in various DC titles throughout the decades, including *The Brave and the Bold,* the team-up title where he frequently joined forces with Batman during the 1970s. In the 1980s and 1990s, Grant's goddaughter, Yolanda Montez, briefly succeeded him as Wildcat in the superteam called Infinity, Inc.

Zoologist Ralph Hardy uncovered a Peruvian artifact in 1961: a belt made from a jaguar's pelt, carrying the inscription, "To be transformed into a human jaguar with supreme power over animals everywhere in the universe, the wearer need only say, 'The Jaguar.'" Hopping into a red uniform with a cat-head chest insignia and spotted boots, Hardy becomes the Jaguar, Archie Comics' Superman-meets-Doctor Doolittle. The Jaguar used prodigious strength and his critter control to fight everything from dinosaurs to aliens in a fifteen-issue run of *The Adventures of the Jaguar* (1961–1963), and was updated in 1991 as part of DC Comics' "Impact" imprint, a short-lived attempt to revive the Archie superheroes.

Animal Man—whose garish costume consists of an orange chainmail bodysuit with a big blue "A" on the front—debuted in DC's *Strange Adventures* #180 (1965). Secretly Buddy Baker, Animal Man can mimic the ability of any creature within close proximity, including felines, a trait he acquired after being irradiated by a UFO. After a smattering of appearances, Animal Man was resurrected in his own monthly comic that ran for an astounding eighty-nine issues (1988–1995). A teenage superhero with similar powers also bowed in 1965: Beast Boy (a.k.a. Changeling), in *Doom Patrol* #99. Garfield Logan survives a rare disease after a genetic experiment imbues him with the ability to transform into animals—and gives him green skin as a side effect. Morphing into green tigers and lions (and other creatures), Beast Boy is now one of DC's Teen Titans.

The peculiar Tiger Boy was introduced in Harvey Comics' *Unearthly Spectaculars* #1 (1965). Paul Canfield was born on Earth to parents who immigrated from Jupiter. He inherits the Jovian power of transmutation and uses it to change into, of all things, a tiger with a boy's head. Tiger Boy originally wants to subjugate Earthlings, but his parents harangue him into changing his stripes and becoming a superhero. Panthea is equally as extraordinary as Tiger Boy. Briefly appearing in Marvel's *Comix Book* #1–#5 (1974–1975), Panthea's parents are an African lion and a human woman, explaining her unorthodox catlike facial features and the tail on her humanoid frame.

Atlas Comics, an ambitious but ill-fated publisher surfacing in 1975 with a line of titles that disappeared within months, published two cat-inspired heroes. *The Cougar,* running two issues, was a gender-switching update of the original Black Cat, Harvey Comics' "Hollywood's Glamorous Detective Star," with a touch of TV's *Kolchak: The Night Stalker* (1973–1975) added. A Tinseltown stuntman moonlighting as a monster-bashing superhero, the Cougar was clad in red with a laced, open-chested shirt similar to Plastic Man's attire. Other than his name and his self-taught acrobatic agility, the powerless Cougar had no catlike attributes. Atlas managed to eke out *three* issues of *Tiger-Man.* Dr. Lancaster Hill isolates a strength-inducing chromosome from a jungle tiger's blood and, after an injection, gains catlike senses and powers. As Tiger-Man, he fights crime in a tiger-striped tunic with clawed gloves and boots.

Several other cat-inspired heroes have pranced through comics and the media over the decades in such numbers as to prohibit a full listing, but notable examples include Streaky the Supercat, the pet of the Silver Age (1956–1969) Supergirl, who temporarily obtains superpowers from kryptonite exposure; *Pumaman,* a low-budget 1980 movie featuring a feral superhero whose powers are derived from a mysterious amulet; *Coyote,* an atypical comic first published in 1981 by Eclipse Comics, starring the Native American trickster god; and Pantha, the vicious she-cat who in the 1990s was a member of DC's New [Teen] Titans. —*ME*

Cat-Man

In 1940, the newsstands were suddenly awash with superheroes, several eminently forgettable. Such characters could be found in the pages of *Crash Comics,* published by the obscure TEM Publications, but issue #4, in between episodes of Buck Burke, Strongman ("the perfect human"), and the Blue Streak, featured the first appearance of Cat-Man, who soon gained a sizeable following. Cat-Man's origin would have been familiar to fans of Tarzan and the recently released Black Condor; while traveling in India (or Burma, according to later issues), young David Merrywether's parents are killed by "jungle wildmen," and the child is left to the tender mercies of an approaching tiger. As wild animals are seemingly prone to do, she raised the child as her own cub and, by the time he emerged from the jungle as an adult, he had developed great strength and leaping abilities, as well as the ability to see in the dark (by shining beams of light from his eyes). Moving to the great metropolis, he becomes appalled at man's inhumanity to man, and quickly rustles up an appealing green costume, complete with large, furry tiger-claw mittens—all the better to fight crime with.

With his superior abilities, Cat-Man was more than a match for any evildoer, but a stray bullet in his first adventure resulted in his untimely death. However, it seems that he had also acquired the nine lives of a cat during his wilderness years, and the great spirit of the tigers conveniently revived him. The trouble-prone hero was also killed in the next two stories, before his editors realized that his nine lives were being rapidly exhausted and so quietly abandoned that idiosyncrasy. By this point, Cat-Man's popularity had demanded that he be given his own title (and a more sensible costume), and in the spring *Cat-Man* #1 was released by the newly renamed Holyoke Company. From the outset, the strip was drawn by Charles Quinlan, in an accomplished if slightly old-fashioned style, and written by Martin Panzer.

After a first-issue battle with terrorists, Cat-Man's comic was soon dominated by the outbreak of World War II, and Merrywether enlisted as a lieutenant in the army, quickly rising to the rank of captain. In between battling Benito Mussolini, Hideki Tojo, and Adolf Hitler (one cover even showed him throttling the Nazi despot), he also gained a young sidekick. In the wake of Robin's enormous success, no self-respecting hero would be complete without his own pal, but only Cat-Man was assisted by a girl. Eleven-year-old orphan Katie Conn is an unwilling accomplice in her evil uncle's life of crime but, when the recalcitrant relative is tackled by Cat-Man, she joins in and helps our hero defeat him. In classic comic-book style, Merrywether adopts her as his ward and she becomes the daredevil fighting girl, the Kitten. Over the ensuing months she also grew up very quickly until, barely a year later, she looked more like a grown woman. Kitten's relationship with "Uncle David" was always rather ambiguous, but incredibly no one ever seemed to notice, and the strip managed to avoid the controversy that surrounded other comics.

The typical *Cat-Man* story involved the pair foiling Axis plots or organized crime, and there was usually a high body count and more than the strip's fair share of sadism. What the feature initially lacked, however, was an arch-villain, a problem that was resolved after the war with the introduction of top-hatted, monocled baddie Dr. Macabre (and face it, with a name like that he was hardly likely to be a saint, was he?). Dr. Macabre and his ward Lenore sailed in from Lisbon, of all places, and set about establishing a crime syndicate—until Cat-Man and Kitten came upon the dastardly pair in the middle of a robbery. Over the following five issues, the evil Doctor acquired the touch of death from a Z-ray gun (which basically meant that anything or anyone he touched suddenly keeled over dead), caused havoc with a band of killer gorillas, and attempted to cook the unfortunate Kitten in a cauldron of molten metal. Macabre was last seen in *Cat-Man* #32, plunging to his death in a deep-sea diving bell, but whether he lived to fight another day fans will never know, as that issue was the last.

In the new millennium, interest in *Cat-Man* has grown as collectors have discovered just how rare the comics are. Evidently, very few copies survived wartime paper drives, and barely ten copies are known to exist for some issues. Longtime enthusiast Bill Black has also revived Cat-Man in his AC Comics line and has added Kitten to the lineup of his long-running Femforce team. Additionally, various AC titles regularly reprint vintage tales from the Holyoke era, keeping interest in the crime-fighting duo alive. —*DAR*

Catwoman

Catwoman, slinking in and out of thievery like a mischievous kitten, has titillated Batman throughout most of the Dark Knight's long career. This "princess of plunder" was envisioned by Batman creator Bob Kane and writer Bill Finger as a female counterpart to the Caped Crusader, and as a means to attract girls to the comics' readership, but through spunk and tenacity she quickly distinguished herself as much more than a copycat. From her first appearance as "The Cat" in *Batman* #1 (1940), Gotham City's most notorious burglar—dressed to the nines (lives?) in a clinging, cleavage-showcasing gown—arouses a side of Batman that the prepubescent Robin finds puzzling. Through each encounter, suggestive repartee between the Bat and Cat intimates that if not for their ethical division, these two would boot the Boy Wonder out of the Batcave and redefine the term "Dynamic Duo."

When compared to the Joker, Two-Face, and other psychopaths in Batman's deadly rogues' gallery, Catwoman, whose penchant for luxuries entices her into a career as a thief, seems tame—but by no means is this lady docile. Wielding a whip with a "cat-o'-nine-tails," a weapon that by the late 1980s acquired sado-sexual connotations, the cun-

ning Catwoman, with her pugilistic prowess and … well, *cat*like reflexes, becomes a fierce combatant when cornered or challenged. She had clawed her way through a decade's worth of stories in random issues of *Batman* and *Detective Comics* before her roots were disclosed. In "The Secret Life of Catwoman" in *Batman* #62 (1950), the villainess reveals her true stripes as she saves Batman's life, taking a blow to the skull in the process. Once regaining consciousness, she emerges from amnesia with the recollection of her past life as Selina Kyle, flight attendant, and no knowledge of her stint as a criminal. Aiding Batman and Gotham City Police Commissioner Gordon in their apprehension of her former partner in pillage, Kyle is exonerated of her felonies and allowed to set up business as a pet-shop operator, but before long her ego, bruised by taunts from the press and former underworld associates, leads her back into larceny as Catwoman.

While her identity was known to Batman and Gordon, Catwoman's mystique stymied her adversaries, particularly her ability to resurface after seemingly perishing—did she, like her namesake, really have nine lives? This raven-haired, wide-eyed "felonious feline" also dazzled Gotham's finest with her wardrobe: Aside from the ghastly full-sized cat-head mask she wore during a few early outings, Catwoman skulked about for more than two decades in a stylish purple dress, green cape, and a cat-eared cowl before streamlining her garb in the 1960s into a form-fitting emerald catsuit that would have made Diana Rigg (TV's Mrs. Peel) green with envy. By 1969, she'd slipped into a skintight blue bodysuit with a long cat tail, before returning to the purple gear in the mid-1970s. She also frequently cavorted about town in a cat-shaped "kitty" car, took to the air in a catplane, hurled a catarang, and even used a *cat*-apult to leap to a helicopter while pulling a heist.

Throughout most of her comic-book career, Catwoman was portrayed as Batman's most likeable villain: Sure, she was a bad girl, but not *that* bad. In the late 1970s, Catwoman's heart of gold led her to

Michelle Pfeiffer portrays Catwoman in a scene from *Batman Returns*.

shed her life of crime and marry Batman—not in the comics' regular continuity, but on "Earth-Two," DC's parallel world where its characters from the 1940s resided. Their union bore a daughter, Helena, who became the Huntress when the Earth-Two Catwoman was murdered.

Back on "Earth-One," Catwoman continued to pillage, even after DC Comics jettisoned its multiple-Earth concept in 1985. Selina Kyle was reinvented, along with the Dark Knight, in Frank Miller and David Mazzucchelli's groundbreaking "Batman: Year One" four-issue story arc beginning in *Batman* #404 (1987). Kyle, it was disclosed, endured an abusive childhood and was on the streets at age twelve, becoming fiercely independent as a result. Segueing into a life of prostitution, this new Kyle was a dominatrix with a butch haircut, who donned a leather

catsuit and used her whips on johns before taking to the rooftops as the burglar Catwoman. More recently, however, Catwoman has given up streetwalking and developed a profound moral sense, albeit one tempered by her hard life. She serves as an occasional ally to Batman and often protects the downtrodden in Gotham City's seediest neighborhoods.

Catwoman's popularity was bolstered in the mid-1960s by Julie Newmar's tantalizing portrayal of the villainess in the popular *Batman* television show. Newmar sunk her claws into the role, playfully frolicking about with moves so sensuously catlike, all eyes were glued to her while she was on camera. Her immediate successors to the part, Lee Meriwether in the *Batman* theatrical movie (1966) and Eartha Kitt in later episodes of the television series, never quite commanded the screen as Newmar did. In director Tim Burton's *Batman Returns* (1992), Michelle Pfeiffer's take on Catwoman rivaled Newmar's, and spawned a long-delayed Catwoman movie, planned for 2004, starring Halle Berry (Ashley Judd and Nicole Kidman were previously considered for the part). Catwoman has also appeared in the numerous incarnations of Batman television cartoon series throughout the years and has been merchandized since the 1960s in items including dolls, action figures, and bubble-bath dispensers. —*ME*

Censorship: *See* **Comics Code**

Challengers of the Unknown

Although still published in the twenty-first century amongst the many thousands of superheroes vying for comic shelf space, the Challengers of the Unknown enjoyed their heyday during the Silver Age of comics (1956–1969). Indeed, after the Flash, Challengers of the Unknown was the second significant superhero creation of this era. After the cancellation of the Justice Society of America in *All Star Comics* in 1951, the newsstands did not carry superhero teams for much of the 1950s until writer Dave Wood and artist Jack Kirby revived the concept in DC Comics' *Showcase* #6 in early 1957. In an origin sequence that lasts all of two pages, Wood and Kirby revealed how four adventurers on their way to a radio show narrowly avoid death when their airplane is struck by lightning. Climbing from the wreckage, the group decides that since they are living on borrowed time they might as well take whatever risks the world can throw at them and literally "challenge the unknown." As motivations go it was perilously shallow, but nevertheless one page later they were a team and already hot on the heels of their first challenge.

The Challenger lineup included Professor Haley, the thinker of the group; pug-nosed wrestler Rocky Davis; ginger-haired daredevil Red Ryan; and jet pilot Ace Morgan. The group soon added an occasional fifth member, plucky June Robbins, whose main role was to be captured by assorted wrongdoers. After four issues of *Showcase* and eight of their own title, Kirby left for Marvel Comics, but by then he had set the pattern for the team's career. Issue after issue featured the intrepid team taking on an endless parade of aliens, monsters, magicians, robots, and all manner of miscreants from deepest antiquity to the furthest-flung futures. By 1959, the purple-jumpsuited band had mysteriously acquired their own secret hideaway in the Rockies, complete with their own jail and a fleet of planes, helicopters, and cars. They also collected a cadre of arch-enemies, led by the mustached Multi-Man, who gradually grew a large bald head and pointed ears—as supervillains are wont to do—as well as an ever-expanding range of deadly powers. As the 1960s progressed, the prison in Challengers' Mountain filled up with the motliest group of evildoers in comics, including Volcano Man, Brainex, and the truly horrifying Spongeman. Somewhere along the line they lost the constantly imperilled June but gained Cosmo the superpet.

Because of a formula that appealed to a wide readership, the Challengers became something of a blueprint for many future superteams, notably Jack Kirby's world-conquering Fantastic Four of Marvel Comics fame: The Challengers had Professor Haley; the Fantastic Four had Reed Richards. Wrestler Rocky Davis was a clear precursor to the muscle-bound Thing. And, much like June Robbins rounded out the Challenger lineup nicely, so too did Invisible Girl for the Fantastic Four.

And what an adaptable superteam the Challengers were. In the late 1960s, DC discovered horror in a big way and, to cash in on the trend, the Challengers began to investigate the mysterious; the giant aliens were replaced by ghosts and ghouls. A June look-alike, Corrinna Stark, briefly

Challengers of the Unknown #3 © 1997 DC Comics.
COVER ART BY JOHN PAUL LEON AND SHAWN MARTINBROUGH.

village below, killing the visitors. Understandably upset by this, the foursome split up and all got a bit peculiar, but thankfully they pulled themselves together again just in time to save the world as usual. For the final Challengers series of 1997, the original team were dumped altogether in favor of a new band of heroes who investigated alien sightings and paranormal phenomena in a transparent attempt to hit the *X-Files* market. Despite some of the comic's finest writing and artwork, the revamp failed to find an audience, but it's always only a matter of time before the Fab Four ride the next trend and return to the shelves—as they did in the much-anticipated period piece *The New Frontier,* a retro epic by writer-artist Darwyn Cooke that impressed readers in 2004. *—DAR*

Charlton Heroes

An unauthorized song magazine sent its publisher to "sing-sing." Such is the origin of Charlton Publications, the Derby, Connecticut, outfit known for everything from crossword puzzle periodicals to superhero comic books.

In the early 1930s, Italian immigrant John Santangelo, a bricklayer, was encouraged by a girlfriend to produce a magazine that printed the lyrics to popular songs. His effort landed him behind bars for copyright infringement. In jail, he got a crash course in copyright law courtesy of fellow inmate Edward Levy, a disbarred lawyer, and the two joined forces upon their release to start a legitimate publishing house, Charlton. They legally obtained the rights to print song lyrics, and in 1945 launched their first magazine—*Hit Parader*—a huge success that became the cornerstone of a line of music titles. Charlton entered the comics business in 1946, mimicking the then-current market trends of funny animals, science fiction, horror, and crime series.

Santangelo's frugality is legend. Charlton—or Capital Distributing Company, its official name—

joined the group, but their heyday was over and the comic was canceled in 1970. A few years later they were back in a short-lived revival that mixed horror and science fiction, presumably going for a crossover market that didn't really exist.

After a very lean spell in the 1980s, the group returned for a couple of startling revamps in the mid-1990s, the first of which saw Challengers' Mountain transformed into a sort of theme park, complete with its own visitors' village. It seems that the group had decided to cash in on their celebrity status by courting the tourist dollar, a plan that was rather undermined when a mysterious villain blew up their hideaway, which then plummeted onto the sliced its production costs by headquartering its editorial, production, distribution, and printing divisions in one plant (Charlton at one time even owned a paper mill). The publisher also paid the lowest page rates in the publishing field, even feeding a few bucks to prisoners for contributions.

This gift for parsimony helped Charlton stay alive during a mid-1950s comic-book market crash. It absorbed properties from other publishers, including Fox Features Syndicate, from which Charlton obtained its first superhero series, *Blue Beetle,* which the company issued briefly during this era before cancellation. Charlton also published the funny-animal superhero comic *Atomic Mouse* beginning in 1953.

Hurricane Diane nearly decimated Charlton's facilities on August 18, 1955, dumping eleven inches of rain on Derby in the course of a day and sending a surge of flood waters into the building. Some employees narrowly escaped, but managed to salvage the printing press during their hasty exodus. Comics inventory, artwork, and reams of paper did not fare as well. "All of the comic books were turned into papier-mâché," remembered former Charlton and DC Comics editor/artist Dick Giordano in his biography, *Dick Giordano: Changing Comics, One Day at a Time* (2003).

Charlton became the third comic-book publisher to release superhero comics during the industry's Silver Age (1956–1969), following DC and Archie Comics' lead. Charlton's nuclear hero Captain Atom was first seen in *Space Adventures* #33 (1960). His stint there did not last long, but he was resurrected in the mid-1960s—as was Blue Beetle, as a gadget-wielding, high-tech crime fighter. Soon, Charlton's two superheroes were joined by some not-so-super friends.

"I always preferred heroes who could do things that *we* supposedly would be able to do," revealed Giordano, who was tapped to edit the Charlton superhero titles. He and his creative teams opted for heroes with skills and talents, not superpowers

(discounting the preexisting Captain Atom), which he called Charlton's "Action Heroes." Steve Ditko, the original artist of Marvel Comics' *The Amazing Spider-Man,* drew *Blue Beetle, Captain Atom,* and the faceless hero the Question, who appeared as the backup feature in *Beetle.* Other Action Heroes: Pete "PAM" Morisi's Peter Cannon–Thunderbolt, who relied upon his "powers of the mind"; the Peacemaker, who loved tranquility so much he was willing to fight for it; Nightshade, "Darling of Darkness," the occasional partner of and backup series in *Captain Atom;* the iron-fisted Sarge Steel, drawn by editor Giordano; and martial artist Judomaster.

Tightfisted Charlton did not market its Action Heroes during this extremely competitive time for superhero comics, and many titles never made it into the distribution web, with never-opened bundles remaining on delivery trucks and then being returned to the company. The Action Heroes titles were canceled after roughly two years. Giordano is favorably remembered by the writers and artists who produced the Action Heroes titles—Denny O'Neil, Jim Aparo, Joe Gill, Roy Thomas, and others—and believes that his uncharacteristic superhero comics would have performed well if Charlton had supported them.

In the 1970s, Charlton made a few additional forays into superhero publishing. The company licensed stalwarts from the King Features Syndicate and published comic books starring space adventurer Flash Gordon and the jungle hero the Phantom. *Underdog,* based on the animated television cartoon featuring a canine do-gooder who gains powers from popping energy pills, appeared in ten issues of his own Charlton series from 1970 to 1972. Also receiving a ten-issue run was *E-Man,* a lighthearted superhero created by Nick Cuti and Joe Staton in 1973.

In the early 1980s, improvements in the quality of comics production and the industry's growing reliance upon the "direct market" (selling preordered titles to specialty outlets) began to squeeze Charlton

Thunderbolt #52 © 1966 Charlton Comics.
COVER ART BY PETE MORISI.

trate the changing distribution network, Charlton Comics went out of business in 1986. —ME

Civilian Heroes

Although "civilian" heroes appeared in the movie serials of the 1940s and 1950s, it was not until the 1970s that the era of civilian superheroes really took hold. Unlike their "true" superhero brothers and sisters who glossed the pages of many Silver Age (1956–1969) publications—complete with an iconic costume or mask and loaded with superhuman powers and/or a secret identity—civilian heroes have had to make do with functioning in the world as, well, civilians. For the most part, they fight crime and subvert evil in their street clothes, living life in one persona. Though they are undeniably heroic in their actions, the popular culture has been reticent to label them superheroes in the most complete sense of the word.

Granddaddy of them all was Steve Austin (played by Lee Majors), the title hero of *The Six Million Dollar Man*. Once an astronaut, Austin was injured in a crash landing. "Gentlemen, we can rebuild him. Better. Stronger. Faster." So said Oscar Goldman (Richard Anderson) at the start of each episode, and rebuild Austin they did, replacing his legs, right arm, and left eye with costly bionic enhancements. Once he recovered, Austin became a secret agent for the Office of Scientific Information (OSI), using his bionics to aid the world against spies, terrorists, and other criminals (although an occasional encounter with deadly robots, aliens, and Sasquatch did figure into later seasons). Debuting on ABC on March 7, 1972, with a telefilm based on Martin Caidin's novel *Cyborg,* the series was picked up the following fall for two more films, and then run as a regular series from January 1974 to fall 1978.

The Six Million Dollar Man not only made a star out of Majors, it also provided an opportunity for a

out of business. Giordano had since become the managing editor, then the editorial director, of DC Comics. DC executive Paul Levitz purchased the rights to the Action Heroes as a "gift" for Giordano in 1983; beginning with *Crisis on Infinite Earths* #1 (1985), DC infused Charlton's characters into its universe, with *Blue Beetle, Captain Atom,* and *The Question* receiving monthly titles. Writer Alan Moore originally wanted to use the Action Heroes as the stars of his twelve-issue series *Watchmen* (1986–1987), but was encouraged by Giordano to create original heroes instead. The Charlton characters have sporadically surfaced in the DC universe ever since.

After a few difficult final years of publishing reprints of its old horror series and failing to pene-spin-off series. After Austin's girlfriend, tennis pro Jaime Sommers (Lindsay Wagner), was injured parachuting, she too was outfitted with bionics to become the Bionic Woman. Appearing first on *The Six Million Dollar Man* in January 1975, Sommers debuted in *The Bionic Woman* on ABC in January 1976. Her series switched networks in the fall of 1977, to NBC, and ended its run in 1978. Like Austin, Sommers fought kidnappers, criminals, and thugs, as well as occasional aliens and "fembots." Between OSI assignments Sommers lived her life as a schoolteacher in Ojai, California, occasionally accompanied by her bionic dog, a German Shepherd named Max. Both *The Six Million Dollar Man* and *The Bionic Woman* were hugely popular with TV audiences, and much licensed material was sold from the properties, including dolls, books, puzzles, and more. Along with an array of lunchboxes and T-shirts, the marketplace welcomed the "Jaime Sommers Classroom" and the "Bionic Beauty Salon." Charlton Comics published comics based on both series. Several reunion movies were shot, including one in which the son of Austin and Sommers required bionic enhancements as well.

Whereas the bionic special effects were relatively easy for producers—even superspeed was shown by using sound effects over *slowed-down* action!—another pair of civilian heroes had a much more difficult time getting seen. *The Invisible Man* (1975–1976) and *The Gemini Man* (1976) were two TV series in which the hero could turn invisible. However, neither hero had a secret identity per se, nor did either have an iconic costume into which they changed. A 1958–1960 series of *The Invisible Man* had been produced in England and aired in the United States, but the 1975 series was different. In the latter show, Dr. Daniel Westin (David McCallum) used his invisibility formula to keep it out of government hands, but found he could not turn visible again. He undertook missions for the KLAE Corporation while searching for a cure. In *Gemini Man,* a government agent for INTERSECT was accidentally exposed to radiation, which rendered him invisible.

Sam Casey (Ben Murphy) finds that he must use a specialized watch to keep himself visible, except when going on dangerous missions. The concept was revived in 2000 when Sci-Fi Channel premiered *The Invisible Man,* starring Vincent Vintresca as a thief and con man who underwent an experiment that rendered him invisible; he was soon blackmailed into helping a secret government organization fight crime. This *Invisible Man* was visible for two seasons.

Two alien-powered heroes appeared at the start of the 1980s. In ABC's *The Phoenix,* Bennu (Judson Scott) was an alien messenger who was trying to help Earth while finding his missing partner. An amulet he wore around his neck gave him special powers to help people and the environment, but although a debut telefilm in September 1981 did well, only four episodes of the series aired the following spring. *The Powers of Matthew Star* was also set to debut in the fall of 1981 on NBC, but an on-set fire badly burned lead actor Peter Barton, delaying production. The series debuted in September 1982, and lasted one season. Barton played Matthew Star, a seemingly normal high school student who was really an alien prince. Watched over by a guardian (Louis Gossett Jr.), Matthew developed his powers of telekinesis, telepathy, and astral projection to help people and the government, all while training to return to his homeworld and overthrow its despotic ruler. A bit later, *Starman* beamed onto TV from the popular movie of same name, for non-costumed, *Fugitive*-like adventures that lasted a single season in 1986–1987.

One of the oddest superhero shows, in the 1983–1984 ABC season, was *Automan.* In it, a police computer expert (Desi Arnaz Jr.) creates a handsome sparkling superhero that jumps right out of his computer! Automan (Chuck Wagner) could walk through walls, affect machinery, and even merge with his creator. They were aided in their crime-fighting adventures by Cursor, an electronic blip that could create fantastic cars or even a tank! Unlike most of the "civilian superheroes," who are regular people (albeit with unusual abilities) all the time, Automan belongs to that odd variety who are, though often costume-less, superheroes all the time.

In 1988, one of syndication's hits was the series *My Secret Identity.* The half-hour series featured the adventures of teen Andrew Clements (Jerry O'Connell) who accidentally gains powers after being exposed to an invention of his wacky scientist neighbor, Dr. Benjamin Jeffcoate (Derek McGrath). Clements develops superspeed and superstrength, limited invulnerability, and the ability to float (even to fly, using aerosol cans for propellant). A lifelong comic book fan, Clements dubbed himself Ultiman, but he never created a costume, and did all his good deeds in such a way that nobody knew it was him. *My Secret Identity* lasted three seasons, until 1991.

DC Comics hero *The Human Target* was translated into a short-lived television series in 1992 on ABC. Produced by Pet Fly Productions, which had earlier done CBS's *The Flash* live-action series, *The Human Target* starred Rick Springfield as Christopher Chance, a hero who would use his high-tech masks and vocal devices to impersonate those targeted for death. Chance flew around the world in a specially designed jet, with three assistants. *The Human Target* ran seven episodes in July–August 1992.

There are those who wear the barest trappings of superheroes, even if they don't have superpowers. Many past versions of *Zorro* on television and in film led to *Sword of Justice* on NBC (1978–1979), in which Jack Cole (Dack Rambo) is a rich playboy who dabbles in crime fighting, leaving a playing card behind at each triumph. A pilot telefilm of Will Eisner's hero *The Spirit* was produced and aired on ABC in July 1986, starring Sam Jones in the title role. Like his comic-book counterpart, television's Spirit was a non-superpowered criminologist. Mike Grell's face-paint-wearing comic-book adventurer Jon Sable was later badly translated to the small screen with Lewis Ven Bergen in the title role. *Sable* aired from November 1987 to January

1988 on ABC. And what to make of Judge Nicholas Marshall (Ramy Zada, then Bruce Abbott), who presided over a courtroom by day but dressed in black, rode a motorcycle, and meted out vigilante justice by night? That was the plot of *Dark Justice,* which ran on CBS from 1991 to 1993, with reruns lasting another full season into 1994.

In today's Hollywood, costumes and assorted superheroic trappings are not nearly as popular as they once were, and lines have blurred when it comes to determining who makes the superhero cut. The X-Men wear leather outfits that would be acceptable in many nightclubs or bars. Young Clark Kent will never wear a costume in *Smallville,* say that series' producers, yet there is no denying young Kent bears the title of coming-of-age superhero. The alien kids of *Roswell* look human but wield their special gifts in defense of good. *Buffy the Vampire Slayer* features several characters with enhanced powers who act heroically, but the show was never promoted as a superhero show. Even the superspy antics of Jennifer Garner on *Alias,* the derring-do of Tomb Raider Lara Croft in her videogames and film franchise, or the impossible martial arts moves of Jackie Chan in any of his films could be classified as superheroic. But because they lack costumes, and in many cases an alter ego, they are—as the public views them—still civilians, like so many heroes before them. —*AM*

Cobra

It is telling that both George Lucas's *Star Wars* and Buichi Terasawa's *Space Adventure Cobra* first appeared in 1977 and went on to redefine their respective media: science-fiction (or in the case of *Star Wars,* science-fantasy) films and manga. Both works went to the past to define their worlds of the future—the "futuristic past" of the pulp-magazine/whiz-bang space opera made famous by E. E. "Doc" Smith's *Lensman* novels but later reaching maturity in the works of such writers as the venerable Robert A. Heinlein (*Starship Troopers*). The manga—and the character of Cobra himself—actually represents a unique fusion of Western pop culture and the storytelling ways of manga and anime.

Cobra was the first major character created by Terasawa, who began work on the manga at the age of twenty-two. Cobra would become Terasawa's "icon" character, much like Astro Boy became associated with Osamu Tezuka (or Captain America with Jack Kirby and Joe Simon). With Cobra, Terasawa established several key elements that would reappear in his later works, such as *Midnight Eye Goku* and *Raven Tengu Kabuto*: One was a world of fantastic technology with designs that careened between the futuristic, the contemporary, and the baroque—even if the series was set in the past. *Kabuto* may have been set in feudal Japan, but *this* feudal Japan had futuristic elements such as robots, helicopters, and fishnet stockings. Another element established by *Cobra* was that of a hero who was a tough guy with a good heart; a kind, gentle romantic who could—and would—use his fists and superpowers (or a superweapon) to get the job done and take down the various villains he would face (each with his or her own bizarre look or backstory).

And finally, a major element was the beautiful women that the hero would meet in his adventures. Some were good, some were bad, but all would be well depicted. Female lead heroes have been used by Terasawa, starting with his 1990 manga *Black Knight Bat* and also *Gundragon Sigma,* which appeared in 1999.

Cobra is a throwback, a hero cast in the Han Solo mold with James Bond and Dirty Harry thrown in to season the mix, although Cobra eschews Harry Callahan's taciturn manner. His look—blond, muscular, wearing a red outfit and with a cigar always in his mouth—is not his real look; his face was changed to avoid the notice of the nefarious Pirate Guild. Although a former space pirate himself, Cobra worked on the side of good, always foiling the Guild's plans until he wanted out and went underground.

Cobra's exploits ran for seven years in Shueisha's *Shonen Jump* magazine; the manga captured the rough-and-tumble action and adventure of pulp science fiction as well as James Bond films and the 1968 Jane Fonda sci-fi romp *Barbarella* (Terasawa is a fan of these films). Like the pulp heroes of the past (although closer to an anti-hero), Cobra has a fast ship (the Turtle); a sidekick (a female android, or "armaroid," named Lady); a trusty sidearm; and an additional ace up his sleeve in the form of the "Psychogun." This weapon is on his left forearm, and when not in use is covered by an artificial hand. It is his most well-known feature, making him a unique standout in a field packed with many strange and bizarre humans, aliens, and worlds. And again, there are the women he meets and romances. Starting with the Royal Sisters in the first story arc, Cobra has had his share of relationships, although like 007 he never settles down, and some relationships end in tragedy—but also serve to push Cobra into stopping the villains once and for all.

When Terasawa began *Cobra* in 1977, he used a hook reminiscent of Philip K. Dick's "I Can Remember It for You Wholesale" (later made into the film *Total Recall*): A bored businessman heads into the "Trip Corporation" to go on a "vacation"—actually a controlled dream trip. The dream actually serves to unlock the man's memories of his previous life as the space pirate Cobra, before he went into hiding. With its mix of science fiction, action, tongue-in-cheek humor, and beautiful women, *Cobra* became a major hit for Terasawa. The manga was collected into eighteen volumes that sold in the millions. Being a fan of Western films, Terasawa often placed familiar icons from those films into the *Cobra* manga; such films include *2001: A Space Odyssey* (1968) and *The Spy Who Loved Me* (1977), and even the late 1970s cult science-

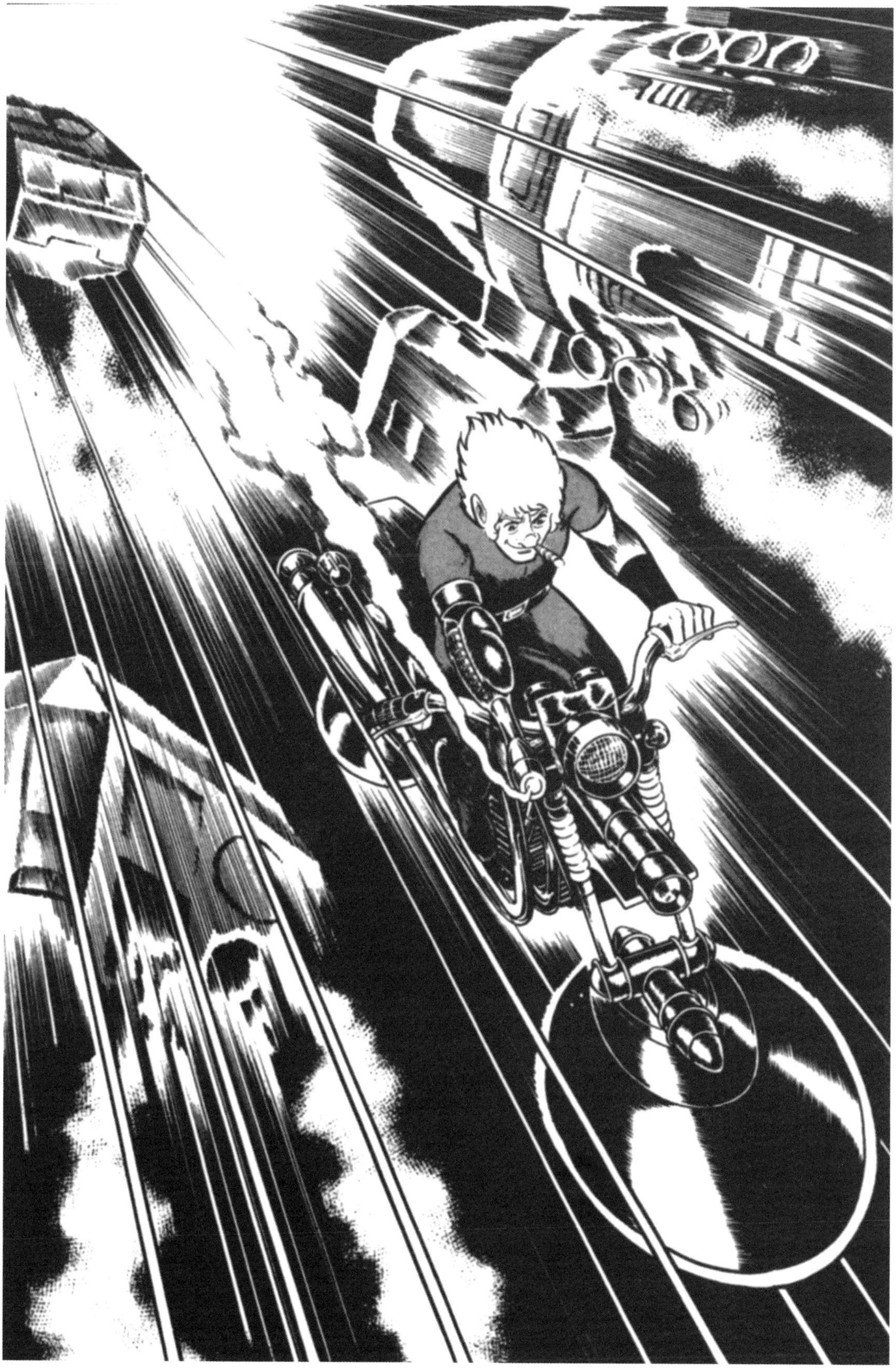

fiction television series *Space: 1999*—and, of course, *Star Wars.* While he adhered to a more realistic, more Western look in terms of his art, Terasawa also followed the storytelling techniques pioneered by his mentor, Osamu Tezuka. The late Tezuka is the man responsible for bringing about the modern age of manga and anime in Japan following World War II.

As was the case for all popular manga, *Cobra* made the leap to movie theaters in 1982; a thirty-one-episode animated television series followed later in the year. Tokyo Movie Shinsha (TMS) produced both the movie and the series, with Osamu Dezaki (*The Professional: Golgo 13, BlackJack*) directing both. While the TV series followed the storylines of the first eight volumes of the manga (with a number of changes), the movie retold the first major story arc involving Cobra and the Royal Sisters—Jane, Catherine, and Dominique—and Cobra's fight against the cyborg agent of the Pirate Guild, Crystal Boy. With a screenplay by Terasawa and Haruya Yamazaki, the film became a sort of metaphysical love story (but didn't skimp on the action), and utilized a unique animation process that gave the film a psuedo-3D look without the need for special glasses or equipment.

Cobra's popularity was such that his 1977 to 1984 run would not be the end; he would return in artbooks, video games, and further manga adventures. The year 1989 saw the release of two CD-ROM games, and the artbooks *Cobra Girls* and *Cobra Wonder* appeared in Japan in 1997. Cobra returned to comics in 1995 with *Cobra: The Psychogun.* This title and the mangas that followed it—*Cobra: Galaxy Knights* and *Cobra: Magic Doll*—were also children of the digital revolution that was sweeping the manga industry at that time. Terasawa was the vanguard in this revolution (starting with *Bat*) and he would use digital coloring and effects to create stunning artwork that won him even more acclaim both in Japan and around the world. Despite his return to these media, Cobra's return to movies was put on hold with the shelving

of the proposed film for *Cobra: The Psychogun,* despite Terasawa's involvement as director, storyboard artist, and screenwriter.

Cobra was well received beyond Japan; the manga was translated into French, Swedish, Tai, Chinese, and English. French television broadcast a dubbed version of the TV series in 1985. In America, Cobra's exploits would reach audiences in two different ways: An English-language adaptation by famed comic writer Marv Wolfman (*Crisis on Infinite Earths, Teen Titans*) released by Viz Comics in 1990 kicked things off. The twelve-issue series covered only the first major story arc of the manga, involving Cobra's "rebirth" and his adventures with the Royal Sisters in the search for the "Ultimate Weapon." One prominent change in the English-language version is that Cobra's Psychogun is now on his right hand, due to the process of reversing right-to-left Japanese art to conform to left-to-right-oriented readers.

Close to a year later, singer Matthew Sweet caused a sensation with the video for the title track of his album *Girlfriend.* The video used clips from the 1982 *Cobra* movie and became one of the most-watched videos on MTV and went into heavy rotation on the video channel. In the late 1990s the movie itself would reach America in an English-language version originally produced by Carl Macek's Streamline Pictures; anime distributor Urban Vision released the film in a limited theatrical run on the "art house" film circuit; both dubbed and subtitled versions were released for the American home video market in 1999.

Only when one takes a step back and sees Cobra for what he is can his appeal be understood. He is the embodiment of the classic hero; he may be rough around the edges, but he is honorable and able to take whatever is thrown at him. His wit and quick thinking—and sometimes his fists—can and will get him out of any trouble. In the end, he will walk away into the sunset or fly off into deep space with the girl and whatever treasure or item was the focus of his search. He does not brood, he acts. In the wildly stylized and imaginative world that Tera-sawa has created, Cobra fits right in. He is, in a sense, the heir to Haggard's Alan Quatermain, Fleming's James Bond, and Bob Kane's Batman (but without the dark elements). Cobra is the quintessential comic book hero, reborn in the Land of the Rising Sun. —*MM*

Comics Code

At the height of comics' Golden Age (1938–1954), industrywide comic-book sales stood steadily at between 100 million and 150 million copies per month, with annual revenues of up to $90 million. Publishers like DC Comics, Marvel, and EC Comics—publisher of *Tales from the Crypt, Crime SuspenStories,* and *MAD*—were enjoying unprecedented success. Into this booming business climate came psychiatrist Fredric Wertham, a doctor who had worked at Bellevue Hospital with juvenile delinquents, and who made a case in his 1954 book, *The Seduction of the Innocent,* that comic-book content was responsible for the decay of America's youth. Though his book targeted the popular crime and horror comics of the day, superheroes didn't escape Wertham's assault, with the good doctor maintaining, "This Superman-Batman-Wonder Woman

group is a special form of crime comics." One of his most well-known claims, still discussed among comic-book aficionados and historians today, is that Batman and Robin were gay.

In response, the Senate Judiciary Committee created a Subcommittee to Investigate Juvenile Delinquency in the United States, which held widely publicized hearings between April and June 1954 to investigate the validity of Wertham's claims. Rather than fall under the wrath of the federal government, in September of that year the comic-book industry created the Comics Magazine Association of America (CMAA), an organization made up of all comic-book publishers that wanted to get their comic books distributed. The CMAA immediately went to work adopting the self-censoring Comics Code Authority (CCA), whose forty-one standards described strict editorial guidelines for depicting sex, crime, horror, and violence within the pages of comics. Its Comics Code seal (boldly proclaiming "Approved by the Comics Code Authority") was placed on those comics that met the requirements of the CCA, namely those that did not "explicitly present the unique details and methods of a crime," and did not show "nudity," "excessive bloodshed," or "disrespect for established authority," but rather fostered "respect for parents, the moral code, and for honorable behavior." To earn CCA approval, a comic had to depict good triumphing over evil and the criminal being punished for his misdeeds "in every instance." By bearing the Comics Code seal, comics promised parents, educators, and the federal government that their content was now "safe" for young, developing minds.

Despite the industry's good intentions in pursing a path of self-censorship, the majority of comics publishers went out of business or canceled entire lines of books during the 1950s (EC's *Vault of Horror* and *Tales from the Crypt* included), with those remaining—most notably, DC—"dumbing down" their stories in an effort to meet the requirements of the code and appeal to a nation in the thrall of repressive moral standards. In 1955, Marvel canceled its superhero division with its final issue of *Sub-Mariner,* and characters like Human Torch and Captain America were shelved in favor of tales of sci-fi monsters (which, unlike EC's popular vampires, werewolves, zombies and witches, were not banned). Other 1950s superheroes to leave the marketplace included minors like Avenger, Captain Flash, Black Cobra, and Strong Man. DC launched a new comic, *The Brave and the Bold,* which featured medieval superheroes, including Robin Hood, the Viking Prince, and the Silent Knight, and as a whole the industry published more romance, Western, and humor comics to replace their now-defunct horror and crime titles. Silver Age (1956–1969) superheroes continued this trend: Heroes of the 1960s lived and fought crime in a world that was noticeably tamer than that of their Golden Age counterparts, thanks in large part to code restrictions that greatly curtailed such comic-book mainstays as gunplay, sadomasochistic subtexts, and displays of cleavage.

In 1971, Marvel's Stan Lee broke new ground when he challenged the code by writing anti-drug stories that appeared in *The Amazing Spider-Man* vol. 1 #96 through #98, all three of which were published without the code's seal of approval. Shortly after their release, the Comics Code language was revised to allow for the depiction of drugs (though not their endorsement), and other restrictions were sufficiently softened to allow the reemergence of the horror comic into the marketplace (though these titles were known as "mystery" comics, because the term "horror" itself remained *verboten*). In the 1980s the alternative comics market began to flourish in an increasingly unfettered creative environment, with maverick creators such as Frank Miller (*Daredevil*) and Alan Moore (*Watchmen*) responding by pushing the envelope of the mainstream superhero genre and crossing characters over into more mature territory, with more realistic examinations of crime, violence, and the extreme

psychology that motivates costumed superheroes. Again the Comics Code language was modified (in 1989) in order to meet the more liberalized mindset of the late twentieth century.

For many years, it was virtually impossible for comics to succeed in the marketplace without the Comics Code seal, since magazine wholesalers would refuse to distribute comics that did not bear the seal on their covers. However, beginning in the mid-1980s many publishers stopped participating in the CCA, primarily due to the emergence of the "direct market," where comics are sold through comic-book stores, reaching older and more sophisticated demographics than ever before. As of 2004, only two major publishers (DC and Archie) continue to participate in the CCA and to print the seal on CCA-approved covers—though some, like Marvel, have adopted a pro forma rating system on their covers and several companies note which comics are "for mature readers." But even for the holdouts, since the CCA review of content is less stringent than it was during earlier decades, its seal of approval is no longer necessarily an endorsement of the "good taste and decency" it was originally created to uphold. —*GM*

The Creeper

When Steve Ditko left Marvel Comics after a row about the direction of his co-creation, Spider-Man, there was no shortage of publishers queuing up to hire him. In the next couple of years, he produced strips for Dell, A.C.G. Tower (Thunder Agents), Warren, Charlton (where he worked on the Blue Beetle and Captain Atom) and, finally, in 1968, DC Comics. At DC he was given the freedom to create and write new superheroes, and he quickly dreamed up the Hawk and the Dove and the Creeper. From a twenty-first-century perspective, the Creeper appears in many ways to be just a variation on the sort of story that had made Spider-Man so successful, but at the

The Creeper #2 © 1968 DC Comics.
COVER ART BY STEVE DITKO.

wearing an absurd green-and-yellow costume, topped off with a voluminous, red fur collar. Ryder succeeds in finding the Professor, who gives him an instant-healing serum (which also endows him with terrific strength) and a molecular rearranger before (inevitably) being mowed down in a hail of bullets; life for a brilliant scientist tends to be perilous in comics.

In his everyday civilian identity, Ryder was a rather dogmatic, straightlaced person, but in his Creeper guise he became reckless and demented, often terrifying criminals with his maniacal laughter and mad behavior. Consequently, he was as distrusted by a baffled police force as he was by the hordes of the underworld—much as Spider-Man had been, of course. Most of the time, the Creeper was found battling Proteus, an identity-changing criminal with a blank face (like the Spider-Man villain, the Chameleon), but he was also pitted against the likes of the Firefly and the wonderfully christened Yogi Bizerk. Undoubtedly, the comic's major selling points were Ditko's energetic pacing and dynamic drawing, which were the equal of anything on the stands at the time. On the other hand, Ditko's characters appeared to inhabit a strange, timeless world in which people wore berets, Stetsons, or polka-dotted clothes that owed nothing to late 1960s America as his readers knew it.

time it was probably just a little too strange for most comics fans.

The first appearance of the Creeper was in *Showcase* #73 (April 1968), where readers are introduced to manic TV interviewer Jack Ryder, just as he is sacked for haranguing a guest. Newly recruited as a network security agent (a sort of cross between an FBI operative and a TV reporter that probably only existed in the mind of Steve Ditko), Ryder embarks on his first mission—tracking down brilliant scientist Professor Yatz and rescuing him from the clutches of "evil commies." For some reason, these commies throw a fancy dress party, which Ryder crashes

Following its introduction in *Showcase,* the strip went on to six issues of its own title, but then it was to be several years before the Creeper was heard from again. The mid-1970s saw a rash of new Creeper stories in various Batman comics, which revealed that the Creeper had moved to Gotham City. Ditko himself returned to the Creeper for a one-shot in 1975, which was followed a few years later by a longer run in the pages of *World's Finest Comics.* As is often the case, the 1980s and 1990s saw occasional short stories (as a backup in *The Flash,* for instance) and guest appearances culminating in a very eccentric 1990s series. In 2003 a radical reinvention was released, inspiring a new generation of fans. The new comic is set in the art world of Paris in 1925, and features a mysterious female Creeper who is as much cat burglar as superhero. —*DAR*

Cutey Bunny

In *The Great Women Superheroes* (1996), historian and comic-book artist Trina Robbins commented on the uniqueness of heroines who grace the pages of self-published comics. "The superheroines who emerge from the pages of these small-press comics tend to be more original than the bad girl clones or the superteam members put out by larger publishers."

Nothing could be truer for Cutey Bunny. Writer and artist Joshua Quagmire introduced the world's first African-American rabbit superheroine, whose name is a parody of the Japanese manga heroine Cutey Honey, in 1982, when she made her debut in Quagmire's self-published *Army Surplus Komikz* #1. Cutey Bunny is really Kelly O'Hare, a tough-talking army colonel who works as a military recruiter. After stumbling upon an ancient Egyptian amulet, she is magically transformed into the flying super-rabbit. Her mentor is the Egyptian solar deity Ra-Harahkte, who gives the hero her "Solar Scarab" amulet, which funnels his solar energy, giving her the powers of superstrength and flight. He also acts as general checker-upper on "the crime-busting cottontail," who distains the god's interference in her superhero career. Her signature expression: "Gosharooty" (second only to "Jeepers" and "Golly wolly").

Bunny is the queen of superhero costumes. She originally had three different outfits encoded in her amulet: an "Aunt Samantha" superpatriot outfit made of revealing stars and stripes; a "Roller Bunny" outfit, complete with motorized skates; and a "Rocket Bunny" space suit accessorized by rockets, a protective force shield, and ample supply of oxygen. None of these were

Army Surplus Komikz #1 © 1982 Joshua Quagmire.
COVER ART BY JOSHUA QUAGMIRE.

acceptable to the ever-serious Ra, who promptly converted them to an Egyptian get-up by issue #4, which Bunny dismissed in favor of her standard leotard, headdress, boots, and white vest. In body-flattering attire, Bunny battled all sorts of comical supervillains during her short-lived run, including the sinister super-spy fox Vicky and the X-Critters (Cycat, Vermin, Zephyr, Clummox, and Night Toddler), ending her day in her downtown Peoria apartment.

Described in a May 1983 issue of *The Comics Journal* as containing a "good, irreverent sense of comics history, with numerous in-jokes, catchphrases, and cameo appearances," Cutey Bunny drew a cult fan base that appreciated Quagmire's unique take on the funny-animal genre. —*GM*

Cutey Honey

Cutey Honey creator Go Nagai is generally known as the *enfant terrible* of manga and anime. The title is not due to Go's personality, but rather his various projects. Born in 1945, Go first broke into the manga industry in the 1960s working as an assistant to the late Shotaro Ishinomori (1938–1998), of *Cyborg 009* fame. Since his initial foray into manga, Go has had a prolific career, but he is better known for manga with darker, more violent themes (not to mention bizarre, grotesque villains and heroes), such as *Devilman* (1972) and *Violence Jack* (1973–1992), and erotic humor like *Kekko Kamen*. In the 1970s, Go created a new genre with *Mazinger Z*: the "drivable robot," which would become a staple of manga and anime for years to come. (Two very famous titles are 1979's *Mobile Suit Gundam* and 1994's *Neon Genesis Evangelion*.) In 1968, Go's manga *Harenchi Gakuen* (Shameless School) garnered a great deal of attention—most of it negative—because of its bawdy humor and violence in a story whose setting was a high school where students matched wits with their oppressive teachers. Elements of this series would make their way into one of Go's most popular characters—Cutey Honey, one of the earliest female superheroes in manga and anime.

Honey is actually an android. While androids were popular in manga and anime at the time of *Cutey Honey*'s publication in 1971, Go went in a different direction with the character's original storyline. Beautiful Kisaragi Honey was created by Dr. Kisaragi as part of the scientist's plan to create the perfect human. At first, Honey was not aware that she was an android; she believed that she was Dr. Kisaragi's daughter. Because the scientist installed a "transformation module" inside Honey, Dr. Kisaragi became the target of the criminal organization

Panther Claw, and with his death Honey sought revenge. In this original manga, the setting of the story was an all-girls Catholic school. Within this typical theme of revenge, Go created innovations: an all-female Panther Claw gang, with Panther Zora being the leader and Sister Jill as her second-in-command.

As for Honey, her transformation module allowed her to change forms to deal with any situation. The forms included "Hurricane Honey" (a motorcyclist), "Scoop Honey" (a photojournalist), and "Cutey Honey," a warrior mode that she used in battle: a red-haired woman wearing a red one-piece leotard, white collar, and black leggings, accessorized with yellow boots and gloves, and with a sword as her main weapon. To change forms Honey would shout, "Honey Flash!" and change … with brief nudity between forms.

Toei Studios produced an animated adaptation of *Cutey Honey* only in Japan and the series ran from 1973 to 1974. While both the manga and anime were popular—especially among teen boys—Go would not publish a sequel until 1990. Known as *Shin Cutey Honey* (New Cutey Honey), the story started after the end of the original manga: Honey had defeated Sister Jill but Panther Zora had gone into hiding after destroying the headquarters of Panther Claw. Unlike the original *Cutey Honey* manga, *New Cutey Honey* was translated into English and released in the United States by Steve Bennett's Ironcat Studio in 1995 under the title *Cutey Honey '90*. The sequel manga was followed in early 1994 by an OVA (Original Video Animation, direct to video) series with the same title, *New Cutey Honey*. This eight-episode series benefited from better animation and action, and opened several years after the end of the original television series. Go Nagai was also much more involved in the production.

This time, the setting was Cosplay City, and Honey fought the forces of Dolmeck, a villain whose ultimate goal was the resurrection of Honey's old nemesis, Panther Zora.

With new allies like teenager Hayami Chokkei and Mayor Light, Honey also had new forms to change into, including an armored form, and a "Chinese Fighter" form (a parody of the character Chun-Li from the *Street Fighter* videogame series). She also had new enemies, predominantly women and with names such as Death Star and Jewel Princess. One male villain, Virtual Hacker, was a character clearly influenced by the cyberpunk movement that had swept through the science-fiction genre in the 1980s and had a major effect on anime (for example, the film *Akira* and the OVA series *Bubblegum Crisis*).

Houston-based AD Vision began releasing English-subtitled versions of the *New Cutey Honey* OVAs in late 1994, only a few months after their release in Japan; in 1998, AD Vision re-released the series, this time dubbed in English. A dual-language DVD was released in 2000.

The success of the *New Cutey Honey* OVAs led to yet another new direction for the character. In 1997, *Cutey Honey Flash* premiered on Japanese television and ran for thirty-nine episodes, with a movie released the same year. Based on the manga written and drawn by Yukako Iisaka (with the blessing of Go Nagai), *Cutey Honey Flash* retained some elements of the original—Honey's various forms and the Panther Claw gang being two in particular. However, the series was much more influenced by *Sailor Moon* (and was even produced by the same creative staff), and was targeted at a younger audience. Bawdy humor and nudity were removed; the result was a romantic action-comedy. Honey was now a human girl attending a boarding school in Tokyo—magic was now the force behind her transformations. She also had a boyfriend, Seiji Hayami (in the original series, he was a reporter who helped Honey track down the Panther Claw gang). One character, a lecherous old man named Danbei Hayami, was also a main character in the original television series and OVAs. As of 2004, the television series was not released in the United States, but the German SAT-1 network ran the show from 2000 to 2001.

In the United States, Cutey Honey's adventures even inspired one of the best-known anime parodies: Joshua Quagmire's 1982 *Cutey Bunny.* She is also a popular "cosplay" character (a favorite anime or manga character that fans often dress up as) at anime conventions in Japan and the United States. Despite the violence, eroticism, and twisted villains, Cutey

Cutey Honey © 2004 Go Nagai.

Honey still stands as one of Go Nagai's most well-known characters thirty years after her debut. —*MM*

Cyberforce

The brainchild of Image Comics partner Marc Silvestri, Cyberforce is a property owned, produced, and controlled by Silvestri's Top Cow Productions, home of such other high-profile characters as *Witchblade*. Introduced in a self-titled, four-issue Image miniseries (1992–1993), Cyberforce is a group of cybernetically enhanced superheroes that stands ever ready to step into the breach to prevent a rapacious multinational corporation called Cyberdata from dominating planet Earth. While Cyberdata routinely engages in various small-scale illicit activities (i.e., industrial espionage), the company's silicon-chip overlords have a far more pernicious long-term agenda: the extermination of all organic life on Earth.

Formerly captives of Cyberdata, the members of Cyberforce see themselves as the only hope humanity has for freedom and even survival, a scenario that pays homage to the artificial intelligence–dominated future dystopia portrayed in the *Terminator* films as well as to the "once more unto the breach, dear friends" foxhole camaraderie that so often characterized Marvel Comics' X-Men during the 1980s (not to mention the corporate-supercriminal/renegade-former-allies premise of Mark Evanier and Will Meugniot's *DNAgents,* itself an homage to the X-Men on some levels); the mutant abilities of the Cyberforce members also serve to reinforce the Marvel mutant parallel. Rootless, homeless, and forever on the run because of the exigencies of their guerrilla war to liberate Earth, the motley Cyberforce members forge tight emotional bonds from their shared adversity. Because Cyberforce routinely finds itself in pitched battles against such powerful adversaries as Cyberdata's private army of half-human/half-machine S.H.O.C. (Special Hazardous Operations Cyborg) troops, everyone on the high-tech superteam employs various bionic enhancements, including artificial limbs, built-in weaponry, and internal cybernetic sensors and computers.

The initial leader is Dylan Cruise (a.k.a. Heatwave), a former Navy SEAL who is also a cybernetically enhanced mutant with the ability to absorb and release solar energy by focusing it into a coherent beam of superheated plasma, a power that also enables him to fly by riding superheated air currents. Heatwave controls this potent and dangerous power by way of a specially built containment suit, à la the visor used by the X-Men's Cyclops. Unfortunately, the sudden onset of his powers (during his teens) resulted in the death of his brother. Working with future Cyberforce members Cyblade and Stormwatch, Heatwave rescues a fourth superbeing, Stryker, from the clutches of Cyberdata. Afterward the four heroes form the nucleus of Cyberforce. Later, after his daughter Dana is killed by terrorists, Heatwave is captured by Cyberdata, whose Borg-like drones transform him, at least temporarily, into one of their obedient S.H.O.C. troopers.

Morgan Struker (a.k.a. Stryker), an alumnus of the U.S. Special Forces and the CIA, is a brilliant fighter, a talent doubtless enhanced by his one mutant characteristic: He was born with four fully functional arms, each capable of operating independently (thus he is often depicted firing four guns simultaneously). Stryker's artificial eye gives him night vision, as well as the ability to pick up both infrared and ultraviolet wavelengths. The targeting computers built into his body make him formidable indeed, as do the four cybernetic arms he acquires later after losing his organic limbs in combat. After helping establish Cyberforce, Stryker went on to found a spin-off group of mercenary mutants known as Stryke Force, seen in *Codename: Stryke Force* and *Cyberforce, Stryke Force: Opposing Force* (both 1995).

Among the other components of Cyberforce are Dominique Thiebaut (a.k.a. Cyblade, a co-founder of Cyberforce), part of the royal family of the small European nation of Chalenne who possesses the mutant ability to project sharp blades constructed of pure psionic energy; Cassandra Lane (a.k.a. Ballistic), a superhuman athlete and markswoman whose abilities are enhanced by her bionic arm; Carin Taylor (a.k.a. Velocity), a cybernetic mutant able run at speeds in excess of 3,300 miles per hour (she is also Ballistic's kid sister and a former S.H.O.C. troop); Impact, a thick-thewed, ironclad powerhouse reminiscent of the X-Men's Colossus; and Robert Bearclaw (a.k.a. Ripclaw), a technologically augmented (with artificial hands) Native-American mutant able to assume the abilities of various animals (think DC's Animal Man crossed with Sasquatch, Snowbird, and Shaman from Marvel's Alpha Flight) and gifted with the power to receive psychic "impressions" from inanimate objects.

Buoyed by the excitement surrounding the advent of Image Comics, the initial *Cyberforce* miniseries in 1992 proved successful enough to spawn (so to speak) further adventures of Silvestri's cyborg crusaders. A second volume of *Cyberforce* began to appear in 1993, running for thirty-five issues before concluding in 1997. As became customary during the first half of the 1990s, several issues of the series sported covers with collectible "enhancements" such as foil embossing and "gold" and "platinum" inks. The team members' origins were revealed in greater detail in *Cyberforce Universe Sourcebook* (1994–1995) and *Cyberforce Origins* (1995–1996), both from Image Comics. Individual Cyberforce members such as Ballistic, Cyblade, Ripclaw, and Velocity proved popular enough to appear in comics of their own between 1995 and 1997, including several crossovers between Cyblade and popular characters from other publishers: *Cyblade/Shi: The Battle for Independents* #1 (1995, Image Comics); *Shi/Cyblade: The Battle for Independents* #1 (1995, Crusade Comics); and *Cyblade/Ghost Rider* (1997, Marvel Comics).

Like many of the superheroes and superteams introduced during the superhero-comics publishing glut of the early 1990s, Cyberforce faded into obscurity during the subsequent lean years. As to whether or when the team will return, only time—and the future machinations of Cyberdata, Mark Silvestri, and Top Cow Studios—will tell. —*MAM*

Daredevil I

Lev Gleason Comics, which developed under the guidance of Leverett "Lev" Gleason and Arthur Bernhardt, was one of the most remarkable companies of comics' Golden Age (1938–1954) both in terms of its success and its approach to its titles. Both Bernhardt and Gleason were avowedly left-wing publishers with strong socialist roots and a pronounced concern for civic values. They also oversaw one of the real powerhouse publishing houses of the 1940s, with sales of its big three titles—*Daredevil, Boy Comics,* and *Crime Does Not Pay*—in the millions. Unusually, for much of the 1940s the company resisted the temptation to expand its line, concentrating instead on producing high-quality comics, though by the early 1950s it had diversified into the Western, romance, and humor genres. Just as Lev Gleason was one of the decade's most successful comic-book companies, it was also among the most controversial, reviled by critics for the brutality and sadism of its comics and accused of being a communist sympathizer.

In its early days, the company went through several names (Your Guide, Rhoda, and Comic House) and several editors (including future Plastic Man artist Jack Cole). Its flagship title in 1939 was

Silver Streak Comics, an unremarkable effort enlivened only by a strip, drawn by Cole, about a monstrous villain called the Claw. Things picked up in issue #6 (September 1940) with the introduction of Daredevil, by the Jack Binder studio and Don Rico. Daredevil's origin seemed to owe more than a little to the recently released Batman strip: Rendered mute by the shock of seeing his parents killed, Bart Hill builds himself up into a strong, fearless fighter to avenge the wrong done to him. Inspired by a boomerang-shaped scar on his chest (which has been branded by his parents' killers), the young lad practices with a boomerang for years until he becomes a deadly master with the weapon (shades of the Batarang). In a somewhat implausible twist, when Hill dons his Daredevil costume he miraculously regains the power of speech.

With little to differentiate it from its many rivals, the Daredevil strip might have faded into obscurity except that editor Cole had other ideas. With issue #7, he took over the feature and reintroduced a memorable villain. Sensing that his terrifying Claw (a giant, yellow-skinned creature of the night with monstrous talons and teeth) needed a worthy opponent, Cole pitted him against Daredevil in a five-issue epic that thrilled his readers. In issue #7, Cole also redesigned Daredevil's costume into a split red-and-blue bodysuit with a spiked belt and a face-covering cowl, and he ditched the mute ploy. Daredevil would go on to star in *Silver Streak* until issue #17, his later tales being illustrated by Don Rico, but before that his publishers had other plans for the hero.

Enraged and affronted by the rise of Adolf Hitler and the terrifying war in Europe, Gleason and Bernhardt were determined to battle fascism the only way they could, and so pitted their top hero against Hitler himself. *Daredevil Battles Hitler* came out in July 1941, five months before the United States entered the war, and launched the boomerang-toting superhero into a fifteen-year solo career. Initial strips were fast-moving affairs, filled to bursting with such villains as the Ghoul, Professor Venom, the Wizard, Fu Tong and, inevitably, the Claw again. Token girlfriend Tonia Saunders was the *de rigueur* damsel in distress. By this point, the feature was being produced by Charles Biro and Bob Wood, who were elevated to joint editorship by the comic's eleventh issue and immediately overhauled its content and direction, deleting most of the title's backup features.

Charles Biro was a limited, if energetic, artist but a sensational writer, and under his direction *Daredevil, Boy,* and *Crime Does Not Pay* (as *Silver Streak* was renamed) were transformed. In *Daredevil* #13, Biro introduced a gang of teenage runaways, the Little Wise Guys—Scarecrow, Pee Wee, Jock, and Meatball—and the strip began to revolve around their adventures. The new strips were incredibly wordy, dense morality tales, frequently dealing with the problems of youth and small-town life that were absolutely engrossing. Reflecting the social concerns of Gleason and Bernhardt, Biro dealt with such issues as crime, juvenile delinquency, alcoholism, child abuse, and doomed romance with gripping energy and a surprising candor. Never afraid to break with convention, Biro killed off one of the Little Wise Guys (Meatball) in issue #13, and replaced him with Curly.

Daredevil was soon given a new name, Bill Hart, and (in issue #18) a new origin, in which he was orphaned by an evil uncle and brought up by aborigines in Australia; it was they who taught him his prowess with the boomerang. During the World War II years, Daredevil and his gang fought the occasional Japanese invasion force but mostly concentrated on homegrown black-marketeers and hoods, in strips very similar to *Crime Does Not Pay,* the company's biggest seller. However, as the Little Wise Guys grew in popularity, Daredevil became increasingly a spectator in his own comic and, by issue #69, he was gone for good—with the exception of a couple of bizarre appearances in issues #79 and #80 where he and the Wise Guys flew to Mars! Biro handled much of the writing himself, with some help from Robert Bernstein, while the artists were Norman Maurer, William Overgard, Al Borth, Tony Dipreta, and others. Biro wanted his strips to look a particular way—as little use of black as possible, to leave the artwork open for the maximum amount of color—and so there is no mistaking one of his strips. His stories were very distinctive as well, full of well-developed, complex characters, convincing dialogue and satisfying plots, and it is no surprise that his comics were so popular.

Lev Gleason comics were among the most criticized of the 1950s, and commentators frequently complained that they glamorized crime, citing numerous examples of violence, sadism, and cruelty. The comics were certainly uncompromising, but Gleason's motives were more honorable than his detractors gave him credit for. Nevertheless, he gave up publishing for good in 1956, with the final issue of *Daredevil* (#134) nestling on the newsstands next to DC Comics' *Showcase* #4, which heralded a new era of superheroics, the Silver Age of comics (1956–1969). Had Daredevil returned to his own title, he might well have enjoyed a great comeback along with the rest of *Showcase*'s heroes, but by that point he was long gone. In recent years, Ace and AC Comics have published a few vintage *Daredevil* reprints (with AC even reviving him for occasional outings under the copyright-secure name of "Reddevil"), but for most fans the character's original name belongs to a more well-known superhero published by Marvel Comics. —DAR

Daredevil II

Daredevil, "The Man without Fear," was the last new major Marvel superhero to come out of the comic company's burst of creativity in the 1960s. It took more than fifteen years for the superhero to become a real fan favorite, but he has enjoyed many fine periods since his introduction. The first Daredevil issue appeared in mid-1964 and the character was the first of Marvel's heroes to be created without the input of either super-artists Jack Kirby or Steve Ditko, but he clearly owed a debt to one of writer/editor Stan Lee's biggest successes, Spider-Man. In a story drawn by veteran comics artist Bill Everett, readers were introduced to a wisecracking, yellow-costumed hero with a big "D" on his chest who swung around the New York City skyline, searching out trouble with his "radar sense"—a scenario that fans of the legendary web-slinger would have found all too familiar. But what differentiates Daredevil from his more famous inspiration is that he has a significant handicap: He is blind.

Daredevil's origin, recounted in that first issue, tells of how put-upon bookworm Matt Murdock is blinded by a radioactive canister while rescuing a blind man from the path of an out-of-control truck from the Ajax Atomic Labs. Young Matt, nicknamed "Daredevil" by his high-school tormentors as a jab at his straggly physique, is the son of washed-up boxer "Battling" Jack Murdock, then on this way back to the big-time through the help of a crooked promoter known, rather suspiciously, as the Fixer. Throughout high school and college, Matt builds himself up physically, aided by his heightened senses (a side effect of the accident that more than compensates for his blindness) and, when his dad is killed after refusing to throw a fight, he dons a costume and becomes Daredevil, vowing to bring his father's killers to justice. In addition to his "razor sharp"

Daredevil #181 © 1982 Marvel Comics.
COVER ART BY FRANK MILLER.

senses that can hear someone else's heart beating, never forget an odor once it is smelled, tell how many bullets are in a gun by its weight, and distinguish color by its feel, Daredevil's innocent-looking blind man's cane contains a grappling hook and cable for scaling walls. On being confronted by the imposing figure of Daredevil, the Fixer promptly dies of a heart attack, so establishing early on the terrifying effect the hero has on criminals.

The first issue also established the strip's supporting cast: Murdock's partner in his law firm, Franklin "Foggy" Nelson, and their beautiful blonde secretary Karen Page; thus was the classic love triangle set in place. Over the following decade, Lee and other writers built up a formidable and bizarre rogues' gallery for Daredevil, including the Owl, Mr. Fear, Stiltman, the Gladiator, the Ox, Kilgrave the Purple Man, the Jester, and Leapfrog, among many others. The strip also boasted some of the finest talents in comics, including Wally Wood (who introduced Daredevil's famous all-red costume in issue #7), John Romita, and Gene Colan, who would draw the feature well into the 1970s. In typical Marvel fashion, where Daredevil was a fast-talking joker, Murdock was tortured and morose, petrified that his secret identity would be discovered and unable to reveal his true feelings to his seductive secretary. Indeed, to cover up his secret life as a costumed hero, Matt created a fictitious twin brother, the obnoxious egomaniac Mike Murdock, whom he impersonated for almost two years. Throughout the deception, Foggy and Page were convinced that Mike was actually Daredevil but by the decade's end Matt finally revealed the truth to Page, who promptly fled to Los Angeles to become an actress.

Throughout the early 1970s, Daredevil acquired a new love, ex-KGB agent and slinky superheroine Natasha Romanoff, a.k.a. the Black Widow, and the pair relocated to swinging San Francisco. After four years of well-crafted crime fighting, including a period when the Widow received equal cover billing, the pair split, with Murdock returning to Foggy in New York and Romanoff joining the short-lived supergroup the Champions. While by no means one of Marvel's top-selling titles, the comic of this period was nonetheless invariably one of the company's most readable books, with consistently fine art from Gene Colan, Bob Brown, and rising star inker Klaus Janson. One 1976 issue (#133) even guest-starred celebrity paranormalist Uri Geller, but a more significant development was the introduction two months earlier of the deadly sureshot villain Bullseye, who could make literally anything into a weapon.

In 1979, *Daredevil* issue #158 saw the introduction of a promising young artist by the name of Frank Miller. He took over scriptwriting two issues later, transforming the comic into a fan favorite and changing its direction forever. Miller's art was both cinematic and atmospheric, with a terrific knack of grabbing the reader's attention and not letting go. Miller's first act as writer was to introduce a mysterious female assassin called Elektra, a deadly Ninja-trained bounty hunter working for the evil Kingpin. But, to confuse things, she had also been Murdock's first love and, over the course of the next few years, their complicated and deadly fascination with each other inspired a fanatical following. What had once been just another comic to most readers was now unquestionably the most talked-about title in the United States. Miller became the first creative star of the 1980s and the strip's searing, dark, violent, explosive direction was mimicked across the comics industry.

From issue #168 to his last hurrah in issue #191, Miller wove an ongoing, elaborate saga involving the Kingpin, Elektra, assorted Ninjas, an increasingly psychotic Bullseye, and numerous lowlifes and gangsters. In his hands (aided greatly by the talented Janson), New York became almost a character in its own right, with Miller delighting in delineating its totemic water towers, forests of skyscrapers, and fetid backstreets. He also greatly expanded the feature's supporting cast, introducing the chain-smoking *Daily Bugle* reporter Ben Urich (who guesses Daredevil's true identity) and the blind derelict known only as Stick, a Zen master who had tutored the teenage Murdock in developing his heightened senses. In the course of the epic, Bullseye went mad and Elektra was killed off, although in a final act Miller resurrected her, much to fans' relief. Elektra's popularity inspired a wildly well-received 1986 miniseries written by Miller and painted by Bill Sienkiewitz, and as of 2004 nine dif-

Opposite: From *Daredevil* #220 © 1985 Marvel Comics.

FOG.

YESTERDAY, A WARM AIR MASS ORIGINATING IN THE CARIBBEAN SUDDENLY VEERED NORTH AND WITHIN HOURS MOVED INLAND TO NEW YORK, WHERE IT TOUCHED THE COLD CONCRETE OF THE WINTRY CITY.

THE RESULT? FOG. THE WORST FOG THE CITIZENS OF NEW YORK CAN REMEMBER.

A CHILLY, ALMOST IMPENETRABLE MIST, THIS FOG -- ONE THAT DEADENS SOUND AND SMELL AND, OF COURSE, MAKES THE HUMAN EYE NOT MUCH MORE THAN A JELLIED MARBLE.

DAREDEVIL DOESN'T CARE ABOUT THAT. HE HASN'T USED HIS EYES SINCE HE WAS BLINDED IN A CHILDHOOD ACCIDENT YEARS AGO. AND HE DOESN'T REALLY REQUIRE HIS EARS AND NOSE, EITHER, NOT USUALLY. HE HAS WHAT HE CALLS HIS RADAR AND THAT'S NEARLY ALWAYS ENOUGH.

ferent Elektra titles (including reprints and mini-series) have appeared.

In 1983, Miller moved over to DC Comics, where he would create another of the decade's standout titles, *The Dark Knight Returns* (also with Janson's inks); Marvel found him a hard act to follow. In time, another emerging artist, future *New Yorker* star David Mazzuchelli, joined the title and soon began to make waves with a beguiling combination of Colan's fluidity and Miller's atmospherics. An increasingly popular run was capped in 1986 by the return of Miller on scripts, resulting in the "Born Again" storyline (in issues #227–#233), which, if anything, surpassed the comic's earlier triumphs. The story saw the return of the long-forgotten Karen Page, now a faded starlet and abject drug addict, who had sold Daredevil's secret identity for the price of a "hit." In the coming months, the Kingpin systematically destroyed Murdock's career, reputation, friendships, and almost his life, but salvation appeared in the form of a nun who rescued the derelict and dying hero. The story's denouement reunited a drug-free Page with Murdock, revealed that the nun was in fact his long-lost mother, and established a new life for America's favorite hero, helping the poor of New York's Hell's Kitchen.

In an ideal world, the comic would have ended there—as close to perfection as any superhero comic has a right to be—but, of course, with high sales and an enthusiastic readership, that was never going to happen. Miller and Mazzuchelli left to create the legendary *Batman Year One* series, and their successors have effectively based their work on this period ever since. In 2003, the live-action feature film *Daredevil* was released to strong box-office and general critical acclaim, particularly from fans who hailed it as one of the most convincing superhero films to date. The film starred Ben Affleck as Daredevil and Jennifer Garner as Elektra; with a supporting cast of Bullseye, the Kingpin, Foggy, and Ben Urich, it is very much based on Miller's vision of the comic.

In the post-Miller era, Ann Nocenti (one of comics' most notable female writers) teamed up with artist John Romita Jr. (whose father had made his Marvel debut with Daredevil some two decades earlier) for a long run on the comic. Nocenti introduced another female assassin, the schizophrenic Typhoid Mary, brought back the Kingpin, and pitted Daredevil against Marvel's own version of the devil, Mephisto. That team's successors, Dan Chichester and Lee Weeks, revisited the "Born Again" era, right down to the comic's artwork, Murdock's mental breakdown, and the villainy of the Kingpin (yet again). In the 1990s, readers were presented with more mental breakdowns, a new Kevlar-armored costume, the return of the hero's mother, his old costume, a brief stint with the secret organization S.H.I.E.L.D., and Daredevil's old pal Stick. By this point, Miller's reinvention of the hero as a dark, tormented, unstable character had permeated the industry to such an extent that strips as diverse as Aquaman, Green Arrow, and Ghost Rider had been given a makeover, and Daredevil was now just one of the crowd.

In 1998, after 380 issues, Marvel decided to relaunch the strip from #1 as part of its more mature Marvel Knights line, and recruited cult film director Kevin Smith as writer and soon-to-be new Marvel boss Joe Quesada on art. Smith and his successor Brian Michael Bendis have succeeded in making fans sit up and take notice by introducing a new twist—possibly unique in the genre—of revealing Daredevil's secret identity to the world. Following an unsuccessful coup attempt against the Kingpin (him again!), former deputy Mr. Silke turned himself in to the FBI, revealing to them the one bargaining chip he had: the knowledge that Matt Murdock is Daredevil. Within a day, news leaked out to the *Daily Globe,* which splashed the revelation to a startled nation. Murdock and Foggy Nelson (who learned of Murdock's secret some years earlier), back together again as law-firm partners, responded with a $400 million lawsuit, but no one was convinced by their denials. With Bendis and the photo-realistic Alex Maleev creating riveting stories and a strong fan following, *Daredevil* has once more become one of the industry's most innovative and talked-about comics. —*DAR*

Daredevil in the Media

Prowling the night, he lives in a world of shadows. Matt Murdock may be a crusading lawyer by day, but when the lights go out, it's time for him to turn vigilante as Daredevil, the "Man without Fear." And although Murdock is blind, his hyper-senses allow him to fight crime with a kind of radar that might make him see just a bit better than his enemies. Daredevil first burst onto the comics page in *Daredevil* #1 (August 1964), co-created by Stan Lee and Bill Everett. Although his costume was originally a garish red-and-yellow creation, it quickly became a sleek red bodysuit.

Daredevil's first media appearance was actually just a glimpse, and not even of the real hero. In the debut episode of 1981's *Spider-Man and His Amazing Friends,* Daredevil's is one of the outfits briefly seen at a costume party. It was his only appearance on television in the 1980s, even though Daredevil's main adversary the Kingpin would bedevil Spider-Man on this series and a concurrent syndicated *Spider-Man* series.

During 1984, Marvel Productions planned a *Daredevil* animated series, and ABC announced it on their fall schedule in Hollywood trade newspapers. Dick Sebast was the producer, but early script development had details such as a van with a cannon-catapult, which Daredevil used to shoot himself to the scene of crimes! When the network wasn't wild about the show's direction, Mark Evanier was brought aboard to rewrite the pilot script, jettisoning the objectionable material. He kept Murdock's seeing eye dog ("Lightning the Super Dog," according to

promo art), but turned the plot more toward the lighthearted crime-fighting stories presented in Daredevil's 1964–1965 adventures as drawn by Wally Wood. Despite the ABC announcement, *Daredevil* didn't make the schedule after all, the victim of company politics.

It was not until 1995 that Daredevil made his real animated debut. In the second-season opening episode of the syndicated *Fantastic Four* (FF) series in 1995—titled "And a Blind Man Shall Lead Them"—Daredevil and Murdock were voiced by Bill Smitrovich, and the hero helped the FF fight master villain Doctor Doom. In September 1996, Daredevil made two appearances in the third season of Fox's animated *Spider-Man* series. In chapters 6 and 7 of the "Sins of the Fathers" storyline, Murdock helps clear Spider-Man of murder charges, while Daredevil helps him fight crime. Edward Albert voiced Murdock/Daredevil, while Roscoe Lee Brown was Wilson Fisk/Kingpin. Those episodes, along with the *Fantastic Four* story, were collected as a *Daredevil vs. Spider-Man* DVD in 2003.

Daredevil made his first live-action appearance in May 1989 in the NBC telefilm *Trial of the Incredible Hulk*. That project, written by Gerald DiPego and directed by Bill Bixby, reunited the cast of *The Incredible Hulk* TV series in a storyline in which David Banner (Bixby) is accused of assaulting a woman on a subway. When he goes to trial, he seeks the help of blind attorney Murdock (film and Broadway star Rex Smith). After Banner "Hulks out," the Hulk (Lou Ferrigno) and Daredevil take on the criminal Wilson Fisk (John Rhys Davies).

Trial was meant as a backdoor pilot to see if NBC wanted to commit to a *Daredevil* TV series. The storyline was fairly faithful to the comics origins of "hornhead," but fans weren't happy that Daredevil's costume was significantly altered. Instead of red togs, the crime fighter wore an all-black outfit that looked more suited to ninja-wear than superhero-ing. At least he still had his radar sense and all-purpose billy club.

Jennifer Garner (Elektra) and Ben Affleck (Daredevil) duel in a scene from *Daredevil*.

In March 2002, shooting began on a *Daredevil* feature film, from New Regency Enterprises and Twentieth Century Fox. Longtime *Daredevil* fan Mark Steven Johnson both scripted and directed the film, concentrating on the comic's origin story and Frank Miller's Bullseye-Elektra storyline (1979–1983), as well as elements from more modern storylines. The plot finds Daredevil (Ben Affleck) up against Kingpin (Michael Clarke Duncan), who had hired psychotic assassin Bullseye (Colin Farrell) to kill the father of Elektra (Jennifer Garner).

The film featured bravura fight scenes and a stunning visualization of Murdock's radar-vision. Fans appreciated the red leather costume that was fairly faithfully realized, as well as the peppering of cameo appearances from real-life comics creators Stan Lee, Frank Miller, and Kevin Smith. Affleck had

little to do but look grim in the Daredevil costume, but as Murdock, he played blindness credibly and presented a sympathetic man who retained a sense of humor despite being physically tortured due to his punishing good deeds. Less popular with fans was the reimagining of Kingpin as an African-American villain instead of a Caucasian crime lord, and the lack of traditional costume for either Elektra or Bullseye. Instead of Elektra's red (or white) ninja gear, Garner wore dark leather, while Farrell's Bullseye traded in blue-and-white tights for a tank top, trenchcoat, and tough-guy forehead scar. Few quibbled with the acting talents of Duncan, Farrell, and Garner, however, with each filling their role—as written—nicely, and reflecting elements of their comics characterization.

While critics gave *Daredevil* a mixed reception, the public liked the film, giving it a record opening weekend in February 2003 and a $102-million-plus domestic box office take. Duncan reprised his role (in voice only) as Kingpin in an episode of MTV's computer-animated *Spider-Man* series in August 2003. Meanwhile, Fox has discussed a *Daredevil* animated series, and deals have been signed for development on a sequel for *Daredevil* and a stand-alone *Elektra* film, with both Affleck and Garner signed to reprise their roles. Clearly, the "Man without Fear" is also the "Man with a Hollywood Future." —*AM*

Dark Horse Heroes

Mike Richardson, owner of a successful chain of comics shops in the Portland, Oregon, metropolitan area, was dissatisfied with the caliber of material being produced in the mid-1980s, and invested in a highly risky venture: publishing his own comic-book line. Dedicated to producing quality projects with diversified subjects, *and* to giving major publishers Marvel and DC Comics a run for their money, his tenaciously named Dark Horse Comics charged out of the gate in 1986 with its black-and-white anthology series, *Dark Horse Presents* (*DHP*). Paul Chadwick's Concrete and Chris Warner's Black Cross were featured in *DHP* #1, two nontraditional strips featuring nontraditional heroes. True to Richardson's vision, those stories were miles above standard B&W fare and rivaled the quality of the best comic books then being published by the majors. Concrete and Black Cross helped Dark Horse define a template that would direct the path of the company's heroes to follow: a nurturing of creators' visions and a drive to be different.

Richardson, abetted by editorial second-in-command Randy Stradley, expanded the Dark Horse line in the late 1980s with licensed titles, continuing the sagas of Twentieth Century Fox's *Aliens* and

Ghost #2 ™ & © 1995 Dark Horse Comics, Inc.
COVER ART BY ADAM HUGHES.

Predator movies in best-selling comic books. The promise of lucrative royalties lured top talent to this upstart's books, and before long big-name creators anxious to break free of the corporate restraints of Marvel and DC Comics were bringing their personal wares to Dark Horse.

John Byrne, a fan favorite from his work on *X-Men, Fantastic Four, The Incredible Hulk,* and *Superman,* came knocking on Dark Horse's door in 1992 with his original superhero concept, *The Next Men.* This series, an homage to Marvel's *X-Men,* featured a quintet of mutates who flee from the top-secret "Project Next Men" and struggle to adjust to the real world while avoiding their pursuers. Byrne followed his thirty-issue stint on *Next Men* with his short-lived *Fantastic Four* pastiche, *Danger Unlimited.*

Also in 1992, Dark Horse picked up *Grendel,* Matt Wagner's bleak but compelling study of aggression that originated in the late 1980s at Comico the Comic Company, for a lengthy run of irregularly published miniseries and one-shots. On two occasions, Wagner's creation encountered the Dark Knight in DC/Dark Horse *Batman/Grendel* crossovers. *Grendel* is in development as a movie, with a release date yet to be unannounced.

Eccentric cartoonist Bob Burden transplanted his bizarre superhero comic books *The Flaming Carrot* and its spinoff *Mysterymen Stories* to Richardson's company in the mid-1990s. The latter property became a movie produced by Dark Horse Entertainment: *Mystery Men* (1999) featured a band of low-rent superheroes, including Mr. Furious (Ben Stiller), the Bowler (Janeane Garofalo), Captain Amazing (Greg Kinnear), and the Spleen (Paul Reubens). Despite its impressive cast and a wickedly satirical script, *Mystery Men* tanked at the box office. Another established independent superhero series that temporarily relocated to Dark Horse was Mike Baron and Steve Rude's *Nexus,* a critically lauded science-fiction concept—inspired in part by Rude's fascination with the television cartoon *Space Ghost*—which featured the exploits of an intergalactic executioner. Similarly, Mike Allred's snappy beatnik-hero concept, *Madman Comics,* was picked up by Dark Horse in the mid-1990s and stayed there until late 2000.

Creator Mike Mignola's *Hellboy,* the story of an orphaned demon, debuted at Dark Horse in 1994. Mignola's stylish, shadowy rendering and his flair for having fun with dark subjects struck a chord with readers. Numerous *Hellboy* miniseries and specials have appeared, as has some merchandising, and director Guillermo del Toro's live-action feature *Hellboy,* starring Ron Perlman (of TV's *Beauty and the Beast*), was released in April 2004—just in time for the character's tenth anniversary.

Dark Horse had made a name for itself publishing *other* people's characters: creator-owned series and licensed titles (*Godzilla, Terminator, Tarzan, Star Wars,* and other properties joined *Aliens* and *Predator*). When Richardson, Stradley, and their editorial staff decided to produce superhero comics all their own, they were determined to create superheroes unlike any other publisher's.

Dark Horse's first company-owned superhero— the Mask—first appeared in *Dark Horse Presents* #11 (1987), quite early in the company's history. A twisted, graphic melding of Bugs Bunny and the Terminator, the original Mask is actually poor schmuck Stanley Ipkiss, who buys a bizarre ancient mask and gains *Looney Tunes*–inspired superpowers, but uses these abilities to slaughter his tormentors. The Mask made repeated appearances, with other unlucky souls gaining the artifact and its dangerous properties, before heading to the big screen (albeit in a watered-down, family-friendly incarnation) with *The Mask* (1994), a film co-produced by Richardson, with Jim Carrey in the lead. *The Mask* was a summer box-office hit, and an animated series and loads of action figures followed.

Brand-new superhero universes flooded comics shops in the early 1990s, the result of a speculator-fueled sales boom. Dark Horse entered this competition for market share in 1993 with its boastfully named "Comics' Greatest World" (CGW), which situated new heroes in four distinctive environments: Arcadia, an art deco–inspired Mecca for mobsters; Steel Harbor, a bombed-out urban landscape overrun by superthugs; Golden City, a picture-perfect megalopolis governed by superheroes; and Cinnabar Flats, the sparsely populated, Southwest desert location of an interdimensional vortex and a top-secret military installation. Sixteen titles (four in each environment), bargain-priced at one dollar each, were released to introduce the cities and their stars.

This baptismal gimmick was succeeded by a quartet of ongoing monthly series, each deeper in content than the standard superfare: *Catalyst,*

Go Boy 7 #1 ™ & © 2003 Dark Horse Comics, Inc.
COVER ART BY FRANCISCO RUIZ VELASCO.

Agents of Change, set in Golden City, dealt with the woes of a utopian gated community, including the U.S. government's suspicions over its autocracy and an influx of persistent would-be immigrants. *X,* the Arcadia title, was a violent study of a lone vigilante's efforts to unravel the city's corruption. *Out of the Vortex,* based in Cinnabar Flats, focused on the dubious motivations of an extraterrestrial called Vortex who emerged from the region's strange whirlpool, as well as the military's efforts to take advantage of alien nanotechnology. Finally, Steel Harbor's *Barb Wire* starred a hard-hitting, motorcycling lady brawler.

Other series and specials were released to help strengthen Comics' Greatest World, featuring super-heroes cut from a more cerebral cloth: *The Machine,* featuring a horrific tech/flesh fusion; *Motorhead,* a heavily tattooed, muscle-bound bar bouncer haunted by voices implanted into his head; *Titan,* an arrogant superman with few mental gifts; *Mecha,* a free-wheeling iron man; *Hero Zero,* a teenage boy who morphed into a Japanese-robot-inspired giant (he even fought the King of Monsters in *Godzilla vs. Hero Zero*); *Division 13,* an *X-Files*-esque task force; *Agents of Law,* a *Catalyst* sequel with Golden City leader Grace deposed from her own city; and *Ghost,* a moody series involving a sexy, gun-toting wraith butchering Arcadia's bad boys.

X, written by Steven Grant, was a modest hit, and Steel Harbor's "babe on wheels" became a movie star—in the ample (and heavily exploited) form of Pamela Anderson—in *Barb Wire* (1996), a poorly received movie borrowing the comic's tag line: "Don't Call Me Babe!" The one success of these Dark Horse heroes was *Ghost.* Initially scripted by screenwriter Eric Luke (*Explorers*) with lushly rendered covers and interior art by comics' most celebrated "Good Girl" artist, Adam Hughes, *Ghost* ran through 2000. Dark Horse produced a Ghost action figure and three crossovers involving the character: *Ghost/Batgirl* (with DC Comics), *Ghost/Hellboy,* and *Ghost and the Shadow.*

Despite Dark Horse's valiant efforts, the comics industry became glutted in the mid-1990s and imploded. After a 1994 attempt to reimagine "Comics' Greatest World" as "Dark Horse Heroes," the titles, save *Ghost,* were canceled, one by one. As a result, Dark Horse continues in the 2000s as a smaller, more tightly run comics machine, counting the *Star Wars* and *Buffy the Vampire Slayer* franchises, *Hellboy,* and American-distributed Japanese manga series like *Ghost in the Shell* as its most successful properties. In 2003, Dark Horse launched a new line of superhero titles under its "Rocket Comics" imprint: *Go Boy 7, Hell, Syn, Galactic, Lone,* and *Crush,* youth-oriented concepts with contemporary themes and in-your-face characters. Given Dark Horse's persistence and flair for originality, Rocket may very well succeed where CGW didn't. —*ME*

Dazzler

Alison Blaire, a young woman with the mutant ability to transform sound into blinding light bursts, holographic illusions, and even intense laser blasts, first flared across the Marvel Comics firmament in late 1979 in an issue of *X-Men* (vol. 1 #130, cover-dated February 1980), the creation of writer Chris Claremont and co-plotter and artist John Byrne. Like most mutants, Blaire's powers do not manifest themselves until her teens, suddenly appearing while she is performing at a high-school dance. Fortunately, Blaire's adolescent audience mistakes her nascent light powers for clever stagecraft. Though her father, Judge Carter Blaire, wants her to pursue a legal career as he did, she enters the world of music instead, using her powers on stage to visually enhance her vocal performances; as during her high-school years, the adult Blaire's audiences attribute her light shows to special effects. As she matures, Blaire develops her abilities—which, incidentally, are useless in a vacuum, or in the complete absence of sound—into formidable offensive and defensive weapons. Her mutant talents (which account for her stage name Dazzler) eventually attract the attention of the villainous Hellfire Club, whose minions attack her, and the X-Men, who try to recruit her. However, Dazzler doesn't opt to join the team until years later, after going on musical tours during which she finds herself using her powers to thwart various undistinguished criminals.

Also known as "the Disco Dazzler," Blaire represents Marvel's attempt to capitalize on the disco craze of the 1970s, though her debut came a little too late to be anywhere near the "cutting edge" of contemporary popular culture. But Dazzler proved popular anyway, and this success prompted Marvel to place the character in her own self-titled monthly series, beginning with *Dazzler* #1 (March 1981),

written by Tom DeFalco with pencils by John Romita Jr. This series was destined to change the face of comics forever—though this was more due to the book's marketing than to its content.

Throughout the mid-1970s, the vast majority of new comics sales occurred on newsstands. But as the decade wore on, news vendors began seeing comics as less profitable than other periodicals, causing steady declines in sales. Meanwhile comics shops across the United States—mostly subsisting from the sales of back issues—had been clamoring to Marvel and DC for new comics made strictly for the comic-shop market (or "direct-sales market," as it is usually called inside the industry). Taking a cue from small upstart publishers such as Pacific Comics—who sold its publications to comics stores at unprecedented deep discounts but also adopted newsstand-antithetical nonreturnable terms—Marvel made its new *Dazzler* title exclusive to the direct market, racking up an impressive 428,000 in sales for the premiere issue. Although newsstand sales remained Marvel's bread and butter for the next several years, *Dazzler* had put the writing on the wall in great, glowing letters: The direct-sales market was here to stay. By the end of the decade, upwards of 5,000 comics shops were thriving across the country, dwarfing Marvel's flat newsstand sales.

Although Dazzler's best days were rather quickly behind her—sales of her series' debut issue may have been inflated somewhat by collector speculation, and the series went bimonthly in 1983 before expiring with its forty-second issue—the character soldiered on, struggling to adapt to changing times. Reinventing herself periodically in Madonna-esque fashion, she redesigned her costume several times, taking her musical career in a more relevant (for the 1980s, at least) techno-pop direction. In the 1984 graphic novel *Dazzler: The Movie,* writer (and Marvel editor-in-chief) Jim Shooter sent Alison Blaire to Hollywood, where a crooked producer named Roman Nekoboh (strangely, that's "Hoboken Namor" spelled backward) takes advantage of her both personally and professionally; instead of benefiting from having starred in a career-boosting biopic, Blaire finds herself "outed" as a congenital super-human, her show-business career essentially destroyed by the general public's hysterical hatred of mutants.

During the late 1980s, Alison rebuilds her life while living and training with the X-Men, under whose tutelage she greatly refines her powers. She meets and falls in love with the extradimensional mutant entity known as Longshot during this time, but fails to kindle a satisfying relationship with him right away because of his romantic tone-deafness, as it were. In the early 1990s, Dazzler is killed during a battle against anti-mutant forces in Dallas, Texas, only to be restored to life by a sorceress named Roma—who confers upon her the dubious "gift" of causing others to lose their memories of her, and gives her a vampire-like inability to be recorded on audio, video, or film; this development is an anathema for one who seeks show-biz immortality.

After helping Longshot rid his other-dimensional realm of Mojo, its tyrannical ruler, Blaire finally settles down with Longshot on his homeworld. Tragedy strikes soon afterward, however, when Longshot goes missing after a battle, and she miscarries his child; a second Mojo reconquers Longshot's world (which is destroyed soon thereafter), forcing Blaire to flee to Earth. As the new millennium dawns, Dazzler is once again a solo act, trying to reconstitute her life and musical career and proving herself to be one of Marvel Comics' most tenacious survivors. —*MAM*

DC Comics

"An adventurer, an author, a teller of tall tales, a dreamer, and perhaps a bit of a rogue, Major Malcolm Wheeler-Nicholson was the individual who created the comic book as we know it today," observed writer Les Daniels in his book, *DC Comics: Sixty*

Years of the World's Favorite Comic Book Heroes (1995). Nicholson, a former cavalry officer, drew from his military experiences when penning fiction stories in the late 1920s and early 1930s for a pulp magazine whose name would soon bear great significance for him: *Adventure.*

In February 1935, the indomitable Nicholson published *New Fun,* a collection of all-new comic strips in a comic-book format. Reprints of strips had been previously collected by other publishers, but *New Fun* was the first *new* comic book. The major's company, National Allied Publications, soon added to its roster *New Comics,* but before long changed the series' titles to *More Fun Comics* and *New Adventure Comics,* respectively.

Comic-book publishers trickled into existence in the mid-1930s. One of them, Harry Donenfeld and Jack Liebowitz's Detective Comics, Inc., partnered with Nicholson's National in 1936, ultimately buying out the major's interest the following year. By endorsing his check, Major Malcolm Wheeler-Nicholson was transformed from an influential innovator to a footnote in the annals of comics history; few readers or fans are aware of his valuable contributions and, stated Daniels, "He died, all but forgotten, in 1968."

THE COMING OF SUPERMAN AND BATMAN

This new publishing house lived, however, and grew. Now officially called National Comics, but better known as "DC" (for Detective Comics, its flagship series), DC produced anthology series that delivered short stories bristling with verve but lacking identifiable characters. When Liebowitz assigned editor Vin Sullivan the start-up title *Action Comics,* the search began for a headlining character.

A young collaborative team from Cleveland, Ohio, writer Jerry Siegel and artist Joe Shuster, had been producing strips for DC's *More Fun* and *New Adventure.* Their labor of love, a brightly garbed champion with amazing powers they called Superman, had earlier been rejected by newspaper syndicates but seemed right for DC's new title. Placing Superman—effortlessly heaving a sedan over his head—on the cover of *Action Comics* #1 (June 1938) was a wise move for DC: This assertive image was unlike anything the comics audience had ever seen. In the History Channel's documentary *Comic Book Superheroes: Unmasked* (2003), filmmaker Kevin Smith remarked, "I'll never have anything approaching the level of the sense of wonder that those first kids who opened up *Action* #1 had." The first costumed superhero was born.

And so was an industry. *Action* sold phenomenally well, and competitors instantly materialized with inventive successors and transparent replications of DC's "Man of Steel." Instead of plagiarizing its own character, DC chose, with its second major superhero, to create the antithesis of Superman. *Detective Comics* #27 (May 1939) introduced the Batman, a grim vigilante created by artist Bob Kane, abetted by writer Bill Finger. With his foreboding guise (chosen to "strike fear" into the hearts of the "cowardly lot" of criminals) and violent methods (Batman killed gangsters early on), the Batman was comics' original anti-hero.

TRAILBLAZER OF THE GOLDEN AGE (1938–1954)

The Batman's gruesome methods made publisher DC nervous, and soon the hero's edge was softened by the addition of the first-ever superhero sidekick: the "laughing young daredevil" Robin the Boy Wonder, heralded as "the sensational character find of 1940" in his *Detective* #38 debut (April 1940). The Batman, shadowy avenger, became Batman, costumed crime-fighting mentor and patriarch.

In the late 1930s, DC formed an alliance with M. C. Gaines' All-American Publications (AA), with Gaines' titles bearing DC's imprint. Gaines published several series that initiated the next wave of superheroes who would become DC Comics mainstays: "The Fastest Man Alive," the Flash, and the winged hero Hawkman first appeared in *Flash Comics* #1 (January 1940), and the power ring–wielding Green Lantern bowed in *All-American Comics* #16 (July 1940). Gaines was instrumental in two other important DC milestones: the creation of comics' original super*team,* the Justice Society of America, in *All Star Comics* #3 (Winter 1940), and the birth of the most popular and enduring female superhero, Wonder Woman, in *All Star* #8 (December 1941–January 1942). DC and AA temporarily parted company in 1944, but by the following year DC had purchased Gaines' properties.

DC, like other American comics publishers, enlisted its superheroes in the war effort during World War II—even before the United States officially entered the conflict. Siegel and Shuster were commissioned by *Look* magazine to prepare a two-page comics story called "How Superman Would End the War," which was published on February 7, 1940. The tale depicted the Man of Steel corralling the "power-mad scoundrels" Adolf Hitler and Joseph Stalin and dropping them off in Geneva to be tried. After the bombing of Pearl Harbor, pro-Allied propaganda became common in DC's titles, particularly on its covers: Batman and Robin sold bonds, Hawkman dropped a bomb on Japan while signing "V for Victory" to the reader, and the Justice Society delivered food to the "starving patriots" in occupied Europe.

DC SUPERHEROES CONQUER POPULAR CULTURE

The Man of Steel became a media sensation in the 1940s. The Fleischer animation studios produced a celebrated series of seventeen *Superman* cartoon shorts beginning in 1941, and the hero spun off into a radio drama, a long-running newspaper strip, and two live-action movie serials. The hero was heavily merchandized throughout the decade, in figurines, board games, puzzles, and other novelties. Superman also moonlighted in product endorsement, pitching everything from Kellogg's Pep cereal to Conoco "N-tane" gas. Other DC stars shone in the media—Batman and Robin starred in two serials and a short-lived comic strip, while Congo Bill, the Vigilante, and Hop Harrigan appeared in movie serials of their own. Yet no DC character of the era could hold a candle to Superman: The Man of Steel was the man of ubiquity.

Once World War II ended, America's love affair with superheroes similarly died, and caped crusaders crashed and burned as quickly as they had premiered a few years prior. By the end of the 1940s and into the 1950s, only Superman, Batman, and Wonder Woman remained in print in their own titles, with a few "B" players (Superboy, Aquaman, Green Arrow and Speedy, and a few others) visible in backup stories. DC pursued new genres in the 1950s: Westerns, funny animals, science fiction, horror, combat, romance, teen- and kid-oriented humor, and even celebrity tie-ins (comedians Jerry Lewis and Bob Hope had their own DC comics for years). With the burgeoning medium of television competing for the attention of comics' young audience, sales slipped. "It was a *real* tough time," penned editor Mike Gold in his introduction to the DC Comics collected edition, *The Greatest 1950s Stories Ever Told* (1990).

Psychologist Fredric Wertham made it even tougher. In his contemptuous book *Seduction of the Innocent* (1954), Dr. Wertham condemned comic books as a gateway to juvenile delinquency and sexual immorality, charging that Batman and Robin were gay and that Wonder Woman was a "frightening image for boys." His book leveraged U.S. Senate hearings against the entire comic-book industry, resulting in the implementation of a censorship board called the Comics Code Authority. Most of DC's content had been innocuous enough to emerge unscathed, but Batwoman and Bat-Girl were introduced to skirt any inkling of homosexuality between Batman and Robin, and Wonder Woman was recast in a less-threatening manner compliant with patriarchal views of feminine roles.

Throughout this tumultuous decade, Superman held strong. He rocketed to television stardom, portrayed by George Reeves on the syndicated live-action series *The Adventures of Superman* (1953–1957). Superman merchandising marched forward, and his comics franchise expanded. Superman aside, DC's sales suffered.

DC DEFINES THE SILVER AGE (1956–1959)

In 1956, editor Julius "Julie" Schwartz revived the Flash—albeit an updated version in a stylized new costume—in the "try-out" series *Showcase* (#4, September–October 1956). The Flash was a hit, returning for more *Showcase* outings before running off into his own series. The Flash's (re)introduction marked the beginning of what would soon be known as the Silver Age of Comics.

Schwartz similarly reworked Green Lantern beginning with *Showcase* #22 (September–October 1959), then made a courageous next step by reimagining the Justice Society in the form of an all-new Justice *League* of America in *The Brave and the Bold* #28 (February–March 1960). Hawkman and the Atom were also revived, and new heroes like Metamorpho, the Metal Men, and the Teen Titans were introduced. Superheroes became a hot commodity, and once again, DC Comics had defined at trend.

"BATMANIA" SWEEPS THE U.S.A.

In 1964, Batman received a makeover under Schwartz's direction: Silly menaces like space aliens and monsters, which had populated the Batman books with alarming frequency, were discarded and the stories became more science- and detective-oriented. Batman's Batmobile was retooled into a stylized hot rod, and the hero's all-purpose utility belt now housed an arsenal inspired by the gadgets of the James Bond movies.

January 1966 marked a milestone in DC Comics history. The colorfully campy live-action television series *Batman* (1966–1968), starring Adam West and Burt Ward, premiered as a twice-weekly program on ABC and became a runaway hit. With its surfin' score, imaginative sets, frenetic pacing, and celebrity-cast villains, *Batman* commandeered the nation's attention. Hundreds of merchandized items, most authorized but some cheaply pirated, flooded toys stores, magazine racks, record bins, clothing outlets, and grocery marts.

Batman's popularity inspired a fad of serious and satirical superheroes during the mid- to late 1960s. DC's sales improved, especially on its Batman titles. Superman also basked in the glow of Batman's acclaim: Reruns of Superman's 1950s TV show were widely syndicated, a new *Superman* animated program premiered, and a stage musical about the Man of Steel hit Broadway. As with all trends, however, Batmania ran its course: The TV series was canceled in 1968 and DC's sales dropped precipitously. The company was being outdistanced in the marketplace by competitor Marvel Comics.

Not that the DC editors noticed. "We were top dog for so long," reflected longtime DC editor Murray Boltinoff, "we became impervious to any criticism or new ideas. We thought everything we did was right." Readers thought otherwise, preferring the quirky, problem-ridden Marvel superheroes like the Fantastic Four, the Incredible Hulk, and the Amazing Spider-Man.

New management certainly took note, though. Kinney National Services bought DC in 1967, beginning a transformation that would eventually evolve into the Time Warner media conglomerate. Corporate higher-ups initiated DC staff changes. "DC needed a kick in the rump. And they brought me on board to do it," revealed Carmine Infantino, former artist of *The Flash,* in the fanzine *Back Issue* #1 (2003). Infantino was hired first as art director, then promoted to editorial director and later publisher of the DC line. Stodgy literary editors were replaced by editors with artistic backgrounds, like Joe Orlando, Dick Giordano, and

Joe Kubert: "I felt the company needed visual people, because comics is a visual medium," Infantino said. In the late 1960s through the mid-1970s, DC, under Infantino's direction, was reborn.

"KIRBY IS COMING!"

New superheroes that defied DC's traditional mold began to appear, among them, the maniacal Creeper and the argumentative Hawk and Dove, two concepts created by Steve Ditko (former artist of Marvel's *The Amazing Spider-Man*). Batman returned to his dark roots, largely thanks to writer Denny O'Neil and artist Neal Adams, and Superman became hipper, with his alter ego Clark Kent shifting careers from newspaper journalist to TV reporter. "Relevance"—explorations of contemporary themes—became vogue in DC's series: Superheroes Green Lantern and Green Arrow hopped in a pickup truck to tackle racism and corporate fatcats as they "discovered" America; Green Arrow's sidekick Speedy got hooked on heroin; and Wonder Woman lost her superpowers and became a fighting feminist (although in a few years she got her supergroove back and starred in a successful live-action TV series with actress Lynda Carter).

DC reinvented horror comics during Infantino's watch, from anthologies like *The House of Mystery* to the sympathetic monster Swamp Thing, and acquired classic pulp and fiction properties like Tarzan and the Shadow for brilliantly illustrated, critically acclaimed runs. DC also went on a superhero shopping spree, acquiring characters from defunct publishers, most notably the original Captain Marvel, who was reintroduced in *Shazam!* #1 (February 1973); ironically, DC had sued the character, who at one time outsold Superman, out of business in the early 1950s for being derivative of the Man of Steel. Exciting new artists like Bernie Wrightson and Michael Kaluta added fresh visual dimensions to the publisher's titles, and in 1975 the previously unthinkable happened: DC and Marvel joined forces to co-produce a tabloid-sized crossover, the best-selling *Superman vs. the Amazing Spider-Man.*

Infantino also helped recruit Jack Kirby—the artist fundamental to so many of Marvel Comics' successes—to DC beginning in 1970. "My job is to involve the reader," Kirby once asserted, and he did just that with his series of separate but interlocking titles *The New Gods, The Forever People,* and *Mister Miracle,* plus the DC mainstay *Superman's Pal Jimmy Olsen.* Kirby's arrival was trumpeted by house ads announcing, "Kirby Is Coming!" His DC efforts failed to generate substantial sales, however, and disappeared after a few years, with Kirby returning to Marvel.

THE NEW DC

A disagreement with upper management forced Infantino out of his job in 1976, and he was replaced as publisher by Jenette Kahn. Kahn had previously spearheaded three successful children's magazines and was hand-picked by Warner Publishing (then DC's parent company) to steer DC Comics into new territory. While Kahn dropped the company's longtime official name, National Periodical Publications, for its more common name, DC Comics, she got off to a rocky start: A rapid expansion of titles and material (the "DC Explosion") led to a 1977 crash (the "DC Implosion") that put numerous creative folk out of work.

DC got a shot in the arm in December 1978 when *Superman: The Movie* was released. Starring newcomer Christopher Reeve, *Superman* was a box-office smash, and its sophisticated (for the time) special effects helped shape the look of fantasy films that followed. But DC's sales, which had stagnated post-Implosion, experienced little improvement from Superman's star status, and the movie's 1980 sequel didn't help either.

So Kahn, not unlike Infantino before her, targeted quality and innovation as the means to distinguish DC in the marketplace. Giordano returned to DC in 1980, first as editor, then as editorial director, and helped groom new talent and massage existing superstars. Abetted by executives

Paul Levitz and Joe Orlando, Kahn and Giordano recruited cutting-edge British visionaries (like author Alan Moore and artists Brian Bolland and Dave Gibbons), implemented new formats (glossier paper and square-bound "Prestige Format" editions), paid royalties to top-selling creators, and elevated the medium's standards with literate, well-illustrated titles like *Camelot 3000* and *The Saga of the Swamp Thing.*

By the mid-1980s, this "new" DC had revitalized what comics could be: Its landmark *Crisis on Infinite Earths* (1985–1986) streamlined its continuity while garnering strong sales, Frank Miller's *Batman: The Dark Knight Returns* (1986) revolutionized the Batman legend, John Byrne's *The Man of Steel* (1986) reworked Superman for a contemporary audience, and Moore and Gibbons' *Watchmen* (1986–1987) depicted ethically ambiguous costumed characters and illustrated that superheroes weren't just for kids. Marvel Comics still, by and large, commanded a larger market share than DC, but DC established new standards for excellence. Innovative series like Neil Gaiman's *The Sandman* (1989–1996) helped DC explore more adult themes, and such series ultimately splintered from the company's mainstream fare into its own "mature readers" imprint, Vertigo (which has forged ahead into the 2000s with critically lauded series like *Preacher* and *Fables*). DC seemed content with its reputation: Being number two isn't so bad when you are number one in excellence.

A GARDEN OF CONCEPTS AND GIMMICKS

In 1989, DC's parent company shifted from Warner Publishing to Warner Bros., the film and television studio, and DC found itself directed to feed a media machine. Its superheroes have since been regularly translated to film and video. Examples include (but are not restricted to) the live-action movie *Batman* (1989) and its three sequels, TV's *The Flash* (1990–1991), the long-running *Bat-*

man: *The Animated Series* (1992) and its continuations, the romantic action/comedy *Lois & Clark: The New Adventures of Superman* (1993–1997), the teen drama *Smallville* (2001–present), and the Cartoon Network's animated *Justice League* (2001–present) and *Teen Titans* (2003–present) programs. In 2004 a legion of DC superheroes is under development or consideration for TV shows and movies, including a relaunch of the *Batman* film franchise, with actor Christian Bale (*American Psycho*) tapped for the lead.

Perpetuating its long-standing publishing history, the DC Comics of the 1990s and 2000s has struggled to find its niche in the industry, and to profitably sell its wares in the marketplace. Numerous big "events," designed to make noise and attract consumers, have been introduced: the death of Superman (1992), the (back) breaking of Batman in the far-reaching "Knightfall" storyline (1993), more character overhauls in *Zero Hour* (1994), and even more character overhauls in the "Our Worlds at War" serial interwoven through numerous DC series in 2001. Yet while its heroes have been slaughtered, maligned, and mutated in recent years, DC has, as it has always done, taken chances along the way. It is the company that defined the comic book, the superhero, and the medium's potential, and will continue to be a trendsetter into the twenty-first century. —*ME*

Deadman #6 © 2002 DC Comics.
COVER ART BY JOSÉ LUIS GARCIA LOPEZ.

Deadman

Despite never gaining the high sales it deserved, Deadman has been one of the most influential and critically acclaimed characters in superhero comics. Deadman was conceived by maverick writer Arnold Drake in 1967 and first appeared in the pages of *Strange Adventures* #205, in what was to be artist Carmine Infantino's last strip before becoming editor-in-chief of DC Comics. Usually, the tale starts with the death of its star, Boston Brand, a daredevil trapeze artist assassinated by a sniper in the

middle of his act. But death is not the end for Brand, as a disembodied voice (of Rama Krishna, a sort of god) tells him that to avenge his death he must roam the earth in ghostly form until he finds his killer. Unfortunately, the only clue to the killer's identity is that he has a hook on his arm, but Brand now has the convenient ability to enter people's bodies and take them over.

The strip was blessed with an unusual setting—Brand's circus with its colorful performers—an intriguing quest at its heart, and an unconventional, complex hero. Brand was an argumentative, egotistical, and somewhat self-pitying character who, despite his powers and stylish costume (as a ghost, he still wore his acrobat's red high-wire outfit, complete with white death's-head mask), was no better than the reader. In 1967, this was revolutionary content and in retrospect Brand can be seen as the first "mature" superhero. Another revolutionary factor in the strip's critical appeal was the art of Neal Adams, who took over the feature for its second instalment. Adams came to the strip from the world of advertising and newspaper strips, and brought a realism to comic books that had never been seen before. He also had a gift for dynamic drawing and stylish design; Deadman was peppered with pop-art effects and witty in-jokes. In short, this was a very cool comic.

Over the next two years, Deadman roamed the country endlessly, tracking down the Hook in what was very much the comic-book equivalent of the 1960s television show *The Fugitive.* In his travels, he came across supervillains (the Eagle), drug pushers, Batman, and a group of killers called the League of Assassins. The strip's complexity and depth were perhaps too much to take for most readers and, after its twelfth installment, the series was canceled. Undeterred by this, Adams went on to draw further Deadman appearances in numerous comics, including *Aquaman, The Justice League, The Brave and the Bold,* and *Challengers of the Unknown.* Editors finally revealed Deadman's killer to be an assassin in the pay of a mysterious criminal called Sensei, and the pair went on to tangle with each other throughout the 1970s.

While it is true that Deadman was then relegated to a relatively minor status, he nevertheless continued to appear in backup spots in *Adventure Comics* and *Phantom Stranger,* which were notable for their high quality. A 1986 miniseries—the first of six relaunches as of 2004—drawn by José Luis Garcia Lopez (Adams' talented successor on the strip) featured a final showdown with Sensei. The strip showed Deadman finally regaining his human form only to lose it again, vowing to continue his fight against evil, wherever it may appear. For a while later on in the decade, DC repositioned him

as a horror character, now looking more like a living skeleton than a well-toned superhero, but recent miniseries have been very much in the intelligent, elegant tradition of Deadman's early days.

As a commercial project, the strip has never rewarded DC's continued faith in it, though the publisher has repackaged the Adams run on several occasions, as have several European publishers; the feature is highly regarded across Europe. But in introducing the concept of "serious" superhero strips, Deadman was clearly the precursor to the likes of *Watchmen* and *The Dark Knight Returns,* and it is now widely viewed as one of the key strips of the 1960s. —DAR

The Defenders

When is a team not a team? When they are a non-team. That, at least, was the logic behind the Defenders, a grouping of Marvel Comics' misfits, loners, and losers that met with unexpected success and acclaim. Like DC Comics' All-Star Squadron, the Defenders characters sometimes belong to other superhero groups, but can still hold membership within the team; however, most Defenders are offbeat and eternally team-less or series-less characters who unite out of necessity and disband at whim. The seeds of the group were sown in two 1970 issues of *Sub-Mariner* (#34 and #35) by writer Roy Thomas and artist Sal Buscema, in which the Sub-Mariner recruits the nearby Hulk and Silver Surfer to help him destroy a rogue weather-controlling device. Naturally enough, the three "collaborators" end up fighting both each other and the Avengers, but the combination of such seemingly incompatible characters struck a chord with both Thomas and the fans. Later the next year, Thomas brought the Sub-Mariner and the Hulk back together, teaming them this time with Dr. Strange as the group the Defenders for a three-issue run in the new *Marvel Feature* title. As in the Sub-Mariner strip, the three superheroes came together to dis-

Giant-Size Defenders #1 © 1974 Marvel Comics.
COVER ART BY GIL KANE AND FRANK GIACOIA.

pose of an Earth-destroying device, in this case the Omegatron, created by dying sorcerer Yandroth. While they parted company at the end of the first issue, the pattern was set for adventures to come.

Shortly after the third issue of *Marvel Feature,* the Defenders were promoted to their own comic (August 1972), with new writer Steve Englehart and Sal Buscema on art (a role that he would hold for the next forty issues). Almost from the outset, the team members—including a returning Silver Surfer—would come and go, with Dr. Strange operating as a *de facto* leader, while the team used his sanctum sanctorum as their rendezvous point. Issue #4 introduced the first new "regular" team

member, Valkyrie, previously seen in *The Avengers* (as a disguise for a Thor villain, Amora the Enchantress) and *The Incredible Hulk* (in which the Enchantress used an unwitting host body for Valkyrie's persona). The current incarnation's host body was Barbara Norriss, a catatonic ex-cult member. As Valkyrie's warlike and stridently feminist persona asserted itself, the quest for her true identity became one of the comic's central themes.

The Defenders fought a variety of Marvel's stock of villains, including Magneto, the Red Ghost, and Attuma, and they were also part of the first extended inter-title crossover, in the so-called "Avengers/Defenders war," which ran across eight issues altogether. Soon afterward, the group was joined by a defecting member of the Squadron Sinister, Nighthawk, a.k.a. wealthy heir Kyle Richmond, who had drifted into a life of crime to relieve his boredom but who would soon become one of Marvel's most complex heroes.

With issue #20 (1975) and the arrival of eccentric genius Steve Gerber as writer, the comic entered its most memorable era. Gerber pitted the team, now reduced to a nucleus of Hulk, Dr. Strange, Valkyrie, and Nighthawk, against a bizarre group of deviant scientists known as the Headmen. One of these had his head transplanted onto the body of a gorilla, while another's head was a large, ruby-red sphere. Gerber also explored Valkyrie's schizophrenic existence, as her host body's husband, Jack Norris, suddenly appeared looking for his wife. Nighthawk, too, was developed as a character when first his girlfriend lost an arm in an explosion and then his own brain was removed by the Headmen. Indeed, identity (and brains) proved to be a recurring theme of Gerber's tenure, as the brain of Headmen member Chondu was transplanted first into an unsuspecting deer and then into a monstrous harpie's body, while Valkyrie's erstwhile husband Jack ended up in Nighthawk's now-vacant body. Add to the mix a new (female) Russian superhero, the Red Guardian, a celestial mind-control cult called the Bozos, a caged heat–style spell behind bars for Valkyrie, and a murderous elf with a gun, and it's no wonder that fans were by turns amazed, amused, and bemused. Gerber left the comic after issue #41; his successor, David Anthony Kraft, sustained something of its strangeness, but by the turn of the decade it was just another superhero title.

The final twist in the team's existence came in late 1982, when most of the group were jettisoned to make way for X-Men alumni the Angel, Iceman, and the Beast, in a failed attempt to cash in on the X-Men's soaring popularity. The fans failed to take the revamp to heart and Marvel, deciding to stick their lucrative stars into a comic with an "X" in its title, canceled *The Defenders* and created *X-Factor* in its place, leaving Valkyrie, Gargoyle et al. in limbo.

Since that time, two subsequent revivals have emerged, the first of which (in 1993) went back to the comic's original premise of the "non-team" by using "The Defenders" as a catchall title to showcase eclectic or underused superheroes. *The Secret Defenders* was based on Dr. Strange summoning the likes of Wolverine, Spider-Man, and the Silver Surfer to combat various mystical enemies, and ran for two years. The 2000 revival, with long-time fan Erik Larsen providing art and also co-scripting with popular writer Kurt Busiek, returned to the classic lineup of the team's early years and was predicated on frantic action and old-style battles. Neither revival matched the popularity or quality of the Defenders' glory years. —DAR

"Dial 'H' for Hero"

From its inception in January 1966, "Dial 'H' for Hero" has been one of DC Comics' quirkiest features. In fact, it was comics' first interactive strip. Readers were first introduced to young Robby Reed in *House of Mystery* #156, in a story written by Dave Wood and illustrated by Jim Mooney. Soon after moving to Littleville, bespectacled science prodigy Reed discovers a strange-looking telephone

dial while exploring an underground cavern. After decoding a strange inscription on the dial, he finds that it was created by aliens and that by dialing the letters H-E-R-O he is transformed into a superhero. In fact, as the strip's subtitle, "The Boy Who Could Change into a Thousand Superheroes," made clear, Reed became a different hero each time he touched the dial.

Like many of DC's mid-1960s features, "Dial 'H' for Hero" was lighthearted, breezy, and attractively drawn, but what set it apart from its competitors were the various superhero guises dreamed up by DC's writers. These were as wonderfully diverse and bizarre a sequence of characters as the comics world has ever seen. Among other peculiar creations, fans were entertained by the likes of Daffy the Great, the Squid, King Kandy, Baron Buzz-Saw, Robby Robot, Balloon Boy, the Human Icicle, Mighty Moppet (a giant baby), and Plastic Man (who was actually the old Quality Comics hero making his DC debut). After seventeen issues, *House of Mystery* dumped the strip and was converted into a horror anthology. Nothing further was heard of Reed until he filled a guest slot in Plastic Man's mid-1970s revival. This appearance starred an embittered, misanthropic Reed reduced to eking out a living as a writer, but by the end of the issue he seemed to be all right again.

In March 1981 a new "Dial 'H' for Hero" strip surfaced in *Adventure Comics* #479, shortly after being previewed in revised form in *Legion of Super-Heroes* #272. Uniquely for a superhero comic, it encouraged readers (including noted science fiction author Harlan Ellison) to contribute ideas for the various characters. This strip starred Christopher ("Chris") King and Victoria ("Vicki") Grant, high-school students from Fairfax, Virginia, who discovered an old chest in King's attic; in the chest were a watch and a pendant, both bearing dials. It seemed that Reed had at some point dialed D-I-V-I-D-E on his original dial, so splitting it in two. The process also split Reed into two characters: the Wizard (who was good) and the evil Master, who plagued the two

Adventure Comics #482 © 1981 DC Comics.
COVER ART BY CARMINE INFANTINO, DENNIS JENSEN, AND DON HECK.

teenagers until he was reunited with his good counterpart. While never quite as silly as their 1960s predecessor, King and Grant nevertheless had several enjoyably ridiculous incarnations, such as Mister Thin, Thumbelina, Hasty Pudding, Frosty, and Ragnarok the Cosmic Viking.

After *Adventure Comics* became a reprint title in 1982, King moved over to the pages of *The New Adventures of Superboy*, but Grant apparently lost interest in being a hero—though she later improbably joined a cult called the Children of the Sun while her dial was picked up by Hero Cruz. In a series of tales throughout the 1990s in *Teen Titans* and *Superboy & the Ravers*, Cruz tackled the brain-

washed Grant (who had somehow internalized her dial's powers) before she eventually came to her senses. At some point her dial must have been donated to a museum, where it was discovered in the twenty-fifth century by one Lori Morning, who then took it back with her to the thirtieth century (are you following this?), where she joined the Legion of Superheroes. In the fine tradition of the strip, her many heroic incarnations included Star-Spangled Lass, Chiller, Blip, and Blobetta.

After a somewhat fallow period, DC once more revived the concept in 2003, for the first time in its own title—now shortened to *H-E-R-O*. The next recipient of a magical dial was Jerry Feldon, who found it in Scoopers' ice cream shop, where it had been left behind by a mysterious female customer. After a few issues, Jerry passed on the dial to family man Matt Allen, who passed it on to others, and it appears as if this latest series will be the most unpredictable to date. —DAR

Doc Savage

With his rippling muscles, extraordinary strength, and genius-level IQ, he could outrun a horse, dodge a speeding bullet, speak in a myriad of foreign languages, and perform life-saving surgery, and then, after saving the world yet again, he would retire to his secluded Arctic hideout, the Fortress of Solitude. No, this is not a description of Superman but is, in fact, Doc Savage, a hero who predated the Man of Steel by five years and who laid the foundation for the superhero explosion that occurred in 1938 with Superman's arrival. In the wake of their successful *Shadow* pulp magazine, Street & Smith publisher Henry Ralston and editor John Nomaric dreamed up their ideal hero, a cross between Tarzan and Sherlock Holmes, as a sort of counterpoint to the darker, sinister Shadow. They handed over the concept to pulp veteran Lester Dent (writing under the pseudonym Kenneth Robeson), and the first issue of *Doc Savage* magazine hit the stands in March 1933. Sales soon rose to 200,000 per issue; the title was a hit.

Clark Savage Jr. had been raised as the perfect man, a master of all things intellectual and physical, and he was given the nickname "Doc" because of his skills as a surgeon. At a wake to mourn his late father, Doc gathers together five friends—all masters in their respective fields—who swear to maintain his father's ideals of travel, adventure, and punishing evil. The group consists of the dapper Harvard lawyer "Ham" Brooks, the strong engineer Renny, the bespectacled and verbose archaeologist Johnny, the electrical expert Long Tom, and Monk, a cantankerous, ape-like chemical genius whose constant baiting of Ham was one of the feature's recurring themes. Operating out of the 86th floor of a certain New York skyscraper (which closely resembles the Empire State Building), the happy band trek around the globe, from exotic location to hidden tribe to evil genius and back again.

Not content with his imposing physique, bronzed skin, fabulous wealth, and secret hideout, the Man of Bronze was a master inventor, and his stories were chock-full of his super-inventions, including a pocket knife that fired sleep-inducing "mercy" bullets from its handle (since Doc did not believe in killing his enemies), a belt with its own grappling hook, miniature bombs, false fingertips fitted with needles that caused unconsciousness, an Atomic disintegrator, Oxygen pills, exploding buttons, and clothes that either held, or doubled as, weapons. Add to this an array of super-gadgetized vehicles—including his Helldiver, capable of sailing under polar ice—and one can easily see that Doc was indeed a hero to be reckoned with. In the course of their adventures, he and his band encountered all manner of weird and colorful adversaries, including the Black Witch, the Annihilist, the Stone Man, the Vanisher, and the Czar of Fear. Dent's prose was punchy, breathless, and fast-moving; it grabbed the reader and did not let go for a moment. With a contract binding him to an output of 70,000 words a month, Dent himself had to be something

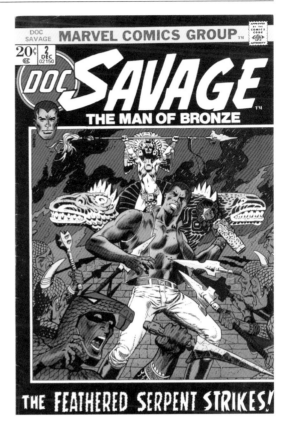

Doc Savage #3 © 1972 Marvel Comics.
COVER ART BY JIM STERANKO.

of a superman! In fact, he not only managed that workload, writing almost every story for 181 issues, but also found time to contribute to other titles to boot. Physically, Dent was an impressive figure—tall, strong, a member of the Adventurers' Club—as well as being a diver, a magician, and a sailor with his own yacht, and so it is not hard to see Doc Savage as an extension of Dent's own persona.

Street & Smith was quick to exploit Doc's popularity with a fan club, portrait, lapel pin, and his own short-lived radio show in 1934. However, when Superman and his hundreds of followers appeared on the newsstands, sales of pulps were gradually hurt across the board, since they largely shared with the new comics the same young readership. Street & Smith itself entered the emerging comic-book market in 1940, only a few months after Marvel and Fawcett, with *Shadow Comics,* which also featured a strip version of Doc Savage, drawn by Maurice Gutwirth. This backup strip lasted five issues but, even before it ended, Doc had emerged in his own comic (in May 1940). Early episodes closely followed the pulp stories, but with issue #5 of *Doc Savage Comics* (August 1941) the Jack Binder studio reinvented the pulp magazine hero into a superhero: Doc acquired a Tibetan sacred hood, armed with a "miracle-working ruby" that could deflect bullets and hypnotize his foes. This bare-chested, hood-wearing superhero (for such he now undoubtedly was) was known as Doc Savage—the Invincible (often simply referred to by his new name, the Invincible); unfortunately, in sales terms he was certainly not the latter, as the comic folded after a mere twenty issues, in 1943. Nevertheless, the superhero makeover of the character continued on in a 1943 radio show.

Returning to the back pages of *Shadow Comics,* Doc's comics adventures continued until that title's demise in 1949, though in those strips he was once more just plain Doc. Doc's comic strips were written by Otto Binder, among others, and were drawn initially by his brother John's studio, though later by Al Bare and Bob Powell. Just as *Shadow Comics* was canceled in 1949, so too was its pulp equivalent, and Doc's pulp magazine as well. The comparison between the demise of the pulp heroes and comics' own superheroes, most of whom had been canceled by the end of the decade, is a fascinating one. Clearly, both were fulfilling the same need for heroes, first during the Great Depression and then later during World War II—a need that apparently no longer existed in a postwar era. Then, just when superheroes experienced their extraordinary rebirth in the 1960s, so too would Doc Savage rise again.

In 1964, Bantam repackaged the first of Lester Dent's Doc Savage stories in paperback. More books followed, and in time the new paperback series became a publishing phenomenon, eventually reprint-

ing all 181 original stories and adding new ones by Philip José Farmer and fan/historian/comic writer Will Murray. With sales running into the tens of millions, it is no surprise that comic-book companies soon took notice, and a Gold Key one-shot comic duly appeared in 1966. Marvel was next in line for the license, releasing two well-crafted series: first a color adaptation of various Dent stories (eight issues, 1972–1974) and then an all-new black-and-white magazine by Doug Moench, John Buscema, and Tony Dezuniga (eight issues, 1975–1977), which has come closest to capturing the spirit of the pulps. A couple of fanciful crossovers also saw Doc and his chums guest-star with Spider-Man (*Giant-Size Spider-Man #3,* 1974) and the Thing (*Marvel Two-in-One #21,* 1976).

The increased interest in Doc Savage as a hero also came to the attention of George Pal, who produced a 1975 movie starring Ron Ely. Critics found the film to be cinematically appealing and Ely the perfect Doc; however, many mentioned its weak script, the tone of which veered dangerously close to camp. Longtime fan and artist Jim Steranko also weighed in with a new fan club, the Doc Savage Brotherhood of Bronze. By the end of the decade, only the paperbacks were left, but in recent years a succession of comics publishers—DC, Millennium, Innovation, and Dark Horse—have released their own versions of the great man. Most of these have been relatively true to the character's pulp roots. DC's 1988 series brought him forward to the present and also featured a crossover with the Shadow. In 1995, Dark Horse Comics released *The Shadow and Doc Savage* miniseries, which has proved to be his last comics outing as of 2004. However, it is undoubtedly true that his legacy lives on to some degree in each and every superhero comic published today. —*DAR*

Doctor Strange

What started as a small backup strip in a 1963 issue of *Strange Tales #110* soon blossomed into one of the cult characters of the decade—one who has been a cornerstone of the Marvel Comics universe ever since. Magicians had been a staple of comics ever since Mandrake in the comic strips of the 1930s and Zatara in *Action Comics* #1, but Doctor Strange potently mixed his sorcery with the energy of superheroes to create something unique. His origin story, however, could have come out of the pulps: Vain, egotistical neurosurgeon Stephen Strange injures his hands in a car crash and winds up on skid row with the other outcasts. In a last-ditch search for salvation, he travels to Tibet to find the fabled "Ancient One" who he hopes will heal his hands. On finding the old sage, he becomes his acolyte and (as each cover proudly proclaimed) "Master of the Mystic Arts!"

Under writer Stan Lee and artist Steve Ditko, Doctor Strange was a strip unlike any other, as the hero traveled to other dimensions and fought unique villains like Nightmare, Eternity, and the dread Dormammu. References to such wonders as the Eye of Agamotto and the Great Book of the Vishanti hinted at almost unimaginable wonders. Lee kept the stories punchy, exciting, and enjoyably florid, while Ditko summoned up inventive images and unique visions that still look innovative today.

Doctor Strange, his acolyte and girlfriend Clea, and his faithful servant Wong operated out of their Gothic "sanctum sanctorum" in the heart of New York City's Greenwich Village, soon to be the epicenter of the city's emerging counterculture. By the time of 1967's summer of love, the Doctor Strange strip had been widely adopted by the hippie movement, and its spells and alternate realities were widely believed to resemble LSD trips. Strange appeared on Filmore Ballroom concert posters and even on the covers of Pink Floyd albums. He was, in effect, the psychedelic superhero—except, of course, his creators were middle-aged professionals with years of comics work behind them, and Ditko in particular was known for his conservative views and distrust of hippies.

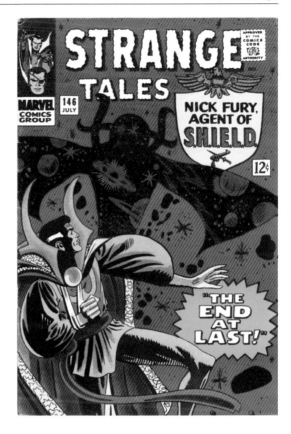

Strange Tales #146 © 1966 Marvel Comics.
COVER ART BY STEVE DITKO.

In 1968, despite Ditko's departure, Doctor Strange was given his own title. His new artist, Gene Colan, produced hallucinatory layouts that were even more experimental than his predecessor's. There was a brief, last-ditch attempt to make Strange more superhero-like by giving him a mask, but it would appear that the character was becoming too far-out for a mass audience. Rather than have a useful character languish in obscurity, Strange was eventually teamed with those other Marvel nonconformists, the Hulk and the Sub-Mariner, as the Defenders. Throughout the 1970s and intermittently ever since, the Defenders have been a newsstand staple and, with Doctor Strange taking a leading role, interest in the sorcerer was rekindled.

Initially in *Marvel Premiere* and then (from 1974 onward) once again in his own comic, Doctor Strange was used by new writer Steve Engelhart as a vehicle to examine the interest in spirituality, self-exploration, and consciousness-raising that was then in vogue. Among all manner of cosmic, surreal adventures, the most extraordinary storyline culminated in Earth's destruction and, one second later, recreation, leaving the almost omnipotent Strange as the planet's only "original" inhabitant. Engelhart left after a couple of years, but the comic continued to be one of the more literate titles in Marvel's line-up for the rest of the decade. Evidently, as readers had grown up with their comics, the more introspective and thoughtful Doctor Strange stories resonated with their maturity. Presumably among those more mature readers were the television executives who commissioned a well-received made-for-TV movie in 1978, aptly titled *Doctor Strange*. Starring Peter Hooten, John Mills, and Jessica Walter and written and directed by Phillip DeGuere, the movie was very true to the spirit of the comic (indeed Frank Brunner, one of the main artists in the comic's revamp, contributed design work to the project), despite changing Doctor Strange's costume. In 1979, Pocket Books published William Rotsler's Doctor Strange novel, *Nightmare*.

In the more materialistic 1980s, on the other hand, there was apparently no place for subtlety or introspection, and so Strange spent much of that decade in cancellation. A revival in 1988 was characterized by an almost constant procession of changes, including Strange being stripped of most of his powers, losing one eye, and abandoning magic only to return to it three issues later. Many 1990s issues were filled with monsters and vampires, and the comic became affiliated with Marvel's hard-hitting "Midnight Sons" storyline. Later innovations, including a completely new Doctor Strange, failed to prevent the comic's cancellation. Doctor Strange has kept appearing, if sporadically, ever since—in a

miniseries for Marvel's mature-readers Marvel Knights line; as a benign spirit in the grim future fable *Earth X* and a cold manipulator in the otherwise upbeat alternate-future MC-2 line; in a short-lived, tongue-in-cheek *Defenders* revival; and as an aide to the Thunder God in the macabrely humorous *Thor: Vikings* miniseries; and elsewhere—which shows Marvel's fondness, if not always the market's enthusiasm, for this unusual character. —*DAR*

Do-It-Yourself Heroes

True to its favored theme of alien planets and parallel dimensions, the field of major superhero publishers has a parallel world all its own, in the output of fanzines, small-press ventures, and self-published writers and artists. Though this world is best known for autobiographical cartooning by quirky outcasts (Phoebe Gloeckner, Daniel Clowes), offbeat fairytale fantasy (Linda Medley's *Castle Waiting*), and other individualistic exceptions to the entertainment mainstream, fan and indie publishing has seen its share of costumed adventurers.

Some of these, like Kevin Eastman and Peter Laird's mid-1980s Teenage Mutant Ninja Turtles, grow into long-running mass-media phenomena, or, like Sara Dyer's mid-1990s Action Girl, hold on as cult empires in an era more hospitable to alternative media. Others, like Biljo White's mid-1960s The Eye and Richard "Grass" Green's contemporaneous Xal-Kor, the Human Cat, remain under-the-radar legends, staying in print through niche publishers like Hamster Press and TwoMorrows and (in The Eye's case) even attracting famous professional talent (including writer Roy Thomas and artist Dick Giordano) to work on occasional stories. Still other small-press publications have presented the pros with an outlet from mainstream restrictions, as with Spider-Man co-creator Steve Ditko, who debuted his controversial moral-absolutist hero Mr. A in the late 1960s "prozine" *Witzend* and (with Robin Snyder) self-published other abstract ethical heroes in a late 1990s string of black-and-white trade paperbacks.

No less impressive do-it-yourself stars have emerged at the turn of the new century. Perhaps the only superhero strip ever to win the respected Xeric Grant (given to help finance first-time self-publishers in the comics field), *The Myth of 8-Opus* is a gripping, pulpy outer-space saga written and drawn by Tom Scioli. It ran for five issues from 2000–2001, attracting guest contributions from industry pros along the way, and continues in a series of graphic novels.

Writer-artist Glenn Whitmore bypassed the periodical route and went straight to the trade paperback graphic-novel form for his Captain Clockwork concept in *Chronicles* (2002), the story of a dynasty of time-manipulating heroes that takes in the style and sensibility of various eras in comics history. Like Scioli, Whitmore has found work in the majors while continuing to publish increasingly popular material on his own.

One of the most charming and literate of the do-it-yourself superheroes is *Dr. Speck* by pop painter and Adelphi University art professor Geoff Grogan. Produced in the mid-1990s, the comic concerns the misadventures of a creature of unstable atomic structure who is capable of Plastic Man–like transformations—and an outlandish sense of humor reminiscent of that classic character's stories. The good Dr.'s comics are as malleable as his body, ranging from a children's storybook style recalling *Tin Tin in Tibet* to hallucinatory episodes evoking Terry Gilliam's animations for Monty Python. It is just one of many convincing examples that, beyond the boundaries of most readers' known comics universe, the do-it-yourselfers know what they're doing. —*AMC*

Doll Man

Although it is rarely mentioned today, the comic books of the 1930s were dominated by newspaper strip reprints, in titles such as *Famous Funnies* and *Ace Comics*. It was the extraordinary impact of Superman that concentrated publishers' minds on the financial benefits of creating new heroes that they would own themselves. Neophyte publisher and owner of Quality Comics Everett "Busy" Arnold was enjoying reasonable success with *Feature Comics,* which was stuffed cover-to-cover with newspaper reprints, but he wanted a chance at the sort of big money that Superman's publisher, DC Comics, was making. Arnold called up the Eisner/Iger comics studio and demanded a hero of his own. Their response was Doll Man, the first in a long line of Quality heroes that would include Plastic Man, Uncle Sam, Blackhawk, Kid Eternity, the Ray, and many more. Doll Man premiered in *Feature Comics* #27 in December 1939 and was only the twelfth superhero to appear on the shelves, beating such bigger names as Captain Marvel, the Flash, and Captain America to the punch.

Studio co-owner Will Eisner himself dreamed up the character, possibly with some input from Arnold, and was no doubt inspired by the tiny Lilliputians from *Gulliver's Travels.* Eisner recruited one of his top artists, Lou Fine, to draw the tale over his layouts, and the result was some of the most handsome art of the era. Publishers were keen to get straight to the action in those days, and there was little room for introspection, but even by the standards of the late 1930s the Doll Man's origin was disappointingly slight.

Brilliant young scientist Darrel Dane creates a super-formula that shrinks him down to a height of just five inches. After drinking it to save his girlfriend, Martha Roberts, from hoodlums, Dane decides to take up life as a caped crime fighter, proclaiming, "From now on, I shall be known as Doll Man, and I pledge myself to fight crime and evil relentlessly." But he doesn't need an antidote to resume his normal size, he simply "wills" it. As the "World's Mightiest Mite"—complete in a blue bodysuit-like costume that boasts bare arms and legs, a short cape, and pixie boots, worn under his street clothes—Doll Man is ready to go. By way of compensation for his diminutive size, Doll Man packs a mean punch and is able to sneak up on villains unannounced, hiding in pockets, bags, boxes—or on cats! Magically, he also gains the telekinetic power to slow moving objects.

Within a couple of issues of the arrival of Doll Man, Arnold lost the rights to many of his newspaper strips, so Doll Man was promoted to cover star and Quality Comics changed its direction for good, switching over to superhero production with gusto. Fine drew the feature for eleven issues and was soon followed by his only real rival at the time, Reed Crandall (who would go on to draw *Feature Comics* #44–#63). Crandall was, if anything, an even better draftsman than Fine, being a master of anatomy, mood, and action. Given the strip's excellent art, it is no surprise that Doll Man was soon given his own quarterly title, which hit the stands in winter 1941. With Crandall busy with Blackhawk, other artists were brought in, including Mort Leav, John Cassone, and Rudy Palais, but it was Al Bryant, Quality's most prolific artist, who drew the bulk of the strips for the rest of the 1940s. Eisner soon left the scripting chores to other hands, including Joe Millard and William Woolfolk.

Most Doll Man stories began with the pipe-smoking Dane relaxing with his girlfriend Roberts and her inventor father Dr. Roberts in their front room. Invariably, the radio would announce some heinous crime and Dane would rush out, shrink, discover the evildoer, and dispatch him—all within ten pages. Over the course of fourteen years, Doll Man encountered an impressive array of villains, including Iron Mask, the Storm, Fat Catt, the Vulture, the Brain, the Phantom Duellist, and Pluvius the Storm Maker. In the 1940s these could be fairly brutal encounters and the miscreants rarely reappeared for a second thrashing, most of them having been callously and fatally disposed of by Doll Man. However, two notable returnees were the dapper, pint-sized Tom Thumb and the "Lord of the Plunder-world," the Undertaker—a theatrically sinister foe who slept in a grave.

The year 1949 was something of an *annus horribilis* for superheroes, witnessing Doll Man replaced in issue #140 of *Feature Comics* by the woefully banal Stunt Man Stetson. Unusually, however, Doll Man's own title was to run for four more years, and there were even a couple of new additions to the comic's supporting cast. First up (in *Doll Man* #31) was a rather pathetic-looking stray mutt called Elmo, which Doll Man befriended and transformed by means of some sort of ray into Elmo, the Wonder Dog, an extra-strong, super-intelligent, crime-fighting canine! Not content with that, six issues later the cast was joined by Doll Girl, a.k.a. Martha Roberts, who had finally acquired the knack of thinking hard enough to shrink. Her red costume was a skimpy counterpart to Dane's blue one and certainly added a touch of glamour to the strip, but perhaps it all came a little too late and *Doll Man* was canceled with issue #47, in 1953.

Quality Comics sold its heroes to DC Comics a few years later, but the company must also have sold some old printing plates to I.W. Comics, as that company brought out a series of Doll Man reprints in the early 1960s. It took DC a long time to realize the potential of the Quality heroes but, following a couple of appearances in the Justice League of America in 1973, Doll Man eventually emerged as one of the Freedom Fighters in 1976, along with Uncle Sam, the Ray, Human Bomb, Phantom Lady, and the Black Condor. Sadly, that group's comic was not a success and the Doll Man returned to obscurity, possibly for the very good reason that DC had a tiny superhero of its own. During the mania for revivals that characterized the early stages of the Silver Age (1956–1969), artist Gil Kane had remembered Doll Man and suggested that DC resurrect its old Atom character as a shrinking superhero. By the 1970s, therefore, DC already had its Atom—and indeed had seen his solo title canceled—and probably saw no point in publishing

Doll Man. Whether or not he surfaces again is anyone's guess. —DAR

Doom Patrol

It's asking a lot of a comic to star "the world's strangest heroes," but the Doom Patrol has delivered on that promise not once but twice. The veteran creative duo of writer Arnold Drake and artist Bruno Premiani introduced the team in the pages of DC Comics' *My Greatest Adventure* #80 (in mid-1963). Their first story relates how the wheelchair-bound genius Niles Caulder (also called "the Chief") summons "three victims of a cruel and fantastic fate" to his brownstone to offer them the chance of adventure—and superhero status. The three are: actress Rita Farr, who, after being affected by volcanic gas, is able to assume a large or small size (Elasti-Girl); Larry Trainor, a test pilot who is doused in cosmic rays, gaining an "energy double" made of negative energy—though this can only survive outside his body for sixty seconds (Negative Man); and Cliff Steele, a daredevil racecar driver whose brain is transplanted by the Chief into a robot body following a cataclysmic crash (Robotman—no relation to the Golden Age [1938–1954] character of the same name).

Drake conceived the team as a response to such emerging Marvel Comics superheroes as the Fantastic Four, which emphasized characterization over the convoluted plots that were then DC's stock-in-trade. In fact, the Marvel superhero team and comic that the Doom Patrol most closely resembled was the X-Men, which shared its lineup of bitter outsiders under a wheelchair-confined leader, a secret hi-tech hideout, and arch-villains with similar names (the Brotherhood of Evil for Doom Patrol, the Brotherhood of Evil Mutants for the X-Men). Indeed, to compound the similarities, Drake would later move to Marvel to write—you guessed it—the X-Men comic. Significantly, however, it was the Doom Patrol that came first (by three months), though, while

Doom Patrol #96 © 1965 DC Comics.
COVER ART BY BOB BROWN.

both strips developed a committed readership, it was the X-Men, of course, that proved the more enduring of the two.

Back in 1963, however, the Doom Patrol comic soon proved popular and, with its 86th issue, *My Greatest Adventure* was retitled *The Doom Patrol,* and ran under that name until issue #121 five years later. The strip had an air of sophistication about it, thanks to Drake's well-rounded characterizations and Premiani's accomplished, European-flavored draftsmanship, which set it apart from its rivals. The lineup was augmented by bizarre figures such as Mento, the wealthy Steve Dayton, who built himself his own (ludicrous-looking) mind-reading hairnet; and the green-skinned Beast Boy, who could change into any animal (and who later joined the Teen Titans). Villains, too, were included in abundance, including the immortal (and very wrinkly) General Immortus; Videx (a giant with see-through skin); an enormous walking jukebox; and assorted monsters and mutants. The aforementioned Brotherhood of Evil was a motley crew consisting of the Brain (who was just that—a brain), the shape-changing Madame Rouge, and Monsieur Mallah, who was a sentient gorilla.

In time, Mento and Elasti-Girl married, and then adopted Beast Boy, while Madame Rouge fell in love with the Chief, but the comic was perhaps too strange for some readers and cancellation became inevitable. The last issue ended with the group sacrificing themselves to save a village, and they stayed dead for a decade but, when DC's *Showcase* comic was revived in 1977, so too was the Doom Patrol. It seemed that Robotman had somehow survived the explosion that killed his teammates, and he joined up with a new group of young outsiders: Tempest, Negative Woman (no relation), and Celsius, who turned out to have been married to the Chief (not that anyone knew). This new team starred in a mere three issues of *Showcase* and had to wait another ten years before being heard of again, when a new Doom Patrol comic premiered in 1987.

This second run reintroduced the original Negative Man, Larry Trainor, and in due course the Chief reappeared, so that only the unfortunate Elasti-Girl seems to have perished back in the 1960s. A couple of years into their new comic, the Doom Patrol acquired a young British writer, Grant Morrison, and became stranger than ever, picking up a more mature, cult audience in the process. Morrison introduced Crazy Jane, a schizophrenic with sixty-four different personalities, while Trainor fused with his energy being and an unfortunate nurse to become the radioactive Rebis. The cast of villains now included the Brotherhood of Dada, the Beard Hunter, and Danny the Street, who was—yes!—a sentient street. For almost four years, Morrison

dreamed up some of the strangest and most imaginative comics ever seen, which managed the seemingly impossible task of combining traditional superheroes with surreal plots and serious topics, such as child abuse. After Morrison's departure, the comic carried on in much the same vein but without his spark of inspiration, and it was canceled with its eighty-seventh issue—nevertheless an impressive run for such a left-field title. —*DAR*

Dr. Fate

Like his fellow supernatural hero, the Spectre, Dr. Fate was born and canceled during World War II, but endless revivals have kept the character in the public eye for decades. Dr. Fate first appeared in May 1940 in *More Fun Comics* #55, under the hands of journeymen creators Gardner Fox and Howard Sherman, and was DC Comics' eleventh superhero (although by this point magicians of various descriptions were already a staple of comic books). With his blue-and-yellow bodysuit and his identity-concealing golden helmet, he was one of the more striking heroes of the time—albeit a rather impersonal one, with his face permanently covered. Dr. Fate was Kent Nelson who, at the age of twelve, had stumbled across some ancient Sumerian ruins while exploring with his archaeologist father. An escaping gas killed the father but the son awakened an ancient energy being called Nabu, who infused him with power, causing him to grow to instant adulthood, and equipping him with mystical artifacts: a helmet, an amulet, and a cape.

Back home in the United States, Nelson's power was almost limitless, which made his initial adventures somewhat predictable; after all, there can be little suspenseful drama if you know that your hero will always be victorious. This deficiency was partly addressed halfway into the character's career when his helmet was shortened, apparently limiting his powers to a degree, but coming up with suitably powerful villains was always a problem for his writers. In his civilian identity, Nelson operated out of an eerie-looking brick tower in Salem, Massachusetts, and courted the society beauty Inza Cramer. In an unusual twist, Nelson soon revealed his secret identity to Cramer, and he later married her. Like most of DC's main heroes of the period, Dr. Fate was inducted into the Justice Society and starred in their first eighteen adventures but, after the cancellation of his own strip in 1944, he was soon removed from the Society, too.

Despite Dr. Fate's early years being generally unexceptional, when the Justice Society was revived in the 1960s the character became an integral part of the group and took part in almost all of their regular Justice League crossovers until the mid-1980s. When *All Star Comics* was brought back in the 1970s, Dr. Fate was in action again and he featured in most succeeding Justice Society outings. In the years since the war, comics had increasingly embraced powerful mystical heroes, and Dr. Fate's cosmic abilities were more and more in keeping with what the fans had come to expect. A 1976 one-shot, drawn by Walt Simonson, was particularly well received (and has been reprinted periodically ever since) but readers had to wait another twelve years before Dr. Fate was given his own title, and by then the helmet already had a different occupant.

This new Dr. Fate was, in fact, two people: ten-year-old Eric Strauss and his stepmother Linda, who merged to become one person; Kent Nelson was reduced to being their mentor. After a couple of years, the mantle of Fate was passed on to Nelson's wife Cramer, as the writers began to develop the idea that the spirit of Nabu, which was what had given Dr. Fate his (or her or their!) power, resided in the helmet and other artifacts—so almost anyone could take over the role. Cramer's Dr. Fate seemed as interested in urban renewal and ecological matters as fighting demons or sorcerers, so there was no place for her in the "nasty nineties" and she was replaced by the character's fourth incarnation.

Jared Stevens was a treasure hunter who found Dr. Fate's helmet, and was thereby summoned back to the tower in Salem. When the tower was destroyed in a mysterious explosion, the various artifacts became merged with Stevens, while Nelson and Cramer disappeared in a puff of smoke. Stevens became, simply, Fate. That the old helmet was now transformed into a dagger was symptomatic of Stevens' unlikeable personality, and few mourned when his incarnation of the character was short-lived. After three years in the wilderness, Fate reappeared in the first issue of a 1999 Justice Society revival, only to be killed off immediately; in a telling editorial comment, he was dispatched with his own knife. However, the comic's next few issues were devoted to the search for a new host for the spirit of Nabu, and in a mind-bogglingly complex plot twist the Silver Scarab (from Infinity Inc.), son of the first Hawkman, was summoned from a dream realm, reincarnated as a newborn baby, suddenly transformed into a fully grown adult, and inaugurated as Dr. Fate the fifth! This latest version of Dr. Fate continues in the pages of *Justice Society of America,* but it would be a reckless fan who would bet that he will be the last. —*DAR*

Dragon Ball

Journey to the West is one of the most beloved tales of China. Based on a novel said to have been written by Wu Cheng'en (1500–1582), the tale recounts the story of Sun Wu Kong (known as the Monkey King) and his companions—Zhu Ba Jie, the pig-headed monk; Sha Seng; Xiao Bai Long, the Dragon Horse; and the monk Tang Seng—as they search for sacred Buddhist writings to bring them back to China. Born from a large stone egg, Wu Kong has simian features such as a tail and an anthropoid face. He is also a mischievous troublemaker who brings chaos to heaven and hell until he is punished by being imprisoned under a mountain for five hundred years. Released by Buddha to help Tang Seng on his quest,

Dragon Ball Z Part 5 #4 (2002) © BIRD
STUDIO/SHUEISHA, Inc.
COVER ART BY AKIRA TORIYAMA.

Wu Kong agrees, but must wear an iron crown on his head; the divinity Kuan Shi-Yin places this upon Wu Kong's head—and if the Monkey King would return to his former ways, a spell would constrict the iron crown. Wu Kong travels long distances on a white cloud; he is also a shape-shifter. A Taoist monk taught Wu Kong the martial arts, and he has an indestructible quarterstaff that can grow to any length upon his command.

The story of *Journey to the West* is called *Saiyuuki* in Japan, and Sun Wu Kong is called "Son Goku." The tale has been used as the basis for many popular manga and anime in Japan; it is well

known throughout Asia. Dr. Osamu Tezuka (*Astro Boy*) and Buichi Terasawa (*Cobra*) are two examples of manga artists who created stories based on *Saiyuuki*. In Terasawa's case, he used a few elements from the story and placed them in a twenty-first-century setting in his cyberpunk manga *Midnight Eye Goku.* A most recent example is the 2000 manga and anime *Gensomaden Saiyuuki.*

The most famous—and most popular—adaptation of the Monkey King legend is Akira Toriyama's manga *Dragon Ball* (1984–1995), which was serialized in *Shonen Jump* magazine (*Shonen Jump* is targeted at teen readers). Known for his 1980 hit manga *Dr. Slump* (which also spawned a successful animated series and movie) and his designs for the videogames *Tobal No. 9* and *Chrono Trigger,* Toriyama not only used many elements from *Saiyuuki,* he also combined science fiction and superhero action (and sometimes destruction on a massive scale). The *Dragon Ball* manga spawned an even more popular animated television series that ran for 250 episodes; seventeen movies; an incredible amount of merchandise; and fans from all around the world. The manga went on to become the best-selling book in the world. *Dragon Ball* and its animated version (which was titled *Dragon Ball Z* after episode 153) have been translated into many languages, and have a large following in the United States.

Toei, one of Japan's oldest animation studios, produced the animated series with Minoru Okazaki and Daisuke Nishio directing the episodes. A sequel series, *Dragon Ball GT,* began running on Japanese television in 1996, after the end of *Dragon Ball Z,* but it ended in 1997, and only had peripheral involvement by Toriyama.

Dragon Ball follows the adventures of Son Goku, a kindhearted—but somewhat naïve—fourteen-year-old boy. Goku has a tail, and knows little about his past; he was raised by the kind Son Gohan, and Goku refrains from killing. Found by a young woman named Bulma, Goku begins a journey to help her find the seven glass spheres known as the Dragonballs.

THE SUPERHERO BOOK

The objects are scattered around the world, and when all are brought together, they can summon the dragon Shen Long, who will grant the holder of all seven Dragonballs a single wish. Joining Goku and Bulma are Oolong and Yamcha, plus Yamcha's cat partner Puar (who is a shape-shifter). The group is aided by Master Roshi, known as the turtle hermit, and along the way encounter Krillin, a martial artist. The main antagonists are the Emperor Pilaf and the Red Ribbon criminal organization.

It is here that one can find similarities between Goku and Wu Kong. Both have tails. While Goku does not transform into many forms, he does change into a gigantic ape during the full moon; only when his tail is removed does the transformation end. Both travel on a white cloud—in Goku's case, it was given to him by Master Roshi; only someone who is pure of heart can ride the cloud. Unfortunately, Master Roshi's lecherous ways prevent him from doing so. Goku and Wu Kong each wield extending, indestructible fighting staffs. Bulma, Oolong, Yamcha, and Puar—Goku's companions—are parallels to the four companions of Wu Kong.

Dragon Ball Z can be called the second stage of Goku's life; several years have passed, and Goku is now a young man, happily married to his wife Chi-Chi and father to Gohan and Goten. What is more evident are the parallels with American superheroes, especially Superman. Goku finds out that he is the last—or one of the last—survivors of an alien race known as the Saiyans; he was sent to Earth in a spaceship. His son Gohan also has Saiyan blood, and both undergo intense training—as a result, both can transform into "Super Saiyans"; their hair turns gold and they become far more powerful. Many more enemies and allies are introduced, including Vegeta, a Saiyan who starts off as a foe but becomes a reluctant ally; Piccolo, a green-skinned alien from the Namekian race who becomes a mentor to Gohan; and Trunks, a time-traveler from the future who is the son of Bulma and Vegeta.

In Dragon Ball Z, the action becomes more and more extreme. There are many martial arts tournaments that are the settings for epic battles. Fights between characters can last several episodes, and the characters become so powerful that the destruction resulting from their battles often devastates the landscape. In one example, Piccolo destroys the Moon to prevent Gohan's transformation into a giant ape (like father, like son …). Characters often die and go to the afterlife, only to train and return to the world of the living—this happens to Goku and, as a result, he is seen wearing a halo. Some characters can even fuse with one another to become a new, powerful being.

Dragon Ball GT begins after the end of Dragon Ball Z, and this time features Goku, an older Trunks, and Goku's granddaughter Pan as the main characters. Emperor Pilaf has also returned, this time with a new set of Dragonballs—and when Goku's wish goes awry, he is turned back into a child. The series follows the search for the new Dragonballs, but this time the setting is outer space.

Dragon Ball was first broadcast in the United States in the mid-1990s; FUNimation Productions attained the rights to the series and adapted it for the syndicated television market. However, changes were made due to broadcast standards; nudity and excessive violence were edited or cut out. In the late 1990s, Cartoon Network began airing the series, this time with less edits, and it went on to became the highest-rated program on the cable channel. The edited and unedited versions of the series were released on home video from FUNimation and Pioneer beginning in 1996 in both subtitled and English-dubbed formats; in April 2003, FUNimation began releasing Dragon Ball GT on DVD. Viz Comics began publishing an English translation of the manga beginning in the late 1990s, but this time published both Goku's early adventures under the title Dragon Ball and his adventures as an adult under the title of Dragon Ball Z.

Yet Dragon Ball already had a fan following in the United States, due to episodes and movies subtitled by fans that were sold at conventions; many could also find the original Japanese manga in specialty bookstores, as well as the merchandise—action figures, models, artbooks, video games, and more. Fans are attracted to the action and super-hero elements and the various characters—some of them truly bizarre—that populate the world created by Toriyama. It is a tribute to his skill as both artist and writer that Toriyama was able to blend so many different elements into a cohesive story that would have failed in lesser hands. The series also made him well known in the United States. It doesn't look like the popularity of *Dragon Ball* around the world will fade any time soon. —*MM*

Eclipse Heroes

Eclipse was one of the first truly independent comics companies, beginning in 1977 and serving as a haven for many of the medium's most thoughtful and edgy talents (like writers Don McGregor and Steve Gerber) when they'd been driven from the majors, while also offering a welcoming creative space for those who remained in the mainstream but sought more substantive outlets (like artists Marshall Rogers and Gene Colan). The company came into being with McGregor's dystopian action saga *Sabre,* and continued for seventeen years with a diverse roster of everything from sci-fi, horror, and manga to satire, postmodern funny animals, and opera adaptations. In the mix, it didn't shy away from the occasional quality superhero series.

In this area, Eclipse is probably best remembered as the Stateside home of Alan Moore's gloomy masterwork *Miracleman.* But there are other fan favorites as well, perhaps chief among them Mark Evanier and Will Meugniot's long-running *DNAgents.* Debuting in 1983 when genetic engineering seemed more than a calendar century away, the book concerns a troupe of specially powered meta-humans created by a global corporation to do its often-questionable bidding—and the questions these characters nonetheless develop about the morality of their missions. Their corporate master, it is amusing to recall, was known as Matrix, and the book tapped into anti-big-business paranoia long before this theme became a staple of pop culture.

The series dealt with uneasy relationships between genetic "cultures" in the way Marvel's X-Men books are known to, as an allegory for real-life friction between nations and races. Stories would revolve around unusual ethical themes, like the one in which a hostile potentate (the Commander) forces the armor-clad DNAgent Tank into a televised battle with a mighty assassin to prove the mutant race's inferiority, but the assassin's mercilessness increases pubic sympathy for the DNAgents instead. The book also took a novel approach to ubiquitous comics conventions of the day, as when *DNAgents* and DC's *Teen Titans* held a "secret crossover" in which the two actual teams never met, but a parallel narrative played out in each series concurrently, with the Agents thinly veiled and cleverly renamed "the Re-Combatants" in the Titan's book and the Titans dubbed Project Youngblood in the Agents'.

DNAgents #5 © 1983 Mark Evanier and Will Meugniot.
COVER ART BY WILL MEUGNIOT AND AL GORDON.

The series ran for some four years and spawned several successful spinoffs, including a miniseries for the team's electricity-generating hot-head Surge and a two-year run for the non-genetical-ly-modified hero Crossfire (also written by Evanier, with artist Dan Spiegle), a Hollywood bail-bondsman by day and costumed vigilante by night who found endless material in Evanier's real-life discontents as a television scriptwriter.

In addition to the veteran creators of these series, Eclipse was known for giving promising new talents their first opportunities, and one such arrange-ment resulted in a series little-noticed at the time but sought after by fans since: *The Liberty Project,* a book

built around the novel concept of incarcerated supervillains given a shot at redemption through a kind of work-release as government-controlled super-heroes. The series was drawn by James W. Fry and written by Kurt Busiek, a writer then known to none but later acclaimed throughout the industry for comics like the groundbreaking *Marvels* and *Astro City.* (In 2003 *The Liberty Project* was put back in print in a collected volume from About Comics.)

Other Eclipse superheroes included the patriot-ic WWII champion Sgt. Strike and his modern coun-terpart Strike!, a black teenager who finds the high-tech harness that gave the Sgt. his superpowers. (These characters' mythos tied into that of Airboy, Skywolf, and other headliners from an unusual 1940s genre of aviator heroes once published by Hillman and revived by Eclipse.) The eclectic stable included such others as the spacefaring superteam the New Wave, and one of Spider-Man co-creator Steve Ditko's strange metaphysical heroes, Static (no relation to the later Milestone Comics star). Big names from the nomadic landscape of creator-owned properties, including Dave Stevens' Rocke-teer, also passed through the company's pages.

Eclipse was committed to quality production val-ues, creative freedom, and full ownership of its books by each one's artists and writers. In this, it set a standard for integrity that not many of the get-rich-quick independents that followed it into comics' mid-1980s to early 1990s boom bothered to match. Eclipse had helped bring about that boom by pioneer-ing the practice of distributing comics directly and exclusively to specialty comic shops with a ready audience. But many comic shops shut their doors, and Eclipse went out of business in 1994. —*AMC*

ElectraWoman and DynaGirl

"ElectraWoman and DynaGirl, fighting all evil deeds. Each writes for a magazine, hiding the life she leads." So began the catchy theme song for *Electra-Woman and DynaGirl,* a popular but short-lived segment of *The Krofft Supershow.* Sid and Marty Krofft, best known for strange (some would say hallucinogenic) live-action Saturday mornings kids' shows, created a ninety-minute variety show for ABC, premiering it on September 11, 1976. Leading its mixture of segments was a pair of female crime fighters.

At its ElectraHeart, *ElectraWoman and DynaGirl* was a campy female version of the 1960s *Batman* series. ElectraWoman (not-yet soap star Diedre Hall) was really Lori, while DynaGirl (Judy Strangis) was Judy, her pigtail-wearing teen sidekick. During the day, they were reporters for *NewsMaker* magazine, but whenever they got a call from Frank Heflin (Norman Alden), the electrical genius at their Electrabase, they rushed off to fight crime. The girls' gadgets included giant-sized wrist-mounted Electra-Comps that fired rays like the ElectraBeam and ElectraDe-gravitator, and they traveled to fight crime in an ElectraCar or ElectraPlane.

The villains they faced were a silly lot whose aims never seemed too evil. The Sorcerer and his beauteous sidekick Miss Dazzle used hypnosis to rob Fort Knox of its gold, while Glitter Rock kidnapped a prince and tried to take over the world with disco. The Empress of Evil and her partner Lucretia, the sinister Ali Baba, the greedy Pharoah, and the curvy Spider Lady were other dastardly doers that ElectraWoman and DynaGirl faced.

Eight half-hour episodes of *ElectraWoman and DynaGirl* were produced and aired during the 1976–1977 season, and then the heroines went away. Though costumes, puzzles, lunchboxes, and some other licensing were released, television would be the only medium that the costumed heroines would appear in. Diedre Hall had just begun starring on the soap opera *Days of Our Lives* in 1976, but Strangis all but disappeared from Hollywood. Despite its short life, the series achieved a kind of cult celebrity. In the late 1990s, episodes were released on video, and an ElectraWoman action figure was released (DynaGirl was never available, however).

In 2000, the Kroffts and Warner Bros. Television filmed a half-hour *Electra Woman and Dyna Girl* (note spaces now in title) TV pilot starring Markie Post as the retired and now-alcoholic Electra Woman, who is brought out of retirement by Judy Bennett (Anne Stedman), a reporter who wants to become the new Dyna Girl. The WB chose not to pick up the series, and it appears that hope is lost—for now—for any revival. ElectraBummer! —*AM*

Elektra

In his initial encounter with Elektra in *Daredevil* #168 (January 1981), Marvel Comics' sightless Man without Fear receives from her the blunt end of a dagger to the back of his head, then a merciless kick across his jaw, proving that issue's cover copy to be no hyperbole: "Once he loved her … now she is his most deadly enemy!"

"Elektra came into existence simply because I wanted Daredevil to have a femme fatale," comments writer/penciler Frank Miller in Les Daniels' historical volume *Marvel: Five Fabulous Decades of the World's Greatest Comics* (1991). Yet "simply" never applies to Miller's complex work. Elektra Natchios, once the college love of law student Matt Murdock, Daredevil's alter ego, retreats from her boyfriend and society after her father, a Greek envoy, is assassinated. Emotionally poisoned by her father's murder, she embarks upon a Zen-like quest to find purpose in her life, receiving martial-arts training first from a teacher in Japan and then, in a mysterious Arctic retreat, from Stick, the sensei who similarly instructed Murdock. Too indignant to become a noble warrior, Elektra allies herself with the Hand, a cult of ninjas that manipulates her into executing her original teacher in a deadly rite of passage. Her life now has direction: Armed with a pair of three-pronged blades called sai, the crimson-clad Elektra becomes an executioner for hire. Single-handedly plowing through throngs of gangsters, assassins, and ninjas alike, Elektra ricochets her sai off of walls with staggering accuracy

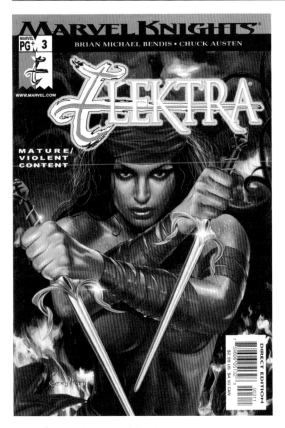

Elektra #3 © 2001 Marvel Comics.
COVER ART BY GREG HORN.

while spinning, ducking, punching, and kicking, leaving no foe standing.

At the time of her debut in late 1980, Elektra defied the stereotype of the classic superheroine, that prim, altruistic mighty maid of previous decades who had slipped into cliché. She represented an escapist take on the global tensions and political cynicism looming over the heads of readers. Elektra was a female character unlike anything comic-book readers had seen before: Determined, self-assured, and vicious, she chose not to veil her identity behind a mask or alter ego—she was Elektra, the assassin, nothing more, nothing less. Although she was a killer, Elektra was a symbol of empowerment: *Women no longer have to be vic-*

tims, her actions spoke. Miller may have been "simply" creating a femme fatale with Elektra, but in the process he redefined the superheroine for the 1980s and beyond. And unlike the female love interests that had previously been introduced in comics, Elektra emerged not as a disposable character, but as an equal to her lover.

Elektra's saga continued throughout intermittent issues of Miller's *Daredevil* run (as well as in a 1981 solo story by Miller in Marvel's black-and-white anthology magazine, *Bizarre Adventures*). The assassin had a heart, readers discovered, as she still loved Murdock, the blind man behind the devil mask, affording her character emotional complexity beyond her brutality. Yet that bond was overpowered by their wills: Elektra was committed to serve as the executioner for Daredevil's foe the Kingpin, while the heroic Daredevil was pledged to stop her. In *Daredevil* #181 (1982), Elektra *was* stopped—by another assassin, Bullseye, who skewered her to regain his position in Kingpin's corner. Mortally wounded, Elektra crawled to Murdock's home and died in her lover's arms. Unable to accept the passing of such a forceful spirit, Murdock exhumed her in the very next issue for firsthand proof that Elektra was indeed dead. A mere five months later, a story written and penciled by Miller—"What if Bullseye Had Not Killed Elektra?"—was published in *What If?* #35, but it merely teased readers with make-believe.

Elektra lived again, however. Miller resurrected her in *Daredevil* #190 (1983), by metaphysically cleansing her soul. The character resurfaced, first in *The Elektra Saga* (1984), a four-issue repackaging (with new material added) of her *Daredevil* appearances, then months later in what would be creator Miller's banner year.

That year was 1986. Miller returned to *Daredevil,* but only as writer, for a brief, critically acclaimed stint, and produced his magnum opus *Batman: The Dark Knight Returns* for DC Comics. *Elektra: Assassin,* launched in August 1986, reunited author Miller with his popular creation in an eight-issue postmodern prequel to her *Daredevil* appearances. Lavishly painted by Bill Sienkiewicz, *Elektra: Assassin* pitted Elektra against a pigheaded federal agent and a demon bent on starting a nuclear war. Sienkiewicz's experimental art style and Miller's scathing political commentary made *Elektra: Assassin* a controversial milestone for Marvel Comics.

By the 1990s, more superheroines had followed Elektra's edgy lead—Avengelyne and Shi, for example—dulling some of the assassin's uniqueness. Yet Marvel consistently maintained a presence for the character. A four-issue *Elektra* miniseries was published in 1995, followed by more reprints of the original Miller material and a crossover with Image Comics' Cyblade in early 1997. In July of that year, Marvel released *Elektra* #1, an ongoing monthly comic. Daredevil guest-starred in the first issue and Bullseye surfaced shortly thereafter. Without Miller's participation, however, and with the embittered Elektra out of place in the mainstream Marvel universe, the series died after nineteen issues.

In the 2000s editorial changes at Marvel Comics helped Elektra regain her stature. Some of the publisher's grittier characters have been allowed to explore explicit themes in the company's Marvel Knights and MAX imprints. After co-starring with the immensely popular X-Man Wolverine in the three-issue *Elektra & Wolverine: The Redeemer* (2001), Elektra was back on the stands in September of that year in a new and appropriately violent series. In her solo adventures, Elektra's marks are clearly criminals; however, despite their wrongdoings, she still assassinates them, making her a villain in the eyes of the authorities in the comics, and from the perspective of some readers.

Elektra's profile received another boost with the release of the live-action movie *Daredevil* (2003), starring Ben Affleck in the lead. *Daredevil* appropriated much of Miller's material from his first run on the comic book, including the hero's relationship with Elektra, portrayed by actress Jennifer Garner. Garner's interpretation of the character captivated viewers, including young girls, elevating Elektra from cult-comic status to mass-media acclaim. An *Elektra* movie and possible film franchise is under development. At the time of the release of *Daredevil,* Garner commented, "I wish that I had read *Elektra* when I was growing up because I think that she's very empowering to young women. I can't pass up the comics now; I have to stop and see if there's a new *Elektra* out." With the promise of an ongoing motion-picture series bolstering the presence of the popular comic book, Elektra truly lives again. —*ME*

Elementals

Earth, wind, fire, water. Element-based superpowers may seem routine in the world of superheroes—Geo-Force, Swamp Thing, Storm, Human Torch, and Aquaman are just a few of the characters who possess them—but in the hands of creator Bill Willingham, they were anything but pedestrian. Premiering in Texas Comics' *Justice Machine Annual* #1 (1984), the Elementals were four ordinary, unrelated people—Tommy Czuchra, a precocious fourteen-year-old orphan; Jeff Murphy, a thrill-seeking professional pilot; Jeanette Crane, a passionate Los Angeles cop; and Rebecca Golden, a pampered heiress—who die. But not for long.

They return from the grave with abilities that connect them to the planet's natural order. Czuchra can transform into the superstrong Monolith, a being of living stone. Murphy becomes Vortex, able to soar at fantastic speeds and project concussive blasts. Crane pyro-kinetically masters fire and heat immunity. Golden—who now has green skin, and webbed fingers and toes—becomes Fathom (no relation to Mike Turner's similarly named heroine), manipulating (and even *becoming*) water. In the first story arc, "The Natural Order," writer/artist Willingham pushes the envelope by delving into subject matter that Marvel and DC Comics (at the time) considered taboo:

Elementals #1 © 1984 COMICO the Comic Company.
COVER ART BY BILL WILLINGHAM AND BILL ANDERSON.

the social and psychological repercussions of resurrection from the dead, and graphic explorations of violence and sociopathic behavior.

Independent publisher Comico the Comic Company picked up Willingham's creator-owned superteam shortly after the Texas Comics debut and issued *Elementals* #1 in 1984. Erratically released at first, *Elementals* garnered a loyal fan base, largely due to Willingham's provocative creative voice. As a writer, he stretched with each installment—over time, he addressed occultism, child abuse, sexual identity, religious obsession, immoral ministers, depression, and suicide, all while delivering well-paced, solidly scripted super-

hero stories. A disciple of folklore, Willingham also introduced fantasy themes into *Elementals,* with storybook and mythological characters appearing, territory he later continued to cover by writing the critically acclaimed series *Fables* (2002–present) for DC Comics' Vertigo imprint. As an artist, Willingham matured with each issue, starting as a competent copycat (while popular *Batman* and *Micronauts* artist Michael Golden's influence is quite obvious in his early work, Willingham commands a firm grasp of storytelling) but blossoming into a remarkably talented illustrator.

But Willingham came and went, and *Elementals* issues written and drawn by others lacked his magic and verve. In early 1989, Comico devised a "best of both worlds" scenario to keep Willingham on the title *and* publish what had become a strong seller for the company on a monthly schedule: *Elementals* was relaunched with vol. 2 issue #1, with Willingham scripting and providing cover art, but with Mike Leeke and Mike Chen on interior art (superstar artist Adam Hughes, then an up-and-comer, guest-penciled *Elementals* #12). This plan worked well—until bankruptcy forced Comico to close its doors in the early 1990s. Not long thereafter, a new financier revived Comico and purchased *Elementals* from its creator. Willingham and the artists and editors involved with the earlier, groundbreaking series chose not to participate in this new venture, and the new publisher pandered to the marketplace with some gratuitously exploitative comics involving the characters (including *Elementals Sex Special* #1–#4 and *Elementals Sexy Lingerie Special* #1). The new Comico was dead by the mid-1990s, and it took *Elementals* to the grave with it, an unfortunate conclusion to a once-celebrated series. —ME

Elongated Man

The perennial backup character the Elongated Man has brightened up numerous DC comics since his introduction in the pages of *The Flash* #112 in 1960 by Gardner Fox and Carmine Infantino. The Elongated Man was Ralph Dibny, who developed a fascination for circus "India rubber men" and eventually discovered that their stretching ability was derived from a soft drink called Gingold. Dibny found that by taking a concentrated drink of the liquid he could alter the cellular properties of his tissue and so stretch any part of his body to incredible length. Gingold's only drawback was its tendency to lose its effect after twenty-four hours, resulting in all manner of hilarious scrapes.

After his first appearance, reader response was so positive that the Elongated Man became a regular guest in the Flash strip for the next couple of years. Not only was the character unusual in his lighthearted approach to life but he had also, by his third appearance, abandoned his secret identity and married his girlfriend, glamorous socialite Sue Deerborn. With a rosy outlook on life matched by a colossal, fame-seeking ego, Dibny decided to earn his living by making personal appearances across the country. Nearly every story started with Dibny and Deerborn driving into a fresh town and coming across a quirky mystery or a robbery of some sort; in a nice touch, his nose would begin to twitch whenever a puzzle was about to present itself.

When Fox and Infantino were recruited to revamp the flagging Batman titles, they brought the Elongated Man with them, and for six years the "stretchable sleuth" was a welcome backup strip in *Detective Comics* (starting in issue #327). The first story set the tone for years to come: When Dibny and Deerborn stumble across a diamond-smuggling racket, the Elongated Man uses his special talent to eavesdrop on the hoods, leading to the immortal line "An ear in the fireplace! He must be up on the roof!" As the strip's run developed, the intrepid duo continued to foil ingenious crimes and to solve complex conundrums, but they never once acquired the lineup of supervillains that plagued other, more serious heroes. In fact, much of the strip's appeal lay in its low-key charm, which was perfectly complemented by Infantino's sophisticated line work.

In the 1970s, Elongated Man enjoyed occasional spots in the back pages of *The Flash* and *Detective Comics,* and finally joined the Justice League of America; his membership had previously been rejected on the grounds that Dibny exploited his powers for monetary gain. It was as a regular member of the Justice League, and later the Justice League Europe, that he gained his greatest popularity, allowing his constant cheerfulness to brighten up an otherwise somewhat dour group. This exposure culminated in the character's own solo comic (in a 1992 miniseries), a full thirty-two years after his first appearance; this proved to be a jolly romp through Europe. He also found a suitably bizarre supervillain of his own, Calamari, who was clad in a giant squid costume. This series did not lead to any further solo outings, but to this day the Elongated Man remains a member of the Justice League, where he is always a welcome sight. —DAR

E-Man

"I think, therefore I am, but what am I?" In a market dominated by neurotic heroes, creatures of the night, bloodthirsty barbarians, and horror comics by the score, E-Man was a breath of fresh air in the mid-1970s. E-Man was the creation of editor/writer Nick Cuti and up-and-coming artist Joe Staton, who were given permission to dream up a new superhero by the unfashionable Charlton Comics, almost as a reward for good work on the company's *Mystery Comics* line. Drawing on their interest in science and love for the legendary Plastic Man strip of the 1940s, the pair concocted a funny, inventive, and genuinely warm-hearted hero who quickly established a cult following.

E-Man #1 (October 1973) reveals how an exploding supernova, off in the furthest reaches of the universe, created a ball of sentient energy that proceeds to float through space for the next thousand years or so, finally stumbling across a passing spaceship, manned by the malevolent "Brain" (perhaps not surprisingly a giant, disembodied brain). The entity hitches a ride. After inadvertently causing the ship to crash on Earth, the energy creature travels through electrical cables to end up in the dressing room light bulb of exotic dancer Nova Kane and assume human form. The newly named E-Man ("E" for energy, of course) is very much an innocent force abroad, albeit a powerful one. Inspired by a poster of Albert Einstein in Kane's apartment, E-Man fashions himself a yellow-and-orange costume with "$E = MC_2$," embroidered on the front, and becomes a superhero. He takes on everyday life in his alter ego of private detective Alec Tronn.

E-Man's powers were seemingly limitless. He could shoot energy bolts from his fingertips, transform himself into any shape he wanted, fly, travel through telephone cables, and sleep in a car battery. He soon encountered a bizarre collection of enemies, including the Battery, the Boar, the Entropy Twins, aliens, hillbillies, and killer theme parks. The third issue of *E-Man* introduced the grime-encrusted, low-life private investigator Michael Mauser, who soon befriended E-Man, much to the disgust of Kane; she preferred her newly discovered boyfriend (the relationship flowered pretty much from their first meeting) to be unspoiled by the world around him. In fact, E-Man's naïve, optimistic, relentlessly cheerful personality, together with Kane's endless reserves of pluck, determination, and flirtatiousness, provided much of the strip's appeal. In time, Kane herself became a superhero—named, appropriately enough, "Nova, the Energy-Being that Walks Like a Woman"—after she became caught in an exploding star (in issue #8), while Mauser starred in his own feature in the *Vengeance Squad* comic. However, despite the best efforts of Cuti and Staton, along with a loyal band of fans, the *E-Man* comic simply failed to resonate with a wide audience.

E-Man's initial run sadly lasted for only ten issues, plus a one-off appearance in the *Charlton Bullseye* fanzine, but eight years later (in 1983) he was back as one of the stars of First Comics' entry into the specialty market. The revival by Staton and new writer Marty Pasko was more of a parody title than an out-and-out superhero comic and included a spoof of the X-Men. Later issues eventually returned to the charming stories of the Charlton era, bringing back Mauser and introducing E-Man's mischievous sister, Vamfire. After twenty-five issues, First pulled the plug but Staton—now with Cuti once again—fashioned further adventures for Comico (in 1989) and Alpha (in 1993), all much in the classic tradition.

Though not published with any consistency since the 1990s, there remains a wonderful freshness and sense of fun in the many E-Man stories, particularly those of the original Charlton run. As late as 2001 E-Man starred in a new strip (in *Comic Book Artist* #12), so there is always hope that his time still might come. —*DAR*

Everyday Heroes

Realism and superheroes. It sounds like an oxymoron, but at least since Stan Lee and Jack Kirby revolutionized the genre in the early 1960s, comics creators have been pursuing the principle.

"Realism" has meant different things to different writers and artists. To Lee, Kirby, and their contemporaries it meant giving believable flaws and self-doubts to character types once known for their impossible purity and confidence, even if the real-life emotions were played out in an alien dimension by people with green and orange skin. Spider-Man was a guilt-ridden neurotic, the Fantastic Four were not so much a superteam as comics' first dysfunctional family, the rageaholic Hulk was the quintessential anti-hero, and so on.

Since the 1990s, "realism" has meant something else: A whole genre has emerged exploring the lives of the ordinary people in the universes superheroes inhabit. These are neither paragons whose problems readers can relate to nor stock sidekicks and girlfriends who have too little personality to identify with, but people with everyday lives, regularly threatened by forces beyond their control.

The genre began in earnest—and was given a daunting model to match—with *Marvels* (1994), a miniseries by two current comics superstars who were then virtually unknown, writer Kurt Busiek and artist Alex Ross. Taking in the whole sweep of the twentieth century, both historical and fictional, *Marvels* presented the Marvel Comics universe as seen freshly through the eyes of a photojournalist, Phil Sheldon. Ross' own dazzlingly photographic style (in which each panel is fully painted and remarkably believable), and Busiek's knowing knack for down-to-earth treatment of incredible subject matter, made readers feel as if they were reading an actual documentary of the imaginary Marvel characters—and the ambivalent mix of awe and fear that such characters (and the real-life conflicts they symbolize) inspire in ordinary people.

Marvels cast a long shadow in which few successors flourished (though Busiek himself has occasionally returned to the series' person-on-the-street structure in his acclaimed independent comic *Astro City,* 1995–present). But by the end of the 1990s it was time for the next landmark in the "everyday heroes" genre. Image Comics' *Powers* (2000–present), by fan-favorite writer Brian Michael Bendis and artist Michel Avon Oeming, is a gripping costumed crime-drama in which the secrets and shortcomings of superbeings are seen from the perspective of the ordinary cops who clean up after their scandals, which range from disillusioning to disastrous. The series is heavy on political paranoia and celebrity-bashing disdain, but also rich in humor from the *Dragnet* dialogue and Mars/Venus interplay between stolid veteran detective Christian Walker and brash rookie Deena Pilgrim.

Bendis single-handedly perpetuated the genre with his own series from 2001 to 2003, *Alias* (no relation to the TV show, which serendipitously debuted at the same time) for Marvel's MAX imprint (with artist Michel Gaydos). The comic concerns

Jessica Jones, a second-tier superhero turned struggling civilian private investigator. The series' plain, cynical heroine is rare for a medium oriented toward uncomplicated babes, and her adventures cover the underbelly of the Marvel universe, from farcical superhero-sidekick impostors to frightening drug-addict thrill-seekers who mainline mutant blood. Resonantly squalid and often surprisingly funny, *Alias* tells the subtly moving story of a powerful woman who, rather than protecting regular people from on high, has chosen to live as they do.

The success of such books opened the spigot on similar concepts, from Marvel's 2002 miniseries *Deadline* (following the misadventures of superhero-hating junior reporter Katherine Farrell, who struggles with a man's world as well as a Superman's), to DC's *Gotham Central* (2003–present), focusing on the police force of Batman's fair city.

Another addition to the genre fizzled out from the most promising of beginnings. After the 9/11 tragedy, Marvel published three interlocking mini-series under the general title *The Call of Duty* (2002), each dealing with a different cast of first-responders (*The Brotherhood* featured firefighters; *The Precinct,* police; *The Wagon,* ambulance teams). Though nominally set in the Marvel universe, with some supernatural and sci-fi elements involved, the books were best at realistically portraying human nature in unusual situations under extraordinary pressures. These were the heroes people wanted to read about, and in a baffling botch, the miniseries were followed by an ongoing (but swiftly canceled) comic (*The Call,* 2003) that turned the everyday stars into more standard superheroes.

But never fear; after that book's demise, Jessica Jones was set to return in *The Pulse!* (also by Bendis and Gaydos), a 2004 series in which she feeds exposés of costumed characters' less-heroic episodes to an investigative reporter, thus bringing the genre full-circle—and no doubt opening up a whole new horizon. *—AMC*

Extreme Studios Heroes

In February 1992, six of the hottest artists in the comics medium announced that they had formed Image Comics, a collective publishing house in which they would own all of their creations, sink or swim. Over the next several years, the artist who would do the most sinking and swimming would be Rob Liefeld, the head of the Extreme Studios imprint. Liefeld first garnered industry attention on DC Comics' *Hawk & Dove* miniseries in 1988–1989, but it was his work on Marvel properties such as *New Mutants* and *X-Force* that won him a hardcore fan base who would follow him anywhere. They liked his ultra-line-filled art, and didn't care that many of his characters—and some of the art—seemed awfully familiar. It was Liefeld's extreme style that caught fandom's attention.

Liefeld's first book for Image was *Youngblood* #1 (April 1992), in which he introduced a group of government-sponsored heroes who were as comfortable being publicity-friendly celebrities as they were stopping supervillains. Badrock is a stony giant with great strength, but inside he is just a teen. Chapel is an African-American marksman with dark secrets. Shaft is the arrow-firing hero who would grow into leadership. Vogue is a Russian gymnast whose deadly aim with throwing weapons is surpassed by her fortunes as the head of a cosmetic empire. Riptide is a water-wielding beauty. Others on the Youngblood roster—which soon split into two books, *Youngblood* and *Team Youngblood*—included werewolf-like Cougar, fire-headed Photon, and armored Sentinel, as well as Brahma, Psi Fire, Combat, and Diehard. The first issue saw the group battling villains such as Strongarm, Gage, Deadlock, and Starbright, and Psi-Fire killed Middle Eastern leader Hassan Kussein.

The *Youngblood* team formed the core of the Extreme universe. Many of the characters had

Supreme #2 © 1993 Rob Liefeld.
COVER ART BY BRIAN MURRAY.

appeared in fan stories illustrated by Liefeld for *Titan Talk,* a *Teen Titans* fan publication in the 1980s; their first comic appearance was actually in *Megaton Comics Explosion* (June 1987). Extreme soon expanded its line and hired artists who could ape Liefeld's style. Books included other hero teams like *Brigade* and *New Men,* and solo series such as the violent *Bloodstrike;* futuristic science fiction hero *Prophet;* comedic space barbarian *Bloodwulf;* and more. Several *Youngblood* characters were given their own titles, which often crossed over with other Image series; *Chapel* was a part of *Spawn* continuity, *Troll* mixed stories with *The Maxx,* and *Badrock and Company* was an actual team-up book featuring Badrock meeting other Image denizens.

The most lasting of the Extreme books is *Supreme,* featuring a lead character that started out as a Superman rip-off, but became a beloved homage once renowned author Alan Moore came aboard to script the stories, beginning with issue #41 (August 1996). Moore took the outrageous elements of Silver Age (1956–1969) *Superman* stories—alternate dimensions, multiple permutations of the hero—and brought them into Supreme's world, with fascinating spins that made the outlandish seem real.

Although many Extreme titles were solid sellers, and action-figure and toy licensing was taking off, Liefeld himself—the highly public face of Extreme—was getting a critical backlash in the industry. When he would take steps forward—he appeared in a Levi's commercial and optioned film and television rights on a regular basis to Tom Cruise's production company, Cruise-Wagner Productions, as well as actor Will Smith and Fox television—the industry would shoot back with tales of his copied artwork, his inability to meet deadlines or keep character costumes consistent, and battles with his fellow Image creators and with animators who worked on a prospective *Youngblood* series. At a time when a near-bankrupt Marvel had farmed out several of its

lead titles to Liefeld and fellow Image creator Jim Lee to produce—*Captain America, Avengers, Iron Man,* and *Fantastic Four* were theirs for a one-year experiment called "Heroes Reborn"—Liefeld's standing in the comics world was unsteady.

In September 1996, Liefeld announced he was stepping down as Image's CEO, and relocating all of his titles to the self-published Maximum Press. Image stated that Liefeld had been voted out of the group non-voluntarily, and a battle of press releases and spin control began. Extreme Studios continued publishing some titles under the Maximum Press banner, including Moore's *Supreme,* and a run of the warrior women series *Avengelyne* and *Glory.* As the new millennium began, Liefeld had mostly stopped publishing his own comics, licensing some titles out, and eventually changing imprints again, to Awesome Comics, then Arcade Comics. Dabbling in work sporadically for Marvel, Liefeld finally released new issues of *Youngblood* in 2003. The return was bittersweet, however; a series of resolicitations and missed shipping dates meant that *Youngblood* did not get distribution from the industry's largest distributor, Diamond. Whether Liefeld and his Extreme heroes can once again regain fan-favorite status is still in doubt, but the effect that Extreme Studios had on the comics industry will definitely be remembered in comic-book history. —*AM*

Fantastic Four

"The World's Greatest Comic Magazine!"—the immodest subtitle displayed above the logo of *Fantastic Four* since its fourth issue—is no mere hyperbole. Still going strong in its fifth decade of publication, *Fantastic Four,* the series that spearheaded the Marvel universe, has become its cornerstone.

Fantastic Four was the product of editorial decree and creative desperation. Beginning in the late 1950s, DC Comics had successfully resuscitated the superhero genre through its reintroduction of classic heroes like the Flash and Green Lantern. The Silver Age of comics (1956–1969) was underway. Martin Goodman, publisher of Marvel Comics, was informed during a golf game with DC's publisher Jack Liebowitz that DC's superhero books were selling exceptionally well, particularly their new *Justice League of America* series, which united Superman, Batman, and other popular characters. Marvel was known mainly for its monster comics, and Goodman realized that his line would benefit from a title starring a supergroup. He ordered his editor, Stan Lee, to create one. This directive came at an opportune time for Lee, who was tiring of writing and editing disposable pap for children and was on the brink of resigning from the company. Lee longed

to script material with more profundity—stories featuring real people, with realistic foibles—and his wife encouraged him to make this mandated superteam the trial project for his aspirations.

Fantastic Four #1 (November 1961) introduced a quartet of new characters: Dr. Reed Richards, a pompous scientist and aerospace engineer; Susan (Sue) Storm, his lovely and somewhat reserved fiancée; Sue's hotheaded teen-age brother Johnny Storm, a car-racing enthusiast; and Richards' beefy and snappish longtime friend, pilot Ben Grimm. This group of four commandeers an untested spaceship of Richards' own design from the U.S. military, in a frantic but unsanctioned effort to beat "the Commies" (as Sue calls them) in the Space Race. Grimm protests, concerned over inadequate research into the effects of space radiation, but is sweet-talked into participation by Sue, for whom he carries an unrequited passion. In orbit, the craft is flooded by cosmic rays ("I warned you about 'em!" yells Grimm) that genetically alter its passengers. Once returning to Earth, the quartet discover that they have been forever changed: Sue can fade in and out of view (and before long, project force fields) as the Invisible Girl; Grimm mutates into a freakish, rock-skinned powerhouse dubbed the Thing; arrogant Richards elongates into a plastic man who calls himself Mr. Fantastic; and Johnny erupts into flame, blazing through the skies as the Human Torch. "Together we have more power than any humans have ever possessed," submits Richards, who persuades this group to join forces as the Fantastic Four (FF).

Author Lee's co-architect was artist Jack Kirby, an industry superstar who, like Lee, was looking for a chance to stretch beyond the monster comics he'd recently illustrated for Marvel. Kirby's energetic and cinematic storytelling ("Nobody drew a strip like Jack Kirby," beamed Lee in his 2002 autobiography, *Excelsior! The Amazing Life of Stan Lee*) earmarked *Fantastic Four* as something new, as did Lee's bouncy dialogue, which often placed the series' teammates in verbal conflict with each other—and physical conflict, too, via the playful ruckuses sparked by practical joker Torch and his target, the Thing. They were more than a team: They were a *family,* and a dysfunctional one at that.

Fantastic Four quickly became a triumph for Marvel, and Lee and Kirby's imaginations burst into hyperdrive. An array of fearsome foes appeared and reappeared, including, but certainly not limited to, the oafish Mole Man, enslaver of a subterranean race; Golden Age (1938–1954) anti-hero Sub-Mariner, also known as Prince Namor of the undersea kingdom of Atlantis, whose hatred of "surface dwellers" was quelled only by his love of the Invisible Girl; the alien Super-Skrull, who possessed *all* of the FF's awesome abilities; the manipulative Puppet Master, who could control the FF via miniature proxies; and the towering Galactus, who gained sustenance by absorbing the life forces of planets. Yet no menace was more insolent than Doctor Doom, whose hideously scarred face was hidden behind an ominous iron mask (it is rumored that Doom was the template for Darth Vader in George Lucas' *Star Wars* movies). Originally Richards' colleague Victor Von Doom, this despotic mastermind habitually returned to plague not only the FF but to engage Mr. Fantastic in intellectual battles, always with dire consequences.

Lee and Kirby ushered the FF—who operated from the Baxter Building, a skyscraper in midtown Manhattan—into a dizzying array of exciting adventures to exotic locales: the center of the earth, the past, the subatomic Micro-World, and the treacherous void called the Negative Zone. Mr. Fantastic's unending array of technological gadgets assisted the FF in their exploits, most notably the aerodynamic Fantasti-car, which in its earliest incarnation resembled a flying bathtub, and the FF's own malleable uniforms, woven from "unstable molecules" that mimicked each hero's power (for example, the fabric stretched with Mr. Fantastic). Despite his brilliance, Richards could never find a permanent reversal of the Thing's tragic condition.

In *Fantastic Four Annual* #3 (1965), Reed and Sue were married (in a wedding crashed by a cadre of criminals), and a few years later their son Franklin was born. The Richards family was far from traditional, however: Franklin displayed dangerous superpowers, and Mr. Fantastic repeatedly ignored his wife and son by spending days holed up in his laboratory. A growing supporting cast was introduced: the Black Panther, Marvel's first African-American superhero; the Inhumans, a race of outcast superbeings; the Watcher, a chronicler of intergalactic events sworn to observe but not participate; and the Silver Surfer, the space-spanning herald of Galactus who turned against his master at the urging of the Thing's blind girlfriend, Alicia Masters. Alicia, the daughter of the Puppet Master, became part of the FF's extended family, and helped soften the Thing's morose demeanor by "seeing" what only she could: the kind inner soul of Grimm.

Two renowned comics catch phrases were born early in *Fantastic Four*'s run: Johnny's "Flame on!," which he exclaimed when soaring into action as the Torch, and the Thing's high-spirited battle charge, "It's clobberin' time!" The Human Torch was the initial breakout member, starring in solo adventures in *Strange Tales* and routinely appearing in *The Amazing Spider-Man,* but as the Thing's personality changed from bitter outsider to lovable grouch, by the mid-1960s Grimm emerged as the FF's most popular player.

In 1967, the FF's acclaim extended beyond comic books. *The Fantastic Four* (1967–1970), an animated television series produced by Hanna-Barbera, borrowed heavily from the Lee/Kirby comics. The cartoon ignited a firestorm of merchandizing, including storybooks, flicker rings, coloring books, Halloween costumes, and puzzles.

In the 1970s, changes disrupted the status quo of *Fantastic Four*. A dispute involving story contributions divided the Lee/Kirby team, and before long both vacated the book. For years, a variety of creators ventured in and out of the title (artist John Buscema distinguished himself by his lengthy run on the series in the 1970s), some making minor contributions to the canon, others leaving a larger mark. The Thing headlined the long-running team-up title *Marvel Two-in-One* (1974–1983), Reed and Sue suffered marital problems, and members came and went from the team, temporarily replaced by heroes like Power Man and Medusa.

By the late 1970s, several Marvel superheroes were starring on live-action television on CBS. The Human Torch was optioned for an unrealized live-action film, precluding his inclusion in the FF's second animated series, *The New Fantastic Four* (1978), on rival network NBC. (A comics urban legend contends that the Torch wasn't allowed on the 'toon due to the network's concerns that impressionable children would set themselves ablaze in emulation.) Johnny Storm was replaced in the show by a comical robot named Herbie. The following season, NBC aired *Fred and Barney Meet the Thing,* a *Flintstones* continuation that included shorts featuring a teenage version of "Benjy" Grimm who transformed into the ever-lovin' Thing by uniting two separated pieces of a ring and shouting, "Thing Ring, do your thing!" Both cartoons strayed too far from the FF source material and died quickly.

Writer/artist John Byrne's 1980s run on the *Fantastic Four* comic book (#232–#292, July 1981–July 1986) spanned half the decade and featured such memorable events as the induction of the She-Hulk as a temporary member, the evolution

Fantastic Four #82 © 1969 Marvel Comics.
COVER ART BY JACK KIRBY AND JOE SINNOTT.

of the once-meek Invisible Girl into the forceful and liberated Invisible *Woman,* the shocking romance between the Torch and the Thing's girlfriend Alicia, and the transformation of Sue into the villainess Malice. Grimm segued from *Marvel-Two-in-One* into his own monthly title, *The Thing* (1983–1986), which took him into the cosmos as a space explorer and into the sports arena as a professional wrestler.

The 1990s did not bode well for *Fantastic Four*. Convoluted story continuity impeded the series, and sales dropped. A 1994 low-budget live-action FF movie was deemed unworthy of release, yanked from distribution, and denied home-video availability, although bootleg copies are common among collectors. (Another FF movie, with Chris Columbus [*Home Alone*] at the helm, was later bandied about but shelved.) At least a new FF cartoon stayed on-air for two seasons, as part of *The Marvel Action Hour,* from 1994–1996.

After rebootings in both 1996 and 1998, Marvel's *Fantastic Four* eliminated some problematic history and returned the series to more accessible and stable ground. In the 2000s, the Human Torch was spun off into his own series, and *Fantastic Four* was restored to its former glory by fan-favorite writer Mark Waid and artist Mike Wieringo. A 2003 corporate decision to remove Waid and Wieringo from *FF* was met by such overwhelming backlash from readers that the move was soon reversed. An alternate-universe title featuring a younger version of the team, *Ultimate Fantastic Four,* premiered in early 2004, and a third ongoing FF series, *4* (a.k.a. *Knights 4*), a harder-edged interpretation produced by the creative team originally contracted to replace Waid and Wieringo, bowed in 2004. A major live-action *Fantastic Four* motion picture has been in development for years, and is targeted for a mid- 2005 release date. Another FF milestone: In continuous publication since 1961, the Invisible Girl/Woman has earned the distinction of being in print longer than every comics superheroine except for Wonder Woman.

Although disagreements and personal quests have often separated the Fantastic Four, their mutual affection inevitably reunites them. It's that bond between Mr. Fantastic, the Invisible Woman, the Thing, and the Human Torch that will always make their series "The World's Greatest Comic Magazine!" —*ME*

Fantastic Four in the Media

They are the world's greatest dysfunctional family. Exposed to cosmic rays while traveling in an experimental rocketship, Reed Richards, Sue Storm, Johnny Storm, and Ben Grimm return to Earth with astonishing powers. The stretchable Richards dubs himself Mr. Fantastic, while the see-through Sue Storm is the Invisible Girl, and her now-flammable brother Johnny is the Human Torch. Poor Grimm gets the raw end of the deal, becoming a superstrong orange-skinned creature known as the Thing. As created by Stan Lee and Jack Kirby for *Fantastic Four* #1 (November 1961), the quartet known as the Fantastic Four would become almost as popular for their squabbling relationships as they would for their efforts to protect the world from such cosmic threats as planet-devouring Galactus, dictator Doctor Doom, angry underwater monarch Sub-Mariner, and the shape-changing alien invaders known as Skrulls.

It would be a mere six years after their comic debut that the Fantastic Four would make their first media appearance. Hanna-Barbera saw that Filmation's DC Comics–based superhero cartoons were popular, as was Grantray-Lawrence's limited-animation *Marvel Super-Heroes* series. Hanna-Barbera quickly licensed *The Fantastic Four* for a cartoon series, basing many of the scripts directly on comic-book storylines of the day.

The Fantastic Four debuted on September 9, 1967, with a half-hour slot. The animation was adequate; though it lacked the power of Kirby's comics, the characters were designed by comics legend Alex Toth and art direction was by Marvel Comics artist John Romita Sr. Voice work was by several popular voice actors of the day, including Gerald Mohr, JoAnn Pflug, Jack Flounders, and Paul Frees. During the series' twenty episodes, the "FF" faced familiar villains such as Doctor Doom, Klaw, the Red Ghost, Galactus, and others. The final show aired on March 15, 1970, though the series would later be revived for syndication.

In late 1975, *The Fantastic Four* was a nationally syndicated radio program, with each weekday segment running a scant five minutes. This was part of a new program called *Marvel Comics Radio Series,* but the show proved costly to produce and was canceled after thirteen five-part episodes of the *FF* were released. Adapted directly from the comics, the radio show is almost completely forgotten by fans, save as a trivia question: Who played the Human Torch on the 1975 *Fantastic Four* radio show? A pre–*Saturday Night Live* Bill Murray!

In the late 1970s, animation studio DePatie-Freleng began work on *The New Fantastic Four,* an animated series revival that debuted on NBC on September 9, 1978. Stan Lee and comics scribe Roy Thomas worked on many scripts, while Jack Kirby did storyboards. Although the stories were relatively faithful to their comic counterparts—if a bit updated for the times—one major change was made: The Human Torch was replaced by a flying miniature robot named HER-B, or "Herbie." Although legend has it the change was made because the producers feared kids would set themselves on fire in an effort to emulate the Torch, the main reason for the switch was that Universal Studios had optioned the Human Torch character for an Irwin Allen–produced live-action feature film. *The New Fantastic Four* lasted thirteen episodes, ending its run on September 1, 1979.

One FF member didn't stay off the air for too long. On September 22, 1979, NBC premiered the new Hanna-Barbera series *Fred and Barney Meet the Thing.* The show was a bizarre mixture, with *Flintstones* stars Fred Flintstone and Barney Rubble having their own adventures, and only really "meeting" the Thing for brief "joke bumpers" between episodes or preceding and following commercial breaks. The twenty-six twelve-minute episodes of *The Thing* (shown two per episode) saw the Thing as a teenager named Benjy Grimm (the voice of Wayne Morton) who had a magic "Thing Ring." When he rams its two separated parts together and chants, "Thing Ring, do your thing," he transforms into the familiar orange-skinned hero, the Thing (Joe Baker's vocalization, doing a Jimmy Durante impression). Most of the Thing's adventures were spent foiling the dastardly plans of the biker thugs known as the Yancy Street Gang. Although the title of the

series changed to *Fred and Barney Meet The Schmoo* on December 8, 1979, *The Thing* episodes continued until the show's ultimate demise on November 15, 1980.

The Fantastic Four had been licensed for a feature film throughout much of the 1980s. After years in development, Neue Constantin Productions was about to lose the rights to make a movie, unless they began production on a feature film by December 31, 1992. They hired low-budget producer Roger Corman to create a $2 million live-action production, written by Craig J. Nevius and Kevin Rock and directed by Oley Sassone. Work on the picture began on December 28, 1992, three days before the license would have expired!

The story showcased the origin of the quartet, with Mr. Fantastic (Alex-Hyde White), the Invisible Woman (Rebecca Staab), the Human Torch (Jay Underwood), and the Thing (Carl Ciarfalio, voiced by Michael Bailey Smith) facing off against Dr. Doom (Joseph Culp) and the Jeweler (Ian Trigger). Although Thing's bodysuit (complete with animatronic head) was impressive, less interesting were Reed Richard's stretching powers, and Johnny Storm "flamed on" only in the film's finale.

Although a movie poster was released and a charity premiere was announced for January 19, 1994, at Minneapolis, Minnesota's Mall of the Americas, *The Fantastic Four* was scuttled before it could be released. It remains unreleased to this day, although bootleg recordings of it flourished throughout the late 1990s.

In September 1994, *The Marvel Action Hour* debuted in syndication, courtesy of Marvel Films and New World Entertainment. The animated series was composed of a half-hour *Fantastic Four* segment combined with a half-hour *Iron Man* series. Stan Lee introduced and narrated the episodes, which utilized stories inspired by the comics. The first season of thirteen episodes saw multi-part stories for the origin of the FF, as well as the introduction of the Silver Surfer, Galactus, and Doctor Doom. The second season featured drastically improved character designs and animation, as well as guest appearances by the Inhumans, Daredevil, Thor, Black Panther, Ghost Rider, the Hulk, and the Impossible Man. The series used lots of stunt voice-casting, including the voice of Dick Clark as himself, as well as Michael Dorn (Gorgon), Kathy Ireland (Crystal), Mark Hamill (Maximus), Ron Perlman (Wizard, Hulk), Richard Greico (Ghost Rider), and John Rhys-Davies (Thor).

Although *The Marvel Action Hour* was canceled in fall 1996, some of the FF characters reappeared in animated form. The Thing showed up in a first-season episode of UPN's *The Incredible Hulk.* In 1997, the Fantastic Four guest-starred in two episodes in the fifth season of Fox's animated *Spider-Man* series. Finally, in 1998, Fox aired one season of *The Silver Surfer,* which featured the title character and Galactus, and would have also featured the Fantastic Four if the in-production second season had not been canceled.

A second live-action *Fantastic Four* feature film has been in development for years at Twentieth Century Fox—as has a *Silver Surfer* movie—but it has been plagued by multiple screenwriters and defecting directors. Scripts have been turned in by Michael France, Chris Columbus, Philip Morton, Sam Hamm, Doug Petrie, and Mark Frost. Although Peyton Reed (director of *Bring It On*) once had a lock on directing, he resigned those duties in 2003. Still, the film has been announced to debut in mid-2005. Will the quartet make their date, or will cosmic rays interfere? Only time will tell. —*AM*

Fawcett Comics: *See* **Bulletman; Captain Marvel Jr.; Captain Marvel/Shazam!; Golden Age of Superheroes (1938–1954); Mary Marvel**

Femforce

The culmination of many long years spent laboring in the vineyards of comics fandom, mainstream

publishing, and independent publishing, Femforce was the brainchild of AC Comics founder Bill Black. Noted by AC writer and editor Mark Heike as being the first successful all-female superhero team, Femforce evolved out of the explosion of inexpensively produced—and for a brief time, highly profitable—black-and-white comics publishing that occurred in the mid-1980s, a period of wild growth for the industry, its publishers, and its direct-market (specialty shop) retailers.

As the market for such titles quickly grew glutted, Black established a unique publishing niche for AC by focusing on a conspicuously underrepresented area of the superhero genre: female protagonists, which, thanks to his earlier publishing ventures, Black possessed in abundance. In 1985, the ongoing *Femforce* series, created largely by utilizing characters from earlier AC comic books, landed on America's comics racks. The title quickly distinguished itself from most other contemporary superheroic fare by portraying its powerful female leads in an appealingly cheesecake "Good Girl" art style, replete with characterization and humor. The regular series also bucked the era's prevailing independent comics trend by printing in full color.

Femforce, which quickly became AC's flagship title, was mainly composed of female characters from the universe of Black's principal superhero, Captain Paragon. The team, whose membership has fluctuated over the years, was led by the blonde, statuesque Ms. Victory, a patriotic heroine. Victory's alter ego, Dr. Joan Wayne, was a U.S. government biogeneticist during the 1940s, when she invented a pumped-up vitamin compound known as V-47. This discovery granted her superstrength and the power of flight, as well as giving her perpetual youth while she was in her superheroine guise, thus affording her an excellent disguise. As the years wore on, Wayne aged into an old woman while Victory remained young. Originally known as "Miss Victory," she adopted the more contemporary "Ms." honorific as the years went on. Kept strong and youthful by the V-47 compound, Ms. Victory (now

Paragon's wife) can look forward to many more decades of service as one of America's most stalwart protectors.

Among the rank-and-file members of Femforce are She-Cat, a free spirit whose feline powers originated from an encounter with the evil cat goddess Sekhmet. Savage and noble natures are constantly at war within She-Cat, and the feline metaphor accurately describes both her razor-sharp claws and her well-honed sexuality. Nightveil (a.k.a. Laura Wright, the Blue Bulleteer), an Earth heroine who gained sorcerous abilities on the extradimensional world of Dark Dhagor, is a brooding woman of mystery and beauty. Evolved from a Fox Comics Phantom Lady look-alike of the 1940s, Nightveil derives her mystic powers partly from her arcane Cloak of Darkness, which she struggles to control and use for good purposes, though she realizes that its dark nature may cause her demise. One of the more popular members of the group, Nightveil has headlined several comics of her own.

Silver-tressed Silva Synn has big hair, big brains, and a major sweet tooth; not only can she teleport using subspatial wormholes, she also has the ability to create mentally generated objects called "synnestrophic constructs" that remain solid as long as she maintains her concentration. "Too Tall" Tara Fremont, an environmentalist, marine biologist, and latter-day "jungle girl" (though not in the Sheena mold, since she never wears animal skins), uses the enormous wealth of her father (industrialist T. C. Fremont) to protect the planet's many endangered species from extinction; thanks to a variant of Ms. Victory's V-47 serum, Fremont has also acquired the power to grow to enormous proportions, à la the 50-Foot Woman of the classic 1950s sci-fi film. Stardust is a pacifist extraterrestrial scientist who hails from the matriarchal world of Rur; her body gathers and concentrates stellar energy, which she can use either as a weapon or as a means of flight. An outsider among humans, "Dusty" continually struggles to understand Earth's aggressive, conflict-ridden culture. Colt (Valencia

Femforce #120 © 2003 AC Comics.
COVER ART BY MARK AND STEPHANIE HEIKE.

Kirk), the diminutive mistress of all manner of weaponry and martial arts, and Rayda (Dyna Morisi), a "human dynamo," are auxiliary members.

Other characters that have seen action as members or allies of Femforce include Kitten, the female partner of Catman (Holyoke Publishing's Golden Age hero, revived by Black), as well as such forgotten Golden Age (1938–1954) heroines as Yankee Girl, Miss Masque, and Jetgirl. Femforce's ranks sometimes swell nearly to Avengers proportions, mainly because of a surfeit of eager and evocatively named villains, including Alizarin Crimson, the Black Shroud,

Capricorn, Darkfire, the Fearforce, Fem-Paragon, Lady Luger, the Shimmerer, and Stella Stargaze, as well as ambiguous sometime-allies who as often as not are foes, such as the antisocial Rad (actually Ms. Victory's daughter) and the giantess Garganta.

By the late 1980s, as independent comics sales declined, Black converted *Femforce* into a black-and-white format; the title (along with its several spin-off miniseries and one-shots) remained AC's only consistently solid seller, both in the direct-sales market and via mail order. By 1990 AC Comics, along with the rest of the industry, was growing steadily. AC's staff grew as well; *Femforce* acquired a new writer-artist known only as "The Count," and artist Brad Gorby also began contributing to the positive fan-reaction the series was receiving. With the further assistance of new associate editor Heike (a major contributing factor as the multi-talented Heike wrote, drew, and inked stories), Black was able to begin releasing *Femforce* on a monthly schedule.

The year 1990 also saw the launch of two new Femforce-related titles: *Good Girl Art Quarterly* (which consisted largely of color reprints of Golden Age cheesecake stories, led by a new Femforce tale, also in color), and *She-Cat* (a black-and-white comic devoted to the feral feline Femforce member). In an effort to improve the quality and consistency of AC's Femforce line, Black took over all the writing chores on the property, even as the rest of the AC stable continued to expand. *Femforce Up Close,* a color title that focused on individual Femforce members, debuted in 1992, complementing *Jungle Girls,* which began its sixteen-issue run in 1988 and presented black-and-white Golden Age reprints as well as new tales of Tara, Femforce's jungle queen. To address the increased demand for Femforce artwork, Black hired veteran Marvel Comics great Dick Ayers, whose work Black had admired for decades.

While sales of most of the AC Comics line declined during the lean times of the mid-1990s, the up-and-coming "Bad Girl" trend—exemplified by such lucrative characters as Marvel's Elektra, DC's Catwoman, Dark Horse's Barb Wire, and Crusade

Comics' Shi—helped keep *Femforce* and its spin-offs afloat. All the while, the property somehow managed to hang onto an upbeat, relatively nonviolent image, despite the increased prevalence of "gritty" superhero fare that was becoming almost *de rigueur* across the comics industry. By 1998, against all odds, Black's relatively tiny company released the one-hundredth issue of *Femforce* (only 228 previous comic-book series have attained the century mark). AC was also reaping considerable profits from Femforce T-shirts, art portfolios, and other paraphernalia bearing the likenesses of AC's well-upholstered heroines.

As the third millennium unfolds, Femforce's future remains bright, due in no small part to Black's nostalgic Golden Age preservationist vision and his continued hands-on involvement with the stories. Still published as an ongoing title today, a summer 2003 story arc titled "Femforce: Superbabes"—spanning issues #120–#122—heated up summer sales. Spearheaded by Heike, who enlisted such artistic luminaries as Joe Staton and Will Meugniot (among others) to contribute stories demonstrating their own creative visions of Femforce-like characters, the three-issue arc proved popular.

Today Femforce fans remain fascinated with Black's unique characterizations of Ms. Victory, Nightveil, Synn, She-Cat, Tara, and Stardust, the core members of the team. Among the newest members of the Femforce creative stable are artists Jeff Austin, Mark Glidden, and Ed Coutts, and writers Paul Monsky and Chris Irving. Meanwhile the company has plans to produce an as-yet untitled independent, direct-to-video *Femforce* feature film spotlighting the exploits of a fan-favorite Femforcer, Nightveil. As of early 2004, principal photography has been completed and the project is in the editing stage. —*MAM*

Feminism

Does the classic superhero headquarters have a glass ceiling? It's certainly true that superheroines have had a mightier task to perform than their male counterparts just to get noticed in the comic-book medium, let alone thrive. Still, over the years the identities of superwomen, even more so than the traditional costumed men, have been subject to change.

After a handful of obscure predecessors, the era of the superheroine entered an auspicious phase with DC Comics' Wonder Woman, who leaped onto the printed page in *All Star Comics* #8 (December 1941–January 1942). Conceived as a draw for female readers (in the days before comics publishers wrote this entire audience off), the character—though like most such heroines, written and drawn by men—was an Amazonian archetype in whose adventures males were decidedly the less capable sex, and in which fantasias of matriarchal rule played out.

Of course, the fact that it was so fantastic may have undermined the empowering effect of the series on little girls reading it, and Wonder Woman would remain one of relatively few stand-alone superheroines for some time. Much more common were female versions of established male characters—and ones seldom with their own books, as Wonder Woman rated. Everyone knows Supergirl and Batgirl, though fewer people remember Bulletgirl and Batwoman—and perhaps that's no accident. The heroines created as diminutives of male heroes seemed to stay afloat; grown women on a potentially equal footing with their counterparts—like the forgotten 1950s Batman colleague Batwoman and the regular teammate of Fawcett Comics' Bulletman, Bulletgirl—sank thoroughly from view.

Of course, times change, and husband-and-wife teams took hold more firmly as the 1950s and 1960s progressed, from DC Comics' Hawkman and Hawkgirl to Marvel's Ant-Man (later Giant-Man) and the Wasp. By the 1970s, superwomen were liberated enough to be portrayed in extra-marital team-ups, including DC's Black Canary with Green Arrow and Marvel's Black Widow with Daredevil—in the

latter case, the woman even took co-billing in the book's title.

But where were the women standing on their own two feet? In the 1950s Marvel had had Venus, a self-reliant career woman who just happened to be the Greek goddess of the same name. But did a gal have to be from Olympus to get star billing? It seemed sadly so, sisters, when, by the 1970s, Marvel tried a brand-new (if Catwoman-derived) heroine in her own book, the Cat. Unusually (and even more so for the time) both written and drawn by women (Linda Fite and Marie Severin, respectively), the series was a moody, intriguing innovation that withered within a few issues.

The gender dynamic *was* slowly changing when the superheroes pulled off their garish work clothes and got home, especially in the case of Spider-Man, whose alter-ego Peter Parker is raised in a matriarchal household by his widowed Aunt May and would end up spending most of his series dating—and later married to—the uncommonly gutsy and independent Mary Jane Watson. But they were still the proverbial women behind the man.

Superheroines were having better luck on the TV screen, from the Saturday-morning live-action Egyptian deity Isis to primetime's Bionic Woman and, again, Wonder Woman. Back in comics, female heroes found a haven in Marvel's more offbeat ensemble books like *The Defenders,* which featured another Amazonian character (this time, of the Northern European variety), the Valkyrie, and a retooled Cat named Hellcat (though this time, empoweringly if a bit surreally, it was Marvel's former prom-queen romance-comic character Patsy Walker under the mask). Team books in general seemed to be a more hospitable workplace for women, with Marvel's mega-popular late 1970s *X-Men* reboot featuring such powerful female images as Storm and Jean Gray (if never democratizing the book's male-centric name).

The latter character is pivotal—the telekinetic Gray, who had been able to take back her name after being called "Marvel Girl" years before, is one of comics' few instances of a heroine whom male and female fans alike admire for her abilities rather than her appearance—a dignified, brainy humanitarian and leader, she gained god-like powers and met a tragic end (though various popular-demand resurrections have inevitably followed) in the *X-Men* book's classic "Dark Phoenix Saga" (issues #129–#137, 1980).

But can a superheroine be powerful and actually live? Some have been trying it. The Wasp has gone from air-headed socialite sidekick in the 1960s to leader of Marvel's team the Avengers in the 1980s and 1990s; in the same time span the Fantastic Four's Invisible Girl finally got promoted to Invisible Woman, and a stronger position in the team (a more permanent change than when she briefly left her husband, Mr. Fantastic, and the book itself in the I-am-woman early 1970s); Catwoman has gone from titillating vamp (and villain of the piece) to champion of the downtrodden (and star of her own book).

Meanwhile, the Amazon archetype introduced to comics by Wonder Woman has marched on, with ambiguous results. These characters always tread a line between role models of power and role players of dominatrix male fantasy, from Marvel's Thundra (a one-shot "Femizon" from a matriarchal future) to Jack Kirby's Barda (steely and scantily clad interdimensional warrior woman) and beyond. A subset of this type has been the sexy assassin. From Gamora in Jim Starlin's mid-1970s Marvel series *Warlock* to Elecktra in Frank Miller's early 1980s *Daredevil,* the line between power and pin-up has always blurred—and all the more so in such characters' modern equivalents, from Buffy the Vampire Slayer to Lara Croft.

Mixed blessings like these have long been superheroines' lot. The elderly Agatha Harkness, strong-willed and somewhat supernatural governess of the Invisible Girl and Mr. Fantastic's son Franklin, was introduced in 1970, becoming perhaps comics' first super senior citizen. Oracle, the contemporary heroine who used to be Batgirl, is a technological mastermind whose abilities are indispensable though the use of her legs has been lost. But neither of these characters is the first woman—in comics or real life—to have her strength and know-how appreciated only after developments (age, disability) that disqualify her as a conventional sex symbol.

Legendary underground cartoonist and feminist comics historian Trina Robbins tried taking matters into her own hands with the 2000–2001 series *Go Girl!* for Image Comics. Written by Robbins and drawn by Anne Timmons, the book follows the adventures of a hip-hop era teen taking up the mantle of her mod seventies-superheroine mom ("Go-Go Girl"!). Aimed at youngsters in an attempt to depict more three-dimensional females in comics and welcome more real ones into the medium's audience, the book wavers a bit between charming and cloying, but is a worthy and refreshing read. Its short, stormy run—previewed with high-profile fanfare and then delayed in its release and downgraded to an infrequent black-and-white due to low preorder interest among comic-shop dealers—said less about the book's quality than about the unsalability of women-starring series that is axiomatic in the industry (if self-fulfillingly so).

It is probably no coincidence that the most famous female comic-book artists have been humorists, deflating the self-importance of a male-centric genre. Marie Severin was known for satire books like *Not Brand Echh!* in the 1960s; Ramona Fradon for wacky heroes like Metamorpho and Plastic Man in the 1960s and 1970s; and Amanda Conner for the outlandish prostitute-turned-super-heroine book *The Pro* in the early 2000s.

That last book's relentlessly unglamorized look at a low-respect female occupation may be a signal of things to come. No-nonsense portrayals of domestic abuse have appeared in Marvel's *Ultimates* and *Spider-Girl* (the latter of which has drawn some fire for its sympathetic characterization of lesbian moms—and drawn a larger female readership than most comics have in years); well-rounded characters like Brian Michael Bendis' Jessica Jones in *Alias* (no relation to the TV show) and Frank Miller's reluctant urban warrior Martha Washington have garnered feminist praise; companies are trying out books starring non-male-derived, non-cheesecake-oriented heroines again (like Alan Moore's acclaimed goddess epic *Promethea* and Peter David's mature and enigmatic noire drama *Fallen Angel*); and even honest-to-gosh women writers like Devin Grayson and Gail Simone are bringing new spins to characters from the Black Widow to Birds of Prey.

High-profile movies like the Halle Berry *Catwoman* and the Jennifer Garner *Elektra* are in the pipeline, which will boost the box office for super-women and may either help or hurt super-sister-hood—but whatever happens, both on the page and behind the scenes, the female population of a male-dominated medium will keep pressing forward, even if it's not in a single bound. —*AMC*

Fighting American

Fighting American #1 © 1966 Harvey Comics.
COVER ART BY JACK KIRBY AND JOE SIMON.

The 1950s comics scene was dominated by horror and crime comics, witch hunts and scare stories, and was characterized by long-established comic-book companies going under. Into this unpromising environment Joe Simon and Jack Kirby launched *The Fighting American* in 1954 (published by Prize Comics), which the creative duo hailed as the first superhero satire in comics history. Interestingly, Marvel Comics had revived Captain America just eight months earlier, and it is intriguing to ponder if Simon and Kirby created the Fighting American as a riposte to their earlier superhero creation. Indeed, the pair's avowed aim was to make the public forget Captain America entirely; clearly, this did not happen.

The first issue of *Fighting American* introduced readers to patriotic television newscaster Johnny Flagg, a war hero much given to warning America about the dangers of communism. Those self-same communist agitators promptly beat him close to death, but on his deathbed he asks his feeble brother Nelson (who had been scripting Johnny's red-baiting speeches all along) to carry on his fight. Days later, the army summons Nelson to a secret lab where Johnny's revitalized body has been dressed in a stylish red-white-and-blue costume. In the ensuing operation, Nelson's brain is transferred to Johnny's body and the fearless Fighting American is born; what happened to Nelson's body is never revealed (and Nelson himself does not refer to the event again).

Just as Captain America had a sidekick, the Fighting American soon acquired his own young assistant, Speedboy, a young pageboy who stumbled across Johnny/Nelson's secret identity and was instantly recruited to the cause. Again like Captain America's 1950s adventures, the Fighting American was rabidly anticommunist, although Simon and Kirby played it all strictly for laughs. Indeed, there has never been a stranger collection of bizarre villains in comics history. Among the varied villains on display, the unsuspecting reader could come across the likes of Invisible Irving, Double Header (with, naturally, his two heads), Hotsky Trotsky, Poison Ivan, Count Yuscha Liffso, Superkhakalovitch, and Square Hair Malloy. Not content with outlandish bad guys, the strip also featured weird guest stars like Uncle Samurai, Shiskabob the Sorcerer, and Yafata's Moustache, along with a bevy of buxom femme fatales including Charity Bizarre, Scarlet O'Haircut, and Lucy Liverwurst.

Simon and Kirby were long-established comics pros but their roots were in the unsophisticated, hard-living slums of New York and the comic reflected this environment. The humor was broad, slapstick comedy, full of joke Yiddish names, ethnic stereotypes, and resolute political incorrectness. In spite of (or because of) this, the feature was genuinely funny. However, the mid-1950s were not a good time for superheroes, and *Fighting American* lasted a mere seven issues. Eleven years later (in 1966), Simon revived the comic during his short-lived stint as an editor at Harvey Comics; this comic combined reprints with strips intended for the old, unpublished eighth issue. Harvey pulled the plug on its superheroes with only one issue released, even though a second issue was ready for printing, but Simon retained his copyright on the character, waiting for the right moment to unleash his hero again.

After a long wait, the character returned in 1989 in a deluxe hardback compilation of his 1950s strips, issued by Marvel Comics. This heralded a decade of bizarre miniseries. The first of these, published by DC Comics in 1994, retold the character's origin story but updated it to the present day, dumping the treacherous commies but

keeping the strange villains (such as the Media Circus and the Gross National Product). The Fighting American's next outing had as convoluted an origin as any comic of recent years. In the mid-1990s, Marvel revamped a host of its comics in a campaign called "Heroes Reborn." One of these—Captain America—was produced by the controversial Rob Liefeld. The Heroes Reborn line was jettisoned after a year but Liefeld had already drawn some more issues that he was determined to use, and so he made some art changes, renamed the hero Agent America, and prepared to release it under his own company, Awesome Entertainment. Marvel immediately sued over the blatant similarities to its legendary Captain America, but Liefeld countered by licensing Fighting American from Joe Simon, changing his leading characters (again) and redrawing the Nazis as communists. Such was the fervor for superheroes at the time that the *Fighting American* miniseries (in 1997) led to two further outings over the next couple of years. Neither added much to the hero's reputation, but the idea that new Fighting American stories came out of old Captain America strips was deliciously ironic.

While no new comics have appeared since 1999, the Fighting American was the inspiration behind Alan Moore's hilarious superhero spoof, "The First American" in *Tomorrow Stories,* and so his legacy lives on. —*DAR*

Firestorm

Created by writer Gerry Conway and artist Allen Milgrom for DC Comics (*Firestorm* #1, 1978), Firestorm is unique among nuclear-powered superheroes, representing a transition between the atomic-generated heroes of the 1960s (mainstays such as Spider-Man and the X-Men, characters for whom nuclear power is a potent yet ultimately benign force) and the distrust of all things nuclear that marked the post–Three Mile Island 1980s. Firestorm stands astride the mushroom clouds of the Nuclear Age's heyday and the postmodern Earth-goddess spiritualism of the 1990s New Age.

On the eve of the opening of the controversial and experimental Hudson Nuclear Facility, the Earth Spirit (known alternatively as Gaia or Maya) selects nuclear physicist Martin Stein to be Earth's latest fire elemental. When radical environmentalist Edward Earhart attempts to destroy the plant, Stein is knocked unconscious. One of Earhart's confederates, a high-school jock named Ronnie Raymond, has a change of heart and tries to stop the sabotage, only to be irradiated along with Stein, to whom Earhart has shackled him inside the main reactor room. Stein and Raymond find themselves combined into a single, nuclear-powered form—that of the flame-headed superbeing known as Firestorm.

Because Raymond is conscious at the time of his melding to the insensate Stein, the teen's impulsive, wise-guy personality dominates Firestorm's consciousness; Stein's calmer, more staid mind runs in the background, lending its expert scientific guidance to Raymond in the use of his power to alter the atomic structure of inorganic matter (Firestorm later forswears this ability because of its tendency to make the objects he transmutes unstable). Firestorm can also fly at light speed, release intense blasts of nuclear-generated fire and heat through his hands and eyes, pass through solid objects, control flames and fire (which he can also use as an energy source to enable him to grow or shrink), and even teleport himself to any open flame on Earth. In addition, he has the ability to transform back into his two human forms—with Stein at first having no recollection of Firestorm's adventures afterward, unlike Raymond. Operating initially as a fairly standard villain-foiling costumed superhero—albeit a hero with an awkward, twofold secret identity—Firestorm at first knows nothing of his status as a fire elemental, and must learn to master his powers gradually over time (with Stein's help). Firestorm's one major weakness is a tendency to suffer mental "attacks" during which the bond between Raymond and Stein suddenly weakens, requiring intense concentration on Raymond's part in order to maintain Firestorm's powers.

Unfortunately for the fused fissile hero, his first series lasted only five issues before succumbing to the so-called "DC implosion" of 1978, a bleak time characterized by slumping comics sales and the cancellation of a multitude of DC titles (the aborted sixth issue of *Firestorm* was published in 1978 under the title *Canceled Comics Cavalcade #1*). Firestorm was subsequently relegated to guest-star status in such series as *DC Comics Presents, Justice League of America, Flash,* and *The Brave and the Bold.* Four years later, the burgeoning comics specialty shop (or direct-sales) market had significantly increased sales across the comics industry, allowing *The Fury of Firestorm, the Nuclear Man* to flourish as a monthly series. Initially written by Conway with pencils by Pat Broderick, this comic (whose title was shortened in 1987 to *Firestorm, the Nuclear Man* with issue #65) lasted until its one hundredth issue (1990), demonstrating a longevity that is remarkable in modern superhero comics. During this run, Firestorm becomes a key member of the Justice League of America and fights such adversaries as Black Bison (a superpowered Native American), Killer Frost (a cold-themed Justice League villain with the ability to freeze her enemies), the Pied Piper (based on the fairy tale), the explosive Plastique, a foul-weather foe called the Typhoon, the nuclear-powered Soviet superhero Pozhar, and even Jack Kirby's nigh-omnipotent conqueror Darkseid.

Under the creative tenure of writer John Ostrander and such artists as Joe Brozowski, J. J. Birch, Ross Andru, and Tom Mandrake, Firestorm (with Stein, now an aware and willing participant in Firestorm's trifold existence, suffering from an inoperable, radiation-induced brain tumor) attempts to disarm the Soviet Union to bring about world peace; this leads to a clash with the Russian hero Pozhar (Mikail Denisovitch Arkadin, who gained his powers during the nuclear mishap at Chernobyl, is introduced in *Fury of Firestorm* #63, 1987), bringing on a "mental attack" that splits Firestorm into his two component entities. Caught in a subsequent nuclear explosion with Arkadin, Raymond becomes melded with the Russian (*Firestorm Annual* #5, 1987). This re-fusion yields a second, all-new Firestorm who resembles an incendiary god out of myth more than a traditional spandex-clad superhero. The revamped champion also has his own independent personality (based upon Stein's), into which Raymond and Pozhar are submerged as Firestorm takes his place among the pantheon of Earth's elemental protectors. He also becomes aware for the first time of his status as a divinely selected fire elemental and becomes increasingly distant from other superheroes; protecting the environment is now his primary focus. Firestorm's new persona is cold and analytical at first, gradually learning over time to trust his developing emotions and "go with his gut" during crisis situations. Despite these radical changes and new priorities, Firestorm never hesitates to assist any human being in distress.

Cured of his brain tumor years later, Stein helps the Raymond-Arkadin Firestorm fight an atomic villain named Brimstone, who tries to use the sun's energies to incinerate Earth. During the battle Firestorm is split into his constituent parts (Raymond and Pozhar), and Stein is caught in a nuclear blast that transforms him into another Firestorm— all by himself, as the Earth goddess had intended all along. The reborn Firestorm ultimately uses a black hole to defeat Brimstone after a fierce contretemps on the surface of the sun itself. Stein/Firestorm then becomes the Universal Fire Elemental, which amounts almost to an ascension to godhood, and leaves Earth behind entirely for cosmic parts unknown.

Bereft of his nuclear powers, the earthbound Raymond retains enough of his superheroic good looks to garner some success as a male model. Unfortunately, Raymond also develops a drinking problem (a result of the years of stress that Firestorm had inflicted upon Raymond and his family, and a common plight of heroes' alter egos) and discovers that his days of nuclear derring-do have left him with a nasty surprise—a rare type of leukemia, echoing Stein's earlier brain tumor. Raymond's illness forces him to seek the help of his old Justice League associates (*Extreme Justice* #1, 1995), which leads to the discovery that Firestorm's powers still lay dormant within his cells. Stein eventually returns to Earth, using his fire elemental powers to reignite Raymond's slumbering abilities, thereby eliminating his cancer and allowing Raymond to return to superheroics (and Justice League reserve status) in Firestorm's original form (appearing more or less as he did in his 1978 debut, while Stein returns to space as a fire elemental). Raymond's alcoholism remains a persistent problem, however, giving the nuclear-powered hero an enduring human dimension. Another difficulty he faces is learning how to use his powers without access to Stein's scientific expertise. To make up for this lack, Raymond calls on superhero colleagues such as Oracle for advice (*JLA* #40, 2000), and enrolls as a physics student at Ivy University, where he is tutored in the mysteries of nuclear science by Ray Palmer, who leads a double life as the Atom (*Day of Judgment* miniseries, 1999).

Though the early years of the new millennium found Firestorm still dispossessed of a series to call his own, the nuclear man continued to appear as what his crime-fighting confrere Batman described as a "heavy hitter" in the current Justice League series (*JLA,* which debuted in 1997), in which writer Joe Kelly hinted that Firestorm may have once again evolved multiple personalities (*JLA* #71, 2002). His future seemed as ambiguous as the real-world prospects of atomic energy, but in spring of 2004 the nuclear man regained his monthly marquee status in an ongoing solo series. —*MAM*

The Flash

In an industry characterized by almost constant change, it is reassuring that the Flash has stayed true to his comics roots, even through his three different incarnations. The first version of the character was as DC Comics' fifth superhero (tying with Hawkman for the honor) and as the first super-speedster in comics history—though of course Superman was also rather quick on his feet. The Flash's origin in *Flash Comics* #1 (January 1940) recounts how student Jay Garrick is experimenting one night in the lab at Midwestern University when he is overcome by hard-water fumes and passes out. Reawakening weeks later, he finds that he can move incredibly fast and is even able to pluck a bullet out of the air. ("Swifter than the speed of light itself—faster than a bolt of lightening in the sky—is the Flash!) In an unusual display of self-aggrandizement, his first action is to play in the college football team, single-handedly winning the game and impressing the socks off his girlfriend, Joan Williams.

The strip's creator, writer Gardner Fox, was inspired by Mercury, the Roman god of speed, and the Flash shared Mercury's winged helmet and boots, combined with a red shirt and blue slacks ensemble, topped off with a lightning-bolt insignia on his chest. For its first few years, the strip was rather lighthearted in tone, reflected in the cartoony art of Harry Lampert and Everett E. Hibbard and adventures that pitted America's beloved hero against witches and fairies. He also acquired some bumbling assistants—the Three Stooges-inspired Winky, Blinky, and Noddy—who eventually got their own strip in *All-American Comics.*

After World War II, the Flash's more comedic elements were downplayed by new editor Julius Schwartz, who, along with writers John Broome and Robert Kanigher, introduced a colorful lineup of supervillains into the strip. These included the Ragdoll, the Thinker, Star Sapphire, the Fiddler, and the flirtatious Thorn (who was deemed too suggestive by DC's management and promptly banished from the feature). Visually, too, the introduction of dynamic young artists Carmine Infantino and Joe Kubert ensured that the strip was one of the most attractive of the Golden Age (1938–1954). The powerful simplicity of the Flash's powers—what kid

The Flash #145 © 1964 DC Comics.
COVER ART BY CARMINE INFANTINO AND MURPHY ANDERSON.

wouldn't want to be the fastest runner in his school, for instance?—made him one of DC's top sellers. In addition to *Flash Comics,* he was also featured in *All-Flash Comics, Comic Cavalcade,* and, as a member of the Justice Society, *All Star Comics,* making almost 200 appearances altogether. Only Superman, Batman, and Wonder Woman made more appearances than the Scarlet Speedster, as he was nicknamed.

Jay Garrick's last Golden Age adventure was in *All Star Comics* #57 in 1951, but a little more than five years later a new Flash hit the newsstands in what was to be one of the pivotal moments in comics history. *Showcase* #4 (September–October 1956) introduced police scientist Barry Allen, who suddenly acquired superspeed powers when a lightning bolt hit his chemical cabinet, drenching him with a cocktail of chemicals. Inspired by an old copy of *Flash Comics,* Allen made himself a red, rubberized costume that could compress itself into a chamber in his ring, and suddenly a new Flash was born. Like Spider-Man's alter ego Peter Parker to come, Allen exemplified the very human faux pas of real life outside of a costume: As the Fastest Man Alive, he could run faster than the speed of light, but as Barry Allen he could never show up for a date on time. After the postwar collapse of the genre, there had been the occasional attempt to revive the superhero concept, but the Flash was the first revival that actually *worked,* and its success single-handedly inspired the Silver Age comics boom (1956–1969).

The team behind the new Flash included the same people who had worked on him before: Schwartz, Kanigher, Broome, and Infantino; all had matured and improved, especially artist Infantino, who brought a sleek sophistication to the strip. After four issues of *Showcase,* the Flash was given his own comic in 1959, resuming numbering at #105—the point at which the previous *Flash Comics* had been canceled. Barry Allen and Jay Garrick shared several common features: they were both scientists, both had girlfriends who knew their secret identities (though Barry kept his girlfriend Iris West guessing for several years), and both were laid-back, mature, almost fatherly figures. As before, the new Flash strip cleverly sustained the lighthearted tone of its stories, mixing humor with adventure in a way that was quite unique for the time.

Again like the Golden Age Flash, the new strip featured villains by the score, more so in fact than just about any other superhero comic. Over three decades, the Flash pitted his wits and his fists against the likes of Mirror Master, Super-Gorilla Grodd, Professor Zoom, the Pied Piper, Weather Wizard, the Top, Captain Boomerang, Abra Kadabra, the Trickster, and Captain Cold. In fact, where most stories embraced "relevance" in the 1970s or became dark and violent in the 1980s, the Flash remained for the most part the same. Similarly, he had a remarkably stable creative team: Infantino drew the strip until 1968 and then returned in the early 1980s, while Irv Novick drew most of the other issues; Broome and Kanigher were replaced by Cary Bates, who then wrote the comic for more than ten years.

While Barry Allen and Iris West never actually had any children (they were married in 1966), the strip nevertheless acquired its own family of sorts. The first arrival was Wally West, Iris' kid brother, who was awarded his own superspeed powers in *Flash* #110, in a repeat of the original accident while he was visiting Barry in his lab. He thus became Kid Flash and accompanied the Flash on numerous adventures, before later going on to join the Teen Titans. Ralph Dibny, the Elongated Man, introduced himself two issues later and teamed up with the Flash on many occasions, as did the Green Lantern and a long-lost friend: Jay Garrick, the original Flash. Garrick re-entered the comics world in *Flash* #123, ten years after his last appearance in print. The popularity of that issue led to the gradual reintroduction of many other Golden Age heroes, including the Justice Society of America. From 1976 on, Garrick has been a stalwart of numerous Justice Society comics and crossovers, and remains a treasured star of the DC universe—which is more than can be said for Barry Allen.

The 1970s were a hard time for a lot of DC's Silver Age warriors and, although the Flash weathered the storm, as the years went by his world began to crumble away. First, his beloved Iris was murdered by Professor Zoom, who in turn was later killed by the Flash, leading to years on the run and a tumultuous court case. In 1985, his comic was canceled (with issue #350) and finally, in the *Crisis on Infinite Earths* miniseries, poor old Barry died trying to save the planet. At this point, DC decided to let the sidekick take over—to date the only time this has happened—and in 1987 Wally West, Kid Flash, became the one and only Flash.

West was a different, edgier, and more youthful Flash; he shared none of his mentor's modesty and reticence. He was brash, bold, and somewhat self-centered—the perfect hero for the 1980s, in fact. West was not as quick as Allen and needed to consume vast quantities of food to keep going, but luckily money was not a problem, since he had won the lottery. While initially trying to steer things away from the old Flash, the comic's various writers, including William Messner-Loebs and Mark Waid, soon found themselves bringing back the old villains one by one, proving that what worked in the 1960s could work just as well in the 1990s.

The new decade also brought with it an entirely unexpected development: *The Flash* television show that ran for twenty-two episodes on CBS in the 1990–1991 season. John Wesley Shipp made a charismatic Flash and Amanda Pays, who portrayed Dr. Christina McGee, a convincing pseudo love interest who knew about the Flash's secret identity. With story editors from the comics industry (Howard Chaykin and John Francis Moore), a budget of $1 million for each hour-long episode, and unprecedented special-effects techniques, *The Flash* redefined the way that superheroes had previously been portrayed on television. Critics cite the poor time slot (opposite NBC's *The Cosby Show* and Fox's *The Simpsons*) as the reason for the show's brief lifespan.

Today's Wally West has surrounded himself with his own cast of thousands, including interdimensional pal Chunk and Asian journalist (and future wife) Linda. For the most part, however, his companions are fellow speedsters, such as Johnny Quick, Jessie Quick, Jon Fox (the Flash of the twenty-seventh century), and the "Zen master of speed," Max Mercury. The most significant hanger-on has proved to be Impulse (introduced in *Flash* vol. 2 #92), a hyperactive speed demon from the thirtieth century, sent back in time to counteract a fatal super-aging disease and to learn how to "chill out" with the help of Max Mercury.

The hyperkinetic Impulse struck a chord with fans and was soon granted his own comic (1995–2002) and a starring role in the Young Jus-tice group (1998–2003), though perhaps his enduring legacy will be as one of the first major DC characters drawn in a manga-inspired style. Impulse may not have had real staying power, but the Flash seems likely to run and run. West has been a long-time member of the Justice League, just as Jay Garrick continues as a mainstay of the Justice Society, and it seems likely that fans will continue to be captivated by the fastest man (or men) for years to come. *—DAR*

Funny Animal Heroes

It's a dog-eat-cat world in the land of animated cartoons. Endangered by falling anvils and ubiquitous dynamite, as well as ravenous predatory toons loony for a meal of a weaker species, anthropomorphic animals need their superheroes, too.

The first big cheese was Mighty Mouse, originating as "Super Mouse" in the theatrical short *The Mouse of Tomorrow* (1942). If Terrytoons animator "Izzy" Klein had his way, this diminutive dynamo would have been "Super Fly." Head honcho Paul Terry, seeing dollar signs in a merger of Mickey Mouse and Superman, appropriated and altered Klein's idea, little realizing that Standard Comics had just beaten him to the punch with its own Supermouse (whose comics ran until 1958), leading Terry to change his character's name. Bursting into action by singing an operatic strain of "Here I Come to Save the Day," Mighty Mouse rescued his sweetie Pearl Pureheart or other random rodents from the clutches of a cagey cat named Oil Can Harry through decades of cartoons and comic books published by St. Johns, Pines, Dell, and Gold Key Comics. He was a staple of Saturday morning television for many years, including CBS's *Mighty Mouse: The New Adventures,* Ralph Bakshi's subversive 1987 interpretation, peppered with double-

Super Mouse from *Super Mouse* #14 © 1951 Standard Comics.

entendres that flew over the heads of children—but not their parents. Watchdog groups incensed over a flower-sniffing sequence that allegedly mimicked cocaine use lobbied Bakshi's *Mouse* off the air.

Hoppy the Marvel Bunny, a Bugs Bunny/Captain Marvel amalgamation, bounced into Fawcett Comics in 1942. Two different Super Rabbits premiered in 1943: the first, an original character

published by Marvel Comics and the second, a Superman parody in a classic Bugs Bunny short. DC Comics' McSnurtle the Turtle, the slow-as-molasses alter ego of the Terrific Whatzit, a funny-animal version of DC's own speedster the Flash, bowed in 1944. From the ashes of the post–World War II atomic age rose Charlton Comics' Atomic Mouse in 1953, joined by spin-offs Atom the Cat and Atomic Rabbit. Cartoonist Henry Boltinoff's Super Turtle, a half-page humor strip, appeared in the 1950s and 1960s as filler in many of DC's titles.

Funny-animal heroes arrived on the budding medium of television in 1948 in the form of *Crusader Rabbit.* This low-budget series starred a clever bunny hero and his lumbering, dim-bulb buddy Rags the Tiger in narrated comical capers with cliff-hanger endings. Sound familiar? Co-creator Jay Ward later recycled this concept with Rocky and Bullwinkle. In the 1960s, the boob tube became a super zoo: Quick Draw McGraw paraded about as the Zorro clone El Kabong, and Bob Kane, the father of Batman, parodied his own creation with *Courageous Cat and Minute Mouse.* "Humble and loveable" Shoeshine Boy popped power pills to change into *Underdog* (1964), spending his series rescuing the demure Polly Purebread; Hyram Fly slipped on his "supersonic glasses" to become lightening-fast hero Fearless Fly on the *Milton the Monster Show* (1965); Hanna-Barbera's invincible insect *Atom Ant* debuted in 1965; *Batfink* (1966) featured a steel-winged rodent with a sidekick named Karate; and Ward's wacky *George of the Jungle* featured Super Chicken (1967), whose powers came from guzzling a concoction called "Super Sauce." More toon titans would follow, including *Hong Kong Phooey* (1974), *Danger Mouse* (1981), and *Darkwing Duck* (1991).

A new crop of caped critters continued to fill comic-book pages through the latter twentieth century. Underground comics artist Gilbert Shelton created Wonder Warthog in 1962, and in 1965 Disney's Goofy donned a blue cape and red long johns as Super Goof, a stint that lasted almost twenty years. Howard the Duck became "trapped in a world he never made" (the Marvel Comics universe) in 1973, enjoying several years of popularity and a 1976 bid for the U.S. presidency before becoming mired in the oil slick of George Lucas' 1986 live-action film adaptation. (To avenge an earlier indignity, Howard creator Steve Gerber teamed with comics-art legend Jack Kirby for *Destroyer Duck* [1982–1984], a farcical allegory of—and fundraiser for—Gerber's court battle to retain ownership of Howard.) DC's *Captain Carrot and His Amazing Zoo Crew,* a funny-animal super*team,* launched in 1982 and Marvel's porcine version of Spider-Man—Peter Porker, the Spectacular Spider-Ham—wallowed into comics in 1983. Stan Sakai's samurai "rabbit bodyguard" Usagi Yojimbo got his start in 1985, and occasionally appears today. But no funny-animal heroes in recent memory have scored a larger success than the Teenage Mutant Ninja Turtles. Premiering in 1984 as a black-and-white comic, these "Heroes in a Half Shell" quickly blasted into a mega-media empire, including television animation, a live-action movie franchise, and a line of action figures. After a period of dormancy, the Turtles returned to the TV screen and toy shelves in 2003. —*ME*

Gay Heroes: *See* **Northstar**

Gen 13

Often seen as the slacker heroes of the WildStorm universe, Gen 13 are a group of teenage superheroes who have Gen-Active powers. Created in the Project Genesis program, a part of the secret government group known as International Operations (I.O.), the teens escape an uncertain future to live as a surrogate family for each other, all while fighting aliens and criminals such as Ivana, the Keepers, Bliss, and Threshold. The Gen 13 team is mentored by an ex-operative for the government, John Lynch, a man with mysterious powers and a shady past. The team lives at his La Jolla, California, home, where he has an android maid named Anna. Eventually, Lynch is revealed as team member Burnout's father. Others in the group include Fairchild, Rainmaker, Freefall, and Grunge.

Fairchild is Caitlin Fairchild, a very tall college student who developed superstrength and an extremely dense body while at Project Genesis. After she helped the others escape, Fairchild became the *de facto* leader of the group. The Amazon-like Fairchild is rarely able to stay dressed, as her clothes are constantly being shredded, vaporized, or otherwise destroyed.

Burnout is Bobby Lane, a sullen high-schooler who is inducted into Project Genesis, gaining the power to generate heat and plasma fire blasts, and to fly. Sarah Rainmaker uses her last name as her code name, and is an Apache who first discovered her powers while on the San Carlos Reservation. Rainmaker is able to fly and control the weather, and uses ampli-bands on her forearms to direct lightning strikes at her opponents. She is openly bisexual.

Freefall is Roxanne Spaulding, a girl who tries to cultivate a "bad girl" image, and who is romantically linked with Grunge. She has the power to levitate herself or almost any mass, negating gravity. Grunge is Percival Edmund "Eddy" Chang, a muscular, immature youngster with a taste for skateboards, surfing, pizza, tattoos, and women. Although stronger than average humans, he has the ability to assimilate properties from anything he touches—steel, water, concrete—and become a living version of that property. He is sometimes able to transform into other people as well, has a photographic memory, and knows multiple forms of the martial arts. His roving eye for romance doesn't sit well with Freefall.

Fairchild, Burnout, and Freefall first appeared in *Deathmate* #2 (a.k.a. *Deathmate Black,* September

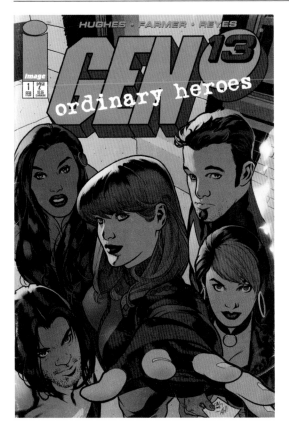

Gen13: Ordinary Heroes #1 © 1996 Jim Lee/WildStorm Productions.
COVER ART BY ADAM HUGHES.

1993) an inter-company crossover between Image Comics and Valiant Comics. Rainmaker appeared in *Stormwatch* #8 (1994), while Grunge made his debut in *Gen 13* #1 (February 1994), the first of a five-issue miniseries from Image imprint WildStorm. Drawn by fan favorites J. Scott Campbell and Jim Lee, and written by Brandon Choi, *Gen 13* was given a regular series starting in March 1995, and a second series, *Gen 13 Bootleg,* ran twenty issues plus an annual from November 1996 to July 1998. The series were very popular not only because of the kinetic art and humorous stories, but also because the book was laden with cheesecake and beefcake; the hormones of the characters rivaled any soap opera stud or vixen, and thongs and shorts seemed acceptable crime-fighting apparel.

In addition to the two regular *Gen 13* series, there were almost twenty one-shot issues and almost as many miniseries. *Gen 13* became one of the hottest properties for WildStorm, leading to crossover stories with *Fantastic Four* and *Generation X* (Marvel), *Monkeyman & O'Brien* (Dark Horse), *Superman* (DC), and *The Maxx* (Image). A planned and partially completed crossover with *Batman* (DC) never appeared. Spin-offs such as *Gen 12* and *Gen-Active* also appeared. Besides spin-offs, *Gen 13* was infamous not just for its cheesecake covers, but also for its alternate ones; issue #1 of the second series would have fifteen different covers total, and it wasn't rare for other issues to have at last one alternate cover and sometimes more.

When WildStorm Studios was bought by DC Comics in 1999, *Gen 13* moved under the DC/WildStorm publishing umbrella with issue #37 (1999). The popularity of the series began to wane—critics often blamed overexposure—and *Gen 13* was finally canceled with issue #77 (July 2002). In that final issue, it appeared that the original teen heroes were dead.

Gen 13 was relaunched with issue #0 (September 2002), written by past *X-Men* author Chris Claremont. Several new multicultural teens showed up to fight evil—Dylan York, Ethan York, Gwen Matsura, Ja'nelle Moorhead, Hamza Rashad—with some of them having gotten their Gen-Active powers from the mysterious Herod. The new team faced villains such as the Triad, Purple Haze, Chrome, and G-Nome. Predictably, Caitlin Fairchild returned, signaling the eventual return of her other previous teammates. By the time the series ended again, the original *Gen 13* team was reinstated. The final issue was #16 (February 2004).

Comics were not the only place that Gen 13 were seen. Assorted action figures and models have been released, as well as three novels. In 1998, an eighty-minute *Gen 13* animated feature film was written and directed by Kevin Altieri. An all-star cast recorded voices, including Alicia Witt (Fairchild), John de Lancie (Colonel Lynch), Elizabeth Daily (Freefall), musician Flea (Grunge), Mark Hamill (Threshold), and Cloris Leachman (Helga). The PG-13-rated film was never released in the United States by Hollywood Pictures (an arm of Disney), though it was shown at some comic-book conventions, and released direct-to-video in England, Australia, Germany, Hungary, Iceland, Brazil, and other countries. A live-action *Gen 13* film, slated to be produced by Courtney Solomon, went through several script drafts before being mothballed at Disney. —*AM*

Ghost Rider

After the enormous superhero boom of the 1960s, the following decade was characterized by a big upswing in horror comics. Marvel Comics responded to this demand with a major line of horror stories, adopting the same sort of continuity and characterization that had made their superhero stories so successful. Only rarely, however, did they combine the two genres to create horror superheroes; Morbius the Living Vampire was their first attempt, although he started life as an out-and-out villain, while the Son of Satan was, despite his name, a genuine hero. However, it was the Ghost Rider who would prove to be by far the most popular of this type of specialty character.

The first Ghost Rider was a macabre Western lawman from the 1950s, inspired by the hit Vaughn Monroe song, "Ghost Riders in the Sky." Despite that character having been created by a rival company (M.E.), Marvel revived the comic in the 1960s, but it was not a great success. Somehow, however, the name still hung around. In 1972, editor Roy Thomas decided to use it for a bike-riding hero that he had been thinking up and, with artist Mike Ploog in tow, the new Ghost Rider was born. With his sleek blue leather costume, custom-built chopper, and blazing skull for a head (Ploog's idea), he was one of the

Ghost Rider #4 © 1974 Marvel Comics.
COVER ART BY GIL KANE AND FRANK GIACOIA.

most visually arresting characters in comics—though Ploog apparently only signed up for the project thinking that it was going to be a Western strip!

The new Ghost Rider was Johnny Blaze, who had been raised since the death of his father by Crash Simpson, a daredevil stunt rider in the circus (as Blaze's father had been). Over the years, Blaze, too, learned to be an expert motorcyclist, but his life changed when he found out that Crash was dying of an incurable disease. Naturally, this being the 1970s, Blaze sold his soul to the devil, though at the last minute his half-sister stepped in and at least partially prevented the spell from working. The result was that, as night fell, Johnny Blaze became a living skeleton, possessed with the power of hell-fire, which he used to battle evil, faced with the dread prospect that he, too, could go over to the dark side at any time.

Soon, leaving the circus behind, he moved to Hollywood and briefly spent time (with former members of the X-Men) in a superhero team called the Champions, before hitting the road as a drifter. Along with most of Marvel's horror stars, Ghost Rider fought all types of grade-Z villains, including his nemesis the Orb, a motorcycling goon who wore a giant eyeball helmet. After a short run in *Marvel Spotlight,* the Rider was given his own title in 1973, but by then Ploog had left. By most measures, Ghost Rider was rarely one of Marvel's better-crafted comics, but somehow it outlasted all the other horror books to run for an incredible ten years. If nothing else, it showed the potency of the horror/super-hero/easy rider hybrid and just how far you can go with a character of truly startling appearance.

As the 1980s turned away from horror, Johnny Blaze more or less vanished from sight. Then, out of the blue, in 1990 a new Ghost Rider comic appeared with a new star. This incarnation was teenager Danny Ketch, who happened upon the Ghost Rider's motorcycle in a graveyard and was transformed into another flaming-skulled hero. Much as before, this Rider was soon enjoying enormous popularity and quickly became very much one of the hot characters of the 1990s. The combination of crunching action and the ultimate in teenage alienation (forget acne, imagine how you would feel if you suddenly became a fiery skeleton!) clearly struck a chord with fans.

It was not long before Johnny Blaze himself returned, this time simply called Blaze, and soon both he and Ketch were co-headlining in a second Ghost Rider comic called *Spirits of Vengeance.* That was followed by another spin-off, *Ghost Rider 2099,* which starred a futuristic, computer-enhanced version of the hero, potently mixing science fiction and horror. For a while, Ketch and his fellow bikers were everywhere—in spin-offs and one-shots, and guest-starring with classic superheroes such as Captain America, Wolverine, and the Punisher. Sometimes, however, you can have too much of a good thing, and this overexposure disheartened fans and eventually led to the comic's cancellation in 1998. A brief comeback in 2001 led to serious discussions regarding *Ghost Rider* the film, due to start shooting in 2004, directed by Mark Steven Johnson (*Daredevil*) and starring Nicolas Cage as Johnny Blaze/Ghost Rider. The endurance of the hero in his various incarnations only shows that each generation of readers needs to have its own Ghost Rider, so fans eagerly await the next time he will ride again. —*DAR*

Golden Age of Superheroes (1938–1954)

In the view of many, the superhero and the comic book are interchangeable, but historically, the comic book came first.

THE FIRST COMIC BOOKS

Collections of newspaper comic strips and cartoons had been published as early as the late nineteenth century, printed on low-grade pulp paper in a variety of sizes and generally distributed as promotional items. The characters featured in these editions—*The Yellow Kid* and *The Katzenjammer Kids* were among the more popular early features—were almost entirely comical, earning the nicknames "the funnies" or "funny papers" (which ultimately morphed into "funny books," a moniker vehemently loathed by many superhero readers and collectors). An anthology of Sunday newspaper strips, *Famous Funnies* #1, debuted as a monthly periodical in May 1934, and is acknowledged as the precursor to the conventional comic book (although this series was preceded a year earlier by two similarly formatted one-shots, *Funnies on Parade* and *A Carnival of Comics*).

Pulp magazines catered to readers craving adventure and thrills. The "pulps," collections of prose short stories published on pulp paper with an illustrated (usually painted) cover image, emerged in the early twentieth century and grew to tremendous popularity, particularly in the 1920s through the 1940s. From anthologies like *Weird Tales* to solo titles featuring mysterious heroes like *The Shadow* (whose pulp series lasted an astounding 326 issues from 1931 to 1949), the pulps offered breathtaking action and chilling suspense.

It was only a matter of time before these two modes of popular culture converged. Major Malcolm Wheeler-Nicholson, a retired soldier and author of pulp stories in the late 1920s and early 1930s, started his own publishing house in 1935—National Allied Publications—and in February of that year released *New Fun* #1, the first comic-book series exclusively consisting of new material; in this case, comic strips. Adventure-oriented comics with new material followed, most notably *Detective Comics* #1, released in March 1937 by Nicholson and his new partners, Harry Donenfeld and Jack Liebowitz, who had previously run Detective Comics, Inc. and then soon bought out Nicholson's interest in his own company, renaming it National Comics—even though it was (and still is) commonly called DC.

THE COMING OF THE SUPERHERO

DC Comics introduced the first costumed superhero, Superman, in *Action Comics* #1 (June 1938). The creation of writer Jerry Siegel and artist Joe Shuster, Superman had unsuccessfully been marketed to newspaper syndicates as a daily strip. Although Superman was chosen by television network VH1 as the second most recognizable figure in its 2003 "200 Greatest Pop Culture Icons" poll, DC took an enormous risk in 1938 by publishing the untried

character, given the depressed economic climate of the day. DC's Donenfeld suspected that the concept would quickly perish: "He felt nobody would believe it, that it was ridiculous—crazy," Sheldon Mayer, a former DC editor and artist, once revealed. Siegel and Shuster's unwavering faith in their superpowered champion never faltered, and readers of the day reciprocated the creators' enthusiasm: *Action* #1 sold phenomenally well; with subsequent issues its circulation figures were boosted to meet reader demand. Superman, the first superhero, was a hit.

At the time, however, Superman was not labeled or marketed as a "superhero," even though he perfectly personified the term as it is defined by many comic-book scholars today: a heroic character with an altruistic mission who possesses superpowers, wears a defining costume, and functions in the "real world" in his or her alter ego. According to author Mike Benton, in his book *Superhero Comics of the Golden Age: The Illustrated History* (1992), "Although the term 'superhero' was used as early as 1917 to describe a public figure of great talents or accomplishments, the early comic book heroes of the 1940s were usually referred to by their creators as 'costumed characters' or as 'long-underwear' or 'union-suit heroes.'" Nonetheless, the superhero had been established, and was about to be cultivated.

IN SUPERMAN'S FOOTSTEPS

Encouraged by Superman's success, DC introduced the Crimson Avenger in *Detective* #20 (October 1938), the Sandman in *New York World's Fair Comics* #1 (April 1939), and Batman in *Detective* #27 (May 1939), and published *Superman* #1, spinning off the "Man of Steel" into his own solo series, in the summer of 1939.

Victor Fox was an accountant for DC Comics who knew a good thing when he saw it. After witnessing the profits generated by Superman in *Action,* Fox quit his day job and started his own publishing company, Fox Features Syndicate. The overly ambitious Fox was sued by his former employer upon the May 1939 release of *Wonder Comics* #1, which featured "the daring, superhuman exploits" of Wonderman, a superpowered character too close to Superman for DC's comfort. Wonderman did not return for a second appearance, but Fox continued to publish comics, introducing the Flame, the Green Mask, and the Blue Beetle.

Entrepreneurs other than Fox also took notice of the success of Superman, and comic-book publishers—from talented visionaries to fly-by-night shysters—sprouted up instantly, with a flood of new "long-underwear heroes" spilling forth, including Lev Gleason Publications' Silver Streak; Quality Comics Group's Doll Man; Brookwood Publications' Shock Gibson; Centaur Publications' Amazing-Man, the Archer, the Iron Skull, and the Fantom of the Fair; and MLJ Publications' the Wizard.

A publisher that would later become DC's chief competitor entered the field in November 1939: Timely Comics. Its first superheroes—the Human Torch, the Sub-Mariner, and the Angel—premiered that month in an anthology that bore the eventual name of the company: *Marvel Comics* #1.

Comic books were the perfect entertainment form for the Depression: Their heroic, larger-than-life characters stirred the demoralized masses, and the very format of the magazines themselves—usually sixty-four pages of original material for a mere dime—was a bargain during those times of economic hardship.

THE SUPERHERO EXPLOSION

The years 1940 and 1941 heralded an eruption of new comic-book superheroes. Included among their legion: DC's the Flash, Hawkman, the Spectre, Hourman, Dr. Fate, Green Lantern, the Atom, Starman, Green Arrow, and Aquaman; radio stars the Green Hornet, the Shadow, and Captain Midnight; Fawcett Publications' Spy Smasher, Bulletman, Ibis the Invincible, and the "World's Mightiest Mortal,"

Captain Marvel; plus Cat-Man, Blue Bolt, Sub-Zero Man, the Black Terror, Hydroman, the Black Owl, the Ray, Plastic Man, Midnight, the Human Bomb, Magno (the Magnetic Man), Daredevil, the Black Hood, the Comet, and the Spirit (who starred in a comic supplement appearing in newspapers).

Superhero sub-genres quickly arose. There were the sidekicks, pre-teen or teenage junior superheroes who worked alongside their adult mentors. Starting this trend was Robin the Boy Wonder, "the sensational character find of 1940," first seen in *Detective* #38. Robin was introduced by Batman creator Bob Kane as a gateway for young readers to live vicariously "inside" the hero's adventures, and as a means to soften the rather gruesome tone of Batman's first year of publication, in which the character, originally more anti-hero than superhero, hurled mobsters off of rooftops. The concept of the superhero sidekick was yet another first for DC Comics, and another success. More kid heroes followed, like Toro, Captain Marvel Jr., Speedy, Davey, and Roy the Superboy. Superheroines began to appear in the man's world of superheroics: Wonder Woman, the Woman in Red, Phantom Lady, Lady Luck, and Black Cat were among the first. These two sub-genres dovetailed with the introduction of female sidekicks to superheroes, such as Flame Girl, Bulletgirl, Hawkgirl, Mary Marvel, and Cat-Man's partner Kitten. And in the winter of 1940, the superteam was born, as the Flash, Green Lantern, Hawkman, and other DC superheroes joined forces as the Justice Society of America.

These early superheroes (except for Timely's anti-hero, the erratic Sub-Mariner, and its flaming android, the Torch) had secret identities; they obtained superpowers through bizarre, often scientifically based occurrences, or through acquisition of power-inducing devices; they hid their actual identities behind a mask, a costume, and, often, a cape; they adopted a flamboyant appellation; they engaged in bizarre or outlandish escapades; and they dedicated their lives and their abilities to fighting crime. Or to fighting Nazis.

SUPERHEROES HELP FIGHT WORLD WAR II

"As World War II spread across Europe in the late 1930s, comic books began to take notice," commented author Ron Goulart in *Comic Book Culture* (2000). Superman, a symbol of American patriotism in his blue-and-red uniform, fought tyrants and dictators, and apprehended both Adolf Hitler and Joseph Stalin in a special comic prepared in 1940 for *Look* magazine—not surprising since the Man of Steel was called "the champion of the oppressed" in his *Action* #1 debut. Captain Marvel and other superheroes also clobbered Nazi and Japanese soldiers on the covers of their comics, even before the December 1941 bombing of Pearl Harbor brought the United States into the conflict.

It was MLJ Publications—the company that would later be known as Archie Comics—that created the first specifically patriotic superhero: the Shield, in *Pep Comics* #1 (January 1940), a red-white-and-blue-garbed crime fighter who used his superpowers, obtained from a secret formula, to protect American soil from enemy saboteurs and spies. The best-known patriotic superhero premiered in March 1941: Timely (Marvel)'s Captain America. "Cap," originally a weakling intensely loyal to his country, took a government-invented "super soldier serum" to permanently transform into the superhero who remains in print as a terrorist-buster in the post–September 11 world of the 2000s. The Shield and Captain America were merely two of a contingent of starred-and-striped heroes who appeared prior to and after America's entering the war: Miss Victory, U.S. Jones, the Star-Spangled Kid and Stripesy (a kid hero with an adult sidekick), Pat Patriot, Captain Victory, the Fighting Yank, Captain Flag, and Minute-Man (the One Man Army) were just some of the superpatriots of the World War II era. Even Uncle Sam, the symbol of U.S. Army recruitment, was a superhero during the 1940s.

A superhero was not required to wear stars and stripes to fight the Axis. The grimly clad Hangman

America's Best Comics #19 © 1946 Standard Comics. COVER ART BY ALEX SCHOMBURG.

punched out Nazis, Batman and Robin sold war bonds, the Black Terror—who bore a skull and crossbones as his costume insignia—rallied to the cause by carrying U.S. flags on his covers, and even the fussy Sub-Mariner—dressed in nothing but green swim trunks—redirected his aggression from attacking New York landmarks toward sinking Japanese subs. Comics became pro-war propaganda, and were even mailed abroad to American servicemen.

The comic-book industry flourished from a mere six comics companies in the pre-Superman days of 1936 to two dozen by the early 1940s, some of them manufacturing comics pages in unsavory, assembly-line conditions that resembled sweatshops. A 1943 *Newsweek* article cited 25 million copies of comic books being sold each month; "They were selling 102 percent; that is, beyond their spoilage rate," former comic-book writer William Woolfolk once revealed. By the mid-1940s, eager would-be publishers were blockaded from entering this expanding field by the paper shortages of World War II. Kids were encouraged to donate their used comics to paper drives, resulting in their rarity in the 2000s, where high-grade copies of 1940s comics command prices, in some cases, of tens of thousands of dollars. Despite paper rationing, the existing publishers continued to produce, produce, produce.

"Every civilization and its arts has a period in history of great accomplishments and flourishing activity," observed comics historian Benton. "From the golden age of Ancient Greece to the golden age of silent movies, there is a time (often enhanced by nostalgia) which is judged to be the best of an era or the seminal period for an art form." Although no one at the time referred to it as such, this era of comics, particularly superhero comics, is considered the medium's Golden Age (1938–1954).

In retrospect, the era is better remembered for its novelty and profusion, not for the quality of its material. Most superhero stories of the Golden Age were primitively scripted and crudely drawn, yet at the time the audience was less discerning, seeking escapism rather than artistic or intellectual engagement.

GOLDEN AGE GREATS

Some Golden Age superhero comics, however, brilliantly exemplify superlative storytelling and artistic excellence. One such series is Quality Comics' *Kid Eternity*. First seen in *Hit Comics* #25 (December 1942), Kid Eternity is rumored to have been inspired by the film *Here Comes Mr. Jordan* (1941), which was later remade into *Heaven Can Wait* (1978) and *Down to Earth* (2001). The "kid"—he is never given an actual name—dies, along with his grandfather, when the merchant marine ships they are on are torpedoed by Nazis. The boy's death is deemed a heavenly mistake, and he is returned to Earth, accompanied by a ghostly guardian, Mr. Keeper. As Kid Eterni-

ty, he commands a magic word ("Eternity!") to become invisible, and to summon famous historical figures into the present to fight crime for him. Several lauded Golden Age artists rendered the character's adventures in *Hit* and in the *Kid Eternity* solo series, including Al Bryant and Alex Kotsky.

Other standouts, highly regarded by collectors and historians: the charming Captain Marvel tales whimsically drawn by C. C. Beck, Kurt Schaffenberger, and other illustrators; Captain Marvel Jr., a character who, under the guidance of artist Mac Raboy, was rendered in a manner much more realistic than Captain Marvel's; Matt Baker's voluptuously rendered "Good Girl" art pinups on *Phantom Lady* and other covers, plus covers drawn by artists extraordinaire Alex Schomburg and L. B. Cole; Jerry Robinson's creepy interpretation of the villainous Joker in his first appearance in *Batman* #1 (1940); Bill Everett's breathtaking underseascapes in *Sub-Mariner;* Jack Cole's ingeniously lively layouts on Plastic Man; Alex Schomburg's bombastically bold covers on *Captain America* and other patriotic series; Will Eisner's groundbreaking splash-page designs in *The Spirit;* and virtually anything drawn by virtuosos Jack Kirby, Reed Crandall, and Lou Fine.

POSTWAR WOES

The end of World War II nearly marked the end of the superhero. With the Axis forces eliminated as the menace *du jour,* "comic-book heroes and heroines had nothing to do," noted Fawcett Comics artist Beck. One by one, superhero titles were canceled. Publishers went out of business, and those that survived did so from the success of new genres like funny animals, Westerns, horror, crime, romance, and science fiction, although those titles sold, at best, roughly half of circulation figures from the World War II boom.

Postwar America, despite its illusion of prosperity, was gripped by the fear of nuclear war and the spread of communism. Comics publishers scrambled to take advantage of the audience's awareness of both. The cover of *Captain Marvel Adventures* #66 (1946) depicts the hero standing amid a decimated city, with warheads sailing his way, its blurb proclaiming, "Captain Marvel Battles the Dread Atomic War!" Similarly, Superman, Fighting Yank, and other superheroes lamented nuclear warfare, while neo-heroes Atomic Man, Atoma, Atoman, and the Atomic Thunderbolt capitalized on it. Radiation-spawned monsters became a recurring theme in superhero comics by the 1950s; Plastic Man fought giant ants, and Batman and Robin were plagued by giant bees. Marvel Comics, which had canceled its superhero comics in the late 1940s, resurrected Captain America, Sub-Mariner, and the Human Torch as "commie busters" in the early 1950s, and superstar artist Jack Kirby and his partner Joe Simon launched a short-lived superhero parody, *The Fighting American,* taking on the red scare with tongue placed firmly in cheek. But readers did not seem to care. Comic-book consumers had a new pastime: the Golden Age of superheroes had given way to the Golden Age of television.

By the mid-1950s, only DC's Superman, Batman, and Wonder Woman continued to star in their own titles, and they were about to meet a real-life supervillain who would endanger them further: Dr. Fredric Wertham. A psychologist, Wertham published a 1954 book titled *Seduction of the Innocent,* indicting comic books for causing juvenile delinquency and moral decay among youth. A U.S. Senate hearing followed that targeted graphic content in horror and crime comics. Sales shrunk even more, as many parents forbade their children from reading comics. It was comics' darkest hour. A censorship board was implemented, more publishers closed shop, and DC's remaining superheroes limped along under stringent new guidelines. The Golden Age of superheroes was over. —*ME*

Good Girl Art

Good Girl art is a genre that dates back to comics' Golden Age (1938–1954), during which a range of

Men of Mystery Spotlight Special #1 © 2001 AC Comics. COVER ART BY ALEX SCHOMBURG AND BILL BLACK.

comic-book heroines were rendered in the Betty Grable and Rita Hayworth pin-up tradition of World War II. Good Girls were a departure from the popular *femmes fatales* of the era, such as the seductive villainess the Dragon Lady. Sporting a spunky attitude and dressed in the provocative sexiness of the 1940s, Good Girls were adventurers, heroines, sidekicks, or girls who stumbled into, and then escaped from, danger. While many of the Good Girls were early superheroines, others came from a range of genres. Classic Good Girls include Sheena, Queen of the Jungle; Señorita Rio, Queen of Spies; Flamingo, the Gypsy Gal; pilots like Flying Jenny and Sky

Girl; and heroines such as Mysta of the Moon, Miss Victory, the Phantom Lady, and Lady Luck. Regardless of origin, all these women share the qualities of beauty, strength, and independence—albeit fighting crime in a scanty evening gown and high heels (or, in Sheena's case, a leopard-skin miniskirt and bikini top with leopard-skin slippers).

Early comics publishers like Fiction House (1938–1954) specialized in Good Girl art within the pages of their *Wings Comics, Rangers Comics,* and *Fight Comics.* Sheena came alive in 1937 when the Jerry Iger/Will Eisner art studio invented the jungle heroine for Fiction House publisher T. T. Scott. Beautiful, strong, smart, knife-wielding Sheena was a heroine who could think on her feet, rescue men, even carry a male sidekick—a novel role reversal for the time. Sheena starred in Fiction House's *Jumbo Comics,* which also featured the zany exploits of Ginger McGuire, whose strip was titled *Sky Girl.* Drawn by popular Good Girl artist Matt Baker, in every story would-be fly-girl McGuire took to the air, revealing a long-leggedness second only to her determination. For the same publisher, Lily Renee and Bob Lubbers drew Señorita Rio, a sexy American spy who operated in Central and South America. Said comic-book historian Ron Goulart in his *Great History of Comic Books* (1986), "In [Fiction House] stories, you encountered amply constructed and sparsely clad young women on the land, on the sea, and in the air. Deep into the jungles, you ran into beautiful blondes wearing leopard-skin undies; off on some remote planet there would be a lovely redhead sporting a chrome-plated bra." Interestingly, many of these "pin-up" strips were rendered by women, at least one of whom (Ruth Atkinson) used a male pseudonym ("Ace Atkins").

After World War II, girly strips continued in comics, with added attention to plunging necklines and high-slitted hemlines, often revealing a fuller, more curvaceous figure than in issues past. Fox Features Syndicate premiered notable Good Girls Phantom Lady and Rulah of the Jungle together in *All Top Comics* in November 1947. The Baker-rendered Phantom Lady embodied the Good Girl tradition—glamorous debutante Sandra Knight fought crime in a halter top, trunks, and cape, touting her "blackout ray" as secret weapon. Women's physical attributes were amplified in Fox's comics, with Rulah's legs often hanging over the panels of the page. Soon the late 1940s Good Girl gave way to the romance heroine, with titles like *My Desire* and *My Love Secret* (both published by Fox) flooding the market. Though it is largely a product of a bygone era, certain artists, such as Rocketeer creator Dave Stevens, pay homage to Good Girl art in their work. Stevens' use of the iconic 1950s model Betty Page as inspiration for *The Rocketeer's* leading lady created a resurgence of general interest in the Good Girl art period during the late 1980s and throughout the 1990s. Even contemporary titles like AC Comics' *Femforce,* still going strong after one-hundred-plus issues, often show the inspiration of the Good Girl tradition.

Although the early decades of the twentieth century were an unenlightened era for women both in and out of the comics pages, some social historians have argued that the introduction of Good Girl art allowed for the emergence of feminism—albeit a stunted version—in print form. Others have maintained that such portrayals of women trivialized feminism and impeded its growth. Despite these conflicting conclusions, early female heroes who possessed superhuman strength, powerful weapons, an independent spirit, and exotic back stories can be found by those social archeologists willing to dig. —*GM*

The Greatest American Hero

Ralph Hinkley (portrayed by William Katt) is not having a good week. As a new teacher at Whitney High School, he is given charge of the worst class in school. But when he takes the teen delinquents on a field trip, Hinkley's life gets weirder. When the school bus stalls in the desert, Hinkley goes looking for help, only to be almost run over by an angry FBI agent named John Mackie (Robert Culp), who is searching for his partner. The two are astonished when a UFO appears, and Mackie's partner—who, unbeknownst to Mackie, is dead—delivers a special red supersuit to Hinkley. He is told that the aliens are giving him this special suit, and only he can use its powers to help humanity!

When Mackie drives off in a huff, Hinkley walks back to the bus, not noticing that he has dropped the suit's instruction booklet in the desert! Shortly thereafter, a reluctant Hinkley dons the supersuit and helps Mackie avenge his partner and stop terrorists. Unfortunately, Hinkley cannot control the powers he has and, when flying, he often crashes into buildings! Mackie and Hinkley form a reluctant partnership, with Hinkley's girlfriend Pam Davidson (Connie Sellecca) keeping them from strangling each other, and the world has a new—if uncoordinated and somewhat reluctant—superhero.

William Katt stars as Ralph Hinkley, reluctant hero, in *The Greatest American Hero*.

Debuting on ABC on March 18, 1981, *The Greatest American Hero* was the creation of Stephen J. Cannell, best known for such action fare as *The A-Team* and *21 Jump Street*. The series mixed humor and action in a fun way, and the lead characters played off each other brilliantly. Culp's pressure-cooker-about-to-blow style and Katt's laid-back help-humanity act were a great mix, and Sellecca balanced them out with the right amount of feminine power.

The Greatest American Hero had one problem right out of the starting gate: On March 30, 1981, John Hinckley attempted to assassinate President Ronald Reagan. The studio and network scrambled to cover their lead character's sound-alike name, and Hinkley suddenly became "Hanley" or "Mr. H" to his students (though his original last name was restored for the second season). To make matters worse, DC Comics threatened legal action over what the company deemed too many similarities to its Superman character, but DC lost in court.

Nevertheless, *The Greatest American Hero* was a hit with audiences. Its theme song, "Believe It or Not," sung by Joey Scarbury and written by Stephen Geyer and Mike Post, rose to number two on the pop music charts in 1981. Geyer and Post also wrote and recorded original songs for twenty-three of the show's episodes. Actor Culp wrote and directed some second-season episodes.

During the third season of the series, Hinkley and Davidson married, and Hinkley got a bit better at using his various superpowers. But ABC's decision to move the series to Friday nights—a death-knell for science fiction–oriented series—proved too villainous an act for Hinkley to triumph over. The show ended its run on February 3, 1983, with four episodes unaired. Those shows later popped up when *The Greatest American Hero* hit syndication, and the series drew good ratings yet again.

With NBC expressing interest in a relaunch, the main cast members reunited in 1986 to film a new pilot, titled *The Greatest American Heroine*. In it, Ralph's secret is exposed to the world, and when the fame goes to his head, the aliens "fire" him. The suit is given to a young girl named Mary Ellen Stuart (Holly Hathaway), who drives Mackie crazy with her grand plans to save the whales and then solve the rest of the world's woes. NBC passed and the pilot never aired, but it was expanded to a full hour and put into the syndication package, alongside the previous forty-three episodes.

Although an animated series was rumored to be in development for years, it was in March 2000 that a feature-film development deal for *The Greatest American Hero* was announced, with Stephen J. Cannell producing for Film Roman productions and Touchstone Pictures. Three screenwriters worked on a script—Paul Hernandez, Abby Kohn, and Marc Silverstein—that found comic-book fan/teacher

Ralph Hinkley given a supersuit by aliens, and facing the prospect that other humans had been given supersuits as well. Whether this potential new version of *The Greatest American Hero* will actually be made into a feature film is probably something that only someone with superpowers can answer. —*AM*

Green Arrow

From the very earliest days of superheroes, there have been "super-archers." While DC Comics' Green Arrow was not the first, he was certainly the longest lived. Created by writer Mort Weisinger and artist George Papp, the Green Arrow first appeared in 1941 in *More Fun Comics* #73, and was from the start a transparent attempt to replicate one of the company's biggest successes. Like Batman, Green Arrow had a wealthy playboy alter ego (Oliver Queen), a plucky kid sidekick called Speedy (Queen's ward, Roy Harper), a secret underground workshop beneath his estate, and his own Arrow car, Arrow plane, and Arrow boats. Where Batman had his seemingly limitless utility belt, Green Arrow had an almost inexhaustible supply of gimmicky arrows, including boxing glove, trip-wire, lariat, jet, tightrope, and acetylene types. His origin, however, was different from other superheroes and very straightforward: After being shipwrecked on a desert island, Queen makes himself a bow and over the following months becomes an expert bowman. After saving a ship that anchors offshore, Queen arrives at his purpose in life: "I knew then, in that split-second, that my existence on the island could now serve a useful purpose! When I returned to civilization, I would fight crime with my trick arrows!" Back home, Queen creates a suitably heroic costume and pairs up with young Speedy, who in "real life" as Roy Harper has been trained in archery by Indians and so is himself an expert archer.

The strip was usually well crafted if a little lacking in personality, but that DC believed in it is clear from its transfer to *Adventure Comics,* where it ran until 1960. A simultaneous backup slot in *World's Finest Comics* lasted several years longer (until 1964). Within a few months of their creation, the intrepid duo were inducted into the Seven Soldiers of Victory in *Leading Comics,* where they enjoyed rather improbable adventures throughout the war. The Emerald Archer, as he was often called, and Speedy tangled with minor villains like the Wizard, Clock King, and the Rainbow Archer throughout the 1940s and 1950s, but the 1960s superhero boom rather passed them by. With little in the way of character development or depth, Green Arrow had to make do with membership in the Justice League of America, while Speedy joined the Teen Titans. However, by the turn of the decade both archers were to become among the most talked-about heroes in comics.

In late 1969, Green Arrow first gained a new costume and goatee beard (courtesy of artist Neal Adams in *The Brave and the Bold* #79), and then lost his fortune to a crooked business partner (thanks to writer Denny O'Neil in *Justice League* #75). In that same issue of *Justice League* he moved to the ghetto and met the Black Canary, who would become his love interest for the next few decades. Finally, he co-headlined with Green Lantern in a series of comics by O'Neil and Adams that tackled such "relevance" issues as race relations, ecology, politics, business corruption, and drugs in an award-winning series of strips that generated vast amounts of publicity. Readers now enjoyed an older Oliver Queen—passionate, belligerent, hot-headed, and radical. Here was a character that had gone from a one-dimensional cipher to an embodiment of the zeitgeist, equal parts hippie, hero, and rabble-rouser. Speedy, on the other hand, personified the era's darker side as he descended into drug addiction in a story that garnered widespread praise (in *Green Lantern/Green Arrow* #85 and #86), including an endorsement from New York City's mayor at the time, John Lindsay.

Despite all this attention, the Green Lantern/Green Arrow partnership lasted only a couple of years, and the archer had to be content with numerous backup features, invariably with Black Canary, in such books as *World's Finest, Action Comics,* and *The Flash,* as well as numerous *Justice League* comics throughout the 1970s. These shorter tales gradually saw a mellowing of the rhetoric and a penchant for wisecracks emerging in its place, but more recent stories have chronicled a steady descent into darkness. Green Arrow was given his first (short-lived) solo comic in 1983, followed a few years later by Mike Grell's hard-hitting *Longbow Hunters* series, which was set in Seattle's mean streets and featured a harrowing sequence in which the Black Canary was brutally tortured.

The *Longbow Hunters* went on to a long-running "mature readers only" series that continued in much the same violent, seedy vein and became a big-selling *cause célèbre* for its grim, violent tone. The Canary and Arrow finally split up and new cast members Shado (a female Japanese assassin) and Eddie Fryes (a sort of dissolute secret agent) were introduced, along with a long-lost—and previously unknown—son, Connor Hawke. As part of its wide-ranging *Zero Hour* series in the mid-1990s, DC killed off Oliver Queen in an airplane explosion, and Hawke became a new, more youthful Green Arrow. Hawke's idealism and inexperience breathed new life into the strip, but few doubted that his father would one day return. True to form, in 2001 new writer (and cult film director) Kevin Smith (*Clerks; Chasing Amy*) duly resurrected him from the dead. Smith was replaced by best-selling author Brad Meltzer and other successors, ensuring that the comic, now starring two generations of Green Arrow, will continue to excite interest for some time to come. —*DAR*

Green Hornet

Heroes who operate on both sides of the law have long been popular in comics and crime fiction. Such a character is the masked mystery man called the Green Hornet, a crime fighter who gamboled with gangsters in order to sting them for apprehension.

The Green Hornet and Kato first appeared in a 1936 radio drama produced by George W. Trendle, whose previous program, *The Lone Ranger,* was a tremendous (and perennial) success. Revisiting *The Lone Ranger's* proven formula—an enigmatic masked hero accompanied by a loyal ethnic partner (in the Ranger's case, his Native American companion, Tonto)—*The Green Hornet* took the concept one step further, linking the two series into a generational saga. Historians acknowledge radio scriptwriter Fran Striker as the principal creator of the Green Hornet.

The Green Hornet is actually Britt Reid, whose father Dan is the Lone Ranger's nephew. The Ranger's penchant for silver bullets (and even his horse's name) was derived from the family's silver mine, which dispassionate Britt inherits and begins to squander as a playboy. He picks up a manservant on an excursion to Japan after rescuing a young man named Kato from peril; Kato returns the favor by dedicating his life to his redeemer. Back in the States, Reid assumes the family business—*The Daily Sentinel* newspaper, which targets organized crime—and rises beyond his flippancy as he matures into its publisher. On a nighttime jaunt to collect evidence against mobsters for a *Sentinel* exposé, Reid and chauffeur Kato are spotted at the scene of the crime in their unique sedan—the Black Beauty—and the car is added to the police's most-wanted list. Reid—abetted by his executive assistant Lenore Case and a handful of confidantes within the police department—preserves that underworld brand by adopting the masked identity of the Green Hornet, and along with Kato, an accomplished martial artist, begins a battle against crime by pretending to be on its side.

The Green Hornet ran on radio for sixteen years, as the hero, clad simply in a trench coat, eye-mask, and fedora, used his steel-piercing, vibrating Hornet's Sting to burst through gangsters' walls and his Gas Gun to render them unconscious. High-kicking Kato was on hand to karate-chop the crooks his partner didn't gas. The heroes' popularity extended beyond the airwaves: They headlined a pair of quickly produced movie serials from Universal Studios—*The Green Hornet* and *The Green Hornet Strikes Again* (both 1940)—and a smattering of comic books from publishers Holyoke, Harvey, and Dell. During the 1940s, a handful of Big Little Books written by Striker were published, including *The Green Hornet Strikes, The Green Hornet Returns,* and *The Green Hornet Cracks Down.*

By the early 1950s, the buzz around the Green Hornet had faded, and Kato parked the Black Beauty in the garage of pop-culture limbo—until September 1966. *The Green Hornet,* a weekly live-action television series, premiered that month, courtesy of producer William Dozier, the man responsible for bringing *Batman* to the tube nine months prior. The show's handsome lead Van Williams was eclipsed by his two co-stars: in the role of Kato, Asian import Bruce Lee, an accomplished martial artist whose proficiency soon kicked off a series of 1970s kung-fu movies; and the Black Beauty, a customized 1966 Chrysler Imperial Crown brimming with a hornet's nest of gadgets including a secret surveillance camera, laser cannon, and smoke screen. The Black Beauty and its costumed occupants were heavily merchandised in the form of trading cards, comic and coloring books, bendable figures, a lunchbox, and miniature cars. Jazz trumpeter Al Hirt's frenetic "Flight of the Bumblebee" theme was a pop-music hit, but the show was not: *The Green Hornet* was swatted from the schedule after one season.

It took more than two decades before the Green Hornet and Kato reappeared. In 1989, Now Comics launched *The Green Hornet,* expanding the legend of both heroes with their sons and daughters assuming their fathers' legacies. While briefly popular, Now's *Hornet* comic books disappeared in late 1994. Since that point, at least two attempts to bring the Green Hornet to the big screen (with George Clooney and Greg Kinnear, respectively, in the title role) have fizzled. Filmmaker Kevin Smith is, as of early 2004, attached to yet another attempt to resuscitate this project, which is partially backed by Dark Horse Comics, the publisher responsible for comics-inspired movies *The Mask, Barb Wire, Timecop,* and *Mystery Men.* —ME

Green Lantern

From humble beginnings, the Green Lantern concept has evolved through numerous revamps (with five Lanterns as of 2004), a complex mythology, and countless spin-offs. The character was first launched in July 1940 by artist Mart Nodell, with additional input from Batman writer Bill Finger, in the pages of *All-American Comics* #16 and immediately became one of DC Comics' biggest and most powerful stars. Like many early superheroes, his origin was based in magic; while working on a bridge, construction worker Alan Scott comes across a green lantern, which he later discovers was made out of a meteor. Somewhat improbably, the lantern speaks to Scott, instructing him to make a ring out of its extraterrestrial material. The ring would transform thought into reality as long as he touched the lantern once every twenty-four hours. Indeed, the power ring enables Scott to fly and take on any kind of superpower. In short order, Scott fashions himself a garish red-and-green costume (duly acknowledging, "I must have a costume that is so bizarre that once I am seen I will never be forgotten") and, as they say, embarks on a career of crime fighting.

Initial stories concentrated on the Lantern's dispatching ordinary hoods, often in a surprisingly ruthless manner, but as his powers became increasingly mind-boggling (from flying to mind-reading and, eventually, imperviousness to bullets) so, too, his villains needed to be more far-fetched. Colorful criminals such as the Sportsmaster and the Harlequin (a female villain who was also in love with Green Lantern) began to predominate, but by far the most remarkable protagonist was Solomon Grundy—a giant reanimated corpse—created by noted science fiction author and regular Green Lantern writer Alfred Bester. By this point, DC had

Green Lantern #171 © 1983 DC Comics.
COVER ART BY GIL KANE.

limited the hero's abilities somewhat by making his ring powerless against wood, but he was still a very potent wish-fulfillment figure (literally) for his fans. In addition to appearing in more than eighty issues of *All-American,* he also starred in his own solo comic for eight years, in *Comic Cavalcade* and in many issues of *All Star Comics* as one of the principal members of the Justice Society until that comic's cancellation in 1951.

Alan Scott continued to appear throughout the 1960s as part of the Justice Society and has been a constant member of the group in its many revivals, rebirths, and relaunches ever since. In fact, as of 2004 he is a regular guest star in the

Green Lantern comic (although he now goes by the name of Sentinel), largely unchanged since his debut sixty years ago, but the Green Lantern concept itself has expanded exponentially in that time.

Following the successful revamp of the Flash in 1956, editor Julius Schwartz (along with John Broome on scripts and Gil Kane on art) turned his sights on Green Lantern. The new Green Lantern premiered in September 1959 in DC's *Showcase* #22, with a new history: Test pilot Hal Jordan chances upon the crashed space ship of an emerald-garbed, red-skinned alien named Abin Sur. With his dying breath, the alien passes on his green ring to Jordan, whereupon he becomes transformed into an identically clothed superhero. Like his predecessor, this Green Lantern could use the ring to make his thoughts reality and he, too, needed a lantern to recharge the ring, but its weakness this time was to anything colored yellow (which inevitably was the cue for countless stories about yellow aliens, villains, and monsters). When the Lantern (nicknamed the Emerald Crusader) recharged his ring every day, he recited an oath that soon became his mantra: "In brightest day, in blackest night, no evil shall escape my sight. Let those who worship evil's might, beware my power—Green Lantern's light!"

It was the ring's background that differentiated the two strips; it seems that the later Green Lantern was but one of many ring-wielding superheroes across the universe—members of a sort of intergalactic police force. The Green Lanterns were picked by small, blue-skinned aliens, known as the "Guardians of Oa," as the bravest individuals on their own planets, and with their almost omnipotent rings they were sworn to uphold justice and defeat evil wherever it may appear. The Lantern stories were dynamic and inventive, often revolving around some alien menace or scientific conundrum, but characterization was not a strong feature. Hal Jordan was based on Gil Kane's neighbor at the time, an up-and-coming actor by the name of Paul Newman, and despite an attractive supporting cast including girlfriend Carol Ferris and best buddy

"Pieface," he was something of a loner. The principal villains were the rogue Green Lantern, Sinestro, and the powerful Star Sapphire—in reality Jordan's schizophrenic girlfriend Ferris.

Green Lantern started appearing in his own self-titled comic in 1960, soon became a regular member of the Justice League of America, and was very much one of DC's top characters throughout the 1960s. Kane developed into one of comics' most exciting artists but, when he left the title to try becoming a publisher himself, Green Lantern's popularity dropped. Eventually the decision was made to boost sales by introducing the Green Arrow in a retitled *Green Lantern/Green Arrow* comic, featuring the creative team of writer Denny O'Neil and artist Neal Adams. Over the course of fourteen issues (#76–#89), the comic became one of the most talked-about titles of the 1970s, tapping into the radical politics of the era and the growth of the counterculture. The Green Lantern was portrayed as the arch-establishment figure whose complacency was constantly challenged by the anti-establishment firebrand, the Green Arrow. As the voice of the streets, O'Neil and Adams introduced the concept of "relevance" to comics, tackling a different social topic in each issue, including race relations, Native American rights, women's liberation, pollution, consumerism, drugs, and campus unrest—subject matter previously untapped in the comic-book world.

Surprisingly, despite enormous media interest, numerous industry awards, college tours, and Adams' outstanding draftsmanship, sales were never strong (though conspiracy theorists have suggested that issues were sidelined by organized crime and sold to fans later) and the comic was canceled in 1972. Backup strips in *The Flash* eventually led to the *Green Lantern* series' revival in 1976, and it continued in various guises until 1988. Green Arrow left the comic in 1979 and it was retitled *Green Lantern Corps* for its last few years, but it was mostly a pale shadow of the pioneering relevance period. *The Green Lantern Corps* retitling reflected the increasing number of Green

Lanterns that had popped up over the years, many of them enjoying success in their own right.

The first of the new Green Lanterns at around this time (though originally appearing in 1968) was Guy Gardner, who was Hal Jordan's replacement should anything happen to him. Gardner later took over Jordan's ring and became a rather bad-tempered (and occasionally villainous) superhero with an appalling, pudding-bowl haircut. The fans loved his bad attitude and in the 1980s he became a regular in the Justice League, which led to his own comic in 1992; this ran for more than four years. The next replacement Lantern to star in a comic was John Stewart—one of the earliest African-American heroes—who first appeared in the O'Neil/Adams period and was portrayed as a proud defender of the black community. From the 1980s to the 2000s, he has periodically taken over the lead role in the Green Lantern comic and has made numerous appearances without ever building up a large fan base (though outside the comics medium he's had a shot at a whole new audience as the Lantern who got the call for Cartoon Network's popular *Justice League* show). Even alien Green Lanterns have broken out of the background, with the pug-faced Kilowog joining the Justice League and another short-lived *Green Lantern Corps* comic running (albeit quarterly) from 1992 to 1994.

In 1989 a miniseries called *Emerald Dawn* was meant to herald a new beginning for the character, but the following years have been almost impossibly complex, so that even the most devoted fan could be forgiven for becoming confused. Hal Jordan developed a drinking problem and then, having seen his home city destroyed, went mad and turned on his overseers, the Guardians of Oa. Not surprisingly, the Guardians resolved to replace him and discovered young artist Kyle Rayner (in *Green Lantern* vol. 2 #48, 1994), who has been DC's main Green Lantern ever since. Jordan, meanwhile, became a character called Parallax and flounced around the universe, killing people before being

killed himself—only to be resurrected several years later as the Spectre.

While longtime fans were outraged at the cavalier treatment of an old favorite, a newer generation of fans has taken to Kyle Rayner, and the younger hero has undeniably reinvigorated the *Green Lantern* strip's popularity. The Guardians of Oa, on the other hand, have not fared quite as well; the Green Lantern Corps has been broken up and replaced by a group called the Darkstars, and the planet Oa itself has been destroyed. As these things tend to go in comics, Rayner acquired the massed powers of the dead Guardians and briefly became rather godlike before rebuilding the planet and returning to his "normal" self. The coming years will doubtless bring more plot twists and more Green Lanterns but, for many fans, Hal Jordan will remain the one true Lantern. —*DAR*

Guardians of the Galaxy

The idea of comrades-in-arms struggling against tyranny is a mainstay of fiction and folklore as old as Robin Hood. Superhero comics have long provided a natural stage for stories of such underdog heroes. The Guardians of the Galaxy, originally created for a one-shot Marvel Comics story (*Marvel Super-Heroes* vol. 1 #18, 1969) by writer Arnold Drake and artist Gene Colan, carries this time-honored tradition forward into the year 3007 A.D. By this time, Earth, the other planets of the solar system, and the human colony at Alpha Centauri have all fallen under the dominion of the Badoon, a hostile race of sentient alien reptiles.

The Badoon invasion brings together a disparate group of humans who hail from points all across the solar system and beyond, echoing Akira Kurosawa's classic 1954 film *The Seven Samurai* (and its 1960 American clone *The Magnificent*

Seven). Charlie-27, a human soldier who has been genetically enhanced (with gigantic muscles and natural body armor) for life on a Jupiter colony, returns from offworld duty to discover his Jovian home overrun by Badoon forces. Teleporting to Pluto, he encounters that world's only survivor, Martinex (a crystalline human, genetically altered to survive the frigid Plutonian environment). To thwart the Badoon occupying Pluto, Charlie-27 and Martinex work together to sabotage the planet's industrial infrastructure before teleporting to Earth, where they meet Vance Astro and Yondu. Astro (a.k.a. Astrovik) is an Earth-born twentieth-century astronaut recently awakened from a cryogenic suspension that has given him powerful psionic abilities while dooming him to live out his life inside a protective suit that keeps him from aging naturally; Yondu is a nonhuman native of Alpha Centauri, and the last of his kind. The pair have just arrived on Earth after fleeing the Badoon-overrun Alpha Centauri system in a commandeered faster-than-light starship. Though Vance and Yondu fall into Badoon hands on Earth, Charlie-27 and Martinex rescue them, whereupon the quartet adopts the collective name the Guardians of the Galaxy (not to be confused with DC Comics' blue-skinned alien Guardians, who presided over the Green Lantern Corps in the Silver Age [1956–1969] and Bronze Age [1970–1979] of superhero comics). The sworn purpose of this small group of crusaders is to drive the Badoon from every one of their strongholds across the entire galaxy. They flit around the Milky Way in a spaceship called *Freedom's Lady*.

Although the Guardians vanished from the comics spinner-racks after their 1969 debut, they reappeared half a decade later (*Marvel Two-In-One* #4 and #5, 1974), under the creative direction of writer Steve Gerber and penciler Sal Buscema. It is now 3014 A.D., and Captain America and the Fantastic Four's Thing (both from the twentieth century) become temporarily embroiled in the Guardians' ongoing battle for freedom, as do the Defenders (also from the twentieth century) a year later

(*Defenders* #26–29, 1975), who help drive the Badoon from Earth's solar system and the adjacent regions of space. Inspired by Captain America (Astrovik is a particularly enthusiastic fan of Cap's wartime exploits), the Guardians name their starship after him and take the craft on an interstellar journey of discovery and adventure.

During these wanderings, the group encounters and inducts other members: Nikki (a human woman genetically engineered to survive the heat of her homeworld Mercury), and a pair of physically/psychically melded Arcturians named Starhawk (a former Defender now caught in a time-loop that forces him to relive his life repeatedly) and Aleta (Starhawk's former wife and present foster-sister, who has the ability to manipulate light energy). Now a septet, the Guardians explore the galaxy and defend it from the Badoon and other superpowered menaces in the pages of *Marvel Presents* (beginning in issue #3, 1976). Unfortunately, writers Steve Gerber and Roger Stern and penciler Allen Milgrom failed to sustain a large enough audience to continue the series, and the Guardians feature died a quick and ignominious death (along with *Marvel Presents* itself, whose twelfth and final issue was released in 1977).

The Guardians subsequently reached their highest 1970s readership levels when they time-traveled back to the twentieth century to help resolve the "Korvac saga" of 1978, a story arc crafted by writers Jim Shooter, Bill Mantlo, and David Michelinie and artists George Pérez, Sal Buscema, and David Wenzel. In this story, the Avengers struggle to prevent the sudden omnipotence of an ordinary man (Michael Korvac) from wreaking havoc across the cosmos (*The Avengers* #167–#168, #173–#177). Before returning to the thirty-first century following Korvac's defeat, Vance Astrovik meets his younger twentieth-century self and talks him out of becoming an astronaut in order to prevent his becoming forever trapped in the containment suit. Unfortunately for both Astroviks, this action creates a psionic backlash between the two men, prematurely awakening the younger man's psychic abilities, thereby allowing him to become Marvel Boy in the later series *The New Warriors* (1990–1996, 1999–2000). This development split the Guardians' future off from Marvel's main timeline, sequestering it in one of comicdom's many "alternate futures." Undeterred by being rendered effectively apocryphal, the Guardians forged a prominent one-shot partnership with Spider-Man the following year (*Marvel Team-Up* #86, written by *X-Men* scribe Chris Claremont with pencils by Allyn Brodsky), but made only infrequent guest appearances during the ensuing decade (*The Avengers* #264, 1986; *The Sensational She-Hulk* #6, 1989).

But the Guardians were not destined for permanent obscurity. In 1990 Marvel placed the team in the hands of writer-artist Jim Valentino, who had previously made his mark in the world of independent comics publishing in 1984 with *normalman* (published first by Aardvark-Vanaheim, and later by Renegade Press), a parody of the superheroes who had become so profuse in the universes of Marvel and DC since the dawn of the Silver Age; normalman is the only individual on Earth (known as "Levram," which is "Marvel" spelled backward) who lacks superpowers and a costume. Later in the 1990s, Jim Valentino would go on to join the ranks of writers and artists working at Image Comics on creator-owned properties (Valentino's semi-autobiographical 1997 miniseries *A Touch of Silver,* which relates the traumatic upbringing of a young comics fan, is undoubtedly his most distinguished and personal work from that period). Of his own work, Valentino has said, "Since my influences are strongly in the DC and Marvel Silver Age—which is from when I was a kid—and then in underground comics when I was a teenager, I have strong influences on both sides. I am just as strongly influenced by Jack Kirby as I am by Robert Crumb; and by Vaughn Bode as I am by Steve Ditko, and neither influence touches me any stronger than the other. I just sort of smoosh them all together."

Valentino's nearly three-year tenure with the Guardians reveals his abiding love for Marvel's

superheroes and their history, delving more deeply than ever before into the motivations of the team's individual members. Returning the Guardians to their alternate thirty-first century, Valentino began the series by taking the team on a quest for the indestructible shield of Vance Astrovik's most revered hero, Captain America (*Guardians of the Galaxy* #1–#6, 1990). The quest succeeds, although the Guardians are faced along the way by such powerful foes as Taserface (whose powers are self-explanatory), Firelord (a former herald of the world-eating Galactus who subsequently becomes a reserve member of the group), and the Stark (aliens who have based their technology and weaponry upon the armored twentieth-century superhero Iron Man, a.k.a. munitions manufacturer Tony Stark).

Valentino's run on the series lasted twenty-nine issues, culminating in a multi-issue 1992 crossover with Marvel's cosmos-spanning *Infinity War* arc, an epic in which Jim Starlin's Thanos attempts to gain absolute power, and in so doing affects the continuity of virtually every title in the Marvel line (a storytelling-cum-marketing tactic that began gaining currency in the mid-1980s with such megasuccesses as *Marvel Super Heroes Secret Wars* and DC Comics' permanently universe-altering *Crisis on Infinite Earths*). Under Valentino the Guardians became less a gang of ragtag freedom fighters and more a band of explorers and adventurers, an amalgam of *Avengers*-type team superheroics and *Star Trek*–style space opera. The Guardians still found the time to overthrow despotic rulers, however, unseating Rancor, a descendant of the X-Men's Wolverine who had taken over a lost human colony called Haven, which is ultimately destroyed by a future version of the world-devouring Phoenix after the Guardians evacuate the planet (*Guardians of the Galaxy* #9–#12, 1991). The Guardians subsequently add a shapechanging Havenite named Replica to their ranks (*Guardians of the Galaxy Annual* #2, 1992). In another memorable story arc, Valentino introduced the team to a futuristic iteration of the Ghost Rider; in addition to being a spirit of vengeance, this skull-headed demon also heads a religious cult whose own clergy he is secretly murdering until the Guardians negotiate a truce with him (*Guardians of the Galaxy #13–#14*, 1991). Thanks to time travel and Valentino's fascination with Marvel's 1970s mythos, the team also revisits the Korvac saga (1991's *Fantastic Four Annual #24*, *Thor Annual #16*, and *Silver Surfer Annual #4*).

After Valentino's departure from Marvel for Image Comics, the Guardians' series continued under writer Michael Gallagher and such artists as J. J. Birch, Kevin West, Dale Eaglesham, Jeffrey

Moore, Yancey Labat, Scot Eaton, Geoff Isherwood, Michael Bair, and Sandu Florea, finally concluding in 1995 with issue #62. But the Guardians weren't quite ready to vanish into four-color oblivion, turning up again as guest stars occasionally during the 1990s in various Marvel titles and headlining in a four-issue miniseries written by Valentino's successor, Michael Gallagher, and penciled by Kevin West and Yancey Labat (*Galactic Guardians,* 1994). Although the Guardians have yet to reach the heights to which Valentino took them in the 1990s, it's a big galaxy, and one that frequently needs defending; someday the Guardians will surely answer the call to arms again. *—MAM*

Hanna-Barbera Heroes

William Hanna and Joseph Barbera were pioneers of television animation. Having learned the ropes by producing *Tom and Jerry* theatrical cartoons for MGM in the 1940s, they adapted their craft to the small screen, devising cost- (and quality-) cutting measures to make animation affordable for mass production (having running characters repeatedly pass the same background images, for example). From the humble beginnings of *The Ruff and Reddy Show* (1957), the Hanna-Barbera collaboration eventually launched a pantheon of cartoon greats (and some not-so-greats) including the Flintstones, Yogi Bear, Jonny Quest, Scooby-Doo, and their first superhero (not counting Quick Draw McGraw's Zorro riff El Kabong, that is)—Atom Ant.

With a battle cry of "Up and at 'em, Atom Ant!" this miniature muscle-mite first buzzed into action in *The Atom Ant/Secret Squirrel Show* (1965). Head-quartered in an anthill with a mailbox bearing his name, *Atom Ant* was a superhero parody, its tiny titan engaging in pun-filled clashes with menaces large (Crankenshaft's Monster) and small (Ferocious

Flea). A swarm of mid-1960s Atom Ant items were produced, including a Soaky figural bubblebath container, coloring book, View-Master reel, push puppet, Gold Key comic, and plush doll. Atom Ant aired, with and without Secret Squirrel, for several years before crawling into occasional syndication, and can be seen, as of 2004, on the Cartoon Network.

Beginning in 1966, superhero mania swept America, ignited by the success of the live-action *Batman* television series (1966–1968). The Hanna-Barbera studios, always willing to capitalize on a trend, quickly cranked out a host of animated superhero shows all their own. Premiering on CBS in September 1966, *Frankenstein Jr. and the Impossibles* was cut from the same tongue-in-cheek cloth as *Atom Ant*. *Frankenstein Jr.* fused giant robots, monsters, and superheroes into one package: a masked and costumed computerized crime fighter who answered to his creator, trouble-prone prodigy Buzz Conroy. Appearing in the same half-hour program was another hybrid—of super-heroes and rock stars—*The Impossibles*. The Impossibles were a trio of pop musicians who, when summoned by their boss Big D via a guitar-based TV monitor, cheered "Rally-ho!" and trans-formed into … the Impossibles, a supergroup composed of Fluid Man, Coil Man, and Multi Man, who zoomed to crime scenes in their Impossicar. The

Impossibles—in their musician identities—performed a token tune in each episode.

Debuting concurrently with *Frankenstein Jr. and the Impossibles* was *Space Ghost and Dino Boy,* also on CBS. Space Ghost, an intergalactic superhero designed by legendary comic-book artist Alex Toth and voiced by Gary Owens (best known as the announcer on *Rowan and Martin's Laugh-In*), was abetted by junior partners Jan and Jayce and their monkey Blip (a staple of Hanna-Barbera adventure cartoons was the inclusion of pets for comic relief; witness Jonny Quest's pup, Bandit). Armed with ray-blasting wrist bands and his Invisibelt, Space Ghost tackled an army of alarming adversaries. Dino Boy was a contemporary kid lost in a dangerous stone-age society that had never evolved beyond its prehistoric state. Unlike Hanna-Barbera's satirical superhero programs, *Space Ghost and Dino Boy* was played straight, an attitude Space Ghost maintained during a 1981 revival. Not so with the spectral hero's 1994 comeback, however: He is now a wacky talk-show host, backed up by former foes Zorak, Moltar, and Brak, in the hilarious *Space Ghost Coast to Coast* program on Cartoon Network.

For the 1967–1968 television season, Hanna-Barbera released an unprecedented amount of original superhero fare, three new shows on CBS alone. *The Herculoids,* another series featuring Toth's designs, was set on the planet Quasar. It starred a family—King Zandor, Tara, and Dorno—who warded off assaulting monstrosities with the help of their unusual allies, the Herculoids: Tundro, a ten-legged rhino; Zok, a laser-beam-firing flying dragon; Igoo, a superstrong rock creature; and the malleable Gloop and Gleep. *Shazzan* also bowed during the 1967 season. It featured a pair of kids from the 1960s, siblings Nancy and Chuck, transplanted into the past, where they and their flying camel Kabooie found themselves in conflict with a variety of thieves and cutthroats, only to be rescued each episode by an omnipotent, sixty-foot genie named Shazzan (while certainly not a superhero show in the strictest sense, *Shazzan* was marketed as

such). Hanna-Barbera also unveiled *Moby Dick and the Mighty Mightor* that year. Mightor was a prehistoric superhero, an homage to the original Captain Marvel. Each of his episodes began with a boy named Tor, who, when raising a magic club into the air (while exclaiming "Mightor!", not "Shazam!"), transmogrified into a powerful superhero. Also on the program, Herman Melville's formerly formidable great white whale became an amiable adventurer, joined by scuba-diving teens Tom and Tub (yes, he was a fat kid) and their seal, Scooby.

On NBC, Hanna-Barbera produced two shows for the 1967–1968 season. *Young Samson and Goliath* offered another tale of wish-fulfillment and transformation, as an ordinary teenage boy and his pet dog were upgraded into the powerful hero Samson and his fierce lion Goliath whenever the lad locked together his wrist gauntlets and proclaimed, "I need Samson power!" Prolific designer Toth was back again with *Birdman and the Galaxy Trio.* The lead feature was a winged superhero, who, with a cry of "Bir-r-r-rdman!", soared into action with his eagle cohort Avenger. (Birdman, like Space Ghost, got a droll facelift in 2001 in Cartoon Network's Adult Swim program package as *Harvey Birdman, Attorney at Law.*) Also appearing in the show was *The Galaxy Trio,* about a mundane team of titans consisting of Vapor Man, Meteor Man, and Galaxy Girl. A more fascinating supergroup was adapted from Marvel Comics to ABC that year by Hanna-Barbera in *The Fantastic Four,* a fondly remembered animated series that borrowed heavily from the Stan Lee/Jack Kirby comics for its adventures of Mr. Fantastic, the Invisible Girl, the Thing, and the Human Torch.

By 1968, superheroes were falling out of vogue. While Batman and Robin twice guest starred with—of all characters—Scooby-Doo in the first season of *The New Scooby-Doo Movies* (1972–1974), Hanna-Barbera didn't produce a superhero program again until 1973—and this time they struck gold. *Super Friends,* a kid-friendly version of DC Comics' *Justice League of America,* began on ABC in September 1973, starring Superman, Batman and Robin, Wonder Woman, and Aquaman, with their "junior Super Friends" teenagers Wendy and Marvin (with Wonder Dog!), later replaced by the shapeshifting alien teens the Wonder Twins (with the monkey Gleek!). In a variety of incarnations, *Super Friends* continued well into the mid-1980s.

The success of *Super Friends* prompted Hanna-Barbera to try its hand at original superheroes again with *Hong Kong Phooey* (1974–1976), a kung-fu superhero canine. Their next effort: *Dynomutt, Dog Wonder,* which began a successful run in 1976. Dynomutt was a laughably clumsy robot with extending paws hero who, along with the no-nonsense, square-jawed Blue Falcon, tackled evildoers in Big City. *Captain Caveman and the Teen Angels* (1977) featured a mumbling, diminutive (and very hairy) stone-age superhero released (by teenage *Charlie's Angels* clones) into the present after a lengthy deep freeze. Captain Caveman (voiced by Mel Blanc, of Bugs Bunny fame) flew into action with a club like Mightor's and a deafening battle shriek ("Captain Ca-a-a-avema-a-a-an!") before being shuttled off his own series into supporting-cast status in *The Flintstones Comedy Show* (1980) and its offshoots. After appearing in their own Hanna-Barbera cartoon program from 1970–1973, basketball stars the Harlem Globetrotters got superpowers in the short-lived *The Super Globetrotters* (1979).

Many of Hanna-Barbera's heroes have enjoyed exposure beyond their television roots. Space Ghost (in his original form and his *Coast to Coast* revamp) has materialized over the decades into comic books from several publishers, and Gold Key's *Hanna-Barbera Super TV Heroes* anthology (1967–1969) spotlighted not only the Ghost but also the Herculoids and several other characters. Space Ghost, Frankenstein Jr., and Shazzan each starred in Big Little Books, and most of the company's superheroes were merchandized in some fashion during the 1960s, from Give-a-Show projector slides to Whitman Publishing Company coloring

books to perhaps the most unusual Hanna-Barbera collectible, the box of Space Ghost and Frankenstein Jr. "Bubble Club" bubble bath soap from Purex. Since the late 1990s, *Space Ghost Coast to Coast* pins, T-shirts, and coffee mugs have been available, as licensing and merchandising have become synonymous with successful animated properties. In the early twenty-first century, action-figure lines have immortalized Space Ghost and his villains; Blue Falcon and Dynomutt; and Birdman. Upscale coldcast porcelain sculptures of Space Ghost and "Harvey" Birdman were also released in 2002 and 2003.

Since the 1980s, reruns of the original cartoons starring Hanna-Barbera's heroes have appeared on television in syndicated anthology shows and on cable's Cartoon Network and Boomerang. With this recurring airplay, it is inevitable that these superheroes will maintain a long-lasting berth in pop culture. —ME

Harvey Heroes

To solely consider Harvey Comics as the home of *Casper* and *Richie Rich* is to undervalue a significant publishing and entertainment empire whose benchmarks far exceed friendly ghosts and poor little rich boys.

Alfred Harvey—born Alfred Harvey Wiernikoff, later changing his surname to his middle name, with his parents, his brother Leon, and lastly, his brother Robert following suit—made his first professional sale as a cartoonist in 1927. He was soon taken under the wing of publisher Victor Fox, and by the end of the 1930s had risen to Fox Features Syndicate's managing editor position, working with Joe Simon, Jack Kirby, and other luminaries, as well as journeymen galore, in the early days of American comic books.

Harvey branched out on his own in 1940, establishing Alfred Harvey Publications. *Pocket*

Comics #1, a one-hundred-page, digest-sized periodical, was Harvey's initial effort, seeing print in
1941, with *Fun Parade,* a cartoon compilation,
becoming the company's second title. *Pocket* was
the home of Harvey's first superhero hit, the Black
Cat. Secretly actress Linda Turner, the Black Cat—
"Hollywood's Glamorous Detective Star"—turned
heads as one of the first superheroines to grace
this burgeoning entertainment medium. Black Cat
was too big a star to be tucked away in Harvey's
Pocket: She soon was awarded her own title, a rarity
for female characters of comics' Golden Age
(1938–1954), with story and art contributions by Al
Gabrielle (the character's creator), Pierce Rice, Joe
Kubert, and Lee Elias, among others.

Harvey's twin brother, Leon, became his partner
in 1942 when Alfred served a military stint. The
company purchased *Speed Comics* from Brookwood
Publications. *Speed* was the home of two rather
generic superheroes: Shock Gibson (a.k.a. the
"Human Dynamo") and Captain Freedom. Shock,
first seen in *Speed Comics* #1 (1939), was actually
Robert Gibson, a wealthy tinker who stumbles
across a means of "humanizing" electricity. Firing
electrical bolts from his hands, Shock Gibson wards
off Japanese invaders and clobbers bad guys as
"America's champion of liberty and justice." Captain
Freedom, a star-spangled stalwart, followed patriotic
heroes like the Shield and Captain America by crack-
ling into print in *Speed* #16 (1941). Behind his red-
white-and-blue garb was Don Wright, a newspaper
publisher, who dons his guise to charge to the aid of
a kid gang known as the Young Defenders.

Another early Harvey series was *Champion
Comics,* later *Champ Comics,* an anthology that ran
through the early 1940s and featured costumed
and noncostumed heroes including the Champ,
Duke O'Dowell, Neptina, the Liberty Lads, Jungle-
man, the Human Meteor, and Doctor Miracle, Master of Magic. Harvey also published *Spitfire Comics*
in 1941, starring the headlining hero, Spitfire, and
other uniformed fighters like the Clown and Fly-Man.
Black Cat and, arguably, Shock Gibson aside, Har-

vey's early superhero comics were rather pedestrian, as were most titles of the era, and no characters attracted much of an audience.

In 1942, Harvey acquired publication rights to
the radio hero *The Green Hornet* (comic books starring the Hornet had previously been produced by a
company called Holyoke). This licensed property
inaugurated a trend for Harvey: Throughout the
1940s, the publisher released titles based on a
host of concepts from newspaper strips, including
*Joe Palooka, Blondie, Terry and the Pirates, Dick
Tracy, Steve Canyon,* and *Li'l Abner.* Most of these
titles sold solidly, anchoring Harvey with profitable
product in the superhero bust that followed World
War II. Simon and Kirby, undeterred by this postwar
attrition of caped crusaders, created another superhero comic for the publisher in 1946: *Stuntman,*
the "New Champ of Split-Second Action," a male
counterpart to Black Cat. *Stuntman* was retired
after three issues.

Throughout much of the 1940s, Harvey was
known in print as Family Comics, a reference to its
innocent subject matter and, quite possibly, a nod
to its familial business union. By the end of the
decade, another brother, Robert, became a partner
in the business. (Joked authors Steve Duin and
Mike Richardson in their 1998 historical tome,
Comics: Between the Panels, "Everything's relative.
Or—as was the case at Harvey—*everyone* is.")
Some historical sources have credited Alfred, Leon,
and Robert as collectively launching Harvey Comics,
but, in a September 2000 letter to *Animation World
Magazine,* heir Alan Harvey wrote, "Harvey was NOT
'founded in 1939 in New York City as a comic book
company by brothers Alfred, Leon, and Robert Harvey,' as your article states. Harvey was founded in
1940 by Alfred Harvey as 'Alfred Harvey Publications.'" The company was dubbed Harvey Publications in 1946, and within a few years bore Harvey
Comics logos on its covers.

In the 1950s, Harvey Comics continued to produce licensed titles based on newspaper strips, but
temporarily veered from its wholesome publishing

Speed Comics #40 © 1945 Harvey Comics.
COVER ART BY RUDY PALAIS.

image by releasing five horror titles, one of which, *Black Cat Mystery,* bumped the book's former starring superheroine into limbo. Historians Duin and Richardson noted that Harvey's horror output exceeded the industry's titan of terror titles, EC Comics: "Between 1951 and 1954, Harvey published 96 horror comics, five more than EC." It was in the 1950s, however, that Harvey defined itself, by obtaining the publication rights for a handful of animated series which it later purchased as its own: *Casper the Friendly Ghost, Little Dot, Baby Huey, Wendy the Good Little Witch, Richie Rich, Sad Sack,* and others. Harvey brought those characters to TV animation in the 1960s, and in the 1990s and 2000s to live-action theatrical films, made-for-TV movies, and direct-to-video movies.

Always willing to experiment with popular trends, Harvey continued to irregularly produce a smattering of superheroes. To capitalize on the 3-D movie craze of the 1950s, Harvey published *Captain 3-D* #1 in December 1953. This rather nondescript superhero had the good fortune of being illustrated by Kirby and Steve Ditko (Ditko would, in 1962, become famous as the artist of *The Amazing Spider-Man*). Kirby's former partner Joe Simon, at one juncture during his long career, worked as a Harvey editor. When the live-action *Batman* television show (1966–1968) ignited a superhero explosion, Simon released such short-lived features as *Jigsaw* (the "Man of a Thousand Parts"), *Spyman* (the hero who employed an "electro-robot hand"), *Unearthly Spectaculars* (an anthology starring the ice-inducing Jack Q. Frost, dubbed "The Coolest Hero in Comics," and Tiger Boy, a teen who could morph into a tiger—while maintaining his human head!), and *Thrill-O-Rama.* The latter series premiered with a Mandrake the Magician clone, "The Man in Black Called Fate," then introduced an Aquaman-like hero named Pirana (the "Deadliest Creature in All the World"). Also during this period, Harvey published two issues of Will Eisner's *The Spirit,* and a one-issue reprint of Simon and Kirby's 1950s cold-war superhero satire *Fighting American.* The publisher concluded the decade with its oddest superhero effort, a one-shot starring a superpowered grocer: *Fruitman* (the "World's Peachiest, Berry Grapest Superhero").

Ultimately existing exclusively on its kid-friendly cartoon characters, Harvey Comics closed its doors in 1982, but reopened shop in 1986 with Alan Harvey at the helm. The company was sold to an outside party in 1989, and focused more on mass-media (mostly film) exposure of the characters, permanently discontinuing its comics line in 1994. The classic Harvey characters are, as of 2004, represented by Classic Media, with the exceptions of Sad Sack and the Black Cat, who are owned and occasionally published by Alan Harvey. —*ME*

The Hawk and the Dove

The Hawk and the Dove could only have sprung from the tumult of the late 1960s, and the pair encapsulated the conflicting ideologies Americans felt about the Vietnam War. The strip was the brain-child of the great comics maverick Steve Ditko, who dreamed up the concept of an aggressive super-hero (the Hawk) teamed with a pacifist partner (the Dove). Ditko both plotted and drew the feature's first appearance in *Showcase* #75 (in 1968) but DC Comics paired him with writer Steve Skeates, who dialogued the strip. The first story introduced read-ers to brothers Hank and Don Hall, students during the time of the Vietnam War, who are transformed into a pair of superheroes by a voice in their heads (later revealed to be the Forces of Order—whoever they might be), the twist being that, while Hank/Hawk is more than happy to weigh in with both fists flying, Don/Dove refuses to fight.

In a delicious irony, the Hawk and the Dove conflict was mirrored by the strip's creative team. Staunch conservative Ditko plotted the stories with the idea that the Dove was essentially a useless weakling, while arch-liberal Skeates sympathized with pacifism and effectively rewrote the tales to favor the Dove. The feature was a hit in *Showcase,* and five months later was given its own title, aptly called *The Hawk and the Dove.* However, Ditko quit after two issues, unhappy with the direction the comic was taking. The dilemma of what to do with a superhero who will not fight eventually came to a head when Ditko's successor, Gil Kane, finally bowed to the inevitable and had the Dove batter some hoods into submission, mistakenly believing them to have killed his brother. Despite this, the public seemed unsure of what to make of the team and the comic was canceled with its sixth issue (in mid-1969), but editor Dick Giordano believed in the concept and took the heroes over to another of his

titles, the *Teen Titans.* After five issues as team members, the Hawk and the Dove were cast aside by an incoming editor and fell into obscurity.

With the exception of a brief return to the *Teen Titans* in 1978, the duo's next significant appear-ance was in DC Comics' house-clearing exercise *Crisis on Infinite Earths.* Among the various heroes killed off in this miniseries was, inevitably, that perennial whipping boy, the Dove—crushed by a falling wall. Surprisingly, the Dove's death seemed to remind DC that it had a good concept going to waste and so, soon after, the husband-and-wife team of Karl and Barbara Kesel revived the strip with a five-issue miniseries in 1988. It seems that the ever-vigilant Forces of Order had noticed the Dove's demise and promptly gave his powers to a new hero, this time a girl: young student Dawn Granger. After his brother's death, the ever-volatile Hawk had become more violent than ever, but even-tually he accepted the new Dove, who in any case was a bit more proactive than the original had been.

The miniseries contrasted crunchingly violent action with some zippy dialogue, and led to a regular series in 1989, but the fates were against it. DC had plans for a title called *Armageddon 2001,* which was to involve Captain Atom turning bad and becoming a villain called Monarch, but at the last minute word got out to howls of fan protest and, in their search for a replacement, the publishers settled on the Hawk. As Monarch, the Hawk was supposed to have killed just about all of DC's heroes, but a character called Waverider traveled back from the future to stop him in the nick of time. Perhaps inevitably, *Armageddon 2001* was followed by yet another earth-shattering miniseries in 1994: *Zero Hour.* Once again, the Hawk/Monarch was back, this time as the even more villainous Extant. In the ensuing battle, Extant killed or maimed various members of the Justice Society in a manner that would surely have horrified his creators.

Never a company to abandon a concept for good, DC revived the *The Hawk and the Dove* title once more in 1997 for a five-issue run with a com-pletely different duo. Once again, the Forces of

Order bestowed their powers on two young people, but this time the genders were reversed, with the Hawk being army cadet Sasha Marten and the Dove a laid-back rock musician called Wiley Wolverton. Another new twist was that, on shouting out the name "Hawk" or "Dove" (the traditional method used by previous Hawks and Doves to transform themselves), the pair sprouted wings and developed piercing shrieks. The inevitable personality clashes were tempered by a growing romance, but the amiable strip did not lead to any further starring appearances from this unique superhero team (though a version of Dove has been seen in the Justice Society of America book *JSA,* and in early 2004 fandom buzzed with the possibility of the duo's return in some form to *Teen Titans). —DAR*

Hawkeye

After a short career as a supervillain, Clint Barton, alias Hawkeye the Archer, has been a nearly constant fixture in the Marvel Comics firmament. His first appearance was in the Iron Man strip in *Tales of Suspense* #57 (1964), which relates how he leaves a successful career as a circus archer for the newly fashionable occupation of superhero. Stumbling across a jewelry heist, he is mistakenly taken by the police to be the gang's ringleader. Embittered by the experience, he turns to crime, spurred on by the deadly Russian spy, the Black Widow. Following several attacks on Iron Man, he sees the error of his ways when the Black Widow is seriously injured by her communist masters. As luck would have it, the Avengers are advertising for new members, and he is duly welcomed into the team. And so began Hawkeye's decades-long association with this superteam.

With his troubled background as an orphan, brought into the circus by the treacherous Swordsman, Hawkeye was something of a rough diamond, initially hot-headed, arrogant, and prone to wisecracking. Inevitably, readers took him to their hearts, and he was one of the Avengers' most steadfast members for a good ten years. While not physically as imposing as his colleagues, he possessed a perfect aim and, with his seemingly inexhaustible supply of trick arrows (acid spray, power blast, suction, deafener, flare, knock-out gas), he made a valuable contribution to the group. However, throughout the 1960s, the ever-present Black Widow (whom he gradually convinced to defect) was a regular presence in the comic and on his mind. At the end of that decade, in order to rescue his beloved, Hawkeye took a swig of growth serum and became the giant-sized Goliath, a role he kept for the next several years.

The next Hawkeye to hit the comics scene was a villain from an alternate Earth and a member of the Squadron Supreme (*Avengers* #85), a kind of anti-Avengers based satirically on DC Comics' Justice League; this Hawkeye later became known as Golden Archer. Despite his own formidable abilities, Clint Barton/Goliath was always vulnerable to a sudden loss of growth serum, and when that finally happened during the renowned Kree-Skrull War (in 1971), he found that his old skills as an archer had not deserted him. Although he was briefly happy as Hawkeye once more, the ensuing decade (and indeed his subsequent superhero career) was a restless one, which saw him leave, rejoin, and leave the team again. During his various absences from the Avengers, Hawkeye joined the Defenders, briefly adopted the Golden Archer's name to pose as a villain and coax a disillusioned Watergate-era Captain America out of retirement, and rode off into the West with the time-displaced cowboy hero the Two-Gun Kid.

In the late 1970s, following yet another stint with the Avengers, he was rejected by a government-appointed advisor and quit superheroing in disgust, ending up as chief of security at Cross Technologies. This period is later described in Hawkeye's first solo outing (in a 1983 miniseries), which was followed by starring roles in *Solo Avengers* and *Avengers Spotlight.* Inevitably, Cross Technologies turned out to be a front for organized crime, but during the ensuing ruckus Hawkeye fell in love with and married the reformed criminal Mockingbird. Together, the pair recruited their own team, the West Coast Avengers (featuring Iron Man, Tigra, and Wonder Man), which contributed to making the 1980s probably Hawkeye's finest hour commercially.

Perhaps reasoning that nothing breeds apathy more than contentment, Marvel then decided to wreck poor old Hawkeye's life. The West Coast Avengers began to fall apart and his beloved Mockingbird was killed by the evil demon Mephisto (an uneven contest if ever there was one). The rest of the group split off to form the Force Works, while Hawkeye retreated to the wilderness to indulge in some serious brooding. Feeling the need for human company, he drifted back to the Avengers before becoming restless once more and deciding to throw in his lot with Marvel's newest team, the Thunderbolts. This was one of the surprise hits of the 1990s, and its premise of a group entirely made up of masquerading ex-criminals was clearly as innovative and tempting to an ex-baddie like Hawkeye as it was to its many fans. In 1998, his second solo comic hit the stands, but by 2003 the Thunderbolts concept was in trouble and the title was radically reworked into a supervillain equivalent of David Fincher's film *Fight Club* (1999). Hawkeye was out of a job once more, though yet another solo series (and Avengers slot) were ongoing as of early 2004.

In an age where the cosmic is commonplace, the notion of a hero armed with nothing but a bow and arrow is almost impossibly quaint, but at the same time rather refreshing. Hawkeye's combative persona may have been a blueprint for generations of dysfunctional anti-heroes, but his essential honesty and charisma will doubtless inspire future writers and readers. —*DAR*

Hawkgirl: *See* **Hawkman**

Hawkman

A regular fixture in the DC Comics universe since his inception in 1940, Hawkman has gone through many changes over the years. The original Hawkman first appeared as a backup feature in *Flash Comics* #1 but soon graduated to cover status, alternating with the comic's other star, the Flash. Hawkman was wealthy amateur archaeologist Carter Hall, who discovers that he is in fact the reincarnation of Prince Khufu, one half of a pair of legendary ancient Egyptian lovers. Searching out his long-lost love, he comes upon Shiera Saunders; their meeting reactivates their memories of the past. As a result, Hall rediscovers the secret of the "ninth metal," which he uses to make an antigravity belt, and then dons a shirtless costume with hawk's-head mask and giant, feathered wings. Saunders is aware of Hall's secret identity from the beginning but has to wait two years before joining her beau (and future husband) as Hawkgirl. Needless to say, she wears a shirt.

The feature was created by the prolific writer Gardner Fox, with art initially by Dennis Neville. The latter was soon replaced by Sheldon Moldoff and subsequently, after World War II, by the teenage prodigy Joe Kubert. It is often said that the character was inspired by a race of Hawkmen prominently featured in the Flash Gordon newspaper strip; true or not, the Hawkman feature proved to be quite a hit in its own right. Hawkman was soon one of the founding members of the Justice Society, later becoming its chairman, and was the only hero to star in all 57 issues of *All Star Comics,* as well as appearing in more than 100 issues of *Flash Comics.* While the concept and artwork were strong, critics have noted that the feature lacked depth and had only a few memorable villains, such as the Human Fly Bandits and the Ghost.

Along with many other DC heroes, the original Hawkman last appeared in 1951 and had to wait ten years before being revived as part of the company's Silver Age (1956–1969) explosion. The new Hawkman was showcased in six issues of *The Brave and the Bold* in very impressive tales by the old team of Gardner Fox and Joe Kubert. After a series of backups in *Mystery in Space,* Hawkman was finally granted his own comic in 1964, though Kubert was then replaced by the elegant Murphy Anderson. As with so many other DC heroes, this new Hawkman was based in science; he was Katar Hol who, along with his wife, Shayera, was a policeman from the planet Thanagar, hot on the trail of shape-changing villain Byth. Once on Earth, the pair decided to stay in Midway City, ostensibly to study local police techniques, and they soon settled down to day jobs as museum curators, in between crime-fighting capers as Hawkman and Hawkgirl.

Like their 1940s predecessors, this pair flew with the help of antigravity belts but differed in being able to talk to birds and in their predilection for ancient weapons, such as bows and arrows, borrowed from the museum. They soon amassed a colorful array of foes, such as the Shadow Thief, the IQ Gang, Matter-Master, the Crocodile People, and winged gorillas. However, unlike Marvel Comics' more three-dimensional heroes, Hol and Shayera were a rather colorless, resolutely middle-class, middle-aged couple (not at all "alien"), and when Anderson left the comic it soon ran into trouble, ending with issue #27 in 1968. Hawkman joined the Justice League of America in the mid-1960s and was a staple of the team for ten years, but he had to be satisfied with backup slots in various DC comics (and a couple of *Showcase* issues) throughout the 1970s.

From the mid-1980s on, DC Comics decided that, come what may, there should be a Hawkman comic out there, resulting in seven completely different revivals. At various points in the 1980s and 1990s, the publisher has tried to simplify the increasingly long and complex history of its main stars, often resulting in sheer confusion for their readers, and nowhere has this been more true than in the case of Hawkman. Following two revivals that pitted the Hawks against an imperialist Thanagar bent on invading Earth, a third title—*Hawkworld*—introduced a different Katar Hol, dressed in a sort of body armour. The success of this miniseries led to a regular title in the 1990s that saw the new

The Brave and the Bold #36 © 1961 DC Comics.

Katar and Shayera Hol travel to Earth as escorts to the Thanagarian ambassador; they were soon exiled as traitors.

DC initially intended this Hawkman to supersede the two earlier (revived) versions—which readers were meant to ignore—but soon enough the previous, Silver Age version was back on the scene, rewritten as an impostor. Fans of the hitherto noble and upright Hawkman 2 had a hard time accepting him as a treacherous spy, and recent writers have tried to forget that unfortunate plot twist. The most recent version of Hawkman follows on from DC's *Zero Hour* series, where all previous incarnations are somehow merged together; the new Carter Hall is once more a reincarnation of Prince Khufu, while

253

his partner Kendra Saunders is somehow a reincarnation of Shiera. However much DC has tested the patience of its readers, the elegance and simplicity of a superhero with wings should continue to entice readers of succeeding generations. —DAR

Hellboy

One of the surprise hits of the 1990s, *Hellboy* mixed horror, superheroics, and the darkest of humor, spawning a mini-merchandising industry in its wake. Throughout the 1980s and 1990s, creator Mike Mignola was something of a journeyman artist, flitting from title to title and slowly evolving an increasingly dark and expressive style. The emergence of Image Comics prompted Mignola, Art Adams, Frank Miller, and other artists to set up their own imprint, Legend, but not wanting to self-publish, they arranged for Dark Horse to become their distributor while they retained ownership of their characters and their imprint. Remembering a sketch he had drawn in 1991 of a striking-looking character that he called Hellboy, Mignola developed the concept further, and by 1993 he was ready to be unleashed.

Hellboy was first introduced to fans at the 1993 San Diego Comic-Con, in a section of a Dark Horse giveaway comic (aptly called *San Diego Con Comics*), and was exposed to a wider audience through a guest shot in John Byrne's *Next Men* title later that year. Hooking up with Byrne as scripter, Mignola brought out the first *Hellboy* comic proper in early 1994, and such was its success that the four-issue miniseries, *Hellboy: Seeds of Destruction,* has been in print ever since.

Hellboy is a large, muscular, red-skinned apparition, half man and half demon, with a tail, horns (which he regularly saws off), and a gigantic, iron-gloved right hand. Much of his background has been left deliberately obscure, but it has been revealed that, during World War II, he was summoned to Earth—as a child—by a cabal of Nazi

Hellboy #1 ™ & © 1994 Michael Mignola.
COVER ART BY MIKE MIGNOLA.

necromancers, in a ceremony that was broken up by allied troops and mystics. Adopted by a British parapsychologist, who was killed in the first story, Hellboy grew up to be a force for good, and his constant battle against his demonic heritage has been very much a feature of the series.

As the comic has progressed, more details of his past have slipped out, including the revelation that he was born to a human mother in hell, and that he is apparently the harbinger of the Apocalypse; this he was not happy to hear. For decades, Hellboy has apparently been a member of an international group of investigators, the Bureau for Paranormal Research and Defense (BPRD), which sends its investigators

From *Hellboy* #1 ™ & © 1994 Michael Mignola.

around the world to research the unknown and the terrifying. Like so many heroes of the 1990s, Hellboy breaks the tradition of the classic superhero, in that he has no alter ego, supercostume, or superheroic trademarks—save for incredible strength, which he metes out on unsuspecting criminals and villains.

The first story, spread over four issues, set the tone for the succeeding tales with its collection of monsters, haunted houses, evil magicians (in this case Rasputin), Nazis, and the threat of world destruction. This and other stories co-starred Hellboy's fellow BPRD members, most notably the pyrokinetic Liz Sherman, Roger the Friendly Homunculus, and Abe Sapien, a scaled amphibian who was originally placed in suspended animation by frightened townsfolk in the nineteenth century. Other episodes have featured werewolves, pig-men, harpies, gorgons, ghosts, giant rats, demons, homunculi (man-made monsters, à la *Frankenstein*), world-destroying worms, and Nazis by the score. In fact, most of the Hellboy tales appear to involve left-over Nazis of some description or another, whether it be Nazi corpses returning from space, disembodied Nazi heads floating around, vampire Nazis, or an endless supply of deformed Nazi scientists. As outré as some of the material is, however, Mignola's mordant humor and taste for the absurd always make it eminently readable.

Mignola has released his tales sparingly in a succession of miniseries, collections, and one-shots, in yarns ranging from a few pages to the epic 1996 five-issue "Wake the Devil" story. As of 2004, more than twenty issues of the comic have appeared, all of which have been collected in book form, and they have proved to be consistent sellers. In the process of writing the comic solo since 1995, Mignola has grown as a writer and artist, constantly paring his dialogue and art down to a striking minimalism. His *Hellboy* style is a mass of dark, menacing shapes, with figures rendered in an almost abstract way, and it has inspired many artists in its wake. Mignola always saw the series as an opportunity to combine his two great loves: the atmospheric horror milieu, full of menacing creatures, crumbling castles, and bleak locales, and the power and excitement of superhero comics. An avowed fan of legendary artist Jack Kirby, Mignola fills his strips with enormously muscular beasts engaging Hellboy in vast fight scenes, often reducing all around them to rubble.

The comic's success has led to all manner of tie-ins, crossovers, and merchandise, almost from its inception. Crossovers have included miniseries with Ghost, Batman, Starman, Savage Dragon, and the little-known Pain Killer Jane. Spin-off titles have ranged from several BPRD series to an Abe Sapien one-shot and *Hellboy Junior.* In addition, noted horror writer Christopher Golden has taken the hero in a new direction with a series of prose novels, illustrated by Mignola: *Hellboy: The Lost Army; Hellboy: Odd Jobs;* and *Hellboy: Bones of Giants.* As if all

that were not enough, a bewildering amount of merchandise has tempted the devoted fan, including Hellboy caps, prints, games, lighters, calendars, watches, lunch boxes, figures, statues, and tumblers. Even so, this is nothing compared to the deluge of tie-ins that accompanied the keenly anticipated *Hellboy* movie. This live-action feature film, whose screenplay was co-written by Mignola, was released in April 2004. Directed by Guillermo del Toro, the film stars Ron Perlman.

Since its inception, *Hellboy* has consistently been one of the most influential and finely crafted titles in the shops, and Mignola is still very much at the peak of his powers. His graphic style has already influenced one major movie: Disney's *Atlantis the Lost Empire* (2001) was clearly created in the image of his strips, Mignola himself consulting on the film's overall design and background settings. With the arrival of the *Hellboy* movie, Mignola's influence in both the comic-book world and American popular culture will undoubtedly grow. —*DAR*

Heroes for Hire

A revival, continuation, and expansion of the "mercenary superhero" concept that Marvel Comics originated in 1972 with its *Luke Cage: Hero for Hire* comic, Marvel's latter-day *Heroes for Hire* series began its brief run a quarter-century later. Written by veteran comic-book fabulist John Ostrander (with the collaboration of the equally august Roger Stern on the premiere issue) with pencils by Paschalis Ferry, Scott Kolins, Martin Egeland, and Mary Mitchell, *Heroes for Hire* reunited Marvel's first "professional" superhero Power Man (Luke Cage) with his 1970s and 1980s crime-fighting partner, the martial arts expert and "living weapon" known as Iron Fist (Danny Rand). In the fondly recalled pages of *Power Man and Iron Fist* (1978–1986), this pair of mismatched yet complementary heroes had founded Heroes for Hire, Inc., which allowed the duo and associates such as the Daughters of the Dragon (female martial-arts adventurers Misty Knight and Colleen Wing) to make a living by selling (or as often by donating) their unique skills as bodyguards, detectives, and superpowered fighters.

Just as Marvel's editorial staff and publishing program had grown exponentially since the premiere of the original *Luke Cage* title, the superteam assembled by Stern and Ostrander for *Heroes for Hire* expanded greatly as well, bringing aboard the Hulk, Hercules (now no longer an immortal), Ant Man (Scott Lang), the Black Knight (Dane Whitman), and the White Tiger (another martial arts hero). As in its predecessor series, *Heroes for Hire* dealt with the conflict between doing good and doing well—the tension that inevitably arises between being heroic for ethical reasons and the need to keep paying the bills.

As the series unfolds, a diverse panoply of other Marvel characters strut across its stage, ranging from second-stringers such as the Golden Age (1938–1954) Human Torch (who joins the team in the second issue); Jane Foster, the human alter ego of Thor's old girlfriend (*Heroes for Hire* #5, 1997); Brother Voodoo (issue #13, 1998); She-Hulk (issue #17, 1998); Quicksilver (*Heroes for Hire/Quicksilver Annual,* 1998); and Shang-Chi, the Master of Kung Fu (issues #18–#19, 1998–1999) to such certified audience draws as the Punisher (issue #9, 1998) and the X-Men's Wolverine (issues #18–#19, 1998–1999). One significant plot thread recounts Iron Fist's misguided effort to bring the mystical city of K'un-Lun, the place where he was raised and trained, to Earth from its native dimension. This plan could have devastated the planet, and is finally resolved in the four-issue *Iron Fist/Wolverine: The Return of K'un-Lun* miniseries (2000–2001), written by Jay Faerber and drawn by Jamal Igle.

Ultimately, *Hero for Hire*'s revived supersquad-for-profit failed to click with comics audiences; the series was given its walking papers in 1999 after a mere nineteen issues. Though the Marvel universe still contains no dearth of wrongs to be righted, the agency established by Power Man and Iron Fist still

has yet to reassemble. But like many real-world entrepreneurs, Power Man, Iron Fist, and many in their circle of working-stiff superheroes are no strangers to the occasional failure, series-cancellation, or even death; at some point in the future, they can be relied upon to bounce back and resume righting wrongs for love and money. —*MAM*

The Hulk

During the 1950s, Marvel Comics' publishing program consisted largely of bizarre monsters with names like Googam Son of Goom, Rommbu, and Fin Fang Foom; the era represents the nadir for the marketing of superheroes. But the immediate success of Marvel's *Fantastic Four* (*FF*) series (which debuted in November 1961) heralded an epochal change in the funnybook business, with costumed heroes supplanting monsters in much the same way mammals began to rule the planet after the dinosaurs died out. The FF's creators (scripter-editor Stan Lee and plotter-artist Jack Kirby) were keen to follow up on their superteam's success, but did so in a counterintuitive manner by launching a bimonthly series titled *The Incredible Hulk,* the first issue of which bears a May 1962 cover date. The Hulk, a misunderstood, superstrong creature spawned by atomic science run amok and driven by rage, is uniquely transitional between the fading era of monsters and the nascent age of superheroes.

In developing the Hulk, Lee and Kirby drew upon three principal sources. One was the Thing, the Fantastic Four's monstrous yet heroic strongman. Another was the laboratory-spawned creature from Mary Wollstonecraft Shelley's *Frankenstein* (or perhaps more precisely, the conception of him from James Whale's 1931 film version). Robert Louis Stevenson's *The Strange Case of Dr. Jekyll and Mr. Hyde* (1886) was the third. "To me," Lee explained, "[Frankenstein's] monster was the good guy. We always saw that mob of idiots with torches chasing Boris Karloff, who played the monster, up and down

Shadows & Light vol. 1, #3 © 1998 Marvel Comics.
COVER ART BY JOHN BUSCEMA AND CLAUDIO CASTELLINI.

the hills until he went berserk, remember? He never really wanted to hurt anybody. So I figured some sort of misunderstood monster would be fun to work with." But unlike the Thing, who was a warmly regarded member of the Fantastic Four's family, the Hulk's unrestrained rage made him a permanent outsider, a fearsome creature capable of evoking humankind's most atavistic nightmares.

In the Hulk's premiere appearance (*The Incredible Hulk* [*IH*] #1), Lee and Kirby introduced the emotionally repressed nuclear scientist Robert Bruce Banner, inventor of the gamma bomb. When teenager Rick Jones sneaks onto the bomb's test site at New Mexico's Desert Base, Banner races into

harm's way to push him into a protective trench, only to absorb a vast quantity of gamma rays when the device detonates. The irradiated Banner consequently begins making nightly transformations into a seven-foot, thousand-pound, gray- (later green-) skinned monster with virtually limitless strength and destructive capability, who embodies the darkest, angriest, and most antisocial aspects of Banner's personality. Lee saw the Hulk's ability to change back and forth between his human form and his (initially quite evil) monstrous aspect as key to the character's success. "Why couldn't a monster have a secret identity? Never done before, far as I knew. At least not in comics. It was wildly successful when Robert Louis Stevenson did it in *Dr. Jekyll and Mr. Hyde*."

The most important members of the series' supporting cast are in place from the very beginning: Air Force General Thaddeus E. "Thunderbolt" Ross, who oversees security at Desert Base and despises Banner, whom he loudly disparages as a gutless "milksop"; Betty Ross, Thunderbolt's mousy daughter, who despite being oppressed by her overbearing father is in love with Banner; and Rick Jones, the only one (at first) to become aware of Banner's dual nature, who repays the tortured scientist by helping to limit the amount of havoc the Hulk can wreak in a world that fears and hates the creature. All of these characters were destined to endure for decades.

But the Hulk's first comic-book series was somewhat less fortunate; it lasted only six issues before being canceled. But audiences were sufficiently intrigued with the title character to justify his continued guest appearances in other Marvel titles. During his early visits to the pages of *The Fantastic Four* (vol. 1 #12, 1963; vol. 1 #25–#26, 1964) the Hulk invariably fights that group's almost-as-strong Thing, and also crosses paths with Spider-Man in the wall-crawler's own title (*The Amazing Spider-Man* vol. 1 #14, 1964). The Hulk even becomes a charter member of another Lee-Kirby superhero team, the Avengers (*The Avengers* vol. 1 #1, 1963), alongside

Ant-Man, Iron Man, Thor, and the Wasp. Not a "team player" by nature, the Hulk leaves the inchoate organization in the series' second issue. Thanks to reader reaction to his sporadic guest appearances, the Hulk garnered a regular feature in *Tales to Astonish* beginning in issue #60 (1964). After sharing the title first with Giant-Man and later with the Sub-Mariner, the Hulk eventually took over the magazine completely. With issue #102 (1968), the title was permanently rechristened *The Incredible Hulk.*

The characterization and appearance of the Hulk have undergone countless changes since the character's inception, and these transformations began almost immediately. In his debut appearance (though not in most reprints of same), the creature has gray skin. "Unfortunately," Lee recalled, "in our first issue the printer had trouble keeping the shade of gray consistent from page to page. On some pages his skin was light gray, on others it was dark gray, and on some it looked black. Too confusing. So for the next issue I changed his skin color to green, a color the printer had less trouble with. Although it was done on a whim, it turned out to be a fortuitous choice because it gave rise to many memorable nicknames for me to employ, such as the Jolly Green Giant, Ol' Greenskin, the Green Goliath, etc."

During the Hulk's Lee-Kirby run, the mechanics of Banner's metamorphosis into the Hulk—during which Banner initially retains his intellect, though his personality becomes warped and evil—also changed fairly early in the character's history. By issue #4 of the first series (November 1962), Jones is helping Banner to trigger his transformations by means of a focused gamma ray beam, which enables the Hulk to fight assorted villains (Tyrannus; General Fang) and invading aliens (Mongu, the gladiator from space; the Metal Master) whenever the need arises. In late 1960s *Tales to Astonish* stories, Banner begins morphing into the Hulk whenever he is roused to extreme anger rather than because of the arrival of nightfall. Throughout the Hulk's first series, his speech contains none of the dumbed-down "Hulk Smash!" locutions that distinguish the character's run in the late 1960s and throughout the 1970s. Initially his language has more of a blue-collar, almost Archie Bunker–like quality (he even calls an attacking soldier a "meathead" in the first series' fifth issue).

As his post–*Tales to Astonish* series progressed, the Hulk's secret identity became common knowledge, and the Green Goliath was increasingly portrayed (by such scribes as Gary Friedrich, Bill Everett, Roy Thomas, Archie Goodwin, and such illustrators as Marie Severin and Herb Trimpe) as a misunderstood, childlike creature of diminished intellectual capacity and limited vocabulary (à la Lenny from John Steinbeck's 1937 novel *Of Mice and Men*) who turns his prodigious strength to mindless destruction most often when hounded by foes such as "Thunderbolt" Ross, who frequently pits the full fury of the United States military against him. And although he is often given to temper tantrums set off by relatively minor provocations, the Hulk can also be peaceful and gentle when left alone, a status he enjoys only rarely. This characterization strikes a sharp contrast to the Hulk's first appearances, in which he appears to be evil and remorseless in his desire to attack humanity; the destruction this middle-period Hulk causes is actually more incidental than intentional. Underlying the Hulk's rage is a theme of mutual emotional repression—with Banner's personality attempting to hold the Hulk in check, and vice versa—that pervades the series from its beginning. Countless scenes depicting the Hulk methodically pounding his way through impregnable walls relentlessly drive the emotional-repression metaphor home.

An artifact of cold war–era nuclear anxieties, the gamma rays that created the Hulk also spawned some of the Jade Giant's most enduring adversaries and allies. *Tales to Astonish* #90 (1967) served up foreign spy Emil Blonsky, whose exposure to gamma rays transforms him into the Abomination, a green-skinned superstrong being who resembles a muscle-bound version of the Creature from the Black Lagoon. As criminally oriented as the Hulk is innocent, the Abomination's subsequent slugfests with the Green Goliath are legion. *IH* #115 (1969) introduced uneducated janitor Samuel Sterns; thanks to gamma rays, Sterns' unrequited desire to be a genius manifested in his transformation into the green-skinned, giant-brained, would-be world-conqueror known as the Leader, another one of the Hulk's long-term foes. Psychologist Leonard Samson subsequently tries to end Banner's transformations into the Hulk by siphoning off some of his body's gamma radiation, and uses it to turn himself into a green-haired, superstrong being (*IH* #141, 1971). For many years, "Doc" Samson continues studying and psychoanalyzing Banner and the Hulk (whom he is sometimes forced to fight) in an unsuccessful effort to find a permanent cure for Banner's affliction.

In one of the most poignant chapters in the life of Marvel's misunderstood man-monster, the Hulk enters the subatomic world of K'ai (*IH* #140, 1971), a realm inhabited by green-skinned humanoids who are ruled by the benevolent Princess Jarella. Here the Hulk finds not only the acceptance he craves (the K'aians regard him as a great hero, not a monster), but also the love of Jarella. Best of all, he manages to retain the intellect and emotions of Banner while using the Hulk's prodigious strength to protect Jarella and her people from various cosmic menaces. This storyline, a product of the fertile mind of fantasist Harlan Ellison and veteran comics writer Roy Thomas, ends with the Hulk/Banner mourning Jarella's death, and inspired later Hulk writers—such as John Byrne in the 1980s and Peter David in the 1990s—to alter the balance between Banner's and the Hulk's personalities, often to tremendous dramatic effect.

With the premiere issue of *Marvel Feature* (December 1971), the Hulk once again tests his misanthropic tendencies by joining a superhero group, the misfit "non-team" known as the Defenders. In addition to the Hulk, the group initially consisted of Doctor Strange and the Sub-Mariner (another outsider who has nearly as antagonistic a relationship with the rest of humanity as does the Hulk). After four issues of *Marvel Feature,* the supergroup moved into its own bimonthly series (*The Defenders* vol. 1 #1, 1972). The Hulk drifted in and out of this loose agglomeration of heroes until its dissolution in 1986, and returned to the group when it reformed years later, in 2001.

With the Hulk's popularity at its zenith thanks to a successful primetime live-action television show starring Bill Bixby and Lou Ferrigno (1978–1982, CBS), in 1980 Lee launched the Hulk's first and only major spin-off with *The Savage She-Hulk* (vol. 1, #1), in which Bruce Banner gives a transfusion of his gamma-irradiated blood to his injured cousin, lawyer Jennifer Walters. For the next twenty-five months, Walters was large, green, and often angry during her highly derivative adventures. The character returned nine years later in a far more innovative series titled *The Sensational She-Hulk* (#1, May 1989), in which writer-artist John Byrne toyed with traditional comic-book tropes in various clever ways, including having the eponymous character break down the "fourth wall" by grabbing panel borders and even addressing the audience directly.

During the Hulk's first two decades, all of his writers kept Banner and the Hulk essentially separate from one another, at least in a psychological sense; no serious, sustained attempt was made to explore the deep connections between these two personalities. Then, in stories that began running in the large-format *Rampaging Hulk* magazine (January 1977–June 1981, known simply as *The Hulk* from the tenth issue forward), writer Doug Moench posited that Banner suffered from multiple personality disorder. Hulk scribes Roger Stern and Peter B. Gillis bolstered this theory by contending that the

Opposite: From *Shadows & Light* vol. 1, #3 © 1998 Marvel Comics.

THE AIR... IS ALREADY PRETTY STALE IN HERE. PROBABLY WOULDN'T TAKE LONG...

NO... NO!

I CAN'T LET IT END THIS WAY!

I CAN'T! I WON'T!!

HEART'S RACING... NO TURNING BACK NOW! I CAN ALREADY FEEL.... THE CHANGE!

ONE THING IS ALWAYS THE SAME... EVERY TIME... IT HURTS!

SO!

THOOM

BANNER THOUGHT HE COULD TRAP ME HERE, DID HE?!

ALWAYS THINKS HE'S SO SMART! THINKS I'M STUPID!

BUT HE'S WRONG! WRONG!! JUST BECAUSE HE COULDN'T BUDGE THE DOOR--!

Hulk and Banner are entirely different creatures who happen to occupy the same body (*IH #227, 1978*). This take on the Hulk changed radically with writer Bill Mantlo's revelation (*IH #312, 1985*) that the Hulk's rage comes not from gamma rays but from the beatings that Banner received from his alcoholic, abusive father during childhood. After Banner's exposure to the gamma bomb, the authoritarian General Ross naturally becomes a lightning rod for the scientist's deep well of repressed anger toward his father. This development made possible some of the most affecting and psychologically complex Hulk stories ever penned, and resonated well with the larger culture's growing interest in the so-called "recovery movement," usually without venturing too far into maudlin whining or touchy-feely New Age excesses.

One of the highlights of writer-artist John Byrne's brief stint on the series (beginning in *IH #314, 1985*) is Banner and the Hulk being split into independent entities in two separate bodies, thereby shining a new light on the original Lee/Kirby Jekyll-and-Hyde concept. Unshackled from Banner's emotional restraint, the Hulk becomes a complete berserker, more dangerous than ever before. Freed of the capricious rages of the Hulk, Banner finally marries Betty Ross, despite the attempts of her father (who has become demented by his encounters with the Hulk) to kill him. But Banner's connubial bliss is short-lived; Byrne's successor, writer Allen Milgrom, quickly placed both the man and the monster back into a single body, finishing up 1986 with a battle royal between the newly reconstituted green Hulk and the original gray Hulk.

The Hulk arguably received his most riveting portrayals—and underwent some of his most significant changes—during Peter David's lengthy writing tenure, which began in *IH #328 (February 1987)* and ended with issue #467 (August 1998). Among the many highlights of David's run is Banner's metamorphosis into the gray Hulk who becomes a Las Vegas mob enforcer known as Joe Fixit, a latter-day Mr. Hyde in an Armani suit. This persona combines Banner's intelligence with the Hulk's strength, while freeing Banner from his inhibition against using violence and trickery, the main tools of the gangster's trade. David (working with such artists as Todd McFarlane, John Ridgway, and Dale McKeown) built upon Mantlo's multiple-personality concept by exploring three distinct personalities: Banner, who despite his emotional scars is capable of experiencing a loving relationship with Betty; the intelligent, scheming gray Hulk, who represses all of his "softer" emotions; and the raging child represented by the traditional green-skinned Hulk. Doc Samson even succeeds in integrating these three personalities into a single being, a sophisticated, intelligent superhero—neither a rampaging brute nor a geeky scientist—who becomes the leader of a supergroup called the Pantheon (*IH #400, 1992*). David's Hulk is also memorable for its clever, incisive dialogue.

In *The Incredible Hulk: Future Imperfect* (two issues, December 1992 and January 1993), David created a grim postapocalyptic future Earth where the Hulk meets the Maestro, his future self—who is also the ruler of this dystopian world. Like the Leader, the Maestro had used guile and intelligence, rather than brute strength, to conquer the human race; the Hulk sees the Maestro as a cautionary wake-up call, a warning that he might become as hateful as his father unless he is very careful. After returning to the present, the Hulk becomes increasingly fearful of becoming the Maestro; consequently, when he becomes angry he turns into plain, powerless Bruce Banner, whose impotent tantrums symbolize the Hulk's latest take on emotional repression (IH #426, 1995). No longer an emotionally stable superhero, the Hulk (with Betty, now his wife, at his side) once again becomes a fugitive, hiding out in small towns all over America. During this period, Betty completes a transformation of her own, evolving from a helpless damsel to be rescued, to a young bride mourning Banner's miscarried child, to an independent, self-actualized woman. Unfortunately, at the end of the 1990s she contracts gamma-radiation poisoning because of years of close proximity to Banner and ultimately dies at the gamma-mutated hands of the Abomination.

Although his long-running series concluded with issue #474 (March 1999), the Jade Giant returned to prominence a month later with a new monthly title (*Hulk* #1), following the creative vision of John Byrne for the first seven issues. As the series unfolds (with stories from such writers as Paul Jenkins, Fabian Nicieza, Sean McKeever, and Christopher Priest, and the illustrative talents of John Romita Jr., Kyle Hotz, Joe Bennett, and Jon Bogdanove), Banner must contend with a new incarnation of the Hulk that represents his intense guilt over Betty's death. This soon leads to the emergence of the "Devil Hulk," a purely evil Hulk who tries to use Banner's illness to gain control of the scientist's body; subsequently, Banner learns that each of his transformations into the Hulk creates an entirely new personality, upping the ante on his multiple personality disorder by a factor of thousands. In the 2000s, the series was simplified and revitalized again with an ominous, film noir-ish treatment by writer Bruce Jones.

Over more than four decades, Banner and the Hulk have received widely varying interpretations as each successive creative team reinvents them to suit the evolving sensibilities of comics audiences. Through all of these nonstop, manifold changes, the essential purity of the Hulk's dual nature—the eternal tension between rationality and emotion, the endless twilight struggle between the id and the super-ego—remains archetypally clear and literarily valid. The series will certainly continue to grow, develop, and fascinate for decades to come. —*MAM*

The Hulk in the Media

Four years after his comic-book debut in *The Incredible Hulk* #1 (1962), the Hulk made his animated premiere as part of the syndicated daily program for tele-

vision called *The Marvel Super-Heroes.* The fall 1966 series was the work of animators and producers Robert Lawrence, Grant Simmons, and Ray Patterson under the company name of Grantray-Lawrence. Each weekday half-hour episode put the spotlight on a different hero with a three-part adventure. *Captain America* was Monday, *The Incredible Hulk* was Tuesday, *Iron Man* was Wednesday, *Mighty Thor* was Thursday (naturally), and *Sub-Mariner* was Friday.

The Incredible Hulk's theme song was frighteningly inept, but strangely catchy: "Doc Bruce Banner, belted by gamma rays, turned into the Hulk, ain't he un-glamorays? Wreckin' the town, with the power of a bull, ain't no monster clown, who is as lovable … The ever lovin' Hulk! Hulk! Hulk!" The animation was even more inept. Through a process called xerography, artwork was transferred directly from Marvel comic books onto animation cels. It was then given a slight movement by jiggling the cel or sliding it across a background. Occasionally, blinking eyes or moving hands would give the illusion of motion. However, because the stories were taken directly from issues of *The Incredible Hulk* and *Tales to Astonish,* the plots and characters remained faithful. After one season of production, *The Marvel Super-Heroes* show was canceled, though it has shown up in syndication and on the video market ever since.

Hulk's next television appearance was not until November 4, 1977. That's the night that CBS debuted *The Incredible Hulk,* a new live-action telefilm from producer Kenneth Johnson and Universal. A second two-hour pilot film was aired later in November, and when ratings came in strongly, a series was commissioned. While the pilot was successfully released theatrically overseas, in the United States the regular television series began on March 10, 1978.

The Incredible Hulk series departed from the comics in several ways. The producers felt the name "Bruce" sounded too gay, and asked Johnson to change it (the "official" story would retroactively become that they changed it to avoid the name's

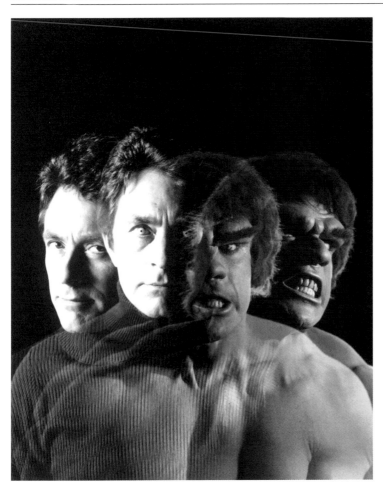

Bill Bixby (Dr. David Banner) and Lou Ferrigno (the Hulk) in *The Incredible Hulk*.

obnoxious reporter Jack McGee, whose pursuit of Banner and his secret brought him close to the Hulk many times.

The Incredible Hulk was a huge hit with audiences, spawning several theme park attractions at Universal Studios, and adding a catchphrase to the English lexicon: Banner's admonishment, "Don't make me angry. You wouldn't like me when I'm angry." Rare for a genre show, *Hulk* even picked up an Emmy Award in 1979 (Mariette Hartley for Best Dramatic Performance). Audiences identified with the tragic Banner and his loneliness, while they also enjoyed the super-id destructiveness of the Hulk.

By the fourth season, *The Incredible Hulk* began to become formulaic. Everyone knew that Banner would end each episode walking down the highway, alone, so what was the draw for fans to tune in the following week? Ratings began to fall, and Universal was also cutting the show's budget. Production on the series finally halted in the summer of 1981. After five seasons—the last of which featured numerous preemptions—*The Incredible Hulk* series left the air on May 12, 1982. Syndication and reruns followed, but the "Greenskin Goliath" was not off the air in new adventures for long.

alliteration); the character became David Banner thereafter. The budget would not allow for supervillains, so Johnson's approach was to have Banner and the Hulk deal with more intimate human issues and traumas. Popular actor Bill Bixby was cast in the title role of Banner, while the young two-time Mr. Universe Lou Ferrigno played the Hulk. Ferrigno endured hours of makeup for each scene he filmed; in addition to his entire body getting painted green, he also wore a prosthetic brow and a green wig. The series' only other recurring character was Jack Colvin as

The Hulk had made a 1981 guest appearance on the animated NBC series *Spider-Man and His Amazing Friends*. Although the live show was over, Marvel Productions put a *Hulk* animated series on the fast-track. On September 18, 1982, *The Incredible Hulk and The Amazing Spider-Man* debuted, as a one-hour series with half-hour segments for its two stars. Stan Lee narrated the Hulk's adventures.

The stories hewed closer to their comic-book origins, putting Banner back with the military, and involving supporting characters such as Rick Jones, Betty Ross, General Thunderbolt Ross, Major Ned (in the comics, Glenn) Talbot, and others. Villains included Doctor Octopus, Spymaster, the Puppet Master, and others who imperiled Gamma Base. The eleventh episode, "Enter: She-Hulk," introduced Jennifer Walters, Bruce's cousin, as the woman who gained Hulk's powers through a blood transfusion (just as happened in 1980 in the first issue of Marvel's comic *The Savage She-Hulk*). Thirteen episodes were produced, and rerun the following year when the show changed titles to *The Amazing Spider-Man and The Incredible Hulk.* That series aired its last on March 31, 1984.

New World Pictures bought Marvel Comics in 1986 and wanted to turn its library of superheroes into television series and feature films. The best way the company felt it could do that was to utilize a known quantity as a "backdoor pilot." The cast of *The Incredible Hulk* reunited for a telefilm that aired on NBC on May 22, 1988. Titled *Return of the Incredible Hulk,* the show saw the live-action debut of Thor (Eric Kramer), the hammer-wielding Norse god. Ratings were high, but interest in a *Thor* series didn't go anywhere.

A second telefilm aired on NBC nearly one year later, on April 30, 1989. *Trial of the Incredible Hulk* featured Banner seeking the services of blind lawyer Matt Murdock (Rex Smith), who just happens to secretly be the superhero Daredevil. Together, the two work to bring down Wilson Fisk/Kingpin (John Rhyes Davies) and clear Banner's name. Ratings were solid, but a *Daredevil* series also failed to materialize.

New World looked into developing further *Hulk* telefilms to introduce She-Hulk, Wolverine, and Iron Man, but decided to alter their plans, partially due to Bixby and Ferrigno's growing restlessness in their

roles. A final telefilm was shot, airing on February 18, 1990. Titled *The Death of the Incredible Hulk,* and directed by Bixby himself, the story found Banner close to a cure for his "condition," but the Hulk must make the ultimate sacrifice to stop terrorists. Reverting to Banner at the end as he dies, his final words are, "I'm a free man now."

Unwilling to fully end the series, New World came up with ways to continue the franchise. A telefilm script titled "Metamorphosis" would have used flashbacks to show how Banner's blood transfusion turned a young woman into She-Hulk. But that project lost steam, as did another telefilm, *The Rebirth of the Incredible Hulk.* Bixby's death on November 21, 1993, meant that any further television reunion plans were now impossible. Another *She-Hulk* project—produced by film director Oliver Stone and starring Ms. Olympia bodybuilding champion Cory Everson—was scuttled after initial network interest.

At the Cannes Film Festival in summer 1991, New World Pictures offered a fold-out sales sheet with photos of actress Brigitte Nielsen painted green, announcing that a *She-Hulk* feature film would start filming soon. Carl Gottlieb wrote the script and Tamara Asseyez was to produce, but the picture was never made.

The Hulk himself next made a trio of guest appearances in animated form: in a third-season episode of Fox's *X-Men* in May 1995; in a second-season episode of the syndicated *The Fantastic Four* in November 1995; and in a second-season episode of the syndicated *Iron Man* in February 1996. These were just a warm-up for an all-new animated series.

The Incredible Hulk debuted on UPN on September 8, 1996. Bruce Banner was back in action, still struggling with his dark/green side as the Hulk on Gamma Base, and still searching for a cure. Lou Ferrigno returned also, to be the voice of the Hulk, while TV and film stars such as Neal McDonough, Genie Francis, Luke Perry, Mark Hamill, Kathy Ire-

A computer-generated Hulk stars in the live-action film *The Hulk*.

land, Richard Moll, and Matt Frewer did regular or guest voices.

Comic-book villains such as the Leader, Abomination, Wendigo, Doctor Doom, and Gargoyle appeared, as did fellow heroes such as Thor, the Fantastic Four, Ghost Rider, and Sasquatch. But the primary guest-star was Banner's cousin Jennifer Walters, blood transfused as She-Hulk. Appearing in two first-season episodes, She-Hulk was promoted to regular co-star with the series' second season, and the title was changed to *The Incredible Hulk and She-Hulk*. A total of twenty-one episodes were produced in the two seasons. A third season saw another title change, to *The Incredible Hulk and Friends,* and a bump to hour-length with the addition of rotating reruns of the syndicated *Fantastic Four* and *Iron Man* episodes. The series was finally canceled on September 11, 1999.

Since the demise of the live-action *Incredible Hulk* series, Universal Studios had put a feature film on the development slate. John Turman developed the first script in 1994, working on the project until 1996. In the late 1990s, Joe Johnston was attached to direct, from a script by Jonathan Hensleigh, but he stepped aside in 1997. Hensleigh was then going to direct the film himself, with special effects by Industrial Light & Magic. Later, Scott Alexander and Larry Karazewski were announced as having come aboard to script, and actors Gregory Sporleder and Lynn Red Williams were signed on to portray villains in the film. Early in 1998, Hensleigh departed, and Michael France came aboard to script, then Hensleigh came back aboard to redraft the project and lower its projected $100 million budget. The start date for shooting came and went, and the film retreated back into further development. In 2000, Michael Tolkin, then David Hayter, took swings at the script.

Early in 2001, Academy Award–winning director Ang Lee came onboard to direct the *Hulk* project, with both himself and James Schamus working on the script. Lee wanted to create a story that explored both the psychological origins of the Hulk and the scientific aspects. "Scientifically, I am doing an academic study on how a cell can expand and how a person can become a Hulk," Lee told *USA Today*. With the part of the Hulk to be completely realized using computer-generated imagery (CGI), casting began on the other leading roles. Australian actor Eric Bana gained the part of Bruce Banner, while Jennifer Connelly took her second comic-book role (after *The Rocketeer*) as Betty Ross. Sam Elliott and Josh Lucas played the parts of General Ross and Major Talbot, while Nick Nolte was written into the hitherto unseen role of Bruce's father, David Banner. Even Stan Lee and Lou Ferrigno were given cameo sequences. On March 18, 2002, filming began.

Less than a year later, the film was wrapping production and expectations were high. The biggest question on the public's collective mind was, "Can they make a CGI Hulk look convincing?" Audiences saw their first glimpses of the creature during the January 26, 2003 Super Bowl, teasing them until later trailers debuted in theaters and online on February 14. The $120 million film was released on June 20, 2003, to great fanfare, following successful releases for *Daredevil* and *X2: X-Men United*.

Audiences were pleased at the realism of the CGI Hulk, at the comic-book-style visuals, and of the surprise element that Bruce's father became the (unnamed) Absorbing Man. Less enthusiasm greeted the glacial pace of the film, the moody drama, the silly "Hulk dogs" that menaced Betty and the Hulk at one point, and the incomprehensible ending battle. Still, *The Hulk* won its opening weekend with a $62 million box office take. It plummeted during its second weekend, though it did pass the $100

million mark. Overseas reactions and box office business were mixed, but were enough to propel the film to over $200 million worldwide, prior to its October 2003 DVD release. In addition, the film spun off a million-dollar merchandising campaign, with *Hulk* tie-in books, games, action figures, noise-making "Hulk fists," and assorted sundries hitting the marketplace in stride. In traditional Hulk fashion, the green giant even offered, "Bones no break when Hulk drink milk," for the popular "got milk?" ad campaign.

Despite the film's mixed critical reception and not-as-high-as-hoped box-office take, a feature sequel to *The Hulk* was announced by Marvel in mid-2003. Although Marvel had previously talked about negotiations for a *Hulk* animated series to follow the first film, that project appears to have vanished from development. Still, despite Kermit the Frog's lament, "It's not easy being green," the Incredible Hulk seems to have smashed his own successful path through Hollywood's media machine. —*AM*

The Human Torch

The Human Torch was one of the "big three" heroes of Marvel (then known as Timely) Comics, along with Captain America and the Sub-Mariner—and one of the most popular Marvel superheroes of the 1940s. Like the Sub-Mariner, he was first seen on the newsstands in *Marvel Comics* #1, in late 1939. Historians believe that the Sub-Mariner came first and that the Torch was created by Carl Burgos as a counterpart to his friend Bill Everett's aquatic hero. Both artists worked in the Funnies Inc. sweatshop and were among several creators involved in packaging together the first of a new comic line for pulp publisher Martin Goodman. The comic, and particularly the Torch and Sub-Mariner characters, proved a hit, and Timely soon grew to become one of the era's biggest companies, finally emerging as the Marvel Comics that readers know today.

As the story in *Marvel Comics* #1 reveals, the Torch is an android created by Professor Phineas T. Horton, which accidentally bursts into flames when exposed to oxygen, due to a design flaw. Disappointed by his failure, Horton buries the poor creature in a glass tomb and sinks it in concrete, but when an explosion accidentally releases the Torch, he rampages through a nearby town, causing chaos wherever he goes. Befriended by a crook called Sardo, the Torch is lured into a life of crime until rescued by Horton, who has his own agenda. Seeing that the Torch can now control his flame, Horton plans to exploit the Torch's powers for his own gain. Disgusted by the professor's greed, the Torch heads off on his own, to right injustices wherever he encounters them, and he soon signs up as a member of the police department (adopting the alter ego Jim Hammond, though this temporary device is not well-remembered today), rushing to the scene of any crime or disaster.

Although he had no tool or weapons to speak of, and his scant bodysuit costume disappeared when he ignited into flames, the Torch's persona as a red-hot flame intrigued readers. He could melt bullets shot his way, fly, and create ropes of flame and fireballs to subdue even the most dastardly ne'er-do-wells. In his Torch persona, the hero was unaffected by electricity and explosions, although the force of a powerful blast was known to knock him over. His number one vulnerability, of course, was water.

In 1939, the superhero was still a very new concept and only nine heroes preceded the Torch and Sub-Mariner, many of them (Wonderman, the Green Mask, the Masked Marvel) eminently forgettable. So Timely's pair made a massive impact. The Torch's regular spot in *Marvel Mystery Comics* (the new name for *Marvel Comics*) was soon joined by his own quarterly solo title and, as the United States entered World War II, the Axis-smashing Torch began to pop up elsewhere as well. Between 1939 and 1949, the Torch starred in almost 300 adventures in such titles as *All Winners, Daring, All-Select, Captain America,* and *Mystic Comics*— almost tying Captain America for the greatest number of stories published for a 1940s Marvel hero.

For *Human Torch* #1, Burgos created a junior sidekick for the hero (possibly inspired by the recent emergence of Robin in *Detective Comics*), a young counterpart called Toro, the Flaming Kid. Following the death of his parents in a train crash, Toro was adopted by a circus fire-eating act that had discovered that he could control fire and was unharmed by it. When the Torch happened upon him, they teamed up and Toro eventually moved in with his mentor as his ward. The pair became inseparable for the rest of the strip's run. Toro later went on to join the Young Allies, who starred in twenty issues of their own comic as well as a lengthy run in *Kid Komics.*

The war was a boost to Timely/Marvel's heroes and they were among the first to take the fight to the Axis powers. While the Torch never really developed any arch-enemies, he was constantly battling the Nazis and Japanese, in between rooting out spy rings and racketeers. Another innovative feature of the Human Torch strip was his many battles with his co-star and rival the Sub-Mariner. The first of these appeared in *Marvel Mystery Comics* #8. The pair's longest battle stretched to an astonishing sixty pages (in *Human Torch* #5) and ranged across the whole planet, taking in Axis plots and vast warring armies. Burgos, Everett, and their Funnies Inc. colleagues would hole themselves up in hotel rooms and work for days on end, churning out these mammoth tales, to meet their fans' insatiable demand. While sometimes crude, these epics have an incredible energy and dynamism to them that still excites today.

Burgos was drafted in 1942 and other creators were brought in to take over his work, including artists Harry Sahle and Don Rico and a promising young writer named Mickey Spillane. After the war, Burgos contributed a few new tales but the strip was in decline and, in mid-1949, *Human Torch Comics* suffered the indignity of being transformed into *Love Tales.* Not even the late innovation of replacing Toro with a distaff assistant—the light-ray-emitting Sun Girl—could halt the sudden collapse of the superhero market. Marvel concentrated on romance, war, and horror comics until the mid-1950s, when they evidently felt that the time was right for a revival of their heroic stars. *Young Men* #24 (December 1953) starred all the big three, with the Torch as cover star, and reintroduced the heroes to a new audience.

The Torch, it seems, had been covered by a flame-retardant solution and buried in the desert by "the crime boss" until, five years later, he was freed by a nuclear test blast. Toro had been captured and brainwashed by the Koreans, and the Torch's first task was to free him from their control. Together again at last, the pair took up from where they had left off, tackling organized crime (and bashing the occasional "red" in the process). Their resurrection led to the revival of the Torch's own comic and to appearances—many by Burgos—in further issues of *Young Men, Sub-Mariner, Captain America,* and *Men's Adventures,* but within a year the Torch was canceled once again. When, in 1961, fans next discovered on the stands a comic starring the Human Torch (*Fantastic Four* #1), it was a totally different Torch, Johnny Storm. Following DC Comics' success with its new superhero line, Martin Goodman decided that the time was right for his own company to re-enter the genre and, when writer Stan Lee and artist Jack Kirby set about dreaming up a new title, someone clearly remembered the first Torch's success. Of course, Storm remains an integral member of the Fantastic Four to this day, but he has rarely enjoyed solo success; his main ventures outside the group have been an early run in *Strange Tales* (issues #101–#134) in the early 1960s (one episode of which was drawn by Burgos), and a new solo series targeted at young readers that flared up in 2003 and had not yet burned out in early 2004.

Fans had not quite seen the last of the original Human Torch and Toro, however. The first Torch reappeared to fight the new version in the 1966

Young Men #25 © 1953 Atlas.
COVER ART BY CARL BURGOS.

Fantastic Four Annual, having been reactivated by the Mad Thinker, while Toro made an appearance in *Sub-Mariner* #14. Sadly, both died. However, over in the *Avengers* comic, the evil robot Ultron acquired the Torch's remains and took them off to Prof. Horton (who had actually been killed off back in 1939; clearly, no one at Marvel had remembered that). Horton then managed to fix the flaw that had caused his creation to self-immolate. Using the new, improved android, Ultron fashioned a new superbeing—the Vision—who soon became an Avenger, as chronicled in *Avengers* #57 and #58 (though his synthetic lineage was not fully revealed until #135, as part of a time-travel saga that also brought the original Torch and his later self face-to-face).

Writer and comics historian Roy Thomas always had a fondness for the first Torch, and in 1975 created *The Invaders* to recount further wartime adventures of the Timely Comics "big three" (including Captain America and Sub-Mariner and adding Toro and Captain America's sidekick Bucky to the group). That title's cancellation in 1979 might have marked the last hurrah for the first Torch. But one should never say never where marketable properties are concerned, and by the late 1980s continuity had been revised so that the original Torch had not been transformed into the Vision and could fly again, first as a member of the West Coast Avengers and later with the Heroes for Hire. Whether readers will see him again is uncertain, though Carl Burgos' inspiration lives on in every issue of *The Fantastic Four.* —DAR

The Huntress

Borrowing her name from a relatively obscure Golden Age villainess, the heroic Huntress first appeared on "Earth-Two"—the parallel world onto which the 1940s incarnations of DC Comics' characters had been relegated—in *All-Star Comics #69* (1977). Envisioned by writer Paul Levitz and artist Joe Staton as the Earth-Two Batgirl, the Huntress is more intriguingly distinguished by her parentage: She is Helena Wayne, the daughter of millionaire Bruce (Batman) Wayne and rehabilitated criminal Selina (Catwoman) Kyle. Helena had recently graduated law school when a former associate of Catwoman's blackmails Kyle back into her feline guise for a heist. Catwoman perishes in a consequent conflict, leading her traumatized husband to burn his cape and cowl in a grim funeral pyre, retiring his Batman identity. Helena swears vengeance against her mother's killer, taking a vow that eerily mirrors her father's some decades prior, and becomes the Huntress, a violet-and-black-clad crime fighter who

carries on the traditions of her parents with athletic prowess and crossbow in tow. The Huntress so enthralled DC readers fascinated by the heroine's lineage and motivation that she spun out of *All-Star Comics* into a successful backup series in *Wonder Woman,* until being defeated by an unstoppable menace: continuity revision. In 1985, DC Comics streamlined its multiple worlds and their respective character variations in its highly acclaimed twelve-issue series *Crisis on Infinite Earths.* Since that series eliminated the Earth-Two Batman, the Huntress was also erased from comics reality.

But the character was too popular to fully jettison from the DC universe, and in April 1989 was reintroduced in *The Huntress #1.* During her childhood, Mafia princess Helena Rosa Bertinelli's family, a Gotham City crime cartel, was executed in a syndicate hit. The sole surviving Bertinelli, Helena forsakes her gangland roots and takes up a quest to dismantle organized crime as the Huntress, aiming her crossbow at the city's mobsters. By day, she works as a teacher, further toiling to undo some of the damage caused by her family ties.

The Huntress' brutal (but nonlethal) methods attracted the attention of the Batman, who initially regarded her as yet another plague on the streets of Gotham, but after several encounters the Dark Knight accepted her as an ally. *The Huntress* was canceled after nineteen issues, but the heroine has maintained a profile through numerous guest appearances in other Batman titles, a membership stint in the Justice League, the issuance of several action figures, and a partnership with Oracle and Black Canary as the Birds of Prey. The Huntress even tangled with Twentieth Century Fox's murderous movie monster in the Dark Horse Comics/DC Comics four-issue crossover comic *Batman vs. Predator II: Bloodmatch* (1995).

The Huntress has twice ventured onto the small screen. Actress Barbara Joyce played the character in two 1979 *Legends of the Super-Heroes* live-action comedy specials airing on NBC, also starring Adam West as Batman and Burt Ward as

Robin. In 2002, a short-lived *Birds of Prey* series ran on the WB network, including in its cast Ashley Scott as the Huntress. While this program adapted the contemporary *Birds of Prey* comic book into episodic television form, it borrowed the Huntress' heritage from the Earth-Two comic-book incarnation, as evidenced by the show's tagline: "Batman's Little Girl Is All Grown Up." —*ME*

Hurricane Polymar

Hurricane Polymar is the third of the "Tatsunoko heroes" shows created by Tatsunoko Productions in the early 1970s. Following on the heels of *Gatchaman* (1972) and *Casshan* (1973), *Polymar* toned down the angst of the previous shows and added a lighthearted feel, making it a popular superhero anime in Japan in the mid-1970s. While it would be almost twenty years later that the character enjoyed popularity in the United States, once there he would become firmly rooted in the anime subculture.

The staff behind *Polymar* included creator Tatsuo Yoshida (one of the founders of Tatsunoko), who also designed the show's characters along with Yoshitaka Amano. Junzo Toriumi was the chief screenwriter, but Akiyoshi Sakai, Masaru Yamamoto, and Junichi Shima also contributed screenplays. Handling the directing duties were Eiko Toriumi, Hideo Nishimaki, and Yoshiyuki Tomino. Years later, Tomino—along with *Polymar*'s mechanical designers Mitsuki Nakamura and Kunio Okawara—would revolutionize Japanese animation with the groundbreaking science fiction series *Mobile Suit Gundam*.

Premiering on the Asahi Network in Japan on October 4, 1974, *Hurricane Polymar* ran for twenty-six half-hour episodes. The storyline revolved around Takeshi, a young police chief who works with the International Crime Division (ICD) of Washingkyo City (an amalgam of Washington and Tokyo). At first, Takeshi was trying to please his father, who is the director of the ICD, and even underwent special martial arts training in an effort to do so, but after frequently butting heads over methods of police work, the chief fires his own son. On his own, Takeshi takes on a solo career, but eventually becomes the assistant to Private Investigator Joe Kuruma.

Unfortunately, Kuruma frequently gets in the way of the police, and is somewhat of a blundering investigator. Takeshi takes on most of the tougher assignments, which leads one night to an assault by several thugs. Putting up a fight, Takeshi is badly injured, but is saved by Professor Oregar. The Professor gives the detective an experimental suit made of an artificial polymer, polimet. The suit is red in color, with white gloves and boots, a short cape, a stylized logo on the chest, and yellow horns on the side of its helmet. It is voice-activated, and is stronger than steel, giving the user incredible strength. In addition, it can transform itself into a super-boat, a super-tank, a super-submarine, and a super-plane, each with its own super-abilities. Now, as the hero Hurricane Polymar, Takeshi battles a bizarre collection of criminals, including the Band of the Doberman, the Band of the Rats, and the Band of the Scorpions. With all of these features, Kuruma as Hurricane Polymar embodies the typical features of the American superhero—superpowers, an identity-changing costume, and an alter ego that sets about functioning in the real world. And like the American superhero, he has a typical dilemma: how to keep his secret identity from love interest Teru Namba.

Polymar was a success in Japan, and was more of a lighthearted, martial arts–influenced series. The show was filled with in-jokes poking fun at earlier Tatsunoko superhero shows. The original series was never released in the United States, but was a popular import on Italian television in the 1980s. As testimony to the show's popularity, Italian fans started websites, circulated newsletters, and developed somewhat of a cult following for the character. Pioneer released the entire series on DVD in Japan in 2001, and Polymar himself was a character in the Japanese-only Playstation game *Tatsunoko Fight* (which also featured the main heroes from the other three Tatsunoko heroes shows). In 2003, the Japanese toy company Takara released action figures of the major characters from the *Tatsunoko Fight* game, including Polymar.

In 1996, Akiyuki Shinbo supervised a remake of *Polymar,* with Yasuomi Umetsu providing the character designs. The remake, now titled *New Hurricane Polymar,* was released in the United States on video by Urban Vision, but this remake only consisted of two thirty-minute episodes. This time, the setting is the artificial island Tokyo Plus. Dr. Oregar creates the Polymar helmet, but is murdered by the vicious Catshark Squad. His assistant, Ryoko Nishida, manages to get the helmet to Takeshi, assistant

to Detective Kuruma, but Nishida too is killed by the Catsharks. Now, as the hero Hurricane Polymar, Takeshi must stop the Catsharks and their leader, Nova, from destroying the Geofront Plan, a major project designed to protect the environment. If this project is destroyed, it will mean the end of the human race.

Hurricane Polymar was the last of the Tatsunoko heroes shows to be remade in the 1990s. While not as well known in the United States, it still stands as an important part of Tatsunoko Productions' efforts to create unique, action-packed superhero stories. In 1998, Tatsunoko produced the science-fiction series *Generator Gawl,* a successor to the studio's superhero anime of the 1970s. —*MM*

Image Comics Heroes

The early 1990s was a watershed period for the creators of Marvel Comics' highest-profile titles. Comic-book artists (who often also wrote their material) such as Todd McFarlane (*Spider-Man*), Erik Larsen (*Amazing Spider-Man; Spider-Man*), Jim Lee (*X-Men; Uncanny X-Men*), Rob Liefeld (*X-Factor; X-Force*), Whilce Portacio (*Longshot; Punisher; Uncanny X-Men; X-Factor*), Marc Silvestri (*Uncanny X-Men; Wolverine*), and Jim Valentino (*Guardians of the Galaxy*) generated unprecedented sales. Riding a wave of success with characters owned by Marvel, these graphic *auteurs* left the company in 1992, joining forces to form Image Comics, a company dedicated to publishing creator-owned properties, principally in the comics industry's dominant superhero genre. During their tenures at Marvel, the Image founders had often felt constrained by corporate editorial edicts; under the Image banner, however, they had free reign to control and develop their own characters, taking them in whatever direction they saw fit. As the 1990s progressed, the fledgling company prospered and its line expanded, successfully weathering the comics industry's mid-decade

sales slump. Today, Image Comics remains a serious competitor to both Marvel and DC Comics, the two publishing houses that had for decades dominated the comic-book business.

At its inception, Image was the home of several distinct comics publishing ventures, including Todd McFarlane's Todd McFarlane Productions (TMP), Marc Silvestri's Top Cow Productions, and Jim Lee's WildStorm Productions. Solely owned by McFarlane, TMP still publishes *Spawn* and its spinoff titles today.

Arguably Image's most successful title, *Spawn*—which recounts the story of a murdered soldier (Al Simmons) who is resurrected as the commander of the armies of hell—began publication in 1992. Despite the hero's rather derivative appearance—Spawn appears to have raided the attics of Spider-Man, Dr. Strange, the Punisher, and Lobo when he assembled his costume—and the title's overemphasis on ultraviolence and its elevation of McFarlane's faddish, extreme art-style over story, *Spawn* was an immediate hit among comics readers and collectors. The series gave rise to a feature film (starring Michael Jai as the macabre hell-warrior) in 1997, developed into an Emmy Award–winning HBO animated series (1997–1999), and birthed a line of collectible action figures from

McFarlane's own toy company (McFarlane Toys). *Spawn* also engendered a pair of spin-off comics series: *Hellspawn* (the tale of a version of Spawn even meaner than the original one) and *Sam & Twitch* (a pair of urban detectives investigating the supernatural in a *Buffy the Vampire Slayer* meets *NYPD Blue* milieu).

Top Cow is wholly owned by Image partner Marc Silvestri, and publishes such titles as *Battle of the Planets, Delicate Creatures, Midnight Nation, Rising Stars, Fathom, Tomb Raider* (based upon the popular action-oriented video game and film property), and *Witchblade* (an occult-themed female action heroine stylistically reminiscent of Marvel's Elektra, and the subject of a successful TNT television series).

The rest of Image's voluminous superhero output—which, over the years, has included such titles as Jim Valentino's *ShadowHawk* (a violent crime fighter cast in the mold of Batman, blended with elements of Marvel's Iron Man and the Punisher); Erik Larsen's *Savage Dragon* (a green-skinned superheroic monster-turned-supercop, who was the subject of a USA animated series from 1994 to 1996); Dale Keown's *Pitt* (a sharp-clawed, super-strong hero, simultaneously evocative of Marvel's Hulk and Wolverine); Whilce Portacio's *Wetworks* superteam; J. Scott Campbell's *Danger Girl* (a squad of "grrl-power" superheroines); Sam Kieth's *The Maxx* (a member of a race of personal guardian angels/spirit guides whose comic book birthed a short-lived MTV animated series in 1994); and Trina Robbins' and Anne Timmons' *Go Girl* (a retro-style superheroine with an upbeat feminist subtext)— falls under the general rubric of Image Central, which is home to all Image titles not owned or produced by a founding Image partner (though the above-mentioned Image Central work of Larsen, Portacio, and Valentino are notable exceptions to this rule). Still, the trademarks and copyrights connected to all of these titles are the property of their respective creators, rather than of Image Comics.

From the beginning, Image Comics stood at the eye of a maelstrom of controversy. Though enor-

mously popular with fans, the company's initial offerings, as typified by titles such as *Spawn* and action-team comics like Silvestri's *Cyberforce* (1992), Liefeld's *Brigade* (1993), and Lee's *Gen13* (1994), received mixed critical reaction. While unquestionably a commercial success, the company drew barbs from detractors who regarded its titles as little more than collections of pinup art, and charged that plot and characterization usually took a back seat to stylistic considerations—which chiefly involved lovingly rendered illustrations of idealized musclemen and improbably upholstered female superheroes, a visual style that dominated superheroes of the 1990s in much the same way that Jack Kirby's pioneering dash had done in the 1960s. During the mid-1990s, veteran Marvel and DC comics writer Peter David quipped that a rival publishing house called "Substance" should be launched, to emphasize story and characterization in the hopes of countering Image's primarily art-driven esthetic.

During the first half of the 1990s, Image blossomed into a surprisingly diverse publisher, branching out into the sophisticated, realistic superheroics of *Kurt Busiek's Astro City* (1995) and presenting *A Touch of Silver* (1997), Jim Valentino's poignant autobiographical miniseries about a young superhero fan growing up during the Silver Age of comics (1956–1969) in a dysfunctional home. Image even provided a home for Matt Wagner's delightful Arthurian fantasy *Mage* (1997), which had debuted to resounding acclaim in 1984 at the defunct independent publisher Comico. Many Image properties have also appeared in successful "crossover" ventures with other publishers; most prominent among these intercompany efforts are team-ups between Spawn and Batman (DC); ShadowHawk and Vampirella (Harris Comics); and Savage Dragon and Superman (DC), the Atomics (AAA Pop Comics), the Teenage Mutant Ninja Turtles (Archie Comics and Mirage Comics), and Hellboy (Dark Horse). Top Cow's *Witchblade* has also shared the four-color page with such Marvel heroes as the Silver Surfer and Wolverine, as well as with Shi (Crusade Comics).

The Image experiment was not a completely successful one, however. Because the company has always been a loose confederation of creator-owned artistic and business entities, relationships within the company were predictably more anarchic than within the more staid corporate confines of Marvel or DC. The difficulty of coordinating and maintaining monthly production and publishing schedules eventually led to creative differences, and to the split-up of some of Image's founders. Consequently, many of Image's editorially interconnected titles—in which characters owned by different Image creators appeared in one another's books in much the same way that the Fantastic Four, Spider-Man, and the Hulk had begun sharing the "Marvel universe" as their four-color commons in the early 1960s—had to be disengaged from one another. Characters abruptly vanished from sight as they left Image for other publishing entities.

To accomplish this complex disentanglement, Image published a miniseries titled *Shattered Image* (1996), a sort of reverse version of DC Comics' *Crisis on Infinite Earths.* While *Crisis* was intended to consolidate several distinct universes into a single coherent narrative strand, Image's goal was to spin many of its characters off to whatever separate destinations their respective owners intended for them. Rob Liefeld left Image in 1997, taking his properties—most notably Supreme (a time-displaced supersoldier, a cross between Captain America and Superman, who was introduced in 1993 in a self-titled series and whose World War II–era exploits were recounted in 1994's *Supreme: Glory Days* miniseries) and Youngblood (an X-Men/Avengers-inspired superteam)—to form Awesome Entertainment. Jim Lee's WildStorm Productions, which put out such superhero action titles as *WildC.A.T.S* and *Stormwatch* under the Image aegis, left the company in 1998 (along with WildStorm's two sub-imprints, Homage Comics and America's Best Comics) to become part of DC Comics. After the dust settled, the "Image universe" was a more sparsely populated place than it had been previously, although the

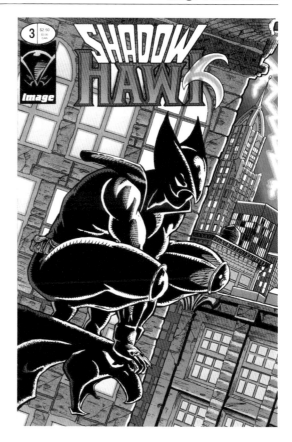

ShadowHawk #3 © 1992 Jim Valentino.
COVER ART BY JIM VALENTINO.

Spawn titles, *Savage Dragon,* and *The Authority* (a superteam descended from the now-absent *WildC.A.T.S* and *Stormwatch* characters) continued to find a profitable home under the Image colophon.

Fortunately for Image, superhero comics tend to grow like kudzu, even during the comics industry's slow periods, such as the late 1990s. Now, in the opening years of the new millennium, Image Comics is still the country's third largest publisher of superhero comics, graphic novels, and trade paperbacks, right behind Marvel and DC. Image began to provide a wide audience for titles originally published elsewhere, such as the daily *Zorro* newspaper strips of writer Don McGregor and illustrators

Tom Yeates and Tod Smith. In addition to its continued successes in publishing and mass-market toys (including McFarlane's action figures based on the Beatles and KISS), Image properties continue to make inroads into the film and television industries today. A sequel to the first *Spawn* feature film was in development in 2004, and television and movie options exist for Image's *Noble Causes: Family Secrets* (the story of the decidedly ordinary widow of a slain superhero who struggles to adjust to life among her superpowered in-laws) and such Image non-superhero properties as *Area 52* (about a group of incompetent soldiers guarding a secret government facility in Antarctica) and *Aria: The Uses of Enchantment* (a sorcery/fantasy series).

Though Image publishes comics in many story genres, superheroes remain the company's bread and butter, an emphasis reinforced by the 2003 advent of such titles as *Firebreather* (a young, hip superhero who is part human, part Godzilla-type monster), *Invincible* (the teenage son of Earth's most powerful superhero, who must cope with his developing powers while living up to his father's daunting reputation), and *Wildguard* (about a group of wannabe heroes auditioning for a superteam whose composition will ultimately be determined by an audience-driven vote, à la Fox TV's *American Idol*). As the first decade of the new millennium unfolds, Image appears to have remained largely true to its stated mission, which is to nurture, develop, and find audiences for unique, well-crafted creator-owned properties. —*MAM*

The Inferior Five

For much of the company's existence, DC Comics had been the comics industry's most conservative publisher, somewhat staid and reserved, but the rise of Marvel Comics and the success of the 1960s camp *Batman* television show changed all that. One of DC's responses to a growing superhero market that could stand a bit of comedy was to introduce the Inferior Five. It was one of the first self-referential strips, taking swipes at the whole superhero genre and its conventions, and—most satisfyingly—actually managed to be funny.

The team was introduced in the pages of *Showcase* #62 (1966) by longtime fan/writer/editor E. Nelson Bridwell and artist Joe Orlando, and soon graduated to its own title. The story begins with the aging (and less-than-athletic) members of the Freedom Brigade being summoned by the Megalopolis police force to defend the city from the menace of a mad scientist. Quickly realizing that their crime-fighting days are well behind them, the Patriot, Lady Liberty, and their fellow Freedom Brigade members decide to send their children instead. Sadly, the younger generation lack their parents' awesome crime-fighting skills, but nevertheless decide to band together as the aptly named Inferior Five.

The team's leader was young cartoonist Myron Victor who, as the comic declared, "used to be a ninety-seven-pound weakling before losing weight." With no powers whatsoever, Victor dressed himself in a jester's costume, to illustrate the futility of his crime-fighting career, and went by the inappropriate name of Merryman. Rotund Herman Cramer was the Blimp ("He flies like a bird with the speed of a snail") who sadly did not inherit the incredible running prowess of his father, Captain Swift. The politically incorrect Dumb Bunny ("stronger than an ox … and almost as intelligent!") was beautiful but vacant model Athena Tremor, who wore a bunny-girl costume, complete with fluffy tail and ears. The team's strongman was beatnik beach-bum Leander Brent ("more powerful than a locomotive, but always getting derailed"), whose accident-prone bumbling earned him the name Awkwardman. Rounding out the group was the White Feather ("the only bird who's chicken!"), also known as glamour photographer William King, whose archery skills were somewhat undermined by his abject cowardice. The group communicated using telephones known as the Lukewarm Line, and rode about the city in their jalopy, the Inferi-Car.

Bridwell had a real talent for humor, which meant that the comic emphasized laughs over thrills. Indeed, with villains like Dr. Gruesome, the Sparrow, and the Masked Swastika (an armor-clad Napoleon Bonaparte look-alike), the title was always lighthearted. Another unusual aspect of the comic was its wholesale lampooning of Marvel's all-conquering heroes, who involuntarily guest-starred in many strips, frequently as rather pathetic villains. The Hulk became the Man Mountain, the Sub-Mariner was Prince Nabob the Submoron, and the Fantastic Four were the Kookie Quartet, while Spider-Man, Thor, the X-Men, and Iron Man were also affectionately parodied. Marvel replied with its own spoof comic, *Not Brand Echh,* but in that book by-and-large concentrated on satirizing its own characters (presumably being reluctant to give publicity to its rivals).

Perhaps the strip's most ambitious moment was in issue #6, in a bizarre story titled "How to Make a Bomb," which featured the Five taking a tour of DC's offices, and starred pretty much the company's full editorial team. Among other incidents, artists Carmine Infantino and Mike Sekowsky were shown having a fight, and DC owner Irwin Donenfeld was depicted as a lollipop-sucking child! Sadly, the comic got lost in the camp craze and, after ten issues of its own title, it was canceled, leaving in its wake a small but enthusiastic cult following. —*DAR*

The Inhumans

Like so many Marvel Comics characters the Inhumans were a creation of writer Stan Lee and artist Jack Kirby, first appearing in a late 1965 issue of *The Fantastic Four* (#45). In fact, one of the Inhumans—Medusa—had been featured in the comic several months earlier as one of a motley group of villains called the Frightful Four, though her criminal career was short-lived. The Inhumans themselves were a carnival-show collection of strange-looking people unlike any other superteam, although "team" in this case is something of a misnomer, since they were effectively a race apart. Their origin was revealed in several later issues of *Thor,* which described how, centuries ago, a force from the all-conquering Kree Empire had visited Earth and genetically engineered a hybrid human/alien race. Over the years, these had evolved and mutated, far from the gaze of humankind, before they came out of hiding in the 1960s.

The Inhumans were probably several thousand in number and lived in isolation in the ultra-modern city of Attilan, hidden deep in the Himalayas (or Andes or Alps, depending on how good the writer's memory was!). The small group that ventured into the outside world were in fact the Royal Family, a powerful and fancifully garbed collection of uniquely mutated individuals. Their leader and king was Black Bolt, who could control molecular motion (whatever that meant) and whose voice could destroy everything in earshot with the merest whisper. Needless to say, he did not speak very often and conveyed his wishes through future wife Medusa, who could control her incredibly long, animated, red hair. Other members of the group were the grotesque Gorgon, who could cause earthquakes with a stamp of his cloven hoof; diminutive martial-arts expert Karnak; scale-covered amphibian Triton; and the winsome young Crystal, who could control the elements.

Crystal soon fell for the fresh-faced charms of the Human Torch and, when the Invisible Girl went on a seemingly interminable maternity leave, Crystal took her place in the Fantastic Four (FF). Crystal could whiz back and forth between the two groups with the help of her colossal, teleporting pet bulldog Lockjaw. In time, after the Invisible Girl left again (not for another baby but a marital separation), Crystal ran off with the Avenger Quicksilver, and Medusa briefly became an FF member in what was clearly a sort of job-share scheme for superheroes. The Inhumans as a whole regularly guest-starred in *Fantastic Four* and other comics (notably *The Hulk*) and in

1970 finally got their own feature in *Amazing Adventures*—though it only lasted ten issues. In the mid-1970s, they were given their own comic, but that survived for only twelve issues. Both attempts were well crafted, with an interesting mixture of radical Black Power politics (in *Amazing Adventures*), alien intrigue (in the 1975 *Inhumans* comic) and entertaining villains such as the Mandarin and Blastaar, yet neither venture proved popular enough to continue.

Perhaps the problems with the Inhumans were their outlandish appearance and somewhat detached personalities, or it might have been that they were mostly fighting a single enemy: Black Bolt's evil-genius brother, Maximus (in full, Maximus the Mad—which rather gave the game away). Maximus seemed to dedicate himself to overthrowing Black Bolt and the ruling Inhumans, who were endlessly taken in by him: "Oh no, he has betrayed us again!" However, following a lengthy fallow period, the Inhumans enjoyed something of a revival in the 1990s, with several specials and graphic novels, and a self-titled series under the Marvel Knights imprint in 1999. This series saw the group under siege from humankind, while the following year's miniseries featured the return of the Kree, who literally picked up and carried away the experiment they abandoned so many years earlier. The story culminated with the massed Inhumans deciding to stay in space and banishing the Royal Family to Earth, no doubt bound for intrigue and action (in another ongoing series and, probably, beyond). —*DAR*

Insect Heroes

"Don't you realize that people hate spiders?" asked an incredulous Martin Goodman, the publisher of Marvel Comics, when hearing author Stan Lee's pitch for the Amazing Spider-Man. Goodman may have been right, but people also find spiders—and other insects—utterly beguiling. Especially people who create—and read about—superheroes.

Wall-crawling "Spidey" was not the first superhero to adopt a spider guise. Before there were comic books there were "pulps"—inexpensive magazines featuring prose adventure tales under illustrated, usually painted, covers—like *The Spider*, premiering in 1933 from Popular Publications. Its hero, playboy Richard Wentworth, a.k.a. the Spider, metes out vigilante justice in a black facemask, hat, and cloak. On his missions he brandishes pistols, his fists, and his "Spider Web" climbing cord, leaving behind a spider-shaped seal as a calling card. Abetted by makeup artist Ram Singh (Wentworth's Sikh valet) and his chauffeur Jackson, the Spider coldly kills criminal vermin with a swift bullet to the head. His magazine ran until 1943, with 118 installments published, and he headlined two movie serials starring actor Warren Hull: *The Spider's Web* (1938) and *The Spider Returns* (1941). Elements of the Spider reportedly inspired the creation of Batman in 1939.

Quality Comics introduced its own Spider, also a playboy with a servant, in *Crack Comics* #1 (1940). This Spider, garbed in a yellow shirt and blue tights, also employs a trademark "spider seal"—although his are affixed to arrows, his weapons of choice—and cruises the streets in his ultra-fast car, the Black Widow. A hero called the Spyder—a *billionaire*, upping the ante from his millionaire forerunners—appears once in *WonderWorld Express* #1 (1984). Tony Brooks is a CEO and a practitioner of "Gung-Fu," which he uses to topple traitors while wearing blue tights with a spider chest emblem, yellow webbing highlights, and a helmet.

Black widow spiders have long been a popular theme in superhero lore. Dianne Grayton, yet another social butterfly, hides her good looks behind the façade of a hag as the Spider Widow, commanding black widows to do her bidding, in Quality's *Feature Comics* #57 (1942). Marvel Comics has, in the course of its lengthy history, published two characters named Black Widow. Claire Voyant pays the ultimate price to gain superpowers: her life. In *Mystic Comics* #4 (1940), Voyant is killed and descends to Hades, where Satan—one of comics' most enduring supervillains—gives her the "touch of death" and returns her to Earth to execute criminals as the dark-clad Black Widow. This Black Widow holds the record for another distinguishing characteristic: the darkest eyebrows of any character in comic-book history. Marvel's second Black Widow, Natasha Romanoff, is a Russian spy when first seen in *Tales of Suspense* #52 (1964), but ultimately defects to the United States and becomes a superheroine, fighting criminals with her debilitating "widow's bite" blasts (and, in the late 1990s and early 2000s, fending off a successor, Yelena Belova). Black Widow is a name used at least twice for supervillains: Tallulah Bankhead played the Black Widow, a crime queen with a paralyzing spider toxin, in episodes 89 and 90 (aired March 15 and March 16, 1967) of television's live-action *Batman* (1966–1968), and the animated superhero Space Ghost has occasionally tangled with an intergalactic villainess known as Black Widow over the years.

Superhero mythology's fascination with arachnids does not end there. In Archie Comics' *Zip Comics* #42 (1942), criminologist John Raymond sports a green-and-yellow costume with a web-mesh cape as the Web, outsmarting criminals with calculated entrapment. The Web has resurfaced throughout the decades in subsequent revivals of Archie's superheroes, including *The Web* #1–#14 (1991–1992), part of DC Comics' "!mpact" imprint, reimagining the Web as a network of high-tech operatives. DC's Tarantula, creeping into *Star Spangled Comics* #1 (1941), is Jonathan Law (yes, John Law), a mystery writer who dons a purple-and-yellow masked costume and aims a web-firing "webgun" to snare Nazi saboteurs. (Marvel borrowed the name Tarantula in the 1970s for a Spider-Man villain. DC returned the favor by introducing the Black Spider, a Batman foe. To complicate matters further, the short-lived mid-1970s Atlas Comics headlined a cursed man-spider anti-hero also called the Tarantula, and in the 2000s Marvel's Spider-Girl has encountered a crimelord called the Black Tarantula.)

The Spider Queen's ephemeral crime-fighting career began in Fox Features Syndicate's *The Eagle*

Double-Dare Adventures #2 © 1967 Harvey Comics. COVER ART BY JOE SIMON.

#2 (1941), and ended after three issues. The original Spider Woman, a one-shot character in publisher Harry "A" Chesler's *Major Victory* #1, is trapped in a web of obscurity, but the second Spider-Woman (note hyphen) has fared better, originating in *Marvel Spotlight* #32 (1976) and becoming a mainstay in the Marvel universe, even starring in a 1979 animated TV series. Several new Spider-Women have succeeded the original in Marvel's comics, and Spider-Girl—"The Daughter of the True Spider-Man!"—received her own monthly series in 1998. On the CBS Saturday-morning cartoon *Tarzan and the Super 7* (1978), a farmer named Kelly Webster is awarded a ring bearing a black-widow hourglass by a dying extraterrestrial she attempts to rescue.

The ring grants her insect powers and control over bugs as Web Woman. This character's origin is a verbatim retread of that of DC's Insect Queen. In *Superboy* #124 (1965), the Boy of Steel's girlfriend Lana Lang assists an imperiled, six-armed alien, from whom she receives a "Bio-Genetic" ring as a token of gratitude. The ring enables Lang to mimic insect abilities—although the same insect's powers cannot be engaged more than once in twenty-four hours—and as the half-human, half-bug Insect Queen, she becomes a part-time superheroine and a reserve member of the Legion of Super-Heroes.

Flies are also popular inspirations for superheroes. The original Fly-Man, as seen in *Spitfire Comics* #1 (1941), is only a few inches high, with the strength of a normal-sized man (traits displayed earlier by Quality's Doll Man and much later by DC's Atom and Marvel's Ant-Man). Fly-Man buzzed (on orange wings) through two adventures before being swatted out of print. *The Adventures of the Fly* #1 (1959) presents Thomas Troy, a young orphan who discovers a fly-insignia magic ring. The boy is chosen to become the champion of the Fly People, an ancient race. Stroking the ring and saying "I wish I were the Fly" transforms him into an adult superhero, the Fly, in a green-and-yellow costume with transparent wings. With his stinger-blasting "buzz gun" and his female sidekick Fly-Girl, the Fly—called Fly Man during the 1960s—is one of several Archie superheroes prone to habitual reintroductions. Marvel Comics published seventeen issues of *The Human Fly* beginning in 1977. Its protagonist (though purportedly based on a real-life daredevil) is a nameless individual, crippled in an automobile accident, who rehabilitates his body and embarks upon superheroics. "Mag-clamp" boots and gloves allow him to climb walls, and jet boots give him an extra boost through the air.

Other insect superheroes include the Green Hornet, a crime-crusher who pretends to be a masked mobster to trick ganglords into traps (and when his smarts fail, his electrical "Hornet's Sting" helps, as does his martial-artist aide, Kato); Mar-

vel's Ant-Man and the Wasp, both able to shrink and fly (Ant-Man also communicates with ants), and Ant-Man's later identity, Yellowjacket; the Yellowjacket-like Buzz, an ally of Marvel's Spider-Girl; the original Wasp, a fedora-topped masked man in a suit and cape, who appeared twice in *Silver Streak Comics* (1939); three incarnations of the Blue Beetle, each having little, if anything, to do with insects other than the heroes' appellations; DC's Spider-Girl, a Legion of Super-Heroes supporting-cast member, who manipulates her hair's length and density; and *Hit Comics* #1's Red Bee, clad in a red-and-yellow striped suit, who sics irate bees on his foes. In Jack Kirby's early 1970s *New Gods* the writer-artist introduced an entire society of insect-like creatures, known collectively as "The Bug," that evolved from biological-warfare organisms on Kirby's mythic world of New Genesis. Marvel's mid-1970s *Champions* superteam title featured the unusual villain Swarm, whose body is composed of myriad insects with a collective mind. And one of the major creations of Michael Chabon's fictional 1940s writer-artist team in his novel *The Amazing Adventures of Kavalier & Clay* (2000) is the scandalous and surreal superheroine Luna Moth.

Some obscure insect heroes have buzzed under the radar of most fans. Harvey Comics' Mosquito Boy, first seen in *Harvey Hits* #110 (1966), is a surly teen with see-through wings and a cowl with a stinger beak (his unique weakness is insect repellent). B-Man, another Harvey hero (from *Double-Dare Adventures* #1, 1966), is an ex-astronaut named Barry E. Eames (note his initials) who gains super-metabolism after being stung by alien bees and fights crime from his Bee Hive. The Butterfly—who first appeared in Skywald Publishing's *Hell-Rider* #1 (1971)—is a soul singer-turned-superhero (albeit with an enigmatic origin) who flies thanks to her supersuit, and Beetle Boy and Butterfly Girl are tiny superheroes who appeared on the Japanese anime program *Microid S* (1973). Americomics' Dragonfly zips through the air on gossamer wings (while wearing fashionable shades), and Scarlet

Scorpion is a red-clad hero with a long stinger tail (similar in appearance and power to Spider-Man's enemy, the Scorpion). In its short publishing history, Atlas Comics twice used the name "the Scorpion" in 1975: for a pulp-like hero created by Howard Chaykin and for a Spider-Man ripoff who climbs buildings with a grappling hook. The short-of-stature-and-temper Bug Boy is a sometime cast member of Bongo Comics' satirical *Radioactive Man*. Finally, there is the Moth, a little-known costumed crusader debuting in *Mystery Men* #9 (1940). Not little-known at all due to what can only be called a loud fan buzz, a new Moth, co-created by artist Steve Rude (*Nexus, World's Finest*) and inker/scripter Gary Martin, bowed in spring of 2004 at Dark Horse Comics. —*ME*

International Heroes

If one were to believe the news in comic books, not only is New York City the center of the universe, but it is also the center of superhero and supervillain activities. Sure, sometimes the superbeings are in Metropolis, Gotham City, Opal City, Keystone City, or even real urban centers like Chicago or Los Angeles, but what about other countries? Don't they have superheroes, too? Independent American publishers are not terribly global, but both Marvel and DC have international heroes, many of whom critics deride as countrywide cultural stereotypes.

DC's biggest group made up mostly of foreign nationals is called the Global Guardians. The group is led by African shaman Doctor Mist, and includes the following members and represented countries: lizard-powered Bushmaster (Venezuela); long-haired Godiva (England); flaming spitfire Green Fury (Brazil), later a member of the Justice League as Fire; frost-powered Icemaiden (Norway), later a member of the Justice League as Ice; speedy

The Freedom Collective #1 © 2002 Rough Cut Comics.
COVER ART BY DOMINIC REGAN AND COLIN BARR.

Impala (South Africa); magic lantern-powered Jack O'Lantern (Ireland); mutant Atlantean Little Mermaid (Denmark); Golden-Fleece-wearing the Olympian (Greece); flying Native American Owlwoman (Oklahoma); solar-powered Rising Sun (Japan); Biblically blessed hero the Seraph (Israel); gay lycanthrope and future Justice League member Tasmanian Devil (Australia); vocal screamer Thunderlord (Taiwan); time-seeing third-eyed Tuatura (New Zealand); and Viking barbarian Wild Huntsman (Germany).

The Global Guardians are not the first of DC's international hero groups, nor the last. The first would likely include the "Batmen of All Nations"

from January 1955's *Detective Comics* #215 (England's Knight and Squire, Australia's the Ranger, Italy's the Legionary, South America's the Gaucho, and France's the Musketeer). In 1988, DC debuted the weekly *Millennium* miniseries, which introduced ten heroes from across the globe who would usher in the next era of humanity as the New Guardians. Its members included Betty Clawman, Extraño, Floro, Gloss, Harbinger, Jet, and Ram. The 2000 annuals for DC introduced yet another line of international heroes in a multi-part storyline called "Planet DC," most of which have since been relatively unseen—such as samurai-like Bushido (Japan); magical swordswoman Janissary (Russia); shape-shifting Aruna (India); Manhunter-related swordswoman Nemesis (Greece); strong swordswoman Sala (Tunisia); The Boggart (England); the animalistic eight-hero team The Super-Malon (Argentina); and the armored trio Iman, Acrata, and El Muerto (Mexico).

Marvel's international characters have sometimes been perceived as villains or antagonists by the company's American heroes (from the incorrigibly French Batroc the Leaper to the definitive Eastern European despot Dr. Doom), though many, like Russia's supergroup Soviet Super-Soldiers (Darkstar, Crimson Dynamo, Gremlin, Titanium Man, Ursa Major, and Vanguard) were clearly fighting for their country's beliefs. Many Marvel heroes already hail from other countries and continents, such as Black Panther (Africa), Captain Britain (England), Spitfire (England), Union Jack (England), Banshee (Ireland), Storm (Africa), Nightcrawler (Germany), Sunfire (Japan), the Black Widow (Russia), Gypsies Quicksilver and the Scarlet Witch (Europe), Wolverine (Canada), and the team Alpha Flight (Canada).

Marvel made an attempt to diversify its slate in *Marvel Super-Hero Contest of Champions* (June–August 1982), featuring the debuts of power-suited Peregrine (France), Talisman (Australia), Shamrock (Ireland), electrical-powered Blitzkrieg (Germany), quill-firing Sabra (Israel), armored Defensor (Argentina), and sword-swinging Arabian Knight (Saudi Arabia). Few of them have been used often in the two decades since, though Marvel published *Excalibur,* a long-running counterpart to its popular X-Men set in the United Kingdom, in the late 1980s and early 1990s, and tried out an amusing, corporate-created team of Japan-based superbeings, Big Hero 6, in a 1998 miniseries. (The Contest of Champions was repeated as farce in 2003, with Marvel's satirical mutants X-Statix squaring off against the superteam Euro-Trash, and in 2004 was set to take a grimmer form, as Marvel's edgy Avengers variation, the Ultimates, mobilized against international heroes created to offset America's unrivaled real-life superpower status.)

Lest anyone think that international heroes are solely the purview of major American comic-book publishers, rest assured that even though superheroes are not as popular in other countries, they do exist. Red-and-white clad adventurer Captain Canuck is one of Canada's most famous heroes, while Canadian gay hero Go-Go Boy is a bit more obscure, and Canadian heroes the Jam, Northguard, and the heroine Fleur de Lyse fall somewhere in the center. Following are a number of other countries, and the heroes that are represented in comics there.

AUSTRALIA

Due to a ban on imported publications throughout the 1940s and 1950s, Australian comics had a chance to grow. Golden Age (1938–1954) heroes included Crimson Comet, the Phantom Ranger, Captain Atom, Sir Falcon, Silver Starr, Blue Ray, and many others. Most Australian comic-book companies ceased publication by 1960, since the import ban was lifted and American comics were now flooding their market. Cyclone Comics revived some older heroes in the 1980s in the pages of *Southern Squadron* (Lieutenant Smith, Dingo, Southern Cross, and Nightfighter) and other books. Further heroes included an adventurer called the Jackaroo, energy-wielding Dark Nebula, heroine Australian Maid, and a parody of American heroes called the A-Men (including the Americano, America Man, and others). Phosphorescent Comics published *The Watch,* with team members Fallout, Adapt, Xenia, Bones, Jack, the Fisher, and others. Other Aussie heroes include Bug Man and Roachboy, Pizza Man, Brainmaster and Vixen, and the groups the Olympians and Forerunners.

ENGLAND

Marvel's Captain Britain first appeared in British comics in 1976, but Marvelman (called Miracleman in the United States) was a much older hero, having first appeared in the 1950s before his 1980s revival by Alan Moore. Costumed heroes first appeared in the 1920s and 1930s pulps, including Invisible Dick, Blackshirt, Waldo the Wonder Boy, the Black Whip, and the Night Hawk. Some 1940s comic-book heroes—such as the Bat—resembled American counterparts, while Captain Magnet, Electro Girl, the Falcon, Maskman, Tornado, Mr. X, and Wonderman were less obvious homages. The 1950s brought in Black Shadow, Electroman, spoof hero Super Stooge, and the bizarrely named Robot Archie. Heroes from the 1960s included Gadgetman and Gimmick-Kid, Captain Miracle, contortionist Janus Stark, Miniman, and the Phantom Viking. The weekly *2000 AD* brought violent helmeted police officer Judge Dredd and others into the 1970s, while Aquavenger, Marksman, Leopardman, evangelist hero Hotshot, and Birdman and Chicken prowled the comics, and actor Dave Prowse donned the costume of the Green Cross Code Man to teach kids about road safety (years before he played Darth Vader in the *Stars Wars* saga). Revisionist hero comics *Zenith* and *New Statesmen* were released in the 1980s, before their creators were whisked away to write revisionist American comics, while the 1990s saw Marvel U.K. titles like *Clan Destine, Hell's Angel, Knigths of Pendragon,* and *Death's Head.* Paul Grist's *Jack Staff* (April 2000) became popular enough that in 2003 Image republished it in the United States.

FRANCE

Early heroes included Fantax and Atomas, while Tenax, Felina, and bug-powered Mikros came later. French publisher Semic brought back some older heroes and mixed them with new creations to construct a shared universe that included Starlock and the Strangers, and superteams Kidz and Hexagon. Alien astronaut Homicron 1, gold-armored peace officer Le Gladiateur de Bronze, and "man of light" Photonik are among other francophilic heroes, while sexy trapeze artist Felina and insect-powered Saltarella are two of the relatively few original heroines. Gay heroes Lift, Volt, Seal, Phase, and Tiger starred in 2001–2002's *Ultimen.*

INDIA

There are numerous Indian superheroes including robotic Fauladi Singh, high-tech hero Abhay (and his higher self Agniputra), and live-action television hero Shaktimaan. The heroes of the company Raj Comics include Jupiterian Vinashdoot, cyborg Inspector Steel, acrobatic Super Commando Dhruva, patriotic Tiranga, and blue-skinned goddess avatar Shakti.

ITALY

Created in 1962 but still going strong, Diabolik is probably Italy's most famous super-character, though this masked man preys on the underworld as a Robin Hood–like criminal. Down Comix's Capitan Italia makes fun of his American counterparts, while *Pumaman* was a 1980 film about an animal-powered paleontologist who becomes a badly dressed avenging hero (tan pants, a black shirt, and a red cape). Zorry Kid, created in 1968, was a parody of *Zorro.* Leo Ortolani, a hilarious Matt Groening–inspired cartoonist, writes and draws the long-running *Rat-Man.* Published by Marvel Comics' Italian imprint Cult Comics, it spoofs the stereotypically diminutive stature of Europe and its comics, as well as the stereotypically brawny self-assurance of both Marvel's American heroes and America itself.

MEXICO

There are hundreds of *luchadores enmascarados* (masked fighters/wrestlers) in Mexico who fight villains in the comics, the movies, and the real-life wrestling rings. The three most famous ones are Santo, the Blue Demon, and Mil Mascaras. Other Mexican heroes include Flyman, Zooman, Supervolador, La Llanera Vengadora and her brother sidekick Fausto, giant Zor, and El Hombre Invisible. More modern characters include the teen hero Meteorix, Cygnus Comics' Creaturas de la Noche, superduck Ultrapato, and anthropomorphic heroes the Valiants. Ka-Boom Estudio has released *Nemesis 2000: La Alianza,* the ghostly Spectrum, and marine group *Hibridos del Mar.*

PHILIPPINES

Heroes include El Gato, Japanese Bat, Kapitan Aksiyon, Captain Barbell, Maskarado, and the longest-running (since 1950) heroine, the buxom Darna. There are several Philippine superhero movies as well, including *Super Islaw, Super B,* and the campy gay hero *She-Man: Mistress of the Universe.*

SPAIN

Many heroes in Spain are published by Planeta's Libertino imprint, including the groups Triada Vertice (Mihura, Estigma, and Cascabel) and Iberia Inc. (Dolmen, Trueno, Lobisome, Drac de Ferro, Aquaviva, Trasnu, and Melkart), as well as solo heroes Gavilan and Le Loup Garou. Some 1940s heroes include the female vigilante La Entorcha and masked crime fighter El Encapuchado. The 1970s saw the birth of comedic superhero Super Lopez, whose adventures continue today and include other parody heroes such as La Chica Increible (Wonder Girl), El Mago (the Wizard), and Capitan Hispania.

Super Pumby, a flying cat, hailed from a 1964 kids' comic.

OTHER COUNTRIES

Denmark has heroes Dukse Drengen (Hero Boy) and Natte Ravnen (Night Owl), while the former Yugoslavia published the scantily clad heroine Cat Claw. Israel is represented by Sabraman, first published in 1978, while Nigeria has the flying Powerman. And as if to show that all international borders could be crossed, in 2002 Scotland's Rough Cut Comics released the satirical publication *The Freedom Collective,* imagining a Silver Age Marvel-style comic as if it were published in the Kremlin at the height of the cold war. The Collective is made up of members Mig-4, the Krimson Kommisar, ice goddess Ajys, rocky Homeland, and the monstrous Mastodon.

Superheroes may have started out as an American pleasure, but as the preceding information shows, the rest of the world loves ultra-powered men and women in tights, armor, and capes as well. —*AM*

The Invaders

Considering how all-pervasive superhero teams have become since the 1960s, it is surprising that there were so few around in the 1940s. DC Comics had the Justice Society of America and the Seven Soldiers of Victory, and Fawcett had the Marvel Family, but Marvel Comics itself managed to produce precisely two stories of its sole adult team, the All-Winners Squad (though, of course, their kid gangs, such as the Young Allies and the Tough Kid Squad, thrived). The All-Winners Squad appeared in *All-Winners Comics* #19 and #21, in late 1946. The comic consisted of Marvel's "big three" heroes, the Sub-Mariner, the Human Torch, and Captain America; the latter two's sidekicks Toro and Bucky; and two lesser-known heroes, the Whizzer and Miss America. Years later, longtime fan and writer Roy Thomas remembered how effective the combination of the big three had been, and used them again in a time-travel issue of *The Avengers* (#71, 1969), pitting the 1940s and 1960s heroes against each other.

In 1975, looking around for a new project, Thomas decided to revive the concept of the All-Winners Squad, minus the Whizzer and Miss America, and to create new, untold tales of the heroes in their World War II prime. Thomas used the team, now christened the Invaders (which he reasoned sounded less embarrassing than "All-Winners Squad") to fill in gaps or correct lapses in old continuity, reintroduce forgotten heroes of the Golden Age (1938–1954), and create his own wartime characters. The result was one of the most action-packed, hero-packed, and fun-packed comics of the 1970s.

For art, Thomas turned to industry veteran Frank Robbins, who had been drawing the Johnny Hazard newspaper strip for decades and could provide just the right mixture of authentic period detail and slam-bang action. The team's first adventure appeared in *Giant Sized Invaders* #1 but, soon after, the decision to reduce its page count to that of a regular comic meant that its second issue was just plain *Invaders* #1; back then not many comics could boast of having two #1 issues! The team's origin was quite simple: All five members meet by coincidence, hot on the trail of the Nazis' answer to Captain America, Masterman (the first of many wonderfully kitsch villains), and are persuaded to stay together as a team by none other than Winston Churchill.

Over the course of forty-one issues, one annual, and several crossovers and guest appearances, the Invaders traveled the world, from the home front to a blitzed London to Egypt, Berlin, and even the Warsaw ghetto. Among the outlandish villains they trounced were Brain Drain, U-Man, Baron Blood (an aristocratic vampire), Blue Bullet (a man wearing a giant bullet costume), Warrior Woman, Frankenstein and—of course—Adolf Hitler. The first new heroes to appear, the Liberty Legion, were in fact a round-up of some of Marvel's many short-lived (not to say forgettable) wartime zeroes: the Red Raven, the Thin Man, Jack Frost, the Patriot, and Blue Diamond.

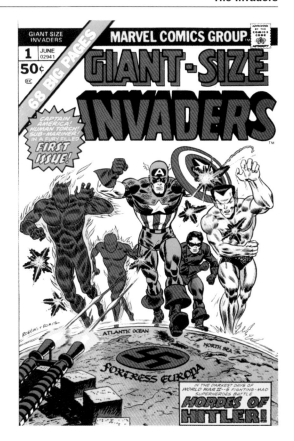

Giant-Size Invaders #1 © 1975 Marvel Comics.
COVER ART BY FRANK ROBBINS AND JOHN ROMITA.

These were joined by those leftover All-Winners, Miss America and the Whizzer. The Legion were actually introduced in 1976 in *Marvel Premiere* #29 and then crossed over to the *Invaders* before guest-starring with the Thing for a couple of *Marvel-Two-in-One* yarns. Plans for their own comic went as far as drawing up a first issue but that was abandoned, though much later the Whizzer and Miss America were promoted to full-time Invaders, thus reuniting the original All-Winners Squad.

Other Thomas creations included Lord Farnsworth, a.k.a. Union Jack (a British hero of World War I), his daughter Jacqueline (who gained super speed to become the Spitfire), and her brother Brian, who was first the Destroyer—another Golden Age Marvel hero—before taking over the Union Jack costume from his now aged father. One of Thomas' most outré heroes was the superpowered Golem, conceived as a kind of Jewish Hulk—an indication of the tightrope walk between innovation and high camp that Thomas was walking on the Invaders project. Toward the end of the comic's first run, Thomas created a new, racially mixed kid group called the Kid Commandos, composed of Bucky, Toro, the Human Top, and Golden Girl. This particular Golden Girl was no relation to Captain America's erstwhile companion; she was, rather, comics' first Japanese-American heroine. Indeed, this team's creation grew out of one of the war's most controversial episodes: the internment of America's Asian community.

Frank Robbins left the *Invaders* at the point of creation of the Kid Commandos, in issue #28, which was a blow from which the title never recovered; it was canceled with issue #41 in late 1979. Thomas returned for one last hurrah with a 1993 *Invaders* miniseries, which added the Thin Man to the team and re-introduced two of the company's longer-lasting Golden Age superheroes: the Angel and the Blazing Skull. Although it has been unfairly left in limbo by Marvel, the *Invaders* remains one of the company's most fondly remembered titles. —*DAR*

Iron Fist

Historically on the prowl for new pop-culture fads to seize upon, Marvel Comics began exploiting kung fu films in the early 1970s, beginning with their hero Shang-Chi, Master of Kung Fu (*Special Marvel Edition* #15, 1973). The early success of Shang-Chi—a fairly straight adaptation of the martial arts film hero, mixed with elements of Sax Rohmer's pulp stories of the 1910s and 1920s—convinced Marvel to try integrating such characters into the ranks of its costumed superheroes. Iron Fist (Daniel Rand), the creation of writer Roy Thomas and artist Gil

Kane, represented the first such attempt (*Marvel Premiere* #15, 1974).

Wealthy businessman Wendell Rand, an exile from the interdimensionally hidden Tibetan city of K'un-L'un, dies at the hands of his business partner Harold Meachum while seeking the city of his birth. Rand's wife Heather and their nine-year-old son Daniel end up stranded in the Himalayas; only the boy succeeds in reaching K'un-L'un alive. Inside the mystical realm—which resembles a cross between the Shangri-La of Frank Capra's 1937 film *Lost Horizon* and the eponymous Scottish village of the 1947 Lerner and Loewe musical *Brigadoon*—young Danny is taken in by a martial artist named Lei Kung the Thunderer, who recognizes him as part of the royal line and spends a decade training him in all aspects of the martial arts, both physical and philosophical. At the age of 19, Rand undergoes his coming-of-age ritual by slaying Shou-Lao the Undying, a powerful dragon. The combat leaves Rand with a stylized black dragon tattoo emblazoned across his chest and the Power of the Iron Fist—the ability to focus the power of his spirit (his "chi") into his hand, making it as strong as iron, all but impervious to harm, and capable of delivering devastating blows that crackle with mystic energies. Like the martial arts themselves, Rand's new power has more than one aspect, giving Rand the ability to heal as well as to destroy. His only vulnerability: When Rand uses his Iron Fist, his energy is depleted, and he becomes exhausted for hours afterward.

Intent on avenging his parents' deaths by killing Meachum, Rand leaves K'un-L'un for the United States. But when he confronts the man whom he had hated for the past decade, Rand discovers that vengeance holds no solace and decides instead to settle for taking over his late father's position controlling the Rand-Meachum Corporation—only to witness Meachum's murder at the hands of ninja assassins. The authorities blame Rand for the murder, and it takes several months for him to clear his name, with some help from female adventurer (and future long-term ally) Misty Knight (*Marvel Premiere* #21, 1975).

Iron Fist's "audition" in *Marvel Premiere* (a testing ground for new Marvel heroes, not unlike DC's *Showcase* title of the 1950s and 1960s) proved successful, despite frequent changes of creative personnel through 1974 and 1975, and landed the character in a self-titled series (*Iron Fist* vol. 1, 1975) written by Chris Claremont and penciled by John Byrne. This creative team, though destined for fame in the early 1980s on *X-Men,* couldn't keep the series running past its fifteenth issue (1977), by which time the sun had set on the kung fu movie fad. But Claremont and Byrne continued presiding over Iron Fist's brief stint on Marvel's guest-star circuit (*Marvel Team-Up* #63, 1977; *Power Man* #48, 1977), as well as the first several issues of his lengthy tenure as half of *Power Man and Iron Fist* (formerly titled *Power Man*), which began in issue #49 (1978). After Claremont and Byrne left to concentrate on *X-Men,* a raft of creative talent rotated in to replace them, including such writers as Ed Hannigan, Mary Jo Duffy, Bob Layton, Steven Grant, Mike W. Barr, Dennis O'Neil, Kurt Busiek, Archie Goodwin, Alan Rowlands, Jim Owsley, and Tony Isabella, and such pencilers as Mike Zeck, Sal Buscema, Lee Elias, Trevor Von Eedon, Marie Severin, Kerry Gammill, Greg LaRocque, Frank Miller, Denys Cowan, Keith Pollard, Ernie Chan, Geoff Isherwood, Richard Howell, Steve Geiger, and Mark Bright.

Working together, Iron Fist and Power Man (Luke Cage) establish a business venture called Heroes for Hire, Inc., and their disparate temperaments—Rand's reserved wisdom and Cage's mercurial anger—prove to complement each other well (combined in a single title, these heroes ended up lasting far longer than either of them had done on their own). Of the innovation that the Power Man/Iron Fist character dynamic represented when it first appeared in the 1970s, latter-day Iron Fist writer Jay Faerber said, "Well for one thing, I think it was refreshing to see a white guy paired with a black guy. And they were equals. Luke wasn't

Danny's sidekick or his driver. Luke's stories took center stage just as often as Danny's did, and that give and take was like a breath of fresh air, even if I was too young to recognize that appeal when I was originally reading the book." Despite their contrasts, some of which were occasionally played for laughs, one commonality that unites both heroes is their keen sense of conscience, a tendency to place the hero ethic above profits; they frequently work for free, despite being in high demand as detectives and bodyguards.

One of Iron Fist's most significant travails occurred during the last few issues of the series; after Danny Rand's inadvertent destruction of his beloved K'un-L'un unhinges him, he turns evil (symbolized by the transformation of his usually green-and-yellow costume into a red-and-yellow one, a development that echoed the 1980 Claremont/Byrne *X-Men* "Dark Phoenix"). All efforts to purge Rand of this evil streak end up failing. In the final issue of the series in 1986 (*Power Man and Iron Fist* #125), Iron Fist apparently dies at the hands of a character named Captain Hero (not to be confused with Jughead's superheroic alter ego at Archie Comics), and Power Man is framed for Rand's murder. "[Iron] Fist's death was supposed to be shocking and senseless," writer Owsley said in a 1999 interview. "It wasn't bad writing. The fact that thirteen years after the fact people are still annoyed about it speaks to the quality of the work, the impact of which has apparently not diminished over time."

But thanks to John Byrne's exercises in retroactive continuity (known in the comic-book trade as a "retcon"), the dead Iron Fist later turns out to have been a mere doppelgänger, with the real Rand imprisoned back in K'un-L'un (and still struggling to control an evil side of his character). Rand's martial arts instructor Lei Kung joins forces with Prince Namor the Sub-Mariner and the Daughters of the Dragon (Heroes for Hire veterans Misty Knight and Colleen Wing) to free Rand and return him to New York City (*Namor, the Sub-Mariner* #23 and #28, 1992). Iron Fist subsequently starred in a self-titled (and critically panned) two-issue miniseries in 1996 (written by James Felder and drawn by Robert Brown) before returning to a greatly expanded Heroes for Hire, Inc., which includes not only Power Man and Iron Fist, but also the Hulk, Hercules (his immortality now a thing of the past), Ant Man (Scott Lang), the Black Knight (Dane Whitman), and the martial artist known as the White Tiger (*Heroes for Hire* #1–#19, 1997–1999, written by Roger Stern and John Ostrander, with pencils by Paschalis Ferry, Scott Kolins, Martin Egeland, and Mary Mitchell).

Iron Fist surfaced again in another three-issue miniseries during this period (*Iron Fist* vol. 3, 1998), with stories by Dan Jurgens and art by Jackson Guice; Iron Fist assisted Quicksilver and the Inhumans in "The Siege of Wundagore," thanks to Ostrander and Ferry (*Heroes for Hire/Quicksilver Annual* 1998). At the turn of the millennium Iron Fist crossed paths with the X-Men's Wolverine (*Iron Fist/Wolverine: The Return of K'un-L'un* #1–#4, 2000–2001, written by Jay Faerber and drawn by Jamal Igle). He was back again to wrestle with more personal demons and with the Black Panther in the latter's series (vol. 2 #38–#40, 2002), and regained an ongoing title of his own in 2004, in the first comics work by writer Jim Mullaney of the *Destroyer* paperback series. Over the course of nearly three decades, Danny Rand has transcended not only death, but also the comics medium itself; a live-action Iron Fist motion picture reportedly starring Ray Park (the agile Darth Maul from *Star Wars Episode 1: The Phantom Menace*) has been announced for a 2006 release. —*MAM*

Iron Man

Ever since his creation in early 1963 (in *Tales of Suspense* #39), Iron Man has been one of Marvel Comics' heavy hitters, a consistent seller in his own title and a regular guest in other comics, including *The Avengers.* In his alter ego of Anthony (Tony) Stark, wealthy playboy inventor, owner of Stark Inter-

national, and (let's not beat about the bush here) an international arms manufacturer, he was an unlikely figure for young readers to identify with. In Marvel's early days, much was made of the company's creation of "heroes with problems," and Stark's was potentially fatal: While demonstrating some new weapons in the jungles of Vietnam, he is injured by a bomb and captured by a Vietcong warlord. With his life ebbing away, Stark is forced to work for his captors, creating new weapons, but unknown to them he secretly builds himself a high-tech suit of armor that will both keep him alive and make him a walking arsenal.

Once in the gray, clanking suit, Stark defeats the warlord and returns to the United States to assume the role of a superhero, but his tragedy is that he can never remove the chest plate that keeps him alive. (Indeed, Stark admits, "The name of Iron Man makes strong men tremble! But, what good does it do me?? I can never relax … never be without my chest plate—never lead a normal life!") To compound his dilemma, the armor needs constant recharging and has the unfortunate tendency to run out of power at the most inconvenient moments, usually in the middle of a pitched battle. With many of his stories taking place in the vast Stark International complex, readers were soon introduced to Iron Man's rather morose chauffeur, "Happy" Hogan; perky secretary "Pepper" Potts; and the inevitable love triangle. Hogan loved Potts but knew that he would never be good enough for her; Potts loved Stark but he was her boss; and Stark loved Potts but was held back by the prospect of his keeling over dead at any moment.

As very much the establishment superhero, it is perhaps no surprise that Iron Man was Marvel's premier red-baiting strip for its first decade, sometimes even showing Soviet premier Nikita Khrushchev plotting against Stark. Almost all Iron Man's major villains were communists of some hue or nationality, including Titanium Man, an armor-wearing Soviet giant (later immortalized by singer Paul McCartney in a song on his *Venus and Mars* album). Notable exceptions were the Melter, the Black Knight (one of many Black Knights in comics), Count Nefaria, the Maggia (an all-purpose crime cartel), and the extraordinary Firebrand, who was a sort of costumed agitator specializing in leading demonstrations. By the late 1960s, Potts had given up pining for Stark and had married the nearest man—who just happened to be Hogan. So Stark embarked on a series of doomed, tragic romances. The first of these, Whitney Frost, turned out to be the mysterious leader of the Maggia, but then became Madame Masque after her face was scarred. Happy Hogan was periodically called in to help Iron Man and invariably managed to turn himself into a bald giant called the Freak. There's no doubt about it: Knowing Tony Stark was dangerous business.

Throughout the 1960s and 1970s, Iron Man was a mainstay of Marvel's output—appearing in all sorts of consumer merchandise, featured in the *Marvel Superheroes* television cartoon show from 1966 to 1968, and taking a bow as the hero in William Rotsler's novel *And Call My Killer … Modok* (1979). The character was one of the charter members of the Avengers and has maintained a regular presence in that superhero group ever since. Stark's millions have come in handy, for instance, for funding the plush Avengers' mansion, and his technical wizardry has enabled him to devise all manner of means for getting the team out of trouble. That same technical brilliance also created an ever-evolving suit of armor, and his hulking gray costume was soon transformed into a sleek, shining red-and-gold number bristling with gadgets and ordnance. For his six-year run in *Tales to Astonish,* Iron Man was predominantly written by his co-creator, Stan Lee, and drawn by Don Heck or Gene Colan, and when he was given his own title in 1968 George Tuska became his artist for most of the next one hundred issues. With that sort of creative stability, fans generally knew what to expect and, if truth be told, this most middle-aged of heroes was occasionally rather dull.

That all changed in the 1980s, when the young writing team of David Michelinie and Bob Layton,

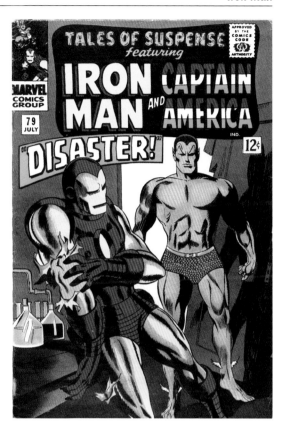

Tales of Suspense #79 © 1966 Marvel Comics.
COVER ART BY GENE COLAN AND JACK ABEL.

along with artist John Romita Jr., decided to shake up the comic. Under the new regime, things began to go very wrong for Iron Man, as Stark International was hit by industrial espionage. A despairing Stark took to the bottle and had to draft in one of his employees (and best friend), Jim Rhodes, as a stand-in Iron Man. Were the fans ready for an alcoholic superhero? They certainly were, and for the first time in its existence, the feature actually started winning awards. However, once the creative team left for other projects, the awards dried up and the comic entered a period of almost constant change.

Rhodes regularly took over the Iron Man mantle (in response to Stark falling off the wagon) and eventually struck out on his own as War Machine, a sort of ethical world policeman, suited up in Iron Man armor. Stark's company collapsed, and he had to start again from scratch. He was paralyzed by an assassin's bullet (but recovered three issues later), got drunk again, died and came back to life, and got drunk once more. Throughout, readers noticed how *Iron Man* stories depicted the contrast between Stark's vulnerability in his civilian identity and his invincibility as a superheroic modern knight in shining armor. One well-received interlude in Stark's troubled times was a storyline called "Armor Wars," which revealed that various Marvel villains had been ripping off Stark's technology for years for their own weapons.

In the 1990s, Marvel decided to put Stark out of his misery and killed him off (*Iron Man #325, 1996*). However, one issue later a younger Stark was plucked from an alternate dimension and began where the original left off (although without the alcohol). The second Tony Stark revels in his role as a playboy with the ego to match, and his comic shows all the signs of continuing for years to come. —*DAR*

Isis

Three thousand years in the past, the Egyptian royal sorcerer Hapsethsut gave his queen, Isis, a magic amulet that endowed her—and her descendants—with the powers of the animals and the elements. "You will soar as the falcon soars, run with the speed of gazelles and command the elements of the sky and the earth," he said. In 1975, science teacher Andrea Thomas excavated the amulet of Isis and found she was heir to its secrets. Now, by holding the amulet and exclaiming "Oh mighty Isis!" Andrea becomes the superheroine Isis, "dedicated foe of evil, defender of the weak, champion of truth and justice."

With the live-action *Shazam!* show a hit on CBS, producers Lou Scheimer and Norm Prescott wanted a second superhero show to freshen up the second season. Taking a cue from the Egyptian origins of Captain Marvel, they created a female counterpart in Isis. They cast exotic beauty Joanna Cameron in the lead roles of Andrea Thomas and Isis, and outfitted her in a skimpy white tunic and miniskirt, platform boots, and Egyptian jewelry.

The Shazam!/Isis Hour debuted in September 1975, with sixteen half-hour episodes produced in the first season. Other cast members for the Filmation series included fellow teacher Rick Mason (Brian Cutler) and students Cindy Lee (Joanna Pang) and Renee Carroll (Ronalda Douglas), none of whom ever figured out that Thomas was Isis. Thomas also had a pet crow named Tut who would sometimes aid her in emergency situations. By reciting rhyming couplets such as "O zephyr winds which blow on high, lift me now so I can fly," Isis could fly, gain super strength, and even stop time!

Isis guest-starred in three episodes of *Shazam!*, and Captain Marvel reciprocated in three of the six second-season *Isis* episodes. Another seven *Isis* scripts were completed, but were never filmed. Although *The Shazam!/Isis Hour* was canceled in September 1977, *Isis* continued on as a solo series of reruns for another year (some sources call the series *The Secrets of Isis*). From 1976 to 1977 DC Comics licensed the character and published eight comic books with her (written by Denny O'Neil, Steve Skeates, and Jack C. Harris and illustrated by an array of artists, including Ric Estrada, Wally Wood, Mike Vosburg, Vince Colletta, and Frank Giacoia); other licensing included dolls, puzzles, costumes, coloring books, and more.

In 1978, Filmation produced *Tarzan and the Super 7* for CBS. The ninety-minute animated show featured rebroadcasts of *Batman* and *Tarzan* episodes, as well as five other rotating segments. One of these segments was *Freedom Force,* a team of historical heroes that included Isis, Hercules, Super Samurai, Sinbad, and Merlin. Isis was voiced by Diane Pershing in the five produced episodes. The *Freedom Force* episodes were later released on video.

THE SUPERHERO BOOK

A *Legend of Isis* one-shot comic book was released in 2002 from Image Comics, but although the heroine was similarly dressed, it wasn't the TV character. Filmation's assets have been sold and resold multiple times since *Isis* went off the air in the United States, and although the series has been seen in foreign countries, neither programming chiefs nor zephyr winds have brought mighty Isis back to American fans. —*AM*

Justice League of America

"Just imagine! The mightiest heroes of our time … have banded together as the Justice League of America to stamp out the forces of evil wherever and whenever they appear!" So screamed the text of a DC Comics house advertisement in 1960, promoting *The Brave and the Bold* #28 (March 1960). In that story, the first superhero team of the Silver Age (1956–1969) was established, and Wonder Woman, Aquaman, Flash, Green Lantern, Martian Manhunter, and even Superman and Batman came together as a group to fight crime. Their legacy would last well over forty years to the modern day. And the current Justice League of America, now known as JLA, still contains the same members, even if some faces behind the masks have changed.

The Justice League was the brainchild of DC editor Julius Schwartz, who saw the smash revivals of Flash and Green Lantern as a time to update and reintroduce one of DC's most venerable older superhero groups, the Justice Society of America. Schwartz wanted the new group to have a different name, as he related in *The Amazing World of DC*

Comics #14 (1977) when he said, "To me, 'Society' meant something you found on Park Avenue. I felt that 'League' was a stronger word, one that the readers could identify with because of baseball leagues." Schwartz assigned famed Golden Age (1938–1954) sci-fi writer Gardner Fox to script the new series, and artists Mike Sekowsky and Bernard Sachs to illustrate the book. After two further issues of *The Brave and the Bold,* the JLA was awarded its own title with *Justice League of America* #1 (November 1960).

The early *Justice League of America* stories showcased the creative team's ability to introduce exciting new villains, such as Starro the starfish alien conqueror; power-stealing android Amazo; mesmerizing three-eyed alien Despero; tubby Professor Fortune; magician Felix Faust; Dr. Light; the Royal Flush Gang; Queen Bee; and many others. At the group's mountain hideaway "Secret Sanctuary"—outside Happy Harbor on the East Coast—hot DC stars were welcomed in as new members. Green Arrow joined in issue #4 (May 1961), while the Atom came along in #14 (September 1962). The team even had a hip-speaking teen sidekick named Snapper Carr, who managed to help his super-buddies often.

The origin of the JLA wasn't revealed until issue #9 (February 1962), wherein the team members

Justice League of America #200 © 1982 DC Comics.
COVER ART BY GEORGE PÉREZ.

fought alien champions from the planet Appellax. But the most memorable stories from the Justice League's early days came with issues #21–#22 (August–September 1963), which saw the heroes reuniting with their forebears, the Justice Society of America. As had been seen in *The Flash* #123 (September 1961), the JSA lived on Earth-Two, while the JLA lived on Earth-One. Piercing the barrier between the Earths enabled the two teams to fight super-criminals together. The team-up proved so popular that the stories—most of which included the word "Crisis" in their titles—became a yearly event in *Justice League of America.*

Fox and Sekowsky left the series in 1968, and writer Denny O'Neill and artist Dick Dillin came

aboard as replacements. Dillin penciled 120 consecutive *League* issues until his death in 1980, whereupon George Pérez and other artists took over. More heroes joined or were offered honorary memberships in the JLA, including Hawkman, Black Canary, Elongated Man, Red Tornado, Hawkgirl/Hawkwoman, Zatanna, Firestorm, the Phantom Stranger, Adam Strange, the Creeper, Metamorpho, Sargon the Sorceror, and others. Some resigned or took leaves of absence, including Green Arrow and Wonder Woman. The team moved their headquarters from the mountain to an orbiting satellite, constructed using Thanagarian technology (from Hawkman's homeworld) and requiring members to use transportation tubes to gain entrance.

In 1984, the *Justice League of America* series was radically revamped. The team disbanded after a Martian attack, and then reformed with Aquaman as the leader. Headquartered in a bunker in an abandoned Detroit factory—and later in the original mountain base—this Justice League was full of newcomers such as animalistic Vixen, second-generation strongman Steel, chameleon-like Gypsy, breakdancer Vibe, and a few old-timers. The team didn't click with readers for very long, and *Justice League of America* was canceled with issue #261 (April 1987).

During 1987's *Legends* miniseries, some of the "Detroit" Leaguers were killed, and a new JLA was formed. Members of the new *Justice League* series (debuting May 1987) included Batman, Martian Manhunter, Black Canary, Blue Beetle, Mr. Miracle, Green Lantern Guy Gardner, Captain Marvel, and new heroine Dr. Light. Joining shortly thereafter were Booster Gold, the Creeper, Captain Atom, Ice-Maiden/Ice, Green Flame/Fire, Big Barda, Dr. Fate, and Russian hero Rocket Red. A mysterious benefactor named Maxwell Lord helped run the team, getting them international diplomatic status.

The new series proved popular with the fans, largely because of the humorous ways its creators played with the heroes. J. M. DeMatteis and Keith Giffen never took the characters too seriously, and penciler Kevin Maguire proved adept at facial reactions that conveyed more than dialogue ever could. The popular series was renamed *Justice League International* with issue #7 (November 1987), and then *Justice League America* with #26 (May 1989). Multiple spin-offs were soon published: *Justice League Europe* (1989–1993), which became *Justice League International* (1993–1994); *Justice League Quarterly* (1990–1994); *Justice League Task Force* (1993–1994); and *Extreme Justice* (1995–1996) filled the stands, with each book spotlighting a different crew of superheroes operating from Justice League embassies throughout the world. Eventually though, the various series' popularity tapered off, and with *Justice League America* #113 (August 1996), all the Leaguers were out of work.

A few appearances passed by, and another series was launched with a shorter-titled *JLA* issue #1 (January 1997), though the characters in the book still referred to their group by its full title most of the time. This time the big guns were brought back to confront earth-shaking menaces and galaxy conquerors as they had at the beginning; unlike the one-issue Silver Age tales, however, these stories usually took four to six issues to tell. "Hot" creators came and went on the series; *JLA* held its own in sales. This time the lineup included Superman, Batman, Wonder Woman, Aquaman, Flash, Green Lantern, and Plastic Man, although membership would grow and expand to include many of DC's large roster of heroes, including Huntress, Steel, Zauriel, Aztek, Tomorrow Woman, Orion, and many others. More recently, Hourman, Faith, and Manitou Raven (a redesign of cartoon *Super Friends* member Apache Chief) have joined. This League operates from the Watchtower, a high-tech base on the moon; ex-Batgirl Oracle helps them with information for their missions.

With its own series a solid seller for DC Comics, *JLA* has been free to branch out again. A maxi-series of *JLA: Year One* (1998) retold the formative year of the team, retroactively inserting Black Canary in Wonder Woman's spot, according to revised DC continuity. In 2003, a miniseries called *Formerly Known as the Justice League* reunited the "comedy-era" team of DeMatteis, Giffen, and Maguire to relate new adventures of the second-rate squad. The series was a surprise sales hit, and further volumes were announced. Writer Paul Dini and painter Alex Ross also delivered a treat to fans with the tabloid-sized *JLA: Secret Origins* (2002) and *JLA: Liberty and Justice* (2003). And a new comic-book series based on the popular *Justice League* cartoon series debuted in January 2002 for younger audiences, titled *Justice League Adventures*. After forty-three years, it seems that the fans still thrill to see the mightiest heroes of our time banding together as the Justice League of America … and as long as there are DC superheroes and villains, perhaps they always will. —*AM*

Justice League of America in the Media

DC Comics' mightiest heroes may have banded together to fight evil in the pages of comic books, but their history in the media has been a bit more fractured. Until the early 2000s, the Justice League of America had only made a handful of appearances on television, and none in the movies. And yet, if the average person looked at the membership of the JLA, he or she might classify them easily: as the Super Friends.

The first appearance of the Justice League was in animated form on Filmation's *The Superman-Aquaman Hour of Adventure.* Debuting on September 9, 1967, the hour-long show featured two *Superman* adventures and a *Superboy* story in one half-hour, and two *Aquaman* adventures and a guest-hero in the other half-hour. Each of the guest-heroes had three seven-minute stories. Guest heroes included

Legends of the Superheroes stars (from left to right): The Flash (Rod Haase), Robin (Burt Ward), Black Canary (Danuta Rylko-Soderman), Hawkman (Bill Nuckols), Huntress (Barbara Joyce), Retired Man (William Schallert), Batman (Adam West), Captain Marvel (Garrett Craig), and Green Lantern (Howard Murphy).

similar to the core of the JLA, Hanna-Barbera's animated *Super Friends* series, which began on ABC in September 1973, was not technically the Justice League. The group was known as "the Super Friends" to civilians and villains alike on the series. Even in later episodes, when other JLA members such as Green Lantern, Hawkman, Hawkgirl, Flash, and Atom joined for adventures, the team retained its friendly sobriquet in all but a few instances when the name "Justice League" crept in. By 1984, when Kenner's *Super Powers* toy line was going strong, the Super Friends became the Super Powers Team, and Firestorm joined.

There has never been a first live-action appearance of the *Justice League* on television, but that wasn't for lack of trying. On January 18 and 25, 1979, NBC aired Hanna-Barbera's *Legends of the Super-Heroes,* a two-part story subtitled "The Challenge" and "The Roast." In the first part, the heroes were represented by Batman (Adam West), Robin (Burt Ward), Captain Marvel (Garrett Craig), Black Canary (Danuta Rylko-Soderman), Flash (Rod Haase), Huntress (Barbara Joyce), Green Lantern (Howard Murphy), Hawkman (Bill Nuckols), and H-B creation Scarlet Cyclone/Retired Man (William Schallert). In a plot involving a bomb, they faced the villains gathered against them, which included Mordru (Gabriel Dell), The Riddler (Frank Gorshin), Dr. Sivana (Howard Morris), Sinestro (Charlie Callas), Solomon Grundy (Mickey Morton), Weather Wizard (Jeff Altman), and Giganta (A'leisha Brevard).

the Flash, Hawkman, Green Lantern, the Atom, Teen Titans, and Justice League of America. This latter team consisted of Superman, Flash, Hawkman, Green Lantern, and the Atom. The guest-hero entries were repeated the following year when the series split; *The Adventures of Aquaman* aired from September 1968 to September 1969.

Although the lead characters—Superman, Batman, Robin, Wonder Woman, and Aquaman—were

In "The Roast," emcee Ed McMahon hosted a roast of the heroes while they sat around and were ribbed by villains and other superheroic colleagues. Added to the mix this time were heroes Ghetto Man (Brad Sanders) and the Atom (Alfie Wise), plus villainess Aunt Minerva (Ruth Buzzi). Neither of the *Legends of the Super-Heroes* specials ever aired again. But at least they aired once, which is more than the next set of *Justice League* telefilms got a chance to do.

In 1989 and 1990, Lorimar and Magnum Productions were working on a two-hour television pilot for *Justice League of America.* Hampered by the fact that Superman, Batman, Wonder Woman, Flash, and Green Lantern were already optioned, they were forced to use less-known characters. Taking several pages from the JLA series of that time period (the humorous one), they chose Martian Manhunter, Blue Beetle, Booster Gold, Fire, Ice, Mister Miracle, Big Barda, Maxwell Lord, and Oberon, in a convoluted and silly plot against a Lord of Chaos. Four script drafts were produced by James Caape, David Arnott, and Jeff Freilich before the project was scrapped.

The next *Justice League of America* telefilm project actually was produced in 1997 as a pilot for CBS, directed by Felix Enriquez Alcala and an uncredited Lewis Teague, and scripted by Lorne Cameron and David Hoselton. Again following the humorous League stories, it featured a rotund Martian Manhunter (David Ogden Stiers), Green Lantern/Guy Gardner (Matthew Settle), the Flash (Ken Johnston), the Atom (Jon Kassir), Fire (Michelle Hurd), and Ice (Kim Oja). Operating out of their underwater base—Manhunter's Martian ship—the JLA tries to protect New Metro from a villain called "the Weatherman" (Miguel Ferrer). The characters were treated as slackers, the costumes were dreadful, and the story was trite; small wonder that CBS passed on the project and it never aired in the United States. It did air in other countries—England, Germany, Brazil, Israel, and others—in two different forms. One was a straight-ahead narrative, while the other was presented pseudo-documentary style, splicing in interviews with the heroes to the action footage!

It would take animation for the proper *Justice League* to be seen again on television. First, WB's *Batman Beyond* would guest-star the futuristic Justice League Unlimited in two November 2000 episodes. Then, following the success of *Batman: The Animated Series* and *Superman: The Animated Series,* Bruce Timm, Paul Dini, and Alan Burnett pitched a new *Justice League* series in 1998. The following year, Warner Bros. commissioned the show for the Cartoon Network. Not aimed at young audiences, *Justice League* played it straight when it debuted on November 1, 2001. The core group included Superman, Batman, Wonder Woman, Green Lantern/John Stewart, Martian Manhunter, Flash, and Hawkgirl. The heroes banded together in a three-part "Secret Origins" tale, and then had mostly two-part adventures from then on. Episodes were aired first in full-screen, and secondly in widescreen, with black bars obscuring the top and bottom of the picture (the producers originally wanted to do the series in widescreen).

The Justice League heroes work out of the Watchtower, a satellite in geosynchronous orbit around the Earth. They have fought an impressive array of comic-book villains, including Lex Luthor, the Joker, Kanjar Ro, the Manhunters, Deadshot, Felix Faust, Mongul, Gorilla Grodd, and Vandal Savage. They have also teamed up with other heroes such as Aquaman, Metamorpho, the Green Lantern Corps, the Blackhawks, the Demon, and Sgt. Rock. Many well-known Hollywood talents have lent their voices to the series, including *Smallville*'s Michael Rosenbaum, *Mad TV's* Phil LaMarr, Mark Hamill, Gary Cole, John Rhys-Davies, Robert Englund, Patrick Duffy, and even David Ogden Stiers (though he played Solivar instead of Martian Manhunter).

In March 2003, the Justice League guest-starred on two episodes of the WB's animated *Static Shock!* cartoon. Later that fall, *Justice League* was moved to a one-hour block, and the two-part

297

shows were combined. Due to outside licensing, it seems unlikely that a *Justice League* film or live-action series will ever be produced, but fans are happy with the animated series, which finally gives the Justice League of America the show it deserves. —*AM*

Justice Society of America

It's a rare superhero team that can be said to have created a whole genre, but the Justice Society of America (JSA) did just that in the pages of *All Star Comics.* Simply put, they were the first superteam in comics history—the first time that superheroes banded together to fight a common foe. The team's origin has its roots in the confusing development of DC Comics or, to be more precise, in the creation of its sister company, All-American Publications. In 1939, DC owner Harry Donenfeld joined forces with industry pioneer Max (M. C.) Gaines to form an off-shoot called All-American, which would have its own editorial base (led by chief editor Sheldon Mayer) and its own characters. Within two years of the company's creation its self-titled publication *All-American Comics* had amassed a formidable roster of heroes, including the Flash, Hawkman, Johnny Thunder, Green Lantern, the Atom, and Dr. Mid-Nite.

All Star Comics was one of many Golden Age (1938–1954) anthology comics stuffed to the gills with superheroes, but with its third issue (Winter 1940) the decision was made to put them all together into a team. Mayer and writer Gardner Fox combined their own All-American heroes with some of DC's characters, notably Dr. Fate, Hourman, Sandman, and the Spectre, and the Justice Society of America was born. For its first few years, the strip featured individual adventures of the various heroes (often drawn by their regular creative teams), usually pitted against a common foe, culmi-

nating in the group all meeting up in the last few pages. With a length of up to fifty-eight pages, the tales had an epic quality that captivated readers, despite the occasionally crude artwork on show. The momentum of World War II only increased the comic's excitement as the team took on the Axis hordes and even went so far as to join the army (where they were also occasionally known as the Freedom Battalion).

Early on, management decided to showcase those heroes without their own comics (which is why Batman and Superman were notable absentees) and, as Flash and Green Lantern gained their own titles, they were eased out, as was Hourman (to make way for DC's big hope of 1942, Starman). Issue #8 saw the first appearance anywhere of All-American's biggest star, Wonder Woman, who was inducted into the group a few issues later, although she mostly had to make do with being the team secretary until issue #39! In late 1944, the comic witnessed a bigger upheaval when All-American owner Gaines split from DC over a row with DC owner Harry Donenfeld (who had given half of his share of All-American to DC's accountant, Jack Liebowitz). Consequently, DC regulars the Spectre and Starman were booted out (joining recent evictees Sandman and Dr. Fate, who had just seen their own solo series canceled). A year later, Gaines sold out his share in the company to Donenfeld, and All-American was formally merged with DC. Surprisingly, however, the Justice Society remained wholly made up of All-American heroes to its end.

By the mid-1940s, the comic was at its peak, with the return of the Flash and Green Lantern, improved art from such young talents as Alex Toth, Carmine Infantino, and Joe Kubert, and scripts from Fox, Robert Kanigher, and John Broome. The JSA had also amassed a formidable array of foes, including the Wizard, the Brain Wave, Degaton, Vandal Savage, the Psycho Pirate, and the Injustice Society; they would all serve as the team's principle enemies for decades to come. Wildcat and Mr. Terrific (both from the pages of *Sensation Comics*)

made fleeting appearances in 1945, but it was the Black Canary (introduced to the team three years later, in issue #38) who was to be the last significant new member. DC canceled almost all its superhero books in 1949 but *All Star Comics* hung on for a few years longer as the last refuge for All-American's once-cherished superheroes. Their final appearance came in issue #57 in 1951 and with the following issue the comic was retitled *All-Star Western,* signaling the end of an era.

In the ensuing years, the JSA became the focus for much of comic fandom and were the subject of numerous fanzine articles. When DC started reviving its long-lost heroes in the late 1950s, the team was the inspiration behind the Justice League of America, who in turn inspired Marvel Comics' Fantastic Four. Soon, the clamor for the JSA inspired Julius Schwartz (the JSA's final editor, and then-current editor of the Justice League) to reintroduce the Society in a two-part team-up with the League in 1963. Schwartz and writer Fox rationalized the JSA's reappearance by establishing that they were in fact from a parallel planet—called Earth-Two—which was apparently where all the 1940s and early 1950s DC/All-American adventures had actually taken place.

The Justice League story proved to be so popular that Schwartz decided to make the team-up an annual event, which was to last until 1985. The Justice Society members featured in the team-ups hailed from various periods of the strip, seemingly

All Star Comics #37 © 1947 DC Comics.
COVER ART BY IRWIN HASEN.

chosen at random. Previously little-seen characters, such as Wildcat, Superman (the Earth-Two version), Hourman, and Mr. Terrific became regulars and the Earth-Two Robin was introduced to the team. These crossovers sparked interest in the individual heroes, leading to more guest appearances in such comics as *The Flash, Green Lantern, Atom,* and *The Brave and the Bold,* while the Spectre was given his own, short-lived title (the first of many Spectre series). Finally, the groundswell of affection for the team culminated in *All-Star Comics* being revived in 1976 with issue #58 (ignoring the many issues of *All-Star Western*), twenty-five years after their last Golden Age adventure.

However, the new *All-Star* was no mere exercise in nostalgia. Writer Gerry Conway introduced a new group of younger heroes: the Star-Spangled Kid, Robin, and a new superheroine, Superman's feisty and flirtatious cousin, Powergirl. This new group called themselves the Super Squad. The intergenerational conflict between the aging JSA and the Super Squad enlivened a well-crafted comic, with the grizzled ex-boxer Wildcat, something of a bit player in the 1940s, emerging as a star at last. In its later years, the Justice Society had become a rare showcase for powerful female characters; both Wonder Woman and Black Canary took prominent roles. Similarly, the new *All-Star* featured strong women: In addition to Powergirl, the comic also starred the much darker Huntress (introduced in issue #69), a.k.a. Helena Wayne, later revealed to be the daughter of Batman and Catwoman. The Huntress went on to her own backup in *Wonder Woman* and *Batman Family,* as well as numerous Batman titles, a couple of her own series in the 1990s, and a starring role in the *Birds of Prey* title. Unfortunately, she could not inspire the public to buy *All-Star Comics,* and it was canceled with issue #74, while the JSA briefly moved over to the pages of *Adventure Comics,* where the Earth-Two Batman was killed off. Undeterred by this setback, DC still had faith in the team and, over the next two decades, no fewer than ten Justice Society–inspired titles were launched.

Of the many fans who clamored for the team's revival in the early 1960s, Roy Thomas (then editor of the legendary fanzine *Alter Ego*) was one of the most vocal. In the years that followed, he rose to become the editor-in-chief and one of the top writers at Marvel Comics, but by 1981 he was looking to make his mark at DC and his first project involved his beloved Justice Society, albeit somewhat tangentially. *All-Star Squadron* was set at the dawn of World War II, and over its six-year existence featured pretty much all the JSA at one time or another, but its focus was on those Golden Age stars passed over by *All-Star Comics*. The team contained old DC heroes Johnny Quick, Robotman, Liberty Belle, and the Shining Knight, plus two characters from rival company Quality Comics, Firebrand and Tarantula, and one new creation, Amazing Man—the first African-American hero set in that era. Much as he had done with Marvel's Invaders, Thomas wove ancient strands of comic-book continuity with historical events and military set pieces to fine effect.

The success of these Earth-Two heroes inspired Thomas to revive their contemporary adventures and, possibly piqued by the Super Squad, he created Infinity Inc., together with artist Jerry Ordway. Infinity Inc. characters were the offspring of various superheroes who had been rejected by the "grown-up" JSA. They had banded together to prove their elders and betters wrong. The team consisted of Fury (daughter of Wonder Woman), the Silver Scarab and Northwind (son and godson respectively of Hawkman), Nuklon (godson of the Atom), Jade and Obsidian (Green Lantern's children), and Brainwave Junior, along with disaffected younger JSA-ers Power Girl, Huntress, and Star Spangled Kid. Slick, modern, and fast-moving, the comic was a fine companion to the All-Star Squadron, and later introduced new incarnations of Hawkman, Dr. Mid-Nite, and Wildcat. However, all was not well in the DC boardroom.

The powers-that-be had been wary about the sheer volume of past history that their heroes were carrying, and felt that their whole line needed to be simplified and updated. In the wake of the creation of the Earth-Two concept, several other alternative universes had sprung up, including Earth-X for the heroes bought from Quality Comics, Earth-S for Captain Marvel, and even Earth Prime for our own world. DC decided that they all had to go, and in the 1985 *Crisis on Infinite Earths* miniseries the various worlds were merged, and numerous comics were given "year-one" relaunches. But if the (heroic) world began in 1985, where did that leave the old Justice Society with their Golden Age counterparts of Wonder Woman, Superman, et al.? Thomas countered this confusion with yet another wartime comic—the *Young All-Stars*—starring stand-ins for the now unusable old stars. However, this did not quite catch on. By 1989, the last of the JSA-inspired comics was canceled, killed by the confusion created in the wake of the series that was meant to end confusion.

The early 1990s saw a few tentative steps toward reviving the Justice Society, first in 1991 with a nostalgic 1950s-era miniseries, followed a year later by a last, present-day outing for the original team. (Incidentally, both series were titled *Justice Society of America,* the only time they appeared in a comic with that name.) That second series unflinchingly, lovingly, and wittily starred a team of now elderly heroes. However, this was not what DC wanted to see, and the comic lasted a mere ten issues. In the 1994 miniseries *Zero Hour* (another failed attempt at simplification), numerous group members were either killed off altogether (Dr. Mid-Nite, Hawkman, and the Atom) or aged to doddering infirmity.

Salvation came in the form of British writer James Robinson, who had made a splash with his 1993 miniseries *The Golden Age* (an imaginary story set in the 1940s). He rekindled interest in the old team in 1999 with a series called *The Justice Society Returns*. This was followed immediately by a regular series simply called *JSA,* which began unpromisingly with the death (of old age, for once) of yet another team member, the Sandman, but went on to become not only a success but also a worthy tribute to the venerable group. Original members the Flash, Green Lantern (renamed Sentinel), and Wildcat were joined by new incarnations of Dr. Fate, the Spectre, Dr. Mid-Nite et al., along with Infinity Inc. alumni Brainwave and Nuklon (now known as Atom Smasher) and a female Star Spangled Kid (step-daughter of Stripsey, the original Kid's sidekick).

Fittingly, the new JSA has inherited the same parade of villains (Solomon Grundy, the Injustice Society) and the same sense of honesty and fun that characterized the earliest incarnations. The old heroes (such as the Flash, Wildcat, and Hawkman) may have been simplistic by contemporary standards, but they personified an uncomplicated, heroic, essentially moral sense of the world—quite refreshing in the twenty-first century. In its various forms, the JSA and its offshoots have proved to be remarkably resistant to the periodic waves of "relevance" and nastiness that have afflicted the comics world from time to time. In some respects, the group represents DC's past (and that of comics in general), and as much as the company may try to kill off the characters or in some way expunge the ponderous baggage of their long history (more than sixty years and counting), somehow they keep on coming back, enriching new generations of readers. —*DAR*

Kryptonite

Any person even remotely familiar with Superman lore has heard of this superhero's number-one vulnerability: kryptonite.

First introduced on the *Superman* radio show in 1945 before making its way into the comic-book pages of *Superman* #61 (1949), kryptonite is used in the Superman mythology to denote any portion of material that survived from Superman's exploded planet, Krypton. The material, described as "the only thing the Man of Steel has to fear in the entire universe" in *Action Comics* #291 (1962), scattered throughout space and "laden with cosmic energy," emits a deadly radiation to which Superman and other surviving natives of Krypton are vulnerable. Because kryptonite fragments still float in space, they make their way to planet Earth buried in meteors.

There are five unique types of this planetary matter, the nuances of which only the most die-hard Superman fan has committed to memory. *Green* kryptonite, the most common variety and the one traditionally discussed in comics stories of the Golden (1938–1954) and Silver (1956–1969) Ages, is the only type potentially fatal to the hero. If not removed "in time" from Superman's midst, death follows the loss of his superpowers and a general state of inertia. While large quantities produce the most drastic effects, even a piece the size of a jawbreaker can bring Superman to his knees. Though the Man of Steel has often circumvented the effects of green kryptonite by using the heat of his X-ray vision to melt away small chunks of the substance, this Super-plan-of-attack doesn't work with larger quantities.

Though not fatal, *red* kryptonite imposes temporary (usually twenty-four hours), strange, and random results, such as when it turned Superman into a giant ant, drove him insane for forty-eight hours, or made it impossible for him to write or speak in any language other than his native Kryptonese. As a general rule, once Superman is exposed to the strange effect, he becomes immune to it, forcing his writers to come up with new and interesting ways of afflicting the hero. *Gold* kryptonite permanently steals Superman's superpowers; *white* kryptonite affects only plant life; and *blue* kryptonite is hazardous only to Bizarro (a Superman "replica" hero built by supervillain Lex Luthor as "a grotesque imitation of Superman" in *Action Comics* #254 in 1959) and related Bizarro creatures. Kryptonite of the green, red, and gold variety is toxic to any surviving natives of Krypton, including members of the Superman family such as Supergirl and Krypto the Super-Dog.

Over the years *Superman* writers introduced variations like jewel kryptonite and X-kryptonite, the latter of which gave Supergirl's cat Streaky superpowers. The one substance impervious to kryptonite is lead. In 1971, *Superman* editor Julius Schwartz excised kryptonite from the Man of Steel's canon, although it has been used more judiciously since the reworking of the Superman mythos begin-ning in *The Man of Steel* #1 (1986). The glowing substance from a distant planet factors heavily into Superman media, having been used in the 1948 movie serial *Superman,* a half dozen episodes of the *Superman* television series of the 1950s, animated cartoons of the 1960s and 1970s, and the four live-action *Superman* films of the late 1970s and 1980s. —*GM*

Lane, Lois

She's pop culture's best-known damsel in distress, but Lois Lane is one gal who can take care of herself. As a reporter's rival, Superman's girlfriend, and even Clark Kent's wife, Lane has accompanied the Man of Steel through a never-ending string of adventures. Beginning with Superman's first appearance in *Action Comics* #1 (June 1938), writer Jerry Siegel and illustrator Joe Shuster clearly establish that this imprudently ambitious newspaper journalist for Metropolis' *Daily Planet* (called the *Daily Star* in the earliest tales) will go to any length to get a story, being it shimmying along skyscraper ledges, stowing away on speeding trucks, or frolicking with hardnosed gangsters. Borrowing their inspiration from the Hollywood heroine "Torchy Blaine," a saucy female newshound from a 1930s movie franchise, Siegel and Shuster regularly place Lane in perilous predicaments—she faces a dictator's firing squad, is booted from a speeding sedan, and freefalls without a working parachute—but in a flash of red and blue Superman always arrives for a daring rescue. Lane is so aggressively industrious, however, one suspects that she could save herself if the Man of Steel didn't show.

But show he did, usually because Superman's alter ego, reporter Clark Kent, accompanied his audacious *Planet* colleague on many of her assignments, forging a formula that ran for decades: Lois ditches Clark to scoop him, she gets in trouble, Clark sneaks away to become Superman, Superman rescues Lois. With each encounter with the Man of Steel, Lane became suspicious as to why Superman and Kent never appear together ("intrepid girl reporter," indeed). Thusly, she spent much of the next thirty years ferreting out clues, perpetrating hoaxes, and even setting traps to prove that Kent and Superman were the same. Yet the Man of Steel was always one step ahead of Lane, outsmarting her each time while frequently concluding comic-book stories and animated television episodes with a winking aside to the reader/viewer.

For decades, Lane treated Kent as a professional adversary, and sometimes with contempt, criticizing him for being timid. She occasionally found him charming, though, as in a *Superman* daily newspaper strip (April 24, 1941) where she revealed, "Odd, Clark—half the time I can't make up my mind whether you're a swell fellow or a heel...." Conversely, it didn't take long for Lane to develop a fascination with Superman beyond an appreciation of his astonishing abilities. She longed to be Mrs. Superman; in *Action Comics* #245 (1958), when the Man of Steel commented to Lane about their friendship, she sighed to herself, "I ... I wish I were more than a

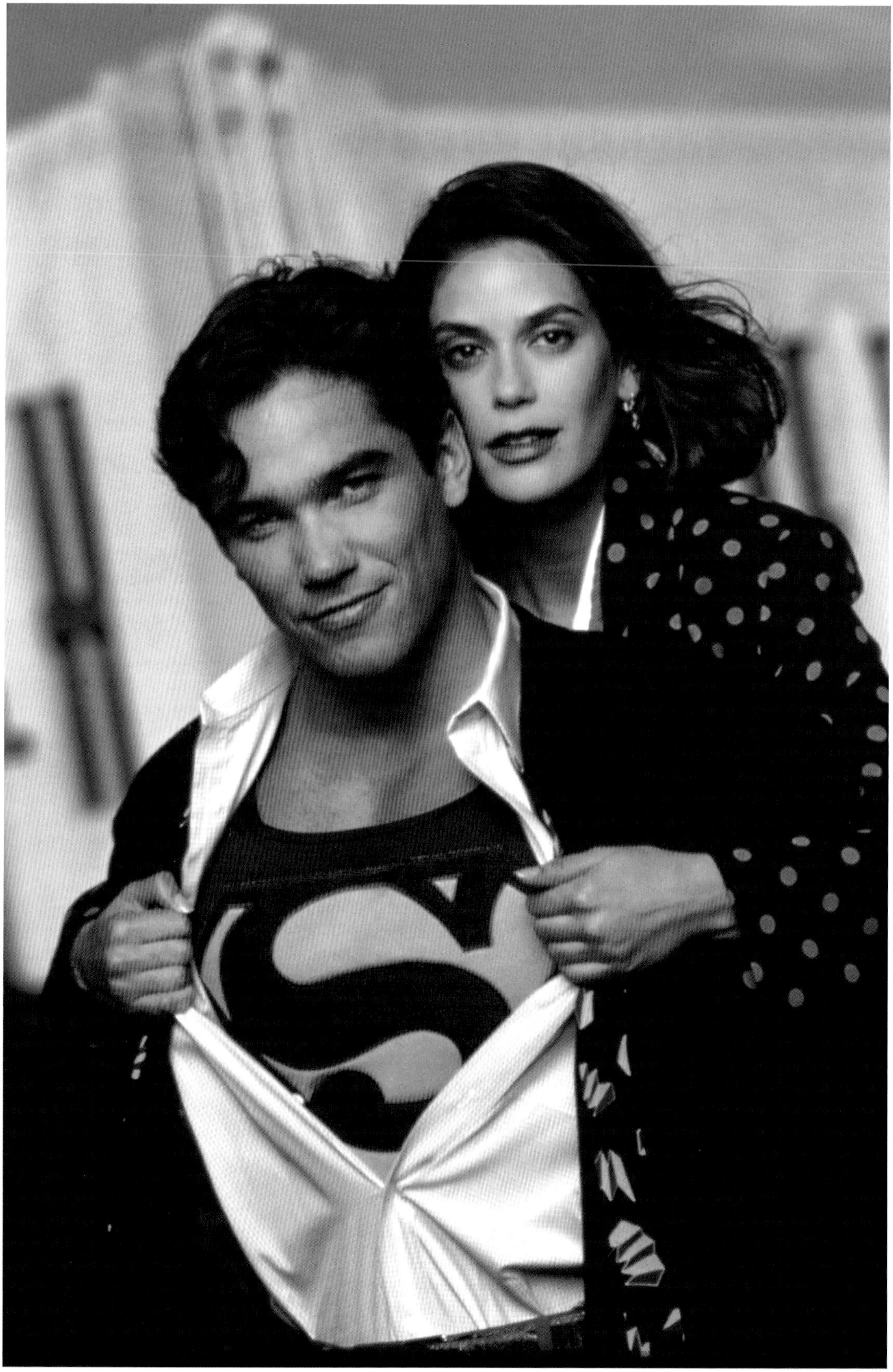

close friend … his wife!" Her love was to remain unrequited for decades, although "imaginary" stories in the 1960s frequently placed Lane in the role of Superman's spouse, and sometimes the mother of a super-son or super-daughter.

Superman did carry the torch for Lane, but his duties as the world's greatest superhero prohibited him from walking down the aisle with her. Other suitors for Lane came and went, including millionaires, superheroes from other worlds, mobsters, Batman (the reporter became Mrs. Bruce Wayne in a 1969 imaginary tale), and even Superman's foes Bizarro and Titano the Super-Ape. During the 1960s and 1970s, Lana Lang, Super*boy's* sweetheart from the Man of Steel's hometown of Smallville, reentered the picture as a competitor for Super*man's* affections.

Lane has always stood as an advocate for gender equality. American women may have marched out of the factories and back into the kitchen at the conclusion of World War II, but not Lane—she remained a working gal, dedicated to her career. Her exposés on Metropolis' gangland earned her kudos and assassination attempts. Through all this excitement, she remained a fashion plate, reflecting each decade's styles with impeccable flair—Lane sported tailored business suits in the 1940s, pillbox hats in the 1950s, miniskirts in the 1960s, and pantsuits and hot pants in the 1970s.

As the Man of Steel's popularity mushroomed throughout the 1950s, in part due to the success of the syndicated television program *The Adventures of Superman* (1953–1957), Lane earned her own comic-book title in 1958, *Superman's Girl Friend Lois Lane,* after a pair of issues of DC Comics' try-out book *Showcase.* Her series, which ran through 1974, was a favorite among girls, with stories of female empowerment (Lois goes undercover, Lois gains powers as Superwoman), female fantasy (Lois becomes a witch, Lois becomes a crone), and female domestication (Lois fantasizes over marrying Superman).

When writer/artist John Byrne spearheaded the overhaul of the Superman mythos beginning with DC Comics' *The Man of Steel* miniseries in 1986, Lane also received a facelift. Pining and pettiness were no more: Lane, now a military brat adept at hand-to-hand combat, returned to her roots as a hardcore journalist. For the next decade, the reporters' rivalry between Lane and Kent blossomed into a profound friendship, and DC Comics, recognizing the maturity of its audience, allowed the previously unthinkable to happen in 1996: Lane finally became Mrs. Superman, or actually, Mrs. Clark Kent, marrying the Man of Steel (and of her dreams) in a highly promoted event taking place in the comics and on live-action television in the series *Lois & Clark: The New Adventures of Superman* (1993–1997).

Lane has joined Superman in each of the hero's multimedia adaptations in theatrical animated shorts, a radio program, movie serials, several cartoon and live-action television series, and four theatrical motion pictures. The most popular interpretations of the character were provided by spunky Noel Neill in seasons two through five of television's *The Adventures of Superman* (1953–1957); by firebrand Margot Kidder in the film franchise, most notably *Superman: The Movie* (1978) and *Superman II* (1981); and by fetching Teri Hatcher in television's *Lois & Clark.* —ME

Legion of Super-Heroes

Every kid needs friends, and Superboy, the prodigious youth starring in DC Comics' "Adventures of Superman When He Was a Boy," was certainly no exception. Enter the Legion of Super-Heroes (LSH):

Opposite: Dean Cain (Superman) and Teri Hatcher (Lois Lane) set hearts aflutter in *Lois & Clark: The New Adventures of Superman.*

Superboy #204 © 1974 DC Comics.
COVER ART BY NICK CARDY.

the magnetically powered Cosmic Boy, the mind-reading Saturn Girl, and the electricity-generating Lightning Boy, materializing in DC Comics' *Adventure Comics* #247 (1958). Hailing from the future—the thirtieth century, to be exact—this teenage trio time-travels to Superboy's era to recruit him into their club. Thanks to the Legion's time *bubble,* the Boy of Steel finds himself in his hometown of Smallville, one thousand years hence, where his new superpals are only part of a larger clique (although the other young heroes' faces are shadowed) whose headquarters (their clubhouse) is an upside-down spaceship resembling a prop from a late 1950s sci-fi movie. The Legion's entire depiction of the future smacks of the post–atomic age's vision of the world of tomorrow: Robot factories, jet packs,

and yes, even flying cars abound! After proving himself a "super-good sport" by surviving a rigged initiation (hoaxes were popular story gimmicks during this era in the Superman comics), Superboy is sworn in as a Legionnaire and returns home to proudly show his father, Pa Kent, a prize ribbon decreeing him "Super-Hero Number One."

Mort Weisinger, editor of the Superman family of titles, intended *Adventure* #247's tale "The Legion of Super-Heroes" as nothing more than a throwaway. Readers had other ideas, however, and mail demanding that the Legion return flooded the DC offices. Twenty issues later, they were back (with Lightning *Boy* rechristened as the alliterative Lightning *Lad*), and before long the LSH also encountered Supergirl on yet another recruitment mission. The Legion's roster expanded with more superteens whose heroic names easily identified their powers: Chameleon Boy, Colossal Boy, Invisible Kid, Phantom Girl, and Triplicate Girl. Issues cover-spotlighting LSH members sold so well that "Tales of the Legion of Super-Heroes" bumped "Tales of the Bizarro World" out of *Adventure* and became a regular monthly feature beginning with issue #300 (September 1962), and before long the Legion ultimately seized the entire title from co-star Superboy.

Soon the Legion became truly that, with an enormous cast including, but not limited to, Ultra Boy, Superboy's "brother" Mon-El, Brainiac 5 (the descendent of Superman's android enemy), Sun Boy, Star Boy, Shrinking Violet, Lightning (later Light) Lass, Bouncing Boy, and, believe it or not, Matter-Eater Lad, as well as standbys the Legion of Substitute Heroes and the Legion of Super-Pets. Science remained a major element in the tales, with some upgrades along the way, like the Legion's original jet packs being replaced by anti-gravity belts. And a rogues' gallery, including the Time Trapper, the Legion of Super-Villains, and even the twentieth century's Lex Luthor, began to appear and reappear.

While simple in concept, the early Legion of Super-Heroes series was surprisingly complex for its time. Its pretense as a superhero "club" veiled its true message of brotherhood—members of the LSH migrated from a variety of worlds across the galaxy, which had banded together as the United Planets and shared a common language, Interlac. This interplanetary harmony, however, reflected the Anglo-centric thinking of the late 1950s and early 1960s: Despite their otherworldly origins, every Legionnaire was white, except for the orange-skinned, pointy-eared Chameleon Boy and the green-skinned Brainiac 5. Basing itself in thirtieth-century Metropolis (not Smallville, as in the LSH's initial outing), the Legion was often aided in its protection of Earth by the high-tech Science Police. The LSH operated under a strict constitution, which stipulated, among other things, a maximum age of eighteen, the annual appointment of an acting leader (who was chosen by the vote of the readers), and an expulsion provision (several Legionnaires were debarred in solemn hearings). Weisinger printed stories that revealed the dangerous consequences of superheroics: In an early battle, Lightning Lad lost an arm, and later his life (although he soon returned from the dead), and one of Triplicate Girl's three bodies was destroyed by the menacing machine called Computo, leaving her Duo Damsel.

Throughout the mid-1960s, the Legion's popularity grew, and the series cultivated a loyal and often vociferous fan base, including a teen named Jim Shooter. Shooter lobbied editor Weisinger for work by pitching crudely illustrated but boldly imaginative stories, and soon the young scribe was authoring the LSH feature in *Adventure.* Frequently paired with penciler Curt Swan, best known as "the" Superman artist of the 1960s (who disliked drawing LSH because of its sizeable cast and asked that his Legion stories feature smaller numbers of characters), Shooter's LSH run in *Adventure* was noteworthy due to its development of the young heroes' personalities: Each cast member was individually and consistently characterized, from Lightning Lad's impulsiveness to newcomer Princess Projectra's (actual royalty!) snobbishness. The Legionnaires often referred to each other by their

otherworldly civilian names—some examples: Cosmic Boy/Rokk Krinn, Chameleon Boy/Reep Daggle, and Shrinking Violet/Salu Digby—and as the series progressed, more was revealed about their parents, siblings, and home planets. Under Shooter's tenure, Legion mainstays like flight rings, the merciless magician Mordru, and the fearsome Fatal Five entered the lore. By the late 1960s, Shooter and Swan vacated the thirtieth century, bringing the Legion's first glory days to a close, and the series hobbled along with no true creative direction until being ousted from *Adventure Comics* by Supergirl beginning in issue #381 (June 1969) and temporarily demoted to the backup spot in *Action Comics* before being retired.

The Legion didn't lay dormant for long, returning in 1971 as a backup in *Superboy* before later taking over the title. The LSH enjoyed its second heyday in the 1970s: Hot new artists like Dave Cockrum and Mike Grell became fan favorites on the series, the heroes' garb was modernized (Phantom Girl wore bell bottoms and Element Lad sported a perm), and new characters like Wildfire and Tyroc (the first black member to break the LSH's color barrier) joined the team. The Legionnaires aged to their late teens, and romances took root, with several members even getting married. Science-fiction influences intensified, and the dated futuristic vision of the 1960s was replaced by technological marvels, including an expansive headquarters with a full training facility and warring alien races that defied the laws of the United Planets. With its intricate themes and scientific inspirations, *Legion of Super-Heroes* became the comic-book equivalent of *Star Trek,* and continued to boast a loyal fan following.

Writer Paul Levitz began a lengthy run on *Legion* in 1982, and along with artist Keith Giffen made the series DC's second best-selling title, trailing the company's top hit, *The New Teen Titans.* Levitz and Giffen's most celebrated Legion storyline, "The Great Darkness Saga," employed twentieth-century villain Darkseid as the future team's antagonist. Legionnaires came and went, married and had children, and the series matured, evolving away from its unsophisticated original concept of a club for superkids. But throughout myriad changes, one constant remained: Superboy, a recurring and popular member. Then came John Byrne.

Writer/artist Byrne was Marvel Comics' "fix-it" man, having resuscitated several failing titles for DC's chief competitor. Hired by DC to orchestrate a highly anticipated Superman relaunch that commenced with the miniseries *The Man of Steel* (1986), Byrne excised Superboy from the Superman mythos, forcing the Legion to readjust without its core member. It was explained that a Superboy from an alternate, "pocket" universe was the Legion's teammate, not the younger self of the "real" Superman, before the young hero flew into comics limbo. With this revision, perceived as contrived by some, convoluted by others, the Legion began to stray even further from its kid-friendly roots. Frequent tie-ins to twentieth-century continuity, including team-ups with Superman and a spinoff series called *L.E.G.I.O.N. '89* (later *'90,* then *'91,* etc., before getting the boot in 1994), made the LSH franchise harder to follow.

A 1989 *Legion of Super-Heroes* reboot featured an older and less optimistic Legion, sans costumes and codenames, in a densely plotted series occurring immediately after a then-unexplained "five-year gap" in story continuity (although details would later emerge). Giffen was the chief architect of this version of *Legion,* applauded by sci-fi aficionados for its intricacy but ignored by readers yearning for softer, more accessible fare. In this incarnation, the future Earth was destroyed, and a more reader-friendly team featuring teen versions (presumed to be clones) of the now-adult Legion spun off into their own title in *Legionnaires* #1 (1993). This younger, hipper group kept some classic character names (Cosmic Boy and Saturn Girl) as a historical nod, updated others (Lightning Lad became Live Wire and Triplicate Girl, Triad), and introduced a new wave of members. Yet *Legion-*

naires and its companion title *Legion of Super-Heroes* continued to build upon decades of already cluttered continuity, and readers—as well as editors and writers—were hopelessly confused. House-cleaning was in order.

Zero Hour: A Crisis in Time (1994) was DC's answer. This crossover, appearing throughout many of the publisher's superhero titles, readjusted DC's timeline, allowing for revisions including a restarted Legion. As of 2004, the LSH's comic is titled simply *The Legion,* and borrows the best rudiments of the *Legionnaires* redux in a science-heavy tapestry considerably darker in tone than the original concept.

Beyond its sales peak in the early 1980s, the Legion of Super-Heroes has never risen to A-team status, probably due to its cumbersome cast and rich history. But the concept has commanded perhaps the most dedicated fan base of any DC series. Legion fans, over the decades, have grown up with the characters, and, like the Legionnaires, in some cases have married.

On two occasions, Legion characters have appeared on television: Villainous Mordru was played for laughs in a pair of *Legends of the Super-Heroes* live-action specials (1979), and the Legion itself guest-starred on the animated series *Superman* (1996). A smattering of Legion merchandise has appeared over the years, including a line of action figures and a PVC figurine set sold in a box resembling the classic Legion clubhouse. *—ME*

Lobo

The "grittification" of the comic-book superhero—which began with Marvel Comics' Punisher in the 1970s and continued building toward an artistic peak in 1986 with DC Comics' *Batman: The Dark Knight Returns*—went deliberately over the top in 1983 with the creation of Lobo. The misbegotten, chalk-white, black-clad brainchild of writer Roger Slifer and artist Keith Giffen, Lobo (who debuted in

DC's *Omega Men* #3) embodies all that is nasty, raucous, and unsavory in the world of superpowered beings. Lobo, an anti-hero whose speech is peppered with ersatz expletives such as "frag," "fraggin'," "bastich," and "Feetal's Gizz!" (a reference to the gizzard of a particular individual), despises every decent thing usually associated with the typical comic-book hero, including (but not limited to) short hair, square jaws, democracy, equality for women, equality for men, basic rights, flags, and the notion that good always trumps evil. He is extremely powerful, possessing enough raw strength to go toe-to-toe with members of the Green Lantern Corps (*L.E.G.I.O.N.* #4, 1989) and even Superman himself, which he has done at various points throughout the 1990s and early 2000s.

Lobo has the ability to survive the rigors of airless space, the capacity to track individuals across thousands of light-years of empty space, and possesses his people's inborn power to clone himself from small amounts of tissue; this last ability, coupled with his rapid healing, renders him effectively unkillable, short of complete vaporization. It has been said that Lobo can never die permanently because he is considered too nasty to be admitted either to heaven or to hell (*Lobo's Back* #4, 1992). His "turn-ons" include drunkenness and mindless violence. Although he has demonstrated frightening mastery of all manner of weapons, sometimes going into combat with guns and grenades, Lobo is a street-brawler at heart, preferring to use either his fists or a large metal chain with a hook at one end. His most serious weakness is his tendency to continue a fight long past the point at which any rational person would retreat. But since most other beings in the universe fear Lobo, this seldom presents a serious problem for him. Because of the moral ambiguity that characterized many superhero comics published on the cusp of the new millennium, Lobo's status as a superhero (as opposed to a supervillain) is highly debatable; but his reluctant association with legitimate superhero teams—and the fact that he often does battle against miscreants who are even worse than he is—often places him on the side of the good guys, however marginally or unintentionally.

Born in 1599 A.D. on the distant, idyllic planet Czarnia, a world that had never known conflict or strife of any kind, Lobo is pure, distilled evil; indeed, his name is Khundish for "one who devours your entrails and thoroughly enjoys it" (any resemblance to a terrestrial word meaning "wolf" is completely fortuitous, as it turns out). Moments after his birth, Lobo makes his first attempt to live up to his name by biting off four of his midwife's fingers, driving the poor woman insane; Lobo then grabs a scalpel and attacks several doctors. Although no one on his homeworld knows for sure how or why such a malevolent serpent could appear in the Garden of Eden that is Czarnia, some theorize that Lobo's evil is a perhaps statistically inevitable counterbalance to an otherwise perfect, "evil-free" environment.

As Lobo matures, his evil steadily grows in intensity and sophistication. Consequently, the Czarnian body count rises in a steady tide. All attempts to appeal to Lobo's better nature fail simply because he lacks one (a claim Lobo himself often makes); all efforts to threaten Lobo fail because no one on Czarnia possesses any proficiency whatsoever in arms, violence, or even intimidation. As a toddler, Lobo forces Wolfman Wilf, the DJ of Cosmic Rock Zombie Radio, to play one song continuously: "I Killed My Folks (No Accident)" by Oedipus Wrecks. Lobo then commandeers a medical facility and forces its staff to implant a radio receiver into his brain, giving him unlimited exposure to the Wrecks' not-so-dulcet tones; he murders the doctors afterward and burns their clinic to the ground. At the tender age of five, Lobo rips out the throat of Egon N'g, his elementary school principal, during a fit of pique. "My faith in the natural goodness of the scheme of things has been severely shaken, if not totally destroyed," the dying principal writes to his countrymen, in his own blood (*Lobo* vol. 1 #1, 1990). "I rejoin the Universal One.

Farewell, paradise! P.S.—For your own sake, create the concepts of police, punishment, and prison."

As a teenager, Lobo forms his own heavy metal band (The Main Man and the Several Scum-Buckets), which competes at the All-Czarnia 9-Octave Chime-Haiku Festival; the band's deadly decibels end up killing all of Lobo's musical sidemen, electrocuting the contest's judges, and wreaking fiery mayhem on the audience—leaving Lobo peeved at his failure to take first prize. When Lobo reaches the age of eighteen, his evil finally engulfs all of Czarnia when his desire to be unique in all the universe leads him to genetically engineer an insidious flesh-burrowing flying insect that (very painfully) wipes out his entire species—except, of course, for Lobo himself, who merely laughs at the horrific carnage he has wrought (*Lobo* vol. 1 #1 and #4, 1990–1991; *Lobo* vol. 2 #0, 1994; *DC Universe Heroes Secret Files* #1, 1999).

Hopping onto his spacegoing motorcycle (actually a customized SpazFrag 666 single-seater superluminal spacecraft with a miniaturized turbocharged seventeen-liter power plant and a large-fanged skull mounted on the front), Lobo abandons his murdered homeworld to become the galaxy's most feared bounty hunter and assassin, a calling he pursues with great relish. At first, he specializes in "Dead or Alive" warrants, far preferring the former to the latter. He also sells his services to private clients, but can be relied upon to murder double-crossers and prospective clients who make insulting offers, or those who set him to tasks he finds boring; in Lobo's "plus" column, he tends to "stay bought" once hired, and the more violence a job entails, the likelier he is to work cheaply or even for free (he likes to chase people).

During his many unsavory manhunting missions, Lobo's few arguably redeeming characteristics become evident: his strict adherence to whatever promises he makes (he would prefer to kill the promisee than to renege on the promise itself), and his undying affection for his "fishies" (Lobo's term of endearment for the space-dwelling dolphins that

accompany him in his interstellar travels), whose safety he protects using all the considerable violence at his disposal; Lobo calls the creatures his "cutesy-wutesy flying cosmic-type dolphin buddies." After Garryn Bek of L.E.G.I.O.N. (Licensed Extra-Governmental Interstellar Operatives Network) accidentally kills one of Lobo's dolphins, the assassin comes after Bek, intent on slowly torturing him to death (*L.E.G.I.O.N.* #3, 1989).

Lobo eventually catches up to Bek and breaks his legs (*L.E.G.I.O.N.* #6, 1989), but along the way, he encounters L.E.G.I.O.N. member Vril Dox II, the adopted son of Superman's android nemesis Brainiac. Although Lobo and Dox, being of similar temperament, get along at first, they inevitably come to superhuman blows. Distracted by the sudden disappearance of Cosmic Rock Zombie Radio from the radio built into his brain, Lobo loses the fight and is forced to accept the consequences of a wager he'd made with Dox: L.E.G.I.O.N. membership (*L.E.G.I.O.N.* #4, 1989). After exploiting Lobo's self-cloning powers by using several duplicate Lobos to defeat a galactic drug kingpin named Kanis-Biz, Dox poisons Lobo and his clones, de-powering them and removing their duplicative abilities. Lobo and one of his clones escape destruction by Dox's missiles, however (*L.E.G.I.O.N.* #7, 1989), and Lobo faces his last remaining clone in single combat on the planet Kannit; the original Lobo is presumably the winner, though the matter of the victor's identity isn't settled definitively (*Lobo* vol. 2 #9, 1994). Lobo (or his clone) later joins R.E.B.E.L.S. (the Revolutionary Elite Brigade to Eradicate L.E.G.I.O.N. Supremacy), a group formed by Dox after his renegade son Lyrl takes over L.E.G.I.O.N. (*R.E.B.E.L.S.* #1, 1994).

After Lyrl Dox's defeat, Vril Dox II releases Lobo from R.E.B.E.L.S. (*R.E.B.E.L.S.* #6, 1995), whereupon the assassin resumes concentrating on freelance bounty hunting and personal business. When the radio station to which his brain-mounted receiver is tuned changes to an all soul-music format (deep-sixing Lobo's omnipresent favorite song), Lobo sells his soul (as sullied as it is) to a villain named Neron in exchange for having the radio receiver removed from his cranium; Lobo then shoots the disk jockey responsible for this crisis and immolates the radio station (*Lobo* vol. 2 #22, 1995).

Throughout the 1990s, Lobo's image was everywhere, appearing on countless trading cards, T-shirts (images of Lobo saying "Bite Me, Fanboy" were quite popular), figurines (including a beautiful sculpture based upon art by fan-favorite British Lobo artist Simon Bisley), buttons, and posters. He found his way into numerous best-selling comics miniseries and one-shot comics, including pairings with such DC mainstays as Superman, Batman, Deadman, and other companies' characters (such as Dark Horse's the Mask, Fleetway-Quality's Judge Dredd, and even an unholy one-issue merger with Marvel's Howard the Duck). Perhaps a victim of his own overexposure, Lobo's own ongoing series finally ended with issue #64 in 1999 (though a miniseries written by Giffen, *Lobo Unbound,* appeared in 2003 and 2004).

During Lobo's subsequent years on the guest-star circuit, variant replicas of the character have appeared, such as L'il Lobo, a "cute kid" version of the assassin (*Young Justice* #20, 2000), and Slo-Bo, a slower, weaker, genetically defective "wimpy" redaction of the much-feared assassin (*Young Justice* #38, 2001); these "tweaked" takes on Lobo were conceived by veteran comics writer and novelist Peter David and artist Todd Nauck as a way of fixing what David has characterized as one of the "worst characters of all time." But these recent radical changes weren't the first ones Lobo has undergone; in 1992, he had been briefly reincarnated as a woman, and was even transformed into a squirrel for a short time (*Lobo's Back* #3). But whatever alterations Lobo's many creative handlers may have in store for him in the future, one core principle remains as dependable as the assassin's penchant for bad behavior: his dogged persistence. When Lobo is on the job, he allows absolutely nothing and no one to stand in his way. *—MAM*

Love Interests

"Comic books are for boys," chimed the traditional mindset during the infancy of the comics medium, its illustrious Golden Age (1938–1954), hence the overwhelming number of *male* superheroes. Outside of the occasional superheroine gender-bending the locked doors of this muscular boys club, in the earliest superhero adventures women were depicted as damsels in distress or femme fatales. Matters romantic were of no interest to the lads looking for escapism amid the turmoil of the Great Depression and World War II.

Yet romance remains an integral component of heroic fiction—what is Tarzan without Jane?—and the purveyors of this nascent entertainment form realized that love makes the world go 'round, even for those who occupy their spare time swooping from rooftops in capes and cowls. The majority of Golden Age superheroes in both comics and pulps were assigned significant others by their writers—the Shadow's Margo Lane, the original (not the Marvel Comics character) Daredevil's Tonia, and the Flash's Joan Williams (whom he later married)—but these characters were largely confined to the background.

SUPERMAN'S GIRLFRIENDS

Not so with Lois Lane, however. When Jerry Siegel and Joe Shuster introduced Superman—the character that defined the superhero in popular culture—in *Action Comics* #1 (1938), Lane was along for the ride. She was conceived as the Man of Steel's romantic interest, but not portrayed as such, the creators steering clear of such "sissy stuff." But the subtext was there: Each time the brash young Superman rescued the gallant "girl reporter" from peril, he outwardly admonished her recklessness, but inwardly admired her spunk and courage. Theirs was a taboo love, and a flirtatious one, for many decades. Everyone thought of Lois Lane as "Superman's girlfriend," but during the

1950s and 1960s she showed her affection by either trying to expose the hero's Clark Kent identity or by publicly pining for him.

During the 1970s and 1980s, women's lib and the sexual revolution may have loosened the shackles on ladies in the real world, but Superman still kept Lane at arm's length, married instead to his duty. When the two consummated their relationship in the live-action film *Superman II* (1981), their passion came with a price: Superman (temporarily) forfeited his powers, and superpowered villains from his homeworld nearly decimated planet Earth while the former Man of Steel redecorated his Fortress of Solitude into a lover's pad.

By the time DC Comics rebooted Superman in *The Man of Steel* (1986), readers were mature enough to accept a full-blown relationship between the hero and the reporter—although it was Kent with whom Lane fell in love, having dismissed him as a nebbish in the previous continuity. Kent finally revealed his Superman identity to Lane in 1991 and married her in 1996. (The Superman of "Earth-Two," an alternate reality once housing DC's Golden Age heroes, married his world's Lois Lane in *Action Comics* #484 [1978], and the couple starred in the backup feature "Mr. and Mrs. Superman.")

This is not to say that Superman has only had (X-ray) eyes for Lane. Lana Lang was introduced as part of the hero's Superboy mythos as teenage Clark Kent's girlfriend, although no romantic relationship was ever explored: Lang was merely a *girl* who was a *friend.* In the Silver Age (1956–1969) and Bronze Age (1970–1979), the adult Lang periodically appeared in the Super*man* comics, and a Lois vs. Lana rivalry for Superman's (non-) affections ensued, a theme crucial to the plot of the movie *Superman III* (1983). Lang was redefined as Kent's high-school sweetheart in *The Man of Steel* (1986), and has received an increased profile in TV's *Superboy* (1988–1992) and *Smallville* (2001–present). Superman has had other passing relationships over the years, including a mermaid named Lori Lemaris, whom he dated in college. And in *Action* #600

(1988), the Man of Steel locked lips with Wonder Woman! (This idea was picked up on—and then some—in the popular alternate-universe series *Kingdom Come* [1996] and *The Dark Knight Strikes Again* [2001–2002], in which the pair conceive children.)

WONDER WOMAN'S ROMANTIC WOES

Her smooching with Superman aside, Wonder Woman's life has been relatively loveless. Colonel Steve Trevor, the "Lois Lane" to Wonder Woman's "Superman," was absolutely smitten over the star-spangled Amazon, overlooking the obvious: that she worked with him, each and every day, hiding her looks and statuesque form behind the cat-eyed glasses and military uniform of yeoman Diana Prince. But ever the good soldier, for years Trevor stormed the frontlines of love, hinting, suggesting, and falling short of begging for intimacy from the Amazon Princess. Wonder Woman was interested in Trevor, but reminded him that an Amazonian creed called "Aphrodite's law" forbade her to marry, else she would lose her powers and status among her exclusively female community.

In *Wonder Woman* comics from the 1940s and 1950s, the Amazon Princess was obviously stronger than Trevor (stronger than *twenty* Trevors, actually), but social mores often backed her into a corner of domesticity. She deflected bullets with her bracelets and heaved tanks with a mere shrug, then found time to pen personal advice to her readers in her letters column. Wonder Woman became even "softer" during the post–World War II romance comics boom, when publisher DC Comics attempted to attract girls to the character's comics. In his book *Wonder Woman: The Complete History* (2000), historian Les Daniels remarked of the cover to DC's *Sensation Comics* #94 (1949): "Wonder Woman was suddenly surrounded by mush, and she was in danger of sinking herself: the cover showed Steve Trevor carrying a simpering and seemingly helpless Princess Diana across a narrow stream."

In the 1960s, a succession of unorthodox suitors—amoeba-men, bird-men, mer-men, and space-men—traipsed through the *Wonder Woman* series. She stayed single, and Trevor stayed interested. Wonder Woman and Trevor actually *married* in 1986, as the heroine's title was canceled as part of DC's companywide "housecleaning" project, *Crisis on Infinite Earths*. The Amazon Princess was erased from existence in *Crisis* #12 (1986), and when she was introduced anew in 1987, Trevor had also been altered: He was now older and no longer a love interest, their previous marriage wiped away from continuity. In the years that have followed, other potential paramours—including fellow Justice Leaguers Aquaman and Batman—have waltzed through her life, but Wonder Woman remains the iconic single superheroine.

Among the superheroines who have fallen in love with normal men are two DC characters. The Silver Age Supergirl dated fellow student Dick Malverne while in her assumed identity of Linda Danvers, but Malverne went ga-ga over the Girl of Steel. And the Golden Age Black Canary, secretly flower-shop proprietor Dinah Drake, was sweet on hard-boiled private eye Larry Lance. Lance's sleuthing often dropped him into trouble, and Black Canary rushed to his rescue. It was later established that Drake and Lance had married, and that Lance had died. Shortly after Black Canary hopped from Earth-Two to the parallel reality of Earth-One, she encountered her new world's counterpart of her ex in her team-up with Batman in *The Brave and the Bold* (*B&B*) #91 (1970). But this Lance was not to be trusted, although lovesick Black Canary was oblivious to his shadiness. Batman warned her of his suspicions, but she scoffed, "I'm a woman first—and a super-heroine second! Don't try to ruin my new life!" Batman was right—Lance was no good—but soon the Canary was singing a new tune, in the arms of fellow Justice Leaguer Green Arrow.

ROMANTIC SIDEKICKS

The introduction of Batman's partner Robin the Boy Wonder in *Detective Comics* #38 (1940) inspired a host of superhero sidekicks, and some of them were actually the girlfriends of their male counterparts. Cat-Man, an adult male superhero, enlisted a prepubescent girl he called Kitten as his sidekick. Over the years, Kitten matured into quite the cutie, sparking catty commentary from more astute readers. The tiny hero Doll Man spent much of his time rescuing his partner Doll Girl from spider webs, but on the few occasions Doll Man has been seen since the Golden Age, Doll Girl has been mostly ignored. A more famous diminutive duo is Ant-Man and the Wasp, who buzzed through Marvel's *Tales to Astonish* in the early 1960s before becoming charter members of "Earth's Mightiest Heroes," the Avengers. Their relationship has not been easy—Henry Pym, the man behind the antennaed ant-helmet, has lived a life fraught with costume changes (he has also been known as Giant-Man, Goliath, and Yellowjacket) and mental illness.

Hawkgirl, Hawkman's companion, has earned her wings and remained alongside her feathered partner throughout numerous reinventions over the decades. During the Golden Age, she was mostly window dressing, sometimes flying alongside Hawkman on his escapades. But during Hawkman's Silver Age revival in *B&B* #34 (1961), Hawkgirl was reintroduced as more than a hanger-on—she was now Hawkman's wife and equal partner. While Hawkgirl presented an empowering female figure for the times, she did not restrain her jealousy in their origin story when an attractive lady naturalist set her claws into her hubby: "Could I see you for a moment, *please?*" her icy word balloon dripped when this intrusive vixen made her move.

Bulletgirl, partner to the Golden Age hero Bulletman, was no dud: When she discovered that her boyfriend was actually a superhero, she demanded to be let in on the fun. The Owl and Owl Girl? Contemporary readers would coo, "Who?" as that pair of heroic lovebirds has fluttered into oblivion. The Flame and Flame Girl have similarly flickered out, as have most of the similar male/female teams of the 1940s.

In 1956, Batman was assigned a superheroine love interest—heiress Kathy Kane, who adopted the masked guise of Batwoman—to allay charges of a homosexual relationship between the Caped Crusader and his young ally Robin. Before long, the teenage Bat-Girl appeared as a date for the Boy Wonder. But no romance ever blossomed between these heroes and heroines, and the ladies retired from crime fighting after only a few years in costume.

MILLIONAIRE PLAYBOYS

Batman and his alter ego, millionaire Bruce Wayne, have enjoyed a bevy of beauties as companions over the decades, but, like Wonder Woman, Batman remains a loner. As Wayne, the hero pretends to be a playboy, navigating the social circles of Gotham City as a ruse to create a persona in stark contrast to his grim cowled guise. Wayne's first girlfriend in the comics of the Golden Age was socialite Julie Madison, who disappeared before long—but made an appearance in the flesh, in the live-action movie *Batman & Robin* (1997). Vicki Vale had more staying power in the Batman mythos. She first made her presence known in Gotham in 1950, snapping news photos and interacting with both Wayne and Batman. Her persona was similar to Lois Lane's: a savvy, headstrong newshound with suspicions of Batman's secret identity. She reappeared sporadically in later decades, and was the love interest in the blockbuster film *Batman* (1989).

On Bruce Wayne's yacht in *Detective Comics* #469 (1977), the dapper playboy, wearing an ascot, makes his way through the crowd, encountering a glamazon with stark white hair. "Ah! The mysterious Mr. Wayne!" she calls, continuing, "I don't believe we've met! I'm Silver St. Cloud!" "I'll bet you are!" responds the playboy, not his snappiest come-on line, but it works—they're soon an item. When St. Cloud happens across a battle between Batman and the assassin Deadshot in issue #474 (1977), she gets a good look at the masked Dark Knight, and thinks, "It was Bruce!" The following issue, she

ponders whether or not to tell him she knows his secret, musing, "You're really my boyfriend, Batman! I can see what others would never notice—because I've spent so many evenings studying your jaw!" By *Detective* #476, after watching Batman nearly lose his life combating the Joker, St. Cloud confronts him with her knowledge of his dual identity, confesses her love, then leaves him, admitting she couldn't live with "never knowing what each night would bring." Silver St. Cloud was embraced by readers during her short stint in the Batman legend, but left the series with the departure of her creator, writer Steve Englehart. In the DC Comics continuity of the 1990s and 2000s, women in Batman's life have included Dr. Shondra Kinsolving and Vesper Fairchild, the latter of whom was murdered, with Wayne framed as the killer.

Bad girls have sometimes tempted Batman. The playful pilferer Catwoman has strutted in and out of the hero's life since her introduction in *Batman* #1 (1940). Their attraction has transcended comics, in the campy *Batman* TV series (1966–1988)—where actors Adam West and Julie Newmar relished their sexy on-screen romps in tights (with rumored off-screen romps *out* of tights)—and in the motion picture *Batman Returns* (1992). Talia, the fetching daughter of the international ecoterrorist Ra's al Ghul, has often invited Batman to hang up his cowl and become her mate, but other than occasional kisses, the hero's iron will has kept him from a relationship. In the graphic novel *Batman: Son of the Demon* (1987), Talia, in lingerie, seduces Batman by urging him to "Forego your control, your discipline … just once, let yourself go … and take me with you." He does, the end result being their child, who is given up for adoption. DC Comics courageously published this story, then later stepped away from acknowledging or reprinting it due to its controversial content. Other villainesses that Batman has found attractive include Poison Ivy, Nocturna, and the TV Bat-foe the Siren.

Marvel's Iron Man is actually industrialist Tony Stark, and has worn on his arm more trophy dates than Bruce Wayne could ever imagine. Pepper Potts was Stark's first girlfriend, and lasted longer in the stories than others who followed. While no millionaire, Wally West—who started his career as Kid Flash, before growing into the role of the Flash—is as fast with women as he is as a superhero: He has had more girlfriends than space allows to list. Another rich-man-by-day, masked-man-by-night is the Green Hornet, abetted in his day job (as a newspaper publisher) and his nightlife by his secretary, Lenore Case.

MR. AND MRS. SUPERHERO

Superman and Lois Lane may be the most famous husband-and-wife duo in the superhero world, but they aren't alone, and certainly weren't the first. DC's Aquaman married Mera, a crimson-haired beauty from a watery dimension, and together they ruled the undersea kingdom of Atlantis as king and queen. Frequent misfortunes tore apart their relationship, and at one time, in a deranged state, she tried to kill him. Marvel's underwater anti-hero, Prince Namor the Sub-Mariner, married his water-breathing, blue-skinned love Lady Dorma after a royal courtship, but her death left the avenging son of Atlantis even more vengeful.

Before Lady Dorma, another beauty won Namor's heart: Sue Storm, the Invisible Girl (later Woman) of the Fantastic Four. Sue was the girlfriend of "FF" team leader Reed Richards, a.k.a. Mr. Fantastic, but each time she saw the near-naked, powerful form of Namor, her heart pitter-pattered. In *Fantastic Four* #6 (1961), she defends the subsea man after another of his rampages: "Oh, he isn't our enemy! I just know it! He's so full of pain and bitterness that it blinds his better instincts." Sue's wandering eye finally focused on Richards, and they were wed in *FF Annual* #3 (1965), in which she beams to her husband, "We're married, at last! And nothing will ever part us, my beloved."

The Elongated Man, the ductile detective whose expansive ego led him to publicly reveal his true

identity of Ralph Dibny, is joined on his adventures by his jetsetting wife Sue. Sue has grown to enjoy her stretching hubby's nose for mysteries, and helps manage his superheroic affairs. Earthman Adam Strange traveled light years through space to the planet Rann to be with Alanna, the lovely daughter of that world's chief scientist. Originally, his treks were the result of the otherworldly "Zeta Beam" that teleported him through the cosmos, but eventually he spent more time on Rann with Alanna as his bride. Kit Walker, the latest in the long ancestral chain of jungle heroes known as the Phantom, married the feisty Diana Palmer, with whom he has had two children. Kit Jr., their son, is destined to replace his father in the purple garb of the "Ghost Who Walks." After a lengthy engagement, slowpoke Barry Allen—better known as the Silver Age Flash—married Iris West, but did not reveal his dual identity to her until some time later. And Tempest, DC's hero once known as Aqualad (sidekick to Aquaman), was in love with Tula, a.k.a. Aquagirl, but after her unfortunate death found himself walking down the aisle with Dolphin, a former lover of Aquaman. Hawkeye, the bowman of Marvel's Avengers, was led astray into crime by the Russian spy Black Widow. Hawkeye went straight, and after meeting the superheroine (and also reformed outlaw) Mockingbird, cupid's arrow struck and the two were married.

Another famous couple in the superhero community is Mr. and Mrs. Peter Parker, or Spider-Man and Mary Jane Watson. As a teen, Parker was a hopeless geek before a bite from an irradiated spider made him one of the most famous superheroes in the world. Through the soap opera injected into his series, *The Amazing Spider-Man* vol. 1, by writer Stan Lee and artist/co-plotter Steve Ditko, Parker engaged in several romances before marrying Mary Jane. His first love was Betty Brant, the secretary of Parker's boss, *Daily Bugle* publisher J. Jonah Jameson. Though slightly older than Parker, Brant was impressed with the youth's intellect and sensitivity, but her own personal problems interfered with their becoming a couple. Liz Allan was the girlfriend of

Parker's high-school nemesis, the bully Flash Thompson. Allan had a crush on Parker, recognizing the same attributes that Brant did.

When Parker started college and met Gwen Stacy, he could keep his mind on little else. His Aunt May pressured him to meet her friend's niece, Mary Jane, but Parker resisted, and a series of comical near-misses ensued through numerous issues of *Amazing Spider-Man.* When Parker could no longer duck out on his aunt's machinations and finally met Watson, he was floored to find a gorgeous, lively redhead standing on his doorstep: "Face it, tiger. You hit the jackpot," she audaciously grinned. He was interested in Watson, but remained in love with Stacy. In *Amazing Spider-Man* #100 (1971), Parker reflects, "Maybe I'm beginning to realize there's more to life than being a corny costumed clown. So I might as well admit it! I know what I want. And Gwen Stacy is it." He creates a serum to eradicate his spiderpowers, in hopes of living a normal life, but the untested potion causes him to grow four extra arms, making him even more a spider-man! That problem was soon rectified, but he shortly lost his beloved Gwen at the hands of the villainous Green Goblin. He later began dating, then married, "MJ," although their relationship has been nothing short of tumultuous.

WORKPLACE ROMANCES AND HEARTACHES

Team-ups have long been a staple of superhero stories, and at times the connection between two heroes has gone beyond a shared mission. The aforementioned Ant-Man/Wasp and Green Arrow/Black Canary liaisons were forged in camaraderie, as was the love between Scott Summers, a.k.a. Cyclops, and Jean Grey, a.k.a. Marvel Girl (and later Phoenix), of Marvel's X-Men. For years they were inseparable, but after Grey had apparently died, Summers married and became a father. Their relationship was part of a romantic triangle in the live-action movies *X-Men* (2000) and *X2: X-Men*

United (2003), including a strong, almost feral attraction between Grey and the roguish Wolverine.

Doctor Strange, Marvel's "Master of the Mystic Arts," became involved with the sorceress Clea. DC's futuristic superteam the Legion of Super-Heroes, a virtual army of powerful teens, has long bred romance among members; A few examples include Lightning Lad and Saturn Girl, Brainiac 5 and Supergirl, Bouncing Boy and Duo Damsel, Star Boy and Dream Girl, and Ultra Boy and Phantom Girl. When Gotham City's Dick Grayson fought crime alongside Batman as Robin the Boy Wonder, he met the second Batgirl (Barbara Gordon), and over time formed a partnership with her out from under his mentor's wing. Maturing into the solo hero Nightwing, Grayson and Oracle—the information broker that Gordon has become—have sometimes been an item.

Pity poor Norrin Radd—once Radd sacrificed his humanity to spare his planet Zenn-La from the hunger of Galactus by becoming his herald the Silver Surfer, he bade a tearful farewell to his beloved Shal-la Bal. She laments, "Never has there been … never will there be … another … such as you!" This scene, playing out in Marvel's *Silver Surfer* vol. 1 #1 (1968), did not end after the Surfer streaked into the depths of outer space: He pined and whined for her through numerous subsequent adventures. Hal Jordan, the Silver Age Green Lantern, was similarly unlucky in love. His girlfriend (and employer), Carol Ferris, was corrupted into supervillainy as Star Sapphire.

For some superheroes, love is blind. Heiress Sapphire Stagg seems unbothered by the fact that her boyfriend, adventurer Rex Mason, has been mutated into the freakish DC hero Metamorpho the Element Man. Wyatt Wingfoot, a strapping, Native American friend of the Fantastic Four, was not bothered by the fact that his girlfriend was a green giantess: She-Hulk. And Marvel's mutant enchantress called the Scarlet Witch married the synthetic humanoid known as the Vision.

Perhaps no superhero has had a thornier love life than Marvel's Man without Fear, Daredevil. When secretary Karen Page trips and falls into the arms of blind lawyer Matt Murdock in *Daredevil* #7 (1965), Murdock—secretly Daredevil—wishes, "If only—you could stay this way—forever!" He changed his tune in the 1980s, when Page, then a strung-out junkie, sold the secret of his Daredevil identity for the price of a fix. His next girlfriend, the Black Widow, had since relin-

quished her villainous ways and they shared a relatively normal rapport. When Elektra, Murdock's former college lover, returned to his life, the results were disastrous—Elektra had become an assassin, on a collision course with the law-abiding Daredevil. —*ME*

Luke Cage: *See* **Power Man**

Madara

Madara is the title character of *Spirit War Madara,* an action/adventure fantasy that first appeared in Japan in 1987. First serialized in *Famicon Journal,* the series later expanded to an OVA (Original Video Animation) series and video game; together, all three elements made up the multimedia franchise called the "Madara Project." In the world of *Madara,* magic and technology co-exist—characters sport cybernetic enhancements but can also perform spells of varying power. It is also a tale of a son's revenge against his father.

Madara appears to be a normal, rambunctious teenager, the son of Tatara, the Holy Elder of a small village. Beneath the surface is a tragic beginning: Madara is actually the son of Emperor Miroku and Princess Sakuya, but he was sacrificed by his father to Mazoku (a powerful demon on par with the devil) to forestall a prophecy that foretold Miroku's downfall. Miroku did not stop there—he divided the infant Madara's *chakkera* (the points of energy within the body) among his generals. The ninth *chakkera*—Madara's spirit—was stolen by the kind-hearted Hakutaku and, in a manner similar to Moses, was placed in a basket on a river, later to be found by village Elder Tatara.

Tatara fashioned a bionic "gimmick" body for Madara and raised him.

Years later, now a teenager, Madara receives a new gimmick body, but this is a "Battle" gimmick, equipped with blades and electrified cables. When Miroku's troops invade his village, Madara fights them with the power of his gimmick body and the magical sword Shinken Kusanagi. When Tatara is mortally wounded, he tells Madara of his origins, and that he can only regain his real body by killing Miroku's generals who have his eight *chakkera.* As each general is killed, Madara regains parts of his real body, but he grows physically weaker. In terms of experience and mental strength, he grows stronger, for he will need these skills to confront and defeat his father.

Madara is a cyborg, a hybrid of humanity and technology. The use of cyborgs as superheroes first appeared in Japan in the 1960s in works created by Shotaro Ishinomori. His works—primarily *Cyborg 009, Kamen Rider* (Masked Rider), and *Jinzo Ningen Kikaider* (Artificial Human Kikaider)—have cyborgs as the main characters. Like the heroes of Ishinomori's works, Madara wants to regain his humanity. While his cyborg abilities make him stronger than the average human, they also make him different, an outcast, and he longs to be a "normal" human being. One could take this as a commentary on Japanese culture, with its emphasis on being a part of the whole, or working for the good of all. Renegades or those who stand out have a very difficult time in what is largely a homogeneous society.

During his quest, Madara gains several important allies, including Kaze Hime ("Wind Princess") and the powerful warriors Majin Souen and Gufu. Miroku's generals include the giant batlike creature Kajula, On Kai Yoma (who resembles a gigantic eyeball with tentacles), and Jyato. Despite his appearance—he looks like a walking, talking rabbit—Jyato is evil to the core, and was Tatara's killer. Due to his bloodline, Madara can utilize the spiritual energy within himself, and using the power of the Shinken Kusanagi causes the image of a dragon to appear on his forehead. The image also marks him as the legitimate heir to Miroku.

The original concept for *Madara* was credited to Eiji Otsuka, but the art and story for the manga was done by Sho-u Tajima (who would later create the more contemporary manga *Brothers*). At times, Hidetomo Aga assisted with monster designs. The concept of *Madara* was similar, however, to Osamu Tezuka's 1967–1968 manga *Dororo,* except that the latter was set in feudal Japan, with the hero Hyakimaru fighting monsters based on Japanese mythology. *Dororo* was made into an animated series in 1969. *Madara* itself was a success; in the 1990s an OVA series based on the manga was made, as well as a video game for the Super Famicon (the original Japanese name for the Super Nintendo) video game system. Bandai Entertainment and MOVIC Studio were responsible for the animation. In May 2003, the anime distributor Media Blasters released the OVA series in the United States. —*MM*

Madman

Of the scores of new superheroes introduced during the 1990s, Michael Dalton Allred's Madman is one of the hippest and most stylish. Rendered in a sim-

ple yet expressive manner—running decidedly counter to the stoic, overembelished, and exaggeratedly muscular style that became endemic to mainstream *fin de siècle* superhero comics—Madman's premiere issue (*Madman* #1, Tundra, 1992) gave the world its first glimpse of Frank Einstein, the man behind the mask of Madman. Allred's creation, beautifully colored by his wife Laura, was one of the first superheroes designed for the ironic sensibilities of twentysomething postmodern comics readers—an audience that would undoubtedly show little interest in standard superhero fare.

Reanimated after death by Dr. Egon Boiffard and Dr. Gillespie Flem, a pair of mad scientists worthy of inclusion in the cast of *Buckaroo Banzai,* the man destined to become Madman awakens with almost no memories. Unable to recall his real identity, he adopts the name Frank Einstein (which sounds a little like "Frankenstein" if spoken too quickly); he also finds himself gifted with unpredictable psychic powers (including prophetic dreams and an intermittent sense of danger or security that Einstein describes as "spiritual inner eye awareness"), heightened agility, an apparently instinctual ability to survive being attacked, and an irrational hatred for beatniks. Clearly, Einstein's life isn't as simple as that of most mainstream superheroes. For starters, he is full of unanswered (and perhaps unanswerable) questions about his identity prior to his death. And being a reanimated corpse, he is rather unattractive. Einstein's personal insecurities and neuroses drive him to garb himself in a pajama-like white costume with a red lighting bolt/exclamation point motif; the outfit includes a white mask, intended for vanity's sake rather than for the protection of a secret identity. Despite his extraordinary abilities and his mask—worn only to bolster Madman's poor self-esteem—Einstein does not think of himself as a superhero.

After Dr. Boiffard dies at the hands of Monstadt, a lunatic seeking immortality, Einstein embarks on a desperate quest to restore life to his friend and benefactor, while also fighting to rescue his girlfriend Joe (Josephine Lombard) and Dr. Flem from some menacing monsters. Succeeding in his mission, Einstein discovers his innate propensity for heroism, and begins routinely defending Snap City—an ultrahip urbis that lies somewhere between the 1939 World's Fair retrofuturity of Scott McCloud's *Zot!* and the quotidian skyline of the Mort Weisenger–era Superman (not to mention Allred's own post–Grunge Pacific Northwest *milieu*)—from every imaginable super-menace. Because of his death-addled memory, Snap City is the only place Einstein can even vaguely remember having called home; he loves the town, describing it as "a groovy place where just about *anything* can happen."

Immediately dubbed "the Madman of Snap City" because of his weird, corpselike appearance and his strange turns of phrase (fairly typical of Einstein are such utterances as "Meanies never win. And you can quote me on that."), Einstein finds himself regularly squaring off against rogue robots, late-show monsters (including a vomit-beast known as the Puke), and crazed beatniks, with a little help from gal-pal Joe and an alien called Mott (a native of the planet Hoople, a reference to one of Allred's favorite 1970s bands). Unlike virtually anyone else in the superhero trade, his signature weapons include a hollowed-out, lead-filled Duncan yo-yo and a slingshot, lending a fair amount of credence to the "Madman" moniker.

After producing six issues of *Madman* in 1992 series for small-press publishers Tundra and Kitchen Sink (winning the 1993 Harvey Award for Best New Series), and three issues of *Madman Adventures* for Tundra in 1993, Allred took his concept to Dark Horse Comics, a haven for creator-owned properties since its founding in 1985. Dark Horse furnished Allred's stylishly bizarre hero with a much larger audience than ever before with a new series, *Madman Comics,* which debuted in 1994. Madman's new outing was well received despite frequent and lengthy lapses between issues, especially toward the end of its twenty-issue run (December 2000). Madman teamed up—and briefly switched

Madman #1 © & ™ 1992 Michael Allred.
COVER ART BY MICHAEL ALLRED.

bodies—with DC Comics' Superman in *Superman/Madman Hullabaloo!,* a three-issue miniseries released in 1997. Two years later, Dark Horse released *Madman/The Jam,* a two-issue miniseries that paired Allred and his character with another postmodern hero (with the participation of Bernie Mireault, the Jam's creator).

After nearly dying at Monstadt's hands in the horror-detective yarn presented in *Madman Comics: The G-Men from Hell* (four issues, 2000), Madman became part of Snap City's first superhero group in *The Atomics* (AAA Pop Comics, 2000). Allred wrote and drew this title with obvious affection for the Silver Age (1956–1969) artistic powerhouse Jack

Kirby, though filtered through a postmodern, somewhat tongue-in-cheek lens. In *The Atomics,* Madman finally makes peace with the beatniks he has fought over the years, and helps change several of them from alien spore–infected mutants into a fledgling team of mismatched heroes nostalgically reminiscent of early issues of Marvel Comics' *Fantastic Four* or *Avengers.* Among Madman's new super-companions are the stretchable Mister Gum (better known by Snap City's populace, unfortunately, as the Booger), the Slug (a purple mutant with protuberant eyestalks), the Iron Man–like Metalman, and the enigmatic and acne-afflicted teenage time-traveler known as Zap-Man. *The Atomics* concluded its run in 2001 after fifteen issues.

Unable to remain within the confines of comics and trade paperback reprints, Madman's likeness has found its way onto T-shirts, candy bars, lunch boxes, action figures, and even Zippo lighters. Hollywood has also taken notice of the character, with the release of *G-Men from Hell* (2000), a Madman-based film directed by Christopher Coppola (brother of actor Nicolas Cage and nephew of director Francis Ford Coppola), from a screenplay written by Richard L. Albert and Michael Allred himself. Various Atomics characters and Madman himself have returned for one-shots from 2002 to the present, and another, big-budget *Madman* film from director Robert Rodriguez has been in development since the early 2000s. —*MAM*

Mai, the Psychic Girl

During the 1980s, the comic-book industry in America experienced what could only be called a creative renaissance. New companies—the independents—arose and offered titles, such as *Mage* and *American Flagg!* that went far beyond the typical superhero fare. Even the venerable DC universe underwent a major revision with the *Crisis on Infinite Earths* miniseries that led to revamped versions of major heroes including Superman, Batman, and Wonder Woman. Writer/artist Frank Miller brought a gritty, hard-edged tone to Marvel's *Daredevil* and went on to create the dark, futuristic Batman tale *The Dark Knight Returns.* From England, writer Alan Moore delivered two groundbreaking titles, *Miracleman* and *Watchmen.*

Another revolution was slowly beginning during that time: the influx of Japanese manga into America, adapted into English. First Publications began publishing a translated version of the classic *Lone Wolf and Cub* by Kazuo Koike and the late Goseki Kojima. In 1987, Eclipse Comics joined with Viz Communications to publish three manga titles (later expanded to four) that introduced many readers into the diverse world of Japanese comics. The titles were *The Legend of Kamui; Area 88; Mai, the Psychic Girl;* and *Heavy Metal Warrior Xenon.* Viz had been founded as an American subsidiary of Shogakukan, one of the largest publishers of manga. The titles released by Eclipse and Viz had originally been published in Japanese by Shogakukan in either the bi-weekly comics magazines *Big Comics* or *Shonen* (Boys) *Sunday Comics.* *Big Comics'* target audience was adult males, with teenage boys being the primary audience for *Shonen Sunday.*

Of the four titles, *Mai, the Psychic Girl* by Kazuya Kudo (story) and Ryoichi Ikegami (art) is the closest to a "superhero" tale, but the title goes beyond the standard superhero story. *Mai* at its core is a coming-of-age story, with a young schoolgirl dealing with a tremendous power, and facing an organization that believes in nothing less than the destruction of the world to suit a nefarious purpose. The title has its origins in Shogakukan's *Shonen Sunday* comic magazine. This in itself is unusual, because the primary character is a girl. Another unusual element is the presence of both a writer and artist; normally, it is the artist who both draws and writes in manga. Kazuya Kudo himself is a popular writer (another title written by him, *Pineapple Army,* was later translated into English and released in America by Viz). Ryoichi Ikegami is well known in Japan for his realistic art style, and counts American comic artist Neal Adams as an important influence. Beginning with *AIUEO Boy* and *Otoko Gumi* (Male Gang) in 1973 and 1974, respectively, Ikegami would collaborate with many of the top manga writers. Strangely enough, in the 1970s, Ikegami created the art for a *Spider-Man* manga, which was released in America in the 1990s by Marvel Comics.

Mai ran for fifty-three chapters in *Shonen Sunday.* Mai Kuju, on the surface, is a typical fourteen-year old Japanese schoolgirl who hangs out with her friends, is slightly boy-crazy and is facing the trials of puberty. She lives with her father, Shuichi, an executive of the Marubishi Trading Company. Mai's mother Maki had passed away some years earlier. Below the surface, however, lies a secret: Mai possesses great psychic powers, the strongest being psychokinesis. The powers were passed on to her by her mother, and while at the start of the story Mai uses them in a playful manner—such as dropping pinecones or stopping a baseball thrown by a pitcher—the story soon takes a serious turn. The Wisdom Alliance, a secret international organization headed by Shogen Ryu, has targeted Mai and four other teenagers with psychic powers—Baion Yuwon, David Perry, Turm Garten, and Grall Hong—and has placed them under surveillance. Shuichi Kuju, returning from a trip to America, has uncovered this, as well as the Wisdom Alliance's ultimate goal. He flees with Mai, pursued by the agents of the Wisdom Alliance, but he and Mai are separated, and Mai believes that her father is dead. She is helped by a college student named Intetsu, and by Senzo Kaieda—a former ally of the Wisdom Alliance who turns against them to protect Mai—and Kaieda's monstrous bodyguard Tsukiro.

The Wisdom Alliance sends the other four psychic children to find Mai and capture her by any means possible. Eventually, Mai does find her father, who reveals the Wisdom Alliance's ultimate goal: to start a worldwide nuclear war at 9:09 A.M. on September 9, 1999, and use the psychic children to start a new race of humans. In a final battle over the city of Tokyo, Mai must confront David Perry and Baion Yuwon in a fight to the death; she alone will decide Earth's destiny by promising Shogen Ryu that she will do everything in her power to prevent the Wisdom Alliance's goal of nuclear war.

For American readers, Kudo and Ikegami's story certainly was not the typical superhero fare; Mai does not wear a costume, and is, at times, made brutally aware that using her powers has consequences. One sequence in particular shows Mai saving a young puppy, Ron, with her power, but at the same time causing a major traffic accident. Along with telekinesis and telepathy, Mai's powers also include psychic blasts of immense power, and she is capable of flight. Mai also matures as a character, despite her young age. Ikegami's art was a major draw for the series, with a more realistic look than most manga. Many of the characters have a tragic secret in their past, such as Kaieda, who reveals late in the series that Tsukiro is his own son, turned into a beast-man due to an experiment that he himself approved.

Eclipse and Viz began publishing *Mai* as a fifty-three-issue bi-weekly series in 1987. James D. Hudnall (*Strikeforce: Moritori*) and Satoru Fuji translated and adapted the series into English, and Wayne Truman performed the art touch-up and lettering. Some scenes featuring nudity were cut from the earlier issues, but were restored when Viz released a four-volume graphic novel collection of the series from 1989 to 1990. A three-volume "Perfect Collection" was released by Viz in 1996. *Mai* was well received by critics and readers in America—more so than in its native land; many praised the series for avoiding typical superhero clichés and for also introducing many readers to the world of manga. The series was translated into several other languages, including French and Spanish. While there was never an animated adaptation, there were plans for a live-action film, but they never came to fruition.

Mai stood as an important first step in the gradual popularity of manga in America. Today, dozens of manga titles are available in bookstores and comics shops around the United States, and Viz has become one of the largest companies adapting manga for American readers. Ryoichi Ikegami is one of the most popular manga artists among American readers, and translated versions of his later works, such as *Crying Freeman* (with Kazuo Kioke), *Samurai Crusader,* and the eerily accurate political thriller *Sanctuary* (written by Sho Fumimura), have been very successful. He was a featured guest at the 1995 San Diego Comic-Con, where he was awarded the prestigious Ink Pot Award. It was also at that year's Comic-Con that Ikegami participated in a panel discussion with his idol, Neal Adams. —*MM*

The Man from Atlantis

After a severe storm, the body of a man is found on the beach. Dr. Elizabeth Merrill tries to help save the man at the U.S. Navy hospital, only to find that he has gills, and webbed hands and feet! The man revives in water, and consents to weeks of tests at the Naval Underwater Center; after all, he cannot remember who he is or where he came from. Merrill dubs him "Mark Harris," and learns that he has extraordinary strength and speed in the water, although he'll die if he stays out of the water for too long. Soon, Harris is dragooned into aiding the navy look for a missing submarine, in the process crossing paths with the dangerous megalomaniacal scientist Dr. Schubert. Eventually, Harris agrees to continue aiding Dr. Merrill and the scientists of the Foundation for Oceanic Research. Traveling in the specialized submersible dubbed "Cetacean," Merrill and her crew help Mark fight danger and villains, as well as look for clues to his origins … which may well be connected to the lost city of Atlantis!

The Man from Atlantis debuted on NBC as a two-hour pilot film on March 4, 1977. Relative unknown Patrick Duffy starred in the title role, often wearing little but swim trunks marked with a curlicue symbol. When underwater, he swam with an undulating style that resembled the swimming of dolphins, contributing to his otherworldliness. Belinda J. Montgomery played Merrill, who had a low-key romantic interest in Harris, while Victor Buono played recurring villain Schubert. The character of Mark Harris was similar enough to that of Marvel Comics' Sub-Mariner to negatively affect plans to develop that property as a series; ironically, in 1978, Marvel published a licensed *Man from Atlantis* comic book that ran for seven issues! Four tie-in novels were also published.

Because ratings were strong for the pilot film, NBC commissioned three further telefilms to air in May and June 1977, all featuring the same cast. A semi-regular *Man from Atlantis* series showed up in the fall, but NBC scheduled it haphazardly, preempting it constantly and changing nights that it aired. The *Man from Atlantis* stories ranged all over the map, with aliens, mad scientists, natural disasters, alternate dimensions, giants, doubles in a time-shifted Wild West, and even Romeo and Juliet taking roles in the ongoing saga! Whether the victim of bizarre stories or headache-inducing scheduling from NBC, after four telefilms and thirteen hour-long episodes, *Man from Atlantis* sank below the waves, never to be heard from again. —*AM*

Manhunter

In a career that has spanned some sixty years and featured more changes than a chameleon, Manhunter's finest hour is still considered to be a revered but brief seven-part revival in the mid-1970s. Manhunter was launched in the already overcrowded pages of *Adventure Comics* #58 in 1941, as a sort of plain-clothes private eye who specialized in tracing missing persons. Those stories about Paul Kirk (the Manhunter of the title) were engaging enough, but the fans wanted superheroes, which is exactly what the incoming writer/artist team of Joe Simon and Jack Kirby delivered. Following the death of a policeman friend, Kirk vows to avenge him and—between panels—conjures up a red costume with a blue mask, and sets about beating up all and sundry.

For the next eight issues, Simon and Kirby served up page after page of nonstop action, with the Manhunter taking on hoods, lowlifes, and the occasional Nazi. There were rarely any attempts at characterization or exposition; readers never learned what Kirk does to earn a living beyond being either a big-game hunter or young sportsman and, as long as the stories were exciting, they didn't care. However, when Simon and Kirby left the strip to concentrate on the Boy Commandoes, the life went out of the strip and it was soon canceled.

Thirty years later, in 1973, editor Archie Goodwin and young artist Walt Simonson started work on a series of short stories in the back of DC's *Detective Comics*, once again starring Paul Kirk, Manhunter. This revival recounted how Kirk had been injured in 1946 and kept in suspended animation by a secret cabal of scientists, until he was revived twenty-five years later as a sort of super-mercenary. Goodwin and Simonson had become fascinated with Japanese culture, and the strip is full of black-clad Ninjas, Shuriken throwing stars, and innovative multi-paneled storytelling. Even Manhunter's costume was revolutionary—a cross between a Samurai suit and an exoskeleton, complete with Mauser pistol and vicious knives. The story revolved around Manhunter turning on his masters and trekking halfway around the globe, through the Himalayas, Marakesh, and Constantinople, ending up in Gotham City in an inevitable tangle with Batman.

Mixing filmic influences, tight plotting, exciting art, and international espionage, the strip was an immense critical success, winning numerous fan awards. Fearful of lesser talents picking up the strip at a later date, Goodwin had the courage to kill off his Manhunter in a literally explosive finale. Even so, each decade since the strip's demise has fittingly seen a new collection, keeping it in print for successive generations of readers. As of 2004 Kirk stayed dead but, of course, that does not guarantee that fans have heard the last of the Manhunter name—far from it.

Barely a year after the *Detective Comics* series, Kirby dreamed up a new Manhunter, public defender Mark Shaw (appearing in 1975's *First Issue Special* #5), who was recruited into a secret society of superlawmen. Kirby's reinvention clearly owed a lot to the Phantom in its vision of a race of law enforcers stretching back through the centuries, but it was to be this Manhunter's only appearance—for a few years, at least. The Manhunter cult was revived in a late 1970s issue of *Justice League,* and the 1980s saw a flurry of Manhunters, initially starring in the complex *Millennium* comic in which android Manhunters attacked just about every DC character in print. This led to a continuing Manhunter comic for the first time in the character's history, which followed up *Millennium* in an equally bewildering way. Clearly believing that you could never have too many Manhunters, DC brought out yet another version in 1994, but this incarnation was a musician who appeared to have been possessed by a supernatural creature called the Huntsman. Its edgy approach included the beloved hero selling his soul to the devil (cue the sound of the fine, upstanding Paul Kirk turning in his grave) and, perhaps unsurprisingly, the strip failed to find an audience.

Meanwhile, since only a few years after the original Kirk was in that grave, writers have been picking up on the Goodwin/Simonson series' device of antagonistic clones made by the same shadowy organization that revived Kirk. First, a renegade clone led the short-lived mid-1970s *Secret Society of Super-Villains* in their comic, and much later a less dastardly Kirk duplicate joined the commercial superteam *The Power Company* in the early 2000s. However, come and go as Manhunter(s) undoubtedly always will, it is Goodwin and Simonson's masterpiece that will forever have a place in the hearts of true comics fans. —*DAR*

Manimal

Professor Jonathan "J. C." Chase (portrayed by actor Simon MacCorkindale) appeared to be a suave and sophisticated professor teaching animal behavioral sciences at New York University, or aiding the police investigations of animal-related crimes. But at night—or in times of danger—he could utilize a superpower he had inherited from his father, turning from man into animal, becoming the superhero known as Manimal. Often becoming a panther, a hawk, a snake, a horse, or a cat, Chase would use his shape-changing abilities to stop criminals, such as smuggling ambassadors, Russian spies, and horse thieves. His secret was known to only two people: an African-American Vietnam veteran friend of his named Tyrone C. Earl (first Glyn Turman, later Michael D. Roberts), and a pretty police detective/budding love interest named Brook McKenzie (Melody Anderson).

One of the most unusual superhero shows to air on television, *Manimal* debuted on NBC on September 30, 1983, with an extra-length pilot film. The show was created by Glen A. Larson, no stranger to either the noncostumed superhero genre or the sci-fi/horror realm. *Manimal* featured excellent special effects and makeup work, as a huffing and puffing Chase would transform into animals on-camera, mostly through quick-cut close-ups. Unfortunately, even the large budget didn't allow for many exotic changes, meaning viewers were shown the same transformation scenes in various episodes. Despite its slick look and cool premise, *Manimal* was canceled after one telefilm and seven episodes.

The character didn't completely disappear, however. In worldwide syndication the show was a hit, particularly in France. And in 1998, Larson was doing well with the second season of the syndicated superhero series *NightMan*. In a November episode titled "Manimal," NightMan met Jonathan Chase and his daughter, Teresa Chase (Carly Pope). She discovered that she had inherited her father's powers, and a knack for fighting crime as well. Professor Chase was on hand to help NightMan and his daughter catch a time-traveling Jack the Ripper! Unfortunately, neither Manimal nor his daughter (Womanimal?) proved successful enough to growl up a new pilot, and *Manimal* retreated back into the zoo of obscurity. —*AM*

Martian Manhunter

Although the debut of DC Comics' second Flash (*Showcase* #4, 1956) is universally regarded as the start of the Silver Age of comics (1956–1969), J'onn J'onzz the Martian Manhunter—a second-string superhero—predates the Flash by nearly a year. Created by writer Joe Samachson (scripter of many Seven Soldiers of Victory and Sandman tales for DC) and artist Joe Certa (who had drawn DC's Robotman and Fawcett's Captain Marvel Jr.) as a backup feature for Batman and Robin (*Detective Comics* #225, 1955), the Manhunter is accidentally teleported to Earth from his native Mars by Professor Mark Erdel, whose "robot brain" has locked onto him from across the unknown depths of time and space. Terrified by the sudden appearance of J'onn J'onzz—a thick-browed, nearly seven-foot, 300-pound green humanoid—the professor immediately keels over dead, leaving the Martian stranded on Earth. Altering his appearance with his natural shape-changing abilities, the Martian assumes human form, anglicizes his name to "John Jones," and takes on a day job as a terrestrial police detective, using his innate telepathic powers to trick his human colleagues into believing that they already know him. In his spare time, J'onzz uses his other talents—invisibility, flight (derived from telekinesis), superstrength, superspeed, and "Martian vision" (similar to Superman's heat-vision)—in a relentless war against both street criminals and costumed villains. His major weakness is fire; just as kryptonite is Superman's Achilles' heel, the Manhunter is powerless in the presence of open flames.

During his first few years on Earth, J'onzz uses his invisibility power to conceal his superheroics, and relies mainly on his detective skills to solve crimes (his feature *was* in *Detective Comics,* after all). This changed in 1959 (*Detective Comics* #273), when he lost his ability to use his other powers while invisible. His existence subsequently becomes common knowledge, and he becomes widely known as the Martian Manhunter. This leads to his eventual decision to ditch not only his "John Jones" identity (at first in favor of whatever human form the crisis *du jour* requires him to take) but to stop adopting human guises altogether in favor of full-time superheroics in his alien form. His demeanor is distant and logical, a classic "outsider" personality that anticipates *Star Trek*'s Mr. Spock by more than a decade.

With J'onzz's identity changes still underway during his *Detective* run, J'onzz found himself in the hands of writer Gardner Fox and artist Mike Sekowsky, serving double duty as a charter member of the Justice League of America (*The Brave and the Bold* #28–#30, 1960; *Justice League of America* #1, 1960), DC editor Julius Schwartz's wildly successful revival of the defunct 1940s superteam the Justice Society (also written by Fox, this feature had ended in *All-Star Comics* #57, 1951). It is only in this capacity—as a supporting character in an ensemble title—that the Martian Manhunter finally began appearing on comic-book covers. While J'onzz remained a major player in the JLA, his *Detective Comics* run ended in 1964 with issue #326, with the Elongated Man (a future JLA member) taking his place; two months later, the Man-

hunter's feature resurfaced in the pages of *The House of Mystery* (beginning in issue #143), a title that had previously run only anthology-style horror, science-fiction, and fantasy tales. Now helming his own feature and commanding a spot on each issue's cover, J'onzz had definitely moved up in his adopted world. Unfortunately, the character proved not to be quite the draw DC had hoped, and he lost his cover slot to a new lead feature, *Dial 'H' for Hero* (*House of Mystery* #156, 1966). The following year, J'onzz found himself bereft of even back-page status (as of *House of Mystery* #174) and had only the Justice League's headquarters to call home.

Thanks to the flybys of Mars performed by the Mariner spacecraft in the 1960s, planetologists—as well as the comics readership—became aware that the real Mars was incompatible with sentient life such as the Martian Manhunter. DC therefore had to engage in some judicious "retconning" (retroactive continuity) to better explain J'onzz's origins. When the Manhunter finally returns to his homeworld (*Justice League of America* #71, 1969), he makes the horrific discovery that something has purged the Red Planet of all life. He also learns that his people had fled whatever menace had killed the Martian biosphere, and leaves the JLA—and the four-color page—to find them. His quest is ultimately successful, and he eventually returns to Earth and his fellow heroes (*Justice League of America* #100, 1972).

During the 1980s and 1990s, J'onn J'onzz continued to be a stalwart member of the JLA and Justice League International, becoming almost a father figure for some of the younger and brasher members of the team, such as the Blue Beetle, Booster Gold, Fire, and Ice. In fact, he has been integral to every incarnation of the Justice League from the very beginning. Under such writers as Keith Giffen, J. M. DeMatteis, Dan Jurgens, Gerard Jones, and Mark Waid, J'onzz loosens up a little emotionally, developing a dry sense of humor, though he is still often played as a silent, stolid straight man for banter-prone characters such as the Blue Beetle. During the 1990s, the Manhunter becomes the Justice League's chairman; his leadership skills are praised by no less a personage than Batman himself (JLA #2, 1997), who says J'onzz has "the best grasp of group dynamics of anyone I've ever met."

As has happened with many superheroes, the Martian Manhunter's origin story has been embroidered greatly during the last two decades, making him increasingly complex and more relevant to modern audiences. In 1988 J'onzz starred in a four-issue *Martian Manhunter* miniseries, in which writer DeMatteis and artist Mark Badger plagued the Manhunter with a vision of H'ronmeer, the Martian god of death, fire, and lies. This culminated in several shocking discoveries, including the fact Dr. Erdel still lives. Erdel reveals that the Manhunter, grief-stricken over the deaths of his wife, daughter, and entire species from a plague, had lashed out in pain and destroyed Erdel's teleportation apparatus, thereby stranding himself on Earth. The Manhunter's vulnerability to fire turns out to be purely psychosomatic, a post-traumatic manifestation of J'onzz's repressed memories of his dead world's funeral pyres. To heal J'onzz's shattered psyche, Erdel had implanted happy memories of Mars based on old pulp science-fiction stories—the Manhunter's Martian appearance is one such piece of implanted information. Erdel then faked his own death to leave J'onzz free to adapt to his new life on Earth. Using Erdel's rebuilt equipment, the Manhunter returns briefly to Mars, where he bids farewell to everything he has lost. When he returns shortly to Earth, he regards it as his home more now than ever before.

Working with artists Tom Mandrake, Eduardo Barreto, and Jan Duursema, writer John Ostrander helmed an open-ended *Martian Manhunter* series that ran for thirty-six issues (1998–2001). Noting J'onzz's conspicuous lack of the "rogues' gallery" so typical of other superheroes, Ostrander embellished the character's backstory further by introducing his evil brother Ma'alefa'ak J'onzz (who is better known by his supervillain moniker, "Malefic"), the

architect of the plague that destroyed the Martian people. Ostrander also intertwined the history of Mars and the J'onzz family with Jack Kirby's New Gods characters, revealing that the Martian Manhunter has long been an enemy of the diabolical and supremely powerful quasi-deity known as Darkseid. In *Martian Manhunter 1,000,000* (1998), Ostrander and Mandrake served up a possible future in which the Martian Manhunter is alive and performing heroic deeds on Mars in the year 85,271 A.D.

"[J'onn J'onzz is] the alien on Earth who still remains alien," Ostrander has said of the taciturn extraterrestrial hero. "And thus he's the most classic in terms of a detective as well—if he remains the classic outsider, unlike Superman, who was raised to almost think of himself as human. J'onn always has known that he's the alien and yet, at the same time, he feels very close [to] and very identified with the people of Earth." Today he remains a key player in the Justice League, a long-lived character whose alien-ness remains both intact and intriguing. —*MAM*

Marvel Boy

For a company founded on a title called *Marvel Comics,* the temptation to create a hero called Marvel Boy was always going to be hard to resist, and there have been many incarnations of that name over the years. The first Marvel Boy was Martin Burns, who enjoyed two different origins in just two appearances. In the first (in *Daring Mystery* #6, 1940), he becomes the reincarnation of Hercules, who had been driven to return to Earth by the growing Nazi threat. In his second origin (in *USA Comics* #7, 1941) he inadvertently knocks over a mummy— "Hercules' mummy," as per the myth-mash that characterized all of this Marvel Boy's stories—during a museum trip and some of the mummy extract (whatever that might be) enters a cut in his skin; presto, instant superhero! In both cases, young Martin is presented with a (different) costume by an animated shadow that just happens to be lurking nearby.

Fast-forward a decade and, following the collapse of the superhero genre, up popped a new Marvel Boy: Bob Grayson, son of intrepid genius scientist Professor Matthew Grayson. Frightened by growing instability in Europe, the professor had fashioned a nuclear-powered spaceship and spirited his young son away to safety on Uranus. Now in futuristic 1950, the grown-up Grayson returned to Earth in a Roman-style, bare-legged costume, popping uranium pills and dazzling hoods with his "light jewel," which fired a beam of light that was temporarily blinding. The Marvel Boy stories were enjoyably scatterbrained, as he flitted from Uranus to Earth and back, tangling with aliens, commies, and swamis. After two issues, his *Marvel Boy* comic was retitled *Astonishing,* and beautifully drawn Marvel Boy stories (by Russ Heath and Bill Everett) continued to appear until issue #6, after which it was converted to a horror comic.

In a move to retain copyright on the name, Marvel Boy strips were reprinted in the 1960s and 1970s, and the hero himself was revived by writer Roy Thomas in a *Fantastic Four* issue (#164 in 1975). Grayson had apparently been in suspended animation and woke up with crime on his mind, renaming himself Crusader. He was defeated by the Fantastic Four and promptly died. His armbands (tiny generators filled with the energy of miniature stars) were passed on to Stark Industries, where a young would-be S.H.I.E.L.D. spy called Wendell Vaughn tried them on, fought off some enemy agents, and duly became Marvel Man (in *Captain America* #217). Adding blue tights to the original costume, Marvel Man next met the Hulk, changed his name to Quasar, and flew off to Uranus where, after three years of sleep, he was told he was the universe's new protector. Flying back to Earth, he would go on to enjoy a healthy run in his own comic for six years (1988–1994) as a sort of lighthearted Green Lantern.

But if Marvel Man became Quasar, that name was now going spare again, and so … enter Vance Astrovik, a.k.a. Marvel Boy, in the pages of the *New Warriors* in 1990. (This character was a "real world" variant of Guardians of the Galaxy leader Vance Astro, after the arbiters of Marvel Comics continuity decided that he hadn't left the twentieth century to join that futuristic team after all.) Rejected by the Avengers, the telekinetic Marvel Boy was recruited by Night Thrasher to join his fellow tyro heroes in the New Warriors, which proved to be one of the surprise hits of the 1990s. In an unusual move that very much mirrored the increasingly violent state of life in the late twentieth century, storylines revealed that Marvel Boy was an abused child, and in issue #20 he killed his father after a particularly savage beating. As a result, he was sent to jail where he changed his name to Justice and fought for the cause of prisoners' rights. In due course, Justice was released and, together with new Warriors girlfriend Firestar, went on to get accepted into the Avengers this time. All of this meant that there was another vacancy in the Marvel Boy department.

The fifth Marvel Boy duly arrived in 2000, courtesy of cutting-edge writer Grant Morrison with the talented J. G. Jones on art, as part of the company's more mature Marvel Knights line. This time around, Marvel Boy was Noh-Varr, the sole survivor of a crashed spaceship of the Kree race, and the strip's premise was effectively a retelling of the early (1968) Captain Marvel strip, right down to the design of Marvel Boy's costume. Over six issues, Noh-Varr (effectively a living weapon) came up against Mr. Midas (a billionaire dressed in Iron Man's old armor, for some reason), S.H.I.E.L.D., Nexus the Living Corporation, a beautiful killer called Oubliette, and pretty much the whole planet. Noh-Varr is undoubtedly the least sympathetic Marvel Boy so far, albeit the best crafted, but almost inevitably there will be more. —*DAR*

Marvel Comics

Martin Goodman was a publisher of pulp magazines—inexpensive collections of prose short stories packaged under illustrated covers—who, in the 1930s, oversaw a periodicals line including *Complete Western Book, Marvel Science Stories,* and *Star Detective* (the latter of which, in a 1937 edition, featured a tale with the prophetic title "The X-Man"). In the late 1930s Frank Torpey, representing a consortium of popular fiction authors and illustrators calling themselves Funnies, Inc., persuaded Goodman to enter a promising new entertainment medium: comic books. Goodman's first effort was *Marvel Comics* #1 (1939), an anthology title spotlighting the adventures of the Angel (not the version who would appear decades later in the company's *X-Men* title), the jungle hero Ka-Zar, the Western character the Masked Raider, Bill Everett's Sub-Mariner (listed on the cover as "Submariner"), and Carl Burgos' Human Torch, who was depicted on the cover melting through a steel wall. The issue sold extremely well, and Goodman's company, calling itself Timely Publications (or Timely Comics), was now in the comic-book business. An important editor was Joe Simon, who also wrote and drew many of the publisher's earliest efforts.

WHEN TITANS CLASH

After the success of competitor DC Comics' Superman and Batman, new superheroes inundated the marketplace as an exponentially expanding arena of publishers scurried for a piece of the pie. Timely experimented with new characters, most of which failed to connect with an audience: The Blue Blaze, Flexo the Rubber Man, the Phantom Reporter, and Timely's first superteam, the 3 Xs, were so short-lived that they escape mention in many historical volumes. Goodman struck gold, however, whenever he highlighted the Human Torch and the Sub-Mariner. And when he paired them in a three-part summer 1940 serial in *Marvel Mystery Comics,* the superhero "crossover" was born, and circulation exploded, giving birth to two new ongoing series: *The Human Torch* (Fall 1940) and *Sub-Mariner* (Spring 1941). In late 1940 Goodman hired

his wife's young cousin as an editorial assistant to help manage Timely's growing line. This seemingly nepotistic choice proved to be the most important personnel decision Goodman ever made: The teenager was Stanley Martin Lieber, who, as Stan Lee, would one day be the publisher's driving force.

THE COMING OF CAPTAIN AMERICA

In March 1941, as Adolf Hitler's campaign of conquest was pushing the world into war, editor/writer Simon and artist Jack Kirby introduced a new superhero comic that helped distinguish Timely as one of the major publishers. Simon recalled, in Les Daniels' *Marvel: Five Fabulous Decades of the World's Greatest Comics* (1991), "We were looking for a villain first, and Hitler was the villain." Simon and Kirby's antithesis of this real-life menace was their paragon of patriotism, Captain America. Once the United States entered World War II, *Captain America, The Human Torch,* and other titles regularly featured the heroes combating Axis enemies—for example, the cover of *Captain America* #13 (April 1942) depicts "Cap" punching a grossly caricatured Japanese soldier while proclaiming, "You started it! Now we'll finish it!" Readers embraced the superhero war effort, with many comic books selling hundreds of thousands of copies per issue. In December 1943 Captain America became a matinee idol by starring in the first installment of a live-action, fifteen-chapter Republic Pictures movie serial. Funny-animal titles like *Super Rabbit* joined Timely's publishing line, and the staff increased to handle the workload. Stan Lee assumed a larger editorial role, even writing some stories, and many artists accepted salaried staff positions to draw comic books.

Then the war ended, sounding the death knell for the first wave of superheroes. Some comics publishers withered away, and those that stayed in business canceled or diminished their superhero lines. By the end of the 1940s Timely's remaining superhero titles—*Sub-Mariner, The Human Torch,* and *Captain America*—were axed, the latter bearing the insult of piggybacking the burgeoning horror trend with its last issue: In *Captain America's Weird Tales* #75 (February 1950), the hero appeared in name only. Logos reading "Marvel Comics" sometimes appeared on the covers of late 1940s books, hinting at the name the company would one day adopt.

By the late 1940s the publisher's funny-animal comics were accompanied by crime, romance, girl's adventure, and Western titles; a sampling of Timely series from this era includes *Komic Kartoons, All True Crime, My Romance, Cowgirl Romances, Millie the Model, Patsy Walker,* and *Two-Gun Kid.* As the United States slipped into the post–World War II atomic age, the optimistic vehemence of the 1940s—when readers rallied behind *Captain America* and other comics that became more propaganda than entertainment—gave way to a new era of suspicion and paranoia.

ATLAS SHRUGS

In 1950 the Korean conflict inspired a slew of war series like *Battle* and *War Adventures,* featuring gritty portrayals of the brutality of human combat. The company was gutted in the early 1950s by a sweeping personnel layoff, a cost-cutting measure initiated by Goodman to maximize profits as part of a new distribution pact that added the imprint "Atlas" onto each of the company's covers. Failed 1953–1954 attempts to revive *Captain America* (as a "Commie Smasher!"), *Sub-Mariner,* and *The Human Torch* resulted in the publisher's avoidance of superheroes for the balance of the decade (though some elegant and now largely forgotten attempts at reviving the genre with newer characters like Venus and Marvel Boy had been made earlier on). Atlas added explicit horror titles to its line, a decision it regretted during the 1954 United States Senate witch hunt that attacked graphic comics content and almost extinguished the entire industry. Sales declined, publishers folded, page rates shrunk, and writers and artists were out of work.

By the end of the 1950s Goodman managed to keep his comics house alive by brokering a deal with Independent News Co. to distribute Atlas' periodicals, but there was a catch: The company could produce no more than eight titles a month, not a surprising limitation considering that its new distribution source was owned by its competitor, DC Comics. The company dropped the Atlas label and went nameless for a brief period. Disgruntled and on the brink of resignation, editor/writer Stan Lee sadly surveyed what was left of a once-thriving line: A smattering of monster titles featuring characters with childish names like "Torr," "The Thing That Shouldn't Exist," and "Fin Fang Foom."

THE MARVEL AGE OF COMICS

An early 1960s golf game between Goodman and DC's publisher Jack Liebowitz offered Lee an epiphany, at least indirectly. Liebowitz remarked of the stellar sales generated by DC's new *Justice League of America* title—the most recent addition to its line of successfully reworked superheroes—and Goodman then directed Lee to produce a superteam for their own company's comics line. Lee took this as a challenge to create a series with emotional resonance—"I was really interested in the characters as people," he commented—the result being *Fantastic Four* #1 in November 1961. The "FF" consisted of a family (a snobby scientist, his reserved fiancée, her impulsive brother, and an irascible friend) that gains superpowers and becomes a force for good. This family was a dysfunctional one, however, filled with bickering but united by love. The novelty of this new breed of heroes, along with Lee's dialoguing verve and the energetic artwork of Jack Kirby, made *Fantastic Four* a runaway success. The Marvel Age was born.

The publisher, now calling itself Marvel Comics, continued to strike with unpredictable, problem-plagued, self-consumed, and unlikely superheroes, an exciting universe of characters all co-existing in the same fictional world. The Incredible Hulk, Thor, Spider-Man, Ant-Man, and Iron Man came along, as did supergroup titles *The Avengers* and *The X-Men*. Lee wrote and edited the burgeoning line, and managed his workload by formulating the "Marvel method" of scripting: He'd craft a terse plot that the penciler would illustrate, with Lee scripting pages after they were drawn. This shortcut not only helped the writer/editor manage more titles, it also vested the artists in their storytelling. Lee provided a "voice" to Marvel Comics, speaking colloquially to his readers in his letters pages (and awarding selected letter writers a coveted "No-Prize," which was just that: a specially designed envelope containing *nothing* inside) and in his hype-laced "Stan's Soapbox" columns. He created intimacy between readers and comics professionals by humanizing his fellow creators with nicknames: Jack "King" Kirby, "Genial" Gene Colan, "Jazzy" Johnny Romita, and his own alias, Stan "The Man" Lee. Doctor Strange, Sgt. Fury (later to become Nick Fury, Agent of S.H.I.E.L.D.), and Daredevil joined the line, as did additional writers, artists, and editors.

Although the distribution deal with Independent News/DC strangled Marvel at its eight-title maximum throughout most of the 1960s, anthology books like *Strange Tales* and *Tales to Astonish* allowed more characters their venue. Marvel's superhero comics enjoyed growing sales, mass-media exposure through TV cartoons and merchandising, a company-generated fan club (the Merry Marvel Marching Society, or M.M.M.S.), and counter-culture acceptance on college campuses. As of 1968 the distribution restriction was lifted and a barrage of new characters and titles appeared. And throughout the decade, readers never knew what to expect in a Marvel title: Captain America was discovered frozen in ice, the Green Goblin exposed Spider-Man's identity, Galactus threatened to engulf the entire planet, and visionary artists like Jim Steranko drew for Marvel while DC Comics expatriate Neal Adams relocated there. Lee had created a so-called

"House of Ideas," and his drive to produce superheroes with realistic resonance became a core philosophy that steered the company for years to come. Industry giant DC lumbered through the 1960s, not considering this upstart Marvel a threat until it was too late—as the 1970s began, Marvel was now comics' best-selling publisher.

THE HOUSE OF IDEAS

DC struck back, however, under the leadership of editorial director Carmine Infantino. Superstar artist Kirby defected to DC (for a few years, before he returned to Marvel), and the companies waged content and market-share war for several years. Marvel helped define new genres like sword-and-sorcery (through its acquisition of Robert E. Howard's *Conan the Barbarian* as a comic-book property), horror (via gripping titles like *The Tomb of Dracula* and *Man-Thing*), and martial arts (*Master of Kung Fu* and *Iron Fist*). DC countered with innovative alternatives, but Marvel controlled the 1970s.

Marvel introduced two iconic anti-heroes, the Punisher in *The Amazing Spider-Man* #129 (1974) and the clawed mutant Wolverine in *The Incredible Hulk* #181 (1974), then followed with an all-new incarnation of an old standby in *Giant-Size X-Men* #1 (1975). Marvel and DC even shook hands long enough to co-produce the wildly successful one-shot *Superman vs. the Amazing Spider-Man* (1975). Marvel milestones during the second half of the 1970s include *Howard the Duck*, *The Incredible Hulk* live-action television show, *Star Wars* comics adaptations, and clones of Marvel's two most visible heroes in *Spider-Woman* and *The Savage She-Hulk*. Lee was booted upstairs into executive management before vacating the House of Ideas for Hollywood in 1980, where he helped bring Spider-Man, Fantastic Four, and other characters to animated television. He was succeeded at Marvel by a revolving door of editors in chief, including Jim Shooter.

Appointed in 1978, Shooter, perceived by many as a taskmaster, elicited love/hate reactions from staff and freelance creators. Early in his near-decade-long tenure, Marvel released some of its most celebrated, creator-driven successes: Walt Simonson's *Thor,* Chris Claremont and John Byrne's collaboration on *X-Men,* the "adult fantasy and science fiction" magazine *Epic Illustrated,* Byrne's popular run on *Fantastic Four,* the expansion of *X-Men* into a franchise beginning with *The New Mutants* graphic novel (1982), and Frank Miller's dark take on *Daredevil,* the latter of which introduced the popular assassin Elektra in 1981.

After the publication of the toy tie-in superhero crossover *Marvel Super Heroes Secret Wars* (1984), a critically lambasted but highly profitable limited series that sold roughly 750,000 copies per issue, Shooter reportedly initiated a heavy-handed editorial presence that soured many writers and artists; other creative personnel embraced his vision and stood steadfastly in his corner. Despite his controversial management style, Shooter as editor in chief helped direct Marvel toward a period of commercial success.

AN EMPIRE CRUMBLES

Changes within Marvel's financial infrastructure occurred in 1986, when New World Pictures bought Marvel with an eye toward media development of its characters. More new titles were produced, including a line of comics (including *Star Brand, Nightmask,* and *Psi Force*) in a separate reality from the Marvel superheroes called the "New Universe," an experiment that flopped. Shooter left the company in 1987, replaced by Tom DeFalco, who continued to help the line grow. The Punisher now starred in his own series, as did Wolverine. The House of Ideas produced so *many* ideas that characters strayed from their source material. Some books grew so dense with continuity that they were inaccessible for anyone other than the devotee. But they still sold well.

In 1989 Revlon chief and investor supreme Ron Perelman bought Marvel and took it public. To ensure shareholder profits, Marvel exploited gimmicks like variant covers, cover enhancements, rampant franchising, and its cadre of young, hot artists—Todd McFarlane, Rob Liefeld, and Jim Lee, among others. Marvel cultivated then manipulated a speculator boom that pushed sales of some titles into the millions. Most of Marvel's output was pedestrian at best, pandering at worst, piggybacking on the success of collector and speculator sales. Before long Marvel became part of a conglomerate that included action-figure manufacturer Toy Biz and trading-card company Fleer. Corporate raider Carl Icahn attempted a hostile takeover of the company, and his struggle with Perelman merited a book on the subject: Dan Raviv's *Comic Wars: How Two Tycoons Battled Over the Marvel Comics Empire … And Both Lost!!!* (Broadway Books, 2002). In 1993 Marvel strong-armed its own distribution network and continued to feed the speculator frenzy, but by the mid-1990s—after McFarlane and friends had jumped ship and formed their own publishing company, Image Comics—the excessive glut of product forced the bottom to drop out of the market. Speculators fled, and on December 27, 1996, Marvel Entertainment Group, Inc. filed for bankruptcy.

MARVEL COMICS REBORN

After floundering for several years, with industry naysayers predicting its demise, Marvel Comics was creatively rejuvenated: Chief creative officer Avi Arad appointed Bill Jemas as president and Joe Quesada—an extremely popular comic-book artist—as editor in chief. A leaner, more streamlined Marvel has since focused on a core line of exciting, accessible characters, with successful creators like Brian Michael Bendis, Grant Morrison, Bruce Jones, and others reshaping the Marvel universe for the twenty-first century. Best-selling titles have included *Ultimate Spider-Man* and, now as before, *X-Men* and *The Incredible Hulk.* Marvel emerged from bankruptcy after the unparalleled financial success of Sam Raimi's live-action theatrical blockbuster, *Spider-Man* (2002). Reinforced by the success of additional blockbuster movies starring Marvel characters—including *X-Men* (2000), *X2: X-Men United* (2002), and *Daredevil* (2003)—Marvel Comics has reclaimed its title as the "House of Ideas." —*ME*

Marvelman: *See* Miracleman

Mary Marvel

Perhaps fearing that success inevitably inspires imitation, Fawcett Comics seemed to have stolen a march on its competitors by copying its all-conquering Captain Marvel itself. First, they created Captain Marvel Jr. and then, in one genre-spanning month in late 1942, they hit both the funny animal market with Marvel Bunny and the largely untapped female market with Mary Marvel. Writer Otto Binder and artist Marc Swayze introduced Mary in *Captain Marvel Adventures* #18, in a tale that reveals that Captain Marvel's young alter ego, Billy Batson, has a long-lost twin sister, Mary (Batson) Bromfield, separated from him at birth and brought up by a wealthy foster family. As luck would have it, Mary is then promptly kidnapped, giving Captain Marvel senior and junior ample opportunity to show off their powers by soundly thrashing the kidnappers. Somehow, the miscreants escape, defeat the superheroes, and turn on Mary who, upon uttering a plaintive cry of "Captain Marvel," is magically transformed into the red-mini-skirted Mary Marvel—apparently, she had never spoken his name aloud before. Like her brother, the super-powered Mary can fly and is possessed of almost unlimited strength, and so she makes short work of dispatching her captors.

Fawcett was never overly concerned with explanations for its heroes' powers, and readers had to be satisfied with the ubiquitous, long-bearded wizard Shazam popping up to say that this was simply what was meant to happen. In any case, logical or

Mary Marvel #2 © 1946 Fawcett.
COVER ART BY JACK BINDER.

not, the three heroes pledge to fight crime together, and the following month Mary graduated into her own feature in *Wow Comics* #9, displacing the bizarrely named Mr. Scarlett and Pinky from the cover spot. Swayze was deemed too important to draw a new feature such as Mary's and was returned to the Captain Marvel feature, leaving the new strip to be drawn by Jack Binder, brother of the strip's principal writer Otto; this made them one of the few brother teams in comics history.

Unlike Billy Batson, who was transformed into a muscular adult, his sister Mary was still only a young girl after uttering the magic words, possibly in an attempt to appeal to a young readership. Indeed, for Mary Otto Binder deliberately downplayed the heroics typical of the other Fawcett comics, preferring instead more human-interest stories. (In fact, unlike her contemporary, Wonder Woman, Mary was very much unliberated, content to be helping out her male family members.) However, Mary did have her share of villains, including Georgia Sivanna (from the ever-increasing Sivanna family of mad scientists), Mr. Night, and Nightowl, but she was just as likely to spend her time frolicking with gnomes or rescuing lost puppies. In addition to her wealthy foster parents, the supporting cast included hayseed best pal Freckles, who occasionally donned a costume to become (wait for it) Freckles Marvel, and whose main purpose was to be rescued. Another costumed cohort was Uncle Marvel, a con man who persuaded Mary to sell her heroic services for cash but soon reformed to become a nuisance in many later strips of all the Fawcett characters.

Sales were strong enough during World War II to warrant Mary's own title, and *Mary Marvel* #1 appeared in 1945, while a line of Mary Marvel dresses sold in the thousands. The next year saw the launch of the Mary Marvel fan club but sales soon started to slump (possibly as the result of a maturing audience switching over to romance titles) and in 1947 *Wow* became a Western comic. Barely one month later, Mary's own title was transformed into *Monte Hale Western* and she had to make do with a berth in *Marvel Family* until the 1950s superhero slump killed that off in 1954.

By the time of her initial demise, Mary had become a teenager, and when she was revived by DC Comics some thirty years later she was still a teenager. As part of the *Shazam!* title, Mary starred in occasional *Marvel Family* adventures as well as a few solo backups. In these tales, usually featuring Mary surrounded by a gang of teenage girlfriends, she was portrayed as a would-be Nancy Drew, solving quirky mysteries—and with beautiful art by Bob Oksner she never looked better. Captain Marvel went on to become a regular fixture in the DC lineup but for much of the 1980s and 1990s Mary languished in obscurity, her last appearance made in

1999. For a readership lacking in young girls it would seem that there is now no audience for the innocence and simplicity of Mary Marvel. —*DAR*

The Mask

Superheroes have always offered vicarious empowerment to the average, the meek, and the disenfranchised. When orphan whelp Billy Batson transforms into the mighty Captain Marvel by shouting "Shazam," for example, one thinks, *If only I had such a gift.*

Stanley Ipkiss might disagree with you. This human doormat is the lowest of losers—until he buys an ancient mask in a curio shop. Donning the eerie visor, he is transmogrified into a mischievous oddball with a green cranium and a devilish, toothy sneer—plus malleability, invulnerability, and the power to pull objects (especially weapons) out of thin air. Meet the Mask, or "Big-Head," as he is known in public, who embarks upon a mission of revenge against his tormentors. Premiering in *Dark Horse Presents* #10 (1987), the Mask is a vengeful, human Bugs Bunny with an "R" rating—unlike that "wascally wabbit," however, when the Mask blows up someone, he or she stays dead. As the body count increases in Big-Head's wake, resolute cop Lt. Kellaway is determined to stop this crazy killer, and the heat is on hapless Ipkiss.

The Mask was envisioned by Dark Horse Comics president Mike Richardson, writer Randy Stradley, and artist Chris Warner, but given life by writer John Arcudi and illustrator Doug Mahnke. Dark Horse published multiple storylines featuring the mask (the object) falling into the hands of (make that onto the faces of) a variety of people, with the moral to the story (if there was one) being, vengeance carries a price. Each person who has worn the mask has been intoxicated by its power, but eventually beset by disaster. From his *Dark Horse Presents* appearances the Mask clobbered his way into a four-issue miniseries titled *Mayhem*

Adventures of The Mask #1 ™ & © 1996 Dark Horse Comics, Inc.
COVER ART BY BRUCE TIMM.

(1989), then into a succession of miniseries and specials all his own, including *The Mask* (1991), *The Mask Returns* (1992), *The Mask Strikes Back* (1995), and *The Mask: Toys in the Attic* (1998).

A nonlethal, kid-friendly version of the character became a movie icon in *The Mask* (1994), a box-office smash starring rubber-faced comedian Jim Carrey as Ipkiss/Mask and featuring a scene-stealing dog named Milo. (*The Mask* is also noted for its breakout performance by Cameron Diaz as a femme fatale turned Ipkiss' love interest.) A hefty special-effects budget brought to life the Mask's implausible *Looney Tunes*–inspired antics, and Carrey in the role coined a short-lived catchphrase: "Ssssmokin'!" A

spate of merchandising accompanied the film, and *Son of the Mask* made it to movie houses in 2004. *The Mask,* promoted as "From Zero to Hero," spawned a television cartoon spinoff (1995–1996) in both syndication and on Saturday mornings, which in turn inspired a Dark Horse comic book in the "animated" style, *Adventures of the Mask* (1995–1996). Other animation-based and traditional *Mask* comics followed for a few years, including a four-issue Dark Horse/DC crossover teaming Big-Head with Batman's arch foe in *Joker/Mask* (2000). —*ME*

Master of Kung Fu

If the 1960s was the decade of superheroes in the comics world, the 1970s was definitely the decade of fads. Among the horror, sword-and-sorcery, and science fiction genres that captivated fandom, the rise of the kung fu comic was one of the fastest and most unexpected. The popularity of Bruce Lee's movies and David Carradine's *Kung Fu* television show inspired all the major comics publishers—DC, Atlas, Charlton, and Marvel—to jump onto the martial arts craze. Marvel married the concept of the Far East martial arts hero with the traditional American superhero, and a genre was born.

The first of Marvel's superpowered martial artists, who initially saw the light of day in *Special Marvel Edition* #15 in December 1973, was Shang-Chi, Master of Kung Fu, whose name means "the rising and advancing of a spirit." It seems that Marvel had held the rights to comics' version of Sax Rohmer's legendary fictional Chinese criminal genius Fu Manchu for some years and, while looking for a premise for its first kung fu strip, decided to join the two properties together. Consequently, the comic opens with Shang-Chi, Fu Manchu's "living weapon" son, on a mission to assassinate his father's great enemy, Dr. Petrie.

Having seemingly done the deed, Shang-Chi was confronted by Dr. Petrie's longtime colleague Sir Denis Nayland Smith and told the terrible truth about the father whom he had believed was only interested in world peace. Teaming up with Sir Denis and his fellow Fu-hater, Black Jack Tarr, Shang-Chi dedicated his not inconsiderable skills to defeating his father's dastardly plans. In the strip's early days, creators Steve Englehart and Jim Starlin (soon to be replaced by Doug Moench and novice artist Paul Gulacy) concentrated on page after page of martial arts action as the team countered Fu Manchu's endless quest for power. The comic neatly tapped into the public's insatiable hunger for all things kung fu, and Marvel had a hit on its hands.

Throughout 1974, Marvel unleashed a torrent of kung fu–related titles: *Special Marvel Edition* was renamed *Master of Kung Fu* with issue #17; a black-and-white magazine called *Deadly Hands of Kung Fu* was launched; a new hero, Iron Fist, followed in *Marvel Premiere;* and, in September, a quarterly *Giant Sized Master of Kung Fu* comic was added. In Britain, Shang-Chi stories were reprinted in *Avengers Weekly,* and soon the demand for new strips to be reprinted meant that the U.S. office was effectively drawing episodes for the United Kingdom, to be printed later in the United States. At the heart of what was a genuine publishing phenomenon, the *Master of Kung Fu* comic itself gradually improved as the talents of Moench and Gulacy matured.

Moench started adding new characters to Shang-Chi's band of Fu Manchu-fighters: Clive Reston (part Sherlock Holmes, part James Bond), the Marlon Brando look-alike Larner, and Leiko-Wu, Asian trouble-shooter and love interest. With issue #29, Shang-Chi and company began working directly for British intelligence and started to encounter other foes in a succession of Bond-inspired extravaganzas. The likes of Velcro and Mordillo lived up to their Bond-villain inspiration with their secret islands, private armies, femmes fatales, and plans for world domination. The new direction built to a climax with the whole cast battling Fu Manchu and

Master of Kung Fu #17 © 1974 Marvel Comics. COVER ART BY JIM STARLIN AND ERNIE CHUA.

his evil daughter Fah Lo Suee on a vast space station, with the fate of the entire planet Earth at stake. In the end, Fu Manchu escaped, Larner died, and Gulacy moved on to other, more lucrative areas, having established his reputation as one of his generation's brightest stars.

As the 1970s progressed, the kung fu craze inevitably waned, and one by one the various martial arts books folded. Shang-Chi was the last hero standing, having built up enough of a following in his own right. The comic lasted until 1983, buoyed by lengthy runs from artists Mike Zeck and Gene Day (who died soon after leaving the feature), and the redoubtable Moench, who stayed almost to the bitter end. In its last few years, old favorites such as villains Shockwave, Razorfist (who had blades instead of hands), the Cat, and Pavane reappeared with regularity, as did Fu Manchu (inevitably), but critics agree the comic's main selling point was the sensitivity of Moench's characterizations.

Following a lengthy hiatus, Shang-Chi was revived in a few issues of *Marvel Comics Presents* (collected in the 1991 title *Bleeding Black*) and a *Moon Knight* special. Fans then had to wait another decade before being reunited with Shang-Chi, this time in a 2002 miniseries by Moench and Gulacy. Despite these rebirths, ultimately the *Master of Kung Fu* was a quintessentially 1970s concept. —*DAR*

Metal Men

Born out of necessity and desperation, the Metal Men were one of the more inventive concepts of the 1960s. The strip was created over the course of one weekend in 1962 by writer/editor Robert Kanigher and artist Ross Andru, to fill the pages of *Showcase* #37 when a previously scheduled feature suddenly fell through. Kanigher dreamed up a group of robots, each made out of a different metal and each having powers and personality reflecting its particular metal. The origin story recounts how brilliant, pipe-smoking government scientist Dr. Will Magnus creates six robots in his giant, secret laboratory and fits each with a Responsometer, which gives them human characteristics. During their creation, the robots are affected by a powerful Aurora Borealis event, which somehow gives them the personalities and emotions of real people.

The robots' abilities were as distinct as their "personalities." For example, Gold—the leader—could stretch for miles and was brave and serious. Mercury could melt at room temperature and was a real hot-head. Platinum (or Tina as she called herself) was tough and resilient, and could weave herself into all sorts of constructions; she was also in love with Doc Magnus. Lead acted as a barrier and

Metal Men #48 © 1976 DC Comics.
COVER ART BY WALT SIMONSON.

was large and slightly slow-witted, while Iron was incredibly strong, if slightly dull, and Tin was a rather weak, timid, stuttering character who tried his best but lacked the powers of his teammates.

Kanigher was an endlessly creative writer, often basing his stories on gimmicks or plot twists; with the science-based Metal Men his writing occasionally resembled a chemistry lesson. The team were in some ways the ultimate establishment heroes, funded by the Pentagon and operating out of an army compound at the government's behest, but for all that, what made the strip so enjoyable were the robots' clashing personalities, particularly the cantankerous Mercury. Readers also immediately responded to the timid but plucky Tin who, like them, had no real powers, but the focus of the strip was more often on the doomed love of Platinum for her all-too-human creator.

Right from the beginning, the Metal Men's foes were often robots themselves, be they giant robots, wooden robots, dinosaur robots, or even robot termites. The group also had a cadre of chemical opponents, including the Gas Gang and the giant, walking chemical vat, Chemo. Uniquely, the Metal Men often died in their stories, only to be resurrected by Doc Magnus in the next issue, but after a while their Lazarus-like rebirths began to wear thin. In 1963, after four issues of *Showcase,* the Metal Men were given their own title, which was also produced by the Kanigher/Andru team, but when artist Andru left to take over the Flash, the comic's direction began to change. Andru's replacement, Mike Sekowsky, soon became editor and writer, too, and introduced a darker element, with a storyline involving the characters becoming hunted outcasts while Doc Magnus went into a coma.

With issue #37, the Metal Men effectively dispensed with their "superhero" identities altogether, much as the Teen Titans and Wonder Woman had. They met up with wealthy financier Mister Conan and assumed human identities. Donning synthetic skin, Gold became jet-set swinger Guy Gideon; Tina was Tina Platt, a model; and Lead and Tin became Ledby Hand and Tinker—a sort of Simon and Garfunkel singer/songwriter duo. Iron assumed the form of builder Jon "Iron" Mann, while Mercury became the red-haired artist Mercurio, whose wild appearance and savage temper apparently echoed Mike Sekowsky's. Sadly, the new direction, which touched upon the supernatural and involved an insane Doc Magnus bent on world domination, was to prove stillborn as the comic was soon canceled (with issue #41 in 1970).

After a lengthy fallow period, several guest slots with Batman in *The Brave and the Bold* and three reprint issues in 1973 resulted in a second chance for the team when their series was revived (with issue #45 in 1976). The human identities had gone, Doc Magnus was cured of his megalomaniacal tendencies, Chemo was rampaging again, and all was right with the world. Over the following twelve issues, the Metal Men battled Eclipso, the Plutonium Man, and Dr. Strangeglove. They squabbled, fell in love, and died a couple of times. Even so, the public sadly failed to warm to them and, astonishingly, in the years since then the group has largely faded from view, with the exception of a 1993 miniseries, which revealed that Doc Magnus himself had been a robot all along—a twist that genuinely no one saw coming. With regular revivals of almost every obscure vintage DC strip, it has surprised fans and critics alike that this staple of the Silver Age of comics (1956–1969) has been so neglected. *—DAR*

Metamorpho

Throughout the 1960s, DC Comics used its *Showcase* and *The Brave and the Bold* titles to introduce new characters, and as the decade progressed these heroes became stranger and stranger. Metamorpho the Element Man first appeared in *The Brave and the Bold* #57, in 1965, from editor Murray Boltinoff and writer Bob Haney, with art by DC's sole female artist at that time, Ramona Fradon. Metamorpho was originally dashing, reckless soldier of fortune (and occasional Grand Prix racer) Rex Mason, who was besotted with wealthy, blond heiress Sapphire Stagg. Sadly, Stagg's father, Simon Stagg, disapproved of their romance and sent Mason on a deadly quest to an Egyptian pyramid to bring back the famed Orb of Ra. This being a comic book, the Orb somehow rearranged Mason's chemical makeup so that he could control the elements in his body, and he found that he could do the most extraordinary things. He now had the strength of marble and a knockout punch with the power of cobalt. He could transform himself into a slide made of calcium, change into gas

The Brave and the Bold #58 © 1965 DC Comics.
COVER ART BY RAMONA FRADON.

or fire, and assume just about any size or shape you could imagine.

The downside to all this was that Mason was now incredibly ugly, his whole body being a mass of hideously pasty and textured skin in a variety of orange and purple hues. As a result of this, Mason more or less moved in with the Staggs, as the disgruntled Simon Stagg vainly tried to reverse the Orb's effects. Curiously for comics, the smitten Sapphire was still as much in love with Mason as ever. Unfortunately, another resident of the Stagg mansion, the brutish bodyguard Java (in fact a caveman somehow revived by Stagg *père* on one of his many expeditions), was also in love with Sapphire, resulting in all manner of plots to dispose of the afflicted Mason.

Following two successful issues of *The Brave and the Bold,* Mason—now calling himself Metamorpho—graduated to his own comic, which went on for seventeen issues. A typical Metamorpho story involved Mason, the Staggs, and Java traveling around the world, from one luxury villa to another, and somehow blundering into an inevitable tangle with bizarre wrongdoers. Among this motley band of villains were the likes of Stingaree, the Balkan Brothers, Dr. Destiny, Achille le Heel, and Mason's female counterpart Urania, the Element Girl. As their names suggest, this was a superhero strip with its tongue firmly lodged in its cheek and, despite his macabre appearance, Metamorpho was usually one of DC's more lighthearted heroes. In fact, with its settings on the French Riviera, in Africa, and in America's high society, the strip was reminiscent of that staple of swinging 1960s cinema, the caper movie.

Much of the feature's appeal derived not just from Haney's entertaining writing but from Fradon's charmingly inventive artwork, and when she left comics to raise a family, the comic suffered a slow decline, finally going under in 1968. Metamorpho's savior was to be editor Murray Boltinoff, who had a tendency to stick the character into whichever comic he happened to be working on at the time. This meant that Metamorpho guest starred in numerous adventures with Batman and Superman, as well as enjoying short runs as a backup feature in *Action Comics* and *World's Finest.* In the 1980s, he became something of a superteam specialist, joining first the Outsiders and then the Justice League. In one mid-1980s issue of *The Outsiders,* Metamorpho and Sapphire finally married, a satisfying resolution to one of DC's more enduring (and endearing) courtships. In *Justice League Europe* he was stationed in France and was very much the star of the team, enjoying a series of suitably quirky adventures and fraught tussles with the locals. This exposure led to a short-lived series in the 1990s that misguidedly adopted a darker approach and failed to engage the fans. —*DAR*

Mighty Morphin' Power Rangers

A group of multicultural high-school students, guided by their mentor, an interdimensional being named Zordon, guard the universe against evildoers and miscreants. Each of the teens—Jason Lee, Zack Taylor, Billy Cranston, Kimberly Hart, and Trini Kwan—is given access to "extraordinary powers drawn from the ancient creatures [known as] dinosaurs." When they are in danger, they point their Morphers to the sky and call out the names of their "dinosaurs": Mastodon! Pterodactyl! Triceratops! Sabertoothed Tiger! Tyrannosaurus! The teens then morph into "a formidable fighting force known to one and all as the Power Rangers."

Armed with Power Coins, Power Crystals, Blade Blasters, colossal fighting machines called Zords (that connect to form one colossal Megazord), and the ancient secrets of martial arts, the Mighty Morphin' Power Rangers (MMPR) followed the success of the Teenage Mutant Ninja Turtles as the next karate-kicking defenders of the world. As Power Rangers, they are superstrong, super-fast, and super-determined. Donning high-tech racecar driver–like bodysuits and plastic masks and helmets, they are primary-colored heroes well versed in combat skills. In fact, most fans identified the original five rangers by their colors: the Red Ranger (Jason), the Black Ranger (Zach), The Blue Ranger (Billy), the Pink Ranger (Kim), and the Yellow Ranger (Trini). Though the Rangers' names and colors have changed over the years—and their look updated to a high-tech style featuring space and astronomy themes—they are still a fun-loving group of teens sworn to save the earth from destruction.

The Mighty Morphin' Power Rangers were introduced in Japan in 1975 as *Secret Task Force Goranger,* a children's television show produced by Toei Company Ltd., one of Japan's largest movie studios.

Haim Saban, founder and former executive producer of Saban Entertainment, encountered a live-action "Dinosaur Task Force" series in 1992, while he was traveling in Japan, and decided to repackage the show for a U.S. audience as *The Mighty Morphin' Power Rangers.* (Toei still holds the rights to the Power Rangers in Asia and produces the Japanese version of the heroes.)

Since the Power Rangers premiered on the Fox network in 1993, they have "built one of the most passionate groundswells of devotion in the history of kids' entertainment," said *San Francisco Examiner* writer Peter Stack. The *Mighty Morphin' Power Rangers* show ran for three seasons, from 1993 to 1996, in which the Rangers battled the likes of Rita Repulsa, Goldar, Finster, Squatt and Babo, Scorpina, Lord Zedd, Ivan Ooze, Rito Revolto, and Mastervile.

Twentieth Century Fox released the Saban Entertainment–produced *Mighty Morphin' Power Rangers: The Movie* in 1995. In this live-action feature, the super-warriors face off against Ivan Ooze, a centuries-old evildoer out to destroy Zordon. Though critics panned the film (despite its $40 million worth of special effects), kids loved it, finding comfort in the familiar. Licensed children's books, action figures, masks, T-shirts, bed sheets, a comic-book series from Hamilton Comics, and other merchandise enjoyed healthy sales in the retail market—the action figures alone ranking within the top three boys' character toys on the U.S. market. Until the arrival of the Power Rangers, it was almost unheard of for Japanese character merchandise to dominate the American retail market; at its height, trade publications reported annual U.S. sales of Power Rangers merchandise of $100 million.

By 1996, the popularity of the Power Rangers had waned. But because toy sales were still strong and the television show was near the top of the ratings list, Saban executives decided to reinvest in the property in an effort to attract a younger generation of viewers. A massive licensing and merchandising program was kick-started and the Power Rangers look was updated. Multiple changes were

The masked cast of *The Mighty Morphin' Power Rangers*.

made to the TV show's title, which became *Power Rangers Zeo* (1996); *Power Rangers Turbo* (1997); *Power Rangers in Space* (1998); and *Power Rangers Lost Galaxy* (1999). By the end of the 1990s, the Rangers had a new lease on life, the Nielson Galaxy Explorer hailing *Power Rangers* as the "most popular kids show of the 1990s."

The 2000s saw more name changes to the series, including *Power Rangers Lightspeed Rescue* (2000); *Power Rangers Time Force* (2001); *Power Rangers Wild Force* (2002); *Power Rangers Ninja Storm* (2003); and *Power Rangers Dino Thunder* (2004). Despite this seeming confusion and the concerned cries of parents who claimed the superteam promoted violence through its extensive portrayals of physical combat, the show has continued to increase in popularity during the new millennium. —*GM*

Milestone Heroes

It is common for comics companies to give themselves exalted names, but in the case of Milestone the point was particularly well taken. Debuting in

1993, it was the first comics company established by African Americans and devoted to superheroes of color. Seeking strength—and normalcy—in numbers, Milestone's founders (writer Dwayne McDuffie, artist Denys Cowan, business writer Derek Dingle and, briefly, Michael Davis, future head of Motown Animation) decided to launch an entire line rather than a single character, aiming to reflect the range of real life rather than put one more token "minority" superbeing on the shelves.

This ambitious scope helped guarantee that none of Milestone's comics would seem to be a gimmick, even as the creators' perspective helped assure a certain uniqueness, presenting ideas and issues seldom seen in mainstream superhero comics (and hardly ever handled as credibly as Milestone did). Milestone had standards of quality, and a level of freshness and wit, that stood above much else that was produced during an early to mid-1990s glut of new (though not often original) superheroes.

The comics' setting itself is unusual for the New York–centric norm of superhero stories; Milestone's tales take place in the fictional Midwestern metropolis of Dakota. Many of Dakota's superbeings appear after a single catastrophic event, in which a major gang rumble ("The Big Bang") is broken up by the authorities with a mysterious gas that kills many and mutates the survivors (and unwitting bystanders) into superheroes and villains. (Milestone's comics were notable for uncommon touches of realism, and even this fantastic event was eerily restaged by Vladimir Putin at a Moscow theater in 2002, with much less glamorous results.)

The best known of these "Bang Babies" was Static (featured in a comic of the same name from 1993 to 1997), a teen who acquires electromagnetic powers and has since starred in the popular Kids WB! network cartoon *Static Shock*. Static's book was emblematic of Milestone's realism: a bullied schoolkid, Static's alter-ego Virgil Hawkins can't do much more about it after gaining his powers than he could before, for fear of revealing his superhero

Blood Syndicate #17 © 1994 DC Comics/Milestone Media.
COVER ART BY CRISSCROSS.

identity; his tendency to run off when duty calls costs him even the most menial of occupations (it seems that only white *Daily Planet* reporters get better job security); the outcast kid has to deal with his own homophobia when a friend comes out; and after Static recognizes a dealer in a drug bust as another close classmate's boyfriend, he lets him go. (Moral shadings were commonplace for "The Dakota universe," in this book and no less in *The Blood Syndicate* [1993–1996], about a team of super-thugs who form a kind of underground United Nations from the fragments of their former gang factions, with no one but each other to turn to.)

Not all Milestone's heroes were "Bang Babies," though. Hardware (starring in his own book from 1993 to 1997) was a high-tech armored warrior whose alter ego, Curtis Metcalf, rebels against the white corporate mentor who won't give the brilliant black inventor credit for his creations. The CEO turns out to be running a criminal enterprise as well as an unethical business, and over the course of the series Hardware finds a way between his legitimate indignation and his self-sabotaging rage.

Icon (starring in his own book from 1993 to 1997) was the modern superhero name of an alien whose ship crashed in the American South in 1839; seeking to blend in, he takes on the appearance of the earthlings he sees, who unfortunately happen to be African-American slaves. Blessed (or cursed) with a superhuman lifespan among other strange powers, the alien has assumed the identity of a wealthy conservative lawyer in Dakota by the 1990s, and is convinced to use his powers for justice by an idealistic teen who becomes his sidekick, Rocket. The book intriguingly examined the spectrum of black ideology (from the assimilated-in-more-ways-than-one Icon to the rebellious Rocket, who becomes comics' first unwed teen mom superhero). There is also a poignant undercurrent of pride in Icon's selection of a black identity regardless of the consequences.

As Milestone enjoyed an initial flush of success, the line expanded in 1994, with *Shadow Cabinet* (a creepy secret society of superheroes that resonates with post–September 11 questions of civil rights versus national security), *Xombi* (a weird and irreverent series about a slain Asian-American scientist reanimated by his own experimental nano-machines), and *Kobalt* (a somewhat satiric white superhero series).

In its heyday, Milestone introduced some of comics' most successful and interesting new artists (including Humberto Ramos and John Paul Leon), counted famous fans from Clarence Thomas to Chuck D, and published over 200 comics in four years. The company ran several issues without Comics Code approval, pushing the envelope of edgy subject matter in a way that Milestone's establishment distribution partner, DC Comics, honored by carrying every book (and probably growing in the process).

Sadly, a contracting market took Milestone with it, and the company's comic-book production ceased by mid-1997. However, the broader Milestone Media operation soldiers on, and hasn't run out of victories: There has been the *Static Shock* cartoon (2000–present), a 2001 comic miniseries (again published by Milestone and distributed by DC) to tie in to in, and another interesting Static Shock story (dealing with prejudice against Arab Americans) in volume 2 of the industrywide benefit compilation *9-11* (DC Comics, 2002). Milestone Media has put out children's books on African-American history makers, and at least one scholarly treatise has been published on the company's comics (*Black Superheroes, Milestone Comics, and Their Fans* by Jeffrey A. Brown). It may still be a long time before this milestone fades from view. —*AMC*

Miracleman

Newspaper reporter Mike Moran dreams of flying children and of exploding spaceships. When he is caught in a hostage situation in real life, Moran sees the backward reflection of the word "atomic," and it triggers something in his brain. Whispering the word "Kimota," Moran is transformed into Miracleman, a superstrong, nearly indestructible being. With the return of his long-forgotten alter ego, Moran begins to unravel the memories and secrets of his past, including the fate of Kid Miracleman and Young Miracleman, his sidekicks in the 1950s, who have similarly disappeared in the years since. But one of them is now a malicious tycoon with no conscience or scruples, and he'll stop at nothing— even the destruction of London—to stay on top of the world. And even as Moran explores his past, and fathers a very *special* daughter, his real life is unraveling around him, and the scientist responsible for his creation has other plans.

In the post–World War II economy in England, the comics business was booming. Publisher Len Miller was doing well reprinting the adventures of American hero Captain Marvel, until 1954, when Fawcett Publications settled with DC Comics and agreed to stop publishing the adventures of the Shazam!-shouting hero. Suddenly left without a main character, Miller instructed comics writer/artist Mick Anglo to create a knock-off of *Captain Marvel.* Anglo and his studio created Marvelman, whose magic word was "Kimota!" He was accompanied on many of his adventures by Kid Marvelman and Young Marvelman, and often faced the evil genius Emil Gargunza, aliens, and strange thugs. Marvelman became the first true British superhero, and his popularity soared for nine years. But the business changed, and in 1963, the last *Marvelman* adventure was published.

In 1981, ex-Marvel U.K. editor Dez Skinn was striking out on his own to create a new anthology of creator-owned comics, and he planned to bring Marvelman back. Impressed by a proposal by new writer Alan Moore, Skinn commissioned the first new *Marvelman* story for *Warrior* #1 (March 1982). Moore's story, combined with detailed art by Garry Leach, blew readers' minds. Moore took the 1950s concept and brought it into the 1980s, posing the question, "What effect would a real superpowered character have on *our* world?" As *Marvelman* continued, Alan Davis took over as artist, and the strip became *Warrior*'s most popular feature. But creator and financial problems behind the scenes—as well as a threatening letter from Marvel Comics when Skinn published a *Marvelman Special* (1984)—led not only to the end of *Marvelman* in *Warrior,* but the eventual closing of the magazine itself. *Marvelman* had won British comics' Eagle Awards, and attracted attention in the United States, but it was now out of a home.

Skinn approached U.S. publishers about picking up the *Warrior* properties, but both DC and Mar-

Miraclean #1 © 1985 Eclipse Comics.
COVER ART BY GARRY LEACH.

vel declined *Marvelman*. Pacific Comics eventually agreed to publish the series, but went bankrupt before it could appear. Pacific's assets were bought by Eclipse Comics, and *Marvelman* finally had a publisher again. After a controversial name change to avoid litigation from Marvel Comics, the new *Miracleman* #1 debuted in August 1985. The series was an immediate critical and sales hit. Issues #1–#6 featured reprints of the *Warrior* material, but new material—drawn by artist Chuck Beckum (now known as Chuck Austen)—also began appearing in issue #6 (February 1986). As the publishing schedule began to fluctuate, artists Rick Veitch and John Totleben finished the stories for Moore's run on the series, concluding with *Miracleman* #16 (December 1989).

Moore's stories were universally praised, and are often cited as the inspiration for such later series as *Watchmen* (also by Moore), *Marvels,* and DC's *Kingdom Come*. Despite the acclaim, two *Miracleman* issues raised retailer concern in the United States. Issue #9 (July 1986) featured explicit scenes of childbirth, resulting in some retailers refusing to carry the book, or placing it in their adult section. The violence of *Miracleman* #15 (November 1988)—in which Kid Miracleman causes the destruction of half of London and the deaths of more than 10,000 people—was not nearly as boycotted, but comics historians do note it as one of the most violent mainstream comics published to that date. As he left the series, Moore gave his successor a storytelling challenge: Miracleman had now reshaped planet Earth into a utopia, presiding over it as a benevolent supergod.

Hand-picked by Moore, writer Neil Gaiman took to the challenge with relish. He planned three story arcs called "The Golden Age," "The Silver Age," and "The Dark Age." Gaiman's scripts were interpreted by artist Mark Buckingham, who used a different art style for every story. Issues #17–#22 (June 1990–August 1991) comprised "The Golden Age," telling stories of the people in the new utopia, and how they viewed or interacted with Miracleman. Two more *Miracleman* issues were published, and another completed, but #24 (August 1993) was destined to be the final *Miracleman* from Eclipse; the company closed shop shortly thereafter. In addition to the two dozen *Miracleman* issues, Eclipse had released five trade paperback collections; the miniseries *Miracleman; Apocrypha* (which featured out-of-continuity stories by outside writers and artists, 1991–1992); *The Miracleman Family* (featuring reprints of 1950s Anglo material and released in 1988); and the stand-alone *Miracleman 3-D*. Miracleman also appeared as a character in the crossover miniseries *Total Eclipse* (1988–1989).

In April 1996, Image Comics co-creator Todd McFarlane bought Eclipse's assets, planning to bring back several of the properties, including *Miracleman*. Unfortunately, the ownership of the rights to the character is in question, with Gaiman and Buckingham owning a portion, and the once Eclipse-owned rights on shaky ground, keeping future *Miracleman* comic-book material in doubt. Despite this, McFarlane featured Mike Moran in cameo scenes in *Hellspawn* #6–#7 (February–April 2001), and released limited-edition artwork of Miracleman, as well as *Miracleman* statues. Whether Miracleman will ever shout "Kimota!" again in comics, or whether the excellent and much-sought-after material by Moore, Gaiman, and their artistic cohorts will ever appear in print again, is an answer only the future holds. —*AM*

Miss Fury

Several superheroes started life in comic books before going on to be adapted for newspapers. These include heroes that are household names today: Superman, Spider-Man, and Batman. Unusually, Miss Fury's creation was the other way around. Her first newspaper appearance was in April 1941, and she is considered the first major costumed superheroine in comics history, beating the likes of Wonder Woman, the Black Cat, and many others into print. Her creator, Tarpe Mills, was a pioneer herself, being almost certainly the first woman to work on a superhero strip and certainly the first to create one. She was involved in some of the very earliest comic-book series in the late 1930s, working on the likes of *The Ivy Menace, Drama of Hollywood,* and *The Purple Zombie* for titles such as Centaur's *Amazing Mystery Funnies* and *Star Comics*. Mills was born June Mills but adopted the more ambiguous forename Tarpe so that her predominantly male readership would not realize that their favorite strips were drawn by a woman.

Like Mills, Miss Fury had an alter ego; in civilian life she was (in best Bruce Wayne fashion)

wealthy socialite Marla Drake, who makes a fateful decision when on her way to a costumed ball: Discovering that someone else is going to the ball wearing the same costume as hers, she desperately hunts for a suitable replacement and settles upon an African ceremonial costume made out of a panther skin that had been used in magic rituals. The figure-hugging, all-black outfit, with ears, claws, and a tail, was certainly one of the most striking to be seen in the early days of comics. Right from the start, it brings our heroine adventure and peril. With athletic prowess, keen detective skills, and a super-costume bar none, Miss Fury is equipped to take on America's hoodlums and crooks.

In her first few months of publication, the superheroine met the dashing detective Dan Carey and the seductive spy Erica von Kampf as well as assorted criminals, con men, and damsels in distress. At the outset of World War II many of Miss Fury's adventures were set in Brazil, where she fought the bald, monocled General Bruno—the very personification of a Teutonic villain—and his Nazi battalions, hidden in a hollow mountain. Another frequent nemesis was the glamorous Era, with her guerrilla fighters, and the ever-present von Kampf could always be relied upon to pop up with an evil scheme or two. But Miss Fury was every bit the femme fatale herself, and had a string of allies including Gary Hale, Fingers Martin, Albino Joe, and her admirer from afar, Detective Cary.

Mills may not have been as polished as some of her contemporaries but she was nonetheless a fine storyteller, and her never-ending cliff-hangers (in many ways, the strip was one long narrative) moved along at a frantic pace. Mills appreciated glamor, and the feature was characterized by its succession of beautiful women in elaborate, fashionable, and often risqué clothing. She was something of a glamour girl herself, posing seductively for press releases, complete with her ever-present white cat, and she closely resembled the star of her strip, Marla Drake. With its bold linework and action-filled plots, the Miss Fury series was a natur-al for the burgeoning comic-book industry, and Timely Comics (better known now as Marvel Comics) released eight issues of *Miss Fury* reprints between 1943 and 1946, with pinups and cutout dolls thrown in for good measure.

Miss Fury ran for a very respectable ten years, outlasting most of its superhero rivals but also courting controversy. In the strip's later years, Marla Drake adopted a child rescued from the clutches of the evil Doctor Diman, little knowing that he was the son of her weak-willed ex-fiancé, Hale, and her arch-nemesis von Kampf. Just as daring was one 1947 exotic costume that was so revealing (by the standards of the day) that thirty-seven newspapers promptly canceled the strip. At the height of its popularity, the feature was printed in hundreds of newspapers across the United States as well as in Europe, South America, and even Australia, but in 1952, like many other adventure strips, it was finally laid to rest. The taste in newspapers was increasingly leaning toward sophisticated soap-opera strips and humor features, and Mills retired from comics.

In recent years, Miss Fury has been introduced to curious newcomers through further reprints, including a 1979 book collection from Archival Press and a short-lived series from Adventure Comics in 1991. —*DAR*

Modern Age of Superheroes (1980–Present)

By the advent of comics' Modern Age (1980–present), American society in the real world had responded to escalating crime, violence, and ethical deterioration with cynicism, and could no longer relate to the traditional, altruistic do-gooder. "Superheroes needed a *reason* to be superheroes," stated television screenwriter James Grant Goldin in the 2003 History Channel documentary *Comic Book Superheroes: Unmasked,* when referring to post-1980 costumed crime fighters. And thus was born the "new" superhero, motivated into action by stimuli other than "saving the day."

NEW DIRECTIONS AND THE DIRECT MARKET

As the writer/artist of Marvel Comics' *Daredevil* during the early 1980s, Frank Miller transformed what was once a second-banana comic book into a compelling study of one man's struggle against a vast and seemingly unstoppable network of crime. In late 1980, Miller introduced Elektra as Daredevil's former lover turned assassin-for-hire. Like many comic-book characters, Elektra had survived the murder of a parent, but instead of focusing her emotions into benevolence, she mastered martial arts and sold her services as a professional killer. While her marks usually represented the scum of the earth, Elektra executed them efficiently, without compunction—and readers applauded her bluntness. Elektra joined the Punisher and Wolverine, both of which were introduced in 1974, as Marvel's anti-heroes. Yet in the early Modern Age their brutal methods were toned down due to the censorship of the industry's watchdog board, the Comics Code Authority (CCA).

The art form of superhero comic books matured through its Golden (1938–1954), Silver (1956–1969), and Bronze (1970–1979) Ages, but its presentation remained essentially the same: a 64- or 32-page periodical published on inexpensive newsprint paper. That format began a metamorphosis in 1981. Comics venues were dwindling, as newsstands, drug stores, and other outlets stopped selling them due to their low profit margin. Specialty shops—described in *Comic Book Superheroes: Unmasked* as "private clubs catering to a hardcore base of comic-book fans"—began carrying new titles, offering comic-book publishers a fresh lease on life.

This "direct sales" market, where retailers ordered a finite number of copies of each series, offered three benefits: it helped the industry distribute its product straight to the consumer, it eliminated the return of unsold copies, and it sidestepped the approval of the CCA. DC Comics was the first major publisher to explore the direct market with "direct only" one-shots including *Madame Xanadu* (1981). DC experimented with offset printing, which offered richer, more vibrant colors on a brighter paper stock. Graphic novels—epic stories in one longer, and sometimes larger, package—were introduced to help the medium nurture storylines too complex for monthly serialized periodicals.

CREATOR-OWNED COMIC BOOKS

"Independent" publishers that catered to the direct market entered the business. San Diego, California–based Pacific Comics opened shop in December 1981 with *Captain Victory and the Galactic Rangers* #1, written and illustrated by the legendary Jack "King" Kirby (co-creator of Captain America, the Fantastic Four, the Hulk, and countless other superheroes), the first "creator-owned" comic book, allowing Kirby to retain copyright of the characters. Despite this distinction, the majority of Pacific's subsequent content shied away from superheroes, favoring horror and science fiction instead.

Creator ownership, the absence of Comics Code restrictions, and upscale printing created an alluring scent that attracted visionary and reactionary comic-book writers and artists to deeply invest themselves into their work. More independents arose—like Capital Comics, Eclipse Comics, Comico the Comic Company, First Comics, and Dark Horse Comics—and creator-driven, cutting-edge superheroes premiered from these houses, including Mike Baron and Steve Rude's *Nexus,* Matt Wagner's *Grendel* and *Mage,* Bill Willingham's *Elementals,* Mark Evanier and Dan Spiegle's *Crossfire,* Evanier and Will Meugniot's *DNAgents,* Dave

Stevens' Rocketeer (in the *Pacific* [Comics] *Presents* anthology), Neal Adams' *Ms. Mystic,* John Ostrander and Tim Truman's *Grimjack,* Mark Verheiden and Chris Warner's *The American,* and Mike Grell's *Jon Sable, Freelance.* Many of these new superheroes scoffed at historic mores and pushed the medium into grittier, sexier, and more thought-provoking terrain.

Howard Chaykin's *American Flagg!* (1983–1989), published by First, illustrates this superheroic shift. Set in the near future, where mega-corporations and the United States government have escaped Earth's civil and moral collapse by relocating to Mars, *American Flagg!* starred a washed-up actor named Reuben Flagg, who trades on his media image to gain employment as a security agent. Fans related to the storyline, having recently witnessed the election of U.S. president Ronald Reagan, who parlayed his former movie and television career into a public persona that appealed to a disgruntled, post-Carter America. Flagg's ego-driven motivation was only one pioneering element of this series: Its language and sexual content skirted R-rated territory in a marketplace traditionally accustomed to Disney-esque values, making *American Flagg!* unusually controversial. Chaykin's *American Flagg!* stands firm as a benchmark of the new superhero.

WHERE HAVE ALL THE GOOD GUYS GONE?

By the mid-1980s, the Comics Code became more relaxed, and Marvel published *Wolverine* and *The Punisher* titles, and examined racial prejudice in *X-Men.* DC revamped its old-guard superhero line in its continuity-altering twelve-issue series *Crisis on Infinite Earths* (1985–1986), which included the deaths of two major characters, Supergirl and the Flash. Readers discovered in the pages of *The New Teen Titans* that team member Speedy had a child out of wedlock, and over at Marvel, author Bill Mantlo pinpointed child abuse as the root of the Incredi-

ble Hulk's uncontrollable anger (a theme appropriated in director Ang Lee's 2003 blockbuster film, *The Hulk*). Frank Miller returned to superheroes with *Batman: The Dark Knight Returns* (1986), in which a surly Batman takes up arms to save Gotham City from rampant crime. These were not your father's superheroes: No longer men in capes who flew around saving the day, the superhero had become a reflection of the world around him: dark, determined, and no-nonsense.

Superhero subject matter could no longer be neatly resolved in one 22-page story. Nowhere is this better evidenced than in DC's *Watchmen* (1986–1987), a densely plotted and rendered twelve-issue series by writer Alan Moore and artist Dave Gibbons, two of a contingent of British creators who entered American comics in the 1980s. *Watchmen* portrays the personal struggles of a discordant superteam and their foibles—which include sexual impotence and strategic genocide—and stripped superheroes of any innocence they may have still held in the eyes of a comic-buying public.

Superhero titles like *Watchmen* and *Dark Knight* created a more literary climate in the comics business. Writer Neil Gaiman, another Brit, entered the field in the late 1980s and rose to acclaim with his award-winning DC title *The Sandman* (1989–1996), featuring the dream lord Morpheus. While the events of Sandman transpired within the so-called DC universe, uniformed superheroes (beyond robed deities) were absent: "I don't know any people who wear costumes," Gaiman remarked in 2003 on *Comic Book Superheroes: Unmasked.* The lyrical *Sandman* series fascinated a cult audience, and issue #19 of the series was the first— and *only*—comic book to ever win the World Fantasy Award for "Best Short Story." Gaiman's series was the cornerstone of DC's imprint, Vertigo, which has featured avant-garde anti-heroes like Hellblazer and Preacher. Pioneering protagonists like James O'Barr's disturbing Crow, who rose from the dead to become a crime fighter, and Concrete, an Earthman whose brain was grafted into a rock-hard alien body, surfaced from independent companies and continued the reinvention of the superhero. At this point it was clear that there were no "rules" to be followed, no set of criteria that determined whether a character really was or was not a hero.

THE GIMMICK AGE

By the early 1990s, comic-book sales were shrinking. Literary kudos aside, comics did not appeal to most kids, who by this time were distracted by a cornucopia of entertainment options. Additionally, the era of the provocative superhero had created a level of sophistication beyond the interest of most children—hyperactive computer games and violent movies offered more eye candy.

Comics received a temporary financial booster shot from a speculation frenzy, predicated upon the revelation that rare Golden Age comic books were, in the 1990s, commanding prices of thousands of dollars. *There's money in collecting comic books,* the thinking went, and kids of all ages poured into comics shops buying and hoarding comics. Variant covers and cover enhancements lured consumers into buying multiples of the same book, and sales of special issues climbed into the millions, making some royalty-earning or rights-holding artists deliriously wealthy. Heavily armed counterterrorists, disenfranchised street fighters, and demonic entities became the norm in the world of superheroes. "Events" shook up the status quo for longtime superheroes, like the (temporary) death of Superman in 1992.

During this period of explosive growth, superhero universes sprouted from a variety of companies: Dark Horse revealed its "Comics' Greatest World," with *Barb Wire, X, The Machine,* and *Ghost;* Malibu Comics' "Ultraverse" introduced *Prime, Prototype,* and *Hardcase;* and Valiant (later Acclaim) Comics published *Solar, Rai, Magnus Robot Fighter,* and *Bloodshot.* The major newsmaker of the era was Image Comics, founded when Marvel's best-selling artists (including Todd McFarlane, Jim Lee,

and Rob Liefeld) left the company to create their own company and publish their own material (*Spawn, WildC.A.T.S,* and *Youngblood*). Two other hot Marvel artists soon defected to Image, the results being Erik Larsen's *The Savage Dragon* and While Portacio's *Wetworks.*

Speculators finally got wise and defected from the fold in the mid-1990s, causing an abrupt collapse that so depressed the marketplace, Marvel Comics filed for bankruptcy in 1996. *Comic books are dead,* the skeptics cried.

MULTIMEDIA SUPERHEROES

But superheroes lived. Beginning with director Tim Burton's blockbuster movie *Batman* (1989), superheroes have maintained constant visibility in film, on television, in video games, on apparel, as toys, and on Internet sites. To the public at large, the concept of the superhero is universally known, but its source material, the comics, are not. The line dividing the "action hero"—the imperfect but determined non-costumed protagonist of movies and games—and the superhero has blurred, though the latter name is not usually applied to some of its most obvious heirs. Due to their larger-than-life acrobatics and cultural symbolism, action heroes like Lara Croft, the Terminator, Charlie's Angels (of the movies), and even the alien-busting Men in Black could clearly be called superheroes, although none of these characters adhere to conventional superhero trappings likes masks, costumes, or secret identities.

This media awareness has hindered and helped superhero comic books. Negatively, superheroes in mass media feed the entertainment options that have lured consumers away from comics reading. Positively, the income generated by the licensing of comics characters has allowed the comic-book business to stay alive; Marvel paid off its creditors and emerged from bankruptcy after reaping huge profits from the blockbuster film *Spider-Man* (2002).

In the 2000s, the audience for superhero comic books is small but remarkably loyal. Sales of collected editions have been encouragingly healthy, however, with the public's familiarity with superheroes helping sell trade paperbacks to the bookstore market. The path of Future Comics, a 2002 startup company, typifies this: After a difficult first year of trying to find an audience for its comics *Freemind, Deathmask,* and *Metallix,* in 2003 Future abandoned the production of monthly titles and moved exclusively to releasing trade paperbacks and pursuing movie development.

The look, shape, and content of comic books will undoubtedly continue to evolve in the years to come, to match the changing tastes of consumers. But, given its mass-media popularity, regardless of the naysayers, the superhero—and, no doubt, the superhero comic book—will continue to endure. —*ME*

Moon Knight

Ever since the creation of Batman in 1939, that character has been a constant source of inspiration both for DC Comics and its competitors. Marvel Comics' most transparent Batman clone was Moon Knight, who built up a sizeable cult following of his own, despite his obvious debt to the Caped Crusader. Moon Knight's first appearances came in two issues of *Werewolf by Knight* (#32 and #33) in late 1975, by writer Doug Moench and artist Don Perlin. Within a year, reader reaction was so strong that the character fought the Werewolf once more and starred in his own solo strip in *Marvel Spotlight* #28 and #29.

In his civilian life, Moon Knight was three people —or, more accurately, three separate personalities/personas of one rather schizophrenic man. Initially, there was just one man, Marc Spector, an academic's son who rejected his father's restrictive way of life and followed his own, more reckless path, first with the CIA and then as a mercenary under the vicious, tattooed Ronald Bushman. During one mission, Spector stumbles upon Bushman looting an archaeological dig in Sudan and about to kill the daughter of his recent victim, the dig's leader, Dr. Alraune. Spector saves the daughter, Marlene, but seemingly at the cost of his own life. However, local followers of the Egyptian moon god Khonshu drag his lifeless body to a nearby temple, and there he is miraculously resurrected. Back in the United States, with new love Marlene and old mercenary pal John Paul Duchamp ("Frenchie") in tow, Spector vows to turn his back on his past misdeeds and begin his life anew as a force for good.

Spurred on by either schizophrenia or brilliance, Spector adopted two new personalities to aid him in his new calling: Steven Grant (millionaire philanthropist) and Jake Lockley (a rough-edged cab driver, always on the lookout for tips from his underworld informer, Crawley). As Moon Knight, Spector/Grant/Lockley donned a white, caped, hooded costume (almost an inverse of Batman's black getup) and scoured the night sky from his mooncopter, piloted by Frenchie. The many similarities to Batman are unmistakable: the same creature-of-the-night ploy, millionaire playboy alter ego, loyal servant, helicopter, mansion, and driven personality. In addition, longtime artist Bill Sienkiewicz was an obvious follower of legendary Batman artist Neal Adams. However, Sienkiewicz (who came aboard for Moon Knight's first, extended solo series as a backup in *Hulk* magazine from 1978 to 1980) was also the strip's saving grace, as he pushed and transformed his initially derivative—if attractive—artistry into one of the medium's most incendiary talents.

After the *Hulk* series and a solo outing in *Marvel Premiere,* Moon Knight was finally awarded his own title in late 1980 (aptly called *Moon Knight),* which Moench and Sienkiewicz gradually built into a fan favorite. Within a couple of years, Sienkiewicz had taken elements from a wide range of sources, including illustrators Bob Peake and Bernie Fuchs and cartoonist Ralph Steadman, to make his work on the comic the most daring and innovative on the stands. The comic featured regular villains such as the Werewolf, Bushman, and the Midnight Man, but it was the literate tone and experimental art that readers loved. However, while the title was a critical success, it was never an enormous hit with the wider readership and, with issue #15 in 1981, it was one of the first comics to be distributed solely to specialty shops, a bold move that would later be adopted across the comics industry.

Sienkiewicz left the comic with issue #30 and it was canceled eight issues later, but over the following two decades the title was revived four times by a variety of creators. The longest-lasting of these—*Marc Spector, Moon Knight*—ran for sixty issues and featured guest appearances from Marvel's edgier heroes, such as the Punisher and Ghost Rider, whose hard-hitting strips the new comic was trying to emulate (right down to a bullet-proof Kevlar costume). Moon Knight was also an occasional member of the Defenders and of both East and West Coast branches of the Avengers, but he has always made more sense on his own.

Following success in the early 1980s, Moon Knight's creative team has gone on to further great achievement—Sienkiewicz with *The New Mutants* and *Elektra: Assassin* among many others and Moench (ironically) with numerous Batman titles. Moon Knight himself last appeared in a 1999 miniseries, his best days long behind him. However, he will no doubt enjoy occasional forays into the Marvel universe in the future. —*DAR*

Ms. Marvel

For a long time, Marvel Comics has been ever-vigilant in its quest to preserve ownership of characters and names. This has led to a host of female counterparts to male stars, such as Spider-Woman and She-Hulk, and a plethora of heroes with the word "Marvel" in their names. Having secured copyright on the names Captain Marvel (some three

Ms. Marvel #1 © 1977 Marvel Comics.
COVER ART BY JOHN ROMITA.

decades after the Fawcett star first hit the stands), Marvel Boy, and Marvel Girl, it was Ms. Marvel's turn at stardom. The job of fleshing out the new character's identity fell to writer/editor Gerry Conway. In the first issue's editorial (*Ms. Marvel #1*, January 1977), Conway fell over himself to stress his feminist credentials and practically apologized for not being female but, rhetoric aside, this liberated heroine was cast very much in the typical, action-packed Marvel mold.

Ms. Marvel was Carol Danvers (also Supergirl's last name, by the way), previously seen as a NASA security chief in the early days of the 1960s Captain Marvel strip, but now branching out into magazine editing, as the Gloria Steinem of the Marvel universe. Unbeknownst to her, during a heated battle years earlier while she was caught in an explosion next to Captain Marvel, some of his alien genetic structure had melded with hers, creating a Kree/human hybrid. This manifested itself in blackouts during which she donned a more revealing, navel-baring version of the Captain's duds and flew off to batter ne'er-do-wells. In time, her two personalities merged and she acquired a family, a new writer (the X-Men's Chris Claremont), a (navel-covering) costume revamp, and her own villains. The latter included future X-Men villain Mystique (in issue #16), Deathbird, Steeplejack, and Hecate. Later developments included a guest appearance by Captain Marvel in issue #19 and a zippy new black costume in the following issue. However, by its twenty-third issue, the comic was dead; the unpublished issue #24 would have debuted another future X-Men regular, Rogue.

Despite (or because of) the comic's cancellation, Ms. Marvel immediately resurfaced in *The Avengers* (from #181) and experienced the first of many traumatic events, when she suddenly became pregnant by an interdimensional admirer called Marcus (son of occasional Avengers foe Immortus). Within a week, she gave birth to an infant Marcus; it turned out to be a confusing plan to allow him to escape his otherworldly imprisonment, as he instantaneously grew to maturity and the two went off into the sunset, hand in hand. Except, of course, it was all an evil mind-control plot, and an embittered Carol Danvers reappeared a year later, only to be zapped by Rogue, who stole her powers and mind. The X-Men's Professor X restored some of her consciousness but, after convalescing with the team for a while, she was captured by evil aliens, the Brood, who experimented on her, ultimately unleashing her full, Kree-engineered cosmic power. Confused? You will be….

Now calling herself Binary (in *X-Men* #164, 1982) and drawing almost limitless power from a "white hole," she punched Rogue into orbit and,

overcome with remorse, hooked up with a bunch of intergalactic pirates called the Star Jammers, leaving the known universe for the rest of the 1980s. On eventually returning to Earth, she rejoined the Avengers, put on her earlier costume, and started calling herself Warbird for no obvious reason. As a reasonably settled member of the Avengers, the future should have been secure for Danvers but, as her powers inexplicably began to wane, she turned to the bottle and was eventually court-martialed out of the team for reckless behavior. Post-millennial developments included a move to Seattle, where the soused superheroine hit rock-bottom and joined Alcoholics Anonymous. This led ultimately to a recall (her third) to the Avengers, where she looks set to stay for the duration. —*DAR*

Multiculturalism

During comics' Golden Age (1938–1954), the nascent medium of superhero comic books was overrun with cultural stereotypes, a manifestation of societal prejudices widely, and sometimes innocently, held at the time. Captain Aero's "little Chinese pal," Chop Suey; the Lone Ranger's "faithful Indian companion," Tonto; and Mandrake the Magician's obedient African aide, Lothar, were among the characters that marginalized the value of minorities.

THE DAYS OF "KRAUTS" AND "JAPS"

To be fair, there was no bigoted Star Chamber orchestrating these characterizations. Comic books, like movies, novels, and radio, simply reflected America's perception of non-whites as second-class citizens—and minorities were in no position to argue at the time. Interestingly, Germans—other than Adolf Hitler, a short, comical-looking man ripe for caricature—were rarely stereotyped physically, given their physiological similarities to Anglo Americans. Yet they spoke with thick accents and were referred to by the derogatory term "Krauts." However, the Japanese—"Japs"—were rendered with fangs or with buck teeth, colored with yellow skin, and sometimes represented with pointed ears. An offensive stereotype by contemporary standards, granted, but to the U.S. mindset in the early 1940s, these were the devils that bombed Pearl Harbor, so they "got what they deserved" with these depictions.

And they "got what they deserved" from the superheroes. Comics covers routinely showed their stars attacking Japanese (and Germans, and on a few occasions, Italians), but perhaps no cover was more graphic in its anti-Japanese sentiment than Timely (Marvel) Comics' *The Human Torch* #12 (1943), presenting the flaming hero *burning* off the arm of a fanged Japanese torturer. Take that, you rat!

The Torch's acrimonious foe-turned-ally, Namor the Sub-Mariner, was comics' first mixed-race superhero, the offspring of a land dweller and a water breather. His multicultural heritage was often referenced in passing but never fully explored during the Golden Age. Some comics historians have theorized that Namor's patented anger stems from his crossbreeding—he never felt truly accepted by either of his races, leading him to take out his frustrations on others.

"Oriental" menaces, representing the "Yellow Peril" fear of world conquest, were a 1930s staple of the "pulp" magazines, with characters like Shiwan Khan from *The Shadow* and author Sax Rohmer's Fu Manchu inspiring comic-book villains like the Claw. First seen in Lev Gleason's *Silver Streak Comics* #1 (1939), the Claw was a sharp-toothed, insidious monster, with pointy ears, razor-sharp fingernails, fiery breath, and the ability to grow to humongous proportions. World War II only worsened the Asian stereotype. Kato, the Japanese houseboy and high-kicking companion to the Green Hornet, became a Filipino after the Pearl Harbor bombing.

On the rare occasions they appeared in print, African Americans were shown as manservants or comic-relief sidekicks. Mexicans were filthy bandits, as Zorro and other Western heroes were constantly

reminded. Native Americans grunted in broken English, as did Chief Skullface, nemesis of the Golden Age hero Black Owl, who routinely threatened to "scalpum" his feathered foe.

EARLY MULTICULTURALISM

Yet favorable multicultural depictions did occur during the Golden Age, most notably in *Blackhawk*. Premiering in Quality's *Military Comics* #1 (1941), the Blackhawks were a squad of international fighter pilots, crusading for the Allied forces but pledging allegiance to no single country—although their number included a buck-toothed and portly cook, Chop Chop. Chinese typecasting was nowhere to be seen, though, in "Carnival of Fiends," the Torch tale in *All Winners Comics* #1 (1941): Chinese are referred to as Chinese Americans, and they rally behind the Allied war effort.

After World War II and into the 1950s, superheroes evoked a more unified world viewpoint. Tonto received his own comic book from Dell (1951–1959), which appeared on the stands with Magazine Enterprises' *Straight Arrow* (1950–1956), starring a Native American protagonist who fought rustlers and white thieves. Superman and Batman joined England's Knight and Squire, France's Musketeer, "South America's" Gaucho, and Italy's Legionary in "The Club of Heroes" in *World's Finest Comics* #89 (1957). This trend spilled over into radio and television as well. "The most explicitly progressive [radio] series was *[The Adventures of] Superman,* which had its hero fighting racial and religious bigotry for several years after the war," commented author J. Fred MacDonald in *Don't Touch That Dial: Radio Programming in American Life from 1920 to 1960* (1979). Wrote MacDonald: "The appearance of the non-Anglo-Saxon heroes—the Indian brave, Straight Arrow; the Latino avenger, [TV's] Cisco Kid—also guided postwar youngsters toward tolerance."

There were exceptions to this growing depiction of diversity: Blacks mostly disappeared from comics. The spread of Communism made villains of Russians and Chinese, trends that continued into the 1960s. Prize Comics' *Fighting American* (1954–1955) lampooned Soviets with bad guys like Poison Ivan. Marvel even devoted a short-lived series to an "Oriental" villain: *The Yellow Claw* (1956–1957), starring a sinister mastermind who embodied every negative stereotype ever assigned to Asians: He was bald, slant-eyed, yellow-skinned, pointy-eared, and had long fingernails and a "Fu Manchu" goatee. In contrast, this series introduced a positive Chinese American character: FBI agent Jimmy Woo, a highly trained and resourceful lawman dedicated to bringing the Yellow Claw to justice.

THE 1960S SPARK ENLIGHTENMENT

After writer/editor Stan Lee inaugurated the Marvel universe with the publication of *Fantastic Four* #1 (1961), he placed his superheroes in New York City instead of a fictional metropolis, and Marvel's artists started drawing people of color into the comics. At first, the multicultural inclusions were subtle, like a black pedestrian in the background, but by the mid-1960s, non-whites ascended to positions of prominence. *Fantastic Four* #50 (1966) introduced Native American Wyatt Wingfoot, who became a long-standing supporting-cast member of the series, and issue #52 (1966) premiered Prince T'Challa, better known as the black superhero called the Black Panther. And agent Jimmy Woo returned in Marvel's *Nick Fury, Agent of S.H.I.E.L.D.,* engaging in high-tech (for the times) espionage epics that borrowed heavily from the James Bond movies.

None of Lee's series better advocated cultural tolerance than *X-Men*. First seen in 1963, the X-Men were mutants—the next step on the evolutionary ladder—who fought to protect the humans who distrusted them. While a groundbreaking metaphor for racial harmony, *X-Men* originally played it safe, making each of its mutant characters Caucasian.

Despite the multicultural inroads paved by Lee and other Marvel writers during the 1960s, cold-war pigeonholing had yet to fade: Iron Man's origin was rooted in the Vietnam War, and the hero battled the Chinese troublemaker Mandarin and a Vietcong villain named Wong Chu. Despite occasional non-flattering portrayals, Marvel's comics depicted a world of color and diversity, even with the company's misfit heroes, the green Hulk and the orange Thing.

When ABC's live-action *The Green Hornet* (1966–1967) TV show debuted, its producers expected its lead—clean-cut Caucasian hunk Van Williams—to become a heartthrob, but were blindsided when Asian import Bruce Lee, playing sidekick (emphasis on the kick) Kato, stole the show with his dazzling martial arts abilities. Lee was one of the few non-white actors on television at the time, but before long people of color became more visible.

Through most of the 1960s, DC Comics' series stayed exclusively Caucasian, with the exception of a handful of aliens like the green-skinned Martian Manhunter (who became a white man in his secret identity of John Jones) and through one-page public-service announcements extolling the virtues of ethnic tolerance. DC changed its stripes in *Justice League of America* (JLA) #57 (1967), with "Man, Thy Name is—Brother!" by scribe Gardner Fox, acknowledged among some comics historians as a selfless humanitarian. "One man is very much like another—no matter what the name of the god he worships—or the color of his skin," Fox's opening caption begins. The tale involves the intervention of three Justice Leaguers—the Flash, Green Arrow, and Hawkman, plus the JLA's "mascot" Snapper Carr—into the personal lives of three non-white Americans—a young black, a Native American, and a native of India—who struggle against barriers spawned by racial prejudice. The issue's cover, by artists Carmine Infantino and Murphy Anderson, depicts the heroes and their friends of color clasping hands before the symbol of the United Nations.

DC continued to take slow but deliberate steps to portray non-Caucasians in their superhero comics, with varying results. *The Brave and the Bold* (B&B) #71 (1967) introduced Batman's "old friend" John Whitebird, a Native American, but contains a wealth of unintentionally offensive references, including Batman's greeting of Whitebird ("Holy Peacepipes! Are you going on the warpath again?"). Four issues later, *B&B* #75 (1967) takes place in Gotham City's Chinatown, a borough that embraces its native heritage and modern Westernisms (Chinese American teens beam "Cool!" and "Marv!"), and largely avoids the stereotypes seen in issue #71, although issue #75's villain is a Yellow Claw–like conqueror called Shahn-Zi.

MAINSTREAM MULTICULTURALISM

In the late 1960s through the early 1970s, multiculturalism hit the American mainstream. Nonwhite actors appeared on TV programs as diverse as *Star Trek* (1966–1969) and *Hawaii Five-O* (1968–1980), and in movies like *Shaft* (1971). Superhero comics followed suit: the African American Falcon became the partner of Captain America, Wonder Woman learned martial arts from a Chinese teacher named I-Ching, Spider-Man mediated campus unrest, Batman encountered a league of international assassins, and Green Lantern and Green Arrow hopped into a pickup truck to traverse the American landscape seeking solutions for racism and other social cancers.

Luke Cage, Hero for Hire #1 (1972) was the first American comic book starring a black superhero, but numerous others followed, including *Black Goliath, Black Panther,* and *Black Lightning.* Marvel then premiered a headlining Chinese superhero, Shang-Chi (a.k.a. Master of Kung Fu) in *Special Marvel Edition* #15 (1973). Shang-Chi was a hero of great nobility and determination, but his father, the archetypical Fu Manchu (yes, *that* Fu Manchu), added yet another sinister Chinese conqueror to contemporary comics. Compelling characterization, memorable storytelling (first by Steve Englehart and Jim Starlin, then by Doug Moench and Paul Gulacy), and an international film and TV kung fu craze made

Shang-Chi a hit: *Special Marvel Edition* was renamed *Master of Kung Fu* (*MOKF*) with issue #17, and kept kicking for 125 issues.

MOKF's success spawned a fistful of martial-arts titles from a variety of publishers, some of which featured white heroes in Asian settings (Marvel's *Iron Fist* and DC's *Richard Dragon, Kung Fu Fighter*). Marvel's *The Deadly Hands of Kung Fu,* a black-and-white magazine-sized comic, introduced the Sons of the Tiger, a multiethnic group of martial artists, and the White Tiger, the first Puerto Rican superhero. Also bowing during this period were Marvel's Daughters of the Dragon—fighting PIs Colleen Wing (a Chinese American) and Misty Night (an African American)—and Mantis, a Vietnamese member of Marvel's conventional superteam the Avengers (appearing in print, quite unusually, at the height of the Vietnam War). In subsequent years, Asians as martial artists (and, narrowing the trend, Japanese as ninjas) have become a staple of comics, with DC's Lady Shiva and Valiant's Rai among their number.

THE INTEGRATED SUPERHERO UNIVERSE

By the mid-1970s, superhero comic books had become fully integrated. The X-Men were reintroduced in *Giant-Size X-Men* #1 (1975) with a new, multicultural roster: Cyclops (Anglo American), Colossus (Russian), Storm (African), Banshee (Irish), Wolverine (Canadian), Sunfire (Japanese), Nightcrawler (German), and Thunderbird (Native American). The X-Men's original message of cultural tolerance became even more profound given the team's color mix, a theme that has yet to fade: Despite their differences, these mutants work together as a unit and live together as a family. Sir Ian McKellen, the distinguished British actor who portrayed the evil mutant Magneto in the live-action blockbusters *X-Men* (2000) and *X2: X-Men United* (2003), remarked favorably of the X-Men's message of harmony at the 2003 British Independent Film

Awards: "X-Men and its story about mutants, about people who feel disaffected with society, and whom society is hard on, appeals most to young blacks, young Jews, and young gays."

The cultural composition of the X-Men established a template upon which the contemporary superhero team has been built. Numerous super-groups created or revived in the wake of *Giant-Size X-Men* #1 have contained a multicultural mix (some including extraterrestrials for good measure), such as the New Teen Titans, the Outsiders, Infinity Inc., Gen 13, WildC.A.T.S, Generation X, the Legion of Super-Heroes, the New Mutants, Ulraforce, the Suicide Squad, the New Warriors, X-Force/X-Statix, and Cyberforce.

Other teams have been built specifically around ethnicity, or a cultural connection. DC's Global Guardians are just that: superheroes assembled from around the world, like Israel's Seraph and Brazil's Green Flame (a.k.a. Fire of the Justice League). Marvel's Alpha Flight is a group of Canadian superheroes whose roster includes Marvel's first gay hero, Northstar. TV's *Captain Planet and the Planeteers* (1990) assembled a group of teenage environmental protectors, summoned from different regions of Earth by the goddess Gaia. A 1996 CD-Rom comic unveiled the Jewish Hero Corps, led by Menorah Man, and Mystic Comics' *Tribal Force* #1 (2002) introduced a little-known group of Native American superheroes.

Occasionally, non-Anglo superheroes have starred in their own comics, including, but by no means limited to, El Diablo, the Butcher, Blade, Shaloman, and Spawn. Ethnic superheroes and supporting cast members have become common: Superman's titles, for example, have included in their cast the African American hero Steel and his niece, who assumed his name in 2003, and the Hispanic hero Gangbuster. And whites and non-whites have formed teams, like Cloak (black) and Dagger (white), and Power Man (a.k.a. Luke Cage, black) and Iron Fist (white).

Prejudice and discrimination have been commonly explored through these tales of integrated heroes. For example, Amazing-Man, a black superhero retrofitted into the 1940s cast of *All-Star Squadron* with issue #23 (1982), stood up for racial equality at a time when Hitler preached ethnic cleansing. Despite cultural taboos, some interracial romances have occurred, including DC's (black) Bronze Tiger and (white) Gypsy and Marvel's (green, formerly white) She-Hulk and (Native American) Wyatt Wingfoot. No mixed relationship has raised more eyebrows than the marriage of the Avengers' Scarlet Witch (a white mutant) and Vision (a synthetic human)!

Through the meeting of its many cultures—and alien and artificial races—the superhero world inspires real-life humans to overcome their petty differences and live and work together as one. —*ME*

Namor: *See* **Sub-Mariner**

The New Gods

Jack Kirby was undoubtedly one of the most important creators ever to work in comics. Comics historian Mike Benton called him "the American artist who best represents what comic books are all about." Kirby's many creations (with writer Stan Lee) for Marvel Comics in the 1960s reinvigorated the entire industry. When DC Comics boss Carmine Infantino hired Kirby away from Marvel in 1970 with the promise of total artistic freedom, it was surely the coup of the decade. Kirby set himself up with his own editorial office in California and effectively created his own line of interconnected comics, which have now come to be known as the Fourth World series. Three titles premiered in 1971—*The New Gods, The Forever People,* and *Mister Miracle*—to which was added Kirby's eccentric vision of *Superman's Pal Jimmy Olsen,* which he had picked up at DC's insistence. Every two weeks, one of the four titles would hit the streets with a new installment of its story, written, drawn, and edited by Kirby at a punishing work rate that only he could have met.

The New Gods would become the central book of the tetralogy, with a story in issue #7, "The Pact," at last explaining how the various comics all knitted together. The story details the stormy conflict between two far-off planets: the Eden-like New Genesis and the monstrous Apokolips. To cement peace between the two worlds, their leaders—Highfather of New Genesis and Darkseid of Apokolips—exchange newborn sons, Scott Free and Orion, as hostages against hostilities ever resuming. Some years later, Darkseid learns of something called the anti-life equation (about which Kirby was always rather vague; suffice it to say that it was something terrifying), which was hidden on Earth, and he heads off with numerous evil (and bizarre) minions in tow to find it, setting off a new war of the "gods" with humanity in the balance.

The four comics each had different approaches to the ongoing tale. *The New Gods* starred Orion, recently arrived on Earth with his devil-may-care colleague Lightray, and was the most wide-ranging and bombastic of the Fourth World series, featuring colossal battle scenes and panoramic artwork. As the son of the evil Darkseid, Orion was an unusually complex, savage hero, despite his peaceful upbringing on New Genesis, and *The New Gods* explored his constant battle with both his father's minions and his own explosive lineage. The other exchanged son, Scott Free, also came to Earth, fleeing his militaristic upbringing on Apokolips, and assumed the

The New Gods #10 © 1972 DC Comics.
COVER ART BY JACK KIRBY AND MIKE ROYER.

eccentric of the titles. In it, Jimmy and Superman teamed up with a new Newsboy Legion and Guardian (made up of the sons of the 1940s kid gang of that name and the clone of their superhero protector), and with renegade bikers called "the Hairies," to fight Darkseid's scientists. It was Kirby's most prophetic series—anticipating developments in DNA research, cloning, and the Internet—as well as his most bizarre, featuring alien vampires, miniature Jimmy Olsens, the Loch Ness monster, and comedian Don Rickles.

The Fourth World was the most complete expression of Kirby's limitless imagination and the finest example of his monumental, explosive art. The comics were replete with double-page spreads, panoramic cosmic vistas, almost unimaginable creatures, and kinetic fight scenes. Kirby peopled the strips with as strange a collection of villains as comics have ever seen: Granny Goodness, Vermin Vunderbarr, Glorious Godfrey, Mantis, Desaad, and the Black Racer (a man in armor who propels himself through the air on skis!). Some readers hailed the series as a masterpiece, but others found it was more than they could take in, and sales were not what DC had hoped for. The series came to an end in 1972, except for *Mister Miracle,* which carried on until 1974. Kirby's series *Kamandi, The Last Boy on Earth* (which premiered in November 1972) proved to be more popular initially, but it has been his Fourth World stories that live on in the imagination.

Five years later, in 1977, both *The New Gods* and *Mister Miracle* were creditably revived (though not by Kirby), with the latter in particular proving to be of the highest quality, but both were gone again within the year, setting the pattern of revivals for years to come. The first run of *The New Gods* was collected together in a glossy miniseries in 1984, with Kirby providing the ending that he was not allowed to complete twelve years earlier. There was always the suspicion that he was making the story up as he went along, and certainly the new material satisfied no one, least of all Kirby himself. That same year, Mattel launched a series of toys called the Super Powers

identity of top escape artist Mister Miracle. Complete with cantankerous and diminutive assistant Oberon and statuesque, ex-stormtrooper girlfriend (and future wife) Big Barda, a fellow Apokolips escapee, *Mister Miracle* was a more lighthearted and traditional superhero title.

The Forever People were five happy-go-lucky teenagers from New Genesis: Mark Moonrider, Beautiful Dreamer, Big Bear, Vykin the Black, and Serifan. They could merge together to form a super-powered fighter called the Infinity Man. Like Orion and Mister Miracle, the Forever People were on Earth to fight Darkseid, but they were younger and more idealistic, and in some ways were Kirby's take on the hippy movement. *Jimmy Olsen* was the most (which spun off into a series of comics also drawn by Kirby), featuring numerous DC characters, including Darkseid. Kirby had wanted to end his series with a sequence of deaths, but the toy company was against the idea. Nevertheless, the toys and the *Super Powers* comic demonstrated that Darkseid himself may have been Kirby's greatest gift to DC, as the great, all-purpose villain that the company had so patently lacked before. Subsequent battles with the Legion of Super-Heroes and Superman, among others, have only served to confirm that conclusion.

From the late 1980s to 2004, there have been four *New Gods/Orion* series, two *Mister Miracle* revivals, and a single series of *The Forever People,* all with varying commercial and critical success. What none has been able to do is to build substantially on Kirby's originals. In fact, he created so many characters that there is still scope for further exploration for many years to come, as more and more fans of his work become professionals. Two fans, Paul Dini and Bruce Timm, introduced the Fourth World concepts into their acclaimed Warner Bros. cartoon, *The Adventures of Superman,* which used parts of *The New Gods* #7 in its storyline; later on, Timm's creative team showcased more Fourth World characters on the *Justice League* animated series. Some writers have also suspected that the Fourth World was the inspiration for an even more famous property, *Star Wars.* George Lucas is a known comics fan, and the similarities between the two series are striking, with the dark, evil father Darth Vader/Darkseid, fighting his long-lost son Luke Skywalker/Orion, who was trained by a benign, bearded mentor, Obi-Wan Kenobe/Highfather. Even the *Death Star* had a more than passing resemblance to Apokolips, but until Lucas confirms or denies the connection it must remain merely an intriguing theory. —DAR

Nick Fury

Sergeant Nick Fury was first conceived in 1963 as a bet, to see if Stan Lee and Jack Kirby's new

Nick Fury, Agent of S.H.I.E.L.D. #4 © 1968 Marvel Comics.
COVER ART BY JIM STERANKO.

approach to superheroes could work on a comic set in World War II. It did, and *Sergeant Fury and his Howling Commandos* was a successful strip for many years. Then, following the popularity of James Bond movies and the television show *The Man from U.N.C.L.E.,* Lee and Kirby decided to create their own spy—a superspy, if you will—and who better to fill that role than Nick Fury again? His first contemporary appearance (in *Strange Tales* #135) reveals how Fury was recruited to take charge of the secret global peacekeeping organization S.H.I.E.L.D. (originally an acronym for Supreme Headquarters International Espionage Law-Enforcement Division, but altered in 1989 to Strategic Hazard Intervention

Espionage Logistics Directorate), which circled the planet in a vast heli-carrier, almost like an airborne Pentagon. The agency's rationale for Fury's selection was that the tough, cigar-chewing war vet had the sort of street smarts that the organization needed to tackle the evil, green-pajama-wearing hordes of Hydra, a rival group made up of international terrorists.

For the next couple of years, Fury and S.H.I.E.L.D. took on Hydra and like-minded cartels, such as A.I.M. and T.H.E.M., with a vast array of handy gadgets and weapons (flying cars, Fury's robot doubles) in a series of frantic strips. With a large cast list, including Fury's fellow ex-commandos Dum-Dum Dugan and Gabriel Jones, über-geek Jaspar Sitwell, and regular guest star Captain America, the S.H.I.E.L.D. strip was soon full to overflowing. At the end of 1966, young writer/artist/actor/historian/escape artist Jim Steranko took over the feature and soon made it one of the talking points of the 1960s. Like Kirby, Steranko knew how to draw an exciting comic, but he also mixed in a modern, hip sensibility with references to pop art, surrealism, and psychedelia. He also finally got Fury out of his suit and into a black leather costume, bulging with muscles and weaponry, though his trademark eye patch and stogie survived the makeover.

A lengthy battle with the Yellow Claw introduced even more S.H.I.E.L.D. members and climaxed in a four-page spread, which readers needed two copies of the issue to read properly. Soon after, in 1968, Fury finally got his own comic, with Steranko at the helm, introducing Nick Fury's evil brother, Scorpio. The title was a potent force but within a year Steranko was gone, though his groundbreaking stories have been regularly reprinted ever since. By the turn of the decade, the whole spy scene had faded from popularity and the comic lost direction.

Although it would be the late 1980s before a regular Nick Fury comic was released again, both he and S.H.I.E.L.D. were a constant presence in all sorts of other Marvel comics. Throughout the 1970s, Captain America was a member of S.H.I.E.L.D., often teaming up with Fury to take on Hydra, A.I.M., or some other group of wierdos. Since Iron Man's alter ego, the ever-useful industrialist Tony Stark, was S.H.I.E.L.D.'s main idea man, the group frequently interacted with the *Iron Man* or *Avengers* comics, often popping up on flying sleds in the nick of time. Probably S.H.I.E.L.D.'s strangest guest shot was in Marvel's late 1970s *Godzilla* comic, in which a division led by Dum-Dum Dugan attempted to stop the not-so-jolly green giant that was leveling Manhattan each month. For those who wondered how a man who would be in his sixties could still look so good, a controversial one-shot in *Marvel Spotlight* revealed that Fury had been taking a (very convenient) youth serum for all those years.

From 1988 to the present comic fans have been awash with Fury and S.H.I.E.L.D. series, specials, collections, and guest appearances. These have variously introduced and killed off numerous S.H.I.E.L.D. agents, have pitted Fury against aliens, the Red Skull, and Hydra (over and over again), and have even suggested that S.H.I.E.L.D. was part of an intergalactic plot (an idea that Marvel later decided to forget). One particularly enjoyable series featured Fury attending Smokestoppers Anonymous and included a handy secret message decoder. A 1996 issue of the *Punisher* apparently killed off the great man for good, but the deceased turned out to be one of seemingly thousands of Fury robots. In print at least, Nick Fury is now almost indestructible, and looks set to battle Hydra and its ilk for years to come.

Picking up on his popularity, in May 1998 Fox television aired a two-hour telefilm titled *Nick Fury, Agent of S.H.I.E.L.D.* David Hasslehoff played the title character, who pulls out of a self-imposed retirement to fight the forces of Hydra, led by the seductive Viper. Comics scribe David Goyer wrote the fairly faithful script, but the lackluster telefilm—which had been intended as a backdoor pilot years prior—did not do well enough in the ratings to merit any follow-ups. —*DAR*

The Night Man

Musician Johnny Domino is having a good morning in San Francisco, until an alien energy bolt strikes a trolley car, sending a chunk of metal into his head. After he recovers, he learns that he does not need to sleep, his eyes are permanently dilated (making light painful), and that he can telepathically "hear" other people's evil thoughts inside his own head. Using his aikido training, Domino garbs himself in a costume and prowls the city rooftops after dark as the Night Man, to stop the crimes he *knows* are going to happen.

Created by writer Steve Englehart, the *Night Man* comic was part of Malibu Comics' Ultraverse line, and its lead was destined to become the best-known character from the line as far as the general public was concerned. Interconnected with other series, *The Night Man* was most attached to Englehart's *The Strangers* (in the first issue of that series he received the head injury). *The Night Man* #1 debuted in October 1993, and in the first story, the Night Man pursued Deathmask, the murderer of Domino's friend. Other villains he faced included Mangle, lead villain J. D. Hunt, hypnotist murderess Rhiannon, werewolf Nikolai Apocaloff, the Silver Daggers gang, and villainess BloodFly.

The Night Man series would last until issue #23 in August 1995, around the time Malibu was bought by Marvel Comics. After a *The Night Man vs. Wolverine* crossover special (August 1995), a relaunch was produced with *The Night Man "Infinity"* (#0) in September 1995, but this version only lasted until issue #4. The hero appeared again in *The Night Man/Gambit,* a three-issue miniseries in early 1996. He has not appeared in comics again since that time.

The Night Man did appear on television, however, in both animation and live action. DIC produced an *Ultraforce* animated series as part of their *Amazing Adventures* syndicated block in September 1995.

Thirteen episodes of *Ultraforce* were produced—concurrent with a Galoob toy line—and the fifth episode (airing November 12, 1995) featured the Night Man.

A live-action series called *NightMan* (note name change) debuted in syndication the week of September 20, 1997, the creation of producer Glen A. Larson. The two-hour pilot established a slightly revised origin. Jazz musician Johnny Domino (Matt McColm) was now struck by lightning, which re-routes his neural pathways. He dons an experimental suit created by an ex-high tech weapons inventor named Rollie Jordan (Derek Webster) to fight crime in Bay City. The prototype suit has anti-gravity and stealth capabilities, a targeting laser eyepiece, and is bulletproof. Domino doesn't tell his ex-cop father Frank Dominus (Earl Holliman) his secret, which causes friction between the two.

Although there were not really any other costumed supervillains or other heroes in his TV foray, NightMan faced down an array of terrorists, thugs, powered civilians such as telekinetic Chrome, and occasional magical villains. In one episode, he teamed up with Manimal, the animalistic hero of a previous short-lived Glen Larson series of 1983, while a female version of the title character, Night-Woman, appeared in both the first and second seasons. *Night Man* creator Steve Englehart wrote three episodes of the series; fittingly, his first, "You Are Too Beautiful," was the hero's most rerun and most popular episode. *NightMan* aired its last new episode the week of May 23, 1999, but the series remains in syndication and on the air in 2004. —*AM*

Nightwing

DC Comics' Nightwing—formerly Robin the Boy Wonder—toiled for forty years under the shadow of the Batman as comics' premier sidekick. First appearing in April 1940 in *Detective Comics* #38, Dick Grayson, the junior member of the Flying Graysons circus family, witnesses his parents'

Nightwing #41 © 2000 DC Comics.
COVER ART BY GREG LAND AND DREW GERACI.

gram, *The Batman/Superman Hour,* cut from the same campy cloth.

Then came the 1970s. Licking its wounds from marketplace outdistancing by Marvel Comics, former top dog DC implemented a host of sweeping editorial changes in an effort to win back readers. Among them was returning Batman to his roots as a "creature of the night" in a movement largely orchestrated by writers Frank Robbins and Dennis O'Neil, artist Neal Adams, and editor Julius Schwartz. Batman—rechristened "the" Batman as in days of old—now preferred the shadows to the limelight of television, displacing his spirited Boy Wonder in the process.

In *Batman* #217 (December 1969), Grayson, who by this point had matured to his late teens, moved from his home in Gotham City and entered Hudson University. As Robin the "Teen" Wonder, the hero floundered through the 1970s in irregular guest appearances and backup stories. Designed as a cheerful counterpoint to Batman's darkness, Robin without Batman didn't seem to work (notwithstanding some lighthearted solo stories in more innocent earlier decades). He grew introverted, struggled to cultivate his own identity, and became estranged from Batman in the process. In October 1980, Robin was included as the leader of the revamped New Teen Titans (a group he'd been shunted into in its previous incarnation), and under the watch of writer Marv Wolfman and artist George Pérez began to emerge as a character in his own right.

When Jason Todd was introduced as the new and younger Robin in the 1983 Batman titles, Wolfman and Pérez took it upon themselves to reinvent the original Boy Wonder.

Grayson, they discovered, was a cipher, with little individuality outside of Robin's.

So they appropriated the basic components of his heroic guise—his acrobatic flair and detective skills—and made the Teen Wonder a natural leader. As the Titans' tactician, Grayson was now a man, and it was time for him to be Robin no more. In

deaths in a sabotaged trapeze incident. This murder is also observed by millionaire Bruce (Batman) Wayne, who as a child had similarly watched his own parents die. Grayson becomes Wayne's ward, and soon, after months of rigorous training in the subterranean Batcave, joins Batman as his crime-fighting ally, Robin the Boy Wonder. Clad in bright red, green, and yellow, Robin's bubbly demeanor softened Batman's harder edge, and for decades this Dynamic Duo blazed through hundreds of adventures in comic books, movie serials, radio shows, newspaper strips, and the nonsensical live-action *Batman* television series (1966–1968), succeeded in the fall of 1968 by an animated pro-

THE SUPERHERO BOOK

Tales of the Teen Titans #39 (February 1984), he permanently retired his crimson tunic, becoming the ebon-clad, blue-feathered Nightwing five issues later.

Nightwing led the Titans through myriad escapades, falling in love with and almost marrying teammate Starfire. In the lengthy "Knightfall" serial that ran through the Batman comics beginning in late 1992, the rift between Nightwing and Batman intensified when the Dark Knight, after being crippled by the villainous Bane, selected someone other than Grayson to succeed him. Nightwing felt that he should have been chosen to inherit the "mantle of the Bat" and deeply resented his mentor. Nightwing and Batman ultimately came to grips with the reasons behind their emotional separation, and Wayne embraced Grayson as his son, even asking him to temporarily adopt the Batman guise in the "Prodigal" storyline (1994–1995).

Through these appearances, Nightwing had become a fan favorite, and readers clamored for the character to headline his own title. DC Comics hesitated, stayed by the stigma of Grayson's longtime sidekick status, but tested his wings in 1995 first with a one-shot, then with a four-issue miniseries. Critical and commercial reaction to both was strong, and in October 1996, Dick Grayson—one of comics' most recognizable characters—was at last awarded his own ongoing title with the release of *Nightwing* #1. The hero now patrols the streets of Blüdhaven, a woefully corrupt city near Gotham, in a dual capacity: Armed with glove gauntlets (replacing the utility belt he wore as Robin), night-vision lenses, martial-arts mastery, and unbreakable "Escrima sticks" in his guise of Nightwing; and with a badge as Blüdhaven police officer Richard Grayson. He still frequents Gotham City when summoned by Batman, Robin, or Oracle, the latter of whom is his former ally and girlfriend Barbara (Batgirl) Gordon, and during the summer of 2003 rejoined several of his former Titans teammates as the leader of the all-new Outsiders.

Despite the labors of talented DC Comics writers and artists, Dick Grayson remains Robin in the minds of the public at large. Actor Chris O'Donnell portrayed a twentysomething Grayson/Robin in the movies *Batman Forever* (1995) and *Batman & Robin* (1997), although the former film includes the character mentioning "Nightwing" as a possible heroic name. In the late 1990s, Grayson finally broke free of the bonds of pop-culture restraints and appeared on television as Nightwing in the animated *New Batman/Superman Adventures*. —ME

Northstar

Although he was not the comic-book world's first openly gay superhero, Marvel Comics' Northstar is certainly the most well-known homosexual in comics. First appearing in *X-Men* #120–#121 (April–May 1979) with a team of heroes called Alpha Flight, Northstar was described as "Jean-Paul Beaubier, Olympic and professional ski champion." His mutant powers included flight and superspeed, and when he clasped hands with his sister Aurora (Jeanne-Marie Beaubier), they could create brilliant bursts of light.

Northstar would appear a few more times with the Alpha Flight team prior to the first issue of their own comic book debuting in August 1983. There, readers learned that Jean-Paul and Jeanne-Marie were orphans who were raised separately. Jean-Paul had run away from his foster family, joined a circus, traveled through France, and eventually developed his mutant powers. He also became involved with Raymonde Belmonde, an older man who became his mentor and trainer (and perhaps lover). Later, Beaubier joined a radical separatist organization of Quebec Nationalists known as *Front de Liberation du Quebec* (FLQ), but he left when their activities turned violent.

By the time he was recruited to join Alpha Flight, Jean-Paul Beaubier had become a wealthy world-class skiing champion, full of ego, rudeness, and unexplained grumpiness. He became a member of the superhero group, reuniting with his trou-

Uncanny X-Men #414 © 2002 Marvel Comics.
COVER ART BY STEVE UY.

bled sister, who had developed a split personality. He also developed an unrequited crush on his teammate, Walter Langkowski, a.k.a. Sasquatch. In *Alpha Flight* #41 (December 1986), Beaubier's "secret identity" as a mutant superhero was revealed to the world, and he was disgraced in the competitive skiing community.

Shortly thereafter, Northstar began to develop a seemingly incurable illness. Writer Bill Mantlo planned to reveal that the illness was AIDS—and planned to have Northstar die—but his editor Carl Potts, and Marvel's editor-in-chief, Jim Shooter, put a halt to that storyline, forcing Mantlo to change the disease to a curable magic-based health problem.

Mantlo made a public outcry about the subject to newspapers and magazines; reporters investigating found that many Marvel freelancers said that Shooter had reportedly declared a "no gays in the Marvel universe" policy. After Shooter's departure from Marvel, new editor-in-chief Tom DeFalco said no such policy ever existed, nor was ever enforced. Still, despite hints about Northstar's sexual orientation dropped by both John Byrne and Mantlo over the years, writers were not allowed to have him come out of the closet.

That finally changed with *Alpha Flight* #106 (March 1992), in a story called "The Walking Wounded." In it, Northstar adopts a young baby girl infected with AIDS, but upon her death—and a fight with Canadian hero Major Maple Leaf—Beaubier came out as a gay hero to the world. The story got a huge amount of publicity, prompting Marvel to back-pedal, fearing controversy (editors were reportedly instructed to refer reporters to DC Comics rather than comment!). A 1994 *Northstar* miniseries barely made mention of the character's sexuality, though by the late 1990s, mention of his homosexuality became almost *de rigueur* for any story in which he appeared.

Although he can lay claim to being Marvel's first openly gay superhero, Northstar is not the industry's first. Alan Moore introduced gay heroes in his groundbreaking *Watchmen* series (1986–1987) and also revealed that one of the Miracleman family members was gay (*Miracleman* #12, September 1987). But it was in DC's *Millennium* and *New Guardians* (1988) that Gregorio—one of ten "chosen" to become the next step in humanity's evolution—became the first major gay superhero, Extrano. Since that time, many heroes have come out as gay, lesbian, bisexual, or transgendered: Pride in *Gay Comics;* Fade in Milestone's *Blood Syndicate;* Hero in DC's *Superboy and the Ravers;* Spectral in Malibu's *The Strangers;* Josiah Power in DC's *The Power Company;* Amazon in Marvel's *Thunderbolts;* Flying Fox in Homage's *Astro City;* Pied Piper in DC's *The Flash;* Cobweb in ABC's *Tomorrow Stories* and Jack

Phantom and Jetman in ABC's *Top Ten;* and perhaps the most infamous in today's comics world, Apollo and Midnighter in Wildstorm's *The Authority.*

Given its history, it is ironic that in the modern era of Marvel Comics the company features more regularly seen gay and lesbian superheroes than any other company. The *X-Men* books alone feature several, making the corollary between social pressures on gays and mutants more obvious. Even the 2003 film *X2: X-Men United* features a character "coming out" to his parents about being a mutant, while in *New X-Men* #134 (January 2003), founding member Beast tells Cyclops he is not gay, but, "I might as well be! I've been taunted all my life for my individualistic looks and style of dress … I've been hounded and called names in the street and I've risen above it…. Come on, I'm as gay as the next mutant! I make a great role model for alienated young men and women." *X-Statix* has Phat and Vivisector, *Exiles* has Sunfire II, *New Mutants* has Karma, and *Mystique* has its bisexual title character.

Northstar is no longer alone then, as a gay hero or as a publicly-out mutant. He is also more high-profile today; after some guest appearances in 2001—in which it was revealed that he had written an autobiography titled *Born Normal*—Northstar joined the cast of *Uncanny X-Men* with issue #414 (December 2002). At Professor Charles Xavier's school for mutants, he supposedly teaches Business, Economics, and Flight. But mostly, Northstar doles out well-meaning lessons of tolerance to mutants, when not pining over unavailable straight teammates. —*AM*

Nova

In many ways, *Nova* signaled the end of an era. The comic was an avowed attempt to recapture the innocence and excitement of the early days of the all-conquering 1960s *Spider-Man* comic. In the 1970s the tide of comics was turning, however, and

Spider-Man was swept away in the wave of X-Men mania, although he was fondly enough remembered to make several spirited comebacks. Nova was dreamed up in the 1960s by would-be comics pro Marv Wolfman, who was finally able to make his dream a reality when he became editor-in-chief of Marvel Comics. The *Nova* comic's first issue in 1976 introduced readers to underachieving high-school zero Richard Rider, who stumbles across a dying alien (shades of Green Lantern's origin) by the name of Rhomann Dey, from the planet Xandar, who presents him with a golden helmet. In the time-honored tradition, the helmet gives the startled teen fantastic abilities, including amazing strength and the power of flight. In the guise of Nova the Human Rocket he can do the impossible.

The comic's high-school milieu would have been familiar to any longtime Spider-Man fan, but at least Rider had a reasonably functional family—as much a rarity in comics then as now. With solid artwork from veterans such as Sal Buscema and Carmine Infantino, the title was always attractive, and a bizarre mix of villains usually guaranteed the reader a good time. In addition to arch-foe the Sphynx, Nova also tussled with bargain-basement bozos such as Diamondhead, the Condor, Powerhouse, Mega Man, and the Corruptor. *Nova*'s twenty-five-issue run ended with our hero, along with fellow crime-fighters the Comet and Crime Buster (Team Nova, anyone?), in pitched battle with the Sphynx and assorted hoods, en route to Xandar.

The storyline was concluded in a few issues of *The Fantastic Four* (issues #208–#212), in which Nova and pals defended Xandar from a Skrull invasion, cosmic anti-hero Galactus battled it out with the Sphynx, and Nova was awarded the title of Xandar's Protector. After a while in space, Rider felt homesick and was allowed to return, but at the expense of his powers—or so he (and readers) thought. After a decade in the wilderness, forgotten by his readers and now a depressed high-school dropout, he resurfaced in the *New Warriors* in 1990, courtesy of writer Fabian Nicieza. Nova rediscovered his powers in the most dramatic way possible—by being dropped from a tall building (by would-be team leader Night Thrasher) and finding, as he hurtled to the ground, that his former powers kicked in, much to everyone's relief. The New Warriors team, made up of sidekicks and rejects, proved to be one of the hits of the 1990s, renewing interest in Nova and inspiring a second stab at solo success in 1994.

Through a mistaken newspaper report in the team's early days, Nova became widely known as Kid Nova, much to his chagrin and his teammates' merriment—an incident typical of the *New Warriors*' humorous undercurrent. Sadly, after the exuberance of the comic's first few years, darker elements began to encroach on the fun and, in the last issues of his own (second) comic (issue #18 in 1995), Nova lost his powers (again). He had failed to answer a call to arms from the long-forgotten planet Xandar, and so an evil character called Nova

Omega stripped the hero's abilities. Rider eventually recovered his powers two years later, in the last issue of *New Warriors,* only to endure another period in the comics wilderness before Image founder Erik Larsen gave him one last try.

The Larsen-scripted *Nova, The Human Rocket* (1999), began with the New Warriors disbanding and then set about returning Nova to his roots, complete with revived villains the Sphynx, Diamondhead, and others. Now, more than twenty years after his first appearance, Rider had finally become a college student and, much as before, the comic was a mélange of misfit angst, rollicking adventure, and a zeitgeist-defying optimism. It lasted seven issues. Ever since, Nova fans have had to be content with sporadic guest shots from a grown-up Rider in the future- (and alternative-universe-) set *Spider-Girl* comic, at least until the powers-that-be decide to disinter him once more. —*DAR*

Olsen, Jimmy

It's not easy being Superman's pal. For Jimmy Olsen, his friendship with Metropolis' Man of Steel has led to frequent mutations and imperilments. But let's not overlook the fringe benefits: celebrity status, occasional superpowers, lots of dates, and a bulletproof bodyguard. Not bad for a freckle-faced, red-haired, all-American kid.

Olsen's life in fiction didn't start out so exciting, though. Like that other venerable mainstay of the Superman mythos, kryptonite, Olsen first appeared on the 1940s radio show based on the comic, and there as in his 1941 comic-book debut, he was a rather insignificant *Daily Planet* copy boy with dreams of becoming a newspaper journalist. His idol was reporter Clark Kent, secretly Superman, who quickly took notice of Olsen's promise. Nor did much time pass before DC Comics' editors realized that in Olsen they possessed the same benefit for Superman that the recently introduced Robin the Boy Wonder provided to Batman: a teenage sidekick to whom younger readers could relate. Jimmy was promoted to "cub reporter," sporting his trademark bowtie and joining Kent and Lois Lane on a host of often dangerous escapades, along the way encountering—and usually being res-

cued by—Superman. His staunch loyalty to the Man of Steel made Olsen Superman's pal, a friendship that sometimes placed him in harm's way when targeted by the hero's enemies.

In the live-action television program *The Adventures of Superman* (1953–1957), Jack Larson's comically spirited portrayal of the cub reporter made Olsen a household name, becoming comics' most famous supporting-cast member. DC promptly capitalized on this recognition, and in 1954 released the first issue of *Superman's Pal Jimmy Olsen,* the entry-level book in Superman's burgeoning periodicals franchise. In a run lasting a remarkable twenty-eight years, Olsen's colorful series sometimes took him undercover as a master of disguise (he masqueraded as Robin to fool Batman, and even appeared in drag as a gun moll!), into pop-culture parody (Jimmy was "as popular as Ringo" as "The Red-Headed Beatle of 1,000 B.C." and made Superman "cry U.N.C.L.E." as a secret agent), and occasionally into conflict with his superfriend (under the influence of the "Helmet of Hate," Olsen zapped the Man of Steel with a kryptonite beam). It was Olsen's peculiar transformations, however, that made his magazine so memorable. His mishaps with alien weapons and his ill-advised sips of unusual potions caused Olsen to mutate, at one time or another, into a giant turtle man, a human porcupine, a werewolf, a future man, and even an obese version of himself!

Olsen's favorite conversion was his serum-induced change into the elongating superhero Elastic Lad, a role he so frequently slipped into that he earned reserve-member status in the Legion of Super-Heroes. The Legionnaires weren't the only superheroes with whom Olsen fraternized: He sometimes joined Superman on adventures with Batman and Robin in *World's Finest Comics,* himself forming a recurring partnership with the Boy Wonder.

To summon his powerful pal in times of crisis—once an issue, at least, it seemed—Olsen was given by Superman a signal watch emitting a frequency that only the Man of Steel could hear. Olsen was idolized by Metropolis teens who formed a fan club in his honor, and he dated airline attendant Lucy Lane (Lois' sister) and a bevy of other beauties. This fame sometimes overfed Olsen's ego, but his friend Superman was always there to help him learn humility.

Industry superstar Jack Kirby took the creative reins of *Superman's Pal Jimmy Olsen* in 1970 for an imaginative but short-lived stint that proved too sophisticated for readers of the time. In 1974, Olsen's book absorbed the sagging *Superman's Girl Friend Lois Lane* and *Supergirl* series into a giant-sized comic retitled *The Superman Family,* where the junior journalist's adventures continued until cancellation in 1982. Olsen returned to his supporting-cast roots, maintaining his position as Superman's ally in the current DC Comics continuity, rebooted in 1986.

The glory days of his own wacky comic may be long gone, but Olsen rose again as the star of the moody twelve-issue "maxi series" *Metropolis* (2003–2004). And he has been immortalized on screen and radio by a host of actors in each of Superman's media interpretations, as well as in song: The Spin Doctors' hit "Jimmy Olsen's Blues" from their *Pocket Full of Kryptonite* CD (1993) is Olsen's ballad of unrequited love for Lois Lane. —*ME*

One-Hit Wonders

Superman, Batman, Spider-Man, Wonder Woman—they're the heavy hitters, powerful enough to make *People* magazine's "200 Greatest Pop Culture Icons" list for 2003. Then there's what many would categorize as the B-list: Iron Man, Green Lantern, Thor, and Green Arrow, heroes popular among comics fans, but never quite crossing the line into the general public's consciousness. Let's not forget the more minor titans like the Scarlet Witch, Blue Beetle, Ant-Man, and Metamorpho, heroes only a mother (or a die-hard comics fan) could love, whose shots at stardom come and go.

And then there are the one-hit wonder women and men who just never quite cut the mustard, and would be spreading it on burgers at a fast-food joint were out-of-work superheroes considered employable. Heroes who make a lone appearance in comics, then ride off into the sunset quicker than you can say, "One strike, and yer out!"

Believe it or not, the amazing Spider-Man almost suffered this discomfiting fate. In 1962, Marvel Comics head honcho Martin Goodman rejected writer Stan Lee's concept of a teenage superhero with *spider* powers—everybody hates spiders, after all!—but Lee badgered Goodman to publish the character in the last issue of an anthology series on the chopping block, *Amazing Fantasy* #15. Lee's uncanny intuition for heroes with reader resonance was right on target—the issue sold like mad and Spidey became Marvel's most popular character. Similarly, DC Comics' long-running characters the Legion of Super-Heroes premiered as one-time guests in the Superboy story in *Adventure Comics* #247 (1958), but readers demanded their return. The Legion and Spider-Man got lucky.

Not so with the superheroic guise of Spidey's (or his alter ego, Peter Parker's) relative, dear old Aunt May. In *Marvel Team-Up* #137 (1984), May was selected by the omnipotent world-eater Galactus to be his cosmically powered herald. Encased in a gleaming exoskin, geriatric May became—are you ready for this?—Golden Oldie. May's still around, but Golden Oldie was retired to a home for has-been heroes.

In comics' boom period, the Golden Age (1938–1954), publishers introduced new characters virtually every month, mostly in anthology titles, testing the marketplace to see what clicked. Action-starved readers embraced unique newcomers like the Sub-Mariner and the Spectre, but not every hero was a winner. Remember Commandette, the movie star by day, female commando by night? Or the futuristic fighter called Atoma? Probably not. They were attempts to parrot the success of DC Comics' Wonder Woman, and each appeared once, Commandette in Superior Comics' *Star Studded Comics* (1945), a two-issue series that, curiously, featured *no* issue numbers, and Atoma in Harvey's *Joe Palooka* #15 (1947).

By the 1950s, the superhero comics market had shrunk, and DC Comics was looking to franchise its remaining characters. Wonder Girl clicked in *Wonder Woman,* but Superman sidekicks Skyboy, who flew into *World's Finest Comics* #92 (1958), and Super-Girl (who preceded Superman's cousin Supergirl by one year), from *Superman* #123 (1958), fizzled after one story each. Aquagirl, who teamed with Aquaman in *Adventure Comics* #266 (1959) four months before the introduction of Aqualad, also sank after a single outing. Those failed fighters' names, however, would later be recycled by DC for wholly different characters.

Try-out titles, like DC's *Showcase* (1956–1970, with a 1977–1978 revival) and *First Issue Special* (1975–1976) and its competitor's *Marvel Premiere* (1972–1981) and *Marvel Spotlight* (1971–1977), were staples for more than twenty years, offering exposure to new characters in hopes of launching their own series. For every Metal Men and Iron Fist that made the cut, there were losers: Witness (if you dare) B'Wana Beast, who somehow got *two* appearances in *Showcase* #66–#67 (1967) to ply his jungle justice;

Atlas and the Dingbats, from DC's *First Issue Special* #1 and #6, respectively (both 1975), neither of which is considered a jewel in the crown of writer/artist Jack "King" Kirby; the freakish superteam the Outsiders (not to be confused with Batman and the Outsiders and its successors), in *First Issue Special* #10 (1976); and the forgettable Thor spinoff Warriors Three in *Marvel Spotlight* #30 (1976).

Occasionally, a one-hit wonder from a try-out title would resurface years later. Dolphin, the charming undersea heroine created by romance-comics artist Scott Pike, may have floated through only one issue of *Showcase* (#79, in 1968, although she *did* have a brief cameo, along with every other *Showcase* star, in 1978's anniversary issue, #100), but in the 1990s she joined the cast of DC's *Aquaman*. Kirby's Manhunters instantly disappeared from view after their debut in *First Issue Special* #5 (1975), but by the late 1980s were a villainous force in many DC titles. And another *First Issue Special* flunkie, a blue-skinned alien called Starman from issue #12 (1976), was woven into the fabric of author James Robinson's historically rich, all-new *Starman* series beginning in 1994.

Some champions got one shot at stardom—*literally.* The supple Sentinel, premiering in Megaton Comics' *Megaton* #1 (1983), took a fatal bullet first time out of the gate. Detroit's own superhero, the Crusader, busted into action on page six of DC Comics' *Aquaman* #56 (1971); several pages later, as he leapt across rooftops, anticipating a victory that would elevate him beyond "two-bit superhero" (his own words) status, the poor guy tripped over wires and fell to his death.

In other cases, one-hit wonders were never intended to appear more than once, but, unlike Sentinel or Crusader, were allowed to fade away peacefully. Two examples: The pink-garbed Ant was actually an acrobat tricked into crime to battle the Teen Titans in issue #5 of their series (1966), and Captain Thunder, an homage to the original Captain Marvel, whizzed into battle with the Man of Steel in *Superman* #276 (1974).

A one-hit wonder of the early 2000s was a mega-hit, by comics standards, and turned heads—as well as tricks! Image Comics' *The Pro* (2002) was the outrageous saga of a superpowered prostitute and the straight-laced heroes she scandalizes. The salacious subject-matter attracted national news coverage, and the working girl wonder woman hooked both superhero fans intrigued by the taboo theme *and* casual readers who enjoyed a comic starring a heroine who finds superheroes as silly as they do. The Pro was sacked after her one-and-only outing, perhaps because the creators knew they would never get away with it again. In any case, the story was another notch in edgy author Garth Ennis' typewriter, and was the breakthrough book for gifted cartoonist Amanda Conner, helping to ensure that *The Pro*'s makers would be anything but one-hit wonders themselves.

Merchandising gimmicks have spawned their share of one-shot characters, like Generic Super-Hero, who debuted in Marvel's *Generic Comic Book* #1 (1984). Originally an anonymous man who gained superpowers after exposure to radium, this one-timer, clad in nondescript action garb, was a futile attempt at cashing in on the trend of "generic" versions of major product brands. Countless one-shot superheroes have been created as product spokesmen: Their number includes Hallmark Cards' Captain Laser (1984); the Neal Adams–illustrated Captain Cash, muscular mascot of the 1977 Connecticut State Lottery; and the New York State Health Department's health-conscious Nutri-Man and Vita-Woman (1983).

To these and the plethora of additional one-hit wonders, atomic also-rans, and fantastic failures, superhero fans salute you for a job *not* so well done! —*ME*

Oracle: *See* **Batgirl; Birds of Prey**

The Outsiders

DC Comics spent the 1970s reinventing Batman, returning him to his 1939 roots as a brooding "creature of the night" and distancing him from the campy persona made famous by actor Adam West in the television series *Batman* (1966–1968). By the early 1980s, the Caped Crusader had become the Darknight Detective, his grim demeanor making Batman an outsider among his Justice League of America (JLA) teammates. When the JLA refuses to intervene in an international crisis involving the kidnapping of an associate of philanthropist Bruce Wayne (alter ego of Batman), Batman does the unthinkable: He quits the JLA! "I've had *enough* of your two-bit Justice League!" he snarls on the cover of *Batman and the Outsiders* #1 (1983), as he chooses sides with his "new partners." These Outsiders, a merging of heroes old and new, infiltrate the politically unstable European nation of Markovia to liberate Wayne's friend in a covert mission orchestrated by tactician Batman, actions in direct defiance of the JLA and the U.S. State Department. And thus, these Outsiders are introduced as a fighting force willing to go beyond conventional means to exact justice. (Incidentally, DC had previously used the name "Outsiders" twice in the 1970s, for a group of bikers in Jack Kirby's *Superman's Pal Jimmy Olsen* run and for a grotesque superteam appearing only once in *First Issue Special*.)

Joining Batman were old-timers Metamorpho the Element Man, gruesome in appearance but comical at heart, a chemical combatant who had oozed in and out of comics limbo since his premiere in 1964; and Black Lightning, a street-smart African-American hero (a DC rarity at the time) with electrical powers, who briefly headlined his own comic in 1977. Fleshing out the group were the indomitable Katana, a female samurai wielding a soul-absorbing sword; the spirited Halo, a teenage amnesiac who was one of a race of energy beings called the Aurakles; and the regal Geo-Force, the Earth-manipulating brother of Terra from *The New Teen Titans*. Under the guidance of writer Mike W. Barr and artist Jim Aparo, *Batman and the Outsiders* promptly became one of DC's best-selling series, as the team tackled myriad menaces with amusing names like Baron Bedlam, the Force of July, and the Bad Samaritan. Barr's energetic scripting was rife with character development and subplots, and Aparo's (and later Alan Davis') artwork helped elevate *Batman and the Outsiders* to fan-favorite status. In 1985, the book split into two separate titles—the newsstand-distributed "softcover" *The Adventures of the Outsiders* series and the direct-sales (sold exclusively to comics shops on a nonreturnable basis) "hardcover" *The Outsiders,* with Batman defecting and newcomer Looker joining the group. Two titles a month was too much of a good thing: By February 1988 both were no more.

The Outsiders, minus Batman but with a handful of new recruits including Wildcat and the Atomic Knight, returned with little fanfare in 1994 for a two-year stint. In the summer of 2003, a new version of *Outsiders* premiered, a monthly comic written by Judd Winnick (an original cast member on MTV's *The Real World*). This band of twenty-somethings specializing in "taking on threats no one else will" (according to DC's promotions) is fronted by Batman's former protégé Nightwing, and features a familiar blend of heroes new and established: Arsenal (once Speedy of the Teen Titans), Metamorpho, Black Lightning's daughter Thunder, the Golden Age Green Lantern's daughter Jade, a futuristic android called Indigo, and a superwoman named Grace. With popular Nightwing at the helm, perhaps this incarnation of the Outsiders will enjoy the longevity denied its predecessors. —*ME*

The Phantom

Comics scholars generally agree that Superman was the first true superhero of the comic books, clearing marking the entrance of a new kind of hero into the marketplace. Though Superman wears an iconic costume, he was not the first heroic character to do so. That honor goes to the Phantom, a mystery-man hero type who clearly ushered in the superhero genre. Written by Lee Falk (who earlier had success with the newspaper strip *Mandrake the Magician*) and drawn by Ray Moore, the Phantom first appeared in King Features Syndicate on February 17, 1936.

Readers first see the Phantom rising out of the sea to rescue beautiful Diana Palmer from peril, thus putting in motion events that will be repeated endlessly over the coming decades. With his purple bodysuit (though readers had to wait for a Sunday strip added in May 1939 to actually see the costume in color), striped trunks, hood, blank-eyed mask, and black leather gun belt bearing a "death's head" skull, the Phantom's costume defined his persona as a masked avenger. Preceding Superman by two years, it is here that the

superhero blueprint was first fully established: a physically impressive, costumed character, complete with secret identity (Kit Walker), imperiled girlfriend, and secret hideout (the Skull Cave). In addition, the Phantom came equipped with his super-weapons and super-gadgets, including two revolvers, homing pigeons he dispersed to send and receive messages, and a "skull" ring worn on his left hand, the imprint of which clearly meant that a person was struck by the hero.

The Phantom's origin lays hundreds of years in the past—the sixteenth century, in fact—when pirates raid a merchant ship, killing the crew and captain and leaving only his young son alive. Washed up on a beach in an unspecified jungle setting, the child is befriended by a local tribe and swears an oath to "devote my life to the destruction of piracy, cruelty, and greed, and my sons will follow me!" Early versions of the origin name the child's father as Sir Christopher Standish, a British nobleman, but later versions name him as Kit Walker, and his descendants appear to think of themselves as American. The child thrives under the tutelage of the tribe and creates the Phantom costume, inspired by a native idol, to strike fear into the hearts of his enemies. Each generation of Walkers is trained to take over the mantle of the Phantom and, since all wear the same costume, local legend has it that he is in fact the same man 400 years later, hence the nickname, "the Ghost Who Walks."

Over the years, the Phantom accumulated a wide cast of characters, including Guran, leader of the tribe; trusted friend Bandar; foster son Rex; trusted wolf Devil; and horse Hero. After dating love interest Palmer for decades, he married her in 1977 and she later gave birth to twins, Eloise and Kit, the latter destined to become the twenty-second Phantom. The supporting cast and constantly changing storyline have kept the strip fresh. The Phantom's adventures have taken him around the globe, and many episodes (particularly in the comic books) have related tales of earlier Phantoms, even including a nineteenth-century lady Phantom.

Newspaper strip artist Phil Davis fell ill in 1942 and his assistant, Wilson McCoy, gradually took over the strip, working completely solo from 1947 to 1961. His successor, comic-book veteran Seymour "Sy" Barry, then produced the feature for an extraordinary thirty-two years, before his assistant, George Oleson, finally took up the reins in 1994. If the work of Davis and McCoy now appears quaint, Barry's has consistently been attractive and polished, and it is his Phantom that invariably appears on merchandise to this day.

With any successful comic strip there is an inevitable flood of tie-ins and merchandise, and the Phantom has been no exception, appearing in or on everything from novels (twelve pulp-style paperbacks from Avon published in the early 1970s and co-authored by Falk), watches, and games to mugs, dolls, and rings. In 1943, he was brought to the silver screen by Columbia Pictures in a fifteen-chapter serial starring Tom Tyler (previously seen portraying Captain Marvel). A promised follow-up fell into licensing difficulties and was hastily rejigged into *The Adventures of Captain Africa,* starring John Hart. More successful was a 1996 Paramount movie (simply titled *The Phantom*), directed by Simon Wincer and starring Billy Zane and Catherine Zeta-Jones. Longtime fans praised the film for capturing the spirit of the strip.

If the Phantom's celluloid outings have been rare, his comic-book life has been long and fruitful, starting in 1938 when the David McKay Company began reprinting his newspaper strip in Ace Comics, King Comics, and Feature Books. McKay printed Phantom strips throughout the 1940s, and then Harvey Comics took over the reins in the 1950s. In the 1960s, editor/writer Bill Harris and courtroom artist Bill Lignante produced new Phantom comic books for the first time, for Gold Key from 1962 to 1966 and for King Features (the syndicating company, thereby getting into the comics business for themselves) from 1966 to 1967. Charlton took over the franchise for the next eight years, initially producing a very handsome-looking *Phantom* comic by the future Aquaman team of Steve Skeates and Jim Aparo. Charlton's run met with mixed opinions, not least from King Features, but it ended on a high in 1977 after a beautiful sequence of issues from artist Don Newton.

There was then a decade in the wilderness for the Phantom before DC Comics tried its hand at a title or two in 1988, and since then various companies (including Marvel, Wolf, Moonstone, Manuscript Press, and Tony Raiola) have kept the Ghost Who Walks in the public eye. Two of Marvel's short-lived attempts were based on slightly eccentric Saturday morning cartoons: the 1986 *Defenders of the Earth,* which co-starred King's other main heroic properties, Mandrake the Magician, Flash Gordon, and Prince Valiant; and the 1994 futuristic *Phantom 2040,* starring the twenty-fourth Phantom.

The Phantom is far from being a solely American phenomenon. The character has achieved enormous success across the world and has been enjoyed in more than sixty countries. Foreign Phantom comics first appeared in Italy in 1938, in fact preceding their American equivalent, but it is in Scandinavia and Australia that he has been most successful. The jungle hero has been a national institution in Sweden since World War II, and Stockholm even has its own Phantom theme park. While the 1970s and 1980s saw a decline in U.S. comic books featuring the masked avenger, Sweden's Semic Press was producing two new stories a month for the Scandinavian market, mostly drawn by Spanish artists. These Semic strips have tended to explore the Phantom's earlier incarnations, including the fifth Phantom (who fought Blackbeard), the thirteenth Phantom (who fought in the 1812 war) and the sixteenth Phantom (who was apparently a cowboy!).

If the Phantom is popular in Scandinavia, then he is a genuine obsession in Australia, dominating the comic-book scene there just as Superman, Spider-Man, and the X-Men have in the United States. Since 1948, the Frew Company has been publishing a combination of newspaper strips and European reprints in a variety of formats, every couple of weeks. As of 2004, Frew has produced more than 1,300 editions of its *Phantom* comic and it is still going strong. If the American comic book is no longer a significant presence on U.S. newsstands, the newspaper strip itself is still in fine health, appearing in more 500 papers across the country. The Phantom would seem to be one of those very few heroes whose popularity transcends all boundaries, and he should be stalking the world's landscapes for years to come. —*DAR*

The Phantom in the Media

The Phantom is *killed* as Columbia Pictures' *The Phantom* (1943) opens. Your hero's dead in the first reel…. *How do you continue a fifteen-chapter movie serial?,* wondered the viewers, on the edge of their seats.

Enthralling the ticket buyers was the name of the game for movie makers during the challenging times of the Great Depression and World War II. Producers were on the lookout for exhilarating, high-profile characters whose adventures could be quickly and inexpensively developed into movie serials (fifteen- to twenty-minute shorts released in weekly chapters). King Features Syndicate's successful newspaper strip

The Phantom—starring a hero who was masked mystery man and jungle swashbuckler in one—was the perfect candidate for a serial, and to ensure an action-packed product, Columbia put former stuntman "Breezy" Eason behind the camera as director.

The Phantom quickly resolves its chapter one dilemma as the son of the murdered hero assumes his father's masked identity, maintaining the immortality myth of the "Ghost Who Walks." The plot: The Phantom (Tom Tyler) aids an expedition of adventurers seeking an elusive key to the lost city of Zoloz, as another party with suspicious motivations repeatedly takes measures to stop them. This meager premise withstands the fifteen-chapter duration thanks to briskly paced cliffhangers, and the Phantom's understated costume adapts well to the screen. Tyler commands a believable presence in the garb, which isn't surprising, since he had experience in tights two years prior in the serial *The Adventures of Captain Marvel.*

The Ghost Who Walks next leapt before the cameras in *The Phantom,* a 1961 teleplay and unsuccessful TV series pilot directed by Harold Daniels. Roger Creed played the mystery man and his alter ego Mr. Walker (from the comic strip), backed by a strong supporting cast featuring Lon Chaney Jr. and Richard Kiel.

Nursing his wounds from his 1961 failure, the Phantom avoided television until 1986, when he returned—with friends. *Defenders of the Earth,* a thirty-minute animated program produced for daily syndication, teamed the hero with King Features' Flash Gordon, Mandrake the Magician, and Lothar, plus their teenage offspring. Despite an ambitious marketing campaign including an action-figure line and a Marvel Comics series, *Defenders of the Earth*'s limited scope—protecting the planet from Ming the Merciless—was not compelling enough to extend its sixty-five episodes, and the show was canceled after only one season. *Phantom 2040* (1994–1996), another animated television series appearing in syndication, transplanted the hero into

An animated rendition of the Phantom in *Phantom 2040.*

the urban jungles of Metropia, one of a few Earth cities to survive a ravaging of the planet's resources. The Phantom struggled against a corrupt corporation and terrorists with conflicting ecological agendas, and was hunted by a police officer who happened to be the girlfriend of his alter ego, Kit Walker. Stylish animation and competent scripts helped *The Phantom 2040* foster a loyal cult audience that was, unfortunately, too small to sustain the series past two seasons.

Paramount Pictures was optimistic that its live-action blockbuster *The Phantom* (1996) would score big at the box office, as had the previous summer's superhero release, Warner Bros.' *Batman Forever* (1995). Paramount's movie had a body-sculpted hunk (Billy Zane) ably filling the purple tights, two sexy co-stars (Kristy Swanson and then-newcomer Catherine Zeta-Jones), a *Raiders of the Lost Ark* atmosphere, and a catchy tag line ("Slam Evil!"). The studio thought that nothing could go wrong.

Think again. Director Simon Wincer's *The Phantom* couldn't attract an audience. The Phantom lacked the iconic stature of Batman, the movie had no bankable stars, and the story, a period piece prone to frequent camp, failed to connect with film-goers of the 1990s. Hollywood hasn't given up on the Ghost Who Walks, however; a new movie version of *The Phantom,* with a script worked on by *Die Hard* screenwriter Stephen E. de Souza and Olympic gold medallist turned scriptwriter Mel Stewart, is in development. —*ME*

Phantom Lady

The Phantom Lady started life in 1941 as just one of many bit players hiding in the pages of *Police Comics* #1 (published by Quality Comics), but she went on to become one of the most controversial characters of the 1940s. The strip, like much of *Police Comics,* was put together by Jerry Iger's comics studio (or sweatshop) in 1941, and was fairly unsophisticated at this stage. The Phantom Lady was "Washington society's pampered darling" Sandra Knight, Senator Henry Knight's beautiful daughter, whose life revolved around the theater, dinner parties, and dates with her fiancé, Don Borden. However, in true superhero fashion, she had a habit of stumbling into trouble, whereupon she would change into a very fetching yellow bathing costume, green cape, and boots, and would emerge ready to fight crime. With no superpowers to speak of, she had to make do with a pocket-sized blacklight "blackout ray," which would temporarily blind her quarries while she tied them up. Dedicated to defending her country, she was known to say, "America comes first, even before Dad!"

Probably the most remarkable aspect of these stories was that none of the characters ever recognized Phantom Lady as Sandra Knight, despite the fact that she didn't wear any sort of mask! Quality persevered with the Lady for two years before Flatfoot Burns replaced her, but evidently Iger (for one) thought that there might well be life in her yet. In 1947, the notorious publisher Victor Fox contacted Iger in the hope of launching a new line of characters (this, despite owing Iger thousands of dollars from a previous collaboration). Iger agreed and, along with the likes of Rulah, Zegra, and a revamped Blue Beetle, the Phantom Lady was reborn. It seems that Fox had noticed the pinup strips that Iger's studio had been churning out for rival publisher Fiction House and wanted more of the same for himself—and that's what he got, in spades!

The first issue of the Phantom Lady's own comic (confusingly numbered 13 on the cover) hit the stands in late 1947 and, right from the start, it was clear that things had changed. The new Phantom Lady was all flowing hair, beguiling curves, and legs that went on forever. Her costume was now a matching blue halter-top and shorts, with a large red cloak and hood, topped off with a dainty little purse for her blackout ray. Her new artist was Matt Baker, one of the first African-American artists in comics (and at the time certainly the most important), who was gaining a reputation as the king of pinups. His rendition of the heroine seemingly owed a lot to the legendary model Bettie Page, and the strip was full of glamour poses with ladies in their underwear or taking a bath. In fact, the Phantom Lady herself was forever bathing, undressing, or getting into catfights, much to the alarm of observers such as comic-book critic Frederic Wertham. In his devastating indictment of the comics industry, *Seduction of the Innocent* (1954), Wertham singled out the character, cit-

Big Girl Adventures #1 © 2002 AC Comics.
COVER ART BY MATT BAKER.

ing the cover of *Phantom Lady* #17 (where she is shown giving the reader a smoldering look while straining against imprisoning ropes) as being particularly perverse.

Ironically, the writer of this "depravity" was a woman, Ruth Roche, whose scripts were inspired by her husband who worked for the police. Like the *Police Comics* episodes, Roche's scripts still revolved around the wealthy Sandra Knight and her rather dim-witted fiancé, but they were now peppered with stabbings, shootings, and strangulations, largely directed at women. Despite this, some feminist critics (including noted superhero author and cartoonist Trina Robbins) have suggested that the Phantom Lady was a rare example of a strong, positive role model for girls, an indomitable heroine who never gave up. Victor Fox, however, did give up and, in 1949, the controversial comic became the much more sedate *My Love Secret.*

As is often the case, occasional revivals followed, including a much tamer version from Ajax Comics in 1955 and a few reprints from I.W. Comics a decade later. In the 1970s, DC Comics (now the owners of the rights to Quality Comics' superheroes) included her as part of the Freedom Fighters, a team who started life in a Justice League story and then spun off into their own short-lived series. This was the more demure (and less pneumatic) *Police Comics* version of the Lady, having now mysteriously acquired the ability to become intangible—a real phantom. In fact, DC briefly brought her back in the 1980s as well, and then promptly dropped her (probably due to poor sales), never publishing her again.

However, that's not the end of the story. It was a fan, publisher Bill Black, who was to be the Lady's savior. He first drew her in a new story in his *Fun Comics* in 1982, presumably unaware that DC still owned the rights (even though his update was based on Fox's blue-costumed incarnation). Clearly enamored of her, Black changed her name to Nightveil, gave her mystical powers, and included her in his glamorous, all-girl superheroine group, Femforce. Nightveil went on to her own comic, a number of specials, and a devoted following all her own—proving that you can't keep a good (or bad) girl down. —DAR

Phantom Stranger

Throughout the 1940s and 1950s, comics were peppered with all kinds of mysterious storytellers, masked, cloaked, or hatted—narrators such as the

Mysterious Traveler, the Man in Black Called Fate, Mister Mystery, Dr. Drew, and DC Comics' Phantom Stranger. The DC series ran for only six issues, from 1952 to 1953, each issue presenting several short mystery tales starring the trench-coat-and-hat-wearing Stranger. In fact, "starring" is probably too strong a word, since the Stranger had the disconcerting habit of popping up out of nowhere (and only "where I am needed") and apprehending evildoers in the nick of time. His creators never made it clear who he was or where he came from, his tell-all quote being, "I do not foresee the future, I merely *act* upon it."

In the late 1960s, following the successful relaunch of the Spectre and the burgeoning popularity of its horror comics, DC decided in 1969 to revive the Phantom Stranger in *Showcase* #80. By the summer the hero was starring in his own comic. Those early tales mostly featured him materializing on street corners wherever groups of young children were gathered to tell them scary stories, occasionally starring himself. He was joined in this somewhat dubious pursuit by Dr. 13 who, like the Stranger himself, had enjoyed a brief outing in the early 1950s (when he was known as the Ghost Breaker). Dr. 13's sole purpose in life appeared to be to disprove "evidence" of the supernatural, and for the next few years he doggedly trailed the Stranger's every move. In a way, their relationship was something of a forerunner of the *X-Files,* with Dr. 13 resembling the doubting Scully and the Phantom Stranger as a precursor to Mulder.

Until the fourth issue, the Phantom Stranger had defeated his enemies with his fists and wits, but that issue pitted him against an enchantress called Tala, Queen of Darkness and, rather conveniently, he suddenly became incredibly powerful—with attributes including the ability to create heat, to cause temporary blindness, and to talk to animals. Tala regularly popped up for the next couple of years, developing something of a crush on the Stranger—in between trying to destroy him, of course, as did another evil witch called Tanarok. As the strip became more popular, its star appeared in a couple of Batman strips and was also inducted into the Justice League of America. From that point on, whenever DC's writers put their characters into particularly tricky situations, they could always summon up the Phantom Stranger to get them out of trouble.

Much of the comic's success was due to its writer, Len Wein, and artist Jim Aparo. Together, they took the Stranger around the world, to other dimensions and, finally, to an all-out battle with Tala that saw her trying to summon up the Four Horsemen of the Apocalypse. However, when the creative team's popularity promoted them to other comics, the Stranger gradually declined as he returned to his 1950s roots as a bystander in his own stories. Some late adventures with Deadman were not enough to stave off cancellation in 1976, but further guest slots with Batman, Superman, and Deadman kept him in the public eye. A 1980s backup slot in a new *Swamp Thing* comic led to appearances in the main strip and finally an issue of *Secret Origins,* which set out to explain where he came from—a mere twenty-five years after his first series.

For a character that had "lived" this long without an origin story, management decided that just one tale would do less than justice, and so DC served up four potential explanations. In the first, the Phantom Stranger turned out to be the Wandering Jew who betrayed Jesus, and who had been condemned to walk the earth for eternity. In another version, he was the sole survivor of Sodom and Gomorrah, given powers by an angel, while in a third variant he was an angel himself, cast out of heaven. In the fourth take, he absorbs power from the end of the universe, and tracks back in time to the beginning—or something like that. Then again, of course, the Stranger's true origin might well be none of the above!

In the 1990s, he was reduced for the most part to being a bit player in other characters' comics, with one final, valuable role to play. In the *Books of Magic* miniseries, the Stranger was one of four DC heroes chosen to oversee the emergence of a new, powerful sorcerer, who would control all the magic in the world. This was the young, spikey-haired, bespectacled boy wizard, Tim Hunter, whose similarity to the somewhat better-known (and later developed) Harry Potter is striking. —*DAR*

Plastic Man

Plastic Man was one of the real stars of the Quality Comics lineup of superheroes in comics' Golden Age (1938–1954), thanks to the madcap genius of his creator, Jack Cole. Cole had led a colorful life, including cycling across America at the age of eighteen, before deciding to dedicate himself to his true passion of cartooning and moving to New York in 1935. After a fitful start as a gag cartoonist, he found himself in at the beginning of the nascent comics explosion, working for Centaur Publishing and Lev Gleason Publications before being headhunted by Quality Comics owner Everett "Busy" Arnold. In mid-1941, Arnold asked Cole to create a new hero for Quality's upcoming new *Police Comics* title—something in the tradition of Will Eisner's Spirit. But Cole responded with his own sort of super-detective, a hero who always got his man in his own way: Plastic Man.

In August 1941, the first issue of *Police Comics* introduced an unsuspecting public to a disreputable hoodlum called Eel O'Brian, hard at work cracking a safe at the Crawford Chemical Works. Disturbed by a guard, O'Brian and his gang flee the building, but a stray bullet hits a large chemical vat, showering the thief with acid. Injured and desperate, O'Brian runs for miles before reaching a mountain retreat called Rest-Haven, where he is tended to by kind monks who shield him from the police. Inspired by their trust in him, he decides to turn over a new leaf and vows to change his ways. Only then does he discover that the acid has affected his body in such a way that he can now stretch it into any shape he can think of. Thrilled by that discovery ("Great guns!! I'm stretchin' like a rubber-band!"), he dons a red body-

Penny, Plastic Man, and Baby Plas in the animated *Plastic Man Comedy-Adventure Show*.

suit, trimmed with a yellow belt and topped off with wraparound sunglasses, and begins his new life's work as a crime fighter.

Under Cole's infinitely creative direction, Plastic Man soon developed into one of the wittiest, most inventive superheroes on the stands. Originally Cole wanted to call his hero the India Rubber Man, but was persuaded by Arnold to take advantage of the consumer's new fixation with plastic, which advertisers had just termed the "miracle material" and which was quickly making its way into dozens of new household products. Plastic Man—or Plas, as his friends referred to him—could stretch himself into any shape or size. He could roll himself into a ball, roll off a skyscraper and bounce right back up off the street below. He could make himself into a giant sail and fly through the air, and he was so pli-

able that bullets just bounced right off him. He could disguise himself as a chair, a boat, a lasso, a bag full of money, a blimp, a net—in fact, anything that Cole's fertile mind could dream up. Plas could also change his features to impersonate anyone, from a beautiful woman to Adolf Hitler himself. But while he was seemingly invulnerable enough to withstand being flattened by a steamroller, he was badly affected by intense heat (which caused him to melt) and cold (which stiffened him like a board).

Traditional superheroics—the battle between good and evil—were hardly the strip's principal concerns. Rather, Cole used Plastic Man's adventures as excuses to showcase his zany brand of humor. As an artist he had an outwardly simple style but was able to animate his characters with a manic zeal, and each panel was crammed with weird char-

THE SUPERHERO BOOK

acters, slapstick gags, or Plastic Man's increasingly bizarre contortions. Even today, when many of the strips from this era appear quaint or crude, Cole's Plastic Man seems fresh, vibrant, and hilarious.

Feeling the need for a sidekick for his "stretch-able sleuth," Cole introduced the polka-dot-shirted, rotund Woozy Winks in *Police Comics* #13 (November 1942), and the strip rose to even greater heights of lunacy. Having rescued a drowning swami, Woozy was rewarded with the gift of invulnerability to become "the man who cannot be harmed," and he decided to use his great gift for evil by turning to crime. When Plas tried to stop him, the great crime fighter was attacked by lightning, giant hailstones and instantly sprouting trees, but he finally defeated the indolent thief by making him feel guilty: "Think of your mother—what would she say if she knew about your crime career?" The newly contrite, if barely repentant, Woozy instantly became Plas' ever-present crime-busting companion and comic foil, a bumbling, always ravenous, leering, cynical layabout who naturally stole the hearts of his devoted readers.

Plastic Man soon became the cover star of *Police Comics* and starred in the title for 102 issues, only being ousted when the title was revamped into a true-crime comic in 1950. Plas was also given his own comic in 1943, and this flourished until Arnold sold the whole company to DC Comics thirteen years later. The in-demand Cole was co-opted into helping out on *The Spirit* newspaper feature when that series' creator, Will Eisner, was drafted, which meant that he soon needed help of his own to keep up production of his beloved *Plastic Man.* By all accounts, Cole was heartbroken that he could not handle all the work on his own, but various Quality staffers, including Gwenn Hansen and Bill Woolfolk on scripts and artists Al Bryant, Gill Fox, and Charles Nicholas, all pitched in.

Cole was at his peak after World War II. His kinetic style was now more fluid than ever and each page overflowed with sight-gags and increasingly bizarre characters. Plastic Man (who was by now an FBI agent) never developed a regular cast of bad guys but Cole delighted in inventing ever more eccentric and bizarre wrongdoers for his hero to dispatch. Among many peculiar fellows, Cole created Bladdo the Super Hypnotist, the Sinister Six, Amorpho, Abba and Dabba, and Wriggles Enright—in fact, each story could boast someone memorable. But as successful and creative as his work on the strip was, Cole always craved more and had been moonlighting as a gag cartoonist for years, finally leaving the strip in 1954. Freed from his comics workload, Cole soon found fame and wealth as the leading cartoonist in the newly launched *Playboy* magazine, and a few years later began work on the newspaper strip *Baby and Me.* Tragically, the intense and complex Cole killed himself at the height of his success, in 1958, for reasons that have never been clear, thus robbing comics of one of its true giants.

In 1956, while DC was keen to keep publishing such newly purchased Quality titles as *Blackhawk* and *GI Combat,* they inexplicably chose to ignore Plastic Man, and the character was soon forgotten by the company. Indeed, it was not until a decade later, when DC was approached by an agency wanting to use the hero in a magazine advertisement, that anyone in the company realized that it owned the character at all. After a tryout in the "Dial 'H' for Hero" strip, DC revived Plas for a new series in 1966, but without Cole's inspiration the comic was a disastrous mélange of tired TV parodies and camp superheroics. A decade later, in 1976, DC tried again, with art by the Cole acolyte Ramona Fradon, and produced a very attractive series that nevertheless never quite realized the heights of the strip's golden years. This was followed by a 1980 run in *Adventure Comics,* with art by Joe Staton, which was probably the truest to Cole's original vision of any of the revivals and was prompted by the unexpected arrival of a Plastic Man TV series (titled *The Plastic Man Comedy-Adventure Show,* which ran on ABC in 1979–1980 for a total of thirty-two episodes.)

These ill-fated attempts illustrate a pattern in which DC would resurrect Plastic Man each decade (for example, in 1988 and 1999) for a well-crafted miniseries or one-shot, which singularly failed to find an audience. DC's most recent attempt at a series, in late 2003, involved the left-field talents of the inventive Kyle Baker and might yet prove to be successful. Over the years, however, the company has met with greater success when it has used the hero as a bit-player in its superhero universe, teaming him with Batman numerous times in titles such as *The Brave and the Bold* or inducting him into the Justice League of America. In fact, in a 2002 JLA storyline, it was revealed that Plastic Man had a long-lost son!

In addition to the well-received series by Baker, DC has tried to keep the character in the public eye with occasional reprints of the strip's glory years, culminating in a series of hardbacked "archives," collecting Plastic Man strips from his very first appearance onward. Another late-breaking development was the publication in 2001 of the trade paperback *Jack Cole and Plastic Man: Forms Stretched to Their Limits* by Art Spiegelman and Chip Kidd. Though the hero may not regain the level of popularity and acclaim he enjoyed in the 1940s, the revival of interest in Cole and his flexible hero is a long overdue and welcome acknowledgment. —*DAR*

Power Man

Not to be confused with Erik Jolsten, a superstrong Caucasian Marvel Comics villain that splashed into the pages of *The Avengers* in the mid-1960s, the African-American superhero known as Power Man (Luke Cage) represents a breakthrough in racial diversity from Marvel's first great period of publishing expansion in the early 1970s. While Power Man wasn't Marvel's first African-American superhero—that honor goes to T'Challa, the Black Panther, who was introduced in 1966 (*Fantastic Four* #52)—he blazed other, arguably even more significant pop-cul-

Power Man #39 © 1977 Marvel Comics.
COVER ART BY BOB BROWN AND JIM MOONEY.

tural trails: (1) Luke Cage is the very first black superhero to star in a regular series bearing his name (beginning in *Luke Cage: Hero for Hire* #1, 1972); (2) his crime-fighting name does not contain the adjective "black" (à la Black Lightning, Black Goliath, and the Black Panther); and (3) he is Marvel's first mercenary superhero.

Conceived by writer Archie Goodwin and penciler George Tuska, Power Man starts life as a streetwise Harlem native known only as "Lucas," a character whose derivation from the protagonists of contemporary "blaxploitation" films such as *Shaft* (1971) represents a real innovation for the superhero genre. Framed for the crime of heroin trafficking by a former friend named Willis Stryker, Lucas finds himself incarcerated in the Seagate maximum security prison, where his self-righteous belligerence provokes the ire of Albert Rackham, a racist prison guard. Lucas' sole ally is Dr. Noah Bernstein, who believes the prisoner's claims of innocence and arranges for him to receive parole in exchange for Lucas' participation in a hazardous chemical experiment intended to catalyze human cell regeneration and to counteract old age and disease. Hoping to kill Lucas, Rackham interferes with Bernstein's experiment when it reaches a critical juncture, and the resulting chemical accident leaves Lucas with superhuman muscle and bone mass, incredible strength, and steel-hard skin. Lucas' principal weakness is his hot temper.

Unaccustomed to his new abilities, Lucas lashes out at Rackham, leaving him apparently dead (thus enabling Rackham to return later as a vengeful badguy). Now believing himself to be a murderer, Lucas escapes from Seagate, smashing through its walls with his fists. Although the authorities think Lucas has died during his breakout attempt, he makes it to New York City, where he intends to confront Stryker. Unfortunately, Lucas also has no means of support and lives in fear of being recognized and recaptured. But after a restaurateur gives him a cash reward for thwarting a robbery, Lucas finds his niche: engaging in heroics in exchange for money. He also adopts the name "Luke Cage" (an amalgam of his real first name and his recent state of confinement) and a costume that prominently features an open-chested, yellow polyester shirt and a belt made of heavy chain (also a symbol of incarceration). Cage goes on to get revenge on Stryker, who was also responsible for the death of his girlfriend, Reva, and begins confiding in Dr. Bernstein, who now runs a New York City free clinic (*Luke Cage: Hero for Hire* #2, 1972). Soon, Cage is actually scraping out a marginal living via commercial superheroics (*Luke Cage: Hero for Hire* #3, 1972), though he is generally as likely as not to right wrongs in the world purely out of unremunerated conscience.

During the first four issues of *Luke Cage: Hero for Hire,* Goodwin did the lion's share of the writing, with assists from Roy Thomas. Tuska and a young African-American artist named Billy Graham provided most of the art (Graham was one of the few blacks then working in the comics industry), and writer Steve Englehart penned most of the next dozen issues. Len Wein (co-creator of the 1970s X-Men revival) took over the writing chores with issue #17 (1974), by which time the series was retitled *Power Man,* reflecting Cage's attempt to make his enterprise more marketable by emphasizing his professional moniker. In fact, Cage is forced to fight the aforementioned villainous Power Man (Erik Jolsten) over the right to use the name (*Power Man* #21, 1974). After a brief stint as a member of the Defenders in 1975 Cage temporarily replaces the Thing as a member of the Fantastic Four the next year. During the 1970s, the hero's exploits caught the attention of an enthusiastic young comics reader named Nicolas Coppola, who years later achieved movie stardom using a Power Man–inspired stage name: Nicolas Cage.

As "blaxploitation" films receded over the cultural horizon along with the kung fu craze, in *Power Man* #48 (1977) Marvel sought to salvage its investment in both genres by introducing Power Man to Iron Fist (Daniel Rand), a martial arts hero whose own series had recently been canceled. Under the creative guidance of the future *X-Men* team of Chris Claremont (writer) and John Byrne (artist), Power Man's two-fisted directness and Iron Fist's disciplined rationality proved to be a good mix. The pair go into business together under the name of "Heroes for Hire, Inc." and the book's title was changed yet again (*Power Man and Iron Fist* #49, 1978). Writer James C. Owsley has called *Power Man and Iron Fist* the best "buddy book" Marvel Comics ever produced, describing it as "a dysfunctional version of DC Comics' venerable *World's Finest* series [which teamed Superman and Batman]. It was [a] fairly standard opposites-attract dynamic: the hardened cynic and the philosopher from [mystical city] K'un-L'un. The humor was largely based on Luke's reaction to Danny, and the inexplicable bond that grew between the two men."

The reconstituted series prospered under writers such Bob Layton, Mary Jo Duffy, Steven Grant, Chris Claremont, Mike W. Barr, Dennis O'Neil, Kurt Busiek, Archie Goodwin, Alan Rowlands, James C. Owsley, and Tony Isabella, and such artists as Kerry Gammill, Greg LaRocque, Denys Cowan, Keith Pollard, Ernie Chan, Geoff Isherwood, Richard Howell, Steve Geiger, and Mark D. Bright. As the stories unfolded, various writers allowed Cage to evolve, letting his slangy, stereotypical ethnic speech become more realistic. "Issue #123 had a fabulous panel," said writer Owsley (an African American), "something I can't believe I got away with, where Luke reveals [that] his 'Loud Angry Negro' routine was just a put-on. It is difficult, by and large, for white America to understand [that] the tribal slang that is stereotypical of black America is an affectation and not a handicap. We can turn it on and off. One minute, we're Don Blake, the next, we're Thor. Luke can, absolutely, turn his slang on and off."

Power Man and Iron Fist ended in 1986 (though still selling well, it was canceled to make room for Marvel's New Universe titles), along with the life of Iron Fist, who dies at the hands of a character named (absurdly) Captain Hero; Cage is blamed for Iron Fist's death (*Power Man and Iron Fist* #125) and lives as a fugitive until his name is formally cleared several years later. A true example of comics publishing synergy, Power Man and Iron Fist lasted longer together than either of them had as solo heroes anchoring series of their own.

After more than half a decade as an occasional guest star in other titles, Power Man earned another series, simply titled *Cage* (1992). Despite Marvel's efforts to make the book relevant in the age of Rodney King (writer Marcus McLaurin is African American), the series lasted only until issue #20 (1993). Though weary of superheroics-for-profit, Power Man reluctantly allows himself to be talked into rejoining the mercenary-hero business he had

started in the early 1970s; the new monthly *Heroes for Hire* series (1997) not only brings Cage together with such fellow superentrepreneurs as the Hulk, Hercules (who is now no longer an immortal), Ant-Man (Scott Lang), the Black Knight (Dane Whitman), and the White Tiger (another martial arts hero), it also resurrects the late Iron Fist, bringing him into the group. Because Power Man has spent years on the run, falsely blamed for Iron Fist's death, he harbors some resentment toward his old partner, and the two have to work at patching up their relationship. Unfortunately the new supersquad failed to click with readers, getting the ax in 1999 after nineteen issues.

A more successful latter-day update of Luke Cage came in 2002 from writer Brian Azzarello, legendary artist Richard Corben (best known for his colorful and expressive work in *Heavy Metal* during the 1970s), and painter Jose Villarrubia. Part of Marvel's adult-oriented MAX line, this series (also titled *Cage*) dispenses with the character's 1970s canary-yellow "superpimp" shirt in favor of gray vests, black stocking caps, and sunglasses—a look that is far more consonant with modern inner-city, hip-hop, and gangsta rap sensibilities. The series' R-rated language, though far rougher than anything the industry's self-censoring Comics Code Authority would approve even today, is likewise far more realistic and authentic in comparison with earlier Power Man tales. This had not been Cage's first appearance in the MAX line; a similarly believable (if somewhat less gruff) version had guest-starred as the iffy love interest of *Alias*' super-private-eye star. After both Cage's own MAX miniseries and *Alias* ended their runs, Cage and *Alias*' headliner Jessica Jones moved over to *The Pulse!* (2004–present), in which they are revealed to be expectant parents! Though much "grittier" than any of his predecessors, today's Power Man makes it clear that this character is more than capable of transcending the times that spawned him and the unique circumstances of his creation. —*MAM*

Power Pack

During the early 1980s, mainstream superhero comics such as Frank Miller's *Daredevil* were becoming increasingly "gritty" and "hardboiled," a trend of escalating violence that would reach its apotheosis with such series as *Batman: The Dark Knight Returns* (also by Miller, 1986) and *The Punisher* (1986). But *Power Pack,* created in 1984 by Marvel Comics writer-editor Louise Simonson (an alumnus of such Warren horror magazines as *Creepy* and *Vampirella*) and artist June Brigman (also known for her work on *Supergirl* for DC Comics and the syndicated *Brenda Starr* newspaper strip), followed a decidedly different trajectory.

Power Pack is the tale of a quartet of siblings, four young children who receive superhuman abilities from a benevolent, horselike alien named Aelfyre Whitemane, who with his sentient spaceship seeks to thwart the invading reptilian Snarks. Alex, Jack, Julie, and Katie Power are the children of Margaret Power and Dr. James Power, who had invented a technological device that the Snarks sought to possess. To prevent this, Whitemane gives twelve-year-old Alex the power to make objects lighter or heavier (hence his superhero name "Gee," as in gravity), bestows superspeed upon ten-year-old Julie ("Lightspeed"), confers upon eight-year-old Jack the ability to expand and contract his body's molecules, thus enabling him to alter his body's density at will (and justifying his nickname "Mass Master"), and empowers five-year-old Katie with the ability to unleash powerful energy blasts from her hands (she calls herself "Energizer," thanks to the inspiration of a well-known television commercial). As the oldest of the siblings, Alex becomes the group's natural leader, carefully looking out for the younger kids (especially the emotionally volatile Katie, to whom Julie often refers affectionately as "Katie-bear").

Although many enthusiasts of the era's traditional superhero fare (primarily adolescent males) disdained *Power Pack,* younger readers and those who were themselves the parents of small children found the series enchanting. Simonson's scripts blended fairy tales with science fiction and children's books (the evil alien Snarks, for example, were straight out of Louis Carroll), juxtaposing the backdrop of outer space with the real-world setting of New York City, and presented relatively realistic characterizations of children and their sibling relationships. Brigman's art had a gentle, expressive, and whimsical quality that brought Simonson's words and imagery to vivid life. The reason for the distinctiveness of Brigman's illustrations may have been her relative unfamiliarity with the comics medium prior to working on *Power Pack;* being largely unacquainted with the conventions and clichés of the superhero genre, she wasn't enslaved by them. While *Power Pack*'s unusual content may have put the series at a competitive disadvantage in terms of sales, it provided seven years of highly original comic-book storytelling. *Power Pack* evidently found its unorthodox audience right away; though originally conceived as a miniseries, Marvel quickly decided that the concept was strong enough to sustain an open-ended monthly series.

During the first half of *Power Pack*'s run, the kids' adventures don't involve their parents, who are at first entirely ignorant of their children's superheroic double lives. The group eventually expands to encompass a nonfamily member, four-year-old Franklin Richards, the son of the Fantastic Four's Mr. Fantastic and Invisible Woman. Franklin, who becomes an honorary team member, adopts the supermoniker "Tattletale" because of his ability to see events from five minutes in the future, thus "telling on" bad guys before the fact (he also frequently quarrels with the headstrong Katie). The Powers also have a number of adventures with Kofi, the son of Whitemane, the source of the group's powers. During these adventures, the team is frequently at odds with their father's former boss, who becomes a supervillain whose name is calculated to strike fear into the hearts of children: Bogeyman. In addition, they frequently face big-league villains, such as the fearsome mutant known as Saber-tooth, their series taking part in such world-threatening multiseries crossovers as *Secret Wars II* (1986), *The Fall of the Mutants* (1988), *Inferno* (1988), and *Acts of Vengeance* (1990).

Over the years the series also played host to numerous high-profile Marvel guest stars, such as Spider-Man, Cloak and Dagger, the X-Men, Wolverine, the New Mutants, the Fantastic Four, the Avengers, the Punisher, and even the all-but-omnipotent eater of entire planets, Galactus. On one occasion, Marvel used the *Power Pack* characters in a special public service-oriented giveaway comic dealing with child sexual abuse (*Spider-Man/Power Pack,* 1984).

After Simonson's departure from the series with *Power Pack* #40 in 1988, numerous other writers took custody of the Power kids, including Steve Heyer, Jon Bogdanove, Judith Kurzer Bogdanove, Julianna Jones, Terry Austin, Dwayne McDuffie, and Michael Higgins, and the art chores passed from Brigman to Mary Wilshire, Brent Anderson, Scott Williams, Bob McLeod, Terry Shoemaker, Sal Velluto, Whilce Portacio, Ernie Colón, Jon Bogdanove, Tom Morgan, and Steve Buccellato. While *Power Pack* was being published, a TV pilot based on the property was produced, intended to launch a Saturday-morning cartoon series on NBC during the 1991–1992 season. Unfortunately, the show died on the drawing board, just as the comics series—its audience weary of so many creative-team changes—was gasping its last.

During the run of the series, the superabilities of the Power children were swapped around among the four siblings on more than one occasion. The first time this occurs (*Power Pack* #25, 1986), Alex receives Katie's "zap" power, prompting him to change his name to "Destroyer"; after getting Jack's density-powers, Julie changes her nickname to "Molecula"; Alex's original gravity-control powers go to Jack, who becomes "Counterweight"; and Julie's superspeed jumps to Katie, who is subsequently known as "Starstreak." The Powers' powers

received yet another random reshuffle three years later (*Power Pack* #52, 1989) only to be restored to their original owners in *Power Pack Holiday Special* #1 (1992), the oversized magazine-format comic in which the series concluded (the regular monthly title had ended in 1991 after a sixty-two-issue run).

But permanent obscurity wasn't in the cards for the Power family, lest Marvel risked losing its trademarks on the characters. Under the name "Powerhouse," a slightly older Alex Power joined the 1990s motley misfit superteam known as the New Warriors (*The New Warriors* vol. 1 #64, 1995). In this incarnation, Alex bears the powers of all four Power Pack members. The rest of the Power siblings recovered their abilities a few years later, however, when the original Power Pack team reassembled in a four-issue miniseries (*Power Pack* vol. 2, 2000), written by Shon C. Bury and penciled by Colleen Doran (whose beautifully rendered science-fiction comic, *A Distant Soil,* makes her an ideal *Power Pack* illustrator). Today Power Pack remains alive, well, and charged with fond memories. Though underemployed now, the Power kids stand ready to return whenever the superhero readership seems ready for kinder, gentler storytelling. —*MAM*

The Powerpuff Girls

Imagine a fairytale gone awry: When Professor Utonium accidentally knocks over a vial of Chemical X, his superheroine trio, the Powerpuff Girls, is born. Originally designed to be a family of perfect sisters concocted, literally, from the ingredients "sugar, spice, and everything nice," instead these super-powered kindergartners kick butt as they combat evil and advance the forces of good—all while mastering their ABCs. The team consists of Blossom (the leader of the group and brains of the operation), Bubbles (the overly sensitive and bubbly one who avoids sibling rivalry at all costs), and Buttercup (the tomboy of the group, always willing to fight first). Blossom's element is everything nice, Bubbles' element is sugar, and Buttercup's is spice. Since their core elements vary, so do their superpowers: Blossom has ice breath, Bubbles can speak to animals and has a Super Sonic Scream, and Buttercup can create a tornado and shoot laser beams from her hands. All three can fly.

As the girls' creator, father figure, and *de facto* mentor, Professor Utonium raises and trains the super-trio. Based in the city of Townsville, where the mayor is able to call the girls on his hotline whenever trouble arises, the girls attend kindergarten by morning and combat villains such as Mojo Jojo, Him, the Amoeba Boys, the Gang Green Gang, Roach Coach, Elmer Sglue, Seduca, and the Rowdyruff Boys by afternoon. They are also guided by their teacher, Ms. Keane, who educates them in kiddy curriculum and the benefits of peaceful resolution at Pokey Oaks Kindergarten.

One of Cartoon Network's original animated series, *The Powerpuff Girls* is the inspiration of animator Craig McCracken, who first conceived of the superheroine trio as a project for a college class at the California Arts Institution in 1992. Three years later Cartoon Network executives saw McCracken's concept and gave the girls their first pilot in 1995; a second pilot soon followed. By 1998, *The Powerpuff Girls* was a television series, raved about for its rich blend of action, engaging storytelling, and smart humor. Behind-the-scenes talent includes McCracken (who also serves as the show's executive producer), *Dexter's Laboratory* creator Genndy Tartakovsky (who often directs), and the voice talents of Catherine Cavadini (Blossom), Tara Strong (Bubbles), and Elizabeth Daily (Buttercup). Since landing their own gig, the Powerpuff Girls have fared well for themselves, drawing strong ratings, winning awards, and branding themselves on a wide array of girl merchandise, including clothing, lunchboxes, jewelry, dolls, and toys.

Catering to a grade-school-age girl demographic, *The Powerpuff Girls* is successful because it provides young girls with an example of dynamic female superheroines—girls just like them—who are empowered and empower*ing*. With unique abilities, minds of their own, and strong character traits—the antithesis of their names—these girls are forces to be reckoned with. In 2002, the super-trio segued from television to the silver screen with their own self-titled animated feature film. With their popularity at its peak, the perky threesome shows no signs of slowing down. —*GM*

Powers: *See* **Everyday Heroes**

Project A-ko

For a period of about ten years, starting in the late 1970s, anime went through what can only be called a "Golden Age" in Japan. Television and movies were joined by the OVA (Original Video Animation) format, which offered advantages over television or film animation. Titles such as *Mobile Suit Gundam, Dr. Slump, Macross,* and *Urusei Yatsura* became multimedia hits, from comics to animation to merchandising. Studios were breaking away from traditional stories or taking them in different directions.

Of course, such a Golden Age was ripe for parody.

Perhaps the best-known parody of that time was released in Japanese theaters in 1986. The makers of the film would never have guessed, however, that the film would become popular not just in Japan, but in many other countries as well, including the United States. The film was *Project A-ko,* released by APPP. There is a strong, coherent story to *Project A-ko,* despite the fact that nearly every element of anime is satiriz*ing* in it. First, the title is a spoof of the 1983 Jackie Chan film *Project-A.* Among other things satirized are: Giant robot (*mecha*) shows such as *Macross;* alien invasions; Captain Harlock, the classic space pirate created by Leiji Matsumoto; the red, white, and blue "sailor suit" Japanese schoolgirl uniform; post-apocalyptic anime and manga such as *Hokuto no Ken* (*Fist of the North Star*); and even American superheroes.

This last one is not evident until the end of the film. In short, the film is an action-packed comedy/parody, in some ways reminiscent of the 1980 film *Airplane!* This made it a runaway success in Japan and a favorite among American anime fans (*otaku*), despite the language barrier.

Project A-ko opens with a mysterious meteor (possibly an alien craft) hitting Graviton City, destroying it completely. Sixteen years later, as the Earth probe Constellation is launched from Space Station L-III, the focus is back on the rebuilt Graviton City, constructed from advanced technology reverse-engineered from the alien spacecraft. None of this matters to A-ko Megami, who is late for her new school and rushes there—at rather incredible speed—with her friend C-ko Kotobuki in tow. Compared to the red-haired, serious, and superstrong A-ko, C-ko is a bubble-headed blond crybaby, and worst of all, cannot cook. At the school, the Graviton Institute for Girls, both of them (who happen to be wearing the wrong uniforms) are introduced by the teacher, Miss Ayumi … but also watching is B-ko Daitokuji, a violet-haired, spoiled rich girl who has it in for A-ko and wants C-ko for herself. With her minions, B-ko uses her fortune and her aptitude for mecha design to send a variety of machines to defeat A-ko. A-ko, with her super-strength, defeats all of B-ko's creations.

Finally, B-ko, in frustration, unleashes her ultimate weapon, the "Akagiyama 23" armed with "Super High Grade Missiles." This weapon only gets laughs from the girls at the school, for it resembles a dark-purple bathing suit with a helmet. That only makes B-ko angrier, and she unleashes a furious assault on A-ko. The two end up battling through the school and the surrounding city, causing massive damage (of course, remember that this *is* a comedy). However, there is an even greater threat … an approaching alien ship, crewed by women, is searching for a lost princess who disappeared sixteen years earlier. Their spy, "D" (who looks masculine but is a female, a fact on display near the end of the film when [s]he fights A-ko with a sword and shield,

dressed in a bikini), has been observing A-ko and C-ko, but is always run over by A-ko. The alien captain Napolipolita (resembling a transvestite version of Captain Harlock) is also an alcoholic, and takes her vessel further into Earth's atmosphere, following "D"'s confirmation that the lost princess is on the planet and is C-ko. Earth's military forces launch a desperate counterattack, but are nearly decimated.

(It should be noted at this time that the front of the alien ship resembles Captain Harlock's famous vessel, the *Arcadia.* Remember, this *is* a parody.)

A-ko and B-ko, still fighting, run right into the invasion, and C-ko is kidnapped and taken aboard the alien ship. The antagonists call a temporary truce and head off to the ship. A-ko nearly doesn't make it, but gets aboard using a swarm of alien missiles as stepping-stones. On board, A-ko, B-ko, and C-ko end up in a no-holds-barred battle against each other, the alien crew, "D", and the Captain (who is going through withdrawal and just needs *one* more drink), resulting in the destruction of most of the vessel, with the remains coming to rest on top of Graviton City's military base. The next day, wearing the right school uniform, A-ko leaves as her parents Clark Kent and Diana Prince watch. Together, her and C-ko head to school as the two most popular girls....

The fact that A-ko's strength is owed to her famous parents—who happen to be American superheroes—is a major plot twist in the film. It certainly took many American otaku by surprise. Superman and Wonder Woman are not unknown characters in Japan (the former being a large influence on the manga *Dragonball Z,* and its animated adaptation), but one must wonder if DC Comics is even aware of the use of two of their major characters in such a manner as depicted in *Project A-ko* and its sequels. Despite being the child of two great costumed superheroes, A-ko herself does not change into a typical "superhero" costume.

An argument can also be made that the conflict between A-ko and B-ko satirizes the relationship between the United States and Japan, with one side being the strongest member of the club, and the other trying to knock them down using knowledge and application of technology.

The staff for the film included director Katahiko Nishijima, producer Kazufumi Nomura, and Yuji Moriyama, who did triple duty as screenwriter, animation director, and character designer. Moriyama had previously worked on such titles as the *Urusei Yatsura* TV series and the movie *Only You,* as well as the *Crusher Joe* anime property; after *A-ko* he would work on the classic anime film *Wings of Honneamise, Royal Space Force* for the iconoclastic anime studio Gainax. In a rare move, all the songs for the film are performed in English, with Americans Richie Zito (*Flashdance*) and Joey Carbone (*Star Search*) creating the soundtrack. Moriyama himself would become a popular animation director in both Japan and the United States; in the late 1990s, he would also become a favorite speaker at American anime conventions. Strangely enough, he would direct another comedy involving a super-strong teenager (albeit an android one)—the anime adaptation of Yuzo Takada's manga *All-Purpose Cultural Catgirl Nuku-nuku.*

With the success of *Project A-ko,* it was only a matter of time before sequels arrived. Three sequels were made, but all eschewed the movie theater for the OVA format. Moriyama worked on these sequels, including the last one, entitled *Project A-ko: Final.* The title was not entirely accurate; a fourth sequel of sorts, the two-part OVA *Project A-ko Versus* was released in 1990 with the parts labeled "Grey Side" and "Blue Side." The OVA itself was a major retelling, or more accurately, a major revision: A-ko and B-ko are older "gun for hire" partners, and C-ko is the rich daughter of a wealthy magnate. There are also more elements of space opera present. What was not present was Moriyama; for him, *Final* was the truly the last. None of the sequels attained the success of the original film, for fans found that, while funny and action-packed

in their own right, the sequels lacked the unique charm of the first film.

With the rise of anime fandom and appreciation, the *Project A-ko* film and sequels would soon see official release in the United States and elsewhere. The New York–based distributor Central Park Media (CPM) gained the rights to the A-ko franchise in the early 1990s and from 1992 to 1995 released them in both subtitled and dubbed formats (which were broadcast on the Sci-Fi Channel as well). When it came to merchandising, CPM did not disappoint. The domestic version of the soundtrack for the original movie was released by CPM, which was no doubt a relief to many fans; they no longer had to pay a high price for the original Japanese release. CPM went even further, releasing comic book adaptations of the film and OVAs. The first film was adapted by Tim Eldred, with Ben Dunn providing the art. This adaptation was released as a four-issue series by Malibu Comics, then released as a graphic novel "Director's Cut" by CPM. Eldred would return to do adaptations of the sequels for CPM as part of Studio Go!; he provided both script and art with assists from John Ott. The Montreal-based publisher Ianus Publications released *Project A-ko: The RPG,* a role-playing game that also functioned as a major source of background information regarding the world that A-ko and friends inhabited. Since nothing of the sort had ever appeared in Japan, the comic adaptations and the RPG were unique to North America. The popularity of *Project A-ko* among American otaku is such that the film is listed as an essential title to see, or is ranked very high on the list of "most popular." This fact amazed Yuji Moriyama, who admitted that he was surprised to hear of the series being so popular among English-speaking fans.

Such was *Project A-ko*'s popularity in both Japan and America that it is easy to miss out on one curious fact: one of the studios that did animation for the film was Gainax, which would also release its own wildly popular satire of anime and anime fandom, *Otaku no Video.* A descendant, in a sense, of *Project A-ko* would be the 1999 anime series *Excel Saga;* one could also count Gainax's own *FLCL* as well. Both shows, like the first A-ko film, do have a firm storyline, but are filled with madcap comedy and plenty of anime references that are satirized. And again, both shows are very popular among English-speaking otaku. —*MM*

Promethea

Even by the innovative standards of writer Alan Moore's ABC comics line, *Promethea* is one of the most unusual superhero series ever published, a fantasia of compelling quests and mystical transformations that rivets the reader with scarcely a punch being thrown.

Debuting in 1999, the book's storylines concern the fabric of the supernatural and the nature of creativity itself, exploring the world of the imaginary and drawing together many spiritual beliefs in a surprisingly unified mythos. Promethea is the name of a little girl in fifth-century Roman Egypt who is saved by her sorcerer father as Christian zealots close in on him. While the father and his way of life fall, the girl is spirited to the Immateria, a heaven-like dimension that all creatures of the imagination spring from and return to. Since legends don't die like humans, the girl's spirit survives, manifesting in the real world to creative people who channel her essence or project it onto others.

In the modern day, young college student Sophie Bangs is researching a character called Promethea who has oddly recurred through history in seemingly unconnected popular fiction, from florid romantic poetry to pulps and comics. Visiting Barbara Shelley, the widow of the last man to write a Promethea comic, she is rebuffed before learning the woman's secret: Used as the model for her husband's stories, she took on the Promethea identity, as did her forebears through other means (including painters inhabiting their own imagery). Bangs gets

Promethea #1 © 1999 America's Best Comics.
COVER ART BY J. H. WILLIAMS III AND MICK GRAY.

caught up in Shelley's losing battle with a group of demons (the middle-aged, unglamorously-built heroine being one of many uncommonly realistic portrayals of women in the series), and, at a crucial moment, Bangs realizes that she is to be the next Promethea, whom she first turns into by scrawling a poem about the legendary heroine.

Shelley dies as Bangs takes over, defeating the demons and embarking on an apprenticeship with Promethea's previous incarnations (who still reside part-time in the Immateria). This leads to an amusing sequence of issues in which these varied popular reflections of womanhood, from Orphan Annie–esque airhead to protofeminist 1920s tough-gal and beyond, take Sophie through their worlds. The newly trained Promethea returns for a rematch with the demons, who have possessed New York's mayor en masse and control him in turn, leading to even more inconsistencies than the average politician.

Dispatching the demons again, Bangs decides she must travel to the afterworld for a proper farewell to Shelley (who has chosen not to rest in the Immateria but to try and join her late husband). Leaving her brash best friend Stacia Vanderveer in charge of the earthly plane as a substitute Promethea (with both humorous and hair-raising results), Bangs begins a lengthy quest through multiple levels of reality, finding Shelley's spirit and traveling onward to the essence of God itself. The worlds they visit along the way offer some of the most intriguing and moving reflections on mortality and eternity in any medium, a philosophical odyssey that most comics writers would be thought mad to attempt.

Having successfully explained the universe and depicted God with neither bombast nor cliché, Moore turned to the small task of envisioning the end of the world, selecting *Promethea* as the setting for the apocalyptic conclusion to the whole ABC line in 2003–2004.

In every issue, artist J. H. Williams III matched Moore's intricate writing with ornate page designs based on mystical charts and M. C. Escher-esque visual paradoxes, which dazzled without ever confusing the reader. The series could veer from uproarious satire to touching pathos; entire issues would be written in verse or illustrated in paint; all-in-all, it was that rare comics series with both beautiful art and experimental formats that never sacrificed clear and captivating storytelling. Even if the book ends forever, it will, like its heroine, undoubtedly live on. —*AMC*

The Punisher

Anticipating such "grim and gritty" 1980s superhero fare as *Batman: The Dark Knight Returns* and

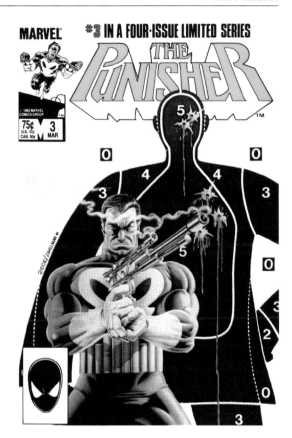

The Punisher #3 © 1985 Marvel Comics.
COVER ART BY MIKE ZECK AND PHIL ZIMELMAN.

Watchmen by more than a decade, Marvel Comics' Punisher is one of the medium's quintessential antiheroes. Created by regular Spider-Man writer Gerry Conway and Marvel art director John Romita, Sr. (and unveiled in *Amazing Spider-Man* vol. 1 #129, 1974), the Punisher captures a 1970s vengeance-against-crime zeitgeist best exemplified in the larger culture by the gunplay-laden *Dirty Harry* films of Clint Eastwood, the *Death Wish* cinematic bloodbaths of Charles Bronson, and Don Pendleton's men's adventure paperback hero, *The Executioner.* Indeed, the original Punisher concept was for an *Executioner*-like hero, whom Conway dubbed the Assassin. Both editor-in-chief Stan Lee and the

Comics Code Authority, however, vetoed that name as too amoral and violent. The newly renamed Punisher sported a distinctive, skull-emblazoned black costume (designed by Romita) that recalled the garb of the Black Terror, a Golden Age (1938–1954) hero from Standard Comics.

Though originally conceived as an adversary for Spider-Man, the Punisher is no mere garden-variety criminal; rather, he views himself as a crusader against all criminals, many of whom don't survive their encounters with him. Long before Frank Castiglione first takes up the formidable weaponry and body armor of the Punisher, he plans on entering the Catholic priesthood, only to abandon his clerical aspirations after learning that forgiveness is not his strong suit. Leaving his seminary studies behind, he falls in love with Maria Falconio, and the two are soon married and begin raising a family. Castiglione also enters the U.S. Marines, where (as Frank Castle) he receives training in land, sea, and airborne combat and becomes proficient in underwater demolitions. Rising to the rank of captain while serving on various combat fronts, Castle earns the nickname "Punisher" because of his tenacious pursuit of the enemy (*The 'Nam* #52–#53, 1991), eventually becoming a military training instructor.

While on leave, Castle takes his family on a picnic outing in New York's Central Park, where they inadvertently witness a gangland execution. The mobsters next gun down Maria and the Castle children, Frank Junior and Christie. But Castle himself survives, deserts the Marine Corps, and brings all of his considerable military expertise to bear in a one-man war against the underworld (the Punisher's oft-retold origin, which is very like that of the Executioner who served as his template, first appears in *Marvel Preview* #2, 1975). Unlike the typical comic-book crime fighter, the Punisher utilizes a varied arsenal of both lethal and nonlethal weapons, including an automatic M-16 rifle, pistols, concussion bombs, tear-gas grenades, and a fully armed and armored battle-van. Although Castle never hesitates to use lethal force against the criminals he

stalks, he maintains a strict military code of honor that eschews the use of violence against innocent parties, including civilian police forces, which he allows to arrest and incarcerate him (briefly) without resistance. Despite his extralegal, overly violent methods, the Punisher regards himself as a protector of the helpless and the innocent.

Nevertheless, the Punisher's extreme worldview puts him on an ethical collision course with Spider-Man in their first encounter back in the 1970s, during which the two stake out highly polarized positions in American society's eternal law-and-order debate. The wall-crawler sees the Punisher as a dangerous loose cannon who should not be allowed to roam the streets; Castle regards Spider-Man as a foolish idealist who lacks the strength and resolve to give criminals the harsh treatment they deserve. Spider-Man survives this initial clash largely because the Punisher does not entirely believe the bad press the *Daily Bugle* newspaper routinely gives the wall-crawler (editor J. Jonah Jameson sees Spider-Man in much the same way that Spidey does the Punisher). Probably because 1970s comics audiences (to say nothing of comic-book editors) were not yet ready for the Punisher's moral ambiguity, the character spent the next several years as a mere guest star, primarily in the *Amazing Spider-Man* comic.

But the Punisher was not destined to languish for long on Marvel's back bench, and arguably owes much of his far greater success in the 1980s to two influential men: Ronald Reagan, the embodiment of the nation's tough, rightward swing during this period; and Frank Miller, the innovative young writer-artist who began using the take-no-prisoners Castle as a foil for his gritty, film noir version of Daredevil (which he introduced in *Daredevil* vol. 1 #182–#184, in 1982). Miller's Punisher is still clearly a criminal, though treated sympathetically; his code of honor and his calculating nature receive more emphasis than do his violent, vengeance-inspired lawbreaking. But Miller makes no bones about the Punisher's goals. "The Punisher is an avenger," said the cartoonist. "He's Batman without the lies built in. They come from the same root. They're created by the same fears. The same kind of fear that I feel every time I ride the subway." Portrayals of the character by writers other than Miller varied widely during this period; for example, *Spectacular Spider-Man* #82 (1983) portrays a Punisher who is so maniacally obsessed with small legal infractions that he shoots at litterbugs and red-light runners (happily without hitting them).

As a (largely unfounded) fear of increasing street crime gripped the nation throughout the conservative Reagan era, comics audiences were increasingly receptive to the lethal vendetta of the Punisher, who finally landed his own five-issue miniseries in 1986 (cover-dated January–May). Marvel followed this successful effort with *The Punisher,* an ongoing monthly title debuting in July 1987. Such was the character's expanding success that November of the following year saw the introduction of *The Punisher War Journal* (a new monthly title); a third series, *The Punisher: War Zone,* began its run in March 1992. The Punisher also headlined a plethora of miniseries and graphic novels, some of which featured as guest stars such popular Marvel characters as the Black Widow and Wolverine. During the late 1980s and early 1990s, a Punisher guest appearance in any sluggish-selling Marvel title all but guaranteed significant additional sales. The Punisher even graced the pages of two inter-company crossovers with DC Comics' Batman (*Punisher/Batman: Deadly Knights,* and *Batman/Punisher: Lake of Fire,* both in 1994)—and even turned up in a crossover with Archie of Riverdale High (*The Punisher Meets Archie* #1, August 1994)! The Punisher's vengeful legacy even survives into the far future with the monthly *Punisher 2099* series (its thirty-four-issue run began in February 1993), in which Public Eye Special Operations agent Jake Gallows wages war against criminals as an armored, high-tech vigilante.

During this period of intensive Punisher publishing, the character achieved increasing complexity, revealing more of his inner motivations. Not only does Frank Castle harbor a hatred for criminals of the sort that slew his family, he also hates being the Punisher—just as he despises himself for having failed to protect his family when it mattered most. But Marvel's overexposure of the character clearly took its toll as readers seemed to tire of Castle and his grim mission. July 1995 saw the end of all three of the main ongoing Punisher series. Still, the Punisher subsequently made a comeback as part of the highly successful *Marvel Knights* superteam series (vol. 1), which began in July 2000, and can also be seen in numerous miniseries, one-shots, and guest appearances since the turn of the millennium.

The Punisher made it to the silver screen in 1989 (courtesy of New World Pictures) with Dolph Lundgren starring, fresh from the role of He-Man in *Masters of the Universe* (1987). The movie's quality and fidelity to the original were lax—the hero's skull-emblem was removed because the filmmakers deemed it "too comic-booky"—though it spawned a Marvel comic-book adaptation (*The Punisher Movie Special,* June 1990) and the premiere (in September 1989) of *The Punisher Magazine,* a large magazine-format monthly series that lasted only sixteen issues. The Punisher's cinematic future includes a second feature film released in 2004, with Thomas Jane (of *Face/Off, Boogie Nights,* and *Dreamcatcher* fame) starring as the eponymous artilleried avenger, proudly displaying the skull emblem across his chest. Produced jointly by Artisan Entertainment and Marvel, the film's teaser campaigns describe the Punisher as a former U.S. Marine and special agent turned vigilante, emphasizing his real-world superheroic skills, such as his finesse with explosives, large caliber guns, tactical weapons, and hand-to-hand combat. Overexposed or not, the grim crusade of the Punisher will doubtless continue for many years to come. —*MAM*

Radioactive Man: *See* **Bartman**

Relevance: *See* **African-American Heroes; Anti-drug Series; Bronze Age of Superheroes (1970–1979); Green Arrow; Green Lantern**

Rising Stars

The night skies above the small town of Pederson, Illinois, are illuminated by a bright flash of extraterrestrial light in 1969, and the lives of 113 soon-to-be-born individuals are changed forever. The children born after "the flash" (as the event came to be known) are genetically enhanced, each bearing superpowers. The government monitors the "Specials," quarantining them at Camp Sunshine for observation, treatment, and training. After a counselor is killed by one of the children, the government tries to keep the lot of them in custody, but the parents sue. When the case reaches the Supreme Court, a compromise is set: Dr. William Welles will both aid and supervise the children, and if any are determined to be dangers, they will be taken into custody.

Years later, most of the Specials are adults. Some have become celebrities, while others are virtual unknowns. Some are superpowered protectors

of the law, while others are criminals. Those who leave Pederson are tracked by the government. But when low-powered Specials begin showing up dead, it appears a serial killer is stalking the Specials. John Simon, the hero known as the Poet, is dispatched to find the murderer, but stopping the crimes may not be so easy—especially when it is revealed that every time a Special dies, the others gain something. And by 2032, only one Special remains, and he has a story to tell …

Rising Stars is one of a number of critically acclaimed series—including *Watchmen, Powers, Astro City, Marvels,* and a handful of others—which examine how superheroes might affect the real world, and how real people would react to superpowered beings living among them. Although there are 113 Specials, the series mainly focuses on about two dozen of them. These include Matthew Bright, a tough police officer with strength and flight powers; Elizabeth Chandra, a superstrong model who appears to everyone as the ideal woman; Laurel Darkhaven, a telekinetic assassin with a specialty of killing terrorists; Randy Fisk, a.k.a. Darkshadow, a street vigilante with flight, strength, tracking powers, and a computer-equipped Shadowcave; Lee Jackson, a pyrokinetic with a deadly secret in his past; Joshua Kane, a.k.a. Sanctuary, a hermaphroditic televangelist who hides his true, female form

Rising Stars #1 © 1999 J. Michael Straczynski and Top Cow Productions.
COVER ART BY KEU CHA, JASON GORDER, AND LIQUID!

from everyone; Stephanie Maas, a.k.a. Critical Maas, a woman with multiple personalities and the ability to mind-control other Specials; Jason Miller, a.k.a. Patriot (and Flagg), a strong masked superhero working as a corporate spokesperson; and John Simon, a.k.a. the Poet, the withdrawn narrator of the *Rising Stars* story and the most powerful of all the Specials.

A twenty-four-issue maxi-series, *Rising Stars* is the creation of writer J. Michael Straczynski (also creator of the popular TV series *Babylon 5*). Wanting total creative freedom and ownership of his properties, Straczynski brought *Rising Stars* to Top Cow, an imprint of Image Comics. The first issue

appeared in August 1999. Additionally, a *Bright* miniseries saw print in 2003, and a pair of *Rising Stars* novels were published in 2002, written by Arthur Byron Cover. A series of action figures was released by Palisades in 2001. Straczynski also wrote the feature film script for *Rising Stars: Born in Fire* in late 2000, adapting the first story arc for an MGM and Atlas Entertainment movie. After the script was drastically revised by Anthony Russo and Joe Russo, tensions flared between Straczynski and Top Cow, and the future of the film deal is now in question. Still, the comic-book series stands as a critical and fan favorite, and a landmark in the synergy between comics and other media (with Straczynski's crossover from the world of TV mirroring that of screenwriter/director Kevin Smith from the world of film to comics) like Marvel's *Daredevil* and DC's *Green Arrow*. Clearly, Straczynski caught the comics bug—literally—going on to write Marvel's prestigious *Spider-Man* among other comics, including the somewhat *Rising Stars*–like hit *Supreme Power,* also for Marvel. —AM

Robin

Imagine swooping from the rooftops and rushing into peril alongside a dark-cloaked crusader, crushing criminals while having the time of your life. Such is the appeal of Robin the Boy Wonder, Batman's death-defying junior partner, who epitomizes the designation "sidekick" more so than any other comic-book superhero. Touted as "the sensational character find of 1940" in his inaugural appearance in *Detective Comics* #38, Robin, premiering a scant eleven months after the debut of his cowled mentor, was envisioned by Batman creator Bob Kane as a hero with whom juvenile readers could identify. Kane's hunch was correct: the Boy Wonder's introduction not only instantly elevated the already-popular Batman's sales, it also spawned a legion of imitators, including the Shield's Dusty, Captain America's Bucky, and Green Arrow's Speedy.

Val Kilmer (Batman) and Chris O'Donnell (Robin) team up as crime-fighting partners in *Batman Forever*.

Robin the Boy Wonder was actually Dick Grayson, the youngest of a family of circus aerialists, who witnessed his mother and father plunge to their deaths from a sabotaged trapeze. This murder was also observed by millionaire Bruce (Batman) Wayne, who as a child had similarly watched his own parents die. Batman took this vengeful youngster under his wing, training him as his partner. And thus the most famous of superhero teams—Batman and Robin, the Dynamic Duo—was born. But while both Wayne and Grayson's childhoods were shattered after seeing the executions of their parents, the heroes' parallels ended there. Batman was brooding and grim, demonically clad in shadowy hues. But Robin was buoyant and robust, ostentatiously outfitted in a red tunic; green shorts, boots, and gloves; and a yellow cape. With gymnastic flash and the crime-fighting arsenal in his utility belt, the Boy Wonder laughed in the faces of his foes, punning while pummeling. Before long, the line dividing the Dynamic Duo's styles began to blur, with Batman's attitude becoming more jovial and Robin learning detective skills from his teacher.

Robin accompanied Batman on a host of 1940s and 1950s escapades in *Detective, Batman,* and *World's Finest Comics,* protecting their home of Gotham City against routine thugs and a growing contingent of colorful psychotics including the Joker, Catwoman, and the Penguin. The characters' acclaim became so immense that their comic-book adventures soon spawned a short-lived newspaper strip, a guest sequence on the *Superman* radio program, and two movie serials, *Batman* in 1943 and *Batman and Robin* in 1949. Robin the Boy Wonder was even awarded his own series in *Star-Spangled Comics,* beginning in 1947 and continuing for several years thereafter.

During those innocent times, no one pondered the threat of child endangerment facing young Dick Grayson each time he leapt into action as Robin (although the theme would be addressed in 2000 in the flashback miniseries *Robin: Year One*). Real-life psychiatrist Fredric Wertham, however, perceived a different menace to the Boy Wonder and to the boys reading *Batman* and other comic books. In his 1954 indictment of the comics industry, *Seduction of the Innocent,* Dr. Wertham labeled the relationship between Batman and Robin as "homosexual," and the resulting backlash sparked U.S. Senate hearings that nearly put comics out of business. Batman and Robin limped along through the late 1950s and early 1960s, plagued by mundane, often ridiculous stories and by the inclusion of the "Batman Family" (Batwoman, Ace the Bat-Hound, Bat-Mite, and the original Bat-Girl, the latter of whom was Robin's sometime-girlfriend, devised to erase the notion of a gay partnership between the Boy Wonder and his adult companion). Sales dropped precipitously and the Batman titles teetered on the brink of cancellation.

In 1964, editor Julius Schwartz revitalized the Batman franchise with a movement called the "New Look." Robin was now clearly a teenager, and while still an enthusiastic juggernaut of justice, he began to come into his own, joining other powerful adolescents as the Teen Titans. In 1966, ABC-TV's wildly successful, campy *Batman* series made the Dynamic Duo pop icons and catapulted actor Burt Wart into instant stardom in his role of Robin. Ward's earnest portrayal of the Boy Wonder birthed a national catchphrase: "Holy [insert your favorite noun here], Batman!" Millions of boys wanted to be Robin, masquerading as the young hero for Halloween and playing with the plethora of Robin (and Batman) merchandising that permeated the mid-1960s retail market. And millions of girls went gaga over the groovy Boy Wonder—Ward was a teen idol, his masked visage gracing the covers of *16* and *Tiger Beat* fan magazines.

By late 1968, the television series sputtered out of steam and the comic books were returning Batman to his darker roots as a "creature of the night." Robin emerged from Batman's shadow: He became the "Teen Wonder" and Dick Grayson vacated the Wayne mansion and the Teen Titans for Hudson University. In the early 1970s, Robin appeared in a series of relevant (for the times) backup stories in *Batman* and *Detective,* fighting corporate fatcats and student unrest instead of supervillains. After a decade of sporadic appearances, Robin the Teen Wonder fronted a new incarnation of the Teen Titans that launched in 1980, and fell in love with team-mate Starfire. In February 1984, Dick Grayson permanently shed his red tunic, ultimately adopting a new superhero guise as Nightwing. Despite these changes in the comics, television and movies preserved Grayson in the role of Robin: Via a variety of Batman animated programs from the late 1960s through the early 1990s; in the long-running *Super Friends* TV series; and twice on the big screen, with actor Chris O'Donnell playing Grayson/Robin in director Joel Schumacher's *Batman Forever* (1995) and *Batman & Robin* (1997).

Even though Dick Grayson sported a new heroic name, the legend of Robin the Boy Wonder lived on, fueled by tradition and copyright protection. Succeeding Grayson as Robin in 1983 was Jason Todd, a troubled teen who, after a largely unpopular stint as Batman's aide, was slaughtered by the Joker in a 1988 event stemming from a DC Comics–sponsored phone-in contest where readers decided the new Robin's fate. A new, female Robin appeared in writer/artist Frank Miller's *Batman: The Dark Knight Returns* in 1986, although this four-issue series occurred outside of the regular DC Comics continuity. In 1989, a tech-savvy teen named Tim Drake entered the life of Bruce Wayne—having cleverly inferred Batman's true identity—lobbying to become the new Boy Wonder. Reluctant to mentor another partner for fear of repeating Jason Todd's ghastly demise, Batman resisted, but eventually Drake adopted the Robin identity, albeit in a new, modernized uniform. The Drake version of Robin has, as of 2004, twice made the leap into animation: first in *The New Batman/Superman Adventures* (1997), then in the *Teen Titans* series airing on the Cartoon Network in 2003. In his subsequent comic-book adventures with and without Batman, the new Robin has begun to question his commitment to crime

fighting, and realizes that it's probably not his life's work. If Tim Drake ever hangs up his mask and cape, it is inevitable that another Robin will take his place. —*ME*

Robotman

Robotman was one of the little jewels in the DC Comics superhero lineup of the 1940s and, while he never graduated beyond backup status, he is still fondly remembered by comics historians to this day. Dreamed up by Superman creator Jerry Siegel, Robotman premiered in *Star Spangled Comics* #7 (1942) with an unusually dark and gritty origin story that gave little indication of the type of yarn that would come to typify the feature. While working late one night, scientists Bob Crane and Chuck Grayson are disturbed by hoods, and in the ensuing mêlée Crane is fatally shot. By luck, the pair had been working on a prototype robot, and Grayson toils through the night to transplant his stricken colleague's brain into the body of their experiment. With the operation seemingly a failure, Grayson is hauled away by the police, but the next day Crane wakes up as the apparently invincible Robotman. Donning a synthetic facemask and hands, Robotman adopts the pseudonym of Paul Dennis and tracks down his "killers" before freeing his hapless colleague.

In a slightly macabre twist, our hero kept the Dennis identity, attended his own funeral and struck up a romance with his grieving girlfriend, Joan Carter. It would be a year later before she found out that her old and current boyfriends were one and the same, when his true identity was revealed during a trial (in issue #15) to determine whether he was really a human being. That issue was a turning point in the series, as the tone gradually lightened from then on, the creative team was changed, and editors introduced a new companion. From its inception, the strip had been written by Siegel and drawn by members of his Superman co-creator Joe Schuster's Art Shop, including Paul Cassidy. With issue #25, veteran newspaper artist and Western devotee Jimmy Thompson was the unlikely choice as new artist, but he rose to the task magnificently. Thompson had an elegant, sophisticated style with a well-developed design sense and the lightest of touches—he even did his own lettering. Much of the feature's enduring appeal is due to Thompson's graphic mastery, although a lot of its success at the time was due to Robotman's new assistant, Robbie the Robodog.

Editors introduced Robbie (in issue #29) to give Robotman someone to talk to, but he soon developed a feisty personality of his own. Much like his creator (Robotman himself), Robbie could venture into the outside world disguised in a convincing outer skin, albeit covered in fur. He also fancied himself as something of a detective and was a keen fan of Sherlock Holmes, often depicted with his nose stuck in one of Doyle's novels. These were the strip's glory years, but everything changed when the feature was moved to *Detective Comics* in 1948. Gone were supporting cast Joan Carter, Chuck Grayson, Robbie, and even Jimmy Thompson, and in their place were a succession of colorless hoodlums and the rather less exciting art of Joe Certa. Robotman's 1950s strips were characterized by robotic enemies (Robot Robber, Robot Crook); an ever-changing robotic body, complete with outlandish gimmicks; and a less humorous tone to the stories. However, while it may have lacked the exuberance of its early years, the series enjoyed a creditable run up to 1954 (finishing in *Detective Comics* #202) for an impressive total of 139 episodes—far more than many of its more lauded competitors.

The next time readers came across a Robotman (in the early 1960s) it was Cliff Steele of the Doom Patrol, who shared a similar origin to the Crane/Dennis character but was a far more edgy, embittered individual. In the 1980s, longtime Robotman fan Roy Thomas reintroduced his childhood favorite into comics when he included him in the lineup of the *All-Star Squadron* in a series of wartime stories, which occasionally retold some of his original adventures (such as his trial). In the All-Star Squadron, Robotman was very much a bit-part player, with little of his original humor. Nonetheless, his six-year run with the team was a welcome coda to his early triumphs. Prior to his success, robots had often been portrayed as cold, sinister, and villainous (with the exception of Otto Binder's pulp hero Adam Link, a clear inspiration), but Robotman opened the way for other synthetic heroes to come, including Marvel Comics' Vision. —DAR

Rock Superheroes

The first KISS comic book hit the newsstands on June 28, 1977. The comic won accolades for its publisher Marvel Comics, which sold hundreds of thousands of copies to the supergroup's fans. However, it was not the first appearance of the band in comic-book form (that came with a guest shot in Marvel's *Howard the Duck* #12 earlier that year), nor was it to be the band's last. And though KISS's success in comics is perhaps the most well known (and oft-cited), it is not a unique phenomenon for rock musicians, who have often guest-starred in both real-life and superheroic form.

Pre-KISS rock phenomena to appear in comics include Elvis Presley in *I Love You, Featuring Elvis* (Charlton Comics, 1966) and the Beatles, who appeared in several one-shots over the years, including *The Beatles: Complete Life Stories* (Dell, 1964) and *Girls' Romances* (DC Comics, 1965). Riding on the Fab Four's guitar strings were the Monkees, whose 1967–1969 Dell series lasted seventeen issues. The Monkees series was the first to feature a band in superhero form—as the Monkeemen—though not in every issue. The supergroup premise came from the successful *Monkees* TV show, where in several episodes the Monkees leaped into a phone booth to become the Monkeemen, four superheroes in identical costumes who possessed superstrength and the ability to defy the laws of nature. DC must have been watching the show—and the comic's sales figures— before it brought out *Maniaks,* a short-lived series about a fictional mod-rock quartet that dabbles in superhuman stunts and campy adventures (*Showcase* #68, #69, and #71, 1967).

During the 1970s, publishers like Marvel tried their hand at adapting the rock-and-roll genre to comics, with mixed success. In addition to its best-selling *KISS* comic, Marvel published an unauthorized "Beatles Story" biography in *Marvel Comics Super Special* #4 (1978), a second KISS appearance in *Marvel Super Special* #5 (1978), and Alice Cooper's debut in *Marvel Premiere* #50 (1979). Shortly thereafter, Marvel introduced original rock-music-based superheroes with its *Dazzler* series (March 1981), about a roller-skating rock-disco singer whose mutant ability to turn sound into brilliant light comes from her singing voice; and then with its *Nightcat* series in early 1991, based on an album released through RCA Records featuring singer Jacqueline Tavarez, about a rock singer who gains catlike powers after being injected by a secret cat serum at the hands of an evil scientist. (In the almost-super category, for years Marvel's longtime supporting-cast member Rick Jones picked up a guitar and toured folk clubs in between stints as the company's number one superhero sidekick, while late 1970s followers of Shang-Chi, Master of Kung Fu could often count on the hero puzzling over Fleetwood Mac lyrics or meditating to blasting Rolling Stones albums in between bouts of martial-arts mayhem.)

Other publishers to emerge with their own rock and roll heroes include the short-lived Skywald Publishing, whose superhero Butterfly was a soul singer in her alter ego of Marian Michaels (*Hell-Rider* #1, 1971). In 1987 Eclipse Comics published a one-shot *Captain EO* comic, the official 3-D comic-book adaptation of the George Lucas 3-D movie/rock video directed by Francis Ford Coppola. Only available for viewing at Disney theme parks, the seventeen-minute-long short and the comic starred Michael Jackson as a futuristic space hero. Practically every rock star from the 1950s onward cameoed in Mike Allred's *Red Rocket 7* (Dark Horse Comics, 1997–1998), the saga of a prophetic extraterrestrial rocker.

Amongst these blips on the screen emerged and endured KISS, whose larger-than-life stage personae make for perfect comic-book characters. With the 1977 *KISS* comic, Marvel mixed band members' blood with the red ink that was used to print the first run. Never ones to pass up a marketing opportunity, band members complied with the promotional ploy invented to ignite sales of the first edition, even showing up at the printing plant to donate blood. In 1997 Todd McFarlane Productions published *KISS: Psycho Circus.* Influenced by the vision of *Spawn* creator and Image Comics co-owner Todd McFarlane, this series "was born with a decidedly darker edge to it," according to KISS frontman Gene Simmons. Dark Horse Comics launched its own KISS comic (*KISS* #1) in July 2002, written by *X-Men*'s Joe Casey, with art by Mel Rubi (of Joss Whedon's *Angel*), and covers by J. Scott Campbell (*Danger Girl*) and Leinil Francis Yu (*X-Men, High Roads*). A superteam aesthetic drives this new series, with "lots of fun, over-the-top villains," according to Simmons, who also calls the series "the Fantastic Four of the twenty-first century" in a Dark Horse press release.

Overseen by Simmons, Dark Horse's *KISS* series turns these rock-and-roll icons into the ultimate superhero team. Years after the split-up of these four superpowered warriors, each member has followed his own path. The Demon (Gene Simmons) is a bounty hunter; the Starchild (Paul Stanley) is an artist who lives with a race of women warriors in South America; the Spaceman (Ace Frehley) is an intergalactic loner adrift in the solar system; and the Catman (Peter Criss) is almost all beast, with very little humanity left in him. The heroes band together in an effort to save their bestial brother from his destructive rampages, and a new comic book is born....

Besides KISS, a long list of rock groups—from Led Zeppelin to Aerosmith—have appeared in Revolutionary Comics' Rock 'n' Roll line. Even Billy Ray Cyrus appeared in a Wild West comic-book adventure in 1995 from Marvel's short-lived Marvel Music line, launched in 1994 with licensed titles that featured musicians such as KISS (again), Alice Cooper, AC/DC, KRS-One, and Bob Marley. Many of the comics tied in with album releases and videos or were packaged with CDs, cassettes, and other merchandise. Malibu Comics graphic-novelized the careers of bands like Black Sabbath in the company's early 1990s Rock-It line, and in the 2000s shock-rocker Rob Zombie masterminded the hit *Rob Zombie's Spookshow International* comic from MVCreations. In the world of manga, rock and movie star Courtney Love is the inspiration for TOKYOPOP's *Princess Ai,* a 2004 series featuring an outspoken young heroine who disguises herself as a nightclub performer modeled after Love.

And to discuss another outlet for superheroic antics, several well-known rock music videos feature superhero takes: Prince's 1989 "Batman" features Prince as a half-Batman/half-Joker, with Batmen and Jokers performing as background dancers; Eminem's 2002 video "Without Me," presented in classic Batman comic-book style, showcases the hip-hop artist impersonating Batman's sidekick Robin; and Shania Twain displays superheroic action in her semi-animated "I'm Gonna Getcha Good" video from 2003.

These aren't the only examples of the rock-to-comics crossover reversing from comics into rock— the nucleus of David Bowie's legendary Spiders from Mars band was an early 1970s outfit called Hype in which Bowie and his bandmates dressed as superheroes onstage; Todd McFarlane has illustrated album covers for KORN and others; myriad alternative-rock favorites convened in 1999 for a "soundtrack album" to the *Witchblade* comic; and a number of bands of all genres have taken their names from superhero secret identities, from Peter Parker to David Banner. —GM

The Rocketeer

In 1991 few moviegoers would have been aware that *The Rocketeer* had been a comic book before it was a film, but in fact the character had been a cult favorite in print for years before he appeared on the silver screen. The character's genesis was inauspicious, to say the least: Artist Dave Stevens was approached at a comic-book convention by upstart publishing house Pacific Comics to fill a couple of six-page gaps at the back of their new *Starslayer* comic. Pacific was desperate and simply did not care what Stevens came up with, but to their undoubted surprise the resulting strip provoked a torrent of rapturous acclaim. With a blank canvas to work on, Stevens decided to indulge his love of 1930s movie serials, especially the ones featuring Commando Cody a.k.a. Rocketman (*King of the Rocketmen, Radar Men from the Moon,* and *Zombies of the Stratosphere*), and created a beautifully rendered homage to a more innocent age.

The story, set in 1938, begins with a couple of hoods on the run from the law, who stash a stolen rocket pack in the cockpit of stunt pilot Cliff Secord's plane. Discovering the strange contraption (effectively a small rocket with a harness to attach it to the pilot's back), Secord seizes on it as the chance for him to become a star at his local airfield, earning him lots of money and impressing his girlfriend Betty. With the help of his curmudgeonly pal Peevy (based on Jonny Quest creator Doug Wildey), he fashions himself a costume of brown breeches, flying jacket, and metal-plumed steel helmet and flies into action. As a normal human being with no superpowers or superweaknesses to speak of, Secord as the Rocketeer relies on his superfast rocket pack to help him save the day. Inevitably, the hoods who had stolen the jet pack in the first place (Nazis, of course) want it back, as does the FBI and its mysterious inventor (a thinly veiled Doc Savage, complete with cohorts Monk and Ham). This initial story appeared in *Starslayer* #2 and #3 (1982) and the strip was promoted to the lead feature in the first two issues of *Pacific Presents,* before being wrapped up two years later in a *Rocketeer* special edition from Eclipse Comics after Pacific went under.

Stevens had two trump cards: First, he was a fantastic artist, whose mastery of brushwork was second only to his mastery of the female form—which brings us to the comic's second selling point, Secord's girlfriend Betty. Stevens based Betty's appearance on a largely forgotten 1950s pinup model, Bettie Page and, as fans devoured the comic and bought up posters of the fictional Betty in droves, interest was revived in the character's original inspiration. From forgotten model to major twentieth-century icon, Bettie Page's re-emergence as a sex symbol, with a merchandising machine to match, stemmed almost entirely from the pages of *The Rocketeer*. If Betty was a remarkable comic-book character, so too was the artist's depiction of the 1930s milieu surrounding her adventures with Secord. Stevens delighted in delineating the eccentric architecture of prewar Hollywood, its stylish cars and airplanes, and its sense of fun.

However, Stevens' burgeoning career as a comic-book artist was matched by his successful life in Hollywood's movie world as a storyboard artist and designer, which meant that it was four more years before a second Rocketeer adventure was serialized. This new tale appeared in 1988, from new publisher Comico. Then Comico went bust after only two issues of the comic, and it was an astonishing six years before the final installment crept out, published by Dark Horse Comics. The new yarn was, if anything, even more majestically drawn than the earlier episodes, and featured hard-boiled gangsters and old-time carnivals and freak shows, not to mention the Shadow (in all but name), complete with autogyro.

Both stories did well in comic-book form but, long before the first tale had even been completed, *The Rocketeer* was optioned by Hollywood and eight years later (in 1991) the live-action feature film finally appeared, from the unlikely stable of Disney. *The Rocketeer* was directed by Joe Johnston, a long-time friend of Stevens, and starred Billy Campbell and Jennifer Connelly. Connelly's role, significantly, was as a new damsel-in-distress, and not Betty (Dis-

Rocketeer Adventure Magazine #1 © 1988 Dave Stevens. COVER ART BY DAVE STEVENS.

ney was wary of the character's connection with the real-life Page and her pinup background). The film was reviewed as a breezy family entertainment film with great special effects. Careful viewers noted the multiple Hollywood references, such as an effective villain (played by Timothy Dalton) that was clearly based on early film actor Errol Flynn. Disney saw the project as a merchandising bonanza, but its loving re-creation of a bygone era failed to connect with a young audience, and so the merchandise was abandoned and the option for two sequels was not executed.

Since the Rocketeer, Stevens has largely left comics behind, preferring to concentrate on covers, paintings, and film work. However, his character will doubtless live on in its old comics, with their charming storyline and luxurious artwork continuing to entertain and inspire. —*DAR*

Ronin Warriors

Five teenagers are granted superhuman powers to battle an evil leader and his minions. The heroes often interact with mythical figures, and while the five are powerful as individuals, they are an unstoppable force when united. This is a typical scenario for popular anime in Japan. In the 1990s, an example of it first appeared on American television in the form of the series *Ronin Warriors.*

The English-language version of *Yoroiden Samurai Troopers, Ronin Warriors* was first broadcast on syndicated television in the United States from 1995 through 1996. The name *Ronin Warriors* was chosen to avoid confusion with two live-action shows running on American television at that time—*VR Troopers* and *Samurai Cyber Squad.* In its original Japanese version it first aired on Japanese television in 1988 and ran for thirty-nine episodes. The show's popularity in Japan led to three sequel OVA (Original Video Animation) series, merchandise, and a 1992 manga *Shin Yoroiden Samurai Troopers* (New Legendary Armor Samurai Troopers). There was also a special laser disc collection released in Japan in the early 1990s. The series was produced by Sunrise, a studio better known for its giant robot shows such as *Mobile Suit Gundam* and *Heavy Metal L-Gaim.* In fact, the series supervisor for *Samurai Troopers* was Sunrise veteran Ryosuke Takahashi, more famous for creating and directing *mecha* (giant robot) series such as *Armored Trooper Votoms* and *Gasaraki.*

Many Americans were aware of the show's Japanese look, but not its origins; nor did they realize that the show was part of a unique subgenre of anime, the "Magical Armor Team." Two other shows were part of this category—*Saint Seiya* (1986) and *Legend of the Heavenly Sphere Shurato* (1989). All three shows had common elements: a core group of five good-looking male teenagers with powerful armor that possesses magical properties; each suit being essentially the same in design while each has its own individual color; and a single, powerful evil overlord that the team has to defeat or else all is lost. The overlord also has his own lieutenants that do his dirty work for him, and these enemies have their own special abilities. The five heroes can transform from their civilian identities into their armor; this is accomplished in an often-repeated animated sequence. There is also a strong female character that helps the heroes, as well as an older character that acts as both a guide and a sage. There are many violent battles between the main characters and the forces of evil. A final ingredient is mythology—each series is based on a particular one, with a great deal of liberties taken. *Saint Seiya* was based on Greek mythology; *Shurato* took Buddhist and Hindu lore. *Samurai Troopers*—and thus *Ronin Warriors*—used Shinto symbolism.

The use of five team members as major heroes had been a staple of anime and *sentai* (live-action science fiction shows featuring special effects and actors in costumes portraying both heroes and evil monsters) since 1972; that was the year that Tatsunoko Studio's *Science Ninja Team Gatchaman* premiered on Japanese television and changed anime forever with the introduction of its five main characters. They would set a standard that would be duplicated, expanded upon, and reimagined over the following years. One prominent example is the popular 1990s *shojo* ("girls' comic") manga and anime versions of *Lovely Soldier Sailor Moon,* which employs five teenage girls instead of boys as the main heroes.

Graz Entertainment and the Ocean Group handled the English-language adaptation; with only a few changes—mostly regarding the names of characters and the music—*Samurai Troopers'* storyline was left relatively untouched when it became *Ronin*

Warriors. Talpa, a powerful and possibly immortal sorcerer, seeks to conquer the human world. He has tried before, but one thousand years ago, the Ancient One thwarted him. Ever on guard for the Dark Lord's return, the Ancient One created nine suits of mystical armor—resembling stylized samurai garb—from Talpa's own armor. When Talpa returns in modern-day Japan, four of the mystical "Armor Gears" are used by his lieutenants Cale, Anubis, Sekhmet, and Dais. These "Dark Warlords" are opposed by five teens using the remaining Armor Gears—Ryo, Kento, Sage, Cye, and Rowen. Their allies are the Ancient One, the white tiger White Blaze, a teenage girl named Mia Koji, and Ully, a courageous nine-year-old boy. The five teens, as the Ronin Warriors, go into combat against Talpa and his army, with nothing less than the fate of the world at stake.

Each Ronin's armor represented a particular element from nature, and each hero had a *kanji* symbol on his forehead that represented a specific Shinto virtue. Power came not just from the armor, but from the courage and will of the five teens themselves; in later episodes, Ryo would use the White Armor of Hariel which drew its power from his four friends.

Ronin Warriors' popularity was high among males (the series, after all, had a great deal of action), but the show was also very popular among female viewers, especially teenage girls—no doubt a result of five good-looking male leads! Yet the series was also very strong on characterization; each character was given more than a paper-thin personality. Villains that might have been cardboard cutouts were complex beings, and in the cases of Anubis and Lady Kayura, honorable to the point of changing sides and joining the heroes in their quest. By the final episode, all the heroes and villains joined forces to defeat Talpa once and for all—at least, one hoped so. Only by joining forces could the heroes hope to stop the enemy (in fact, a tactic used by Talpa was to separate the five heroes and send his Dark Warlords to take each Ronin out one at a time). Personal egos had to be put aside for the greater good.

After the syndicated run, the thirty-nine episodes were rerun on the Sci Fi Channel. Bandai Entertainment released the series on DVD starting in 2002, but with episodes from both *Ronin Warriors* and *Samurai Troopers* on each DVD. Merchandising was far below the level of *Samurai Troopers,* but action figures of the main heroes and villains were released in America during the series' run. The English-language voice actors became popular guests at American anime conventions in the late 1990s, and Sakura Con 2002 featured Norio Shioyama, the series' character designer, as a guest. As of early 2004, the sequel OVAs have not been released in the United States. —*MM*

Sailor Moon

In 1972, Tatsunoko Productions' *Science Ninja Team Gatchaman* ushered in a new concept in anime—the five-member superhero team. Since then, that concept has been featured in anime such as *Yoroiden Samurai Troopers* (Ronin Warriors in the United States), *Saint Seiya, Shurato,* and *Golion* (the Voltron Lion Team). Yet the main characters were almost exclusively male; there was only one female member. Twenty years after *Gatchaman,* however, the team concept was changed again, and the result brought an entirely new energy to manga and anime. The series responsible for this change was *Sailor Moon.*

Lovely Soldier Sailor Moon began as a short-lived manga created by Naoko Takeuchi called *Codename Sailor V* in 1991. The main character was a mask-wearing heroine whose costume was modeled after the "sailor suit" uniform worn by Japanese schoolgirls. Yoshio Irie, the new editor of the monthly *shojo* ("girls' comic") magazine *Nakayoshi,* latched onto the possibility of using the manga as the first step in a multimedia franchise—one that could be launched simultaneously in comics, television, and merchandising. Takeuchi reworked *Codename Sailor V,* creating new characters and adding new elements to the story. She also drew from her love of superheroes and *sentai* (live-action sci-fi/fantasy) series. What emerged was a *shojo* title that was a superhero adventure, with the main characters being five teenage girls—something unheard of at the time. In January 1992, *Bishojo Senshi Sailor Moon* began running in *Nakayoshi,* but in February the animated series began airing on Japanese television. Normally, there would be a period of several months, or even years, between the manga's initial run and its anime adaptation. In the case of *Sailor Moon,* the manga and anime were running concurrently, another first in the Japanese pop-culture world.

The staff involved in the production of the *Sailor Moon* animated series included directors Kunihiko Ikuhara and Kazuhisa Takenouchi and character designers Kazuko Tadano and Ikuko Ito, among others. Toei Animation produced the animation for the series in Japan, which would eventually run for more than two hundred episodes over five years. Each season also had a different title; after season one's *Sailor Moon,* there was *Sailor Moon R, Sailor Moon S, Sailor Moon Super S,* and *Sailor Moon Sailor Stars,* the final season, which ended in 1997. The manga's run also ended that year. The popularity of the series led to the production of

Sailor Moon #1 © 1998 Naoko Takeuchi.
COVER ART BY NAOKO TAKEUCHI.

ets: Sailor Mercury (Ami Mizuno), Sailor Mars (Rei Hino), Sailor Jupiter (Makoto Kino), and Sailor Venus (Minako Aino). Each heroine wears a "sailor suit" of a particular color, and each has powers based on the "elements" of fire, water, wood, and love. The team must face a growing threat to the universe in the form of Queen Beryl and her master Queen Metallia. The Sailor Warriors' main allies are Luna, Artemis (a magical white cat), and the mysterious Tuxedo Mask, who is actually the girls' classmate Mamoru Chiba. Mamoru is also the reincarnation of Endymion, Princess Serenity's beloved.

While the manga and anime did have humor and action, both also had strong storylines, well-developed characters, and a strong element of romance. In addition, the five heroines were always victorious when working together—an important component of the "five-member team" anime concept, and one that appealed to a girl audience. To fans, the characters were "real"—they had typical teenager issues; one can easily see parallels with Spider-Man's alter ego, Peter Parker. "The attraction of Sailor Moon is that it enables young girls to fantasize themselves as powerful as their brothers' macho superheroes, without losing any of their femininity," notes Maurice Horn's *The World Encyclopedia of Cartoons* (1999).

True to form, the series did not shy away from killing off major characters—in fact, the first season of the anime series ended with the main cast being killed off during the final assault on Queen Beryl's lair (but they were revived at the episode's end). Even the courageous Tuxedo Mask had to be saved by the Sailor Warriors on several occasions. Usagi accepts her role as the leader of the Sailor Warriors and grows in experience and maturity. Over the next four seasons, more villains would be introduced, but also new Sailor Warriors—Saturn, Uranus, Neptune, and Pluto. One major new character was Chibi Usa, young girl from the future … who happens to be the future daughter of Usagi and Mamoru. In the course of the series, it is revealed that Usagi and Mamoru become the future rulers of the Silver Mil-

three animated theatrical films that were released in Japan—*Sailor Moon R* (1993), *Sailor Moon S* (1994), and *Sailor Moon Super S* (1995).

The manga and anime followed the adventures of Usagi Tsukino, who by all appearances is a cheerful teenage girl. She is also lazy and a whining crybaby, ignoring her schoolwork and daydreaming. Everything changes when she meets a talking black cat named Luna, who is searching for the reincarnation of the Moon Princess Serenity. Usagi is told that *she* is Princess Serenity, reborn. Using magical items that include a wand and a tiara—plus powers given to her by Luna—Usagi transforms into superheroine Sailor Moon, who becomes the leader of the Sailor Warriors; the remaining four are named after planlennium; as Queen Serenity and King Endymion, both rule peacefully over thirtieth-century Earth, where all have eternal life and beauty.

The success of the manga, anime, and merchandising for *Sailor Moon* made it one of the most popular anime franchises of the 1990s. The series had high ratings and drew an audience that was predominately female, but also attracted males. It was inevitable that an American release would soon follow. DiC produced an English-language version of *Sailor Moon* for release on American syndicated television in 1995. Names were changed—Usagi became "Serena," and the Sailor Warriors became the "Sailor Scouts"; a new English-language theme song was created. Unfortunately, the attempt nearly ended as a major failure. Many stations broadcast the series at time slots that were too early in the morning for viewers; others simply did not know the target audience. The triad of manga-series-marketing push that had been successful in Japan was not repeated in the United States. Also, the series was heavily edited to remove elements that were regarded as too mature or sophisticated for children; whole episodes essentially had their stories radically altered. The series was canceled after its first season in 1996—yet all was not lost.

In Canada, the first two seasons were aired successfully on the YTV network. In the United States, an Internet-based movement called S.O.S. —Save Our Sailors—was organized to create petitions and appeal to network executives to bring the series back to television. The campaign was a resounding success; *Sailor Moon* was aired briefly on the USA cable network in 1997, and was picked up by the Cartoon Network in 1998. With a better timeslot and full-fledged promotion, the series became the network's highest-rated show. To the delight of fans, the first four seasons of *Sailor Moon* were aired on television. TOKYOPOP/Mixx Entertainment produced the English translation of the manga; first for the comic magazine *Smile* and then as an ongoing series. The company also released original novels based on the series written

by Lianne Sentar. Guardians of Order produced a role-playing game and a collectible card game (CCG) and Irwin Toys of Canada produced toys and dolls. Sailor Moon and her team appeared in books, on apparel, on mugs, and in calendars, just about everywhere that the pop-culture eye roamed. The series was also parodied, most notably by American writer-artist Adam Warren in his 1998 three-issue miniseries *Gen 13: Magical Drama Queen Roxy.*

In 1999, Pioneer began releasing subtitled and dubbed versions of the three *Sailor Moon* movies. The movies were uncut and unedited (although the initial English-language release on VHS was edited for content). ADV Films began releasing the edited English-language version produced by DiC on DVD in 2002, but in 2003 the company released an uncut, subtitled version of *Sailor Moon*'s first season on DVD, with plans to release the entire five seasons in the future.

Sailor Moon triggered a new wave of manga and anime that combined *shojo* and action; among the titles were *Fushigi Yuugi, Magic Knight Rayearth, Card Captor Sakura, Escaflowne,* and *Revolutionary Girl Utena* (created by Kunihiko Ikuhara, one of *Sailor Moon*'s directors). Naoko Takeuchi was a guest at the 1998 San Diego Comic-Con International. Even though it ended in 1997, the show is still popular in Japan and around the world. In the United States, the Sailor Scouts are popular "cosplay" characters, in a branch of fandom in which both males and females dress up as members of the team at conventions and other events. —*MM*

Samurai Troopers: *See* **Ronin Warriors**

Sandman

When he first appeared in the summer of 1939 (in *Adventure Comics* #40) the Sandman was only the fourth superhero in comics history, and the third published by DC Comics (then National Publications) after Superman and Batman. However, he did not possess any superpowers. Like Batman's alter ego, Bruce Wayne, Wesley Dodd was a millionaire playboy who put on a costume to confront hoodlums and ne'er-do-wells, armed only with his fists and wits—and a rather handy gas-gun. Dodd's costume, such as it was, consisted of a purple cape, a slouch hat, a smart suit, and a gold gas mask (necessary because his modus operandi was to gas his foes into slumber with the pull of his trigger). Unusually for superheroes of the period, the Sandman's elegant society girlfriend, Dian (also Diane) Belmont, knew his secret identity and had a habit of helping him out on assignments, invariably dressed in a diaphanous ball gown.

The men responsible for these early episodes were prolific writer Gardner Fox and the young but talented artist Bert Christman. Sadly, Christman left the strip to seek adventure of his own as one of General Claire Chenault's legendary Flying Tigers, and was later killed while flying over China in the early days of World War II. His replacement was the equally talented Craig Flessel but, despite the strip being one of the best-crafted features of the era, DC decided to spice it up by giving the Sandman a yellow and purple superhero costume and a young sidekick named Sandy Hawkins. A few issues later, the transformation was complete when Joe Simon and Jack Kirby, recently defected from Marvel Comics, took over the creative reins (with issue #72) and turned it into an all-action slugfest.

The Simon and Kirby Sandman punched first and thought later, and the strip became a frenetic display of all-out battles and daredevil heroics. Unlike other wartime features, the Sandman and Sandy generally fought organized crime and the occasional Norse god rather than the Third Reich. The strip was the cover feature of *Adventure Comics* throughout the war, but its quality suffered when its creative team was drafted (as creative teams often were at the time) and, in February 1946, it became one of the first casualties of the peacetime comics slump and lost its place to Superboy. At the peak of his popularity in both his guises, the Sandman was featured in comics such as *World's Finest, World's Fair,* and, as a member of the Justice Society of America, in *All Star Comics;* it was the latter group that would prove to be his savior.

While the Silver Age (1956–1969) superhero boom of the 1960s saw a whole range of new characters, it also revived some of the old favorites and, for many years, the Justice Society appeared in an annual crossover with the Justice League of America. Between 1966 and 1974, the Sandman was a frequent member of the Justice Society in those team-ups, though it was always in his earlier, gas-mask costume. The last of those stories revealed, somewhat implausibly, that for many years Sandy had been lurking around, transformed into a giant sand creature. Things got even stranger for our hero when Simon and Kirby created another Sandman (published in January 1974 as the one-shot titled *Sandman* #1 and later picked up as a brief mid-1970s series), a yellow-suited hero who lived "somewhere between heaven and earth" in a secret hideout where he monitored people's dreams. Complete with monstrous assistants, Brute and Glob, this Sandman battled the likes of Dr. Spider, the Sealmen, General Electric, and various frog people. Perhaps inevitably, it was just a short-lived experiment but it served, some years later, as the inspiration for yet another Sandman, who premiered in 1989.

This radical reinvention, written by Neil Gaiman, was a fantasy series starring Morpheus (the Sandman of the title, also known as Dream, the Prince of Stories), an angelic-looking girl named Death, and numerous other characters from the realm of dreams. While Morpheus had little to do with previous incarnations of the Sandman character, the comic's enormous critical and commercial success—*Sandman* #19 won the World Fantasy Award for Best Short Story in 1991—rekindled interest in the character. The Sandman comic sold more than 1 million copies per year, and Gaiman was heralded as the creator who reignited a medium, with Norman Mailer proclaiming, "Along with all else, *Sandman* is a comic strip for intellectuals, and I say it's about time." This excellence of writing, in fact, attracted acclaimed guest-talent, including Clive Barker, Sam Keith, and Todd McFarlane. Ten Sandman short-story collections have appeared as of 2004; and Warner Bros. has optioned Sandman for a movie. Though the series ended in 1996, Gaiman has returned to it for such special events as the hardback collection *Endless Nights* (2003), and a number of spinoffs by other creators have appeared.

In 1993 the original Sandman returned in the *Sandman Mystery Theatre* comic. This *Sandman* spin-off series effectively retold the story of Wesley Dodd and Dian Belmont from their very first adventures, and featured guest stars such as Blackhawk and Hourman. It ran for seventy issues—much longer, ironically, than its 1940s forerunner—and ended in 1999 with Dodd and Belmont heading off for wartorn Europe. As if that wasn't enough, yet another Justice Society revival starred an elderly Dodd, still wearing the gas mask, in modern-day adventures, one of which told of how he died. In the 2000s he has been replaced by "Sand" (actually an incarnation of side-kick Sandy!), a gas-masked hero who can transform into his namesake substance (like the Marvel Comics Spider-Man villain also named Sandman); a sure sign of a concept and character durable enough to with-stand the sands of time. —*DAR*

THE SAVAGE DRAGON
image
4
SEPT
$1.95
2.45 CANADA

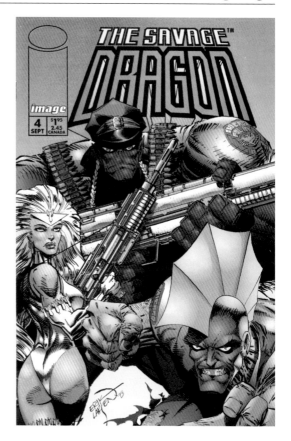

The Savage Dragon #4 © 1993 Erik Larsen.
COVER ART BY ERIK LARSEN.

The Savage Dragon

Discovered naked in a burning empty lot in Chicago, an amnesiac green man with fangs and a fin on his head is taken to the hospital. Named "Dragon" by a nurse, the man bonds with Lieutenant Frank Darling of the Chicago Police Department. Later, when Dragon helps stop some super-criminals at the harbor, Darling tries to get Dragon to join the police force to help fight the rising tide of super "freaks." After surviving a tragedy partially engineered by the criminal gang known as the Vicious Circle, Dragon becomes a Chicago PD officer with a penchant for fighting crime, getting his shirt torn off, and romancing the ladies.

Comic creator Erik Larsen had started in the independent comics trenches, which is where his childhood creation, the Dragon, first saw print (in *Megaton* #3, February 1986). Larsen worked his way up through the comics ranks, eventually becoming a fan favorite on Marvel Comics such as *Amazing Spider-Man* and *Nova.* Larsen left Marvel with six other popular creators to form Image Comics in 1992. *The Savage Dragon* #1 debuted a three-issue miniseries in July 1992, and the regular series has appeared monthly (mostly) ever since its first issue in June 1993. Larsen has written and drawn every issue to date, though other creators came onboard to create special issues, spin-off miniseries, and crossovers with books as diverse as *Destroyer Duck, Marshal Law, Teenage Mutant Ninja Turtles, Superman,* and *Megaton Man.*

The Savage Dragon has incredible strength, and can jump huge distances. He is nearly invulnerable to flame, plasma, explosions, and gunfire, though he has been hurt, cut, and even maimed by maces, knives, and other weapons. His healing power is also advanced; he has regrown entire limbs in the past, after battles with supervillains. The most dangerous villains he faced in the past worked for the OverLord in the Vicious Circle. Villains included SkullFace, Hardware, Abner Cadaver, Arachnid, Clawedd van Damage, Phathead, Stigma, and the waste-spewing Dung. After the death of OverLord, a more charismatic leader named Cyber-Face took over the Circle, and bedeviled Dragon anew, even succeeding in getting him fired from the police department.

For a time, Dragon worked with a government-sponsored Special Operative Strikeforce, but after facing a personal tragedy on his wedding day, Dragon semi-retired. Some time later, after Dragon killed an infant who would have grown up to be the villain Damien DarkLord, he caused a disruption in the timestream, and discovered he was now living in a new "Savage World," similar to the old Earth, but different enough to be dangerous. He was forced to figure out friend from foe, and deal with the many surprises that this new life threw at him.

During his run, Dragon has teamed up with a variety of heroes—many of whom have had their own spin-off series or miniseries—including star-spangled cyborg SuperPatriot, the funky weirdos known as Freak Force, the squabbling Deadly Duo, gender-switching Mighty Man (whose secret identity is a female), and more. Unmatched in this capacity by most of the other Image creators, Larsen has singularly created a vast universe of characters that have an internal consistency. He has also managed to crossover with other series; besides those in specific titles previously mentioned, and other Image heroes, Savage Dragon has interacted with Hellboy, FemForce, E-Man, Zot, Vampirella, the DNA-gents, and others.

Whether fighting crime in Chicago on the Image Earth, or fighting supervillains in the Savage World universe, the Savage Dragon remains popular with fans. In October 1995, USA Network debuted a *Savage Dragon* animated series. The series lasted two seasons, ending in the fall of 1996 after twenty-six episodes. Multiple action figures of Dragon and his friends and enemies have been produced, as well as statues, posters, trading cards, and more. Larsen also has an aggressive trade paperback program, so that fans can read all of the Dragon's adventures even if they can't find the back issues.—*AM*

The Scarlet Witch and Quicksilver

Longstanding Avengers members the Scarlet Witch and her twin brother Quicksilver have gone through as convoluted and protracted an origin as any characters in comics, and have endured many indignities in the process. Despite or perhaps because of this, the Scarlet Witch is one of the longest-lived female supporting characters in the Marvel universe. The twins first appeared as members of Magneto's Brotherhood of Evil Mutants in *X-Men* #4 (in 1964) but were almost from the start reluctant villains. After a year of regular battles with the X-Men, their creators, writer Stan Lee and artist Jack Kirby, evidently felt that the pair deserved a chance at the big time and, after a speedy renunciation of their criminal past, they were duly inducted into the Avengers (*Avengers* #16, 1965).

As Avengers, the twins were a cornerstone of the group's glory years through the 1960s and 1970s, while never quite building up enough of a following to encourage Marvel to launch them into solo careers. Initially, all that was known about them was that they were mutants. Wanda Maximoff, a.k.a. the Scarlet Witch, possessed a form of magic ("hex power"), while her brother Pietro, known as Quicksilver, was (as his name suggests) a super-speedster with a short-fused temper to match. Their first origin involved them fleeing persecution in their native Transia (one of Marvel's all-purpose Balkan backwaters) into the arms of Magneto, but there was much, much more to come.

In 1975 editors suggested (in *Giant-Size Avengers* #1) that Wanda and Pietro's parents were 1940s heroes the Whizzer and Miss America, who had given birth after a nuclear accident. Miss America died and the Whizzer fled in grief, leaving the twins to be brought up by a highly evolved cow (one of the *Island of Dr. Moreau*–like characters from Marvel's mythical complex called Wundagore). Some years later, however, this explanation was superseded by an even more startling revelation. This newer version (in *Avengers* #185) suggested that Miss America's twins had died and that Wanda and Pietro were actually born to a gypsy named Magda, who had subsequently killed herself rather than reveal their whereabouts to their father Magnus, later known as … Magneto. The cow-lady midwife later gave the children to a gypsy family, the Maximoffs, who brought Wanda and Pietro up until they were killed by a mob, whereupon the twins were rescued by Magneto—which is where readers came into the storyline with *X-Men* #4.

The 1970s were a romantic decade for the twins, as the Scarlet Witch fell in love with her android teammate, the Vision, and Quicksilver fell for Crystal of the Inhumans. Both couples married, and Quicksilver went off to live in the Inhumans' Himalayan refuge (and later on the moon), while his sister settled down to cozy domesticity in Leonia, New Jersey. (The Vision and the Witch starred in a couple of mid-1980s miniseries, *Vision and Scarlet Witch,* by writer Steve Englehart and artist Richard Howell.) But whereas Quicksilver gained a child, Luna, and was largely written out of the Avengers,

Marvel writers had a different fate in store for the Scarlet Witch. During the company's *Secret Wars* series, the Vision was controlled by aliens, and a while later the couple left the Avengers for their West Coast branch. There Wanda became pregnant and gave birth to twins, William and Thomas; it later transpired that these were demon offshoots of the evil Mephisto. Then an increasingly unbalanced Vision was dismantled before being reconstructed without any emotion, and the couple tragically divorced, although the Vision's "half-brother" Wonder Man (on whose brain patterns the android's mind was based) unhelpfully declared his undying love for Wanda.

Things got even worse for Wanda in the 1980s, as she was reclaimed by Magneto after becoming a bride of Set, and went over to the "dark side." Quicksilver returned to rescue her, but she was soon claimed by another Marvel baddie, Immortus, who had been influencing her actions for years. Confusingly, it seems that she was in fact not a garden-variety mutant but a nexus being—"someone who belongs to all realities." In later issues of *West Coast Avengers* she became the group's leader, a position she continued to hold in Force Works, a team of former West Coast Avengers (1994), but there was more upheaval to come. In the "Onslaught" storyline, she died along with the other Avengers but was resurrected soon after. Wonder Man died, came back, died, came back as an energy being and died again, still proffering his undying love, even though it was his robotic half-brother who was Wanda's most enduring paramour.

Perhaps feeling that they have wrung every last plot twist from the unfortunate girl, Marvel's writers have been somewhat kinder to the Scarlet Witch in the new millennium. Back in the Avengers after a decade away, with the Vision restored to his full range of emotions, and with romance possibly back in the air, the future looks promising. Although she has made only one solo outing (in a four-issue 1994 miniseries), as one of the Avengers' longest-serving members, the Scarlet Witch will almost certainly feature in Marvel's plans for years to come. —*DAR*

The Secret Identity

You can't have wishes without drab realities, and that's where superheroes' secret identities come in. These characters were, after all, created by artists and writers who felt vulnerable in every situation but the fantasies they fashioned. In his Pulitzer Prize–winning novel about the origins of the American comic book, *The Amazing Adventures of Kavalier & Clay* (2000), Michael Chabon is not the first to note the alchemy of promise and desperation that led two Depression-era Jewish youths to create Superman, characterizing the superhero genre's purpose as being "to express the lust for power and the gaudy sartorial taste of a race of powerless people with no leave to dress themselves." The Supermen of the new medium were what its creators and readers aspired to; the Clark Kents were what they identified with, and thus the secret identity was born.

This concept was actually one of comics' deft carryovers from earlier adventure literature; everyone from Zorro to the Shadow had fought injustice under cover of idle rich daytime identities. One of the Superman character's many innovations was to make the hero's cover identity a common man, or at least one with common flaws. This was a populist development that fit the New Deal era, even though wealthy paragons like President Roosevelt himself would persist in the person of heroes like Batman, a masked avenger by night and a suave millionaire by day.

In contrast, Superman's alter ego Clark Kent was shy and awkward, a supposed coward and weakling. The legendary cartoonist and commentator Jules Feiffer, in his classic work *The Great Comic Book Heroes* (1965), explained the Clark Kent persona as a satire of human foibles, a kind of noncostumed drag with which Superman has a private laugh at the ordinary humans he serves. In more recent treatments of the Superman mythos like Marvel Comics' *Supreme Power* series (2003–present), the omnipotent character Hyperion, a government-raised alien superbeing recognized by all, longs to establish a secret identity just so he can know what it's like to be ordinary. One thing that is certain is that superheroes' secret identities have always provided a buffer between the everyday reader and the superpowered exploits that reader is asked to believe.

Of course, most superheroes don't have to pretend they're ordinary Joes and Janes; it's typical for a superhero to be born after some strange magical phenomenon or scientific accident thrusts great power onto some unsuspecting everyman or -woman (the lightning bolt that hits scientist Barry Allen's chemicals, turning him into the Flash, or the nuclear explosion that transforms Bruce Banner into the Hulk being two familiar examples). Some of the grimmer heroes transform *themselves* into crime fighters after the intervention not of a miracle but a tragedy, like the murder of his parents that makes Bruce Wayne become Batman. And as comics have gotten more realistic, their heroes' feet-of-clay alter egos have become progressively flawed; Clark Kent's occupation as a *Daily Planet* reporter put him in a position to learn of crimes and disasters as they happen and then save the day, while Spider-Man's true identity, Peter Parker, takes a job as a crime photographer so he can make ends meet by selling photos of himself to the *Daily Bugle*.

Notwithstanding these touches of realism, almost from the start comics have prominently featured characters of such an alien nature or mythic stature that they dispense with secret identities altogether. Back when it was called Timely Comics, Marvel's very first heroes (and hits) were Namor, the Sub-Mariner, a prince from the sunken kingdom of Atlantis who went by his own unusual name, and the Human Torch, a combustible android created only as a sideshow curiosity.

Timely's characters were renowned for running much more to the weirder end of the superhero spectrum than those of Superman's home, DC (originally known as National), and in the early 1960s resurgence of superheroes, Marvel would lead the way in introducing characters who are former regular guys and gals, but make their identities known to the world. As Fantastic Four co-creator Stan Lee remarked in his 1974 book *Origins of Marvel Comics,* "I was utterly determined to have a superhero series without any secret identities. I knew for a fact that if I myself possessed a super power I'd never keep it a secret. I'm too much of a show-off. Why should our fictional friends be any different?"

This concept for Marvel's flagship series would be extended to other heroes, some of whom even go by their civilian names like Luke Cage, Hero for Hire (only later changed to "Power Man," but switched back to the hero's given name in current comics). However, Lee's other idea for modernizing the superhero—that the Fantastic Four would not wear costumes—lasted all of one issue, and the secret identity itself has remained alive and well for many heroes.

It is often a kind of currency carefully guarded by the superbeings. Everyone is familiar with Lois Lane's repeated attempts to "out" Clark as Superman (though in modern comics he has confided in and married Lane), and anyone who saw the feature film of Marvel's *Daredevil* (2003) knows the story (adapted from comics written by Frank Miller in the early 1980s) of muckraking reporter Ben Urich discovering the hero's secret and then self-sacrificingly keeping it for the good of those Daredevil protects. In 2000s Daredevil comics there has been an extended storyline revisiting this concept, as a tabloid reveals the hero's identity and his lawyer alter ego fights to repudiate it in court. Marvel's Captain America has also unmasked himself on international television, so that a terrorist opponent could focus his fight on Steve Rogers rather than all Americans.

It may be far-fetched when compared to everyday life, but as both historical and modern examples show, the secret identity is a device that exposes dramatic shades of psychology in the superhero genre, and is unlikely to be removed anytime soon. —*AMC and GM*

The Sentry

The Sentry is a character central to the Marvel Comics universe, though almost nobody's ever heard of him—and that's the point. In 2000, comics fans were used to the scarcity of new characters being added to the bankable Marvel mythos, so it came as no surprise that the "newest" character to be introduced that year might actually be the oldest. Starring in a self-titled miniseries from 2000–2001, the Sentry was said to be a rejected character found in some old Marvel files, historic for being a concept by Marvel founder Stan Lee and artist Artie Rosen that predated Lee and artist Jack Kirby's creation of *Fantastic Four* in 1961. The latter event went on to be considered the landmark that inaugurated an era of more hip and literary superhero comics, while the Sentry languished on the discard pile as Marvel's Pete Best.

Reimagined for the "Marvel Knights" line of edgy books about the company's more offbeat characters, the Sentry, originally a kind of Marvel counterpart to Superman, was portrayed as a demigod too powerful for his own good. The character first appears as what seems to be an alcoholic delusion suffered by suburbanite Bob Reynolds, but little by little Reynolds realizes that he was the omnipotent Sentry before being consigned to amnesia for mysterious reasons. Readers gradually learn that the Sentry's addiction to the very serum that gave him his superpowers released a malign, apocalyptic opposite, the Void, from his own subconscious, considered a standard archenemy by an unknowing public—and the denial-ridden hero.

The only solution is for the Sentry himself to cease to be, which is impossible physically but achieved by wiping his and all the world's memory of his career. In the present day, the Void has returned with Reynolds' memories, and the Sentry "defeats" him once more—by finally becoming at peace with his existence as an ordinary, imperfect human. With a subtle, sensitive script by Paul Jenkins and moody, atmospheric art by Jae Lee, the series was a poignant comment on the loss of heroic illusions and the poisoning tendencies of power. And, for longtime Marvel fans, it was a fascinating trip down the road not taken.

The only trouble was, what might have been never could have to begin with—the Sentry's 1960s creation was a hoax planted in the fan press, "Artie Rosen" a fictional character himself. Lee fully participated in the gag, which satirized his own famously faulty memory about what was created when. Marvel's "lost" character was really one of its few (and best) new ones after all, and the company had managed the kind of performance-art put-on unheard of in the pulpy realm of comics. It added an extra dimension to the series' own theme of mass amnesia, replacing the usual side-merchandising of characters with a kind of "conceptual tie-in." This was only fitting for a series that marked one of the few cases of a comics company tinkering with its history to make an artistic statement rather than just rewarm a brand. As one of only two "superhero novels" (along with Marvel's *Earth X*) to come close to the standards of Alan Moore's *Watchmen, The Sentry* was guarded well. —*AMC*

The Shadow

"Who knows what evil lurks in the hearts of men? The Shadow knows!" A generation of pulp readers and radio fans grew up knowing by heart that chilling oath, recited by the mysterious scourge of the underworld, the Shadow.

The Shadow's origins lie in radio, where in 1930 pulp publishers Street & Smith were sponsoring a show to promote their *Detective Story* magazine. The weekly program, *Detective Story Magazine Hour,* was a mystery show narrated by a menacing-

The Shadow #12 © 1975 DC Comics.
COVER ART BY MICHAEL KALUTA.

sounding announcer known only as the Shadow. When Street & Smith realized that this "Shadow" character was creating a lot of interest, they rushed to bring out a pulp magazine by that name before anyone else thought of the idea. To that end, they grabbed a painting that was lying around—the only one they could find showing someone's shadow—to use as a cover, and recruited a young journalist and magician called Walter Gibson. Gibson's brief was to write 60,000 words a month (soon to rise to twice a month) about this Shadow character and to make it a success. Gibson duly obliged.

The first issue of *The Shadow* hit the newsstands in 1931 and introduced an eerie figure swathed in a large, black cloak and hat, with a scarf covering most of his face—a genuine man of mystery who was sworn to punish evildoers of each and every persuasion. It also introduced the first of his many assistants, Harry Vincent, who was about to commit suicide by jumping off a bridge until the Shadow prevented him from doing so. In time, the Shadow collected a band of assistants, including cabbie/chauffeur Moe Shrevnitz, reporter Clyde, switchboard operator Burbank, and African strongman Jericho, among others. The Shadow himself had many identities, including police station janitor Fritz, the aged Phineas Twabley, Henry Arnaud, and George Clarendon, but it was millionaire playboy Lamont Cranston to whom he most often returned. In fact, these were all fictitious identities (except for Cranston, who was a real millionaire whom the Shadow persuaded to leave the country in the magazine's second issue, so that he could assume Cranston's identity), as the Shadow was in story reality Kent Allard, a noted explorer and aviator.

The Shadow stories gradually became faster and harsher as the decade progressed, with Gibson adding layers of colorful background to the feature. (The *Detective Story Magazine Hour* radio show was canceled in 1935.) While it is true that the Shadow is mostly identified as a masked mystery man of the pulps, his stories—especially toward the end of the 1930s and into the 1940s—contained many super-hero elements and conventions. In print, the Shadow operated out of Cranston's fantastic mansion, which came complete with radio tower and a hangar for his autogyro (a super-helicopter) and limousine. Typically, Burbank would discover some wrongdoing and wire the Shadow and his gang, who would then race into action. The Shadow became increasingly cavalier toward his foes, effectively acting as judge, jury, and executioner, meting out justice with his two blazing .45s while laughing maniacally the whole time. Outside of his various automobiles and aircraft, his only gadgets were suction cups that slipped onto his hands and feet, allowing him to scale walls and tall buildings.

Motivated by a desire to see evil of all manner dismantled, the Shadow quickly amassed a colorful rogues' gallery of foes, including Grayfist, the Robot Master, the Wasp, Murder Master, the Creeper, Voodoo Master, and the Green Terror, as well as such sinister organizations as the Green Hoods and the Silent Seven. While these bizarre antagonists rarely lasted beyond a single story's end, one villain—the self-styled Ruler of Tibet, Shiwan Khan—kept coming back enough times to be considered the Shadow's major nemesis.

The pulp's success sparked a mini merchandising industry that produced pins, costumes, books, games, disguise kits, and much more. Just as the Shadow was inspired by radio, he fittingly returned there for his own show, which thrived until 1954 and starred, among others, Bill Johnstone, Bret Morrison and—most memorably—Orson Welles. On the radio, the Shadow's alter ego was Lamont Cranston, who had acquired all manner of powers, including mind-reading, hypnotism, and even invisibility, through years of study in Tibet. He rarely used the pulp's band of comrades but did acquire a pretty young assistant (and potential love interest), Margo Lane. On the radio, she was voiced by veteran actress Agnes Moorehead.

Lane made it into the pulps by the early 1940s, but the title was in decline by that point, young fans having switched to the more wholesome, patriotic heroes of the comic books. Comics readers were introduced to the Shadow in early 1940, when the first issue of *Shadow Comics* (also published by Street & Smith) hit the newsstands. Later that year, a moody Shadow newspaper strip, put out by the Ledger Syndicate, began a two-year run (from June 1940 to June 1942). It was written by Gibson and well drawn by Vernon Greene. Gibson also wrote the comic book for six years (with art by the Jack Binder studio, among others), adapting a lot of his pulp stories, interspersed with reprints of the newspaper strip. These comic strips were very true to the spirit of the pulps, featuring the supporting cast and even Shiwan Khan. Ironically, the comic's artistic high point came after Gibson had left, with a long run by artist Bob Powell from 1946 to its cancellation in 1949. The Powell years featured fanciful fare such as flying saucers and the Shadow Junior, but they were nevertheless masterpieces of dramatic, atmospheric storytelling.

Street & Smith were hit hard by the postwar move away from the superhero genre—that was precisely what their pulp and comics empires were built on. In 1949, both the comic and the pulp were canceled, the pulp appropriately ending with three issues written by a returning Walter Gibson, with covers by longtime pulp artist George Rozen. The radio show lived on past the death of the pulps until 1954; since then its syndicated reruns have periodically resurfaced in radio shows across the country (as well as various lines of nostalgic audiocassettes). At its height, the Shadow phenomenon inspired a number of films and serials, launched by a pair of Grand National movies starring Rod La Rocque: *The Shadow Strikes* in 1937 and *International Crime* a year later. In 1940, Columbia Pictures released a fifteen-chapter serial simply called *The Shadow,* starring Victor Jory, while Monogram Pictures released three Shadow movies in 1946, all starring Kane Richmond. The 1950s were a poor decade for the character but, out of nowhere, in 1958 Republic produced a Shadow movie called *The Invisible Avenger,* starring Richard Der.

In 1963, in the wake of the James Bond phenomenon, publisher Louis Silberkleit picked up the Shadow license and commissioned Walter Gibson to write a spy-themed Shadow novel for his Belmont Books line. The paperback was not a success, but Silberkleit decided to make the most of his investment by moving the franchise over to his rather more successful comics division, Archie Comics. The first couple of Archie *Shadow* comics in 1964 were fairly pedestrian retreads of the pulp stories, but with his third issue the character was inexplicably transformed into a superhero. This Shadow wore a green-and-blue costume with a mask and cape, complete with boot-jets and sonic whistle. In his alter ego of Lamont Cranston, he was a bespectacled businessman, while Lane became his unsus-

pecting secretary. The strips, written by Superman co-creator Jerry Siegel and drawn by Paul Reinman, have become famed for their poor craftsmanship; there was little attempt at character development, plot, or narrative. The superhero Shadow amassed a rogues' gallery of Grade Z no-hopers, such as Dr. Demon, Elasto, Attila the Hunter, Brute, and Radioactive Rogue, as well as the now inevitable Shiwan Khan. The comic was canceled after only eight issues.

While Silberkleit's 1960s reworkings were unsuccessful, a renewed interest in pulps during the 1970s brought forth a whole slew of high-quality revivals. A number of paperback houses successfully reissued old Gibson Shadow stories, including Pyramid, which commissioned comics star Jim Steranko to paint a series of striking new covers. DC Comics contacted Steranko to helm a new Shadow title for them, but the honors eventually went to writer Denny O'Neil and talented young artist Mike Kaluta. DC's series went through three artists (with Frank Robbins and E. R. Cruz also contributing) in only twelve issues, and it was not the commercial success that the company had hoped for. Nonetheless, the comics were an outstanding example of the medium at its finest. Whereas that 1970s series was faithful to its pulp origins, a 1986 reinvention by Howard Chaykin was anything but. Chaykin's miniseries was set in contemporary New York and, in addition to the old cast, starred Harry Vincent's daughter Mavis as a critical sparring partner for the increasingly bloodthirsty Shadow—and his two Tibetan sons! Longtime fans were outraged at the strip's mix of sex and violence, yet it was successful enough to inspire a regular series in 1987 (running for nineteen issues) which, if anything, was even more bizarre.

A third DC series of the 1980s, *The Shadow Strikes,* was once more set in the 1930s, as were five mid-1990s outings from Dark Horse Comics, which arrived in the wake of 1994's Universal *Shadow* movie—the most lavish to date. The film, directed by Russell Mulcahy and starring Alec Baldwin, looked fabulous and had all the elements of the pulp's glory years. However, it had none of the original's heart or intelligence, and suffered from a poor script. Nevertheless, the Dark Horse titles once more teamed the Shadow with his definitive comic artist, Mike Kaluta. If little has been seen of the character since the last of these strips in 1995, his influence remains immense. The notion of the creature of the night, operating from his millionaire's mansion, striking terror in the hearts of wrongdoers, has held enormous sway over generations of comics heroes, from Batman and the Black Terror to Moon Knight and beyond. Fittingly, Batman and the Shadow have teamed up twice (in *Batman* #253 and #259) during DC's first, mid-1970s run with the pulp hero, and they made a fine pairing. —*DAR*

ShadowHawk

At first, he appeared to be a particularly brutal vigilante, moving through the shadows of the New York City night. Wearing a silver helmet, clawed gloves, and a dark armored costume, and with a propensity to break the backs of those who had murdered others, everyone wondered, "Who is ShadowHawk?" Not even the readers of the *ShadowHawk* comic knew the answer to that question at first, as writer/artist Jim Valentino had created the series with a mystery at its core. Coming off successful runs on Marvel's *Guardians of the Galaxy, What If?,* and other series—and with the legendary superhero spoof *normalman* (1984–1985) behind him—Valentino joined six other popular creators to form Image Comics in 1992.

The debut book to appear from Valentino at Image was *ShadowHawk* #1 (August 1992), the first of a four-issue miniseries. The initial storyline set up the mystery of who the character was, providing lots of supporting-cast suspects for readers to choose from. In *ShadowHawk* vol. 2 #1–#3 (May–July 1993), the secret was revealed. ShadowHawk was really Paul Johnstone, an African-

American man who had been infected with the HIV virus. Johnstone used the suit to avenge those who had been killed unjustly. Villains that ShadowHawk fought included a racist named Hawkshadow, the hedonist group Regulators, an acidic alien named the Liquifier, and a female kingpin of crime known as Vendetta.

Although AIDS had been seen in comics before—*Megaton* #4 (April 1986) contains the comics world's first reference to the disease—ShadowHawk was the first superhero to suffer from the disease. Valentino chose not to sensationalize the subject, and actively tried to dispel stereotypes and misconceptions about AIDS while telling his stories. Johnstone succumbed to the illness in *ShadowHawk* Vol. 3 #18 (May 1995), the final issue of that series.

The New ShadowHawk #1 debuted in June 1995, written by Kurt Busiek. In it, the "ShadowHawk energy" was dispersed between three people and a robot. Combined with a tale told by superstar writer Alan Moore in *ShadowHawks of Legend* (November 1995), Busiek's stories noted that there had always been ShadowHawks throughout time, in different lands and eras. The energy was actually the essence of an ancient Egyptian shaman who worshipped Horus (an extraterrestrial from Sirius). When the shaman was murdered, his spirit became ShadowHawk and sought revenge for those murdered unjustly. The ShadowHawk essence lived within the silver helmet that Johnstone had worn.

In a series of stories that ran through various titles from Extreme Studios (an Image sub-imprint run by Rob Liefeld), seventeen-year-old Eddie Collins became the latest ShadowHawk. Able to channel power from the gods, and sharing the memories of all the previous ShadowHawks, Collins is also aided by the morphing suit; it enhances his strength and agility, gives him infrared vision, and allows him to shoot grappling hooks from his gauntlets.

Although *ShadowHawk* was never a top seller for Image, the character continues to appear semi-regularly, often as a guest star. ShadowHawk has appeared on numerous licensed products, including two action figures, card sets, posters, T-shirts, statues, hats, and even a full-cast audio drama. —*AM*

The She-Hulk

Conceived during the run of the highly successful *Incredible Hulk* CBS television series (1978–1982), the She-Hulk sprang from the brow of Stan Lee (the co-creator of the original Hulk, the Fantastic Four, Spider-Man, the X-Men, and most of Marvel's seminal early 1960s heroes) and artist John Buscema (who was associated closely with the first *Silver Surfer* series and *Conan the Barbarian*). Created in 1979 principally to prevent competitors from trademarking their own female version of the Hulk—and in the hopes of spawning a television series that never came to fruition—the She-Hulk was Lee's last major creation for Marvel before he relinquished his editorial duties in favor of developing the company's many properties in Hollywood.

The Savage She-Hulk, a monthly series that began its twenty-five-issue run in early 1980, introduced female lawyer Jennifer Walters, a cousin of Robert Bruce Banner (the Hulk's alter-ego). As children, Walters and Banner (who is five years her senior) are very close, though they choose very different life paths later on; while the bookish Banner pursues a career in high-energy physics that culminates in his invention of the gamma bomb that transforms him into the Hulk, the mousy Walters enters UCLA's law school and ultimately becomes a criminal defense attorney. Years later, Banner visits his cousin, to whom he confides the torments he suffers as a consequence of being the Hulk. During this period, Walters is defending a client named Lou Monkton, who has been framed for murder by a mobster named Nicholas Trask. After one of Trask's hit men shoots and wounds Walters, Banner saves her life by giving her an emergency transfusion of his own (gamma-irradiated) blood. Walters soon finds herself transformed into a 650-pound, 6' 7" tower of exquisitely-muscled emerald outrage.

Although the She-Hulk initially possesses a real streak of savagery (hence the title of her comic), she quickly becomes quite different from the character that inspired her. Unlike Banner, who becomes a ravening beast when his suppressed anger transforms him into the Hulk, Walters retains her intellect as She-Hulk and can change back to her ordinary human guise at will. She also contrasts sharply with Banner in that she has little desire to return to her human form; the same gamma rays that release Banner's repressed rage also allow Walters to free herself of the prim "lady lawyer" personality that had shackled her throughout her professional life. While Banner is perpetually tortured by his transformations into the Hulk, Walters exults in her newfound power, enjoying her crime-fighting adventures and imbuing them with verve and passion. If the Hulk is a study in emotional repression and mania, his distaff counterpart embodies instead the liberated, upwardly-mobile professional woman of the early 1980s, attractive, quick of wit, and unintimidated by anyone's glass ceiling. When exposure to radiation traps her permanently in her She-Hulk form (during the 1984–1985 twelve-issue *Marvel Superheroes Secret Wars* miniseries), Walters hardly gives her buttoned-down human persona a second thought.

Like many a refugee from a canceled Marvel series (her first one ran twenty-five issues), the She-Hulk becomes a member of a supergroup, joining the Avengers (*Avengers* vol. 1 #221, July 1982) before temporarily replacing the Fantastic Four's Thing during his extended off-planet leave of absence (*Fantastic Four* vol. 1 #265, April 1984). Even after the Thing's return more than two years later, the She-Hulk (or "Shulkie" as her friends often call her) remains a close friend of (and sometime babysitter for) the FF family.

In 1989, the She-Hulk once again became a monthly series headliner with the debut of *The Sensational She-Hulk*. Written and illustrated by John

Byrne (famed for his work on *The Uncanny X-Men* and *The Man of Steel,* the 1986 "reboot" of DC Comics' Superman), this series made much better use of the character's obvious comedic potential than did the previous one. Not only does Jennifer Walters still enjoy being a superpowered jade giantess, she is also keenly aware of the absurdities inherent in the superheroic life. Moreover, she is wryly cognizant of the fact that she is a comic-book character, often driving the point home by grabbing panel borders, chasing bad guys by tunneling through the pages of her comics, and speaking directly to the audience (and sometimes even to writer/artist Byrne) in a manner reminiscent of television's *It's Garry Shandling's Show* (1986–1990) or *The Burns and Allen Show* (1950–1958). She-Hulk isn't the only "self-aware" character in the series; Marvel's golden-age Blonde Phantom joins the supporting cast (issue #4) in a deliberate effort to take advantage of the slow aging process that all comic-book heroes seem to enjoy—but only as long as they are featured in a monthly comics magazine.

Following a squabble with Marvel, Byrne left the series with issue #50 in April 1993 (having left and returned after another squabble from issue #10 to issue #31, an interim in which, among other writers and artists, Howard the Duck creator Steve Gerber stepped in for a well-regarded run), and the book limped to its finish exactly ten issues later. Since that time the She-Hulk has been ubiquitous on Marvel's "guest-star circuit," racking up appearances from the mid-1990s forward in such titles as *Nova* (vol. 2), *Fantastic Force, Thunderstrike, The Avengers* (vols. 1 and 3), *The Fantastic Four* (vols. 1 and 3), *Iron Man* (vol. 2), *Heroes for Hire,* and *Captain America* (vols. 1–3). She finally regained a fixed address with a new ongoing series in 2004, and remains one of Marvel's most consistently merchandised characters, her image appearing on everything from drinking cups to apparel. Created as an exercise in trademark building, the She-Hulk even now continues to fulfill her primary function—generating green—while seeming to laugh all the way to the bank. —*MAM*

Shi

Despite the venerable tradition of depictions of overendowed women in superhero comics, powerful female characters have steadily risen to prominence over the past two decades or more. Though some of these are arguably icons of funnybook feminism, crime-fighting women are still the objects of adolescent male fantasies. One of the more popular superheroines to arise in recent years from this schizoid comics tradition is Shi. Taking her superhero name from the Japanese word for "death" rather than from her gender, Shi is a heroine who clearly owes as much to monomaniacal crusaders like Batman and to films such as *The Seven Samurai* as she does to the time-honored comic-book tradition of "Good Girl art" cheesecake (though her swords-and-scanty-clothing visuals place her firmly in the latter camp). Regardless of where one stands in this debate, it is beyond doubt that Shi has far outlasted the dire predictions of detractors who pronounced her a fad when she first appeared in 1994.

The creation of writer, artist, filmmaker, and former paratrooper William Tucci, Shi premiered in *Shi: The Way of the Warrior* #1 (1994), a series from Crusade Comics that ran for twelve issues (1994–1997) and generated a decade-long dynasty of sequels and merchandise. Shi was born Ana Ishikawa, the daughter of Shiro Ishikawa, a member of a clandestine, millennium-old Japanese samurai order engaged in a centuries-long shadow war against a rival order. Shiro had abandoned his secret society in order to marry Ana's mother, Catherine, a Catholic missionary; this prompted Shiro's order to dispatch an assassin named Masahiro Arashi to kill him. Though Shiro nearly succeeds in besting his attacker, he is distracted at a critical moment by his young daughter Ana; because of this unfortunate happenstance, Ana's father, mother, and brother Toro are slain before her eyes.

Despite her mother's pacifist teachings, the teenage Ana undertakes training in *sohei* (the

Japanese martial disciplines of the samurai and the assassin, including the mastery of swords) under the tutelage of her grandfather, guardian, and first *sensei*, Yoshitora Ishikawa. Spending her nights in intensive martial training, Ana's days are filled with classes at the Inagaki School of Art and Design in Kyoto, which afford her a convenient "secret identity" of sorts. Finally deeming herself ready to avenge her murdered family, Ana takes up her samurai sword, girds herself in a scarlet battle suit, and paints her face white to emulate a revered ancestor, Yuri Ishikawa, who had adopted the name *Tora No Shi* (the Tiger of Death) during feudal Japan's 1637 revolution.

Ferocious and tenacious, Ana tracks down Masahiro Arashi, her family's killer, earning the sobriquet "Shi" ("Death") along the way. Though her original purpose had been to assassinate the assassin, her conscience restrains her, and she settles for having the Arashi imprisoned. Ana subsequently forswears indiscriminate violence and vengeance, devoting herself instead to running New York's Oike Gallery. Though opposed to wanton killing, Ana continues to adopt the Shi persona in her new home of New York City, donning the costume and makeup and drawing her sword whenever innocent people are in need of rescue or protection.

Following Shi's debut series—and with the assistance of various scripters—Tucci continued the saga of his sword-wielding super-samurai in a raft of Crusade miniseries and one-shots, including: *Shi: Senryaku* (1995); *Shi: Kaidan,* a one-shot volume of Japanese ghost stories (1996); *Shi vs. Tomoe* (1996); *Shi: The Blood of Saints* (1996); *Shi: Rekishi* (1997); *Shi: Nightstalkers* (1997); *Shi: The Series* (1997–1998); *Shi: Heaven and Earth* (1997–1998); *Shi: East Wind Rain* (1997–1998); *Shi: Black, White, and Red* (1998); *Shi: Masquerade* (1998); *Shi: Year of the Dragon* (2000); *Manga Shi 2000* (2000), which was rendered in an authentically Japanese "big-eyed character" style; and *Shi: Through the Ashes* (2001), a tribute to the valiant police and firefighters who died in the September

11 terrorist attacks on New York City. Still more *Shi* titles followed as the new millennium continued.

In addition to accumulating a superhero's usual rogues' gallery of villains (which has included the assassin known as Gemini Dawn and the now-deceased telekinetic-telepathic killer called Headrush), Shi has also forged friendships with many superheroes published by other comics companies, such as Grifter from Jim Lee's WildC.A.T.S (originally an Image title, currently published by WildStorm). In a pair of one-shot comics, *Cyblade/Shi: The Battle for Independents* #1 (1995) and *Shi/Cyblade: The Battle for Independents* #1 (1995), she formed an alliance with Cyberforce's prickly psionic heroine Cyblade. Shi later fought alongside Marvel Comics' Daredevil in *Shi/Daredevil: Honor Thy Mother* (1997). Tucci's heroine even shared the stage with Harris Comics' Vampirella in *Shi/Vampirella* (1997) and gained the respect of Marvel's Wolverine in *Wolverine/Shi: Dark Night of Judgment* (2000).

Tucci produced a new black-and-white, eight-issue miniseries titled *Shi: Poisoned Paradise* (2002) for Avatar Press, a small-press publisher. Disappointed by the series' lackluster sales, Tucci decided to avail himself of the marketing and publicity resources of a larger publisher and took Shi to Dark Horse Comics. "Well, if you can't beat 'em, join 'em!" Tucci has quipped on an Internet bulletin board, referring to the move to the more high-profile company. Tucci's newest publisher has already successfully released a collectible Shi statuette for the direct-sales market, and in the spring of 2004 released a new miniseries: *Shi: Ju-Nen,* the latest tale of the female samurai who stands astride both East and West and embodies both vengeance and conscience.

Since Shi's inception, Tucci's Crusade Fine Arts Ltd. has published Shi stories in four languages, with more than 4 million copies now in print. Shi's publishing and merchandising ventures have generated more than $25 million in sales over the past decade. In 2002, Shi entered the world of prose in *Shi: The Illustrated Warrior,* writer Craig Shaw Gardner's novelization of the superheroine's origin story, a volume adorned with Tucci's elegant and kinetic illustrations. Hollywood may loom in Shi's future as well; in the summer of 2003, Mandolin Entertainment purchased a film option on the character. Far from being a mere fad, Shi's prospects seem as bright as her flashing blades. —*MAM*

Sidekicks and Protégés

After Superman's debut in DC Comics' *Action Comics* #1 (June 1938) set off an explosion of comic-book allies and imitators, cartoonist Bob Kane realized that these colorful caped crusaders were all *adult men*—including his own creation, the Batman—while *young boys* were comics' target audience. Just one month shy of Batman's first anniversary, Kane introduced "the sensational character find of 1940" in *Detective Comics* #38, April 1940: Robin, the Boy Wonder! Robin was circus aerialist Dick Grayson, who witnessed the murder of his parents. Sympathetic Batman took the youth under his wing and trained him to be his crime-fighting partner. "I visualized that every kid would like to be a Robin … a laughing daredevil," Kane said. "It appealed to the imagination of every kid in the world." Not the entire world, perhaps, but certainly American boys during the Great Depression. *Detective* doubled its circulation, thanks to Robin—and the superhero sidekick, comics' ultimate vehicle for wish fulfillment, was born.

Robin's uniqueness was short-lived. Other creators and publishers took notice of the sales punch packed by comics' first sidekick, and before long boy wonders abounded. Six months after the premiere of Robin, Marvel Comics unveiled Toro, the partner of the Human Torch. Toro was, like Grayson, a circus performer—a *fire-eater*—who could, without explanation, combust into living flame. In its fervor to copy Robin, Marvel sacrificed originality for timeliness—not surprising, as the company's original name was Timely Comics.

Appearing in the same month as Toro was Roy, the Super-Boy, the protégé of Archie Comics' the Wizard. *The Official Overstreet Comic Book Price Guide* 32nd edition speculates that Roy, not Toro, may be comics' second sidekick—Roy's first appearance was *Top-Notch Comics* #8, September 1940, while Toro debuted in *The Human Torch* #2, cover dated Fall 1940—but falls short of making this a definitive statement since both comics appeared at roughly the same time. Ace Magazines' Magno, the Magnetic Man was joined by the magnetic boy named Davey in November 1940, and Archie Comics' the Shield teamed with Dusty, the Boy Detective in January 1941.

When Marvel's Captain America was first seen in March 1941, he was not alone. In *Captain America* #1, writer Joe Simon and artist Jack Kirby unite "Cap" with Bucky Barnes, the mascot of the regiment with which Steve Rogers, Captain America's alter ego, is stationed. The lad stumbles across Rogers changing into his patriotic garb, muttering, "Gosh … gee whiz … golly!! I … I never thought!" After threatening to "tan his hide," Cap gives Bucky Barnes a mask and ushers him onto the front lines as … Bucky!

Curiously, this first wave of post-Robin superhero sidekicks—Roy, Davey, Dusty, Bucky, even Toro—used their first names while in action. One might speculate that the creators of these characters wanted to strengthen the appeal of their sidekicks by assigning them names familiar to their readers. While it's unlikely there were many boys named "Toro" reading comics during the early 1940s, *Captain America* co-creator Simon claimed that Bucky was named after an old school chum. These earliest sidekicks share another characteristic: They were orphans, and needed the guiding hand of a caring mentor. In each of these relationships, the senior member was always in charge, with the junior member learning the ropes of superheroics from the seasoned pro.

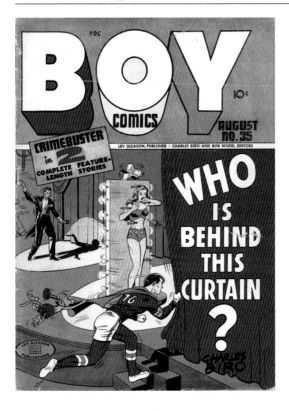

Boy Comics #35 © 1947 Lev Gleason.
COVER ART BY CHARLES BIRO.

No publisher was more enamored of junior heroes than DC, the company that started the trend: Green Arrow, like Captain America, debuted with a junior partner, the young archer Speedy (whose real name was *not* Speedy, incidentally, but Roy Harper). DC overhauled its once-mysterious Sandman, hatboxing his Shadow-inspired fedora and cloak and dressing him in extravagant yellow-and-purple tights, with his protégé Sandy by his side; similarly, the Crimson Avenger—a Green Hornet–like midnight man who preceded Batman's *Detective Comics* #27 debut by five issues—was redesigned in 1941 and appointed a protégé named Wing.

Fawcett Comics followed suit with Mr. Scarlet and Pinky, and the publisher's Captain Marvel was accompanied by *two* sidekicks: Captain Marvel Jr.

and Mary Marvel. Captain Marvel wasn't the only Golden Age (1938–1954) hero who socialized with girls: Holyoke's Cat-Man gained the homeless pre-teen Kitten as his companion. Observes historian Mike Benton in his book *Superhero Comics of the Golden Age* (1992), "By the end of the series, the coquettish and fully developed Kitten and her Uncle David (her pet name for Cat-Man's alter ego) could certainly provide rich fodder for small-minded gossips." Society was more innocent during those simpler times, however, and improprieties between adult and junior superheroes, regardless of their genders, were never implied by their creators or considered by their readers. Parents of readers also never seemed bothered by the threat of child endangerment faced by these junior heroes when they blazed into danger with their costumed big brothers.

Nor were they concerned when superkids went solo. Young heroes headlined their own titles or strips, like Golden Lad, Kid Eternity, and Merry, Girl of a Thousand Gimmicks. Some formed teams, like the Young Allies (sidekicks Bucky and Toro with a group of nonpowered boys known as the Sentinels of Liberty), the Boy Commandos, and the Newsboy Legion (the Commandos lacked superpowers, but compensated with an abundance of patriotism and attitude; that goes for the Newsboys too, though their strip tuned the tables by having a grown-up superhero, the Guardian, as both mascot and mentor). And Lev Gleason Publications made no secret of its target audience by releasing *Boy Comics,* starring a teen titan named Crimebuster. Robin the Boy Wonder continued to work with Batman but moonlighted in his own series in *Star-Spangled Comics,* the comic book that also featured the Star-Spangled Kid, the only teenage superhero with an *adult* sidekick working under him: Stripesy. And while DC didn't give its flagship character, Superman, a junior partner during the Golden Age (1938–1954), it did the next best thing by publishing stories starring Super*boy,* "The Adventures of Superman When He Was a Boy."

An interesting variation on the sidekick theme also occurred during the Golden Age: the partnering of adult male superheroes with adult female superheroines. In April 1941 Susan Kent learned that her boyfriend, Jim Barr, was actually Bulletman, and demanded that he make her a superhero, too. Thus Bulletgirl was born. Her confidence and verve made her a valuable ally to Bulletman, despite the fact that her superheroic title did not suggest her maturity. "Even their names told the reader who was the stronger and who was the weaker of the pair," observed historian Trina Robbins in her book, *The Great Women Superheroes* (1996). With Hawkman's Hawkgirl, the Flame's Flame Girl, Lash Lightning's Lightning Girl, and Doll Man's Doll Girl, the woman was banished to a secondary role, often being rebuked by the male for her impetuousness, or for just putting on the costume in the first place. Most of these sidekick superheroines also doubled as damsels in distress, but Hawkgirl enjoyed the ultimate revenge: In the 2000s she has flown the coop, serving as a popular member—*without* Hawkman!—of DC Comics' Justice Society in the *JSA* comic book and of that group's counterpart on the Cartoon Network's *Justice League* animated series.

After World War II, however, when superheroes were no longer required to help bolster the nation's patriotism, kid sidekicks started to disappear, along with their adult cohorts. By the mid-1950s only a handful of superhero comics remained in print. Robin stuck around with Batman, Speedy and Green Arrow remained in backup series in various DC anthologies, and newcomer the Fighting American was joined by Speedboy for a very brief stint on the stands. Jimmy Olsen was elevated from supporting cast status to a pseudo-sidekick role with Superman, getting his own long-running title, *Superman's Pal Jimmy Olsen*. Olsen became Superman's actual sidekick in a number of adventures inside the Bottle City of Kandor when the pair fought Kryptonian crime as the Batman-and-Robin-inspired Nightwing and Flamebird.

In his contemptuous book *Seduction of the Innocent* (1954), real-life psychiatrist Dr. Fredric Wertham charged that the comic-book industry was morally corrupting impressionable young readers with graphic depictions of violence, gore, and sexual impropriety. The original superhero sidekick was also besieged, as the author impeached Batman and Robin's relationship as "a wish dream of two homosexuals living together." Wertham helped fuel the U.S. Senate's attack on the comic-book industry, which as a result homogenized its content under the auspices of the watchdog guild called the Comics Code Authority. Wertham, however, proved an unintentional ally for the kid sidekick in comics: In the mid- to late 1950s more superpowered protégés were introduced, to strengthen the lead heroes' paternal (or maternal) roles. Superman got Supergirl, Aquaman got Aqualad, Batman's new ally Batwoman got Bat-Girl (DC made sure it sidestepped the gay allegations by adding not one but *two* females to Batman's cast), and Wonder Woman got Wonder Girl (and Wonder Tot, to boot!).

The role of the superhero sidekick underwent a transformation throughout the Silver Age of comics (1956–1969). The traditional sidekick was still in action at DC Comics, with Kid Flash joining the Flash as the publisher's newest protégé, but Marvel Comics pushed young heroes into autonomous roles. Marvel's *Fantastic Four* #1 (1961) introduced a new Human Torch, an adolescent named Johnny Storm, clearly characterized as an equal member of the team, not merely an exuberant add-on—the Torch even solo-starred in *Strange Tales*. A free-spirited teen named Rick Jones became the voice of reason to Marvel's rampaging Incredible Hulk, and the publisher's Amazing Spider-Man—its runaway sensation who premiered in *Amazing Fantasy* #15 (1962)—was an introverted high-schooler overburdened with personal problems … just like his readers.

Marvel audaciously charted new territory with its young characters: *X-Men* #1 (1963) introduced a band of mutant teens, genetic flukes that represented the next step in human evolution. Of course, most of Marvel's heroes were adults, but its new breed of independent superteens stood their own alongside the grown-ups instead of following in their footsteps. DC's bravest and boldest move with its sidekicks during the 1960s was to ally them as a team: Robin, Kid Flash, and Aqualad were first united in *The Brave and the Bold* #54 (1964), then picked up Wonder Girl in two more tryout appearances before being awarded their own title with *Teen Titans* #1 (1966). As the 1960s drew to a close, DC had continued to follow Marvel's lead by creating new teen heroes—like argumentative brothers the Hawk and the Dove and the prehistoric hero Anthro—who were stars of their own series, not toiling under the shadow of a big brother.

Changing social and political climes throughout the 1960s and 1970s changed the American teen, and as kids matured, so did superhero sidekicks. By the early 1970s the members of the Teen Titans had graduated out of their mentors' titles, now fully on their own, and Robin had become the *Teen* Wonder, having left Batman's tutelage for college. Spider-Man's alter ego of Peter Parker was also a college student. More "relevant" themes crept into comics, affecting some teen characters: Both Parker's friend Harry Osborn and Green Arrow's ex-sidekick Speedy wrestled with (but overcame) drug addictions, and in the early 1980s, it was disclosed that Speedy had also fathered a child out of wedlock. Grayson hung up his red Robin tunic in 1984, adopting the new guise of Nightwing. Before long, his fellow Titans also discarded their sidekick identities: Wonder Girl became Troia, Aqualad became Tempest, Speedy became Arsenal, and Kid Flash became the Flash. The superhero sidekick had grown up.

Only one sidekick has remained in that traditional role: Robin the Boy Wonder—a *new* Robin, that is. Jason Todd became the Boy Wonder in 1983, in a move largely inspired by DC Comics' desire to merchandize its famous character. This second Robin fared poorly with readers, and in 1989 was killed in the comics as the result of a 1-900 phone-in vote with readers choosing between the character's life or death. DC promptly replaced him that year with Tim Drake, who has endured into the 2000s as Batman's new protégé, also starring

in his own successful comic book (running uninterrupted since its 1993 premiere).

While teen heroes have been and continue to be popular in comics since the 1970s—Nova, Firestorm, Cyborg, Speedball, Impulse, and Spyboy are just a few of the adolescent characters appearing in print—they have been presented either as solo players or members of a larger (usually teen) team. As a changing and demanding world continues to expect youngsters to grow up faster, it is unlikely that the traditional superhero sidekick will ever return to prominence. —*ME*

Silver Age of Superheroes (1956-1969)

It was 1955, and the comic-book industry was imperiled. Postwar circulation figures had plunged, psychologist Fredric Wertham had impeached comics' content in his book *Seduction of the Innocent* (1954), and the U.S. Senate had imposed upon the industry a censorship board called the Comics Code Authority. Superheroes were passé, save the Man of Steel, a media star thanks to *The Adventures of Superman* (1953–1957), a syndicated program appearing on the medium that had robbed comics of much of its audience: television.

To survive, comics diversified away from superheroes into the Western, romance, mystery, teen humor, funny animal, and TV tie-in genres. Science fiction also proved a popular theme. Technological advancements spawned during the atomic age piqued Americans' imaginations, while the red scare fomented rampant paranoia. Science and cold war mistrust melded in November 1955 when DC Comics introduced—with absolutely no fanfare—the first new superhero in roughly ten years: the Man-

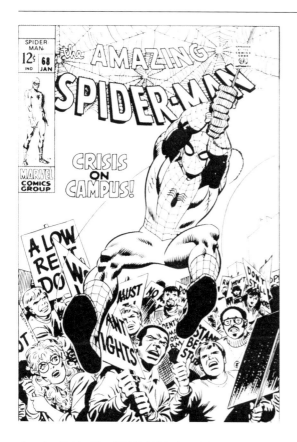

Amazing Spider-Man #68 © 1969 Marvel Comics.
COVER ART BY JOHN ROMITA.

hunter from Mars. First seen as the backup feature to Batman and Robin in *Detective Comics* #115, J'onn J'onzz (pronounced "John Jones"), a green-skinned superman, is teleported to Earth by an American scientist. Unable to return home, J'onzz employs his shape-shifting ability to conceal his true looks from an unwelcoming population and masquerades as a Caucasian human detective named … John Jones. The Manhunter from Mars would eventually be better known as the Martian Manhunter.

THE FASTEST MAN ALIVE

In 1956 DC Comics, struggling to find new concepts that might attract readers, introduced a "try-out" title, *Showcase*. "The first three *Showcases* flopped," editor Julius "Julie" Schwartz recalled in his autobiography, *Man of Two Worlds: My Life in Science Fiction and Comics* (2000), "and we were at an editorial meeting trying to decide what to do in number four when I suggested that we try to revive the Flash." This renewal was given the green light despite the trepidation of other editors still battle-weary from the demise of superheroes several years earlier.

Schwartz steered the project into a fresh direction. Jay Garrick, the Flash of comics' Golden Age (1938–1954), was ignored—for a time, at least—and a new character, police scientist Barry Allen, obtained superspeed in his initial excursion in *Showcase* #4 (September–October 1956). Given a sporty costume by artist Carmine Infantino, the Flash mixed action, style, and imagination, an attractive alternative to DC's other series and to then-current television fare, where special-effects limitations made such superactivity impossible (or laughable when attempted). Brisk sales warranted three more *Showcase* appearances before the "Fastest Man Alive" sped into his own magazine.

At the time, DC, Schwartz, Infantino, and original Flash writer Robert Kanigher merely had in mind the creation of a new product that would generate readers and profit. Their efforts, and the Flash's runaway success, marked a vital moment in comic-book history: the beginning of its eminent Silver Age (1956–1969). Without the success of the Flash, publishers might have given up on superheroes, leading the genre into extinction.

POST-FLASH DC SUPERHEROES

In 1958, Schwartz's colleague Mort Weisinger, editor of DC's Superman franchise, guest-starred the Legion of Super-Heroes—one of the first times the term "superheroes" was used on a comics cover—in the Superboy strip in *Adventure Comics* #247. Cosmic Boy, Saturn Girl, and Lightning Boy (later renamed Lightning Lad) were superpowered teenagers from a thousand years in the future who traveled to the past to recruit the Boy of Steel into their club of heroes. Weisinger added a new super-powered member to Superman's family in May 1959, when *Action Comics* #252 introduced the Man of Steel's cousin Supergirl, a survivor of the planet Krypton.

Schwartz's next volley was the reintroduction of Green Lantern, another DC Golden Age great. As he did with the Flash, Schwartz took the superhero's name and power—in this case, his power *ring,* the source of Green Lantern's almost limitless abili-ties—and premiered a new version of the character in *Showcase* #22 (September–October 1959). Robust reader response to the hero led to the release of *Green Lantern* #1 in 1960.

With the acclaim for the Flash and Green Lantern, Schwartz took an ambitious step in *The Brave and the Bold* #28 (1960) by combining them, along with DC's other major superheroes—Super-man, Batman, Wonder Woman, Aquaman, and the Martian Manhunter—into a team called the Justice League of America, another revamp, this time of the Golden Age's Justice *Society* of America. Continuing Schwartz's winning streak, the "JLA" was a smash, and the editor next overhauled both Hawkman and the Atom in 1961. Also that year, he published the momentous "Flash of Two Worlds" in *The Flash* #123, introducing the concept of a parallel world— "Earth-Two," where the Golden Age Flash still oper-ated, while the current version of the Flash existed on "Earth-One." Over the next few years, Schwartz offered exposure to more Earth-Two heroes, along-side their Earth-One counterparts: meetings between the Silver Age and Golden Age Flashes, Green Lanterns, and Atoms became common, and the Justice Society began annual crossovers in the pages of *Justice League of America.* Beyond those appearances, Starman and Black Canary teamed up in *The Brave and the Bold* #61 and #62 (1965), Dr. Fate and Hourman joined forces in *Showcase* #55 and #56 (1965), and the Spectre was revived

in his own solo series beginning with *Showcase* #60 (1966).

BATMAN'S "NEW LOOK"

Batman and *Detective Comics* teetered on the brink of cancellation in 1964, stagnant from years of mediocre stories and art. DC's editorial director Irwin Donenfeld assigned the books to Schwartz with the mandate of "saving" them. Schwartz realized that Bat-man had, in his own words, "strayed away from the original roots of the character." The editor returned the element of mystery to Batman's tales, incorporating clues into the stories that invited the reader to solve the whodunit along with the superhero. Schwartz's most commercial alteration was in Batman's appear-ance: The Caped Crusader's costume was stream-lined, and a yellow oval was added around his chest insignia, simulating the look of the sky-illuminating Bat-signal. The Batmobile was souped up into a stylish hot rod, and Robin the Boy Wonder became hipper in the process. This facelift, called "The New Look" Batman by fans and historians, sold solidly and rescued the "Dynamic Duo" from the chopping block.

Although these new Silver Age superheroes generated stronger sales than DC had been earning on many of its titles, circulations were still consider-ably lower than during the medium's heyday. "By 1962 less than a dozen publishers accounted for a total annual industry output of 350 million comic books, a drop of over 50 percent from the previous decade," reported author Bradford W. Wright in his book, *Comic Book Nation* (2001).

THE MARVEL AGE

Julius Schwartz indirectly contributed to a yet another substantial event: the advent of the Marvel Age of comics. *Justice League* was commanding such strong sales in 1961 that it afforded bragging rights to DC publisher Jack Liebowitz during a golf game with his contemporary, Martin Goodman. Goodman, the publisher of Marvel Comics—then limping along in the marketplace with a handful of monster and thriller series—ordered his staff editor/writer Stan Lee to create a group of superheroes. Lee had considered resigning from Marvel at the time of Goodman's directive, but was encouraged by his wife to challenge himself to try something new with this assignment. "For once I wanted to write stories that wouldn't insult the intelligence of an older reader, stories with interesting characterization, more realistic dialogue, and plots that hadn't been recycled a thousand times before," explained Lee in his biography, *Excelsior! The Amazing Life of Stan Lee* (2002). Lee, along with artist Jack Kirby, created Marvel's premier superteam, and its flagship title, in *Fantastic Four* #1 (November 1961).

The Fantastic Four's complex characters—smug scientist Reed Richards, a.k.a. the malleable Mr. Fantastic; his sheepish fiancée Sue Storm, the disappearing Invisible Girl; her fiery-tempered teen brother, Johnny, better known as the Human Torch; and Richards' brusque friend, ace pilot Ben Grimm, the grotesque man-monster called the Thing—each had personality quirks that frequently thrust the "FF" into verbal and physical conflict, yet they set their differences aside in times of crisis. They were a family, and the most realistically portrayed comicbook superheroes readers had ever seen. *Fantastic Four* instantly became Marvel's best-seller.

The Fantastic Four may have been inspired by the Justice League of America (JLA), but they shared no other traits. The FF was the JLA through a refractive lens: The Justice Leaguers exemplified camaraderie and teamwork, its members (except for Aquaman) concealed their true identities behind their colorful superguises, and its heroes lived in fictional cities (Metropolis, Gotham City, Central City, and others); on the other hand, the FF bickered incessantly, they saw no reason to conceal their superpowers behind alter egos, and they resided in the "real" world city of New York.

Over the next few years, Lee—with Kirby, Steve Ditko, and other artists—unleashed a plethora of problem-plagued powerhouses, including the gamma-irradiated Incredible Hulk; the mighty Thor, god of thunder; the occult-based Doctor Strange; the sightless superhero Daredevil; and the outcast society of mutants known as the X-Men. Golden Age stalwarts Sub-Mariner and Captain America were rejuvenated and fought against and/or alongside the newer Marvel characters. The breakaway superhero in the burgeoning Marvel universe was the Amazing Spider-Man, who, behind his webbed mask, was actually a self-centered teenage nebbish named Peter Parker. Marvel's offbeat, flawed superheroes were embraced by the 1960s counterculture, particularly on college campuses.

With each new series, the differences between Marvel's and DC's titles became progressively apparent. "DC's comic books were the image of affluent America," noted Wright, while Marvel's plopped its heroes onto the dirty streets of Manhattan—and sometimes its boroughs—where average Joes were often frightened by or angered at these strange beings. DC's villains were usually stereotyped scofflaws with gimmicky weapons, where Marvel's bad guys were cold war spies, grandiloquent warlords, and rotten rabble-rousers with superpowers of their own. There was little, if any, damage on the streets of DC's faux cities during its superhero-versus-supervillain battles, while Marvel's New York withstood the brunt of smashed autos and imploded pavement. DC's heroes usually met as allies when battling a common enemy, but Marvel's heroes generally clashed within moments of an encounter. DC's stories were more traditionally based good-versus-evil yarns, where Marvel sometimes dealt with issues like campus unrest and corrupt politicians. Even the editorial tone between the two publishers varied: DC's letters columns featured articulate, sometimes chiding, and usually faceless responses to readers, while Marvel's—generally in Lee's voice—were amiable and teeming with hyperbole. DC's stories were largely uncredited, but Marvel's creative staff, from the writer down the chain to the colorist, got their due in print, with endearing nicknames attached (Stan "The Man" Lee, Jack "King" Kirby, and "Jazzy" Johnny Romita, to name a few).

SUPERHERO-A-GO-GO

Comic-book history repeated itself during the Silver Age. The success of a new DC superhero—in this case, the Flash—motivated other companies to publish their own costumed crusaders, just as Superman's 1938 introduction had produced super-successors. Similarly, World War II was a catalyst for an immeasurable amount of new superheroes, and the Vietnam War also inspired an outbreak of superheroes—not as patriotic icons, as in the 1940s, but as engines of escapism. Protests against the Vietnam War made it a delicate and rarely seen topic in comics stories.

Superheroes originating, or returning to action, during the Silver Age include Charlton Comics' Captain Atom; Dell Comics' atomic ace Nukla, and its trio of superhero titles based on movie monsters: *Frankenstein* (Boris Karloff-meets-the Man of Steel), *Dracula* (who looked more like Batman than Bela Lugosi), and *Werewolf;* Gold Key Comics' *Magnus Robot Fighter* and *Dr. Solar, Man of the Atom* (revived in the 1990s by Valiant Comics); ACG (American Comics Group)'s Magicman and Nemesis, starring in the anthologies *Forbidden Worlds* and *Adventures into the Unknown;* fly-by-night M.F. Publications' Captain Marvel, an appropriation of a classic appellation, featuring a superhero who split his body into separate parts by yelling, of all things, "Split!" (similarly, M.F. ripped off other Golden Age heroes' names for its villains: Plastic Man and Dr. Fate); Harvey Comics' Spyman (who fought bad guys with his "electro-robot hand"), Jigsaw (a "splitting" hero, like M.F.'s Captain Marvel), icy Jack Q. Frost, and aquatic Pirana, plus reprints of legendary superhero series *The Spirit* and *The Fighting American;* Archie Comics' Mighty Crusaders, the Fly (later Fly-Man), and Jaguar, as well as superhero versions of its teenage characters, *Archie as Pureheart the Powerful* and *Jughead as Captain Hero* (Archie's girlfriend Betty even donned a guise to

become Superteen!); and *MAD* magazine's superhero parody, Don Martin's *Captain Klutz.*

Two small comic-book publishers distinguished themselves with thought-provoking takes on the superhero genre. Tower Comics' lauded T.H.U.N.D.E.R. Agents, which featured artwork by renowned comics artist Wally Wood and starred superheroes like Dynamo, No-Man, Menthor, Raven, and Lightning; and Charlton Comics' "Action Heroes" line, which included Blue Beetle, Captain Atom, Sarge Steel, Nightshade, the Question, Judomaster, and Peter Cannon-Thunderbolt. Dick Giordano, the editor of most of Charlton's Action Heroes series, revealed in his 2003 biography, *Dick Giordano: Changing Comics, One Day at a Time,* "That name was not an accident. I chose that term. Superman never did anything for me. Batman did. I always preferred heroes who could do things that *we* supposedly would be able to do." The nuclear-powered Captain Atom aside—a hero already in print when Giordano came on board but whose powers were weakened by the new editor's dictate—Charlton's heroes used acquired skills, mental disciplines, or weapons in their war against injustice.

"BATMANIA" INSPIRES TV SUPERHEROES

1966 was the year of the superhero. *Batman* (1966–1968), the kitschy sendup starring Adam West in the title role, premiered on ABC in January of that year to instant acclaim. The show satisfied a wide demographic spread—children, mesmerized by its action; teens, especially girls, for the fashions and heartthrob Burt Ward as Robin the Boy Wonder; and adults, in tune with the camp humor and double-entendres that eluded kids' understanding. Universal exploitation of Batman made "Batmania" an inexorable phenomenon.

Superheroes dominated the television airwaves during the mid-1960s: *Captain Nice, Mr. Terrific, Space Ghost, Birdman and the Galaxy Trio, The Lone Ranger, The Green Hornet, The New Adven-*

tures of *Superman,* and *Aquaman* were among the live-action and animated entries. Many of Marvel's characters starred in cartoon programs: Captain America, Iron Man, Hulk, Thor, and Sub-Mariner rotated days on the syndicated *Marvel Super Heroes,* and both *Fantastic Four* and *Spider-Man* appeared on Saturday-morning TV, and in a wealth of toy and product licensing.

MARVEL TAKES THE LEAD

The superhero craze fizzled by 1968, driving some smaller publishers out of business. Even the oldest comics company got a rude awakening, as DC was overtaken by Marvel as the industry leader. Popular artist Carmine Infantino was instated as DC's art director, with the mission of making the line's covers more appealing to the potential consumer. Infantino was soon appointed to editorial director, and elected to take on Marvel to regain his company's former stature. He shook up the status quo in some of the superhero books—Wonder Woman was stripped of her superpowers; *Amazing Spider-Man* artist Steve Ditko defected to DC to launch the offbeat superhero comics *Beware the Creeper* and *The Hawk and the Dove;* and superstar artist Neal Adams began to transmute Batman from a masked detective to a creature of the night. At the same time, the company blindsided Marvel with its groundbreaking, commercially popular horror comics like *House of Mystery.*

But Marvel's superheroes continued to outsell DC's by the end of 1969. DC ended the Silver Age with the same dilemma it faced at the beginning of the era: how to make its superhero comics popular again. —*ME*

The Silver Surfer

Though first introduced into an issue of *Fantastic Four* as an afterthought, the Silver Surfer has become one of the great icons of comics and is an enduring cult favorite. In early 1966, *Fantastic Four*

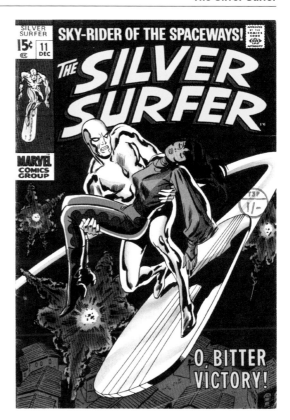

The Silver Surfer #11 © 1969 Marvel Comics.
COVER ART BY JOHN BUSCEMA AND JOHN VERPOORTEN.

#48 was originally intended to feature the superhero team in pitched battle with a new enemy, the colossal, planet-eating alien Galactus. But when Jack Kirby presented his penciled page, writer/editor Stan Lee had a real surprise: Kirby had dreamed up a new hero—a bald, silver man flying through the sky on a silver surfboard, possessed with cosmic power and apparently acting as Galactus' herald—and simply inserted him into the story. Whatever his genesis, the public (and Lee) took the "Sentinel of the Spaceways" to their hearts, and more appearances in *Fantastic Four* followed soon after.

The initial *Fantastic Four* story ended with the Surfer, touched by the humanity he saw on Earth, turning on Galactus and persuading him to leave the planet alone. Galactus agreed, but punished the Surfer by erecting a barrier around Earth that would keep him restricted to the planet, ensuring years of heartbreak, angst, and mourning for the tortured herald. In the psychedelic 1960s, both the fans and the growing counter-culture movement adored the Surfer, seeing in his James Dean-esque emoting a reflection of their own insecurities and confrontations with society. Indeed, the Surfer himself had much to say about the hot topics of the 1960s—namely, war and peace—Lee himself admitting that he wrote his "most obvious moralizing" through this character. By 1968, the clamor for the hero had grown to fever pitch and Lee bowed to the inevitable by giving the Surfer his own comic, complete with a long-delayed origin story and (much to the surprise of Kirby) a new artist, the elegant John Buscema.

The Surfer's origin, detailed in *Silver Surfer* #1 (1968), tells of how Norrin Radd from the planet Zenn-La offers to become Galactus' superpowered scout in order to save his people from the planet-guzzling titan's terrible appetite. Radd has become dissatisfied with his undemanding life on the paradise-like Zenn-La and jumps at Galactus' offer of a life in the stars, reasoning that he could find uninhabited planets for his master to devour and save countless civilizations in the process. ("On and on he soars, dodging meteors—skirting around asteroids—rocketing from planet to planet—with entire galaxies as his ports of call.") However, in accepting a future at Galactus' side, he has to leave the love of his life, the beautiful Shalla Bal, behind, inducing centuries of wistful pining, as the people of his home planet are conveniently immortal.

Under the great classicist Buscema, *Silver Surfer* was one of the decade's high points. Exciting, dynamic, and expansive, each issue was a treat for the eyes. However, readers soon became aware that Lee was unsure where to take the title, and Marvel's decision to launch it in an expensive sixty-eight-page format put many potential buyers off.

Issue #3 introduced the Surfer's nemesis, Mephisto—Marvel's answer to the devil himself, complete with pointed ears, sharp teeth, red skin, and flame-filled Stygian lair. Lee had Mephisto tempt the increasingly Christ-like Surfer with riches, power, and women, finally offering him a life with Shalla Bal if he would only join him in a career of evil. Inevitably, the Surfer rejected these temptations only to see Shalla Bal whizzed off back to Zenn-La; Mephisto would regularly drag the poor girl into his plans over the next couple of years. As the Surfer's moanings and posturings continued to escalate, fans deserted the comic, and after eighteen issues Marvel threw in the towel. Lee had seen the title as an outlet for his musings on American consciousness, and had reveled in the opportunity to indulge his taste for Shakespearean speeches, but possibly at the expense of the fans' yearning for action and characterization.

Throughout the 1970s, the Silver Surfer was a regular guest star in numerous issues of the Fantastic Four's comic and was a popular member of the Defenders, as well as being a potent iconic symbol for the cognoscenti. In 1978, Lee and Kirby were reunited for a final time on an all-new *Silver Surfer* trade paperback, published by Simon & Schuster—one of the first graphic novels. The story was an alternate take on the Surfer's first journey to Earth, excising the Fantastic Four from the proceedings, and was possibly intended to be the blueprint for a Silver Surfer movie. Rumors persisted throughout the late 1970s that a Silver Surfer film, starring pop singer Olivia Newton John as Shalla Bal, was imminent, but it never materialized and there was a sense that the character's popularity was on the wane.

A long fallow period in the 1980s, punctuated by a 1982 one-shot, unexpectedly came to a close in 1987 with a new Silver Surfer series, which this time was a resounding success. Writer Steve Englehart immediately freed the Surfer from his reluctant exile on Earth, correctly seeing that fans would love to explore the wider universe out there. For its first few years, this second series featured all sorts of aliens, the warring Kree and Skrull empires, Galactus, and, inevitably, Shalla Bal. In an intriguing twist, the Surfer was finally able to propose to his beloved but she rejected him, feeling that the pair had grown apart over the centuries. The 1990s tied the Surfer into new writer Jim Starlin's menagerie of cosmic stars, including Captain Marvel, Warlock, Pip the Troll, and the villainous Thanos.

While never the critics' favorite that he had been in his early days, the period starting with the Englehart series was the Surfer's commercial high point, resulting in a stream of specials, graphic novels, toys, and merchandise. Lee enjoyed occasional reunions with his old favorite, including a 1988 collaboration with the legendary French artist Moebius on a short book called *Parable.* In the Surfer's own title his writers began to play around with his history, including a revelation (in issue #48) that, back in the distant past, Galactus had tampered with his soul so that he would agree to become his herald. Other plot twists included the death of Shalla Bal and the destruction of Zenn-La (both inevitably reborn later) and a showdown with Mephisto (again).

The comic's last years were perhaps not its finest, and included Shalla Bal falling in love with the Surfer's (previously unmentioned) half-brother and the unconvincing revelation that Zenn-La had been destroyed thousands of years earlier and had been an illusion ever since. The sense that, after ten years in the limelight, the character had finally run out of steam was confirmed by the comic's cancellation in 1998 with issue #146.

However, the same decade saw him make it to America's TV screens if still not its multiplexes, as a well-regarded *Silver Surfer* animated series ran from 1998–1999. A co-starring role in Marvel's early 2000s *Defenders* revival was followed by an atmospheric new comic of his own, self-described as a more mysterious, M. Night Shyamalan treatment of the hero (2003–present). Time will tell if this new concept clicks with fans. But in any case, constant reprints of the Silver Surfer's first series (now fondly regarded as a classic) and of his early encounters with the Fantastic Four, as well as high-priced collectibles such as statues and action figures, will doubtless ensure his status as one of America's most memorable heroes. —DAR

Space Ghost

Although he calls himself Space Ghost, there is no data to say whether or not the interstellar superhero (and later talk show host) is an *actual* ghost. Wearing a white, red, black, and yellow costume and cape, the hooded Space Ghost's origin and real name have never been revealed (though his booming voice was originally portrayed by radio announcer and cartoon veteran Gary Owens). What is known is that his suit and his powers are incredible. An Inviso-Belt allows him to disappear, while his suit also gives him the power of flight at great speeds, the ability to breathe underwater or in the vacuum of space, and even to teleport! Also aiding Space Ghost in his missions against interstellar bad guys are his Power Bands (worn on his forearms), which have an astonishing variety of functions, including hypno force rays, destructo rays, heat intensifier rays, freeze rays, battering ram rays, electro shock rays, and even force fields!

With this much power, it's surprising that Space Ghost needs any help, but he does traverse the spaceways in his Phantom Cruiser (sometimes known as the Ghost Ship), a spaceship equipped with a variety of weapons including an inviso ray, freeze mist, heat-seeking missiles, and the ability to reach hyperspeeds. The Phantom Cruiser is docked at the Ghost Planet Headquarters, hidden behind a defensive force shield on the Ghost Planet.

Space Ghost mentors two twin teens who dress in blue, black, and yellow costumes—sister Jan (voiced by Ginny Tyler) and brother Jayce (voiced by Tim Matthieson)—and their monkey Blip (voiced by Don Messick). The kids and Blip use a jetpack to fly, have an Inviso-Belt, and use the Space Ghost emblem on their chest as a communication device.

Late-night superhero Space Ghost in *Space Ghost Coast to Coast.*

The teens have their own vehicle, the interstellar Space Coupe, which can double as a submarine! They aid Space Ghost in policing the universe.

Over the years, Space Ghost has amassed a number of interstellar enemies in his rogues' gallery. They include insectoid Zorak; catlike pirate Brak; the Spider Woman (also known as the Black Widow, and not to be confused with other popular superheroines of each name); heat-inducing Moltar; robot master Metallus; the Creature King and his nightmare beams; giant locust Lokar; and many others.

CBS executive Fred Silverman wanted a morningful of superhero shows for the 1966 season, and he asked Hanna-Barbera animation studios to develop a serious superhero series (unlike previous comedy shows). Legendary comic artist Alex Toth

created and designed Space Ghost, and production began on the series. *Space Ghost and Dino Boy* launched on September 10, 1966. *Space Ghost* had two eight-minute adventures per episode, while *Dino Boy* only had one short story. Thirty-six episodes of *Space Ghost* were produced in the first year, and another six stories were added for the 1967–1968 season. These six stories were significant because they crossed over with other Hanna-Barbera characters such as the Herculoids, Mightor, Shazzan, and Moby Dick.

Eight years after its cancellation, the series was repackaged with another Hanna-Barbera series, and aired on NBC. *The Space Ghost/Frankenstein Jr. Show* aired during the 1976–1977 season. On September 12, 1981, *Space Ghost* returned to the air with twenty-two new episodes as part of the hour-long anthology *Space Stars* (the series was hand-chosen by Fred Silverman, now at NBC). There were also eleven "Space Stars Finale" stories that teamed Space Ghost and his crew with the Herculoids and Teen Force against various evil invaders and galaxy scoundrels. The *Space Stars* series ended in 1982.

Often in syndicated and cable reruns, *Space Ghost* is a cult favorite among animation fans, largely due to its sleek look and its slightly off-kilter action. The Cartoon Network revived the character in April 1994 as the host of a late-night talk show called *Space Ghost Coast to Coast*. The show was surreal, featuring an animated Space Ghost constantly bedeviled by band-leader Zorak and show director Moltar, as well as other past foes, as he attempts to run a talk show from the Ghost Planet. Live celebrities including Dr. Joyce Brothers, Jim Carrey, Mark Hamill, Hulk Hogan, Elvira, and others would appear on a hanging television monitor to be interviewed by Space Ghost (now voiced by George Lowe), but the hero's non-sequiturs and strange questions made each interview bizarrely unique. The series finally ended on New Year's Eve 2003, though it led to spin-off series such as *Cartoon Planet* (1997–1999), *Brak Present the Brak Show Starring Brak* (2000), and *The Brak Show* (2001–2004).

Space Ghost appeared on a variety of licensed products in the 1960s and 1970s, including a Big Little Book, costumes, puzzles, coloring books, patches, and even bubble bath! His comic book adventures have been few and far between: *Space Ghost* #1 from Gold Key in March 1967 (and four anthology appearances in 1968–1969); one appearance in *The Funtastic World of Hanna-Barbera TV Stars* #3 from Marvel in December 1978; one issue from Comico in December 1987; one issue from Archie Comics in March 1997; and irregular issues of *Cartoon Network Presents* from DC Comics from 1997 to 2004. (However, in early 2004 it was announced that a non-humorous comic-book miniseries giving a kind of prequel to

the character's original cartoon adventures—and answering long-standing questions about who he is and where he comes from—was on the way from DC.) In the years since *Space Ghost Coast to Coast* premiered, the character's cult status has grown, resulting in action figures, statues, T-shirts, lithographs, books, soundtracks, and other material. Whether as superhero or talk show host, Space Ghost is definitely *not* dead. *—AM*

Space Heroes

Space may be the final frontier, but some superheroes traverse the intergalactic skyways and explore perilous planets, boldly going where the Terran hero has never gone before.

Buck Rogers and Flash Gordon, the headstrong Earthmen who rocketed into futuristic and/or otherworldly adventures, are the prototypical space heroes. Both originated in newspaper comic strips—Rogers in 1929, and Gordon in 1934—and were immortalized beyond the funnies in movie serials, Big Little Books, motion pictures, television series and cartoons, View-Master reels, action figures, and comic books. (Brick Bradford, their contemporary, starred in a comic strip from 1933 to 1987, as well as in other media, but never quite reached the cultural zenith of Buck or Flash. Also largely forgotten today is the earth-bound Flash-and-Buck variant named Blue Bolt, who fought outlandish menaces and secret societies *underground* and, in 1940, became the first character collaborated on by the soon-to-be-legendary Joe Simon and Jack Kirby team.)

The colorful costumes, exotic locales, and larger-than-life menaces in the *Buck Rogers* and *Flash Gordon* comic strips were a major influence upon the first superhero, Superman—actually a "strange visitor from another planet" himself—and upon the burgeoning comic-book industry. During comics' Golden Age (1938–1954), Fiction House published

Planet Comics (1940–1954), an anthology spotlighting "weird adventures on other worlds—the universe of the future." Each issue of *Planet* teemed with electrifying epics starring handsome heroes and fetching females cut from the Rogers/Gordon cloth—Reef Ryan and Princess Vara, Mars (God of War), Auro (Lord of Jupiter), Flint Baker, the Red Comet, Gale Allen and the Girl Squadron, Mysta of the Moon, the Star Pirate, and the Space Rangers—discharging their ray guns against freakish extraterrestrial monstrosities and interplanetary warlords.

Other publishers zoomed into the fray. Rex Dexter of Mars, a laser-blasting space hero who soared on steel wings, was one of the features premiering in *Mystery Men Comics* #1 (1939), the same comic that launched the career of the superhero Blue Beetle. A pulp-magazine character named Captain Future—a crossbreed of Flash Gordon and Doc Savage—blazed into action in 1940 with his proton pistol and superior intellect. An entirely different character called Captain Future appeared in *Startling Comics* #1 (1940), but had no futuristic gimmicks, only an appropriation of the name. Spacehawk, the star-faring marshal first seen in *Target Comics* #5 (1940), was a surprisingly grim strip from a cartoonist best known for madcap, Basil Wolverton. Starring in the short-lived *Miracle Comics* (1940–1941) was Sky Wizard, the "Master of Space," whose garish red-and-green uniform went unappreciated by colorblind readers. *Superworld Comics*—the product of publisher Hugo Gernsback, originator of *Amazing Stories,* the first sci-fi pulp—starred Mitey Powers, an adventurer who battled "Martians on the Moon." Captain Dash, a blue-cowled aero cop who patrolled the thirty-first century, appeared—only once—in *Comedy Comics* #9 (1942).

In its four-year run, *Wonder Comics* (1944–1948) included the forgettable Dick Devins ("King of Futuria") and the leggy, redheaded space pirate named Tara, who brandished a sci-fi saber instead of a ray gun. Lance Lewis, Space Detective flew into *Startling* #44 (1947). Clad in red togs (bearing a blazing blue comet chest insignia) with orange-and-blue striped epaulets, Lewis fired his ray blaster at renegade robots with a penchant for kidnapping scantily clad ladies. And DC Comics' Tommy Tomorrow of the Planeteers' bumpy but lengthy ride in print began in the "real science" series *Real Fact Comics* #6 (1947). Tomorrow was used to depict the man of the future in educational strips, then matured into a full-fledged space-adventure series beginning in *Action Comics* #127 (1948). In his purple outfit with short pants, Tomorrow navigated the stars in his ship the Ace of Space.

American paranoia fueled by the spread of Communism and the threat of atomic warfare metaphorically played out in popular culture through invaders from outer space in films like *The Day the Earth Stood Still* (1951), and soon the new medium of television featured a galaxy of futuristic heroes. TV viewers were enthralled by *Captain Video and His Video Rangers* (1949–1955), featuring the "Guardian of the Safety of the World," a self-proclaimed planetary protector who stunned his adversaries (including Mook the Moon Man, Kul of Eos, and Tobor the Robot [read that name backwards]) with his Cosmic Ray Vibrator; and *Tom Corbett, Space Cadet* (1950–1952), who patrolled the cosmos in the starship Polaris with the fellow members of the Space Academy. Space heroes stormed into other media: Commando Cody a.k.a. Rocketman, the "Sky Marshal of the Universe," was one of the last characters to headline a movie serial as that art form was dying out due to the emergence of television; and comics publisher Ziff-Davis' *Crusader from Mars* (1952) featured the alien Tarka, deported from the red planet for a crime and determined to redeem himself by performing good deeds on Earth, over which he hovered in his soundless "Whirling Disc-craft."

With Julius "Julie" Schwartz—the founder of science-fiction fandom and a former sci-fi literary agent—in the editorial pool of DC Comics, space heroes dotted DC's publishing starscape of the 1950s. *Strange Adventures* #9 (1951) premiered Captain Comet, actually Adam Blake, an evolutionary fluke—comics' first *mutant*—centuries ahead of his time. Captain Comet fought crooks and aliens with ESP, flight, and psychokinesis; for example, in *Strange Adventures* #28's (1953) "Devil's Island in Space," Comet's "super-normal senses detect danger," but his eyes cannot see the invisible invaders encircling him. The Knights of the Galaxy, DC's ultramodern interpretation of King Arthur's Knights of the Round Table, bowed in *Mystery in Space* #1 (1951), fighting mundane menaces like the conqueror Korvo. The Atomic Knights, a group of far-flung (set *way* off in 1986) champions, debuted in *Strange Adventures* #117 (1960). Gardner Grayle led his defiant militia—each dressed in an ancient suit of armor—in opposition to the despotic Black Baron and other menaces threatening the nuclear-ravaged "future" Earth. Schwartz's titles included additional space characters (Star Hawkins, Space Cabbie, and the Star Rovers, among others), but the editor's best-remembered—and most enduring—sci-fi superhero is the jetpacked Adam Strange, premiering in *Showcase* #17 (1958) and sporadically appearing in myriad comics, including *Justice League of America.*

DC editor Jack Schiff unveiled the Space Ranger in *Showcase* #15 (1958). The Ranger had a secret identity—business heir Rick Starr—and donned a red-and-yellow spacesuit with a bubble helmet and a rocketpack to fight futuristic bad guys (the Jungle Beasts of Jupiter and the Alien Brat from Planet Byra, among others) with a cutesy alien pal, Cryll, by his side. Ultra the Multi-Alien—commencing in *Mystery in Space* #103 (1965)—was a bizarre DC hero whose ragtag body was composed of four ethereal life forms.

The "space race" between the United States and Russia encouraged a trend of star-spanning superheroes during the 1960s. Marvel Comics' Silver Surfer flew into the pages of *Fantastic Four* #48 (1966) first as the herald to the world-eating Galactus, then as a superhero in his own right. Mar-Vell, a military officer from the Kree empire, trekked to Earth in *Marvel Super-Heroes* #12 (1967), where he

became known as Captain Marvel, fighting aliens and supervillains for years before dying of cancer and being succeeded by his son, Genis. The Guardians of the Galaxy—Vance Astro, Charlie-27, Yondu, Starhawk, Martinex, and Nikki—was a superteam that premiered in *Marvel Super-Heroes* #18 (1969), waging war against serpentine soldiers that enslaved future Earth. In 1967, Hanna-Barbera introduced the animated hero Space Ghost, who used his power bands to battle Brak, Moltar, and other galactic antagonists. Wham-O, the makers of the popular Frisbee toy, produced a one-shot comic—*Wham-O Giant Comics* #1 (1967)—starring Galaxo, a space policeman for the United World Interstellar Agencies, who communicated with various races via his Computo-Translator. Also during the 1960s, Gold Key Comics published two series starring sci-fi heroes: *Magnus, Robot Fighter* and *M.A.R.S. Patrol.*

From the 1970s to the present, science-fiction heroes have frequently launched their careers, some blazing eternally, others going supernova within a few appearances. Among their number: the ABC Warriors, robotic combatants from the British comic *2000 AD;* Alan Moore's social-commentary star-trooper saga *The Ballad of Halo Jones* (one of the relatively few series of this type with a female protagonist); Deathlok, Marvel's cyborg soldier—and a precursor to Robocop—with 75 percent of his body boasting cybernetic enhancements, first seen in *Astonishing Tales* #25 (1974); First Comics' Grimjack, a freelance assassin who chose a sword over technological weapons; Britain's popular Judge Dredd, Mega City's "Lawman of the Future," from a host of comics, Batman crossovers, and a poorly received 1995 live-action movie starring Sylvester Stallone; *Kamandi, the Last Boy on Earth,* written and drawn by the legendary Jack Kirby, a post-apocalyptic DC Comics series heavily inspired by the film *Planet of the Apes;* and creator Jim Starlin's Dreadstar, an opposition leader embroiled in a conflict between the Church of Instrumentality and the Monarchy. (Starlin is perhaps the foremost practitioner of the "cosmic" hero as well, a protagonist who mixes interstellar adventure with mind-expanding mysticism, as in the case of another character most associated with Starlin, the space-faring swashbuckler Adam Warlock.)

Other futuristic favorites: Killraven, seen in Marvel's *War of the Worlds* series (appearing in the title *Amazing Adventures*), a continuation of H. G. Wells' classic, featuring a former gladiator turned leader of a rebellion against Martian tyranny; Frank Miller and Dave Gibbons' Martha Washington, an African-American freedom fighter warring against a fascist-controlled near-future where the poor are incarcerated; Mike Baron and Steve Rude's Nexus, the fusion-generating hero who dreamt of mass murderers, then sought them out to execute them; another Kirby concoction for DC Comics, *OMAC: One Man Army Corps,* actually Global Peace Agent Buddy Blank, answering to the all-seeing satellite Brother Eye; the *X-Men* spinoff Star Jammers, Marvel's crew of interplanetary pirates; writer/artist Walter Simonson's Star Slammers, a space militia for hire; America's Best Comics' bawdy time-travel series *Jonni Future;* and the Wanderers, a superteam 1,000 years in the future first seen as supporting-cast members in DC's Legion of Super-Heroes series before spinning off into their own comic in the 1980s. Most of these characters' realities are bleak and oppressive, with the space heroes acting as resistance soldiers to liberate themselves and/or others. —ME

Spacehawk

As superheroes began to dominate the newsstands, more publishers entered the comics market including, in 1940, Curtis, owners of the *Saturday Evening Post,* at the time one of the country's leading magazines. Their first title, *Target Comics,* featured a mixed bag of strips including Manowar, the White Streak, and Bulls-Eye Bill, but it was not until the introduction of Spacehawk in the fifth issue (June 1940) that the comic really took off. Spacehawk was

the creation of one of comics' most maverick talents, Basil Wolverton, whose bizarre, extraordinary artwork has earned him a cult following to this day. Wolverton had long held an affection for space heroes, stretching back to his creation of Marco of Mars in 1928, and he had worked on such strips as Meteor Martin, Shack Shannon, and a group called the Spacehawks throughout the 1930s. Spacehawk (singular) differed from his predecessors in combining the science fiction setting of Flash Gordon or Buck Rogers with the superpowers of the recently launched Superman.

Like Superman, Spacehawk traveled from a distant, alien planet to Earth's solar system to patrol the spaceways as a sort of intergalactic policeman, traveling anywhere he sensed "vibrations of hatred." He wore a bulky spacesuit with heavy metal boots covered in rivets, was armed with a ray gun, and, in his first few appearances, sported a rather ugly mask resembling melted Jello. While he could not fly under his own power (he had his own somewhat lumpen spaceship), he was nonetheless unnaturally strong, had a telepathic mind, and possessed a steely determination in dealing with the various bandits, space pirates, and menacing aliens whom he came across. In fact, as heroes go he was unusually ruthless, often disposing of his foes in a casually brutal manner, frequently shooting them dead. He was also, apparently, 800 years old but looked remarkably well preserved for his age.

In its first year, the strip was filled with the strangest array of Martians, Saturnians, and Uranians that one could hope to find. Wolverton was a master of the "spaghetti and meatball" school of illustration (as he was once so memorably described) and his aliens were a bizarre looking bunch, seemingly constructed from warts, tentacles, frankfurters, and spikes. Strangely, they shared a fondness for the letter G in their names: Glak, Glork, Grubb, Gorvak, Grebo, Galar, and so on. In this rather macho world of boiler suits, guns, and monsters, there was usually little room for the fairer sex, though Queen Haba of Mercury provided the occasional dose of romance.

Even as early as 1940, some parents' groups were putting pressure on publishers to tone down the more outré elements in their comics, and Wolverton's editors regularly asked him to rein himself in. On the outbreak of World War II, they insisted that Space-hawk be brought down to Earth to fight the enemy and that the strip be cleared of its troublesome aliens. Spacehawk was made to reflect the growing patriotic sentiment of the day, and for most of 1941 fought invading Japanese, an enormous Nazi subma-rine, and a dictator named "Moosler" (you figure it out). Wolverton reluctantly complied with these edito-rial shifts, but by then the strip had lost much of its special appeal, despite such innovative touches as a Japanese fifth column hiding in asteroids. On Earth, "an interplanetary feature couldn't survive," Wolver-ton later recalled. Nevertheless, our hero soon acquired an arch-villain, the bullet-headed, bald, moustachioed Prussian man-mountain, Dr. Gore, who wreaked havoc with his dastardly paralyzing ray. At one point, Dr. Gore was captured and carried off into the Martian desert by one of Spacehawk's alien pals (the unfortunately named Dork) but he soon returned in his own spaceship to fight again.

As Wolverton had feared, once the feature was shorn of its space setting it got lost among the crowd of other superheroes, and it was canceled after thirty adventures; its last appearance was in *Target Comics* vol. 3 #10 in late 1942. Wolverton's influence lived on, however, and his detailed, grotesque pen work can be clearly seen in the art of R. Crumb and others from the 1960s under-ground comics movement. Spacehawk has been reprinted on several occasions, in self-titled book form in 1978 and as a regular series of comics from Dark Horse in 1989. —DAR

Spawn

Of the many creator-owned superhero properties that sprang from the 1992 advent of Image Comics, Spawn is without doubt the most influential. Con-

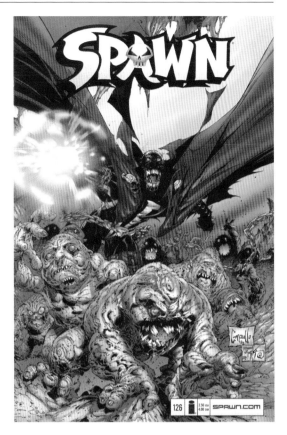

Spawn #126 © 2003 Todd McFarlane.
COVER ART BY GREG CAPULLO AND DANNY MIKI.

ceived, written, and illustrated by Image co-founder Todd McFarlane—best known previously for writing and drawing Marvel Comics' multiplatinum-selling *Spider-Man* series (1990–1991)—*Spawn* #1 (1992) begins the story of former U.S. Marine Corps soldier Al Simmons (a character named after one of McFarlane's college friends) who progresses to a brilliant career as a covert intelligence opera-tive after distinguishing himself by saving the presi-dent of the United States from an assassin's bullet. Simmons subsequently discovers that his mentor and superior, Jason Wynn, is presiding over a web of international intrigue and corruption. Wynn protects his secrets by sending an operative named Chapel (a character from fellow Image partner Rob Liefeld's

Youngblood series) to murder Simmons by burning his face off with a laser.

Simmons finds himself not only dead, but also doomed to an eternity in hell because of the many crimes he had committed as a covert government operative. But Simmons has never taken defeat well; at the precise moment of his death, he makes a deal with Malebolgia, the demonic overlord of a Dantean "eighth sphere of hell." Thanks to this unholy bargain, Simmons gains the power to return to the world of the living, where he can see his beloved wife again—and, as the hellborn creature known as Spawn, now has an opportunity to wreak vengeance on the man who engineered his death. Spawn's hell-haggled supernatural powers include teleportation, superhuman strength and endurance, and the ability to transform his facial features—left in horrific ruins by the laser Chapel used to kill him—on a temporary basis. Added to his skills as a trained killer, these new gifts make Simmons all but unstoppable in combat.

Spawn's resurrection wasn't the first such occurrence in the annals of superhero comics. McFarlane's demonic hero embroidered on such ectoplasmic predecessors as the Spectre (a powerful and vengeful shade who originated in DC Comics' Golden Age [1938–1954]) and Deadman (who haunted DC's Silver Age [1956–1969] *Strange Adventures* anthology title) by exploring the consequences that flow from bargains made with the forces of darkness. After agreeing to be transformed into Spawn, Simmons finds himself back on Earth—where he learns that five years has passed since his death, and discovers that he is free to use his powers to do battle against minions of hell and other evildoers. But he also finds that he is expected to command Malebolgia's demon armies in a war against the forces of heaven. Even more painfully, he learns that his wife has remarried and is now raising a family with her new husband. Unwilling to cause his widow further grief by re-entering her life—and not wishing to frighten her by allowing her to see his horribly scarred visage—

Spawn opts to live out his days in the world's back alleys, among the dregs of humanity. Determined not to use his abilities to enhance the power of evil in the world, Spawn turns against Malebolgia, whom he sees as having betrayed the spirit of their bargain. Spawn subsequently commits himself to bringing the powerful demon down, while simultaneously trying to redeem himself for his prior misdeeds as a covert intelligence operative. Like Marvel's Punisher and DC's Batman, Spawn is separated from his family by forces beyond his control and responds to his trauma by waging an eternal one-man war against all the evil he encounters.

Despite his good intentions and dogged determination, Spawn must also contend with some sharp constraints against the use of his preternatural abilities—his battle against hell is hampered by the fact that killing the bad guys he encounters merely sends more evil souls into Malebolgia's employ, thus increasing the "evil quotient" of the universe. Also, every time he uses his abilities he places himself in danger of permanently returning himself to hell by depleting his finite supply of eldritch energy. On top of that, his cloak and some of the other pieces of his way-cool, heavy-metal costume are sentient, parasitic entities with agendas of their own. Simmons' life is further complicated by the unwanted presence of the Violator, an evil, sadistic clown sent by Malebolgia to act as Spawn's "chaperone" on Earth—a sort of "guardian demon" who might have been conceived by a Satanic Frank Capra.

Because the series combined the twin *zeitgeists* of its time—a reliance on the "gritty" ultraviolence that became the *lingua franca* of many superhero comics of the late 1980s; and an emphasis on aesthetics that sometimes overshadowed its storytelling—*Spawn* became an immediate hit among comics readers, collectors, and speculators. Spawn's appeal, which is strongest among teens and heavy metal enthusiasts, stems in no small part from his appearance, which is derivative of many of the superheroes—and rock bands—McFarlane grew up with. Spawn's costume clearly shows the influence of Marvel's Spider-Man, Doctor Strange, and the Punisher, along with liberal dollops of DC's Batman and Lobo. Spawn's visual appeal arguably transcends the milieu of the violent postmodern superhero; he wouldn't look at all out of place playing rhythm guitar with such rock bands as KISS or Gwar.

The unrelentingly grim tone of *Spawn* might have stalled the series creatively fairly early in its run, had McFarlane not decided to bring in some new blood. Fan favorite writer Alan Moore, who gained international prominence after penning DC's seminal 1986–1987 *Watchmen* miniseries, wrote *Spawn* #8 (1993), and subsequent issues were authored by Neil Gaiman (best known for DC/Vertigo's long-running *Sandman* series), Frank Miller (of *Batman: The Dark Knight Returns* fame), Dave Sim (creator and writer-artist of *Cerebus the Aardvark*), and Grant Morrison (DC's *Animal Man*). Thanks in part to the efforts of these creators, Spawn's mythos evolved significantly in sophistication and expanded to include such new personages as the Hellspawn (earlier incarnations of Malebolgia's minions), Cogliostro (a powerful ally to Spawn, whose immortal nature and lengthy history are evocative of DC's Phantom Stranger), an angel known as Angela, and an antagonist called the Anti-Spawn.

As the 1990s progressed, not only did *Spawn* become a popular stop for talented guest writers, the character also guest-starred in such intercompany "crossover" comics as *Batman-Spawn: War Devil* and *Spawn-Batman* (both 1994 Image Comics/DC Comics co-productions). *Spawn* also engendered several comics spin-offs, including *Spawn Blood Feud* (four issues, 1995); *Spawn: Blood and Salvation* (a 1999 one-shot); *Spawn: The Undead* (1999–2000); and such long-running titles as *Sam & Twitch* (1999–present), about a pair of urban detectives investigating the supernatural in a *Buffy the Vampire Slayer* meets *NYPD Blue* setting; *Spawn: The Dark Ages* (1999–2001); and *Hellspawn* (2000–present), the latter two of which feature versions of Spawn (Malebolgia's other

demonic military commanders) that are even meaner than the original 1992 incarnation. Taking on a life of his own during his first half-decade of existence, Spawn also became the subject of a 1997 feature film (*Spawn,* starring Michael Jai and directed by Mark A. Z. Dippé), gave rise to an Emmy Award–winning HBO animated series (1997–1999), and provided a major impetus to Todd McFarlane's toy company (McFarlane Toys), which generated huge sales with its line of action figures based not only upon Spawn, but also on such licensed properties as KISS, *Shrek, The X-Files,* Austin Powers, *Army of Darkness, Alien, Predator,* and the Beatles.

Comics, toys, films, and television series aside, the greatest contribution that Spawn—and McFarlane—have made to the superhero genre may be in encouraging comics creators either to retain ownership and control of their creations, or to obtain better payment for their work. Like artist Neal Adams, whose crusades in the late 1960s and early 1970s on behalf of creators' rights pressured comics publishers to offer better terms to artists and writers than those found in the industry's thenstandard "work- for-hire" contracts, McFarlane exerted a similar influence on the publisher-creator dynamic during the 1990s and beyond; indeed, McFarlane was one of Marvel's highest-paid creators at the time he was still writing and drawing *Spider-Man.*

Whether McFarlane's aesthetic effect on comics was equally salutary will no doubt be debated for many years to come, however. But for good or ill, Spawn's "grittification" of the storytelling and design of many other superhero comics published over the past decade is undeniable, showing up clearly in such Image titles as *Witchblade* (1995), *The Darkness* (1996), *Violent Messiahs* (1997), and *Rising Stars* (1999). The darkness and otherworldly violence that characterize Spawn can also be seen in comics such as *30 Days of Night* (Idea Design Works, 2002) by Steve Niles and Ben Templesmith (who collaborated earlier on McFarlane's *Hellspawn*) and in *Criminal Macabre* (also by Niles and Templesmith, from Dark Horse Comics, 2003); and *The Authority* (1999, DC/WildStorm).

Having successfully weathered the myriad ups and downs of the comics business since *Spawn*'s inception—including the 1996 breakup of the core Image Comics partners and an ultimately successful (and costly) defamation lawsuit filed against McFarlane in 1999 by hockey player Tony Twist, who objected to having one of Spawn's villains (a gangster) named after him—Todd McFarlane still runs Todd McFarlane Productions (TMP) in 2004. TMP oversees Spawn's considerable licensing empire and continues to publish the original, ever-durable *Spawn* title, as well as its current spin-offs, which employ numerous other artists and writers. Whatever criticisms its detractors may have, Todd McFarlane's *Spawn* represents one of the most phenomenal success stories in the history of superhero comics. —*MAM*

The Spectre

Within a year of Superman's first appearance, DC Comics followed up with Batman and the Sandman. Soon after, among a flood of colorful crime fighters, Superman creator Jerry Siegel invented the first supernatural hero, the Spectre. Drawn by young artist Bernard Baily, Siegel's first Spectre story was featured in *More Fun Comics* #52 in early 1940, and it is safe to say that young comics readers had never seen anything quite like it. The story opens with tough cop Jim Corrigan attending a party celebrating his engagement to socialite Clarice Winston. Following a tip-off, Corrigan rushes to a nearby race course where a bunch of local criminal "Gat" Benson's hoods are attempting a robbery. Corrigan rounds them up single-handedly, but later an enraged Benson kidnaps Corrigan, shoves him into a concrete-filled barrel, and throws it and Corrigan into a river.

Naturally, this being a comic, death is hardly an impediment to a hero's career, and so at the gates

Adventure Comics #432 © 1974 DC Comics.
COVER ART BY JIM APARO.

of Eternity the voice of God tells Corrigan that his work is not yet complete, and he is returned to Earth, where he destroys the gang of crooks. This new "avenging Spectre" has almost limitless powers, including a death stare (by which criminals are literally frightened to death), and the ability to read minds, heal wounds, grow to an immense size, and even travel back in time. Sensing, quite understandably, that he is not quite the same as other men, Corrigan breaks off his engagement to Winston and goes home to sew himself a green hooded costume.

Over the next couple of years, the Spectre struck terror into the hearts of crooks everywhere and was in many ways a figure of horror himself. He was effectively God's executioner and, whether it was a common hood or an exotic weirdo such as Zor, the Blue Flame, Xmon, or the Black Doom, he dispatched each foe with cold efficiency. Love interest Winston made regular appearances in order to give the Spectre someone to rescue, but the Spectre's creators perhaps felt that their character was becoming too unsympathetic. After the character lost the cover slot on *More Fun,* Baily tried to humanize his hero by introducing a comedy sidekick, Percival Popp the Supercop, whose sole purpose was to get into trouble. The only outcome was a steady erosion of the Spectre's unique appeal, and in 1945 the strip was canceled.

For much of the early 1940s, the Spectre was also a regular member of the Justice Society but, while many group members were enjoying successful revivals in the 1960s, the Spectre was conspicuous by his absence. Following a campaign by fans, the Spectral Avenger was finally brought back in three 1966 issues of Showcase Comics, which soon led to a regular series. Wary of returning to the original incarnation's rather bloodthirsty personality, the new strip played up the character's mystical side, resulting in a series of rather cosmic, psychedelic adventures. However, this Spectre still lacked the sort of emotional depth that was making Marvel Comic's superheroes so popular, and it was not until the horror-obsessed 1970s that the strip attained any real popularity.

Legend has it that after editor Joe Orlando was mugged in New York he envisioned a new Spectre who could wreak the vengeance that he felt so powerless to mete out. With inventive horror writer Michael Fleisher and artist Jim Aparo on board, the new Spectre debuted in the February 1974 issue of *Adventure Comics* #431 to a mixture of acclaim and disbelief. Fleisher had gone back to the Spectre's avenging roots and relished dreaming up new and inventive ways of killing villains. These included turning a hood to wood and sawing him up, cutting someone in half with a colossal pair of scissors, skewering a cell of terrorists with giant protractors, and causing a crime lord to be devoured by a twen-

ty-feet-tall duck! Jim Corrigan himself was now a chain-smoking police detective in the Dirty Harry vein, harder than hard and as cold as the grave. From the start, fan reaction was divided; some loved the hard-hitting stories while others felt the strip was little more than an exercise in sadism. When DC's executives heard of the fuss, they took a look at the comic and were so appalled that they canceled it on the spot, despite its encouraging sales. Fleisher and Aparo had their revenge years later, however, when the whole series was collected in a deluxe package, complete with the unprinted stories completed before the axe fell. Apparently, what was once shocking was now a classic.

Recent years have seen three more series, which have largely picked up where the 1970s series left off—with varying degrees of success. A lengthy 1990s run was particularly well received, and daringly even brought back Percival Popp, the Super Cop. The latest, post-millennium incarnation (which has since been canceled) had rather radically revived long-deceased Green Lantern Hal Jordan in the guise of a kinder, gentler Spectre. The "Spirit of Redemption" had incarnations all over the universe, with almost untold power; although this was apparently all too confusing for some, it was nevertheless a sign that Jerry Siegel knew what he was doing when he devised the character all those years ago. —DAR

Speed Racer

Speed Racer. A name that conjures up images of fast cars, death-defying action, a gadget-packed supercar that puts superspy James Bond to shame, and a daring eighteen-year-old dark-haired hero dressed in a blue shirt, white pants, and penny loafers—a hero with nerves of steel but harboring a family secret. For many American children growing up in 1967—the year Speed's adventures first aired on syndicated television in the United States—*Speed Racer* was unlike anything they had ever seen. He had no superpowers to speak of, but he still had adventures that matched any superhero from Marvel or DC Comics. Speed was in his teens—in a sense, he was closer in age to the audience—and he was both human and fallible. He would often find himself in situations that were too much for him to handle alone. Finally, as a member of his father's Go Team, Speed would travel the world race circuit driving the Mach 5, an advanced prototype equipped with an array of special features that were activated by corresponding buttons on the car's steering wheel.

Members of the Go Team included Speed; his father, Pops Racer; Sparky, Speed's friend and a top mechanic; Speed's mother; his younger brother (and troublemaker), Spritle; and chimp mascot Chim-Chim. Rounding out Go Team was Speed's girlfriend, Trixie, who was also a helicopter pilot and a martial artist.

Since its initial broadcast, *Speed Racer* has grown in popularity, gaining more fans over the years. The show is clearly one of the most popular animated shows ever seen in the United States. Yet what many fans of the show did not know—at first— was that *Speed Racer* was one of the earliest anime to be imported from Japan to the United States. For many, it was their first look at this art form.

To find the origin of *Speed Racer,* one has to go back several decades and across the Pacific Ocean, to Tatsunoko Productions (*Science Ninja Team Gatchaman*) in Japan. The late Tatsuo Yoshida, a popular manga artist and one of the co-founders of Tatsunoko, wanted to make an animated adaptation of his manga *Mach Go Go Go.* The title itself is also a pun on "go," which means "five" in Japanese. *Mach Go Go Go* would be Tatsunoko's first full-color animated series. Jinzo Toriumi was both the planner and head writer, Hiroshi Sasagawa was the chief director, and Yoshida was the show's overall supervisor. *Mach Go Go Go* chronicled the adventures of Go Mifune, a young racecar driver who drove the Mach Go racer—and who had a strict moral code that often came into conflict with his

racing career. His elder brother Kenichi had left the racing circuit after a bitter disagreement with his father, and Go would clash with his father as well. Throughout his adventures, Go's girlfriend Michi would remain at his side. The series was also influenced by the "spy craze" of the 1960s. The manga and eventual series, which premiered in 1967 and ran for fifty-two episodes, were popular in Japan and spawned a wave of merchandise.

The American company Translux bought the rights to all episodes of *Mach Go Go Go,* but allowed Tatsunoko to have a role in the English-language adaptation of the series. Peter Fernandez, a voice actor and screenwriter who had previously worked on *Astro Boy* (the American version of *Tetsuwan Atom*), supervised the writing and dubbing for the series, now given the name *Speed Racer.* Fernandez also provided the voice for Speed and the mysterious Racer X. Names and locations were changed, but the music remained the same. Even the music for the catchy opening theme was the original background music, with only the words rewritten, starting with "Here he comes, here comes Speed Racer / He's a demon on wheels." Go Mifune became Speed Racer—but the "G" on his shirt remained, leading to years of speculation by fans. Michi Shimura became Trixie (voiced by Corinne Orr, who also provided Spritle's voice). Rounding out the cast were Jack Grimes (Sparky) and Jack Curtis (Pops Racer). Another change occurred during the adaptation process—Speed became the main focus of the show; in the original *Mach Go Go Go,* there had been more focus on the car.

One memorable aspect of *Speed Racer* was the cast of secondary characters and villains, many with somewhat bizarre names, such as Inspector Detector the Interpol agent, who would show up to help Speed solve a case. Another was Racer X—in reality Speed's brother Rex—the champion masked racer, the driver of the black and yellow Shooting Star, and a secret agent. Major villains from Speed's rouges' gallery included crime bosses Tongue Bloggard and Cruncher Block, and the sinister hitman Ace Duecey.

All fifty-two episodes of *Speed Racer* ran on syndicated television in the United States starting in 1967, and became the first anime series that many viewers had seen. The show's fast-paced adventure, races, and characters were unlike anything viewers had experienced before, and many fans did not forget the series as they grew older. Throughout the 1970s and 1980s, Speed's adventures would be shown in many other countries and in different languages, eclipsing its original version in recognition. In the late 1980s Now Comics published a *Speed Racer* series written by Len Strazewski with art by Gary Thomas Washington. A second series followed in the early 1990s. Stories from the original *Mach Go Go Go* manga were translated into English and released under the title of *Speed Racer.* The 1990s also marked a revival of interest in the TV series. MTV began airing episodes in the mid-1990s, and a compilation film called *Speed Racer: The Movie* toured film festivals and art houses around the United States. Volkswagen even used the characters in an animated commercial. The Children's Safety Network organization sponsored the construction of a full-sized Mach 5; Peter Fernandez and Corinne Orr went on tours around the country with the car in order to promote their campaign for children's safety.

The entire series was released on home video, and in April 2003 Family Home Entertainment began releasing the series on DVD. A best-selling book written by Elizabeth Moran titled *Speed Racer: The Official 30th Anniversary Guide* was published in 1997. Two years later, WildStorm released a three-issue comic miniseries written and drawn by Tommy Yune. The series detailed the origins of the Mach 5 and Speed's entry into the world of racing. It was popular enough to have a sequel of sorts released in 2000; this time Rex Racer was the focus, with the series detailing his journey toward becoming Racer X. Yune would return to write the series, with Jo Chen providing the art. Combined with a new wave of merchandising, all of these projects brought Speed's adventures to a new generation.

Not all of the revival projects worked. In 1993, Fred Wolf Films (responsible for the *Teenage Mutant Ninja Turtles* animated television series) produced a new Speed Racer television series called *The New Adventures of Speed Racer,* but it was not well received and was not successful in the end. Too many fans felt that the show—which featured updated designs for the characters and vehicles—lacked the essence and charm of the original. In Japan, Tatsunoko Productions produced an updated version of *Mach Go Go Go* in 1997, in time for the show's thirtieth anniversary; the series ran for thirty-four episodes. An English-dubbed version under the title of *Speed Racer* ran on the Nickelodeon cable channel starting in 2002. While the series was better than the earlier, ill-fated revival attempt, it still was not as popular as the original, either in Japan or America. The lightening, it seemed, could not be caught in the same bottle twice. —*MM*

Spider-Girl: *See* **Spider-Woman**

Spider-Man

Spider-Man is easily the most widely recognized character in Marvel Comics' four-color pantheon, and has been an American pop-culture mainstay for more than four decades. He was a radical departure from the staid conventions of the comic-book superhero of the 1950s—a teenage character that wasn't relegated to sidekick status beside an older, more experienced hero. Creators Stan Lee (editor-scripter) and Steve Ditko (artist-plotter) loosed Spider-Man on an unsuspecting world in 1962 in *Amazing Fantasy* #15, portraying a scientifically brilliant but socially maladroit teen named Peter Parker—a high-school everyman—who receives a fateful bite from a radioactive spider during an atomic science demonstration. Parker consequently finds himself in possession of the proportional abilities of an arachnid, including heightened strength, speed, agility, the ability to cling to walls and ceilings, and a precogni-

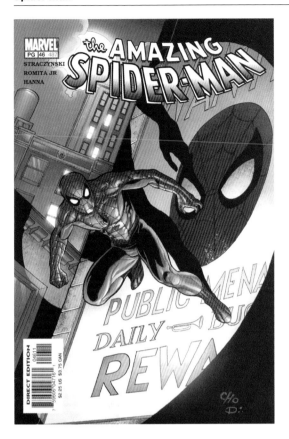

Amazing Spider-Man vol. 2, #46 © 2002 Marvel Comics.
COVER ART BY FRANK CHO.

tive "spider sense" that alerts him to approaching dangers. Using his inborn scientific talents, Parker synthesizes a unique adhesive "web fluid"—though superstrong it dissolves after an hour's exposure to the open air—and builds a pair of wrist-mounted web-shooters that enable him to shape the webbing into various useful forms. He also designs and sews the web-festooned red-and-blue costume that would quickly become "Spidey's" most visible trademark, and a ubiquitous sight along Manhattan's skyline (hence the immortal and oft-repeated tag-line, "Your friendly neighborhood Spider-Man").

In addition to possessing superpowers atypical for his era—heroes with arthropod-like abilities were relatively uncommon in the early 1960s—Spider-Man also departs from the background typical of other "long-underwear" characters. Instead of hailing from another world like Superman, inheriting millions like Batman, or having the godlike advantages of Wonder Woman, Spider-Man is essentially an ordinary guy whose alter ego lives a basically normal life prior to gaining his extraordinary abilities. Co-creator Lee has described him as "an orphan who lived with his aunt and uncle, a bit of a nerd, a loser in the romance department, and who constantly worried about the fact that his family barely had enough money to live on. Except for his superpower, he'd be the quintessential hard-luck kid. He'd have allergy attacks when fighting the villains, he'd be plagued by ingrown toenails, acne, hay fever, and anything else I could dream up." However, Lee's publisher Martin Goodman wasn't initially receptive to the idea of a teen hero taking center stage, nor did he want to accept Spider-Man's neuroses, romantic deficiencies, and chronic concerns about money. Goodman also thought that the audience would be repelled by the character's spider motif. Fortunately, Lee's instincts prevailed; Spider-Man's debut in *Amazing Fantasy* was an immediate and resounding success.

From the beginning, Spider-Man's behavior deviates significantly from the prevailing superheroic norms as well. Instead of selflessly dedicating his superhuman gifts to crime-fighting or the general betterment of humankind, the newly empowered Spider-Man cashes in on his talents by becoming a television celebrity. After his first performance before the cameras, he refuses to bother to stop a robber from stealing the television station's studio box-office receipts. During the days that follow, Spider-Man's fame grows, though Peter Parker wisely keeps his identity concealed. But his world abruptly collapses a few days later when a burglar murders his uncle, Ben Parker, leaving Peter's Aunt May a widow (Ben and May Parker had raised young Peter after the boy's parents, Richard and Mary Parker, died while performing espionage on behalf of the U.S. government). The grief-stricken Spider-Man tracks down Uncle Ben's killer, collaring his first criminal—only to make the horrible discovery that the murderer is the very same robber he'd allowed to escape from the television studio. "My fault," a tearful Peter Parker soliloquies after catching the killer. "All my fault! If only I had stopped him when I *could* have. But I *didn't*—and now—Uncle Ben—is dead …" Spider-Man's debut story closes with a somber narration that permanently sets the series' moral tone: "And a lean, silent figure slowly fades into the gathering darkness, aware at last that in this world, with great power there must also come—great responsibility!"

Although Spider-Man's one-shot comics "pilot" in *Amazing Fantasy* #15 soon led to an ongoing series that began with *The Amazing Spider-Man* (abbreviated *ASM*) vol. 1 #1 in March 1963, the eponymous character immediately became integral to the ever-burgeoning "Marvel universe" as well, interacting (and sometimes exchanging blows) with such mainstays as the Fantastic Four, that group's Human Torch (another teen hero), Daredevil, and the Incredible Hulk. Spidey also quickly developed a colorful, soap opera–worthy supporting cast of his own, including: the rabidly anti-vigilante *Daily Bugle* newspaper publisher J. Jonah Jameson; girlfriend Gwen Stacy (to be replaced later by hipster "party girl" Mary Jane Watson following Stacy's untimely death); high-school jock bully Flash Thompson, who would later become part of Parker's circle of friends; college roommate Harry Osborn; and a roster of costumed adversaries such as the Chameleon; Mysterio; the Tinkerer; the Vulture; Doctor Octopus; the Sandman; the Lizard, Electro; the Enforcers; the Green Goblin; Kraven the Hunter; the Ringmaster and His Circus of Crime; the Scorpion; the Beetle; Spencer Smythe and the Spider-Slayers; Crime-Master; Molten Man; Master Planner; the Looter (later known as the Meteor Man); and the Kingpin. Like most of the superheroes of his time, Parker takes great pains to conceal his secret crime-fighting life from everyone around him; he is largely successful,

despite being unmasked on more than one occasion. Stacy's father (NYPD Captain George Stacy) and Watson also figure out his secret on their own, but keep it to themselves. In 2001, even Peter's Aunt May discovers his secret.

Parker is beset by chronic personal and financial difficulties from the outset, such as having to earn enough money to pay his ailing Aunt May's medical bills; she had been poised at death's door virtually from the beginning of *The Amazing Spider-Man,* and even experienced "fake deaths" on two notable occasions. For many years, Peter Parker earned the money he needed to keep his aunt alive by selling photos of himself in action as Spider-Man (taken surreptitiously with an automatic camera, usually webbed to a wall) to his unsuspecting newsprint nemesis, Jameson. But Parker's earnings are barely sufficient to keep body and soul together, let alone properly maintain his Spider-Man costume; on one memorable occasion (*Spectacular Spider-Man* magazine #1), Parker had to make do with a knock-off Spider-Man uniform borrowed from a costume-shop window; on another (*ASM* vol. 1 #258, November 1984), he had to wear a paper bag over his head—and a Fantastic Four uniform lent to him by the Human Torch—while waiting for his Spidey suit to dry in a public Laundromat. Despite the myriad mundane problems Parker faces, he generally approaches life—and crime fighting—with an upbeat attitude and a sly sense of humor that often manifests as wisecracks delivered in the midst of battle.

As *The Amazing Spider-Man* developed through the 1960s, the series distinguished itself with a sense of moral ambiguity that the vast majority of its contemporaries lacked; thanks largely to the inflammatory editorials of *The Daily Bugle*'s Jameson, Spider-Man spends many years as a fugitive from the law, though all the while he is attempting to do good in the world. Spidey's reputation isn't helped when he is blamed for the death of George Stacy, who had actually been killed by Dr. Octopus (*ASM* vol. 1 #90, November 1970). The wall-crawler's first ongoing series is also unusual in that Parker and his supporting cast are not completely frozen in time in the manner of many competing comics. Issue #28 (September 1965) presents Parker's high school graduation. By issue #31 (December 1965) he begins his physics studies at Empire State University, where he meets Gwen Stacy, the first major love of his life, who would later be slain by the first Green Goblin. By issue #185 (October 1978), Parker graduates from college. And in *ASM Annual* #21 (1987), Parker marries the second great love of his life, Mary Jane Watson; in an alternate universe first glimpsed in *What If?* vol. 2 #105 (February 1998) and explored more thoroughly in the monthly *Spider-Girl* series (which debuted in October 1998), Parker and MJ eventually have a daughter named May "Mayday" Parker who inherits Dad's powers and takes up the family business of costumed crime fighting.

Steve Ditko, the artist who originated Spider-Man's characteristic lean, "spidery" look, left the series with issue #38, after which penciler John Romita took over the illustration chores, adding a dash more realism to the character's still-developing milieu and greatly affecting the look of the rest of the Marvel line as well (Romita eventually became the company's art director). It was Romita who provided the visuals for Spider-Man's climactic battle with the first Green Goblin in 1966, which broke another long-standing superhero taboo—both characters learn one another's secret identities (the Goblin is really Norman Osborn, the industrialist father of Parker's college roommate, Harry). Issues #96–#98 (May–July 1971) broke more new ground by portraying substance abuse by Harry Osborn. Although these three comics (written by Stan Lee and illustrated by Gil Kane) weighed in negatively on illegal drug use, the subject matter was sufficiently ahead of its time to prompt the Comics Code Authority (an industry self-censorship board) to withhold its seal of approval.

Many other Spider-Man artists and writers followed in the creative footsteps of Lee, Ditko, and Romita throughout the 1970s, including such scribes as Gerry Conway, Len Wein, and Marv Wolfman, and such illustrators as Gil Kane, Ross Andru, and Keith Pollard. Even prior to this period, Spider-Man was already a fast-expanding franchise, unable to be contained between the covers of a single monthly publication. Not only had the character crossed over into numerous other Marvel titles (this "shared universe" was always one of Marvel's most appealing features), but he spun off briefly into a large-format magazine titled *Spectacular Spider-Man,* which lasted only two issues (July and November 1968). Spidey's frequent crossovers with other Marvel characters led to a bimonthly title dedicated to this idea, *Marvel Team-Up,* which began in March 1972 and ran for 150 issues. The debut issue teamed Spider-Man with the Human Torch, and the series eventually paired him with nearly every high-profile character in the Marvel universe (the series was replaced by the *Web of Spider-Man* monthly series, which started in April 1985; *Marvel Team-Up* had a second incarnation, an eleven-issue run that began in September 1997).

A new monthly series called *Spidey Super Stories,* intended for younger readers, began publication in October 1974 and lasted for fifty-seven issues. As the 1970s continued, Spider-Man's adventures expanded into a fourth ongoing comic series (a monthly intended for the mainstream Spidey audience) titled *Peter Parker: The Spectacular Spider-Man* (later shortened to *The Spectacular Spider-Man*), which debuted in December 1976 and ran for 263 issues. Marvel parodied the character in such series as *Not Brand Echh* (1967–1969) and *Peter Porker, Spider-Ham* (a bimonthly that began in May 1985 as part of Marvel's kid-oriented Star Comics line). Spider-Man even left the confines of the Marvel universe itself when he took part in the first crossover between the heroes of Marvel and DC Comics in the large-format ("treasury-sized") *Superman vs. the Amazing Spider-Man* (1976), which heralded several more eagerly-anticipated intercompany crossings during the next several years. By April 1978, an unrelated character (Jessica Drew) became the star of Marvel's monthly *Spider-Woman* series, which ran for fifty issues and spawned two more brief series in the 1990s.

Although Spider-Man's editorial teams blazed fewer new trails than did either the Lee-Ditko or Lee-Romita pairings as the hero gained increased exposure during the late 1970s and early 1980s, this era still enjoyed some high-quality stories. Roger Stern's "The Kid Who Collected Spider-Man" (*ASM* vol. 1 #248, January 1984) is arguably the finest example. In this haunting, poignant tale, Spider-Man reveals his closely guarded secret identity to a young fan. It isn't until the last panel that readers discover the reason for this revelation—it is a gift to a child who is fated very soon to die from a terminal illness.

Spider-Man's most significant departure from tradition came more than two decades into his run. *ASM* vol. 1 #252 (May 1984) garbs Peter Parker in a new, black-and-white costume, which he acquires on a distant planet during the large-scale multi-hero/multi-villain twelve-issue *Marvel Super Heroes Secret Wars* crossover miniseries (May 1984 through April 1985). This living costume, which supplies its own web-fluid and morphs itself into street clothes in response to Parker's thoughts, turns out to have its own evil, manipulative intellect. After Parker realizes that the symbiotic costume is controlling him rather than vice versa, he discards it; the jilted costume subsequently "possesses" a former newspaper reporter named Eddie Brock. The costume and Brock—whose reputation was smeared after he had falsely accused Spider-Man of being the serial killer known as the Sin-Eater—join forces to settle their respective scores with the wall-crawler as Venom (*ASM* vol. 1 #300, May 1988). Venom resembles a supermuscular version of the black-and-white-clad Spider-Man, with the addition of hundreds of razor-sharp teeth and a long, prehensile tongue. This creature subsequently becomes one of Spider-Man's deadliest recurring villains. Venom also gives rise to the villain Carnage, who comes into existence when a piece of the symbiotic costume

bonds with a deadly convicted killer named Cletus Kasady (*ASM* vol. 1 #361, April 1992). Carnage subsequently comes into conflict with both Venom and Spider-Man on several occasions.

Another significant, if temporary, change Spider-Man experiences occurs during what is popularly known as the "cosmic Spidey saga," which ran in *Spectacular Spider-Man* #158–#160 (December 1989 through January 1990, written by Gerry Conway and penciled by Sal Buscema), *Web of Spider-Man* #59–#61 (December 1989 through February 1990, written by Gerry Conway and penciled by Alex Saviuk), and *ASM* vol. 1 #328 (January 1990, written by David Michelinie and illustrated by Todd McFarlane). In this arc, Parker's accidental exposure to an unknown energy source at an Empire State University lab increases his power-level by orders of magnitude; Spider-Man soon discovers that he possesses hyperacute senses and can shoot devastating blasts of force from his fingertips. However, Spider-Man also learns that with this even greater power comes even greater responsibility. A cosmic struggle to prevent a superpowered robot called the Tri-Sentinel from causing a meltdown at a nuclear reactor ultimately bleeds off Spidey's excess power, restoring him to his "normal" Spider-powered self.

The title that launched Spider-Man into the 1990s was called, simply enough, *Spider-Man,* and debuted in August 1990. *Spider-Man* showcased the writing and illustrations of fan-fave artist and *Spawn* originator Todd McFarlane, whose eye-grabbing, rococo style drew unprecedented fan attention to the character. Particularly noteworthy are the detailed renderings of "Ditko-esque" poses and the ornately braided "spaghetti webbing" that flow from Spidey's web-shooters. The first issue of *Spider-Man* also inaugurated Marvel's soon-to-be-ubiquitous practice of releasing a single comic book with multiple covers, a marketing maneuver that arguably appealed more to collector-speculators than to readers; nevertheless, that issue set a benchmark for sales, pumping more than 3 million copies into direct-market comics shops and news-stand venues around the world, a record that wouldn't be broken until the new *X-Men* title premiered the following year. November 1992 saw the release of the first issue of *Spider-Man 2099,* part of a group of titles set in the Marvel universe of the late twenty-first century. This future Spider-Man, whose real name was Miguel O'Hara, received his powers—which included a biologically extruded webbing that anticipated Sam Raimi's cinematic wall-crawler by a full decade—as a result of exposure to genetic-engineering treatments. *Spider-Man 2099* was published monthly until August 1996 (issue #46). *Spider-Man Unlimited* began its quarterly, twenty-three-issue run in May 1993, part of an aggressive Spidey publishing program that lasted throughout the 1990s, even though comics sales in general softened greatly as the decade wore on. Numerous limited series, graphic novels, and reprint collections continued to appear throughout this period.

One of the biggest shakeups in Parker's 1990s adventures was a story arc commonly known as "the clone saga," which began in the Spidey comics that bore October and November 1994 cover dates. This arc reveals that Peter Parker is actually a clone of Spider-Man made way back in *ASM* vol. 1 #149 (October 1975) by the Jackal (Miles Warren, one of Parker's college professors), while the real Peter Parker—who had been mistaken for a clone thought killed in an explosion along with the Jackal—returns in the guise of Ben Reilly (a combination of Ben Parker's first name and May Parker's maiden name). (*ASM* vol. 1 #150 [November 1975] had established that the "Peter Parker" left standing had never definitively learned whether he was the clone or the original.) After Reilly (a.k.a. Parker) returns to New York, the clone Peter Parker decides to leave behind his Spider-Man identity, allowing Reilly to take over as Spider-Man. This controversial development is regarded by many critics as one of the most significant editorial missteps in Spider-Man's checkered history because it was confusing and repudiated two decades of settled continuity.

The story arc was finally undone by the later revelation that Reilly was, in fact, *not* the original Peter Parker; the entire situation had been engineered by Norman Osborn, the original Green Goblin, who was back from the dead (*Spider-Man* #75, December 1996). Rather than committing wholesale revisionism on the Spidey milieu as the "clone saga" had, *Untold Tales of Spider-Man* (a twenty-five-issue series, beginning in September 1995) instead embroidered the existing web-slinging legend. Written with obvious respect and affection by acclaimed comics scribe Kurt Busiek, these stories were set very early in Spider-Man's timeline, "between the panels" of the earliest Lee-Ditko stories.

Every superheroic icon that endures for several decades is bound to accrete an unwieldy amount of backstory, and Spider-Man is no exception. In an effort to "scrape off the barnacles," Marvel broke with tradition yet again by ending *The Amazing Spider-Man*'s run with issue #441 (November 1998), as part of the "Final Chapter Arc," which continued in *Spider-Man* #97, *Spectacular Spider-Man* #263, and *Spider-Man* #98 (the final issues of those venerable series as well), preparatory to a controversial "reboot" of the character. In *Spider-Man: Chapter One* (which began in December 1998), writer-artist John Byrne—renowned for his complete rewrite of the history, origin, and powers of DC's Superman a dozen years earlier—updated Spider-Man's origin story, as well as his first year as a spandex-clad crime fighter, to mixed reactions. January 1999 saw the start of *Peter Parker, Spider-Man,* a new ongoing series, as well as the first issue of volume 2 of *The Amazing Spider-Man,* the revival of Spider-Man's flagship title. This series has run parallel to a reboot in *Ultimate Spider-Man* (which debuted in October 2000), in which writer Brian Michael Bendis retells the entire Spidey saga from a beginning moved up to the 2000s.

The Amazing Spider-Man vol. 2 #36 (December 2001), written by J. Michael Straczynski (the creator of the *Babylon 5* television series) and drawn by John Romita Jr., dealt with Spider-Man's reactions to the September 11, 2001 terrorist attacks on New York's World Trade Center, thereby gaining national media attention. Consistent with his "everyman" viewpoint, Spider-Man sees the non-superpowered police and fire personnel who risked—and lost—their lives during the catastrophe as the real heroes of the day. The carnage of September 11 forces Spider-Man to honestly confront the limits of his ability to thwart evil.

Now more than four decades into his existence, Spider-Man is still going strong, both as a storytelling vehicle and as one of the enduring icons of American popular culture. The principle new storylines can be found today in *Amazing Spider-Man* (vol. 2) and *Peter Parker: Spider-Man.* Reacting to the glutted, depressed comics market of the late 1990s, Marvel's editorial staff has taken great pains to ensure the quality of these titles, as well as producing several well-executed ancillary ones, including *Ultimate Spider-Man* (the previously referenced retelling of older tales from the Spidey canon); *Tangled Web,* whose stories emphasize off-beat perspective on various events and characters from Spider-Man's lengthy past; and a second *Spider-Man Unlimited* comic, which essentially replaced *Tangled Web* in 2004 and spotlights talents new to producing Spidey stories. High-profile writers who have signed exclusive contracts with Marvel to write about the enduring superhero include Straczynski and Kevin Smith, writer, producer, and director of such cult-classic films as *Clerks, Mallrats,* and *Chasing Amy.* With *ASM* highly popular and *Ultimate Spider-Man* releasing eighteen issues annually as of 2004, the wondrous wall-crawler clearly shows no sign of slowing down. And thanks to the mass exposure achieved by Raimi's 2002 megahit film *Spider-Man* and its many merchandising tie-ins, there is now no dearth of highly motivated Spidey readers. Although today's Spider-Man titles sell at nowhere near the multimillion-copy levels that characterized McFarlane's 1990 *Spider-Man* premiere, Marvel's friendly neighborhood forty-something arachnid is clearly not about to hang up

his webs any time soon, nor lose sight of the awesome responsibilities his powers bring. —*MAM*

Spider-Man in the Media

"Spider-Man, Spider-Man, does whatever a spider can. Spins a web any size, catches thieves just like flies, look out, here's comes the Spider-Man." So start the lyrics of one of the most famous superhero theme songs in history. Peter Parker was first bitten by the radioactive spider that gave him superpowers in *Amazing Fantasy* #15 (August 1962), but Stan Lee and Steve Ditko's creation would surge in popularity in 1967, with the debut of ABC's animated *Spiderman* series (without the official hyphen).

Following their work the previous year with the syndicated daily animated program called *The Marvel Super-Heroes,* animators and producers Robert Lawrence, Grant Simmons, and Ray Patterson—under the company name of Grantray-Lawrence—debuted the *Spiderman* cartoon on September 9. Opening the show was the catchy, jazzy theme song by Bob Harris and Paul Francis Webster. Viewers expecting the limited animation of *Marvel Super-Heroes* were treated to better visuals—even if much of the web-slinging scenes were reused over and over again—by animators including Disney artist Shamus Culhane and a young Ralph Bakshi.

The *Spiderman* stories hewed closely to their comic-book counterparts. Villains included Doctor Octopus, Electro, Mysterio, the Green Goblin, and the Lizard, and also newly created villains such as the Imposter and Dr. Zap. Canadian actors were used to fill the voice roles; Bernard Cowan played the hero for the first season, while Peter Soles became his voice for the second season. A total of 52 half-hour shows were completed, with 50 eleven-minute stories and 27 twenty-two-minute stories included. *Spiderman* was popular enough to last

Tobey Maguire portrays the web-slinging hero in *Spider-Man*.

until September 1970, and has been a hit in syndication markets ever since.

The next place Spidey appeared was a surprise for fans. Children's Television Workshop had a public television series called *The Electric Company*. The educational show started in 1971, but it was during the 1974–1977 seasons that it had a special guest-star. A live-action Spider-Man appeared in almost thirty short segments, fighting Dracula, the Wall, a Yeti, worms, and assorted nasty people. The shorts taught young viewers life lessons, though the always-silent Spider-Man (Danny Seagren) wasn't his usual talkative self; instead, thought balloons above him expressed what he was thinking.

With the exception of some full-cast audio adventures and a "rock opera" released on record and tape, Peter Parker's alter ego was down for

another few years, until Stan Lee hit Hollywood. There, Lee sold CBS on the idea of a *Spider-Man* live-action series. Charles Fries was soon producing the show, and on September 14, 1977, *Spider-Man* premiered in primetime with a two-hour pilot film. Nicholas Hammond (Friedrich von Trapp in *The Sound of Music*) snared the dual role of Peter Parker/Spider-Man, while David White (of *Bewitched* fame) played the blustering J. Jonah Jameson. The younger Aunt May was played by Irene Tedrow, while Michael Pataki played the new Police Captain Barbera, a constant thorn in Spider-Man's side.

Although *Spider-Man* did well in the ratings—and a semi-regular series called *The Amazing Spider-Man* ran in spring 1978—CBS failed to greenlight a regular series. Eight more episodes spottily aired from September 1978 through July 1979, before the network chopped Spidey's web-line in two. Although the series did not feature any costumed villains, and the web-shooting effects were cheesey, the wall-crawling scenes with stuntmen subbing for Hammond were excellent.

Spidey's next media appearance was never seen by U.S. audiences (except on bootleg videos). A Japanese *Spider-Man* (pronounced "Soupaidaman") ran on TV Tokyo from May 7, 1978 through March 14, 1979. There were forty-one total episodes, produced by the famous Toei Company. In this version, motocross racer Yamashiro Takuya (Kayama Kousuke) was given a special bracelet by a dying spider-alien. Using his new powers to stick to walls and spin webs, Spider-Man was also equipped with a flying car called the Spider Machine GP-7, a flying fortress called "The Marveller," and a giant robot called "Leopardon" which would throw its sword to stop evildoers. Invariably, Spider-Man would face alien creatures from the Iron Cross Group, all of which could grow to be giant-sized monsters. Leading the Iron Cross was Professor Monster (Andou Mitsuo) and Amazoness (Kagawa Yukie).

Back in the States, animation beckoned again, and Spider-Man answered the call, appearing as a guest-star on ABC's *Spider-Woman* series from DePatie-Freleng during the 1979–1980 season. That company would also develop a new spider-series for NBC, debuting *Spider-Man and His Amazing Friends* in September 1981. With smooth animation that echoed comic-book artist John Romita's style, the series teamed Spidey with fellow crime fighters Iceman and Firestar, a female character created especially for the show. "Spider-Friends," as the show was called by fans, often guest-starred other superheroes such as the X-Men, Captain America, the Sub-Mariner, Dr. Strange, the Black Knight, and even little-known jungle heroine Shanna the She-Devil! Villains included the Red Skull, Mysterio, Green Goblin, Chameleon, and Loki.

In September 1982, the series expanded to an hour, with new adventures of the Hulk taking half the time slot for *The Incredible Hulk and the Amazing Spider-Man.* The third and final season of the series in 1983–1984 found the billing reversed and the show became *The Amazing Spider-Man and the Incredible Hulk.* Concurrently with the first Spider-Friends series, a syndicated *Spider-Man* solo series ran in some markets. The twenty-six episodes had actually been completed prior to *Spider-Man and His Amazing Friends,* but aired in the 1981–1982 seasons. Because they were not syndicated in all areas of the country, this is one of the least-known versions of *Spider-Man* on television. In this series, the plots again stayed close to their comics roots, and Spidey battled Dr. Doom, Electro, the Lizard, Doctor Octopus, Green Goblin and Kingpin. In 1988—the year after the web-spinner debuted as a giant balloon in the Macy's Thanksgiving Day parade—the *Spider-Man* solo episodes were re-syndicated as part of the *Marvel Action Universe* series.

In November 1994, Fox aired a preview episode of a new animated *Spider-Man* series (often called *Spider-Man: The Animated Series,* though not in the credits), but the series proper did not begin until February 1995. After comic-book writer Martin Pasko left the show in its developmental stages, animation veteran John Semper stepped in to finish development and get the show on track. Although the first season started out with single-part stories that had some character continuity, by the end of the season, and into the next, the show had multi-episode story arcs. The creators brought in many aspects of the *Spider-Man* comic-book universe, including the black alien costume, and friends and foes such as Venom, Morbius the Living Vampire, the Punisher, Rocket Racer, Hydro Man, Dr. Strange, Daredevil, Carnage, Kraven, Black Cat, and more. By the end of its high-rated fifth season in 1998, sixty-five adventures had been produced, giving this *Spider-Man* the record for highest amount of Spider-time on television.

In October 1999, Fox decided to relaunch Spidey in a new milieu. In *Spider-Man Unlimited,* the web-spinning hero was accidentally trapped on Counter Earth, a parallel world like Earth except for beastmen bred by the High Evolutionary, though Spidey also faced Venom and Carnage there. Attired in a new costume and aided by Machine Man X-51 and good versions of Vulture and Goblin, Spider-Man fought to protect the people of Counter Earth. Although the series was intended to run at least three years, *Spider-Man Unlimited* flopped in the ratings. Taken off the air with only four episodes shown, the series finally returned in December 2000 for the remainder of its initial thirteen episodes.

Part of the reason that the concept of *Spider-Man Unlimited* was so far away from its comic-book reality was that the *Spider-Man* feature film was *finally* about to get underway. It had been a long time in coming. A movie version of the web-spinner's adventures was first announced in the early 1980s, with *Poltergeist* helmer Tobe Hooper originally slated to direct a big-budget pic for Cannon from a script by Leslie Stevens. Then Hooper bowed out and the film was announced for Christmas 1985, directed by Joseph Zito (*Missing In Action III*) with a script by Ted Newsom and John Brancato. Further announced dates included Christmas 1986, Easter 1987, and Christmases 1987, 1988, and 1990. Multiple scripts were written, by Joseph Goldman, Barney Cohen, Don Michael Paul, Ethan Wiley, Frank LaLoggia, and Neil Ruttenberg. Even the movie company changed, with the collapse of Cannon; movie mogul Menahem Golan's 21st Century Productions picked up the rights, and Golan planned to have *Captain America* feature-helmer and B-movie man Albert Pyun direct.

Through the 1990s, scripting or getting attached to the "upcoming" *Spider-Man* film production seemed almost a cottage industry. A pilot script was written for a new ABC TV series by Manny Coto, working for New World (which owned Marvel). On the film front, *Terminator* and *Aliens* director James Cameron wrote a treatment and planned to direct the proposed feature. The web became even more tangled as Golan sold pieces of the rights to Vicaom, Carolco, and Columbia Tri-Star, and Carolco eventually sold their rights to MGM. In 1993 and 1994, multiple lawsuits were filed by all the companies claiming to own the *Spider-Man* rights. The battles finally ended in 1999, and on March 1 of that year, Sony Pictures Entertainment and Marvel Enterprises announced a deal to develop *Spider-Man* for film, television, and merchandise.

Work began on a new script, with David Koepp adapting Cameron's treatment, then Scott Rosenberg and Alvin Sargent coming aboard. Practically every young male actor in Hollywood (and a few older ones) were rumored to be testing for the role of Peter Parker/Spider-Man, and multiple hot film directors were rumored to be helming. In 2000, the dust settled, and Sam Raimi was announced as the director, with Tobey Maguire as Spider-Man. Other cast members included Willem Dafoe as the Green Goblin, and Kirsten Dunst as girlfriend Mary Jane Watson. As rumors flew fast and furious on the Internet, the most controversial element of the film was that Spider-Man's webshooters would be organic, with the webbing coming directly from Parker's wrists.

By the time of its release on May 3, 2002, *Spider-Man* was one of the most widely anticipated films of the new millennium. Merchandising was omnipresent, and opening weekend netted over $114 million! The film would eventually top over $400 million in the United States alone. Critics adored the film, and fans did as well, thanks to a pleasant story, good acting, incredible special effects, and a costume that made real Spider-Man's red-and-blue comic-book threads.

Even as filming for *Spider-Man 2* was underway, in July 2003 MTV debuted a new computer-animated *Spider-Man* series that took its continuity not only from the *Spider-Man* feature film, but also from 2003's *Daredevil* movie (with a guest-appearance by the Kingpin). Acclaimed *Ultimate Spider-Man*

Opposite: Tobey Maguire (Spider-Man) and Kirsten Dunst (Mary Jane Watson) share a tender moment in *Spider-Man*.

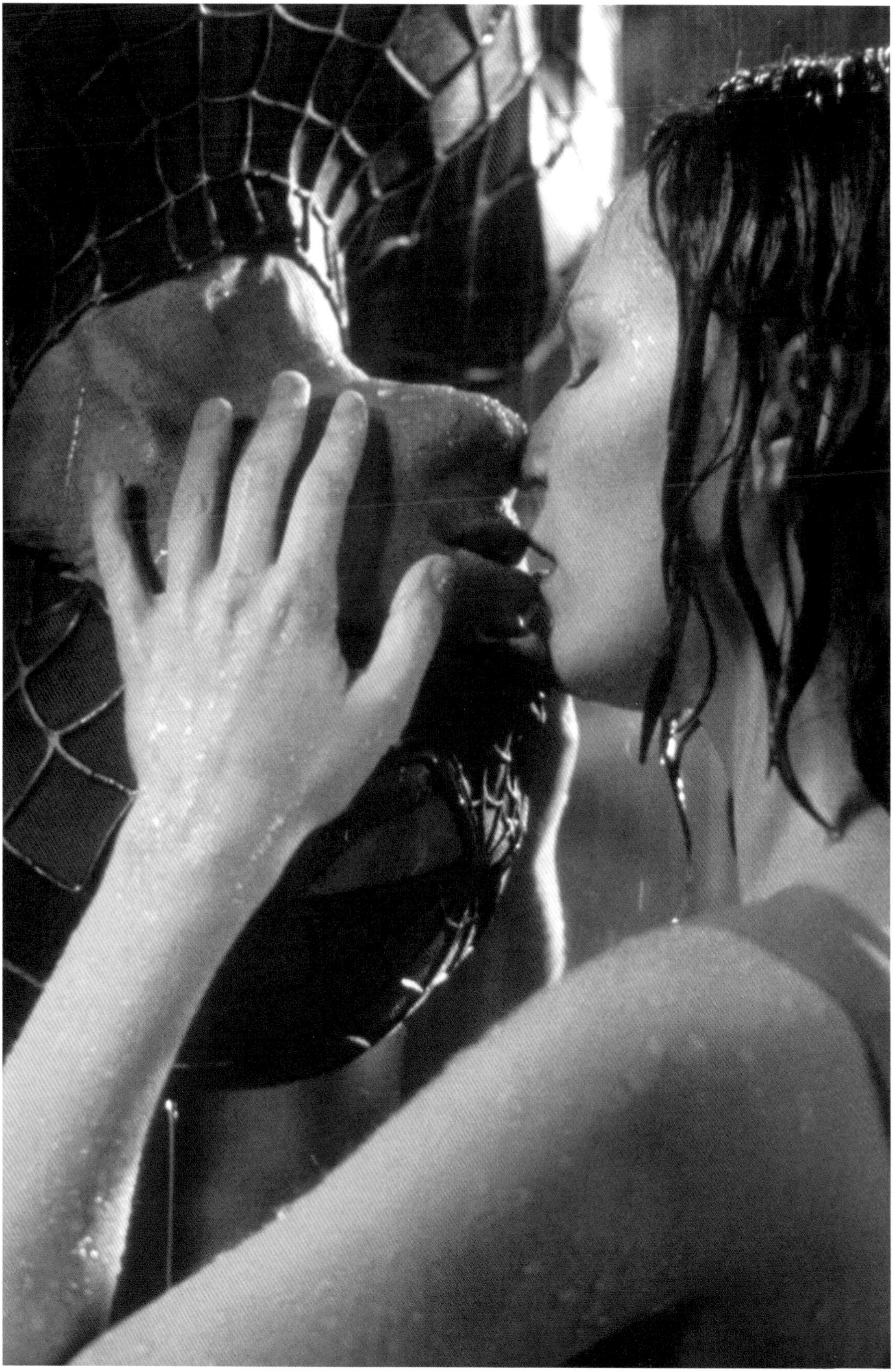

comic-book writer Brian Michael Bendis took an active part in developing the series, which skewed older than its animated predecessors. Stars aplenty dropped by to voice characters: Neil Patrick Harris took on the title role, with Lisa Loeb as Mary Jane, while guests included Gina Gershon, Ed Asner, Rob Zombie, Jeffrey Combs, and Michael Clarke Duncan. Only thirteen episodes of the MTV series were produced.

Announced to debut on June 30, 2004, *Spider-Man 2* sees many returning cast members from the first film, including Maguire, Dunst, James Franco as Harry Osborn, Rosemary Harris as Aunt May, and J. K. Simmons as J. Jonah Jameson. New to the cast this time is the pre-Lizard scientist Dr. Curt Connors (played by Dylan Baker), and the mechanically armed villain Dr. Octopus (Alfred Molina). With Sam Raimi back in the director's chair as well, and a script by Koepp, Sargent, Alfred Gough, Miles Millar, and Michael Chabon, the web-slinger is again poised to make a multi-million-dollar mark in theaters and in the licensing arena. Uncle Ben may have warned Peter that "with great power comes great responsibility," but as Spider-Man's media appearances have shown over the years, with good spider-stories come great paychecks as well. —AM

Spider-Man Villains

The greatness of any superhero is determined by the quality of the adversaries he or she must overcome, and Marvel Comics' Spider-Man is no exception to this axiom. Over the course of more than four decades, supervillains such as Dr. Octopus, the Green Goblin, Kraven the Hunter, the Kingpin, and Venom have become enduring icons of roguery, constantly challenging both Spider-Man and his writers to make their heroic best efforts.

The principal distinguishing characteristic of Spidey's most enduring nemesis, Dr. Octopus (created by scripter Stan Lee and plotter-artist Steve Ditko), is four superstrong, lightning-quick, prehensile metal tentacles; like his principal foe, Spider-Man (Peter Parker), Dr. Octopus styles himself after an eight-limbed creature, and his origin story from 1963 (in *The Amazing Spider-Man* vol. 1 #3) bears similarities to that of the wall-crawler as well.

Shy and bookish as a child, young Otto Octavius excels at his studies, eventually earning a doctorate in physics and becoming a brilliant nuclear scientist. Dr. Octavius toils ceaselessly at scientific endeavors, becoming not only nationally famous but also extremely egotistical, keeping his co-workers literally at arm's length with the mechanical-arm harness he wears when handling hazardous materials—until an accidental lab explosion permanently bonds the metal limbs to his body and gives him mental (rather than merely mechanical) control over them. He can extend each limb from about six to twenty-five feet in length, moving them even more quickly and easily than he can his four natural limbs. But the accident also unhinges the self-absorbed Octavius, who turns his talents to superpowered crime, largely of the "rule-the-world-and-avenge-my-many-previous-humiliations" variety.

Although Dr. Octopus occasionally menaces the Fantastic Four, Spider-Man has always been "Doc Ock's" principal foe. Dr. Octopus is the first villain to publicly unmask Spider-Man, though without exposing the hero's true (teenage geek) identity, which no one, least of all Ock, finds believable. Ock also causes the death of NYPD Captain George Stacy, the father of Gwen Stacy, Peter Parker's first serious girlfriend, and later hides out from the police in a room rented from Parker's Aunt May, whom he nearly marries, to Parker's enormous chagrin. Ock later unmasks Spidey a second time and cures the hero of a lethal virus, only to be killed shortly thereafter by the cloned Spidey villain known as Kaine—and is briefly replaced by a female Dr. Octopus named Carolyn Trainer. Proving the axiom

Spider-Man and the Hobgoblin square off in the animated show *Spider-Man*.

that death in comics is largely only an inconvenience, Octavius is soon restored to life by the Hand, a mystical Asian crime syndicate; afterward, Ock has no recollection of having discovered Spider-Man's secret identity. Dr. Octopus remains one of Spidey's most lethal foes to this day.

The Green Goblin, another classic Lee-Ditko creation from a 1964 issue of *The Amazing Spider-Man* (vol. 1 #14), is another mainstay of Spider-Man's rogues' gallery. Norman Osborn, growing up watching the many failures of his inventor father (Amberson Osborn), becomes obsessed with amassing power and wealth at an early age. Pursuing collegiate studies in business, chemistry, and chemical engineering, Norman Osborn forms Osborn Chemical in partnership with Dr. Mendel Stromm, one of his professors. After having the

embezzling Stromm arrested and taking over his interest in the company, Osborn discovers in Stromm's notebooks a chemical formula capable of greatly increasing human strength and intelligence. Unaware that his young son Harry has innocently rearranged some of the chemicals in his lab, Norman tries to use Stromm's formula on himself, only to cause a violent explosion. After recovering from his injuries, it becomes evident that Osborn's experiment has made him superhuman—but has also rendered him criminally insane.

After outfitting supervillains such as the Scorcher and the Headsman to help expand his wealth, Osborn develops the Green Goblin's demonic costume, the turbine-powered Goblin Glider he will fly into battle, and an arsenal of explosive pumpkin bombs. Thus equipped, he attempts to establish his own underworld credentials by trying to kill Spider-Man. His presence concealed by a compound that dulls Spider-Man's danger-detecting "spider sense," the Goblin discovers the hero's secret identity and imprisons Parker in a secret hideout, where he reveals his own true identity to Parker. During a climactic battle, Osborn runs afoul of high-voltage wires, which leave him amnesiac and prompt the kind-hearted Spidey to leave him alone.

Osborn's memories soon return, culminating in several clashes between the Goblin and Spider-Man. During the most memorable of these 1970s contretemps, the Goblin kidnaps Gwen Stacy and hurls her to her death from the top of the George Washington Bridge, only to impale himself (apparently fatally) on his own Goblin Glider shortly thereafter in an attempt to murder Spider-Man. To protect his father's reputation, Harry Osborn hides the Green Goblin's costume and equipment and buys a coroner's silence about the presence of the Goblin formula in the elder Osborn's blood. After accidentally discovering that Spider-Man is actually his roommate Parker, the mentally unstable and drug-addicted Harry assumes the Goblin's identity and begins waging his own battles against the wall-crawler, though he is later rehabilitated by Dr. Barton Hamilton, a psychiatrist who eventually becomes the third Green Goblin. Years later, in 1983, the ruthless fashion designer and business-man Roderick Kingsley takes up the Green Goblin's mantle as the Hobgoblin.

Harry Osborn later reprises his role as the Green Goblin after exposing himself to a lethally toxic Green Goblin formula. While dying of chemical poisoning, Osborn menaces Spider-Man and his wife, Mary Jane Watson-Parker, but ultimately sacrifices himself to prevent the death of his son, Normy. Unknown to everyone during this period, Norman Osborn's chemically spawned powers have enabled him to survive his apparent death. After years of living underground, the original Green Goblin emerges in the 1990s to perform some of his most heinous acts: He takes over Kingsley's corpo-ration; cruelly fakes Aunt May's death; murders Ben Reilly, Spider-Man's clone; and complicates Parker's life even further by purchasing his workplace, the *Daily Bugle*—thus reclaiming his original position as one of the premier bad guys in the Spider-Man mythos. Norman Osborn later begins trying to force Parker into becoming the heir to his criminal enter-prises, as told in the popular *Revenge of the Green Goblin* miniseries, which ran from October through December 2000. Like Doc Ock, death can scarcely slow the Green Goblin down.

Kraven the Hunter sprang from the fertile minds of Lee and Ditko in *Amazing Spider-Man* vol. 1 #15 in August 1964. Descended from the van-ished Russian aristocracy, Sergei Kravinoff garners a reputation as the greatest hunter in the world and seeks out an unusual trophy—Spider-Man's head. His strength, reflexes, and senses greatly augment-ed by exotic jungle elixirs, Kraven hunts Spidey on numerous occasions, and finally succeeds in bury-ing him alive. Taking possession of Spider-Man's late (and unlamented) black costume, Kraven briefly takes the wall-crawler's place—defeating the rodentlike villain known as Vermin—to prove his superiority over his vanquished foe before taking his own life in accordance with his twisted sense of honor. Kraven's son Vladimir Kravinoff (created by writer Howard Mackie and artists Tom Lyle and Scott Hanna) followed in his father's footsteps, tak-ing on the guise of the Grim Hunter. He fought Spidey (unsuccessfully) only once (in *Peter Parker: Spider Man* #47, June 1994) before being killed by the villain Kaine not quite a year later.

In 1967, Stan Lee and artist John Romita Sr. created Wilson Fisk, the crime boss known as the Kingpin, a man distinguished by his ruthlessness (he commits his first murder at the tender age of twelve), his huge size, his expensive suits, a ciga-rette holder, and a diamond-studded laser-blasting walking stick. Though he appears to be grossly fat in his introduction in *Amazing Spider-Man* vol. 1 #50, the Kingpin is actually a deceptively quick pow-erhouse whose bulk is composed of solid muscle, and he fights Spider-Man to a standstill on many occasions; in the 1980s he becomes the principal enemy of Daredevil. Apart from the occasional turf war, the Kingpin—who was once the supervillain known as the Brainwasher in the late 1960s—has long been considered the leader of New York's underworld, and numbers most of the city's other mob bosses among his enemies. Despite his toughness, the Kingpin's strong-willed wife Vanessa exerts a powerful influence over him. Their adult son Richard also enters the family business, adopting the personae of the underworld figures known as the Schemer and the Rose, who becomes one of the Kingpin's greatest criminal rivals.

The Kingpin's reign over the underworld comes to an end in 1992 when Daredevil, several other crime bosses, and the criminal organization called Hydra (run by the Red Skull) defeat him. Undeterred, Fisk quietly rebuilds his illicit empire and mounts simultaneous attacks on such criminal rivals as Norman Osborn, Hammerhead, Silvermane, Caesar Cicero, and Don Fortunato. The Kingpin once again claws his way back up by 1998, only to be shot, dumped into a river, and struck blind by a gunshot to the face fired by a Fisk employee named Echo, whose father the Kingpin had murdered. Later Richard Fisk and a Kingpin employee named Silke stage a coup against the Kingpin, who has agreed to drop a dime on his fellow crime bosses to prevent his beloved Vanessa from leaving him. Vanessa foils this plot, saving the Kingpin's life and killing Silke's men as well as Richard, her own son. Leaving the Kingpin's empire divided, Vanessa flees with her husband to Europe, where he convalesces.

The serpent-tongued, shark-toothed creature known as Venom is truly the stuff of nightmares. He was brought to eerie life by writers David Michelinie and Tom DeFalco, writer-artist Todd McFarlane, and artists Ron Frenz and Brett Breeding in the late 1980s, a time when supervillains were becoming darker, grittier, and more vicious than ever before. After Spider-Man shreds his costume during the *Marvel Super Heroes Secret Wars* crossover mini-series (May 1984 through April 1985), he adopts a new jet-black costume that turns out to be a sentient alien life-form that feeds on his adrenaline. Spidey wears the costume for the next several months, taking advantage of its convenient ability to transform itself into civilian clothing. Spidey's subsequent discovery of the alien costume's desire to bond permanently with him leads him to ditch it. The jilted costume later joins with the suicidal ex-*Daily Globe* reporter Eddie Brock, who hated Spider-Man for ruining his career with the revelation that his biggest news story—which purported to reveal the identity of the late murderer known as the Sin-Eater—was a fraud. United in their antipathy toward Spider-Man, Brock and the alien symbiote costume begin a rampage through New York as the grisly, violent composite creature called Venom.

Seeing Spider-Man as evil, Venom believes himself to be "protecting" innocent people from the hero's depredations. Venom also finds himself at odds with Carnage, an even more horrible, violent creature who comes into being after a piece of the alien symbiote bonds with a criminal named Cletus Kasady, who made his debut in 1992 in *Amazing Spider-Man* vol. 1 #361. Though he actually behaves in a heroic fashion on several occasions, Venom's belief that people he regards as "evil" (including Peter Parker) should be killed places him squarely in the "villain" column.

Venom later fights Spider-Man's clone, Ben Reilly, who manages to separate Brock from the symbiote temporarily. Afterward, Brock and the alien costume rejoin, becoming more violent, crazy, and dangerous than ever before. After Spider-Man's 1998 "continuity reboot," Venom (now somehow unaware of Spidey's secret identity) becomes part of the Sinister Six, along with such Spidey mainstays as Electro and Sandman, both of whom he attacks savagely. After calling a truce with Spidey, then declaring war again, the emotionally unstable Venom is once again split back into his component beings by the part human/part alien Senator Stewart Ward. The symbiote was next seen in a popular version in the parallel-universe *Ultimate Spider-Man* series in the early 2000s, and in a 2003 *Venom* series from the Tsunami line of youth-oriented reboots. Like any good Spidey villain, Venom can't stay out of the fray—or avoid starring in a new self-titled series—for long. —*MAM*

Spider-Woman

Given the number of women in the Marvel universe who have taken on the mantle of Spider-Woman, one might think that the role was charmed. On the contrary, it is more cursed. One of Marvel Comics' most recognizable heroines in the 1970s, Spider-Woman is now retired, and the various people who have filled the persona are now a score of supporting characters, even as Spider-Girl, a futuristic version of her, hangs onto her own series with the sticky tenacity of a wall-crawler. Pull back the webs, and take a look at the twisting history of Spider-Woman.

Concerned that someone in either animation or comics would create a female character whose name played off its most popular property, Spider-Man, Marvel's then-president Stan Lee backed the decision to debut a femme fatale named Spider-Woman. Writer/editor Archie Goodwin created the character for *Marvel Spotlight* #32 (February 1977), working with artist Sal Buscema. In this story, the character was an agent for the villainous organization Hydra, assigned to kill Nick Fury, agent of S.H.I.E.L.D., and her origin involved her being mutated from a real spider! A four-issue guest-stint in *Marvel Two-In-One* (#30–#33, August–November 1977) ended with the now-heroic Spider-Woman learning she actually had a different backstory....

Spider-Woman's "true" origin was revealed in *Spider-Woman* #1 (April 1978). Jessica Drew learned that she had been exposed to radioactive uranium while a child, and that her scientist father had injected her with an experimental serum made of irradiated spider's blood to cure her. Put in cryogenic stasis,

Jessica aged slowly, and was later released. Jessica discovered that she could fire bio-electric "venom blasts," had the ability to stick to walls, had superhuman strength and speed, was immune to most toxins, and could secrete pheromones that made men desire her and women fear her. Her red-and-yellow costume also had a pair of glider wings that allowed her to approximate flying.

In the *Spider-Woman* comic-book series, Drew lived for a while in Los Angeles, and became known to the public as a superpowered bounty hunter. She faced villains such as the sixth-century sorceress Morgan le Fay, Gypsy Moth, the Brothers Grimm, Viper, and others. Eventually, she moved to San Francisco and became a private detective as well. Along the way, Drew romanced S.H.I.E.L.D. agent Jerry Hunt, and worked with both wheelchair-bound criminologist Scotty McDowell and a dark hero named the Shroud.

After a rotating series of writers, including Michael Fleisher, Chris Claremont, and Ann Nocenti, *Spider-Woman* was a muddled mess. Her powers were faltering, her supporting cast had changed numerous times, and her origin had been revised and expanded upon until it confused even longtime fans. *Spider-Woman* ended at issue #50 (June 1983), with a story that appeared to have her body killed, her astral self trapped in limbo, and all memory of her erased from the Marvel universe.

The ending of *Spider-Woman* was an odd choice for so visible a character. After Filmation created an animated heroine named Web-Woman for the CBS animated series *Tarzan and the Super 7* (1978–1980), Depatie-Freleng sold ABC a *Spider-Woman* animated series. Debuting September 22, 1979, the show lasted one season, with sixteen episodes (including a Spider-Man guest appearance). The show followed comic-book history very loosely. Jessica Drew was now the publisher of *Justice Magazine,* using her enhanced spider-sense to warn her of dangers around the world. Spinning in a circle like Wonder Woman, Drew (the voice of Joan Van Ark) would become Spider-Woman and fly to danger. Often, she would also have to rescue *Justice* photographer/love interest Jeff Hunt and her smarty-pants nephew, Billy Drew; they would travel to sites of trouble in the Justice Jet Copter. The heroine faced mummies, Vikings, Dracula, and a few comic-book adversaries such as Kingpin and Dormammu. While *Spider-Woman* was on the air, she enjoyed a healthy licensing run, appearing on T-shirts, costumes, underwear, school supplies, stickers, Slurpee cups, and more. Once the show disappeared, her appearances on licensed product grew less frequent.

Jessica Drew didn't stay dead for long, thanks to the Avengers and Dr. Strange, who helped revive her in the comic books, even though she lost her powers in the process (*The Avengers* #240–#241, February–March 1984). Drew continued her life as a private detective in San Francisco, though she later worked in the East Asian city of Madripoor, a job which brought her into contact with Wolverine numerous times. In modern stories, Drew has worked alongside and even mentored her counterparts, and it appears that some of her superpowers have returned. (Behind the scenes, writer Brian Michael Bendis wanted Drew to be the heroine of his Marvel MAX series *Alias;* when he could not use her, he created ex-heroine Jessica Jones instead, and later had her meet Drew in a memorable storyline that also involved the third Spider-Woman.)

The second Spider-Woman was Julia Carpenter, a single mother from Denver, Colorado. First glimpsed in *Marvel Super-Heroes Secret Wars* #6 (October 1984), this Spider-Woman wore a black costume with white boots and gloves, and a white spider-symbol across her chest. Her powers— gained from secret exposure to spider venom by the evil Commission—included the ability to psionically stick to walls and ceilings, as well as to create strong "psi-webs" of energy. She also had enhanced strength and speed. She became a member of Freedom Force, a government-sponsored group that captured super-criminals such as the Brotherhood of Evil Mutants. Spider-Woman aided

Spider-Woman #1 © 1978 Marvel Comics.
COVER ART BY JOE SINNOTT.

the Avengers as well, and later joined Avengers West Coast and Force Works, but her career was cut short when a villainous opponent—also calling herself Spider-Woman—stole her powers. Prior to starring in *Avengers West Coast* and *Force Works,* Carpenter appeared in her own four-part *Spider-Woman* miniseries (November 1993–February 1994). She also appeared as one of the semi-regular characters in the syndicated 1994–1996 series *Iron Man,* part of Marvel Films and New World Entertainment's animated *The Marvel Action Hour.*

The third heroine to wear the Spider-Woman mantle was actually a teen girl named Martha "Mattie" Franklin. Taking her father's place in a mystical ceremony, tomboy Franklin gained great strength. A fan of Spider-Man, Franklin took on the name Spider-Woman, until she lost her powers to Charlotte Witter, an evil woman who was aided by Doctor Octopus in stealing the powers of all three Spider-Women. Franklin eventually stole the powers back, gaining her immediate predecessor's powers and more—flight, super strength, venom blasts, psionic webbing, psychic powers, and adhesion—in the process. Franklin faced villains such as Shadrac, Nighteyes, and Flesh and Bones in the third *Spider-Woman* series, which lasted eighteen issues (July 1999–December 2000). Franklin turned up in the same *Alias* storyline (#16–#21, January–June 2003) as Drew, where it was discovered that she was addicted to drugs, and that her pusher was using her blood to give his own drugs a super-boost.

Although she does not bear the name Spider-Woman yet, one girl in a potential Marvel future might one day take on that name. In a not-too-distant future, Peter Parker has retired his life as Spider-Man to live with his wife, Mary Jane, and daughter, May Parker. Shortly after May exhibits signs of superstrength and speed, Peter is forced into a battle against the Green Goblin's vindictive grandson. Learning her father's secret, May takes one of his spare costumes and web-shooters and battles the Goblin, saving her father's life and embarking on a career as Spider-Girl. First appearing in *What If?* #105 (February 1998), May garnered her own series debut in *Spider-Girl* #1 (October 1998). In the ensuing years, she has fought old-time spider-villains such as Venom, as well as new and updated villains such as Dragon King, Mr. Nobody, Crazy Eight, Spyral, and Raptor. Although the *Spider-Girl* series has been on the brink of cancellation many times since, a vociferous fan base has always rallied for the series and saved it, making it the longest-running solo series starring a female character in Marvel history. It seems that, not unlike cats, *Spider-Woman* and *Spider-Girl* may have nine lives. —*AM*

The Spirit

In the early days of comic books, aspiring artists could look to Lou Fine's work on the *Black Condor* for tips on anatomy, to Jack Kirby's *Captain America* for excitement, and to Bob Kane's *Batman* for mood. For storytelling, drama, inventiveness, characterization, and pacing, they turned to one of the medium's true innovators, Will Eisner, and his legendary newspaper feature, *The Spirit.* Eisner came into comic books in the mid-1930s and, together with Jerry Iger, created one of the first packaging firms—the Eisner/Iger studio—producing comics for the many companies entering the nascent field. Along with Fiction House and Fox, one of the studio's clients was Quality Comics, and it was Quality owner Everett "Busy" Arnold and the Des Moines Register and Tribune Syndicate who offered Eisner a partnership to produce for syndication a sixteen-page comic-book insert for Sunday newspapers, which would compete with the increasingly popular superhero comics springing up in the wake of *Superman.* After selling his half of Eisner and Iger, from early 1940 to 1942 Eisner and his new studio created a host of features for such Quality titles as *National, Smash, Blackhawk, Uncle Sam* and *Military Comics,* as well as the ground-breaking newspaper section, *The Spirit.*

The Spirit was marketed through the Des Moines Register and Tribune Syndicate, and the feature was eventually sold to approximately twenty newspapers, reaching a readership of 5 million. *The Spirit* section itself was a separate, sixteen-page, coverless insert, consisting of a lead seven- or eight-page *Spirit* strip by Eisner and two backup strips: *Lady Luck* (a detective feature by Chuck Mazoujian) and *Mr. Mystic* (a magician created by Bob Powell). The Spirit himself appeared in a daily newspaper strip from 1941 to 1944, and on-air in a short-lived radio show.

Appearing in June 1940, the first *Spirit* section introduced readers to the dashing private detective and criminologist Denny Colt, who is given a tip-off about mad scientist and all-round bad guy Dr. Cobra by his curmudgeonly friend, Central City Police Commissioner Dolan. Colt tracks down Cobra to catacombs beneath Chinatown but is accidentally drenched by a strange chemical. When Dolan and the police find him later, he is pronounced dead at the scene and buried in Wildwood Cemetery. However, when Colt shows up two days later at Dolan's police-headquarters office, Colt reveals that the liquid had merely induced a temporary state of suspended animation. The newly resurrected Colt decides to let the world carry on believing in his demise as a cover for his pursuit of the mad doctor, under the guise of "The Spirit." With Dolan in tow, and donning a blue business suit, gloves, hat, and domino mask as a "costume," the Spirit finally tracks down Cobra, who dies in a hail of bullets. Afterward, the hero decides to stay "dead," declaring, "There are criminals and crimes beyond the reach of the police, but the Spirit can reach them."

Arnold and the Syndicate had wanted a superhero to rival Superman, but Eisner had dreams of creating a more complex strip for the older, sophisticated newspaper readership, one that was not cut from the same superhero cloth as the Man of Steel. Eisner's compromise was to give the Spirit a small mask, covering his eyes, and a uniform (of sorts)—a white, long-sleeved shirt, blue suit, fedora hat, and gloves—which was (almost) ever-present over the feature's twelve-year existence. With his *de facto* costume and dual identity, though no superpowers of which to speak, the Spirit became one of the first detective heroes to stick with audiences. Over the strip's first few weeks, Eisner introduced the hero's slightly macabre hideout—a well-appointed laboratory (for his clever inventions, such as smoke pellets and the short-lived car and plane) underneath Wildwood Cemetery—and the strip's colorful supporting cast. Principal among these were Commissioner Dolan's beautiful, blonde daughter Ellen, whose main goal in life appeared to be to marry the Spirit, and Ebony White, a plucky

The Spirit #48 © 1988 Will Eisner.
COVER ART BY WILL EISNER.

young black cabbie who soon became the hero's driver, comic foil, and *de facto* sidekick.

In its first few years, the feature was a more or less a traditional detective comic, albeit one laced with humor and the sort of energy found only in the comic books, but what set it apart from its rivals were Eisner's sophisticated storytelling, his inventiveness, and his ability to cram a witty, intelligent whodunit into seven pages. A lifelong fan of the movies (counting the films of Orson Welles, Alfred Hitchcock, and Man Ray among his influences), Eisner played around with "camera angles," page layouts and pacing, and changing panel shapes, sizes, and viewpoints to affect how his audience read the strip. If he wanted to slow a sequence down or speed it up, he had the visual tricks to do it, and to a large extent he was inventing the visual language of the medium as he drew, in the process inspiring generations to come; Eisner's 1985 book, *Comics and Sequential Art,* is still the definitive word on how to draw comics. An example of his playful inventiveness was the way in which, on his splash pages, he would spell out the word "Spirit" on bits of paper blowing in the breeze, on shop signs, in puddles, on the bars of a window, on steps, or in countless other ways.

Soon after America entered World War II, Eisner was drafted, and for the duration of the conflict the strip was handled by quality staffers such as William Woolfolk, Manly Wade Wellman, and Bill Millard on scripts and Jack Cole and Lou Fine on artwork. It was still immaculately crafted but lacked the spark of genius that Eisner brought with him, a spark that was resolutely rekindled on his return in late 1945. After a couple of episodes that employed penciler John Spranger, Eisner really hit his stride in the late 1940s, fashioning a succession of dazzlingly witty and creative stories. His years in the army had matured him as an artist, revealing a more fluid, cartoon-influenced style that delighted in creating memorable characters and atmospheric action sequences. Where the prewar episodes had starred a succession of matinée villains, such as the Black Bow and Mr. Midnight, the later Spirit stories featured a more picaresque array of protagonists. Together with his increasingly influential new assistant Jules Feiffer (later a legendary cartoonist for the *Village Voice* and the *New Yorker*), Eisner explored the lives of Central City's losers, con-men, petty criminals, weirdos, outsiders, and corrupt officials, who rejoiced in such names as Bottles McTopp, Stuffer Balot, Snagg Debbin, P. T. Bumble, Tempus J. Fujit, Sven Galli, Stud Sharpe, and Rattsy Trapp. That is not to say that Eisner had abandoned arch-villains entirely, however; two recurring foes were the eccentric Mr. Carrion (with his pet buzzard Julia) and the mysterious Octopus, whose face was never seen but whose identifying trademark was his two purple gloves with three white stripes.

More often than not, the Spirit's most memorable opponents were women—*femmes fatales* of the deadliest, most seductive variety. Inspired by such movie sirens as Lauren Bacall, Ava Gardner, and Bette Davis, Eisner fashioned a wildly entertaining parade of pouting assassins, including Nylon Rose, Dulcet Tone, Sparrow Fallon, Powder Pouf, Plaster of Paris, Autumn Mews, Thorne Strand, Flaxen Weaver, and Sand Saref. The Spirit's female foes were as likely to kiss him as try to kill him and, indeed, his first significant foe—Silk Satin—had been his childhood friend when they ran together in Central City's Slum Gulley. Satin eventually renounced her life as a thief, but less repentant was the man-eating P'Gell. Named in honor of Paris' notorious Pigalle district, P'Gell had left a string of wealthy and deceased husbands in her wake, and sported lips that would have been the envy of Jessica Rabbit. In one of the strip's most memorable lines, she introduced herself with the immortal announcement: "I am P'Gell and this is not a story for little boys."

Another example of Eisner's postwar creativity was the expansion and development of the series' supporting cast. Commissioner Dolan, Ebony White, and Ellen became integral, witty elements of the feature rather than mere plot devices to rescue, or be rescued by, its hero. Indeed, in many stories Eisner used the "crime of the week" as a hook on which to hang the exploration of his characters' personalities, rather than as the stories' focal point. Ellen became more than just a would-be spouse and ultimately became Central City's mayor, while Dolan softened to become the Spirit's friend and confidant. For contemporary readers, White was more problematic. While he was a brave and fearless companion for the Spirit, he was also rather too broadly caricatured; his Southern black dialogue ("Yassuh, Mr. Spirit Boss!") and stereotyped features became decidedly un–politically correct. Although he was always well intentioned, Eisner eventually bowed to the trend and replaced Ebony with the less controversial—and Anglo—Sammy, Willum, and PS, three kids straight out of the popular kid group the Little Rascals.

Eisner had always prided himself on being as much a businessman as an artist (his studio had already made him financially secure by the age of twenty-five) and by the early 1950s, his outside interests had largely curtailed his involvement in *The Spirit,* leaving it in the hands of his studio. During these years, Eisner was aided by such notable artists and writers as Jules Feiffer, Wally Wood, and Tex Blaisdell. In late 1952, the feature was finally abandoned. But that was not to be the last anyone saw of the character. Busy Arnold had begun reprinting *Spirit* stories in *Police Comics* as early as 1942, and added a regular *Spirit* title in 1944. Both of these disseminated *Spirit* stories to comics fans for the rest of that decade. Despite the feature's newspaper demise, Fiction House reprinted vintage tales in their own *Spirit* comic from 1952 to 1954, and IW Comics released its own title a few years later. Harvey Comics introduced a new generation of fans to the Spirit in 1966, but its revival only lasted two issues despite some new *Spirit* additions from Eisner himself. However, the 1970s proved to be more receptive to the character, as first Kitchen Sink Press and then Warren Publishing Company revived him.

The Warren magazines reprinted up to ten classic adventures from the postwar period in each issue, topping them off with lavishly painted covers. After sixteen issues, Kitchen Sink once again took over the title, going on to print *Spirit* stories for the next sixteen years. Throughout the 1980s and early 1990s, *Spirit* stories could be found in black-and-white magazines, lavish hardbacks, and a regular, full-color comic that ran for almost 100 issues. In addition, the masked hero entered into television for the first time when a pilot telefilm was produced and aired on ABC in July 1986, starring Sam Jones in the title role. By the time of Kitchen Sink's collapse in the late 1990s, almost every *Spirit* story had been reprinted—some many times—and Eisner had assumed the role of

comics' great genius. After more than twenty years of publishing instructional comics for industry, schools, and the military, Eisner introduced a succession of well-received graphic novels, none of which starred the Spirit, but all of which intended to develop comic books as a mature medium.

For the many reprint series, Eisner drew literally hundreds of new covers but always resisted the temptation of drawing new *Spirit* stories, preferring to concentrate on his graphic novels. However, in 1997 Kitchen Sink finally persuaded him to let other, contemporary creators produce new *Spirit* tales—the first for decades. With such talents as Alan Moore, Neil Gaiman, and Dave Gibbons, the series promised much but, despite the high level of craft on show, the results lacked the spark of the originals. In the 2000s, DC Comics has taken up Kitchen Sink's mantle as *Spirit* publisher, releasing a series of hardback "archives" volumes, reprinting in series the entire run of stories. In spite of its origins in the transient world of newspapers, *The Spirit* has become one of the most reprinted series in comics history and has secured its place as one of the medium's cornerstones. —*DAR*

Starman

Starman is an interesting example of a character that was initially considered a relative failure but that has, after a very long wait, eventually achieved critical success. Starman was dreamed up by DC Comics as something of a successor to Superman, and the company launched him with much fanfare in 1941, through full-page advertisements in their comics, a cover and lead slot in *Adventure Comics* #61, and membership in their top-selling *Justice Society of America* strip. Starman's creators were among the company's best: Sandman and Dr. Fate creator Gardner Fox, and artist Jack Burnley, the first person to draw both Batman and Superman outside of their creators' studios. Even Starman's powers—flight and strength—and costume were similar to those of Superman, although the costume had different colors and a hood. And still the strip never quite caught on.

Starman was wealthy American astronomer Theodore ("Ted") Knight, who had constructed a Gravity Rod (a.k.a. Cosmic Rod) that could harness the energy of the stars and effectively give him almost unlimited powers—including the ability to fly, create energy fields, and melt steel. Fox, and later writer Alfred Bester (the noted science fiction author), peopled the strip with a fine selection of villains, including Electron, Dr. Droog, and their star rogue, the Mist, who coated himself (and his henchmen) with an invisibility paint, leaving only his head eerily visible. Burnley was by some margin the best draftsman at DC Comics and, as a 2002 reprinting of all his Starman strips has shown, the old episodes still look impressive today. Yet the strip lacked individuality, and DC's high hopes for its success and impact were never realized. Starman's cover slot was soon usurped by Manhunter, Green Lantern replaced him in the Justice Society, and the strip was concluded in 1946 with a change to another top artist, the great Mort Meskin.

Like most Justice Society members, Starman was featured in numerous *Justice League* guest appearances in the 1960s and 1970s, and co-headlined with Black Canary in two attractive 1965 issues of *The Brave and the Bold*. In fact, he had more adventures in the revived Justice Society than he had had in the 1940s and, while writers were rarely able to develop his personality very much, he made a decent enough team player. In the revived *All Star Comics* in 1976, his Gravity Rod was temporarily requisitioned by the Star-Spangled Kid (who then turned it into a belt) but this device was short-lived. Throughout the 1980s, Starman was an occasional presence in the *All Star Squadron,* one issue of which finally gave him the proper origin that his creators had forgotten to write: It seems that he was inspired to become a hero after seeing Batman in action—an origin that some fans say was hardly worth waiting thirty years for!

In spite of their early disappointment, the DC creative team must have thought that Starman was too good a name to waste on a bit-part player, and since the 1970s they have periodically tried to pass the title on to another character—or, to be precise, five other characters (so far). The first of these (Starman number two) was a blue-skinned alien attired in a sort of disco-era jump suit who starred in *First Issue Special* #12 (1976); he was met with complete indifference by a bemused public. Starman number three, who ran throughout 1980 in *Adventure Comics,* was a futuristic superhero from another galaxy, and the strip featured art by Spider-Man's Steve Ditko. More successfully, the fourth Starman premiered in his own title toward the end of the 1980s and enjoyed four years of relative popularity, though curiously he is almost forgotten today. This incarnation was Will Payton, who somehow inherited immense powers (flight, strength, and the ability to change his features) siphoned off from the previous Starman. In an interesting twist, this Starman bumped into yet another one: David Knight, son of the now aged first Starman, who had taken on his father's mantle (or, rather, cape).

Readers next come across Knight in the first issue of yet another Starman project (in 1994) only to see him abruptly killed off and the Gravity Rod passed to his brother, Jack. This latest Starman (the sixth) was a reluctant superhero, preferring to rummage through junk for his antiques shop rather than tackle the likes of the Shade or the Mist, who perennially popped up in the comic. In a device that anticipated the post-millennial move away from costumes, he opted to go into battle wearing a trenchcoat and goggles and, even more revolutionarily, he never bothered to adopt a secret identity. Much of the comic's appeal came from the interplay between two generations of superheroes, as father passed on advice to his novice son, and its quirky, reserved style gradually garnered the sort of praise that DC had hoped for back in the 1940s. Neophyte writer James Robinson became a star through his Starman scripts and then surprised everyone by canceling the comic after eighty issues, declaring that he had told all the stories he wanted to tell—a unique ending to a unique comic. —*DAR*

Static Shock

During the day, Virgil Hawkins is a fourteen-year-old African-American teen attending Dakota Union High School with his best friend Richie Foley. But when he's not in school—or when trouble strikes—Hawkins dons a black, blue, white, and yellow costume with a trenchcoat, white face mask, and goggles and zaps crime with his electrical powers as Static. Technologically gifted Foley aids Static, by wearing his own superhero suit and using his brilliant gadget inventions to fight crime as Gear. But can the pair of teen heroes really keep Dakota City safe from the "Bang Baby" meta-human villains that are stealing and looting?

Co-created by African-American comic-book veterans Dwayne McDuffie and Denys Cowan, *Static* was originally a part of the minority-owned and diversity-based Milestone line distributed by DC Comics. *Static* #1 was released in June 1993, and the forty-seven-issue series followed the adventures of young Hawkins after he inhales a strange gas that the police used against a gang. The gas changes him, making him capable of throwing shock-powered taser punches at his enemies, and enabling him to fly on an electromagnetically charged garbage can lid. Hawkins' secret is known by Frieda Goren, his best friend and the hottest babe at Ernest Hemingway High. While dealing with school, his lower-income family, and his racing hormones, Static must also knock knuckles with bruisers, gang-bangers, and supervillains such as Hotstreak, Tarmack, Puff, Coil, and others.

The WB network debuted a series called *Static Shock*, based on the comic, on September 23, 2000. Several members of its production team had moved over from the popular *Batman: The Animated*

Series and *Superman* shows but, wisely, Cowan was also hired as a producer and McDuffie as a story editor and writer for the series. Because of its Saturday morning time slot, *Static Shock* is a bit toned down from its gritty comic origins: guns aren't used as often; Foley is no longer a gay teen; Hawkins' mother is dead; and both the costume and Static's use of his powers are different. Perhaps most interesting though is that Static now exists in the larger "DC universe," as guest appearances from Batman, Superman, the Justice League, Green Lantern, and even a futuristic visit with the cast of *Batman Beyond* have occurred.

On the series, Static has fought other characters that received superpowers from the same mutagenic gas he inhaled. These so-called "Bang Babies" (named for the rumble, or "Big Bang," that the police used such unnatural force to put down) include Ebon, shadowy leader of the Breed (Talon, Shiv, D-Struct, Kangorr, and Aquamaria), as well as the flaming F-Stop/Hotstreak, blowhard Slipstream, bounty hunters Onyx and Puff, duplicate-maker Replay, and brother-sister act Boom and Mirage. Static and Gear are sometimes aided by other heroes, including the stretchable Rubberband Man, and genetically engineered Shebang.

Still on the air as of 2004, *Static Shock* is an important stride forward for animation. Static was not the first African American superhero on television; *All New Super Friends Hour's* character Black Vulcan (1977), *The Young Sentinel's* Astraea (1977), *Tarzan and the Super 7's* Superstretch & Microwoman (1978), *The New Fat Albert Show's* The Brown Hornet (1979), and *Kid Super Power Hour's* Misty Magic (1981) had all predated him. But *Static Shock* was the first series centered around an African-American superhero, with a diverse cast both on-screen and behind the scenes. African-American comedian Phil LaMarr has voiced Static, and guest-stars galore have lined up to either play themselves—as in the case of NBA legend Shaquille "Shaq" O'Neal, Backstreet Boy A. J. McLean, and rapper Lil' Romeo—or perform character voices, as in the case of Terence Trent D'Arby, Neil Patrick Harris, David Faustino, Carl Lumbly, Coolio, Malcolm Jamal-Warner, and Alfre Woodard.

Like its comic-book predecessor, *Static Shock* tackles issues both multicultural and urban. While one story might be about gang violence, another explores both the Chanukah and Christmas seasons (in-between superbattles of course). An episode called "Jimmy" (May 2002) dealt with teen gun violence. That episode was given the prestigious Humanitas Prize in 2003, an award recognizing film and television writers whose work both entertains and enriches the viewing public. At its best, *Static Shock* provides solid superheroic entertainment and a role model and promotion of diversity for not only African-American viewers, but audiences of all colors and ages. —AM

Steel

John Henry Irons' life is one of second chances. His backstory: As an engineer for munitions manufacturer AmerTek, Irons becomes disenchanted with his role as a designer of weapons of mass destruction when one of his creations is usurped by an enemy force. He destroys his technology, incurring his employer's wrath—to the extent of a death warrant. Taking the alias of construction worker Henry Johnson, he hides out in Metropolis until being saved from a near-fatal fall by Superman, who admonishes him to make something of his life. After Superman "dies" in *Superman* #75 (1992), Irons is one of "The Reign of the Supermen," a quartet of successors to the Man of Tomorrow (the others being Superboy, the Cyborg Superman, and the Eradicator). In his sterling debut in *The Adventures of Superman* #500 (1993), he forges for himself a suit of high-tech armor and sledgehammer, and, memorializing the fallen hero with a metal-plated "S" on his chest and a red cape, takes to the Metropolis skies as the new Man of Steel: Steel!

Superman didn't stay dead for long, and upon his return, Steel stepped aside. But when weapons he designed were being used on the streets of Metropolis' Suicide Slum, Irons donned the armor again, busting bad guys with his sledgehammer. In February 1994, Steel was awarded his own monthly comic book written by Louise Simonson and illustrated by Jon Bogdanove, as part of a dual agenda by publisher DC Comics: Expand the Superman franchise and develop a headlining black superhero. Some readers criticized DC for shielding the face of Irons, an African American, behind a chrome countenance, but the hero's multi-ethnic cast—including Steel's younger brother Crash, the evil Dr. Villain, and a mob enforcer called Skorpio—was a welcome departure from the mostly white series dominating the publisher's line.

Steel, commanding both remarkable intellect and gallant heroism, aided Superman on many occasions, as well as Supergirl and Superboy, all joining forces as "Team Superman." He was recruited into the roster of DC's Justice League of America (JLA), becoming the group's techno-whiz, and also used his talents to construct Superman's private retreat, the Fortress of Solitude. A wave of post-"Death of Superman" merchandising included Kenner Toys' production of Steel action figures, and Steel appeared on the WB network's *Superman* animated television series (1996). The character—sans the Superman connection—was the star of *Steel* (1997), a poorly received live-action feature film starring basketball legend Shaquille "Shaq" O'Neal in the title role. The promos for *Steel* played upon Shaq's massive size: "Heroes Don't Come Any Bigger." Ultimately, his comic-book series folded with *Steel* #52 (1998), and Irons was relegated to guest-star status.

In 2001, Imperiex, a destroyer of planets, unleashed an intergalactic conflict in DC Comics' multi-part "Our Worlds at War" storyline that ran through a variety of the publisher's superhero series. Steel, having outlived his usefulness as a DC "B" player, perished in the battle. Yet the iron

Shaquille O'Neal stars in *Steel*.

man was not banished to the scrap heap: The villainous Darkseid restored life to Steel's form, encasing him inside alien armor called the Entropy Aegis. *Action Comics* #806 (2003) revealed that the *soul* of Irons apparently inhabits his hammer: It "speaks" to his niece, Natasha—"I chose to be Steel because I was given a second chance by Superman … it is a gift that should not die with me"—and in a blinding explosion, Natasha Irons is transformed into the new Steel, ready to continue the family tradition of "hammer time."

It must be noted that John Henry Irons was not the first DC superhero named Steel. DC published a short-lived series titled *Steel the Indestructible Man* (1978–1979), starring a World War II–era superpatriot with striking similarities to Marvel Comics' Captain America. In the 1980s, this hero, also called Commander Steel, appeared in the pages of *All-Star Squadron*. His grandson, the second Steel, was a member of the Justice League

of America during the team's brief stint in Detroit, Michigan. *—ME*

Stripperella

Erotica Jones is an exotic dancer by night, crime fighter by … later night. With "a heart of gold, a passion for animal rights, and a weakness for fashion," according to the plug she received on Spike TV's website, when she's not busy pole dancing Jones lends a helping hand and sympathetic ear to the other dancers at the Tender Loins strip club. When her belly ring vibrates, Erotica jumps into action as superhero/secret agent Stripperella.

As an agent for the organization T.H.U.G.G., Stripperella battles supervillains Dr. Cesarian (a plastic surgeon who injects beautiful models with deadly implants that make them obese), Pushy

Galore (a former genetic physicist who breeds animals with designer logos on their skin), and Cheapo (a dime-store-rate villain). In between, she dodges the catty looks and subversive plans of fellow dancer Catt, and spends time exercising her superpowers: floating to safety via her superpowered hair, doing the Scissor-ella (which involves knocking out bad guys with her thighs), and playing with the super-gadget lie-detector she conceals in the chest area of her costume.

Stripperella is the brainchild of Spider-Man co-creator and all-around Marvel Comics genius Stan Lee, who modeled the stripper-turned-superhero after actor Pamela Anderson, who voices the part of Jones/Stripperella. The animated show debuted in June 2003 on Spike TV (the revamped network formerly known as TNN). Joining executive producer Lee behind the scenes are director Kevin Altieri, known for his work on the highly acclaimed *Batman: The Animated Series,* and writers Kevin Kopelow and Heath Seifert (Nickelodeon's *All That*), who came aboard to give the show its comedic twist. Kid Rock provides the theme song. Regular and guest voices are courtesy of Mark Hamill, Kid Rock, Kristin Davis, Maurice LaMarche, and Dee Bradley Baker. —*GM*

Sub-Mariner

Bill Everett's Sub-Mariner was the first of Timely/Marvel Comics' "big three" superheroes to be created, back in early 1939, and proved to be one of the company's most enduring characters, as well as being the first anti-hero in comics. The Sub-Mariner was dreamed up by Everett for a promotional comic called *Motion Picture Funnies Weekly,* packaged by Funnies Inc.—the art studio of which he was co-owner and art director. The project was not a success; only eight copies are known to exist, suggesting that few copies were ever circulated to the general public. However, later that year, when Funnies Inc. was contracted by pulp publisher Martin

Goodman to package a comic, Everett recycled his original Sub-Mariner story, adding a short origin sequence, and so *Marvel Comics* #1 was born, hitting the newsstands in October 1939. The comic, co-starring the Human Torch, the Angel, and Ka-Zar (the latter two have no relation to their later namesakes), was retitled *Marvel Mystery Comics* with its second issue, and soon became one of the nascent industry's best-selling books. At the time of the Sub-Mariner's creation in April 1939, the only costumed superhero on the stands was Superman, making Everett's character genuinely groundbreaking.

The Sub-Mariner's brief origin relates how explorer Leonard McKenzie leads a scientific expedition to the Antarctic and, during exploratory explosions on the ice shelf, accidentally damages an undersea kingdom. The settlement (later christened Atlantis, inevitably) sends up one of its blue-skinned inhabitants—Princess Fen—to bargain with the men, and she ends up having an affair with McKenzie, who nevertheless carries on with his dangerous experiments, killing most of the kingdom's inhabitants in the process (albeit unwittingly, it seems). It takes the Atlanteans twenty years to rebuild their numbers, but by 1939—led by the product of the union between McKenzie and Fen, Prince Namor the Sub-Mariner—they are ready to unleash their wrath on the unsuspecting surface-dwellers. The half-human Namor was pale-skinned and sported winged feet, pointed ears, and a somewhat triangular head. He possessed extraordinary strength (swimming 60 miles per hour and lifting 75 tons underwater) and could even fly out of water—however, he weakened after several hours of not being wet and needed to immerse himself at least once a week.

In his earliest *Marvel Mystery* tales, the Sub-Mariner was to prove a menace to humankind in general, rampaging through cities and striking terror into American hearts (indeed the name Namor means "avenging son"), but he soon turned his attention elsewhere. In Spring 1941, he was given his own comic, in which the Nazis rashly attacked Atlantis, and for the rest of World War II Namor was to prove their nemesis, at least in those stories in which he was not pummelling his erstwhile co-star, the Human Torch. As the war progressed, he began to star in other Timely titles, including *USA, Daring, All Winners, The Human Torch,* and *All Select,* but by this point Everett was long gone, having been drafted in early 1942. Everett was a skilled, fluid artist with a genuine love of the sea, and though his successors (including Carl Pfeufer and Syd Shores) did not share that same enthusiasm, the strip thrived in his absence.

The postwar Sub-Mariner was an altogether tamer beast since, having defeated the Axis hordes, he seemed to regard himself as a *de facto* Ameri-can, helping the police and hanging out with the beautiful Betty Dean, while rarely returning to Atlantis. As sales began to decline, the company introduced his shapely cousin Namora as a sort of companion-in-arms (first appearing in *Marvel Mys-tery* #82 in 1947) and she was soon spun off into her own short-lived comic. More importantly, Everett returned to the strip that year, a much improved artist, but even he could not halt the industrywide slump and, by mid-1949, both *Marvel Mystery* and *Sub-Mariner* were canceled.

By late 1953 Marvel (now known as Atlas) decided to try out the superhero genre once more and, following a couple of issues of *Young Men,* all three of the company's principal heroes were given their own comics again. Whereas *Captain America* and the *Human Torch* proved to be short-lived, a proposed Sub-Mariner television series (which never materialized) persuaded Martin Goodman to keep Namor's title afloat for ten issues. With Everett (and Namora) back on board, it was as if nothing had changed, and all of the 1950s Sub-Mariner yarns are a joy, particularly since Everett had improved still more, marrying a winningly car-toony touch with delicate, detailed rendering. There was also less of the rampant commie-bashing prevalent in the other revivals. Barely a year after the final issue of the series (#42, 1955), DC Comics brought out *Showcase* #4, starring the

Sub-Mariner #57 © 1973 Marvel Comics.
COVER ART BY BILL EVERETT.

Flash, meaning that Marvel only just missed out on starting the big superhero revival of the Silver Age (1956–1969). As it was, readers had to wait until 1962 to enjoy the Sub-Mariner again.

The action in *Fantastic Four* #4 opens with the latter-day Torch (in his unrelated Johnny Storm ver-sion) burning the stubble off a Bowery bum and dis-covering the Sub-Mariner underneath. In a piece of retro-fitting from later in the decade, it was revealed that a character called Destiny had destroyed most of Atlantis and that Namor had just survived, but he was stricken with amnesia. When his memory was restored, the newly angry Subby went on the ram-page, swearing revenge on humankind—much as he had done in his early days. For the next couple of years, he was a regular (unwelcome) guest in the pages of *Fantastic Four* (where he developed a crush on the Invisible Girl) and popped up all over the Marvel universe. After a particularly memorable rampage through New York City in *Daredevil* #7, it became obvious to Marvel that Sub-Mariner was too strong a character to be wasted on occasional guest shots, and he was finally given his own series again.

Namor's new berth was *Tales to Astonish*. In issue #70 (1965) he ousted the moribund Giant-Man strip and, under the guidance of writer Stan Lee and artist Gene Colan, it was a handsome feature. As in the 1940s, the company found it hard to sustain a strip centered on an outright villain, and so the feature concentrated on Namor's regal side in Atlantis. It introduced a supporting cast of love interest Lady Dorma; the steadfast, bearded vizier Vashti; and the plotting warlord Krang. Within a few issues, Namor had graduated from prince to king. In 1967, Bill Everett once again (temporarily) returned to his favorite son, though his hard-living lifestyle had taken its toll and critics generally agree he was not at his best. Nevertheless, a year later the Sub-Mariner was promoted to his own title and began a successful run of more than seventy issues.

The new title introduced a new creative team—Roy Thomas (on scripts) and John Buscema (on art for the first year)—and a dynamic new approach. Indeed, the early issues were almost underwater sword-and-sorcery stories. The comic soon settled down to a more traditional superhero look and introduced a succession of fishy villains, including Tiger Shark, Stingray, Commander Kraken, and Orka the Human Killer Whale, in addition to Marvel's all-purpose underwater thug, Attuma. The 1970s fully re-established the Sub-Mariner at the heart of the company and he also starred in *The Defenders, The Invaders,* and *Supervillain Team-up.* In his own comic he suffered a number of tragedies, including the death of Lady Dorma, the loss of his throne, and the departure of Thomas (after four years). On the plus side, he tracked down his long-lost father

(last seen in *Marvel Comics* #1) and was reunited with his (other) creator, Bill Everett, one last time.

By 1972, Everett had conquered his personal demons and was once again at his quirky, intricate best, and he immediately introduced a new element into the strip in the form of the perky, teenage Namorita, daughter of the long-forgotten (and now regrettably deceased) Namora. Everett's tenure was to be brief (from #50 to #61), and he died four pages into a new episode. By the decade's end, all the Sub-Mariner's various titles either had been canceled or (in the case of *The Defenders*) had written him out of their lineup. The 1980s were an even less promising era for Subby, reducing the character to the status of "villain of the issue" in scattered *Fantastic Four* numbers; why the public had tired of him remains something of a mystery.

A new decade brought an old fan—industry favorite John Byrne—a new comic called *Namor* (sixty-two issues between 1990 and 1995), and a move in a darker direction. Much like Aquaman, his DC Comics counterpart, Namor became caught up in the trend toward darker, harsher heroes and he grew his hair long and sported a beard (never a good sign in comics). A revival of his romance with the Invisible Girl (now Invisible Woman) went nowhere, but he did gain a son along the way, courtesy of the previously villainous Llyra. The same year that the *Namor* comic was initiated also saw the birth of a new superteam, the *New Warriors,* starring Namorita. The *New Warriors* was a far more lighthearted venture and, against the received wisdom of the day, proved more popular than *Namor*'s supposedly more cutting-edge nihilism.

By the millennium, both Namor and Namorita were homeless once more, but a 2003 series proves that there is life under the sea yet. With a hero who should realistically now be in his eighties, Marvel decided that their new comic—once again called *Namor*—would feature untold tales of his youth, and its charmingly gentle approach has heralded another innovative chapter for the Prince of the Seas. —*DAR*

Super Friends

For thirteen years, they protected the Earth from within their headquarters, the Hall of Justice. If they had kept their title the same, ABC and Hanna-Barbera's group of superheroes would have been among the longest-running animated series in history, but even though they always got along, the *Super Friends* got new series titles on a regular basis. The core team always remained Superman, Batman, Wonder Woman, Robin, and Aquaman, although multiple other heroes and sidekicks often joined them for adventures.

Superheroes had fallen out of favor with networks as the 1970s began, but in 1972, a pair of CBS *New Scooby-Doo Movies* with guest stars Batman and Robin, and two episodes of ABC's *The Brady Kids* which guest-starred Superman and Wonder Woman, changed the minds of development executives at ABC. Soon, the alphabet network commissioned Hanna-Barbera to create a new supergroup to entertain on Saturday mornings, but they wanted the adventures to be moralistic and nonviolent. Hanna-Barbera picked five of DC Comics' top heroes—Aquaman was included over Flash or Green Lantern because he had already had his own animated series—and saddled them with teen sidekicks Wendy, Marvin, and Wonder Dog. Simple but elegant designs by comics master Alex Toth gave all the characters a dynamic flair.

Super Friends debuted on September 8, 1973, with an adventure in which the heroes had to stop energy thieves who came from an energy-depleted planet. Of the sixteen episodes produced, other adventures included guest-stars Green Arrow, Flash, and Plastic Man, and saw the Super Friends battle a super-computer called G.E.E.C., dastardly polluters, and alien balloon people. Although *Super Friends* did well in the ratings—and actually received primetime promotion—it was dropped from the air in August 1975, only to return again in February 1976. Half-hour edited versions of the shows ran from December 1976 to September 1977.

The first title change for the series came on September 10, 1977, when *The All New Super Friends Hour* debuted. This version altered the format, showing four adventures over the hour (one half-hour story, and three mini-adventures). Interspersed between each story were Safety Tips, three-part Decoder Clues games, and alternating Crafts or Magic Tricks short segments. The other major change for the series was that Wendy, Marvin, and Wonder Dog were dumped for new sidekicks: alien teens from Exxor named Zan and Jayna, and their space monkey, Gleek. Zan and Jayna were the Wonder Twins, and when they pushed their fists together and yelled "Wonder Twin powers, activate!" Zan could form anything made of water or ice, and Jayna could become any animal from Earth or another planet.

The short stories tended to feature one or two characters teaming up to stop disasters or villains, and many of them guest-starred other heroes from the DC Comics universe: Hawkgirl, Hawkman, Rima the Jungle Girl, Green Lantern, Flash, and the Atom. Created for the series were the new multicultural heroes Black Vulcan (an African-American man with electrical powers), Apache Chief (a Native American man who could grow to be a giant), and Samurai (an Asian man who could spin his lower torso into a tornado). The final of fifteen episodes also featured the first supervillain adapted from the comics: Hawkman's foe Gentleman Jim Craddock, the Gentleman Ghost.

On September 9, 1978, ABC debuted what would be the most popular incarnation of the series ever: *Challenge of the Super Friends.* In this series, the Super Friends were now regularly joined by Flash, Green Lantern, Hawkman, Black Vulcan, Apache Chief, and Samurai, leaving Wonder Woman the sole female heroine (the Wonder Twins were gone for these stories). Fighting against them was the Legion of Doom, whose members included well-known comic-book villains Lex Luthor, Brainiac, Cheetah, the

Riddler, the Scarecrow, Toyman, Sinestro, Black Manta, Captain Cold, Bizarro, Gorilla Grodd, Solomon Grundy, and Giganta. The Legion of Doom met in the Hall of Doom, a building that resembled Darth Vader's helmet and was built in a swamp.

Although the villains were out to conquer the world, and often caused major problems, they just as often escaped justice at the end of each half-hour adventure. When television's Standards and Practices arm objected, the Legion were caught in some episodes, only to be miraculously free the next week. Not only did the show feature many comics characters, several episodes showcased the origins of the heroes and villains, including Superman, Wonder Woman, Green Lantern, Lex Luthor, Giganta, and the Legion of Doom itself.

Since *Challenge of the Super Friends* was a one-hour show, and the Legion of Doom stories only took half that time, separate half-hour stories filled the rest of the hour. These sixteen stories *did* feature the Wonder Twins, fighting evil alongside the crew from the previous season's adventures. These stories were a little more cosmic in nature, with Mr. Mxyzptlk, Dracula, the Greek Gods, and dangers from Exxor, Krypton, and other planets stressing out the Super Friends. *Challenge* proved so popular that the show was expanded to ninety minutes from November 1978 to September 1979, with older reruns added in to fill the time.

Another name change came in 1979, and the show became *The World's Greatest Super Friends.* Though the series was an hour, only eight new episodes were produced. Fantasy ruled these episodes as the heroes battled space knights of Camelon and the Frankenstein monster, took a trip to the Planet of Oz, and faced their evil *dopplegängers.* Gone were the extra heroes, though the Wonder Twins stuck around.

The 1980–1981 season saw the title simplified to *The Super Friends Hour.* Eight new half-hour shows were produced, though each was split into a trio of seven-minute short stories. Eight new Safety Tips, Magic Tricks, and Crafts shorts were produced as well. The cast returned to its wider reach, as guest-stars Apache Chief, the Atom, Flash, Hawkman, Hawkgirl, Rima, and others stopped by to lend a helping hand. Villains included Mr. Mxyzptlk and Bizarro, in addition to non-comic-book menaces such as the Voodoo Vampire, the Termites from Venus, and the Incredible Crude Oil Monster.

Things got a bit complicated for the heroes over the next several years. In September 1981, the series was renamed *The Super Friends,* and more short adventures were produced (three per half-hour), adding a new Hispanic hero named El Dorado to the mix. Six new half-hours (eighteen stories) were produced and aired in the 1981–1982 season, but 1982–1983 featured all reruns. Eight more half-hours (twenty-four stories) were produced for the 1983–1984 season but did not air in the United States. Thus, for viewers, the 1983–1984 season was also all reruns.

Concurrent with a new line of action figures from Kenner known as *Super Powers,* ABC and Hanna-Barbera changed the title of the series again with the September 8, 1984 episode. *Super Friends—The Legendary Super Powers Show* featured Superman, Batman, Robin, Wonder Woman, Aquaman, Green Lantern, Flash, Hawkman, Atom, Black Vulcan, Apache Chief, Samurai, and the Wonder Twins. Also introduced into the stories was teen hero Firestorm.

The Legendary Super Powers Show started out as a thirty-minute series, but by December it had been expanded to an hour. The stories were either two separate eleven-minute tales, or a two-part storyline; in addition to eight new half-hours, two half-hours from the missing 1983–1984 episodes were also aired. Darkseid and others of Jack Kirby's Fourth World characters (Kalibak, Desaad, the Para-Demons) were the main antagonists, while familiar comic villains such as Brainiac, Mr. Mxyzptlk, Mirror Master, and Lex Luthor also bedeviled the heroes.

In September 1985, the series changed titles once again, losing its *Super Friends* connection once and for all as it was renamed *The Super Powers Team: Galactic Guardians,* and the character designs were changed to reflect the templates drawn by Jose Luis Garcia Lopez in the *DC Comics Style Guide* for licensors. Eight more half-hours were produced, with some of them cited by fans as the best stories of the entire run.

While the team remained functionally the same, African-American teen hero Cyborg was added to the mix, perhaps testing the waters for a proposed *Teen Titans* series, of which he would have been a part. Lex Luthor, Darkseid, Brainiac, and Bizarro were back to cause trouble, while new-comers the Royal Flush Gang (with Joker in tow) and Felix Faust appeared. But it was in an episode called "The Fear" that fans got a real "first": the story of Batman's origin was told for the first time on television or in film! Another story bucked television tradition and harkened back to a much-loved Silver Age (1956–1969) Man of Steel comic-book story: "The Death of Superman" was one of the rare cases that the word "death" ever appeared in an animation title.

Galactic Guardians ended its run on September 6, 1986, closing out thirteen seasons of the various *Super Friends* series. The show was later sent to syndication, then to USA Network (where all the missing 1983–1984 episodes were finally shown), and finally to Cartoon Network, where it resides today. Well-remembered by older fans, and embraced by younger viewers, *Super Friends* began a resurgence of popularity after the turn of the century. Cartoon Network produced newly animated promos featuring the characters (and brought back many of the original voice actors), and even featured Black Vulcan and Apache Chief on its *Harvey Birdman, Attorney at Law* series.

Justice League, the successor to *Super Friends,* began airing on Cartoon Network in November 2001. DC Comics launched a nostalgia-laden campaign in 2002, publishing the first of two *Super Friends* trade paperbacks, and following them later with action figures, posters, statues, and other lim-

ited edition materials. The Wonder Twins have shown up in recent years in the pages of *Extreme Justice* and *Young Justice,* and even Apache Chief was reborn as Manitou Raven in the pages of *JLA.* Warner Bros. also began to release *Challenge of the Super Friends* DVDs, to surprisingly high sales. It seems that the Hall of Justice may be retired as headquarters for DC's greatest superheroes, but the popularity of the *Super Friends* goes on. —*AM*

Super-archers

Comic-book publishers were scrambling to create new costumed crime fighters in the wake of Superman's instantaneous success in *Action Comics* #1 (June 1938). Since the wildly popular Errol Flynn movie *The Adventures of Robin Hood* was attracting long lines at the box office during that summer, the notion of pitting a contemporary bowman against villains armed with guns was too good for comics creators to ignore.

Centaur Publications struck the first bull's eye with the Arrow, comics' original super-archer—*and* the first costumed hero to appear in print after Superman. Bowing in *Funny Pages* (September 1938), the Arrow, written and drawn by Paul Gustavson, mixed the archery motif of Robin Hood with the mystique of pulp hero the Shadow. The Arrow was a masked enigma—even the readers weren't privy to his identity. His adventures routinely pitted him against thugs and deviants, whom he would disable, and sometimes even destroy, with a well-aimed arrow and absolutely no compunction. The Arrow graduated into his own title in October 1940, where he was unmasked—for readers—and revealed to be a United States federal agent named Ralph Payne. Removing the mystery around the hero also removed his appeal, and *The Arrow* was canceled after its third issue.

Fawcett Comics' Golden Arrow was the next super-archer, drawing aim in *Whiz Comics* #2 (February 1940). Raised by a prospector in the 1940s American West, Golden Arrow was actually Roger Parsons, who became a master bowman to avenge the murder of his parents. Golden Arrow was far from the traditional costumed crusader: He dressed in nondescript garb and wore no mask. Nonetheless, he continued to target criminals throughout comics' Golden Age (1938–1954), appearing both in *Whiz* and in six issues of his own title. Three months after Golden Arrow's debut, Quality Comics premiered its own super-archer, the Spider—in a strip titled *Alias the Spider*—in *Crack Comics* #1 (May 1940). Dressed in a vibrant yellow shirt and blue tights, the Spider, secretly wealthy playboy Tom Hallaway, took crime prevention into his own hands as a bowman whose quiver contained a "spider seal" arrow he fired into the hands of gun-wielding mobsters.

The next super-archer of note was the first uniformed villain to challenge Superman: the Archer, who appeared in *Superman* #13 (November–December 1941). This rogue was a green-clad, masked assassin, piercing victims' hearts with perfectly aimed shafts. Once Superman caught him, the Archer was revealed as a big-game hunter who admitted, "I thought hunting human beings would prove more profitable!" While the Arrow and Golden Arrow may have impressed comics readers, the Archer missed the mark, his weapons seeming trivial against the superhero who was "more powerful than a locomotive."

Appearing concurrently with the Archer was DC's Green Arrow, inarguably comics' best-known bowman. First seen in *More Fun Comics* #73 (1941), "GA" was more than DC's answer to Robin Hood: He was a clone of the publisher's own Batman! Behind his domino mask and emerald costume was millionaire playboy Oliver Queen. Living with Queen was a young ward named Roy Harper, who fought alongside his mentor as the superhero sidekick Speedy. While most adult superheroes first established themselves as solo crime fighters before adopting sidekicks, Green Arrow and Speedy debuted as a team. This dynamic duo was head-

quartered in an Arrow Cave, drove an Arrow Car, took to the air in an Arrow Plane, and relied upon an amazing arsenal—not gadget-filled utility belts like Batman and Robin used, but quivers brimming with regular and trick shafts: the boomerang arrow, the boxing-glove arrow, the super-sensitive-sonar arrow, even a fountain-pen arrow!

Despite their lack of originality, Green Arrow and Speedy commanded a long-running presence in comics: They survived the 1950s, the decade when most superheroes disappeared from print, and the 1960s, when GA joined the Justice League of America and Speedy hooked up with the Teen Titans. Green Arrow was reinvented in 1970: Queen lost his fortune and became a bearded leftist, using his tongue more frequently than his bow in a series of critically acclaimed adventures with Green Lantern. This relevant take on GA made him one of DC's most popular characters throughout the 1970s, but by the mid-1980s he was overhauled again, beginning in a miniseries entitled *Green Arrow: The Longbow Hunters.* Queen was now a grizzled vigilante, not unlike the original super-archer, the Arrow. The character died in the mid-1990s and was succeeded as Green Arrow by his bowman son Connor Hawke. Speedy, no longer a teen sidekick, matured into his own as Arsenal, firing concussive arrows among a varied cache of weapons. In 2001 the 1970s version of Green Arrow was resurrected from the dead in a new monthly series, originally written by filmmaker Kevin Smith (*Dogma, Chasing Amy*). Curiously, in his lengthy career, Green Arrow has encountered a variety of adversaries, but has never developed a recognizable rogues' gallery or even a signature villain.

The other major super-archer of note is Marvel Comics' hotheaded bow-slinger Hawkeye. Beginning with his first appearance in *Tales of Suspense* #57 (1964), ace sideshow marksman Clint Barton set his sights on becoming a superhero, but got shafted when the police misinterpreted his actions. After flirting with a life of crime alongside a Russian spy called the Black Widow, Hawkeye salvaged his reputation and joined Marvel's mightiest superteam in *The Avengers* #16 (1965). Hawkeye's quiver is loaded with an array of trick arrows, but instead of the preposterous weapons in Green Arrow's employ, Vibranium arrows, stun-arrows, and other scientifically enhanced barbs help this Avenger in his war on crime. Readers have followed Hawkeye through myriad Marvel team books including *The Defenders, West Coast Avengers,* and *Thunderbolts.* Unlike Green Arrow, Hawkeye has hit the mark less often as a solo player, with two limited series in 1983 and 1994 and an ongoing one starting in 2003 that fans may or may not embrace long-term. However, his impulsiveness and staunch loyalty to his teammates will no doubt save him a place in readers' affections no matter which comic he lands in.

Other super-archers have come and gone, from White Feather in DC's superhero parody *The Inferior Five* to the Amazon Artemis in the pages of *Wonder Woman* and the grim-and-gritty Shaft in Rob Liefeld's *Youngblood.* Marvel's Bullseye may not shoot arrows, but he throws any object with deadly force and accuracy. In the 2000s archery is depicted in fantasy comic books like CrossGen's *Sojourn,* but as real-life science creates technologically astounding weaponry, superhero stories, which have always been required to stay one step ahead of reality, have begun to steer away from the traditional bowmanship inspired by Robin Hood. One exception to this rule is Arrowette, an adolescent archer first seen in *Impulse* #28 (1997), who later joined the teen team Young Justice. *—ME*

Superboy

Superman was approaching his seventh birthday in 1945 and had proven himself a phenomenal sales success as the star of *Action Comics, World's Finest Comics,* and his own title. Beginning with *More Fun Comics* #101 (January–February 1945), publisher DC Comics found a new way to milk its

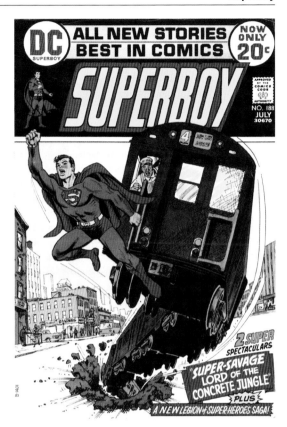

Superboy #188 © 1972 DC Comics.
COVER ART BY NICK CARDY.

Kryptonian cash cow—"The Adventures of Superman When He Was a Boy"—Superboy!

When Superman first took flight in *Action Comics* #1 (June 1938), creators Jerry Siegel and Joe Shuster established that this "strange visitor from another planet" had delayed his crime-fighting career until adulthood, upon the death of his adopted Earth parents. Funny how the prospect of exploiting a lucrative franchise can inspire reinvention: With Superboy, Superman's origin was retrofitted to offer readers a pint-sized superhero. The Superboy series, backdated roughly a dozen years from the Man of Steel's adventures, took the hero who would one day protect the bustling city of Metropolis and plunked him down in a hick town appropriately called Smallville. Enthusiastic younger readers made Superboy a hit, and the hero burst out of *More Fun* into the lead spot in *Adventure Comics* and his own long-running title.

The basic story of Superboy remained the same as Superman's—childless Jonathan and Martha Kent discover a humanoid baby in a crashed rocketship and adopt him as their son, Clark, guiding him to use his otherworldly powers (flight, superstrength, invulnerability, superspeed, supervision, superhearing, and, yes, superbreath) to benefit humankind—but then the variations began. Superboy's blue-and-red suit was sewn by "Ma" Kent from the very blankets into which the infant was swaddled. He frolicked about the sky with another survivor of Krypton, his superdog Krypto. Lana Lang, not Lois Lane, was his headstrong female companion (and neighbor). Instead of an Arctic Fortress of Solitude, the Boy of Steel operated out of a secret headquarters underneath the Kents' modest home.

Initially, Superboy appeared to be a pre-teen, but before long the strip's writers made him a teenager at Smallville High School. Young Kent perfected his "mild-mannered" persona to deflect any suspicion of his S-chested identity, but that didn't fool nosy Lang, who spent years trying to prove that the boy next door was the Boy of Steel. Teenage Kent struck a more resonant chord with the readership than his adult counterpart: His angst closely mirrored the growing pains experienced by his readership. While the writers expertly characterized young Kent, they rarely explored the Boy of Steel's immaturity with his superpowers—Superboy was essentially Superman in a smaller package.

By the 1960s, Superboy had developed a rogues' gallery including Bizarro, the Kryptonite Kid, and classmate-turned-evil-scientist Lex Luthor, who blamed Superboy for the permanent loss of his hair (!). He regularly encountered a bevy of young superfriends, most notably the Legion of Super-Heroes, a club of teen champions from a thousand years in the future. Youthful versions of a pre-Batman Bruce Wayne, Aquaman, Green Arrow, and Lois Lane even stopped by Smallville, as did the time-traveling Robin the Boy Wonder and a cadre of other crusading kids in one-shot appearances.

Superboy never matched the ubiquitous merchandising muscle of Superman, but a handful of items bearing his likeness have been produced over the years, from a model kit and board game in 1966 to an action-figure two-pack with Supergirl in 2002. On three occasions, the Boy of Steel has starred in television series: in *The Adventures of Superboy* unsold pilot (1960) starring Johnny Rockwell; in Filmation Studios' 1966 Superboy animated cartoon (part of *The New Adventures of Superman* series); and in the live-action *Superboy* syndicated program (1988–1992) starring John Haymes Newton in season one and Gerard Christopher in the remaining three seasons. *Smallville,* a live-action, teen-oriented hour-long drama that premiered in 2001 on the WB network, updated the Superboy legend (sans costumed identity), with a young Clark Kent (Tom Welling) on a journey of super-discovery.

Superboy was expunged from DC Comics' continuity in 1986 in writer/artist John Byrne's *Man of Steel* miniseries, which re-established Superman's inaugural appearance as transpiring during the hero's adulthood. In the aftermath of DC's highly publicized "Death of Superman" storyline in 1992, a new Superboy—a cloned proxy for the deceased Man of Steel—was introduced in *Adventures of Superman* #500 (1993). Kryptonian DNA doesn't lend itself to replication, discovered the geneticists at Metropolis think tank Project Cadmus, so their test-tube titan was grown from a scientist's heritable matter and programmed to parrot Superman's powers. Superboy's abilities are accredited to "tactile telekinesis": He can fly, he is invulnerable, and he is strong like the Man of Steel, but he also commands the power to disassemble any object. After Superman returned from the grave, he accepted "The Kid" (as Superboy is often called) into his super-"family," bestowing upon him the Kryptonian name of Kon-El. Hip, brash, and fashion-conscious, this Superboy starred in a healthy run of his own title from 1994 to 2002, as well as the short-lived spinoff *Superboy and the Ravers*. Superboy was a member of Young Justice before settling, in the summer of 2003, into the roster of a revamped Teen Titans. —*ME*

Superboy in the Media

What was Superman like as a boy? Since 1945, fans have known the answer. Superboy first appeared in *More Fun Comics* #101 (January–February 1945), and starred there for a while until moving on to headline *Adventure Comics* the following year (with #103, April 1946). In his comic-book adventures, Superboy loved redhead Lana Lang, palled around with Pete Ross, zipped around the skies with Kryptonian superdog Krypto, and helped Martha and Jonathan Kent—Ma and Pa Kent to everyone—on their Smallville farm. But what about Superboy's media appearances?

The Boy of Steel *almost* made his first television debut in 1961. Following the death of TV Superman actor George Reeves, in 1959, producer Whitney Ellsworth wanted a super-spin-off. In April 1961, Ellsworth attempted to recreate the hit show *The Adventures of Superman*, using the same stylistic touches to tell stories of the Boy of Steel. Ellsworth commissioned a total of thirteen scripts, though only the first was ever filmed. "Rajah's Ransom" adapted the story "The Saddest Boy in Smallville" from *Superboy* #88 (April 1961). Clark Kent/Superboy was played by John Rockwell—who bore a strong resemblance to Reeves—while Lana Lang was played by Bunny Henning. The live-action black-and-white pilot never aired.

A few years later, CBS began showing Filmation's animated *The New Adventures of Superman*.

The series consisted of two short *Superman* stories and one *Superboy* story per half-hour. Many of the *Superboy* stories were written by comic-book writers, including Bob Haney, George Kashdan, and Leo Dorfman. Bob Hastings voiced Superboy and young Clark Kent, while Janet Waldo was Lana Lang, and Ted Knight narrated. The series ran from September 10, 1966, to September 2, 1967, when it became the *Superman-Aquaman Hour.* In September 1968, the series became the *Batman-Superman Hour,* and ran until September 6, 1969. Thirty-six *Superboy* stories were produced, in which Superboy and Krypto averted natural disasters, sea dragons, alien invaders, and the occasional super-criminal such as Mighty Lad.

In December 1978, Warner released a big-budget live-action feature called *Superman—The Movie.* Although he did not wear the familiar costume, young actor Jeff East portrayed teenage Clark Kent in Smallville, who was struggling with hiding his superpowers and with the death of his foster father, Jonathan Kent (Glenn Ford). Ma Kent was played by Phyllis Thaxter, while Diane Sherry played the briefly seen Lana Lang. The Smallville scenes— along with sequences set on Krypton before its destruction—formed one-third of the film.

Young Clark Kent next appeared (at various ages) in Ruby-Spears new animated *Superman* show for CBS (1988–1989). In addition to an eighteen-minute action-oriented *Superman* lead story, each episode featured a four-minute backup story entitled *Superman's Family Album,* detailing Kent's years from Smallville baby to young noncostumed hero-to-be to his first adult appearance in costume in Metropolis.

Following the relative failure of the feature film *Superman IV: The Quest for Peace,* Cannon Films gave up the live-action rights to the *Superman* family. Previous *Superman* movie producers Alexander and Ilya Salkind snapped them up again and sold Viacom on a half-hour syndicated series featuring Superman as a teen. The week of October 8, 1988, *Superboy* premiered with unknown actor John Haymes Newton

John Haymes Newton is the Boy of Steel in *Superboy.*

Sherman Howard was the new Lex Luthor, fresh from cosmetic surgery. DC villains Metallo (Michael Callan), Bizarro (Barry Meyers), and the Yellow Peri (Elizabeth Keipher) appeared, as did Kryptonian parents Jor-El and Lara (George Lazenby and Britt Ekland). In the third season, the series was renamed to *The Adventures of Superboy,* and Kent began to intern for the Bureau for Extranormal Matters. In the series' fourth and final season (1991–1992), Kryptonite Kid (Jay Underwood) appeared, and Jack Larson and Noel Neill (from *The Adventures of Superman*) guest-starred in an episode. Although there was talk of a TV movie, *Superboy* was gone after 100 episodes. The series has not been syndicated in the United States since.

in the lead role. Stacy Haiduk played Lana Lang, and other series regulars were Jim Calvert, as Clark's college roommate and Perry White's son, T. J. White, and Scott Wells as the young Lex Luthor. The series centered around Shuster College in Siegelville, a nod to Superman's creators. Initially signed for thirteen episodes, the show grabbed top ratings, and was renewed for a second set of thirteen episodes. Comic-book characters such as Mr. Mxyzptlk (Michael J. Pollard) and Ma and Pa Kent (Salome Jens and Stuart Whitman) appeared, and Jackie Cooper (Perry White in the films) directed an episode. *Superman* comic-book editor Mike Carlin and *Justice League* editor Andy Helfer wrote many episodes.

For the second *Superboy* season in 1989, Newton, Wells, and Calvert were dumped. Gerard Christopher became the new Boy of Steel, while

The Boy of Steel was off the air for nearly a decade, until the WB network debuted Warner's *Smallville* on October 16, 2001. This one-hour live-action drama series features the adventures of teenage Clark Kent (Tom Welling) and Lana Lang (Kristin Kreuk), as well as a slightly older Lex Luthor (Michael Rosenbaum). The cast is rounded out by John Schneider as Jonathan Kent, Annette O'Toole (the adult Lana Lang in *Superman III*) as Martha Kent, Sam Jones III as Clark Kent's friend Pete Ross, Allison Mack as teen reporter Chloe Sullivan, and John Glover as the Machiavellian father, Lionel Luthor. Comic-book authors Mark Verheiden and Jeph Loeb are on board the *Smallville* production team to script episodes and help oversee the series, but the producers, Alfred Gough and Miles Miller, have promised "no tights, no flight," saying that Kent will never fly on the series, nor wear the well-known Superman costume.

Although the first *Smallville* season dealt too much with kryptonite-created villains—Smallville had been the site of a kryptonite meteor shower that killed Lang's parents, drove Luthor bald, and brought Clark Kent to Earth—the show was still a hit. The producers changed tactics in the second season, bringing an edgier set of stories into play and touching on moments that foretold the future of Kent and Luthor's relationship; now they are friends, but eventually they will be bitter enemies. Kent's powers have begun to develop more, including X-ray vision, heat vision, and moments where he seems to defy gravity. He also learns more about his origins from the spaceship that brought him to Earth and the cryptic Dr. Virgil Swann (Christopher Reeve), and has visited Metropolis. *Smallville*'s third season in 2003–2004 continued the trend, beginning with a red-kryptonite-influenced Kent calling himself "Kal" and committing not-so-super acts.

Although he hasn't had Krypto to trail along since the demise of his animated cartoon, Superboy has done pretty well for himself. In fact, combined with his adult adventures as Superman, the last survivor of Krypton has had more media adventures than any other superhero in history. And as *Smallville* has taught its wide audience, for Superboy, compared to high school and love triangles, kryptonite is a breeze. —*AM*

Supercities

Golden Age (1938–1954) and Silver Age (1956–1969) comic-book writers devoted their energies to inventing their new superheroes' powers, weaknesses, supporting casts, and rogues' galleries. In their ambitious pursuit of building characters and storylines, they left many of their characters' cities requiring urban development. Superheroes' municipalities of those eras bore different names, but a reader would be hard pressed to find any diversity between the Golden Age Flash's Keystone City and the Silver Age Flash's Central City

other than their heroic occupants. If captions didn't inform readers that Green Lantern lived in Coast City or that Hawkman called Midway City home, most fans wouldn't know the difference. Even Gotham City, Batman's base of operations, suffered an identity crisis until the 1970s. This metropolis' appellation had certainly become legend, being coined in *Batman* #4 (Winter 1941), but other than its allure to garish psychotics, little made Gotham unique from other superheroes' locales (although it *was* home to an usual amount of giant props during the 1950s).

Then came DC Comics' reinvention of Batman in the 1970s, when the hero was returned to his original "creature of the night" reputation. Gotham City was renovated into a dark and foreboding megalopolis where misconduct ran rampant. The site where young Bruce (Batman) Wayne witnessed the gangland slaying of his parents was christened Crime Alley, and Arkham Asylum, an institution for the criminally insane, supplanted the run-of-the-mill prison that had previously incarcerated Batman's rogues. Soon, Gotham's very architecture appeared more … gothic (from the efforts of talented interior and cover artists like Neal Adams and Michael Kaluta), with minacious spires, gargoyles, and parapets.

Visionary Anton Furst designed the cinematic Gotham City for director Tim Burton's film *Batman* (1989), blending the urban density of *Blade Runner* into the mix and earning an Academy Award for his efforts. In "No Man's Land" (1999), a multi-chaptered story arc serialized throughout DC Comics' Batman franchise, Batman's turf was leveled by an earthquake and rebuilt by Metropolis billionaire Lex Luthor (from the pages of *Superman*) into a city of glass, with radiant new skyscrapers juxtaposed alongside surviving structures from Gotham of old. Homages to former Bat-artists, writers, and editors were introduced, including Robert Kane Memorial Bridge, Cape Carmine (Infantino), and (Jim) Aparo Park. In the DC continuity of the 2000s, Gotham City is the home of a host of heroes: joining Batman as Gothamites are Robin, the Huntress, Oracle, Batgirl, Catwoman, Plastic Man, and even the private eye Slam Bradley.

If Gotham represents the City of Yesteryear, then Metropolis is its antithesis: the City of Tomorrow—but where else would the *Man* of Tomorrow, Superman, call home? Even during Superman's earliest appearances in the late 1930s, Metropolis clearly stood unique among supercities. Artist Joe Shuster and writer Jerry Siegel, creators of Superman, were heavily influenced by filmmaker Fritz Lang's vision of the future in his film *Metropolis* (1927), which they saw as children. The luminous structures of DC Comics' Metropolis stretched boldly to the heavens, parroting humankind's eternal reach for improvement, a trait personified in Superman himself.

The focal point of Metropolis has always been the *Daily Planet* building, home of the newspaper where Superman is employed in his alter ego of Clark Kent. During the Silver Age, Kent's home, 344 Clinton Street, apartment 3D, was an occasional setting; upon returning home from work each evening, he tossed his hat onto a bust of former *Superman* comics editor Mort Weisinger, which he called "Morty," and kept a few Superman robots secreted behind a hidden closet partition.

When Superman's history was reworked beginning with the miniseries *The Man of Steel* (1986), the twin towers of Luthor's LexCorp became a familiar site, a haunting image in the wake of the real-life destruction of New York's World Trade Center towers on September 11, 2001. In 2000, Superman's foe Brainiac upgraded himself *and* the city by downloading a supervirus into a computerized Metropolis. Today's Metropolis is the technological nucleus of the DC universe.

The enduring legend of Superman inspired a real-world city, Metropolis, Illinois, to "adopt" the Man of Steel as its native son in 1972, a move sanctioned by DC Comics. In an official ceremony on January 21 of that year, Carmine Infantino, then the publisher of DC, ventured to Metropolis and

spoke before a crowd of hundreds of area children and citizens and representatives from the media. Infantino introduced "Superman" (as portrayed by local Baptist minister Rev. Charles Chandler), who was awarded the key to the city. A theme park, the Amazing World of Superman, was started but scrapped halfway through due to a shortage of funds. In the 2000s, the Metropolis, Illinois, Chamber of Commerce continues to use Superman as its not-for-profit mascot, and a statue of the Man of Steel proudly overlooks its town square.

Erected in stark contrast to DC Comics' Metropolis, Clark Kent's hometown Smallville is a quaint Midwestern farming community where, in the good ol' days of the Silver Age, Ma and Pa Kent operated a general store. In current DC Comics continuity, Superman often returns to the homestead to seek advice from his parents on the family farm. This dichotomy between Superman's two Earth cities also illustrates the hero's dual personalities: "Anytown, USA" Smallville represents Kent, the personification of everyman, while Metropolis symbolizes the realization of ideals and dreams, just as Superman does.

Several other supercities have evolved from Superman's mythos. The Man of Steel's scientifically advanced native planet, Krypton, has provided three splendorous cities with globe-shaped skyscraper spires and flying cars, employing an image of the future originating in the 1930s comic strips *Buck Rogers* and *Flash Gordon*: Kryptonopolis, birthplace of Kal-El (Superman's Kryptonian name); Argo City, which survived the planet's destruction; and Kandor, which was miniaturized by Brainiac and held as a trophy in a giant bottle. On at least two occasions Superman has sought solace in cities other than Metropolis and Smallville: In *Action Comics* #179 (1953), Superman temporarily sets up shop in the hamlet of Mapleville, which is then renamed Supermanor, but Super*mania* surrounding the hero's residency ultimately makes the Man of Steel the town's least-liked neighbor; and in Jack Kirby's *The Forever People* #1 (1971), Superman's encounter with a group of godlike teens lures him to the remarkable city of Supertown, home of a race of superpeople, on the planet New Genesis.

DC Comics' Paradise Island (a.k.a. Themyscira), an oasis of lush forests and ancient Greek architecture, has remained hidden from the rest of the world for centuries and is the habitat of a race of physically superior females called the Amazons. Amazonian Princess Diana bested all challengers in a competition of warriors for the right to travel to "Man's World" as Wonder Woman. In the Marvel universe, there exists at the end of a rainbow bridge the city of Asgard, the home of the Norse gods. Asgard is ruled by the all-powerful Odin, whose sons, the god of thunder Thor and the god of evil Loki, have respectively assisted and plagued humankind for many years.

Atlantis, the lost continent of yore, appears in both DC and Marvel comic books as an undersea city. DC's Atlantis is protected by a huge dome, although its populace, at one time governed by the superhero Aquaman, has adapted to breathing underwater. Sorcery was introduced to the mythos of DC's undersea kingdom beginning in the 1980s, and Garth, once known as Aquaman's sidekick Aqualad, is now a powerful mystic called Tempest. Marvel's version of the aquatic civilization is inhabited by blue-skinned warriors who have often been led to attack the surface world by their wrathful ruler, Prince Namor the Sub-Mariner. These assaults began in the earliest years of comics' Golden Age, but the Sub-Mariner, Marvel's first anti-hero, has grudgingly grown to accept the surface dwellers, even joining forces with some of Marvel's superheroes to fight against common threats.

While a handful of DC Comics superheroes—the Teen Titans; Green Lanterns Kyle Rayner, John Stewart, and Guy Gardner; some members of the Justice Society of America (JSA); and even Wonder Woman—have called or call New York City home, the bulk of Marvel's characters reside there. This concept was fathered in the early 1960s by writer/editor Stan Lee, who wanted a realistic environment for the company's legion of superheroes. From the humble beginnings of a mere handful of crusaders like the Fantastic Four (whose headquarters, the Baxter Building skyscraper, is located in midtown Manhattan), the Mighty Thor, and the Amazing Spider-Man (although Spidey's alter ego, Peter Parker, lived in Forest Hills, Queens, when he was a teen), soon an entire universe of champions—Daredevil, Iron Man, the Avengers, Captain America, Doctor Strange, and many, many more—were peppering the skies and streets of the Big Apple, though often in distinctive settings that amounted to mini-cities (Daredevil's Hell's Kitchen, Doctor Strange's Greenwich Village).

In Marvel's continuity, New Yorkers are usually portrayed with stark realism—brusque and self-preserving, but able to unite in times of crisis. Marvel's Manhattan has for more than forty years been a magnet for mayhem, with alien invaders, destructive monsters, and lunatic supervillains striking without notice. *Marvels* (1996), a celebrated four-issue miniseries written by Kurt Busiek and painted by Alex Ross, adroitly retells Marvel Comics' milestones through the eyes of people on the street. When the terrorist attacks of 9/11 leveled the World Trade Center and rocked the real world, Marvel addressed this tragedy, as the twin towers also collapsed in the comics, with Spider-Man, Captain America, and other superheroes—as well as "average" New Yorkers—rallying to assist the fallen. Publishers DC, Image, and Dark Horse also dealt with this horrific event by releasing several special comic books, the proceeds from which benefited the tragedies' victims and their families.

The X-Men operate from the Xavier Institute for Higher Learning in the wooded confines of Westchester County, New York, offering these mutants, held suspect by so many homo sapiens, safe haven from the bigotries of city dwellers. The Inhumans, another race of outcast superheroes, first settled on a North Atlantic island named Attilan before hiding out in the Himalayas, and eventually establishing the lunar colony of New Attilan.

Another unique supercity is Astro City, from the award-winning comic-book series of same name created by Busiek. Astro City's history is rich with superpowered friends and felons like the Samaritan and Jack-in-the-Box. Dark Horse Comics' immodestly named "Comics' Greatest World" consists of four distinctive environments: Arcadia, an Art Deco–inspired Mecca for mobsters and the base for anti-heroes X and Ghost; Steel Harbor, a bombed-out urban landscape overrun by superthugs, where Barb Wire and the Machine protect the weak; Golden City, a picture-perfect, gated megalopolis where superheroine Grace and her agents of change Catalyst inspire the masses; and Cinnabar Flats, the sparsely populated, southwest desert location of an interdimensional vortex and a top-secret military installation—as well as the stomping grounds for Hero Zero and Division 13. Like Dark Horse's Arcadia, DC's Fawcett City is an architectural testament to Art Deco design. Fawcett City is home to Captain Marvel, Mary Marvel, and CM3 (formerly known as Captain Marvel Jr.).

DC's contemporary superheroes continue the publisher's long-standing tradition of spanning the continental United States in mostly fictitious bergs. A 2004 survey of DC cities and their superpowered residents includes: Blüdhaven (where Batman's prodigal son, Dick Grayson—the original Robin the Boy Wonder—fights crime both as a police officer and as the costumed hero Nightwing); Portsmouth City (home of Dr. Mid-Nite of the JSA); Star City (home of Green Arrow); St. Roch, Louisiana (home of Hawkman and Hawkgirl); Salem Tower, Massachusetts (home of Dr. Fate); Pittsburgh, Pennsylvania (home of Firestorm, the Nuclear Man); Bette Noire, the shadowy, somewhat supernatural Gulf Coast home base of Fallen Angel; and Z'onn Z'orr, Antarctica (home of J'onn J'onzz, better known as the Martian Manhunter).

Even real-life cities can seem exotic in the New York–centric comics world; it was big news when Marvel actually situated a superteam in Los Angeles (the Champions, in the 1970s), and just as novel when the company started a long-running

West Coast counterpart to its popular Avengers team in the 1980s. Chicago, America's "Second City," has played perennial host to the superhero world's second string, including Marvel's mysterious Cat and satirical Hawk-Owl and Woody and Jack Kirby's Ninth Men, with one bona fide star, Erik Larsen's Savage Dragon, also calling the city home.

Still, fantasy cities remain an essential ingredient of superhero lore. The mid-1990s Milestone line centered its multicultural heroes in the fictional Midwestern metropolis of Dakota, and Alan Moore's ABC titles have given the made-up supercity a new lease on life. *Tom Strong* takes place between the traditional/technological island of Attabar Teru and the utopian town of Victorian skyscrapers, Millennium City; *Top Ten* is set in the dizzying sci-fi city of Neopolis, a kind of sprawling superhero ghetto; *Greyshirt* and *Cobweb* confine their adventures to the twilight-toned, natural-gas-powered Indigo City; and many of the heroes of the parallel Earth called *Terra Obscura* ply their trade in Invertica City, a metropolis built into a crater in which "everywhere is downtown."

A recurring trend for comics writers has been to relocate superheroes to actual cities—Barbara Gordon (Batgirl, later Oracle) was once a congresswoman in Washington, D.C., and fought crime there at night; Green Arrow vacated Star City in the 1980s and 1990s and aimed for Seattle; at one time the Justice League of America was headquartered in Detroit; Wonder Woman temporarily set up digs in Boston; and for a while Supergirl hung her cape in Charlotte, North Carolina—in efforts to pique reader interest with fresh, new environments. Outside of the sporadic insertion of geographic landmarks, however, these (and other) real-life locations have seemed surreal on the comics page. —*ME*

Supergirl

"It … uh … must be an illusion!" stammers Superman as he witnesses "a youngster flying, dressed in a supercostume," zipping from a crashed spaceship. It's Supergirl, the cousin of Superman, arriving on Earth in *Action Comics* #252 (May 1959). Superman discovers that this ebullient, golden-haired teen is Kara, a survivor from his homeworld of Krypton. When the planet exploded years ago—the horrific event that led to baby Superman being sent to Earth—the entire megalopolis of Argo City survived, hurled from the explosion and existing on a chunk of planetary debris. As a meteor shower decimates the floating city and its populace, scientist Zor-El—brother of Jor-El, Superman's biological father—rockets his daughter Kara to Earth to join her cousin. Given the tragedy from which she has just emerged, Supergirl's giddiness seems rather callous as she soars about in a blue-skirted version of Superman's uniform, but this was a time of innocence for publisher DC Comics' characters.

Superman concealed Kara's existence from the world, covertly instructing Supergirl on how to use her powers (slightly weaker versions of his own). Disguising herself with a brunette wig and taking the Earth name Linda Lee, Supergirl resided at an orphanage in the hamlet of Midvale, eventually being adopted by the Danvers family. After almost three years (in real time) of laboring in the shadows as her cousin's secret weapon, Supergirl was introduced to the world by Superman in a televised ticker-tape parade in *Action* #285 (February 1962).

Throughout the 1960s, Supergirl starred as the backup strip in *Action Comics,* sometimes cover-featured as a guest star to her top-tiered cousin. Unmistakably, the character was created as an attraction for young girl readers, and while most boys reading comics shunned DC's *Wonder Woman* title, they read Supergirl's stories since they shared space in *Action* with the immensely popular Man of Steel. Supergirl soon had her own supporting cast—Linda Lee Danvers' boyfriend Dick Malverne, her adopted parents, Streaky the Super-Cat, and Comet the Super-Horse, plus the thirtieth century's Legion of Super-Heroes, particularly member Brainiac 5, who carried a torch for the

Supergirl #3 © 1973 DC Comics.
COVER ART BY BOB OKSNER.

Girl of Steel—but the super-cousin herself never quite evolved past second-banana status. Her *Action* stories were lighthearted fluff, generally dealing with teen-age heartache or a campus-based mystery. In June 1969, Supergirl assumed the lead spot in *Adventure Comics,* but despite frequent costume changes (including a hot pants ensemble she donned for most of the 1970s) and two attempts at headlining her own title, it became obvious to readers that she had never really developed her own personality. Still, publisher DC Comics kept the character in print in one fashion or another, trading on her licensing potential through a variety of dolls, pencil cases, purses, and other products targeting young girls.

In the early to mid-1980s, Supergirl, having shed her hot pants for a skirt and a headband right out of singer Olivia Newton-John's "Physical" music video, was headed for the big time—and for disaster. Writer Marv Wolfman, while pitching to DC his twelve-issue comic-book opus *Crisis on Infinite Earths,* suggested that Supergirl be killed to give more emotional resonance to this continuity-reshaping series. Editorial director Dick Giordano agreed, calling Supergirl "Superman with boobs." The company's other executives hesitated, as Supergirl was about to star in a summer 1984 movie from the producers of the first three Superman movies. The theatrical *Supergirl,* featuring Helen Slater in a charming title performance with Faye Dunaway hamming it up as a campy witch antagonist, tanked at the box office, and the decree was made: Supergirl would die. And she did so in *Crisis* #7 (October 1985), valiantly sacrificing herself to save other heroes. By the end of the *Crisis* series, the Girl of Steel had been removed from the rewritten DC mythology.

In 1986, author/artist John Byrne revamped the Superman legend in his six-issue *Man of Steel* series, and by 1988, a new Supergirl was introduced. Created from protoplasm in an alternate reality known as the "pocket universe," Supergirl, originally called "Matrix," ventured to Metropolis to recruit Superman's aid in overcoming a menace from back home. Making Earth her adopted planet, the new Supergirl's career has been fraught with change. After merging her body with that of the dying Linda Danvers, she upped the super-ante by becoming an angel with fiery wings before morphing yet again, experiencing a makeover into a cutesy blonde with a bare midriff and lace-up boots.

In late 2002, DC Comics came full circle when Super*girl* encountered a youngster, flying, dressed in a supercostume, zipping from a crashed spaceship, just as Super*man* had done in 1959. This was the Kryptonian Supergirl Kara, the cousin of Superman and a survivor of Argo City—but from a parallel universe, to which she soon returned. Beginning in the pages of *Superman: The 10-Cent Adventure*

(2003), yet another Supergirl—a buxom babe in a black swimsuit and blue, flowing cape—entered DC continuity, claiming to be the daughter of Superman. These continual changes illustrate what's right and wrong with the twenty-first-century Superman franchise: While it's exciting to see new spins on classic themes, frequent reinventions make the continuity so confusing that it is inaccessible for the casual or new reader. That may be why, in early 2004, DC brought back a contemporary version of the "real" Kara Zor-El, best known to the general public and best loved by longtime fans, in issue #8 of the hit *Superman/Batman* series.—*ME*

Superhero Cartoon Shows

Animation has been a staple of television almost since the medium's inception, although superheroes were not quick to catch on. Early cartoons—relegated mostly to Saturday mornings or after-school timeslots—were generally repeats of theatrical comedy shorts strung together into half-hour blocks. Early examples of superhero cartoons included all funny-animal characters such as *The Mighty Mouse Playhouse* (1955–1966), the Bob Kane–created *Courageous Cat and Minute Mouse* (1960), shoe-shine boy turned superhero *Underdog* (1964–1973), and insect and rodent heroes *The Atom Ant/Secret Squirrel Show* (1965–1968).

1965 saw the debut of the first two animated superheroes who were played for adventure instead of comedy. *The Eighth Man* (syndicated, 1965) was a Japanese import show about an android crime fighter, while Grantray-Lawrence's *The Marvel Super-Heroes* (syndicated, 1965) featured five days of superhero programming (*Captain America, The Incredible Hulk, Iron Man, Mighty Thor,* and *Sub-Mariner*).

New heroes were created for American television in 1966. *Frankenstein Jr. and the Impossibles*

The animated show *Iron Man.*

(CBS, 1966–1968) featured a trio of rock-and-rolling crime fighters known as Fluid Man, Multi-Man, and Coil Man. CBS's *Space Ghost and Dino Boy* (CBS, 1966–1968) gave top billing to a space-bound crime fighter with powerful gauntlets. *The Super Six* (NBC, 1966–1969) starred heroes defined by their names: Granite Man, Super Scuba, Elevator Man, Magnet Man, and Captain Whammy. Ralph Bakshi's *The Mighty Heroes* (CBS, 1966–1967) were an odd quintet named Diaper Man, Cuckoo Man, Rope Man, Strong Man, and Tornado Man.

1967 was a banner year for animated heroes. *Batfink* (syndicated, 1967) was a parody of a certain other Bat-hero, and was accompanied by sidekick Karate. *Birdman and the Galaxy Trio* (NBC, 1967–1968) featured stories with Birdman, Birdboy, and their pet eagle Avenger as they fought

crime, while Vapor Man, Galaxy Girl, and Meteor Man were the trio of the title. Galaxy Girl shared with Invisible Girl of Hanna-Barbera's *The Fantastic Four* (ABC, 1967–1970) and Mera of Filmation's *The Superman-Aquaman Hour of Adventure* (CBS, 1967–1968) the title of the first animated superheroines. Grantray-Lawrence again checked in with an ultra-popular *Spiderman* series (ABC, 1967–1970), while *Super President* (NBC, 1967–1968) saw the country led by a crime-fighting Commander in Chief.

The following several years debuted few new hero shows, largely because the others were popular enough to go to second or third seasons. Filmation's *The Batman/Superman Hour* (CBS, 1968–1969), *Aquaman* (CBS, 1968–1969), and *The Adventures of Batman* (CBS, 1969–1970) were extensions of previous shows. In 1973, Hanna-Barbera teamed several of DC Comics' top heroes together as *Super Friends* (ABC, 1973–1977), while police janitor turned kung fu hero *Hong Kong Phooey* (ABC, 1974–1976) rode to crime sites in his Phooeymobile. Old heroes got a new life in *The Space Ghost/Frankenstein Jr. Show* (NBC, 1976–1977), and comedy dog hero Dynomutt joined with Blue Falcon to fight crime in *The Scooby-Doo/Dynomutt Hour* (ABC, 1976–1977).

1977 saw the format of *Super Friends* altered for *The All-New Super Friends Hour* (ABC, 1977–1978), while Batman played double duty, also starring in Filmation's *The New Adventures of Batman* (CBS, 1977) and later *The Batman/Tarzan Adventure Hour* (CBS, 1977–1978). The following year, the show was changed to *Tarzan and the Super 7* (CBS, 1978–1980), and several superhero elements were added: *Freedom Force* featured Isis, Hercules, Merlin, Super Samurai, and Sinbad; *Web Woman* featured a heroine given spider powers and accompanied on her adventures by an alien pet named Spinner; *Manta and Moray* showcased the last survivor of an underwater civilization and his girlfriend; and *Super Stretch and Microwoman* featured African Americans Chris and Christy Cross who could shrink and stretch to fight crime. Rumored legal trouble from both DC and Marvel led to few episodes (and fewer reruns) of the latter three series.

1978 also saw *Dynomutt, Dog Wonder* (ABC, 1978), another new title for Hanna-Barbera's *Challenge of the Super Friends* (ABC, 1978–1979), and a trio of familiar Marvel heroes—plus a clownish robot sidekick—in *The New Fantastic Four* (NBC, 1978–1979). The following year was a banner year for heroes, though several of them were comedy oriented. *The Super Globetrotters* (NBC, 1979–1980) refashioned the basketball-playing Harlem Globetrotters into the superheroes Multi-Man, Sphere Man, Gizmo Man, Spaghetti Man, and Fluid Man. *The Plastic Man Comedy-Adventure Show* (ABC, 1979–1980) featured the Quality/DC stretchable

character, as well as a segment called *Mighty Man and Yukk* featuring a tiny hero and the world's ugliest dog fighting crime. Hanna-Barbera debuted a new series called *Fred and Barney Meet the Thing* (NBC, 1979), teaming characters from *The Flintstones* with one member of the *Fantastic Four*. Another Marvel character made her debut in Depatie-Freleng's *Spider-Woman* (ABC, 1979–1980), and the DC superteam got another new incarnation with *The World's Greatest Super Friends* (ABC, 1979–1980).

Format changes resulted in more name changes for older series in 1980: *The Super Friends Hour* (ABC, 1980–1981), *Batman and the Super 7* (NBC, 1980–1981), and *The Plastic Man/Baby Plas Super Comedy* (ABC, 1980–1981). Hanna-Barbera mixed monsters and teens to become the superheroes Drak, Frankie, and Howler and pitted them against Dr. Dred and O.G.R.E. in *Drak Pack* (CBS, 1980–1982). The following season saw the return of Space Ghost in *Space Stars* (NBC, 1981–1982), and another name change for *The Super Friends* (ABC, 1981–1984). Marvel's web-spinning hero appeared on the network show *Spider-Man and His Amazing Friends* (NBC, 1981–1982) and in a syndicated solo version called simply *Spider-Man* (1981–1982). Prescott-Scheimer's *Kid Super-Power Hour with Shazam!* (NBC, 1981–1982) featured animated adventures with the Fawcett/DC Marvel Family (Captain Marvel, Mary Marvel, Captain Marvel Jr.), as well as adventures of the teen heroes who attended Hero High (Captain California, Gorgeous Gal, Dirty Trixie, Misty Magic, Rex Ruthless, Weatherman, and Punk Rock).

The following several years mainly featured name and format changes for a few continuing series: *The Incredible Hulk and The Amazing Spider-Man* (NBC, 1982–1983), which added a half-hour *Hulk* component; *The Amazing Spider-Man and the Incredible Hulk* (NBC, 1983–1984); and *Super Friends—The Legendary Super Powers Show* (ABC, 1984–1985). A British comic strip was brought to the United States with *Bananaman* (Nickelodeon,

1985–1987), in which a banana-eating wimp becomes a superhero. That year also saw the final name change and final incarnation for Hanna-Barbera's venerable Super Friends with *The Super Powers Team: Galactic Guardians* (ABC, 1985–1986).

Defenders of the Earth (syndicated, 1986–1987) featured King Features' comic-strip heroes the Phantom, Flash Gordon, Mandrake the Magician, and Lothar as they protected Earth's future from Ming the Merciless. A family of bionic-powered heroes fought Dr. Scarab in *Bionic Six* (syndicated, 1987). An old heroic mouse reappeared for funny—and sometimes controversial—new stories with *Mighty Mouse: The New Adventures* (CBS, 1987–1989), while comic-dom's hero supreme reappeared in a new Ruby-Spears series with *Superman* (CBS, 1988–1989). The universe's cuddliest hero arrived in the form of a superpowered teddy bear, set to battle Skeleton, Bulk, and Texas Pete in *The Further Adventures of Super-Ted* (syndicated, 1988–1989).

As the 1990s began, superheroes had all but disappeared from the airwaves, though that would soon change. Environmental heroes faced villainous polluters and strip miners in *Captain Planet and the Planeteers* (syndicated, 1990–1995), while Disney produced its first hero cartoon with the adventurer known as *Darkwing Duck* (Disney Channel and ABC, 1991–1995), who protected the city of St. Canard from evildoers. Musician M. C. Hammer donned magic shoes to become a superhero in *Hammerman* (ABC, 1991–1992), but by the following year, weird heroes were in vogue. DIC produced a short-lived *Swamp Thing* cartoon (Fox, 1991), while bizarre and deformed Troma movie creations Toxic Crusader (toned down from Toxic Avenger), double-craniumed Headbasher, Junkyard, and No Zone fought against evil polluters and mutants such as Zarzoza from the planet Smogula, Bonehead, Psycho, and Dr. Killemoff in *Toxic Crusaders* (syndicated, 1991–1992). The following year, two excellent comic-book adaptations began their long runs on Fox: *Batman: The Animated Series* (1992–1994) and *X-Men* (1992–1997).

1994 was the biggest year for superheroes in history with eight new series debuting, and one going through a name change: *The Adventures of Batman & Robin* (Fox, 1994–1997). Marvel's web-spinner debuted with a brand new show in *Spider-Man* (Fox, 1994–1998), while New England Comics' big blue hero arrived in *The Tick* (Fox, 1994–1997), and Image saw representation with both *Jim Lee's WildC.A.T.S* (CBS, 1994–1995) and *The Maxx* on *MTV Oddities* (MTV, 1994–1995). Two Marvel series were combined for *The Marvel Action Hour* (syndicated, 1994–1996), with *Fantastic Four* and *Iron Man* sharing the screen. Animation met live-action in the wacky talk show *Space Ghost Coast to Coast* (Cartoon Network, 1994–2003), and a purple-clad King Features hero saw more futuristic adventuring against environmental villains in *Phantom 2040* (syndicated, 1994–1996).

Several more comic book properties reached TV screens in 1995, with DIC's production of Malibu's *UltraForce* (syndicated, 1995–1996), Image's *Savage Dragon* (USA Network, 1995–1997), and Dark Horse's movie spin-off *The Mask* (CBS and syndicated, 1995–1997). Also on tap were the zany antics of a computer geek turned rubber-boned superhero in *Steven Spielberg Presents Freakazoid!* (WB, 1995–1996). Superhero action figures came to life in the *Kablam!* segment *Action League Now!!!* (Nickelodeon, 1996–1999), with short segments featuring the Flesh, Stinky Diver, Thundergirl, the Chief, and Melt Man. The following year DC produced the critically acclaimed *Superman* (WB, 1996–1997) and Marvel's green-skinned Goliath returned in *The Incredible Hulk* (UPN, 1996–1997). Both series changed titles and gained fellow heroes the next season, with *The New Batman/Superman Adventures* (WB, 1997–1998) and *The Incredible Hulk and She-Hulk* (UPN, 1997–1998). Aimed squarely at mature audiences, *Todd McFarlane's Spawn* also debuted in latenight timeslots (HBO, 1997–1999).

In 1998, Marvel's angst-ridden space hero debuted with *The Silver Surfer* (Fox, 1998–1999), and a trio of cute girl heroines debuted with their own series (though two earlier cartoons had aired in 1995 and 1996). Bubbles, Buttercup, and Blossom are *The Powerpuff Girls* (Cartoon Network, 1998–present) and they fight such enemies as evil monkey Mojo Jojo, Fuzzy Lumpkins, Princess More-bucks, and others. The following year, a futuristic relaunch of Marvel's top hero tanked in the ratings with *Spider-Man Unlimited* (Fox, 1999), while a futur-istic version of DC's dark hero soared with *Batman Beyond* (WB, 1999–2002). Even cute and addictive kids series *Spongebob Squarepants* (Nickelodeon, 1999–present) got into the hero business with undersea crime-fighters Barnacle Boy and Mermaid Man appearing as Spongebob's favorite TV heroes.

An old Hanna-Barbera hero was revived for the bizarrely funny *Harvey Birdman, Attorney at Law* (Car-toon Network, 2000–present), in which the ex-hero took on legal cases from other cartoon characters. Milestone's African American teen hero Static debuted in his own series called *Static Shock* (WB, 2000–present), while Marvel's popular mutants were revived in *X-Men: Evolution* (WB, 2000–present). *Bat-man Beyond* spun off a fugitive hero character into its own series with *The Zeta Project* (WB, 2001–2002), while DC's top heroes reunited for a well-received *Jus-tice League* (Cartoon Network, 2001–present), which aired in both widescreen and full-frame formats. *Ren & Stimpy* creator John Kricfalusi created *The Ripping Friends* (Fox and Cartoon Network, 2001–2002), a quartet of strange musclebound heroes—Rip, Slag, Crag, and Chunk—who "ripped" criminals ranging from wormy Flathead and egg-stealing Ovulator to sen-tient wads of chewing gum. The series proved too odd for Saturday mornings. And speaking of odd, *The Fair-ly Oddparents* (Nickelodeon, 2001–present) features Timmy, a boy whose wishes can bring his favorite comic-book heroes to life, including Crimson Chin (voiced by Jay Leno) and Cleft the Boy Chin Wonder, as well as Crash Nebula. Timmy also becomes Turbo Timmy in one episode.

In 2002, Disney produced a show in which young kids become the superheroes Captain Cran-dall, Skate Lad, and Rope Girl in *Teamo Supremo* (ABC and Toon Disney, 2002–present), fighting vil-lains such as Baron Blitz, Mr. Inflato, the Sinister Stylist, and the Birthday Bandit. An anime-inspired version of *Teen Titans* (Cartoon Network, 2003–pre-sent) debuted, with the teen heroes opposing the Fearsome Five, Terminator, Trident, and others. On the adult front, Pamela Anderson's *Stripperella* (TNT and Spike, 2003–present) doffed clothes and bat-tled villains, and *Spider-Man* returned (MTV, 2003) for a set of computer-animated adventures based on the feature film.

Besides the clearly superhero-related series, many animated shows feature adventurers, fantasy heroes, or space characters who don't quite fit the superhero mold: Boys are represented by *Marine Boy, Jonny Quest, GI Joe, Masters of the Universe, Flash Gordon, Buzz Lightyear of Star Command,* and *Men in Black;* girls have such heroines as *Jem, She-Ra: Princess of Power,* and *Aeon Flux.* As the above history shows, while the twenty-first century moves forward and computer-generated animation becomes more commonplace, superhero cartoon shows will remain an integral part of the television landscape. —*AM*

Superhero Confidants

Confidentiality and superpowers are usually bedfel-lows—superheroes' identities *are* called "secret," after all—requiring the superhero to solve personal crises alone, with no one to talk to. But not all superheroes are doomed to this solitary fate. Walk-ing in and out of the lives of superheroes, lending their sympathetic ears, have been sidekicks (includ-ing Captain America's Bucky, Green Arrow's Speedy, and Plastic Man's Woozy Winks), significant others (like the Elongated Man's spouse Sue and the Fan-tastic Four's husband/wife duo Mr. Fantastic and the

Invisible Woman), super friends (Kitty Pryde of the X-Men touched embittered Wolverine's heart, and the Justice League's Blue Beetle and Booster Gold are the best of "buds"), godlike guardians (the Keeper spectrally watches over Kid Eternity, and Thor answers to his all-knowing father, Odin), kindly relatives (Billy Batson—Captain Marvel—talks to both his sister Mary and his Uncle Dudley), and stereotyped ethnic companions (the Lone Ranger's Tonto, the Green Hornet's Kato, Captain Aero's Chop Suey, and Green Lantern's Pieface, among others).

Some confidants have become crucial to their superheroes' mythology. The character who defined the genre—Superman—may have lost his Kryptonian birth parents when his home planet exploded, but is adopted on Earth by "Ma and Pa" (Martha and Jonathan) Kent, who eagerly offer him their wisdom. In Superman's 1938 origin, the Kents instruct the young extraterrestrial to conceal his super-strength while in his guise of Clark Kent, and to wisely channel his might: Ma Kent advises, "… when the proper time comes, you must use it to assist humanity." This sentiment is echoed in director Richard Donner's *Superman: The Movie* (1978), when actor Glenn Ford as Pa Kent assures teenage Clark (Jeff East), "You are here for a reason." When Superboy ("The Adventures of Superman When He Was a Boy") was retrofitted into Superman continuity in 1945, Ma and Pa Kent appeared as supporting cast members, helping their teenage son help conceal his identity from nosy next-door neighbor Lana Lang. The Kents eventually passed away, triggering Clark's move from Smallville to Metropolis to become Superman. When the Superman mythos was rebooted with the miniseries *The Man of Steel* (1986), Superboy was eliminated but Ma and Pa Kent remained alive, specifically to mentor their adult super-son. In the 2000s, Superman frequently soars home to seek advice from his parents.

Lang was also altered as a result of *The Man of Steel*: As Clark Kent's high-school sweetheart, she anticipates marrying him after graduation. He takes her into his deepest confidence and reveals to her his superpowers, then leaves her behind to pursue his career as Superman. Lang's love for Kent remains unrequited. She weds classmate Pete Ross, who later becomes the U.S. vice president, but eventually separates from him and moves to Metropolis, presumably to be closer to Kent.

On television's live-action *The Adventures of Superman* (1953–1957), the public believes that the Man of Steel's confidant is *Daily Planet* reporter Clark Kent, the perception being that Kent can contact the Man of Steel during crises. In the DC comic books of the Silver Age (1956–1969), cub reporter Jimmy Olsen is Superman's "pal." The Man of Steel entrusts young Olsen with kryptonite, alien weapons, and interplanetary artifacts, but never reveals his Kent identity to the lad for his own protection against criminals who might harm him for that information. The Silver Age Superman and Batman share many secrets, including knowledge of their dual identities and access to their private headquarters, the Fortress of Solitude and the Batcave, respectively. Superman's most unusual Silver Age confidant is President John F. Kennedy, who actually fills in for Kent on an occasion when Superman and his alter ego must appear simultaneously.

"Lois, for the past few years I've lived a double life," confesses Kent to the woman he loves, Lois Lane, in *Action Comics* #662 (1991). Five years later, Kent and Lane become husband and wife. Mrs. Kent assists her husband in grappling with the enormous responsibilities of being the planet's premier superhero.

Batman, emotionally scarred since childhood after witnessing the brutal slayings of his parents, is a more introverted character than Superman. For the first year of his career, beginning in 1939, Batman is wanted by the Gotham City police and lives alone as millionaire Bruce Wayne. When his ward Dick Grayson (Robin the Boy Wonder) enters his life in 1940, the lad's *joie de vivre* permits some sunshine to seep into the Dark Knight's dour existence, yet Batman keeps his feelings at arm's length from his junior partner. In the 1980s, Batman's obsession divides the Dynamic Duo, but they ultimately reconcile when Wayne confesses that he regards Grayson as his son.

Once Alfred Pennyworth—better known as "Alfred the Butler"—joins the Wayne household in 1943 as a gentleman's gentleman and stumbles across his employer's dual identity, Wayne is forced to accept Alfred into his inner circle. Over the decades, Alfred undergoes a gradual transformation from a superhero's valet—dusting the Batcave and laundering tights and cowls—to Wayne's guardian angel. Alfred reminds his resolute boss of his engagements, ensures that he eats and sleeps, and nurses his wounds, both physical and emotional. Wayne may consider Grayson his son, but privately admits that Alfred is his "father."

While Batman's inhospitality may be unpalatable among his teammates in the Justice League of America, one man has called the Dark Knight "friend": Gotham City police Commissioner James Gordon. They meet as adversaries, however, in Batman's very first appearance, when Gordon orders his officers to fire at the shadowy vigilante, a scene replayed over the decades in revisions of Batman's history, including Frank Miller and David Mazzucchelli's "Batman: Year One" (1987) and Tim Burton's motion picture *Batman* (1989). Over time, Gordon realizes that Batman and he are playing on the same team. From the 1940s through the 1960s, Commissioner Gordon views Batman as his (dark) knight in shining armor, using the Bat-signal to summon the hero when needed—a dependency played for laughs on TV's campy *Batman* series (1966–1968), in which it seems that Gordon's inept police force can handle no threat without the aid of Batman and Robin. During Batman's 1970s return to his ominous roots, Gordon and Batman are allies, with the commissioner often spooked when the Caped Crusader stealthily steps out of the shadows into his office. As Batman's stories grew even grittier beginning in the mid-1980s, the rapport between he and Gordon became strained, but

they maintain a mutual respect that continues in the 2000s, despite Gordon's retirement.

Gordon's daughter, former Batgirl Barbara Gordon—known among the superheroes of the DC universe as the mysterious information broker Oracle—is often a voice of reason or friendship to the street operatives who use her services, including Black Canary, the Huntress, the new Batgirl, and Nightwing. Oracle's uncanny fluency as a hacker makes her privy to virtually any data stored in computer networks, and thus she knows or has discovered the secret identities of many of DC's heroes. While she routinely offers counsel, the austere, self-reliant Oracle seeks information, not advice, from others. For most of her Bargirl career, she kept her costumed guise a secret from Commissioner Gordon (although he deduced the truth), and in the 2000s she similarly shields her covert Oracle activities from her father.

For years, lawyer Matt Murdock—Marvel Comics' blind superhero, Daredevil—shoulders the burden of his dual identity alone, but once his law partner Foggy Nelson discovers the truth, Murdock gains a trusted confidant. Daredevil has divulged his alter ego to three former girlfriends: The Black Widow guards his confidence, but an addled Karen Page sold Murdock's secret identity for drugs, and his college sweetheart—the assassin-for-hire Elektra—tried to kill him. Throughout his one-man crusade against New York City crime, Daredevil frequently crosses paths with the amazing Spider-Man. The two are now staunch allies and sometimes talk heart-to-heart on rooftops.

Two other confidants are snared within Spider-Man's personal web. Mary Jane Watson, wife of the hero's alter ego Peter Parker, dated Parker for years before walking down the aisle with him. The demands of her career as a model and his moonlighting as a crime fighter lead to their separation, but as of 2004 they remain romantically attached. Parker's sickly Aunt May doted on him during his adolescence, with the teen living in perpetual fear of his Spider-Man identity being exposed to her. His worst nightmare nearly comes true in the landmark *The Amazing Spider-Man* #39 (1966), when the insidious Green Goblin unearths Spidey's true identity and attacks Parker where he is most vulnerable—outside of his home, with Aunt May inside! Years later (in 2001), Aunt May inadvertently discovers her nephew's dual identity when she finds him in bed, bloodied and bruised from a supervillain tussle, a tattered Spider-Man uniform by his side. Aunt May surprises Parker by supporting his superhero career. —*ME*

Superhero Creators

Superheroes as diverse as Wonder Woman and Spawn share one characteristic: They were originally conceived by a spark of an artist's or writer's imagination. Each of the costumed characters unveiled since the debut of Superman in *Action Comics* #1 (June 1938) has his or her own story of evolution, with innovative folk behind the scenes who thought, hoped, and dreamed that their creation would be the next Man of Steel.

To the superhero and comic-book aficionado, names like Jack Kirby and John Byrne are as important as Clark Kent and Peter Parker. A complete survey of the individuals who have produced the adventures of the superheroes chronicled in this volume is too extensive to include, but some creators' legacies are so embedded in superhero history that they must be mentioned.

(There are numerous legendary comics artists and authors who have not, or have rarely, produced superhero work. So as not to diverge from the focus of this encyclopedia, industry legends such as Alex Raymond, Harvey Kurtzman, Bernie Krigstein, Jack Davis, Frank Frazetta, Hal Foster, Al Williamson, George Evans, Carl Barks, Joe Orlando, John Severin, Russ Heath, Robert Crumb, Richard and Wendy Pini, Harlan Ellison, and Dave Sim are not discussed, but are acknowledged here for their superlative contributions.)

GOLDEN AGE OF COMICS (1938–1954)

The Golden Age of superhero comics was an era of assembly-line production. Publishers shoved hordes of young, enthusiastic artists into sweatshops and pressured them to produce, produce, produce, with ambitious businessmen like Harry "A" Chesler, Malcolm Wheeler-Nicholson, Charles Biro, Martin Goodman, and "Busy" Arnold always looking over their shoulders. Most of the stories printed during the Golden Age were crude, but some writers and artists emerged as talented draftsmen, pioneering visionaries, or, in a few cases, both. During their day, however, they were largely ignored by the public who devoured their work.

"In 1940, comic-book artists, if they were regarded at all, were not [well] regarded," said cartoonist Will Eisner. Eisner's *The Spirit* appeared not in traditional comic books, but in the newspapers as a comic supplement, from 1940 to 1952. "Comics before (*The Spirit*) were pretty much pictures in sequence, and I was trying to create an art form," Eisner once commented. And that he did: With his dramatic storytelling, contrasting lights and darks, and ingenious splash pages (which often incorporated the Spirit's name as an artistic element), Eisner raised the bar for other illustrators. Beyond *The Spirit,* Eisner has contributed to mainstream comics (including Quality's *Uncle Sam*), illustrated numerous graphic novels, and authored a tome many comics professionals regard as the industry's premier textbook: *Comics & Sequential Art.* Eisner is the patron saint of comics professionals—the industry's top awards, presented annually at the San Diego Comic-Con, bear his name.

Writer Jerry Siegel and artist Joe Shuster, high-school buddies from Cleveland, Ohio, created Superman in the early 1930s, first as an illustrated prose story, then as a proposed newspaper strip. They had such faith in their concept, they ambitiously promoted their creation as "The Smash Hit Strip of 1936," but the syndicates rejected the series. In 1938 their hero finally saw print in a DC Comics start-up title called *Action Comics,* and the rest, to borrow a cliché, is history. Siegel and Shuster sold DC the rights to Superman for a reported $130, but in subsequent decades they, and their heirs, have contested copyright ownership in court.

Illustrator Bob Kane commanded more business savvy than did Siegel and Shuster: Kane brokered a deal to be listed as the sole credited creator of Batman, first published in *Detective Comics* #27 (May 1939). Historians have long contested Kane's claim, as writer Bill Finger was the artist's partner and contributed much to Batman's canon. Along with Finger, artist Jerry Robinson worked under Kane's wing and eventually assumed a larger profile as a Batman illustrator. Robinson once said of Finger, "Unlike most of the writers in the early comic-book industry, Finger wrote very visually. His stories were well-plotted and paced." The controversy of Batman's authorship aside, Kane was largely responsible for the look of the series: "I wanted my style a little cartoony," he said, "a cross between Dick Tracy and illustration." Kane's studio, which included stalwarts Dick Sprang and Jack Burnley, continued to produce Batman stories, with and without Kane's participation, well into the 1960s.

Charles Clarence "C. C." Beck was in his mid-twenties when he was hired as a house artist by Fawcett Publications in the late 1930s. Beck was paid a biweekly wage of $55 to crank out cartoons and spot illustrations for Fawcett's magazines. When his employer entered the comic-book business, Beck was tapped to draw their new Captain Marvel series that premiered in *Whiz Comics* #2 (1940). His clean, simple style helped make Captain Marvel the best-selling superhero of the Golden Age. In the 1950s the character was sued off the stands by DC Comics, but Beck ultimately returned to Captain Marvel in the 1970s when DC revived the hero in the title *Shazam!*

Cartoonist Jack Cole had been in the comics trenches for a while before bouncing to prominence with his creation, Plastic Man, in *Police Comics* #1 (1941). Cole's art was a wild blend of comedy and drama: His storytelling was impeccable, his splashes rivaled Eisner's, and he used his malleable hero's stretching ability to lead the reader's eye from panel to panel. Chagrined by the lack of respect afforded comic-book artists, Cole, in the 1950s, became an acclaimed artist for *Playboy* magazine and realized his dream of launching a syndicated newspaper strip, *Betsy and Me.* At the pinnacle of his success, Cole took his own life, a suicide that his surviving family members still find puzzling decades later.

Joe Simon was a multi-talented gent: He wrote and drew comics, but through his editorial position at Fox Comics he met and partnered with Jacob Kurtzberg, better known as Jack Kirby. Kirby was a street-smart kid who grew up in New York's rough-and-tumble Lower East Side during the Great Depression. Simon and Kirby formed comics' most celebrated writer/artist team of the Golden Age. Together, they produced Fawcett's *Captain Marvel Adventures* #1 (1941) and a variety of strips for DC Comics, but in 1941 struck gold (for the publisher, alas, not for themselves) with Timely (Marvel) Comics' *Captain America.* As a team, Simon and Kirby pioneered new ground with a host of horror, Western, and other titles—they even co-created the romance-comics genre—until parting ways in the late 1950s. Simon went on to invent *Brother Power the Geek* and *Prez* for DC, while Kirby became "King" as the visual architect of the Marvel Age of Comics in the 1960s: Kirby co-created the Fantastic Four, the Incredible Hulk, the X-Men, Thor, and many other characters with Stan Lee. In the 1970s Kirby created the vast "Fourth World" for DC Comics in series including *The New Gods,* but never completed his epics due to the titles' cancellations—"It's an unfinished symphony," observed Kirby's protégé Mark Evanier. Kirby later returned to Marvel, then illustrated independent comics, animation model sheets, and toy designs. Simon and Kirby's lives during the Golden Age inspired author Michael Chabon's Pulitzer Prize–winning novel *The Amazing Adventures of Kavalier & Clay.* In the 2000s Kirby's work is examined in the quarterly fanzine *The Jack Kirby Collector* from TwoMorrows Publishing.

Alex Toth, a cutting-edge illustrator who emerged during the late Golden Age, ignited the comics page in the 1950s and beyond with experimental art techniques that challenged his contemporaries. Toth has always been intensely committed to his craft: "I respond to honesty of skill, motive, talent, and preparation," he once said. Toth's superhero work was sporadic in later decades, but when it occurred, it was highly lauded, including his Atom/Flash team-up in *The Brave and the Bold* #53 (1964). Toth was also the designer behind three popular animated TV series: Hanna-Barbera's original *Space Ghost, Fantastic Four,* and *Super Friends.*

Other Golden Age greats include Lou Fine (Doll Man, the Ray, Black Condor), who learned to draw while bedridden with polio as a teen; Tarpe Mills, a rarity for the era, a female comics artist (of the character that's arguably the first major superheroine, *Miss Fury,* originally a newspaper strip and later reprinted in comic-book form); Mac Raboy, whose stunningly realistic style contrasted his *Captain Marvel Jr.* work from Fawcett's cartoonier Captain Marvel house style; Bill Everett, creator of the Sub-Mariner, whose vivid underwater scenes and intimidating star made Marvel's first anti-hero a huge success; Carl Burgos, whose flaming hero the Human Torch became Marvel's best-selling character; Wayne Boring, who helped Shuster by illustrating *Superman* stories during the hero's Golden Age boom and continued drawing the character into the 1960s; Sheldon Mayer, DC editor (of *All Star Comics*) and artist of the first superhero parody, the Red Tornado, in the *Scribbly* backup series; cover artists extraordinaire Alex Schomburg ("I always felt Alex Schomburg was to comic books what Norman Rockwell was to *The Saturday Evening Post,*" noted Stan Lee) and Matt Baker (whose *Phantom Lady* covers are prized

among collectors of "Good Girl" art); William Moulton Marston, a psychologist who created both the lie detector and Wonder Woman; and Sheldon Moldoff, an unsung journeyman who illustrated countless Batman and Hawkman tales for DC.

SILVER AGE OF COMICS (1956–1969)

DC Comics editor Julius "Julie" Schwartz is credited as the father of the Silver Age of comics. In the 1930s Schwartz was one of the founders of science-fiction fandom, and later worked as a literary agent for sci-fi authors Ray Bradbury and Alfred Bester before becoming a DC editor in the 1940s. Superheroes dwindled in popularity after World War II, their series supplanted by other genres including funny animals, horror, TV adaptations, and romance, and by the mid-1950s Schwartz was editing, not surprisingly, science-fiction comics like *Strange Adventures.* After the first three issues of DC's tryout title *Showcase* failed to capture the audience's imagination, Schwartz in 1956 proposed to his fellow editors that the Flash be revived in issue #4. "Some of my co-workers were incredulous and asked me why I thought Flash would succeed now, having failed so dismally a few years before," Schwartz recalled in his autobiography *Man of Two Worlds* (2000). He countered that the comics' audience replenished itself every few years, and while the editors remembered the Flash, the character would be new to most readers. Schwartz won his argument and was tapped to edit the revival, which became a reworking, as the Silver Age Flash was an entirely new character. The new Flash was a tremendous success, prompting Schwartz to continue the trend by revamping Green Lantern, the Atom, Hawkman, and other characters, resurrecting the entire superhero genre in the process. Schwartz enjoyed a lengthy career at DC, charting the courses of Batman and Superman for many years, retiring in the mid-1980s but continuing with the company as a consultant and "goodwill ambassador."

Carmine Infantino, who had started his comics career by drawing random strips during the Golden Age, was, like most other artists employed during the 1950s, illustrating cowboy, mystery, and science-fiction comics when Schwartz tapped him to be the artist for the relaunch of the Flash in *Showcase.* Infantino became DC's artistic star of the 1960s, visible on *The Flash, Batman,* Adam Strange in *Mystery in Space,* the Elongated Man in *Detective Comics,* and many of the company's most vibrant covers. Outside of the mid-1960s success with *Batman,* DC's sales were outdistanced by Marvel's. "DC needed a kick in the rump," claimed Infantino in a 2003 interview in *Back Issue* magazine. "And they brought me on board to do it." Infantino was hired as DC's art director in late 1966, and before long was booted upstairs to editorial director and later president. During his ten-year tenure, he steered the company to new creative heights and higher sales.

Schwartz recruited Gil Kane for his new versions of Green Lantern and the Atom. Kane was a young artist during the Golden Age, working largely unnoticed until earning the spotlight with his 1960s work in *Green Lantern.* Famous for his dynamic rendering style and unusual camera angles, Kane eventually drew *The Hawk and the Dove, Captain Action* (which he also later scripted: "I've always maintained that the best art came out of a continuity, either wholly created, of at least broken down dramatically, by the artist himself," he wrote in 1969 in the letters column of *Captain Action* #5), and *Superman* for DC, and *The Amazing Spider-Man* and *Captain America* for Marvel, among many other credits.

Writer Gardner Fox and artist Joe Kubert were selected for Schwartz's revival of Hawkman, the winged superhero, not a surprising selection since that team was also responsible for many of the Golden Age Hawkman's adventures. Kubert's lithe, sinewy figures made him perfect for the character's graceful aerial moves. Later in the Silver Age, Kubert spearheaded DC's war titles, most notably Sgt. Rock in *Our Army at War,* and in the 1970s wrote and drew DC's

critically acclaimed *Tarzan* comic. In 1976 he opened the Joe Kubert School of Cartoon and Graphic Art, an industry institution at which many gifted illustrators have studied. Fox also wrote *Justice League of America* and other series for Schwartz.

Other creators in editor Schwartz's corner: author John Broome (*The Flash, Green Lantern*), also a Golden Age carryover; penciler Mike Sekowsky, the original artist on *Justice League,* and Dick Dillin, the illustrator who replaced him; and artists Curt Swan and Murphy Anderson. Penciler Swan, whose first published comics work was in 1946, had been illustrating various Superman titles since the 1950s, working under iron-fisted editor Mort Weisinger; in the 1960s he ascended to the position of Superman artist supreme by illustrating, at various times, *Superman, Action Comics, World's Finest Comics, Superboy,* the Legion of Super-Heroes in *Adventure Comics,* and *Superman's Pal Jimmy Olsen.* Anderson launched his comics career in the 1940s and later enjoyed a stint illustrating the *Buck Rogers* syndicated newspaper strip. Schwartz regularly employed Anderson throughout the 1960s, as a solo artist on *Hawkman* and *The Spectre,* and as a regular cover inker for Infantino and Sekowsky. During a 1970 updating of *Superman,* Schwartz united Swan and Anderson on the series, a perfect meshing of two clean styles in collaboration nicknamed "Swanderson."

THE MARVEL AGE

If Julie Schwartz engineered the Silver Age, Stan Lee was its hijacker. In 1961 writer/editor Lee and co-conspirator artist Jack Kirby produced *Fantastic Four* #1 for Marvel Comics. With its unique take on realistic superheroes, *Fantastic Four* put Lee and Marvel on the map. Lee quickly followed with a universe of problem-ridden characters, including the Incredible Hulk, Spider-Man, Daredevil, and the X-Men. Through innovation and Lee's knack for hyperbolic self-promotion, Marvel steamrolled over DC in the 1960s and became the industry leader.

Jack Kirby penciled most of Marvel's original titles with Lee, but other artists were on board as the line expanded. Steve Ditko drew *The Amazing Spider-Man, The Incredible Hulk,* and Doctor Strange in *Strange Tales.* Ditko's peculiar illustrative style, with his flair for frenetic movement and equilibrium-bending perspectives, made his work visually unique. The Ditko/Lee partnership eventually severed over disagreements about *Spider-Man* character and storyline authorship. Throughout his illustrious career, Ditko has drawn *Blue Beetle* for Charlton, *Beware the Creeper* for DC, and *Mr. A,* a study of the struggle between good and evil. Once Ditko left *Spider-Man,* he was replaced by an artist with a dissimilar style but one who managed to catapult the series into a different yet equally popular course: John Romita, Sr., fresh off a stint on Marvel's *Daredevil.* Ultimately Romita's energetic approach would become Marvel's house style: He was a frequent cover artist and designed two of the company's most popular characters, the Punisher and Wolverine.

John Buscema distinguished himself on *The Silver Surfer* and *The Avengers* in the late 1960s, then *Fantastic Four* and *Conan the Barbarian* in the 1970s. His brother Sal was another Marvel mainstay, having illustrated, in a career spanning decades, virtually every title at the company. Gene Colan had served tours of duty at several comics publishers before landing at Marvel in the mid-1960s. His lengthy run on *Daredevil* is fondly remembered, as is his stint on *Sub-Mariner* in the late 1960s and his 1970s turn on Marvel's groundbreaking *Tomb of Dracula* series. A dependable penciler on series like *Sub-Mariner* and a gifted cartoonist on the satire comic *Not Brand Echh,* Marie Severin was also Marvel's main colorist and cover designer for years, an essential yet largely unsung role that mirrored that of women in society at the time. Roy Thomas worked briefly as assistant editor to DC's Mort Weisinger in 1965 before jumping ship to Marvel, where he honed his writing and editing skills under Lee's tutelage. A Golden Age historian,

Thomas at one time was Marvel's editor in chief, and is best known as the author of Marvel's *The Avengers* and *Conan the Barbarian* and DC's *All-Star Squadron.* In the 2000s he continues to edit and co-write his long-running fanzine *Alter Ego.*

Artist Walter Simonson beamed in Steve Duin and Mike Richardson's *Comics Between the Panels* (1998): "His work was like unto a God for a lot of us." Simonson was referring to Wally Wood, an immeasurably versatile illustrator perfectly fluent with humor, science fiction, horror, and superhero comics. Rising to prominence in the 1950s on a host of E.C. Comics, Wood is venerated among comics fans for his superhero parodies in *MAD* magazine, his run on Marvel's *Daredevil,* and his *T.H.U.N.D.E.R. Agents* for Tower Comics. In 1982 Wood, soured by failing health and embittered by being put out to pasture by younger artists, committed suicide.

Other noteworthy Silver Age superhero creators: Ramona Fradon, one of the few female illustrators working during this period, who drew DC's Aquaman in *Adventure Comics,* as well as *Metamorpho the Element Man, Super Friends,* and *Plastic Man* (she confessed, "I had serious difficulty relating to superhero subject matter, the staple of the comic-book industry"); Joe Gill, a prolific but rarely recognized writer of hundreds of Charlton Comics series, from superhero to romance; writer/editor Robert Kanigher, who guided, among many 1960s series, DC's *Wonder Woman* and *Metal Men,* along with artists Ross Andru and Mike Esposito; Kurt Schaffenberger, artist of *Superman's Girl Friend Lois Lane* and Supergirl in *Action Comics;* and Nick Cardy, whose drawings of striking women and serio-comic layouts made DC's *Bat Lash, Teen Titans,* and *Aquaman* fan favorites.

COMICS' FIRST "ROCK STARS"

A pair of visionaries rocketed to acclaim in the late 1960s. There was Jim Steranko—deemed "the first 'rock star' artist of comics" on the History Channel's two-hour special *Comic Book Super-*

heroes: Unmasked (2003)—who exploded onto the scene with his surrealistic style in Marvel's *Nick Fury, Agent of S.H.I.E.L.D.; Captain America;* and *X-Men* series. His work was the storytelling equivalent of pop art: impressionistic, cinematic, and fully alive. Artist Paul Gulacy commented in the book *Comics Between the Panels* (1998), "I look at Kirby as being the architect, Steranko building the framework, and the rest of us doing the finish work." Steranko's contributions to comics have been rare, but permanently imprinted onto the medium. He has authored two *Steranko History of Comics* volumes and painted dozens of paperback covers (including lauded covers for *The Shadow*).

The other profoundly influential illustrator of the late 1960s was Neal Adams. He started as an ad-agency artist in his late teens, then illustrated the *Ben Casey* newspaper strip before segueing to DC Comics in 1967—drawing, oddly enough, the company's licensed *The Adventures of Jerry Lewis* and *The Adventures of Bob Hope* books. The powers-that-be at DC quickly recognized his talent, and Adams began to make his mark on the Deadman strip in *Strange Adventures* and on *The Spectre* with his photorealistic rendering style and his imaginative layouts that whisked the reader from panel to panel; "… when you look at the page as a whole … it should never be a burden," he contended in Vanguard Productions' *Neal Adams: The Sketch Book* (1999). "What we're doing is telling stories." By the late 1960s Adams had lobbied to draw Batman in the team-up title *The Brave and the Bold,* where he visually transformed the character from campy caped crusader to mysterious creature of the night. Soon he was the hottest artist in comics, drawing *Batman, Detective,* and the award-winning *Green Lantern/Green Arrow* series. A staunch advocate for creators' rights, Adams helped lobby for the return of original artwork, royalties, and pensions for Superman creators Siegel and Shuster. Among comics artists, Adams is both revered and feared. His harsh critiques of artists' portfolios have encouraged some, and intimidated others.

BRONZE AGE OF COMICS (1970-1979)

Superhero comic books grew up during the 1970s, in content and in appearance. Adams continued to trailblaze throughout the decade, forming his own company, Continuity Associates, with his inking partner, former editor, and friend Dick Giordano. "Dick's inking pretty much set the standard," Adams revealed in the biography *Dick Giordano: Changing Comics, One Day at a Time* (2003). Giordano quietly grew from assembly-line inking during his youth in the early 1950s to lauded editorial stints at Charlton and DC in the 1960s. An accomplished solo illustrator (*Batman,* the Human Target in *Action Comics,* romance comics, and *Wonder Woman*), Giordano is best known as Adams' inker ("The Lennon and McCartney of comics," noted Giordano biographer Michael Eury) and as DC Comics' editorial director during its decade of innovation, the 1980s.

Adams and Giordano's Continuity Associates was the Mecca for comics artists of the 1970s. Continuity located work for seasoned professionals, but is best known for attracting young artistic wannabes. "People would sleep on the floor or even in the hall by the elevator," recalled Giordano. "Since so many people came and went, my policy became, 'if he's here a month from now I'll ask him what his name is.'"

Some of the young associates of Continuity who blossomed into popularity during the 1970s and beyond include Howard Chaykin, who started on sword-and-sorcery comics before making his mark on random *Batman* stories and with the sexploitative sci-fi epic *American Flagg!;* Terry Austin, a Giordano protégé who embarked upon a successful inking career; Marshall Rogers, who, with writer Steve Englehart, produced a critically acclaimed sequence of Batman tales in *Detective* that helped reinvent the Joker; Michael Golden, who followed his innovative Batman work with science fiction (*The Micronauts*) and war (*The 'Nam*) comics; Klaus Janson, renowned as Frank Miller's inker on *Daredevil,* who later enjoyed enduring success as a solo illustrator; Bill Sienkiewicz, who quickly abandoned a Neal Adams homage (on Marvel's *Moon Knight*) to chart new territory with his experimental rendering on *The New Mutants* and *Elektra: Assassin;* and Walt Simonson, yet another newcomer who garnered notice on Batman then blossomed in the 1980s on such strips as *Thor* and the Marvel/DC *X-Men/New Teen Titans* crossover.

Batman transmogrified into darker territory throughout the 1970s, partially due to moody covers by Bernie Wrightson (also known for *Swamp Thing*) and Michael Kaluta (who became a superstar by illustrating DC's *The Shadow*). No one was more influential in Batman's transformation than writer Denny O'Neil, who penned many of the character's 1970s adventures as well as *Superman, Green Lantern/Green Arrow,* and other revolutionary efforts. After editing at Marvel in the late 1970s, O'Neil returned to DC in the 1980s and supervised the Batman franchise as its group editor and as a frequent writer. After the highly publicized—and controversial—"Death of Robin" storyline in 1989, O'Neil was verbally accosted in a New York City deli: "Hey, this is the guy that killed Robin!" yelled an employee, which made him realize the far-reaching importance of his job. In the television special *Comic Book Superheroes: Unmasked,* O'Neil reflected that the Batman and Superman editors are "custodians of folklore."

Other creative forces to ascend during the 1970s: Jim Aparo, once a Charlton artist hired by Giordano to draw *Aquaman* at DC, then a dominant *Batman* artist for two decades; Archie Goodwin, a much-loved writer/editor for DC, Marvel, and Warren Publications; Barry Windsor-Smith, a British transplant who started in the United States on random Marvel superhero work before soaring to acclaim on *Conan the Barbarian;* Marv Wolfman, a popular writer (*Tomb of Dracula, The New Teen Titans, Crisis on Infinite Earths*) who served a stint as Marvel's editor in chief and also has worked in Hollywood;

Len Wein, scripter of *Batman, Swamp Thing,* and *X-Men,* creator of Wolverine, and yet another former Marvel editor in chief; Dave Cockrum, fan-favorite artist of *Superboy Starring the Legion of Super-Heroes* and the 1975 revamp of *X-Men;* Mike Grell, who started as the *Legion* artist before growing into his own as the writer/artist of *The Warlord, Jon Sable: Freelance,* and *Green Arrow: The Longbow Hunters;* Jim Starlin, artist/writer who popularized Marvel's Captain Marvel, then killed the hero (of cancer); and George Pérez, jumping from *Fantastic Four* to *The Avengers* in the late 1970s to *Justice League of America* and *The New Teen Titans* in the early 1980s.

THE GROWING STATURE OF ARTISTS

By the 1980s comics publishers realized the importance of their creative personnel. Superstar artists, and sometimes writers, were producing higher sales, and DC and Marvel bowed to pressure to accord top performers royalties for their efforts.

Noteworthy superhero creators during the 1980s include author Chris Claremont, whose lengthy run on *X-Men* is unparalleled; artist/writer John Byrne, who started in the 1970s on minor Charlton titles (like *Wheelie and the Chopper Bunch*) before illustrating Marvel titles (*Marvel Team-Up, The Uncanny X-Men*) and ultimately writing and illustrating a host of series (*Fantastic Four, The Incredible Hulk, Superman,* and *The Sensational She-Hulk*); Frank Miller, who grabbed readers by their throats with his gripping take on *Daredevil,* then followed with his magnum opus *Batman: The Dark Knight Returns;* Keith Giffen, who began as a penciler for random DC titles in the late 1970s before rising to prominence in the early 1980s as the artist of *Legion of Super-Heroes,* and becoming the driving force behind 1980s hits like *Lobo* and the revamped *Justice League;* Arthur Adams, who became a frequently imitated fan favorite from his illustrations on *Longshot* and *X-Men;* David Mazzucchelli, an accomplished stylist whose brief fling with mainstream comics included two eminent projects with writer Frank Miller, "Batman: Year One" and "Daredevil: Born Again"; Jerry Ordway, a triple-threat writer/penciler/inker whose art on *The Adventures of Superman* helped redefine the hero for the decade; and second-generation artists: Joe Kubert's sons Andy and Adam, and John Romita's son John Jr., who developed into talented illustrators in their own rights.

Smaller "independent" publishers sprouted in the 1980s, some growing out of a mid-decade boom of black-and-white (B&W) comics, others dedicated to producing quality color work. From the throng of companies achieving some degree of prominence during the 1980s (Pacific Comics, Comico the Comic Company, First Comics, Now Comics, and others), only Dark Horse Comics, which started in 1986, remains an industry leader in the 2000s. Several immensely gifted talents got their starts at these companies, including artist Steve Rude, who rose to acclaim on *Nexus* and later illustrated more mainstream work including Superman and Batman in *World's Finest;* Matt Wagner, whose groundbreaking *Grendel* and *Mage* series later led to opportunities to write and draw Batman and other high-profile characters; Bill Willingham, creator of the provocative superteam comic *Elementals;* and Dave Stevens, whose lavishly rendered *The Rocketeer* became a live-action movie in 1991. Kevin Eastman and Peter Laird experienced the decade's most lucrative financial success: Their cheaply produced *Teenage Mutant Ninja Turtles* B&W title took the marketplace by storm, spawning counterfeiters, copycats, and a cottage industry that has included a film franchise, TV cartoons, and action figures.

During the 1980s, more female creators began to distinguish themselves in comics than in previous decades. Historian and book author Trina Robbins dabbled in mainstream comics by drawing the 1986 miniseries *The Legend of Wonder Woman,* which was also written, lettered, and colored by women (Lee Marrs, Lois Buhalis, and Shelley Eiber, respectively). Artists Colleen Doran and Jill Thompson gained prominence, as did Louise Jones Simonson, X-Men editor and writer of *Power Pack.* Other women comics editors to emerge in the 1980s were Karen Berger, Diana Schutz, Barbara Kesel, and Bobbie Chase.

American comics professionals were looking over their shoulders in the 1980s, many concerned that they would be squeezed out of the industry, as the British were coming, the British were coming! A wave of writers and artists from Britain penetrated the U.S. domestic comics market during the 1980s, mostly landing at DC. Foremost was Alan Moore, heralded by many as comics' greatest writer, who effortlessly leapt from *Saga of the Swamp Thing* to *Superman* stories, dazzling readers all the way. Other Brits to make an impression during the decade were artist Dave Gibbons, who followed a successful stint on *Green Lantern* by partnering with Moore on *Watchmen,* the twelve-issue series that redefined superheroes for a new, jaded generation; Brian Bolland, artist of writer Mike W. Barr's *Camelot 3000,* who later illustrated (with author Moore) *Batman: The Killing Joke* and numerous DC Comics covers; and daring new writers like Peter Milligan, Grant Morrison, and Neil Gaiman. Much of these creators' work bore an edgier voice than DC's traditional fare, and the publisher began a "mature readers" line that grew into its Vertigo imprint. One of those titles, Gaiman's award-winning *Sandman,* premiered in 1989.

SPECULATORS AND IMAGE

In the early 1990s a speculation boom inflated comics' sales to figures unheard of since the Golden Age. Gimmick covers and multiple editions sold in the hundreds of thousands—and in a few cases, the millions—enabling hot comics creators to flex their muscle. Artists Todd McFarlane, Jim Lee, and Rob Liefeld were the first Marvel artists whose popularity allowed them to jettison their writers from their series and ultimately tell their own stories. After reaping fortunes from relaunches of *Spider-Man, X-Men,* and *X-Force* that sold in huge numbers to speculators and fans, that trio, along with Jim Valentino, Whilce Portacio, Erik Larsen, and Marc Silvestri, cut their apron strings from Marvel in 1992 and founded Image Comics, where they published their own material (McFarlane's *Spawn,* Lee's *WildC.A.T.S,* Liefeld's *Youngblood,* Larsen's *The Savage Dragon,* and others).

In 1993 the market imploded when the speculator demand withered. Many artists and writers found themselves out of work. Marvel and DC courted in-demand creators with lucrative exclusive contracts and smaller companies tried to keep up, but the mid-1990s were a bleak period for the industry. There were artistic highpoints: Adam Hughes' gorgeous rendering on *Ghost* and his posteresque covers for *Wonder Woman;* writer Kurt Busiek and painter Alex Ross' remarkable miniseries *Marvels;* Ross' follow-up, DC's *Kingdom Come,* with author Mark Waid; Scott Campbell's impressive *Gen 13;* Joe Quesada's stunning artwork on *Ash* and *Daredevil;* and the prominence of painted portrait covers, which have, in the 2000s, threatened to supersede line-art drawings as the norm for cover art.

THE FUTURE OF SUPERHERO CREATORS

In the late 1990s the comics business took a collective deep breath to rebound from the blow of the market collapse. Publishers began to put aside sales stunts and dedicated themselves to publishing quality material. Since that time, writers from other media—including screenwriters Kevin Smith and Jeph Loeb, television writer and *Babylon 5* creator J. Michael Straczynski, crime novelist Greg Rucka, and Judd Winnick, one of the original cast members from MTV's *The Real World*—have been lured to comics. The 2000s have, to date, been dominated by newer creators—Brian Michael Bendis, Joe Kelly, Gail Simone, Brian Azzarello, Amanda Conner, Ed McGuiness, Alex Maleev,

Michael Allred, John Cassaday, and Scott McDaniel are just some of the writers and artists popular as of 2004—while Gaiman, Byrne, Pérez, Giffen, and Miller continue to command an audience of loyalists and newcomers. American superhero comic-book art as of 2004 is heavily influenced by Japanese manga and by the "animation" style popularized on such TV cartoons as *Batman: The Animated Series, Superman,* and *Justice League.* As superhero comics continue to morph to find their role in a fast-changing world, their creators will continue to strive for ways to create the next Man of Steel. —*ME*

Superhero Headquarters

"Beneath a harmless-looking Gotham City residence, a unique cavern lies hidden from the world!" announced *Detective Comics* #205 in 1954. Batman and Robin's subterranean headquarters, located underneath alter ego Bruce Wayne's mansion, has become so ingrained in America's consciousness that one only has to say the word "Batcave" in order to conjure up images of this top-secret underground labyrinth. Although the Batcave's appearance has varied over the years according to comic-book artists' (and film and TV set designers') interpretations, some of its more well-known features include the crime lab, the crime-file room, a garage and repair shop for the Batmobile, a hangar for the Batplane and Batcopter, docking facilities for the Batboat, a Bat-costume vault, a trophy room, and a fully equipped workshop. Thanks to its portrayal in the *Batman* TV show (1966–1968) and the *Batman* live-action film franchise of the 1990s, the Batcave is an icon: Alternately accessible via a spiral staircase, Batpole, and secret elevator from the Wayne mansion (depending upon the era of the story), Batman and Robin often retreat to their laboratory apparatus and crime-detection equipment in order to solve a mystery, referencing their "electronic data analyzer" and "DNA Spectograph" in order to unearth information on Gotham's criminals. The Batcave also contains mementoes of some of Batman's previous cases, including a replica of a giant penny, a giant Joker playing card, and a statue of a T-Rex, all salutes to Batman stories from the 1940s and 1950s but visuals maintained in Batman comics in the 2000s.

Sorry, that was *then.* Fast-forward to *now,* an era wherein only die-hard Batman fans know that the Batcave as much of America has come to know it no longer exists. The "New Batcave," constructed in the aftermath of the earthquake that demolished Gotham City in the lengthy "No Man's Land" serial that ran throughout the Batman titles in 1999, is a self-contained, eight-level, underground lair for the Dark Knight. This ultra-high-tech hideout boasts a state-of-the-art massive computer system and hologram projector, as well as much-updated renditions of Batman's library, training facilities, forensics laboratory, and vehicle ramps, dockers, and hangars. Bedecked in cool steel structures with retractable walkway bridges, there is no mistaking the New Batcave for anything other than the ultimate superhero sanctuary.

Another Gotham City resident, Oracle, sits perched in the city's Clocktower, ready to dispatch any one of her Birds of Prey "field operatives" upon the city's villainous. Working high above the crime-ridden streets, Oracle stays posted at her computer—actually, six Yale super-computers—acting as information broker to Gotham's heroes, including Batman, Nightwing, and the Justice League. With her genius-level intellect, photographic memory, and research and analytical skills, she is Batman's trusted confidante, a necessary part of the Dark Night's inner circle. Her secret hideaway—though difficult to reach for most—is, of course, wheelchair accessible for the heroine's special needs.

In stark opposition to the Batcave, Superman's Fortress of Solitude lies inside a dimension of unlimited space. Though originally built "deep in the core of a mountainside in the desolate Arctic wastes," this location proved to be too vulnerable a

hideout for the Man of Steel. It was here, according to *Action Comics* #241 (June 1958), that the Man of Steel conducted "incredible experiments," kept "strange trophies," and pursued "astounding hobbies"—in addition to just putting his feet up. First mentioned by name in the comics in 1949, his secret sanctum was originally conceived as a hidden repository for showcasing Krypton's culture and artifacts, and as such housed Superman's workshop, trophy room, and super-laboratory, where Superman put in overtime in search of an antidote for kryptonite. In addition, the Fortress contained a gym; a bowling alley; an interplanetary zoo (housing wildlife from a variety of distant planets); a Hall of Interplanetary Monsters; the Bottle City of Kandor (a city of Superman's home planet, Krypton, which was reduced to microscopic size by the villain Brainiac); special "hyperspace radios" for communicating with various distant galaxies and alien dimensions (housed in a communications room that also included "hotline" channels to the United Nations, the White House, and the Metropolis Police Department); and a number of assorted weapons and scientific apparatus.

In the Superman comics continuity of the 2000s, the Fortress is a high-tech wonderworld bearing little resemblance to the version popularized during the Silver Age of comics (1956–1969). Though fans might find a Krypton memorial, it is in the form of twin holographic images of Superman's Kryptonian parents, Jor-El and Lara. And though Kandor is still preserved, the crystalline diorama of Kandor's capital, Kryptonopolis, is more likely to catch visitors' eyes. Fans stumble upon Kryptonian power crystals; radiation-depleted chunks of Lex Luthor-contrived synthetic kryptonite; and a model of a Kryptonian skyship, a glider from ancient Krypton. The Fortress also houses the Last Son of Krypton's holographic archive, the holographic encyclopedic library that chronicles Superman's life; a Central Computer Nexus; the Phantom Zone Portal, which provides an entrance into that extradimensional space; and a Phantom Zone Control, which monitors the energy sources and all movement inside and outside the Phantom Zone. In addition, the Fortress is home to Ned, the sole remaining Superman robot; Superman's faithful robotic servant, Kelex; and Krypto, Superman's dog.

Few heroes enjoy such elaborate bases of operations as Batman and Superman, although the X-Men headquarters is a site to be reckoned with. Marvel Comics' mutant band of superheroes spend most of their time at their mentor Professor X's mansion, located in Westchester County, New York. Xavier's estate houses the X-Men's training facility, the Xavier Institute for Higher Learning, which fronts as an Ivy League–like school. It's here that the telepathically and telekinetically inclined fine-tune their intellectual skills and learn to strengthen their powers. Some of the mansion's more interesting features include the Medi-Lab, an advanced medical facility that provides full-scale medical treatment for the mutants; the Cerebro computer system, an elaborate system of machines that Professor X designed to locate mutants by tracking their psionic energy; a subterranean Danger Room, where the X-Men hone their athletic and combat skills by pitting themselves against super-robots in combat-training classes; and a subterranean War Room, which houses computers that collect top-secret global information. The property boasts such extravagances as an underground hangar and runway, specially designed for the X-Men's Blackbird jets; an ultra-fast monorail carries the X-Men from the mansion to the hangar in only twenty seconds. Finally, all manner of internal and external high-tech security (courtesy of wealthy industrialist Tony Stark, a.k.a. Iron Man) protects the mansion from would-be intruders.

Just a train-ride away from upstate Westchester lies New York City, home to many Marvel superheroes. The Fantastic Four (FF) battle crime in the Big Apple from Four Freedoms Plaza, located in midtown Manhattan. Just a stone's throw from the United Nations headquarters, Four Freedoms Plaza was built on the former site of the Baxter Building, the Fantastic Four's previous headquarters before it was destroyed by the villainous Thunderbolts. Designed by FF leader Reed Richards (a.k.a. Mister Fantastic), Four Freedoms Plaza is a forty-five-story office building topped off by the FF's four-story base of operations—a self-sustaining, heavily armored barricade, containing both the superteam's meeting place and individual members' living quarters. Relying heavily on computers, guard robots, and other high-tech devices to maintain security, this ultra-cool command post houses several major state-of-the-art research laboratories, complete with one-of-a-kind mechanisms permitting entry into the Negative Zone and a duplicate of Doctor Doom's time machine.

Quarantining the FF headquarters from the rest of the building is a buffer zone of top-security equipment; if the Fantastic Four's HQ should come under attack, emergency security devices seal the headquarters area off from the rest of the building. However, most visitors prefer to enter via the more traditional first floor, through elevators guarded by Mr. O'Hoolihan, the trusty doorman who serviced the superteam at the Baxter Building. Although permission for entry is required from none other than the FF themselves, visitors who are admitted take an elevator up to the reception room, attended by Roberta, a robot receptionist that appears human from the waist up.

The Avengers Mansion is one of the few hero hideouts to carry an exact street address—890 5th Avenue—and comes complete with all the accoutrements hard-living heroes need to unwind at the end of a long day: an Olympic-sized pool, workout facilities, even a combat simulation room, though it doesn't benefit from the interstellar Shi'ar technology that creates virtual environments for the X-Men's Danger Room. The Teen Titans do business from the T-shaped Titans Tower. Still other heroes simply prefer to live life in the apartments of their alter egos: Peter Parker and Matt Murdock are content to hang out in their New York City brownstones when they aren't swinging and leaping from rooftops as Spider-Man and Daredevil, respectively (though

Spidey's alternate-universe daughter, Spider-Girl, has operated out of an abandoned historic meeting-hall refitted with high-tech equipment and renamed—what else?—the Web Site).

Far away from New York City lies the moon-based headquarters of the Justice League of America. The Watchtower is the most advanced command post of DC's superteam, who have in days past convened in the mountain-top base of their "Secret Sanctuary" near Happy Harbor, Rhode Island, as well as in an underground "Bunker" in Detroit, Michigan. (Perhaps the team's longest-running redoubt was a satellite orbiting Earth, homaged in the 1990s and 2000s by Honor Guard's hovering mobile command center in *Astro City* and the Five Swell Guys' own space satellite, "High Five," in *Promethea*.) The Watchtower, a high-tech solar station, boasts all the accoutrements of a five-star hotel, including living suites, a well-stocked kitchen, and training and work-out facilities. Of course, this *is* outer space, so all types of super-equipment make it possible for the team and its visitors to come, go, live, fight, and breathe: landing docks and entry ports; a teleport tube; an armory loaded with "last resort" weapons; a deep-bore ice miner; a deep water tank; and a hydroponic forest. —*GM*

Superhero Movie Serials

Return to the days of yesteryear, long before television. Cinema fans who lived in cities with movie theaters could thrill every week to motion picture serials. Along with newsreels and cartoons, serials were short action-adventure films that played prior to feature attractions. Often running ten to thirteen episodes, serials were told in chapter form. To keep the audience hooked on returning to see the next chapter, the serial writers and directors ended each one with a "cliff-hanger"; the heroes or heroines of the story were often caught in dire peril, with no discernable means of escape. How did they survive? Viewers had to come back next week to find out. Hundreds of serials were produced during the film industry's silent era, beginning in 1912, but few have survived to today. Modern audiences generally think of 1930s–1940s serials, most of which *have* been preserved, and many of which featured superheroes, in addition to Western heroes, jungle heroes, and crime dramas.

In 1936, Universal released the first *Flash Gordon* serial, based on the science fiction comic strip, and in 1937, Republic issued *Dick Tracy*. Universal was one of the main companies in the serial business of that era; Republic and Columbia were others. While some Hollywood leading men and women appeared or got their start in serials—John Wayne did several before becoming a star—the majority of serial actors did a lot of serial work. And why not? Weeks of steady work and exposure on the big screen meant job security and the potential to move up in the Hollywood food chain.

The first superhero serial was *The Green Hornet* (Universal, November 1939). Based on a popular 1936–1953 radio drama created by Fran Striker and George W. Trendle, the serial Green Hornet was played by Gordon Jones (radio alter ego Al Hodge provided Hornet's voice), while sidekick Kato was played by Keye Luke. In the thirteen chapters, Hornet and Kato fought underworld crime boss the Leader, whose identity was kept secret until the final episode. A fifteen-part sequel, *The Green Hornet Strikes Again,* was released in September 1940, with Warren Hull taking over the title role. This time out, danger came in the form of underworld crime boss Crogan (Pierre Watkin) and his cronies. Both serials featured such Hornet staples as the theme music ("Flight of the Bumblebee" by Nikolai Rimsky-Korsakov), the gas gun, and the buzzing car known as Black Beauty.

Comic-strip and pulp characters also got their own serials in 1939: *Mandrake the Magician* (Columbia, 1939, twelve chapters) and *The Shadow* (Columbia, January 1940, fifteen chapters). But it was Fawcett Comics' red-and-gold-clad hero who became the first comic-book superhero to garner his own starring serial. Republic's twelve-chapter story, *The Adventures of Captain Marvel,* debuted in March 1941. Heroic leading man Tom Tyler was cast as Captain Marvel, with his radio announcer alter ego Billy Batson played by Frank Coghlan Jr. When not escaping deathtraps—or rescuing others from them—Captain Marvel did his best to stop the evil machinations of the Scorpion. With excellent flying effects and an engaging storyline, *The Adventures of Captain Marvel* remains one of serial history's most popular adventures.

A fellow Fawcett comic-book character got his own serial the following year. *Spy Smasher* (Republic, April 1942, twelve chapters) starred Kane Richmond in the title role, helping to stop spies and saboteurs during World War II. This became a common theme for serials during this time period. In *Batman* (Columbia, July 1943, fifteen chapters), lead actors Lewis Wilson as Batman and Douglas Croft as Robin fought the evil machinations of the villainous Japanese spy Dr. Daka (Caucasian actor J. Carroll Naish). Comic-book hero *Captain America* headlined his own serial (Republic, December 1943, fifteen chapters), but instead of following his comic-book Nazi-fighting adventures, here Cap was secretly District Attorney Grant Gardner (Dick Purcell), who fought criminals—and the deadly Scarab—with a gun and his fists.

Africa's purple-clad hero made his film debut in *The Phantom* (Columbia, December 1943, fifteen chapters), though no one could see that Tom Tyler was in purple because the serial was black and white. At least his costume was better than that of the Western comic-book hero in *The Vigilante* (Columbia, 1947, fifteen chapters), who hid his secret identity behind a neckerchief. Ralph Byrd portrayed the Vigilante, fighting against the mysterious X-1 in a plot to recover cursed "Tears of Blood" rubies. Fellow *Action Comics* adventure hero *Congo Bill* (Columbia, 1948, fifteen chapters) appeared the following year, starring Don McGuire in the title role as a jungle adventurer.

The comics world's most famous superhero finally made his serial debut in *Superman* (Columbia, July 1948, fifteen chapters). Handsome actor Kirk Alyn was in the lead, with young actress Noel Neill in the part of Lois Lane, and former *Our Gang* star Tommy Bond as Jimmy Olsen. Here, the Man of Steel had to use his powers to stop the "Queen of the Underworld," Spider Lady (Carol Forman), from gaining control over the ultra-powerful Reducer Ray. A sequel, *Atom Man vs. Superman* (Columbia, June 1950, fifteen chapters), introduced a hooded villain who was eventually revealed to be Lex Luthor (Lyle Talbot).

Fellow National/DC hero Batman also got a sequel with *Batman and Robin* (Columbia, May 1949, fifteen chapters), but it was scraping the bottom of the budget-barrel, and fans weren't happy. Replacing the original heroes, Robert Lowery played Batman and John Duncan played Robin, while Jane Adams was a comely Vicki Vale and Leonard Penn was the villainous Wizard.

By the 1950s, the popularity of serials was declining, and no more superheroes made the leap to weekly theater bookings. Although serials themselves would last a few more years afterward, the final comic book-inspired one was *Blackhawk* (Columbia, 1952, fifteen chapters), starring ex-*Superman* star Kirk Alyn in the title role of the costumed pilot hero and once again pitting him against the evil plans of Carol Forman and others. And with *Blackhawk*'s final chapter, the age of comic-book heroes in serialized form was relegated once again to the pages of comics and a newer medium: television. —*AM*

Superhero Nicknames

Some superheroes' nicknames are so ingrained in America's consciousness that hardcore fans and the general public alike often use the nickname to refer to the character. How many times has "The

Man of Steel" been used to describe Superman? Or "The Caped Crusader" for Batman? What about the Dynamic Duo (Batman and Robin)? Spider-Man is Spidey or the web-slinger to most, while few can instantly recall his other (less complimentary) name, Web-Head. Fewer still remember the World's Smallest Superhero (it's the Atom, of course). Some heroes' nicknames are so catchy they are reminiscent of fairy-tale ideals or popular advertising campaigns (think the Hulk's sobriquet, Jolly Green Giant). But these are just a few examples of comic-book creators' ingenuity and of names both popular and long-forgotten that have served costumed crime fighters well.

Early comic-book references to DC Comics' ominous hero, Batman, have hailed him as the Masked Manhunter, Master of Darkness, the Dark Night, and the World's Greatest Detective. This last phrase comes from the fact that Batman is an ingenious mystery-solver (a "supersleuth," if you will) and "ace criminologist." Indeed, *Batman* #14 (December 1942) calls the hero "a stunt man … an acrobat … a superb athlete … a lion-hearted fighter—and a sleuth … all rolled into one." As protector of one of America's most crime-ridden cities, he is the Guardian of Gotham.

The other half of Batman for most of his fighting career, Robin, the Boy Wonder, was a wondrously dexterous ex–circus performer turned America's most popular sidekick—also described as Batman's "daredevil young aide" and a "young, laughing Robin Hood of today" in the early 1940s. Coming into his own as Nightwing, he fights crime in nearby Blüdhaven—though time, not miles, has separated his counterpart character Batgirl from perhaps the most unforgettable (and unforgivable?) of superhero nicknames, straight from the camp-crazed 1960s: the Dominoed Dare-Doll.

DC champion Superman is heralded as both the Man of Steel and the Man of Tomorrow—both fitting for a futuristic demigod who can bend steel in his bare hands and withstand being struck by steel girders. Mid-1950s issues of *Action Comics* called

him the "champion of the underdog," "eternal foe of the underworld," and "the world's mightiest hero." The comics pages have also referred to him colloquially as a "colorfully-costumed, mighty-sinewed man of might," "mankind's foremost crusader for good," and "a fighting champion of justice" who is "famous the world over." In the high-tech 1990s and 2000s he has sometimes been known, with apologies to IBM, as "Big Blue." Following in the footsteps of Superman's most popular nickname, Superboy is the Boy of Steel; Supergirl, the Girl (or Maid) of Steel.

Sobriquets for other costumed heroes include Amazing Amazon, aptly embraced by DC's Wonder Woman, who has also enjoyed such honors as "Aphrodite's agent," "America's Guardian Angel," "disciple of peace and love," and "invincible enemy of injustice." Marvel Comics' Ant-Man is also known as the Ant-Size Avenger, and as Giant-Man has been referred to as High-Pockets. DC's Elongated Man was often called the Ductile Detective. DC's Aquaman is none other than Marine Marvel or King of the Seven Seas. Marvel's undersea counterpart, the Sub-Mariner, is called the Prince of the Seas. Marvel's Captain America goes by Cap, the Star-Spangled Avenger, or—are you ready for this?—Winghead (depending upon who is doing the name-calling).

Marvel's blind superhero, Daredevil, is simply referred to as the Man without Fear—his supersensory powers enabling him to fight crime with a super-level of confidence. DC's favorite speedster, the Flash, has been termed (most appropriately) the Fastest Man Alive, the Scarlet Speedster, and the Sultan of Speed. DC's Green Arrow is simply the Emerald Archer; the Green Lantern is the Emerald Crusader or the Green Gladiator. Marvel's Doctor Strange is the Master of Mystic Arts. DC's birdlike hero Hawkman is dubbed the Winged Wonder or the Flying Fury. Marvel's Iron Man has fondly been called the Golden Avenger, the Golden Gladiator, Bullet Head, and Shell Head. DC's green-skinned Martian Manhunter prefers to be called either Manhunter from Mars or Martian Marvel (no ego there!).

Marvel's ultra-cool Silver Surfer rides intergalactic waves as the Sentinel of the Spaceways. Marvel's Iron Fist has been called the Living Weapon. Finally, who could forget Marvel's Norse God of Thunder, the mighty Thor—who has been called both the Son of Odin and the less immortalizing Goldilocks?

Teams don't escape nicknaming either. Marvel's superteam, the Avengers, has been called Earth's Mightiest Heroes. DC's superteam, the Justice League of America, is named the World's Greatest Super-Heroes. Marvel's mutant X-Men are, most appropriately, the World's Strangest Superheroes. —*GM*

Superhero Radio Series

Riding on the coattails of the ever-popular *Shadow* and *Lone Ranger* radio shows that were aired several times weekly beginning in 1932 and 1933 respectively, superhero radio series made their way into the hearts of an audience enamored of the medium and its melodrama. Loaded with sound effects, distinctive introductions, and memorable musical ditties, radio series drew their inspiration from comic strips and comic books, and before long Doc Savage, the Green Hornet, Superman, Batman, the Blue Beetle, and Mandrake the Magician all had a presence on radio. One character, Captain Midnight, first appeared on radio before successfully parlaying himself into his own comic book.

"Radio heroes, like most champions in American popular culture, were symbols of truth, justice, honor, and other bourgeois values," observed J. Fred MacDonald in *Don't Touch That Dial!* (1979), a survey of radio programming from 1920 to 1960. As such, these heroes were loved, especially by children, who voraciously absorbed their programs in the after-school hours, in the early weekday evenings, and on Saturday mornings. Many were action-adventure serials, a fifteen-minute program

that ran three, sometimes five, days per week. The popularity of the radio programs fed the sales of the print material, giving comic books a boost.

One of the first comic-book hero shows to air, *Doc Savage* engaged listeners in a short-lived 1934 radio drama, from which little solid information remains. No cast list or recordings exist, just *Doc Savage* pulp writer Lester Dent's personal carbon copies of the scripts of twenty-six episodes. An entirely different Doc—the magic-hooded superhero version of the character that was portrayed in the post–August 1941 Street & Smith *Doc Savage Comics*—was the star of a 1943 radio series.

The Green Hornet's signature introduction was the buzzing of a hornet and the sound of the hero's supercar, Black Beauty, racing away. *The Green Hornet* debuted in January 1936 on local Detroit station WXYZ before moving to the Mutual radio network for national broadcasting. Fran Striker, a writer of *The Lone Ranger,* wrote all of the scripts for *The Green Hornet* until April 1944, after which several other writers scripted the show. In the beginning, the shows typically ran thirty minutes twice a week; they were later broadcast once a week. Britt Reid, newspaper publisher of the *Daily Sentinel* by day and the masked crime fighter Green Hornet by night, was voiced by Al Hodge for about half of the show's run, which ended in 1953.

Announcer Don Gordon signaled the start of a mysterious aviator's show with the tolling of a bell, the roar of a plane, and his signature "Captainnnnn Midnight!" prelude. *Captain Midnight* debuted in 1938 as a regional, fifteen-minute serial sponsored by Skelly Oil. Captain Midnight (a code name for young Air Corps officer Captain Red Albright) flew off to adventures around the world with his ward, Chuck Ramsey, and young aviatrix Patsy Donovan. Ripe for adventure, Captain Midnight (voiced by Bill Bouchey) buttoned up his black bodysuit and donned his aviator's cap and goggles to pursue international criminal Ivan Shark. In 1940, the show was sponsored by Ovaltine and broadcast nationally by Mutual and other networks for almost a decade.

Captain Midnight (now voiced by Ed Prentiss) was recruited to head the Secret Squadron, a top-secret government organization created to fight espionage and sabotage. Listeners were invited to join the Secret Squadron by sending in Ovaltine labels, at which point they would receive a Code-O-Graph to decipher Secret Squadron Signal Session messages at the end of each show, giving code-breakers a clue about the next show's escapades.

Probably the most well-known and best received superhero to be broadcast was Superman, who hit the airwaves in February 1940, and was broadcast three times a week in fifteen-minute time slots. By 1942, *The Adventures of Superman* was being broadcast every day of the week. Only a handful of diehard Superman fans know that Jimmy Olsen (voiced by Jackie Kelk) was created as a device to replace the missing "thought balloons" so prevalent in print. Whenever Superman (voiced by Bud Collyer) needed to explain something "off panel," he confided in Olsen on-air. The Superman radio show also added kryptonite, which, along with Olsen, made its way into comic-book stories. Batman and Robin's radio escapades, which took place in 1945, were part of the *Superman* radio series. The Dynamic Duo never received their own radio show.

In the wake of *Superman*'s success, *The Blue Beetle* radio show ran twice weekly for forty-eight episodes, from May through September 1940. For the first thirteen episodes actor Frank Lovejoy voiced Blue Beetle; later episodes are uncredited. Running first at thirty, then at fifteen, minutes long, this "thrilling drama of the avenging gang smasher," conjured up intrigue and adventure for listeners both young and old. Similarly, stage magician/crime fighter Mandrake the Magician (voiced by Edward Johnson), who used his superpowers to fight crime, starred in his own show on Mutual between November 1940 and February 1942. Begun as a thrice-weekly serial, *Mandrake the Magician* soon moved to daily air time in 1941.

Superman left radio in March 1951, but arrived on television the following year. With America's growing fascination with the new medium, many

radio series lost the support of their sponsors or audience or both, and began to disappear. While experiments with superheroes on the airwaves have appeared sporadically since the Golden Age of radio (the mid-1970s saw the short-lived *Marvel Comics Radio Series,* for example), none have had the kind of longevity or appeal of the programs of the 1930s and 1940s. —*GM*

Superhero Role-Playing Games

Fantasy role-playing games—mostly tabletop wargame-variants in which three or more players take on the personalities of characters they have developed for use in fantasy combat or treasure-hunting situations—can trace their origins to the advent of *Dungeons and Dragons* (1974, TSR Games). An individual *Dungeons and Dragons* (*D&D*) game session, generally a part of a larger game cycle known as a *campaign,* is moderated by a *dungeonmaster* (or gamemaster), who designs the game milieu—the castle to be stormed, the dragon's hoard to be raided, and the monsters to be fought. The players bring into the game characters whose basic abilities (numerically quantifiable traits such as strength, intelligence, wisdom, dexterity, constitution, and charisma) are determined by means of random die throws. Polyhedral dice, whose sides can number anywhere from 4 to 20, generate the random numbers that govern the outcome of the game's many variables, including the number of points of damage sustained or inflicted during combat, the efficacy of magic spell-casting or weaponry, the chance that a character's actions will attract an enemy or activate a booby trap, and even character mortality.

Building on the fantasy worlds of J. R. R. Tolkien and others, *D&D* spawned a vast role-playing game (RPG) industry, which supports many competing gaming systems. Some RPGs have complex rule systems that emphasize realism and control nearly every conceivable game variable, while others place a higher premium on ease of play, storytelling values, and character evolution. During the 1970s and 1980s, RPGs were devised for a wide variety of story backdrops and storytelling genres, including space-opera science fiction, postapocalyptic science fiction, international espionage, Lovecraftian horror, the Western—and comic-book superheroes.

During the early 1980s, three RPGs came to dominate the superhero gaming audience: *Champions* (Hero Games; Gold Rush Games), *Superworld* (Chaosium), and *Villains and Vigilantes* (Fantasy Games Unlimited). Not surprisingly, each game system had its own distinctive approach to superhero gaming, with unique strengths and weaknesses.

Designed to closely simulate the world of a mainstream, four-color superhero universe, *Champions* boasted a flexible character-generation system that allowed players to build their superheroes' abilities around a theme (say, "insect powers") rather than forcing them to rely too heavily on the random results of die-rolls. Combat was typically "kinder and gentler" than in *D&D;* though characters were often knocked unconscious during the game's combat simulations, death was an uncommon occurrence, reflecting the superhero comics of the time. The *Superworld* RPG was written as part of a short-lived multigenre gaming system called *Worlds of Wonder,* whose rules encompassed not only superheroes but also Tolkienesque fantasy and space-borne science fiction; *Superworld*'s game mechanics worked particularly well for simulating the established heroes of the Marvel and DC universes. Another popular early 1980s game, *Villains and Vigilantes,* also had an authentically "comic-booky" feel, thanks in large part to the interior artwork of Jeff Dee; some players have observed, however, that *V&V*'s character-generation rules were more dice-based—and therefore less flexible—than the other systems. Because of the game's reliance on die-generated character traits, it was far too easy to

create groups of characters whose power levels weren't a good fit (imagine the difficulties inherent in forcing DC's Batgirl and Marvel's world-devouring Galactus to share an adventure). The game was also plagued by large numbers of rules errata, which the publisher corrected by inserting update sheets into the rulebooks. Bits and pieces of the worlds and rules of *Superworld, Champions,* and *Villains and Vigilantes* made their way into a successor game titled *Havoc* (1984, Reality Storm: When Worlds Collide), a superhero RPG that remains in print today.

It was only a matter of time before superhero RPGs, which owed their existence to superhero comics, begat some comics of their own. *Champions'* signature superteam (the Guardians) became the basis for two *Champions* comics series (Eclipse, 1986–1987; Hero, 1987–1989). Two *Villains and Vigilantes* "game modules" (game scenarios published for use by gamemasters in RPG play) by Bill Willingham inspired the artist's compelling superhero team comics series, *The Elementals* (Comico, 1984–1989; 1989–1994; 1995), which borrowed the villainous Destroyers directly from the game. Eclipse Comics also produced a four-issue miniseries (1986–1987) based upon a *V&V* game module titled *Crisis at Crusaders Citadel,* created by the game's originators writer Jack Herman and illustrator Jeff Dee. Several of the superheroes developed by award-winning science-fiction writer George R. R. Martin and others for the *Wild Cards* paperback fiction anthologies (some of which Marvel began adapting into comics in 1990) grew out of campaigns played within these three game systems. Clearly, the superheroes of the games and those of comics and prose literature have had powerful mutual influences.

As the networks of comics-oriented and gaming-oriented specialty shops expanded throughout the 1980s, several more superhero-oriented RPGs followed the original three, including Palladium Games' *Heroes Unlimited,* which debuted in 1984 for use with the generic (and still extant) RIFTS fantasy gaming system; a version of *Heroes Unlimited* remains in print today. Palladium followed this with an RPG based upon Kevin Eastman's and Peter Laird's popular and durable superhero/martial arts parody comic book, *Teenage Mutant Ninja Turtles.* Following on the heels of these successful games were several also-rans, such as *Justifiers* and *Guardians* (StarChilde Publications), both of which were plagued by confusing rules, a flaw mitigated somewhat by the games' cheap purchase prices and their "comic-book format" presentation.

By the late 1980s, the major comics publishers had taken note of the burgeoning superhero RPG market; to satisfy the rising demand for game systems based upon their characters, Marvel Comics and DC Comics sold RPG licenses, each of which resulted in well-crafted, slickly-produced, and generally well-received game rulebooks and modules. By the end of the decade, Mayfair Games was publishing the *DC Heroes Role-Playing Game* and the *Batman Role-Playing Game,* while TSR (of *D&D* fame) was producing *Marvel Super Heroes* as well as a line of small lead figures intended for use as game tokens (à la the war games that preceded the emergence of the first true RPG). Both of these gaming systems were widely praised for their well-described, carefully quantified characters, their ease of play, and their usefulness as reference tools for the comic books themselves.

As is true in the comics industry, the RPG market is a volatile one; publishers come and go, or end up mergered out of existence. Specific RPG properties either vanish forever, or evolve into something new. Despite a surfeit of competing modern pastimes—i.e., electronic media such as the Gameboy, the X-Box, or MMORPGs (Massive Multiplayer Online Role-Playing Games, campaigns conducted over the Internet by dozens or hundreds of players)—a small but enthusiastic audience for traditional tabletop pencil-and-paper superhero RPGs still existed in the late 1990s and persists today. Steve Jackson Games' GURPS (General Universal Role-Playing System) *Supers* appeared in the early

1990s and remains in print. This game system's emphasis on combat realism—inasmuch as the concept makes sense in a superhero milieu—places players' characters at considerable risk of injury or death. 1995 saw the release of *Cosmic Enforcers* (Myrmidon Press), an RPG in which superhumans protect the Earth from invading arachnoid aliens. A revised, simplified version of *Champions*—including much improved interior artwork—appeared in 1998, and remains in print today; some of the changes made to the game proved unpopular, thus prompting a re-release of the original rulebook. Also in 1998, Mayfair lost the license to produce *DC Heroes,* which moved to Task Force Games. At roughly the same time, UNI Games issued *Living Legends,* a superhero RPG based upon the venerable *Villains and Vigilantes* game.

While few of the many superhero RPGs introduced over the past three decades have proved as durable as the mass-marketed *Dungeons and Dragons*—which is still going strong today as both *Dungeons and Dragons* and *Advanced Dungeons and Dragons,* both under the aegis of Wizards of the Coast—several still have substantial followings today. The recent profusion of superhero RPGs, most of which are available only through specialty vendors, includes such attractively-packaged entries as: the light-hearted *Superbabes* (1997, TriCity Games), which emphasizes the pulchritudinous powerhouses of Bill Black's AC Comics line; *Nemesis: A Perfect World* (2001, Maximum CNG), which blends superheroics with postapocalyptic science fiction; *Mutants and Masterminds* (2002, Green Ronin Publishing) a game system set in the appropriately heroic-sounding "Freedom City"; *Silver Age Sentinels: The Ultimate Superhero RPG* (2002, Guardians of Order, Inc.), a game supported by a line of miniature tabletop figurines and whose slick, detailed rulebook is reminiscent of that of *Advanced D&D; Godlike* (2002, Hobgoblynn Press), which chronicles the clash between the superheroes of the Allies and the Axis in an alternate World War II; *Heroes by Gaslight* (2002, Web of Horrors/Web of Heroes), which places superheroes in the Victorian Age; *Judge Dredd* (2002, Mongoose Publishing), a game centered on Britain's over-the-top protector of Megacity One; *Cartoon Action Hour* (2003, Z-Man Games, Inc.), which delivers superheroic action in the mold of such 1980s animated kid-vid as *G.I. Joe, Thundercats, Transformers,* and *Masters of the Universe;* the *DC Universe Roleplaying Game* (1999, 2002, West End Games); and the *Marvel Universe* RPG (Marvel Comics, 2003). This abundance suggests that the market for superhero RPGs is as healthy today as it has ever been. —*MAM*

Superhero Slogans

Superhero slogans, catchphrases, words of wisdom, and general declarations and utterances have flooded the popular consciousness since the dawn of comic books. Delivered via word balloons, actors' mouths, or radio and television voice-overs, one cannot deny the power of superhero speech.

Although Superman first appeared in *Action Comics* #1 in 1938, much of the mythology of the hero originated in his radio escapades. On his radio show, which premiered in February 1940, DC Comics' press agent Allen Ducovny and Robert Joffe Maxwell, a former pulp fiction author, scripted the opening of the show that would be recited—and varied—countless times: "Faster than an airplane, more powerful than a locomotive, impervious to bullets! Up in the sky—look! It's a giant bird! It's a plane! It's SUPERMAN!" The actor hired to portray both Superman and Clark Kent on-air, Bud Collyer, gave super-oomph to phrases like "Up, Up, and Awaaay!" and "This looks like a job for Superman!" The Man of Steel left the radio airwaves in 1951, quickly moving into a live-action television show starring George Reeves. It's here that Superman became "Faster than a speeding bullet! More powerful than a locomotive! Able to leap tall buildings in a single bound!" In a continuing variation on the opening lines from the show's radio counterpart, a

baritone voice announced, "Yes, it's Superman—strange visitor from another planet who came to Earth with powers and abilities far beyond those of mortal men. Superman! Who can change the course of mighty rivers, bend steel in his bare hands, and who, disguised as Clark Kent, mild-mannered reporter for a great metropolitan newspaper, fights a never-ending battle for Truth, Justice, and the American Way!"

Though the comic-book pages are filled with such wholesome Superman phrases as "Great Guns!" and "Great Scott!" it's Superman's first words on the printed page that perhaps best set the tone for years of adventures to come: Living in Smallville with his adopted parents, the Kents, Superman's first words are, "Try again, Doc!" uttered when a physician tries to give him a shot from hypodermic needles that keep breaking on his impervious skin (*Action Comics* #1, 1938). In the television show *The Adventures of Superman* (1953–1957) actor George Reeves came up with many pointed lines as both alter ego Clark Kent and the Man of Steel. In the 1955 episode "The Big Freeze," for example, Kent admonishes citizens to get out and *vote* for the city's next mayor, rather than rely on Superman to step in and "save the election" from a gangster crook who is running for office: "Sometimes, Lois, it's not wise for the people to depend on Superman to keep their own house in order."

As the "Master of darkness" and "foe of all evil" Batman's expressions are always of the serious, contemplative sort. The hero dissects complicated mathematical formulas with as much finesse as he quotes multiple poetic stanzas. But it is Batman's original pun-loving sidekick Robin who is the better remembered of the two for his nimble-tongued epithets, often sending super-criminals like the Joker to near defeat. "Put me in jail … anyplace … so I won't have to listen to Robin's puns anymore," the Joker bemoans in a 1947 issue of *Batman*. Indeed, Robin's expressions received ample airplay in the *Batman* TV show (1966–1968), with actor Burt Ward reciting such lines as "Holy Long John Silver!" and "This Brassy Bird has us Buffalo-d" with deadpan delivery. Producer William Dozier delivered the pompous narration, coining such phrases as, "Same Bat time, same Bat station," to invite viewers to tune in to the second half of the weekly aired cliff-hangers. Superimposed over the show's fight scenes were words like "Pow!" "Thwack!" and "Pop!," themselves becoming as iconic as the shows' lead characters.

Other heroes' expressions may not be as well known as those of the Boy Wonder, yet merit mentioning. In comics' Golden Age (1938–1954), Fawcett Publishing's young newsboy Billy Batson simply recited the name "Shazam!" and he became the grown-up Captain Marvel, embarking on adventures in the pages of *Whiz Comics* with the wisdom of Solomon, the strength of Hercules, the stamina of Atlas, the power of Zeus, the courage of Achilles, and the speed of Mercury. So well known is this catchphrase (in part made popular by the mid-1970s live-action TV show of the same name) that people often mistake "Shazam" for the hero's name. A Silver Age (1956–1969) favorite, the Green Lantern, recited an oath every time he recharged his ring, persevering through several comic-book writers and editors: "In brightest day, in blackest night, no evil shall escape my sight. Let those who worship evil's might, beware my power—Green Lantern's light!" Oaths, magical spells, and super-incantations flooded Golden Age comic-book stories, including those of Doctor Fate, Ibis the Invincible, and Wonder Woman, whose Amazon Code ("Govern yourselves with love, kindness, and service to others") and "Aphrodite's Law" are used to signify the set of carefully defined moral and religious tenets that govern Wonder Woman's and her fellow Amazons' behavior.

Stan Lee, Marvel Comics' creative impetus during comics' Silver Age, was influenced by Shakespeare and the Bible when he wrote for the Mighty Thor, dousing the strip with "Whither goest thou?" and similar phrases. With Silver Age star Dr.

Strange, Lee blended magical incantations and oaths, the most oft-used being "by the hoary hosts of Hoggoth," which preceded every serious Dr. Strange sentiment. Lee's moralizing Silver Surfer became, as comic-book historian Mike Benton calls him, "the voice of conscience for a 1960s generation," as Lee spoke to his readers about war and peace, politics and environmentalism, through his silver-skinned space hero's soliloquies. Other Silver and Bronze Age heroes with super-epithets include the monosyllabic Hulk ("Hulk Smash!"); the ever-enthusiastic Avengers ("Avengers Assemble!"); the gruff Thing ("It's Clobberin' Time!") and hotshot Human Torch ("Flame On!") from the Fantastic Four; and the super-rhyming Isis.

Certain heroes, however, really *own* their words, even developing mottos. Spider-Man's message to readers—to act responsibly and be accountable for your actions—comes straight out of his origin story in *Amazing Fantasy* #15 (1962): "With great power, there must also come—great responsibility!" —*GM*

Superhero Vulnerabilities

Without adversity or weakness—or the "supreme ordeal," as myth-master Joseph Campbell contends in *The Hero with a Thousand Faces* (1949)—a hero cannot truly be challenged.

"Kryptonite! Oh … getting weak … (Gasp!)" murmurs the Man of Steel as his routine rescue of a collapsed train trestle is upended by "vengeful criminals" who drop a glowing green meteor on him in *Superman* #123 (1958). This is just one of the hero's numerous encounters with kryptonite, radioactive fragments from the hero's home planet Krypton. Over the years Superman has writhed in pain from kryptonite exposure, turned tail and run from kryptonite meteor showers (actually, he flew), and shielded himself from it with lead, the only substance that can impede kryptonite radiation.

Superman is also vulnerable to magic, and foes like the mischievous Mr. Myxzptlk have used incantations and sorcery to plague the Man of Steel. Kryptonian technology and otherworldly science have harmed Superman: The supervillain Brainiac's shrinking ray made the hero a tiny titan, and weapons from Darkseid's planet of Apokolips have pummeled and even enslaved him. Alien diseases, particularly the Kryptonian Virus X, can kill Superman: In *Superman* #156 (1962), the hero thinks he has contracted the illness, but on his death bed his pal Jimmy Olsen discovers a tiny speck of kryptonite is actually the culprit for his malady. When Superman actually does contract Virus X, in a serialized tale in *Action Comics* #363–#366 (1968), his skin turns green and mummifies. Fortunately, his funeral pyre, the sun, is his salvation, as its radiation kills the virus. A later exposure to a meteor-borne Kryptonian fungus almost does the Man of Steel in again in *DC Comics Presents* #85 (1985), before the plant-sensitive Swamp Thing is able to defeat the source of Superman's sickness. The rays of Earth's yellow sun feed Superman's powers, and once he ventures from this energy source he weakens. In *Superman* #164 (1963), his arch nemesis Lex Luthor goads the Man of Steel into hand-to-hand combat on a world with a red sun, where Superman is mortal. In the revision of Superman's mythos beginning with the miniseries *The Man of Steel* (1986), Superman, slightly de-powered from previous decades, requires a breathing apparatus when flying through space.

Superman's greatest weakness is also his most admirable virtue: his compassion. The Man of Steel's enemies have captured his beloved Lois Lane, his foster parents Jonathan and Martha Kent, and his friends Lana Lang, Jimmy Olsen, and Perry White to lure the hero into traps.

While a lifesaver when blocking kryptonite rays, lead exposes a frailty of Superman's: His X-ray vision cannot see through it. This weakness is minor when compared to Mon-El's reaction to lead. This member of DC Comics' Legion of Super-Heroes becomes deathly ill when exposed to the ore. Mon-El spent one thousand years in ghostly exile to protect himself from the common substance, until Legionnaire Braniac 5 created an antidote for Mon-El's vulnerability. Another member of the Legion, Ultra Boy, has a peculiar weakness: He possesses ultra-strength, ultra-vision, ultra-speed, and invulnerability, but can only use one power at a time.

Wonder Woman commands two amazing superweapons: her magic lasso, which forces captives to tell the truth, and her bracelets, with which she repels bullets. Those weapons can work against her: Wonder Woman can be bound by her own lasso, and she is robbed of her Amazonian strength if her bracelets are linked by chains. Green Lantern's miraculous power ring can fly him through space, protect him from harm, and create anything its wearer can imagine, but it has one major imperfection: It is ineffective against anything made of the color yellow. In *Justice League of America* #21 (1963), supervillain Chronos stops "GL" merely by spraying him with a "golden mist." The power ring wielded by the original Green Lantern, who appeared during comics' Golden Age (1938–1954), had an equally unusual flaw: It wouldn't work against wood. The Justice League's Martian Manhunter is vulnerable to fire, while the Flash's weakness with food extends far beyond the waistline woes of the average person: His hyper-fast metabolism burns calories so quickly, Flash must eat frequently to maintain his energy.

Aquaman, DC's Sea King, can only breathe out of water for an hour. On the cover of *Aquaman* #44 (1969), the hero is tied to a pier by gangsters, who sneer that the tide will be up "in about an hour!" Wide-eyed Aquaman shrieks, "But … but if I don't have water … *I die in two minutes*!!" This Sea King is not the only superhero who is a sixty-minute man: Witness the Golden Age hero Hourman, whose Miraclo Pill imbued him with enhanced strength and stamina—but only for an hour, as his name suggests.

Billy Batson transforms into Captain Marvel at his mere utterance of the magic word "Shazam!" Once his foe Dr. Sivana realizes this, however, he frequently binds and gags young Batson, thereby keeping the World's Mightiest Mortal from materializing. In the Golden Age, Captain Marvel was often joined in action by Captain Marvel Jr. (later called CM3) and Mary Marvel—the Marvel Family—with each superhero relatively equal in power. Since being revamped by writer Jerry Ordway in DC's *The Power of Shazam!* series (1995–1999), Junior and Mary now borrow superpowers from Cap when they say their magic words, making teamwork more important given their diminished abilities.

Batman is, like many superheroes, mortal—a serious vulnerability for a superhero constantly in the line of fire. His flesh is a mass of scar tissue, from years of gunshots, stab wounds, and burns sustained in the line of duty. This Dark Knight has been preoccupied with justice since his childhood after witnessing the murder of his parents. This obsession has often embittered him, straining his relationship with his inner circle (his protégé Nightwing, his sidekick Robin, and his butler Alfred). Still, he is vehemently opposed to using guns, which constantly endangers him as he swoops into action on Gotham City's mean streets.

Many superheroes in the Marvel universe wrestle with a variety of vulnerabilities. Daredevil is blind, but the Man without Fear does not regard this as a handicap. He is gifted with a "radar sense" that enables him to "see" objects around him. Spider-Man's "spider sense" affords him a warning of impending danger, but it isn't infallible: In *The Amazing Spider-Man* #39 (1966), the villainous Green Goblin penetrates Spidey's line of defense when a common cold blunts the hero's unique perceptive power. The arrogant Sub-Mariner has been vanquished by fire, and the Human Torch's flame-based powers can be snuffed out with water or a lack of oxygen. The stretching ability of the Torch's teammate, Reed Richards, a.k.a. Mr. Fantastic of the Fantastic Four, has its limits, as does the resiliency of his pliable body. Richards' wife, the Invisible Woman, can project force fields, a defense mechanism that cannot endure repeated or enormous blasts. The Incredible Hulk's gamma-spawned strength increases with his rage, and the destruction caused by his rampages often torment his alter ego, Bruce Banner. Iron Man is plagued by his weakened heart, which requires energizing from his armor. His alter ego, industrialist Tony Stark, once struggled with another weakness: alcoholism. After excessive drinking led Stark to several mishaps while in armor, he confronted his problem in the classic tale "Demon in a Bottle" in *Iron Man* #128 (1979).

The uncanny X-Men may be the world's mightiest mutants, but they are not without their vulnerabilities. Cyclops' optic blasts are so formidable he cannot control them without his ruby quartz visor. Rogue can siphon the abilities and memories of those she touches, denying her human contact with her loved ones, and Iceman is endangered by heat. Wolverine's feral impulses must be tempered with self-control so that he does not kill his opponents, but maintaining this focus sometimes lessens his effectiveness in combat. Wrote Les Daniels in *Marvel: Five Fabulous Decades of the World's Greatest Comics* (1991): "(Wolverine) must walk forever on a razor's edge."

A common weakness among superheroes is electricity—Spider-Man has been zapped by Electro and the Shocker, and the Electrocutioner has tried to fry Batman. Archie Comics' Jaguar, who communicates telepathically with wildlife and appropriates their attributes, can be stunned by a serious jolt of electricity. Cybernetic heroes like the Teen Titans' Cyborg and Marvel's Deathlok can be short-circuited, and they and armored characters including Iron Man, the X-Men member Colossus, and Steel are in danger during encounters with villains with magnetic powers like Magneto and Dr. Polaris.

A familiar vulnerability among many superheroes, particularly Marvel's, is self-absorption. Contemplating his personal problems—from his Aunt May's failing health to family financial difficulties—

has often impeded Peter Parker in his battles as Spider-Man. Reed Richards boasts remarkable intellect, and an ego to match, which is his greatest weakness: In *Fantastic Four* #500 (2003), it impedes the master scientist from learning the magic spells needed to free his teammates. Elektra may be the world's deadliest assassin, but her love for Matt (Daredevil) Murdock has softened her edge. While their superpowers and motivations make superheroes awe-inspiring, their jealousies, animosities, and other foibles make them human. —ME

Superheroes and Celebrities

There are few people who don't wish they could either have superpowers or be a celebrity. But comics history is speckled with occasional combinations of the two which remind everyone to be careful what they wish for.

These uncommon meetings between real people and mythic characters are always hard for comics fans to forget, while often being the only comics the general public even hears about. Among such books, the all-time champion, fittingly, involves a hero of the boxing ring: DC Comics' much-publicized 1978 one-shot, *Superman vs. Muhammad Ali.*

Though nowadays white America has caught up with black America in seeing Ali as an icon of defiant individualism, back then fewer people could see through his personal promotion to his political significance, and the book was viewed by many as a crass new low for the medium (along with Marvel Comics' licensing of KISS, another now-respected group of celebrities who were then considered the end of civilization as we know it). In any case, there was something *Space Jam*-ishly weird about seeing the ubiquitous real-life champ and the definitive two-dimensional titan interact. This mismatch was mirrored by the combination of beautiful imagery from one of comics' most phenomenal innovators, artist Neal Adams, with an off-the-rack space-opera storyline involving some sort of intergalactic boxing tournament, giving the effect of an Ed Wood flick with George Lucas production values.

But while the Ali-Superman bout may be the most unlikely celebrity-superhero pairing, it is by no means the most bizarre. That title may go to the several-issue appearance of insult comedian Don Rickles and his fictional, even eviler twin, "Goody," during Jack Kirby's early 1970s run on *Superman's Pal Jimmy Olsen* (issues #139–#141, 1971). That meeting was itself a bit surprising—Kirby is acknowledged as the king of superheroic spectacle, and the bland super-supporting-character was a strange choice of subject matter—but the "Goody" Rickles story topped it, inexplicably immortalizing the abrasive talk-show staple (though, yes, Superman himself figures into this storyline, too).

In fact, Superman finds his way into many of the most-remembered celebrity-superhero summits, a term that can be taken literally in the case of the notorious mid-1960s comic which has become a kitsch classic and a high-priced flea-market fixture: the issue (*Superman* #170, 1964) in which the Man of Steel promotes President Kennedy's physical fitness program (produced before the president's assassination, abruptly pulled, and then sheepishly published a bit later, reportedly at Lyndon Johnson's request).

DC's celebrity team-ups tended toward mainstream icons like the martyred leader; an early 1970s Robin story, "The King From Canarsie" (*Batman* #252, 1973), features a thinly veiled variant of beloved entertainer Danny Kaye. The more-rebellious Marvel tended toward the underground, with appearances like that of *Rolling Stone* founder Jan Wenner in the hundredth issue of *Daredevil* (1973), for reasons that seemed obscure even at the time (though scripter Steve Gerber, who also wrote the first KISS comic, had a longstanding interest in raising comics' hipness with references to the then-revolutionary realm of rock).

Continuing this partnership with edgy pop-culture pioneers who are now institutions, an issue of *Marvel Team-Up* (#74, 1978) had Spider-Man meeting the John Belushi–era Not-Ready-for-Prime-Time Players, while a 1984 issue of *The Avengers* (#239) starred David Letterman. (Letterman fared better there than in Frank Miller's classic dystopian Batman series *The Dark Knight Returns,* in which the Joker ensures ratings supremacy by mass-murdering the host and his audience on live TV—though to be fair, he does seem to spare Paul.) As if to offer belated equal time, a tiresome "team-up" between Spider-Man and Jay Leno was serialized in the back pages of many Marvel comics in mid-2002.

Also in the 2000s, both Freddie Prinze Jr. and Shannon Elizabeth have had less-than-flattering walk-ons rubbing elbows with the celebrity superheroes of Marvel's *The Ultimates* (2002–present), who have been seen sitting around speculating on who could play them in a movie (while it's no contest with team leader Nick Fury—a reworking of the classic Marvel superspy—who in this incarnation is a dead ringer for Samuel L. Jackson).

That book also belongs to an emerging subgenre of George W. Bush cameos, which range from the surprisingly positive (he's seen as a blunt but savvy horse-trading pragmatist in *Black Panther*'s "Enemy of the State II" story arc, issues #43–#45, 2002), to the mildly caricatured (he's the hapless frontier mayor in the 2003 *Rawhide Kid* miniseries—not a superhero comic, but a widely publicized one), to somewhere in-between (the vigorous if unreflective cheerleader-in-chief of *The Ultimates* and *The Order* [2002], also from Marvel).

On-target, warts-and-all portrayals of presidents Jimmy Carter, Bush Sr., and Bill Clinton appear in Marvel's *Supreme Power* (2003), a reality-oriented superhero saga written by a celebrity in his own right, *Babylon 5* creator J. Michael Straczynski—with a nod to the writer's Hollywood roots from a

character (Dr. Spectrum) explicitly modeled on Robert Redford. Also crossing the genre barrier by getting more notice in the rock press than in comics fandom, Mike Allred's miniseries *Red Rocket 7* (Dark Horse Comics, 1997–1998), concerning a messianic alien musician, features affectionate cameos from a number of rock legends, including (for obvious reasons) David Bowie.

But perhaps the most high-profile celebrity/superhero meet-and-greet of recent years is, paradoxically, one that didn't end up happening. The entertainment media was abuzz when Marvel announced that its book *X-Statix* (formerly *X-Force*), itself a media satire of super-celebrities drawn by Allred and written by the iconoclastic Peter Milligan, would run a story arc featuring a resurrected Lady Di in combat with a murderous royal family. Images were widely circulated, as were legal threats, and a censored (if still hilarious) version, with Di renamed and stuck in a black wig, ran in late 2003.

Only Hollywood can make you a star, and only the comics can make you super. The co-production of the two has met with mixed success, but you can bet it's far from over. —*AMC*

Superheroes and the Popular Culture

Writer Jerry Siegel and artist Joe Shuster had unwavering faith in their Superman creation, even when newspaper syndicates of the mid-1930s balked at their outlandish concept. Despite their confidence, Siegel and Shuster could not, in their wildest dreams, have imagined that one day, kids and consumers would be eating Superman peanut butter,

Opposite: From *Captain America* #113 © 1969 Marvel Comics. ART BY JIM STERANKO.

A MAN CAN BE DESTROYED, A TEAM OR AN ARMY CAN BE DESTROYED, BUT HOW DO YOU DESTROY AN *IDEAL*--A *DREAM*? HOW DO YOU DESTROY A LIVING *SYMBOL*--OR HIS INDOMITABLE *WILL*--HIS UNQUENCHABLE *SPIRIT*? PERHAPS *THESE* ARE THE THOUGHTS WHICH THUNDER WITHIN THE MURDEROUS *MINDS* OF THOSE WHO HAVE CHOSEN THE WAY OF *HYDRA*--OF THOSE WHO FACE THE *FIGHTING FURY* OF FREEDOM'S MOST FEARLESS *CHAMPION*--THE GALLANT, RED-WHITE-AND-BLUE-GARBED FIGURE WHO HAS BEEN A TOWERING SOURCE OF *INSPIRATION* TO LIBERTY-LOVERS EVERYWHERE! HOW CAN THE FEARSOME FORCES OF EVIL EVER HOPE TO DESTROY THE UNCONQUERABLE *CAPTAIN AMERICA*?

wearing Superman underwear, and playing Superman video games.

But such is the public's fascination with the superhero. Beginning with the arresting image of Superman hoisting a sedan over his head on the cover of *Action Comics* #1 (1938), the superhero has captured the attention of the masses, earning a position of permanence in the social psyche.

THE 1940S: OUT OF THE COMICS AND INTO THE WORLD AT LARGE

Action was an instant success, prompting publisher DC Comics to open a floodgate of merchandising bearing Superman's likeness, from the expected (figurines, bubble-gum cards, and the like) to the atypical (a table-top lighter for cigarette smokers). Superman quickly flew into cultural omnipresence. The first public "sighting" of the Man of Steel took place in 1939, when Broadway actor Ray Middleton impersonated the hero at the New York World's Fair. That very year, the "Supermen of America" fan club was launched, extolling the virtues of "Strength, Courage, and Justice," and a Superman newspaper strip began a decades-long run. The hero was soon the star of a dramatic radio program, theatrical cartoons, a paperback novel, and, at the close of the 1940s, two live-action movie serials.

Of course, the burgeoning comic-book industry consisted of other superheroes—Plastic Man, the Human Torch, the Black Terror, Cat-Man, and countless other masked adventurers were among their colorful legion—and some were translated to the big screen via live-action movie serials, including *Spy Smasher* (1942), *Batman* (1943), *Captain America* (1944), and *Congo Bill* (1948). Outside of Superman, however, few were licensed into other areas. A handful of Captain Marvel retail items (including a paper glider, a tin car, and figures) were produced. Captain America endorsed a fan club that not only promoted his Marvel (then known as

Timely) comic but American patriotism itself: the Sentinels of Liberty, with members receiving a tin badge. "Apart from the Sentinels of Liberty badge," wrote Bill Bruegman in his book, *Superhero Collectibles: A Pictorial Price Guide* (1996), a youth-sized Captain America costume produced in the mid-1940s "is the only known child's product made from a Timely character."

Sales of superhero comics nose-dived in post–World War II America and titles rapidly disappeared from the stands. At the end of the 1940s, one might have suspected that superheroes were merely a flash in the pan born of the Great Depression and the war's thirst for inspirational figures. Only a few survived.

THE 1950S: THE AUTHORITY FIGURE OF STEEL

During the 1950s, the frigid fingers of the communist threat gripped the United States in a cold war, and the Man of Steel helped break the ice. Superman became a national symbol of the American Way, most notably in the wildly successful live-action television series *The Adventures of Superman* (1953–1957), starring George Reeves. Reeves made numerous personal appearances as the Man of Steel, and also played Superman in a short film promoting U.S. Savings Bonds, in a commercial for Kellogg's Grape Nuts cereal, and in a fondly remembered episode of *I Love Lucy*. As evidence of the Man of Steel's impact upon popular culture, a 1953 *Superman* newspaper sequence guest-starred bespectacled television personality Steve Allen, with a storyline addressing Allen's physical resemblance to Superman's alter ego, Clark Kent.

Superman was perhaps the only ray of hope in the world of superheroes of the 1950s. The comics business altered its content to address changing tastes, and many titles, particularly horror and crime series, became outrageously graphic. Comics transformed into what some historians have deemed boys' "dirty little secret," taboo material read with flashlights under bedcovers. The comics industry fell under denunciation in the mid-1950s at a U.S. Senate subcommittee hearing that foisted upon publishers a censorship board called the Comics Code Authority (CCA), a crippling move putting many players out of business. The History Channel documentary *Comic Book Superheroes: Unmasked* (2003) reported that the industry suffered a 50 percent drop in sales between 1954 and 1956, due to the budding prominence of television, as well as rock and roll music, "the new teen thing."

To portray to skeptical parents the wholesomeness of its product, DC Comics published in its titles one-page public-service announcements (PSAs) in comic-book form, featuring Superman (and occasionally other DC characters like Batman and Robin) in mini morality plays. In a Superman PSA called "Safety First," for example, the Man of Steel spouts traffic-accident statistics to a careless jaywalker ("32,300 people were killed and 1,150,000 injured in traffic accidents in a single year!").

THE 1960S: "POP" GO THE SUPERHEROES

In the 1960s, the superhero commandeered popular culture, and did so with a "Pow!" The decade started as did the two prior, with Superman as the superhero big cheese. Marvel, which had abandoned superheroes in the 1950s, introduced its "heroes with problems," offbeat, self-absorbed characters like Spider-Man, Daredevil, the Hulk, and the X-Men. By the mid-1960s, the Hulk and Spider-Man were counterculture icons, appearing alongside real-world civil-rights crusader Malcolm X on lists of figures most admired by college students.

Batman (1966–1968), a campy live-action television series starring Adam West and Burt Ward as Batman and Robin, became an overnight ratings smash. Mere months after the show's premiere, a quickly produced *Batman* movie was filmed ("I worked just over 30 days," recalled West in an interview on the film's 2001 DVD edition), promoted with

a trailer featuring Ward as Robin buoyantly beaming, "Soon, very soon, Batman and I will be bata-pulting right out of your TV sets and onto your theater screens!" An ensuing wave of "Batmania" slapped the Dynamic Duo's faces, both photographed and illustrated, on almost every product conceivable, including knife-and-fork sets, bubble-bath dispensers, apparel galore, model kits, and lunchboxes. "Batman makes a mighty leap into national popularity" announced the cover of the March 11, 1966 edition of *Life* magazine. Recording artists Jan and Dean released a *Jan and Dean Meet Batman* album, and Neal Hefti's surfing-inspired "Batman" TV theme became stamped onto the public's musical mind. *Batman*'s fight-scene graphics—boisterous comic-esque sound effects like "Crunch!" and "Zowie!"—became part of the American vernacular to such a degree that in the twenty-first century, many journalists employ these exclamations when referencing contemporary comics-related material.

Batman's popularity sparked a superhero boom of unprecedented proportions. 1940s superheroes like Captain America and Plastic Man bounced back to life, and TV networks raced to create their own superheroes, live-action and animated, including Captain Nice, Space Ghost, and Mr. Terrific. Superhero parodies flourished, from *MAD* magazine's Captain Klutz to the animated series *Underdog*. Several licensors' characters (Batman, Spider-Man, and the Green Hornet, among others) were funneled into Ideal's Captain Action toy line, featuring a host figure that "transformed" into other heroes by donning their uniforms (each sold separately). Superman enjoyed a surge in popularity, spinning off into an animated TV show and a Broadway musical, *It's a Bird, It's a Plane, It's Superman*.

The superhero continued to serve as a super-pitchman. Superman endorsed New Jersey's Palisades (amusement) Park in comic-book ads that included a ticket for a free ride on the Batman slide. ABC-TV commissioned a promotional comic book to plug its Saturday fare: *America's Best TV*

Comics (1967) was an eighty-page giant with the Jack Kirby–drawn Mr. Fantastic (of the Fantastic Four) on the cover, along with Spider-Man, Casper the Friendly Ghost, and other cartoon stars. Marvel's comic books hyped a line of peripherals like inflatable Spider-Man pillows and Fantastic Four sweatshirts. The short-lived TV series *The Green Hornet* (1966–1967) inspired a brief but impressive spate of merchandising, including playing cards, a kite, a paint-by-number set, and walkie talkies.

Real-life painter Roy Lichtenstein interpreted comic-book panels into a series of "pop-art" portraits incorporating word balloons, primary colors, and Ben-Day dots, mimicking the primitive four-color printing techniques of the day. Lichtenstein's comics-inspired works helped legitimize comics as an art form and remain popular in the twenty-first century.

THE 1970S AND BEYOND: SUPERHEROES, SUPERHEROES, EVERYWHERE!

As an entertainment force and a licensing vehicle, the superhero soared to new heights in the 1970s. After decades of increasing media saturation, Superman had grown into an icon, immortalized in music (Jim Croce warned, "You don't tug on Superman's cape" in his hit "You Don't Mess around with Jim" [1973], and Barbra Streisand released an album titled *Superman* [1977]), in politics (a popular poster released in 1971, during the height of the Vietnam War, depicted Superman flashing the "peace sign"), and even in junk food (Superman Pretzels and Superman Peanut Butter). And the Man of Steel wasn't alone in such impact: The coveted cover shot for the inaugural issue of *Ms.* Magazine in 1972 was won by Wonder Woman.

A blitz of products bearing the likenesses of Marvel and DC superheroes inundated retail markets, and their characters continued to pitch other products, including a fondly remembered but rather odd mid-1970s campaign by baker Hostess selling

its wares to comic-book readers through one-page illustrated adventures (an example: a *Shazam!* installment in which Captain Marvel investigates the "strange disappearance of cup cakes around the world"). Superheroes flourished on TV, from new creations like Isis and ElectraWoman, to DC's kid-friendly *Super Friends* cartoon, to primetime dramas starring the Hulk, Wonder Woman, and Spider-Man. The box-office muscle of the live-action *Superman: The Movie* (1978) elevated the superhero to multi-million-dollar blockbuster status, and the then-emerging video-game industry ushered the Man of Steel (and later, many other comics heroes) into this exciting new world.

These merchandising trends continued throughout the 1980s, and the phenomenal success of director Tim Burton's *Batman* (1989) only cemented the superhero's role as a mass-media force (and as a cash cow). By the 1990s, generations of consumers had been exposed to superheroes through film, TV, cartoons, video and computer games, action figures, apparel, snack and breakfast food, fast-food kids' toys, and even amusement parks (various theme parks feature rides based on Batman, Superman, Spider-Man, the Hulk, and the X-Men, with actors wearing superhero costumes intermingling with park-goers). As confirmation of his iconic status, an animated Superman teamed with comedian Jerry Seinfeld in a 1998 television commercial for American Express. Seinfeld, not the Man of Steel, is the commercial's real hero, coming to Lois Lane's aid when she finds herself trying to buy groceries without any cash. The licensing of superheroes has become big business for comic-book publishers; so big, in fact, that revenues generated by merchandising far exceed profits earned by the comic books themselves, posing the ultimate irony: The popularity of superheroes through competing media has adversely affected the appeal of the superhero's source material, the comics.

While comics publishers of the 2000s explore new methods of attracting readers, vintage comic books, particularly those of the Golden Age

(1938–1954) and Silver Age (1956–1969), are becoming increasingly rare—the better the condition (or grade), the higher their value. In "Big Bucks in Collectible Comics," an August 4, 2003 CBS News.com report, investor Bob Storms revealed that in 2002 he sold a copy of Marvel's *Amazing Fantasy* #15 (the first appearance of Spider-Man) for $32,500—a comic he bought four years earlier for $20,000. Baltimore, Maryland, businessman Steve Geppi, President and CEO of Diamond Comic Distributors, issued an October 31, 2003 press release announcing, "I'll pay at least $25,000 for an unrestored, complete copy in good condition, and up to $1 million for a genuine, 'near mint' condition copy of *Action Comics* #1."

Profits aside, comics collecting often inspires mockery from the masses: The nebbish "Comic Book Guy" is a recurring character on Fox's animated series *The Simpsons* (1989–present), and the September 29, 2003 episode of the CBS sitcom *Yes, Dear* categorized guest star Tim Conway's newfound hobby of comic-book collecting as a peculiarity. Similarly, a young girl fascinated by the Marvel superhero Thor received some ribbing in the movie *Adventures in Babysitting* (1987), as did a preschooler who always wears a Flash costume in the Eddie Murphy comedy *Daddy Day Care* (2003).

But thousands of superhero (and comic-book) fans remain undaunted by the taunts. The San Diego Comic-Con, an international Mecca for matters fantastic, attracts tens of thousands of attendees each year and has become so important that major Hollywood stars now make appearances to promote their superhero and action films (included among the guests of the 2003 show were actors Angelina Jolie, Halle Berry, Hugh Jackman, Quentin Tarantino, and Alfred Molina). Grade-school kids have superheroes all their own, like the star of Dav Pilkey's *Captain Underpants* books, and preschoolers are amazed by *Sesame Street*'s Super Grover. And lest one regard superheroes and comics as juvenile pap, Michael Chabon's 2000 novel, *The Amazing Adventures of Kavalier and Clay* (loosely

based on the lives of the Golden Age's classic team of comics creators, Joe Simon and Jack Kirby), won a Pulitzer Prize and is being adapted into a motion picture. Noting the cultural importance of superheroes, former *Batman* editor and writer Dennis O'Neil remarked, on the *Comic Book Superheroes: Unmasked* program, that the editors of *Batman* and *Superman* comic books have become "custodians of folklore." Their venues may be forever changing, but superheroes are here to stay. —ME

Superheroes in Prose

The adaptation of superheroes into prose fiction goes back to the very genesis of the superhero genre. Indeed, Philip Wylie's 1930 science-fiction novel *Gladiator*—the tale of an invincible superpowered man who lives among normal humans—predates the advent of Jerome Siegel's and Joe Shuster's *Superman* by eight years. Just four years after debuting in 1938's *Action Comics* #1, and two years after gaining national prominence via the *Superman* radio program, the last son of Krypton starred in his first novel: *The Adventures of Superman* by George Lowther (1942), a book that introduces the current spelling for the name of Superman's Kryptonian father Jor-El (as opposed to Jor-L). A steady stream of pictureless superhero text narratives followed over the ensuing decades, almost all of them based upon heroes that originated in the comics. Superman and other high-profile DC Comics heroes, such as Batman and Wonder Woman, and flagship Marvel Comics characters like Spider-Man and the Hulk, all became prose protagonists, often due to the efforts of comic-book writers.

Among the more memorable superhero novels were a pair of Bantam releases from the 1960s: 1967's *The Avengers Battle the Earth-Wrecker* by science-fiction writer Otto Binder (Binder also wrote scores of Captain Marvel stories for Fawcett during the 1940s and 1950s) and *Captain America: The Great Gold Steal* by Ted White (1968). Armed with the editorial expertise of Len Wein (co-creator of DC's *Swamp Thing* and Marvel's "new" X-Men) and Marv Wolfman (co-creator of DC's *New Teen Titans* and Marvel's Blade the Vampire Slayer), Pocket Books picked up the Marvel license in the late 1970s, releasing a short fiction anthology (*Stan Lee Presents the Marvel Superheroes, featuring the Hulk, the Avengers, the X-Men, and Daredevil,* 1979) and a raft of short novels, all of which are long out of print.

Among these out-of-print gems are: *The Amazing Spider-Man: Mayhem in Manhattan* by Len Wein and Marv Wolfman (1978); *The Incredible Hulk: Stalker from the Stars* by Len Wein, Marv Wolfman, and Joseph Silva (1978); *The Incredible Hulk: Cry of the Beast* by Richard S. Meyers (1979); *Captain America: Holocaust for Hire* by Joseph Silva (1979); *The Fantastic Four: Doomsday* by Marv Wolfman (1979); *Iron Man: And Call My Killer … Modok!* by well-regarded science-fiction author William Rotsler (1979); *Doctor Strange, Master of the Mystic Arts: Nightmare,* also by Rotsler (1979); *The Amazing Spider-Man: Crime Campaign* by comics writer Paul Kupperberg (1979); *The Avengers: The Man Who Stole Tomorrow* by *Avengers* and *Iron Man* writer David Michelinie (1979); and *The Hulk and Spider-Man: Murdermoon* by Paul Kupperberg (1979). Meanwhile, DC's stable of heroes was also beginning to make inroads into text-only storytelling with *Superman: Last Son of Krypton,* a novelization of the 1978 *Superman* motion picture by Superman comics writer Elliot S. Maggin (1978). Maggin followed this up with *Superman: Miracle Monday* (1981), a novel set in the far future, when mankind has colonized the entire solar system—but still sets aside a day to commemorate the life and achievements of Earth's mightiest hero. Maggin also penned *Starwinds Howl* (1997), a novella about Superman's boyhood pet, the Kryptonian super-dog Krypto, who had been "retconned" out of existence (removed from the Superman mythos by means of "retroactive continuity") in 1986 (*Action Comics* #583).

Also in 1986, Marvel and role-playing game (RPG) manufacturer TSR collaborated on the *Marvel Adventure Gamebooks,* a series of short paperback novels that straddled the worlds of prose fiction and RPGs. In titles such as Jeff Grubb's *Amazing Spider-Man: City in Darkness* and Jerry Epperson and James M. Ward's *Wolverine: Night of the Wolverine,* the reader could "steer" Spider-Man through various story scenarios, keeping tabs on the protagonists' power levels and fighting ability by means of custom "stat cards" bound into the books. DC's heroes began ramping up their literary appearances by the decade's end, with novelizations of the 1989 Warner Bros. *Batman* film and *Batman Returns* (1992), both by Craig Shaw Gardner.

Buoyed by the success of these films and their merchandising, the Caped Crusader and members of his supporting cast soon starred in several original Warner Books novels, including: *The Batman Murders* by Craig Shaw Gardner (1990); *Batman: To Stalk a Specter* by Simon Hawke (1991); *Batman: Captured by the Engines* by award-winning horror novelist Joe R. Lansdale (1991); and *Catwoman: Tiger Hunt* by fantasists Lynn Abbey and Robert Asprin (1992). Several anthologies of short fiction dedicated to DC's highest-profile superheroes and villains, all edited by Martin H. Greenberg, also appeared during this period, including: *The Further Adventures of Batman* (1989); *The Further Adventures of the Joker* (1990); *The Further Adventures of Batman Volume 2: Featuring the Penguin* (1992); *The Further Adventures of Batman Volume 3: Featuring Catwoman* (1993); *The Further Adventures of Superman: All-New Adventures of the Man of Steel* (1993); and *The Further Adventures of Wonder Woman* (1993).

In the late 1980s, superheroes with no prior experience on the comics page were being introduced in "shared world" prose novels. *Wild Cards* was a series of "mosaic novels," assembled by a large group of writers working in tandem. The series began publication in 1986 with *Wild Cards,* a tale that presented superheroes originally conceived for use in superhero role-playing games by a group of distinguished science-fiction authors spearheaded by George R. R. Martin (the series' editor) and Melinda M. Snodgrass (the assistant editor since the sixth volume), with stories contributed by Edward W. Bryant, Pat Cadigan, Michael Cassutt, Chris Claremont, Arthur Byron Cover, Leanne C. Harper, Stephen Leigh, Victor Milán, Gail Gerstner-Miller, John J. Miller, Laura J. Mixon, Kevin Andrew Murphy, Lewis Shiner, Walton Simons, Howard Waldrop, Sage Walker, Walter Jon Williams, William F. Wu, and Roger Zelazny.

The central conceit of *Wild Cards* is that an alien organism (the Wild Card virus) is released over New York in 1946, randomly killing 90 percent of the city's population; those who died are said to have drawn the Black Queen from the Wild Card virus' genetic deck. Of the 10 percent who survive the infection, 90 percent of these become horribly mutated and disfigured—genetic "Jokers." The virus bestows comic-book-style superhuman powers upon the small remainder, who are known thereafter as "Aces," and also gives fantastic abilities to some of the Jokers. The Aces and Jokers quickly sort themselves out into bands of heroes, like the super-strong Golden Boy, the thunder-throwing Black Eagle, Fortunato the Tantric magician, the body-switching Sleeper, and the Great and Powerful Turtle, or become villains like the mind-enslaving Puppetman, the lethal-handed Demise, the bloodthirsty Carnifex, or the brain-eating Deadhead. The term "Joker" is considered pejorative, and those who have never been exposed to the virus (the vast majority of the human species) are known as "Nats."

The story spans several decades as the Aces and Jokers face the McCarthyism of the 1950s, endure the social upheavals of the Vietnam period, and fight the good fight against renegade Jokers during the Reagan-Bush years and into the 1990s. The first *Wild Cards* novel series ran twelve volumes, fin-

ishing up in 1993. Marvel produced comics based upon the *Wild Cards* novels in 1990 and 1991, and a second cycle of *Wild Cards* novels (whose first volume was titled *Card Sharks*) began in 1993.

American superhero comics made an enormous impression on English writer Neil Gaiman (best known as the creator of the DC/Vertigo comics series *Sandman*), inspiring him to co-create and co-edit the prose-based *Temps* series (with co-creator, co-editor, and contributor Alex Stewart). *Temps* (1991) and *Euro Temps* (1992) set up the saga of the British League of Superheroes and the villains who bedevil them, presenting the familiar-yet-alien history that results from the presence of superhumans in the United Kingdom and in Europe. Like the *Wild Cards* volumes, the Temps books occur in a shared world, a literary quilt created from the short fiction of such science-fiction writers as Christopher Amies, Tina Anghelatos, Molly Brown, David V. Barrett, Storm Constantine, Anne Gay, Colin Greenland, Graham Higgins, Liz Holliday, Jenny Jones, Graham Joyce, Roz Kaveney, David Langford, Marcus L. Rowland, Brian Stableford, and Jack Yeovil.

Back in the States, Superman grabbed international headlines by dying at the hands of the ultra-powerful villain Doomsday (*Superman* vol. 2 #75, 1993). Fortunately, the Man of Steel's demise proved only temporary, and dovetailed with a hard-cover novel titled *The Death and Life of Superman* by Superman comics writer Roger Stern (1993). Not to be outdone, Batman sustained and overcame grievous injuries in a 1993–1994 DC Comics story arc titled "Knightfall," which inspired the hardcover novel *Batman: Knightfall* by veteran Batman comics writer Dennis O'Neil (1994).

Marvel's superheroes experienced what was arguably their greatest prose renaissance from 1994 until 1999, during the joint publishing program of the now-defunct Byron Preiss Multimedia Company and Berkley Boulevard Books, a team-up that was initially under the direction of editor and writer Keith R. A. DeCandido. This prolific alliance yielded forty-five novels and seven short fiction anthologies, covering a wide pallet of Marvel heroes ranging from the X-Men to Nick Fury, Agent of S.H.I.E.L.D.

Among the most memorable titles were: *Iron Man: The Armor Trap* (1995) by Greg Cox, who is perhaps best known as a *Star Trek* novelist; *The Incredible Hulk: What Savage Beast* (1995), an immensely popular hardcover novel by Peter David, who has written Hulk's comics adventures longer than anyone else, and has established critical backstory for the Hulk and his supporting cast (in the novel and in the comics) that is now considered as canonical as the original Stan Lee/Jack Kirby material from the early 1960s; *The Ultimate Super-Villains* (1996), a short-fiction anthology edited by Marvel pioneer Stan Lee; *X-Men: Smoke and Mirrors* by eluki bes shahar (1997), a tale that successfully evokes the best *Uncanny X-Men* comics work Chris Claremont and John Romita Jr. did in the 1980s; *The Incredible Hulk: Abominations* (1997) by Jason Henderson, one of the most dramatic, character-driven, and action-packed Hulk/Abomination clashes ever executed in any medium; *Untold Tales of Spider-Man,* a short-fiction anthology edited by Stan Lee and Kurt Busiek (1997); *The Fantastic Four: Countdown to Chaos* by Pierce Askegren (1998); *The Fantastic Four: Redemption of the Silver Surfer* by Michael Jan Friedman (1998); *Spider-Man: Venom's Wrath,* a suspenseful police procedural tale by Keith R. A. DeCandido and José R. Nieto (1998); *Generation X: Crossroads* by J. Steven York (1998); *The Ultimate Silver Surfer,* a short-fiction anthology edited by Stan Lee (1999); and science-fiction writer Adam-Troy Castro's critically-acclaimed trilogy of Spider-Man novels, *The Gathering of the Sinister Six* (1999), *The Revenge of the Sinister Six* (2000), and *The Secret of the Sinister Six* (2002).

Because of legal disputes between the publishing partners and Marvel's bankruptcy woes, this line of books was temporarily shut down in 1999, though Berkley Books picked up the reigns solo and issued the remaining titles between 2000 and 2002. Marvel's mutants even teamed up with the crew of the *U.S.S. Enterprise-D* in Michael Jan Friedman's *Star Trek: The Next Generation and the X-Men: Planet X* (1998), a novel that grew out of a superhero-*Star Trek* crossover in Marvel's then-current *Star Trek* comics line.

During the 1990s, DC's superpowered pantheon maintained its visibility in the world of letters by gracing the pages of several more hardcover novels. Batman turned his attention to the horrific crime of pedophilia in *Batman: The Ultimate Evil,* penned by crime writer, children's advocate, and attorney Andrew Vachss (1995). *Kingdom Come* by Elliot S. Maggin (1998) engages a graying Justice League of America from an alternate future in a final apocalyptic battle, based on DC's *Kingdom Come* comics miniseries (1996). *Batman: No Man's Land,* by *Detective Comics* story sensation Greg Rucka (2000), adapts into prose a 1999–2000 DC Comics story arc in which Gotham City sustains horrendous earthquake damage, prompting Batman to embark on a mission of mercy. DC has further added to fans' bookshelves in the 2000s with a series of paperback novels on individual Justice League members from Pocket Books.

The crowning literary achievement for the comic-book hero is doubtless Michael Chabon's original novel, *The Amazing Adventures of Kavalier & Clay* (2000). This story of two young Jewish boys coming of age during the gritty Great Depression years and finding success in the fledgling comics business with their escape-artist superhero creation ("the Escapist, Master of Elusion, whom no chains could hold nor walls imprison") won the Pulitzer Prize in fiction in 2001—and went a long way toward making comic-book superheroes respectable in the jaundiced eyes of the bluenosed literary orthodoxy. —*MAM*

Superheroes with Disabilities

In the time it will take to read this entry, real-life superheroics will occur. A blind woman will safely cross the street. A teenage boy whose body is crippled with cerebral palsy will rise unassisted from a chair. Physically and mentally challenged individuals who refuse to be handicapped by their conditions overcome adversity in virtually every facet of their lives. Superheroes *do* exist.

Some fictional superheroes face impediments that make their feats of bravery even more Herculean. Daredevil, Marvel Comics' "Man without Fear," leaps fearlessly off of metropolitan rooftops in pursuit of criminals, and pounces into armies of heavily armed gangsters—awe-inspiring actions that truly flabbergast when one considers the hero's *blindness.* The accident that robbed his alter ego, lawyer Matt Murdock, of his vision—exposure to a radioactive isotope—heightens his other senses and imbues him with a "radar sense" that allows him to perceive nearby objects, helping compensate for his lack of sight.

Daredevil may be the most recognized blind superhero, but others preceded him. The Black Bat, a hero originating in 1934 in the pulp magazines— periodicals published on inexpensive "pulp" paper and featuring prose adventure stories—loses his vision when, in his true identity of district attorney Terry Quinn, acid is splashed in his eyes by criminals attempting to destroy evidence. Quinn receives a transplant from an eye donor, and emerges, strangely, with the capacity to see in the dark. He conceals this enhancement from the world, maintaining a blind façade as Quinn, but taking to the streets at night as the crime-crushing Black Bat. The comic-book hero called the Mask (not to be confused with the offbeat Dark Horse Comics character portrayed by actor Jim Carrey in the 1994 blockbuster film of same name) is a district attorney who loses his sight, then regains it and becomes a costumed vigilante. It's interesting to note that he, the Black Bat, and Daredevil all share the same vocation—law— and all are blind. The original Mask debuted in Better Publications' *Exciting Comics* #1 (1940).

In DC Comics' *All-American Comics* #25 (1941), readers first encountered surgeon Charles McNider, who is blinded in a mishap but discovers

that he possesses perfect night vision. Accompanied by Hooty, an owl, he becomes the nocturnal superhero Dr. Mid-Nite, later joining the Justice Society of America (JSA). The hero was succeeded in the guise in 1985 by Beth Chapel, an African American medical student who also was robbed of her ability to see. She became Dr. Midnight (different spelling), and served with Infinity, Inc. before dying in a battle against the lord of darkness, Eclipso. In 1999, yet another physician, Pieter Cross, was engaged in unorthodox medical experiments that cost him his sight, adopting the name (and original spelling) of the first Dr. Mid-Nite. This version of the hero is among the roster of the 2000s incarnation of the JSA. Other vision-challenged heroes include the X-Men's Psylocke, who lost her eyesight but received cybernetic eyes, and Marvel's Shroud, a dark-clad vigilante who willingly allowed himself to be blinded to receive the "gift" of extrasensory perception from the goddess Kali.

A few superheroes are vertically challenged—or, in less politically correct terminology, *short.* In *All-American Comics* #19 (1940), Al Pratt, long ridiculed for his five-foot stature, undergoes physical training to become the pint-sized pummeling powerhouse, DC's original Atom. "Shorty" Wilson, a former football player of diminutive height, wears a cloak and fedora and tackles criminals as the Shadow homage called the Black Dwarf in publisher Harry "A" Chesler's *Red Seal Comics* #14 (1945). Rackman, bowing in 1947 in Hillman Periodicals' *Clue* #12, is a little person who walks on stilts when fighting crime. Tom Thumb is a purple-and-green-dressed tiny titan in Marvel Comics' Squadron Supreme, and Eugene Milton Judd—barely three feet tall—is a beefy former nightclub bouncer who is better known as Puck of Marvel's Canadian superteam Alpha Flight.

Some superheroes have overcome amputations. DC's Aquaman lost a hand in a 1994 conflict, replacing it with a hook. In 2001, his hand regenerated— but as living *water,* not flesh—due to a spell from the mystical Lady of the Lake. Most of Victor Stone's body was destroyed in an accident and replaced with cybernetics. As Cyborg, he has used his artificial sub-stitutions, including interchangeable hands with different combative functions, as one of the Teen Titans. Originally resentful of his plight, Stone accepted the change and became an aide to children with disabilities after meeting a young boy with a prosthetic arm in the landmark tale "A Day in the Life" in DC Comics' *The New Teen Titans* #8 (1981).

Sensory impairment has affected, but not stopped, a few superheroes. Cyborg's Teen Titans teammate Joseph Wilson (Jericho) was mute. The son of the Titans' arch nemesis Deathstroke the Terminator, Jericho had the ability to possess others' bodies, and communicated with his friends via hand signals, but ultimately died at the hand of his father. Assassin David Cain taught his daughter Cassandra only one language: violence. The mute teen, trained to follow in her father's footsteps, was shown guidance by Gotham City's heroes Batman and Oracle, and became the new Batgirl. Batgirl has since developed verbal communicative abilities thanks to her support network. Hawkeye, the ace archer of Marvel's mightiest heroes, the Avengers, sustained a profound hearing loss in an accident and is dependent upon digital hearing aids.

Mental illness bears a stigma in modern society, yet some superheroes have fought crime despite psychological problems. The schizophrenic Badger, appearing in print in the 1980s, brutally targeted ne'er-do-wells who harmed animals and spat on sidewalks. In DC's six-issue *Rose & Thorn* miniseries (2003–2004), Rhosyn Forrest's psyche is severed by rage after her father's murder, creating two wholly separate personalities: the docile Rose and the vengeful superheroine Thorn. *Rose & Thorn* updated the split-personality crime fighter who debuted in *Superman's Girl Friend Lois Lane* #105 (1970). In 2000, DC Comics published *Realworlds: Batman,* a poignant tale about a mildly retarded young man who believes he is Batman, and tackles street punks dressed in a makeshift superhero costume, nearly dying in the process.

There are superheroes whose alter egos lack the ability to walk unassisted. Both Freddy Freeman and Dr. Don Blake were "lame," requiring a single crutch or cane to walk. Yet they became ambulatory—and superpowerful!—after transforming into their amazing identities of Captain Marvel Jr. and the mighty Thor. Similarly, war journalist John Mann, a former soldier who lost his right leg in combat, was first seen in Charlton Comics' *Mysteries of Unexplored Worlds* #46 (1965). While standing amid the ruins of a Roman temple, he shrieks to the heavens, lamenting the bloodshed of human conflict, and is transported by a bolt of lightning to Olympus, where the gods transform him into the superstrong Son of Vulcan. Freemind, the premier superhero from the 2002 startup publisher Future Comics, is "a brilliant man in a useless body," a quadriplegic who transfers his mind into a superheroic form (a concept previously seen in Marvel's It, the Living Colossus, a stone giant possessed by a wheelchair-bound master). Silhouette, a crippled member of Marvel's teen team the New Warriors, has used crutches in combat.

Marvel's Human Fly is an unnamed man who is injured in an automobile accident and informed that his legs are now useless in *The Human Fly* #1 (1977). He beats the odds through rehabilitation and determination, not only regaining the ability to walk but also perfecting his body. In a red-and-white suit and cowl, with magnetic-grip gloves and boots, he raises awareness and money for the handicapped as the Human Fly. His adventures ran for nineteen issues.

Perhaps the most famous disabled hero is Charles Xavier, or Professor X, founder of the mutant assemblage the X-Men. An accident robbed him of the use of his legs and permanently placed him in a wheelchair, but thanks to his uncanny telekinetic powers and his proven leadership qualities, his authority is never questioned. Niles Caulder, the "Chief" of the Doom Patrol, also directs DC Comics' "world's strangest heroes" from a wheelchair.

Barbara Gordon, who once fought alongside Batman and Robin as Batgirl, became a paraplegic after being shot by the Joker. Initially despondent over her paralysis, she later channeled her energies into the cultivation of a vast computer network, secretly becoming Oracle, the information broker for numerous DC superheroes. Batman, Robin, Nightwing, and the Suicide Squad are among those who have relied upon her ability to ferret out valuable data, and she works closely with heroines Black Canary and the Huntress as the point person of the covert team Birds of Prey. Oracle has proven to herself, and to others, that she need not walk to be an asset to justice. "Barbara is stronger than she knows, and this is, perhaps, her only great weakness," wrote DC Comics scribe Devin Grayson in *Wizard* magazine's 1998 Batman special edition. "Hyper-defensive about her disability, she has, if anything, over-compensated. However, her very determination to remain self-reliant, though admirable and inspiring, has made her less willing than ever to accept support or aid of any kind."

The disabilities experienced by most of the aforementioned superheroes have largely been gimmicks—the "blind" hero, the "short" hero—or shunted aside after a magical transformation (i.e., crippled Freddy Freeman converts, with a bolt of magic lightning, into the superboy Captain Marvel Jr.). And their handicaps were preexisting, as in the case of Professor X (he was in his wheelchair when readers first met him in *X-Men* #1 [1963]), or introduced as part of their origins (Matt Murdock lost his sight in *Daredevil* #1 [1964]). As Oracle, however, Gordon stands tall as the most empowering disabled superhero. Readers witnessed her tragedy, and watched her rise above it.

Arguably, two other heroes with disabilities are equally empowering, if not more so. "Never underestimate the powers of the handicapped" asserted Damon Wayans' Handi-Man, the physically challenged superhero seen on Fox-TV's *In Living Color* (1990–1994). While played for laughs, Handi-Man, and his diminutive sidekick the Tiny Avenger, crusaded for the rights of the disabled. And actor Christopher Reeve, who catapulted to fame starring as the Man of Steel in the franchise of four live-action *Superman* movies between 1978 and 1987, was seriously hurt in a 1995 horse-riding accident, becoming a paraplegic. In the years since his injury, Reeve has advocated for severed spinal-cord research, raising money, awareness, and hope for the cause. He is more a superman in actuality than he ever was on screen. —*ME*

Superheroines

Superheroes, no matter their media of presentation, have always held a mirror to society and offered a reflection of cultural attitudes. No better example of this can be found than with super*heroines*.

Jerry Siegel and Joe Shuster were teen nebbishes when they created Superman, and their brazen Man of Steel clearly embodied the male adolescent power fantasy: He was handsome, self-assured, in control, and robust, attributes most insecure teenage boys can only covet. Little did Siegel and Shuster realize that they were paving a societal super-highway with their character. Following Superman's phenomenally lucrative 1938 debut, a heroic brotherhood quickly appeared: Batman, Captain Marvel, Sub-Mariner, the Human Torch, Captain America. Even the teenage sidekicks, like Robin the Boy Wonder and Bucky, were high-spirited males. The burgeoning business of superhero comics was the publishing equivalent of the "He-Man Woman Hater's Club" from the *Little Rascals* film shorts. When women did appear in comics, they were damsels in distress. It's no wonder that girls found this new genre of comic books unattractive.

THE FIRST FEMALE SUPERHEROES

Comics publishers of this era tried to attract a female audience—they just didn't try very hard. Four significant female heroines, although not *super*heroines in the strictest sense, all showed up in

1940. First came Fantomah, Mystery Woman of the Jungle, an unabashed attempt to milk the success of *The Phantom* and *Sheena, Queen of the Jungle.* Bowing in Fiction House's *Jungle Comics* #2 (February 1940), Fantomah wore no mask, but instead transformed her appearance from a beautiful blonde to a skull-faced monstress (keeping her flowing golden locks in the process), using her supernatural powers to combat evil. During her four-year career, she was confined to *Jungle Comics'* backup strips, almost as if Fiction House was ashamed of her. On his Toonopedia website, Don Markstein observed, "From beginning to end, Fantomah was obscure almost to the point of vanishing."

The Woman in Red, the first *costumed* heroine, originally donned her disguise in Standard Comics' *Thrilling Comics* #2 (March 1940). She was actually police officer Peggy Allen, but by night she sported a crimson hood, mask, and cloak—as well as a revolver—to mop up crime without the judicial restraints that tied her hands in her day job. Fighting gangsters and thugs until 1945, the Woman in Red fared slightly better than Fantomah: While she was never cover-featured on *Thrilling,* her headshot was squeezed onto the covers of *America's Best Comics* #1 and #2 (1942). Largely unknown other than for her historical significance, the Woman in Red managed to resurface in 2001 in an homage by Alan Moore in the pages of ABC's *Tom Strong* (and in a related 2003 miniseries, *Terra Obscura*), and appears among AC Comics' vast stable of reclaimed characters from comics history.

On the heels of the Woman in Red came Lady Luck, first seen in the June 2, 1940, newspaper comic-book supplement, *The Spirit.* Lady Luck was the feminine answer to the Green Hornet—she even had her own "Kato," a chauffeur named Peecolo. She was actually a bored socialite, Brenda Banks, who at night concealed her identity with a green veil and caught criminals for kicks. Like the Hornet, Lady Luck was wanted by the law, complicating Banks' relationship with the police chief.

In November 1940 readers were introduced to the first cross-dressing superhero: Red Tornado. Strictly played for laughs, Red Tornado was actually Ma Hunkle, a stout matron who dressed up in red long johns and a cooking pot for a helmet in the *Scribbly* series appearing in DC Comics' *All American Comics,* starting with issue #20.

The first supervillainess also premiered in 1940. In the pages of *Batman* #1, Batman and Robin encountered a natty cat burglar slinking about in a form-fitting green dress. Batman was smitten by this kitten calling herself "The Cat," but before long she would be renamed Catwoman, and would begin a lengthy career as a sometime-thief, sometime-heroine.

As evidenced by the low profile afforded Fantomah and the Woman in Red, comic-book publishers weren't convinced that a superheroine could sell a comic. Newspaper syndicates were more courageous, and in April 1941 a vivacious costumed heroine dressed in a skintight leopard suit began fighting crime in a Sunday newspaper comic strip. This was Miss Fury, a character whose series "combined intelligently written mysteries with cinematic action sequences shown from multiple viewpoints," according to superheroine historian Trina Robbins in her book *The Great Women Superheroes* (1996). Miss Fury feared no man, slapping and scolding bad guys, even whipping them with her tail. Her adventures were written and drawn by a real-life woman of wonder: Tarpe Mills, one of the first successful female creators to render superheroines for the printed page. Mills was, like her character, glamorous. *Miss Fury* was a popular strip, enjoyed by both sexes, and Mills basked in the glow of celebrity its acclaim brought her.

Comic-*book* publishers impressed with *Miss Fury's* success tested the waters with more superheroines, but cautiously stuck only one toe in. The Black Cat, dressed in a black swimsuit and a pointy-topped eye mask, started her career in Harvey Comics' *Pocket Comics* #1. She was secretly movie star/stuntwoman Linda Turner, who used the tricks of her trade and gimmicks from movie sets as "Hollywood's Glamorous Crime Fighter," solving mysteries in Tinseltown. The Phantom Lady's adventures transpired on the opposite coast, in Washington, D.C. Premiering in Quality Comics' *Police Comics* #1, Phantom Lady, decked out in a bathing suit and cape, thwarted political assassinations and other crimes with her blackout-ray projector, which she wore as a bracelet. Probably the first superheroine to bring together the holy trinity of costume, secret identity, and superpowers to the comic-book page was Bulletgirl, the elixir-powered, airborne companion of Fawcett Comic's Bulletman; Bulletgirl's first appearance (in early 1941) predates those of Wonder Woman, Mary Marvel, and even the Black Cat, though her sidekick status seems to prevent this from being often recognized.

SUPREMA STARTS A TREND

Dr. William Moulton Marston, eminent psychologist and inventor of the lie detector, created for DC Comics the most famous of all superheroines: "Suprema, the Wonder Woman." Marston's concept underwent obvious name-doctoring, and Wonder Woman, the beautiful red-white-and-blue-clad Amazon who fearlessly deflected bullets with her bracelets, first saw print in *All Star Comics* #8 (December 1941–January 1942)—just as the bombing of Pearl Harbor dragged the United States into World War II. DC had more faith in this superheroine than its competitors did in theirs. Wonder Woman busted onto the cover of *Sensation Comics* #1 (January 1942), and by that summer she was also awarded her own title. Wonder Woman embodied feminine and masculine traits: She was a compassionate feminist who would fight when necessary. A favorite of girls, *Wonder Woman* also sold to boys during the war, as the heroine epitomized patriotism—*and* had a great pair of legs (comics have never been shy about the sexual exploitation of the feminine form).

World War II empowered American women. While men were overseas, their wives, sisters, and mothers took over back home. They worked in the factories and played professional baseball, all while raising the children. A nation of wonder women.

This gender strengthening augmented the status of comics superheroines, and the stands were soon filled with them. In addition to Bulletgirl, Fawcett Comics had Mary Marvel, the supergirl sibling of Captain Marvel, who, like her brother, said "Shazam!" to gain her mighty powers. DC Comics introduced the streetwise Black Canary, the battling blonde in fishnets who became a valuable member of the Justice Society of America; Hawkgirl, the feathered fury who flew into action with her companion, Hawkman; the adventurous freedom fighter named Liberty Belle; and the assiduous Merry, Girl of a Thousand Gimmicks. Even Superman's girlfriend, the intrepid reporter Lois Lane, was a superheroine in her own right: She fearlessly scaled skyscraper ledges and infiltrated mobs, all for a newspaper story.

Marvel (then Timely) Comics published Miss America, a character historian Mike Benton called "a fair sex Captain America," who punched bad guys and bad girls alike ("Sorry, sister! Hate to do this, but you invited it!" she once said while kayoing a woman) and eventually made her way into the All Winners Squad with Captain America, Sub-Mariner, and the Human Torch. Another Marvel superheroine who turned heads was the Blonde Phantom, a yellow-haired detective in a shimmering crimson gown and black mask.

Superheroines appeared from other publishers as well. Kitten was the flirtatious sidekick to Cat-Man, Quality's diminutive Doll Girl fought crime with Doll Man, and Fox's web-swinging Spider Queen employed a "spider-web fluid" two decades before Spider-Man. Commandette was an actress/stunt-woman heroine (and a ripoff of the Black Cat), making only one appearance in 1945, while Pat Parker, War Nurse, teamed with the Girl Commandos. Some superheroines were ace pilots, cut from the same cloth as real-life aviatrix Amelia Earhart: The Black Angel feigned weakness in her real identity of

Sylvia Lawton but protected her native England from the "Nazi cobra of the skies, Baroness Blood," and Black Venus was a physical therapist by day, costumed air fighter by night.

Some ladies skirted the supernatural realm, like the original Black Widow (whose real name was Claire Voyant), Lady Satan, and Ghost Woman. There were masked mysterywomen and flag-waving Nazi-busters galore, too many to chronicle in full detail, but Pat Patriot, Yankee Girl, the Silver Scorpion, USA ("The Spirit of Old Glory"), Flame Girl, Miss Masque, Golden Girl, Invisible Scarlet O'Neil, Rocketgirl, Owl Girl, Atoma, Moon Girl, Lady Fairplay, and Miss Victory were among their number. Wonder Woman, Mary Marvel, and a few others aside, these superheroines were featured in anthology titles, were partners to a male superhero, or were tucked away in backup series. Publishers still lacked faith in superheroines as cover-featured stars.

HEADLIGHTS AND HEARTTHROBS

Superheroines, like their male counterparts, fell out of fashion after World War II. Comic-book sales dropped, publishers folded, and genres like crime, funny animals, and Westerns supplanted superhero material. In the real world, men returned home from the war and resumed their jobs, displacing the women who had so ably filled their shoes. Some women willingly reverted to domestic roles, some did so unwillingly.

As circulations spiraled downward in the mid- to late 1940s, the comic-book industry adopted extreme measures to make superheroines appealing to its male readership. Superheroines were often depicted in titillating pin-up poses, sometimes in bondage, with an abundance of cleavage exposed—Matt Baker's "Good Girl art" *Phantom Lady* covers of the 1940s are highly prized collectors' items in the 2000s—in an exploitive trend called "headlights." In 1948 Marvel ambitiously tried a line of superheroine comics targeted specifi-

cally at young girls—*The Blonde Phantom* being joined by *Venus, Namora,* and *Sun Girl*—but these books were canceled after short runs. By the mid-1950s only *Wonder Woman* survived, and only barely at that. Girls were now reading romance comics, a genre started in 1947 by legendary creators Joe Simon and Jack Kirby with *Young Romance* #1, featuring tales (written and drawn by males) centered on immature, sighing women fawning over Mr. Right (and sometimes Mr. Wrong). Superheroines had hung up their capes and donned aprons.

THE NEW SUPERHEROINES OF THE 1960S

DC Comics introduced Batwoman in *Detective Comics* #233 (1956). She appeared not as an attempt to attract a female readership, but to counter allegations by psychiatrist Dr. Fredric Wertham that Batman and Robin were homosexuals. Batwoman was actually Kathy Kane, an heiress who dated millionaire Bruce Wayne (Batman's alter ego). Garbed in a garish red-and-yellow batsuit, Batwoman fought boredom by fighting crime, but never developed a personality beyond giddiness. By 1964 she and her sidekick Bat-Girl (a love interest for Robin) were retired.

In *Action Comics* #252 (1959) DC introduced Supergirl, the teenage cousin to Superman. Supergirl, who also survived the destruction of the Man of Steel's homeworld Krypton, packed power like her relative, but was innocent and genial. When Superman introduced her to the world in 1962, he commented, "Physically, she's the mightiest female of all time! But at heart, she's as gentle and sweet and as quick to tears—as any ordinary girl!" Supergirl's adventures accompanied Superman's in *Action* throughout the 1960s. Readers both female and male watched her mature as a heroine and a woman. For the first time in a generation, young girls had a new superheroine to emulate. Yet Supergirl's appeal wore thin over time. Attempts to expand her personality beyond her original naiveté failed, and she died—valiantly, at least, while saving the world—in *Crisis on Infinite Earths* #7 (1985).

History repeated itself in the 1960s. Superheroes were hot properties and by mid-decade commandeered popular culture. Marvel Comics was fundamental in reinventing the concept of superheroes—"heroes with problems"—but its initial wave of superheroines still preserved the concept of women in roles shaped by patriarchal standards. The Invisible Girl premiered in *Fantastic Four* #1 (1961), and was shy and often endangered. The telekinetic Marvel Girl (a.k.a. Jean Grey), first seen in *X-Men* #1 (1963), was mostly a love interest for X-Man Cyclops, and the self-absorbed Wasp, the only woman in Marvel's Avengers, was an affluent fashion plate who loved to shop.

Other superheroines emerged during the 1960s: A sampling includes Wonder Woman's apprentice Wonder Girl, who go-go danced with her fellow Teen Titans; Fly Girl, the clinging partner of Archie Comics' Fly Man; Elasti-Girl of the Doom Patrol, who could expand her body to humongous proportions but could not grow beyond her restrictive domestic role; Mera, the wife of Aquaman and mother of Aquababy; Marvel's magical Scarlet Witch, who was persuaded to join the Brotherhood of Evil Mutants before exerting her own free will to become a heroine; Platinum (a.k.a. Tina) of the Metal Men, a lady robot whose faulty "responso-meter" caused her to go ga-ga over the human scientist who created her; and the all-new Batgirl, a high-kicking 1967 addition to both the *Batman* comics and TV show, who allowed a run in her tights to distract her from helping Batman and Robin. These characters may have put females back in action roles, but their dependent and/or indecisive personalities rooted them in stereotyped behavior.

SUPERHEROINES GET SAUCY

It took a Brit to help wedge American superheroines from this trap of tradition. In the early 1960s actress Diana Rigg played Mrs. Emma Peel on the popular English television series *The Avengers* (not to be confused with the Marvel superteam title). Mrs. Peel was an intellectual well trained in physical combat. Leggy Rigg often wore skin-tight catsuits in the role, and her balance of beauty and brawn made Peel a bold new type of superheroine. Peel caught the American eye in 1966 once *The Avengers* was imported to the United States, where the character made her imprint upon superhero creators. DC's Catwoman, although a villain, went the Peel catsuit route, especially through fetching Julie Newmar's coquettish portrayal of the character on TV's live-action *Batman* series (1966–1968). The sultry Russian spy Natasha Romanoff, premiering in the *Iron Man* feature in *Tales of Suspense* #52 (1964), was one of Marvel's first female characters to exhibit a forceful personality—but she was playing on the wrong team! Soon, however, she defected to the United States, donned a form-fitting costume, and disabled villains with her "Widow's Bite" blasts as the superheroine Black Widow.

In 1968 DC Comics borrowed heavily from TV's Emma Peel and reinvented its Amazon Princess. Wonder Woman was stripped of her superpowers and had to rely upon her newly acquired martial-arts training to survive. Wearing white jumpsuits, Diana Prince (alter ego of Wonder Woman) embarked upon globe-spanning exploits involving international thieves and assassins. This transformation was criticized by women's rights activist Gloria Steinem, who complained that DC had de-powered its principal superwoman. Other feminists joined Steinem's chorus. Dennis O'Neil, writer of *Wonder Woman* during this period, confessed in 2003, "Years later, I absolutely see what they were talking about."

In the real world, the sexual revolution of the 1960s enabled women to exert themselves physically, and the burgeoning women's rights movement afforded them political and cultural might. Women's liberation swept America: Bra burnings, sit-ins, walkouts, and demonstrations transpired to free females from societal shackles.

THE SWINGING SEVENTIES

In the 1970s women became bolder, reflected on TV with female-centric sitcoms like the workplace heroine Mary Richards on *The Mary Tyler Moore Show* and the boisterous, opinionated title character in the *All in the Family* spinoff *Maude.* Comics followed suit: Marvel gave the Invisible Girl more confidence and introduced a sisterhood of new superheroines. The iron maiden Valkyrie debuted as a sword-wielding feminist who became a member of the Defenders; two women creators—writer Linda Fite and artist Marie Severin—produced a short-lived series called *The Cat,* a crime-fighting alternative to DC's villainous Catwoman; and Black Widow took over half of *Amazing Adventures* (an anthology title shared with stories about the sexually egalitarian Inhumans), then co-starred in the pages of *Daredevil.*

When Marvel launched the all-new X-Men in 1975, among its cast of mutants was Storm, an ethereally beautiful African woman with long white hair. Storm was a survivor, an orphan who once supported herself with thievery. This weather manipulator became one of the X-Men's most popular members, and remains a favorite in the 2000s, particularly through actress Halle Berry's portrayal of the character in the live-action films *X-Men* (2000) and *X2: X-Men United* (2003).

In the 1970s Marvel cranked out clones of its best-selling characters—Spider-Woman and She-Hulk, as well as Red Sonja, the female counterpart to Conan the Barbarian—and fashioned new superheroines like the disco-spawned Dazzler. DC gave Supergirl her own series, published *Rima the Jungle Girl,* unveiled the mysterious Black Orchid in *Adventure Comics,* introduced "Earth-Two" (alternate reality) versions of Supergirl and Batgirl in the busty Power Girl and the brooding Huntress, and produced a comic book based on the popular Saturday-morning show *Isis* (1975–1977). ElectraWoman and DynaGirl were TV superheroines during the 1976 season of *The Kroft Supershow,* and *Charlie's Angels* (1976–1981), *The Bionic Woman* (1976–1978), and *Police Woman* (1974–1978) were successful primetime TV series starring female heroes. And then there was *Wonder Woman.*

Lynda Carter, a stunningly gorgeous, five-feet-ten-inch tall former Miss World USA, rocketed to instant stardom on TV's live-action series *Wonder Woman* (1976–1979). This hour-long action-drama was originally set in the 1940s, with Wonder Woman battling Nazis and extraterrestrials, then shifted to the present day with the 1977 season, at which point Wonder Woman's alter ego Diana Prince sported the grooviest pantsuits and fashions of the era. For the second half of the 1970s, Wonder Woman was TV's number-one superhero, and a spate of Wonder Woman merchandising flooded the marketplace. Girls adored the Amazon Princess, and college boys and men tuned in to admire Carter's attributes.

The 1970s was the decade of the liberated superheroine. Despite this cultural step forward, these superheroines were characterized with frailties, be they emotional attachment to boyfriends, husbands, children, jobs, or even their hair. That would soon change.

SUPERHEROINES GET TOUGH

The first new superheroine of the 1980s had no such "weaknesses." She was Elektra, an assassin for hire wielding three-pronged daggers (called sai), first seen in Marvel's *Daredevil* #168 (1981). Elektra Natchios, like many fictional characters, survived the death (in her case, the political assassination) of a parent, her father, a Greek ambassador, and redirected her life as a result. Instead of fighting crime, as Batman did once his parents were killed, Elektra chose execution, a reaction catering perfectly to what historian Robbins called America's "get tough on crime mood" of the 1980s. As a paid killer, she sought out and eliminated the worst of the worst, and while her marks were generally criminals, her methods were decidedly anti-heroic. She captivated the audience of the early 1980s, and has commanded a steady presence in comics ever since.

Actress Jennifer Garner was cast as Elektra in the live-action movie *Daredevil* (2003), and is pegged to star in a proposed Elektra solo film. Garner's physical prowess, honed pre-Elektra by her acrobatics on her television series *Alias* (2001–present), impressed her *Daredevil* costars: "She did this stunt where she kicks off the wall and does this split, and I was ready to marry that woman right there," gushed actor Michael Clarke Duncan to *TV Guide* in 2003.

Comics publishers didn't realize at the time that the emergence of Elektra signaled the end of cheerier, more colorful superheroines. DC's *Amethyst, Princess of Gemworld,* part-superhero, part-Alice in Wonderland, enjoyed an initial blip of success, then cascaded to cancellation. (Syndicated TV's animated *She-Ra: Princess of Power* [1985–1988] experienced a similar fate.) Marvel's pre-teen supergroup Power Pack also contained two girls in its cast. Like *Amethyst, Power Pack* was critically embraced, but did not connect commercially with an audience large enough to sustain its publication (though it hung on for seven years, an impressive feat in an increasingly depressed market).

Conversely, superheroines with a darker edge netted higher returns. Marvel's Dagger, of the team Cloak and Dagger, attacked evildoers with piercing shards of light. Spider-Man soon cavorted with the Black Cat (not the original Harvey character), a naughty but vivacious thief, and the Invisible Girl was liberated to the Invisible Woman, and temporarily became a supervillainess named Malice. While Marvel's 1980s superheroines got tougher, so did women in the real world: Self-defense classes were the rage.

During the 1980s some fans accused DC Comics of misogyny due to its treatment of its superheroines. Supergirl was killed (beaten to death, incidentally), Wonder Woman was erased from existence in 1986 (but was resurrected the next year), Black Canary was criminally assaulted in *Green Arrow: The Longbow Hunters* (1987), and Batgirl was debased and crippled by the psychotic villain the Joker in *Batman: The Killing Joke* (1988). Other DC superheroines became decoration, like Fire and Ice in the pages of *Justice League America,* important more for sex appeal than story substance.

GOOD GIRLS GO BAD

In 1992 Michelle Pfeiffer's mesmerizing turn as Catwoman in director Tim Burton's *Batman Returns* popularized the concept of a "bad girl" heroine. Pfeiffer's Catwoman was fundamentally a villainess, but while her motivations were anti-heroic, her plight was sympathetic. Deep down she had a soft spot, questioning her actions against Batman as she fell for his true identity of Bruce Wayne. Her alter ego Selina Kyle was battered and abused, but as the sultry Catwoman she took charge, letting no man interfere with her goal—revenge against her male tormentor. Pfeiffer's pulchritude made Catwoman the sexiest screen character of the year. As Catwoman she carried the torch lit by Elektra and helped transform the superheroine: Superwomen could now have looks *that* kill, and the power *to* kill.

Post–*Batman Returns,* the comic-book business—which once avoided superheroines in starring roles—has produced dozens of titles with sexually exaggerated women in the lead (a survey of DC and Marvel comic-book titles published in September 2003 included a remarkable sixteen titles [not including superteams] starring women). Many have shamelessly parroted Elektra, even equipping their characters with knives, swords, and mystical gauntlets: Avengelyne, Glory, Cyblade, Witchblade, and Shi. Other such characters have fortified themselves with an arsenal: Ghost, Tank Girl, Shotgun Mary, Barb Wire, and Silver Sable. Still others use supernatural powers to stop or eradicate their foes: Lady Death, Darkchylde, and Vampirella (a mainstream-comics revival of the extraterrestrial bloodsucker from Warren Comics' legendary 1970s line of magazine-sized, ostensibly mature nonsuperhero titles). Not all contemporary superheroines kill, but some of them come dangerously close. Even Wonder Woman has developed a warrior's edge.

Beautiful "bad girl" protagonists with martial-arts mastery have transcended comics into mass-media omnipresence. Video games are filled with them, most notably Lara Croft of *Tomb Raider* fame. Sexy "action heroines" have replaced the Arnold Schwarzenegger/Bruce Willis action hero archetype in 2000s cinema. These action heroines are not superheroines in the strictest sense of the word, but—thanks to wires and special-effects wizardry—they display spellbinding feats of superheroics: Witness Cameron Diaz, Drew Barrymore, and Lucy Liu in the *Charlie's Angels* movies; Angelina Jolie in the *Tomb Raider* film franchise; Carrie-Anne Moss as Trinity in *The Matrix* series; Uma Thurman as a vengeful bride in *Kill Bill: Vol. 1* (2003) and *Vol. 2* (2004); and Halle Berry, stepping beyond her Storm role to upstage James Bond as Jinx in *Die Another Day* (2002) and succeeding Michelle Pfeiffer as *Catwoman* (2004). Numerous live-action television series have featured "chicks who kick," like *Buffy the Vampire Slayer, Xena Warrior Princess, Dark Angel,* and the comics-based *Birds of Prey* and *Witchblade.* Aggressive superheroines have also invaded the world of children's pop culture, particularly in the case of the Cartoon Network's *Powerpuff Girls,* who usually level the city of Townsville in their violent efforts to "save" it.

Since the latter decades of the twentieth century, men (enlightened men, that is) have grown less threatened by the concept of powerful women. In the case of superheroines, titillation has been employed as an incentive to attract the support of males. Some comic-book covers featuring superheroines border on softcore pornography, with impossibly proportioned women in pin-up poses. "It has been said that the comics industry has given nothing to girls but misogynist sewage from the underdeveloped noggins of pig-eyed little men whose idea of a strong woman is 'She Who Can

Bear the Weight of Her Enormous Boobs'," wrote *Amazons!* editor Jessica Amanda Salmonson in her introduction to Robbins' *The Great Women Superheroes.* Indeed, a subculture has developed that regards the superheroine as a sex object, attested to by a host of websites featuring photos of partially clad actresses in costumes.

Those extremes aside, superheroines have, like real-life women, clawed their way from subservience to prominence. Should future cultural climes alter the societal position of women, the characterization of superheroines will naturally follow. —*ME*

Superman

Superman is widely regarded as the first superhero. That's not entirely true: The Shadow, the Phantom, Doc Savage, the Spider, and a handful of others preceded him in the mid-1930s. Those costumed or superpowered crime fighters may have beaten Superman out of the gate, but not to the punch. This "Man of Steel" and his astounding abilities caught an unsuspecting readership by surprise in 1938. Generations later, Superman has become indelibly etched into the annals of American folklore. Today, most historians call Superman the first superhero because he defined a distinct hero type, clearly breaking away from the masked adventurers who preceded him.

Superman's origin is nearly as recognizable as the hero himself. Moments before the planet Krypton explodes, its chief scientist rockets his infant son to safety. The baby's spaceship lands on Earth and is discovered by the Kents, a childless couple that adopt the tiny extraterrestrial. The boy exhibits astonishing powers, and the Kents teach the lad, whom they name Clark, to use his abilities to "assist humanity." Upon adulthood (and the death of his Earth parents), Clark Kent dons a caped uniform as Superman, "champion of the oppressed."

This tale was first revealed in *Action Comics* #1 (June 1938), published while the United States was in the stranglehold of the Great Depression. In his earliest outings, Superman was enormously brazen as he caved in walls, slapped dictators, and spanked sharp-tongued heiresses. By stark contrast, his alter ego, the bespectacled Kent, was outrageously diffident, and on this dichotomy hinged the hero's audience appeal: Kent was the downtrodden "everyman," while Superman personified physical power. Superman was an unabashed intimidator you could cheer for, a figure of hope when many Americans felt hopeless. Readers found in Superman a hero who represented "truth, justice, and the American way," and his colorful escapades, told in the vibrant new medium of comic books, captured their imaginations. Superman not only initiated his own career with *Action* #1, but single-handedly launched a new industry—comic-book publishers sprouted instantly, and scores of new superheroes followed, truly exemplifying the "American way" (capitalism).

And to think, Superman started on the wrong side of the law. Throughout the early 1930s, his creators, author Jerry Siegel and illustrator Joe Shuster, high-school chums from Cleveland, Ohio, were habitually rejected by professional publishers. So they started their own mimeographed fanzine, *Science Fiction,* in which they printed Siegel's prose story "The Reign of the Superman," about a misshapen human who acquires superpowers and turns evil. Siegel and Shuster later modified the concept into a proposal for a newspaper strip featuring a caped Superman with an "S" on his massive chest who uses his powers—augmented strength and stamina, bulletproof skin, and the ability to leap an eighth of a mile—for good. They ambitiously marketed their creation as "The Smash Hit Strip of 1936," but the syndicates balked. Maintaining unwavering faith in their concept, the persevering pair submitted their Superman idea to comic-book publisher Detective Comics, Inc. (DC), who took a chance on the property for their start-up title, *Action.* Siegel and Shuster sold DC the rights to Superman for a reported pittance of $130, but they didn't mind—it was a gig, and, most importantly, their hero was in print.

Superman #1 © 1939 DC Comics.
COVER ART BY JOE SHUSTER.

Action Comics starring Superman sold phenomenally well, and DC Comics wasted no time in exploiting the character. In January 1939, Siegel and Shuster realized their earlier dream by producing a Superman syndicated newspaper strip. Distributed by the McClure Syndicate, the feature ran successfully through the 1940s. Siegel and Shuster (before turning the reigns over to writer/artist Wayne Boring in 1940) expanded the hero's origin by giving the baby a Kryptonian name (Kal-L, later Kal-El), and by naming his biological parents (Jor-L and Lora, later Jor-El and Lara). The Man of Steel was awarded his own title with *Superman* #1 (Summer 1939), and soon began appearing in *World's Best* (later *World's Finest*) *Comics.* In a few short years, Superman rocketed into ubiquity. DC introduced a "Supermen of America" fan club and licensed the character's likeness to manufacturers of toys, puzzles, novels, coloring books, bubble gum—almost every product imaginable. The Man of Steel burst into radio in 1940 in the long-running *The Adventures of Superman* program, with actor Bud Collyer lending voice to the hero, and into movie theaters in 1941, in a celebrated series of seventeen animated shorts from the Fleischer Studios. Superman became big business. Some joked that the "S" emblazoned across his chest should be changed to a "$."

Superman's superpowers grew with his acclaim: Soon he was flying instead of leaping, he became invulnerable, and supersenses like X-ray vision and superhearing were added. Of course, every hero needs a weakness, and Superman's was kryptonite, radioactive meteorites from his homeworld, a story element that first appeared on his radio program. He quickly developed a rogues' gallery including Lex Luthor, the Ultra-Humanite, and the Prankster. Upon the advent of World War II, Superman was anointed as DC Comics' standard-bearer of patriotism, and on several occasions even took on the Axis forces.

Superman's Kent identity was Siegel and Shuster's in-joke. As a reporter for the *Daily Planet* (originally the *Daily Star*) in the city of Metropolis, Kent frequently winked at his readers to acknowledge that *they* were in on the gag (the first comic-book hero to do this, by the way): that the people around him couldn't see through his flimsy disguise of eyeglasses and a business suit. His spunky colleague Lois Lane wasn't fooled for long, however. Suspicious over Kent's disappearances during Superman's feats, she spent decades unsuccessfully trying to prove that Kent and Superman were one and the same. Kent's association with the newspaper placed him on the ground floor of breaking events in which Superman's presence might be required—and often that meant rescuing the daring Lane from danger. Kent's boss in the earliest tales was George Taylor, who soon morphed into crusty managing editor Perry White, a cigar-chomping, old-

school newshound often agitated by the antics of his staff. Jimmy Olsen, a copy boy (and later "cub reporter") whose enthusiasm frequently got him into trouble, became famous as Superman's pal.

Most superheroes withered from view after World War II, but the Man of Steel kept going strong. In 1945, DC amended its continuity with the creation of Superboy, "The Adventures of Superman When He Was a Boy." His wholesome adventures took place in Smallville, a geographical slice of America's heartland, where young Kent lived with his parents, Jonathan and Martha. Neighbor Lana Lang was introduced as the teenage equivalent of Lois Lane. Meanwhile actor Kirk Alyn brought Superboy's adult counterpart to life in a pair of live-action movie serials, *Superman* (1948) and *Atom Man vs. Superman* (1950), the latter of which adapted Luthor to the big screen. During this period of super-profit, Siegel and Shuster lost a legal battle to regain the rights to their creation.

In the 1950s, as Americans enjoyed postwar prosperity and pride, Superman was redefined from the burly bully of comics' Golden Age (1938–1954) into a helpful scoutmaster, instilling virtues into the childish Lane and Olsen—and the readers. Actor George Reeves, who portrayed the Man of Steel in the live-action theatrical release *Superman and the Mole Men* (1951), starred in the movie's syndicated television spinoff *The Adventures of Superman* (1953–1957). Reeves became beloved in the role: He pitched Kellogg's Corn Flakes as Superman and appeared on *I Love Lucy* as the Man of Steel (Who could forget the episode in which he flies in to save Lucy from her high-rise window-ledge shenanigans?). A *Superman's Pal Jimmy Olsen* comics title was launched in 1954, followed by *Superman's Girl Friend Lois Lane* in 1958, and Superman and Batman formed a regular partnership in *World's Finest*. Superman was developing a family. Enter the family superdog, Krypto, another survivor of the hero's homeworld. The Man of Steel was DC Comics' best-selling and flagship character, so important to the publisher that it changed its company logo to

"Superman–DC Comics." As the decade closed, the atomic age zapped science fiction into a place of prominence in Superman's comics: Luthor flourished high-tech weapons against the Man of Steel; new villains like the android Brainiac were established; the time-traveling Legion of Super-Heroes joined the supporting cast; and Superman's cousin, Supergirl, showed up in a Kryptonian spaceship.

The 1960s were a turbulent decade of escalating global tension, civil unrest, a bloody and unpopular war, and social disorder—and for much of the decade, Superman turned a blind eye to it all (tough to do with his super-*vision*). Mort Weisinger, editor of the Superman comics, continued to expand the Man of Steel's family: Joining the already cumbersome cast were mermaid Lori Lemaris; loopy inventor Professor Potter; superpets Beppo the Supermonkey, Streaky the Supercat, and Comet the Superhorse; Superman's biological parents Jor-El and Lara (via frequent flashbacks and time-travel tales); Kryptonian survivors in the Phantom Zone and in the miniaturized Bottle City of Kandor; and a whole world of wacky Superman mutates called Bizarros. Traces of the real world occasionally crept into his comics—President John F. Kennedy's assassination was too big for even Weisinger's Super-sanitized Man of Steel to ignore—but mostly, the Superman titles offered an escape from, not an exploration of, matters political. And no one seemed to mind: Superman's fame reached global status, as translations of his comic books were being gobbled up in numerous countries. He was the king of all media long before Howard Stern, appearing on television (through reruns of Reeves' 1950s series and an animated cartoon in 1966), in toy stores, in popular song (Donovan's trippy 1966 release "Sunshine Superman"), and even on Broadway in a musical comedy, *It's a Bird, It's a Plane, It's Superman* (1966).

By the mid-1960s, Curt Swan's crisp penciling style helped him emerge from a pack of talented illustrators as "the" Superman artist, a title Swan held until the 1980s. Superman's comics may have *looked* good, but they didn't *read* well: The burgeoning ensemble of superpeople and superanimals was neutering the hero's individuality. Weisinger and his writers were running out of ideas, resorting to gimmicks rather than characterization for Superman's adventures. "Imaginary" stories—tales appearing outside of the regular continuity—became commonplace, allowing Superman to die, to marry, and to have offspring, but return to the status quo with the next adventure. His superpowers intensified to an inane level: Superman gained microscopic vision, heat vision (previously he had melted objects with the heat from his X-ray vision), and even super*ventriloquism*! As Superman's faculties increased, his enemies simply could not pose a credible threat, and his stories lost dramatic intensity. Only the energy-siphoning Parasite, the creation of writer Jim Shooter, gave Superman a run for his money, but he surfaced too late to stop the hero who was "more powerful than a locomotive" from derailing: By the end of the decade, Superman's adventures had grown stale and his titles' readership had dwindled. Similarly, the *Superman* newspaper strip was canceled in 1967.

Carmine Infantino, former artist of *The Flash* and *Batman,* had recently been appointed DC's editorial director and was revitalizing the company's line. The Man of Steel was slated for an overhaul, with editor Julius Schwartz, who had successfully resuscitated the Batman titles from near-cancellation in 1964, assigned to helm the revisions. In 1970, DC house ads trumpeted an impending change: "There's a New Kind of Superman Coming!" *Superman* #233 (January 1971) was where it began: Kent, now bolder and hipper, became a *television* news reporter, kryptonite was eliminated, and Superman's powers were weakened. Pioneering young writers like Denny O'Neil, Elliot S! Maggin, and Cary Bates invigorated the tales with realism and new villains. None of this mattered to the world at large, however, where Superman's status was now iconic: His "S" insignia was appropriated by the lead character (a Christ allegory) in the rock opera *Godspell* (1971); singer Jim Croce immortalized the Man of Steel as a tough guy in his 1973 hit, "You Don't Mess around with Jim" (with the recurring line, "You don't tug on Superman's cape"); and Superman was featured as one of television's animated *Super Friends* (1973).

Halfway through the 1970s, two major events occurred: DC joined forces with competitor Marvel Comics to co-publish a best-selling crossover, *Superman vs. the Amazing Spider-Man;* and film producers Alexander and Ilya Salkind signed a deal to produce a big-budget movie (and a sequel) starring the Man of Steel. The impending film and its promise of profit inspired Neal Adams, superstar illustrator and advocate for artists' rights, to lobby DC to provide financial restitution to Superman's architects Siegel and Shuster, both of whom teetered on the brink of destitution. DC and parent company Warner Bros. obliged, bowing to media pressure, and established pensions for both and inserted their names into all Superman comics as the creators of the character. In 1977, as part of a promotional campaign for the upcoming motion picture, the *Superman* newspaper strip was revived, beginning a sixteen-year run. The Salkinds' *Superman: The Movie* was the blockbuster film of 1978: It made actor Christopher Reeve a megastar and raised the special effects bar by several notches.

As with any successful film, sequels followed, and the first half of the 1980s for Superman was demarcated by Reeve's interpretation of the hero—the Man of Steel as a "friend," a sincere Boy Scout who never told a lie, earning his merit badge by saving the world. Editor Schwartz's Superman comics suffered during this period. The radical changes he implemented in the early and mid-1970s had been jettisoned, and the resulting stories were reminiscent of the material he'd been hired to eliminate. Superman needed a shot in the arm.

As DC Comics reinvented itself in the mid-1980s with its continuity-altering *Crisis on Infinite Earths* series (in which Supergirl died valiantly), Marvel Comics writer/artist John Byrne was hired to recreate the hero. Byrne's opening volley was *The Man of Steel*

(1986), a six-issue, biweekly miniseries that cleaned the slate for the character while preserving the best aspects from previous incarnations (mostly the movies). Superboy was no more, Krypton was antiseptic, and Luthor became the 1980s version of evil incarnate: a corporate CEO. Byrne's Reeve-like Superman would kick ass when necessary. There were also significant changes involving Kent's personal life, perhaps the biggest being that his parents, Jonathan and Martha, were now still alive, lending compassionate support to their adult super-son.

Since Superman's 1986 reintroduction, an army of writers, artists, and editors have expanded upon the revised mythology, reintroducing classic concepts and characters (with new twists) and introducing potentially lethal menaces to imperil the Man of Steel, usually in lengthy and sometimes inaccessible story arcs. Three highly publicized events affected the character in the 1990s: his January 1993 death (at the hands of a brutish behemoth appropriately called Doomsday) in *Superman* #75 and subsequent resurrection (surprise!); his controversial transformation into a pure energy being with a different costume than the bankable classic (another headline-grabbing but short-lived innovation); and Kent's 1996 marriage to Lois Lane in *Superman: The Wedding Album* #1.

Since *The Man of Steel,* Superman has maintained a consistent television presence: in two animated *Superman* cartoons (in 1988 and 1996) and on the Cartoon Network's *Justice League* (2001–present); in the live-action programs *Superboy* (1988–1992), *Lois & Clark: The New Adventures of Superman* (1993–1997), and the teen-oriented *Smallville* (2001–present); and as a regular topic of discussion among the characters of the 1990s sitcom *Seinfeld.* His movie prospects haven't fared as well since the failure of Reeve's *Superman IV: The Quest for Peace* (1987). The revival of the Superman movie franchise has passed through multiple hands, with a script by screenwriter Jeffrey Abrams still in development in 2004. His theatrical woes aside, Superman ranked in second place on VH1's

2003 list of the "200 Greatest Pop Culture Icons," with only Oprah Winfrey besting the Man of Steel.

In 1999, a legal ruling granted the heirs of Superman co-creator Jerry Siegel 50 percent of the Superman copyright. Since Joe Shuster died with no heirs, DC Comics retained his half of the copyright, and owns the Superman trademark in full. The long-range effects of this decision, if any, remain to be seen.

Thus far in the twenty-first century, Superman comic books have reflected contemporary cultural trends, with a Japanese manga–influenced art style being in vogue as of 2004. It is inevitable that future market and societal shifts will spark further alterations in the Superman canon. No matter what's in store, the Man of Steel will endure as a symbol of hope and inspiration. He *is* Superman, after all! —*ME*

Superman in the Media

Look, up on the screen! It's a bird, it's a plane, it's Superman! Since his creation in 1938, Superman has traveled into the heart of generation upon generation of readers, moviegoers, and television fans. In the last sixty-plus years, Superman has been the star of movie serials, live-action and animated TV shows, radio programs, and several movies. Rocketed to Earth from a dying planet, Kal-El may be the last son of Krypton, but Clark Kent and Superman have been portrayed by more than a dozen actors, and the Man of Steel has appeared in more media interpretations that *any* other superhero.

THE 1940S: CARTOONS AND SERIALS

Although Republic Studios had bid against them, Paramount gained the rights to bring National Comic's best-selling hero to life in an animated *Superman* cartoon series in 1941. Fleischer Studios, noted for their popular *Popeye* and *Betty Boop* cartoons, planned the series with an astonishing attention to detail, utilizing *Superman* co-creator Joe Shuster's powerful character designs along with incredible special effects and vibrant colors. A process known as "rotoscoping"—tracing the animation over live-action models—gave the art a startling realism.

The seventeen original *Superman* cartoons were shown regularly at movie theaters, from September 9, 1941 to July 30, 1943. Even today, the cartoons are considered classic animation; Superman and Lois Lane looked as if they had literally walked off of the comic-book page and into a three-dimensional world. The late Clayton "Bud" Collyer was the voice of Clark Kent, whose voice dropped a few octaves whenever he became Superman. Collyer was also portraying the Man of Steel in the popular Mutual Network *Superman* radio show (1940–1951). There, he originated the phrase "Up, Up, and Away" because listeners could not see their hero flying off. In the cartoons, Superman fought mechanical monsters, mummies, spies, robots, and "Japoteurs."

Although they publicly announced (twice) that they were bringing *Superman* to live-action, Republic Studios was outbid again, in 1947, by Columbia Pictures. Serials were 15- to 30-minute mini-movies with cliff-hanger endings; theaters ran a new chapter each week. Republic was the serial king, but Columbia was noted for its other comic adaptations, including National characters such as *Batman* (1943, 1949) and *Vigilante* (1943). Under the auspices of low-budget producer Sam Katzman, production began on the *Superman* serial in late 1947, with handsome leading man Kirk Alyn in the lead, young actress Noel Neill in the part of Lois Lane, and former *Our Gang* star Tommy Bond as Jimmy Olsen.

The debut *Superman* serial (1948) contained fifteen chapters, with the opening showing the first media-related origin sequence on Krypton. Although the young Clark Kent was raised in the serials by

Eben and Sarah Kent (rather than the more familiar "Jonathan and Martha"), the adult Clark Kent still worked as a reporter in Metropolis. As Superman, he kept the dreaded "Queen of the Underworld," Spider Lady (Carol Forman), from gaining control over the ultra-powerful Reducer Ray. Acting in the serials was strong, but the special-effects flying sequences were inadequate; to fly, Alyn would leap over the camera, and suddenly become an animated figure!

Superman became the most popular—and profitable—serial ever done. A second serial, *Atom Man vs. Superman* (1950), was soon underway, featuring the same heroic cast, but a new villain. The Atom Man was a hooded menace who terrified Metropolis and Superman with his synthetic kryptonite, a flying saucer, a torpedo, and the dreaded sonic vibrator. Superman eventually unmasked the Atom Man, only to find his arch nemesis, Lex Luthor (Lyle Talbot in a bald skull-cap). *Atom Man vs. Superman* was not as successful as its predecessor, despite live flying sequences, but it brought enough money in for talk of a third serial. But the days of the great movie serial were coming to an end with the dawning of a new era of entertainment: television.

THE 1950S AND 1960S: MOVIES, TELEVISION, AND STAGE

In 1951, production began on *Superman and the Mole Men,* the Kryptonian hero's first full-length motion picture. After Kirk Alyn turned down the role, producers Tommy Carr (who had directed parts of the first *Superman* serial) and Robert Maxwell chose leading man George Reeves (best known at that time for his role of Stuart Tarleton in *Gone with the Wind*) to play Superman. Lois Lane was also recast, with budding screen actress Phyllis Coates taking over the role. Filming began on July 30, 1951, on an RKO lot, the new crew little knowing that their work would have implications for many generations to come, and eventual shattering consequences for their new Superman.

The story in *Superman and the Mole Men* concerned a small mining town whose drilling broke through the earth's crust into an underground civilization, bringing forth a race of glowing midgets. Superman defends the "Mole Men" against the fearful mob, who want to kill the strange beings. Despite the fact that America was in the grip of McCarthyism, with the "Red Scare" finding a Communist under every bush, *Superman and the Mole Men* held an unlikely but powerful message for tolerance of the unknown, and a peaceful co-existence with the other inhabitants of the planet.

With theaters packed, producer Maxwell had already begun filming episodes for a new television series called *The Adventures of Superman.* Reeves and Coates returned, supported by young actor Jack Larson as Jimmy Olsen, John Hamilton as *Daily Planet* editor Perry White, and the newly created Police Inspector Henderson role played by Robert Shayne. The actors worked hard and fast—six days a week, averaging four episodes in ten days—shooting most scenes in one take! Although twenty-six episodes of *The Adventures of Superman* were filmed in 1951, release was delayed by Superman's owner, National; however, when Kellogg's decided to sponsor the show in 1953, the debut was set. *The Adventures of Superman* premiered on ABC on February 9, 1953, and soared in the ratings.

New *Superman* episodes were commissioned, but changes were mandated. First, Bob Maxwell, whose episodes were deemed too violent, was replaced as producer by the gentler Whitney Ellsworth. Second, the budget had to be strictly adhered to. And third, Coates had found other work and could not reprise her role as Lois Lane. Recasting the role seemed simple, and the serial Lois, Noel Neill, was brought back. As the show moved on, other problems popped up; most important was Reeves' growing dissatisfaction with the slowness of production (initially, only thirteen episodes were scheduled to shoot over four years' time) and the typecasting he was feeling from the popular role. Still, with a pay raise, he chose not to hang up his cape.

In 1954, the series converted to color, requiring new sets, makeup, and costumes; in addition, action sequences were trimmed to a minimum, mainly due to budgetary constraints. The show wobbled in format, but stayed popular until its end—after 104 episodes and a guest spot for Superman on *I Love Lucy*—in 1957. Reeves himself directed the 102nd through 104th episodes, his first directing assignments. Syndication began immediately.

On June 16, 1959, Reeves was found dead in his bedroom from a gunshot wound to the head. Although suicide was ruled the cause, and newspaper headlines shouted "Superman Kills Self," the death has been seen as suspicious and remains one of Hollywood's dark mysteries to this day. National had been talking to a typecast and despondent Reeves about returning for more *Superman* episodes, but now they began to develop other spin-off properties. A *Jimmy Olsen* show was talked about, with footage mixed in from the previous *Superman* shows, but Jack Larson refused to consider the project. Whitney Ellsworth filmed a 1960 live-action pilot called *Superpup*, starring a superpowered dog who masqueraded as Bark Bent and a cast made up of midgets, who roamed around a miniaturized set. Ellsworth also produced a pilot episode of *The Adventures of Superboy*, but neither project was ever aired.

Superman next appeared in a Broadway musical-comedy titled *It's a Bird, It's a Plane, It's Superman.* With music by Charles Strauss and lyrics by Lee Adams, the script was written by David Newman and Robert Benton, who would later do the same for the first modern *Superman* film. The original cast included Bob Holiday as Superman, and pre-*Alice* Linda Lavin as Lois Lane. The 1966 musical was later filmed by ABC-TV, and shown in 1975, with David Wilson as Superman. Two decades later, in 1997, Michael Daugherty would release a full-scale orchestral work known as *Metropolis Symphony*.

CBS aired Filmation's animated *The New Adventures of Superman* from September 10, 1966 to September 2, 1967, when it became the *Super-man-Aquaman Hour.* The series consisted of two short *Superman* stories and one *Superboy* story per half-hour, and included comic-book villains such as Luthor and Brainiac. In September 1968, the series became the *Batman-Superman Hour,* and ran until September 6, 1969. Bud Collyer reprised his role from both the radio shows and the earlier cartoons as the voice of Superman, as did Joan Alexander as Lois Lane.

THE 1970S AND 1980S: CARTOONS AND MOVIES

Superman did not have any new television adventures on his own for quite some time, but after a 1972 guest-shot on ABC's *The Brady Kids* cartoon, he showed up as the main member of Hanna-Barbera and ABC's *Super Friends* series on September 8, 1973. Teamed with Batman, Robin, Wonder Woman, and Aquaman, Superman fought aliens and an occasional supervillain. Superman's voice was now provided by Danny Dark, since Collyer had died in 1969.

Super Friends evolved almost yearly, changing titles and formats as it went. It became *The All-New Super Friends Hour* (1977–1978), *The Challenge of the Super Friends* (1978–1979), *The World's Greatest Super Friends* (1979–1980), *The Super Friends Hour* (1980–1981), *The Super Friends* (1981–1984), *Super Friends—The Legendary Super Powers Show* (1984–1985), and, finally, *The Super Powers Team: Galactic Guardians* (1985–1986). Many Superman concepts made it onto the small screen, including Mr. Mxyzptlk, Lex Luthor, the Phantom Zone, Brainiac, and kryptonite.

"You'll Believe a Man Can Fly" was the tag-line on teaser ads for the Warner Bros. live-action *Superman: The Movie,* and since the audiences were still reeling from the impact of the blockbuster hit *Star Wars,* the movie had to impress. Filmmakers had worked on the film for two years before its premiere on December 15, 1978. Although several major stars such as Robert Redford, Bruce Jenner, and Arnold Schwarzenegger were considered for the lead role, relatively unknown stage actor Christopher Reeve was cast instead. Other parts were soon cast: Marlon Brando was Jor-El, Gene Hackman was Lex Luthor, Jackie Cooper was Perry White, Margot Kidder was Lois Lane, Marc McClure was Jimmy Olsen, Ned Beatty was Luthor's bumbling henchman Otis, and Valerie Perrine was Luthor's consort, Miss Eve Teschmacher. Even Kirk Alyn and Noel Neill made a cameo appearance as the parents of the young Lois Lane.

Superman: The Movie was a success on almost all levels. The story, by Mario Puzo, David Newman, and Robert Benton, stuck closely to the original Superman legend. The special effects were Academy Award–winning, and theater-goers *did* believe that a man could fly. John Williams provided the lush soundtrack and score, earning a 1979 Academy Award nomination for his work. Director Richard Donner, working with producers Ilya Salkind and Pierre Spengler, created what in many viewers' eyes was the definitive *Superman* film, largely because the cast played the film straight. No camp or winks to the audience; this Superman was real. *Superman: The Movie* was a top-grosser at the box office, and the sequel was already in production.

The filmmakers had filmed a large portion of footage for *Superman II* concurrently with *Superman,* but much of Donner's footage was reshot by new director Richard Lester. The plot contained a super-confrontation between Superman and three survivors from the Phantom Zone (Terrence Stamp, Sarah Douglas, and Jack O'Halloran). It also featured a dramatic resolution of sorts to the Clark Kent–Lois Lane–Superman love triangle that had been present for over forty years, when Lane discovers Kent's identity, and their night of passion has disastrous consequences. *Superman II* debuted in 1981 and was another success; critics would call the first and second *Superman* films the best examples of the superhero genre.

Lester, producers Alexander and Ilya Salkind, and scripters David and Leslie Newman developed a plot for *Superman III* (1983), which dealt with a mad computer genius (Robert Vaughn) and his super-computers, and co-starred comedian Richard Pryor. The regular supporting cast was gone, with Superman visiting Smallville where he was reunited with old girlfriend Lana Lang (Annette O'Toole). The film was played too much for laughs, and it bombed in theaters. Christopher Reeve made a public announcement that he would never play Superman again.

On November 23, 1984, Warner expanded its franchise with the first *Supergirl* movie. Ilya Salkind returned to produce, with Jeannot Szwarc directing. The part of Kara Zor-El/Supergirl went to young unknown, Helen Slater, while the supporting cast was peppered with more seasoned performers: Faye Dunaway and Brenda Vaccaro as the villainesses, and Peter O'Toole and Mia Farrow as Zor-El's parents. Marc McClure was brought in as Jimmy Olsen, providing a bridge between the two movie series. Despite Slater's appealing performance and some excellent flying sequences, *Supergirl* failed at the box office, and no sequels followed.

With *Superman's* fiftieth anniversary in 1988, Warner wanted a new *Superman* film. In 1986, Christopher Reeve agreed to return after being granted script approval and a much higher salary, and other main cast members also returned: Kidder, Hackman, Cooper, and McClure. Reeve worked with Larry Konner and Mark Rosenthal on a script that concerned Superman dealing with a young schoolboy's question: If Superman is so powerful, why doesn't he get rid of all of the nuclear weapons on the earth? Unfortunately, production company Cannon Films didn't have the budget that the Salkinds had worked with, and the script morphed into Superman battling a pair of Luthor's two solar-powered super-creations. Special effects were subpar, and stock footage from the previous three

Opposite: Christopher Reeve stars as the Man of Steel in *Superman: The Movie.*

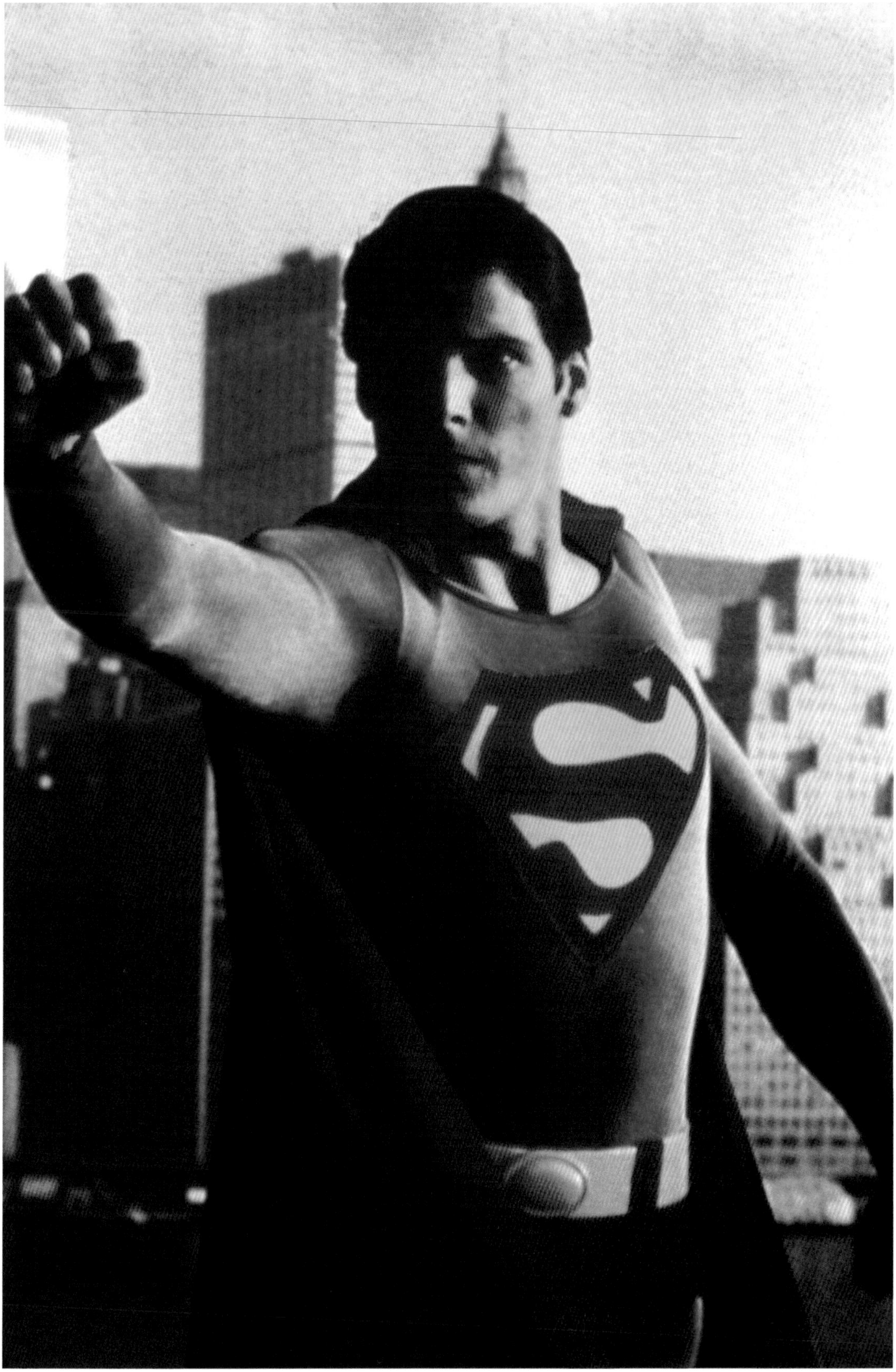

movies was used for some flying sequences. When a preview audience panned the film in early 1987, director Sidney Furie edited the two-hour-plus film to ninety minutes, muddling the story completely. *Superman IV: The Quest for Peace* was released in 1987 with little promotion, and with disappointing—and disappointed—audiences. Cannon Films announced plans for *Superman V,* due out in the summer of 1989, but the movie never took flight.

THE 1980S AND 1990S: BACK TO TELEVISION

Superman celebrated his fiftieth birthday February 29, 1988, in the middle of Warner's and DC's media push. NBC aired a primetime *Superman's 50th Birthday Special,* produced and directed by *Saturday Night Live* producer Lorne Michaels. The campy special included cast members from the serials and television shows in cameo roles, but also Jan Hooks as a woman who had birthed Superman's "love child," and Dana Carvey as the villainous Brainwave.

Warner also worked with Ruby-Spears on a new animated *Superman* show, which premiered on CBS on September 17, 1988. Famed comic writer Marv Wolfman—at that time the scripter of the *Adventures of Superman* comic—became story editor, in charge of developing the show, and writing the series bible. He hired other comic-book writers to work on the series, as well as veteran artist Gil Kane to design the show. Each episode contained an eighteen-minute action-oriented *Superman* lead story, and a four-minute backup feature entitled *Superman's Family Album,* detailing Clark Kent's years from Smallville baby to his first appearance in costume in Metropolis. Villains included Lex Luthor, the Prankster, General Zod, and Wild Sharkk, and heroine Wonder Woman guest-starred in one episode. Animation on the show was strong, and the John Williams' film theme was modified for musical use, but the series was retired after thirteen episodes.

After Cannon gave up the live-action rights to the *Superman* family, Alexander and Ilya Salkind produced a half-hour syndicated series for Viacom, featuring Superman as a teen. *Superboy* premiered the week of October 8, 1988. In 1990's third season, the series was renamed *The Adventures of Superboy,* and it lasted two more seasons, ending in 1992. Following *Superboy,* the Salkinds wanted to start production on *Superman: The New Movie,* for a Christmas 1991 release, with a Superman versus Brainiac script by comic writer Cary Bates. The film project lost steam, however, and died in 1993.

That same year, Lorimar and ABC worked out a deal for an all-new live-action *Superman* TV series titled *Lois & Clark: The New Adventures of Superman.* Deborah Joy Levine developed the series, which balanced lighthearted romance with superheroic action. Dean Cain was cast as Superman, with sexpot Teri Hatcher grabbing the role of Lois Lane. Michael Landes was cast as Jimmy Olsen, but he was replaced after the first season by Justin Whalen. Eddie Jones and K Callan played an earthy and elderly Jonathan and Martha Kent, while Lane Smith had the perfect bluster as Perry White. John Shea came onboard as the villainous-but-charming Lex Luthor.

Lois & Clark debuted on September 12, 1993, and was a hit with audiences. It lasted four seasons, bringing in a handful of comic-book and previous TV concepts, including kryptonite, Metallo (Scott Valentine), Inspector Henderson (Richard Belzer), Jor-El (David Warner), the Prankster (Bronson Pinchot), the Toyman (Sherman Hemsley, Grant Shaud), Mr. Mxyzptlk (Howie Mandel), and Lana Lang (Emily Procter). The final two seasons played around too much with a will-they-marry-or-not? story between Lois and Clark, and fans began to desert the show. *Lois & Clark* finished in 1997, after eighty-eight episodes had aired.

TURN OF THE CENTURY: MOVIES, CARTOONS, AND TV

Even as *Lois & Clark* was winding down, the WB was planning a companion show to its popular *Batman: The Animated Series.* Utilizing most of the same team that had made that series a success, Warner commissioned *Superman*. Debuting on September 6, 1996, with a three-part origin story, the animated show lasted four seasons. On *Superman*, Timothy Daly voiced the title character, while Dana Delaney voiced Lois Lane, David Kaufman was Jimmy Olsen, and Clancy Brown was Lex Luthor.

Extremely faithful to its comic-book origins, *Superman* included such villains as Lex Luthor, the Parasite, Bizarro, Darkseid, Lobo, Maxima, Toyman, Livewire, Mr. Mxyzptlk, and others. It also debuted a newly styled Supergirl, and saw guest-appearances from Batman, Robin, Green Lantern Kyle Rayner, Aquaman, Flash, Steel, the New Gods, Dr. Fate, and the Demon. One popular third-season episode even saw members of the Legion of Super-Heroes coming back in time, marking their first and only appearance on television. *Superman* was combined with episodes of *Batman* in 1997 under the title *The New Batman/Superman Adventures,* and new episodes aired until February 2000.

New adventures of Superman as a team member are seen weekly on the Cartoon Network's animated *Justice League* series, from the same crew that worked on the *Batman* and *Superman* shows. *Justice League* debuted on November 17, 2001, and new episodes continue to air in 2004. George Newbern provides Superman's voice.

The Kryptonian adventures have not ceased in live-action, however. The WB airs Warner's *Smallville,* which began on October 16, 2001. The popular one-hour drama series focuses on the adventures of teenage Clark Kent (Tom Welling) and slightly older Lex Luthor (Michael Rosenbaum), but the producers have promised "no tights, no flight," saying that Kent will never fly on the series, nor wear the well-known Superman costume. Still, the series is not without its touchstones to the *Superman* mythos; besides kryptonite, the voice of Jor-El has been heard, and familiar sights such as the *Daily Planet* offices, and characters like policewoman Maggie Sawyer, crime boss Morgan Edge, and editor Perry White have appeared. Even Christo-

pher Reeve has guest-starred, as Dr. Virgil Swann, a cryptic man who knows something about Krypton.

As Superman has reached more than two-thirds of a century in print, another feature film may be in the wings. Producer Jon Peters hired Jonathan Lempkin in 1995—then Gregory Poirier—to script a new movie. Kevin Smith wrote drafts of a 1997 script titled *Superman Lives,* but when director Tim Burton came aboard in 1997, he jettisoned the story and cast Nicolas Cage in the title role. After costume fittings and location scouting was complete, Burton stepped out of the picture in 1998, and Cage left the project shortly thereafter. Since then, multiple scripts have been written by Wesley Strick, Dan Gilroy, Alex Ford, J. Ellison, William Wisher, Paul Attanasio, and J. J. Abrams. Multiple directors have also climbed aboard, including McG (*Charlie's Angels*), Brett Ratner (*Rush Hour*), and McG again in 2003. The film even has multiple titles, including *Superman Reborn* and *Superman: The Man of Steel.* A *Superman/Batman* film was also in development during 1999/2000, written by Andrew Kevin Walker.

In a March 1988 *Time* magazine story, Christopher Reeve said, "Siegel and Shuster created a piece of American mythology. It was my privilege to be the onscreen custodian of the character in the '70s and '80s. There will be many interpretations of Superman, but the original character created by two teenagers in the '30s will last forever." For two-thirds of a century, the public has had a media-related *Superman* to enjoy, in addition to the comic-book stories. As long as there is a sky to look up to and see neither a bird nor a plane, whether on film or television, in live-action or animation, the Man of Steel will be there, defending the principles of "Truth, Justice, and the American Way." —*AM*

Superman Villains

He can "change the course of mighty rivers.... Bend steel in his bare hands." And that description of the

Man of Steel, from the introduction of *The Adventures of Superman* television program (1953–1957), barely scratches the surface of the hero's vast abilities, which poses the problem: What kind of menace can threaten a character who borders on omnipotence? Not that this question bothered Superman's creators—writer Jerry Siegel and artist Joe Shuster—in the hero's earliest excursions in *Action Comics,* beginning with issue #1 (June 1938). Since the Man of Steel was the progenitor of superheroes, the sheer novelty of a "super" man was enough to amaze readers as he heaved bulky sedans over his head and smacked gangsters across the room.

Mad scientist the Ultra-Humanite bears the dishonor of being Superman's first recurring enemy, bowing in *Action* #13. Boasting, in his own words, "the most learned brain on Earth," the Ultra-Humanite's knack for transferring his own mind into other bodies stymied his superfoe. The Man of Steel's best-known adversary, Lex Luthor, debuted in *Action* #23 (1940). This evil genius' legendary bald pate was nowhere to be seen as the original Luthor sported a mane of shocking red hair. While the Ultra-Humanite and Luthor battled the Man of Steel with brain power, Superman's next major opponent, the Puzzler, matched *wits* with the hero. On his heels were the Prankster and the Toyman, both more daffy than dangerous, who were little more than an annoyance to Superman. In *Superman* #30 (1944), the bedeviling imp Mr. Mxyztplk first popped into Metropolis to pester Superman with his magical powers. And thus the super-conflicts tromped, rather predictably, for two decades: Luthor would try to eliminate the Man of Steel with a death ray, and the Toyman would attack him with toy soldiers that fired real ammo. Superman's ego swelled as he considered his battles with these bad guys as little more than mere diversions. This plot predictability made Superman's adventures wholesome, entry-level reading material, which was the objective of his editors during the Golden Age of comic books (1938–1954).

Science-fiction-based villains crept into the Superman titles with the advent of comics' Silver Age in the late 1950s, and for the first time in his career Superman began to face actual risks. Brainiac, a space-faring android, employed both sophisticated science and a miniaturization ray to plague the Man of Steel. A mutated monkey called Titano the Super-Ape konged through Metropolis, zapping Superman with kryptonite vision. Metallo, a cyborg whose robotic body was powered with a kryptonite heart, pummeled and poisoned Superman. The Phantom Zone was introduced as a ghostly dimension incarcerating villains from the late planet Krypton, some of whom, including General Zod and Jax-Ur, occasionally escaped and imperiled Metropolis with powers that rivaled Superman's.

By the early 1960s, Superman had established himself as not only the Metropolis Marvel but also the galaxy's greatest hero, enticing a band of interplanetary enemies to join forces as the Superman Revenge Squad. In *World's Finest Comics* #142 (1964), the Composite Superman, commanding the powers of the entire Legion of Super-Heroes, gave the Man of Steel and his superfriends, Batman and Robin, the biggest challenge of their lives. The Parasite, the last great Superman villain of comics' Silver Age (1956–1969), was introduced in 1966 and came close to killing the Man of Steel with his ability to siphon the hero's very life force. Luthor's hatred of Superman intensified throughout the 1960s, and the mastermind—usually wearing prison grays—regularly constructed devices or plans to eliminate his enemy. With all this meanness in Metropolis, Bizarro, an imperfect duplicate of the hero played strictly for laughs, and a renamed Mr. Mxyzptlk (note the spelling change) regularly dropped by to keep the overall tone light. By the time the 1960s closed, Superman's writers and editors had run of out new ideas, and his villains had once again become humdrum.

Publisher DC Comics overhauled its flagship character in 1970, and new and more challenging super-adversaries were introduced. Writer/artist

Jack Kirby's Darkseid, the despotic and immeasurably powerful ruler of the planet Apokolips who over time emerged as DC's most formidable foe, was first seen in, of all places, *Superman's Pal Jimmy Olsen* #134 (1970). Working behind the scenes with Darkseid was Intergang, a Metropolis crime network. In the landmark *Superman* #233 (1971), an explosion that (temporarily) transformed all kryptonite into iron also created a "Sand-Superman," a rogue replication of the Man of Steel. In 1972, Luthor, still loathing Superman after all these years, created the Galactic Golem to attempt to destroy his foe, and Terra-Man, a desperado from the Wild West transplanted into contemporary times rode— make that *flew*—into town on a winged horse for the first of several showdowns with the Action Ace. Other new additions to Superman's rogues' gallery during the 1970s—the high-tech Toyman II, the ion-charged Blackrock, and the insipid Microwave Man—didn't fare as well, deservingly being put out to pasture after a few appearances.

In the early to mid-1980s, DC Comics pumped up the villainous volume by introducing newer and more powerful super-foes. World enslaver Mongul was almost more than Superman could handle, and the hero was imperiled by demonic forces courtesy of Lord Satanis. Not to be outdone by upstarts, Luthor donned a cyber-suit and Brainiac was retooled into a new robotic form. When the entire Superman franchise was reinvented in *The Man of Steel* (1986), previous incarnations of the super-foes were discarded as the hero's entire continuity slate was wiped clean. Old favorites were repackaged in newer, darker forms. Luthor was re-established as a corporate megalomaniac with criminal ties whose power reached such heights that in the 2000 election he became president of the United States. Brainiac, Bizarro, Parasite, Mr. Mxyzptlk, Metallo, Toyman, and even the Prankster were upgraded (and ethically degraded) into dangerous, credible threats. And a lethal legion of new villains has since been introduced to endanger the Man of Tomorrow: the mercenary Bloodsport, the she-fury

The Adventures of Superman #441 © 1988 DC Comics. COVER ART BY JERRY ORDWAY.

Rampage, the unstoppable Dreadknaught, and the bounty hunter Massacre, as well as Riot, Dominus, Imperiex, Ignition, and Kancer, super-rogues whose very names evoke danger and potential death. None has been so fatal, however, as the behemoth Doomsday, who actually *killed* Superman in 1992 before the hero rose from the dead not long thereafter. Although his "never-ending battle" against these increasingly dangerous adversaries has forced the Man of Steel to get down and dirty, Superman remains an inspirational symbol of hope.

As the Man of Tomorrow leapt onto screens small and large, Luthor has, more than any of his foes, joined him for the ride: in the movie serial

Atom Man vs. Superman (1950); in animated incarnations of Superman in 1966, 1988, and 1996, plus the long-running *Super Friends* series; in three of the four *Superman* movies, with Gene Hackman in the role; and in the live-action television series *Superboy* (1988), *Lois & Clark: The New Adventures of Superman* (1992), and *Smallville* (2001). —*ME*

Superman's Weapons and Gadgets

In a never-ending battle for "truth, justice, and the American way" that has spanned sixty-plus years, Superman has designed, invented, and utilized his fair share of super-paraphernalia. While the Superman mythos of the twenty-first century allows for much more high-tech gadgetry than initially accompanied Superman's early career, all told there is a super-list of apparatus that accessorizes the Man of Steel.

Superman's secret hideout, the Fortress of Solitude (described in detail in *Action Comics* #241 [1958] and given larger-than-life status in the *Superman* live-action films of the late 1970s and early 1980s), originally housed one of the most well-stocked superweapons chambers in comic-book history. This might seem like a dichotomy to some, for in his battle for "truth, justice, and the American way," the hero's violence is never cruel, malicious, or initiated by him. Noted a *Time* magazine cover story on Superman when the hero turned fifty, "His greatest powers are exerted to deflect violence, by stepping in front of bullets, say, or moving huge objects out of harm's way." More times than not, Superman's powers of superspeed, super-strength, flight, and virtual invulnerability overrule the need for the Man of Steel to defend himself with anything other than his inborn, alien powers. Why resort to weaponry when you can bend steel

with your bare hands? But even America's most beloved hero sometimes needs an extra line of defense; in these situations, items like the War-suit—an ultra-high-tech suit of armor housed in the new Fortress—come in handy.

Once inside the Warsuit, Superman can cocoon himself in the chest cavity and, linked telepathically to a techno-brain, manipulate the armor shell as if it is an extension of his own body. The suit also acts as a protection device, sheltering Superman from the effects of kryptonite, radiation, and other harmful substances. Equipped with super-gadgets like environmental scanners, fusion reactor pads, and ion pulse cannon gauntlets, supervillains don't stand a chance against the Man of Steel when he assumes his protective shell. The Warsuit is one of the few weapons stored safely in the hero's hide-out, replacing such Golden Age (1938–1954) and Silver Age (1956–1969) staples as the Lex Luthor–created "fourth dimensional ray machine"; the duplicator ray that Luthor used to create the faux-Superman named Bizarro; the enlarging ray used by Kandorian scientist Zak-Kul; and the portable shrinking ray that Superman once confiscated from supervillain Brainiac.

Within the Fortress' impenetrable walls lies other noteworthy super-apparatus. Once upon a time, dummies and robots, in the likeness of both Superman and his alter ego, Clark Kent, awaited their super-orders. Called upon to carry out various super-tasks, the robots showed human emotion and possessed amazing powers. Summoned by Superman's X-ray vision or by voice command, the remote-controlled machines allowed Superman to experiment vicariously with kryptonite and participate in pitched battle with numerous supervillains. Today's Fortress houses only "Ned," the sole remaining Superman robot, whose number one task is to care for Superman's dog, Krypto, who also calls the secret sanctuary home. Since the 1990s Superman has also sometimes been seen floating amidst a vast 360-degree complex of video screens feeding him information about wrongs in need of righting worldwide.

As "champion of the oppressed," the Man of Tomorrow has wielded some far-fetched tools and equipment. He has used a super-blowtorch to burn off dirt from his invulnerable costume; snapped pictures with his krypto-raygun, a combination camera/projector in the shape of a raygun straight out of *Flash Gordon;* whipped out his kryptonite detector (that's "K-detector" to friends and family) to locate these powerful planetary fragments; and applied his selective amnesia-inducer to erase the knowledge that Clark Kent is really Superman from the minds of Batman and Robin. In the wake of Superman's revamping in *The Man of Steel* comic book (1986), most of this weaponry no longer exists. Instead, Superman dons the Mother Box, an ultra-advanced armband computer (of a type originally seen in Jack Kirby's "Fourth World" comics) that summons dimension-spanning Boom Tubes, heals injuries, and outfits Superman's costume for battle. He overlays his aquanaut suit for deep-sea exploration. He bedecks himself in a device known as a Phantom Zone Projector, created by John Henry Irons (a.k.a. the superhero Steel) to allow Superman to see Krypton's past. For otherworldly adventures, Superman uses his super-oxygen mask, a deep-space breathing apparatus useful in non-oxygenated atmospheres.

Whether calling upon these or an array of his backup gadgets, Superman frequently consults the expertise of S.T.A.R. Labs, Metropolis' innovative super-laboratory, and has sought advice from super-inventors like Irons and Professor Emil Hamilton. Besides providing super-gizmos, these resources allow the hero a safety net when the villainous grow too gigantic for even the Man of Steel to battle alone. —*GM*

Supermedia

Next to the number-one occupation of millionaire playboy, the day job most heroes embrace is somehow media-related. A quick rundown reveals that, when not out saving the world, many heroes spend their time on the air or behind the scenes of radio and television stations, or other media outlets.

In 1936, the Green Hornet carved out a niche when his alter ego, Britt Reid, founded the *Daily Sentinel,* using his newspaper to fight for law and order. In 1938, *Detective Comics* #20 unfolded the cloak-and-mask-wearing Crimson Avenger, whose alter ego, Lee Travis, is a newspaper reporter for the *Daily Globe-Leader.* Like apparently so many other men in this field, Travis gleans great satisfaction working outside the law in his heroic guise. Probably the first hero to hit the airwaves premiered in Columbia Comics' *Big Shot* #1 in 1940: Tony Trent, a radio announcer for station WBSC, becomes disgusted by the reports of criminal activity he hears daily on the air, and decides to fight crime as the terrifying, rubber-masked hero, the Face. The following year, Harvey Comics' *Speed Comics* #13 hit the stands, featuring newspaper publisher Don Wright, writer of editorials by day and crime fighter (Captain Freedom) by night, and *Smash Comics* debuted the hero Midnight, who, as Dave Clark, announces the news at radio station UMAX. One of the most popular characters to emerge from this era was Captain Marvel, who first appeared in *Whiz Comics* #2 (1940). His alter ego, Billy Batson, is an orphaned newsboy before he turns into the Shazam!-shouting hero. In his first adventure, Batson shows off his investigative skills to the head of WHIZ radio station, earning himself the position of roving radio reporter.

While Captain Marvel would endure for years to come, other heroes have become yesterday's news. Though one version or other of the character has come around from his debut to the current era, few readers are familiar with Johnny Quick, the super-speedster who ran in *More Fun Comics* and *Adventure Comics* for thirteen years beginning in 1941, a cameraman for "Sees-All, Tells-All News" in his civilian guise as Johnny Chambers. Or what about Marvel Comics' the Patriot, who bowed in *Human Torch* #3 (1941), as reporter Jeff Mace? Though well known among hardcore fans, the general public is none too acquainted with Marvel Comics' the Destroyer, who appeared in nine different comic books from 1941 to 1946, as reporter Keen Marlow, or Prize Comics' Fighting American (1954), who broke stories as a TV newscaster-commentator at station U.S.A. in his everyday life as Johnny Flagg.

Despite these predecessors and colleagues, the media man bar none is bespectacled *Daily Planet* reporter Clark Kent, alias Superman, who made headlines in *Action Comics* #1 (1938). For years, the *Daily Planet* trio helped round out Superman's cast of characters: tough-boss publisher Perry White; Superman's pal and the newspaper's photographer, Jimmy Olsen; and love interest and fellow reporter Lois Lane. (In fact, Lane is one of the rare strong, female role models in this field; other superheroines whose civilian lives have been anchored in the media include Golden Age [1938–1954] favorite Liberty Belle and Bronze Age [1970–1979] stalwart Ms. Marvel.) When the Superman mythos was revamped in the mid-1980s the *Daily Planet* roster expanded, introducing gossip columnist Catherine "Cat" Grant and fellow reporters Ron Troupe and Dirk Armstrong. Kent is now a foreign correspondent for the leading Metropolis newspaper, making it easier for him to slip out of the newsroom when duty calls. Along the way, Lane picked up a Pulitzer Prize and Kent's hand in marriage.

The Silver (1956–1969) and Bronze Ages of comics also had their fair share of media moguls and beat reporters. Witness DC Comics' vigilante the Question, whose alter ego Vic Sage is a TV newscaster for World Wide Broadcasting; DC's the Creeper (who premiered in 1968, and surfaces occasionally today), whose alter ego Jack Ryder is a security investigator for the TV station WHAM; and the Steve Ditko–created Mr. A, who, as *Daily Crusader* reporter Rex Graine, fights mobsters in the press until he is forced to take them on as the metal-masked hero. Outshining these journalists is Peter Parker, a freelance photographer who keeps the *Daily Bugle* well stocked with candid photographs of Spider-Man in action. Few know that

another masked hero, Archie Publications' the Fox, functioned in the real world as Paul Patton, staff photographer for the *Daily Globe,* twenty-plus years before the web-slinger came along. Patton is the first to use a concealed camera to take news pictures of himself in action as the Fox, a gimmick solely credited to Parker. And lest anyone think that Lane is the only non-superpowered newshound to become a comic-book star in her own right, there's also Ben Urich, Daredevil's confidant in the 1980s and a leading character of the newspaper-themed Marvel Comics series *The Pulse!* in the 2000s.

Other twentieth-century heroes have a nose for news. DC Comics' first Green Lantern, who appeared in 1940, started his noncostumed career as construction engineer Alan Scott before becoming a radio announcer for WYZX and eventually president of Gotham Broadcasting. DC's Green Arrow, who debuted the following year, was known for the events of alter ego playboy Oliver Queen, who eventually became a reporter when his millions ran out.

The most obscure character of this genre to come out of the late twentieth century was Captain Kentucky, who first appeared in Street Enterprises' *The Comic Reader* in 1980. His alter ego, Lancelot Pertwillaby, is a reporter for the *Louisville Times.* While covering a story on radioactive sewage, he accidentally swallows a rare form of chemical waste and instantly gains superstrength and the ability to fly. But his powers aren't permanent, and Pertwillaby must partake of the gooey compound whenever he needs his powers. He was aided by his pet beagle Cleo, who as Captain Cleo, Hound Hero, often joined Captain Kentucky in saving the day. —*GM*

Supernatural Heroes

When the dark forces of the underworld threaten to scare up trouble for humankind, paranormal protec-

Dick Durock stars in *Swamp Thing.*

tors—many with modus operandi drawing from the same sinister sources as their enemies'—stand ready to vanquish vampires, demons, and wizards.

King Features' Mandrake the Magician, an illusionist sporting a top hat and tails, first used his mystical attributes to fight crime in the June 11, 1934 unveiling of his long-running newspaper strip. Over the decades Mandrake and his assistant, Lothar, have appeared in a 1939 movie serial, Big Little Books, comic books, a 1979 TV movie, and the animated series *Defenders of the Earth* (1986). DC Comics' debut of Dr. Occult predated the industry's eminent Golden Age (1938–1954). Originating in 1935, this amulet-wearing investigator of the arcane has materialized off and on in DC's titles over the decades but has never achieved tremendous acclaim. Dr. Occult's creators, Jerry Siegel and Joe Shuster, scored a larger success with their next character, Superman, first seen in *Action Comics* #1 (1938), the same issue that introduced Zatara the Magician, the crime-fighting showman who voiced backward incantations ("raeppasid" = "disappear").

Zatara's daughter, Zatanna, surfaced in the 1960s, eventually joining the Justice League of America with her own backward-spoken spells. In 1940, Egyptian Prince Amentep emerged from a four-thousand-year sleep to become Fawcett's Ibis the Invincible, the red-turbaned titan who wielded a magic wand—his Ibistick—against evil. A chilling superheroine named Madame Satan had a short lifespan in 1941 at the publisher that would ultimately be known for its squeaky-clean characters—Archie Comics—and Fox Features Syndicates' the Wraith, a ghostly guardian parroting DC's successful supernatural hero, the Spectre, faded from view after a mere five stories that same year. The Heap, Hillman Periodicals' mindless, lumbering behemoth, first tromped from the mire in 1942, putting the squeeze on Axis officers and criminal vermin that stumbled across his path. Other supernatural superheroes seen during the 1940s were Dr. Fate, Mr. Mystic, and Sargon the Sorcerer.

Horror comics were the rage in the early 1950s, through gruesome anthology titles like EC Comics' *Tales from the Crypt.* During this trend, two noteworthy supernatural heroes arose at DC. There was Dr. Thirteen, a.k.a. the "Ghost-Breaker," a skeptic sleuth who flushed out the truth behind supposed paranormal perils, and the Phantom Stranger, a trench-coated enigma who guided passersby through the supernatural realm in a short-lived series bearing his name. The Stranger was a moderate success, inspiring copies like Charlton's Mysterious Traveler and

Harvey's Man in Black. The Phantom Stranger returned to his own title from 1969 to 1976—with Dr. Thirteen occasionally included as a backup feature—and continues to wander in and out of various DC titles in the 2000s.

The content sanitization of comics in the wake of mid-1950s U.S. Senate subcommittee hearings temporarily retired supernatural references. Two of DC's spooky heroes eventually resurfaced in the 1960s: the Spectre returned in 1966 and spun off into a ten-issue run of his own title, and Dr. Fate received occasional outings in the pages of *Justice League of America.* Marvel's master of the mystic arts, Doctor Strange, first peered into his all-seeing Eye of Agamotto in 1963, fending off magical menaces like Baron Mordo, and in 1966 Dell Comics launched three superhero titles based on famous monsters: *Frankenstein, Dracula,* and *Werewolf.* DC's Deadman, originating in 1967, was circus aerialist Boston Brand before an assassin's bullet ended his life and began his postmortem quest: to find his killer. While dealing with matters mystical, these 1960s creepy crusaders were squarely rooted in the mainstream.

The same cannot be said of Vampirella, the scantily clad, voluptuous vampire, who originally flashed her fangs (and other attributes) in 1969 in her self-titled series from Warren Publishing. *Vampirella*'s black-and-white magazine-sized format sidestepped the stringent restrictions imposed upon color comic books, and her stories were replete with gore and eroticism. A native of Drakulon, a planet of bloodsuckers, Vampirella took stake against her evil brethren that wrought havoc on Earth. Her title lost its bite in 1983, but she did not lay dead for long. Harris Comics resurrected the character first with a 1988 reprint, followed in 1991 by a new comic-book series (and an altered origin) that continues in print as of 2004. Vampirella starred in a 1996 movie that was mercilessly slaughtered by critics, but the world's sexiest vampire remains undaunted: Live models, including *Playboy* Playmates, have popularized the heroine through personal appearances and cover photo shoots. As of 2004, model Kitana Baker wears Vampirella's slinky red costume.

In the 1970s, the Comics Code Authority censorship board eased its restrictions against occult references, and a plethora of paranormal heroes crawled forth. DC revived the Spectre (again) in the pages of *Adventure Comics,* pushing graphic storytelling to its limits with the hero's bloodcurdling means of disposing of criminals, including dismemberment by giant scissors and transmutation into mannequins. Legendary comics artist Jack Kirby expanded DC's mystical mythos in 1972 with *The Demon,* a series starring demonologist Jason Blood. Blood, an immortal, is the human host to Etrigan, a chaotic, yellow-skinned devil who once served in the court of Camelot. Channeled by Blood through an incantation, the Demon speaks in rhyme and has fought magical threats in myriad appearances, including team-ups with Batman.

Marvel Comics embraced the macabre with a host of horrifying heroes all bowing in the 1970s. Morbius, the "living vampire," was a geneticist whose treatment of his own blood disease triggered scientifically created vampirism, which he employed to fight demonic menaces—after some early skirmishes with Spider-Man, that is. Another Spider-Man spinoff was Man-Wolf, an astronaut mutated into a white-furred beast by a moon rock. Jack Russell sprouted fur as Marvel's Werewolf by Night, a hip young lycanthrope who, after initial uncontrollable rages, channeled his bestial abilities into battling bad guys. Other Marvel supernatural heroes premiering during this era include the Ghost Rider, the flame-headed motorcyclist/superhero who gave a new definition to the term "Hell's Angel"; Moon Knight, Marvel's answer to DC's Batman; the half-man/half-vampire Blade, who has headlined a successful franchise of live-action movies from the late 1990s to the present; Brother Voodoo, an African-American character mixing Hougan mysticism and superheroics; the Son of Satan, a.k.a. Daimon Hellstrom, who, with a pentagram birthmark on his chest and a trident that emit-

ted "soul fire" in hand, waged war against his unholy father; and lesser-known characters like Satana (Hellstrom's sister), the Living Mummy, the Monster of Frankenstein, Manphibian, Gabriel the Devil Hunter, and the Golem.

Marvel's Man-Thing and DC's Swamp Thing both premiered at roughly the same time in 1971 and have become immortalized in comics lore. Both were humans transmogrified by the marsh, both were slimy plant-men, both pitted their newfound strength against wrongdoers, and both have regularly encountered superheroes. Swamp Thing is better known, with two live-action movies (1982 and 1989), a live-action TV series (1990–1993), a Kenner toy line, an animated cartoon program (1992), and several successful Vertigo (DC's "mature readers" imprint) series under his belt, but *Man-Thing,* a small-budget motion picture slated for 2004 release, should afford a higher profile to this misunderstood beast whose touch burns those who fear him.

Beginning in the 1980s, "real-world" society grew more violent, and the supernatural heroes of popular fiction followed suit. Perhaps no character better exemplifies this than creator James O'Barr's bleak angel of vengeance, Eric Draven, popularly known as the Crow. In the character's 1989 origin from Caliber Comics, the mortally wounded Draven watches helplessly as his fiancée is brutalized and murdered by street punks. The trauma of this event prohibits him from resting in the afterlife, and on the first anniversary of his death he is resuscitated by a crow and given paranormal abilities, including an empathic touch and augmented agility, in a mission of vengeance against those who cut short his life. His iniquitous methods have transcended his cult-favorite comic book and have been adapted to cinema via a franchise of films beginning with *The Crow* (1994), and a syndicated TV series, *The Crow: Stairway to Heaven* (1998).

Top Cow Productions' NYPD detective Sara Pezzini was first seen in 1995 on an implacable expedition to destroy the mobster who ritualistically eliminated those closest to her. Once she unearthed Joan of Arc's enchanted gauntlet—called the witchblade—Pezzini donned the glove and symbiotically bonded with it. As Witchblade, she wields the glove's powers—the creation of daggers, the deflection of bullets, and an extrasensory perception—in a brutal vendetta against organized crime. A live-action *Witchblade* TV movie (2000) and weekly cable series (2001–2002) starred Yancy Butler.

Characters like the Crow, Witchblade, and Buffy the Vampire Slayer are non-masked fighters that elevate the classic concept of the superhero to a more realistic level, despite their fantastical settings. "Buffy could be seen as qualifying as a superhero," wrote Peter Coogan in his 2002 dissertation "The Secret Origin of the Superhero." Coogan also observed, "She has a mission; she has superpowers; Buffy has an identity as the Slayer." Buffy and her supernatural ilk—Steven Hughes' Lady Death, Dark Horse's Ghost, and DC's Vertigo heroes (like Sandman, Death, Hellblazer, and Preacher)—have reinvented the concept of the dark hero for a new generation. —*ME*

Superpatriots

Marvel Comics' shield-slinging Captain America is, bar none, the most famous of the star-spangled freedom fighters known as the superpatriots. But he was not the first superhero to wear the colors of Old Glory.

The Shield was the first superpatriot. *Pep Comics* #1 (January 1940) introduced Joe Higgins, a man who avenges his father's murder by applying dad's secret formula "SHIELD" (an acronym for Sacrum, Heart, Innveration, Eyes, Lungs, and Derma) to his skin. The formula is activated when Higgins wears a specially designed outfit—which just happens to be star-spangled—that boosts his strength, speed, and stamina, making him the Axis-busting superhero, the Shield. The Eagle promptly parroted the Shield by flying into print in *Science* #1

(February 1940). Secretly Bill Powers, the Eagle, dressed in a blue suit with a golden eagle chest logo and red-and-white striped cape, fights the Nazis and their American sympathizers. Manowar, a superpatriot *android,* also premiered in February 1940, in *Target Comics* #1.

Uncle Sam—*the* Uncle Sam, the top-hat-wearing, white-goateed icon painted by James Montgomery Flagg in his immortal military recruitment poster—became a superhero in *National Comics* #1 (July 1940) in a tale by Will Eisner, creator of the Spirit. Imbued with patriotism-induced super-strength, Sam is more than a match for Nazis and saboteurs. *Uncle Sam,* a 1997 miniseries published under DC Comics' Vertigo imprint, features a dispirited Sam, muttering madly as the America he once knew has fallen apart.

Private Jack Weston was a true patriot, but not a *superpowered* one, which did not deter his zeal: In a red-and-white-striped shirt with blue sleeves dotted with white stars, he blazes onto the frontlines as Minute-Man, the "One Man Army," in *Master Comics* #11 (February 1941). One month later, in March 1941, comic-book readers witnessed two flag-furled firsts: *Captain America* #1, by Joe Simon and Jack Kirby, and *Feature Comics* #42's USA—"the Spirit of Old Glory"—the first star-spangled superheroine. Both debuted nine months before the United States entered World War II.

SUPERPATRIOTS FLOURISH

A survey of 1941 comic books would lead one to suspect that America was already at war. Publishers barraged readers with a surfeit of superpatriots, each clad in democratic duds that would warm Betsy Ross' heart. Some carried guns, some were supported by sidekicks or kid gangs, some were superstrong, and virtually all were indistinguishable from each other: the American Crusader; Captain Battle (dubbed the "One-Man Army," the difference from Minute-Man's moniker being a mere hyphen); Captain Courageous; Captain Fight ("America's #1

Defender"); Captain Flag; Captain Freedom (aided by the Young Defenders, a patriotic street gang); the Conqueror; the Defender (a Captain America clone by Cap's own creators, Simon and Kirby); and the Flag (who, as an infant, bore a U.S. flag birthmark, predestining his fate as a superpatriot).

Joining them were Flag Man, Lady Fairplay, the Liberator, Major Liberty, Major Victory, Man of War (who received a flaming sword from Mars, the god of war), Miss America (granted the superpower of matter alteration by the Statue of Liberty in *Military Comics* #1), Miss Victory (often spied winking and flashing the "V for victory" sign at her readers), Mister America, and the Patriot (joined by his girlfriend Miss Patriot). Also originating in 1941: "War Nurse" Pat Patriot (accompanied by the Girl Commandos, "five fearless freelance fighters of the United Nations"); the Sentinel; the Skyman; the Spirit of '76; the Star-Spangled Kid and Stripesy (a kid hero with an adult partner); the Unknown Soldier; and the no-nonsense U.S. Jones (one of his earliest stories in *Wonderworld Comics* was titled "Traitors Die Fast!"). By the time Stormy Foster—a.k.a. "the Great Defender"—premiered in *Hit Comics* #18 (December 1941), all the good superpatriot costumes (and names) had been taken: Below the belt Foster wore white briefs with no leggings, looking as if he had left his pants at home. Another superpatriot debuting that same month had better fortune in fashion and longevity: Wonder Woman.

In *Startling Comics* #10 (1941), the Fighting Yank receives superpowers while wearing an ancestral cloak from the American Revolution. His tri-corner cap and buckle shoes differentiated him from other superpatriots. Likewise, from his first appearance in *Mystic Comics* #6, the Destroyer is clearly no average star-spangled hero. His grim blue face and piercing yellow eyes terrorize the Nazis, as does the foreboding white skull insignia on his black shirt. Many of the Destroyer's earliest stories were written by a teenage Stan Lee, who later became the driving force behind Marvel Comics.

More comic-book superpatriots appeared after the United States entered the war: American Avenger, American Eagle, Captain Commando, Captain Red Blazer, Commando Yank, Crimebuster (a young hero), Liberty Belle, a different Miss America (this one from Timely/Marvel Comics, a female Captain America who remained in print for several years), the Phantom Eagle, Super-American, V-Man (with his young aides, the V-Boys), Yank and Doodle, Yankee Doodle Jones, Yankee Boy, Yankee Girl, and Yankee Eagle. Superpatriot sidekicks were common, including Dusty (partner of the Shield), Buddy (the Eagle), another Buddy (Uncle Sam), Bucky (Captain America), Dandy (Yankee Doodle Jones), Sparky (Captain Red Blazer), and Rusty (Flag Man). The Axis could not stop these invincible superpatriots, but the end of World War II could: Peacetime almost instantaneously put them out of business, although some limped along until the early 1950s.

FROM RED, WHITE, AND BLUE TO RED SCARE

Pack leader *Captain America* suffered an ignoble fate in 1950, being ousted from his own series as it briefly became a horror comic (*Captain America's Weird Tales*) before being discontinued. Timely revived *Captain America* in 1954 with a new agenda: fighting Communism, as Captain America, "Commie Smasher." Within several issues, however, the character and series were once again retired.

Yet Communism remained a new threat to explore in superhero comics, and the next superpatriot to combat it plied a different weapon: satire. With tongue rooted firmly in cheek, Simon and Kirby melted the cold war in Prize Comics' *Fighting American.* Issue #1 starts harshly, though, as an American Adonis, blunt-tongued broadcaster Johnny Flagg, is executed by Russian agents. The life force of Flagg's meek brother, Nelson, is transferred into his slain sibling's "revitalized and strengthened" body, and he resumes the Commie Smashing abandoned after *Captain America*'s cancellation. As the Fighting American, he and teenage sidekick Speedboy tackled broadly portrayed Red menaces like

Super Khakalovich and Poison Ivan. During this era of rampant paranoia, however, *Fighting American*'s cavalier approach was rejected by readers and the series died after seven issues (though similar spoofs in the 1990s and 2000s, like AC Comics' retooled Fighting Yank and Alan Moore's First American, have shown that the strip was simply ahead of its time).

The next superpatriot to materialize bore a familiar name: the Shield. In Archie Comics' *The Double Life of Private Strong* #1 (1959), by Simon and Kirby, Army private Lancelot Strong ventures down three familiar superpatriotic paths: He is orphaned; his late father, a scientist, leaves behind data that helps Strong develop superpowers; and he adopts a red-white-and-blue supersuit and battles the United States' enemies. This Shield incarnation lasted a mere two issues.

Another superpatriot appeared in DC's Revolutionary War series, *Tomahawk* #81 (1962): Miss Liberty. In her debut tale, the "Frontier Heroine," clad in red, white, and blue, rescues the magazine's heroes, Tomahawk and Dan, from British soldiers by chucking explosive powder horns at the Redcoats. Miss Liberty stuck around as a member of the *Tomahawk* cast off and on throughout the 1960s.

SUPERPATRIOTS OF THE VIETNAM ERA

The Revolutionary War heroine Miss Liberty aside, superpatriots lay dormant for several years after the Shield's disappearance. America was embroiled in the controversial Vietnam War, and heroic characters could no longer rouse the nation's spirit. In Marvel Comics' *Avengers* #4 (1964), "Earth's mightiest heroes" discover the most famous superpatriot literally frozen in ice. Captain America is thawed into an uneasy existence as an anachronistic superpatriot (his "Commie Smasher" stint is conveniently forgotten). Cap's Archie Comics *doppelgänger*, the Shield, resurfaced again in *Mighty Crusaders* #1 (1965), this time as the son

of the 1940s Shield. This version of the character enjoyed a brief blip of popularity during a superhero boom of the mid-1960s, but soon hung up his star-spangled togs. Meanwhile, Charlton Comics used the name Captain USA for a hero who could fly at the speed of light in a one-shot tale in *Charlton Premiere* #3 (1968).

In the 1970s, Captain America, having mostly ignored Vietnam, diverted his attention to the urban streets, partnering with the African American superhero the Falcon. In his essay "The Vietnam War and Comic Books," from James S. Olson's *The Vietnam War* (1993), scholar Bradford Wright observed, "The Captain America of the 1970s symbolized a nation, weary of confusing and painful overseas adventures, that had turned inward to confront serious domestic ills, brought on, in part, by a decade of war." Captain America soon rejected his patriotic persona, becoming Nomad, but before long was in the red, white, and blue once more.

The 1976 American bicentennial renewed interest in patriotism, but instead of wading into potentially polarizing waters, comic-book publishers returned to safe ground: World War II, where the menace, the Axis, was clear. Captain America headlined Marvel's *The Invaders* (1975–1979), a series retrofitted into the 1940s; Uncle Sam joined other superheroes in a 1970s-set title called *Freedom Fighters* (1976–1978); and *Wonder Woman* temporarily published "untold" tales set during World War II, mimicking the setting of the then-popular television series starring the superheroine. DC also introduced a new title starring a 1940s superpatriot, *Steel the Indestructible Man,* lasting only five issues in 1978.

VIGILANTISM AND THE NEW SUPERPATRIOT

By 1980, American cynicism rooted in the Vietnam War and the Watergate scandal had triggered a transformation: The anti-hero was displacing the altruistic caped crusader. Superheroes representing traditional values had no place in this harsh new world, and a new breed of superpatriot was born.

In DC's *Batman and the Outsiders Annual* #1 (1984), the American Security Agency's Force of July—Major Victory, Lady Liberty, Mayflower, Silent Majority, and Sparkler—toe the line for the government, but once his teammates die in battle, the Major reevaluates his loyalty. In 1986, Dark Horse Comics introduced a conflicted superpatriot, forged in the fires of conspiracy. The American (no relation to the 2000s hero of same name from Com.X), serialized in the anthology *Dark Horse Presents,* was a jingoistic juggernaut, genetically enhanced to protect the United States' foreign and domestic interests against terrorist threats. The public was led to believe that the American was a sole individual, and did not suspect that he was actually an army of interchangeable soldiers, one always ready to replace another who died in action. When the latest American decides to go public to honor his predecessors who perished while fighting terrorists, he is thrust into conflict with a tight-lipped U.S. government. DC's Agent Liberty storms into *Superman* vol. 2 #90 (1991) brandishing firearms, retractable gauntlet blades, and an energy shield. An expertly trained operative for the CIA's covert squad the Sons of Liberty, Agent Liberty questions his employers' motivations after encountering Superman and members of the Justice League of America. Image Comics' superpatriot, appositely named Superpatriot, is a hard-hitting freedom fighter first seen in the pages of Erik Larsen's *Savage Dragon* series in 1993.

In 1986, Marvel introduced into *Captain America* a former soldier named John Walker, publicly known as the grandstanding guardian Super-Patriot. With augmented strength and a well-oiled publicity machine backing him, this superpowered yes-man leveraged Steve Rogers out of his job as Captain America. Rogers eventually returned to his guise and Walker became USAgent, a bounty hunter of supervillains employed by the U.S. Commission on Superhuman Activities. Captain America suffered through several subsequent reboots, with varying

degrees of success, until being renewed by a real-life catastrophe: the September 11, 2001 terrorist attacks on America, after which the hero was reinvented into a kind of "terrorist smasher." Taking a cue from the American and Agent Liberty, however, the post–September 11 Cap is suspicious of the government he is sworn to defend. —*ME*

Superpets

Joseph Campbell, author of *The Hero with a Thousand Faces* (1949) and respected interpreter of heroic lore, noted that heroes often have helpers along their mythic journey. Though the traditional sidekick has often fulfilled this role through comics history, the "superpet" has occasionally proved to be a hero's best friend in perilous circumstances.

Probably the best known of all superpets is DC Comics' super-pooch, Krypto the Superdog. As the beloved canine companion of Superman, Krypto was first introduced in *Adventure Comics* #210 (1955) as the teenage Superman (a.k.a. Superboy)'s dog, who had drifted down to planet Earth many years after being launched off into space as a "test" by Superman's scientist father, Jor-El. He has all of Superman's powers (including X-ray vision, superstrength, and flight), is vulnerable to kryptonite, and retires to his Doghouse of Solitude when the going gets tough. The comics often refer to Krypto as the Dog of Steel. During his many adventures, Krypto wears a red cape detailed with the letter "S."

A few years later, in *Action Comics* #261 (1960), DC introduced Streaky the Super-Cat, pet feline to Supergirl. She was an average cat before being exposed to a strange strain of "X-kryptonite" (accidentally created by Supergirl while experimenting with the common green kryptonite), after which the cat gains the ability to fly, with matching red cape. In her heroic form, Streaky has a yellow lightning-bolt streak on either side of her body. A few years later Supergirl also acquired a white stallion, Comet the Super-Horse, in *Action Comics* #293 (1962). Unlike the other pets in the Superman mythos, Comet didn't quite start out as an animal. A former centaur from ancient Greece with powers of mental telepathy, he locates Supergirl, who takes him under her wing and adopts him as her equine companion. To complicate matters, he also has the power to temporarily take on human form, changing into a handsome young man (with the identity of cowboy "Bronco" Bill Starr) each time a comet passes through the solar system. In his adventures, Comet is bedecked with (are you sitting down?) a red and yellow cape. Beppo the Super-Monkey, a Kryptonian lab animal who was a stowaway on the rocketship that carried Superman to Earth, made his first appearance in *Superboy* #76 (1959). As Superman's pet, he wears a yellow and blue costume and enjoys many of the same powers as his master. Proty II is a native creature of the planet Antares who can change into any shape he chooses. He is the pet of Chameleon Boy, and—along with Krypto, Streaky, Comet, and Beppo—does double-duty as a member of the Legion of Super-Pets. A nonhuman superteam who often came to the aid of the thirtieth century's Legion of Super-Heroes, the Legion of Super-Pets enjoyed about a dozen adventures over the 1960s, after which they pretty much disappeared from the DC mythos. Only the careful comic-book reader noticed that Streaky and Beppo were given cameos by British comics writer Grant Morrison in a 1990 *Animal Man* story (issue #23).

Outside of the Superman storyline, other DC superpets include Ace the Bat-Hound, Bruce Wayne's household pet and Batman's courageous crime-fighting companion. Wearing a bat insignia on his collar and a tight-fitting eye mask intended to conceal distinctive markings that would otherwise reveal him as Wayne's pet, Ace accompanied Batman and Robin on many adventures from the late 1950s through the mid-1960s. He was occasionally joined by Bat-Mite, a magical, elf-like creature described as a "mischievous mite from another dimension" in a 1960 story from *Detective Comics* (issue #276).

While the superpets phenomenon is primarily restricted to DC's lighter moments, a few other characters come to mind. Captain America's partner the Falcon has a real falcon "partner" of his own, Redwing. A trained bird of prey, Redwing developed a paranormal mental link with Falcon and often aids his master in defeating various criminals. Marvel's Red Wolf, a Native American hero with mystical powers and a smattering of adventures in both the Old West and the present day, has a trusted companion, a wolf named Lobo. The most notable superpet of late, however, might just be Radar, canine companion to the strongman Supreme, as recreated by British comics scribe Alan Moore in 1996 for the now-defunct Maximum Press Comics. In Moore's homage to the Superman myth, Radar takes the Krypto role, with a radio collar to amplify his translated doggy thoughts. Though he shares the cape and superpowers of his predecessor, Radar can terrorize the neighborhood and get his master in the doghouse in ways the comics of a more innocent era would never have depicted—both a nostalgic and satirical reminder of how far comics have roamed from the superpet's golden age. —*GM*

Superpowers

Superheroes, the contemporary extension of the ancient gods, represent ideals to which we all aspire.

Well, that looks good on paper, and to a degree, it *is* true. The fundamental explanation, however, for the enduring popularity of superheroes—from the granddaddy of them all, Superman, to the Man of Steel's more recent successors like Witchblade—is *envy*. People wish they could do the amazing things that superheroes do. Young children tie towels around their necks and pretend to fly, or stage ninja battles in their backyards, before graduating to less visceral, more vicarious means of simulating superpowers: engaging in computer and role-playing games, reading comics and fantasy books, and watching superheroes on film.

Two superpowers fascinate people most: flight and invisibility. In his report for National Public Radio's *This American Life,* in a segment entitled "Invisible Man vs. Hawkman" (February 23, 2001), commentator John Hodgman surveyed a handful of participants on their preference between those abilities. Flight, the ultimate symbol of freedom and happiness, is a common theme in nighttime dreams, while invisibility denotes stealth and even insecurity. To no surprise, many men revealed their transparency by opting for invisibility. What flabbergasted Hodgman was that each of his interviewees' motivations was purely selfish: They wanted to fly to Paris, or to sneak into the women's locker room. *No one* said they'd use their powers to help others—they'd only help themselves.

Humans may covet the gift of flight, but flying is so routine within the supercommunity, it's easier to hail an airborne hero than a taxicab. DC Comics' Superman, Supergirl, Captain Marvel and the rest of the Marvel Family, and Martian Manhunter fly effortlessly. Marvel Comics' Thor is pulled through the air by hurling his magic hammer. The Fantastic Four's Human Torch and the Teen Titans' Starfire scorch the skyways, leaving behind flaming trails. Iron Man's armor, Starman's cosmic rod, and Green Lantern's power ring propel them. The Silver Surfer rides his space-spanning surfboard throughout the deepest regions of the Marvel universe. DC's Hawkman and Hawkwoman, X-Man Archangel, the Wasp of the Avengers, and TV hero Birdman flap their wings, and Sub-Mariner, his winged ankles. Doctor Strange, Marvel's Master of the Mystic Arts, floats with his Cloak of Levitation, while Jean Grey of the X-Men levitates via telekinesis. Justice Leaguers Wonder Woman and the Atom glide on air currents, and Gen13's Freefall manipulates gravity. Members of the Legion of Super-Heroes, the teenage adventurers living one thousand years in the future, all

have *flight rings.* And while the X-Men's Nightcrawler can't fly, he can do the next best thing: teleport.

That *other* superpower, invisibility, is not as prevalent among superheroes as one might think. The Invisible Woman of the Fantastic Four (formerly the Invisible Girl before changing times liberated her) can disappear (as could her possible model, the 1940s newspaper-comic heroine Invisible Scarlet O'Neil). The Legion's Invisible Kid gained admittance to the team by pulling a vanishing act, and the cartoon hero Space Ghost relies upon his Invisi-belt to fade away. Then there are the phasers, phantom superheroes whose ghostly appearances spook their foes, or allow them to walk through walls: Dark Horse Comics' Ghost, the Legion's Phantom Girl (a.k.a. Apparition), the Justice Society's Obsidian, the X-Men's Kitty Pryde (a.k.a. Shadowcat), and Top Ten's Jack Phantom display this trait, as do deceased DC Comics heroes like Deadman and the Spectre. The android member of the Avengers, the Vision, has absolute mastery of his density, through thick and thin.

Superstrength is the superpower supreme, however, found among more characters than any other. There are the infinitely strong, like Superman, who can push asteroids, or the Hulk, whose strength is fueled by rage. Other mighty men and women registering high on the muscle meter are Marvel's Thor, Hercules, Iron Man, She-Hulk, Gladiator, and the Thing; DC's Captain Marvel and Supergirl; and Image (later Awesome) Comics' Supreme. The next level down includes Wonder Woman and Troia (the original Wonder Girl); America's Best Comics' Tom Strong; Gen 13's Fairchild; Marvel's Sub-Mariner and Spider-Man, who can heave cars; and Acclaim's Magnus, Robot Fighter, who can karate chop through rogue cyborgs. They're not alone: Dozens of other superheroes have varying grades of enhanced strength. Being able to bench-press tons sometimes carries a hefty price: Ben Grimm lost his humanity when cosmic rays mutated him into the Thing, and the gamma-irradiated Bruce Banner cannot control his incredible alter ego, the Hulk.

Most superstrong heroes are also bolstered by invulnerability, or superdense skin. The Hulk can shrug off mortar shells, while Superman can withstand even greater blasts. The Avenger Iron Man's armor and X-Man Colossus' steel skin keep them safe from most attacks, and Ferro (a.k.a. Ferro Lad) of the Legion of Super-Heroes can transmute into iron. The Invisible Woman's force fields protect her and her Fantastic Four teammates. The accident that turned Luke Cage into Marvel Comics' "hero for hire" called Power Man buffered his skin into the organic equivalent of Kevlar. The X-Men's Wolverine may not be invulnerable, but his mutant healing ability allows him to rebound quickly from wounds.

Size *does* matter among superheroes. Many can grow, like Dark Horse's Hero Zero, Marvel's Black Goliath, the Doom Patrol's Elasti-Girl, the Legion's Colossal Boy, and the ghostly Spectre, who once expanded to such heights that he clobbered a similarly sized opponent with a planet! Then there's Henry Pym, the size-changing Avenger known as Giant-Man … and Goliath (and Yellowjacket!). Pym started his career by getting small as the astonishing Ant-Man, then teaming up with another tiny titan, the Wasp. The world's smallest superhero, DC Comics' Atom, can shrink to microscopic size, as can the Legion's suitably named Shrinking Violet, and Golden Age (1938–1954) freedom fighters Doll Man and Doll Girl clobbered crooks despite their Barbie-esque statures.

Other heroes shift their shapes in the line of duty. Created in 1941, the first morphing superhero was Plastic Man, who not only stretches his body but also disguises himself as anyone or any object—pliable "Plas" has snared many a felon by pretending to be a chair or a lamp. Ralph Dibny, DC Comics' sleuthing Elongated Man, drinks a liquid called Gingold for his powers, and has frequently snuck an extended ear into a room to get the goods on bad guys. The malleable Mr. Fantastic's primary attribute is his intellect, but he'll bounce and bend with the Fantastic Four when necessary. Superman's pal, Jimmy Olsen, has been known to guzzle

his "elastic serum" to become Elastic Lad, and in 2000, the Atomics' Mr. Gum joined the ranks of the rubbery heroes. Stretching characters aside, the Rapunzel-like Medusa of Marvel's Inhumans can turn her flowing red hair into entrapping tentacles or harmful projectiles. Beast Boy (a.k.a. Changeling) of the Teen Titans monkeys around in a variety of animal forms. The Super Friends' junior allies the Wonder Twins trigger their abilities by joining together their rings and chanting, "Wonder Twin powers, activate!"—Jayna, like Beast Boy, transmutes into creatures, but her brother Zan can become … liquid (a superpower lampooned by the Cartoon Network in a 2002 commercial featuring Zan as water in a mop bucket). The multi-powered Martian Manhunter is also a shape shifter, and employs this ability regularly—the bald, green form he uses as a Justice League member disguises his true extraterrestrial appearance, which unnerves most Earthlings.

Superspeed covers a lot of ground among superheroes. The Marvel mutant Quicksilver is blindingly fast, as are Marvel's Golden Age speedster the Whizzer and the T.H.U.N.D.E.R. Agents' Lightning. DC Comics is so enamored of fast heroes that it has a stable of them, including three generations of Flashes (Wally West, Flash III, got his start as Kid Flash, swift-footed sidekick to Flash II); two generations of Johnny Quicks; a Lady Flash; the racing Russians called the Kapital Kouriers; teenage speedster Impulse; his mentor Max Mercury; and the villainous Professor Zoom. One thousand years from now, the Tornado Twins, descendents of Flash II (Barry Allen), will zip alongside the Legion, as will one of their children, XS. These heroes are all linked by an extradimensional energy supply known as the Speed Force.

Some superheroes possess supersenses. Wolverine is able to sniff out friend and foe alike, while Superman can adjust his hearing to pick up voices from miles away and decipher frequencies generally inaudible to the human ear. The Man of Steel also boasts a range of optic powers: heat, X-ray, telescopic, infrared, and microscopic visions. X-

Men member Cyclops can't regulate the devastating laser blasts from his eyes without his ruby-quartz visor. Marvel's Daredevil lost his sight, but compensates with a "radar sense" that allows him to perceive nearby objects, while Spider-Man's "spider sense" warns him of impending danger—and he can cling to walls, to boot! Captain Mar-Vell is in tune with the Marvel universe thanks to his Cosmic Awareness, an ability *Wizard: The Comics Magazine* once called "spider sense on steroids." Rogue's superpower involves touch: She absorbs the abilities and memories of those she encounters, a mutation that keeps her at arm's length from her friends in the X-Men.

Some superheroes snap, crackle, and pop with electrical energy. Siblings Spark (formerly Lightning Lass), Live Wire (a.k.a. Lightning Lad), and their villainous brother Lightning Lord possess this shocking trait in their futuristic adventures with the Legion, as does DC's Black Lightning and Milestone's Static (a.k.a. Static Shock). Then there's Thunderbolt, the mystical being who is *living* lightning. Thunderbolt fought crime in the 1940s when summoned by Justice Society of America member Johnny Thunder, and is called into action in the 2000s by Jakeem Thunder.

Elemental powers are also widespread among superheroes. Storm of the X-Men and Rainmaker of Gen 13 manipulate the weather, Marvel's Iceman is a human popsicle who can form ice and snow, DC's Red Tornado commands the wind, and the Human Torch and Gen 13's Burnout are able to create flame. The purviews of Comico's Monolith, Vortex, Morningstar, and Fathom are earth, air, fire, and water, hence their superteam name: the Elementals. H_2O-breathers Aquaman and Sub-Mariner are kings of DC and Marvel Comics' seas. DC's Metamorpho the Element Man emulates the properties of the periodic table, transforming his body into a wide array of gases and chemical compounds. Marvel's Scarlet Witch "alters probabilities" to create seemingly supernatural phenomena, while other matters arcane fall under the jurisdiction of sorcerers such as Mar-

vel's Doctor Strange and Clea, and the spirit-channeling mutant Dead Girl; and DC Comics' Dr. Fate, Tempest (formerly Aqualad), and father-daughter magicians Zatara and Zatanna, the latter of whom speak their spells backwards (or "sdrawkcab").

And then there are the superbrains: The Legion's Saturn Girl reads minds and Justice Leaguer Aquaman telepathically speaks with fish. Professor Charles Xavier and Jean Grey are the X-Men's resident telepaths. Professor X can, like Saturn Girl, scan minds, but can also implant thoughts and telekinetically manipulate objects. His protégé Grey is able to project powerful mental bolts.

Many superheroes received their superpowers through scientific accidents: Peter Parker was bitten by a radioactive spider and became Spider-Man, while Barry Allen (and later, Wally West) was simultaneously doused with chemicals *and* struck by lighting (what are the odds of that happening once, much less twice?) to gain superspeed as the Flash. Fluke accidents like these are unlikely to create anything other than body-bag filler in the real world, but science is striving to create artificial superpowers. *Wired* magazine's "Super Power Issue" (August 2003) revealed the latest technological advancements in replicating invisibility (with optical camouflage) and teleportation (an Australian physicist successfully teleported a laser beam in June 2002), as well as weather control, x-ray vision, and other amazing abilities. Journalist Paul Eng's June 4, 2003 ABC News report "Super-Hero Tech" covered the efforts of the U.S. Army's National Protection Center at the Soldier Systems Center—which sounds like an agency lifted from a superhero comic book—to design protective "LECTUS" (Law Enforcement/Corrections Tactical Uniform System) battle gear. Eng's opening comment: "Batman would be jealous."

Actually, the jealousy is ours. Until LECTUS suits and camouflage cloaks are available at the mall, we'll have to rely upon superheroes to be super for us.

It is interesting to note how the *representation* of the superpowers themselves has changed over the decades. In the 1940s and 1950s, the solution to any superhero's problem was clear: Punch the bad guy in the face (the sure-fire method to use against thugs, mad scientists, Nazis, monsters, alien invaders, and Communist spies). In the 1960s, the superpower ante was upped to satisfy an audience jaded by tumultuous world events. Simple fisticuffs no longer sufficed. Old-timers like Superman grew stronger and almost unstoppable, while the new breed of heroes introduced by Marvel Comics boasted powers unlike anything ever seen before, from Spider-Man's uncanny ability to climb walls to the Silver Surfer's almost-godlike "Power Cosmic." For the next three decades, superpowers got bigger and bolder as comic books amped up to complete with special-effects-laden movies, TV shows, and video games: Some superheroes, like Jean Grey (a.k.a. Phoenix), became corrupted by power, while omnipotent menaces like the Anti-Monitor (in DC Comics' 1985 maxiseries *Crisis on Infinite Earths*) threatened to erase all of existence.

As of September 11, 2001, superpowers detoured into realms more realistic: Mighty heroes still battle mighty villains, but newer characters empowered only by determination have become the icons of the twenty-first century. Marvel's *411* (2003) involved "real-world" peacemakers who have no superpowers, and DC's *Gotham Central* (2002–present), stars the cops on the beat in Batman's hometown. —*ME*

Superteams

When the din of the competition threatens to drown companies out of the marketplace, they have to make more noise. That's what DC Comics did in the winter of 1940 when, to give itself a viable edge on the mounting number of new superhero comic books appearing, it made the unprecedented move of combining many of its superstars into one package, introducing comics' first superteam: the Justice Society of America (JSA).

In the ensuing decades, superhero teams have come and gone, some more respected and enduring than others, most with membership rosters too long to cite. Individual heroes, too, have flitted about, joining various teams throughout their careers. Since the JSA splashed onto the pages of *All Star Comics* #3, superteams have evolved into a variety of archetypes.

THE PATRIOTIC TEAM

DC's primary intention with the JSA was to spotlight characters—the Flash, Hawkman, the Atom, the Sandman, the Spectre, Hourman, Dr. Fate, even the lighthearted Johnny Thunder—who were featured in only one other title (which explains why Superman and Batman, who starred in two series each, appeared only as honorary members). This showcase concept created a revolving door for superheroes, with Dr. Mid-Nite, Wonder Woman, Starman, Black Canary, Wildcat, and Mr. Terrific stepping in and out of the group.

Before long, however, the Justice Society received a loftier calling than circulation boosting. Once the United States entered World War II, the JSA became a symbol of teamwork, encouraging readers to unify to support the war effort. They were the first patriotic superteam, poster children for American propaganda. Others followed: Marvel Comics' Young Allies (featuring sidekicks Bucky and Toro, who stormed into action with their boisterous battle cry of "Yahoo!") and All Winners Squad (Captain America, Human Torch, the Sub-Mariner, the Whizzer, and Miss America, with Bucky and Toro thrown in for good measure), and DC's second-string JSA, the Seven Soldiers of Victory (also known as the Law's Legionnaires). Many comics covers starring these characters featured the heroes attacking Axis soldiers, or fighting Adolf Hitler himself.

The Justice Society, like most superheroes, faded into oblivion in the early 1950s, but was resurrected in the 1960s in annual team-ups with their contemporary counterparts in the pages of DC's *Justice League of America.* Subsequent resurrections in ongoing titles and miniseries, beginning with a short-lived 1970s revival of *All Star Comics,* have kept the JSA in print every few years.

Patriotic superteams resurfaced in the 1970s when Marvel published *The Invaders,* a retro series starring Captain America and company, who boldly fought the Axis powers during World War II, sometimes alongside counterparts the Liberty Legion (on America's home front) and the Crusaders (in Britain). In the 1980s DC published *All-Star Squadron,* a conglomeration of champions summoned by President Franklin D. Roosevelt to assist the overtaxed Justice Society of America after the Pearl Harbor bombing. Both *The Invaders* and *All-Star Squadron* (and a variety of spinoffs) were masterminded by writer Roy Thomas. When DC acquired the rights to Quality Comics' classic superheroes like Uncle Sam, the Phantom Lady, the Ray, and Doll Man, the publisher combined them in a 1970s series called *The Freedom Fighters.* Then there's Femforce, the most widely known super*heroine* team, featuring Ms. Victory, Blue Bulleteer (later Nightveil), She Cat, and Rio Rita.

Patriotism isn't confined to American soil: Marvel's Alpha Flight (Northstar, Puck, Snowbird, and others) are Canadian superheroes, and for a while England was protected by Excalibur, consisting of Captain Britain, transplanted X-Men Nightcrawler and Shadowcat, and other mutants. DC's Global Guardians is an international team with diverse heroes like Ireland's Jack O'Lantern, Australia's Tasmanian Devil, and Denmark's Little Mermaid.

THE SUPER-FAMILY

Many superteams are more than allies: They share a close bond, which in some cases is blood. Fawcett's legendary Marvel Family featured brother and sister Captain Marvel and Mary Marvel, plus extended family Captain Marvel Jr., Uncle Marvel,

and even the three lieutenant Marvels. They fought the Monster Society of Evil and other troublemakers for nearly a decade in eighty-nine issues of *Marvel Family* (December 1945–January 1954).

A snooty scientist, his reserved fiancée, her hot-headed brother, and their irascible friend gained superpowers in November 1961 and became Mr. Fantastic, the Invisible Girl (later Woman), the Human Torch, and the Thing—the Fantastic Four. The "FF" bickers constantly, and has had its share of divisive spats, but their love for each other always reunites them. They consider themselves family first, superheroes second. The Baxter Building, a gleaming skyscraper in the heart of Manhattan, serves as the Fantastic Four's home and base of operations. It houses a vast laboratory where Reed Richards (Mr. Fantastic) conducts bizarre experiments, and, as the HQ of the FF, has attracted numerous attacks from supervillains, much to the chagrin of the building's other tenants.

In the 1960s the Teen Titans were just a bunch of sidekicks (Robin the Boy Wonder, Kid Flash, Aqualad, Wonder Girl, and later Speedy) who got together for fun, and to help teens in need. In 1980 they gained new teammates Cyborg, Raven, Changeling, and Starfire as the New Teen Titans, and their union matured: "I was accused of trying to do DC's X-Men," claims *New Teen Titans* writer/co-creator Marv Wolfman. "And that was about as far from the truth as possible. I was trying to do DC's Fantastic Four." The Titans, and its television incarnation on the Cartoon Network's *Teen Titans* animated program (2003–present), operate from the T-shaped Titans Tower in New York City.

Marvel's Power Pack is family in the truest sense: Siblings Alex, Julie, Jack, and Katie Power all have superpowers. Blossom, Buttercup, and Bubbles are genetically engineered sisters as the Cartoon Network's *Powerpuff Girls.* The strangest superfamily is the Metal Men—Gold, Iron, Lead, Mercury, Platinum, and Tin—a group of robots with human personalities. They are known for their arguments, but are fiercely loyal to one another.

THE SUPER-ALLIANCE

Most superhero groups gather together for the common good. In Fawcett's *Master Comics* #41 (August 1943), Captain Marvel Jr., Minute-Man, Bulletman, and Bulletgirl teamed as the Crime Crusaders Club. That quartet was dwarfed in size by the team of teenage heroes from 1,000 years in the future, the Legion of Super-Heroes. First appearing in a throwaway story in DC's *Adventure Comics* #247 (1958), the Legion—originally Cosmic Boy, Saturn Girl, and Lightning Boy (later Lightning Lad)—traveled to the past to recruit Superboy into their "Super Hero Club." Reader demand brought the Legion back, and over the decades the team has grown to an army (with Chameleon Boy, Ultra Boy, Phantom Girl, Shrinking Violet, and Matter-Eater Lad being just a few who have called themselves Legionnaires), with backups (the Legion of Substitute Heroes) and furry companions (the Legion of Super-Pets). The Legion's headquarters was originally their "clubhouse," a yellow-and-red, upside-down rocket ship. Over time their command center expanded and reflected a more technologically realistic vision of the future. Several requirements govern Legion membership, including age (teens only) and superpower restrictions (no artificial abilities, please). The Legion operates under strict bylaws, and upon induction members are issued a flight ring. In the 1990s the Legion received an updating: outmoded names were modernized (Lightning Lad became Live Wire, Triplicate Girl became Triad) and the series' tone took a darker turn. From 1990 to 1995, Marvel published its own futuristic superteam, with a much smaller cast than *Legion: Guardians of the Galaxy,* featuring characters like Starhawk and Yondu.

Perhaps the best-known group of heroes is the Justice League of America (JLA), which debuted in *The Brave and the Bold* #28 (1960). An updating of the Justice Society, the Justice League merged DC Comics' best-known characters Superman, Batman, Wonder Woman, Aquaman, the Flash, Green Lantern, and Martian Manhunter into a superteam supreme. The roster has changed frequently over the decades: Green Arrow, the Atom, Hawkman, Zatanna, the Elongated Man, Blue Beetle, Dr. Fate, and Plastic Man are just a few of the heroes who have marched through JLA stints. The JLA headquarters is a satellite base, orbiting Earth; members must teleport in and out. JLAers rotate through monitor duty, surveying possible or credible threats and either dispatching smaller teams or uniting the group *en masse.* The Justice League has occasionally established outposts, like the Justice League Europe and Justice League International, but no matter where it's located, the JLA stands ready to protect not only America but the entire world.

The Avengers is Marvel Comics' counterpart to the JLA. Originally the team consisted of Thor, Iron Man, Ant-Man, the Wasp, and reluctant member the Hulk, and over the years, Captain America, Scarlet Witch, the Vision, Hawkeye, She-Hulk, and expatriate X-Man the Beast are just some of the heroes who have been called Avengers. The team operates from a New York City mansion—although a West Coast satellite branch was established for several years—with their butler Jarvis assisting when needed. Captain America has frequently served tours of duty as team leader, and has rallied his titanic troops together with the cheer, "Avengers Assemble!" The Avengers met DC's Justice League in a four-issue, best-selling crossover in 2003 and 2004. In the 2000s Marvel's alternate-reality *Ultimates* series features a decidedly different take on the Avengers. During a comics boom of the mid-1970s, Marvel also published *The Champions,* a hodgepodge team featuring former Avengers (Hercules, Black Widow), X-Men (Angel, Iceman), and Ghost Rider thrown in for good measure. In the late 1980s and early 1990s a role-playing game appropriated the name *The Champions* for a module starring a team that also appeared in several comic books—Flare, the Rose, Malice, and the Marksman were included in this group.

Almost every comics company has combined its heroes into teams. Archie Comics' Fly Man, the

Shield, the Black Hood, and other superheroes became the Mighty Crusaders; Malibu's Ultraforce counted Prime, Prototype, and Hardcase among its roster; and even King Features' Flash Gordon, the Phantom, and Mandrake the Magician joined forces as the Defenders of the Earth. A more provocative examination of the superhero group concept began in 1999 with WildStorm's *The Authority,* featuring a team taking on repressive regimes and a corporate power base. Among the Authority's lineup are Apollo and Midnighter, gay versions of Superman and Batman.

THE OUTSIDERS

There are groups of superheroes that are unwelcome in society, usually due to humankind's fear of their differences. No team better embodies this than the X-Men, Marvel's mutant heroes. In *The X-Men* #1 (September 1963) Professor Charles Xavier, a wheelchair-bound telepath also known as Professor X, located five troubled but unique young people with remarkable superpowers and assured them that they were not alone. They were mutants: The next step in human evolution. From Xavier's School for Gifted Youngsters, Professor X trained them as the X-Men, and this original group of five—Cyclops, Marvel Girl, the Beast, Iceman, and the Angel—epitomized the hope for harmony between humans and mutants. Xavier's rival, Magneto, recruited his Brotherhood of Evil Mutants to ascend to societal dominance.

The X-Men's struggles against Magneto, and against racial intolerance, were a modest success in the 1960s comics. *X-Men* was canceled in 1970, but revived shortly thereafter as a reprint book. *Giant-Size X-Men* #1 (1975) debuted a new version of the team, with an ethnically diverse, harder-edged roster including Wolverine, Colossus, Night-crawler, Storm, and others joining Cyclops and Professor X. From that point countless mutants have been introduced, and the concept has mushroomed into a franchise of comics (including, over the years, *X-Factor, X-Force, Wolverine,* and *X-Statix,*

among others), several animated TV series, dozens of action figures, and two successful live-action movies (with the promise of more to follow).

Three months before the premiere of the X-Men, DC's Doom Patrol debuted in *My Greatest Adventure* #80 (June 1963). The similarities between Marvel's mutants and DC's "world's strangest heroes" are undeniable: Paraplegic mastermind Niles Caulder (the Chief) assembled a trio of powerful outcasts (Robotman, Elasti-Girl, and Negative Man) to work together as a team. The Doom Patrol never fared quite as well as the X-Men eventually did, although the "DP" has been revived on several occasions, the most recent being a new *Doom Patrol* series that began in 2001.

The Inhumans are an artificially constructed race of superpeople (Black Bolt, Medusa, and many others) who, like the X-Men, are often shunned by the "real" populace within Marvel's comics and live away from humans in the extraordinary lunar city of Attilan. The Defenders were originally called Marvel's "non-team": The anti-heroic Incredible Hulk and Sub-Mariner, and the Master of the Mystic Arts Doctor Strange, found themselves united by common goals, but divided by motivational differences. The Defenders added numerous non-teammates to its non-roster over the years, from the Silver Surfer to the Valkyrie to former X-Men and Avenger member the Beast. *The Next Men,* creator John Byrne's homage to Marvel's *X-Men,* featured a quintet of mutates who flee from the top-secret "Project Next Men" and struggle to adjust to the real world while avoiding their pursuers.

THE SPECIALISTS

Some superteams are well-trained combatants, "the best at what they do." Marvel's super-spy organization S.H.I.E.L.D. features a host of agents working under the orchestration of former soldier Nick Fury. In 1982 Batman had a falling out with the Justice League and assembled his own task force: the Outsiders (Geo-Force, Metamorpho, Black Lightning,

Katana, and Halo), a team that has morphed into various incarnations over the years. In 2003 Batman's protégé Nightwing (the original Robin the Boy Wonder) began fronting an all-new Outsiders featuring Arsenal, Thunder, returnee Metamorpho, and other heroes. Nightwing's friend Oracle (the former Batgirl) sends her operatives Black Canary and Huntress into urban action as the Birds of Prey. DC Comics has also published several versions of the Suicide Squad, the most popular being the 1987–1992 incarnation, an expendable collection of heroes and villains (Bronze Tiger, Enchantress, Captain Boomerang, the Vixen, and even Oracle) who were sent on missions by their tough-as-nails boss Amanda Waller.

In the 1960s Tower Comics introduced its T.H.U.N.D.E.R. Agents (Dynamo, No-Man, Menthor, and others) as a disparate group of superpowered figures gathered to serve as The Higher United Nations Defense Enforcement Reserves. Beautifully illustrated by superstar artist Wally Wood, the original *T.H.U.N.D.E.R. Agents* comics were reprinted in the 2000s by DC Comics. The Green Lantern Corps is another group of super-specialists: They are intergalactic police, representing every sector of space and protecting the universe with their power rings, the infinitely mighty weapons with one weakness: Ineffectiveness against anything *yellow.* One more group of super-professionals is *Top Ten,* the name of a precinct of cops in a city populated solely by superheroes.

The extreme superteam Youngblood was one of the first of a new wave of hero groups that premiered starting in 1992 when a cabal of popular artists/writers defected from Marvel to form their own company, Image Comics. Boasting heavily armored anti-heroes with take-no-prisoners attitudes and a bottomless munitions cache, *Youngblood* spawned similar series, from Image and other publishers, with impulsive, heavily weaponed characters: *Cyberforce, Brigade, Tribe,* and *Wetworks,* to name a few, most of which have fallen by the wayside. The most enduring superteam to emerge from this trend was *WildC.A.T.S: Covert Action Teams,* counting hotshots like Grifter and Spartan among its number.

WildC.A.T.S continues in print into the 2000s, and was an animated TV series in the mid-1990s.

THE NEXT GENERATION

There are superteams consisting of younger heroes who will one day replace their adult mentors (and in some cases, super-parents), or simply become the next heroic wave. The super "family" of Teen Titans was originally considered the "junior Justice League" before maturing out of their guides' shadows. Infinity, Inc. (published by DC Comics from 1984 to 1988) was a second-generation Justice Society (with Jade, daughter of the original Green Lantern, plus Fury, the Huntress, Northwind, and others, all JSA descendants), and in the 2000s the Justice Society tradition continues in the pages of *JSA,* featuring a hybrid team of classic and new superheroes. DC's superteam parody *The Inferior Five* (Merryman, Awkwardman, Dumb Bunny, White Feather, and the Blimp) were the hapless offspring of superheroes who couldn't quite fill their parents' shoes (or boots). A latter-day Avengers, *A-Next,* followed in its predecessors' flight-paths for one memorable year (1998–1999), and still occasionally appears in the similarly themed *Spider-Girl.*

Marvel has introduced teams of young characters, with *X-Men* spinoffs *The New Mutants* (including Cannonball, Warlock, Wolfsbane, and Sunspot), *Generation X* (with Husk, Jublilee, Mondo, and others), and *X-Statix* (featuring the Anarchist, Phat, U-Go Girl, and Dead Girl), as well as its 1990s version of the Teen Titans, *The New Warriors* (Speedball, Night Thrasher, Namorita, Firestar, Marvel Boy, and Nova). In WildStorm Productions' *Gen 13,* the U.S. government planned to create its own S.P.B.s (superpowered beings) through DNA manipulation, the result being a group of superkids including Fairchild, Burnout, Rainmaker, and Grunge. A similar theme was explored in the mid-1980s series *DNAgents*: "Science made them … but no man owns them" read a tag line for this comic starring Tank, Surge, Rainbow, Sham, Amber, and Snafu.

THE NEXT ORDER

Finally, there are superteams that exhibit god-like traits, no better example being the New Gods, created for DC Comics by the celebrated "King" of comics, artist/writer Jack Kirby. Orion, Lightray, Metron, the Black Racer, and other superpowered beings answer to the all-knowing Highfather on the peaceful planet New Genesis. The New Gods' paradise is constantly disturbed by New Genesis' dark *doppelgänger* world, Apokolips, ruled by the tyrannical Darkseid and his evil minions. For DC Kirby also produced the Forever People (Mark Moonrider, Beautiful Dreamer, Big Bear, Serifan, and Vykin the Black), hippie-ish young superbeings who reside in the amazing city called Supertown; while for competitor Marvel he created the New Gods–like Eternals (Makkari, Thena, Sersi, and Ikaris).

Some superteams consider themselves gods. Marvel's *Squadron Supreme,* at face value a Justice League riff—Hyperion was its "Superman," Nighthawk, its "Batman," Power Princess, its "Wonder Woman," Golden Archer, its "Green Arrow," etc.—was a mid-1980s limited series that explored a superteam's benevolent rule of its society, and a resistance group that plotted to overthrow the Squadron's quiet tyranny. DC's groundbreaking twelve-issue *Watchmen* (1986–1987) covered similar territory via its society of dysfunctional superheroes (Dr. Manhattan, Rorschach, Nite Owl, and others). Dark Horse's mid-1990s series *Catalyst: Agents of Change* chronicled the demands placed upon a superteam (Grace, Titan, Rebel, Mecha, and others) who took it upon themselves to manage the utopian Golden City.

Then there was the New Guardians, a group of dissimilar characters who arrived in the DC universe after *Millennium,* a 1988 crossover threaded throughout most of DC's superhero titles. Their agenda was to propagate their unique genetic strains, but with an odd cast containing Harbinger, Ram, Floro, and the flamboyantly gay stereotype Extraño, readers rejected the series and it died after twelve issues.

Other superteams have come and gone, and some that have gone will surely be back. From the original concept of an assemblage of costumed favorites to the more contemporary interpretation of argumentative rebels, the superteam will continue to exist as long as superheroes do. —*ME*

Supervehicles

"Chicks love the car," observed the Dark Knight (Val Kilmer) in director Joel Schumacher's *Batman Forever* (1995). Guys do, too: For decades, the Batmobile has won the race to be the premier superhero vehicle.

After tooling around Gotham City's mean streets for two years in a variety of unidentifiable autos, in 1941 DC Comics' Batman drove his first stylized Batmobile, a steel-reinforced roadster with a bathead-shaped battering ram, batwinged tail fin, and bulletproof windows. In 1950, the car was lengthened into a sedan with a bubble top, spotlight, and interior crime lab, and got plenty of mileage until the mid-1960s when Batman and Robin traded it in for an open-topped sports car with dual batwinged fins and a batmask hood insignia. The most recognizable version of the Batmobile careened onto television in the campy *Batman* live-action show (1966–1968). Car customizer George Barris converted a 1957 Ford Futura into a batfinned hot rod with mag wheels and orange racing stripes, equipped with a rear parachute for quick stops, a dashboard radar, and a beeping Batphone to police Commissioner Gordon—all clearly labeled. Multiple Batmobiles were created for the program, but the unwieldy vehicles proved awkward to handle. Stunt driver Victor Paul remarked, "That thing was a deathtrap.... The steering would break on it." Maneuvering difficulties aside, the TV Batmobile was a smash, and replicas—from tiny diecasts to plastic model kits to kid-sized pedal cars—were (and still are) popular items. To this day, Barris' Batmobiles tour the United States in auto shows and at comics conventions. In the comics, with each passing decade, Batman has swapped his Batmobile for a newer model: a sports coupe in the 1970s, a drag racer in the 1980s, and a heavily armored rolling arsenal beginning in the late 1980s, inspired by another Barris custom, for director Tim Burton's *Batman* (1989).

The Batmobile is only one vehicle in the expansive Batcave: Batman and Robin have taken wing in the Batplane (which has also undergone many transformations, including the Batwing, in the 1989 *Batman* movie), Batcopter, Batgyro, Whirly-Bat, Bat-Glider, Bat-Missile, and even the Flying Batcave; ridden the waves in the Batboat and Bat-Sub (a.k.a. the Batmarine); and avoided traffic jams in the Batcycle (with a sidecar for the Boy Wonder) and the Bat-humvee! Robin tried rocket-propelled roller skates in 1941 before eventually hopping onto a motorcycle of his own, a mode of transit he maintains in his identity of Nightwing.

Not to be outdone, Bat-foes Joker and Catwoman have sped around Gotham in their own villainous vehicles, the Jokermobile and Kitty Car, and early in their careers, Green Arrow and Speedy cruised the highways and skyways in their golden Arrow Car and Arrow Plane. Ideal Toys' Captain Action, who appeared in his own DC Comics series (1968–1969), zoomed over land and sea in his missile-launching Silver Streak, but the Spy Smasher, a Golden Age great, one-upped the Captain with his Gyrosub: plane, helicopter, speedboat, and submarine, all in one vehicle! The Green Hornet and his sidekick (and chauffeur) Kato patrolled the streets in a sleek sedan dubbed the Black Beauty. Loaded with crime-crushing devices ranging from a surveillance camera to a steel-piercing laser, the Black Beauty was a hit in television's *The Green Hornet* (1966–1967); customized by Dean Jeffries from a 1966 Chrysler Imperial Crown, this supervehicle was profitably merchandised. Even Superman, comics' foremost flying hero, was bitten by the car bug: He took his aerodynamic Supermobile, complete with lead lining for kryptonite protection and retractable giant fists, for several spins in his

1970s comics. Meanwhile, Superman's pal Jimmy Olsen and his young allies the Newsboy Legion rocketed about in a souped-up supercar called the Whiz Wagon, in a series of 1970s comics stories written and illustrated by Jack Kirby. Aquaman, DC Comics' king of the seven seas, usually swam the ocean depths (or hopped a ride from an equestrian-sized seahorse or another of his undersea friends), but once on TV's *Super Friends* he used an Aquasled; his underwater counterpart at Marvel, Namor the Sub-Mariner, commanded his Imperial Flagship to navigate the seas.

Since most of Marvel Comics' superheroes reside in the dense urban environs of New York City, few drive vehicles. Look up, however, and you may see the Fantastic Four's sky-soaring Fantasti-car, or Nick Fury, Agent of S.H.I.E.L.D.'s airborne automobile called the Hovercar. Fury's organization of super-cops also uses a flying headquarters dubbed the Helicarrier, loaded with myriad countermeasures against psionic and telekinetic attacks. Down below, the Punisher seeks human vermin in his shatterproof battle van, and the web-slinging Spider-Man once grabbed the keys to a dune buggy called the Spider-Mobile for a brief ride in the 1970s. Marvel's eerie Ghost Rider prowls the night streets on a motorcycle (with flaming tires!), and he's not alone: DC's Huntress, Black Canary, Wildcat, and cowboy crusader Vigilante are also bikers. (In fact, the Vigilante's cycle has a unique gyro system that allows it to remain stable no matter how the rider leans, and it packs destructive missiles that are activated by a "trigger-mech" in the handgrips.) On the *Batman* television show, Batgirl (Yvonne Craig) puttered about on a purple cycle adorned with lace and a big yellow bow (born to be *mild?*)!

While virtually every superteam from the X-Men to the Legion of Super-Heroes owns a stealth jet or space cruiser, some heroes use even more extraordinary means to travel. Metron, the dimension-crossing couch potato of DC's New Gods, traverses the final frontier in his Mobius Chair, while Marvel's "sentinel of the spaceways," the Silver Surfer, hangs ten on his cosmic surfboard. DC's resident spaceman, Adam Strange, and writer/artist Dave Stevens' Rocketeer, use jetpacks to fly into action. Wonder Woman's invisible plane is the most unusual of all superhero vehicles. Even though her jet is transparent (perceptible to the reader's eye in outline form), Wonder Woman herself is not—the *seated* Amazonian Princess is clearly visible each time she pilots her plane!

With the technological advances of the late twentieth and early twenty-first centuries, sleek, computerized vehicles have rolled out of the exclusive domain of superhero mythology and into the real world: On-board mapping systems, voice-automated instructions, and even televisions with DVDs have become common features in the "family car." As a result, the supervehicle of the comics is no longer the awe-inspiring novelty it was during the Golden (1938–1954) and Silver (1956–1969) Ages of comics. —*ME*

Supervillains

At the advent of comics' Golden Age (1938–1954), readers were dazzled by the audacious exploits and flashy ensembles of the first wave of superheroes. Very quickly, however, the novelty of these men and women of steel became endangered from battles with generic gunmen and mouthy mobsters, menaces borrowed from the pages of newspapers of the day. Comic-book editors, writers, and artists were challenged to create super*villains* against whom their heroes could maintain their mythic status.

MEDIA INSPIRATIONS

Some comics creators looked to the movies for inspiration. Mad scientists, a staple of popular cinema of the 1930s, soon unleashed their diabolical machinations against many of the first superheroes. Dr. Death, a run-of-the-mill evil genius, posed a minor threat to Batman, but Professor Hugo Strange proved a deadlier menace: He terrorized the hero's home of Gotham City with mutated monsters and noxious gas. The first two major foes to challenge Superman boasted tremendous intellects: the Ultra-Humanite, who could transfer his mind into other bodies; and Lex Luthor, a mastermind who took on Superman with a destructive arsenal and became so popular with readers that he has endured to this day. Captain Marvel, the "World's Mightiest Mortal" of Fawcett (and later DC) Comics fame, was habitually harassed by the dastardly Dr. Sivana. Similarly, Professor Torture bedeviled the Angel (no relation to the popular X-Men member), Dr. Psycho confronted Wonder Woman, the Thinker challenged the Flash, Brainwave tried to outsmart the Justice Society of America, Dr. Riddle took on Bulletman and Bulletgirl, and Mr. Who used his "Z solution" to annoy Dr. Fate. Many of these characters apparently patronized the same tailor, given their preference for lab coats.

Movie monsters scared up big box office receipts during this era, and inspired ghoulish supervillains in comic books. In one of his earliest tales, Batman fought—and killed!—vampires, then later met Clayface, a serial killer patterned after horror star Boris Karloff, and Two-Face, a grotesquely scarred Jekyll-Hyde gangster. The undead Solomon Grundy lumbered out of the swamps to become a foe of Green Lantern; Captain America and Bucky battled the "walking dead" called the Hollow Men; and the serpentine saboteur Cobra put the squeeze on Magno, the Magnetic Man.

Another early supervillain trend—costumed criminals—netted mixed results. Bad guys with colorful garb did not always make enduring adversaries: Doll Man's pint-sized pest Tom Thumb and Bulletman's nemesis the Black Rodent (whose uniform included a rat's-head mask and a tail) are remembered today only by the most dedicated historians. Superman's first enemy to don a disguise, the Archer, also failed to strike a bull's eye with readers. Most of the menacing masqueraders added to Batman's rogues' gallery, however, combined compelling modus operandi with garish attire to imprint themselves upon comics readers: The ghastly, grinning Joker's shock of green hair and pasty-white face frightened fans, as did his penchant for inducing a smile upon murdered victims; the fetching Catwoman's sexy purple gown and flowing ebon locks belied her wicked fluency with her "cat-o'-nine-tails" whip; and the pillaging Penguin's portly waddle made him look comical, but his deadly bumbershoots were no laughing matter.

THE EVIL THAT MEN DO

World War II produced real-life "supervillains" who shocked the world. Despicable acts of bloodshed, torture, and conquest perpetrated by the Axis powers filled the papers and newsreels, proving too sinisterly seductive for the comics to ignore. In the early 1940s, German and Japanese soldiers, spies, and saboteurs were regularly depicted as comic-book menaces: Superman tackled Adolf Hitler and Joseph Stalin in a 1940 *Look* magazine supplement, and Marvel's own Captain America, who bowed in March 1941, owes his very origin to the advent of Nazi spies. Once the December 1941 bombing of Pearl Harbor drew the United States into this global conflict, the anti-Axis sentiment became even more overt. Actual comic-book supervillains swathed in Swastika cloth set their diabolical sights on superheroes: The Red Skull became Captain America's principal adversary; Captain Marvel Jr. squared off against Captain Nazi; MLJ Publications' Steel Sterling battled Baron Gestapo, and its dark hero the Hangman was the sworn enemy of Captain Swastika; and a cretin called Satan, decked out in a robe decorated with a Swastika, fought Harvey Comics' Spirit of 76. Japanese villain Captain Nippon took on Captain Marvel Jr.; the yellow-skinned, fang-toothed Claw, an "Oriental" supremacist who could grow to humongous proportions, fought the Golden Age Daredevil (not to be confused with the Marvel Comics hero of the same name); and the Shield and his sidekick Dusty wrangled with the heinous Hun. Hitler himself appeared regularly in comics and on comics covers of the era, including Gleason Publications' 1941 classic, *Daredevil Battles Hitler* #1.

Golden Age superhero comics did not exclusively rely upon the Axis threat for villainous fodder, however: Each publisher consistently churned out a bevy of bad guys (and gals) to fight their superheroes. Noteworthy no-goodniks of the era include Captain Marvel's (and the Marvel Family's) foe Mr. Mind (a brainy worm who wore thick-lensed eyeglasses), the robotic Mr. Atom, the savage Ibac, and the problematic Monster Society of Evil (a villainous superteam led by Mr. Mind); Green Lantern's enemies the Icicle, the Gambler, the Sportsman, the Huntress, and the Harlequin; the Shark, who swam into the pages of *Amazing-Man Comics;* Dr. Fate's mystical menace Wotan; and the Riddler, Tweedledee and Tweedledum, the Mad Hatter, and the Scarecrow, yet more hazardous threats to Batman and Robin.

Other memorable Golden Age supervillains include the Hangman's foe, the Executioner (who wielded an icepick as an artificial hand); Flash rogues Star Sapphire, the Fiddler, and Thorn; Magno, the Magnetic Man's pesky Clown; the villainous Valkyrie, who was a thorn in Airboy's side; the armored God of War Mars and the spotted pest the Cheetah, who made life tough for Wonder Woman; the sentient ventriloquist's puppet called the Dummy, arch foe of DC Comics' Western superhero the Vigilante; Hawkman's dastardly dapper nemesis the Gentleman Ghost; Superman's headaches the Puzzler, the Prankster, the Toyman, and Mr. Mxyztplk (later Mr. Myyzptlk); the cloudy criminal called the Mist, who mystified Starman; a different villain calling himself the Mist, who clashed with MLJ's Black Hood, as did Panther Man, the Skull, and the Crow; and a handful of enemies of DC Comics' Justice Society of America—Vandal Savage, Per Degaton, the Psycho-Pirate, and the evil assemblage the Injustice Gang of the World. Most of these supervillains were content to use their powers or weapons to plunder, or just to irritate their enemies, but a few—including Mars, Vandal Savage, and the Claw—were true tyrants, bent on domination.

Once the most popular superheroes jumped from comic books to other media, their rogues usually failed to accompany them. Sivana was nowhere to be seen in the movie serial *The Adventures of Captain Marvel* (1941), nor did the Red Skull join his foe in *Captain America* (1944). Likewise, the Man of Steel's enemies from the comics were absent from the seventeen *Superman* animated theatrical shorts produced by the Fleischer Studios (1941–1943), but Luthor appeared on screen in the live-action serial *Atom Man vs. Superman* (1950). In their two movie serials, Batman and Robin tangled with villains specially tailored for the limited budgets of the medium, but in their daily and Sunday newspaper strips, arch-nemeses Joker, Penguin, and Catwoman were menacing mainstays.

POSTWAR VILLAINS

While World War II was a boon for superhero comics, the war's conclusion proved disastrous for the genre, and most superheroes and supervillains were systematically retired. For the handful of superheroes who remained in print, their adversaries continued to reflect the headlines of contemporary newspapers. Readers predisposed toward believing the Roswell alien-landing story appreciated Captain Midnight's 1947 struggles with Jagga the Space Raider and Xog the Evil Lord of Saturn; in 1948 the Fighting Yank clobbered Ku Klux Klan–like robed foes; and the Fighting American, one of the few superheroes (albeit a parody of the medium) to premiere in the 1950s, fought Communist adversaries like Poison Ivan and Hotsky Trotsky.

By the mid-1950s, almost all superheroes had hung up their capes, save DC's Superman, Batman, and Wonder Woman, who tangled with alien invaders, a handful of watered-down versions of their Golden Age foes, and a few new additions to their rosters of enemies—Angle Man took on Wonder Woman, and a new, morphing Clayface mucked up Batman's life, as did minor-league menaces Doctor Double-X, Calendar Man, and Signalman. When the

Man of Steel flew onto the small screen in the live-action syndicated television series *The Adventures of Superman* (1953–1957), he corralled hoodlums and petty thieves, with nary a supervillain in sight.

One major supervillain did surface to plague comic-book superheroes in the 1950s: Dr. Fredric Wertham. This well-intentioned, real-life psychiatrist linked juvenile delinquency to comics reading in his book *Seduction of the Innocent* (1954), inciting U.S. Senate hearings that inflicted upon the industry a censorship board (the Comics Code Authority, or CCA). The few post-code supervillains that still appeared in print were nonthreatening—and boring.

DC COMICS SUPERVILLAINS OF THE SILVER AGE (1956-1969)

The introduction of the all-new Flash in DC Comics' *Showcase* #4 (1956) heralded a superhero comeback. The Flash over time garnered one of the most imaginative rogues' galleries in comics, felons each employing technological gadgets or scientific weapons to take on the Fastest Man Alive: The Mirror Master teleported and created illusions with trick mirrors, Heat Wave melted the pavement under the Flash's feet with his heat ray, Captain Cold put the Flash on ice with his freeze gun, and the Weather Wizard manipulated blizzards and winds with his weather wand. Other Flash foes of the era include Captain Boomerang, the Top, the Trickster, Pied Piper, Abra Kadabra, Professor Zoom (a.k.a. the Reverse-Flash), Dr. Alchemy (a baddie who sometimes appeared in a different guise, as Mr. Element), and the telepathic, super-intelligent simian, Gorilla Grodd.

Green Lantern followed the Flash with his *Showcase* #22 (1959) reinvention, and likewise attracted science-spawned adversaries: Sinestro, Doctor Polaris, the Shark, Sonar, the Black Hand, Hector Hammond, the Tattooed Man, and a new Star Sapphire (who happened to be the hero's girlfriend under her pink mask). DC continued to rework its Golden Age heroes into Silver Age incarnations, and added ultramodern (for the time) menaces to the mix: The Atom fought Chronos and Plant-Master; the Shadow Thief challenged Hawkman; Ocean Master, Black Manta, and the Fisherman splashed into the pages of *Aquaman;* and the Justice League of America was plagued by Starro the Conqueror, the Queen Bee, Amazo, Felix Faust, Doctor Light, Doctor Destiny, Despero, the Key, the Shaggy Man, and Kanjar Ro. Eclipso, deemed hero and villain in one man, temporarily became the star of the anthology series *House of Secrets*. The Teen Titans tumbled with the tousle-haired Mad Mod, whose Carnaby Street fashions foreshadowed the coming of the movies' Austin Powers; and Chemo, a giant that spewed toxic chemicals, was a recurring threat to the robot heroes the Metal Men.

Science-based menaces were also introduced into the Superman comics, including the android Brainiac, who used his reducing ray to shrink and collect cities from across the universe; Titano the Super-Ape, a King Kong pastiche, who paralyzed Superman with kryptonite vision; Metallo, the man with the robotic body powered by a kryptonite heart; Bizarro, a superpowerful but dimwitted duplicate of the Man of Steel; the multipowered Composite Superman, who nearly eliminated the Man of Steel *and* Batman; and the Parasite, who could siphon Superman's energy. The Legion of Super-Heroes—the team of super-teenagers living one thousand years in the future—also developed an impressively insidious roster of enemies including Computo, Doctor Regulus, the Fatal Five, the Time Trapper, Mordru the Merciless, Universo, and the Legion's dishonorable *doppelgängers,* the Legion of Super-Villains (Cosmic King, Saturn Queen, and Lightning Lord).

While Batman encountered a few science-based opponents—like the chilling Mr. Freeze (called Mr. Zero in his initial 1959 appearance), the dizzying Spellbinder, and the aforementioned Composite Superman—most of his new foes emerging during the Silver Age were more down to earth: The sultry Poison Ivy seduced Batman and Robin into conflict, the hulking Blockbuster's rage could only be quelled by a glimpse of the face of Bruce Wayne (Batman's alter ego), and Batman discovered the existence of a vast international crime network called the League of Assassins. The Caped Crusader's rogues' gallery became television stars in the live-action *Batman* (1966–1968), which featured Hollywood's hottest (and a few has-beens) as villainous guest stars. Some examples: Cesar Romero as the Joker, Burgess Meredith as the Penguin, Frank Gorshin (temporarily replaced by John Astin) as the Riddler, Vincent Price as Egghead, Roddy McDowell as the Bookworm, Milton Berle as Louie the Lilac, and Victor Buono as King Tut. On Saturday morning TV, Brainiac, Luthor, Mr. Mxyzptlk, and the Prankster fought Superman on his cartoon show, while, conversely, most of the other animated episodes featuring DC superheroes pitted them against stereotyped extraterrestrials.

DC's supervillains of the Silver Age shared more in common than flamboyant costumes and scientific weaponry. Most were motivated by greed, and their rivalry with their superheroes was a byproduct of their thievery. Few DC villains of this era could be categorized as inherently evil. Exceptions include Grodd, who held no regard for humans, and Luthor, whose hatred of Superman had intensified to such a boiling point that he was no longer content with matching minds with the Man of Steel; He wanted Superman dead.

MARVEL COMICS SUPERVILLAINS OF THE SILVER AGE

Marvel Comics approached both superheroes and supervillains differently from competitor DC. Marvel's heroes possessed traits previously considered anti-heroic, such as selfishness and narcissism, and its villains went even further, many being despicable despots or egomaniacal enslavers.

The Fantastic Four (FF), the originators of the Marvel universe, protected New York City from an

Silver Surfer and the evil Galactus in the animated show *The Silver Surfer.*

onslaught of menaces including the hideous subterranean dictator called the Mole Man; Super-Skrull, an alien commanding each of the FF's abilities; and the emotion-manipulating Hate Monger; plus Blastarr, Diablo, Dragon Man, Psycho-Man, the Molecule Man, Puppet Master, and Annihilus. The FF's most challenging adversaries were Galactus, a skyscraper-sized alien who consumed the lifeforce of planets, and Doctor Doom, the collegiate rival of the FF's leader Reed Richards (a.k.a. Mr. Fantastic), whose machinations nearly toppled the Four time and time again. Even the Sub-Mariner, Marvel's popular anti-hero from the Golden Age, resurfaced as a villain in early *Fantastic Four* issues, although his

motivation for striking against humankind—retribution for surface dwellers' encroachment upon his undersea kingdom—made him a sympathetic foe.

Some Marvel menaces' names unambiguously conveyed a thirst for domination, or an evocation of terror: the Avengers' antagonists Kang the Conqueror and Ultron; the Incredible Hulk's bitter enemies the Leader, the Abomination, and the Absorbing Man; Captain America's foe Baron Zemo; the armored adversaries of Iron Man, the Titanium Man and the Crimson Dynamo, plus the insidious instigator the Mandarin; the god of thunder Thor's powerful enemies the High Evolutionary, Grey Gargoyle, and

Ulik; and Dormammu and Baron Mordo, the sinister sorcerers casting evil spells on the Master of the Mystic Arts, Doctor Strange. The Silver Surfer battled the lord of the underworld, Mephisto, and when not warring against pummeling powerhouses, Thor matched wits with his evil half-brother Loki. Daredevil's rogues' gallery lacked the omnipotence of some of Marvel's other 1960s villains, but still, the Beetle, the Owl, the Stilt-Man, and the Gladiator were no pushovers (actually, pushing over the Stilt-Man *was* one way to defeat him …).

Marvel's X-Men, a society representing humankind's next evolutionary step, waged a civil war with evil mutants like Magneto, the Juggernaut, the Blob, the Toad, and Sauron. Spider-Man, Marvel's oft-misunderstood superhero, was regularly branded a bad guy by the media and police, while targeted by supervillains like Kraven the Hunter, the Kingpin, the Scorpion, the Shocker, Electro, the Vulture, the Lizard, the Sandman, the Rhino, and Mysterio. Spidey's most problematic Silver Age villains, the sneering Green Goblin, who sailed over the New York cityscape on his goblin glider, and the mechanical-armed madman Doctor Octopus (a.k.a. "Doc Ock"), stood out among this pernicious pack. The Hulk, Marvel's monstrous superhero, was a frequent combatant of most of Marvel's heroes, particularly the Fantastic Four's Thing.

In the mid- to late 1960s, many of Marvel's characters were translated to television cartoons, and their villains joined them, wreaking terror on the tube. These translations were truly literal in the case of TV's *Marvel Super Heroes* (1966–1968) and *Fantastic Four* (1967–1970), with the former's limited-animation episodes being shot directly from the Marvel comics and the latter's scripts closely based on them.

OTHER SILVER AGE SUPERVILLAINS

The popularity of superheroes during the 1960s triggered an upsurge of costumed crime fighters from a variety of comic-book publishers and television producers. Moltar, Zorak, the Black Widow, and Brak were among the foes of the Saturday-morning TV superhero Space Ghost, and Captain Action of Ideal Toys (and DC Comics) fame clashed with the otherworldly scientist Dr. Evil. While Charlton Comics' "Action Heroes" were inventive alternatives to DC and Marvel superheroes, their supervillains ranged from unique (the Madmen, who battled the Blue Beetle, plus the Ghost, Punch and Jewelee, and Dr. Spectro, foes of Captain Atom) to derivative (Peacemaker's flaming foe Mr. Blaze, Judomaster's agile adversary the Acrobat, and Son of Vulcan's egotistical enemy King Midas).

DARKSEID USHERS IN A NEW BREED OF EVIL

Supervillains became bolder, blacker, and bleaker in the 1970s. So did superheroes. The anti-hero—the hero with personality flaws, or with questionable motivations—was popularized during the decade, in response to a youth culture desensitized over an unpopular war, civil unrest, and dishonest politicians.

In 1970, Jack Kirby, the artist for many of Marvel's most popular characters of the 1960s, jumped ship to DC, producing four interlocking "Fourth World" titles that shared one central villain: Darkseid (pronounced "Dark-side"), a genocidal demigod who subjugated the dismal planet Apokolips. Darkseid craved the elusive Anti-Life Equation, and with malevolent minions like his brutish offspring Kalibak, the duplicitous Desaad, and the sadistic Granny Goodness, Darkseid brought a new depth to DC villainy. Had Kirby introduced Darkseid into the Marvel universe, the villain's impact may have been weakened by the publisher's other omnipotent warlords. But at DC, Darkseid was truly unique, and singularly vile. His machinations ultimately spread beyond Kirby's "Fourth World," and over the decades he has challenged everyone from Superman to the Legion of Super-Heroes.

Another daringly different DC villain that originated in the early 1970s was Batman's adversary, the immortal Ra's al Ghul, an international terrorist spreading global chaos long before anyone in the real world had heard of Osama bin Laden. Also in the 1970s, one of Batman's most enduring enemies, the Joker, reverted from his mischievous Clown Prince of Crime persona to his original murderous ways, leaving grinning corpses in his wake. The Joker became so popular during the decade that he was awarded his own magazine, albeit one in which restrictions imposed by the CCA censorship board made his portrayal more comical than homicidal.

Another chilling Batman foe to debut during the 1970s was Man-Bat, a chemically mutated scientist who sprouted powerful batwings. The CCA eased its limitations that formerly prohibited the depiction of the undead in comics, and monster villains (and some heroes) soon crept forth. Morbius, the Living Vampire and Man-Wolf fought Spider-Man, and Batman tangled with the muck-monster Swamp Thing.

Urban violence intensified in the real world of the 1970s, and comics supervillains reflected that trend. The street smart Hero for Hire, Luke Cage (later called Powerman), got shafted by superpowered enforcers Diamondback, Mace, Lionfang, and Big Ben; hired gun Deadshot took aim at Batman; and by decade's end, Bullseye was hired by the Kingpin to take down Daredevil. The most famous assassin of the decade, Marvel's Punisher, began his career in 1974 as a Spider-Man villain, then segued into his own solo adventures, as well as two live-action movies (in 1989 and 2004). The bestial Wolverine, added to a revamped version of the X-Men in 1974, so embodied violent anti-heroics that the X-Men's villains grew more savage in response, like the feral Sabretooth (who, for the record, first surfaced in conflict with the martial-arts superhero Iron Fist). Even the most traditional of superheroes, Superman, witnessed a darkening of some of his rogues' gallery during the 1970s: Luthor amped himself in battle armor, the killer cowboy called Terra-Man flew (on a winged horse!) into Metropolis to take down the Man of Steel, and the Atomic Skull and the Sand-Superman made life difficult for the hero.

Comic-book villains discovered that there was safety in numbers during the 1970s: Doctor Doom and Sub-Mariner joined forces in *Super-Villain Team-Up* (1975–1980), and DC combined Captain Cold, Sinestro, Grodd, and other scalawags in its *Secret Society of Super-Villains* series (1976–1978). On television, more DC villains (Luthor, Grodd, Black Manta, the Scarecrow, and others) united as the Legion of Doom in the animated *Challenge of the Super Friends* (1978–1979) and the Riddler, Mordru, Dr. Sivana, and several other DC bad guys were brought to life—and lampooned—by comedians in two campy 1979 live-action *Legends of the Super-Heroes* TV specials. However, in the dramatic, primetime adaptations of superheroes airing during the 1970s—ABC's *Wonder Woman* and CBS's *The Incredible Hulk* and *The Amazing Spider-Man*—none of the heroes' supervillains appeared.

UPPING THE ANTE

Starting in the 1980s and continuing into the 2000s, real-world street gangstas, serial killers, and international terrorists have made the comic book's costumed bank robber of yesterday seem ludicrous by comparison. The fictional world of superheroes has darkened, and supervillains have slipped even further into evil and depravity.

Old-time menaces have become more contemptible—Lex Luthor was reinvented into an egomaniacal corporate executive who executed a power play to the U.S. presidency; the Joker crippled Batgirl and massacred the second Robin the Boy Wonder in 1988, then killed Gotham City police Commissioner Gordon's wife in 1999; and readers were shocked by the intensity of Doctor Doom's hatred of Reed Richards when Doom disfigured the hero's face in 2003—and newer villains accomplished previously unthinkable acts: Doomsday beat Superman to death in 1992 (although he rose from the dead), and Bane broke Batman's back in 1993.

Even the very names of supervillains introduced since the 1980s invoke a more dystopian worldview.

Examples include Typhoid Mary and Shotgun, foes of Daredevil; Spider-Man rogues Venom (a talking Venom action figure actually spoke, "I want to eat your brains!"), Carnage, Carrion, and Hobgoblin; X-Men enemies Dark Phoenix (formerly founding team member Marvel Girl), Stryfe, X-Cutioner, Mr. Sinister, Deadpool, and Apocalypse; Fatality, killer of inter-galactic Green Lanterns; Brother Blood, who has ter-rorized the Teen Titans and the Outsiders; Justice League menaces Mageddon (a.k.a. the Primordial Annihilator), Neron, and Soultaker; Spawn's nemesis the Violator; Superman rogues Dominus, Imperiex, Massacre, and Kancer; and Batman villains Killer Croc, Anarky, Brutale, and Cain.

Many of these villains, particularly the rogues' galleries of superstars Spider-Man, Batman, the X-Men, Superman, and the Justice League, have joined their adversaries on television and in the movies. Blockbuster superhero films, however, tend to spice their villains with camp humor—as one of many exam-ples, consider Jim Carrey's over-the-top take on the Riddler in director Joel Schumacher's *Batman Forever* (1995). Willem Dafoe's unsettling interpretation of the Green Goblin in Sam Raimi's *Spider-Man* (2002), how-ever, signaled the arrival of sinister supervillains in Hollywood, a dark trend that has continued with Nick Nolte's abusive David Banner in *The Hulk* (2003).

Superheroes, the contemporary counterparts of the ancient gods, traditionally represented the lofty ideals to which humankind aspired. As society slipped more into violence, so did its heroes. Consequently, supervillains have continued their descent into the darkest recesses of the human soul, with little hope for rehabilitation. But such is villainy. As the editors of Marvel's trade paperback *Bring Back the Bad Guys* (1998) pondered, "What is good without evil?" *—ME*

Superweapons

Not every superhero is faster than a speeding bullet or able to leap tall buildings in a single bound. That's when superweapons become a necessity.

Since his first mission in Gotham City's violent streets in *Detective Comics* #27 (May 1939), DC Comics' Batman has cornered the superweapons market with an array of crime-crushing gadgets that would make 007's "Q" green with envy. The Dark Knight's utility belt houses his miniaturized line of defense: A retractable Batrope, a grappling hook, grenades, smoke and gas capsules, a penlight, an acetylene torch, a respirator, and a first-aid kit are just some of the weapons he keeps close to the hip. Batman is proficient with his bat-styled boomerang—his Batarang—which he flings with expert accuracy, as well as his Batblades, skin-piercing, batwinged projectiles.

Belts also have significance to other super-heroes: Batman's ally Robin the Boy Wonder carries a similar arsenal in his own utility belt, Hanna-Bar-bera's Space Ghost vanishes by pressing a button on his Invisibelt, and Dynamo of the T.H.U.N.D.E.R. Agents uses his belt to become supercharged. DC's 1970s superstar the Thorn stored thorns of every conceivable dimension in her belt—blackout thorns, painful dart thorns, flare thorns, and electric-shock "thistle stingers"—in addition to her whip, coiled up and ready to release on a moment's notice. The orig-inal Robin (Dick Grayson), now called Nightwing, has retired his utility belt for glove gauntlets, loaded with gizmos not unlike Batman's, including customized Batarangs, gas pellets, and "de-cel" jumplines. Nightwing also wields unbreakable "Escrima sticks" with unnerving speed and accuracy. His mask's eye-pieces are equipped with night-vision lenses, as are Batman's and the current Robin's.

Wristbands or gauntlets are fashionable weapons among superheroes. After science student Peter Parker gained the ability to crawl up walls like an insect, he created wrist-mounted shooters to secrete a thin webline for swinging from building to building as the amazing Spider-Man (though in director Sam Raimi's blockbuster *Spider-Man* [2002], Parker gains the organic ability to shoot webs). Several other Marvel Comics superheroes bond with bands: The Wasp and Yellowjacket use their wristbands to fire electrical stings, the Black Widow discharges debilitating "Widow's Bite" blasts from her gauntlets, and the warrior from the planet Kree, Mar-Vell (a.k.a. Captain Marvel), has cosmically imbued Mega Bands. Space Ghost fires a variety of blasts—including a beam that levitates objects—from his power bands. The most famous wrist gear in the superhero world is worn by Wonder Woman: She deflects oncoming bullets with her bracelets—and forces captives to speak the truth with her other superweapon, her magic lasso. Top Cow Comics' Witchblade became a superheroine once she donned an enchanted steel glove that, like Wonder Woman's bracelets, repels bullets. Witchblade's gauntlet can do much more, however: It morphs into a variety of deadly edged blades and commands unusual supernatural properties.

When fighting crime with gadgetry in the world of Marvel Comics, nobody does it better than Nick Fury, Agent of S.H.I.E.L.D. Fury fronts this high-tech police force with a sophisticated arsenal including magnetic cuff links capable of supporting a human's weight, explosive cigars, bulletproof and flame-retardant clothing, shirt buttons that are secretly oxygen pellets, an eyepatch that doubles as a slingshot, and an expansive array of firearms shooting everything from traditional bullets to concussive blasts.

Industrialist Tony Stark covers his entire body with one of the most awesome superweapons in the Marvel universe: the high-tech armor that empowers him as the Invincible Iron Man, placing flight, repulsor blasters, a uni-beam, and super-strength at his command (other armored heroes include Valiant's X-O Manowar, Dark Horse's Mecha, Marvel's War Machine and Future Comics' Metallix). Cyborg of the Teen Titans and Marvel's cybernetic supersoldier Deathlok take the armor concept a dramatic leap further: Both are part-man, part machine. Cyborg, in fact, has interchangeable hands that perform a variety of functions, including the emission of sonic discharges. On a smaller scale, the Avenger Ant-Man's antennae-helmet makes ants do his bidding.

Captain America, Marvel's stalwart patriot, uses his mighty red, white, and blue shield, forged of shatterproof vibranium, to deflect incoming blasts. Cap also hurls his shield to plow through adversaries, and often suckers them by ricocheting the shield in sneak attacks. Even more durable than vibranium is the synthetic metal adamantium, of which the X-Men's Wolverine's retractable claws and entire skeleton are made. His claws can slice through virtually any object. His acquisition of this superweapon did not come easy: Wolverine's bones were replaced with adamantium in an agonizing surgical process. Sarge Steel, a hard-boiled crime crusher who started his career at Charlton Comics in the 1960s before joining the DC universe in the 1980s, has a metal hand that packs quite a punch.

The mighty Thor, Marvel's god of thunder, wields the hammer Mjolnir. The resilient hammer, made of the mystical metal uru, can only be lifted by one deemed worthy by Thor's father, Odin, king of the Norse gods. Thor uses Mjolnir to fly, and to smash objects and enemies. Superman's ally Steel hoists a sledgehammer in his street-level crime-busting in Metropolis. Several members of DC's Justice Society of America have employed a "cosmic rod" in their crime-fighting endeavors: In the 1940s, the original Starman created his "gravity-rod" to siphon stellar radiation to allow him to fly and emit powerful blasts. He later renamed the device the cosmic rod and in the 1970s passed it down to the Star-Spangled Kid. When the 1990s Starman arose to carry on the astral tradition, he did so with a similar superweapon, a cosmic staff, which in the 2000s was inherited by Stargirl. The Master of the Mystic Arts, Doctor Strange, exploits the arcane properties of his all-seeing Eye of Agamotto to locate supernatural threats lurking within the Marvel universe. Blind hero Daredevil enlists the aid of his billy club: Guided by his uncanny radar sense, Daredevil tosses his club at foes and swings from rooftops on its retractable line.

Perhaps the most legendary—and omnipotent—superweapon is DC Comics' Green Lantern's power ring. Alan Scott, the Golden Age (1938–1954) Green Lantern (GL), carved his ring from a meteor and used it to fire mystical energy bolts. A dying alien named Abin Sur gave fearless test pilot Hal Jordan his power ring, the weapon of the intergalactic peacekeeping force, the Green Lantern Corps. As the Silver Age (1956–1969) GL, Jordan used his ring to vanquish global and space-faring threats. Green Lantern reservists Guy Gardner and John Stewart have also worn power rings, and the 2000s ring bearer and newest GL is Kyle Rayner. A Green Lantern's power ring's abilities are nearly limitless, its only boundaries being the wearer's imagination and (up to Rayner's tenure, at least) the ring's sole weakness, ineffectiveness against any yellow object. GL's will power enables him to use the ring to create anything, from a giant green fist to a glowing emerald spacecraft. The power ring's energy source is a battery—shaped like a green lantern—and the ring requires recharging after twenty-four hours.

Expert marksmen Green Arrow (GA), his son Connor Hawke (also known as Green Arrow), and the first GA's former sidekick Speedy (now called Arsenal) all aim arrows from bows, as do Marvel's Hawkeye, DC's Amazon Artemis, and CrossGen Comics' Arwyn the Archer from the series *Sojourn*. Some of their arrows are electrical, explosive, or trick in some capacity (boxing-glove arrows were an old favorite of GA's). The Huntress pins gangsters with a crossbow. Another sureshot superhero is the X-Men mutant Gambit, who infuses biokinetic energy into inorganic objects, making anything he touches a deadly weapon—Gambit gets a charge out of throwing explosive playing cards.

Some superheroes' superweapons aren't super at all. Hawkman and Hawkgirl prefer ancient arms like maces, swords, and shields; the Golden Age's Shining Knight, one-time Avengers Swordsman and Black Knight, and Valkyrie of Marvel's Defenders have used a similar arsenal. Elektra brandishes three-pronged daggers called sai, and the Master of Kung Fu, Shang-Chi, backs up his

martial arts with nunchakus and throwing darts (as does the Green Hornet's ally Kato). The Teenage Mutant Ninja Turtles, those heroes in a half-shell, are also experts at swordplay. And watch out for Catwoman! This sultry streetfighter lashes out at her enemies with her cat-o'-nine-tails whip. The Western superhero the Vigilante, who fought crime during the 1940s and 1950s in DC Comics, often used a lariat to corral his foes.

Making the list of superheroes armed with the wackiest weapons are Harvey Comics' 1960s-era Spyman, with his "electro-robot" hand and his gun-belt filled with additional, screw-in fingers that accomplish amazing feats—from producing a smoke screen to creating a supersonic shock wave; undersea hero Pirana, who packs an undersea blowtorch neatly tucked away in a pocket; and Neal Adams' short-lived (1983) hero Skateman, a former roller derby athlete turned hero, who uses his roller skates as a weapon.

Finally, a horde of heroes new and old wield conventional firepower in battle. DC's Deathstroke the Terminator blasts (as well as slices) away at his foes, as does that *other* Terminator, the futuristic cyborg assassin from a franchise of live-action movies and Dark Horse comic books. Tomb Raider Lara Croft backs up her martial arts prowess with awesome aim as an expert sharpshooter. The vengeful Punisher unleashes his lethal war on crime with a bottomless munitions cache that his altruistic ally Spider-Man finds distasteful. Spidey would no doubt prefer the Green Hornet's or the Golden Age Sandman's firearms, meant to disarm, not destroy: Both use gas guns to knock out their foes (Sandman's former partner Sandy, called Sand as of the 2000s, carries on his mentor's tradition), and the Green Hornet's vibrating Hornet's Sting rips through steel. Still others rely solely on their respective superabilities, preferring not to use weapons of any sort: When you're pliable like Plastic Man, as fast as the Flash, as strong as the Hulk, or can burst into flame like the Human Torch, superweapons serve no purpose. —ME

Tank Girl

Reminiscent of the tough, super-mobile punk babe that became a staple in such science-fiction novels as Neal Stephenson's *Snow Crash* (1992), Tank Girl is the 1990s incarnation of the punkster tomboy superheroine. An Australian tank pilot turned outlaw, Tank Girl is the quintessential "bad grrrl." The tough-talking Generation X-er showcases a partly shaved head and a bad cigarette and beer habit, and is described succinctly by British comics historian Roger Sabin as an outcast "with a knack for gratuitous violence." In her adventures in the Australian outback, Tank Girl always seems to be looking for a fight, and is often aided by friends Jet Girl and Sub Girl, white-haired Aborigine Stevie, and her significant other, Booga, a half-human kangaroo. Her supervehicle of choice is a stolen tank, hence her moniker.

Tank Girl is the creation of UK comic-book artists Jamie Hewlett and Alan Martin. She first appeared in a 1990 issue of the British comic magazine *Deadline,* where she became an underground favorite, her stories reprinted in the United States by maverick comic-book publisher Dark Horse Comics. The U.S. comic-book publisher published two series of four books, *Tank Girl* (1991) and *Tank Girl 2* (1993). Though her position as a true superheroine is debatable, her cult status is not, and as Tank Girl grew in popularity—on both continents—she could be seen plastered on a variety of hipster merchandise, including T-shirts, skateboards, and upper right arms.

Directed by Rachel Talalay, the celluloid interpretation of the character, *Tank Girl,* hit the big screen in 1995. The futuristic live-action thriller starred Lori Petty in the title role, with Naomi Watts as Jet Girl, Ann Cusack as Sub Girl, and Malcolm McDowell as arch-villain Kesslee. A gang of half-human, half-kangaroo mutant warriors called the Rippers rounded out the cast. Described by reviewer Scott Rosenberg in the *San Francisco Examiner* as a film that "takes [the] militant feminism of the *Thelma & Louise* school and weds it to the punk nihilism of the *Mad* Max school," Tank Girl was dismissed by comics' true fan base as a superficial treatment of the heroine. Though it tanked at the box office, the film was adapted into a graphic novel by DC Comics, which then published two four-issue miniseries, *Tank Girl: The Odyssey* (June–August 1995, with art by Hewlett) and *Tank Girl: The Apocalypse* (October 1995–January 1996) under its adult-themed Vertigo imprint. —GM

Lori Petty as the hard-edged heroine in *Tank Girl.*

Team-ups and Crossovers

Superhero comic books, originally an American art form, epitomize escapist entertainment, but have, since their inception in the late 1930s, represented another American principle: capitalism. In June 1940 when Marvel Comics—then known as Timely—paired its two most popular characters in one story, the publisher succeeded in enthralling its audience while reaping huge profits.

THE FIRST SUPERHERO CROSSOVER

The superheroes were the Human Torch, the artificial human who could burst into flame, and the Sub-Mariner, the defiant Prince Namor from the ocean depths. This was a clash of elemental fury: Fire vs. Water! The Torch/Sub-Mariner meeting was brainstormed by Bill Everett, artist of *The Sub-Mariner,* and Carl Burgos, illustrator of Marvel's best-selling title, *The Human Torch,* to curry reader interest within a marketplace exponentially expanding with new superheroes. With writers John Compton and Hank Chapman, Everett and Burgos' epic was serialized in three consecutive issues of *Marvel Mystery Comics* (#8–#10). Namor demolished New York City landmarks in chapter one, building toward chapter two's 22-page slugfest and a cliffhanger ending, with the Torch trapped in a "translite tube," his flame extinguished. Readers anxiously returned the next month to see the combat end in a standstill, cleverly arranged by Marvel so as not to upset fans from either camp. With this momentous meeting of Namor and the Torch, the superhero crossover was born. MLJ Publications (later Archie

Comics) quickly copied Marvel's idea by having the Shield guest star with the Wizard in *Top-Notch Comics* #7 (1940).

THE FIRST SUPERTEAM

Competitor DC Comics took the concept to the next level in the winter of 1940 by introducing comics' first super*team* when the Justice Society of America (JSA) premiered in *All Star Comics* #3, combining the Flash, the Sandman, Hawkman, the Spectre, Hourman, the Atom, Dr. Fate, and Johnny Thunder (with more heroes signing on later) as a super-squad. Marvel countered in the summer of 1941 with *Young Allies,* starring a group of super*kids*: Bucky (Captain America's sidekick) and Toro (the Human Torch's partner), plus a pack of patriotic youths called the Sentinels of Liberty. *Young Allies* #1 also marked the historic first meeting between mentors Captain America and the Torch, who continued to appear in cameos throughout future issues. Lev Gleason Publications' *Daredevil Comics* #1 (not to be confused with the superhero from Marvel Comics) in July 1941 got into the act by having the heroes from *Silver Streak Comics*—Lance Hale, Cloud Curtis, Dickey Dean, Pirate Prince, and, of course, the Silver Streak and Daredevil himself—merge in a multi-chaptered conflict against the supervillain Claw and a menace borrowed from the real world, Adolf Hitler.

In 1941 Martin Goodman, Timely Comics' publisher, decreed to Everett and Burgos that a rematch between the Sub-Mariner and the Human Torch take place—and gave them a mere 72 hours to produce 60 pages of material. The illustrators orchestrated an artistic "jam" session—"All done in my apartment on 33rd St., with six writers, four artists, and a case of booze," remarked Everett in a 1961 letter—running the course of a three-day weekend. Everett recalled "Joey Piazza lying in the bathtub, fully clothed, writing up a storm" while the other artists and authors labored frantically, shouting story ideas back and forth. Irate neighbors com-

plained about the noise, even siccing the police on the annoying comics clan, but despite these interruptions and insurmountable odds, their mission was accomplished: The Torch/Sub-Mariner battle was completed in three days! This "life and death struggle," Marvel's second superhero crossover, was published in *The Human Torch* #5 (Fall 1941). The climax entailed a graphic image that, in the post–September 11 real world, is disturbingly chilling: Namor unleashes a massive tidal wave to flood New York City, with buildings and bridges toppling. Just as prophetic, however, was the accompanying caption: "But the spirit of the populace stays up!" New Yorkers escaped watery deaths by donning diving helmets and seeking solace in shelters below the subways.

Despite the phenomenal sales of the Human Torch/Sub-Mariner meetings, superhero crossovers were relatively uncommon during the Golden Age of comics (1938–1954). The illusions of superhero team-ups were often presented, however, as characters appearing in anthology titles often interacted on comics covers: Fawcett's *Wow Comics* #21 (1944), for example, depicted Mary Marvel, Mr. Scarlet and Pinky, Phantom Eagle, and Commando Yank in action together; and similarly, on artist Alex Schomburg's energetic cover to Marvel's *All Select Comics* #2 (1944), the Human Torch and Sub-Mariner resolved their spat and teamed up—along with their new ally, Captain America—to thwart a Japanese attack. While that scene didn't play out inside, those three heroes (along with the Whizzer, Miss America, Toro, and Bucky) ultimately joined forces as the JSA-like All Winners Squad in *All Winners Comics* #19 (1946).

YOUR TWO FAVORITE HEROES ... TOGETHER!

Although they shared cameo status in *All Star Comics* #7 (1941), DC Comics' two most popular heroes teamed up for the first time in the mid-1940s—but not in the comics! Batman (along with

Robin the Boy Wonder) made occasional guest appearances on the Man of Steel's weekly radio drama *The Adventures of Superman.*

Once World War II ended, superheroes fell out of marketplace favor. By the 1950s only a few survived, mainly at DC. Batman crossed over into the pages of *Superman* #76 (1952), laying the groundwork for a partnership that would resume two years later. Having appeared in separate stories for more than ten years in *World's Finest Comics,* Superman and Batman were combined as the lead feature with issue #71 (1954), making *World's Finest* the first actual team-up title. While the terms "crossover" and "team-up" are often used interchangeably, technically their definitions differ. Editor Mike Gold, in his introduction to DC Comics' *The Greatest Team-Up Stories Ever Told* (1989), explained: "… a crossover is when a hero or a group of heroes meet in another hero's book … A team-up is when two heroes (or two groups) meet in a special title." Batman appeared in print with Superman throughout *World's Finest*'s long run— the series was discontinued in January 1986 with issue #323—although Batman was temporarily bumped from the book in the early 1970s to make way for Superman team-ups with the Flash, Green Lantern, Aquaman, and others. Notwithstanding *World's Finest*'s obvious objective of bonding DC's most lucrative franchises (for years the blurb "Your Two Favorite Heroes, in One Adventure *Together!*" appeared on each story's title page), over the course of the decades Batman and Superman became the best of friends. Characters from each of their respective series would sometimes enter the pages of *World's Finest,* from villains (including Lex Luthor and the Joker, who also teamed up to fight their foes) to sidekicks (Robin was usually on hand, and sometimes, Superman's pal Jimmy Olsen) to supporting cast members (Supergirl, Batgirl, Lois Lane, even the Legion of Super-Heroes). Meanwhile, throughout the 1950s a smattering of crossovers took place in DC's titles—for example, Robin appeared in Superboy's series in *Adventure*

Comics #253 (1958), and Aquaman and Green Arrow visited each other's strips in *Adventure* #267 (1959)—but the concept of superhero team-ups was poised to explode into ubiquity in the 1960s.

THE SILVER AGE (1956-1969)

First, however, came the reemergence of the super*team,* with the Justice League of America (JLA) in *The Brave and the Bold* #28 (1960), mingling the recently introduced new versions of the Flash and Green Lantern with Superman, Batman, Wonder Woman, Aquaman, and Martian Manhunter. During a golf game, Marvel's Goodman discovered how profitable the JLA was for his competitor and commissioned his editor/writer Stan Lee to create a superteam for their company. The result: *Fantastic Four* #1 (1961), marking the coming of a new Marvel Age.

Crossovers began to occur more frequently at DC. The Golden Age Flash returned in *The Flash* #123 (1961), where readers discovered that the JSA still existed on a parallel world called Earth-Two. The first Marvel crossover since the mid-1940s took place in 1962 as the antisocial Sub-Mariner (*him* again!) appeared in *Fantastic Four* #4. At DC, the entire Justice Society returned for annual meetings with their contemporary counterparts, commencing with "Crisis on Earth-One" in *Justice League of America* #21 (1963), while Marvel's second superteam—Thor, Iron Man, Ant-Man, the Wasp, and reluctant member the Incredible Hulk— merged as the Avengers.

Before long, both companies were crossover crazy. At DC, the Flash guest-starred in *Green Lantern* (and vice versa), and Hawkman appeared in *The Atom.* At Marvel, the Hulk fought the Thing in *Fantastic Four,* and the Human Torch and Spider-Man were rivals. These crossovers illustrated a major difference between the publishers' editorial styles: DC's heroes met as allies, where Marvel's fought each other. Granted, many of the tiffs between Marvel's heroes were resolved by story's end (with the exception of the conflicts involving the Hulk and the Sub-Mariner, who couldn't get along with anyone), but the unpredictability of these new, quirky Marvel superheroes made them popular with readers, and made DC's heroes seem stodgy by comparison.

THE BRAVE AND THE BOLD

In late 1963 DC's *The Brave and the Bold* (*B&B*) shifted from its try-out format to team-ups, connecting two (and sometimes more) superheroes in a single adventure, their logos appearing side-by-side on the covers: Green Arrow and the Manhunter from Mars in #50, Aquaman and Hawkman in #51, and so on. When TV's live-action *Batman* series struck ratings gold in 1966, DC's Caped Crusader usurped the permanent lead spot in *B&B* beginning in 1967 with #74's Batman/Metal Men story, and continuing a remarkable run of nearly twenty years that ended with issue #200 (1984). Batman's versatility made him the perfect teammate, adapting to traditional superhero tales (with the Flash, Hawkman, and the Atom), mysteries (with the British sleuths the Bat-Squad and the ghostly guardian known as the Spectre), horror (he encountered the muck-monster called Swamp Thing and even went into the House of Mystery), space epics (with Green Lantern and Adam Strange), time travel (with the Western hero Scalphunter and Kamandi, the Last Boy on Earth), war stories (with Sgt. Rock and the Unknown Soldier), globe-spanning adventures (he ventured to South America with Wildcat and to the undersea kingdom of Atlantis with Aquaman), and even team-ups with his enemies (the Joker, Ra's al Ghul, and the Riddler). Green Arrow was Batman's most frequent *B&B* co-star, with nine appearances total.

Green Arrow is better known for his team-ups with fellow Justice Leaguer Green Lantern. The Emerald Archer packed his quiver and moved into Green Lantern's magazine beginning with *Green Lantern* #76 (1970), and the title became *Green Lantern/Green Arrow* (*GL/GA*)—but on the covers only; the indicia still read *Green Lantern*. The "All-

New! All-Now!" *GL/GA* was DC Comics' first major attempt at producing comics as social commentary. Green Arrow was characterized as "the voice of the streets, of the left," according to writer Denny O'Neil, while GL, an intergalactic cop accustomed to following orders, represented rigid conservatism. Despite their idealistic clashes, the heroes bonded, traveling across America in a pickup truck and tackling problems that were eroding the soul of the nation: racism, pollution, and economic displacement, among others. The celebrated, oft-reprinted *GL/GA* was ahead of its time, so much so that it failed to attract an audience large enough to sustain it, and *Green Lantern* was canceled with issue #89 (1972); the series was revived shortly thereafter, however, with a more traditional superheroic direction. (Two other superhero series featured mergers of two characters into one book: In 1968 DC canceled *Hawkman* and relocated the winged hero into *The Atom,* retitling the series *The Atom and Hawkman,* and in the 1980s Marvel's *Power Man and Iron Fist* shared a series for a lengthy run.)

THE 1970S TEAM-UP TREND

There may have been a gasoline shortage during the 1970s, but team-up comics were abundant. Marvel's characters had mellowed from their 1960s spats and usually worked together in their encounters. *Marvel Team-Up* (*MTU*) premiered in 1972, with Spider-Man (bumped out of the lead by the Human Torch on a handful of occasions) starring in a remarkable thirteen-year run that produced 150 issues and seven annuals. From high-profile heroes like Iron Man and the X-Men, to more obscure characters like Tigra the Were-Woman and Brother Voodoo, almost every Marvel superhero imaginable crossed paths with Spidey, whose flexibility as a teammate rivaled Batman's. The Thing spun out of *Fantastic Four* into his own team-up series, *Marvel Two-In-One* (1974–1983), which lasted 100 issues and seven annuals. The publisher's cads and cowboys even paired off, in the short-lived *Super-Villain*

Team-Up, which premiered in 1975 and ran for seventeen issues, and *Western Team-Up* #1 (and only), published in 1973. DC's *World's Finest* and *B&B* were joined in 1975 by *Super-Team Family,* featuring everything from a Creeper/Wildcat tale to an Atom/Aquaman/Captain Comet trio, and by *DC Comics Presents,* Superman's answer to *B&B,* which launched with Superman and the Flash in #1 (1978) and ran for 97 issues, until its 1986 cancellation.

THE GREATEST SUPERHERO TEAM-UP OF ALL TIME

The ultimate superhero team-up also took place in the 1970s: *Superman vs. The Amazing Spider-Man,* a tabloid-sized one-shot co-published by DC Comics and Marvel Comics in 1976. "The person in charge of Marvel at that time came to DC with the crossover idea," Carmine Infantino, then-editorial director of DC, reflected in *Back Issue* magazine #1 (2003). "I was opposed to it, but since I had no choice, I insisted, 'Let us do it properly.'" Infantino, an accomplished artist (*Batman, The Flash*) who had served as DC's art director prior to ascending into company management, picked the project's creative team—author Gerry Conway and penciler Ross Andru, who had previously worked on both *Superman* and *The Amazing Spider-Man*—and designed the dynamic cover featuring the Man of Steel and the web-slinger in dizzying action above New York's skyscrapers. *Superman vs. The Amazing Spider-Man* garnered media attention and sold phenomenally well, but the publishing rivals parted ways for five years before producing a sequel. In the meantime, DC used this same oversized, "All-New Collector's Edition" format for a handful of team-ups with Superman: *Superman vs. Wonder Woman, Superman vs. Shazam!* (Captain Marvel), and the oddest of all, *Superman vs. Muhammad Ali.*

Marvel and DC's flagship characters reunited in 1981 in *Superman and Spider-Man,* quickly followed by *Batman vs. The Incredible Hulk* the same year, both in the tabloid-sized format. These best-sellers enticed the publishers into a pact to produce more cross-company crossovers, albeit in the regular comic-book size, with an umbrella title of *Marvel and DC Present.* Issue #1, featuring the X-Men and the New Teen Titans, was released in 1982, with the first-ever meeting of the Justice League of America and the Avengers scheduled for #2 in 1983. George Pérez, the superstar artist who had previously illustrated both *The Avengers* for Marvel and *Justice League of America* for DC, was committed to draw the project, but editorial miscommunications between publishers led to plot rejections, verbal allegations of misconduct, and a brouhaha in the comics fan press. Pérez, operating in good faith under direction from DC, illustrated twenty-one pages of the book, but due to mounting disagreements between the companies the project was never completed and was officially axed in 1984. The resulting ill will severed ties between the publishers for many years to follow.

THE COMING OF THE MEGA-CROSSOVER

Both DC's and Marvel's long-running team-up titles were canceled in the 1980s, one by one. The format had grown tired—how many times could Batman and Green Arrow team up, after all?—and readers' tastes had changed, with material growing darker and more violent. Mundane menaces were no longer interesting, and the notion of altruistic camaraderie had also grown stale. But readers still clamored for superhero team-ups. Marvel's editor in chief Jim Shooter, in Les Daniels' history *Marvel: Five Fabulous Decades of the World's Greatest Comics,* commented that "every day a bunch of readers would say [in mail], 'Why don't you have one big story with all the characters in it together?'"

Marvel Super Heroes Contest of Champions, the company's first limited series, was Shooter's response in 1982. This three-issue tale combined most of Marvel's superheroes into a largely routine adventure, but succeeded in taking team-ups to the next level: the mega-crossover. In 1984 the company published the twelve-issue *Marvel Super-Heroes Secret Wars* on the impetus of toy manufacturer Mattel, who approached Marvel with the *Secret Wars* concept for a line of superhero action figures. *Secret Wars* sold 750,000 copies per issue, the largest sales seen in the industry since World War II. The series brought together Spider-Man, the Hulk, the Fantastic Four, the X-Men, and the Avengers to fight a common menace, the omnipotent Beyonder. The repercussions of *Secret Wars* were witnessed in the regular Marvel comics, most notably Spider-Man's garment change to an eerie black-and-white costume.

DC's first mega-crossover was 1985's *Crisis on Infinite Earths,* a massive housecleaning in which their parallel worlds were streamlined into one and outdated characters were killed or retired. Almost every DC Comics character imaginable joined forces to stop the destructive might of the Anti-Monitor. Perishing in this cataclysmic conflict were Supergirl ("She's Superman with boobs," remarked DC editorial director Dick Giordano when lobbying for approval of her demise) and the Flash, in addition to a legion of lesser names. Even Wonder Woman was expunged from continuity in *Crisis,* but quickly reintroduced in a new *Wonder Woman* series.

The former world's finest team of Superman and Batman severed their ties in 1986. Frank Miller, author/illustrator of DC's gritty *Batman: The Dark Knight Returns,* portrayed an aging, angry Batman as a loner against a corrupt Gotham City, placing him into conflict with the Man of Steel. "I'll gleefully take credit for breaking up the Batman/Superman friendship," Miller remarked. The heroes' ideological divisions continued in DC's post–*Dark Knight* titles, and despite frequent encounters and a new *Superman/Batman* series that premiered in 2003, the two remain uneasy allies at best.

Throughout the 1990s, mega-crossovers continued, most often in DC's and Marvel's giant-sized summer annuals, usually with such apocalyptic designations as *Atlantis Attacks* and *Armageddon*

2001. Traditional guest appearances continued, as well, especially with the ever-popular Batman and Spider-Man popping up in DC and Marvel titles needing a sales boost. Newer lines of superheroes from independent comics publishers also employed crossovers to cross-pollinate their characters and strengthen their "universes": Turok was introduced in Valiant's *Magnus Robot Fighter* #12 (1992), Firearm blasted into Malibu's *Prime* #10 (1994), Barb Wire appeared in Dark Horse's *Ghost* #4 (1995), and Spawn crept into the pages of Image's *The Savage Dragon* #30 (1996).

CROSS-COMPANY CROSSOVERS

Cross-company crossovers evolved from lauded events to commonplace occurrences during the 1990s. Almost every publisher got into the act, with team-ups including *Superman vs. The Terminator; ShadowHawk/Vampirella; Hulk/Pitt; Spider-Man/Gen 13; Superman vs. Aliens; The Savage Dragon/Teenage Mutant Ninja Turtles; The Joker/The Mask; Azrael/Ash; JLA; Superman/Madman Hullabaloo!;* and perhaps the strangest of all team-ups, *Archie Meets the Punisher.* Batman reigned as the consummate teammate (or combatant), appearing with (or against) Spawn, Tarzan, Aliens, Grendel (twice), Predator (thrice), and Judge Dredd (in *four* separate team-ups!).

Marvel and DC mended fences during the 1990s: *Batman/Spider-Man, Green Lantern/Silver Surfer, Batman/Daredevil, Superman/Fantastic Four,* and *The Incredible Hulk vs. Superman* were just some of their cross-company team-ups, which have, as of 2004, been reprinted in a series of four *Crossover Classics* trade paperbacks. In 1996, the publishers went at it (fictionally) in the four-issue miniseries *DC vs. Marvel/Marvel vs. DC* (issues #1 and #4 were published by DC, with DC receiving top billing; Marvel took the lead for issues #2 and #3). Superhero slugfests transpired, with their outcomes selected by the votes of fans: Batman beat Captain America, Spider-Man defeated Superboy, etc. The *ulti-*

mate crossover transpired as a result of this series: The DC and Marvel universes temporarily merged into one, during which time the companies—under the Amalgam banner—published heroic hybrids of their characters. Amalgam superhero titles included *Super Soldier* (a Superman/Captain America composite), *Doctor Strangefate* (Doctors Strange and Fate as one), *Spider-Boy* (a Spider-Man/Superboy blend), *JLX* (a Justice League/X-Men fusion), and *Speed Demon* (the Flash plus Ghost Rider). A 1997 follow-up produced similar crossbreeds, including oddities like *Bat-Thing* (Man-Bat/Man-Thing) and *Lobo the Duck* (Lobo/Howard the Duck)!

In the early 2000s Marvel editor in chief Joe Quesada initiated talks with DC to revive the long-stalled crossover between the Avengers and the Justice League of America. After several false starts, the co-publishing project was given the green light—with George Pérez, the artist emotionally wounded in the political crossfire of the first incarnation of the crossover, on board to illustrate. Touted by many as the comics event of the decade, *JLA/Avengers,* a four-issue miniseries, was published in late 2003 to astounding commercial acclaim. While embraced by new fans and welcomed by longtime readers who had anxiously waited twenty years for this meeting, *JLA/Avengers,* as well as the *Marvel vs. DC* stunts of several years prior, may have killed the team-up concept: Once you've pitted DC's and Marvel's powerhouses against each other, then united them to fight a common threat, any future team-ups may seem lackluster by comparison.

TV AND MOVIE TEAM-UPS

Superhero team-ups have also enjoyed popularity in television interpretations of comics characters. The Green Hornet and Kato crossed over onto TV's *Batman* in 1966, and Thor and Daredevil appeared in two late 1980s *The Incredible Hulk* telefilms. Virtually every animated incarnation of DC and Marvel superheroes—from *Super Friends* to *Spider-Man and His Amazing Friends* to *X-Men* to *Justice League*—has featured guest appearances by other superheroes. The crossover phenomenon has not yet burst onto the big screen, however. *Batman Forever* (1995) featured Robin and *Batman & Robin* (1997) included Batgirl, and *Daredevil* (2003) counted Elektra among its cast, but those additional heroes were already a part of the host characters' "families." In 2001 producer Jon Peters bandied about a *Batman vs. Superman* movie as a means of resuscitating each hero's film franchise. The Hollywood buzz ran rampant through 2002, with Collin Farrell as Batman and Jude Law as Superman among myriad casting considerations. *Batman vs. Superman* began to stall later that year and remains dormant, with a high-fanfare new Batman film shooting in 2004 and perhaps indefinitely putting off Hollywood's first superhero team-up movie. —*ME*

Teen Titans

They were not the first group of teen sidekicks to join together to fight crime, but they are the most famous. Robin, Kid Flash, Wonder Girl, Speedy, and Aqualad were the original Teen Titans in 1964, and almost forty years—and many code-name and costume changes later—they and their legacies live on. Created by writer Bob Haney at the behest of DC Comics editor George Kashdan, the group first appeared with no name in *The Brave and the Bold* #54 (June–July 1964), wherein Robin, Kid Flash, and Aqualad joined forces to stop the villainous Mr. Twister. Wonder Girl joined as the group gained their name a year later in *The Brave and the Bold* #60 (June–July 1965). Another appearance in *Showcase* that year preceded *Teen Titans* #1 (January–February 1966).

Green Arrow's sidekick Speedy guest-starred in issue #4 (July–August 1966), while *Doom Patrol*'s animalistic shape-changer Beast Boy showed up in #6 (November–December 1966). Other young heroes joined the Titans for various stories as the book continued its bimonthly run, including Russian powerhouse Starfire, mysterious psychic redhead Lillith, squabbling brothers the Hawk and the Dove, water-breather Aquagirl, and African-American hero Mal Duncan. Along the way, the teens faced villains ranging from monsters, witches, and interdimensional kidnappers to fashion disaster Mad Mod and the robotic killer called Honey-Bun. For a brief time, the Titans gave up their costumes, in penance for a murder they were framed for; during this time, a philanthropist named Loren Jupiter helped mentor them. Wonder Girl's origin was told in the first "Who Is Donna Troy?" story in issue #23 (September–October 1969), though it would later be revised repeatedly. Embarrassingly "hip lingo" was used in the dialogue, but the gorgeous art—by Nick Cardy and others—and youthful exuberance of the stories really set them apart.

Teen Titans came to an end with issue #43 (January–February 1973), but it was revived in November 1976 with issue #44, a story which introduced Duncan with the codename of the Guardian. The Titans were soon fighting criminals such as Dr. Light, the Fiddler, Two-Face, and many others. New characters joined up, including the original Bat-Girl, Hawkman protégé Golden Eagle, Duncan (now Hornblower), Duncan's sting-blasting girlfriend Bumblebee, Beast Boy, the Hawk and the Dove, Lillith, and a crazed woman called Harlequin who kept claiming to be the daughter of various supervillains. Some members eventually split to form a new group called Titans West, but the final issue of the series loomed. *Teen Titans* #53 (February 1978) revealed the heretofore untold origin of the Titans, as they battled their Justice League mentors who were controlled by Antithesis.

Writer Marv Wolfman and artist George Pérez previewed *The New Teen Titans* in issue #26 of *DC Comics Presents* (October 1980), then launched an all-new series the following month. This team consisted of Robin, Kid Flash, Wonder Girl and Changeling (formerly Beast Boy), and an African-

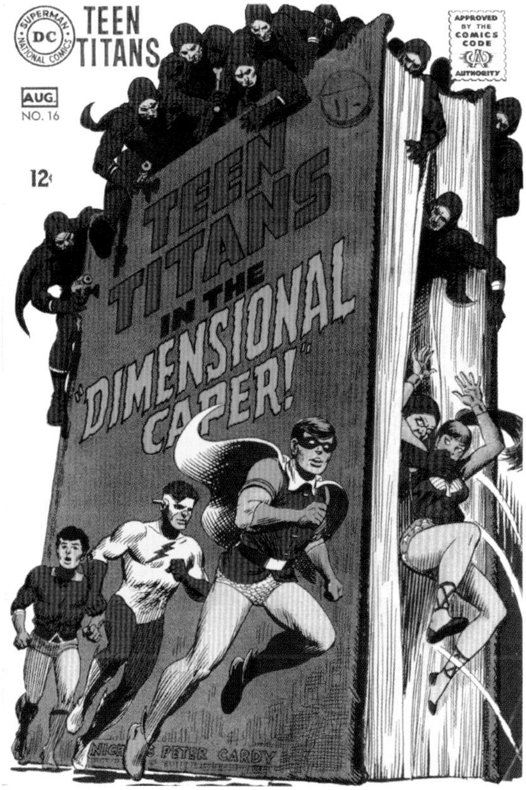
TEEN TITANS
DC
SUPERMAN NATIONAL COMICS
AUG.
NO. 16
12¢
APPROVED BY THE COMICS CODE AUTHORITY
TEEN TITANS IN THE "DIMENSIONAL CAPER!"
NICK & PETER CARDY

Teen Titans #16 © 1968 DC Comics.
COVER ART BY NICK CARDY.

American man-of-metal named Cyborg, all gathered together by a dark teleporting empath named Raven, ostensibly to save alien princess Starfire from alien Gordanians. But Raven *really* brought the team together to fight her father, the ultra-demon Trigon.

The New Teen Titans was an almost instantaneous hit, and was at the top of DC's sales in no time. Wolfman's deft characterization combined with Pérez's awesomely detailed art had fans agog, and the plots (eventually by both creators) moved from serious examinations of the plight of runaways to interstellar civil wars, pausing occasionally for "A Day in the Lives" stories. The Titans operated from Titans Tower on an island in the harbor of New York City. They also amassed their own rogues' gallery, including the Brotherhood of Evil, powerful religious cult leader Brother Blood, amoral mercenary Deathstroke the Terminator, Starfire's evil sister Blackfire, assassin Cheshire, and others.

The popularity of the series caught the eye of First Lady Nancy Reagan and other politicians, and three anti-drug issues of *New Teen Titans* were created for elementary schools (as was an animated television commercial using the characters). In April 1984, the main series split into two. The retitled *Tales of the Teen Titans* continued its numbering with issue #41, while a second *The New Teen Titans* #1 debuted as well, on Baxter paper stock. The idea was that the Baxter issues, sold only in the direct comic market, would be reprinted a year later in the newsstand *Tales* series. This proved a tricky arrangement, but a memorable one for fans, since *Tales* was about to embark on its most infamous storyline ever. In "The Judas Contract" (issues #42–#44 and Annual #3, May–July 1984) teen earth-moving heroine Terra betrays her Titans teammates to Deathstroke and the H.I.V.E., shocking fans everywhere. The story also saw Dick Grayson set aside his Robin costume and codename for the darker gear of Nightwing, and introduced a new Titan, Deathstroke's son Jericho, who could enter and take over anyone's body!

Both *Titans* series continued for several more years, although the loss of artist Pérez (who moved over to illustrate *Crisis on Infinite Earths* and *Wonder Woman*) was a blow to sales. Still, DC produced *Titans* spin-offs such as *Teen Titans Spotlight,* featuring solo stories of cast members and Titans past. Stories in this run showcased return engagements for Trigon, Brother Blood, and the Fearsome Five, as well as two further origins for Donna Troy/Wonder Girl, leaving her with the new codename of Troia. New Titans would join in the form of crystal-powered Kole, angelic Azrael, and adolescent telekinetic Danny Chase. The team also lost allies; Aquagirl, Kole, and Dove were killed in *Crisis*. With issue #50 of the Baxter series (December 1988), the title changed to *The New Titans* and welcomed Pérez

back for a spell of issues, while *Tales* had already ended with issue #91 (July 1988). More members joined—Red Star (the renamed original Russian Starfire), catlike Pantha, a baby Wildebeest, Arsenal (Speedy renamed), and the ghostly telekinetic Phantasm (Danny Chase disguised)—or were killed; Golden Eagle, Danny Chase, and Jericho were slain in a battle against the Wildebeest Society.

In *The New Titans* #79 (September 1991), a team of young heroes from the future—calling themselves "Team Titans"—appeared, gaining their own series in September 1992. *Team Titans* included flying girl Redwing, another Terra, shape-shifting Mirage, vampiric Dagon, electrical being Kilowatt, computerized Prestor John, and gruff leader Battalion. Their initial purpose was to stop Donna Troy from delivering her baby—who would become the tyrannical Lord Chaos in the future—but once that mission was scrubbed, they stayed in the past until their series ended with issue #24 (September 1994) and all but Terra II and Mirage were wiped from existence. During this time, over in *The New Titans,* Arsenal led a team composed of himself, Darkstar (an again-renamed Troia), Supergirl, Green Lantern (Kyle Rayner), speedster Impulse, explosion-causing Damage, Mirage, and Terra II. This team lasted until issue #130 (February 1996), and the series was canceled.

In October 1996, a new *Teen Titans* #1 debuted, showcasing another tyro team of heroes, all unknown save for team leader the Atom. They included plasma-energy-throwing Argent, hyper-adrenalized Risk, heat-powered Joto, and light-capturing Prysm, though later members included Captain Marvel Jr. and hulking fighter Fringe. Despite stories that featured these Titans fighting dinosaurs, aliens, and their predecessors, the series was canceled with issue #24 (September 1998). Fans would not have to wait long, however, as a three-issue series called *JLA/Titans* (December 1998–February 1999) brought back every living Titans character in anticipation of yet another new series.

The Titans #1 premiered in March 1999, featuring Tempest (Aqualad renamed), Starfire, Cyborg (now in a morphing gold body), Flash (Kid Flash renamed), Argent, Nightwing, Troia (back to her old name), Arsenal, speedster Jesse Quick, and Damage. The group operated out of headquarters on the same New York harbor island, though this tower was a hologram and the actual quarters were underground. Familiar villains such as Deathstroke, Blackfire, H.I.V.E., and Cheshire (the mother of Arsenal's daughter) appeared, alongside new villains such as Marilyn Manson lookalike Goth, and supervillain group Tartarus. Distressingly, Donna Troy received a *fourth* major origin revision. *The Titans* never quite caught sales fire though, and ended with issue #50 (February 2003).

Following the July 2003 *The Titans/Young Justice: Graduation Day* miniseries that angered fans by callously killing off both Lillith and Donna Troy, a new *Teen Titans* series was launched in September 2003. Starfire, Cyborg, and Beast Boy (the reverted Changeling) now act as mentors to the former *Young Justice* members who now fight as the Teen Titans. Members include Kid Flash (the former Impulse), Superboy (the Kon-El version), Robin III (the Tim Drake version), and Wonder Girl (the Cassie Sandsmark version), though Raven and Jericho quickly became a part of the mix as well. These new Titans are headquartered in a new Titans Tower in San Francisco Bay, and their battles against Deathstroke, Brother Blood, and others leave them hurting. The 2003 *Teen Titans* was a sales smash, with four separate printings of the first issue produced.

The Teen Titans appeared in a trio of animated short adventures as part of Filmation's animated *Superman-Aquaman Hour* (CBS, 1966–1967), but other than the anti-drug commercial, Cyborg's appearance in *The Super Powers Team: Galactic Guardians* (ABC, 1985–1986), and a proposed animated series in the mid-1980s, the popular group did not make any television appearances. But on July 19, 2003, the Cartoon Network debuted a half-hour *Teen Titans* animated series. The high-rated show features Robin, Starfire, Cyborg, Raven, and Beast Boy, as well as familiar heroes and villains such as Aqualad, Thunder & Lightning, Deathstroke, H.I.V.E., and others.

While still airing new shows on Cartoon Network, *Teen Titans* also debuted on WB's Saturday mornings to further high ratings. Although some older fans chafe a bit at the blatant anime stylings of the show, most fans young and old enjoy *Teen Titans*. In early 2004, even as the second *Teen Titans* animated season was beginning, a third and fourth season were announced, and multiple toy lines and licensed items began to appear in the summer of that same year. DC caught on to the show's popularity quickly, launching *Teen Titans Go!*, a kids comic series based on the animated version, in November 2003. It would be the first time in nearly a decade that two *Titans* series shared the stands at the same time.

The debut 1966 issue of *Teen Titans* proclaimed, "They just couldn't wait to start their own mag!" Almost four decades later, the Cartoon Network's press materials for *Teen Titans* state "The kids are all fight!" Clearly, DC's second-longest-running teen superhero group has lived up to its name. In comics or on television, they are Titans. *—AM*

Teenage Mutant Ninja Turtles

Four turtles fall into the sewers of New York City and are befriended by Hamato Yoshi, a Japanese man who lives in this subterranean refuge. One day Yoshi encounters a strange green glow of sewer sludge, which transforms him into a giant mutant rat named Splinter and the four turtles into humanoid creatures. Master Splinter dedicates his time to teaching the skills of the ninja to the turtles, who have become superpowerful from the radioactive waste floating in the sludge, and thus the Teenage Mutant Ninja Turtles (TMNT) are born.

These "Heroes in a Halfshell," as they have fondly been called, were created by Kevin Eastman and Peter Laird, who started their self-published

From *Teenage Mutant Ninja Turtles* #1 © 1984 Mirage Studios USA.
ART BY KEVIN EASTMAN AND PETER LAIRD.

black-and-white comic book, *Teenage Mutant Ninja Turtles,* on a shoestring budget in 1984. In an off-the-wall creative session, the duo came up with the concept of a group of four turtles with a ninjitsu mentor, or *sensei,* whose origin story loosely parodies various elements of Marvel Comics' Daredevil. Eastman and Laird experimented with different looks for each Turtle, but finally agreed on a singular, unified costume for all. Each Ninja Turtle was named after a renowned Renaissance artist: Raphael, Donatello, Michelangelo, and Leonardo.

"When we created the Turtles, we wanted to spoof the world of superhero characters and poke good-natured fun at the heroic but not-so-funny characters that dominated the business," said Laird on the official TMNT website. "The Turtles are fun heroes with an attitude. Basically, they act and think like average teenagers." Indeed, these wisecracking, fun-loving youngsters live life as "normal" adolescents would, stepping out to battle various miscreants in between binges on pizza and ice cream. Raphael provides the comic relief, delivering one-liners in the midst of heated battle; Donatello is resourceful and wise; Michelangelo (originally spelled "Michaelangelo") is a fun-loving, perpetual kid; and the group's de-facto leader, Leonardo, displays the heroic feats and moments of wisdom that any great leader possesses.

Though the comic's first print run was a humble 3,000 copies, within a few months new issues were regularly being printed in quantities of 50,000 or more. Eastman and Laird's company was christened Mirage Studios, and the two set about publicizing their mutant terrapins. In a stroke of good timing, a reporter from UPI wrote a story about the Turtles that was picked up on the national wire and ran in dozens of newspapers across the country. The rest, as they say, is history. What started out as a creative fluke was parlayed into a $4.5 billion worldwide phenomenon.

Palladium Books produced a pen-and-paper role-playing game featuring the Turtles, Dark Horse Minia-

tures produced sets of TMNT lead figures for the role-playing gamers, and First Comics produced full-color reprint volumes of the original series. In December 1987, CBS aired the animated *Teenage Mutant Ninja Turtles,* which ran until 1996. This highly rated television series saw the Turtles facing off against Splinter's arch enemy, Shredder, a mysterious ninja clan called "the Foot," and Krang, an alien from Dimension X—all the while aiding confidante April O'Neil, a reporter for Channel 6 News.

The success of the show—and the exposure it gave the Turtles—triggered a Playmates toy line, an Archie Comics licensed comic book (which hit the stands in 1988), a daily newspaper strip (launched in 1990), and a big-screen live-action debut, with animatronic characters from Jim Henson. *Teenage Mutant Ninja Turtles: The Movie* debuted in theaters in 1990, followed by *Teenage Mutant Ninja Turtles 2: The Secret of the Ooze* (1991), and *Teenage Mutant Ninja Turtles 3* (1993). In the midst of this licensing bonanza, merchandise galore appeared on retailers' shelves, including Turtles T-shirts, Halloween costumes, lunchboxes, stationery, calendars, and coffee mugs. Turtles colloquialisms like "Cowabunga" became the slogan of choice among all playground-dwelling four-year-olds.

In September 1997, *Ninja Turtles: The Next Mutation,* a live-action spin-off of *TMNT,* aired on Fox Kids, but lasted only one season. Though critics commented that the Turtles were mainly a merchandising phenomenon of the early 1990s, in the 2000s the band of ninja mutants made a comeback. In February 2003, the Turtles returned to television in an all-new animated series as part of Fox's Saturday-morning lineup, supported by a Playmates action-figure line and assorted merchandise. —*GM*

Tekkaman

During the 1970s, the animation studio Tatsunoko Productions, founded by manga artist Tatsuo Yoshida and his brothers Kenji and Toyoharu, created a group of unique animated shows for Japanese television. Fresh from the success of their show *Mach Go Go Go* (released as *Speed Racer* in the United States), Tatsunoko's purpose was to create more ambitious and sophisticated science-fiction anime that would appeal to an older and mature audience of teenagers instead of preteens or younger children. The resulting shows became known as the "Tatsunoko heroes." These programs represented an atypical fusion: all the elements of animation created in Japan (anime), but also the costumes and larger-than-life action and adventure that were typical of American superhero comics—albeit with darker themes, and much more violence. The shows also showcased designs by Yoshitaka Amano, who had joined the studio in 1967 and would later go on to become one of Japan's premier fantasy artists.

Space Knight Tekkaman was the fourth of the major shows of the Tatsunoko heroes line, the others being *Gatchaman, Casshan,* and *Hurricane Polymar.* The series premiered on Japanese television in July 1975 and ended in December of the same year, running for a total of twenty-six episodes. The series chronicles Earth's battle against an alien invasion in the twenty-first century. The aliens, known as the Waldastar, have nearly decimated the planetary forces, leaving only the small band of adventurers—the Space Knights—as Earth's last hope. Johji Minami, Hiromi Tenchi, and Andrew Umeta comprise the Space Knights, but their primary weapon, aside from their spaceship *Blue Earth,* is a special combat suit that transforms Johji into the lethal fighting machine, Tekkaman.

In this armored suit, Minami resembles a stylized, high-tech red and white samurai, reborn in a future age, complete with a weapon that could be compared to a sword or halberd. With Tekkaman leading the way, the Space Knights take the battle to the Waldastar on the ground and in space. A secondary storyline involves the crew of the *Blue Earth* searching for an earthlike planet for humans to colonize and thus escape the environmentally ravaged first Earth. Humanity, then, faces two forces bent on their destruction—the Waldastar and possibly their own planet.

In the early 1980s, about thirteen episodes were dubbed into English and released on video in the United States, but as with the majority of anime brought to the United States at that time, the episodes were heavily edited, with violent scenes removed and the story and dialogue rewritten. The dubbed episodes failed to find an audience and were quickly forgotten.

In Japan, Tatsunoko began to remake several of their most popular shows during the 1990s, and *Tekkaman* was one of these. As the first of the four major shows of the Tatsunoko heroes line to be remade, *Tekkaman Blade* was also the only one to be remade as a television series; the remakes of the other shows—*Gatchaman, Casshan,* and *Hurricane Polymar*—were released as OVAs (Original Video Animation series, direct to the home market), consisting of only three or four episodes. Story coordinators Mayori Sekijima and Satoru Akahori took only a few elements from the original series, and added family tragedy, teen angst, hard science-fiction elements, better animation, and possibly (as careful observers have noted) elements from the cult 1969 British science-fiction series *UFO.* Hirotoshi Sano (who would later work on the science-fiction anime *Bounty Dog*) provided the character designs, and Rei Nakahara and Yoshinori Sayama created the mechanical designs, including a new design for the Tekkaman armor. The updated armor retained the same basic shape and color scheme of the original, but was also given a sleeker look and powerful shoulder-mounted cannons called "voltekkers."

The result was a much more exciting animated series than the original, set against a backdrop of tragedy and war. *Tekkaman Blade* first aired in Japan in 1992 and ran for forty-two episodes. The new series is set in the Year 192 of the "Allied Earth Calendar" (possibly 150 to 200 years in the future), with Earth under attack by an insectoid race called the Radam and their mysterious armored warriors called Tekkamen, with Tekkaman Omega coordinating the invasion. The Radam attack Earth's Orbital Ring and rain down spores on the planet that begin to terraform Earth into a world suitable for the Radam—but not for humans.

The beleaguered Space Knights find themselves fighting the war on two fronts: battling the Radam and bickering with the Earth Defense Force (EDF) and their leader General Colbert. Hope arrives in a most unusual fashion—a rogue Tekkaman named Blade who falls to Earth and is found by the Space Knights. All are shocked to discover that underneath the alien armor is a human being, a young man who cannot remember his name. Given the name "D-Boy" (Dangerous Boy) by Noa and Aki of the Space Knights, Blade joins their fight against the Radam, but his help comes at a terrible price. First, he cannot stay in his armored form for more than thirty minutes; after that, he will go insane and attack friend and foe alike. Second, the EDF wants to use Blade for their own nefarious purposes. Third, and most tragic of all, the opposing Tekkamen Blade faces—Dagger, Evil, Lance, Sword, Ax, and Omega—are his family and friends. As revealed later in the series, D-Boy and his original family, members of a deep-space exploration mission, were transformed into Tekkamen after being captured by the Radam; only D-Boy escaped. After shifting to an "on the road" tale in its latter half, the series concludes with the final battles between Blade and the Tekkamen Evil and Omega.

Tekkaman Blade was a hit in Japan, with coverage appearing in anime magazines such as Out, NewType, and Animage. Also successful was the merchandising effort that, while not on the massive level of Mobile Suit Gundam (the giant robot franchise that many have compared to Star Trek in terms of merchandising and influence in Japan), gave fans artbooks, models, and videogames. In 2000 a videogame was released called "Tatsunoko Fight" which used the characters from the four main shows; also in 2000, the original Tekkaman series was released on DVD.

Tekkaman Blade eventually caught the attention of the U.S. media company Saban Entertainment, which in 1995 dubbed Tekkaman Blade into English and released it on television in the United States as Teknoman. Despite the changes in the music, character names, and in one case, even gender—D-Boy became "Slade" and the male or transsexual character of Rebin was changed to the female Maggie Matheson—the story remained intact. Despite favorable ratings, only the first twenty-six episodes were shown on television even though Saban had completed work on adapting all the episodes of the original Japanese version.

The reaction to Teknoman was mixed. Those who had never seen Tekkaman Blade before were drawn to the show's strong storyline and animation (and would later look for the original version), but fans of the original Tekkaman Blade were split between those who hated the adaptation outright and those who felt that the changes to the show did not detract from the overall mood or story. The latter also felt that the show's appearance on American television could bring new fans into the growing anime fandom movement in the America.

In Japan, Tekkaman Blade II was released as an OVA in 1994, with the same creative staff from the previous series, consisting of six episodes. The OVA was well received, but was not as popular as the original Tekkaman Blade. Urban Vision released Tekkaman Blade II in the United States four years later. In the end, Tekkaman Blade proved to be more popular, both in Japan and abroad, than its predecessor, Tekkaman. —MM

Thor

Just as DC Comics has the all-powerful Superman, Marvel has the Mighty Thor, literally a god with extraordinary powers and, like his Kryptonian counterpart, with an earthly alter ego. Integrating themes from the warrior heroes of Norse mythology, Marvel introduced Thor as its fourth superhero. He appeared in late 1962, in the same month as Spider-Man's debut, and he has been one of the company's most enduring stars ever since.

His first adventure was chronicled in *Journey into Mystery* #83, which introduced readers to the frail, lame Doctor Don Blake, vacationing in Norway. Stumbling across an alien invasion force of the Stone Men of Saturn (who bear an uncanny resemblance to the statues on Easter Island), the startled doctor takes refuge in a nearby cave. There, hidden in a deep chamber within, he finds a cane, which he strikes against the wall, only to find himself transformed into a blond, long-haired Adonis wearing a Viking costume (of sorts) and wielding a magic hammer, called Mjolnir. Blake becomes the Thunder God Thor because, as an inscription on the hammer declares, "Whosoever holds this hammer, if he be worthy, shall possess the power of … Thor." As Thor, Blake can fly (with the help of his hammer) and control the elements, and he possesses extraordinary strength. The hammer also returns, like a boomerang, after being thrown; when the handle is hit twice on the ground it allows Thor to bring on a storm of any type or magnitude; and it makes for one mean weapon in a superhero battle. However, if the hammer is out of Thor's grasp for more than one minute, he reverts to his civilian identity as Blake. Having summarily dispatched the Stone Men back to Saturn, Blake/Thor heads home and on to a long career as a superhero.

Thor was created by Marvel editor/writer Stan Lee and artist Jack Kirby, but neither was consistently able to fit the feature into their schedules for its first few years, so Lee's brother Larry Leiber scripted much of the early material. After several issues, Kirby moved on to the new *X-Men* and *Avengers* titles, but not before contributing to the strip's nascent supporting cast. Having returned to New York, Dr. Blake set up a practice with a pretty young nurse called Jane Foster—think Lois Lane and Clark Kent—with whom he promptly fell in love. In true comic book style, revealing to her that he was really a superhero was strictly forbidden by Thor's father Odin, ruler of the Norse gods in far-off Asgard. Issue #85 introduced Thor's villainous half-brother Loki, the God of Mischief, who was to be a perpetual thorn in the hero's side and the feature's arch-villain, always plotting to take over Asgard.

For its first couple of years, the strip was much like any other comic, with regular forays down to Earth by the treacherous Loki, interspersed with occasional communist plotters and local hoods, such as the Grey Gargoyle, Radioactive Man, the Cobra, and Mister Hyde. Gradually, however, the series began to evolve as Lee and Kirby returned (with issue #97 in late 1963) and changed the strip's focus from earthbound crime-fighting to the more expansive, imaginative realm of fabled Asgard. The pair introduced a new backup series, "Tales of Asgard," which adapted Norse legends and integrated them with the lead strips' growing band of Asgardians. Among the most important new characters were the dashing Balder, a brave, sword-wielding fighter; and Volstagg, Fandral, and Hogun, collectively known as the Warriors Three. Then there was Heimdal, guardian of the Rainbow Bridge to Asgard, and the beautiful and plucky Sif—a future love interest.

The Norse legends had fascinated Kirby since childhood and, coupled with his almost boundless imagination, they inspired some of his greatest art: astonishing battle scenes (often featuring the massed armies of Asgard), vast cosmic vistas, and extraordinary creatures. With issue #126 (in early 1966), *Journey into Mystery* was retitled *Thor,* and the comic entered its most creative period with a stream of new stars and villains. A lengthy narrative introduced the Greek god Hercules (later to join the Avengers), his father Zeus, and the ruler of the Netherworld, Pluto. This was followed by an excursion into a far-off galaxy with the Colonisers of Rigel and Ego, the Living Planet. Later stories featured the High Evolutionary (a sort of Dr. Moreau for the space age); the grotesque Ulik and the Rock Trolls; Hella the Goddess of Death; and the two great beasts, Surtur and Mangog, bent on bringing about Ragnarok—the destruction of Asgard and all around it. Amidst all the rest, of course, there were regular plots and schemes by Loki.

This was heady stuff, and Kirby's narratives (it is widely accepted that he was the guiding force in the project) were complemented by Lee's flowery, almost Shakespearean language—all "thees," "thous," and "forsooths." In issue #124, Jane Foster discovered that Thor and Don Blake were one and the same and, unable to cope with the enormity of it all, was gone within the year, to be replaced by the rather more heroic Sif. The creators used the Blake identity less and less and, by 1970, it had largely been abandoned. That year was a watershed for the feature, as it witnessed Kirby's departure for arch-rival DC Comics, where he would create the New Gods, very much in the same imaginative tradition as Thor.

Within a year, Lee, too, had gone, but his replacements Gerry Conway and Len Wein, with artist John Buscema, carried on in much the same tradition as Kirby and Lee. Indeed, it is a hallmark of the strip that for the next three decades—the 1970s, 1980s, and 1990s—it rarely strayed too far from the Lee/Kirby blueprint. Trends from "relevance" to hard-boiled action to the darker 1990s came and went, but Thor was invariably toughing it out with Loki in Asgard, traveling through space or preventing Ragnarok—again. Buscema was the principal artist throughout much of the 1970s, combining his peerless draftsmanship with a strong sense of action. In lesser hands, however, the strip has struggled.

Following one such thin period, fan favorite Walter Simonson took over the comic in 1983 (with issue #337) and revisited the original premise that a worthy bearer of the hammer shall possess the power of Thor, by giving it to a bizarre-looking alien called Beta Ray Bill. Over the next four years, Simonson—a Kirby devotee—recaptured the

Thor #151 © 1968 Marvel Comics.
COVER ART BY JACK KIRBY AND VINCE COLLETTA.

grandeur of his idol's vision, reviving some of the old favorites and even turning the original Thor into a frog! Thor soon got his hammer (and body) back, but while Simonson was on the comic almost anything he did was received with rapture by its readers. In the late 1980s Simonson left *Thor,* and the former *Amazing Spider-Man* creative team of Tom DeFalco and Ron Frenz took his place.

In the early 1990s (in issue #433), DeFalco and Frenz combined Thor's essence with a new human host, the architect Eric Masterson, to create effectively a new Thor, who had to learn to be a superhero all over again. In time, the old Thor reappeared and the Masterson incarnation (complete with beard and ponytail), now known as Thunderstrike, spun off into his own, short-lived series (1993–1995). Thunder-strike also teamed up with Beta Ray Bill and a Thor of the future called Dargo, in the wonderfully named (if ephemeral) *Thor Corps.* After issue #502, as part of a companywide late 1990s restructuring plan known as *Heroes Return,* the *Thor* comic restarted its numbering at issue #1, and readers were introduced to yet another new Thor.

In the wake of *Heroes Return,* a stricken Thor was given a new mortal incarnation—Jake Olsen, an emergency paramedic—but new writer Dan Jurgens did not stop there. After a period of finding his feet, the new Thor was split apart from his human host by Odin, who feared that his son had become too attached to planet Earth. Odin then died and his almost limitless power was transferred to his son, who became (as a new cover legend proclaimed) Thor, Lord of Asgard. As Thor climbed the ladder of godhood, Asgard was transported to Earth and, in a daring move on Jurgens' part, the strip saw the emergence of a new religion: Thorism. As lowly earthlings attempted to cope with the gods who now walked among them, effectively creating world peace in their wake, it was left to Olsen to question the wisdom of Thor's actions.

As of 2004, the comic has yet to recapture the commercial heights of the Simonson era. Jurgens' run has been by far the most radical of the strip's existence, and perhaps only posterity will reveal how successful he has been in revitalizing the series. By contrast, critics have long considered the Kirby era one of Marvel's finest achievements and these comics have been extensively collected in oversized "Treasury Editions," hardback "Masterworks" anthologies, and paperback "Essentials" compilations. Since 1963 Thor has been a regular star of *The Avengers,* and periodically appears in numerous Marvel comics as well as in merchandise and toys. Occasional rumors of a feature film have come to nothing, but movie technology has now advanced to such a point that Kirby's extraordinary imagination might just be captured on film at last. —*DAR*

T.H.U.N.D.E.R. Agents

Of the many second-division publishers that sprang up in the 1960s, inspired by the sudden success of Marvel Comics, Tower (with its principal title *T.H.U.N.D.E.R. Agents*) is among the most fondly remembered. The precise origins of Tower Comics are still somewhat vague, but the company seems to have sprung from the Midwood and Belmont line of paperbacks owned by Harry Shorten and Archie Comics co-owner Louis Silberkleit. Teaming up as Millwood-Tower, they created Tower Comics and recruited the great artist Wally Wood, fresh from a popular stint on Marvel's *Daredevil,* to put together a comics line for them. Thrilled at the prospect of control over his own work, Wood gathered together his friends and studio members, and created the T.H.U.N.D.E.R. Agents.

The first issue of *T.H.U.N.D.E.R. Agents* came out in late 1965 and, unusually, had twice the page count of other comics at that time, sixty-eight pages, but at twenty-five cents it was also twice the price as well. The comic starred the supersecret heroes Dynamo, NoMan, Menthor, Raven, and Lightning. All of them worked for the clandestine T.H.U.N.D.E.R. organization—The Higher United Nations Defense Enforcement Reserves—in a battle against any evil foe who might threaten the earth.

The characters' origin story reveals how T.H.U.N.D.E.R. operatives arrive too late to save the brilliant Professor Jennings from agents of the dreaded Warlord, but find three fantastic new inventions in his apartment. One of these is given to each of three brave T.H.U.N.D.E.R. Agents. Len Brown (a.k.a. Dynamo) is given an "electron molecular magnifier belt," which gives him Superman-like strength and a body as hard as steel. Dr. Dunn, an aged colleague of Jennings who devised a way of transferring his mind into the body of an android (one of many which he had built), is given a cloak of invisibility to become NoMan. John Janus (a.k.a. Menthor) is given a cybernetic helmet that amplifies his brain power to such an extent that he can read minds and master telekinesis. (This character was also originally a double agent, working for the Warlord, but he soon saw the error of his ways.) The T.H.U.N.D.E.R. Squad (Guy Gilbert, Weed, Kitten, and Dynamite) were regular agents who popped up in various stories to help their super-powered colleagues defeat a variety of aliens, zombies, and dictators.

In what was clearly a combination of Marvel-style superheroics and *Man from Uncle*/James Bond–style spy thrillers, the T.H.U.N.D.E.R. Agents regularly came up against sinister secret societies, such as the Warlords; Overlord and his Subterraneans; the Red Star Group; and SPIDER. Other dastardly (though perhaps rather routine) villains included Dynavac, Vibraman, the Tarantula, Dr. Sparta, and Demo and the Submen. Two of the publisher's most memorable villains had an unusual depth to them—Iron Maiden and Andor. The armor-clad, beautiful but deadly Iron Maiden was Dynamo's top enemy but was also in love with him and would go to some lengths not to kill him. Andor had been experimented on by the Subterraneans since childhood, to make him a deadly opponent for the T.H.U.N.D.E.R. Agents, but he was a tormented soul who soon turned against his masters.

Each issue of *T.H.U.N.D.E.R. Agents* was a treat for the eyes. Wood was at the peak of his powers on the series and was prominently featured in each issue, while such artistic talents as Reed Crandall, Gil Kane, Mike Sekowsky, and Steve Ditko also contributed notable work. Scripts were provided by Wood himself, Steve Skeates, Bill Pearson, Larry Ivie, and Len Brown. The latter's name had been appropriated (much to the writer's surprise) by Wood as Dynamo's alter ego.

Tower's ambition to compete with Marvel and DC was great, but it was also the company's undoing. In 1966, it released a second superhero title,

T.H.U.N.D.E.R. Agents #3 1966. © & ™ John Carbonaro.
COVER ART BY WALLY WOOD.

Undersea Agent, and later spun-off Dynamo and NoMan into their own short-lived series. In addition, it launched a war comic—*Fight the Enemy*—and a couple of titles starring Tippy Teen in an attempt to tap into the Archie Comics market. All of the comics were double-sized and cost twenty-five cents each, and ultimately they overstretched the publisher's talents and readership. At double the price of other comics on the stands, readers were put off. In any case, as beautiful as the comics were, they lacked Marvel's personality and excitement. Tower had its innovative ideas (killing off Menthor in issue #7, for instance) but the company was occasionally too eager to copy more successful superheroes. For example, T.H.U.N.D.E.R.

Agents Lightning and the Raven were transparently based on the Flash and Hawkman. So most of these new titles were dead by 1967, while *T.H.U.N.D.E.R. Agents* staggered on with an increasingly erratic schedule until issue #20 in 1969. *Tippy Teen,* on the other hand, proved to be the publisher's most successful comic, running for twenty-seven issues until 1970.

Despite its relatively short life span, there have been numerous official and unofficial *T.H.U.N.D.E.R. Agents* revivals. Throughout the 1980s, rival comic-book companies published competing T.H.U.N.D.E.R. Agents comics, with certain publishers believing that they had bought the rights to the heroes, while others claimed they were in the public domain. According to the July 2001 issue of *Comic Book Artist* magazine, eight different titles from five companies either presented new strips or reprinted original *T.H.U.N.D.E.R. Agents* comics before the copyright situation was remedied. Interestingly, in the United Kingdom much of the Tower line was reprinted in black-and-white titles such as *Creepy Worlds* and *Uncanny Tales* by the Alan Class Company, and was continuously reprinted from the 1960s up to the mid-1980s, making these titles as familiar to British readers as many Marvel or DC comics. The 1990s even saw a bootleg British *T.H.U.N.D.E.R. Agents* comic clearly photocopied from American issues.

By the mid-1990s the legal complexities had been ironed out and a regular *T.H.U.N.D.E.R. Agents* series was announced by—of all people—*Penthouse* magazine. However, while many issues had been completed, only one story appeared, in the pages of *Omni Comix* #3, before Penthouse canceled its nascent comic line. Fans could have been forgiven for thinking that the characters were forever doomed, but in 2003 DC Comics announced plans to resurrect the Tower line. A much-anticipated new series never made it to the market, but an Archives series of the classic stories and a line of collectible statues, each from DC, preserve the legacy for posterity. —*DAR*

The Tick

Bounding over the rooftops of The City, the big blue ball of justice known as the Tick faces naughty evildoers with fearlessness, gusto, and a rallying cry of "Spoon!" The absurd superhero is often aided in his adventures by the portly Arthur, whose all-white moth-winged costume and easily spooked attitude do not generally strike fear into the hearts of criminals. The spawn of crankiness may churn a bitter butter of evil, but The City has its heroes in Tick and Arthur … and a few of their equally odd superhero friends.

Created as an absurdist parody of superheroes by cartoonist Ben Edlund, the Tick first appeared in the pages of comic store New England Comics' newsletter with issue #14 (July-August 1986). In the story, the character escapes from Evanston Asylum on a mission to protect The City. After a number of newsletter adventures proved popular with fans, a limited edition of *The Tick* #1 was published in March 1988. It was later reprinted in a nationally distributed edition, and the saga of *The Tick* began. In the years since, several dozen series, miniseries, specials, and one-shots for *The Tick* have been published in color and black-and-white. Spinoff series for supporting characters have also appeared, including *Man-Eating Cow* and *Paul the Samurai*. Although Edlund wrote and illustrated most of the original *Tick* adventures, many other creators came aboard for later stories.

Although the Tick first fought crime alone, in *The Tick* #4 (March 1989), he met Arthur, a shy and portly accountant who wanted to become his side-kick. Arthur bought a moth-like outfit that more closely resembled a rabbit, but the two were soon inseparable. The Tick doesn't really have a secret identity (though he once masqueraded as Neville Nedd, crossword-puzzle creator for the Weekly World Planet), and the duo has its headquarters in Arthur's apartment (though a Tick Cave on the outskirts of New York was later seen). Other heroes with whom Tick and Arthur are acquainted include female ninja Oedipus, baker Paul the Samurai, patriotic heroine American Maid, bat-dressed hero Die Fledermaus, color-changing Crusading Chameleon, cannon-firing Human Bullet, stinky hero Sewer Urchin, and World War II–era heroes the Decency Squad (Captain Decency, Johnny Polite, Suffra-jet, Living Doll, and Visual Eyes).

The Tick villains are an equally odd lot. Crime boss Chairface Chippendale has a piece of furniture for a head. The deadly Chainsaw Vigilante wants to get rid of all the superheroes of The City. El Seed is a sentient plant with a daisy-head that wants to take over the world with the Plant Kingdom. Brainchild is an evil genius who is really a grade-schooler with an enlarged brain. The Breadmaster commits baking crimes with his sidekick Buttery Pat. Other villains include the Evil Midnight Bomber What Bombs at Midnight, the Red Scare, Dinosaur Neil, Pineapple Pokopo, the Terror, Omnipotus the Eater of Planets, Thrakkorzog, and the forces of Villainy, Inc.

What are the Tick's powers? Well, he's "nigh-invulnerable," though that seems to mean only that he can withstand a lot of punishment. He also has increased strength, speed, and jumping ability, and the feelers on his mask keep him balanced. Arthur's moth suit enables him to fly. The Tick's rallying cry is "Spoon!", while Arthur's more plaintive battle cry is "Not in the face!" Tick rarely uses super-gadgets, but he does have a Secret Crime ViewFinder (a View Master toy), the Mighty Diner Straw, the Pez Dispenser of Graveness, and a Hypnotic Secret Identity Tie.

On September 10, 1994, Fox debuted an animated series of The Tick for Saturday mornings. The characters closely followed their comic incarnations, and the multi-layered, parodically inclined stories were enjoyed by adults as well as children. Townsend Coleman provided the voice of the Tick, while ex-Monkees star Mickey Dolenz was Arthur (replaced by Rob Paulsen in season two). In an odd state of affairs for the time, Comedy Central picked up the rights to The Tick in 1996 and began showing the new episodes at night, while Fox reran the

The animated show The Tick.

new shows mixed with older episodes. The series attracted an intense cult following among college students and adults; it also led to a line of action figures, bendable toys, plastic figurines, fast-food premiums, games, apparel, videos, trading cards, and other successful licensing. The animated Tick ended in 1997 after thirty-six episodes, though multiple scripts for a fourth season were written; Fox talked about airing Tick primetime specials, but none ever appeared.

In 2000, a live-action pilot for The Tick was created, produced, and directed by Barry Sonnenfeld (Men in Black). The resulting series starred Patrick Warburton in the title role, and he perfectly replicated the cartoon version. Animatronic feelers and a seamless blue latex suit gave Warburton a cartoony look. David Burke played Arthur, while two characters similar to those in earlier series incarnations also appeared regularly: Nestor Carbonell was the perpetually hyper-hormonal lothario Bat Manuel (the new version of Die Fledermaus), while Liz Vassey was patriotic heroine Captain Liberty (the new version of American Maid), a woman who constantly made the wrong choices when dealing with men.

The opening narration for *The Tick* set up the show's odd sensibility: "I am the wild blue yonder, the front line in a never-ending battle between Good and Not-So-Good. Together with my stalwart sidekick Arthur and the magnanimous help of some other folks I know, we form the yin to villainy's malevolent yang. Destiny has chosen us. Wicked men, you face the Tick!" Delayed from a midseason replacement in early 2001, and prior to its debut on Fox on November 8, 2001, *The Tick* was given rave reviews by almost every TV critic in print. Despite its high critical marks, the public didn't warm to the show nearly as well—perhaps due to poor advertising, preemptions, and a constantly shifting schedule—and Fox canceled the series before all nine episodes had aired. The final show appeared on January 24, 2002. Fans had to wait until the October 2003 DVD release to see the final *Tick* episode.

Even as *The Tick* comics continue to appear periodically, creator Edlund has spent most of his energies in Hollywood, writing for such TV series as *Firefly* and *Angel,* and films such as *Titan A.E.* He also shepherded an animated script (with Richard Liebmann-Smith) for a big-budget *Tick* feature film; although it is not in active development, the big blue hero may yet reach the big screen, inspiring fans everywhere to yell "Spoon!" once again. —*AM*

Ultraman

The late Eiji Tsuburaya—Japan's greatest special-effects master—was responsible for the visual effects for the early Godzilla films, beginning in 1954 with *Gojira* (*Godzilla, King of the Monsters*). These films, referred to by the Japanese term *kaiju eiga* (literally, "giant monster film"), have grown in popularity and continue to be enjoyed in Japan and around the world, with new Godzilla films being produced. Yet Tsuburaya made his mark not just in the movies, but also on Japanese television, where his work on a unique live-action science fiction series led to the creation of Japan's most popular live-action superhero: Ultraman.

Ultraman's roots began with the television show *Ultra Q*. This twenty-eight-episode black and white science fiction series first aired on Japanese television on January 2, 1966. The premise dealt with three investigators—a pilot, his assistant, and a reporter—who explored strange phenomena that would lead to the revelation of a giant monster or an unknown creature. At the root of the appearances of such creatures would be an explanation grounded in science, such as environmental destruction or extra-terrestrial visitations. Many have referred to the show as a combination of *The*

Twilight Zone and *The Outer Limits* (or one could call it a precursor to *The X-Files*). Not every episode of *Ultra Q* featured a giant monster, but the series scored high ratings, and its popularity would have a strong influence on *Ultraman*.

Tsuburaya's desire was to create a show that had giant monsters and a force powerful enough to defeat them. At the same time, the show had to fit within a thirty-minute time frame. The result of this work, a series titled *Ultraman,* premiered on July 17, 1966, on Japanese television, and was an immediate success. The original *Ultraman* series only ran for thirty-nine episodes, but in the nearly forty years since the character first appeared, the many television shows, movies, comics, and additional merchandise have gained Ultraman a worldwide recognition on par with Mickey Mouse and Charlie Brown.

At first glance, Ultraman appears to be a robot, with his red and silver body, bullet-shaped helmet (and its fin), yellow eyes, and giant stature—he stands forty meters tall and weighs 35,000 tons. However, he is actually a living being, an interstellar law enforcement officer from a planet located in Nebula M-78. He is part of a galactic law enforcement team consisting of many beings similar to him—all are called "Ultras." Each episode is set in the present day or the near future. The first *Ultraman* series began with the title character pursuing the criminal Bemlar to Earth. Ultraman accidentally collides with a craft piloted by Hayata of the Science Patrol, killing him. In response (and as a way to make amends), Ultraman revives Hayata and gives him the "Beta Capsule"; by raising the device and pressing the button, Hayata transforms into Ultraman to battle giant beasts. The hero's main weapon is the "specium ray," an energy beam fired when Ultraman crosses his arms in a "plus sign" manner. There is a catch—Ultraman can only remain in his giant form for three minutes while on Earth. This time limit would become the standard for future shows. The battles between Ultraman and the various enemy creatures were performed by actors in costumes filmed on sets with detailed miniature buildings, hills, and mountains. Prominent villains of the original *Ultraman* series include Baltan-seijin (an insectiod alien monster), Red King, and Zetton, an alien dinosaur.

Ultraman became a major success, scoring high ratings and interest. Children were the show's largest fan group, although older viewers enjoyed the show too; it was also the first color television show in Japan made for children. With his immense size and strength, Ultraman is truly a larger-than-life superhero, a defender of Earth (even if the majority of the action took place in Japan). There are some similarities to American superheroes: Ultraman is a powerful alien who uses a human "disguise" to hide his identity (like Superman), and changes size to battle monsters (like Giant Man of the Avengers).

In 1967, Tsuburaya Productions decided to develop a new series called *Ultraseven*. This series introduced a new agent from M-78 who takes on the human identity of Dan Moroboshi while on Earth. The TDF (Terrestrial Defense Forces) represent humankind's line of defense against alien invaders or monsters. The new series, at forty-nine episodes, was darker in tone and dealt with more serious issues than the original series. (In fact, the twelfth episode caused a major controversy in

Japan and was banned from television due to its portrayal of aliens whose appearance recalled radiation poisoning as in Hiroshima.) Over the next thirty-five years, *Ultraman* would continue through nineteen television shows in Japan as well as more than a dozen live-action theatrical films. Each new series featured a new Ultra, and in *Ultraman Ace,* two people—Seiji Hobuto and Yuko Minami—become Ultraman Ace by touching their "Ultra rings" together.

In 1996, the fifty-two-episode *Ultraman Tiga* introduced an Ultra who uses different "modes" to utilize in combat: a default "Multi type," a more powerful "Power type," and a "Sky type" that is faster, but not as powerful as the previous two modes. Tiga was also the first Ultraman to have colors other than red and silver—his "Sky type" mode is blue in color with silver trim. The series itself is set in the year 2007, but in a different universe than the previous shows in the franchise. *Tiga* was followed by its lighthearted sequel *Ultraman Dyna,* but the next series *Ultraman Gaia* was set in yet another universe different from *Tiga* or *Dyna*. *Ultraman Gaia* focused primarily on the conflicting beliefs of the two Ultras who were the main characters: Gaia wants to save the earth and humanity, but Agul (who is blue in color) wants to save only the planet—he is not particularly concerned if humanity is wiped out in the process. Another change that was apparent in the Ultraman series of the mid- to late 1990s was that the Ultras are not from Nebula M-78, but are instead guardians of Earth.

The most recent series, *Ultraman Cosmos,* ran on Japanese television from 2001 to 2002. With sixty-five episodes—and two movies—it is the longest-running series in the Ultraman franchise (despite a brief interruption in broadcasting). *Cosmos* also represents a shift in attitude toward violence in the media in Japan; as an Ultra, Cosmos has "gentle" and "strong" modes that are used to defeat the enemy, but gone are the bloody fights with enemies being hacked apart that were so popular on the earlier shows.

Despite being a unique Japanese hero, Ultraman is well known in America. The original series was dubbed into English and syndicated on American television in the late 1960s. *Ultraseven* was dubbed into English by Ted Turner's TNT cable channel in 1985, but the bad dubbing and writing was also combined with major edits. While the dubbed version of *Ultraseven* was shown during the early morning hours on TNT, it was not the entire run of the original forty-nine episodes. However, in 1987, a unique project was created by Tsuburaya Productions and Hanna-Barbera Productions. Called *Ultraman: The Adventure Begins* (or *Ultraman USA*), the animated pilot dealt with three U.S. Air Force pilots—Chuck Gavin, Beth O'Brian, and Scott Masterson—who join forces with three Ultras from M-78. Now known as Ultra Force, the three heroes battle alien monsters from the destroyed planet Sorkin. The pilot episode was the first *Ultraman* show to have a female Ultra as a prominent main character.

The joint Tsuburaya/Hanna Barbera pilot episode never made it to a full-fledged television series. However, there were other efforts to create Ultraman shows outside Japan (but with the full cooperation of Tsuburaya Productions). In 1991, *Ultraman: Towards the Future* (the title was changed to *Ultraman Great* when it was shown on Japanese television) ran for thirteen episodes on American syndicated television. This was the first Ultraman series to be made in English, and was filmed in Australia. The live-action series followed the adventures of former astronaut Jack Shindo, now a member of the UMA (Universal Multipurpose Agency) who became Ultraman to battle monsters created by the alien Gudis virus. The series boasted improved visual effects and miniatures, and was backed up by a merchandising campaign that included action figures and a sequel comics series produced by Harvey Comics in 1993, the same year the series was released on home video. Dwayne McDuffie wrote the limited series, with art by Ernie Colón and Alfredo Alcala. Bandai produced a videogame that was released in the United States

Ultraman #1 ™ and © 1993 Tsuburaya Productions Co. Inc. COVER ART BY KEN STEACY.

for the Super Nintendo game console; called *Ultraman,* it featured the main hero and the villains from *Ultraman: Towards the Future.*

A second attempt at an English-language live-action Ultraman series was 1994's *Ultraman: The Ultimate Hero.* While the series' main character, Ken-ichi Kai, is Japanese (making *U: TUH* one of the few American shows to have an Asian American as the main character), the production was primarily done in the United States, under the supervision of Tsuburaya Productions. In this series, Kai is a member of the W.I.N.R. (Worldwide Investigation Network Response) team that defends Earth from malevolent aliens called Baltans. Major Havoc Entertainment in California filmed the principal photography and the creature effects, as well as many of the visual effects. The design for Ultraman was modernized and redefined; his "eyes," while blue (instead of yellow), turn red during periods of intense combat. The series was shot on 35mm film (which is standard for motion pictures, not television). Unfortunately, the thirteen-episode series was never released officially in the United States; it was released in Japan under the title *Ultraman Powered.* Reaction to the series was mixed; while viewers lauded the creature designs and visual effects, many felt that this Ultraman series was a pale remake of the original 1966 series.

There would be no further attempts to make an English-language Ultraman series after *U: TUH,* but *Ultraman Tiga* was dubbed into English by 4Kids Entertainment, and was first broadcast on American television in 2002. Dark Horse Comics adapted the Hong Kong comic book for *Tiga* beginning in August 2003; popular artists Tony Wong and Khoo Fuk Lung created the ten-issue series. Nearly ten years earlier, Dark Horse, as part of its "Comics' Greatest World" line of comics, created the character Hero Zero, an obvious homage to Ultraman. Zero is the alter ego of teenager David MacRae, who becomes the size-changing hero. He can also communicate with a voice that only he can hear. Writers never revealed how David becomes Hero Zero. In the 1990s, Viz Comics released an English-language adaptation of the manga *Battle of the Ultra Brothers,* featuring Ultraman and his comrades against their standard array of villains. —*MM*

Ultraverse Heroes

New superhero universes come and go, but few have had the flash-bulb success of the Ultraverse, a line of titles from Malibu Comics. Its diverse pantheon of heroes, including Prime, Mantra, the Strangers, the Night Man, and UltraForce, would not only garner press attention, but also spawn a line of

toys, a cartoon, and a live-action television series, and set up a buy-out from one of the world's most successful comic-book publishers.

Malibu Comics was founded by Scott Rosenberg in 1986, but the company didn't hit it big until 1992. That's when a distribution deal with the just-beginning Image Comics brought Malibu a huge financial windfall, enabling it to start work on a shared superhero universe to be called the Ultraverse. Unlike Image's art-based comics that sometimes lacked strong storylines, the Ultraverse was built by a group of writers—Mike W. Barr, Steve Englehart, Steve Gerber, James D. Hudnall, Gerard Jones, James Robinson, Len Strazewski, and famed science fiction writer Larry Niven—who worked out how all their concepts and "Ultra" characters would fit together as a seamless whole. The line debuted in June 1993 with *Prime, Hardcase,* and *The Strangers.* Malibu put posters in city bus stops, and advertised on television, both marketing elements which had never been done in the comics world.

Biggest amongst the Ultraverse heroes (in terms of both size and sales) is Prime. Costumed in red and gold, and with hugely muscled arms, Prime is reminiscent of Captain Marvel. The superstrong adult hero is really teenager Kevin Green, whose Ultra-body often becomes unstable and melts into protoplasmic glop. Prime eventually gains a sidekick known as Turbo Charge, an African-American gay teen, and battles villains such as Primevil, Doctor Vincent Gross, Maxi-Man, and the Aladdin organization. *Prime* was translated for video games, and optioned as a feature film by Universal, with scripts having been written by Doug Chamberlin, Chris Webb, Don Calame, and Chris Conroy.

Hardcase is an actor who gained Ultra-powers. Fighting crime for a while with three other Ultras in a group known as the Squad, Hardcase decides to retire when the other Squad members are killed or made comatose by the robotic NM-E. He plays a hero in the movies, but eventually Hardcase decides to become a hero again in real life.

Villains he faces include Rex Mundi, Dirt Devil, and Hardwire.

The Strangers are a group of heroes whose origin is an accident that affects each of them. When a San Francisco cable car is struck by a blast from outer space (known as "the Jumpstart effect"), the people on it gain Ultra-powers. Seven of them join together as the Strangers, including target-hitting heroine Lady Killer, African-American teen speedster Zip-Zap, transforming hero Atom Bomb, shrapnel-shooting hero Grenade, alien woman Yrial, electrical-powered heroine Electrocute, and light-powered gay hero Spectral. One of the others affected by the cable car accident is Johnny Domino, who would develop the ability to "hear" evil thoughts from others, and soon gained his own series, *The Night Man*.

Other heroes soon followed with their own books. *Mantra* featured the adventures of a male sorcerer reincarnated into the body of a modern single mother. *Freex* followed the adventures of a group of underground teenage Ultras who felt disenfranchised from humanity. *Prototype* saw a young video game player taking over the super-armor of a corporate Ultra hero. *Firearm* showcased a tough guy with an uncanny shooting ability; in addition to his own comic, he was featured in a Malibu-produced thirty-minute live-action video adventure.

At its height, the Ultraverse published fifteen monthly titles, including *Exiles, Firearm, Sludge, Solitaire, The Solution, Warstrike,* and *Wrath.* An ageless evil vampire named Rune was also given his own series, written and drawn by comics legend Barry Windsor-Smith.

In November 1994, Marvel Comics purchased Malibu and all of its assets, including characters from the Ultraverse as well as other properties such as *Men in Black,* and a top-level computer-coloring department. For a brief period, it seemed as if Marvel would keep the Ultraverse a popular property, but the company quickly stumbled. Prices rose dramatically higher, and the comics were taken away from newsstand distribution and placed solely in

Prime #1 © 1993 Malibu Comics.

the direct market of comics specialty shops. Editorial interference with the writers and art teams also led to wavering quality. Although Marvel crossed its own characters over into the Ultraverse—titles included *Rune/Silver Surfer* (April 1995), *Night Man vs. Wolverine* (August 1995), and *Avengers/Ultra-Force* (October 1995)—the line began to hemorrhage both sales and fans.

One of Malibu/Marvel's most popular titles was *UltraForce,* a series drawn by fan favorite George Pérez. *UltraForce* teamed up many popular Ultras, including Prime, Hardcase, and Prototype, with newer heroes Topaz, Ghoul, and Contrary. In October 1995, DIC produced thirteen episodes of a syndicated *UltraForce* animated series, with strong ratings. A Galoob *UltraForce* toy line also premiered. Once the Malibu/Marvel merger was complete, however, even deals that were in place prior to it were in danger. Both the series and toys were killed due to internal politics.

As the Marvel Ultraverse titles continued, the quality slipped further. The creators and original writers were replaced. Characters were also replaced—Mantra changed from a mother to a valley girl—and fans rebelled. In 1996, Marvel made a number of drastic cuts, including canceling a number of books. *Prime, Rune,* and *UltraForce* were among the final

hold-outs in publication, but each of them died by December 1996. The final Ultraverse publication was *Ultraverse: Future Shock* (February 1997), a one-shot that attempted to wrap the universe up.

As of early 2004, the last appearance of any Ultraverse hero was *NightMan,* a live-action syndicated television series from Tribune, that aired forty-four episodes from fall 1997 through 1999 (in 2004, it is in syndication in some markets). The Ultraverse is remembered by fans today as an entertaining experiment that could have been big … and almost was. *—AM*

Valiant Heroes

Valiant is a company that looms large in the landscape of 1990s comics as a symbol—depending on whom you ask—of either the best qualities or the worst tendencies of the medium.

At a time when it seemed that every publisher was raiding comics history for dormant characters to build a universe around, Valiant took perhaps the least fashionable of all—the 1960s heroes of the mostly kiddie-oriented Gold Key Comics—and developed one of 1990s comics' slickest and hippest worlds. As it became vogue for comics lines to connect all their books in an intricate "continuity" that often required readers to have bought every issue of a given title—and all the ones related to it—to know what was going on, Valiant worked out an involved, universe- and time-spanning scenario of the type that delights devoted fans but which others blame for driving away comics' more casual mass audience. Valiant also pioneered the simultaneous use of its characters in other properties such as video games, which some see as the future of the medium and others see as a distraction of reader interest and creator talent from the comics themselves.

For the comics, Valiant specialized in both state-of-the-art treatments of popular themes and inventive reworkings of familiar concepts. The three main characters it acquired from Gold Key in 1990 were Solar, Man of the Atom; Turok, Son of Stone; and Magnus, Robot Fighter, 4000 A.D.

Solar had been a scientist who (like Charlton's Captain Atom before him and Dr. Manhattan in Alan Moore's *Watchmen* much later) literally pulls himself together after a catastrophic nuclear accident, and finds he has obtained awesome powers in the process. In Valiant's reworking, these powers get out of hand, resulting in the destruction of his entire universe. He then travels to "ours," determined to make amends by becoming a champion of humanity (and in this he has his hands full, with, among other menaces, a race of "spider aliens" bent on subjugating Earth that he battles across the world and through time).

Turok was originally a pre-Columbian Native American who stumbles upon—and gets trapped in—a mystical valley where dinosaurs still dwell. First appearing in 1954, this scenario can be assumed as the source for everything from the mid-1970s kidvid hit *Land of the Lost* to Marvel's Ka-Zar character, so by the time of the 1993 Valiant relaunch (retitled *Turok, Dinosaur Hunter*) an overhaul was in order. In this version, the valley was actually an alien dimension, where Turok fought technologically enhanced, intelligent "bionosaurs."

X-O Manowar #7 © 1992 VALIANT™, a division of Voyager Communications Inc.
COVER ART BY FRANK MILLER.

Magnus was a citizen of "North Am" (a sprawling high-tech city covering most of the North American continent) in the far future. A highly trained martial artist able to best mechanical beings with his bare hands, he wages war on the renegade robots who have turned against the human race. In Valiant's 1990 version, the "evil" robots turn out to merely be those who have developed free will, and Magnus rebels against the same society that would enslave them.

Among the many new characters Valiant developed to accompany its Gold Key acquisitions, X-O Manowar (debuting in 1992) compensated for his

clumsy name with an elegant twist on the immortal warrior/reincarnated hero concept. Beginning as a fifth-century Visigoth named Aric Dacia, he was abducted by spider aliens seeking to enslave the mighty warrior. When a time-traveling Solar attacks the aliens, Dacia escapes their ship and steals one of their sophisticated weapons, the Manowar Class X-O Armor, which grants enhanced strength, blasts bolts of energy, and supplies almost immortalizing life-support. Unfortunately, 1,600 years have passed on Earth in the subjectively short time Dacia has been on the aliens' faster-than-light ship, and he must adapt to the twentieth century.

Valiant also developed some inventive spins on Marvel's X-Men concept. In Valiant's universe, those who represent the next step in human evolution are known not as mutants but "Harbingers." The powerful telepath Toyo Harada establishes the Harbinger Foundation (in *Harbinger* #1, 1992) to recruit other such superbeings and help him in a vision of saving the human race from suicide by taking it over. Expectedly, there are both Harbingers who side with him and oppose him, along with the "H.A.R.D. Corps" (Harbinger Active Resistance Division), soldiers "recruited" from the ranks of coma patients, who are given special "psi-borg" implants to boost their brain activity and match the mind powers of the Harbingers (whom they battle on pain of being returned to their semi-living state).

The world of Valiant was also crisscrossed by a war between "geomancers" (sorcerers who protect the earth by drawing on its own energy) and Necromancers (their nihilistic opposites).

Valiant prospered, and fixated its fans, with companywide events that would tie all these concepts together in intricate knots. The definitive one was "Unity," a 1992 epic in which Mothergod, a woman from Solar's original reality who gains similar powers in the same accident as he, seeks to rewrite history so that her own universe can live again, at the known Valiant cosmos' expense. In this storyline readers learn that she is the one who first fitted the ordinary dinosaurs of Turok's "Lost Land" with the implants that made them murderous bionosaurs; that Magnus was actually the superstrong child of two twentieth-century Harbingers; that a geomancer then placed him in the year 4000 to protect humankind at a later date—you get the idea.

By 1997, Valiant (and its parent company Voyager Communications) was acquired by Acclaim Entertainment. As the backbone of the company, Acclaim's videogames garnered more of a focus than its comics, and the latter medium started drastically losing audiences to the former. Acclaim's comic output grew sporadic, though all of comics fandom anticipated a new crossover epic called *Unity 2000* (1999), which was projected for six issues but only shipped three.

Today Acclaim's website commits to no more than occasionally issuing "'special edition' comic magazines to support some of our time-valued [videogame] brands," but these games remain valuable indeed—especially those involving Turok, who has starred in several, and remains so highly in demand that in 2002 Acclaim's marketers scored by surreally offering $10,000 in savings bonds to the first child born on Labor Day (what else?) whose parents had agreed to legally name it "Turok" for one year.

Clearly, the Valiant universe's guardians have an interest in keeping the concepts warm for a devoted fanbase that could one day swell into a mass public again. Valiant remains one of the most fondly remembered players in what was, in its heyday, a very crowded field. And as fans nurtured on the company's mythos of time-traveling, death-cheating warriors will tell you, anything's possible. —AMC

Vertigo Heroes

"We've been called horror, mature, sophisticated, dark fantasy, cutting-edge, and just plain weird," editor Karen Berger said in *Vertigo Preview* (1992). "Tired of tired misnomers, and not even having a collective name, we decided to define ourselves." The name

Animal Man #1 © 1988 DC Comics.
COVER ART BY BRIAN BOLLAND.

chosen for DC Comics' imprint of off-kilter books was Vertigo, and its publications were christened a "bold new line of comics for mature readers."

The genesis of Vertigo began in the 1980s when writer Alan Moore revitalized DC swamp monster/sometime-superhero book *Saga of the Swamp Thing,* beginning with issue #20 (January 1984). Moore's take on the story existed in a darker corner of the DC universe, where monsters and shadows were far more horrifying than any supervillain attack. Although Swamp Thing interacted occasionally with DC heroes such as the Justice League, Superman, and Batman, the sentient plant was eventually revealed to be an "Earth elemental," whose powers were akin to a force of nature. With the success of *Swamp Thing,* other avant garde, dark and revisionist takes on DC heroes were soon put into motion, including *Animal Man, Sandman, Black Orchid, Doom Patrol,* and *Shade the Changing Man.* Like Moore, the writers for all of the series came from the British Isles (though Vertigo would eventually employ American writers as well).

Animal Man (1988–1995) starred a nearly forgotten 1960s hero who could take on the powers of animals around him. Reinvented by writer Grant Morrison, family man Buddy Baker attempts to revive his superhero career, discovering that his connection to animals runs deeper than he had previously thought, thanks to his alien-initiated link to a "morphogenic field" generated by all living things. By the end of Morrison's run with issues #25–#26 (July–August 1990), Baker even realized that he was a comic-book character. Future issues continued the exploration of Baker's connection to nature, as well as animal rights issues, suicide, and religion. *Animal Man* became a Vertigo title with issue #57 (March 1993).

Sandman (1989–1996) was the redefinition of a 1942 hero previously redefined by Joe Simon and Jack Kirby for *Adventure Comics,* who had also enjoyed adventures with the Justice Society of America. Revived (in name only) in 1974, the older hero became more of a superheroic guardian of dreams for a short-lived series. When writer Neil Gaiman reinvented *Sandman* in 1989 for another series, he was now Morpheus, the Lord of Dreams, and one of seven supernatural beings called the Endless. Though a few stories touched base with the DC superhero universe—even explaining Morpheus' connection to the previous Sandmans of comic-book history—most of the stories were dark fantasy, myths, and fairy tales, set in many different time periods with ever-changing casts. *Sandman* became a Vertigo series with issue #47 (March 1993), and soon became one of the most prestigious titles in DC's publishing history, winning

Gaiman accolades for his writing, including a World Fantasy Award.

Black Orchid (1993–1995) was the most forgotten of the Vertigo characters when she was revived. Debuting in *Adventure Comics* #428 (August 1973), she was a superstrong flying woman whose identity and origin remained a mystery. Neil Gaiman revived her in 1988 for a miniseries painted by Dave McKean, in which her origins were revealed, and Batman guest-starred. A short-lived Vertigo series debuted in September 1993, and lasted until June 1995.

Doom Patrol (1987–1995) was initially the most famous of the Vertigo-to-be titles, based as it was on a 1963 superhero team of adventurers—giantess Elasti-Girl, radioactive Negative Man, brain-in-a-metal-body Robotman, and wheelchair-bound genius the Chief—from the pages of *My Greatest Adventure* and their own title. The series was revived in 1987 with a partially new cast of super-characters, but with issue #19 (February 1989), writer Grant Morrison arrived to make things more unusual. The Doom Patrol had been called comics' strangest heroes, and Morrison upped that ante, turning Negative Man into the hermaphroditic Rebis, and adding in multiple-personality heroine Crazy Jane, monkey-faced girl Dorothy Spinner (who could bring things from her imagination to life), and Danny the Street, a sentient transvestite street that could teleport! Morrison's run included villains such as the Scissor Men, the Brotherhood of Dada, and the anagram-speaking men from N.O.W.H.E.R.E. Morrison left with *Doom Patrol* #63 (January 1993), and new writer Rachel Pollack took over with the first Vertigo issue, #64 (March 1993). Pollack continued the surrealistic tone that Morrison had by now made infamous with readers.

Shade the Changing Man (1990–1996) was a strange Steve Ditko–created concept from 1977, in which an other-dimensional alien with an illusion-projecting M-vest was on the run. After eight issues it disappeared, but the concept was revived in 1990 by writer Peter Milligan. As before, Rac Shade is on the run, and his M-vest (now called a "madness vest") helps him in his adventures as he traverses America on a strange road trip. Shade inhabits the body of a killer, and his companion on the trip just happens to be the daughter of his victims. The series was surrealistic to begin with, and obsessed with pop culture, and with #33's switch to Vertigo (March 1993), Shade and friends settled down to live in a hotel that attracted strangeness. Inventive to the end, *Shade* remained more of an experimental superhero series than a crime-fighting adventure book.

As with *Shade* and the others, the switch to Vertigo, in fact, almost completely erased the superhero concept from most titles. *Sandman Mystery Theatre* (1993–1999) told adventures of the 1940s hero but was more pulp adventuring than flashy costumes. *Hellblazer* (1988–present) was a *Swamp Thing* spin-off about chain-smoking magician John Constantine and his brushes with the occult; it was released as a 2004 film starring Keanu Reeves in the title role. *The Books of Magic* (1990–1991 and 1994–2000) detail the adventures of bespectacled British pre-teen magician-to-be Timothy Hunter (to whom the later Harry Potter bears a striking resemblance); Hunter was mentored by DC occult heroes such as the Phantom Stranger, Mr. E, Constantine, and Dr. Occult. *Kid Eternity* (1991 and 1993–1994) revived a 1946 Quality Comics adolescent who could summon historic heroes to help him; the series updated him to be a bitter adult whose summonings brought demons instead.

Although Vertigo remains one of DC's most popular imprints, the stories have become less and less connected to the realm of superheroes as time has passed. To name two of the most talked-about series since the line's earlier reinvented-superhero days, psychedelic adventures filled the pages of *The Invisibles*, while *Preacher* presented a man, who can channel the voice of God, sharing adventures with his girlfriend and a redneck vampire. But two constants have remained since Vertigo's founding: Many of the writers are British, and all of the books are as off-kilter as the imprint's name suggests. —*AM*

The Vigilante

It will probably surprise even the most devoted comics fans to learn that one of the longest-lasting heroes of the Golden Age of comics (1938–1954) was not Captain America, the Flash, or the Green Lantern, but the Vigilante. This character was a backup feature in *Action Comics* from late 1941 (issue #42) onward, created by legendary DC editor Mort Weisinger and pioneering artist Mort Meskin. The first adventure relates how Sheriff Sanders is gunned down by a band of outlaws led by one Judas Priest, in the dying days of the Old West. Vowing vengeance, his son Greg Sanders systematically hunts down the killers, one by one, and decides to become a permanent "vigilante." Sanders soon becomes a successful country singer with his own radio show but, by donning a blue cowboy costume topped off with a white Stetson and a red scarf to cover his mouth, the "Prairie Troubadour" becomes the crime fighter known as the Vigilante.

In one of his earliest tales, the Vigilante came upon a crime scene in Chinatown, where a young boy's parents had been killed by gangsters. Our hero quickly decided to adopt the lad—seemingly known only as "Stuff"—as his ward and crime-fighting partner. It is worth noting, incidentally, that "Stuff" was the first significant Asian hero in comics history. The strip was in many ways an updated Western, with Greg Sanders and Stuff roaming the country from one radio show or concert to the next, invariably coming across wrongdoers wherever they went. The Vigilante rode a motorcycle rather than a horse, but relied on his lariat or six-guns to get him out of trouble. In more traditional superhero manner, he built up a stable of his own arch-villains, including the Fiddler, Dictionary, and the murderous, top-hatted midget, the Dummy.

The Vigilante strip had barely started before the character was recruited to the ranks of DC's second superhero group, the Seven Soldiers of Victory (in *Leading Comics* #1–#14 from 1941 to

1945), along with the Star-Spangled Kid, Stripsey, Green Arrow, Speedy, the Shining Knight, and the Crimson Avenger. The team was relatively short-lived, which perhaps indicates that the chief appeal of the Vigilante strip was its punchy brevity. Weisinger came from the pulps and had a real gift for packing his short, ten-page stories with both action and plot, and his strip was usually a highly entertaining read. Meskin was one of comics' first superstar artists, with a true talent for movement, and his artwork really flew off the page.

By the 1950s, Greg Sanders had moved onto television and his Vigilante alter ego had acquired a very modern-looking, jet-powered "vigi-cycle." The strips were still well written and stylishly drawn (by Flash Gordon artist Dan Barry, among others) but in late 1954, after over 150 episodes, the strip was finally laid to rest, a victim of *Action Comics* cutting its page count. The character was reintroduced to comics readers years later in a 1970 issue of *Justice League of America;* it seems that he had simply been in temporary retirement. A few new, well-crafted strips slipped out later in the decade, in the pages of *Adventure Comics* and *World's Finest,* revealing a strangely ageless Sanders still plying his trade on the concert circuit. The last of these stories (which appeared in *World's Finest* #248 in 1978) killed off the unfortunate Stuff (now a grown man) and introduced his son, Stuff Jr., who was last seen riding off into the sunset with the Vigilante.

In 1995, the Vigilante was finally given his own comic—albeit only a four-issue miniseries—although this featured an "untold" tale from the 1940s rather than a new set of contemporary stories. In the interim, another, wholly different Vigilante had risen from the pages of the *Teen Titans* and enjoyed a degree of success in his own self-titled mid-1980s comic. This character was Adrian Chase, an ex-district attorney by day and a ruthless killer by night, hunting down the criminals whom the law could not touch ("It's time for the *little man* to win"). This Vigilante was one of numerous so-called anti-heroes who sprang up in the wake of Marvel's Punisher, but many readers would prefer to remember the gentler, more heroic singing cowboy of the 1940s. —*DAR*

Warbird: *See* **Ms. Marvel**

The Wasp

The Wasp has spent most of her long comics career in the shadow of her (sometime) husband, Hank Pym/Ant-Man, but as a member of the Avengers she has become one of Marvel's more resilient and enduring stars. Whereas companies such as DC Comics and Fawcett had a history of female partners to male superheroes—in the form of such heroines as Hawkgirl and Bulletgirl—Marvel had never created a major one of its own until the advent of the Wasp. She was introduced in *Tales to Astonish* #44 (1963) to pep up the Ant-Man strip, which had become somewhat moribund barely a year into its existence. In the tradition of Robin, Bucky, Kitten et al., creators Stan Lee and Jack Kirby felt that their hero needed someone to talk to—and occasionally rescue.

In the strip itself, the driven, obsessive scientist Hank Pym is feeling the need for a partner, too, and is experimenting with wasp cells, just in case someone promising comes along. Cue fellow scientist Dr. Vernon Van Dyne, looking for help in contacting alien life, and his beautiful but bored young daughter,

Janet. Inevitably, Dr. Van Dyne falls prey to the first alien life form that he connects with—an escaped convict from the planet Kosmos, who kills the poor doctor merely by looking at him. Investigating the crime scene, Ant-Man is struck by Janet's steely determination to avenge her father's death, and then and there offers her the chance to be his partner in crime fighting. Pym implants his willing victim with bioengineered wasp cells just below her skin, and finds that, when she shrinks down to wasp size (with the help of his shrinking potions), she sprouts wings from her back. Fashioning her with a nifty costume, complete with pointy cap, antennae, and wrist stingers, Pym flies off into battle along with Janet (now christened the Wasp), defeating the evil monster. The Wasp thereupon falls head-over-heels in love with her knight in tiny armor.

For the next couple of years, the Wasp shared Ant-Man's adventures in *Tales to Astonish* and the newly formed Avengers (of which she was a founding member), mixing crime fighting with domestic bliss and countless shopping expeditions at fiancé Pym's side. While usually portrayed as a pluckily fearless combatant, albeit not a powerful one, the Wasp was rather clearly a pre–women's lib heroine and was forever fixing her hair and nails between her perpetual costume changes. Following a year's sabbatical from the Avengers in 1965, and the cancellation of their strip in *Tales to Astonish,* Pym (now known as Giant-Man/Goliath) and Van Dyne returned to active membership in the group and were mainstays for the rest of the decade. In issue #60 they married while Pym was undergoing a psychotic episode in the guise of Yellowjacket; clearly, Van Dyne was not going to let a little thing like madness come between her and her man.

By 1970 the couple's domesticity was perhaps wearing a little thin with readers and they left the team, next surfacing in a short Ant-Man series in *Marvel Feature* (issue #4–#10 in 1972), which saw the unfortunate Wasp temporarily turn into a horrific wasp/girl creature. The late 1970s were a kinder period for the Wasp, as she and Pym (back in his Yellowjacket guise) re-entered the Avengers. When her husband left again a few years later, the Wasp stayed, asserting her independence for pretty much the first time. The 1980s were a traumatic decade for the pair, as Pym's constant working and mental instability led to his assaulting her. His subsequent fall from grace (*The Avengers* #213) culminated in divorce (possibly a first for comics). Perhaps in response to this, the Wasp became a stronger character, going on to chair the Avengers for a number of years and taking a prominent role in the popular *Secret Wars* series in 1984; this rather implausibly saw the Wasp defeat the X-Men single-handedly. Later in the decade, the Wasp transferred to the *West Coast Avengers* title for a couple of years, and enjoyed a reconciliation with the semi-retired Pym.

As the 1990s progressed, the Wasp (with Pym, initially as Giant-Man once more) rejoined the main *Avengers* title and settled back into being a team member again. There have been the occasional setbacks—losing her powers and once more transforming into a hideous insect creature, for instance—but Marvel's writers have clearly appreciated the character's resilience, consistently promoting her as an assertive heroine. With the exception of a short-lived backup feature in *Tales to Astonish* (which merely involved her narrating old mystery stories), the Wasp had never starred in her own comic, and indeed might not have had the depth to support one. Nevertheless, she has contributed to making *The Avengers* one of Marvel's top comics, and with any luck will continue to appear in that title for years to come. —*DAR*

Watchmen

The year 1986 was a momentous one for both DC Comics and the comics industry as a whole, thanks to the release of the four-issue miniseries *Batman: The Dark Knight Returns* and the twelve-part *Watchmen,* which sold in enormous numbers and attracted unheard-of critical acclaim. *Watchmen* was the brainchild of the British creative team of writer Alan Moore and artist Dave Gibbons, who were established stars in their home country and were already beginning to make an impact in the United States. The original plan was to produce a twelve-issue miniseries using the Charlton Comics line of superheroes that DC had just licensed, but Moore's radical reworking was deemed too controversial (and too terminal in some cases), so the decision was made to create a miniseries using an all-new cast, set in a separate, subtly different world. *Watchmen* heroes borrow from the Charlton cast, however; for example, hero Rorschach is based on Charlton's the Question. *Watchmen* ran for twelve issues from September 1986 to October 1987.

Moore's script was set in a parallel universe from the early 1940s to the mid-1980s. Opening with a murder mystery and closing with a thwarted nuclear holocaust, *Watchmen* posited what it would be like if superheroes were real, how they would affect the world around them, and how everyday people would react to them. Moore created a world previously unexplored: superheroes who were morally ambivalent. What set *Watchmen* apart from typical superhero comics of the day was the insight of Moore's scripting—though Gibbons' elegant, detailed artwork made an enormous contribution as well. Moore crafted a complex story with layers of meaning and depth of characterization never before seen in the superhero genre, drawing heavily on irony, symbolism, and multiple perspectives to tell his tale. Meant "to be read on a number of levels," according to Moore, "different little threads of continuity are effectively telling the same story from different angles."

In many respects, *Watchmen* was effectively the first postmodern superhero comic, examining the motivations, foibles, and desires that might drive people to don garish costumes and risk their lives each time they went on patrol. When describing his hero Rorschach, Moore admitted he "was to a degree intended to be a comment upon the vigilante super hero, because I have problems with that notion. I wanted to try and show readers that the obsessed vigilante would not necessarily be a playboy living in a giant Batcave under a mansion. He'd probably be a very lonely and almost dysfunctional guy in some ways." The series asked the question, If you had immense power, how would you use it? In the case of the sadistic Comedian and the sociopath Rorschach, power amplified and fed the characters' natural violence. For Dr. Manhattan—a being with almost limitless powers—it led to a growing isolation and indifference toward both his girlfriend (the reluctant superheroine Laurie Juspeczyk, a.k.a. Silk Spectre) and his fellow men; this alienation was well demonstrated by his move to Mars. For the "smartest man alive," Ozymandias, power forced on him the messianic role of the world's savior; indeed, in the series' denouement, he does prevent an impending apocalypse, albeit in a shocking way.

Watchmen was very much a product of its time, set against the background of the cold war and the ever-present real-life threat of nuclear devastation, but nevertheless it is still compelling reading in the twenty-first century. Within a year of the series' completion, it was released as a book and, multiple printings later, is still in print in 2004. Together with *The Dark Knight Returns,* it laid the foundations for the graphic novel explosion and the massive growth of book collections that have transformed the industry. It also prompted the release of

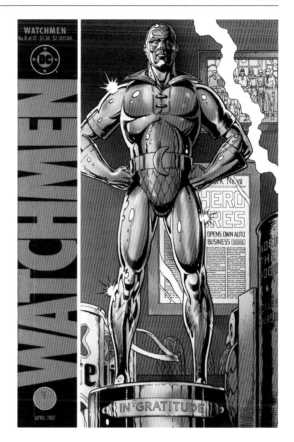

Watchmen #8 © 1987 DC Comics.
COVER ART BY DAVE GIBBONS.

Watchmen posters, portfolios, badges, and T-shirts. There have been persistent rumors of a film, though the comic's complexity is probably too daunting for a motion picture to come to fruition, the critic Douglas Wolk insightfully noting in 2003 that "Watchmen … has been notoriously resistant to attempts to adapt it into a workable screenplay: its narrative about aging superheroes and nuclear panic is so deeply rooted in the comics form that it could no more be filmed than, say, *Citizen Kane* could be adapted into a novel."

Moore and Gibbons became instant celebrities and still enjoy enormous popularity in the field, though both have refused all requests for a sequel, preferring to let the original comic stand on its own. In its wake, however, *Watchmen* has inspired such series as Kurt Busiek's *Astro City,* Alex Ross and Mark Waid's *Kingdom Come,* and countless other comics. Indeed, the *Watchmen*'s deconstruction of the superhero myth was so seductive that it had a profound impact on the industry as a whole. —*DAR*

Watson, Mary Jane

Aside from Peter Parker (Spider-Man)'s indefatigable Aunt May, the woman with the most long-term significance in the life of Spider-Man is undoubtedly Mary Jane Watson. Though she is by no means the web-spinner's first serious romantic interest—that honor belongs to the late, lamented Gwen Stacy—Watson's on-again/off-again relationship with Parker represents the hero's most serious love affair. After several teasing cameo appearances in which she is either "off-panel" (Parker's Aunt May and Watson's custodial Aunt Anna Watson are determined to introduce their respective teenage charges to one another) or is depicted with her face obscured, Watson (often referred to simply as MJ) was finally unveiled in 1966 to an eager comics audience in *Amazing Spider-Man* (vol. 1 #42), the creation of editor-scripter Stan Lee and plotter-artist John Romita, Sr.

MJ quickly assumes far more importance among Spider-Man's *dramatis personae* than her creators could foresee, according to Lee: "Johnny [Romita] and I always planned for Peter to be in love with gorgeous Gwen and one day end up marrying her. But somehow, Mary Jane was the one who seemed to come alive on the page. She crackled with energy, excitement, sex appeal. Much as we tried, we couldn't make Gwen as appealing as MJ." From the start, MJ—who works as a go-go dancer and fashion model—is the epitome of the devil-may-care 1960s "party girl," her flame-topped sex

appeal and innocent hedonism embodying the *zeitgeist* of the era and making an indelible impression on generations of male Spider-fans. Unlike other significant others to superheroes, MJ was never a fawning, demure figure who existed only to be rescued, and her first scene-stealing words to Peter Parker have attained four-color immortality: "Face it, Tiger ... you just hit the *jackpot!*" Although Parker is already seriously dating Stacy at the time, he is immediately smitten after his initial encounter with MJ, who soon becomes the girlfriend of Harry Osborn, Parker's college roommate.

MJ's relationship with Osborn doesn't last, however; she breaks up with him in 1971 shortly before a drug habit threatens to ruin his life. During the months following Gwen's murder by the Green Goblin in 1973, MJ offers the grieving Parker her sympathy, only to be rebuffed. Despite their mutual attraction, both MJ and Parker remain reticent about getting seriously involved with each other for the next several years. But with the inevitability of gravity, the two are eventually drawn together; MJ, whose fun-loving attitude masks her dysfunctional upbringing in an alcoholic home, is apparently both attracted to and frightened by Parker's responsibility-driven stability, while MJ's "party girl" persona represents to Parker an irresistible sense of freedom that he typically can experience only while in wise-cracking, slam-bang action as Spider-Man.

Parker finally "pops the question" to MJ in 1978 (*Amazing Spider-Man* vol. 1 #182); she returns his proffered engagement ring one issue later, explaining that her "free spirit" approach to life won't allow her to settle down with just one man. Afterward, MJ disappears from Spidey's life for several years (to the immense disappointment of legions of male fans), leaving Parker dating women such as the plain-vanilla doormat Debra Whitman and Felicia Hardy, the exciting-yet-dangerous erstwhile second-story woman also known as the Black Cat.

But MJ's estrangement from Parker clearly wasn't meant to last; she returned in 1983 (*Amazing Spider-Man* vol. 1 #242), having lost none of her visual sex appeal under the artistic ministrations of John Romita Jr., the son of the first illustrator to bring her to life on the printed page. MJ and Parker quickly recover their earlier intimacy, growing close enough to prompt her to confide that she has known his secret dual identity for a long time, and to reveal the uncomfortable details of her dysfunctional upbringing. Despite their renewed attachment, Parker dithers for a few more years before again proposing marriage. She refuses an issue later, but changes her mind the issue after that; the wedding takes place shortly thereafter in 1987 (*Amazing Spider-Man Annual* #21), followed by a (decidedly G-Rated) honeymoon (*Spectacular Spider-Man Annual* #7) and domestic bliss in an apartment owned by old friend (and sometime supervillain) Harry Osborn. Reflecting the 1980s and its preoccupation with success and stability, the 1960s "party girl" had at last matured and settled down.

But as longtime readers—and those old enough to remember the late Stacy—are well aware, Spider-Man's milieu is all too frequently incompatible with "happily-ever-afters." About a year after setting up the new Parker-Watson household, Mary Jane is briefly abducted by a wealthy stalker named Jonathan Caesar, who—in spite of being captured and imprisoned—manages to freeze MJ out of the modeling business. A survivor by long habit, MJ (whose visible likeness often resembles a *Melrose Place* cast member more than a 1960s icon) subsequently realizes her lifelong dream of acting by landing a role on a daytime soap called *Secret Hospital.* Again paralleling society as a whole, by the late 1980s and early 1990s the hippie "party girl" continues her maturation into a career-oriented "material girl" who might teach Madonna a thing or two about success. Despite her professional accomplishments, life continues to be complicated for MJ, including a terrifying run-in with the insane, spider-powered villain Venom; a brief almost-affair with a soap-opera colleague; the temporary return of her old smoking habit; and the revelation (later proved false) that her husband was a

mere clone of the "real" Peter Parker. Throughout the latter half of the 1990s, MJ feels herself growing increasingly restive about being married to a danger-loving superhero, a situation analogous to being the wife of a police officer.

Following the resolution to the above-mentioned "clone saga" of the mid-1990s, MJ becomes pregnant, prompting Parker's brief retirement from crime-fighting; the expectant couple relocates to Seattle, Washington, in search of a "normal" existence. This respite from danger turns out to be short-lived, ended by the return of the original Green Goblin and MJ's apparent miscarriage, though the child (named May, after Parker's aunt) appears to have been abducted by an operative of the Green Goblin. MJ and Parker subsequently seek counseling to save their marriage, which later becomes strained both by MJ's increasingly successful return to modeling and by yet another broken promise by Parker to hang up his webs forever. MJ is menaced by yet another stalker, who apparently causes her death in a plane crash in 2000. Spidey later learns that the stalker has actually captured MJ, and rescues her; too traumatized by the incident to continue living a life of danger at Parker's side, MJ leaves and the couple separates in 2001. Though their future together remains up in the air, MJ continues to miss Parker.

Over in the best-selling, youth-oriented *Ultimate Spider-Man* comic the couple (or a teenage parallel-universe version of them) remain together as high-school sweethearts (with MJ already aware of Parker's double life), and in the *Spider-Man* film franchise the romance has barely begun, while in the long-running *Spider-Girl* title, which extends the earlier storyline of the Parkers as parents, MJ and Peter remain happily married, middle-aged suburbanites with a crime-fighting daughter carrying on the family business. MJ's popularity was also shown by her starring role in a prose novel for young adults, *Mary Jane* by Judith O'Brien, in 2003. Clearly, whatever becomes of the famous Spidey-MJ relationship, it is certain that Mary Jane Watson will have an enormous effect on Spider-Man's life (and on his readers) for many years to come. —*MAM*

WildC.A.T.S

Brought together by the multi-billionaire Lord Emp and the mysterious Void, a group of humans, half-humans, and alien Kherubim warriors protect Earth against the host-possessing aliens known as Daemonites. Emp's group, WildC.A.T.S, is a Covert Action Team, and its members include Spartan, Zealot, Maul, Voodoo, Grifter, and Warblade. Millennia ago, the warring Kherubim and Daemonites crashed on Earth, and their battle continues to this day. Now, the WildC.A.T.S will end the Daemonite threat or die trying.

Lord Emp (Jacob Marlowe) was a diminutive homeless man until Void helped him learn his true identity as a powerful Kherubim warrior who had lost his way. Becoming rich and founding HALO, Inc. in New York City, Emp worked with Void to gather the WildC.A.T.S team. Void (Adrianna Terishkova) is the silver-skinned manifestation of a dead Russian cosmonaut, combined with the Void essence which traveled back in time both to warn Marlowe about the Kherubim/Daemonite conflict, and to help him assemble the WildC.A.T.S team. Her computer-like mind, teleportation and telekinetic powers, and limited knowledge of future events are invaluable.

Spartan (Hadrian 7) is actually the soul and memories of a dying Kherubim warrior that has been transplanted into the body of a superstrong cyborg by Void and Marlowe. He can fire biomolecular blasts through his hands, and create plasma shields, and his Central Processing Unit can be downloaded into other bodies, making him nearly unkillable. Zealot is a thousand-year-old Kherubin warrior who is an extraordinarily skilled fighter in the Coda techniques developed by a group of female warriors. She uses her weapons, including the Clef Blade, against the Daemonites.

Maul (Jeremy Stone) is the brilliant son of an archeologist who was really a "Gifted One"/cross-breed: part-human, part-Daemonite. He can grow to immense sizes, but his intelligence and self-control wane the larger he gets. Voodoo (Priscilla Kitaen) is another crossbreed, and was once an exotic dancer. The curvaceous heroine can recognize Daemonites in any form, and can fire mental energies from the focal jewel she wears on her forehead.

Grifter (Cole Cash) is one of the most popular members of the team. With no real superpowers, this ex-con man and intelligence operative has turned his life around as a hero, using his uncanny marksmanship and Coda-trained fighting skills to right wrongs. Green-haired Warblade (Reno Bryce) is a computer-programming crossbreed who can morph his hands into metal claws or other razor-sharp devices.

In their war against the Daemonites, the WildC.A.T.S have used a warplane known as MIRV (Multi-purpose Intercept/Reconnaissance Vehicle). They have also allied themselves with other heroes, including 1960s hero Mr. Majestic, the tactical response team Black Razors, the StormWatch team, gay techno-whiz Noir, Gen 13, and Zealot's sister, Savant. Villains they have faced include Coda assassin Artemis; four-armed Daemonite enforcer Karillion; body-stealing Dockwell and the other Daemonites (whose real appearance is somewhat reptilian); shape-changer Mr. White; the sorceress Tapestry; and Lord Hellspont, the flame-headed telekinetic leader of the Daemonites.

In early 1992, a sextet of extremely popular artists left their books at Marvel Comics *en masse,* and formed their own independent comic book company, Image Comics. One of the most popular of the group was Jim Lee, ex-artist of *Alpha Flight, Wolverine, Punisher,* and *X-Men*. He released his first book, *WildC.A.T.S* in August 1992, providing the art and co-writing with Brandon Choi. Despite plots that were difficult to follow, the series was a success. Fifty issues and an annual were produced by Lee's Image imprint, WildStorm Productions, before the

WILDC.A.T.S: Covert Action Teams #1 © 1992 Jim Lee. COVER ART BY JIM LEE AND BRANDON CHOI.

series was canceled in June 1998; although Lee had quit producing the art, some issues were written by star author Alan Moore, and detailed artist Travis Charest provided a vigorous follow-up for Lee.

The second *Wildcats* series dropped the acronym and periods in its title, debuting in March 1999, after DC Comics bought the WildStorm line. Twenty-eight issues and an annual were published and the series was again retired in September 2001. A third series, *Wildcats Version 3.0,* debuted in October 2002. In this latter series, a retired Spartan heads a multinational company called the Halo Corporation, and deals with the power such a group can wield, for evil or good.

In addition to the regular *WildC.A.T.S* series, numerous sourcebooks, specials, miniseries, and one-shots were produced. Crossovers with other publishers included *WildC.A.T.S/Aliens* (with Dark Horse) and multiple *WildC.A.T.S/X-Men* stories (with Marvel). Spin-off series were also produced, including miniseries for Grifter, Zealot, Voodoo, Backlash, and others. In September 1994, CBS debuted *Jim Lee's WildC.A.T.S* cartoon series, which lasted thirteen episodes and inspired an "animated style" comic book called *WildC.A.T.S Adventures* that ran for ten issues (1994–1995). Merchandising for the various comic-book series has included action figures, T-shirts and other apparel, statues, model kits, and more. —*AM*

WildStorm Heroes

What if a coup were staged and everyone left? That was the question asked and answered in the comics medium in early 1992, when a sextet of extremely popular artists left their books at Marvel Comics *en masse,* and formed their own independent comic-book company, a collective known as Image Comics. One of the most popular of the group was Jim Lee, ex-artist of *Alpha Flight, Wolverine, Punisher,* and *X-Men.* Although his initial offerings did not have a sub-imprint name, and were copyrighted to Aegis Entertainment, Inc., the line of books Lee and his crew oversaw eventually became WildStorm Productions. Unlike some others of the Image group, WildStorm Productions would be incredibly prolific, pumping out dozens of series and spin-offs, all in an increasingly Byzantine and interconnected universe.

Lee's first book, *WildC.A.T.S,* debuted in August 1992, and it set the backdrop of the whole WildStorm universe to come. Millennia ago, the warring Kherubim and Daemonites crashed on Earth, and their battle continues to this day. Kherubim are essentially good warriors, while the Daemonites are reptilian creatures that can take over human host bodies for their nefarious plans. Almost every character that appeared in WildStorm books was somehow related to Kherubim or Daemonites. Those that weren't outright aliens themselves were often half-human crossbreeds, or they were created to fight them or join them. The other cohesive factor of the WildStorm universe was a vaguely sinister secret United States government organization known as International Operations—or I/O—which dabbled in covert special operative teams; bioengineering superhumans with the Gen Factor; and the study of psionics and quantum mechanics.

Besides *WildC.A.T.S* and its various spin-offs—*Voodoo, Zealot, Grifter, Warblade,* and others—WildStorm had special operative books that combined crime, war, and superheroes in one package. These included *Deathblow,* about an elite gun-wielding anti-hero; *Team 7,* about the special ops team that does the government's dirty work; and *Wetworks,* about a group of symbiotically armored operatives who combat the vampire nation. *Gen 13* was originally one of the most popular WildStorm titles, detailing the adventures of a group of Gen-Active teenagers who escaped from I/O's control and fought villains while still trying to fit into the world as semi-normal adolescents.

Union told the adventures of an alien Protectorate member from the planet Aegena who is tricked into going through an astral gate, and is now stranded on Earth. Using his plasma energy staff and powers of flight and strength, he sometimes aids StormWatch. Cosmic radiation from a comet that passed near Earth years ago has imbued many people with unusual powers. A number of them have banded together as the United Nations peacekeeping force known as StormWatch. A later incarnation of *StormWatch* led to the realignment of the team for a book known as *The Authority.*

Periodically, imprint-wide crossovers in the WildStorm universe—"WildStorm Rising," "Fire from Heaven"—shook up the status quo of the various books, resulting in cast changes, power changes, and deaths. The company tried to change with the times as well. Though it had been an early instigator of multiple covers and variant editions, it slacked off those marketing gimmicks by the end of the century. It also tried new ideas editorially, resulting in such experimental series as *Planetary,* with its intricate storylines about "mystery archeologists" who uncover the secrets of the world, many of them involving familiar superhumans of the twentieth century. WildStorm also partnered with superstar writer Alan Moore to create a new sub-imprint known as America's Best Comics (ABC), an ironic sobriquet given that they were created by an Englishman.

In early 1999, DC Comics bought WildStorm and all of its properties. Over the following year, several of the superhero series ended, then were relaunched with new directions and new creative teams. Although the WildStorm offices stayed in California, the imprint now had the selling power of DC Comics, and by extension, the AOL Time-Warner media conglomerate. Today, founder Jim Lee still does a comic every now and then for WildStorm, but the diverse line enjoys success with a very big brother backing it up. —*AM*

Wolverine

The most popular member of the mutant X-Men team, the claw-bearing Wolverine is "the best there is at what he does," according to him, but what he does isn't pretty … just pretty violent. A grumpy loner by nature, Wolverine is short, extremely hairy, and possesses a combination of mutant powers and scientific enhancements. His past has been—until the 2000s—shrouded in mystery, with false implanted memories and a century-plus lifespan complicating matters.

Introduced in *The Incredible Hulk* #180–#182 (October–December 1974), Wolverine was created by writer Len Wein at the behest of Marvel's then editor-in-chief Roy Thomas, who wanted a Canadian hero to bring in more north-of-the-border sales potential. Although artist Herb Trimpe drew the *Hulk* stories, it was Marvel art director John Romita Sr. who designed the costume and clawed look of Wolverine. The yellow-and-blue costume didn't exactly remind readers of the ferocious woodland animal, but the trio of claws Wolverine could pop out of the back of each hand (with a "snikt" sound effect each time), and the character's surly, violent attitude, made him stand out from other new heroes of the time.

As would eventually be shown, Wolverine is a dangerous loner in the tradition of the Western anti-hero; he has no compunctions about killing, and treats the helpless well as long as they don't give him a tougher time. He is, in short, Clint Eastwood with tights and claws. Unlike many traditional heroes, Wolverine is flawed, but it is his battles with those flaws—and an occasional "giving in" to his nastier impulses—that make him a popular charac-ter, especially among male fans.

Wolverine was soon transferred to the pages of the revitalized *X-Men* series with *Giant-Size X-Men* #1 (Summer 1975), where he stayed in the back-ground until artist John Byrne came onboard to work with writer Chris Claremont (*X-Men* #108, December 1977). Claremont and Byrne soon devel-oped the scrappy character further, revealing that his mutant powers included tracking abilities, plus a healing factor that also slowed his growth; those powers had enabled him to survive an as-yet unex-plained process whereby his entire skeleton had been coated in the Marvel Comics über-metal known as adamantium. The creators also showed that he had previously been a Canadian operative of Department H, and that he had worked with the Canadian supergroup Alpha Flight. Wolverine devel-oped a crush on red-headed teammate Jean Grey, although he eventually fell in love with a Japanese woman known as Lady Mariko Yashida. Even as he found love, though, Wolverine still batted to control the violent "berserker rages" that threatened to break out of his unconscious and turn deadly for those near him.

Wolverine #27 © 1990 Marvel Comics.
COVER ART BY JIM LEE.

The Japanese connection was explored further with the first *Wolverine* miniseries in 1982, in a much-lauded story by Claremont and artist Frank Miller. It was clear that Wolverine—whose name had already been revealed to be Logan, and whose costume had been changed to a more animalistic brown and tan—had experienced both martial arts and samurai training in his past. In November 1988, Wolverine was awarded his own regular monthly series, at which point the character spent more time on the Pacific island of Madripoor, run-ning a bar while disguised as a ruffian known as "Patch." The anthology series *Marvel Comics Pre-sents* debuted in September 1988, featuring a

Wolverine serialized story in almost every issue. The most famous of those serials—a story known as "Weapon X"—ran in issues #73–#84 (March–September 1991). This story showed the experiments by which Wolverine's skeleton was covered with adamantium.

Bits and pieces of Wolverine's mysterious past were doled out throughout the 1980s and 1990s, but while many things were established as facts, others were shown to be falsified memory implants. It was clear that Wolverine had fought in the 1937 Spanish Civil War, and that he had also fought alongside Captain America and others during World War II, but he seemed older than that. His frequent foe Sabertooth (alternately spelled Sabretooth), another feral animalistic fighter, was perhaps Logan's father, brother, or teammate, depending on which story fans read.

In *X-Men* #25 (vol. 2, October 1993), the mutant villain Magneto forcibly removed the adamantium from Wolverine's skeleton and claws; the anti-hero struggled without his indestructible skeleton, but used the bone-claws that jutted from the backs of his hands just as effectively. The villain Apocalypse eventually re-bonded adamantium to Wolverine's bones. Still a loner, Logan has taken time out of his brooding, violent solo adventures to mentor some of the younger X-Men members such as Jubilee, Kitty Pryde, and others. He's also continued his pursuit of Jean Grey, much to the frustration of Grey's boyfriend, Scott Summers (better known as fellow X-Men member Cyclops).

Almost thirty years after he first appeared, the backstory for Logan was finally revealed in the six-part *Origin* miniseries (November 2001–April 2002), which was set near the end of the nineteenth century. Born James Howlett in Alberta, Canada, he is the sickly heir to a fortune. With a completely withdrawn mother and a busy father, James is cared for largely by a hired playmate, a red-haired girl named Rose. James has a peculiar relationship with "Dog," the rough-hewn son of the wild-haired family gardener, Thomas Logan, but as

time wears on, the relationship spoils. After the gardener kills James' father, bony claws protrude from young James' hands for the first time, resulting in the death of Thomas (and leading to the suicide of James' mother). To save him from further trauma, Rose takes James to a mining colony to grow up, giving him the name Logan. As he enters puberty, James' mutant powers begin to manifest themselves more, but a later confrontation with the now-feral adult "Dog" leads to tragedy.

While *Origin* gave the foundation for Wolverine's past—including the fact that his healing ability helps to block out memories and mental trauma as well as heal physical wounds—many more questions remained to be answered. Did Dog become Sabertooth? How did Logan become involved with the CIA, covert operations, military forces, and samurai over the next several decades? The Marvel Comics writers and artists will have plenty of time to tell these stories; *Wolverine* and *X-Men* remain among their most popular titles, and guest-appearances by the scrappy Canadian furball guarantee strong sales in any comic. Multiple "alternate future" titles have postulated that Logan will be one of the last survivors among Marvel's heroic pantheon as well. Finally, the popularity of Wolverine in the *X-Men* feature films and animated series, as well as action figures and other merchandising, means that Logan's claws will be popping out for many years to come. —*AM*

Wonder Warthog

The idea of the humorous superhero dates back to the 1940s, with characters like the original Red Tornado and Superduperman of *MAD* magazine fame, but Wonder Warthog became the first regularly published superhero satire strip. Legend has it that Texas cartoonist Gilbert Shelton thought up the character while strolling down New York City's Avenue of the Americas in 1961; he certainly unleashed him on an unsuspecting audience early the next year, in the off-campus humor magazine *Bacchanal.* Wonder Warthog, or the "Hog of Steel" (and sometimes the "Pig of Tomorrow") as he was also known, was an eight-feet-tall, 900-pound fighting machine of sinew and muscle, clad in a dashing red and green costume. Like another well-known crime fighter, he had a secret identity as a mild-mannered reporter, in this case Philbert Desanex of the *Muthalode Morning Mungpie.* He was similarly an alien, cast out of his planet Uranus to find refuge on Earth, though unlike Superman he suffered from one unfortunate deficiency: He was a hideous giant pig with an attitude problem.

Surprisingly, this most unprepossessing superhero began to gather a feverish fan base as he appeared throughout the early 1960s in college magazines and newspapers such as *Yahoo, The Charlatan,* and *The Ranger.* As its fame spread, the strip was soon picked up by the national satire magazine *Help!,* while T-shirts, posters, and rave reviews in *Mademoiselle* and *Esquire* helped make the strip one of the era's hippest comics. Following the sad demise of *Help!,* the strip soon found a regular berth in the cult magazine *Drag Cartoons.* What the fans were picking up on was the fact that Shelton was a terrific cartoonist with a gift for wickedly funny writing. It also helped that the strip specialized in the lamest villains in history, including Pie Man, Superhypnotist, Psuper Psychiatrist, the Zymotic Zookeeper, and Superfool.

After two years of success in *Drag Cartoons,* publisher Pete Miller decided to give the hog his own comic, and the first issue appeared in 1967. As early as 1962, Shelton had used the strip to satirize more controversial subjects, such as segregation in Alabama, and he continued that in *Wonder Warthog* magazine. Unfortunately, the world was not ready for strips about a bare-knuckle-fighting Lyndon Johnson, drug pushers in the ghetto, Vietnam, and the Mafia, and the title sold barely one-third of its print run, bringing down Miller's publishing empire along with it. A chastened Shelton briefly turned to drawing music posters before a copy of R. Crumbs'

legendary *Zap Comix* inspired him to publish on his own, and he became one of the growing band of underground cartoonists.

His comic, *Feds 'n' Heds,* introduced a new creation, the Fabulous Furry Freak Brothers, and featured a new Wonder Warthog strip in which the Hog of Steel travels to San Francisco and meets Janis Joplin. Now something of a counterculture star, the Hog turned up in such "family favorites" as *Radical Amerika Comix, Hydrogen Bomb Funnies* (co-starring one Richard M. Nixon) and even *Zap* itself. In *Zap,* he finally acquires a girlfriend, Lois Lamebrain, but it was his last appearance for quite some time. Shelton concentrated on his million-selling Freak Brothers comic until, in 1977, he brought back the Hog for a series of great strips in *Ripoff Comix.* Stories such as the Pig of Tomorrow's attempt to become a football player and to open his own superhero school showed that he was as relevant in the 1970s as ever, but sadly his paperback, *Wonder Warthog and the Nurds of November* (1980), was to be his swansong. With the Freak Brothers appearing all over the world, there was simply no time for Shelton to draw any more superhero strips, and so after twenty years the Hog of Steel finally hung up his cape. —*DAR*

Wonder Woman

As the legend at the beginning of each story tells readers, she is "beautiful as Aphrodite, wise as Athena, stronger then Hercules, and swifter than Mercury." In her patriotic costume, she has fought the forces of evil since her 1942 debut, whether the threat came from Nazis, aliens, super villains, the Greek pantheon of gods, or those who would seek to oppress womanhood. In her sixty-plus-year history, her adventures have almost exclusively been told by men, and yet she is one of the most recognizable icons of the feminist movement. She is Wonder Woman, Amazon princess from Paradise

Wonder Woman #22 © 1988 DC Comics.
COVER ART BY GEORGE PÉREZ.

Island/Themyscira, and the most famous super-woman in world history.

Wonder Woman was created by psychologist Dr. William Moulton Marston, using the pseudonym of "Charles Moulton." Marston was a bit of a maverick in the scientific community, in which he is credited as the main inventor of the lie detector test, and in his private life, in which he lived with his wife and another woman, and fathered children with both. Marston had written about comics in the early 1940s, and created Wonder Woman thereafter. She first appeared in a backup story in *All-Star Comics* #8 (December 1941–January 1942), then took the

cover spot in *Sensation Comics* #1 (January 1942). She proved popular enough that a second series of her own soon appeared in summer 1942, titled *Wonder Woman.*

Details of Wonder Woman's origin changed many times over the years, but the main plot mostly stayed the same. Air Force pilot Steve Trevor's plane crashes on the uncharted Paradise Island, home of the immortal Amazons. The raven-haired Princess Diana finds Trevor and the Amazons nurse him back to health. A tournament is held, officiated by Queen Hippolyta, for a champion of the Amazons to take the pilot back to "Man's World," but Diana is forbidden to enter. Disguising herself, she engages in the games—including the deadly "Bullets and Bracelets" ritual—winning them and being awarded the costume of Wonder Woman by the queen. Diana takes Trevor back to America in her invisible plane, and trades places with a look-alike army nurse named Diana Prince, who needs money to join her fiancé in South America. The new Diana Prince soon becomes Trevor's assistant, and yet he never suspects that she is also the "beautiful angel" Wonder Woman who constantly helps him on his missions against spies and saboteurs.

In her first forty years of adventures, Wonder Woman wore a red bodice with gold eagle, a blue skirt with white stars (quickly discarded for blue shorts with stars), red boots with a white center stripe and upper edge, a gold belt and tiara, and bracelets on each wrist. The bracelets could deflect bullets or other missiles, while hanging from the belt was a magic golden lasso, which compelled anyone bound by it to tell the truth or obey her commands. Wonder Woman had prodigious strength, speed, and leaping abilities, and could send out "mental radio calls" that a mental radio device received. She was often aided in her adventures by corpulent Etta Candy and her Holliday College sorority sisters, the Holliday Girls.

Wonder Woman was popular with readers for many reasons. For a nation engulfed in World War II, her unwavering patriotism was welcome. Male readers enjoyed adventures with a scantily clad woman who often was put into bondage by male or female villains (and occasionally, by her fellow Amazons). Critics such as Fredric Wertham would later note that not only was Wonder Woman a lesbian fantasy figure, but that the series was rife with bondage; the former point would not be addressed until 1990, while the latter was not even debatable, as almost every story Marston wrote included bondage (sometimes called "loving submission" in the comics). Finally, female readers liked the series because it presented a strong and confidant woman, who often gave lectures to others about the strength and power of womanhood, and the need for a strong sisterhood. In an industry wherein too many superheroines were used as either cheese-cake titillation or adjuncts to their more powerful and popular male counterparts, Wonder Woman was a leader.

Wonder Woman's villains often included women such as Dr. Poison (Princess Maru masquerading as a man), Baroness Paula von Gunther (a Nazi who was later reformed by the Amazons), catlike villain-ess the Cheetah, and female gorilla-turned-human Giganta, as well as males like craggy war god Mars and short misogynist Dr. Psycho. Besides her appearances in her own two series, Wonder Woman was a featured member of the Justice Society of America, over in the pages of *All Star Comics.*

Marston wrote *Wonder Woman* until his death in May 1947, with almost every adventure being drawn by artist Harry G. Peter. Robert Khaniger succeeded Marston as writer in 1948, but the popularity of comics was crashing in the postwar years. The hero-ine last appeared with the Justice Society in *All Star Comics* #57 (February 1951), and was gone from *Sensation* after issue #106 (November–December 1951), leaving her bimonthly series as the sole Won-der Woman adventure source. *Wonder Woman* began featuring her in stories wherein she wrote advice columns, went to Hollywood, faced aliens and dinosaurs, fought to protect her secret identity, and entertained marriage proposals from monsters. Peter

was replaced by artists Ross Andru and Mike Esposi-to, among others.

Khaniger also introduced many elements into the mythos that mucked with established continuity, including adventures of a younger Wonder Woman as Wonder Girl and Wonder Tot, and featuring origins for everything from the robot plane to her magic tiara. Romantic suitors for the various ages of Won-der Woman were no longer limited to Trevor, as Khaniger added Merman/Merboy, Birdman/Bird-boy, and even the gooey Glop. Villains tended toward the bizarre, as in the case of the giant Chinese egg known as Egg Fu, diminutive Mouse Man, wispy Paper Man, or multi-legged Crimson Centipede.

Wonder Woman was a founding member of the Justice League of America, appearing in their first story in *The Brave and the Bold* #28 (February–March 1960). A few years later, Wonder Girl joined the Teen Titans in *The Brave and the Bold* #60 (June–July 1965), though this version of the teen heroine was not a younger Wonder Woman, but a girl named Donna Troy, whom Wonder Woman had rescued as a baby, and who had been raised on Par-adise Island. In 1968, Khaniger left the writing reigns of *Wonder Woman,* and eventually writer Denny O'Neil and artists Mike Sekowsky and Dick Giordano came on board. With issue #178 (Septem-ber–October 1968), Diana Prince was stripped of her superpowers and costume, and she became a mod-dressed undercover adventure heroine partial to wearing white zippered leather suits and thigh-high boots. Mentored by a blind man named I-Ching in martial arts, Prince dealt with the death of Trevor (he was later resurrected, then killed, then resurrected, etc.), fought Catwoman and Dr. Cyber, and dealt with feminist issues of the times. Famed science fiction author Samuel R. Delaney scripted issues #202–#203 (September–December 1972), the lat-ter of which was cover-bannered as a "Special! Women's Lib Issue."

That issue would also prove to be the last of the powerless *Wonder Woman* issues as well. Femi-nist leader Gloria Steinem had cover-featured the heroine on the July 1972 debut issue of *Ms.* magazine, and had helped assemble a 1972 hardcover collection of Wonder Woman's adventures. Her introduction in that book promised, "In 1973, *Wonder Woman* comics will be born again, I hope with the feminism and strength of the original Wonder Woman—*my* Wonder Woman—restored." Issue #204 did just that, reintroducing the heroine's costume and powers; it also introduced a black Amazon named Nubia as a sometime foe of Princess Diana.

Wonder Woman's profile grew during the 1970s, largely due to the media. Besides Steinem's feminist support, Wonder Woman appeared as an animated character on ABC's *Super Friends,* beginning in 1973 and continuing for thirteen seasons. She also appeared in 1974 in a badly received TV movie starring Cathy Lee Crosby that had little to do with the comic-book character; much stronger was the series that began the following year, which starred Lynda Carter. The statuesque former Miss World USA perfectly embodied the Amazing Amazon, and early scripts were very faithful to the World War II comics; later seasons, moving the time frame to the 1970s, were less faithful to their progenitors, but Carter was never anything less than spectacular to watch as she embodied the world's most famous superheroine.

Some of the 1970s *Wonder Woman* comics shifted stories back to World War II to match the television show, but DC continuity established that the World War II Wonder Woman was actually living on Earth-Two, a parallel world on which she had begun her adventures in the 1940s and joined the Justice Society. The Earth-One version was younger, and began her team adventures with the Justice League. Occasionally, the characters would meet, generally in the pages of *Justice League of America.*

In *Wonder Woman* #288 (February 1982), the costume of Wonder Woman was significantly altered. The gold eagle on the bodice was replaced with a stylized double-W symbol. The move marked not only the character's fortieth anniversary, but also the establishment of the new Wonder Woman Foundation, a charitable organization created by DC Comics President Jenette Kahn.

Due to what they felt was increasingly convoluted continuity, DC launched a twelve-issue series called *Crisis on Infinite Earths* in April 1985. The end result of the series was that the DC universe would be "reset" to have only one Earth, and one version of every hero and heroine. *Wonder Woman* #329 (February 1986) featured the wedding of Wonder Woman and Steve Trevor, but it was to be the end of their happiness. *Crisis* wiped out their continuity and existence, and Wonder Woman would be reinvented. A retro-style miniseries called *The Legend of Wonder Woman,* drawn by Trina Robbins, was released in May–August 1986; it was the first time a female artist had drawn a *Wonder Woman* book (Dann Thomas co-scripted February 1983's issue #300, and was thus the character's first female writer).

A grand relaunch of *Wonder Woman* occurred with issue #1 of a new series in February 1987. Superstar artist George Pérez (also the *Crisis* illustrator) signed on to guide the new series, initially working with writers Greg Potter and Len Wein before taking over the writing reigns himself. The relaunched *Wonder Woman* shared a similar origin to her predecessor, though the backstory of the Amazons and involvement of the Greek gods were a stronger part of the series. Here, as before, Queen Hippolyta had formed her daughter as a clay statue, whom the gods brought to life. Diana is raised on Themyscira (the renamed Paradise Island), and possesses gifts given to her by the gods, including superhuman strength and speed, and the ability to fly. When the war god Ares threatens the Earth, the pantheon decrees that the Amazons send a champion out into the world to oppose him; after winning a tournament, Diana becomes that champion. Outfitted with a costume inspired by a female aviator the Amazons had known in the past (Diana Trevor, mother of Steve Trevor), Wonder Woman ventures out into the world.

Pérez and company established a number of new details for Wonder Woman as well. She was now a latecomer to the hero world, joining a later incarnation of the Justice League (Black Canary took her spot in history). She lived in Boston, with Greek history professor Julia Kapatelis and her daughter Cassie. She had no invisible plane, though her "Lasso of Truth" (woven from the Girdle of Gaea) still compelled people to tell the truth. She had no secret identity, but existed as an ambassador from Themyscira to the world, attempting to teach lessons of love, peace, and the power of womanhood. Steve Trevor was now a much older man who eventually married Etta Candy. Although she engaged villains such as Cheetah, Silver Swan, or Doctor Psycho, Diana was just as often in conflict with mythological threats to humankind from Ares, the witch Circe, Eris the goddess of discord, or other forces of evil.

The stories in the revamped *Wonder Woman* were densely plotted, and refused to shy away from controversy. A gay man first appeared in issue #20 (September 1988) before the Amazons' Sapphic sexuality was addressed in issue #38 (January 1990), while issue #46 (September 1990) dealt with the fallout from a teen suicide. Pérez was also keenly aware of the lack of female involvement in *Wonder Woman*'s history; though his editor was a woman, Karen Berger, he also wrote the 1989 *Wonder Woman Annual* stories to be drawn by female artists, and he eventually worked with co-writer Mindy Newell and artist Jill Thompson on the series.

Following Pérez's departure with issue #62 (February 1992), *Wonder Woman* went through a series of creative teams, each of which attempted to put their own mark on the heroine, for better or worse. Brian Bolland signed aboard to do fantastic covers, but the 1992–1995 issues are remembered by most as the era that featured Wonder Woman in space, Wonder Woman taking a job at Taco Whiz, Wonder Woman being replaced by rogue red-headed Amazon Artemis, and Wonder Woman changing from shorts to a star-spangled thong.

Popular writer-artist John Byrne took over the series with issue #101 (September 1995), moving Diana to Gateway City, replacing her supporting cast with similar characters Helena Sandsmark and daughter Cassandra "Cassie" Sandsmark, killing half the Amazons, and pitting her against villains such as Fourth World ruler Darkseid, Arthurian witch Morgan Le Fay, Dr. Psycho, Cheetah, and others. Byrne reintroduced the invisible plane, and turned Cassie into a new Wonder Girl, then killed Diana, had her resurrected as the Goddess of Truth, and had Hippolyta take over her role as Wonder Woman. Continuity was a casualty in the following storylines in which Hippolyta-as-Wonder Woman was inserted backward in time to World War II adventures with the Justice Society, and Donna Troy (the ex-Wonder Girl, now Troia) was given an extraordinarily convoluted origin—the latest in her long line of origin revisions.

Diana became Wonder Woman again in Byrne's final issue (#136, August 1998), followed by a few years of rotating creative teams. With *Wonder Woman* #164 (January 2001), writer-artist Phil Jimenez came aboard to revamp the title yet again, but his stories harkened back to the strength of the Pérez run. Jimenez attempted to straighten out the by-now-again-convoluted history of Wonder Woman, while pitting her against such villains as the Joker, Silver Swan, Circe, a new male Cheetah, Giganta, and others. He also introduced a new male love interest, an African-American man named Trevor Barnes. Unfortunately, Jimenez's work was affected by a number of companywide crossovers mandated by DC, including one—*Our Worlds at War*—which forced upon him the death of Hippolyta. Later, Jimenez reintroduced the concept of Wonder Woman spinning into her costume (a staple of the 1970s comics and the TV series), and even utilized some costume elements from the television show. His final issue, #188 (March 2003) was a virtual love letter to every incarnation of Wonder Woman throughout her sixty-one-year history.

Following a six-issue semi-return to the non-powered jumpsuit-wearing Wonder Woman, the series rebounded with another new creative team. In issue #195, novelist Greg Rucka and artists

Drew Johnson and Ray Snyder came aboard to redefine the character. Gone were elements that the team felt demeaned the heroine, as Wonder Woman published an autobiographical book of essays (titled *Reflections*) and embarked on a proactive stance on making the world a safer and better place. Behind the scenes, Ares, Doctor Psycho, and others are plotting to bring the heroine down, but it is unlikely that DC's female figurehead will be bested easily.

Over six decades, Wonder Woman's likeness and logo have appeared on apparel; dolls and action figures; puppets; puzzles; school supplies; kitchenware; costumes; lunch boxes; candy dispensers; night lights; music boxes; telephones; cake pans; model kits; valentines; Christmas ornaments; and even packaged macaroni. Audio adventures of the heroine have appeared on record and tape in the 1960s and 1970s, while a daily newspaper strip saw print in 1944–1945. Today, she appears weekly in the animated adventures of Cartoon Network's *Justice League,* and a *Wonder Woman* feature film has been in development for years.

Although she is not the first superheroine, Wonder Woman is the most famous, the longest-lived, and the most popular. Appealing to a vast demographic, she is the paragon not just of patriotism, but of womanhood itself. Whether preaching the loving submission and strength of sisterhood of her early years, or the diversity, tolerance, and love for humankind of her current incarnation, Wonder Woman has—as her TV theme asserted—arrived to change the world. And we are all the better for having her in it. —*AM*

Wonder Woman in the Media

"Wonder Woman! Wonder Woman! All the world is waiting for you, and the power you possess. In your satin tights, fighting for your rights, and the old red, white and blue!" No superheroine before her had so dominated the public consciousness, so it seemed that the theme song for ABC's *Wonder Woman* series wasn't strictly hyperbole. All the world *was* waiting for her, but it would be a long time after her January 1942 debut in *All-Star Comics* #8 that Wonder Woman would rule the airwaves.

Although some efforts had been made to interest Hollywood in a *Wonder Woman* serial in the early 1950s, it wasn't until 1967 that any filmed version of *Wonder Woman* existed. With the success of the campy *Batman* series on ABC, in 1966 that series' executive producer William Dozier commissioned a script for a *Wonder Woman* pilot for Greenway Productions and Twentieth Century-Fox Television. Writers Stan Hart and Larry Siegel wrote a silly tale called "Who's Afraid of Diana Prince?" It told not only a revised version of Wonder Woman's origin, but included a plot about computer saboteurs as well.

Director Les Martinson shot almost five minutes of pilot footage, using comedienne Ellie Wood Walker in the title role, with Maudie Prickett as her whiny suburban mother. When the plain Walker would look into the mirror, she saw herself as a gorgeous version of Wonder Woman—the narrator intoned "And who *thinks* she has the beauty of Aphrodite"—played in the mirror by busty actress Linda Harrison. The never-aired mini-pilot wasn't enough to generate interest in a regular series, however, and a live-action *Wonder Woman* would take almost another decade to appear.

Instead of live versions, Wonder Woman did become an animated staple, beginning in 1972. She first appeared in Filmation's *The Brady Kids* on ABC, guest-starring as both Diana Prince and Wonder Woman in a time travel story that found each of the Brady children competing at the ancient Olympics. The following year, Wonder Woman was a founding member of the *Super Friends* on ABC's new Hanna-Barbera superhero team series for 1973. Teamed with Batman,

Lynda Carter stars in *Wonder Woman*.

Super Friends (1979–1980), *The Super Friends Hour* (1980–1981), *The Super Friends* (1981–1984), *Super Friends—The Legendary Super Powers Show* (1984–1985), and, finally, *The Super Powers Team: Galactic Guardians* (1985–1986). A few Wonder Woman concepts made it onto the small screen, including Paradise Island, Queen Hippolyta, the villainous Cheetah and Giganta, and love interest Steve Trevor. The last two incarnations of the series also incorporated the new "double-W" design of Wonder Woman's comic-book bodice, and B. J. Ward took over as Wonder Woman's voice.

Even as *Super Friends* brought young viewers to know Wonder Woman, plans were afoot for a live-action television launch. Unfortunately, the first effort was a worse offering than the 1967 pilot. ABC aired the first *Wonder Woman* telefilm on March 12, 1974, but viewers barely recognized comics' premiere superheroine. Blame fell on producer/screenwriter John D. F. Black, who cast blonde Cathy Lee Crosby in the title role, dressing her in blue boots and tights, and a red-white-and-blue jacket and mini-skirt combination that didn't flatter Crosby or the camera.

In addition to being forced to follow a donkey around to get clues, Crosby faced multiple "perils": twin spies who knew her secret identity (as did everyone else in this film); a melting wall of multi-colored Silly Putty; a rogue Amazon (Anita Ford); and finally Ricardo Montalban as Abner Smith, the villainous leader of a supposed international spy ring.

Robin, Superman, and Aquaman, Wonder Woman fought aliens, androids, and an occasional supervillain. Her voice was provided by Shannon Farnon, and her slightly simplified costume design was by comics legend Alex Toth.

SuperFriends evolved almost yearly, changing titles and formats as it went, but Wonder Woman reamained a constant. It became *The All-New Super Friends Hour* (1977–1978), *The Challenge of the Super Friends* (1978–1979), *The World's Greatest*

Virtually no stunts or special effects were used, and the low budget was painfully obvious. And while plans for further Cathy Lee Crosby as Wonder Woman projects were quickly squashed, ABC remained interested in the concept.

Spurred on by the success of *Police Woman* and the Bionic Woman's appearances in *The Six Million Dollar Man,* ABC ordered up a new telefilm in November 1975. This film's script, meticulously researched by writer Stanley Ralph Ross, was—in most critical and fan opinion—the perfect treatment for *Wonder Woman.* Set during World War II, the movie featured Steve Trevor (Lyle Waggoner), General Blankenship (John Randolph), the Amazon Queen Mother (Cloris Leachman), and Nazis galore. The role of Wonder Woman went to newcomer Lynda Carter.

The nearly six-foot-tall brunette seemed born for the role. Carter was tall, shapely, beautiful, and looked right in the star-spangled costume, which designer Donfeld had taken almost directly from the comics, with the exception of a red-white-and-blue cape Carter wore for special occasions. Carter had been a singer, dancer, variety show performer, and former Miss World USA before landing the role. Although her acting wasn't rock-solid as the series began, Carter gave the role a sense of seriousness; she made the viewer believe she *was* Wonder Woman.

The New, Original Wonder Woman debuted on November 7, 1975, and was an instant success. High ratings told ABC that it was on the right track. It ordered a series of further one-hour specials, keeping the flavor of the 1940s comics; in them, Wonder Woman met Baroness Paula von Gunther (Christine Belford) and Fausta "the Nazi Wonder Woman" (Lynda Day George). There was no shortage of villains, as spies and Nazis were always on the loose, and Steve Trevor was always captured.

The shows had a sense of realism to their superhuman stunts; the heroine deflected bullets with her bracelets, hurled her tiara like a boomerang, and used her magic lasso to rope vil-

lains and force them to tell the truth. Perhaps the most spectacular stuntwork involved the "wonder-jumps," performed mainly by stuntwoman Jeannie Epper. Wonder Woman jumped over tanks, buildings, and other assorted obstacles with the greatest of ease. The invisible plane was used a few times, then abandoned, but one aspect that was kept was Diana Prince's transformation to and from Wonder Woman; she would spin around, and in a burst of light, portions of her civilian clothing would be replaced by her costume.

In the fall of 1976, ABC scheduled the retitled *Wonder Woman* as a regular series. It began with a two-part episode called "The Feminum Mystique," which introduced a new young starlet named Debra Winger in the part of Drusilla, Wonder Woman's younger sister, a.k.a. Wonder Girl (clad in a costume remarkably like that of her comic-book counterpart). Popular with viewers, Wonder Girl appeared again, and a spin-off series was planned, but Winger bowed out, citing difficulties behind the scenes. Another popular episode guest-starred Roy Rogers, but by early 1977, ABC had decided not to renew the show, despite high ratings.

In an unusual move, rival network CBS snapped up the series for its fall 1977 schedule. Under the title *The New Adventures of Wonder Woman,* a new telefilm on September 16 updated the story for a more modern setting. The premiere episode showed young Steve Trevor Jr. (Waggoner again) crash-landing near Paradise Island, to which Wonder Woman had retired almost thirty years prior. Princess Diana once again fell in love and returned to "Man's World" to become a superheroine. There she flew an updated plane, wore an updated costume (skimpier, with a different star-pattern on the shorts and a different chest-eagle and bracelets), and sported an updated hairdo.

Wonder Woman eventually got two additional skin-tight spandex costumes: one for riding a motorcycle and one for swimming. Both were all-blue and star-studded, and she wore either boots or flippers depending on the situation. A skateboarding outfit—

complete with helmet and knee-and-elbow-pads—also made one appearance. The new Diana Prince worked alongside Steve at the Inter-Agency Defense Command (IADC), an intelligence network linked with the White House. She would often go on specialized missions alone, leaving Steve in Washington with the talking IRA (Internal Retrieval Associative) computer.

Although villains on the series sometimes had superpowers, none were from the comics. The heroine fought a vengeful, telekinetic Japanese veteran who was obsessed with her; black Amazonian Wonder Woman counterpart Carolyn (Jayne Kennedy); magician Count Cagliostro (Dick Gautier); insect-controlling Formicidia (popular mime Laureen Yarnell); a psychic disco vampire; the mind-stealing alien Skrills; and a dastardly toymaker who had created an evil, life-size Wonder Woman robot.

Despite strong ratings and a deluge of fan mail, the network put *The New Adventures of Wonder Woman* on hiatus during its second CBS season, airing the final three episodes in the fall of 1979. One episode of the final trio was actually intended as a relaunch for the show's third season, moving Diana Prince to the Los Angeles IADC offices, and dumping Lyle Waggoner for a supporting cast that included a superstrong male co-worker, a cute African-American kid, and a monkey. Given this revamp, perhaps it's best that the third season wasn't produced.

Although not on the air nearly as long as her DC friends Superman and Batman, the *Wonder Woman* series has remained a favorite in syndication and video release, and almost thirty years after its debut, licensed material featuring Lynda Carter as Wonder Woman is still sold. Direct references to the series have shown up on *The Naked Truth* and *Frasier,* and Carter is still a popular guest on talk shows.

Although her live-action adventures ended in 1979, Wonder Woman hasn't been idle in the animated arena. She guest-starred in an episode of 1988's *Superman* series on CBS, in which Themyscira (the renamed Paradise Island) and her post–*Crisis on Infinite Earths* comic-book continuity were referenced. In

1993, producer-director Boyd Kirkland began work on a *Wonder Woman and the Star Riders* pilot, which would have helped promote a series of Mattel toys that teamed the heroine up with Dolphin, Ice, Starlily, and Solara against the evil Purrsia. Only a minute of test animation was produced before the project was canceled (due to low orders for the toys), but Kirkland also developed a more serious *Wonder Woman* cartoon a few years later; it did not sell.

Meanwhile, in 1997–1998, a much-publicized plan to return *Wonder Woman* to live-action for an NBC series was underway. Deborah Joy Levine, who had successfully developed *Lois & Clark: The New Adventures of Superman,* was brought aboard to oversee the series and write the pilot script. Her version found Prince as a UCLA professor of Greek history. A nationwide casting call began, with applicants encouraged to show up at certain Warner Bros. stores in December 1997 and January 1998 with photos and acting resumes. Although casting eventually narrowed down to a few Hollywood newcomers, development on the series was shut down before any filming began.

On November 17, 2001, the Cartoon Network debuted a new animated *Justice League* weekly series, from the same Warner Bros. animation crew that worked on the *Batman* and *Superman* shows. On the series, Wonder Woman (voiced by Susan Eisenberg) is a no-nonsense warrior who has been exiled from her home on Themyscira/Paradise Island. Some episodes have shown Queen Hippolyta, World War II hero Steve Trevor, villainess Cheetah, and renegade Amazon Aresia. New episodes featuring Wonder Woman are still airing as of 2004.

Since the late 1990s, Warner has had plans to shoot a big-budget feature film, with Silver Pictures and producers Jon Peters and Leonard Goldberg. Multiple scripts have been written, including passes by Kimberlee Reed (1999), James R. Harnock and Eve Marie Kazaros (1999), Jon Cohen (1999), Todd Alcott (2001), Becky Johnston (2002), Philip Levens (2003), and Laeta Kalogridis (2003). Ivan Reitman had been set to direct since 1996, but he eventually left the project. Although Jennifer Aniston and several other actresses were rumored for the lead role, the only person the part had been locked to was Sandra Bullock; she eventually dropped out of the project following statements she did not want to wear the traditional costume.

Whenever *Wonder Woman* does reappear in live action, the costume won't be the most difficult aspect for the lead actress to master. The most challenging task will be to replace the image of Lynda Carter as Wonder Woman in the public's mind. Although her time as the character only lasted four years, the appeal of the series cemented Carter's image as the Amazing Amazon for almost three decades. "You're a wonder, Wonder Woman!" indeed. —*AM*

World War II and the Superhero

"Nazis and Japs, you rats! Beware! The Hangman is everywhere!" This copy, grossly politically incorrect by contemporary standards, is plastered above the logo of MLJ Publications' superhero comic, *Hangman* #3 (1942). And no words could better summarize the sentiment of a galvanized nation.

PATRIOTIC PROPAGANDA

Hangman #3 is far from unique. The jingoistic jargon and flag-waving images of dozens of comic-book covers printed before and during World War II rival the pro-war posters displayed in public buildings during the era. Yankee Doodle Jones, Dandy, and Major Victory march toward the reader, playing drums and fife, on the patriotic cover of *Yankee Comics* #2 (1941). The Man of Steel rides a U.S.-dropped bomb (presumably heading toward an Axis nation) on the cover of *Superman* #18 (1942), with a stirring promotional blurb: "War Savings Bonds and Stamps Do the Job on the Japanazis!" *Speed*

Comics #19's (1942) cover depicts Captain Freedom, fists clenched, sneaking up on a yellow-skinned, buck-toothed Japanese soldier donning a Captain Freedom costume. A fortress labeled "Hitler's Berchtesgaden" is stormed by gargantuan versions of Captain America, the Human Torch, and the Sub-Mariner—their size metaphorically symbolizing the superiority of the Allies—on star cover artist Alex Schomburg's *All Select Comics* #1 (1943). Superheroes had only been in existence for a few short years—since the premiere of Superman in DC Comics' landmark *Action Comics* #1 (June 1938)—but comic-book publishers wasted no time in exploiting their greatest superpower: propaganda.

World War II may have a bleak chapter in human history, but for superhero comic books, it was the lifeblood of a period now acknowledged as the Golden Age (1938–1954). As Adolf Hitler's German forces blazed a devastating path across Europe in the late 1930s, Americans fretfully pondered if—or worse, *when*—the conflict would involve the United States. This escalating global conflict, however, offered the budding medium of superhero comics a perfect villain.

INTRODUCING THE SHIELD

"We were fighting Hitler before our government was fighting Hitler," stated Marvel Comics mogul Stan Lee, on the History Channel documentary *Comic Book Superheroes: Unmasked* (2003). German spies tiptoed into the pages of American comics as early as *Pep Comics* #1 (cover-dated January 1940, but hitting newsstands in December 1939, two years before Japan's sneak attack on Pearl Harbor). *Pep* #1, a product of MLJ Publications (soon to be known as Archie Comics) introduces the Shield—the first comic-book character whose costume was patterned after the U.S. flag—the son of an assassinated FBI agent who applies a solution of his father's design onto his person, boosting his strength and stamina. As the Shield, he vanquishes the German infiltrators and engages in Nazi-busting for years to come.

Before long, the Shield was no longer the United States' sole superheroic protector. Guarding the United States from Axis invaders and saboteurs became a recurring theme in comics stories and on comics covers. *Look* magazine published a specially commissioned 1940 comic supplement featuring Superman arresting Hitler and Joseph Stalin for war crimes. Sales of superhero comics had been strong since their inception, but when covers portrayed patriotic motifs, their circulations escalated.

Anti-Axis sentiment exploded from subtlety to ubiquity by 1941. Superman, Captain Marvel, Miss Fury, and Sub-Mariner were among the superheroes encountering German, and soon Japanese, soldiers in their stories. Wrote Maurice Horn in *The World Encyclopedia of Comics, Volume 1* (1999), "The titles of some of the books published in this period suffice to give a clue as to their character: *Spy Smasher, Commando Yank, Major Victory, Captain Flag, The Fighting Yank, The Unknown Soldier …*"

SUPERPATRIOTS IN ACTION

Almost every Golden Age superhero, at one time or another, was an Axis-basher, but none were more blatant than the cadre of red-white-and-blue-clad patriotic superheroes, whose multitude nearly outnumbered the stars on the U.S. flag itself: Uncle Sam, Captain Victory, the Flag, Yankee Doodle Jones, Yankee Eagle, the Star-Spangled Kid and Stripesy, Super-American, Captain Courageous, the American Eagle, the Spirit of 76, American Crusader, Captain Fearless, Flag-Man, Minute-Man, the Liberator, and Mr. America were among their number, as were their female contemporaries, Miss Victory, Pat Patriot, Yankee Girl, Liberty Belle, and Miss America. Fawcett Publications' Spy Smasher's garb was rather mundane when compared to these flashy freedom fighters: He sported an aviator's helmet, Khakis, a bomber jacket, and a crimson cape. But with his noiseless Gyrosub—plane, submarine, helicopter, and speedboat rolled into one—Spy

Smasher crippled saboteurs' vessels and ferreted out enemy agents, flying into his own twelve-chapter movie serial in 1942.

In case any young reader doubted the capabilities of these patriotic paragons, their comics sometimes included reminders that the military was always on watch, as in *Feature Comics* #42's (1941) story starring the superheroine USA (a.k.a. the "Spirit of Old Glory"); as USA is poised protectively on a coastline, the opening caption proclaims, "The security of American shores is well guarded, as our Navy patrols far-flung waters and warns aggressors of the power of democracy." Rest easy, Americans! The superheroes and the U.S. military are here!

The most popular star-spangled superhero of World War II was Captain America, first seen in his own title published in March 1941 by Marvel (then known as Timely) Comics. "The whole reason we put Captain America out was that America was in a patriotic frenzy," recollected Joe Simon, who created the hero (and many others) with Jack Kirby. The cover to *Captain America* #1 has "Cap" delivering a haymaker to the jaw of none other than Hitler himself—and the United States' involvement in the war was *still* almost a year away!

HITLER TAKES ON THE HEROES

The Führer was the perfect patsy and the perfect antagonist for comic book artists of the day. Hitler's pasty complexion, greasy hair, distinctive moustache, and patented furrowed brow made him ripe for caricature. His rather comical proportions and body language stood in ironic contrast to the Aryan ideal that he promoted so vehemently with his Master Race theory. Equally ironic, if not more so, was the image of most of the American superheroes, perfect physical specimens who also epitomized the fascist mindset of the superiority of aggression. Paradoxically, superhero readers and creators did not seem to notice.

Hitler was made aware of the impact of American superheroes, and set his own public-relations machine in motion. Hitler's spin doctor Joseph Goebbels once made anti-Semitic attacks toward Superman's co-creator, writer Jerry Siegel, citing Superman comics as "Jewish propaganda" and calling Siegel "physically and intellectually circumcised."

Real-life German and Japanese soldiers inspired fictional foes in Golden Age comic books, including Captain Nazi, the Red Skull, Baron Gestapo, Captain Nippon, and Captain Swastika. The Claw, a jaundiced "Oriental" with fearsome fangs, appeared in Gleason Publications' *Daredevil* series, as did Hitler himself, in the legendary *Daredevil Battles Hitler* #1 (a.k.a. *Daredevil* #1) in 1941.

Beyond the cover pinups, the Axis was pummeled and ridiculed in the comics stories themselves. Thick, stereotyped accents were afforded to both German and Japanese characters in most Golden Age comics. In "The Human Torch and Sub-Mariner Fighting Side By Side" in *Marvel Mystery Comics* #17 (1941), a Nazi soldier brags, as the unconscious Sub-Mariner is being strung up, "He iss our symbol of victory! Unvard!"

Even the most obscure superheroes fought the enemy, including Marvel's Citizen V: "Single-handed, Citizen 'V' bursts into the Nazi camp and with powerful fists flying, drives his enemies to cover!" reads the opening caption to the hero's adventure in *Comedy Comics* #9 (1942).

COMICS SELL MILLIONS

Golden Age comic books provided amusement and patriotism in one ten-cent, sixty-four-page package. Millions of comics sold each month during World War II. Comic-book houses worked at breakneck pace to meet the demand of a growing audience. Many publishers were akin to sweatshops, with original art pages shuffled down assembly lines of artists, each with his or her own task: One would letter the word balloons, one would ink faces, one would ink figures, and one would ink backgrounds. Artists and writers of the era sometimes huddled collectively into New York City apartments for an entire weekend of all-nighters, grinding out pages at a frantic pace. Many of these creators were happy to have the work, having survived the unemployment of the Great Depression. Others realized the importance of superheroes as mouthpieces of democracy. "I believe in the brotherhood of man and peace on Earth," comic-book and science-fiction author Gardner Fox once asserted. "If I could do it with a wave of my hand I'd stop all this war and silly nonsense of killing people. So I used superheroes' powers to accomplish what I couldn't do as a person. The superheroes were my wish-fulfillment figures for benefiting the world."

Voraciously reading these comics were millions of American boys. The medium spoke to them, its superheroes offering inspiration during a trying time. Captain America, striking an "Uncle Sam Wants You" recruitment pose, was featured in house ads encouraging young readers to join his "Sentinels of Liberty" club, "… and wear a badge that proves you are a loyal believer in Americanism." Not to be outdone, Superman enticed readers to become one of the "Supermen of America." Boys would regularly congregate for "swaps," haggling trades of their well-read comics among one another. Popular titles like *Captain Marvel Adventures, Superman,* and *Captain America* would command more trading value among these young negotiators.

Entertainment-starved American servicemen also read comics. Historian Mike Benton claimed in his book *Superhero Comics of the Golden Age: The Illustrated History* (1992) that a remarkable 44 percent of U.S. soldiers undergoing basic training were regular comic-book readers. "At PXs, comic books outsold *Saturday Evening Post, Life,* and *Reader's Digest* combined by a ratio of ten to one," Benton added. Once these GIs were stationed overseas, superhero comics were sent to them, as part of their care packages from home.

While the war reinforced the popularity of superhero comic books, war-related rationing posed a serious threat to their production. Paper shortages curtailed the expansion of the medium, keeping many would-be publishers from entering the fray, and paper drives led to the donations of used copies of Golden Age comics, explaining their scarcity in the contemporary collectibles market.

D-DAY FOR SUPERHEROES

Americans naturally celebrated when the Allies won their victory, but the war's end delivered a death blow to superheroes. They instantly fell out of favor, and sales steeply plummeted. Titles were canceled, publishers closed their shops, and only the strongest (Superman, Batman, and Wonder Woman) survived.

Superheroes received a second lease on life, beginning with comics' Silver Age (1956–1969). Some of the superheroes who fought for freedom in the 1940s have returned to active duty, and "retro" series set during World War II continue to explore the superhero's role as the superpatriot; examples include Marvel Comics' *The Invaders* (1975–1979) and DC Comics' *All-Star Squadron* (1981–1987). In the 2000s, DC sustains use of a few of its stalwarts of World War II, including the Flash and Green Lantern (now known as Sentinel) in an incarnation of the WWII-era Justice Society called *JSA* (1999–present). —*ME*

X-Men

To the world at large the X-Men have been an overnight success on the back of two well-received movies, when in fact their rise has been a forty-year crawl, punctuated by false starts and protracted editorial caution in initially expanding the franchise.

Since their 1963 introduction the X-Men have served as a metaphor for cultural intolerance. This, though, is predicated on the shaky foundation that the humans populating Marvel Comics' psuedo-Earth are bigoted toward those with inherent superhuman abilities—otherwise known as mutants—while reserving their acclaim for superheroes whose powers were accidentally acquired or technologically conferred. The concept of a mutant as a simultaneously persecuted and amazingly unique creature hit home to readers in the turbulent 1960s, and was a concept that any non-Anglo reader could personally relate to. Created by the prolific Stan Lee and Jack Kirby, the first issue of *X-Men* introduced half a dozen characters still appearing regularly forty years later, and a villain, Magneto, who has been a mainstay of Marvel Comics since his inception.

The guiding light of the X-Men is the distinctively bald and (until 2003) wheelchair-confined Professor Charles Xavier, also known as Professor X. A dis-

ability was of minor consequence to the world's most powerful telepath, who engineered a dream of guiding other mutants to use their abilities for the betterment of humankind. His means for doing so was founding Xavier's School for Gifted Youngsters in Westchester County, New York, away from the prying eyes of the public. His first pupil was Scott Summers, cursed through emitting concussive force blasts from his eyes, beams that are mysteriously contained by the ruby quartz visor he permanently wears. As Cyclops he was field leader of the original X-Men, and plays a major role to this day. In the 2000s he is married to Jean Grey, the first mutant actually treated by Professor X. Now second only to Xavier in terms of extra-mental ability, over the years she's had a rough ride. It was retroactively decided that as Marvel Girl in the original X-Men the Professor had limited her prodigious abilities to telekinesis, considering her not mature enough to cope with the full range of her blossoming powers. She also spent several years cocooned beneath Jamaica Bay, initially replaced by a powerful extraterrestrial entity called the Phoenix Force, over which she maintained an element of psychic control while it masqueraded as her. She eventually convinced it to commit suicide to save the universe. The late 1970s stories featuring Phoenix, as the entity was originally known, are still considered landmark *X-Men* issues.

X-Men #104 © 1977 Marvel Comics.
COVER ART BY DAVE COCKRUM.

Hank McCoy's brutish, almost simian form and athletic ability resulted in his being called the Beast, a code name that belied a prodigious intellect, both artistic and scientific. During a period when the X-Men had disbanded he took a job as research scientist, experimenting on himself with a compound that induced further genetic mutation. He transmuted into a form more in keeping with his name and now resembles an upright blue furry dog. Bobby Drake, alias Iceman, was the mirror image of long-standing Marvel hero the Human Torch. Initially a mobile snowman, he has been refined into a sleeker ice-covered hero, and among other abilities is able to generate sheets of ice from his hands on which he travels. Bizarrely, having no connection with Spider-

Man in the comics, Iceman was one of the "Amazing Friends" from Spider-Man's 1980s cartoon show *Spider-Man and His Amazing Friends*. The original team of X-Men was rounded out by Warren Worthington III. This rich playboy carried a secret in the form of giant wings, which remained strapped to his back in civilian guise. His major trauma was the amputation of his wings, and their subsequent replacement by razor-sharp metal ones courtesy of the villain Apocalypse. It took some while before the original wings re-established themselves.

The original incarnation of the X-Men started strongly, but disintegrated among mediocre plots and never really fired comic readers' enthusiasm. Perhaps the theme of outsiders was inherently off-putting in an early 1960s America where cold war politics were still high on the agenda, and anyone not allowed at the front of the bus was better off not boarding in the first place. Toward the end of the 1960s, though, the comic sported some fine graphic realism from artist Neal Adams, and introduced two intriguing new heroes who never quite lived up to the excitement of their introduction. Alex Summers is brother to Scott, and as Havok channels solar energy into devastating blasts, while his partner, Lorna Dane (who eventually adopted the name Polaris), is able to control magnetic forces, although the reason for her striking green hair remains a mystery.

In the early 1970s *X-Men* survived by reprinting old stories, while the team members made sporadic guest appearances elsewhere, the Beast even maintaining his own short solo run in the pages of *Amazing Adventures*. The lack of activity didn't deter hardcore fans demanding the team's return, and in a period of expansion for Marvel in 1975 *Giant-Size X-Men* #1 appeared with little promotional fanfare. With the X-Men captured, Professor X traveled the globe to recruit a new team of mutants to rescue them. Raised in Egypt, but of deeper African ancestry, Ororo Monroe can fly and control the weather as Storm. Colossus was found on a remote Ukranian farming collective, and the athletic, teleporting

642

Nightcrawler was rescued from a German mob chasing him due to his demonic appearance. The Native American Thunderbird, alias John Proudstar, had superhuman strength, speed, reflexes, and agility, none of which prevented him from being an early casualty, and the pint-sized Wolverine had previously been seen using his metal claws to fight the Hulk with no indication of any mutant abilities. The team was rounded out with two characters who had fought the X-Men in the 1960s. Sean Cassidy, the Banshee, had employed his psionic screams under duress, but the fiercely nationalistic Sunfire resented American imperialism and the atomic bomb that resulted in both his mutation and his mother's death. He flies and fires beams of intense heat, but while no longer an enemy, Sunfire departed after retrieving the original X-Men, and by many is considered very much the third-string hero.

The new characters had largely been designed by artist Dave Cockrum, some having languished in his sketchbooks for years, and while it was Len Wein who plotted the return of the X-Men (after some brainstorming by editor Roy Thomas), he turned over the writing of subsequent stories to his editorial assistant Chris Claremont. An aspiring actor, Claremont never made the stage, but in the manner of many of his characters, discovered an undreamed of talent. He delivered solid soap opera interaction, intriguing plots, and compelling new characters. As time passed his plots would become slimmer, with overwriting the norm, but credit is due Claremont for transforming the X-Men from also-rans to headliners. In the process he can be further credited for finally propelling female superheroes beyond Decoration Girl and Sidekick Lass. Claremont's refrain "Is there any reason this character can't be a woman?" would pass into editorial legend and he was additionally very quick to latch onto the success of *Star Wars* and introduce elements of space opera to *X-Men*. Although uncredited, artist Cockrum and especially his successor John Byrne each contributed ideas, and it was during Byrne's thirty-five issues that the X-Men's inexorable rise to their current stature as marketing monoliths really began.

As soon as the X-Men were restored to their regularly numbered series, editors made a decision to slim down the cast, with all old X-Men other than Cyclops and Jean Grey considered surplus (although the Beast proved popular in *The Avengers*). Of the new characters it was Wolverine who quickly became the favorite, known only by his code name or "Logan." Cynics might claim that comics fans share an affinity with a man cast as a surly, repressed loner, and Wolverine lived out their fantasies by dealing with any trouble that came his way in particularly savage fashion. Much discussion ensued as to whether or not he'd murdered a guard off-panel in one Claremont/Byrne issue, but he subsequently revealed little remorse regarding killing. An aura of mystery surrounded him. It took decades for Marvel to reveal his background, all the while establishing facets, then later revealing the snippets false. His mutant abilities are three-fold: a set of bony claws embedded in each hand, heightened senses, and a body capable of rapidly healing the most severe injuries. This ability has also restrained the natural aging process, Wolverine having been born in the nineteenth century, with recorded experiences dating back to at least the Spanish Civil War. When Wolverine's early life was finally related in the *Origin* series it was a critical and artistic success, and all the more astonishing for being more gothic horror than superhero story. One final element was formative in the Wolverine who is popular today: his unwilling participation in covert, CIA-sponsored "Weapon X" experiments. His skeleton and claws were bonded with an indestructible metal known as adamantium, and he was implanted with false memories, which, over time, have been established as such. His real past, however, remains elusive to him.

Editors introduced the thirteen-year-old Kitty Pryde, able to pass through solid surfaces and walk on air, to restore the idea of youngsters being trained in the best use of their abilities. She played a pivotal role in the Claremont/Byrne team's penultimate story, set in a future where mutants were either murdered or interned in concentration camps. To prevent this scenario the adult Pryde exchanged minds with her teenage counterpart, guiding the X-Men to manipulate pivotal events to ensure her future never occurred. While critics and fans agree it was a great story in isolation, the unfortunate aspect of "Days of Future Past" was that elements would be plundered, expanded upon, and twisted until X-Men continuity was impenetrable to anyone not a regular reader.

While sales, even under Byrne, initially failed to match fan fervor, they did increase to the point that Marvel introduced a second X-Men title in all but name, with *New Mutants* reaffirming Professor X's program of educating young mutants. This was followed by *X-Factor,* launched by retrieving Jean Grey from beneath the sea, in which the original X-Men operated a mutant rescue operation under the pretense of dealing with the mutant "problem." The principal X-Men team also continued to expand, adding Rogue, unable to touch anyone without absorbing their abilities and memories. Her first such encounter was with a heroine named Ms. Marvel, the legacy of which was permanent invulnerability, super strength, and flight. Still not allocated a civilian name, the distinctively southern Rogue has a deep affection for her fellow southerner, the Louisiana-born Remy LeBeau. As Gambit he charges inanimate objects with energy and throws them to detonate on impact. His has a checkered past, having apprenticed as a thief, and he temporarily left the team when it was revealed he'd led a slaughter of tunnel-dwelling mutants known as Morlocks. Writers subsequently revealed he had been under the subtle control of the villainous Mr. Sinister.

Over the years many other heroes joined the X-Men for brief periods. Created in the 1970s to tie in with the disco phenomenon, the Dazzler can transmute sound into light, including holographic images, and started her career on roller skates. She eventually married temporary X-Man Longshot, an other-

dimensional human able to manipulate luck in his favor. Forge is a genius-level inventor with vague shamanic abilities, Stacy X a former mutant prostitute able to exude pheromones that control others, and Cecilia Reyes a doctor able to generate force fields. Two less successful characters are Maggot, who housed two mutant slugs within his stomach from which he could absorb energy, and Marrow, who threw razor-sharp bones she removed from her body. Among the now deceased X-Men are Psylocke, sister of Captain Britain with powerful psychic abilities; Joseph, once believed an amnesiac Magneto, but actually a clone with magnetic manipulation abilities; and Changeling, a shapeshifter who assumed the identity of Professor X for a considerable period. For a relatively obscure character, he was a surprise recurring feature of the animated *X-Men* TV series, albeit in very different form.

Claremont's first, long run on the X-Men gave way to other creators such as dynamic artist Jim Lee, under whom a second *X-Men* title (nominally distinguished from the original by the deletion of the word "Uncanny" from the new one's cover legend) was issued in 1991 to instant success under assorted covers. Collectively it was Marvel's best-selling comic ever, although many were sold to investors possibly still stunned that the issues they stockpiled are commonplace. Although Lee departed for greener pastures soon after, in collaboration with Whilce Portacio he made one lasting contribution to the comic by introducing Bishop, a mutant from the future able to absorb any energy directed at him and return it as force blasts. He grew up idolizing the X-Men, and arrived in the present by accident, aware one of his heroes would betray the team, but not knowing who. It was eventually revealed to be the unlikeliest suspect of all: Professor X.

Having long appealed to the X-Men's arch-foe Magneto to reconsider his ways, Professor X used his powers to close down Magneto's mind, at which point the fury so much a part of Magneto's character was transferred to Xavier. Awakening Xavier's own successfully repressed hostilities, a new consciousness formed within Xavier's mind, taking control with devastating consequences. Only the united force of all Marvel's non-mutant heroes shut down Onslaught. Unfortunately Xavier was once again occupied, this time by the malign intelligence of one Cassandra Nova. While posing as an authority on mutant affairs, Xavier had always guarded the truth of the X-Men, but under Nova's control he revealed the truth to the world at large. Being forced to go public, though, has proved a blessing in disguise. It's enabled Xavier to use his vast personal wealth to set up global branches of X-Corporation throughout the world. Providing a staff position to almost every benign mutant who's had an involvement with the X-Men or affiliated groups, their brief is to offer shelter and aid to mutants in peril.

This storyline was conceived by Grant Morrison, who, as the writer of the newer *X-Men* comic since 2002, has stuffed a wealth of intelligent and radical ideas into the X-Men's world. Morrison's innovative contribution is exemplified by the character he introduced to the team, Xorn. He is a Chinese pacifist who doesn't participate in action missions, and whose skull contains a microscopic star that may somehow be connected with his extraordinary healing abilities, demonstrated when he healed Xavier's legs. Morrison's interpretations of familiar cast members offer new insights, and on occasion his plots have been matched by top-quality artists. Among the best of them is Frank Quitely, whose fine-lined delicacy and well judged poses combine for an extraordinarily expressive style.

As the X-Men franchise has continued to expand, more titles have been added, and the most successful has been *Ultimate X-Men,* a reboot to all intents and purposes, that Marvel kicked off in the new millennium. Under writer Mark Millar and pencil artists Andy and Adam Kubert this comic twists familiar elements into new scenarios, offering a new audience the opportunity to read an X-Men comic unhindered by the baggage of decades of continuity. These X-Men, while sharing the names and identities of the familiar characters, were introduced as if new. The comic began with the founding of the team, mixing the cast from various eras of X-Men, and has since adroitly reworked themes of mutant isolation.

X-titles continue to proliferate like mutant genes, with a publication history that has as many twists as the ongoing super-soap opera's plots; in spring of 2004 the "X-Men: ReLoad" event brought a raft of new or retooled series in the franchise, including a return (though not the first) of Claremont to writing *Uncanny X-Men,* and a new *Astonishing X-Men* series by artist John Cassady and writer Joss Whedon, creator of *Buffy the Vampire Slayer.* —FP

X-Men: Excalibur

A forerunner to the current manifestation of internationally linked groups of X-Men, the hero team Excalibur stemmed in no small part from the work of writer and artist Alan Davis on the U.K. comic book *Captain Britain.* Continuing from the work of Alan Moore there, Davis applied a distinctly British sensibility to the trappings of American superhero comics for an engaging strip starring a character originally conceived as little more than a composite of nationalistic clichés.

Davis dispensed with Captain Britain's pseudo-mystical origin. Instead, he established that the Captain's alter ego Brian Braddock's abilities were a genetic inheritance from his father, a refugee from an other-dimensional world, unimaginatively referred to as "Otherworld." Braddock's lover Meggan was initially shrouded in mystery, and never given a surname. She often modified her appearance, and was eventually revealed as a shapeshifter who instinctively assumed forms offering her protection, whether this be from the elements or from her emotions. Although critically acclaimed, lack of finance ended the *Captain Britain* strip in the United Kingdom, but it had an old friend across the Atlantic in its co-creator, writer Chris Claremont, who had featured Captain Britain in American *X-Men* strips. Significantly, he also used Braddock's twin sister Betsy in *X-Men* titles as the powerful psychic Psylocke.

Excalibur was formed when, believing their X-Men teammates to have been slain, then underused X-Men Nightcrawler, Phoenix, and Shadowcat decided to start afresh by decamping to the United Kingdom, where they became embroiled with Captain Britain and Meggan. The German Nightcrawler had been an early mainstay of the revived 1970s X-Men. His generally jocular personality belies his demonic appearance, complete with forked feet and long tail, essential for the highly developed athletic maneuvers his slight form is capable of. The distinctive sulphurous smell that accompanies his teleporting accentuates his demonic ties, although editors ironically established that Kurt Wagner is a staunch Catholic who has considered taking vows of priesthood. A further ability to become invisible in shadow has been largely sidelined, and it took more than twenty years to establish that Nightcrawler's mother is the similarly blue-skinned shapeshifter, the villainous Mystique.

The Phoenix of this team was not the original X-Men's Jean Grey, but rather Rachel Summers, who arrived from the future in one of the time paradoxes common to X-Men continuity. She was the daughter of X-Men Grey and Scott Summers in a bleak mid-twenty-first century where mutants were hunted and either murdered or confined in concentration camps. Inheriting her mother's mental abilities hadn't prevented Rachel's capture by a mutant-hunter named Ahab, who tattooed her face, permanently identifying her as one of his mutant-hunting "hounds." It wasn't until she escaped to the 1980s that she discovered she could tap into the limitless abilities of the Phoenix Force, which she was able to use to obscure her facial tattoos.

When introduced, Kitty Pryde was the youngest member of the X-Men, only of college age in present-day Marvel Comics continuity, almost twenty-five years after her introduction as a thirteen-year-old who could walk through walls. Characterization appropriate to her age was adroitly handled by Claremont, despite bruising encounters with the vicious alien-like aliens the Brood, and she regularly changed her code name, switching from Ariel to Sprite before settling on Shadowcat. Precociously intelligent, she has a technological affinity, and she honed her original abilities by learning how to partially solidify within machinery to disrupt it and by walking on air. Her acquisition of a miniature alien dragon she named Lockheed further established a unique identity.

The team name evoked Captain Britain's discarded Arthurian origin, but also evoked connections with X-Men titles. Excalibur based themselves at an offshore lighthouse, and the eccentricity of their headquarters was mirrored in the foes they faced. The Crazy Gang were lunatic but dangerous versions of Lewis Carroll's playing card characters from *Alice in Wonderland,* while Arcade constructed elaborate death-traps based on pinball machines and other arcade games. Holy echoes of the 1960s camp *Batman* television show! More threatening was Saturnyne, an other-dimensional conqueror with a close resemblance to Brian Braddock's previous girlfriend Courtney Ross, whom she masqueraded as, and most dangerous of all was Jamie Braddock, brother to Brian and Betsy. His ability to warp reality drove him mad, but he was no less formidable for that.

A notable early adventure was sparked by a fragment of sentient alien technology christened Widget by Pryde. It activated interdimensional and trans-temporal gateways that sent Excalibur on a prolonged tour of space, time and other dimensions. Humor was a significant aspect of the comic, and significantly weaker after Davis departed in 1989, indicating his plotting input. A pastiche of Ronald Searle's riotous public schoolgirls from his *St. Trinians* cartoons was a brief attempt at restoring the humor that only fully returned with Davis' appointment as sole writer and artist in 1991.

The prolific Davis introduced several new characters. Kylun the Barbarian was a British schoolboy transported through Widget to a barbarous world where he grew into an accomplished fighter, although his mutant power to reproduce any sound precisely is hardly an essential combat trait. Cerise was, in effect, an alien recruitment agent for the Shi'ar Empire. Her escape from an overzealous commander brought her to Earth, where an ability to generate malleable energy fields became useful. Feron was a teenage mystic, raised from birth to host the Phoenix Force, and when it passed him by his arrogance became a source of friction within the team. Even Widget finally achieved the fully functional artificial life-form he'd been building toward since arriving on Earth, as a sentient robotic time-portal.

Davis also incorporated characters from his *Captain Britain* days. Inept alien mercenaries Technet turned up for a period as Excalibur's tenants, resulting in slapstick disaster, and police inspector Dai Thomas was a hostile official presence. A recurring plot device, also inherited from *Captain Britain,* was the existence of thousands of extradimensional Earths, each with a counterpart of Captain Britain. On one alternate world the Nazis had won World War II, resulting in a Hauptmann Englande, while other simulacrums included a pith-helmeted Victorian, a hippy, and a reptile! Particularly prone to interfering in the affairs of Captain Britain was Roma, the imperial guardian of Otherworld. While benign, she isn't above indulging in manipulation to produce results her innate sorcery can't affect directly.

Post-Davis *Excalibur* comics entered a protracted five-year decline to cancellation. Davis' creations were largely ignored or completely forgotten, and the characters introduced to replace them were largely cast-offs from other books. Writers transferred the Russian Colossus from the X-Men (long revealed as not dead after all), adding raw power to the team in his organic metal form. Piotr Rasputin was a gentle giant, the object of a teenage crush for Pryde, and an artist as well as a fighter. He would later sacrifice his life to spread the cure for the Legacy Virus. This affected only mutants, lying dormant before activating with fatal consequences, and one victim had been Piotr's sister Ilyana. Former secret service agent Pete Wisdom was a far more cynical and manipulative type than Scottish agent Alistaire Stuart, who'd previously accompanied the team. The chain-smoking Wisdom could fire off "knives" of burning energy from his fingers, and had a sordidly unhealthy passion for the extremely young Pryde, who welcomed his advances. Also incoming, from New Mutants, was British native Rahne Sinclair, alias Wolfsbane.

Making way for the new characters was Phoenix, who was shuffled off into the timestream where she landed in another alternative future and helped to raise X-Force leader Nathan Summers. Here she called herself Mother Askani, and eventually died at a ripe old age. Death, however, has rarely proved a hindrance to Marvel superheroes, and time paradoxes have enabled her subsequent appearance in various incarnations.

Excalibur's last writer was Ben Raab, who was considerate enough to end the comic in 1998 by revealing the whereabouts of all cast members forgotten by interim scripters, and to give the audience what they wanted by featuring the wedding of Meggan to Brian Braddock in the final issue. —*FP*

X-Men: Generation X

The term Generation X, made famous by author Douglas Coupland in his book of the same name, defined an entire generation in the mid-1990s. A shorthand label that acquired pop culture ubiquity, "Gen-X" applied to, in Coupland's words, that twenty-something "category of people who wanted to hop off the merry-go-round of status, money, and social climbing that so often frames modern existence." Often referred to by commentators as

Generation X #61 © 2000 Marvel Comics.
COVER ART BY TERRY DODSON.

"slackers" and "the generation without a name," this core demographic of 47 million was ripe for catering to, lampooning, and generally just trying to figure out. The comic book industry was one that attempted to meet this burgeoning market, and in 1994 Marvel Comics began publishing *Generation X*. With a ready-made title of high recognition that dovetailed neatly with its growing line of *X-Men*-related comics, Marvel soon found an audience for this groundbreaking book.

Generation X reworked a theme established in the earliest days of *X-Men,* that of mutants being schooled in the use of their abilities. Unlike previous attempts at a school environment for mutants,

though, this title had a brazen contemporary perspective. Co-creator Scott Lobdell had honed his writing skills submitting gag material to *The Tonight Show,* and produced snappy dialogue for convincing teenagers while initial pencil artist Chris Bachalo combined appealing character designs with dynamic modern storytelling. His was a talent none of the succeeding pencilers could match.

Xavier's School for Gifted Youngsters was based in the Berkshire Mountains of western Massachusetts, removed from the dangers of the X-Men's Westchester County, New York, headquarters, and the instructors were a decidedly odd couple. The urbane and sexually charged Emma Frost had used her powers of mental manipulation to move within high society, rising to the position of White Queen among the X-Men's foes the Hellfire Club, where she trained a group of villainous mutant teens, the Hellions. Their deaths caused her to re-evaluate her priorities and initiated her reform. The Irish Sean Cassidy concealed his mutant abilities as an NYPD officer before briefly being forced to use his powers of flight and a deafening psionic scream in the pursuit of crime. As the Banshee he is always a reluctant hero, preferring to romance genetic researcher Moira McTaggart, in contrast to his daughter, Siryn, who inherited his abilities and grew to lead X-Force.

The students were a multicultural group. Asian-American orphan Jubilation Lee (Jubilee) accompanied the X-Men and Wolverine before attending the school. Her pyrokinetic powers activated on encountering a mutant-hunting Sentinel, and her sassy and contrary attitude caused tension with Monacan Monet St. Croix, alias M, whose myriad abilities came with a superior social status and attitude. Invulnerable, strong, telepathic, and able to fly, the storyline eventually revealed that the Monet who joined the school was in fact a composite being formed from her two younger sisters, while the real Monet was held captive by their brother, Emplate, Generation X's first and most persistent foe. He siphoned mutant energy and expelled it in deadly

648

fashion, trapping his sister in a silent form that functioned on instinct, not intellect. Emplate's initial encounter with Generation X permitted Monet to escape and join them, subsequently being named Penance. It was some while before writers revealed her true identity, and the cost of regaining her body was trapping her sisters as Penance.

The final female member of Generation X was Paige Guthrie, from a small West Virginia mining community, who calls herself Husk. Her brother Sam Guthrie had been a founding member of the New Mutants as Cannonball. The ambitious Paige accepted her mutant ability to shed skin to reveal different forms beneath. She became romantically linked with her teammate, the eccentrically spelled Jonothon Starsmore from England.

Chamber's force blasts first manifested with a burst that decimated his lower jaw and throat, an area he covered with a scarf. Able to communicate psionically, he grew from a self-pitying loner who considered himself a freak into short-lived status among the X-Men.

The African-American Everett Thomas, code-named Synch, could channel the abilities of any mutant within his vicinity. The team was rounded out by Latino Angelo Espinosa, known as Skin, who was raised in the barrio of East Los Angeles. As a teenager his skin became gray and pliable, and he was able to stretch it to considerable lengths, although no consideration was ever given to whether or not his muscles and skeleton also stretched and, if not, what effects this might have upon him. Resident in the grounds of the Massachusetts academy was Gateway, an enigmatic silent aborigine able to open gates in the sky to elsewhere.

Despite ostensibly being there for schooling, the youngsters were rapidly initiated into combat, although their encounters were as often as not prompted by relations between people at the school. While Emplate was their most persistent enemy, Emma Frost's two sisters proved every bit as manipulative and scheming as she. The younger,

Cordelia, attempted to acquire Emma's former position as White Queen of the Hellfire Club, while the elder, Adrienne, was a deadlier proposition. Able to learn secrets from others merely by "reading" objects they'd handled, she offered necessary financial aid but her true agenda was to see the school destroyed. Ironically she succeeded, but not in the fashion she had intended. These weren't the only antagonists in the series: A human student at the school, Tristan Brawn, had a grandfather possessed of a talisman that surrounded him with an invulnerable force field, and who headed a criminal organization. Banshee's villainous cousin Black Tom Cassidy also appeared several times, and other foes familiar to X-Men readers included Juggernaut and Toad.

As the series progressed, there were additions to the cast. Firstly, the far younger Artie and Leech were relocated from X-Factor under what might be seen as less than the legal requirement for adult supervision. Leech could dampen or siphon away the abilities of any mutant within a certain radius of him. The silent Artie previously lived among a mutant community in the New York sewers, and communicated via sonic "holograms," essentially projecting pictures. Writers sparingly used the pair, although they took a greater role in the spin-off miniseries *Daydreamers*. The other-dimensional, millennia-old Gaia was rescued by the team, hung around for a while, and abruptly departed, having spent more time acting thirteen years old than honing almost limitless powers. The Samoan Mondo was shuffled offstage permanently when he was murdered by the villain Bastion. A generally cheerful guy who could assume the qualities of anything he touched, he was rarely used during slightly more than a dozen issues with the team.

Generation X pushed Marvel's mutants into new territory by presenting a convincing cast with whom the perceived audience could identify. They were not the clean-cut compliant teenagers who had previously occupied Marvel titles, although they tended toward disobedience and mischief rather than outright hostility. The blend was enough to make the comic an instant success in 1994, and the *Generation X* Fox TV movie was fast-tracked, screening in February 1996. While well produced and generally well received by fans, budgetary restrictions necessitated Chamber, Husk, Penance, and Synch being discarded or replaced by substitutes whose powers weren't as costly to simulate for television. The plot centered on a "dream machine" created by Emma Frost (played by Finola Hughes) that enabled telepathic manipulation. Frost had discarded the device, only for the students to rediscover it years later with troublesome consequences.

As the *Generation X* comic continued, the tone became considerably darker, with the abduction of children one topic spotlighted. Synch was killed by Adrienne Frost, and Emma subsequently murdered her sister, an act that left vast residual guilt. With Sean Cassidy also self-absorbed, mourning the death of Moira McTaggart, the students decided their education was suffering, and departed the school, at which point their comic was canceled. Cassidy was next seen heading a mutant militia called X-Corps, brought down in very final fashion by some X-Men villains. He's not been seen since. The remaining cast is involved with the X-Corporation, with Frost, Chamber, and Husk joining the core X-Men team (though Jubilee has occasionally been seen in the alternate-future *Spider-Girl* and related comics as the grown-up leader of the "X-People"). However, the concept, if not the characters, of *Generation X* went back in session as the new series *Academy X* joined many other new or made-over X-titles in Marvel's spring 2004 publishing event "X-Men: ReLoad." —*FP*

X-Men: New Mutants

The New Mutants were the first tentative step toward expanding the X-Men franchise into the marketing behemoth it is today. The original 1960s premise of X-Men was that of a school where those with inherent superhuman abilities, or mutants as they were labeled, would hone their talents away from the public eye for the eventual betterment of humankind. The X-Men as relaunched in the 1970s were a diverse multicultural group, and elements from both incarnations were combined in the New Mutants. They were drawn from the global population of mutants, but their youth and inexperience helped them stand apart from the X-Men, while their similar costumes doubled as school uniforms.

Writer Chris Claremont, then enjoying a sustained creative peak writing *X-Men,* created the cast in 1983. Artist Bob McLeod joined him, and the New Mutants were launched via the then experimental format of the graphic novel, only Marvel Comic's fourth to that point. While their title ran a respectable one hundred issues, none of the original New Mutants really caught the public imagination. The most popular has proved to be Cannonball, able to propel himself through the air with tremendous force, simultaneously becoming invulnerable. His powers manifested under extreme conditions when a cave-in trapped the young Sam Guthrie on his first day as a miner. His initial characterization was as unsophisticated and awed, but nowhere near as reserved and awkward as Wolfsbane, essentially a werewolf who also assumes transitional forms between human and wolf. Her costume shreds during transformation, leading to embarrassing moments for the already shy Rahne Sinclair.

Confidence is no problem for Roberto DaCosta, alias Sunspot, scion of a wealthy Brazilian family whose ability to draw energy from the sun provides prodigious strength and force blasts. The sometimes aloof Native American Dani Moonstar projects three-dimensional images drawn from the minds of others. As the series progressed she also developed a bond with the Valkyries of Norse legend, from whom she inherited a winged horse named Brightwind, and learned to predict imminent death. She never settled on a permanent alias, being known as Psyche and Mirage as often as she was just by her surname. Xi'an Coy Manh was older than her teammates, a Vietnamese immigrant who thwarted her Uncle's aspirations to form a criminal empire via her ability to have others act under her control. As Karma her participation with the New Mutants was sporadic, as her priority was always the welfare of her younger brother and sister.

The initial team was relatively quickly expanded. Ilyana Rasputin, a Russian farm girl and sorceress, was sister to the X-Men's Colossus. As Magik hers was a tragic story with a tragic finale. She had been abducted by an other-dimensional demon named Belasco as a child and grew to puberty within his realm, but when she escaped back to Earth mere seconds had elapsed. She later reverted to her original age, only to succumb to the Legacy Virus, a fatal disease afflicting only mutants. Amara Aquilla was retrieved from what was seemingly the unspoiled Roman civilization Nova Roma secreted within the Amazonian jungle. As Magma she possesses assorted volcanic-related abilities.

The early adventures of the New Mutants were competent, but undistinguished, and it took the appointment of maverick artist Bill Sienkiewicz in 1984 to provide a unique visual identity. In his artistic debut the team confronted a demonic bear that Moonstar believed responsible for the disappearance of her parents. Then heavily influenced by the scratchy distortions of Ralph Steadman, among others, Sienkiewicz's bear was a sinister heaving mass. It transpired that the bear *was* Moonstar's parents, transformed by an ancient evil. Sienkiewicz also concocted the visual template for Warlock, an alien "techno-organic" life-form memorably conveyed as a morphing parade of metallic components. At times Warlock would form a protective suit around Doug Ramsey, whose ability to communicate with machinery as Cypher was ill-suited to combat, although his abilities enabled him to perceive reality as Warlock did when within his protective cocoon. Their relationship grew deeper, and each began to manifest the personality traits of the

other, a fusion halted by Ramsey's death, protecting Wolfsbane. Not comprehending the concept of death, Warlock unsuccessfully attempted to revive Ramsey's corpse.

In the tradition of the X-Men, although ostensibly studying, the New Mutants stumble into plenty of adventures. A recurring playground is Belasco's dimension of Limbo. Bearing many similarities to conventional depictions of hell, it's populated by assorted demons, many of whom have aspirations to control the realm. Writers eventually revealed that Nova Roma was a civilization populated by the abductees of the sorceress Selene, who implanted false memories of a lineage stemming from ancient Rome. Members of the Hellfire Club provided recurring foes, the most prominent among which were the Hellions, mirror images of the New Mutants being trained by the Hellfire Club's White Queen Emma Frost as future mutant enforcers for the Club. They were joined briefly by a group of New Mutants rebelling against the appointment of reformed villain Magneto as their teacher, but came to an untimely end at the hands of a mutant psychopath from the future.

Several mutants introduced in *X-Factor,* and briefly teamed as X-Terminators, later joined the New Mutants. Skids projects a body-encompassing force field, and was romantically entangled with Rusty Collins, who had heat-related powers, but rarely displayed them before his death at the hands of the Mutant Liberation Force. Rictor generates vibratory waves, while Boom Boom creates small parcels of detonating energy. Her later change of code name to Meltdown was well advised. She would develop a relationship with Cannonball. Youngsters Artie and Leech also tagged along before being forwarded to Generation X.

A much-needed boost in profile and popularity came with the appointment of Rob Liefeld first as pencil artist, then as co-plotter, in 1990. Not very much older than some of the characters he drew, Liefeld brimmed with ideas and enthusiasm, and possessed a portfolio of superheroes he'd created since his earliest days reading comics. Foremost among these was Cable. A hulking brute of a man with muscles larger than most people's heads and guns the size of supermarkets, he was an imposing figure with cybernetic body parts and the odd robotic limb. His agenda, though, was not one of harmonious co-existence between mutants: he knew his enemies, and he planned to sort them out before they eliminated him.

The final days of the New Mutants saw the departure of all long-serving team members, with the exception of Cannonball and Boom Boom, as Liefeld introduced more new and extreme characters. One, Shatterstar, dealt with a man restraining him from behind by impaling them both on his own sword. With Cable's proactive policies and the new cast, little was left of the New Mutants, and their title was canceled in 1991 to pave the way for *X-Force*. —FP

X-Men: X-Force/X-Statix

When launched in 1991, *X-Force* was sold enclosed in a plastic bag containing a trading card featuring one of the team members, an additional premium cementing Marvel Comics' biggest new success in years. That it featured grossly distorted artwork and scant plot, both courtesy of creator Rob Liefeld, mattered little to the hundreds of thousands of buyers. Where Liefeld triumphed was with creative enthusiasm. He brimmed with ideas, many of them good, but ineffective editorial channeling of his imagination produced confusing comics. None of this stopped the multitude of scratchy lines and anatomical liberties that comprised his style from becoming *de rigueur* among better selling superhero comics of the early 1990s.

As much as Liefeld stamped his personality on *X-Force* from the beginning, so did his lead character

Cable. Introduced in the latter issues of the X-Men spinoff *New Mutants,* Cable was an instant success. Direct and brutal, with enormous muscles and even bigger guns, Cable's mission was to prevent war between mutants and humankind. His is the type of convoluted origin, slowly released over a period of years, that seems inordinately popular with fans of Marvel's *X-Men*-related titles. Cable's given name is Nathan Summers, and he is the son of the X-Men's Cyclops via a woman Cyclops believed to be his amnesiac true love, Jean Grey. She wasn't, and their offspring was infected with a "techno-organic virus" by X-Men foe Apocalypse. The only alternative to Nathan's death was to send him 2,000 years into the future to a society torn asunder by war between humanity and mutants. While the virus transformed portions of his body into living metal, its spread was halted, and Summers was taught to channel his formidable telekinetic abilities. Additionally, he became the complete soldier.

When returned to the present day as an adult, Cable's self-appointed mission was to seek out and terminate anyone who threatened the persecution of mutants, thus intending to prevent the future he'd experienced. He initially believed this was best achieved leading a team, and so he co-opted Cannonball and Boom Boom from the supergroup New Mutants and added other members. Domino is a successful mercenary with the mutant ability to manipulate luck in her favor, while Feral is a more aggressive and violent version of the New Mutants' Wolfsbane, covered in fur and possessing an animal's heightened senses and speed. She has a mutually belligerent relationship with her sister Thornn, who is similarly gifted, and would eventually join the even more militant Mutant Liberation Front. The Native American James Proudstar blamed the X-Men for the death of his brother Thunderbird, and joined a group of villains in training under his brother's alias. In addition to flying, he performed every athletic feat at superhuman levels, and his anger dissipated, leading to a stint as Warpath in X-Force before joining the X-Corporation. Shatterstar was genetically engineered as the perfect warrior and has an agenda to destroy Mojo, an other-dimensional despot who creates action-driven television spectaculars as a means of controlling his population. Writers have dropped broad hints that Shatterstar is the son of two X-Men, Dazzler and Longshot, who have spent considerable time in Mojo's dimension.

The backstory Liefeld created for Cable provided plenty of foes. These included a cloned version of him sent from the future to ensure mutants and humankind did fight (Stryfe); his evil son Tyler, also snatched from the future (but primarily seen in Cable's own comic); and assorted members of Cable's previous mercenary team Six Pack, of which Domino was a member. In fact the Domino who joined X-Force was a shapeshifting imposter named Copycat, sent to infiltrate the team by Genesis, Tyler Summers.

Cable left the team early on, and Liefeld soon after, and it would be years before any imagination was again applied to the characters. Cannonball, who had grown considerably from the awkward character introduced in New Mutants, assumed the team leadership before temporarily ceding it to Siryn: The Irish Teresa Cassidy is the daughter of X-Man Banshee, who believed her killed as an infant by a terrorist's bomb along with her mother. Inheriting her father's psionic powers, she was raised by his cousin Black Tom Cassidy, who used her as a pawn in his criminal plans. Later exonerated, she assumed a superhero career. Several of the New Mutants returned to X-Force—Rictor believing Cable had murdered his father, Moonstar having served undercover to further Cable's agenda, and Sunspot with increased powers. Former member of Excalibur Pete Wisdom also led X-Force, reinforcing their credentials as a mutant strike force.

The comic coasted until the arrival of writer Peter Milligan and artist Michael Allred in 2001. They dispensed with the entire previous cast, along with the concept of a mutant militia, instead introducing new characters in a broadly based satire of media manipulation and the motivations of superheroes. This X-Force only shared the name with the previous team, and then only briefly as they were relaunched as X-Statix. These mutants were teen idols responsible for generating masses of merchandising dollars via the televising of their carefully chosen missions, always for a hefty fee. The fatality rate was high, and the characters largely arrogant, mercenary, self-serving, and resolutely unpleasant.

The leadership of this in-fighting bunch fell to Guy Smith, code-named Orphan, a depressive who plays a nightly game of Russian roulette. The phrase "acute sensitivity" describes both his mutant ability and nature. He loved the latterly deceased teleporting U-Go Girl, who was an atypical heroine, having given birth as a teenager, then leaving her daughter to be raised by her mother while she pursued a career as a superhero. Anarchist, Tike Alicar, with the unlikely gift of toxic sweat, promotes the agenda of African-American militancy, resenting the whitebread world, but quick to exploit any means of making money from it, to the extent of organizing a stadium tour to rake in some cash. He is joined in this by Dead Girl, who has a mysterious past, awakening in a graveyard after burial. She can "read" corpses for information and can rebuild her own body from any injury, continuing to animate severed limbs. Billy Bob Reilly posed as trailer trash to earn his place on the team, rightly guessing it would render him more media-friendly than his actual middle-class upbringing and an ability to bloat various parts of his body as Phat. He has also discovered his homosexuality via liaisons with teammate Vivisector, a werewolf, that began as attempts to increase their media profile. The most mysterious member of the team is the alien Doop, resembling nothing so much as a flying potato with arms and eyes who communicates via an alien language understood by very few. Editors established that he is known to other Marvel mutants, and within X-Force/X-Statix provides the action video feeds.

X-Statix continues the Milligan and Allred satire, adding Venus Dee Milo to the team, a female composed of pure energy who teleports and sends out energy blasts. Most previous members of X-

Force now have positions within the global X-Corporation. —*FP*

X-Men in the Media

They are the children of the atom, their superpowers manifesting themselves as they enter their teenage years. These uncanny teens are mutants—homo superior—and while they are feared by the non-mutant public, they are also pulled in two directions. Will they join the side of pacifism and good, training under Professor Charles Xavier at his Westchester County private school in New York, or will they allow their anger and displacement to pull them toward the side of Magneto and his Brotherhood of Evil Mutants? So began the saga of *The X-Men,* created by Stan Lee and Jack Kirby, and debuting in September 1963. Mutant heroes Cyclops, Marvel Girl, Angel, Iceman, and Beast were joined in summer 1975's *Giant-Size X-Men* #1 by all-new mutants Wolverine, Colossus, Storm, Nightcrawler, and Thunderbird. And although it would be the latter incarnation that would gain incredible popularity in the comics and the media alike, the original X-Men did appear on television early in their career.

In the fall of 1966, animators and producers Robert Lawrence, Grant Simmons, and Ray Patterson—under the company name of Grantray-Lawrence—debuted the syndicated daily animated program called *The Marvel Super-Heroes.* Each weekday half-hour episode put the spotlight on a different hero with a three-part adventure. *Captain America* was Monday, *The Incredible Hulk* was Tuesday, *Iron Man* was Wednesday, *Mighty Thor* was Thursday (naturally), and *Sub-Mariner* was Friday. One three-part *Sub-Mariner* episode was adapted from *Fantastic Four* #6 (September 1962) and *Fantastic Four Annual* #3 (1965), but the producers could not use the actual *Fantastic Four* characters because another studio owned the animation rights. Instead, the X-Men were brought into the fray, pinch-hitting for the FF. Unfortunately, *The Marvel Super-Heroes* only lasted one season, so this version of the X-Men did not reappear (except in syndicated reruns of the series).

Although the villainous Magneto made an appearance in a 1978 episode of *The New Fantastic Four,* it wasn't until NBC's *Spider-Man and His Amazing Friends* began in the fall of 1981 that the X-Men reappeared in animation. On this series, Spider-Man was teamed with Iceman and newcomer Firestar (who was later integrated into the comic-book Marvel universe in *New Mutants* and *New Warriors*). Several episodes guest-starred the X-Men or their friends and foes, acknowledging both Iceman and Firestar's past. Japanese mutant Sunfire guest-starred once, while Magneto gained control of New York another time. Episodes aired during the 1982–1983 season—when the title was changed to *The Incredible Hulk and the Amazing Spider-Man*—showed the X-Men in the origin stories for both Iceman and Firestar. In the third and final season (1983–1984's *The Amazing Spider-Man and the Incredible Hulk*) the mutants guest-starred again, in a tale entitled "The X-Men Adventure." Present were Professor X, Cyclops, Kitty Pryde, Storm, Nightcrawler, Colossus, and Thunderbird.

Eventually, Marvel Productions felt it was ready for a regular *X-Men* series, and a half-hour *Uncanny X-Men* pilot was made in 1988. "Pryde of the X-Men" related the story of Kitty Pryde's first few days with the team of mutants (who included Professor X, Cyclops, Storm, Wolverine, Colossus, Nightcrawler, and Dazzler), as they fought against Magneto, the White Queen, Juggernaut, Blob, Pyro, and Toad. Marvel Productions hoped to sell the *X-Men* as a series, but no network was interested, and the cartoon went on the shelf. It was shown as part of the *Marvel Universe* syndicated show in 1988, and released on video in 1990.

Carolco optioned the rights to the *X-Men* for use in a feature film in 1991, but shortly after

From left to right: Patrick Stewart (Professor Charles Xavier), Anna Paquin (Rogue), James Marsden (Cyclops), Shawn Ashmore (Iceman), Famke Janssen (Jean Grey), Halle Berry (Storm), and Hugh Jackman (Wolverine) reprise their *X-Men* roles in *X2: X-Men United.*

James Cameron's Lightstorm Entertainment expressed interest in producing the film Carolco ran into money problems, and eventually went under. This film script, *Wolverine and the X-Men,* was written by Gary Goldman, and it detailed teenage Kitty Pryde's first days at the Xavier School for Gifted Youngsters.

Margaret Loesch had worked with Marvel Productions from 1984 to 1990, and when she became head of Fox Children's Network in 1990, she bought a revival of the *X-Men* project she had championed in 1988. Marvel teamed with animation producers Saban Entertainment and Graz Entertainment to produce the new *X-Men,* featuring Marvel's hottest mutants. A trio of animated episodes debuted in October and November 1992, but delays in production—and shoddy work by one of the overseas animation studios—delayed the series. *X-Men* re-premiered in January 1993. The show immediately garnered excellent ratings, and finished its run in 1997, after airing seventy-six episodes.

Fox's *X-Men* series was serialized, with each of the episodes continuing into the next, although most of them also stood alone as separate shows. The main X-Men team was Wolverine, Cyclops, Gambit, Storm, Rogue, Jubilee, and newcomer Morph, though a secondary team of background players included Beast, Professor X, and Jean Grey. Villains included Magneto, the Sentinels, the Morlocks, Mr. Sinister, Lady Deathstrike, and many others. A vast array of X-characters and Marvel superstars showed up over the course of the series.

Perhaps no Marvel series was as completely faithful to its comic-book origins as was this *X-Men*. Some storylines were adapted from the comics, including multi-part adventures detailing Jean Grey's evolution from Phoenix to Dark Phoenix, and her eventual redemption. Character designs and art-work by comic-book veterans Will Meugniot, Larry Houston, and Rick Hoberg (who all previously worked on the "Pryde" pilot) made the characters look like they had stepped off of the comics' pages.

Although Carolco's *X-Men* film languished, pro-ducers Bill Todman and Joel Simon picked up the film rights to a *Wolverine* movie, but it went nowhere. The next *X-Men*-related project was actual-ly based on an *X-Men* spin-off comic-book series. *Generation X* was a live-action pilot telefilm that aired on Fox on February 20, 1996. In this version, Banshee (Jeremy Rathchford) and White Queen (Finola Hughes) ran Xavier's school, helping to train new teen mutants such as Jubilee, Skin, Mondo, and M, as well as non-comics characters Refrax and Buff. Although it fared well in the arenas of story and direction and ratings weren't too shabby, no fur-ther *Generation X* specials were completed.

Marvel's mightiest mutants finally reached live-action status on July 14, 2000, the premiere date of 20th Century Fox's big-budget *X-Men* feature film. Bryan Singer directed, from a story and script by a large group of writers (though credits only showed Tom DeSanto, Singer, and David Hayter). In this gor-geous drama, Charles Xavier (Patrick Stewart) and Magneto (Sir Ian McKellan) lock powers when Mag-neto plots to mutate most of New York. Many of Xavier's star pupils were present: Jean Grey (Famke Janssen), Cyclops (James Marsden), Storm (Halle Berry), and Rogue (Anna Paquin). Newcomer Hugh Jackman stepped into the role of feral Wolverine after actor Dougray Scott was unable to start the film due to scheduling conflicts. Magneto's cohorts included Mystique (Rebecca Romijn-Stamos), Saber-tooth (Tyler Mane), and Toad (Ray Park), while intoler-ant Senator Robert Kelly (Bruce Davison) and his Mutant Registration Act provided even more conflict.

Following a film debut on New York's Ellis Island (a location that had been replicated for the dénouement of the film), *X-Men* was an immediate success. Critics were rapturous, and the public loved the mutants, guiding *X-Men* to more than $157 million in United States box office receipts alone. Jackman in particular went from relative obscurity to immediate superstar status in Holly-wood. A wide variety of licensing was released, including action figures, statues, apparel, posters, and more, and two versions of the DVD were released to tremendous sales. Following the first film's success, an *X-Men* sequel was immediately put into development, but some other X-projects would beat it to the punch.

First out of the gate was a new animated series for the WB network titled *X-Men: Evolution*. Debuting on November 4, 2000, the new series turns back the clock, showing the mutants as younger versions of their film—and comic-book—counterparts. The main group at Xavier's school is now Cyclops, Jean Grey, Wolverine, Nightcrawler, Rogue, Storm, Shadow-cat (Kitty Pryde), and new creation Spyke. Though they initially face Mystique and Magneto's group of nasty teen mutants Toad, Blob, Avalanche, and Quicksilver, these X-Men have also squared off against other familiar faces, including Sabertooth, Juggernaut, Apocalypse, Pyro, and Callisto. Other mutant heroes have joined them over time, including Forge, Iceman, Beast, and Jubilee.

Like its animated predecessor, WB's *X-Men: Evo-lution* was a ratings hit, and fans responded to the clean art style and strong stories. The fourth season began in the fall of 2003. *X-Men: Evolution* has gen-erated toy lines and fast food premiums, as well as apparel and multiple video and DVD releases.

In October 2001, the syndicated *Mutant X* tele-vision series began airing, but even though it is pro-duced by Marvel and based on an *X-Men* comic book spin-off, *Mutant X* does not have anything to do with the *X-Men* continuity. Fox sued production company Tribune twice to make certain that the series would not tread too closely to its film franchise; Fox lost both times, and the series moved forward (though Tribune filed their own lawsuit against Marvel in late 2003). On *Mutant X,* a group of attractive twenty-something non-code-named mutants who are genetically engineered help other mutants come to terms with their powers. The cast includes John Shea, Forbes March, Victor Webster, Lauren Lee Smith, and Victoria Pratt; in its third season, Karen Cliche joined the *Mutant X* cast. A recurring villain on the series is Mason Eckhart (Tom McCamus), the man who murdered the head of the government project that engineered the mutants. *Mutant X* began its third season in fall 2003, and a line of DVDs has been released (oddly, a two-part comic book spin-off flopped).

While *X-Men: Evolution* and *Mutant X* continued on the airwaves, filming on the *X-Men* film sequel was ongoing from spring 2002 forward. Bryan Singer returned to direct, reuniting most of the first film's cast. This time though, Magneto and Mystique are forced to aide the X-Men when insane military leader William Stryker (Brian Cox) invades Xavier's school and captures the mutant-detecting Cerebro device. New mutants Nightcrawler (Alan Cumming) and Iceman (Shawn Ashmore) get some great effects sequences—and some nice characterization—while young Pyro (Aaron Stanford)'s seduction to the side of evil is effective, and Lady Deatshtrike (Kelly Hu) holds her own in a deadly battle against Wolverine in the laboratory where they were both "built."

X2: X-Men United was released on May 2, 2003, to acclaim and high ticket sales. Most critics said that this was one of the rare sequels that actually surpassed its predecessor, and its box office receipts in the United States topped $214 million! As had the first film, *X2* inspired a wide variety of licensing, as well as a deluxe DVD release as 2003 drew to a close.

Although not everyone in the cast is signed to reappear, development work on *X-Men 3* is already underway. Forty-plus years after their comic-book debut, who knew that the mutant underdogs would

one day rule the media? That kind of foresight would take powers greater than those of ordinary humans…. —*AM*

X-Men Villains

While the X-Men heroes have enjoyed a rich history and a dedicated fan following, no less have the X-Men villains made their mark on the pages of *X-Men* and related comics over the past forty years. Making his debut in 1963 along with the X-Men themselves, by far the most majestic and implacable foe the X-Men have faced is Magneto, master of magnetism. He is a complex individual whose thoughts about the co-existence of humanity with mutants veer from militant separatism to benign compatibility. In comics from the early 1990s he was even an ally of the X-Men. Known as both Magnus (to Professor X) and Erik Lehnsherr, both believed aliases, he was the sole member of his family to survive a Nazi concentration camp, and the experience instilled an early belief that mutants could only survive by uniting to enslave humanity. To this end he formed the mutant terrorist group the Brotherhood of Evil Mutants, which numbered among its members the speedster Quicksilver and the Scarlet Witch, who could affect probability, at the time unknown to any party as his children. They later reformed and became mainstays of the Avengers. Creators Stan Lee and Jack Kirby were obviously pleased with their imposing mutant, and he encountered the X-Men in just under half the issues Lee wrote.

Magneto has operated from several bases over the years, notably genetically engineering a group of mutants in an Antarctic jungle, manning a headquarters in the Bermuda Triangle, operating from an asteroid orbiting Earth, and finally establishing the mutant separatist state of Genosha. He was seemingly killed when a cadre of Sentinels slaughtered almost the entire population. Magneto has been presumed dead before though, and it has not hindered his activities.

Hugh Jackman (Wolverine) takes on Stryker's soldiers in *X2: X-Men United*.

Magneto has served as an inspiration to a group of mutant refugees who allied themselves to him as the Acolytes, carrying out his bidding. Their number grew enormously, and all joined him on Genosha, where they presumably died. His concept of a Brotherhood of Evil Mutants has proved surprisingly sustainable under several incarnations. The longest-lived member is Fred Dukes, the Blob, a man who cannot be moved when grounded, and whose enormous bulk defies injury. In the 1960s he was often teamed with Unus, who projected an impenetrable force field, and eventually suffocated when it ceased to admit any air.

After Magneto it was Mystique who revived the team. Inexplicably blue-skinned in her natural form, she is able to morph into any other human shape, and has maintained several long-standing cover identities. Her real name remains unknown, and she spent much of her life infiltrating official organizations, the secrets she disinterred convincing her mutants should conquer humankind. Like Magneto, she is extraordinarily long-lived, having been known as far back as the 1930s. Her Brotherhood included the fire-controlling Pyro; Avalanche, who generated vibrations from his hands; the precognitive Destiny; Post, a heavily armored assassin; and future X-Men member Rogue. A third incarnation of the Brotherhood was organized by the agile but often subservient Toad, a member of the original group. His new recruits were Phantasia, who disrupted mutant powers and machinery; and Sauron, or Dr. Karl Lykos, who had menaced the X-Men alone on several occasions. Driven by a desire to drain the life forces of others to empower himself, in his Sauron form Lykos is a pterodactyl with an almost irresistible hypnotic stare.

Humanity's fear of mutants was exemplified very early on by Dr. Bolivar Trask, who created thirty-foot-tall mutant-hunting robots in attractive shades of purple. Trask didn't survive their first outing, but they've continued to menace mutants for decades. Self-perpetuating on occasions, the robots' greatest strength is their adaptive nature. Other than sheer brute force, one method of destroying an individual Sentinel will never work against another. For the new millennium a new breed of Sentinel emerged. No longer confined to the single form, this new breed incorporates even microscopic Sentinels that access the bloodstream, but are still programmed to destroy mutants.

The deadliest X-Men foe is Apocalypse. Abandoned as an infant five thousand years ago, he made his home aboard an alien vessel he discovered, learning the technology, constructing a suit of bio-armor and becoming, to all intents and purposes, immortal. He has battled groups of mutants several times over the years, often via agents he designated Horsemen after transforming them, including X-Men Angel and Wolverine at different periods. His purpose is to usher in a new era under his control, and he temporarily succeeded in instituting the alternate reality known as Age of Apocalypse, in which mutants dominated North America. Familiar characters were warped here, their motivations altered, but the familiar timeline was eventually restored.

Among those to benefit from Apocalypse's technology was nineteenth-century geneticist Nathanial Evans, whose experiments resulted in expulsion by his peers. He was transformed by Apocalypse into Mr. Sinister, in absolute control of every individual molecule of his body, allowing him to funnel energy blasts and transform his shape. In addition, he is telepathic. Manipulating events that affected the X-Men for years, Mr. Sinister's object was to control the offspring of X-Men Scott Summers and Jean Grey. Thwarted in this, he continues to menace the X-Men, maintaining a hostile collection of mutants known as the Marauders, whose greatest crime included obliterating a group of Morlocks, mutants who lived in the New York sewers. The Morlocks themselves had fought the X-Men several times, temporarily ceasing hostilities when their leader Callisto was defeated in single combat by the X-Men's Storm.

The villain behind one of the most fondly remembered X-Men sequences was eventually revealed to be Mastermind. Physically unattractive, Mastermind began his career as one of Magneto's Brotherhood of Evil Mutants, with his powers of illusion able to affect all senses. Later, disguising his appearance he romanced what he presumed to be the X-Men's Jean Grey. Actually, he was meddling with a fragment of the exceptionally powerful Phoenix Force masquerading as Grey, and his mental tampering unleashed her full powers, rendering him comatose for years. Given the civilian identity of Jason Wyngarde by the creative team of Chris Claremont and John Byrne, his visual appearance was very much based on British actor Peter Wyngarde, best known for his role as the arch-camp secret service agent Jason King. He died, but not before passing on his powers to two daughters. Claremont and Byrne also tapped reality for their villainous Hellfire Club, updating the actual eighteenth-century immorally indulgent organization frequented by bored young aristocrats of the age. The *X-Men* version, under the leadership of the formidable Sebastian Shaw, is more concerned with global domination through political influence. Shaw can absorb and redirect any energy, and fellow members of his Inner Circle have been equally intimidating, if prone to plots resulting in their own downfall.

One of the X-Men's oldest foes, the Juggernaut, reformed in 2003 and joined the team. Cain Marko is step-brother to Charles Xavier, and his abilities were supernaturally rather than genetically conferred when he picked up a mystical gem. He was transformed into an entity more than matching his chosen name, being a match for all but the strongest heroes in sheer physical power. His helmet blocks all telepathic influence, although he has been rapidly defeated on occasions when it has been displaced. Juggernaut has often allied himself with an Irish terrorist and mercenary named Black Tom Cassidy. Rather than having any consistency, his abilities have adapted to suit the plots he has been involved in. While always able to channel heat blasts through a cane he carries, in the 1990s creators portrayed him growing to giant size and controlling plant life. A surprisingly charming parallel-universe series about his son, *J-2,* ran for one year (1998–1999).

Another villain who's experienced periods of reform among the X-Men is the vicious amoral killer Sabretooth, alias Victor Creed, although he has also been affiliated with the Brotherhood of Evil Mutants and the Marauders. Sabretooth has ties to X-Men member Wolverine, with similar heightened senses, healing ability, and indestructible adamantium skeleton and claws, the latter resulting from experimentation at the Weapon X project. At one time writers suggested he was Wolverine's father, which is not the case, but like Wolverine his memories were wiped and false memories implanted at Weapon X. Beyond an abusive father, then, his true background remains unknown to readers.

The X-Men have defeated myriad foes on numerous occasions, but a policy against killing if at all possible results in their inevitable return, and readers wouldn't have it any other way. —*FP*

Resources

PERIODICALS AND FANZINES

Alter Ego. Published monthly by TwoMorrows Publishing, 10407 Bedfordtown Dr., Raleigh, NC 27614. www.twomorrows.com

Anime Insider. Published monthly by Wizard Entertainment, 151 Wells Avenue, Congers, NY 10920-2064. www.wizarduniverse.com

Animerica. Published monthly by Viz Communications, 655 Bryant Street, San Francisco, CA 94107. www.animerica-mag.com

Back Issue. Published bimonthly by TwoMorrows Publishing, 10407 Bedfordtown Dr., Raleigh, NC 27614. www.twomorrows.com

Comic Book Artist. Two-time winner of the Eisner Award. Published bimonthly by Top Shelf Productions, P.O. Box 1282, Marietta, GA 30061-1282. www.topshelfcomix.com

Comic Shop News. Published weekly by Comic Shop News, Inc. Available at comic-book shops or through Diamond Distributors, 1966 Greenspring Drive #300, Timonium, MD 21903. www.csnsider.com

Comics Interview. Published by Fictioneer Books, Ltd., 52 Trillium Lane, Screamer Mountain, Clayton, GA 30525.

The Comics Journal. Published monthly by Fantagraphics Books, 7563 Lake City Way NE, Seattle, Washington, 98115. www.tcj.com

International Journal of Comic Art. Published twice yearly by John A. Lent, 669 Ferne Blvd., Drexel Hill, PA 19026.

The Jack Kirby Collector. Published quarterly by TwoMorrows Publishing, 10407 Bedfordtown Dr., Raleigh, NC 27614. www.twomorrows.com

Newtype USA. Winner of "Best Anime Publication, North America" Award at Anime Expo 2003 from the Society for the Promotion of Japanese Animation (SPJA). Published by A.D. Vision, Inc., P.O. Box 631607, Houston, TX 77263. www.newtype-usa.com

Protoculture Addicts. Published monthly by Protoculture, P.O. Box 1433, Station B, Montreal, Quebec, Canada H3B 3L2. www.protoculture-mag.com

Wizard: The Comics Magazine. Published monthly by Wizard Entertainment, 151 Wells Avenue, Congers, NY 10920-2064. www.wizarduniverse.com

NONFICTION WORKS

Anime

Baricordi, Andrea, et al. Translated from the Italian by Adeline D'Opera and presented by Claude J. Pelletier. *Anime: A Guide to Japanese Animation (1958–1988).* Montreal: Protoculture, 2000.

Clements, Jonathan, and Helen McCarthy. *The Anime Encyclopedia: A Guide to Japanese Animation since 1917.* Berkeley, CA: Stone Bridge Press, 2001.

Kinsella, Sharon. *Adult Manga: Culture and Power in Contemporary Japanese Society.* Honolulu: University of Hawaii Press, 2000.

Ledoux, Trish, and Doug Ranney. *The Complete Anime Guide,* 2nd ed. Issaquah, WA: Tiger Mountain Press, 1997.

McCarthy, Helen. *The Anime Movie Guide: Movie-by-Movie Guide to Japanese Animation.* Woodstock, NY: The Overlook Press, 1997.

Patten, Fred. "TV Animation in Japan." *Fanfare* (May 1980).

Poitras, Gilles. *The Anime Companion: What's Japanese in Japanese Animation?* Berkeley, CA: Stone Bridge Press, 1998.

———. *Anime Essentials: Everything a Fan Needs to Know.* Berkeley, CA: Stone Bridge Press, 2001.

Schodt, Frederik L. *Manga! Manga! The World of Japanese Comics.* Tokyo and New York: Kodansha International, 1983.

Comic Book Academia and History

Benton, Mike. *The Comic Book in America: An Illustrated History,* 2nd edition. Dallas, TX: Taylor Publishing Company, 1993.

———. *Masters of Imagination: The Comic Book Artists Hall of Fame.* Dallas, TX: Taylor Publishing Company, 1994.

Braun, Saul. "Shazam! Here Comes Captain Relevant." In Ray B. Browne, ed., *Popular Culture and the Expanding Consciousness.* New York: John Wiley & Sons, 1973.

Bridwell, E. Nelson. *Batman: From the Thirties to the Seventies.* New York: Bonanza Books, 1971.

———. *Superman: From the Thirties to the Seventies.* New York: Bonanza Books, 1971.

Daniels, Les. *Comix: A History of Comic Books in America.* New York: Bonanza Books, 1971.

DC Comics. *Fifty Who Made DC Great.* New York: DC Comics, Inc., 1985.

Duin, Steve, and Mike Richardson. *Comics Between the Panels.* Milwaukie, OR: Dark Horse Comics, Inc., 1998.

Eury, Michael. *Dick Giordano: Changing Comics, One Day at a Time.* Raleigh, NC: TwoMorrows, 2003.

Feiffer, Jules. *The Great Comic Book Heroes.* 1965. Reprint, Seattle, WA: Fantagraphics Books, 2003.

Goulart, Ron. *Great History of Comic Books.* Chicago: Contemporary Books, 1986.

———, ed. *The Encyclopedia of American Comics.* New York: Facts on File, 1990.

———. *Over 50 Years of American Comic Books.* Lincolnwood, IL: Publications International, 1991.

Harvey, Robert C. *The Art of the Comic Book: An Aesthetic History.* Jackson: University Press of Mississippi, 1996.

Horn, Maurice, ed. *The World Encyclopedia of Comics.* 7 vols. Broomall, PA: Chelsea House, 1999.

Kunzle, David. *The Early Comic Strip.* Berkeley: University of California Press, 1973.

Lee, Stan, and George Mail. *Excelsior! The Amazing Life of Stan Lee.* New York: Fireside, 2002.

Nyberg, Amy Kiste. *Seal of Approval: The History of the Comics Code.* Jackson: University Press of Mississippi, 1998.

Overstreet, Robert M. *The Overstreet Comic Book Price Guide,* 34th ed. New York: Random House, 2004.

Reitberger, Reinhold, and Wolfgang Fuchs. *Comics: Anatomy of a Mass Medium.* Translated by Nadia Fowler. Boston: Little Brown, 1972.

Robbins, Trina, and Catherine Yronwode. *Women and the Comics.* Forestville, CA: Eclipse Books, 1985.

Sanderson, Peter. *Marvel Universe.* New York: Harry Abrams, 1996.

Savage, William W., Jr. *Comic Books and America, 1945–1954.* Norman: University of Oklahoma Press, 1990.

Simon, Joe, and Jim Simon. *The Comic Book Makers.* New York: Crestwood Publications, 1990.

Steranko, James. *The Steranko History of Comics.* 2 vols. Reading, PA: Supergraphics, 1970, 1972.

Wertham, Fredric. *Seduction of the Innocent.* New York: Rinehart and Company, 1954.

Wiater, Staley, and Stephen R. Bissette. *Comic Book Rebels: Conversations with the Creators of the New Comics.* New York: Donald I. Fine, 1993.

Wright, Bradford. "The Vietnam War and Comic Books." In James S. Olson, ed., *The Vietnam War: Handbook of the Literature and Research.* Westport, CT: Greenwood Press, 1993.

———. *Comic Book Nation: The Transformation of Youth Culture in America.* Baltimore: Johns Hopkins University Press, 2001.

Superhero Wit and Wisdom

Beatty, Scott. *Batman: The Ultimate Guide to the Dark Night.* New York: Dorling Kindersley, 2001.

———. *JLA: The Ultimate Guide to the Justice League of America.* New York: Dorling Kindersley, 2002.

———. *Superman: The Ultimate Guide to the Man of Steel.* New York: Dorling Kindersley, 2002.

Benton, Mike. *Superhero Comics of the Silver Age: The Illustrated History.* Dallas, TX: Taylor Publishing Company, 1991.

———. *Superhero Comics of the Golden Age: The Illustrated History.* Dallas, TX: Taylor Publishing Company, 1992.

Bongco, Mila. *Reading Comics: Language, Culture, and the Concept of the Superhero in Comic Books.* New York: Garland, 2000.

Brooker, Will. *Batman Unmasked: Analyzing a Culture Icon.* London and New York: Continuum, 2000.

Brown, Jeffrey A. *Black Superheroes, Milestone Comics, and Their Fans.* Jackson: University Press of Mississippi, 2001.

Colon, Suzan. *Catwoman: The Life and Times of a Feline Fatale.* San Francisco, CA: Chronicle, 2003.

Coogan, Peter. "The Secret Origin of the Superhero: The Emergence of the Superhero Genre in America from Daniel Boone to Batman." Doctoral dissertation, East Lansing, MI: Michigan State University, American Studies Department, 2002.

Daniels, Les. *DC Comics: Sixty Years of the World's Favorite Comic Book Heroes.* Boston: Little, Brown, 1995.

———. *Marvel: Five Fabulous Decades of the World's Greatest Comics.* Special collector's edition. Introduction by Stan Lee. New York: Harry Abrams, 1995.

———. *Superman: The Complete History: The Life and Times of the Man of Steel.* San Francisco, CA: Chronicle Books, 1998.

———. *Batman: The Complete History: The Life and Times of the Dark Knight.* San Francisco, CA: Chronicle Books, 1999.

———. *Wonder Woman: The Life and Times of the Amazon Princess: The Complete History.* San Francisco, CA: Chronicle Books, 2000.

Eury, Michael. *Captain Action: The Original Super-Hero Action Figure.* Raleigh, NC: TwoMorrows, 2003.

Fleisher, Michael L. *The Encyclopedia of Comic Book Heroes: Volume 1: Batman.* New York: Macmillan, 1976.

———. *The Encyclopedia of Comic Book Heroes: Volume 2: Wonder Woman.* New York: Macmillan, 1976.

———. *The Encyclopedia of Comic Book Heroes: Volume 3: The Great Superman Book.* New York: Macmillan, 1978.

Jacobs, Will, and Gerard Jones. *The Comic Book Heroes: From the Silver Age to the Present.* New York: Crown, 1985.

Robbins, Trina. *The Great Women Super Heroes.* Northampton, MA: Kitchen Sink Press, 1996.

DOCUMENTARIES AND FILMS

Comic Book Superheroes: Unmasked. Directed by Stephen Kroopnick. 100 min. Produced by Triage Entertainment for The History Channel, 2003. Documentary.

WEBSITES

AC Comics. www.accomics.com

Anime News Network. www.animenewsnetwork.com

Anime Web Turnpike. www.anipike.com

Animefringe. www.animefringe.com

Animation World Network. www.awn.com

Archie Comics. www.archiecomics.com

Comic Book Resources. www.ComicBookResources.com

Comic Shop News. www.csnsider.com

Dark Horse Comics. www.darkhorse.com

DC Comics. www.dccomics.com

Diamond Comics. www.diamondcomics.com

Don Markstein's Toonpedia. www.toonpedia.com

The Grand Comics Database Project. www.comics.org

Lambiek Comiclopedia. www.lambiek.net

Marvel Comics. www.marvel.com

The Online World of Anime and Manga. www.ex.org

Silver Bullet Comic Books. www.silverbulletcomicbooks.com

World Famous Comics. www.worldfamouscomics.com

ORGANIZATIONS AND FAN CLUBS

The Comics Arts Conference is a conference designed to bring together comics scholars, practitioners, critics, and historians who wish to promote or engage in serious study of the medium, and to do so in a forum that includes the public. Affiliated with the Comic-Con International, the CAC homepage can be found at www.hsu.edu/faculty/duncanr/cac_page.htm

Photo and Illustration Credits

TV AND FILM STILLS CREDITS

page 63: © Warner Bros./DC Comics; page 109: © Universal Television/CBS; page 129: © Warner Bros./Filmation/CBS; page 141: © Warner Bros./DC Comics; page 166: Twentieth Century Fox/Regency/The Kobal Collection/Zade Rosenthal; page 235: © Stephen J. Cannell Prods./ABC; page 264: © Universal Studios/CBS; page 266: Universal/Marvel Entertainment/The Kobal Collection; page 296: © Hanna-Barbera Prods./NBC; page 306: © Warner Bros./ABC; page 344: © Saban Entertainment; page 380: © King Features/Hearst Entertainment; page 384: © Ruby Spears Enterprises/ABC; page 401: © Warner Bros./DC Comics; page 438: © Hanna-Barbera Prods./Cartoon Network; page 456: Columbia/Marvel/The Kobal Collection; page 459: Columbia/Marvel/The Kobal Collection; page 461: © Marvel Productions/Genesis Entertainment/Fox Children's Network; page 473: © Warner Bros./DC Comics; page 484: © Viacom; page 491: © Marvel Productions/New World/Saban Entertainment; page 547: © Warner Bros./DC Comics; page 555: © Universal Television/USA Network; page 577: © Marvel Enterprises/Saban Entertainment/Fox Children's Network; page 584: © United Artists; page 603: © Fox Children's Network/Sunbow Productions; page 633: © Warner Bros./CBS; page 655: © Twentieth Century Fox/Kerry Hayes/SMPSP; page 658: Twentieth Century Fox/Marvel Entertainment/The Kobal Collection/Nels Israelson.

Index

A

668

THE SUPERHERO BOOK

C

THE SUPERHERO BOOK

THE SUPERHERO BOOK

D

E

F

G

THE SUPERHERO BOOK

I

J

K

M

N

THE SUPERHERO BOOK

Q